EC COMPETITION LAW

TEXT, CASES, AND MATERIALS

ALISON JONES

Solicitor, Lecturer in Law, King's College London

AND

BRENDA SUFRIN

Solicitor, Reader in Law, University of Bristol

OXFORD

UNIVERSITY PRESS

OXFORD
UNIVERSITY PRESS

Great Clarendon Street, Oxford OX2 6DP

Oxford University Press is a department of the University of Oxford.
It furthers the University's objective of excellence in research, scholarship,
and education by publishing worldwide in

Oxford New York

Athens Auckland Bangkok Bogotá Buenos Aires Calcutta
Cape Town Chennai Dar es Salaam Delhi Florence Hong Kong Istanbul
Karachi Kuala Lumpur Madrid Melbourne Mexico City Mumbai
Nairobi Paris São Paulo Shanghai Singapore Taipei Tokyo Toronto Warsaw

with associated companies in Berlin Ibadan

Oxford is a registered trade mark of Oxford University Press
in the UK and in certain other countries

Published in the United States
by Oxford University Press Inc., New York

First published 2001

A catalogue record for this book is available from the British Library

Library of Congress Cataloguing in Publication Data

ISBN 0–19–876329–8

3 5 7 9 10 8 6 4

Typeset in Adobe Minion
by RefineCatch Limited, Bungay, Suffolk
Printed in Great Britain
on acid-free paper by
Biddles Ltd., Guildford and King's Lynn

PREFACE

Adherence to a belief in the market economy has led many States around the world to adopt competition laws aimed at preserving and protecting the competitive process and regulating the behaviour of firms as they compete on the market. The competition rules of the European Community have been in force for forty years. In that time the impact of those rules on the conduct of business has increased enormously and competition law has become a major area of legal practice. Competition law has also become a familiar feature in university law schools, at both undergraduate and postgraduate level, where students commonly find the broad sweep of the subject, with its interface with economics and commerce to be challenging and rewarding. The objective of this book is to provide students and others interested in EC competition law with a text which explains the main EC rules and traces their development and also incorporates extracts from relevant legislation, cases, and a broad range of other literature. The literature includes material written by the Commission, lawyers and economists (both academics and practitioners) and competition officials. The aim is to provide the reader with as comprehensive as possible a package of commentary and materials.

Competition law cannot be divorced from economics. In Chapter 1 we therefore set out some basic economic concepts which are essential to understanding the rationale for the competition rules. In the book we note the growing importance of economic analysis in the application of the EC competition rules and have incorporated extracts from economic literature that are accessible to a lay reader. We also discuss in the introductory chapter the objectives of competition law both generally and specifically in the context of the European Community. This early material provides a background which is essential to the comprehension of later chapters of the book in which the principles of the EC provisions are explained and their application to various market situations considered. We do not attempt to deal with the special sectors or with State Aids.

Competition law is a dynamic, evolving subject that has been developing at such a rate that anyone writing in the field is presented with almost insuperable difficulties. The pace of change in the last couple of years in particular, with the reform of the law on vertical restraints, proposals to reform the law on horizontal co-operation and the Commission's proposals for the modernization of the implementing rules, has been breathtaking. One reviewer commented recently that looseleaf format was the only sensible one for a competition book (or, of course, on-line provision). Although students may have access to such publications in the library this cannot, however, replace for them the advantages or their own single bound volume. In the end authors of such books have to predict developments as far as possible, draw a line and publish. We endeavour to present the law up to the beginning of July 2000 but have tried to make reference at proof stage to any major developments occurring between then and November 2000. A particularly important development, which impacts on most Chapters in this book and which we have been unable to integrate fully in the text, has been the Commission's proposal for a Council Regulation implementing Articles 81 and 82 of the Treaty. The Commission adopted this draft Regulation in September 2000 as a follow-up to its White Paper on Modernisation. If adopted by the Council, the new Regulation would effect dramatic changes to the way that the competition rules are enforced and applied. The broad purpose of this Regulation is to end the current centralised notification and authorisation system for agreements set up by Regulation 17, to ensure greater enforcement of the EC competition rules at the national level (without compromising the uniform application of the law), and to free the Commission's precious resources for the detection of the most serious violations of those rules (the draft regulation confers wider powers of investigation upon the Commission in order to facilitate this task, for example, by authorising Commission officials to enter the homes of directors and other employees of the entities concerned and to seal any premises or business records during the inspection).

The draft Regulation also makes some other far-reaching and radical proposals. For example, it expressly confers power on the Commission to impose remedies of a structural nature where necessary to ensure infringements are brought to an end. Entities in breach of the rules may therefore in the future be required to divest themselves of certain assets. In addition the draft Regulation states that Community law will apply to the *exclusion* of national competition law where an agreement or abuse of a dominant position affects trade between Member States. This represents a dramatic departure from the current position and would leave an extremely limited role for national competition law to play. Although it seems unlikely that the changes, if made, will be introduced much before the beginning of 2003 the draft Regulation is of extreme importance and a copy of the proposal is set out in the Appendix to this book.

Finally, we would like to extend our thanks to everyone who has assisted us in the preparation of this book. In particular, we would like to thank Christian Daly, our research assistant at the Centre of European Law, King's College London and the students at Bristol University and King's College who devoted time to proof reading and who made comments on the book in manuscript. We are grateful to Lorraine Dyer for her typing. We would also like to thank Michaela Coulthard and Matthew Cotton of the OUP for their patience, encouragement and efficiency throughout. Finally, we would both like to acknowledge the inspiration and influence of Professor Richard Whish of King's College London with whom we have both taught and collaborated over a number of years.

Alison Jones,
Brenda Sufrin

1 November 2000

OUTLINE CONTENTS

CONTENTS

ACKNOWLEDGEMENTS

We are grateful to the following publishers and authors for copyright material used in this book.

A.B.A. Publishing for P. Jebsen & R. Stevens, 'Assumptions, Goals and Dominant Under-takings: The Regulation of Competition Under Article 86 of the the European Union (1995–1996)'. *Antitrust Law Journal* 443.

Basic Books for Robert H. Bork, *The Anti-Trust Paradox: A Policy at War With Itself*. Copyright © 1978 by Basic Books Inc. Reprinted by permission of Basic Books, a member of Perseus Books, L.L.C.

Blackwell Publishers for W Bishop, 'Price Discrimination Under Article 86: Political Economy in the European Court' in *Modern Law Review* V. 44 (1981). Copyright © Modern Law Review Ltd.

Elsevier Science for Harboard, 'Barriers to Entry' in *International Review of Law and Economics*, Vol 411, 1994.

Fordham International Law Journal for Michael Waelbroek: 'Price Discrimination and Rebate Policies under EU Competition Law' in Hawk (ed). *Fordham Corporate Law Institute* 147; J. Temple Lang: 'Defining Legitimate Competition: Companies' Duties to Supply Competitors and Access to Essential Facilities' (1994). 18 *Fordham International Law Journal*; W. van Gerven: 'EC Jurisdiction in Antitrust Matters: The Wood Pulp Judgment' in B. Hawk (ed), 1989 *Fordham Corporate Law Institute Proceedings* 451.

Hart Publishing, G. Amato, *Antitrust and the Bounds of Power*. Published by Hart Pub-lishing, 1997.

Harvard Law Review for W.S. Comanor, 'Vertical Price-Fixing, Vertical Market Restric-tions and New Antitrust Policy' (1985) in 98 *Harvard Law Review* 983. Copyright © by the Harvard Law Review Association.

Kluwer Law International for L Hancher, 'Casenote on Corbeau' (1994) 31 CMLRev 105; Edward and Hoskins, 'Article 90: Deregulatin and EC Law: Reflections Arising from the XVI FIDE Conference' (1995) 32 *CMLRev* 157; B. Hawk, 'A Bright Line Shareholding Test to End the Nightmare under the EEC Merger Regulation' (1993) 30 *CMLRev* 1155; A.G. Toth, 'The European Union and Human Rights: the Way Forward' (1997) 34 *CML-Rev* ; C.D. Ehlermann, 'Reflections on the ECO' (1995) 33 *CMLRev*; B.E. Hawk, 'System Failure: Vertical Restraints and EC Competition Law' (1995) *CMLRev* 973; V. Korah, 'Concept of a Dominant Position Within the Meaning of Article 86' (1980) 17 *CMLRev*.

Lexecon for *Lexecon Competition Memo*, November 1999.

Michigan Law Review Association for Hovenkamp, 'Antitrust Policy After Chicago' 84 *Mich. L. Rev* 213 (1985).

New York University Law Review for Eleanor M. Fox & Lawrence A. Sullivan, 'Antitrust—Retrospective and Prospective: Where Are We Coming From? Where Are We Going?' 87 *N.Y.U. L. Rev*, 1987.

Sweet and Maxwell for S. Bishop and M. Walker: *The Economics of E.C. Competition Law: Concepts, Application and Measurement.* (1999; C.J. Cook and C.S. Kerse: *E.C. Mer-ger Control 3/e* (2000); C.S. Kerse: *E.C. Antitrust Procedure 4/e* (1998); P.J. Slot and A.

MacDonnell (eds): *Procedure and Enforcement in E.C. and US Competition Law* (1993). For extracts from *European Competition Law Review*: Jones: 'Wood Pulp: Concerted Practice and/or Conscious Parallelism' (1993) 6 ECLR 273; M. Motta: 'E.C. Merger Policy and the Airtours Case' (2000) 2 ECLR 60; R. Whish: 'The Enforcement of E.C. Competition Law in the Domestic Courts of Member States' (1994) 2 ECLR 60; C.D. Ehlermann and B.J. Drijber: 'Legal Protection of Enterprises: Administrative Procedure, in particular Access to the File and Confidentiality' (1996) ECLR 375; F. Montag: 'The Case for Radical Reform of the Infringement Procedure under Regulation 17' (1996) ECLR 428; E. Fox: 'The Merger Regulation and its Territorial Reach' (1999) ECLR 334; D. Ridyard: 'Essential Facilities and the Obligation to supply competitors' (1996) 8 ECLR 438; R.T. Lapp: 'Predatory Pricing and Entry Deferring Strategies: the Economics of AK20' (1986) ECLR 233; M. A. Bergman: 'Editorial: The Bronner Case—A Turning Point for the Essential Facilities Doctrine?' (2000) ECLR 59. For extracts from *European Law Review*: C. W. Baden Fuller: 'Article 86: Economic Analysis of the Existence of a Dominant Position' (1979) 4 ELRev 423; L. Zanon: 'Ties in Patent Licensing Agreements' (1980) 5 ELRev 391; Woulter P.J. Wils: 'The Commission's New Method of Calculating Fines in Antitrust Cases' (1998) 23 ELRev 252.

WEST GROUP for Hovenkamp, *Federal Antitrust Policy: The Law of Competition and Its Practice*. Published by West Publishing Co., 1994. Reprinted by permission of West Group.

TABLE OF CASES

---

[1] See also joint venture and merger decisions on p. LIII.

JOINT VENTURE DECISIONS

MERGER DECISIONS

EUROPEAN COURT OF FIRST INSTANCE

EUROPEAN COURT OF JUSTICE

EUROPEAN COURT OF JUSTICE (numerical)

PERMANENT COURT OF INTERNATIONAL JUSTICE

TABLES OF LEGISLATION

TABLE OF EC/EU LEGISLATION

TABLE OF OECD RECOMMENDATION

TABLE OF NATIONAL LEGISLATION

TABLE OF EU AND EC TREATIES

TABLE OF INTERNATIONAL TREATIES AND CONVENTIONS

TREATY ESTABLISHING THE EUROPEAN COMMUNITY

Previous numbering	New numbering	Previous numbering	New numbering
PART ONE	PART ONE	Section 2 (deleted)	—
Article 1	Article 1	Article 18 (repealed)	—
Article 2	Article 2	Article 19 (repealed)	—
Article 3	Article 3	Article 20 (repealed)	—
Article 3a	Article 4	Article 21 (repealed)	—
Article 3b	Article 5	Article 22 (repealed)	—
Article 3c (*)	Article 6	Article 23 (repealed)	—
Article 4	Article 7	Article 24 (repealed)	—
Article 4a	Article 8	Article 25 (repealed)	—
Article 4b	Article 9	Article 26 (repealed)	—
Article 5	Article 10	Article 27 (repealed)	—
Article 5a (*)	Article 11	Article 28	Article 26
Article 6	Article 12	Article 29	Article 27
Article 6a (*)	Article 13		
Article 7 (repealed)	—	CHAPTER 2	CHAPTER 2
Article 7a	Article 14	Article 30	Article 28
Article 7b (repealed)	—	Article 31 (repealed)	—
Article 7c	Article 15	Article 32 (repealed)	—
Article 7d (*)	Article 16	Article 33 (repealed)	—
		Article 34	Article 29
PART TWO	PART TWO	Article 35 (repealed)	—
Article 8	Article 17	Article 36	Article 30
Article 8a	Article 18	Article 37	Article 31
Article 8b	Article 19		
Article 8c	Article 20	TITLE II	TITLE II
Article 8d	Article 21	Article 38	Article 32
Article 8e	Article 22	Article 39	Article 33
		Article 40	Article 34
PART THREE	PART THREE	Article 41	Article 35
TITLE I	TITLE I	Article 42	Article 36
Article 9	Article 23	Article 43	Article 37
Article 10	Article 24	Article 44 (repealed)	—
Article 11 (repealed)	—	Article 45 (repealed)	—
		Article 46	Article 38
CHAPTER 1	CHAPTER 1	Article 47 (repealed)	—
Section 1 (deleted)	—		
Article 12	Article 25	TITLE III	TITLE III
Article 13 (repealed)	—	CHAPTER 1	CHAPTER 1
Article 14 (repealed)	—	Article 48	Article 39
Article 15 (repealed)	—		
Article 16 (repealed)	—		
Article 17 (repealed)	—		

(*) New Article introduced by the Treaty of Amsterdam
(**) New Title introduced by the Treaty of Amsterdam
(***) Title restructured by the treaty of Amsterdam

Previous numbering	New numbering	Previous numbering	New numbering
Article 49	Article 40	Article 73o (*)	Article 67
Article 50	Article 41	Article 73p (*)	Article 68
Article 51	Article 42	Article 73q (*)	Article 69
CHAPTER 2	CHAPTER 2	TITLE IV	TITLE V
Article 52	Article 43	Article 74	Article 70
Article 53 (repealed)	—	Article 75	Article 71
Article 54	Article 44	Article 76	Article 72
Article 55	Article 45	Article 77	Article 73
Article 56	Article 46	Article 78	Article 74
Article 57	Article 47	Article 79	Article 75
Article 58	Article 48	Article 80	Article 76
		Article 81	Article 77
CHAPTER 3	CHAPTER 3	Article 82	Article 78
Article 59	Article 49	Article 83	Article 79
Article 60	Article 50	Article 84	Article 80
Article 61	Article 51		
Article 62 (repealed)	—	TITLE V	TITLE VI
Article 63	Article 52	CHAPTER 1	CHAPTER 1
Article 64	Article 53	SECTION 1	SECTION 1
Article 65	Article 54	Article 85	Article 81
Article 66	Article 55	Article 86	Article 82
		Article 87	Article 83
CHAPTER 4	CHAPTER 5	Article 88	Article 84
Article 67 (repealed)	—	Article 89	Article 85
Article 68 (repealed)	—	Article 90	Article 86
Article 69 (repealed)	—	Section 2 (deleted)	—
Article 70 (repealed)	—	Article 91 (repealed)	—
Article 71 (repealed)	—		
Article 72 (repealed)	—	SECTION 3	SECTION 2
Article 73 (repealed)	—	Article 92	Article 87
Article 73a (repealed)	—	Article 93	Article 88
Article 73b	Article 56	Article 94	Article 89
Article 73c	Article 57		
Article 73d	Article 58	CHAPTER 2	CHAPTER 2
Article 73e (repealed)	—	Article 95	Article 90
Article 73f	Article 59	Article 96	Article 91
Article 73g	Article 60	Article 97 (repealed)	—
Article 73h (repealed)	—	Article 98	Article 92
		Article 99	Article 93
TITLE IIIA	TITLE IV		
Article 73i (*)	Article 61	CHAPTER 3	CHAPTER 3
Article 73j (*)	Article 62	Article 100	Article 94
Article 73k (*)	Article 63	Article 100a	Article 95
Article 73l (*)	Article 64	Article 100b (repealed)	—
Article 73m (*)	Article 65	Article 100c (repealed)	—
Article 73n (*)	Article 66	Article 100d (repealed)	—

Previous numbering	New numbering	Previous numbering	New numbering
Article 101	Article 96	Article 109q (*)	Article 128
Article 102	Article 97	Article 109r (*)	Article 129
		Article 109s (*)	Article 130
TITLE VI	TITLE VII		
CHAPTER 1	CHAPTER 1	TITLE VII	TITLE IX
Article 102a	Article 98	Article 110	Article 131
Article 103	Article 99	Article 111 (repealed)	—
Article 103a	Article 100	Article 112	Article 132
Article 104	Article 101	Article 113	Article 133
Article 104a	Article 102	Article 114 (repealed)	—
Article 104b	Article 103	Article 115	Article 134
Article 104c	Article 104	Article 116 (repealed)	—
CHAPTER 2	CHAPTER 2	TITLE VIIA (**)	TITLE X
Article 105	Article 105	Article 116 (*)	Article 135
Article 105a	Article 106		
Article 106	Article 107	TITLE VIII	TITLE XI
Article 107	Article 108	CHAPTER 1 (***)	CHAPTER 1
Article 108	Article 109	Article 117	Article 136
Article 108a	Article 110	Article 118	Article 137
Article 109	Article 111	Article 118a	Article 138
		Article 118b	Article 139
CHAPTER 3	CHAPTER 3	Article 118c	Article 140
Article 109a	Article 112	Article 119	Article 141
Article 109b	Article 113	Article 119a	Article 142
Article 109c	Article 114	Article 120	Article 143
Article 109d	Article 115	Article 121	Article 144
		Article 122	Article 145
CHAPTER 4	CHAPTER 4		
Article 109e	Article 116	CHAPTER 2	CHAPTER 2
Article 109f	Article 117	Article 123	Article 146
Article 109g	Article 118	Article 124	Article 147
Article 109h	Article 119	Article 125	Article 148
Article 109i	Article 120		
Article 109j	Article 121	CHAPTER 3	CHAPTER 3
Article 109k	Article 122	Article 126	Article 149
Article 109l	Article 123	Article 127	Article 150
Article 109m	Article 124		
		TITLE IX	TITLE XII
TITLE VIA (**)	TITLE VIII	Article 128	Article 151
Article 109n (*)	Article 125		
Article 109o (*)	Article 126	TITLE X	TITLE XIII
Article 109p (*)	Article 127	Article 129	Article 152
(*) New Article introduced by the Treaty of Amsterdam		TITLE XI	TITLE XIV
(**) New Title introduced by the Treaty of Amsterdam		Article 129a	Article 153
(***) Title restructured by the Treaty of Amsterdam			

Previous numbering	New numbering	Previous numbering	New numbering
TITLE XII	TITLE XV	Article 136	Article 187
Article 129b	Article 154	Article 136a	Article 188
Article 129c	Article 155		
Article 129d	Article 156	PART FIVE	PART FIVE
		TITLE I	TITLE I
TITLE XIII	TITLE XVI	CHAPTER 1	CHAPTER 1
Article 130	Article 157	SECTION 1	SECTION 1
		Article 137	Article 189
TITLE XIV	TITLE XVII	Article 138	Article 190
Article 130a	Article 158	Article 138a	Article 191
Article 130b	Article 159	Article 138b	Article 192
Article 130c	Article 160	Article 138c	Article 193
Article 130d	Article 161	Article 138d	Article 194
Article 130e	Article 162	Article 138e	Article 195
		Article 139	Article 196
TITLE XV	TITLE XVIII	Article 140	Article 197
Article 130f	Article 163	Article 141	Article 198
Article 130g	Article 164	Article 142	Article 199
Article 130h	Article 165	Article 143	Article 200
Article 130i	Article 166	Article 144	Article 201
Article 130j	Article 167		
Article 130k	Article 168	SECTION 2	SECTION 2
Article 130l	Article 169	Article 145	Article 202
Article 130m	Article 170	Article 146	Article 203
Article 130n	Article 171	Article 147	Article 204
Article 130o	Article 172	Article 148	Article 205
Article 130p	Article 173	Article 149 (repealed)	—
Article 130q (repealed)	—	Article 150	Article 206
		Article 151	Article 207
TITLE XVI	TITLE XIX	Article 152	Article 208
Article 130r	Article 174	Article 153	Article 209
Article 130s	Article 175	Article 154	Article 210
Article 130t	Article 176		
		SECTION 3	SECTION 3
TITLE XVII	TITLE XX	Article 155	Article 211
Article 130u	Article 177	Article 156	Article 212
Article 130v	Article 178	Article 157	Article 213
Article 130w	Article 179	Article 158	Article 214
Article 130x	Article 180	Article 159	Article 215
Article 130y	Article 181	Article 160	Article 216
		Article 161	Article 217
PART FOUR	PART FOUR	Article 162	Article 218
Article 131	Article 182	Article 163	Article 219
Article 132	Article 183		
Article 133	Article 184	SECTION 4	SECTION 4
Article 134	Article 185	Article 164	Article 220
Article 135	Article 186	Article 165	Article 221

Previous numbering	New numbering	Previous numbering	New numbering
Article 166	Article 222	CHAPTER 4	CHAPTER 4
Article 167	Article 223	Article 198a	Article 263
Article 168	Article 224	Article 198b	Article 264
Article 168a	Article 225	Article 198c	Article 265
Article 169	Article 226		
Article 170	Article 227	CHAPTER 5	CHAPTER 5
Article 171	Article 228	Article 198d	Article 266
Article 172	Article 229	Article 198c	Article 267
Article 173	Article 230		
Article 174	Article 231	TITLE II	TITLE II
Article 175	Article 232	Article 199	Article 268
Article 176	Article 233	Article 200 (repealed)	—
Article 177	Article 234	Article 201	Article 269
Article 178	Article 235	Article 201a	Article 270
Article 179	Article 236	Article 202	Article 271
Article 180	Article 237	Article 203	Article 272
Article 181	Article 238	Article 204	Article 273
Article 182	Article 239	Article 205	Article 274
Article 183	Article 240	Article 205a	Article 275
Article 184	Article 241	Article 206	Article 276
Article 185	Article 242	Article 206a (repealed)	—
Article 186	Article 243	Article 207	Article 277
Article 187	Article 244	Article 208	Article 278
Article 188	Article 245	Article 209	Article 279
		Article 209a	Article 280
SECTION 5	SECTION 5		
Article 188a	Article 246	PART SIX	PART SIX
Article 188b	Article 247	Article 210	Article 281
Article 188c	Article 248	Article 211	Article 282
		Article 212 (*)	Article 283
CHAPTER 2	CHAPTER 2	Article 213	Article 284
Article 189	Article 249	Article 213a (*)	Article 285
Article 189a	Article 250	Article 213b (*)	Article 286
Article 189b	Article 251	Article 214	Article 287
Article 189c	Article 252	Article 215	Article 288
Article 190	Article 253	Article 216	Article 289
Article 191	Article 254	Article 217	Article 290
Article 191a (*)	Article 255	Article 218 (*)	Article 291
Article 192	Article 256	Article 219	Article 292
		Article 220	Article 293
CHAPTER 3	CHAPTER 3	Article 221	Article 294
Article 193	Article 257	Article 222	Article 295
Article 194	Article 258	Article 223	Article 296
Article 195	Article 259	Article 224	Article 297
Article 196	Article 260		
Article 197	Article 261		
Article 198	Article 262		

(*) New Article introduced by the Treaty of Amsterdam
(**) New Title introduced by the Treaty of Amsterdam
(***) Title restructured by the Treaty of Amsterdam

Previous numbering	New numbering	Previous numbering	New numbering
Article 225	Article 298	Article 240	Article 312
Article 226 (repealed)	—	Article 241 (repealed)	—
Article 227	Article 299	Article 242 (repealed)	—
Article 228	Article 300	Article 243 (repealed)	—
Article 228a	Article 301	Article 244 (repealed)	—
Article 229	Article 302	Article 245 (repealed)	—
Article 230	Article 303	Article 246 (repealed)	—
Article 231	Article 304		
Article 232	Article 305	FINAL	FINAL
Article 233	Article 306	PROVISIONS	PROVISIONS
Article 234	Article 307	Article 247	Article 313
Article 235	Article 308	Article 248	Article 314
Article 236 (*)	Article 309		
Article 237 (repealed)	—		
Article 238	Article 310		
Article 239	Article 311		

(*) New Article introduced by the Treaty of Amsterdam
(**) New Title introduced by the Treaty of Amsterdam
(***) Title restructured by the Treaty of Amsterdam

BIBLIOGRAPHY

The following are comprehensive general works on EC competition law which cover, in varying degrees of detail, the material dealt with in this book. Specialized reading is listed at the end of each Chapter in the 'Further Reading' section.

BAEL, I. van and BELLIS, J-F., Competition Law of the European Community (3rd edn., CCH Europe, 1994, new looseleaf)

BELLAMY, C., and CHILD, G., *EU Law of Competition* (5th edn., Sweet and Maxwell, 2000)

FAULL, J., and NIKPAY, A. (eds.), *The EC Law of Competition* (Oxford University Press, 1999)

FREEMAN, P., and WHISH, R., (eds.), *Butterworths Competition Law* (Butterworths, Looseleaf, updated four times a year)

FURSE, M., *Competition Law of the UK and EU* (2nd edn., Blackstone Press, 2000)

GOYDER, D., *EC Competition Law* (3rd edn., Oxford University Press, 1988)

GREEN, N., and ROBERTSON, A., *Commercial Agreements and Competition Law* (2nd edn., Kluwer, 1997)

KORAH, V., *An Introductory Guide to EC Competition Law and Practice* (7th edn., Hart Publishing, 2000)

RODGER, B., and MacCULLOCH, A., *Competition Law and Policy in the European Community and the United Kingdom* (Cavendish Publishing, 1999)

WHISH, R., *Competition Law* (4th edn., Butterworths, 2001)

NUMBERING OF THE ARTICLES OF THE EC TREATY IN THIS BOOK

Article 12 of the Treaty of Amsterdam, which came into force on 1 May 1999, provides for some substantive changes to the EC Treaty and for the renumbering of its Articles.

The renumbering inevitably causes confusion as pre-existing case law and legislation refer, of course, to the old numbers. All writers on EC law have to adopt some strategy for dealing with these changes. We have tried to do so in a way which makes matters as easy as possible for readers. We have decided therefore to use the new numbers throughout this book, whether discussing cases or events occurring before or after 1 May 1999.

Where Article numbers appear in quotations and extracts we also use the new numbers, putting them in square brackets where the original contained the old number. Thus 'Article [81]' denotes that the original said 'Article 85.' Where the titles of legislative texts and other Community documents are concerned we have left the original numbers but added the new ones in square brackets (for example, Articles 85 and 86 [now 81 and 82]). This is how the Commission refers to pre-Amsterdam documents on its web-site. We have not changed the old numbers in the titles of books and articles. For further clarification the Table of Equivalences at the beginning of the book, which sets out the old and new numbering in full, should be consulted.

One consequence of the method we have adopted, in which we use the new numbers even when speaking historically, is a degree of anachronism which will, we fear, offend purists. However, we believe that this technique makes the text clearer and less cumbersome, rendering it easier to read. Where we mention Articles of the EC Treaty which were significantly changed, we deal with this in the text. Sometimes, for the sake of clarity or where introducing a new provision, we have inserted the old number in brackets after the new number. Thus a reference to Article 81 (ex Article 85) is a reference to the Treaty provision which is now Article 81 but which, prior to the coming into force of the Treaty of Amsterdam, was Article 85.

1

INTRODUCTION TO COMPETITION LAW

1. INTRODUCTION

The first question any book on competition law must address is, what *is* competition law?

The starting point must be that competition law (or, in American terminology, antitrust law[1]) exists to protect the process of competition in a free market economy—that is, an economic system in which the allocation of resources is determined solely by supply and demand in free markets and is not directed by government regulation.

States which adopt a market economy do so because they consider it to be the form of economic organization which brings the greatest benefits to society. The basis of a free market is competition between firms because such competition is believed, for the reasons explored below, to deliver efficiency, low prices, and innovation. At the other end of the spectrum is an economy which is run by central government planning, such as that which existed in Soviet Russia. Adherence to a belief in the market economy leads to great importance being attached to competition policy and the introduction of competition laws. Competition rules seek to promote effective and undistorted competition in the market.

This does not mean that in a free market economy every sector is left to unbridled competition. Areas such as health services or the provision of basic utilities may, for example, be subject to governmental intervention or government controls. In the European Union agriculture is controlled by the common agricultural policy, which employs subsidies, grants, and intervention buying to manipulate the market and is the absolute antithesis to a competitive system. Different States may have different views about how far the free market should be tempered or supplemented by a social component.

The terms competition *policy* and competition *law* are often used synonymously but they are distinct. The former is broader since it describes the way in which governments (or, in the case of the European Community ('the EC'), supranational organizations[2]) take measures to promote competitive market structures and behaviour. Competition *policy* will therefore encompass within it a system of competition *law*. Those rules will of course seek to

---

[1] The American terminology is more aggressive, and has a 'disagreeably negative ring' to it: see F. M. Scherer, *Competition Policies for an Integrated World Economy* (Brookings Institution, 1994) and W. Pape, 'Socio-Cultural Differences and International Competition Law' (1999) 5 *ELJ* 438, 444–5.

[2] In this book we talk about EC rather than EU competition law since the competition rules are contained in the Treaty establishing the European Community and strictly pertain to the EC rather than the EU as such. The distinction between the EC and the EU is discussed, *infra* in Chap. 2. The competition rules also impact on the European Economic Area, *infra* Chap. 2.

implement competition policy by regulating the behaviour of firms as they compete in the market place.[3]

At first sight it might perhaps seem ironic that competition laws seek to control and interfere with the freedom of conduct of firms in the cause of promoting free competition. Similar paradoxes face democratic governments in other spheres: how far should the liberties of individuals be constrained in order to uphold liberty itself?

In the competition context regulatory rules are necessary because, left alone to determine their own conduct, firms are likely to combine and collude in a way which is profitable to those firms but which also distorts the competitive process to the detriment of consumers and consumer welfare as a whole. As early as the eighteenth century Adam Smith[4] described the tendency of those operating within the same trade to conspire to fix prices. Cartels are an age-old phenomenon. Further, the process of competition may result in one firm dominating a market. Competition between firms may produce a 'winner' which dominates the market, or 'natural' monopolies may exist on a market. In these situations it may be necessary for competition law to restrain the dominating firms' behaviour. Monopolies may also be created if competitors are allowed to merge freely with one another. Competition law may thus aim to preclude mergers where necessary to preserve the competitive process on the market.

The discussion above assumes that the sole goal of competition law is to achieve economic goals and to preserve the competitiveness of markets. The position is not this simple, however. Rather, there is much disagreement about what goals should be pursued through the application of the competition rules. Some argue that the economic goals should be the sole objective, others that a wider range of objectives should be pursued. The next section discusses the objectives of competition law.

2. THE OBJECTIVES OF COMPETITION LAW

A. ECONOMIC EFFICIENCY

(i) THE MAINTENANCE OF EFFECTIVE COMPETITION

The prime purpose of competition policy is, in our view, to promote and maintain a process of effective competition so as to achieve a more efficient allocation of resources.[5]

The above extract from an essay by Vickers and Hay suggests that the main objective of competition law should be to achieve efficiency and that competitive markets will achieve the most efficient allocation of resources. This section seeks to show why competition is thought to produce the greatest benefits to society and to achieve efficiency. The branch of

---

[3] The adoption of competition *laws* has, however, sometimes pre-dated the adoption of a discernible policy, see for example the discussion of the Sherman Act in the USA, *infra* 18 ff.

[4] See Adam Smith, *The Wealth of Nations* (1776, reprinted Penguin, 1979).

[5] J. Vickers and D. Hay, 'The Economics of Market Dominance' in D. Hay and J. Vickers (eds.) *The Economics of Market Dominance* (Oxford University Press, Oxford, 1987), 2.

economics we are concerned with here is industrial economics and, in particular, welfare economics. To facilitate the understanding of these issues it is useful to understand some basic concepts of micro-economics. A glossary of economic terms is found at the end of this book.

(ii) BASIC ECONOMIC CONCEPTS

a. DEMAND CURVES AND CONSUMER SURPLUS

Consumers are all different. They place different values on things, have different preferences and different incomes, and will consequently be willing to pay different prices for a particular product. The maximum amount a consumer is willing to pay for a product is his reservation price. In general the greater the quantity the consumer buys the less he will pay for an additional unit. Although suppliers might like to be able to charge each consumer his individual reservation price, in practice this is not normally feasible. The supplier must therefore consider the relationship between the consumer's willingness to pay and the quantity which will bought on the market as a whole. If only buyers with very high reservation prices are supplied, the quantity produced will be smaller than if buyers with lower reservation prices are supplied. Conversely, if greater quantities are produced the price will have to fall to incorporate buyers with lower reservation prices. The relationship between price and supply is represented by the market demand curve. The demand curve normally slopes downwards from left to right.

If we assume that the market price is £50 we can see that some consumers will be paying £50 for a product for which they would have paid more. This results in what is known as

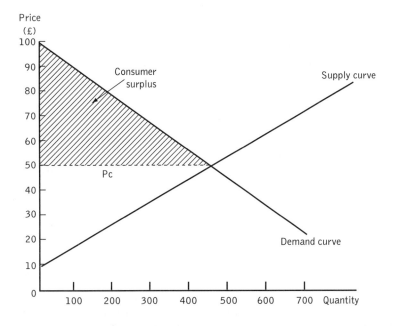

Figure 1 Demand curve and consumer surplus

consumer surplus and is shown by the hatched area in Fig. 1. It is the difference between the buyers' reservation prices and the market price.[6]

b. ELASTICITY OF DEMAND

The amount by which the quantity demanded increases as price reduces (and vice versa) will depend on the market in question and the elasticity of demand for the product.

Price elasticity of demand measures the sensitivity of the quantity demanded to the price. Demand is said to be *inelastic* if an increase in price leads to an insignificant fall in demand. For example, the demand for oil is inelastic since for many of its uses there are no substitutes which perform the same function. If the price of petrol goes up, demand does not fall significantly. Conversely, demand is *elastic* if an increase in price leads to a significant fall in demand. The demand for foreign holidays is elastic.

Technically, price elasticity of demand is the percentage change in the quantity of a product demanded divided by the corresponding percentage change in its price. The result will be a negative figure as the fall in demand will be expressed as a negative figure from the starting point. If demand for widgets falls by 2 per cent as a result of a 1 per cent price increase the change in demand will be expressed as −2 per cent. The demand elasticity is then −2 divided by 1 (the price increase), which is −2.[7] Typically, elasticity falls as one moves down the demand curve, so that at higher prices demand is more elastic. Economic theory puts the dividing line between elastic and inelastic demand at −1. Demand is elastic at a figure below, or more negative, than −1. It is inelastic between −1 and 0. The irony is that in markets where demand is inelastic shortages will lead to higher prices. A bad harvest may be better for food producers than a good one. This was true, for example, when a frost disaster struck the Brazil coffee harvest in 1995.[8]

The position of an individual firm on the market will be different from that of all producers on the market as a whole. Even though the demand for petrol may be inelastic, the price for any individual brand will be elastic. If Esso puts up the price of its petrol but Shell does not, drivers will look for Shell garages and purchase the latter's petrol instead. If, however, all the sellers of petrol collectively agree to increase the price of their petrol the quantity demanded is unlikely to change significantly.

c. CROSS-ELASTICITY OF DEMAND

Elasticity of demand measures the relationship between price of the product and demand for it. In contrast, *cross price elasticity of demand* measures how much the demand for *one* product (A) increases when the price of *another* (B) goes up. It is measured by the percentage change in the quantity demanded of product A divided by the percentage increase in the price of B. Cross-elasticity of demand is crucial to market definition.[9]

Cross price elasticity is positive if the price increase in B leads to an increase in demand

---

[6] The concept of consumer surplus was first described by Alfred Marshall, *Principles of Economics* (8th edn., Macmillan, 1920).

[7] Economists often express this figure without using the minus (as it is always negative). The bigger the negative number the 'higher' the elasticity, for example, elasticity of −5 is higher than elasticity of −1.

[8] D. Begg, S. Fischer and R. Dornbusch, *Economics* (5th edn., Magraw-Hill, 1997).

[9] See *infra* 38 ff.

for A, and this suggests that A and B are substitute products. The Brazil coffee shortage, although leading to an increase in the price of coffee, did not cause consumers to stop purchasing coffee and to purchase tea instead. This indicated that consumers did not consider tea was a substitute for coffee and that the demand for coffee was inelastic. An important point to note is that when considering two products there may be cross price elasticity in one direction and not in the other. Although coffee drinkers may not purchase tea when the price of coffee increases, this does not mean that tea drinkers would not purchase coffee if there was a similar price rise in tea.

If products are complements of each other, rather than substitutes, the cross price elasticity figure will be negative rather than positive. If the price of petrol goes up the demand for big-engine gas-guzzling cars may go down.

d. PROFIT MAXIMIZATION

An assumption is made for the purposes of welfare economics that firms will act rationally and in a way which maximizes profits.[10] Whether firms really do always behave in this way may be doubtful.[11] It will be seen below that, in particular, where a firm has a monopoly the managers may prefer a 'quiet life' to profit maximization. Nevertheless, welfare economics is predicated on this basis. It is certainly a safe assumption that a firm will be concerned not to make long-term *losses*, otherwise it will ultimately have to leave the market. It should also be remembered that a firm which does not deliver profits to its shareholders will be attractive to a predator and so vulnerable to a take-over bid.[12]

e. ECONOMIES OF SCALE

Economies of scale occur when the average cost of producing a commodity falls, the more that is produced. If a widget[13] factory produces only one widget then that widget must bear the whole cost of establishing and running the factory. If it produces 100,000 widgets, however, the costs are spread over 100,000 widgets instead of one. Of course, some costs

---

[10] Profits represent the difference between the total cost of producing goods or providing a service and the revenue earned by selling them.

[11] There is an enormous literature on this subject. The seminal work was A. A. Berle and G. C. Means, *The Modern Corporation and Private Property* (revised edn. 1968, Harcourt Brace and World, 1932). For an extensive discussion see J. E. Parkinson, *Corporate Power and Responsibility* (Oxford University Press, Oxford, 1993), particularly Chaps. 2–4. This doubt arises partly because of the separation of ownership from control in all but the smallest companies. In the layers of complex organization which make up modern businesses, decisions may be made by managers and executives facing uncertain future events and a large number of variables. Their expectations may be misplaced, they may be averse to risk-taking, and they may be most concerned with corporate or individual survival or the growth of the company rather than its profitability. Management may pursue of policy of 'satisficing'. This is a theory of firm behaviour that is contrary to that of profit maximization. 'Satisficing' is when management adopts certain goals for profits, sales, etc. and tries to meet, but not necessarily exceed, them. The goals may not be set high in the first place, so that management will not seem a failure if it does not achieve them, and it is unwilling to be in a position where the shareholders demand ever higher goals in the future. See H. A. Simon, 'Theories of Decision-making in Economic and Behavioral Sciences' (1959) 49 *American Economic Review* 253 and Parkinson, above, 66–7.

[12] See Parkinson, *supra*, n. 11, 113–32.

[13] A widget is traditionally a mythical product with no specific characteristics used in competition law examples. Despite its recent use to describe an article put in drink cans it retains its characterless role as the Everyman of antitrust.

(variable costs) may increase with production (energy and labour for example, although they may well increase less than the cost of producing extra units). However, some costs may not increase at all: if a lorry is delivering widgets, for example, the driver will be paid the same, and the petrol will cost the same, whether the lorry is full or half empty.

Economies of scale result where efficiency in production is achieved as output is increased. There inevitably comes a point, however, when the average cost ceases to fall and economies of scale can no longer be reaped. That point is called the minimum efficient scale (MES). The MES is of great significance for competition law since it has very important repercussions for market structure. Where the MES is very large in relation to the market, i.e. a producer has to supply a large quantity of products on the market before the MES is reached, only a few firms, possibly only one, will be able to operate efficiently on the market. On a competitive market, however, the MES is low in comparison to overall demand so that numerous firms can operate on the market.

(iii) PERFECT COMPETITION

If competition rules are designed to achieve efficiency they should be utilized where there is no effective competition on the market. The theory of perfect competition presents a model of a market on which consumer welfare is maximized and cannot, therefore, be improved by the application of competition rules.

A perfectly competitive market is one in which there are a large number of buyers and sellers (firms with very small market shares can operate at minimal costs since the MES is small in comparison to the size of the market), the product is homogeneous, all the buyers and sellers have perfect information,[14] and there are no barriers to entry or exit. Sellers can come onto, and leave, the market freely.[15] The result of this state of affairs is that each seller is insignificant in relation to the market as a whole and has no influence on the product's price. Consequently, sellers are described as *price-takers*, not price-makers.

In a perfectly competitive market the price never exceeds marginal cost. The marginal cost to a firm is the cost of producing one extra unit of the product. So if it costs £100 to produce ten widgets but £105 to produce eleven, the marginal cost is £5. On such a market the firm will always be able to add to profit where the marginal cost of producing a unit is less than the price. The producer will therefore keep increasing the units it produces until the price charged equals marginal cost. If the price is below marginal cost the firm will have to respond by reducing output.

Where the price charged for a product is at marginal cost this does not mean that the firm makes no profit at that price. It does make a profit, but only a 'normal' one. All the factors of production used to make the product have to be taken into account when computing the cost, and this includes the capital. The firm has to make enough of a return on the capital employed in the business to make it worthwhile staying on the market. When economists talk of zero profits they mean that there is no profit above the 'normal' level, which is assessed in relation to the 'opportunity cost'. An opportunity cost is the value of what has to be given up to do something else. The capital employed in the business must therefore reap a

---

[14] Buyers and sellers know of every change in price or demand and so respond immediately to such changes.

[15] For a discussion of barriers to entry, see *infra* 52 ff.

profit to compensate the business for the profit which would come from a different outlay. If the firm does not do this it will leave the market.

The relationship between marginal and average cost is also an important one. The average cost is the costs of the firm evened out over all the units produced.[16]

F. Fishwick, *Making Sense of Competition Policy* (Kogan Page, 1993), 34–5

At the level of output where average cost is at a minimum, marginal cost and average cost are equal. This is intuitively obvious: if marginal cost were less than average cost, the firm would reduce average cost by increasing output; if marginal cost exceeded average cost, the latter could be reduced by a decrease in supply. For the individual firm under perfect competition, price is equal to marginal cost at a level of output where marginal cost is rising. This implies that price must exceed the variable costs of units of output below the marginal unit, so that the sale of these 'infra-marginal' units makes a contribution to fixed costs. If this contribution exceeds fixed costs the firm is said to be making 'abnormal' profits and this attracts new entrants into the market, depressing market price. So long as some firms are making abnormal profits, this entry process will continue. Existing firms can maintain or increase their profits only by reducing their costs, but, because the model assumes no advantage for the individual firm (and hence compete freedom of access to technology and resources), such cost reductions can immediately be matched by all existing firms and new entrants.

The cumulative effect of free entry and competition through cost reduction is to force price down towards minimum attainable average costs. . . .

The fact that on a perfectly competitive market the market price equals the marginal cost is said to *maximize consumer welfare* by leading to *allocative* and *productive* efficiency.

Allocative efficiency results from the fact that goods are produced in the quantities valued by society. The supplier will expand production to the point where market price and marginal cost coincide. Everyone who values the product at its cost of production will, therefore, be able to purchase it. The supplier will not make more, but neither, if it is acting rationally to maximize profits, will it make less.

Similarly, p*roductive* (or technical) efficiency results from perfectly competitive markets. Goods are produced at the lowest possible cost. Every firm has to produce at minimum cost or it will lose its custom to others, make losses, and eventually will be obliged to leave the market. Given the perfect information in the market any cost-cutting techniques will be copied by the other firms and the market price will be lowered generally.

F. Fishwick, *Making Sense of Competition Policy* (Kogan Page, 1993), 35

The welfare benefits of perfect competition

1. Price is equal to the incremental cost to every firm of supplying the marginal unit. This means that no customer who is prepared to pay the cost of production and delivery of a unit of the product is denied access to it.

---

[16] See further, *infra* Chap. 7 for a discussion of costs in relation to predatory pricing.

2. There is constant downward pressure on costs, because cost-reductions is the only means
    whereby firms can stay in business and increase profits. Because of competition from both
    existing firms and new entrants, such cost reductions are always passed on in lower prices to
    customers.

This resulting state of affairs is *economic efficiency*. 'Efficiency' in welfare economics terms, therefore, bears this special meaning. It is a state in which none of the players, sellers or buyers, could be made better off without someone being made worse off. It is sometimes known as *pareto optimal* after the Italian economist, Vilfredo Pareto, who first developed the theory. *Consumer welfare* is said to be maximized by efficient resource allocation.

Productive and allocative efficiency do not necessarily come as a package, however. It is allocative efficiency that is of greatest importance for competition law.

Despite the fact that the welfare losses arising from productive inefficiency are potentially of equal magnitude to those resulting from allocative inefficiency, most competition inquiries are more concerned with the impact on allocative efficiency. The economic goal of E.C. competition law appears to be concerned with improving allocative efficiency in ways that do not impair productive efficiency so greatly as to produce no increase or a net reduction in total consumer welfare. Given that competition law enforcement should not, in general, be concerned with detailed regulation of industries, this is a sensible policy objective. Of course, increases in productive efficiency generally feed through to consumer welfare by reducing the waste of finite resources and by directly lowering prices . . .[17]

(iv) MONOPOLY

At the opposite end of the spectrum to perfect competition lies monopoly. This is a market where there is only one seller but many buyers. This may be because there are barriers which prevent other firms from entering the market (perhaps legal barriers) or because there is a natural monopoly, as the MES of production means that only one undertaking can operate profitably on the market.

The theory predicts that as the firm is not constrained by any competitors it will price as high as it possibly can. The monopoly price will be above the competitive market price. However, the price that the monopolist charges is still affected by demand and is constrained to some extent by products from outside the market. As the price rises some customers will not purchase the product but will use their resources to purchase something else instead. The firm usually faces a downward sloping demand curve, so the higher the price it charges the lower the demand for its product.

If a monopolist chooses to sell just one unit it may receive an extremely high price for that unit but that price is unlikely to cover its cost. The monopolist will therefore wish to produce more units but each time it sells one more unit it has to lower the price. Unless the monopolist can *price discriminate* between customers, the monopolist must lower the price on *all* units, not just the extra ones. The producer's marginal revenue is the extra amount the monopolist obtains from selling the extra unit, but because it involves lowering the price across the board the marginal revenue is less than the selling price. This means that the monopolist will sell units only up to the point at which the marginal revenue equals

---

[17] S. Bishop and M. Walker, *The Economics of EC Competition Law* (Sweet and Maxwell, 1999), 2.15. The pursuit of allocative efficiency is also considered by the Chicago School to be the only proper goal of antitrust, see *infra* 21 ff.

the marginal cost. A monopolist's marginal revenue is below the market price. This in turn means that the quantity supplied of the product will be less that that which would be supplied on a competitive market. Thus prices are higher than those resulting on a competitive market *and* output is restricted. This is illustrated by the following diagram.

Figure 2 shows that, in the absence of price discrimination, the marginal revenue curve is always under the demand curve.[18] Because price is above the competitive price the monopolist makes abnormal profits and some consumers who would have paid the competitive (marginal cost) price are deprived of the product. The hatched area in the diagram shows the consequent *deadweight loss of monopoly*, the loss of consumer surplus which is not turned into profit for the producer.

According to the above theory therefore the main distinction between perfect competition and pure monopoly is that the monopolist's price exceeds marginal cost, while the

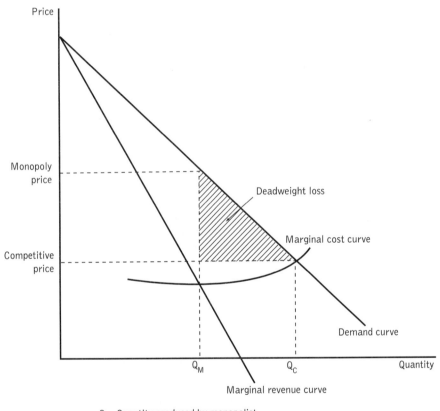

Q_M Quantity produced by monopolist
Q_C Quantity which would be produced in competitive market

Figure 2 The deadweight loss due to monopoly

[18] If the monopolist is able to practise perfect price discrimination, that is, charge each customer his reservation price, the marginal revenue curve and the demand curve are the same.

competitor's price equals marginal cost. This monopoly pricing leads to a transfer in wealth from consumer to producer. It is for this reason that firms operating on a competitive market may wish to emulate the effect of monopoly by colluding, for example, to set their prices at above the competitive level and by reducing output. From an efficiency point of view the transfer of wealth may be immaterial. The behaviour does not, however, simply lead to a redistribution of income but it also results in the misallocation in resources. It is this loss to consumer welfare and efficiency as a whole that is of concern.

This seeming technicality, so trivial at first glance, is the basis of the economist's most general condemnation of monopoly: it leads to an allocation of resources that is inefficient in the sense of failing to satisfy consumer wants as completely as possible.[19]

In economic theory, therefore, the objection to monopoly is not simply the one which is obvious to most people—that the monopolist is able to charge excessively for its product—but that monopoly is inefficient.[20] Consumers who would have bought the product at the competitive price will spend their money on other things and consumer welfare is not maximized (allocative inefficiency occurs).

Another important objection to monopoly is that a monopolist will not have the same pressure as firms operating on a perfectly competitive market to reduce its costs. This was identified by Leibenstein as, and has become known as, the 'X-efficiency'. It describes internal inefficiencies and rising costs due, for example, to high salaries, excessive perks, over-manning, and the lack of need to minimize the cost of production.[21] A monopolist may also waste resources, for example, defending its monopoly position, maintaining excess capacity, and indulging in excessive product differentiation.[22] These inefficiencies will be reflected in higher prices. Another possible inefficiency is that a monopolist not subject to competitive pressures will have little incentive to innovate and to improve its production methods. However, on some markets it could be argued that the opposite will be true. A monopolist may be more willing to bear the risks and costs of invention and technical development precisely *because* they are protected from competition.[23]

(v) OLIGOPOLY

Oligopoly is another type of market structure that lies between perfect competition and monopoly on the spectrum. An oligopolistic market is one on which there are only a few

---

[19] F. M. Scherer and D. Ross, *Industrial Market Structure and Economic Performance* (3rd edn., Houghton Mifflin, 1990) 23.

[20] Economists have often sought to quantify the deadweight loss. The starting point was Harberger's article in 1954 in which he calculated the loss in the USA as less than 0.1% of national income: see A. C. Harberger, 'Monopoly and Resource Allocation', (1954) 44 *American Economic Review* 77–87. In a mass of further studies this has been found to be a great under-estimate (for the literature on this, see Scherer and Ross, *Industrial Market Structure and Economic Performance* (3rd ed) (Boston, Houghton Mifflin, 1990), 661–7). Cowling and Mueller calculated it as 7%: see K. Cowling and D. C. Mueller, 'The Social Costs of Monopoly Power' (1978) 88 *Economic Journal* 724–48, although Scherer and Ross, *supra*, 665 describe these results as 'exaggerated'. In this, as in much else in economics, there are wide differences in views.

[21] H. Leibenstein, 'Allocative efficiency vs. "X-efficiency"' (1966) 56 *American Economic Review* 392–415.

[22] See, e.g., R. Posner, 'The Social Costs of Monopoly and Regulation' (1975) *Journal of Political Economy* 83.

[23] J. A. Schumpeter, *Capitalism, Socialism and Democracy* (Harper, 1942).

leading firms. Given their small number they know each other's identity and recognize that they are affected by the output and pricing decisions of the others. They are not only competitors but rivals too. The result of this mutual awareness may lead on some markets to tacit collusion (that is, understood or implied without being stated) between them. It may also lead them to collude expressly. However, other oligopolistic markets are characterized by fierce competition. Thus in some markets the price appears to be set above the competitive and to approximate monopoly pricing, but in others it is not. A wealth of economic literature has been produced setting out economic models of oligopoly in an attempt to explain why this occurs. The huge differences in behaviour on these markets also cause fundamental problems for those responsible for drafting and applying the competition rules. The mainstream explanations of oligopolistic behaviour and the way in which EC competition law attempts to deal with oligopolistic markets are described in Chapter 11. It is important to note however, that many markets are oligopolistic and that since these markets may also lead to allocative and productive inefficiency they present a major problem for competition authorities.

(vi) PERFECT COMPETITION, MONOPOLY, AND COMPETITION IN THE REAL WORLD

Monopolies and oligopolies do exist. Monopolies may be created and maintained by government regulation (utilities and transport markets, for example) and or may be *natural*. Pure monopoly is rare outside these circumstances but other markets, although not monopolized, may be dominated by one firm which holds a very large share of the market. Other markets may be dominated by two, three, or four sellers. Even though there may be a fringe of smaller sellers on these types of markets, they may present the same concerns for competition law as those arising on a monopolistic market.[24]

The analysis set out of perfectly competitive markets above does, however, present a number of problems. The main problem is that in the real world perfectly competitive markets do not exist. Rather, the model of perfect competition is just that—a model. It is a useful starting point because it demonstrates the concepts of productive and allocative efficiency. In reality, however, markets do not possess all the characteristics of perfect competition, and even if they did, the process of competition would tend to alter it. For example, goods are rarely homogeneous. Rather, players on competitive markets will usually strive to differentiate their products from those of their competitors, by improvements in quality or service, building up a brand image or adding individual features. They will seek to attract customers with better credit terms, delivery terms, or other conditions of sale. Further, it is very unlikely that an infinite number of firms will be operating at identical costs levels, that producers will not benefit from economies of scale, and that sellers and buyers have perfect information across an atomistic market.[25]

Important caveats must thus be attached to the theory that the perfectly competitive market is superior. In particular, in most markets economies of scale make the attainment of perfect competition impossible. On the contrary, in some markets monopolies or different

---

[24] For a more detailed discussion see, *infra* Chaps. 5–7 and Chap. 11.

[25] Where markets are oligopolistic, on the other hand, with only a very small number of firms in the market, the position may be quite different, see *infra* Chap. 11.

structures are 'natural' because of the MES. Further, it is not actually clear[26] that profit maximization is the policy which firms always pursue. In addition, as Scherer and Ross point out, it might not always be wise to rely on the sovereignty of the consumer.

F. M. Scherer and D. Ross, *Industrial Market Structure and Economic Performance* (3rd edn., Houghton Mifflin, 1990), 29–30

For one, the whole concept of efficient resource allocation is built upon the fundamental belief that the consumer is sovereign—that individual preferences are what count in the ledger of social values. . . . If, for example, consumers freely choosing in the market demonstrate that they would prefer at the margin to give up fifty bushels of grain to get an additional twenty hair shirts, we conclude that society is really better off because of the shift. Yet in practice our respect for consumer sovereignty is by no means universal—not, in any event, for infants, convicted criminals, dope addicts, the mentally ill, and others whose preferences cannot be trusted to generate rational choices. And in this age of widespread neuroses and psychoses, the line between rationality and irrationality is not all that easy to draw. One might even entertain doubts about the soundness of consumption decisions made by presumably normal, rational adults whose tastes (assumed in the standard theory of consumer behaviour to be stable) have been remolded under a barrage of advertising messages. Further qualms intrude when we recognize that there are external diseconomies in consumption, for example, that the purchase of a new hair shirt by Mr Willoughby may not only increase his utility, but simultaneously reduce the utility of envious neighbors. All this warns us that the theorems of welfare economics are erected upon sandy foundations. This does not mean that their conclusions are wrong. The demonstration of a competitive system's allocative efficiency makes considerable sense even when complications related to advertising, ignorance, and the like are introduced. But blind faith is also uncalled for.

The reality is that most markets lie somewhere between perfect competition and monopoly, in a state of 'imperfect' or 'monopolistic' competition. The model of perfect competition is nonetheless still useful as a benchmark against which to measure the competitiveness of real markets. The difference between the perfectly competitive and monopolistic market focuses attention on the crucial question: whether the firm or firms have sufficient market power to raise prices above the competitive level and keep them there.

The value of any model lies not in the absolute fidelity of each element to real world phenomena, but in the model's ability to make useful predictions and, more importantly, its ability to give us meaningful verbal accounts of our observations.[27]

Oligopolies also raise competition concerns because of the ability of oligopolists in some markets to exercise collectively their market power.

Despite this important use of the model of perfect competition there would, of course, seem to be little point in designing a competition policy to try to achieve it. Economists have thus identified other models on which to predicate competition policy. Clark in 1940[28]

---

[26] See *supra* n. 11.

[27] H. Hovenkamp, *Federal Antitrust Policy: The Law of Competition and its Practice* (West Publishing Co, 1994), 39.

[28] J. M. Clark, 'Towards a Concept of Workable Competition' (1940) 30 *American Economic Review* 241–56; see also S. Sosnick, 'A Critique of Concepts of Workable Competition' (1958) 72 *Quarterly Journal of Economics* 380–423.

promulgated the theory of 'workable competition': competition policy should aim to produce the best competitive arrangement practically attainable. This too presents its difficulties, however. In particular it may be hard to select criteria by which the workability of competition is judged and hard to assess whether or not those criteria have been fulfilled. Another theory is that of 'contestable markets' which places the main emphasis on freedom of entry to a market. Contestability theory thus attaches importance not on the structure of the market but on its contestability. So long as 'hit-and-run' entry by competitors is possible the behaviour of firms operating on the market will be constrained. The minimum conditions for a contestable market are instantaneous entry and costless exit, and these are not often possible.[29]

B. OTHER GOALS OF COMPETITION LAW

(i) A SOLE GOAL FOR COMPETITION LAW?

Even if one accepts that the goal of competition law is to achieve allocative efficiency and maximize consumer welfare this is only the beginning. There are other problems. A particular problem is to identify whether or not the pursuit of efficiency in the economic sense should be the *only* goal of competition law. Once this has been resolved other problems will arise. In particular, it will have to be decided what competition law should be adopted and *how* it should be applied in pursuit of these goals. We look first at what goals competition law might pursue.

(ii) PRESERVATION OF LIBERTY

The use of the competition rules to preserve competitive markets may achieve economic efficiency but may also uphold the foundations of liberal democracy. Competitive markets will generally preclude the creation of excessive private power.

G. Amato, *Antitrust and the Bounds of Power* (Hart Publishing, Oxford, 1997), 2–3

Antitrust law was, as we know, invented neither by the technicians of commercial law (though they became its first specialists) nor by economists themselves (though they supplied its most solid cultural background). It was instead desired by politicians and (in Europe) by scholars attentive to the pillars of the democratic systems, who saw it as an answer (if not indeed 'the' answer) to a crucial problem for democracy: the emergence from the company or firm, as an expression of the fundamental freedom of individuals, of the opposite phenomenon of private power; a power devoid of legitimation and dangerously capable of infringing not just the economic freedom of other private individuals, but also the balance of public decisions exposed to its domineering strength.

On the basis of the principles of liberal democracy, the problem was twofold and constituted a real

---

[29] Sunk costs, for example, will be a hindering factor, see *infra*. Hovenkamp, *Federal Antitrust Policy: The Law of Competition and its Practice* (West Publishing Co, 1994), 36 states 'contestable market performance deteriorates very quickly in response to market imperfections'.

dilemma. Citizens have the right to have their freedoms acknowledged and to exercise them; but just because they are freedoms they must never become coercion, an imposition on others. Power in liberal democratic societies is, in the public sphere, recognized only in those who hold it legitimately on the basis of law, while, in the private sphere, it does not go beyond the limited prerogatives allotted within the firm to its owner. Beyond these limits, private power in a liberal democracy (by contrast with what had occurred, and continues to occur, in societies of other inspirations) is in principle seen to be abusive, and must be limited so that no-one can take decisions that produce effects on others without their assent being given.

The question whether government regulation or the private power of the firm is more frightening is an ideological one which pervades many arguments in competition law, and is a fundamental dilemma of liberal democracy itself. However, one of the most important arguments in favour of a competitive market structure, where the individual sellers and buyers are insignificant in relation to the size of the market, is that it decentralizes and disperses private power and protects individual freedom.[30]

(iii) FAIR COMPETITION

The preservation of liberty supports competitive markets and may in some markets result in economic efficiency. In other cases the goals may be inimical. Competition laws which are aimed at the dispersal of power as a matter of ideology may favour small businesses and seek to protect them from big business. Instead of protecting competition the tendency may instead be to use the competition rules to protect competitors.

Such a policy may accord with popular sentiment which is distrustful of 'large' firms.[31] It will enable a government to nurture small businesses, and to promote a society in which citizens are encouraged to be their own boss, run their own business, and behave in an entrepreneurial manner. The dispersal of market power also prevents the redistribution of wealth from consumers to firms with market power (individually or collectively)[32] and ensures that consumers have plenty of choice. There may also be a desire for competition to be 'fair'.

(iv) SOCIO-POLITICAL ISSUES

Competition law may also be used to service other policies, such as social, employment, industrial, environmental, and/or regional policy (for example, by prohibiting mergers which will cause job losses or allowing restrictive agreements which will preserve declining industries for a little longer) or the protection of the environment.

(v) THE EC DIMENSION

In the European Community there is an added dimension. The competition rules are set out within the Treaty establishing the European Community. The EC competition rules must

---

[30] See F. M. Scherer and D. Ross, *Industrial Market Structure and Economic Performance* (3rd edn., Boston, Houghton Mifflin, 1990), 18.

[31] See *infra* 27 ff.

[32] Although the transfer of wealth may be economically neutral economists are still concerned by the dead-weight loss caused by a monopolistic market.

therefore be viewed in their context and as one of the tools set out to achieve the aims and objectives of that Treaty. The history of this Treaty and the European Community is explained in Chapter 2. The aims and tasks of the Community and the Treaty competition rules are, however, introduced in section 4 below.

(vi) THE CHICAGO VIEW

In the USA the difficulty in defining a coherent and consistent competition policy and the tendency for it to be politicized led to a call for less intervention by the competition authorities and minimal enforcement of the competition rules. Instead, lawyers and economists, principally of the Chicago School, championed the placement of greater trust in the ability of the market itself to achieve economic efficiency. A brief outline of the US competition law provisions and the Chicago view is set out in section 3 below.

C. CONCLUSIONS

There seems to be consensus that competition law should be adopted and applied in pursuit of economic efficiency. It will be seen in subsequent sections, however, that there is no agreement on how competition law rules can best achieve such efficiency. Further, whether or not competition should seek to pursue goals other than competition such as the protection of competitors, jobs, or the environment is controversial.

The pursuit of these goals may favour small firms, individuals or environmental concerns at the expense of consumer welfare.[33] Supporting small businesses for the sake of it at the expense of more efficient competitors will be a drag on the economy. Similarly, the prevention of a merger which would result in efficiencies on the ground that it may save jobs in the short term may mean that the individual companies are unable to compete effectively on the market in the long run. Similarly, a decision to allow an anti-competitive agreement between firms in an industry in historic decline may ensure the firm's survival for a time but may cause inefficiency. It may be better for nature to take its course. The most efficient will survive and the remaining resources can be used in new industries which will create future prosperity.

It is an unfortunate fact of life that competition produces winners and losers. Efficient firms will flourish at the expense of the less efficient. 'Fair' competition is not necessarily the same as 'free' competition.[34] The problem is that the free market may produce benefits to society as a whole in the long run but cause a great deal of pain to the losers in the meantime.

---

[33] The public may be keen in theory on the idea of protecting small firms from larger competitors, but when faced with the choice of paying more for their groceries at the corner shop than at a supermarket they are likely to get in their cars and drive to Tesco. Similarly, although a society may object to the ability of a large company with market power to make excessive profits at the expense of consumers, the shareholders in the monopolist may be institutions such as pension funds and assurance companies which are investing on behalf of the consumers in their role as workers or policy-holders.

[34] If a thriving takeaway sandwich bar near a university entrance loses its lunchtime trade when a more innovative sandwich bar opens even nearer the entrance this may not seem 'fair' but it simply illustrates the workings of a free market in which the consumer is sovereign.

This is not to say that there should not be social, regional, employment, environmental, or other policies. It is a matter of whether, and to what extent, these may be or should be pursued as part of a *competition* policy and how far competition can be isolated from other policies. A government which wishes to protect the environment by refusing planning permission for out-of-town stores may protect village stores from the competition of larger but more efficient supermarkets. Planning laws may therefore result in the restriction of competition on a particular market. Since such laws are government measures, rather than the actions of private undertakings, they are normally beyond the reach of competition law.[35] The question of what concerns competition law should encompass in addition to efficiency is ultimately a matter of political choice, and we return to it below when looking at the 'Chicago school'.

3. US LAW

A. THE SHERMAN ACT 1890

It is impossible to discuss competition law without some reference to US law because of the influence which American lawyers and economists, working with reference to the American system, have had on competition law thinking.

The USA was the first jurisdiction to adopt a proper 'modern' system of competition law.[36] The US Congress passed the Sherman Act in 1890.[37] It is still in force. Section 1[38] states:

Every contract, combination in the form of trust or otherwise, or conspiracy, in restraint of trade or commerce among the several States, or with foreign nations, is hereby declared to be illegal. Every person who shall make any contract or engage in any combination or conspiracy hereby declared to be illegal shall be deemed guilty of a felony. . . .

Section 2 states:

Every person who shall monopolize, or attempt to monopolize, or combine or conspire with any other person or persons, to monopolize any part of the trade or commerce among several States, or with foreign nations, shall be deemed guilty of a felony. . . .

---

[35] Although note that under EC law (Art. 86 of the Treaty) government measures can be impugned in some circumstances. See Chap. 8.

[36] For a summary of the ways in which throughout the centuries the English Crown created monopolies and the spasmodic action taken against certain business practices, see M. Furse, *Competition Law of the UK and EC* (2nd edn. Blackstone, 2000), 2–5; the UK courts developed a doctrine of restraint of trade at common law, but this never developed into a system of competition law: see R. Whish, *Competition Law* (3rd ed edn., Butterworths, 1993), chap. 2.

[37] 'An Act to protect trade and commerce against unlawful restraints and monopolies', 15 USC, 2 July 1890. It was supplemented by later statutes, the Clayton Act (1914), the Federal Trade Commission Act (1914), and the Robinson-Patman Act (1936).

[38] See also *infra* Chap. 4.

None of the expressions used in the Sherman Act, such as 'in restraint of trade' or 'monopolize' were defined.

The most popular explanation for the passing of the Sherman Act was is that it was to combat the power of the 'trusts'. It had become common for the owners of stocks held in competing companies to transfer those stocks to trustees who then controlled the activities of those competitors and consequently lessened competition between them (this is why it has become known as 'antitrust' law). The activities of the railroad companies gave rise to particular concern. It is also claimed, however, that the Sherman Act was more of a protectionist measure passed in response to pressure by farmers, small businesses, or those desiring to stop the transfer of wealth from consumers to big business.[39] The Chicago school[40] view is that it was passed to preserve economic efficiency, but since the theories of allocative efficiency, dead-weight loss, and pareto-efficiency had not then been invented it cannot have been articulated in exactly this way.[41] It seems quite extraordinary that there should be so much uncertainty about the conception of the very basis of American antitrust law. The argument is not merely about history, however, but is also important when considering what the objective of that law is now and in the 'struggle for the soul of antitrust'. It may seem to the neutral observer that in passing the Sherman Act Congress made a *law* without a discernible policy behind it. Policies, however, emerged later.

The law developed in a series of judicial decisions in the next half-century in a rather ad hoc manner, and reflected the experiences of the American economy as it went through an industrial revolution, the Depression, and the New Deal.[42] In the 1940s and 1950s the 'workable competition' hypothesis[43] was influential.[44] In the 1950s the Structure→Conduct→Performance paradigm was developed by what is called the Harvard School, particularly by J. S. Bain. This led to a belief that markets were fragile and to an antitrust policy which intervened to protect small businesses against large firms. From the 1950s onwards, however, another school of thinking emerged, the Chicago school, which did *not* believe that markets were fragile. Chicago school thinking has had a profound impact on the development of antitrust enforcement in the USA and has influenced the thinking about competition law in Europe. The Harvard and Chicago schools are described in the next sections.

---

[39] See E. T. Sullivan (ed.), *The Political Economy of the Sherman Act* (Oxford University Press, 1991) for a collection of essays written between 1959 and 1989 on the Sherman Act, published to mark the centenary of the Act. The articles display the wide divergence of views between some of the most eminent names in antitrust thinking, as well as historians and Department of Justice officials.

[40] For the Chicago school, see *infra* 21. For Robert Bork's Chicago view of the intention of Congress see R. H. Bork, *The Antitrust Paradox* (Basic Books, 1978, reprinted with a new Introduction and Epilogue, 1993), chap. 2.

[41] Alfred Marshall's *Principles of Economics* (Macmillan, 1890) was first published only in 1890 and Pareto published his theory in 1909.

[42] The New Deal was a federal policy begun under President Roosevelt in 1933 to aid those thrown out of employment in the Depression.

[43] See *supra* n. 28 and accompanying text.

[44] See the Report of the Attorney General's National Committee to Study the Antitrust Laws (1955).

B. THE STRUCTURE→CONDUCT→PERFORMANCE PARADIGM AND THE HARVARD SCHOOL

The S→C→P paradigm is that the structure of the market determines the firm's conduct and that conduct determines market performance, for example, profitability, efficiency, technical progress, and growth. The model thus sought to establish that certain industry structures lead to certain types of conduct which then lead to certain kinds of economic performance. In particular, highly concentrated industries cause conduct which leads to poor economic performance, especially reduced output and monopoly prices.

These views stemmed mainly from work done at Harvard University. The initial work was done in the 1930s, particularly by E. S. Mason,[45] and was developed by his pupil J. S. Bain in the 1950s.[46] The theory was developed through empirical studies of American industries (twenty manufacturing industries were studied in the early 1950s) rather than from theoretical models. The conclusion that market structure dictated performance caused a belief that antitrust should be concerned with *structural* remedies rather than *behavioural* remedies. The focus of attention was, therefore, on concentrated industries. Thus Bain considered that most industries were more concentrated than was necessary (economies of scale were not substantial in most industries); that barriers to entry were widespread and very high and so new firms were prevented from entering markets; and that the monopoly pricing associated with oligopolies began to occur at relatively low levels of concentration.

These influential conclusions coincided with a general trend of US Congressional policies which sought to protect small businesses and which were suspicious of business expansion. This led in the 1960s to an extremely interventionist antitrust enforcement policy.[47] Criticism of the Bainian analysis, led by the Chicago school (below), centred particularly on the fact that the conclusions drawn from the empirical studies were flawed;[48] that they wrongly found barriers to entry to be pervasive and wrongly found economies of scale to be rare. Consequently, the policy of condemning so many business practices as anti-competitive was misconceived. Despite the rise of the Chicago school, the S→C→P paradigm remains a basic tool of antitrust analysis. Although mainstream economists no longer believe that structure *dictates* performance, it accepts that structure is important to the ability of firms to behave anti-competitively. As Hovenkamp says, 'Antitrust without structural analysis has become impossible, thanks largely to S→C→P writers'.[49]

---

[45] See E. S. Mason, *Economic Concentration and the Monopoly Problem* (Harvard University Press, 1957).

[46] See J. S. Bain, *Barriers to New Competition* (Harvard University Press, 1956) and *Industrial Organization* (2nd edn., Wiley, 1968).

[47] e.g. *Brown Shoe Co* v. *United States*, 370 US 294, 82 S Ct.1502 (1962); *FTC* v. *Consolidated Foods Corp* 380 US 592, 85 S Ct 1220 (1965); *FTC* v. *Proctor & Gamble Co*, 386 US 568, 87 S Ct 1224 (1967); *United States* v. *Arnold, Schwinn & Co*, 388 US 365, 87 S Ct 1856 (1967).

[48] *Inter alia*, in that they used accounting rates of return to calculate profits although they are unreliable indicators of monopoly profits.

[49] H. Hovenkamp, *Federal Antitrust Policy: The Law of Competition and its Practice* (West Publishing Co, 1994), 45.

C. THE CHICAGO SCHOOL

'Chicago' is a school of monetarist and free-market economics, called after the University where many of its originators and adherents did their work.[50] Unlike the Harvard school the foundations of its antitrust analysis were rigorously theoretical rather than empirical. Even while the S→C→P paradigm was becoming established as the dominant ideology of the day Chicago antitrust scholars were loudly decrying it. Although the S→C→P model has never been entirely eclipsed, Chicago school economics produced a 'revolution' in antitrust thinking.[51] Although, in its turn, it has been criticized and some of its most treasured shibboleths found not to withstand further analysis, its influence on competition law is indelible. In the USA the ascendancy of Chicago during the 1970s and 1980s led to a change of direction in the application of antitrust law and indeed Chicago thinking was behind the entire 'Reaganomics' of the Reagan administration.

The fundamental Chicago view[52] is that the pursuit of efficiency, by which is meant allocative efficiency[53] as defined by the market, should be the *sole* goal of antitrust.[54] The school does not support sentimentality for small business or the corner store but places trust in the market. The identity of the winners or losers is irrelevant so long as efficiency is achieved. Indeed, since the writers consider that few barriers to entry exist, that industries frequently benefit from economies of scale, and that businesses are profit-maximizers, the Chicago school places much belief in the ability of the market to correct and achieve efficiency itself without interference from governments or antitrust laws.

Hovenkamp sets out the basic tenets of the Chicago school in the following extract from an article written in 1985. Although critical of some of the views, Hovenkamp nonetheless describes himself as a 'fellow traveler' [*sic*].

H. Hovenkamp, 'Antitrust Policy After Chicago' [1985] *Univ. Mich. L Rev.* 213, 226–9

. . . the following discussion summarizes a few of the model's basic assumptions and principles that have been particularly important in Chicago School antitrust scholarship.

(1) Economic efficiency, the pursuit of which should be the exclusive goal of the antitrust laws, consists of two relevant parts: allocative efficiency and productive efficiency. . . . Occasionally practices that increase a firm's productive efficiency reduce the market's allocative efficiency. For example, construction of a large plant and acquisition of large market share may increase a firm's productive efficiency by enabling it to achieve economics of scale; however, these

---

[50] Milton Friedman was a leading figure of the Chicago school. The main proponents of its antitrust ideas include Stigler, Demsetz, Brozen, Posner, and Bork.

[51] See generally R. Posner, 'The Chicago School of Antitrust Analysis' 127 *U Pa L Rev* 925 (1979).

[52] We can only describe here the views of Chicago school adherents generally. There are considerable divergences of view among them and some are far more 'extreme' than others.

[53] Chicago theory holds that the market itself punishes those who are productively inefficient. As the conditions for Pareto-efficiency can rarely be fulfilled, Chicago usually uses 'potential' Pareto-efficiency as the guide, which means a policy whereby the total gains of all those who gain should be greater than the total losses of all those who lose.

[54] Some Chicago adherents would hold that allocative efficiency should be the sole goal of *all* government policies.

actions may simultaneously reduce allocative efficiency by facilitating monopoly pricing. A properly defined antitrust policy will attempt to maximize *net* efficiency gains. . . .

(2) Most markets are competitive, even if they contain a relatively small number of sellers. Furthermore, product differentiation tends to undermine competition far less than was formerly presumed. As a result, neither high market concentration nor product differentiation are the anticompetitive problems earlier oligopoly theorists believed them to be. . . .

(3) Monopoly, when it exists, tends to be self-correcting; that is, the monopolist's higher profits generally attract new entry into the monopolist's market, with the result that the monopolist's position is quickly eroded. About the best that the judicial process can do is hasten the correction process. . . .

(4) 'Natural' barriers to entry are more imagined than real. As a general rule investment will flow into any market where the rate of return is high. The one significant exception consists of barriers to entry that are not natural—that is, barriers that are created by government itself. In most markets the government would be best off if it left entry and exit unregulated. . . .

(5) Economies of scale are far more pervasive than economists once believed, largely because earlier economists looked only at intra-plant or production economics, and neglected economies of distribution. As a result, many more industries than were formerly thought may operate most economically only at fairly high concentration levels. . . .

(6) Business firms are profit-maximizers. That is, their managers generally make decisions that they anticipate will make the firm more profitable than any alternative decision would. The model would not be undermined, however, if it should turn out that many firms are not profit maximizers, but are motivated by some alternative goal, such as revenue maximization, sales maximization, or 'satisficing.'. . . .[55] The integrity of the market efficiency model requires only that a few firms be profit-maximizers. In that case, the profits and market shares of these firms will grow at the expense of other firms in the market . . .

(7) Antitrust enforcement should be designed in such a way as to penalize conduct precisely to the point that it is inefficient, but to tolerate or encourage it when it is efficient. . . . During the Warren Court era,[56] antitrust enforcement was excessive, and often penalized efficient conduct. . . .

(8) The decision to make the neoclassical market efficiency model the exclusive guide for antitrust policy is nonpolitical.

A clear statement of the view that 'efficiency is all' is set out in Robert Bork's celebrated polemic, *The Antitrust Paradox*.

R. H. Bork, *The Antitrust Paradox: A Policy at War with Itself* (Basic Books, 1978, reprinted with a new Introduction and Epilogue, 1993), 90–1

Antitrust is about the effects of business behavior on consumers. An understanding of the relationship of that behavior to consumer well-being can be gained only through basic economic theory. The economic models involved are essential to all antitrust analysis, but they are simple and require no previous acquaintance with economics to be comprehended. Indeed, since we can hardly expect legislators, judges, and lawyers to be sophisticated economists as well, it is only the fact that the simple ideas of economics are powerful and entirely adequate to this field that makes it conceivable for the law to frame and implement useful policy.

[55] For 'satisficing' see *supra* n. 11.
[56] Earl Warren was Chief Justice of the Supreme Court 1953–68.

Consumer welfare is greatest when society's economic resources are allocated so that consumers are able to satisfy their wants as fully as technological constraints permit. Consumer welfare, in this sense, is merely another term for the wealth of the nation. Antitrust thus has a built-in preference for material prosperity, but it has nothing to say about the ways prosperity is distributed or used. Those are matters for other laws. Consumer welfare, as the term is used in antitrust, has no sumptuary or ethical component, but permits consumers to define by their expression of wants in the marketplace what things they regard as wealth. Antitrust litigation is not a process for deciding who should be rich or poor, nor can it decide how much wealth should be expanded to reduce pollution or undertake to mitigate the anguish of the cross-country skier at the desecration wrought by snowmobiles. It can only increase collective wealth by requiring that many lawful products, whether skis or snowmobiles, be produced and sold under conditions most favourable to consumers.

The role of the antitrust laws, then, lies at that stage of the economic process in which production and distribution of goods and services are organized in accordance with the scale of values that consumers choose by their relative willingness to purchase. The law's mission is to preserve, improve, and reinforce the powerful economic mechanisms that compel businesses to respond to consumers. 'From a social point of view,' as Frank H. Knight puts it, 'this process may be viewed under two aspects, (a) the assignment or *allocation* of the available productive forces and materials among the various lines of industry, and (b) the effective *co-ordination* of the various means of production in each industry into such groupings as will produce the greatest result.' . . .

These two factors may conveniently be called *allocative efficiency* and *productive efficiency*. . . . These two types of efficiency make up the overall efficiency that determines the level of our society's wealth, or consumer welfare. The whole task of antitrust can be summed up as the effort to improve allocative efficiency without impairing productive efficiency so greatly as to produce either no gain or a net loss in consumer welfare. That task must be guided by basic economic analysis, otherwise the law acts blindly upon forces it does not understand and produces results it does not intend.

Critics have argued that efficiency could not be the sole pursuit of antitrust without becoming inconsistent with other government policies, such as those pursuing distributive goals.[57] Bork made a riposte to this in the Epilogue to his book reprinted in 1993:

R. H. Bork, *The Antitrust Paradox: A Policy at War with Itself* (Basic Books, 1978, reprinted with a new Introduction and Epilogue, 1993), 426–7

Of the two, the issue of the goals of antitrust seems to have fared somewhat better than the law's capacity to deal with economics. Fifteen years ago, the question of what goals antitrust serves, and hence what factors a judge may properly consider in deciding an antitrust case, had not been addressed in any systemic fashion. The answers given by courts and commentators were hardly more than slogans of a more or less appealing variety, depending on your taste for populist rhetoric. Though the preservation of competition was often cited as the aim of the law, there seemed no agreed definition of what, for the purposes of antitrust, competition is.

'Competition,' the courts assured us, meant the preservation or comfort of small businesses, the advancement of first amendment values, the preservation of political democracy, the preservation of

---

[57] The arguments are summed up in the Hovenkamp article an extract from which is set out *supra* 21–22.

local ownership, and so on ad infinitum. Judges could and did choose among the items they had invented and placed in this grab bag in order to legislate freely. Cornucopias have their attractions but, when it comes to finding and applying a policy to guide adjudication, horns of plenty make anything resembling a rule of law impossible.

The argument of this book, of course, is that competition must be understood as the maximization of consumer welfare or, if you prefer, economic efficiency. That requires economic reasoning because courts must balance, when they conflict, possible losses of efficiency in the allocation of resources with possible gains in the productive use of those resources. In a word, the goal is maximum economic efficiency to make us as wealthy as possible. The distribution of that wealth or the accomplishment of noneconomic goals are the proper subjects of other laws and not within the competence of judges deciding antitrust cases.

By and large, with some ambiguity at times, the more recent cases have adopted a consumer welfare model. Aside from some explicit statements to that effect, the best evidence for the proposition is that courts now customarily speak the language of economics rather than pop sociology and political philosophy. If the conversion from a multi-goal jurisprudence is not complete, it is nevertheless very substantial. Explicit opposition to the consumer welfare thesis comes less from judges than from the academics. The objections are generally of two kinds: denial that an exclusive consumer welfare focus is to be found in the various antitrust statutes; and insistence that such a policy is not desirable.

. . . .

A different line of attack comes from those who observe, quite correctly, that people value things other than consumer welfare, and, therefore, quite incorrectly, that antitrust ought not be confined to advancing that goal. As non sequiturs go, that one is world class. There may be someone identified with the Chicago School who thinks all human activity can be analyzed in terms of economics and efficiency, but that is not true of most Chicagoans and certainly constitutes no part of my argument. No one body of law can protect everything that people value. If antitrust could, we would need no other statutes. If we trace the implications of the proposition, it results in judges deciding cases as if the Sherman Act said: 'A restraint of trade shall consist of any contract, combination, or conspiracy that fails to produce, in the eyes of the court, the optimum mix of consumer welfare and other good things that Americans want.' That is inevitably the result of bringing into judicial consideration an open-ended list of attractive-sounding goals to be weighed against consumer welfare.

Nor is there any force to the argument that the consumer welfare cannot be the exclusive mission of antitrust since that mission will be rendered less effective unless all other government policies pursue the same goal. Of course, antitrust will be less effective in promoting consumer welfare if government simultaneously subsidizes small business. A tariff policy designed to keep American companies viable will be less effective if government allows foreign competitors to set up manufacturing operations in the United States. That fact does not state a reason for a judge to alter the way he construes the tariff laws or other laws that apply to foreign companies' operations here. Many statutory policies conflict to some degree with other statutory policies. Whether or not they should do so, and to what degree, is a subject for legislation rather than adjudication.

In any event, no matter what policy goals or combination of goals one attributes to antitrust, the effectiveness of the law in forwarding those policies will be diminished by other public policies. That fact tells us nothing about how judges should go about deciding cases under the antitrust statutes.

Perhaps the most contentious of all Chicago school claims is that the pursuit of efficiency as the sole goal of antitrust is non-political. The essential argument is that since antitrust policy is dictated only by micro-economics it is ideology-free. The adoption of such a policy is, however, in itself ideological. Chicago proclaims itself as neutral because it believes only in market forces. The idea that this is an apolitical stance is challenged by Fox and Sullivan in the following passages from an article in 1987.[58] In particular, the authors stress that the law should not only be economics. Rather, economics should be used as a tool to support the system which is aimed at supporting consumers and a dynamic system of antitrust. The Chicagoans view of economics itself reflects a vision of what society we should live in.

E. M. Fox and L. A. Sullivan, 'Antitrust—Retrospective and Prospective: Where Are We Coming From? Where Are we Going?' (1987) 62 *New York Univ. Law Review* 936 at 956–9

Economists have both praised and criticized mainstream antitrust law. Many economists, especially those with Chicago leanings, think that because antitrust is about markets, as is microeconomics, antitrust law should *be* economics. They react as though the law is out of kilter whenever it diverges from their particular economic insight; and they so react regardless of whether the law diverges because empirical processes have not validated factual assumptions, or because the law has identified social goals other than or in addition to allocative efficiency.

Law is not economics. Nor were the antitrust laws adopted to squeeze the greatest possible efficiency out of business. Nonetheless, we would not want an antitrust system that hurts consumers rather than helps them. Most people agree that economics is a tool that can help keep the system on course to help consumers and to facilitate dynamic competition. Economic analysts have provided important insights into why business acts the way it does, and what the probable effect of a practice will be on the marketplace. Despite the consensus that economics can play a supporting role, the Chicago School, in the name of law and economics, has waged ideological warfare, assaulting antitrust itself.

Commitment and belief fuel the debate on both sides. While others seem aware that the debate is about values, Chicagoans seem not to be. They often claim the imperative of science for their policy prescriptions. But on points of basic difference between Chicagoans on the one hand and realists or traditionalists on the other, the Chicago assertions are not provable. They are not matters of fact. They cannot be derived from economics. The basic difference between Chicagoans and traditionalists is a difference of vision about what kind of society we are and should strive to be. . . .

. . . .

The Chicago beliefs are compatible with only the most minimal law. In antitrust, the most minimal law, given the existence of the statutes, is law that proscribes only clear cartel agreements and mergers that would create a monopoly in a market that included all perceptible potential competition. Let us review the characteristics that underlie this minimalist approach to antitrust.

First, the Chicago School claims that it has the right prescription for efficiency. This is unprovable; some would say highly suspect, and others would say wrong. Economic experts have intense debates as to what scheme is likely to produce a more efficient or a more dynamic, inventive economy. Economics does not provide a conclusive answer. Within a wide range, the answer is indeterminate. . . .

Second, the Chicago School always opts for norms that presuppose that markets are robust and that firms, imbued with perfect knowledge and risk neutrality, move their resources quickly and easily to the most profitable opportunity. Data about how people actually behave belie these assumptions. . . .

---

[58] One needs only to look at the USA in the 1980s. The economics of Chicago were those of the American Right. Robert Bork was President Reagan's nominee for the Supreme Court, but he was rejected by the Senate (although that had more to do with his conservative views on matters such as abortion than with his views on barriers to entry).

Yet Chicagoans continue to press for legal rules that accept these assumptions as true. . . . It is this mind-set that led Judge Posner to dissent in a recent case in which a prisoner was blinded in jail and sued prison authorities for neglect. . . . A majority of the appellate court thought that appointment of counsel was improperly denied to the prisoner, but Judge Posner disagreed. . . . Assuming the existence of a market for lawyers that would function like a Chicago model market, Judge Posner argued that if the prisoner's case was any good, a lawyer would have taken it on contingency. The fact that no lawyer did 'proved' that the prisoner's case lacked merit. . . .[59]

Third, the Chicago School defines competition in terms of efficiency; defines efficiency as the absence of inefficiency; defines inefficiency in terms of artificial output restraint; . . . and thus concludes that any activity that does not demonstrably limit output is efficient and therefore procompetitive. Thus, it 'proves' that almost all business activity is efficient—a neat trick.

Fox and Sullivan thus question the bases of many of their views on which the Chicago view of efficiency is hung and hence challenge their utter faith in the ability of the market to correct itself. Criticisms have also been made in the Chicagoans' belief that barriers to entry are rare outside government regulation,[60] that potential competition polices the market as well as existing competitors because, in the absence of barriers to entry, monopolists will be challenged by new entrants if they reap monopoly profits, and that most markets are competitive. The Chicago model is criticized for being 'static' and concentrating too much on long-term effects rather than on short-term effects and of competition as a *process*. Above all, the neo-classical market efficiency model of Chicago is too simple to account for or predict business behaviour in the real world.

D. POST-CHICAGO

Whatever criticisms can be and have been made of the Chicago school, it has undeniably changed antitrust thinking profoundly. It placed rigorous economic analysis at the centre of antitrust. After Chicago it is impossible to accept the S→C→P paradigm without qualification, or not to think of efficiency as a central concern. It shed new light on many matters.

More recently, however, there has been more of a *rapprochement* of different strands of thought, and the more extreme Chicago ideas have been tempered. There is a general recognition that economics may give indications of what questions to ask, but does not always yield definitive answers, and certainly not answers which are necessarily value-free. What is sometimes called modern industrial organization theory or new industrial economics stresses the effect that the *strategic conduct* of firms can have in different market situations. It considers that firms may indulge in strategic entry deterrence, for example. So the belief that predatory pricing is rarely rational conduct, as Chicagoans said, is replaced with the idea that it can be adopted as a rational strategy to prevent new competitors entering the market.[61] We have entered a less doctrinaire age. Although there are areas where the Chicago

---

[59] The case concerned was *Merritt* v. *Faulkner*, 697 F 2d 761 (7th Cir). This story rather puts into the shade the classic Chicago school joke (rendered here into an English context). A lawyer and a Chicago scholar walk along the pavement. The lawyer says 'Oh look, there's a £20 note lying on the pavement'. 'No,' says the Chicago scholar, 'there can't be. If there was, someone would have picked it up'.

[60] See the discussion of barriers to entry *infra* 52 ff.

[61] See *infra* Chap. 7.

view is now orthodoxy,[62] for example that vertical restraints are rarely anti-competitive in the absence of significant market power, this does not require adherence to all Chicago views. Bork's views on selective distribution may be accepted without sharing his sanguine belief that what is good for big business is necessarily good for society.

4. EC COMPETITION LAW

A. GENERAL

The Treaty of Rome and the competition rules set within it came into force in 1958. The rules were not enforced however by the Community institutions until Regulation 17 was passed four years later.[63] This was seven decades, therefore, after the birth of the American system. It has been common ever since to discuss EC law with reference to the US law, looking across the Atlantic for comparisons, ideas, and lessons to be drawn from the American experience.

The American influence was seen as quite specific in one respect. On 1 January 1958 not only did the Treaty of Rome come into force but also, coincidentally, did a new German Competition Law system (the *Gesetz gegen Wettbewerbsbeschränkungen*). This was required by the American occupiers before they would return full sovereignty to the new German state. US officials considered that the concentrated and heavy cartelized nature of pre-war German industry had aided Hitler's rise to power and his military conquests and that US-style competition laws would help German democracy. Anti-cartelization statutes were first put into place in 1947. However, there was a domestic as well as an American impetus towards the adoption of a complete new system and Chancellor Adenauer's economics minister, Ludwig Erhard,[64] pushed hard for it, although against strong opposition (which accounted for the delay until 1958).

The GWB (which is still in place today) rapidly acquired an important role in Germany's economic and legal system. The institution primarily charged with enforcing it was (and is) the *Bundeskartellamt* (Federal Cartel Office). One consequence of this was that the German experience and influence were very important as EC competition law began to develop from the mid-1960s onwards.[65] It is easy therefore to draw a connecting line: US antitrust influences Germany: Germany influences the EC. *Ergo*, EC law *has* to be primarily related to US law.

It has always been known that things are not really as simple as that and that EC competition law has been shaped by European, and particularly German, as well as American ideas.[66] Nevertheless, the tendency has been to discuss EC law through the prism of

---

[62] See the reform of EC law on vertical restraints, discussed *infra* in Chap. 9.

[63] [1959–62] OJ Spec. Ed. 87. See *infra* Chap. 2.

[64] Later, from 1963–6 Erhard was himself Chancellor.

[65] Most Directors General of the Competition Directorate-General have been German.

[66] See e.g., V. *Korah, An Introductory Guide to* EC *Competition Law and Practice* (7th edn., Hart Publishing, 2000).

American developments. In a book published in 1998, Daniel Gerber, a comparative lawyer, argues that there is a rich tradition of thought in Europe about what we now call competition law, which has given European domestic competition laws, as well as EC law, a distinctive character of their own. It is not just a counterpoint to things American. Gerber first of all summarizes what he calls the 'Competition Law Story' in Europe.

D. Gerber, *Law and Competition in Twentieth Century Europe: Protecting Prometheus* (Clarendon Press, Oxford, 1998), 6–8

Europeans began to develop the idea of such a general law to protect competition almost a century ago. The idea took shape in the 1890s in Austria, where it was a product of Vienna's extraordinary creative intellectual life. Competition law proposals emerged in order to protect the competitive process from political and ideological onslaughts, and they relied heavily on bureaucratic application of a 'public interest' standard in doing so. One of these proposals gained significant political support, and a competition law was almost enacted—only to be barred by the disintegration of the Austrian legislative process.

Although political events blocked further development of competition law ideas in Austria, such ideas were intensely debated in both intellectual and political arenas in Germany during the decade that bracketed the turn of the century. These conflicts shaped a discourse from which Europe's early competition legislation drew much of its substance and without which its enactment is barely conceivable. Moreover, many elements of this discourse were to become fixtures of European competition law thought.

The first European 'competition law' was enacted in Germany in 1923 in response to the postwar inflation crisis. The system created to implement this legislation became an important factor of economic and legal life in Germany during the 1920s and established competition law as an operational reality rather than merely an idea. It was, however, too weak to withstand the pressures ranged against it, and it was eliminated during the 1930s.

German experience with this system was nevertheless influential in the spread of competition law ideas, and during the late 1920s competition law ideas were widely discussed throughout Europe. By the early 1930s, additional statutes along the lines of the German legislation had been enacted in several smaller European states. More importantly, these discussions and enactments generated a framework for thinking about the roles and characteristics of competition law that was to be used after the Second World War as the basis for competition legislation and that remains influential.

After the end of the war, many European governments turned to competition law as a means of encouraging economic revival, undergirding recently re-won and still fragile freedoms and achieving political acceptance of post-war hardships. Virtually all of these competition law systems were based on the thought and experience of the interwar period. In most of them, however, competition law was imbedded in economic regulatory frameworks that impeded its effectiveness, and it was seldom supported by significant economic, political or intellectual resources. As a result, these systems remained a rather marginal component of general economic policy, and in this respect some have not fundamentally changed even today.

In postwar Germany, competition law took a different turn—one that was to play a key role in the process of European integration and to have extraordinary consequences for the course of postwar European history. This change of direction was prepared during the Nazi period by a group of neo-liberal thinkers who secretly and often at great personal risk developed ideas of how Germany should be reconstituted after the war. In their so-called 'ordoliberal' vision of society, economic freedom and competition were the sources not only of prosperity but also of political freedom. They represented the 'economic constitution' of society, and law, the ordoliberals said, had to protect and implement this constitution. In this view, therefore, competition law acquired a new importance because it was made a basic structure of the political system. It also acquired new characteristics: it was now to operate increasingly according to juridical principles and procedures rather than on the basis of administration discretion.

These ideas eventually fell on fertile soil in the years after the Second World War. Nourished by the desire for new social ideals and supported by the occupation authorities, neo-liberal reformers enacted a competition law in 1957 that achieved new prominence and a vastly greater economic and political role. Despite often intense opposition from 'big industry', competition law has become a 'pillar' of the 'social market economy', and as such it has played a key role in some of the postwar Europe's most impressive economic and political successes.

Gerber thus locates the spirit of European competition law in the ideas of *fin-de-siècle* Austria and in the German concept of Ordoliberalism. In fact, he goes further back, to nineteenth-century liberalism's conception of law being necessary to create freedom by constraining power. In Europe, competition law is to be seen as part of an 'economic constitution' which embraces social justice and is part of the political system.[67] This is not to say that the arguments we have discussed above have no relevance to Europe. They do, but it is useful to be reminded that Europe is not America, and arguments about freedom and the desirability or otherwise of government regulation resound differently in European and American ears.

In the UK, there is even more temptation to take the USA as a point of reference. First there is the language, which makes the enormous mass of American material on antitrust accessible in a way that Continental writings, for most people, are not. Secondly, there is the shared experience of the common law. Thirdly, it can be argued that the UK has, in the recent past at least, shared the American economic philosophy. One commentator has identified a dichotomy between what he calls 'neo-American' capitalism—individualistic, unregulated, based on short-term profits, and with a minimal social component—and 'Rhine model' capitalism—collective achievement, public consensus, social welfare.[68] The Thatcher government eagerly pursued the American model but ultimately the electorate proved more resistant. The British are no more willing than the rest of Europe to abandon the welfare state and accept the survival of the fittest to the extent tolerated in America. Gerber considers that English legal culture led to distinctive features in the UK competition law model, which moved it away from the general 'European model' he identifies. Nevertheless the UK's use of administrative controls produced similarities which are important from the perspective of European integration 'because they have provided a common experiential base that has eased mutual understanding and co-operation within EU institutions and forged important links between Member State governments and officials'.[69]

It is useful to be reminded that, with competition as with other things, not all thinking emanates from the USA. EC competition law uses economic analysis as a tool in

---

[67] For a recent example of the concern of many Member States for the 'social' aspect in competition policy, see the insertion into the Treaty of Art. 16 (ex Art. 7) reiterating the value of 'services of general economic interest' in the Community. See further *infra* Chap. 8.

[68] M. Albert, *Capitalism Against Capitalism* (Whurr Publishers Ltd, 1993).

[69] D. Gerber, *Laws and Competition in Twentieth Century Europe: Protecting Prometheus* (Clarendon Press, 1998), 207.

the application of competition law, as Faull and Nikpay say below,[70] but the context of that law is the aims and objectives of the Treaty of Rome.

B. THE OBJECTIVES OF THE EUROPEAN COMMUNITY AND EC COMPETITION POLICY

(i) THE OBJECTIVES OF THE EUROPEAN COMMUNITY

An examination of the *raison d'être* of the European Community is beyond the scope of a book on competition law. As Craig and de Bùrca state, 'there are and always have been many different views about the aims of the Community, and subsequently the Union, among its political actors, populace, and commentators. A whole range of historical, political, and economic forces and contingencies contributed to creating the entity which exists today'.[71] A brief discussion of the aims and objectives of the Community is, however, essential to understand the context within which the competition rules are set and the impact that these aims and objectives may have on the interpretation and application of those rules.

The objectives of the Treaty of Rome[72] are set out in Article 2. The original Article 2 stated:

The Community shall have as its task, by establishing a common market and progressively approximating the economic policies of member states, to promote throughout the Community a harmonious development of economic activities, a continuous and balanced expansion, an increase in stability, an accelerated raising of the standard of living and closer relations between the states belonging to it.

Article 2 has subsequently been amended, and since the Treaty of Amsterdam came into force on 1 May 1999 states:

The Community shall have as its task, by establishing a common market and an economic and monetary union and by implementing the common policies or activities referred to in Articles 3 and 3a, to promote throughout the Community a harmonious and balanced development of economic activities, a high level of employment and of social protection, equality between men and women, sustainable and non-inflationary growth, a high degree of competitiveness and convergence of economic performance, a high level of protection and improvement of the quality of the environment, the raising of the standard of living and quality of life, and economic and social cohesion and solidarity among Member States.

The Community therefore has a number of wide-ranging and aspirational goals which have expanded during the life of the EC and which it seeks to achieve through economic integration. The creation of the common market is not therefore an end in itself, but a means (along with the establishment of EMU and the implementation of common policies or activities) of achieving the promotion of the matters listed in Article 2. The 'common market', often used colloquially as a synonym for the Community, means an area where

---

[70] See *infra*, 37.

[71] P. Craig and G. de Bùrca, *EU Law: Text, Cases and Materials* (2nd edn., Oxford University Press, Oxford, 1998), 4.

[72] The adoption of this Treaty and its amendments are discussed *infra* Chap. 2.

direct and indirect barriers to trade between Member States are removed and a common import and export policy adopted toward the outside world as far as commercial transactions are concerned. As we see below, in *Metro* v. *Commission*,[73] the Court of Justice said in 1976 that the objectives of the Treaty included the creation of a single market achieving conditions similar to those of a domestic market. The single market is the 'internal' aspect of the common market, and is now defined in Article 14(2):[74]

The internal market shall comprise an area without internal frontiers in which the free movement of goods, persons, services and capital is ensured in accordance with the provisions of this Treaty.

The economic integration of the Member States has now been taken further by progress towards EMU, the third and final stage of which entailed the adoption of a single currency, the Euro,[75] on 1 January 1999. Its foundation, however, remains the core concept of the single internal market.

Article 3 of the Treaty sets out the 'activities' of the Community necessary for the purposes set out in Article 2. This has also expanded since 1958, reflecting the additions to Article 2. The present Article 3 states:

1. For the purposes set out in Article 2, the activities of the Community shall include, as provided in this Treaty and in accordance with the timetable set out therein:

    (a) the prohibition, as between Member States, of customs duties and quantitative restrictions on the import and export of goods, and of all other measures having equivalent effect;

    (b) a common commercial policy;

    (c) an internal market characterised by the abolition, as between Member States, of obstacles to the free movement of goods, persons, services and capital;

    (d) measures concerning the entry and movement of persons as provided for in Title IV;

    (e) a common policy in the sphere of agriculture and fisheries;

    (f) a common policy in the sphere of transport;

    (g) a system ensuring that competition in the internal market is not distorted;

    (h) the approximation of the laws of Member States to the extent required for the functioning of the common market;

    (i) the promotion of co-ordination between employment policies of the Member States with a view to enhancing their effectiveness by developing a co-ordinated strategy for employment;

    (j) a policy in the social sphere comprising a European Social Fund;

    (k) the strengthening of economic and social cohesion;

    (l) a policy in the sphere of the environment;

    (m) the strengthening of the competitiveness of Community industry;

    (n) the promotion of research and technological development;

    (o) encouragement for the establishment and development of trans-European networks;

    (p) a contribution to the attainment of a high level of health protection;

    (q) a contribution to education and training of quality and to the flowering of the cultures of the Member States;

---

[73] Case 26/76, *Metro* v. *Commission (No 1)* [1977] ECR 1875, [1978] 2 CMLR 1, para. 20, see *infra* 34–35.

[74] Previously Art. 7a. The concept of the 'internal market' was first formally enshrined in the Treaty by the Single European Act 1986 (SEA), which provided for its completion by the end of 1992.

[75] For the way in which the 'ECU' referred to in the Treaty became the 'Euro' without an amendment to the Treaty, see S. Weatherill and P. Beaumont, *EU Law* (3rd edn., Penguin, 1998), 776.

(r)   a policy in the sphere of development co-operation;

(s)   the association of the overseas countries and territories in order to increase trade and promote jointly economic and social development;

(t)   a contribution to the strengthening of consumer protection;

(u)   measures in the spheres of energy, civil protection and tourism.

The Community's activities are thus broad, encompassing the pursuit of a large number of policies and activities, including in Article 3(1)(g), 'a system ensuring that competition in the internal market is not distorted'.[76]

Further, Article 4(1), inserted into the Treaty by the TEU in 1993,[77] assumes that economic policies in the Community will be based on an open market economy with free competition:

For the purposes set out in Article 2, the activities of the Member States and the Community shall include, as provided in this Treaty and in accordance with the timetable set out therein, the adoption of an economic policy which is based on the close co-ordination of Member States' economic policies, on the internal market and on the definition of common objectives, and conducted in accordance with the principle of an open market economy with free competition.

This is taken up in Article 157(1) which deals with the Community's industrial policy, and says that Community action shall be 'in accordance with a system of open and competitive markets'.

(ii) THE OBJECTIVES OF EC COMPETITION POLICY

Competition policy has been included in the list of Community activities set out in Article 3 since the inception of the Community in 1958. It was embedded in the Treaty right from the start as a set of wider policy goals oriented towards the objective of European economic integration. It was necessary in order to underpin the internal market aspect of the common market because there was no point in dismantling state measures which divided the Community territorially and compartmentalized the market if private undertakings could erect and maintain barriers to trade between Member States by carving up markets between them and indulging in anti-competitive practices.

This role of competition policy as an instrument of single market integration is absolutely crucial to any understanding of EC competition law. It makes EC law different from any system of domestic competition law, whether in the Member States, the USA, or elsewhere. EC competition law serves two masters, the 'competition' one and (even more demanding) the imperative of single market integration. This second goal has sometimes dictated the entire development of the law, particularly, as we shall see, in respect of vertical restraints.[78]

As the Community has matured competition policy has been seen as absolutely central to its development. This is reflected in the Commission's *Annual Reports on Competition*

---

[76] Until the TEU amendments in 1993 this provision was Art. 3(f) and read: 'the institution of a system ensuring that competition in the common market is not distorted'. It was reworded by the TEU and became Art. 3(g), and was again renumbered by the Treaty of Amsterdam to become the present Art. 3(1)(g).

[77] As Art. 3a.

[78] *Infra*, Chap. 9.

Policy,[79] for example, the *XIIIrd Report* (1993), which discusses, *inter alia*, the relationship between competition policy and industrial policy:[80]

Competition Policy has a central role to play in the Community's strategy for achieving a lasting recovery in growth and employment. The priorities which the Commission has set itself as regards competition are, therefore, largely determined by the contribution which competition policy can make to the Community's objective of growth, competitiveness and employment, as set out in the White Paper[81]. . .

Competition encourages the efficient allocation of resources and stimulates research and development, innovation and investment. It is the mechanism by which resources and jobs are redirected towards growing sectors and away from ones with less promising futures. The importance of this traditional role of competition policy has been reinforced in recent years in two ways. Firstly, its part in making a reality of the internal market which will create jobs, and stimulate growth and competitiveness is widely recognised. Secondly, it is central to the Community's industrial policy. The completion of a genuine internal market and an effective industrial policy have received first priority in the White Paper. This in itself implies the need for renewed vigour in competition policy in areas where it complements and enhances these objectives. . . .

. . . the Commission considers that, far from being the direct opposite of industrial policy, competition policy is an essential instrument, with clear complementarity between the two policies.

In his foreword to the Commission's 1997 *Report on Competition Policy* the then Competition Commissioner, Karel van Miert, considered competition policy in the light of the forthcoming introduction of the single currency. He said that in addition to the 'traditional objectives pursued by the Community through its competition policy (improving the competitiveness of business, both large and small, opening up markets, improving the allocation of resources, increasing consumer choice, etc)' competition policy 'can be expected to play a federating role in the years ahead'.[82] In 1998 the Commission further discussed the role of competition policy in the age of EMU.[83] It said that economic and monetary union would intensify competition for three reasons: first, by reinforcing the positive effects of the single market, as broader geographic markets would offer new opportunities to exploit economies of scale and lead to an increase in mergers and acquisitions; secondly, by increasing price transparency, allowing easier comparisons between prices in different Member States; and thirdly, by reducing the cost of capital, leading to an increase in mergers and to easier entry onto markets for entrepreneurs.

Commission's *XXVIIIth Report on Competition Policy* (E.C. Commission, 1998), 839

In the context of this overall pro-competitive impact of EMU, competition policy has an important role to play in safeguarding or enhancing the flexibility of product and service markets. Companies which are able to protect themselves through anticompetitive behaviour against competitive

---

[79] Published around the middle of each year, reporting on the activities of the Competition Directorate General for the preceding calendar year.

[80] Pt. 10.

[81] The 1993 Delors White Paper on Growth, Competitiveness and Employment: the Challenges and Ways Forward into the 21st Century, COM(93)700.

[82] *XXVIIth Report on Competition Policy* (Commission, 1997), 7 and 10.

[83] *XXVIIIth Report on Competition Policy* (Commission, 1998), Insert 1.

pressures are likely to be less efficient and innovative and hence less well able to adapt in the event of macroeconomic shocks.

Some companies will inevitably experience difficulties as a result of more intense competition. Consequently, Member States are likely to experience strong pressure to protect these companies by means of State aid, notably rescue and restructuring aid. Such aid can lead to serious distortion of competition at the expense of more efficient companies.

The potential for increased competition could also lead to attempts by companies to find ways to reduce the actual level of competition. For example, increased price transparency will create further incentives for parallel trade, but will also increase the temptation for companies to create new obstacles to arbitrage. Similarly, new competitive threats arising from EMU may induce incumbents to enter into vertical or horizontal agreements with the object of foreclosing rivals' markets, or alternatively to seek State aid. Finally, in the longer run, the expected increase in mergers and acquisitions could create oligopolies in some industries. Companies in these industries could be tempted to reduce the competitive pressure either by engaging in tacit collusion or by forming cartels. This will be made easier as the increased price transparency will facilitate the monitoring of competitors' prices. It will also be more difficult to deviate from agreed prices and hide this fact behind exchange rate fluctuations.

Competition policy therefore needs to remain vigilant to ensure that the Euro can deliver its full benefits. Both Community and national competition policy have a vital role to play in ensuring that product and service markets are flexible so that European consumers will truly benefit from the common currency.

It can be seen from the above quotations from Commission Reports that Community competition policy *is* concerned with efficiency and the allocation of resources, although its interaction with other Community policies means that efficiency in the neo-classical sense cannot be seen as the *sole* goal of the law as advocated by Chicago. Rather, competition policy is seen as part of the overall scheme of Community policies. Nonetheless it is important to know what guides the competition authorities in their day-to-day application of the rules. It will be seen from the account of this process in the following chapters that a number of objectives can be discerned. It seems clear that the competition rules have been used to promote allocative efficiency, but it is also true that in some cases the rules have been applied to further other objectives, for example of protecting or favouring small and medium-sized enterprises, keeping markets open, protecting competitors, protecting consumers in a 'non-technical' sense, and allowing co-operative enterprises which will advance European technology. These purposes sometimes conflict, and different ones may be favoured at different times and in different contexts. In 1998, for instance, Advocate General Jacobs reminded the Court that 'the primary purpose of Article [82][84] is to prevent distortion of competition—and in particular to safeguard the interests of consumers—rather than to protect the position of particular competitors'.[85]

European competition law has not nailed its colours to the mast of any particular competition ideology. In *Metro*[86] the Court of Justice said:

The requirement contained in Articles 3 and [81] of the EEC Treaty that competition shall not be distorted implies the existence on the market of workable competition, that is to say the degree of

---

[84] One of the two main competition law arts. See *infra*, in particular, Chaps. 5–7.

[85] Case C-7/97, *Oscar Bronner GmbH & Co KG* v. *Mediaprint* [1998] ECR I-7791, [1999] 4 CMLR 112, para. 58 of his Opinion.

[86] Case 26/76, *Metro* v. *Commission (No 1)* [1977] ECR 1875, [1978] 2 CMLR 1, para. 20.

competition necessary to ensure the observance of the basic requirements and the attainment of the objectives of the Treaty, in particular the creation of a single market achieving conditions similar to those of a domestic market. In accordance with this requirement the nature and intensiveness of competition may vary to an extent dictated by the products or services in question and the economic structure of the relevant market sectors.

The Court's concept of 'workable competition' here is related to what competition is intended to achieve in the Community context.

The best way of describing Community competition policy is to say that it aims to achieve 'effective competition'. This concept is to be found in the EC Merger Regulation. That Regulation provides that concentrations are to be allowed or prohibited depending on whether or not they create or strengthen a dominant position 'as a result of which effective competition would be significantly impeded in the common market'.[87] To understand what is meant by effective competition it is necessary to look back to the theories of competition and monopoly discussed earlier in this chapter.

Micro-economic analysis can explain why and when things happen and can predict outcomes, but it cannot answer questions about when regulators should intervene in markets because those are matters of policy. As Fox and Sullivan point out economics is not law. Economic analysis may provide the tools but the end to which the tools are used depends on the type of society the Community is trying to achieve.

5. TECHNIQUES OF COMPETITION LAW

A difficult question that must be faced by all authorities is how competition law should pursue its goals. The discussion above suggests that appropriate competition rules should be framed:

i   To control the existence of monopoly or other market power and its abuse;

ii   To control oligopolistic markets;

iii   To prevent mergers which lead to a concentration in market power;

iv   To prevent restrictive agreements between competitors (horizontal agreements); and

v   To prevent restrictive vertical agreements.

How such rules are interpreted and applied will also be crucial to the pursuit of those goals.

It is possible to adopt a system of competition law which takes a formalistic prohibitory approach based on the assumption that certain types of conduct are harmful. This was the position taken in the UK's restrictive trade practices legislation,[88] which has now been repealed and replaced by the Competition Act 1998. The legislation proscribed certain types of agreements between certain types of party concerning the matters listed in the Act. The Act did not admit the possibility of looking at the effect of agreements to see if they did in

---

[87] Council Reg. 4064/89 [1989] OJ L395/1, Art. 2(2) and (3).

[88] In its final form, the Restrictive Trade Practices Act (RTPA) 1976.

fact restrict competition. The matter was broadly denuded—deliberately—of economic content and the law reduced to a number of formal propositions. Judges did not, therefore, have to rule on economic matters.[89] The perverse result was a system which caught many harmless and even pro-competitive agreements but, conversely, allowed some which were seriously anti-competitive.[90]

EC competition law does not take this type of extreme formalistic approach. It is essentially an 'effects-based' law. The provisions are drafted in broad terms. Thus Article 81 of the EC Treaty broadly aims to prevent 'restrictive' agreements (see iv and v above); Article 82 broadly aims to prevent abuses of market power, in Article 82's terms a dominant position (see i above); and the Merger Regulation is intended to preclude mergers which lead to the creation or strengthening of a dominant position (or market power, see iii above).[91] Ironically, despite the economic base, the EC competition authorities have often been criticized for failing to take a sufficiently economically rigorous approach to the application of competition law and for having instead adopted a formalistic view. They, too, have sometimes operated on the assumption that certain things should be prohibited as a matter of course because they are bound to have an anti-competitive effect. More recently, the European Commission, which enforces the EC competition rules,[92] has displayed a greater willingness to use economic analysis.

Economic analysis is not, however, a panacea for all problems. It does not necessarily tell the competition authority what the outcome of any given agreement or conduct will be. It has already been seen that economists disagree over many things and economics do not provide the answer to every question. The applicability of a particular law may turn on the question whether or not a particular firm has market power. There may, however, be disagreement about what market that firm operates on (are pink widgets really substitutes for yellow widgets?) and about whether barriers to entry exist[93] to prevent other undertakings entering that market and challenging that firm's strong position. The economic view that monopoly is inefficient presents, therefore, only a starting-point to the application of the law in any particular case. Similarly, economists may disagree about to whether or not a particular agreement is or is not restrictive. A distribution agreement which decreases competition between A and B may in fact increase competition between A and C. Thus a distribution agreement, for example, in which X grants A the sole right to distribute its brand of goods, to the exclusion of B, may encourage A to market the goods actively so that X's product competes vigorously on the market with C's.[94]

It was seen in section 3 that there are fashions in economic theory and schools of antitrust analysis, and that today's orthodoxy may be overtaken by new ideas. Nevertheless, given that

---

[89] The original Restrictive Trade Practices Act was enacted in 1956 and the judiciary did not wish to have to decide such matters.

[90] The best account of the Restrictive Trade Practices Acts is set out in the 3rd edition of R. Whish, *Competition Law* (Butterworths, London, 1993) chap. 5, 123, which states 'the formalism and technical conundra have multiplied and the present law is extremely complex and riddled with anomalies and unanswered questions'.

[91] These Arts. are described in greater detail *infra* in Chap. 2 and are discussed fully in subsequent chaps. It can be seen immediately that EC law does not provide an obvious tool for dealing with oligopolistic market structures: see *infra* Chap. 11.

[92] See *infra* Chap. 2.

[93] See *infra* 52 ff.

[94] For the approach of EC law to this scenario see *infra* Chaps. 3, 4 and 9.

competition policy is concerned with economic structures, conduct, and effects, it must be correct that its application should be as economically literate as possible. Faull and Nikpay (a book written by a team of past and present officials of the EC Commission's Competition Directorate-General) explains the advantages and limitations of economic analysis in competition cases:[95]

J. Faull and A. Nikpay (eds), *The EC Law of Competition* (Oxford University Press, 1999) 4.

1.01 There is a growing awareness among competition policy makers of the importance of eco-nomics for their daily work. In the EU, admittedly with some delay compared to the US, it is now normal to discuss competition cases in terms of market power, entry barriers, sunk costs, etc and to evaluate cases according to their effects on the market. Competition policy is an economic policy concerned with economic structures, economic conduct, and economic effects. It is for this reason that in a book on competition law an introduction to the econom-ics of competition cannot be omitted.

1.02 The growing acceptance and importance of economics in competition policy also raises the question of the usefulness of economics for devising competition rules and deciding on competition cases. A word of caution may be in place in this respect. Economic thinking and economic models have not proven to be perfect guides.

1.03 Economic theories and economic models are built on and around assumptions. These assumptions by definition do not cover (all) real world situations. In addition, when the assumptions are changed the outcomes of the models may look strikingly different, changing for example the price from a monopoly level to a competitive price level. It is for these reasons that economics may often not be able to give a clear and definite answer on what will happen in a market when companies merge, when a company imposes a vertical restriction, or when companies try to collude.

1.04 The best economics can do in general is offer a number of useful concepts and models, exclude certain outcomes, and provide relevant arguments. In other words, it helps to tell the most plausible story. It may be useful by helping to formulate rules, devise safe harbours, indicate under what conditions anti-competitive outcomes are very unlikely or rather likely. In individual cases it will be necessary to find first the concepts and the model that fit best the description of the actual market conditions of the case and then to proceed with the analysis of the actual or possible competition consequences.

All competition laws exist to preserve competition in the market place and to deal in some way with monopoly power. Competition law should be concerned not with *forms* of com-petition for their own sake, but with their *outcome* for society. What *kind* of competitive outcomes the rules aim to ensure in the EC, and the way in which they do it, is the subject of this book.

---

[95] The book is expressed to be the authors' personal opinions, rather than the official position, but is obviously of particular interest because of their connection with the Competition Directorate General.

6. MARKET POWER, MARKET DEFINITION, AND BARRIERS TO ENTRY

A. MARKET POWER

It is clear from the discussion above that competition law is concerned, mainly or partially at least, with controlling the behaviour of firms which impede effective competition on a market and that a key concern is the exercise by firms of market power. It is firms which, individually or collectively, have market power that are able to restrict output, increase prices above the competitive level, and earn monopoly profits. It is this exercise of market power which leads to an inefficient result for society as a whole. In this section we introduce the concepts of market power, market definition, and barriers to entry which are central, and essential, to the discussion throughout this book.

Whether or not a firm has market power is dependent upon the elasticity of demand for its product, that is whether or not it can raise prices without losing sales. This will depend on a number of factors: in particular, whether or not if it raises prices consumers will purchase other products instead from elsewhere (what other products exist on the market), the number of other operators, if any, on the market, their respective market shares, the existence of barriers to entry to that market and the ability of potential competitors to enter the market. Of crucial importance is the determination of the relevant market. Market power arises only in relation to a market. This raises the important question of how a market is identified and defined. This issue is discussed below.[96] Market power also implies that an undertaking is protected from potential competitors who are prevented from gaining access to the market. Thus *barriers to entry* are vital to the determination of market power since it is these barriers which enable a firm already in the market to earn monopoly profits without attracting other firms to enter that market. The definition, identification, and significance of barriers to entry is one of the most controversial matters in antitrust economics. This issue is also discussed below.[97]

B. MARKET DEFINITION AND EC COMPETITION LAW

(i) THE IMPORTANCE OF MARKET DEFINITION

Market definition is a concept that is vital to *all* aspects of competition law. It is only by defining the relevant market that the competitive constraints affecting the firm or firms on that market can be identified and it can be considered whether or not effective competition on a market has been or will be distorted by conduct or threatened conduct. Competition has to be thought of in relation to the *relevant market* (or the 'antitrust market').

The purpose of defining the relevant market is to identify which products and services are

---

[96] See also, in particular, the discussion *infra* in Chap. 6.
[97] See also *infra* Chap. 6.

such close substitutes for one another that they operate as a competitive constraint on the behaviour of the suppliers of those respective products and services. Suppose, for example, you are suspicious that Y, the only producer of yellow widgets, is exercising market power and engaging in monopoly pricing. A preliminary question which must be asked is whether or not the product has substitutes to which customers could easily turn. If it does, then if Y raises prices it will lose customers. If customers can instead buy blue widgets and pink widgets, which are perfect substitutes, from other firms a rise in the price of yellow widgets will lead customers to buy (cheaper) blue and pink ones instead. Saying that Y has a 'monopoly' over the sale of yellow widgets is meaningless in economic terms. Similarly, suppose Y is the sole manufacturer of all colours of widgets. Y will still not be able to raise prices without losing customers if blodgets, which are made by other firms, are perfect substitutes for widgets. The problem of market definition is that it is often difficult to decide which products or services *are* in the same market. It is obvious, for example, that steel beams and chewing-gum are not in the same market, but what about coffee and tea,[98] vodka and whisky, bananas and apples, Eurostar and cross-Channel ferries? A relevant market has a product, geographic, and (sometimes) temporal aspect.

The extract from Bishop and Walker below explains the importance of the relevant market:

S. Bishop and M. Walker, *The Economics of EC Competition Law* (Sweet and Maxwell, London, 1999), 47

3.03 . . . [T]he definition of the relevant market is merely a tool for aiding the competitive assessment by identifying those substitute products or services which provide an effective constraint on the competitive behaviour of the products or services being offered in the market by the parties under investigation. In effect, the relevant market seeks to restrict attention only to those products or services which have a 'significant' impact on competition. As such, the definition of the relevant market represents only an intermediate step in the investigation.

Having established the intermediate role it plays in the competitive assessment, it is then possible to determine the appropriate basis for the definition of the relevant market. The definition of the relevant market can be a useful intermediate tool to aid the competitive assessment only if it is defined on a basis which is consistent with the aims of competition law. . . . One of the goals of E.C. competition law is the maintenance of effective competition. . . . the maintenance of effective competition can consistently be interpreted as preventing the exercise of market power. Whether a firm or firms can exercise market power will depend on the own-price elasticity of demand facing the firm of firms at the price level appropriate for the particular investigation. This in turn depends in part upon the availability of suitable substitutes for the products or services of the firm of firms in question. The definition of the relevant market is concerned with the identification of these substitute products or services. The appropriate basis for defining relevant markets is therefore one that focuses directly on the competitive constraints that products or services impose upon one another. Clearly, the approach to defining a relevant market must be consistent with this. This approach can be summarised by the guiding principle: 'A relevant market is something which is worth monopolising'.[99]

---

[98] See discussion *supra* 7.
[99] B. Owen and S. Wildman, *Video Economics* (Harvard University Press, 1992).

In the next sections we consider how the relevant market has been defined for the purposes of Community competition law. We also outline the way in which the Community institutions go about, or should go about, actually determining what the relevant market is in any given case. Greater detail of the way in which the market has actually been determined by the Community authorities is set out in the relevant chapters later in this book.

(ii) RELEVANT MARKET DEFINITION IN THE CASE LAW OF THE COURT OF JUSTICE

The importance of market definition has been recognized by the European Court. The Court has stressed that in most instances it is necessary to define the relevant market before a breach of the EC competition rules can be established.[100]

The Court of Justice defines the relevant market in terms of substitutability or interchangeability. It has thus adopted a definition of a relevant market which would accord with that given by economist. It describes the market as consisting of products[101] which are interchangeable with each other but not (or only to a limited extent) interchangeable with those outside it. This interchangeability may be with other products (widgets as substitutes for blodgets) or with the same products from elsewhere (widgets from France as substitutes for widgets from England). The relevant market therefore has both a product aspect (the product market) and a geographical aspect (the geographic market).

The Court of Justice has set out the following definitions of the relevant product market:

the definition of the relevant market is of essential significance, for the possibilities of competition can only be judged in relation to those characteristics of the products in question by virtue of which those products are particularly apt to satisfy an inelastic need and are only to a limited extent interchangeable with other products.[102]

The concept of the relevant market in fact implies that there can be effective competition between the products which form part of it and this presupposes that there is a sufficient degree of interchangeability between all the products forming part of the same market insofar as a specific use of such products is concerned.[103]

For the purposes of investigating the possibly dominant position of an undertaking on a given market, the possibilities of competition must be judged in the context of the market comprising the totality of other products which, with respect to their characteristics, are particularly suitable

---

[100] It is an essential component of the finding of dominance which is central to the application of Art. 82 (which, essentially, prohibits abuses of a dominant position) and the EC Merger Reg., Reg. 4064/89 [1989] OJ L395/1, as amended by Council Reg. 1310/97 [1997] OJ L180/1. Broadly, a merger's compatibility with the common market is dependent upon whether or not the merger leads to the creation or strengthening of a dominant position. It also plays a key role in the context of Art. 81 which aims to prevent restrictive agreements.

[101] Or services. The words 'products' and 'product market' encompass both products and services, as appropriate.

[102] Case 6/72, *Europemballage Corp and Continental Can Co Inc v. Commission* [1973] ECR 215, [1973] CMLR 199, para. 32.

[103] Case 85/76, *Hoffmann-La Roche & Co AG v. EC Commission* [1979] ECR 461, [1979] 3 CMLR 211, para. 28.

for satisfying constant needs and are only to a limited extent interchangeable with other products.[104]

In *United Brands* the Court set out the following definition of the geographic market:[105]

The opportunities for competition under Article [82] of the Treaty must be considered having regard to the particular features of the product in question and with reference to a clearly defined geographic area in which it is marketed and where the conditions of competition are sufficiently homogeneous for the effect of the economic power of the undertaking concerned to be able to be evaluated.

. . . .

The conditions for the application of Article [82] to an undertaking in a dominant position presuppose the clear delimitation of the substantial part of the Common Market in which it may be able to engage in abuses which hinder effective competition and this is an area where the objective conditions of competition applying to the product in question must be the same for all traders.

In some cases it may also have a temporal aspect.[106]

It will be seen in later chapters that in some cases the Court of Justice has upheld controversial decisions of the Commission delineating very narrow markets. In *United Brands*, for example, the Court upheld the finding that the market for bananas was separate from the market for other fruit.[107]

(iii) THE COMMISSION NOTICE ON THE DEFINITION OF THE RELEVANT MARKET FOR THE PURPOSES OF COMMUNITY COMPETITION LAW

a. THE PUBLICATION OF THE NOTICE

The European Commission plays the key role in the enforcement of the EC competition rules.[108] It will be seen throughout this book that on many occasions the Commission has been criticized for having failed to take due account of economic arguments and, frequently, for having failed to take a realistic approach to market definition; in particular, that it failed to consider economic principles in defining the relevant market. A welcome step taken in this regard by the Commission has been its publication in October 1997 of a Notice on the definition of the relevant market for the purposes of Community competition law (the 'Notice on market definition').[109] This Notice provides a framework for determining the relevant market which is based on economic principles and which has consequently been welcomed as a progressive and realistic approach to the matter. It has been taken as an indication of the 'modernization of DG IV'.[110]

---

[104] Case 322/81, *Nederlandsche Banden-Industrie Michelin* v. *Commission* [1983] ECR 3461, [1985] 1 CMLR 282, para. 37.

[105] Case 27/76 *United Brands* v. *Commission* [1978] ECR 207, [1978] 1 CMLR 429 at paras. 11 and 44.

[106] See *infra* Chap. 6.

[107] See *infra* Chap. 6.

[108] See *infra* Chap. 2.

[109] [1997] OJ C372/5, [1998] 4 CMLR 177.

[110] See e.g. W. Bishop, 'Editorial: The Modernisation of DGIV' [1997] 8 *ECLR* 481. DG IV was the previous number of the Competition Directorate-General of the Commission: see *infra* Chap. 2.

The Notice states that its purpose is to 'provide guidance as to how the Commission applies the concept of relevant product and geographic market in its ongoing enforcement of Community competition law' (paragraph 1). The Commission states that market definition is a tool to identify and define the boundaries of competition between firms and that it serves to establish the framework within which the Commission applies competition policy (paragraph 2).

The Notice indicates that it seeks to render public the procedures the Commission follows and the evidence which it relies upon in reaching decisions on market definition. By doing this it hopes to increase transparency and assist undertakings (paragraph 3). The Notice thus renders more transparent the Commission's practices and should lead to greater consistency in its decisions.

The Commission's approach set out in that Notice is outlined in this chapter since it describes economic principles which should be used to define the relevant market. It should be noted however that the Notice describes a process which is not evident in many of the Commission's previous decisions or the Court's judgments[111] (in fact at times it seems to be at odds with the existing case law[112]). Rather, it is more reflective of the new emerging practice of the Commission which has developed since the adoption of the EC Merger Regulation.[113] The Notice is not binding, it is not legislation[114] and is 'without prejudice to the interpretation which may be given by the European Court of Justice or the European Court of First Instance'.[115] The case law of the Court of Justice and relevant Commission decisions are described in their own contexts in subsequent chapters. The Commission's Notice is nevertheless of vital importance since it sets out the Commission's current approach to the matter.

b. THE DEFINITION OF THE RELEVANT MARKET

The definition of the relevant market adopted by the Commission in the Notice on market definition is based on that of the Court of Justice set out above.

Commission Notice on the definition of the relevant market for the purposes of Community competition law [1997] OJ C372/5, [1998] 4 CMLR 177

7. ... A relevant product market comprises all those products and/or services which are regarded as interchangeable or substitutable by the consumer, by reason of the products' characteristics, their prices and intended use.

8. ... The relevant geographic market comprises the area in which the undertakings concerned are involved in the supply and demand of products or services, in which the conditions of competition are sufficiently homogenous and which can be distinguished from neighbouring areas because the conditions of competition are appreciably different in those areas.

---

[111] At least in the context of Arts. 81 and 82, see especially Chap. 6.

[112] E.g., the treatment of 'unique suitability' in para. 43 differs from that of the ECJ in Case 27/76, *United Brands* v. *Commission* [1978] ECR 207, [1978] 1 CMLR 429, discussed *infra* Chap. 7

[113] See *infra* Chaps. 6 and 12.

[114] See *infra* Chap. 2.

[115] Commission Notice on market definition, para. 6.

Similar definitions are adopted in other Commission regulations and notices.[116]

c. DEMAND AND SUPPLY SUBSTITUTION

We have seen that the relevant market depends on the determination of which products in which areas are substitutes for one another. If a product has perfect substitutes the sole producer of such a product has no market power, because if that supplier tries to exploit his monopoly by raising the price his customers will turn to the substitutes. There are two aspects to substitutability. *Demand substitution* is concerned with the ability of users of the product to switch to substitute products. *Supply substitution* is concerned with the ability of producers of similar products to produce the product. *Potential competition* is also important. The behaviour of an undertaking on a market will be constrained if potential competitors are easily able to enter the market. Potential competition is, however, ordinarily taken into account not at the stage of market definition but later on in the competitive assessment when considering an undertaking's position on a market.[117]

When defining the relevant market both demand and supply substitutability have to be considered.[118] The Commission's Notice indicates however that the Commission mainly focuses on demand-side substitution.

Commission Notice on the definition of the relevant market for the purposes of Community competition law [1997] OJ C372/5, [1998] 4 CMLR 177

13. . . . From an economic point of view, for the definition of the relevant market, demand substitution constitutes the most immediate and effective disciplinary force on the suppliers of a given product, in particular in relation to their pricing decisions. A firm or a group of firms cannot have a significant impact on the prevailing conditions of sale, such as prices, if its customers are in a position to switch easily to available substitute products or to suppliers located elsewhere. Basically, the exercise of market definition consists in identifying the effective alternative sources of supply for the customers of the undertakings involved, in terms both of products/services and of geographical location of suppliers.

14. The competitive constraints arising from supply side substitutability other than those described in paragraphs 20 to 23 and from potential competition are in general less immediate and in any case require an analysis of additional factors. As a result such constraints are taken into account at the assessment stage of competition analysis.

Demand substitution

Demand substitution identifies which products a consumer considers to be substitutes for another. Unless products are totally homogeneous there will be no perfect substitutes. On the other hand, most products do have substitutes of some kind. Whether or not products

---

[116] See, e.g., section 6 of Form A/B and section C of Form C. Where firms notify agreements or mergers to the Commission they are asked to describe the relevant market on which they believe they operate, see *infra* Chap. 3. These sections define the relevant market.

[117] See *infra* Chap. 6.

[118] Case 6/72, *Europemballage Corp & Continental Can Co Inc* v. *Commission* [1973] ECR 215, [1973] CMLR 199 was lost by the Commission on the issue of demand substitution, see *infra* Chap. 6.

are substitutes for one another is dependent on a number of factors: in particular on customer preference, whether customers can switch immediately or need time to adapt, whether there is similarity in quality or price, and whether substitutes are available. The matter may be complicated if some customers can switch to substitutes but others cannot or if a product has several uses and there are substitutes for some of those uses but not for others. Interchangeability is gauged by measuring 'cross-elasticity of demand', as described above.

The primary method now adopted by the Commission for measuring the cross-elasticity of demand is set out in its Notice on market definition. The Commission relies upon the SSNIP test. This test reflects a more recent realistic approach adopted by the Commission to market definition. Subsequent chapters show that much Community authority is in fact indicative of a less scientific approach which has tended to encourage the adoption of arbitrary and narrow market definitions.[119]

SSNIP stands for a Small but Significant Non-transitory Increase in Price. This test has been adopted by competition authorities around the world: in the USA (where it was pioneered by the Department of Justice in 1982), in Canada, in New Zealand, and in Australia.[120] Its adoption by the Commission is welcomed as an approach which reflects contemporary economic analysis. The test applies as follows: a small (5–10 per cent) rise in the price of widgets is assumed. It is then asked whether this price increase would cause widget customers to purchase blodgets, or to purchase widgets from another area, to such an extent that the price rise is unprofitable. If the answer is yes, then blodgets and/or widgets from the other area form part of the same market.

Commission Notice on the definition of the relevant market for the purposes of Community competition law [1997] OJ C372/5, [1998] 4 CMLR 177

15. The assessment of demand substitution entails a determination of the range of products which are viewed as substitutes by the consumer. One way of making this determination can be viewed as a speculative experiment, postulating a hypothetical small, lasting change in relative prices and evaluating the likely reactions of customers to that increase. The exercise of market definition focuses on prices for operational and practical purposes, and more precisely on demand substitution arising from small, permanent changes in relative prices. This concept can provide clear indications as to the evidence that is relevant in defining markets.

16. Conceptually, this approach means that, starting from the type of products that the undertakings involved sell and the area in which they sell them, additional products and areas will be included in, or excluded from, the market definition depending on whether competition from these other products and areas affect or restrain sufficiently the pricing of the parties' products in the short term.

17. The question to be answered is whether the parties' customers would switch to readily available substitutes or to suppliers located elsewhere in response to a hypothetical small (in the

---

[119] See in particular the criticism of Commission decisions and the case law of the ECJ set out *infra* in Chap. 6.

[120] And in the UK it was approved in the 1992 OFT discussion paper, *Market Definition in UK Competition Policy*, OFT 049.

range of 5 to 10 per cent) but permanent relative price increase in the products and areas being considered. If substitution is enough to make the price increase unprofitable because of the resulting loss of sales, additional substitutes and areas are included in the relevant market. This would be done until the set of products and geographical areas is such that small, permanent increases in relative prices would be profitable. The equivalent analysis is applicable in cases concerning the concentration of buying power, where the starting point would then be the supplier and the price test serves to identify the alternative distribution channels or outlets for the supplier's products. In the application of these principles, careful account should be taken of certain particular situations as described within paragraphs 56 and 58.

18. A practical example of this test can be provided by its application to a merger of, for instance, soft-drink bottlers. An issue to examine in such a case would be to decide whether different flavours of soft drinks belong to the same market. In practice, the question to address would be whether consumers of flavour A would switch to other flavours when confronted with a permanent price increase of 5 to 10 per cent for flavour A. If a sufficient number of consumers would switch to, say, flavour B, to such an extent that the price increase for flavour A would not be profitable owing to the resulting loss of sales, then the market would compromise at least flavours A and B. The process would have to be extended in addition to other available flavours until a set of products is identified for which a price rise would not induce a sufficient substitution in demand.

19. Generally, and in particular for the analysis of merger cases, the price to take into account will be the prevailing market price. This may not be the case where the prevailing price has been determined in the absence of sufficient competition. In particular for the investigation of abuses of dominant positions, the fact that the prevailing price might already have been substantially increased will be taken into account.[121]

The SSNIP test is logical and simple. Its practical problem, however, is actually applying it. How are customers' reactions to the hypothetical price rise to be gauged?

The Commission attempts to answer this question in paragraphs 25–52 of the Notice. It stresses that it has an open approach to empirical evidence and recognizes that the types of evidence which will be relevant and influential will depend on the industry, product, or services in question. The Commission states that it can ordinarily establish the potential market from preliminary information available or submitted by firms involved. Frequently, the matter may boil down to a question as simple as is product A in the same market as product B? Where this is so, the case may be determined without a precise definition of the market being necessary (the outcome will be the same whether or not the markets are separate or the same). Where greater precision in market definition *is* necessary, the Commission may contact the main customers and companies in the industry, professional associations, and companies in upstream markets to ascertain their views. It may address written requests for information to the market players (including asking their views on reactions to hypothetical price increases and on market boundaries), enter into discussions with them, and even carry out visits to or inspections of the premises of the parties and/or their customers and competitors.

The Commission also states in the Notice[122] that it will consider quantitative tests devised by economists for the purpose of delineating markets. These include elasticity estimates, tests based on similarity of price movements over time, causality calculations, and price

---

[121] This is a recognition of the so-called 'cellophane fallacy'. See the discussion *infra* 46–48.
[122] Para. 39

convergence analysis. In particular, it will consider evidence of recent substitution in the past available as a result of actual events or shocks in the market. Indeed, the Commission indicates that 'this sort of information will normally be fundamental for market definition'.[123] Evidence of the consequences of past launches of new products on the sales of existing products is also described as useful.

The Notice indicates that reliance on product characteristics, intended use, and functional interchangeability is unlikely to play an important role in market definition. Such evidence has, however, played an important part in the case law of the European Court and cannot therefore be ignored.[124]

Commission Notice on the definition of the relevant market for the purposes of Community competition law [1997] OJ C372/5, [1998] 4 CMLR 177

36. An analysis of the product characteristics and its intended use allows the Commission, as a first step, to limit the field of investigation of possible substitutes. However, product characteristics and intended use are insufficient to show whether two products are demand substitutes. Functional interchangeability or similarity in characteristics may not, in themselves, provide sufficient criteria, because the responsiveness of customers to relative price changes may be determined by other considerations as well. For example, there may be different competitive constraints in the original equipment market for car components and in spare parts, thereby leading to a separate delineation of two relevant markets. Conversely, differences in product characteristics are not in themselves sufficient to exclude demand substitutability, since this will depend to a large extent on how customers value different characteristics.

The Commission Notice deals with particular problems in demand substitution, such as the chain of substitution (in paragraph 57), the problem where there are primary and secondary markets (paragraph 56), and the situation where products are substitutes for some customers but not for others (paragraph 43). These matters are all considered in Chapter 6.

Another major problem with the SSNIP test is the problem of the 'cellophane fallacy'. Paragraph 19 of the Notice[125] recognizes the difficulties presented by the cellophane fallacy (although it does not refer to it as such). The fallacy is so named after the subject-matter of an American case in which the Supreme Court is said to have failed to recognize it.[126] The cellophane fallacy is described by Bishop and Walker in the extract below.

---

[123] Para. 38. Economics is not an experimental science. The consequences of something happening which really affects the products available on the market (e.g. a shortage arising from a natural disaster) are therefore particularly significant.

[124] See *infra* Chap. 6.

[125] See *supra* p. 45.

[126] *United States* v. *EI du Pont de Nemours & Co*, 351 US 377.

S. Bishop and M. Walker, *The Economics of EC Competition Law: Concepts, Application and Measurement* (Sweet & Maxwell, 1999), 49

3.06 Many commentators have noted a potentially fundamental pitfall in the use of demand elasticities in inferring either market power or the extent of the relevant market. The problem arises from a standard result of economic theory, namely that any profit-maximising firm will always set prices at a level where demand for its product is elastic. As a consequence, with the existence of monopoly power at monopoly price levels, many products may appear to be close substitutes whereas, at a competitive price, substitution would not take place. The degree of substitution between products depends upon current prices of the two products concerned. The mere fact that at the monopoly price, a monopolised product faces demand substitutes does not mean that the firms producing the product has no market power. In other words in non-merger inquiries observed own-price elasticities may well understate the degree of market power.

This is known in competition policy analysis as the *Cellophane fallacy* after the celebrated *Du Pont* case . . . In that case, Du Pont argued that cellophane was not a separate relevant market since it competed directly and closely with flexible packaging materials such as aluminium foil, wax paper and polyethylene. Bus, as many commentator have since noted, the conclusion is a circular one, since *Du Pont*, as the sole supplier of cellophane, it is likely to have set prices for its products at levels where alternative products provide an effective competitive constraint on the pricing of cellophane only if the prevailing prices is the competitive price. The U.S. Supreme Court in this case failed to recognise that a high own-price elasticity may mean that a firm is already exercising monopoly power.

The difficulty is therefore that a profit-maximizing firm will price as high as it can. If X is the sole supplier of widgets it will normally set the price of widgets at a level where other products constrain it. If the marginal cost of a widget is £5 but blodgets, which perform the function as widgets, are sold at their marginal cost of £10, X will sell widgets at just under £10. That way X still makes a supra-normal profit and does not lose out to the blodget manufacturers. At the price of £10 blodgets and widgets are substitutes, and X can argue, as Du Pont did in the *Cellophane* case, that since it cannot raise the price without losing sales it must be operating on a competitive market. The fallacy arises, however, since X is *already* making a monopoly profit. It may have no substitutes at its competitive price of £5. There may be substitutes however at the price of £10. In the *Cellophane* case the Supreme Court found that the market was that for all flexible wrapping materials as other materials competed with cellophane at its current price. It did not ask, however, whether or not cross-elasticity between cellophane and other materials was only high *because Du Pont was already exercising market power*. The Notice recognizes this difficulty. The Commission states that using the prevailing market price as the base figure from which to hypothesize the 5–10 per cent price rise of the SSNIP test may be inappropriate where that price has been determined in the absence of competition. This means that great care will have to be exercised if using the SSNIP test to determine whether or not an incumbent on a market has a 'dominant position' (or market power) for the purposes of Article 82.[127] In contrast, in merger cases it has only to be decided whether or not the merger will create or *increase* market power. The

---

[127] EC law terminology for market power. See *infra* Chaps. 5 and 6.

SSNIP test is thus much more reliable since the prevailing market price is used as the starting point.

Supply substitution

The Court of Justice in *Continental Can*[128] stressed that the market must be defined by reference both to supply side and demand side substitutability. If a manufacturer of one product can easily switch its production to another product then both products may be in the same market. A difficulty here is to distinguish supply-side substitutability from potential competition. The Commission considers this dilemma in the Notice and concludes that it is a question of time scale. If a producer of one product can switch production in the short term to produce another product, without significant cost or risk, then those two products will be found to be in the same market. If a producer can enter the market but only in the longer term and after incurring some cost, then that producer's presence is not relevant at the stage of market definition. Its presence will be crucial, however, when assessing market power. If the producer can enter the market then it is a potential competitor and its existence will have a constraining effect on those operating on the market.[129] Supply substitution is likely to be possible only where producers make similar products which nonetheless are not substitutes for one another from the consumer's perspective. An example, given by the Commission in its notice, is markets for paper.

Commission Notice on the definition of the relevant market for the purposes of Community competition law [1997] OJ C372/5, [1998] 4 CMLR 177

20. Supply-side substitutability may also be taken into account when defining markets in those situations in which its effects are equivalent to those of demand substitution in terms of effectiveness and immediacy. This means that suppliers are able to switch production to the relevant products and market them in the short term . . . without incurring significant additional costs or risks in response to small and permanent changes in relative prices. When these conditions are met, the additional production that is put on the market will have a disciplinary effect on the competitive behaviour of the companies involved. Such an impact in terms of effectiveness and immediacy is equivalent to the demand substitution effect.

21. These situations typically arise when companies market a wide range of qualities or grades of one product; even if, for a given final customer or group of consumers, the different qualities are not substitutable, the different qualities will be grouped into one product market, provided that most of the suppliers are able to offer and sell the various qualities immediately and without the significant increases in costs described above. In such cases, the relevant product market will encompass all products that are substitutable in demand and supply, and the current sales of those products will be aggregated so as to give the total value or volume of the market. The same reasoning may lead to group different geographic areas.

22. A practical example of the approach to supply-side substitutability when defining product markets is to be found in the case of paper. Paper is usually supplied in a range of different qualities, from standard writing paper to high quality papers to be used, for instance, to publish

---

[128] Case 6/72, *Europemballage Corp & Continental Can Co Inc* v. *Commission* [1973] ECR 215, [1973] CMLR 199.

[129] See *supra* 38.

art books. From a demand point of view, different qualities of paper cannot be used for any given use, i.e. an art book or a high quality publication cannot be based on lower quality papers. However, paper plants are prepared to manufacture the different qualities, and production can be adjusted with negligible costs and in a short time-frame. In the absence of particular difficulties in distribution, paper manufacturers are able therefore, to compete for orders of the various qualities, in particular if orders are placed with sufficient lead time to allow for modification of production plans. Under such circumstances, the Commission would not define a separate market for each quality of paper and its respective use. The various qualities of paper are included in the relevant market, and their sales added up to estimate total market value and volume.

23. When supply-side substitutability would entail the need to adjust significantly existing tangible and intangible assets, additional investments, strategic decisions or time delays, it will not be considered at the stage of market definition. Examples where supply-side substitution did not induce the Commission to enlarge the market are offered in the area of consumer products, in particular for branded beverages. Although bottling plants may in principle bottle different beverages, there are costs and lead times involved (in terms of advertising, product testing and distribution) before the products can actually be sold. In these cases, the effects of supply-side substitutability and other forms of potential competition would then be examined at a later stage.

One criticism sometimes made of the Commission is that it places too little emphasis on supply-side substitutability. This may encourage too narrow definitions of the market to be adopted.[130]

The Geographic Market

It is also essential that the geographic market is defined. The Court of Justice in *United Brands* stressed the importance of defining the market from a geographic perspective.[131] Because market definition is determined by reference to substitutability it is possible that even firms producing identical products will not operate in the same market if they operate within mutually exclusive geographic areas. However, where, for example, a customer in England may be able to substitute French widgets for English ones the English producer will not have market power if the small but significant price rise causes his customers to purchase French widgets instead. Whether or not geographic areas are mutually exclusive— whether the geographic market in a particular product is global, local, or something in between—will depend on a number of factors, most notably the cost of transport, the nature of the product, and legal regulation. If transport costs are high relative to the value of the product, as in the case of paving slabs or concrete tiles, a geographic market may be small, perhaps even local.

The Commission sets out its current approach to geographical market definition in its notice and indicates the type of evidence it considers to be relevant to the determination.

---

[130] For a more detailed discussion of this see *infra* Chap. 6.
[131] Case 27/76, *United Brands* v. *Commission* [1978] ECR 207, [1978] 1 CMLR 429.

Commission Notice on the definition of the relevant market for the purposes of Community competition law [1997] OJ C372/5, [1998] 4 CMLR 177

28. The Commission's approach to geographic market definition might be summarized as follows: it will take a preliminary view of the scope of the geographic market on the basis of broad indications as to the distribution of market shares between the parties and their competitors, as well as a preliminary analysis of pricing and price differences at national and Community or EEA level. This initial view is used basically as a working hypothesis to focus the Commission's enquiries for the purposes of arriving at a precise geographic market definition.

29. The reasons behind any particular configuration of prices and market shares need to be explored. Companies might enjoy high market shares in their domestic markets just because of the weight of the past, and conversely, a homogeneous presence of companies throughout the EEA might be consistent with national or regional geographic markets. The initial working hypothesis will therefore be checked against an analysis of demand characteristics (importance of national or local preferences, current patterns of purchases of customers, product differentiation/brands, other) in order to establish whether companies in different areas do indeed constitute a real alternative source of supply for consumers. The theoretical experiment is again based on substitution arising from changes in relative prices, and the question to answer is again whether the customers of the parties would switch their orders to companies located elsewhere in the short term and at a negligible cost.

30. If necessary, a further check on supply factors will be carried out to ensure that those companies located in differing areas do not face impediments in developing their sales on competitive terms throughout the whole geographic market. This analysis will include an examination of requirements for a local presence in order to sell in that areas the conditions of access to distribution channels, costs associated with setting up a distribution network, and the presence or absence of regulatory barriers arising from public procurement, price regulations, quotas and tariffs limiting trade or production, technical standards, monopolies, freedom of establishment, requirements for administrative authorizations, packaging regulations, etc. In short, the Commission will identify possible obstacles and barriers isolating companies located in a given area from the competitive pressure of companies located outside that area, so as to determine the precise degree of market interpenetration at national, European or global level.

    . . . .

44. The type of evidence the Commission considers relevant to reach a conclusion as to the geographic market can be categorized as follows:

45. *Past evidence of diversion of orders to other areas.* In certain cases, evidence on changes in prices between different areas and consequent reactions by customers might be available. Generally, the same quantitative tests used for product market definition might as well be used in geographic market definition, bearing in mind that international comparisons of prices might be more complex due to a number of factors such as exchange rate movements, taxation and product differentiation.

46. *Basic demand characteristics.* The nature of demand for the relevant product may in itself determine the scope of the geographical market. Factors such as national preferences or preferences for national brands, language, culture and life style, and the need for a local presence have a strong potential to limit the geographic scope of competition.

47. *Views of customers and competitors.* Where appropriate, the Commission will contact the main customers and competitors of the parties in its enquiries, to gather their views on the

boundaries of the geographic market as well as most of the factual information it requires to reach a conclusion on the scope of the market when they are sufficiently backed by factual evidence.

48. *Current geographic pattern of purchases.* An examination of the customers' current geographic pattern of purchases provides useful evidence as to the possible scope of the geographic market. When customers purchase from companies located anywhere in the Community or the EEA on similar terms, or they procure their supplies through effective tendering procedures in which companies from anywhere in the Community or the EEA submit bids, usually the geographic market will be considered to be Community-wide.

49. *Trade flows/pattern of shipments.* When the number of customers is so large that it is not possible to obtain through them a clear picture of geographic purchasing patterns, information on trade flows might be used alternatively, provided that the trade statistics are available with a sufficient degree of detail for the relevant products. Trade flows provide useful insights and information for the purpose of establishing the scope of the geographic market but are not in themselves conclusive.

50. *Barriers and switching costs associated to divert orders to companies located in other areas.* The absence of trans-border purchases or trade flows, for instance, does not necessarily mean that the market is at most national in scope. Still, barriers isolating the national market have to be identified before it is concluded that the relevant geographic market in such a case is national. Perhaps the clearest obstacle for a customer to divert its orders to other areas is the impact of transport costs and transport restrictions arising from legislation or from the nature of the relevant products. The impact of transport costs will usually limit the scope of the geographic market for bulky, low-value products, bearing in mind that a transport disadvantage might also be compensated by a comparative advantage in other costs (labour costs or raw materials). Access to distribution in a given area, regulatory barriers still existing in certain sectors, quotas and custom tariffs might also constitute barriers isolating a geographic area from the competitive pressure of companies located outside that area. Significant switching costs in procuring supplies from companies located in other countries constitute additional sources of such barriers.

51. On the basis of the evidence gathered, the Commission will then define a geographic market that could range from a local dimension to a global one, and there are examples of both local and global markets in past decisions of the Commission.

52. The paragraphs above describe the different factors which might be relevant to define markets. This does not imply that in each individual case it will be necessary to obtain evidence and assess each of these factors. Often in practice the evidence provided by a subset of these factors will be sufficient to reach a conclusion, as shown in the past decisional practice of the Commission.

It will be seen in later chapters that the Community authorities' approach to the geographic market has often been criticized for failing to give sufficient attention to substitutability between different geographic areas. As in the case of the product market the geographic market has often been drawn narrowly.

C. BARRIERS TO ENTRY

(i) THE ROLE OF BARRIERS TO ENTRY

'Barriers to entry' are also crucial when determining whether or not a firm is a monopolist or has significant market power on a market. Even if a firm with a 100 per cent share of a market may not, in economic terms, have a monopoly. Market shares tell us nothing about *why* the firm has such a high market share or about potential competition. It tells us only about the current state of competition. A firm will not be able to charge monopoly prices if other firms can freely enter the market and compete with it. It is the monopoly prices which indicate to others that entry to the market is possible. Whether or not a firm really does have a monopolist's power over price is, therefore, dependent on how vulnerable it is to new entrants. Whether or not a market is vulnerable to new entrants is dependent upon 'barriers to entry'. A firm can exercise market power for a significant time only if barriers to entry exist. As Bork states:[132] '[t]he concept of barriers to entry is crucial to antitrust debate. . . . The ubiquity and potency of the concept are undeniable'.

It is difficult to give even the loosest definition of what 'barriers to entry' means without participating in the debate which has raged for many years between different schools of economic thought.[133] To put it as neutrally as possible, however, a barrier to entry may be described as something which hinders the emergence of potential competition which would otherwise constrain the incumbent undertaking. It prevents new entrants entering the market.[134] The difficulty of course is to determine *what* will deter potential competition from emerging in the market.

(ii) THE DEFINITION OF A BARRIER TO ENTRY

As stated above, there is no single accepted definition of a 'barrier to entry'. The seminal work on barriers to entry was that of J. S. Bain[135] who belonged to the Harvard school.[136] Bain described barriers to entry as:

the extent to which, in the long run, established firms can elevate their selling prices above the minimal average costs of production and distribution . . . without inducing potential entrants to enter the industry.

This defines barriers to entry in an effects-based way. In contrast, Stigler, a leading exponent of the Chicago school,[137] adopted a narrower definition, focusing on the differences in demand and cost conditions suffered by incumbent firms and potential entrants respectively. He defined a barrier to entry as:

---

[132] R. Bork, *The Antitrust Paradox: A Policy at War With Itself* (Basic Books, 1978), 310–11.

[133] See *supra* 20–27.

[134] Even these statements are dangerous however, as they could include superior efficiency as a barrier to entry.

[135] J. S. Bain, 'Economies of Scale, Concentration, and the Condition of Entry in Twenty Manufacturing Industries' (1954) 44 *Am.Econ.Rev.* 15, *Barriers to New Competition* (Harvard University Press, 1956), and *Industrial Organization* (2nd edn., John Wiley, Chichester, 1968).

[136] See *supra* 20.

[137] See *supra* 21.

a cost of producing (at some or every rate of output) which must be borne by a firm which seeks to enter the industry but is not borne by firms already in the industry.[138]

The definition of Baumol and Willig[139] followed Stigler:

anything that requires an expenditure by a new entrant into an industry, but that imposes no equivalent costs upon an incumbent.

Von Weizsäcker[140] adopted the Stigler approach but added an economic welfare dimension:

A cost of producing which must be borne by a firm which seeks to enter an industry but is not borne by firms already in the industry and which implies a distortion on the allocation of resources from the social point of view.

Another significant definition is that of Gilbert:[141]

a barrier to entry is a rent that is derived from incumbency. It is the additional profit that a firm can earn as a sole consequence of being established in an industry.

This approach follows Bain but emphasizes 'first-mover advantages', that is the advantage the firm derives simply from being on the market before its potential competitors, rather than absolute costs advantages.[142]

A wide spectrum of definitions has thus been suggested, each having different emphases and each incorporating different things within it. The essential debate still remains, however, over whether the definition adopted by Bain or by Stigler and the Chicago school is more appropriate or accurate. The Bain approach results in many things being identified as barriers. Conversely, the definition adopted by Stigler means that very few things constitute barriers to entry. For example, Bain's approach, unlike Stigler's, accepts that market conduct may operate as a barrier to entry because the definition is effects-based. Further, Bain's definition admits that economies of scale may operate as a barrier to entry, since they deter new entrants and so allow prices to remain above minimum unit cost. Stigler's definition does not, however, accept that economies of scale operate as a barrier since both incumbents and new competitors have to face them at the time they enter the market. There is therefore no asymmetry which the Stigler definition demands.

It is the Bain approach which today has the greatest influence in industrial economics and which is ordinarily used in antitrust decisions in the USA.[143] Herbert Hovenkamp in the extract below explains why this is so.

---

[138] G. J. Stigler, *The Organization of Industry* (Irwin, 1968), 67.

[139] W. Baumol and R. Willig, 'Fixed Costs, Sunk Costs, Entry Barriers and Sustainability of Monopoly' (1981) 95 *Quarterly Journal of Economics* 405, 408.

[140] C. von Weizsäcker, 'A Welfare Analysis of Barriers to Entry' (1980) 11 *Bell J. Econ.* 399, 400.

[141] R. Gilbert, 'Mobility Barriers and the Value of Incumbency' in R. Schmalensee and R. Willig (eds.), *Handbook of Industrial Organization* (North Holland, 1989), 478.

[142] See *infra* 55 ff.

[143] And in the *Horizontal Merger Guidelines* (1992, revised 1997) promulgated by the Department of Justice's Antitrust Division.

H. Hovenkamp, *Federal Antitrust Policy: The Law of Competition and Its Practice* (West Publishing Co, 1994), 40

The difference between the two definitions of entry barriers can be quite substantial. For example, under the Bainian definition economies of scale is a qualifying barrier to entry. If scale economies are significant, then incumbent firms with established markets may have a large advantage over any new entrant, who will enter the market at a low rate of output. As a result, scale economies can permit incumbent firms to earn monopoly returns up to a certain point without encouraging new entry.

By contrast, scale economies are not a qualifying entry barrier under the Stiglerian definition. Both incumbent firms and new entrants had to deal with them at the time of entry; so scale economies are not a cost that applies only to new entrants.

The Stiglerian conception of entry barriers is based on a powerful analytic point: entry barrier analysis should distinguish desirable from undesirable entry. If prospective entrants face precisely the same costs that incumbents faced but still find entry unprofitable, then this market has probably already attained the appropriate number of players, even though monopoly profits are being earned. For example, suppose that minimum efficient scale (MES) in a market requires a 30% market share. Such a market has room for only three MES firms—and a three-firm market is quite likely to perform oligopolistically or else be conducive to collusion. The Stiglerian approach to entry barriers would say that, although monopoly profits are being earned in the industry, entry barriers should not be counted as high because entry by a fourth firm is not socially desirable. Additional entry would force at least one firm to be of suboptimal size, and eventually one of the four would probably exit the market. . . . The socially desirable solution to the problem of oligopoly performance in this market is not to force entry of a fourth, inefficiently small firm; but rather to look for alternative measures that make collusion more difficult.

Nevertheless, antitrust analysis has mainly used the Bainian rather than the Stiglerian definition of entry barriers. The Bainian definition is written into the 1992 Horizontal Merger Guidelines promulgated by the Justice Department's Antitrust Division and the Federal Trade Commission (FTC). . . . In all antitrust decisions except for a few in the FTC, tribunals have relied on the Bainian definition. . . .

Although the Stiglerian approach to entry barriers offers a useful insight into the relationship between market structure and socially desirable entry, there are nevertheless good reasons for antitrust policy to prefer the Bainian approach. In particular, the Bainian definition is free of the value judgment of what constitutes socially desirable entry. This is important because the existence of entry barriers is not itself an antitrust violation. The antitrust policy maker does not use entry barrier analysis in order to consider whether further entry into a market is socially desirable; the market itself will take care of that question. Rather, the question is whether a particular practice is plausibly anticompetitive. This distinction is critically important because we know so little about the minimum efficient scale of operation in any given market.

The debate about barriers to entry is not some theoretical discussion akin to mediaeval theologians debating the number of angels on the head of a pin. It is absolutely vital to the determination of market power. If factors are too readily identified as entry barriers a firm may be wrongly found to have market power and its conduct may then be constrained by competition laws. Similarly a merger between two firms may be prohibited even though it does not lead to the firms acquiring market power. This may mean that the competitive process is actually harmed by competition law since it interferes with and impedes the behaviour of firms operating on a competitive market. On the other hand, if the possibility of entry barriers is too easily dismissed, undertakings which *do* have market power might escape the prohibitions of competition law and mergers which create or strengthen market power might be allowed.

How barriers to entry are conceived is related to industrial organization theory. We have already seen above[144] that Bain was an important contributor to the development of the 'structure → conduct → performance' paradigm. This theory sought to show that certain industry structures dictate that the firms in the industry will engage in certain types of conduct which will in turn lead to a certain kind of economic performance. The paradigm was attacked by the Chicago school. Nonetheless it has had such an enduring influence on antitrust analysis that it is now clear that market structure can never be ignored.[145] However, modern industrial organization (IO) theory stresses the strategic competition of undertakings. This theory looks to the effect which conduct has on structure, rather than vice versa, and considers that whether a new entrant will enter a market will depend, at least in part, on the conditions of competition it will face post-entry. Thus predatory behaviour by the incumbent firm may constitute a barrier to entry. The theory also emphasizes the importance that 'sunk costs' may have on a firm's decision to enter a market. Sunk costs are costs which cannot be recovered on exiting a market.

D. Harbord and T. Hoehn, 'Barriers to Entry and Exit in European Competition Policy' (1994) 14 *International Review of Law and Economics* 411, 413–15

2.2 Strategic Competition and Entry

Modern industrial organization theory, although based upon a large number of particular game-theoretic models and examples, has nevertheless succeeded in isolating a number of crucial factors from which a categorization or 'typology' of barriers to entry may be derived. At the most general level, the message of the new IO is that an analysis of business strategy, or strategic competition, is fundamental to the analysis of particular industries. The Bain paradigm, which analysed industries in terms of a causative chain from structure to conduct to performance, and in which structure was largely determined by technological factors, has been supplanted by an approach that emphasizes the effect of conduct (i.e., strategic interaction) on industry structure and performance. In brief, how firms compete partly determines how concentrated industries will be. Specifically, what is important for entry decisions is the nature of competition post-entry that potential entrants must factor into their decisions.

This has been expressed in a number of ways. Sutton (1991) uses the concept of the 'thoroughness of price competition' in classifying entry conditions in various industries, a concept that describes 'how prices change with market structure.' Bresnahan and Reiss (1990, 1991) suggest a function 'which determines how fast industry margins shrink with entry.' However, the important point is that no analysis of a market or industry, and in particular an assessment of market power and entry barriers, can void an analysis of strategic competition, because it is this that determines entrants' expectations of the profitability of entry, and ultimately their entry decisions. Thus

Lesson I. The analysis of strategic interaction is necessary to an understanding of industry structure and concentration, and in particular analysis of post-entry competition is fundamental to an assessment of entry conditions.

---

[144] *Supra* 20.
[145] *Supra* 20 ff.

2.3 Sunk Costs and Commitments

The second lesson from modern IO theory is the crucial role played by sunk costs in entry (and exit) decisions. Sunk costs are costs that cannot be recovered on exiting an industry, and hence serve to commit a firm or firms to staying in the market. The U.S. Department of Justice Horizontal Merger Guidelines define sunk costs as 'the acquisition costs of tangible or intangible assets that cannot be recovered through redeployment of those assets outside the relevant market.'

There are three important aspects of sunk costs that influence entry and exit decisions. First, sunk costs increase the risk of entering an industry because they cannot be recouped on exiting. Second, sunk costs create a cost asymmetry between entrants and incumbents. Once costs are sunk they are no longer a portion of opportunity costs of production, and hence an incumbent will require a lower return on costs in order to stay in an industry than will be required to enter. Asymmetries of this type have been modelled by Dixit (1979, 1981) and many others. Third, sunk costs can serve as a commitment by incumbent firms not to exit the industry. (For this reason Gilbert (1989) refers to them as 'exit costs.') Thus sunk costs are central to the calculations of potential entrants because if entry involves sunk costs it will be deterred if they are unlikely to be recouped, and incumbent firms may be able to exploit this fact strategically in a variety of ways.

The importance of sunk costs can be seen from a (much-discussed) simple example, which also illustrates the interaction of sunk costs with post-entry competition to create an entry barrier. Consider a market with two potential entrants, each of which face a sunk entry F and constant variable cost per unit of production c (i.e., there are no capacity constraints). If a single firm enters, it will charge the monopoly price P^m and earn monopoly profits. The second firm will then enter if and only if the expected price post-entry P^e, exceeds $c + F/q$, where q is the firm's expected post-entry output. . . .

The above example is simple but illustrates clearly how sunk costs interact with post-entry competition to create a first-mover or incumbency advantage, even in the absence of strategic preemptive behaviour. The recent IO literature has also identified numerous means by which investments involving sunk costs can be used strategically to limit or deter entry in more complex environments. . . . They may be roughly classified as follows.

- investments to lower the incumbent's costs relative to those of potential entrants, that is, capacity, patents, R&D, take or pay contracts with input suppliers, learning-by-doing, etc.
- investments to alter the cost structure of rivals, that is, take or pay contracts, sleeping patents, monopolization of inputs, vertical control, etc.
- investments to favourably alter demand conditions, that is, advertising, brand proliferation, long-term contracts with buyers etc.

In all of these examples commitment is essential, and hence the importance of sunk costs. Thus

Lesson II.   Sunk costs are fundamental to the calculations of potential entrants, and the identification of sunk costs that cannot be recovered on exiting an industry is crucial to the assessment of entry conditions. Strategic behaviour and post-entry competition combined with sunk costs are an important determinant of market structure via their effects on entry and exit decisions.

This industrial organization theory therefore stresses the importance of sunk costs. This means that barriers to entry can be separated into two classes: absolute (cost) advantages and strategic entry barriers. This view is summarized in the conclusions of a 1994 report commissioned by the Office of Fair Trading from London Economics.[146]

---

[146] The article by Harbord and Hoehn quoted above is based on the work done for that report.

Barriers to Entry and Exit in Competition Policy, **OFT Research Paper 2, 57–9**

5.1 Economic analysis of entry barriers

What is the key to the full analysis of entry barriers is therefore the careful appreciation and analysis of the entry conditions in a particular market. . . . [W]e distinguish between two types of asymmetries between incumbent firms and potential entrants which give rise to entry barrier, viz:

(i) *absolute* incumbent advantages, i.e. incumbent access to some factor of production that is denied (on equivalent terms) to potential contracts;

(ii) *strategic* incumbent advantages, typically arising from first-mover advantages in the presence of sunk costs and associated behaviour. These are related to:

- economies of scale
- product differentiation, advertising and goodwill
- capital requirements
- vertical foreclosure and exclusion
- predatory behaviour

5.1.1 Absolute advantages

In considering absolute cost advantages it is important to take account of relevant *opportunity* costs. Some absolute advantages result from public policies designed to stimulate innovation activity. Dynamic incentive effects must also be considered in innovative industries, where an important issue is the degree of competition at the level of innovation.

In so-called '*contestable*' markets there are no absolute asymmetries, no sunk costs, and incumbents are constantly vulnerable to 'hit-and-run' entry threats. The relevance of contestable market theory to public policy is open to question, however, not least because the theory appears to be non-robust to the assumption of zero sunk costs, which will not be a good approximation to the bulk of industries where competition policy concerns are raised.

5.1.2 Strategic entry barriers

Our classification of strategic entry barriers into five groups aids in the identification of factors which may create or strengthen 'first-mover' advantages:

Economies of scale may deter entry, even without strategic behaviour, in particular when these imply that entry:

(i) requires large sunk costs, and,

(ii) would cause tougher price competition. It is for these reasons, which strategic behaviour may add to, that *scale economies* can be entry barriers

However whenever entry involves the sinking of substantial costs, it is the expectations of entrants regarding **post-entry prices** that matter. Incumbents may be able to influence those expectations, in such a way as to deter entry, by altering future incumbents costs, raising rivals costs, future demand conditions, or potential entrants' beliefs about the likely response in the event of entry.

Product differentiation, advertising and goodwill can also be entry barriers, but for deeper reasons than have sometimes been suggested, relating to brand proliferation, scale economy and sunk cost effects of advertising, switching costs, pioneering brand advantages, and information asymmetries. Product differentiation can, of course, also be a means of entry.

Capital requirements more often reflect or are related to other barriers to entry (e.g. those associated with large sunk costs or predatory behaviour) than constituting entry barriers by themselves, though this is possible.

An important class of entry barriers relate to *vertical foreclosure and exclusion.* As was shown by the 'Chicago' school of antitrust analysis, the economics of vertical practices are complex, and superficially 'anti-competitive' vertical practices may in fact be pro-competitive and efficient. However, contrary to the Chicago School, practices such as refusal to supply, exclusive dealing, tying and vertical integration can create entry barriers under a range of circumstances, in particular where there is a horizontal market power in the upstream or downstream market. Such power can be extended vertically by means of vertical practices and hence they call for entry barrier analysis in many cases.

The Chicago School also argued that *predatory pricing* would be non-existent or very rare, on the grounds that it would not be in the incumbent's interests. Recent analysis of predatory behaviour in relation to financial market imperfections and reputation-for-toughness effects has shown that the possibility of predatory behaviour cannot be dismissed in this way.

5.2 Assessment of entry conditions in practise [sic]
Our discussion of the lessons from the theoretical literature of the past 10–15 years has important implications for the design of an appropriate methodology for the assessment of entry conditions in competition policy and practice, in the UK and elsewhere.

There is no single best or easy way to assess entry conditions or entry barriers. No single measure will capture all of the subtleties of strategic interaction, first-mover advantages and the nature of post-entry competition which combine with other factors to influence entry decisions.

We have therefore proposed a stepwise assessment which achieves two things: firstly, it allows for a quick identification of the circumstances in which it is not necessary to carry out a detailed or full evaluation of all factors; secondly, it systematically and comprehensively takes account of the major issues and factors which our overview of the theory and practice has identified as being crucial. These steps are:

Step 1: Market definition and entry by production substitutes
Step 2: Market conditions and historical entry
Step 3: Assessment of absolute (cost) advantages
Step 4: Assessment of strategic (first mover) advantages
Step 5: Vertical foreclosure and exclusion
Step 6: Predatory behaviour
Step 7: Assessment of entry impediments.

The proposed procedure or methodology is both logical and parsimonious, and most importantly is informed by and consistent with the recent theoretical literature on barriers to entry. This subject has received a great deal of attention in the 'new industrial organisation' literature, which has addressed and clarified many of the issues which dominated the earlier debate between rival schools of thought, i.e. that associated with the 'Chicago school' on the one hand, and the so-called 'Harvard school' on the other. . . . It is necessary to examine carefully the individual circumstances of particular markets in order to assess whether or not entry barriers are present, and whether or not a particular type of behaviour by an incumbent or incumbents, may lead to a divergence between private and public interests.

Many of the practices referred to in the above passage are explained in Chapter 7. For the present it should be noted that it is now commonly accepted that a firm's behaviour on the market can constitute a barrier to entry and deter and prevent other firms from entering it.

D. CONCLUSIONS

Market definition and barriers to entry are both vital indicators of market power. The discussion in this section shows the difficulties involved in defining markets and identifying and even defining a barrier to entry. The imprecise nature of these concepts should be borne in mind in all cases where the application of competition rules is being considered. If markets are wrongly defined and barriers to entry imagined competition rules could take a wrong turn and prohibit conduct which might otherwise achieve economic efficiency.

7. FURTHER READING

A. BOOKS

AMATO, G., *Antitrust and the Bounds of Power* (Hart Publishing, 1997)

BAIN, J. S., *Barriers to New Competition* (Harvard University Press, 1956)

—— *Industrial Organization* (2nd edn., John Wiley, 1968)

BISHOP, S., and WALKER, M., *The Economics of EC Competition Law: Concepts, Application and Measurement* (Sweet & Maxwell, 1999), Chapters 1 and 2

BORK, R. H., *The Antitrust Paradox: A Policy at War with Itself* (Basic Books, 1978, reprinted with a new Introduction and Epilogue, 1993)

CAIRNCROSS, A., and others, *Economic Policy for the European Community* (MacMillan, 1974)

CINI, M., and McGOWAN, L., *Competition Policy in the European Union* (Macmillan, 1998)

FISHWICK, F., *Making Sense of Competition Policy* (Kogan Page, 1993)

GERBER, D., *Law and Competition in Twentieth Century Europe: Protecting Prometheus* (Oxford University Press, 1998)

HAY, D., and VICKERS, J., (eds.), *The Economics of Market Dominance* (Oxford University Press, 1987)

HOVENKAMP, H., *Federal Antitrust Policy: The Law of Competition and its Practice* (West Publishing Co, 1994)

JACQUEMIN, A. P., and DE JONG, H. W., *European Industrial Organisation* (MacMillan, 1997)

MERCURO, N., and MEDEMA, S. G., *Economics and the Law: From Posner to Post-Modernism* (Princeton University Press, 1999)

MÖSCHEL, W., 'Competition Policy from an Ordo Point of View' in A. Peacock and H. Willgerodt (eds.), *German Neo-Liberals and the Social Market Economics* (MacMillan, 1898) 142

SAUTER, W., *Competition Law and Industrial Policy in the EU* (Oxford University Press, 1997)

SCHERER, F. M., and ROSS, D., *Industrial Market Structure and Economic Performance* (3rd edn., Houghton Mifflin, 1990) Chapters 1, 2, and 4

STIGLER, G. J., *The Organization of Industry*, (Irwin, 1968)

WILLIAMSON, O. E., *Anti-Trust Economics*, (Basil Blackwell, 1987)

B. ARTICLES

BAIN, J. S., 'Economies of Scale, Concentration, and the Condition of Entry in Twenty Manufacturing Industries' (1954) 44 *Am. Econ. Rev.* 15

Fox, E. M., 'The New American Competition Policy: From Antitrust to Pro-efficiency?' [1981] *ECLR* 439

—— 'The Modernisation of Antitrust: A New Equilibrium' (1981) 66 *Cornell LR*

—— 'Consumer beware Chicago' (1984–85) 84 *Mich. LR* 1714

——, and SULLIVAN, L. A., 'Antitrust—Retrospective and Prospective: Where Are We Coming From? Where Are we Going?' (1987) 62 *NYU LR* 936

FRAZER, T., 'Competition Policy after 1992: The Next Step' (1990) 53 *MLR* 609

HOVENKAMP, H., 'Antitrust after Chicago' (1984–85) 84 *Mich. LR* 213

LEIBENSTEIN, H., 'Allocative Efficiency vs. "X-efficiency"' (1966) 56 *Am. Ec. Rev.* 392

POSNER R., 'The Social Costs of Monopoly and Regulation' [1975] *J. of Polit. Econ.* 83

—— 'The Chicago School of Antitrust Analysis' 127 *U Pa LR* 925

WOOD, D. P., 'The Role of Economics & Economists in Competition Cases' [1999] *OECD Journal of Competition Law & Policy* 82.

2

THE EUROPEAN COMMUNITY AND THE COMPETITION PROVISIONS

1. INTRODUCTION TO THE EUROPEAN COMMUNITY

A. GENERAL

The EC competition rules are set out in the Treaty establishing the European Community. The aims and objectives of this Treaty were introduced in Chapter 1 above. In this Chapter we give a very brief outline of the history of this Treaty, the European Community, and its institutions.[1] We then set out the competition provisions themselves and outline more specifically the way in which those rules are applied and enforced. Procedure and the enforcement of the competition rules are discussed in greater detail in Chapters 14 and 15.

B. THE SOURCES OF COMMUNITY LAW

(i) THE TREATY ESTABLISHING THE EUROPEAN COMMUNITY

Community law is derived from several sources. The most important of these sources are the Treaties, Community acts (secondary legislation and other acts adopted by the Community institutions), the case law of the Court,[2] and the general principles of Community law.[3]

Soon after the Second World War three European Communities were created. The Treaty of Paris in 1951 established the European Coal and Steel Community; the Euratom Treaty in

---

[1] For a more detailed discussion see, e.g. P. Craig and G. de Búrca, *EU Law: Text, Cases and Materials* (2nd edn., Oxford University Press, Oxford, 1998), chapter 1.

[2] The European Court of Justice (ECJ) and since 1989, the Court of First Instance (CFI).

[3] These sources are supplemented by international agreements entered into by the Community itself and by the individual Member States and by public international law.

1957 created the European Atomic Energy Community; and the Treaty of Rome in 1957 established the European Economic Community, now the European Community.[4]

The Treaty establishing the European Community (the 'Treaty') is the treaty of general application (its provisions are not confined to a specific sector) and is by far the most important of the three. It is a framework treaty which sets out what is, effectively, the constitution of the European Community. It provides the legal basis on which the Community operates and sets the limits of the competence of the institutions it creates. At the beginning it sets out the aims and objectives of the Community.[5] These aims and objectives provide an essential backdrop against which the other Treaty provisions and Community acts must be viewed. It is the competition law set out in Articles 81–86 (ex Articles 85–91) of the Treaty which is the focus of this book.

The Treaty has been amended on several occasions. In particular,[6] significant amendments were made to it by the Single European Act of 1986, the Treaty on European Union (the 'Maastricht Treaty'),[7] and the Treaty of Amsterdam.[8] The Maastricht Treaty also established the European Union.[9] It was the Treaty of Amsterdam which effected a complete renumbering of the provisions of the Treaty and the Maastricht Treaty.

(ii) THE EC INSTITUTIONS

The Treaty establishes the Community's autonomous institutions and the rules governing those institutions. It also confers legislative, executive and judicial powers upon them in order that the Community's tasks can be achieved. The five main institutions of the Community are set out in Article 7 of the Treaty: the European Parliament, the Council, the Commission, the Court of Justice and the Court of Auditors. In this section we consider the roles of the Council and the Commission focussing particularly on the responsibilities of those institutions within the sphere of Community competition policy.[10]

THE COUNCIL

The Council, which is comprised of representatives of the individual Member States, is in most respects the most powerful of the Community's political institutions. For example, it takes the final step in the passing of most Community legislation, concludes agreements with foreign countries, and has a key role in the Community budget. In the sphere of Community competition policy it has, however, not played a great part. Rather, it has delegated responsibility for the application and enforcement of the law to the Commission.[11] This has had the advantage that the development of competition policy and the

---

[4] The Treaty on European Union (TEU) (see *infra* n. 7) replaced the term European Economic Community (EEC) with the term European Community (EC).

[5] See in particular Arts. 2 and 3, discussed *supra* in Chap. 1. These aims and objectives have been widened on each amendment of the Treaty.

[6] Accession agreements, for example, also amend the Treaties.

[7] The TEU was signed in Feb. 1992. It entered into force on 1 Nov. 1993.

[8] The Amsterdam Treaty was signed on 2 Oct. 1997. It entered into force on 1 May 1999.

[9] The distinction between the EC and the EU is becoming increasingly blurred: see e.g. Craig and de Búrca, *supra* n. 1, 32–8.

[10] The role of the European Parliament in the legislative process in the sphere of competition policy is generally limited to a consultative role, see *infra* 72 ff.

[11] See *infra* 72 ff.

enforcement of the competition rules has not generally been subject to the delays and compromises that have been encountered in many other of the Community projects. Where the Council plays a significant role, the progress is generally dependent on the political will of the members and the differing views and interests of the individual Member States.

The Commission has been vigorous in its enforcement of the competition rules since the early days of the Community. In contrast, the introduction of the Merger Regulation, which had to be adopted by the Council,[12] took sixteen years to reach the statute book. Even then the Regulation represented a political compromise. The Council declined to hand as much power over mergers to the Commission as had been requested.[13]

THE COMMISSION

The Community Commissioners are unelected individuals[14] who represent the interests of the Community. The Commission has a number of different functions. It formulates most proposals for legislation, mediates between the individual Member States, and is responsible for the enforcement of the Treaty rules. Its role as key enforcer of the competition rules has been a particularly important one. It has power, for example, to take decisions finding an infringement of the Treaty competition rules and fining those responsible. For nearly forty years the Commission has both enforced the competition rules and formulated the policy behind them.

One of the twenty Commissioners is given responsibility for competition. Since 1999 this has been Mario Monti. The two previous Commissioners were Karel Van Miert and Sir Leon Brittan. Administratively the European Commission is divided into separate Directorates-General. Until the summer of 1999 when a new Commission took office, the Directorate-General dealing with competition was known as DG IV. Since then it has been known as the Competition Directorate-General. The Competition DG is headed by a Director-General, and sub-divided into eight Directorates. The responsibilities of each Direcorate are set out below.

Directorate A	General competition policy, co-ordination, international affairs, and relations with other institutions.	Directorate D	Service industries
		Directorate E	Cartel unit, basic industries and energy
Directorate B	Merger Task Force	Directorate F	Manufacturing and food industries
Directorate C	Information, communications and multimedias sectors	Directorate G & H	State Aids

The Competition DG deals with competition matters. Although one Commissioner is responsible for the competition portfolio, formal decisions taken by the Commission (for

---

[12] The legal basis for the Merger Reg., 4064/89 [1989] OJ L395/1, is EC Treaty, Art. 83, which requires a qualified majority, and Art. 308, which requires unanimous approval in the Council.

[13] See *infra* Chap. 12.

[14] The Commissioners are essentially appointed by the governments of the individual Member States but must be approved by the European Parliament: see EC Treaty, Art. 214.

example ordering the termination of infringements of the competition rules[15] and imposing penalties on undertakings in respect of such breaches[16] or permitting or prohibiting mergers[17]) must be adopted by the College of Commissioners as a whole.[18] If a decision has been adopted which does not follow the correct procedures it may be annulled.[19]

Details of the Competition DG, its directorates, and staff can be found on the internet. The website address is: http: //europa.eu.int/comm/competition/index_en.html.

THE ADVISORY COMMITTEE ON MONOPOLIES AND RESTRICTIVE TRADE PRACTICES

This Committee is not a Community institution but was created in 1962 (separate Committees exist for the transport sector and there is an Advisory Committee on concentrations[20]). The Committee comprises representatives from each Member State who are 'officials competent in the matter of restrictive practices and monopolies'. It must be consulted before certain decisions are taken by the Commission, for example, decisions which:

(a) establish the existence of infringements of Article 81 or 82, give negative clearance, or apply Article 81(3);[21]

(b) renew, amend or revoke a decision pursuant to Article 81(3);[22]

(c) impose a fine or periodic penalty payments.[23]

The Commission does not have to follow the Committee's opinion, which is neither published or shown to the parties.[24] The Committee must also be consulted before the Commission publishes a draft block exemption and before adopting a block exemption.[25] It may meet to discuss competition policy generally.

The Commission has suggested strengthening the powers and the position of the Advisory Committee.[26]

---

[15] Council Reg. 17 [1962] OJ Spec. Ed 59–87, Art. 3.

[16] Reg. 17, Art 15.

[17] Reg. 4064/89 [1989] OJ L395/1, Arts. 6 and 8.

[18] Decisions must be passed by a simple majority, EC Treaty, Art. 219. For the effect this may have on the adoption of a decision, see *infra* Chap. 12. The Legal Service of the Commission also plays an important role in competition matters.

[19] Case C–137/92P, *Commission* v. *BASF* [1994] ECR I–2555: see Chap. 14.

[20] Reg. 17, Art. 10. There are separate Advisory Committees for each of the transport sectors and an Advisory Committee on concentrations. The functions of the latter are set out in the Merger Reg. 4064/89, Art. 19. This Committee must be consulted before certain decisions are adopted under the Merger Reg. The Committee can recommend the publication of its opinion and the Commission may decide to carry out such publication: see Reg. 4064/89, Art. 19(7).

[21] Reg. 17, Art. 10(1) and (3).

[22] Reg. 17, Art. 10(3).

[23] Reg. 17, Art. 15(3) and 16(3).

[24] Reg. 17, Art. 10(6) and Cases 100–103/80, *Musique Diffusion Française and others* v. *Commission* [1983] ECR 1823, [1983] 3 CMLR 221 (the *Pioneer* case), paras. 34–36. The decisions of the Advisory Committee on concentrations are sometimes published, however: see *supra* n. 20.

[25] Reg. 19/65 [1965] OJ Spec. Ed. 35, Art. 6, Reg. 2821/71, [1971] OJ Spec. Ed. 1032, Art. 6, Reg. 3976/87 [1987] OJ L374/9, Art. 6; Reg. 1534/91, [1991] OJ L143/1, Art. 6.

[26] White Paper on Modernisation of the Rules Implementing Articles 85 and 86 [now 81 and 82] of the EC Treaty [1999] OJ C132/1, [1999] 5 CMLR 208, para. 106. The Commission suggests that it should have power to discuss important cases whichever national competition authority is dealing with it and to give its opinion on cases dealt with by national authorities.

(iii) COMMUNITY ACTS

Community acts adopted by the autonomous Community institutions (the Council, the Commission, and the European Parliament), such as regulations, directives decisions, recommendations, and opinions, flesh out the basic principles set out in the Treaty.[27] Most general legislative acts, intended to apply in all of the Member States, are adopted by regulation or directive.

A number of Community regulations have been adopted by the Council to ensure that the objectives of the Treaty competition rules are carried out. In particular it has adopted (i) regulations delegating the enforcement and application of the competition rules to the Commission,[28] and (ii) the Merger Regulation, which confers power on the Commission to control mergers.[29]

(iv) THE CASE LAW OF THE EUROPEAN COURT

The ECJ, the court of the European Communities, has the task of interpreting the law set out in the Treaty and secondary legislation and ensuring that the law is observed.[30] 'Its main functions are to ensure that the law is enforced . . .; to act as referee between the Member States and the Community as well as between the Community institutions *inter se*; and to ensure the uniform interpretation and application of Community law throughout the Community.'[31] Since 1989 it has been assisted in certain spheres, including competition law, by the Court of First Instance. The CFI is 'attached' to the Court of Justice.

The means of statutory interpretation adopted by the Court may seem unfamiliar or even unusual to an English lawyer. Because the Treaty is only a framework treaty its meaning is sometimes obscure. Secondly, the difficulties of interpretation faced by the Court are compounded by the fact that each text of a Community provision is relevant to the determination (all provisions are translated into each of the eleven[32] working languages of the Community). Where each text bears a different interpretation a literal interpretation of the provision will be impossible. Each text has equal status and is equally authentic.[33] The approach of the Court is, therefore, to adopt a 'teleological' interpretation of Treaty provisions or Community acts which it construes. The Community provisions are applied against the wider backdrop of the Treaty tasks and activities.[34] On occasion the Court has even gone so far as to ignore clear words of the Treaty or Community act if that construction will

[27] EC Treaty, Art. 249 defines the main characteristics of each of these measures. The ECJ has, however, recognized that other '*sui generis*' acts adopted by one of the Community institutions may be capable of producing legal effects: Case 22/70, *Commission* v. *Council (ERTA)* [1971] ECR 263.

[28] *Infra* 73.

[29] Block exemptions which exempt categories of agreements from the application of Art. 81(1) are also set out in regs. adopted either by the Council or the Commission: see *infra* 73 and Chap. 4.

[30] 'The Court of Justice shall ensure that in the interpretation and application of this Treaty the law is observed': EC Treaty, Art. 220.

[31] T. C. Hartley, *The Foundations of European Community Law* (4th edn., Oxford University Press, 1998), 52.

[32] There is no Irish version of secondary legislation, but there is of the Treaty.

[33] Case 283/81, *CILFIT Srl and Lanificio de Gavardo SpA* v. *Ministry of Health* [1982] ECR 3415, [1983] CMLR 472, para. 18. See the discussion of the meaning of 'affect trade' in Art. 81 of the Treaty, *infra* in Chap. 3, and the discussion of the meaning of an abuse of a dominant position, *infra* in Chap. 5.

[34] Set out in Arts. 2, 3, and 4 of the EC Treaty: see *supra* Chap. 1.

ensure an interpretation which best accords with the broad objectives of the Treaty.[35] A number of instances in which the Court has adopted an extremely broad interpretation of the competition rules or one which does not accord with the clear wording of the text will be seen in this book.[36]

The Court of Justice has no system of precedent. In practice, however, it strives for consistency.[37] It is only on rare occasions that it has seen fit to reverse a previous ruling.[38]

In the context of Community competition law the Court hears two main types of action. First, Article 230 (ex Article 173) of the Treaty specifically provides that the ECJ may review the legality of acts adopted by the Community institutions. This provision thus sets out a procedure for challenging the legality of the Commission's competition decisions.[39] Further, it also allows the challenge to a number of other administrative acts of the Commission which are capable of affecting the interests of individuals.[40] Challenges are generally made, since 1989, to the CFI.[41] Appeals on points of law can then be made to the ECJ.[42]

Secondly, Article 234 (ex Article 177)[43] of the Treaty provides a procedure for a national court or tribunal to request the ECJ to give a preliminary ruling on the interpretation of Community law where such a ruling is necessary to enable that court or tribunal to give judgment.[44] These references are still made directly to the ECJ and are not dealt with by the CFI.[45]

(v) THE GENERAL PRINCIPLES OF COMMUNITY LAW

The ECJ has developed and introduced a body of unwritten law, the general principles of law, as part of Community law. These are rules, based on national laws of Member States and international treaties,[46] especially the European Convention on Human Rights and Fundamental Freedoms, in accordance with which Community law is interpreted. The principles are important when determining the boundaries of proper and lawful action of

---

[35] See e.g. Case C–70/88, *European Parliament* v. *Council* (*'Chernobyl'*) [1990] ECR I–2041, [1992] 1 CMLR 91.

[36] See, e.g. *infra* Chaps. 3, 5 and 12.

[37] Case 4/73, *Nold* v. *Commission* [1974] ECR 491, [1974] CMLR 338. See also A. Arnull, 'Owning up to Fallibility: Precedent and the Court of Justice' (1993) 30 CML Rev. 247.

[38] See, e.g., Case C–70/88, *European Parliament* v. *Council* (*'Chernobyl'*) [1990] ECR I–2041, [1992] 1 CMLR 91; Case C–10/89, *CNL-Sucal* v. *HAG GF AG* (*'Hag II'*) [1990] ECR I–3711, [1990] 3 CMLR 571; and Cases C–267&268/91, *Keck and Mithouard, Criminal Proceedings Against* [1993] ECR I–6097, [1995] 1 CMLR 101, paras. 15–16.

[39] EC Treaty, Art. 230. See discussion *infra* in Chap. 14.

[40] Case 60/81, *IBM* v. *Commission* [1981] ECR 2639, [1981] 3 CMLR 635. See also the discussion, *infra* in Chap. 14.

[41] See EC Treaty, Art. 225(1) and (2). There is an exception to this general rule where the appeal is made by a Member State: see *infra* Chap. 14 and Cases C–68/95 and C–30/95 *France* v. *Commission* [1998] ECR I–1375, [1998] 4 CMLR 829, *infra* Chap. 12.

[42] Protocol on the Statute of the Court of Justice, Art. 51: see Chap. 14.

[43] See *infra* 69.

[44] For a full discussion, see Craig and de Búrca, *supra* n. 1, Chap. 10.

[45] Art. 225(1).

[46] To which the Member States are signatories.

the Community and national institutions (when the latter are acting within the sphere of Community law).[47]

The actions of institutions applying and enforcing the EC competition rules must respect the general principles of law, in particular, the principles of proportionality, legitimate expectations, and fundamental rights. This point is of special importance to the Commission which must ensure that when conducting competition investigations its administrative procedures comply with principles of human rights, rules of natural justice, and rights of defence, for example the right to be heard and to know the case against one. In many appeals from a Commission's competition decision the parties have alleged that the Commission has failed to observe these principles.[48]

The principle of subsidiarity, which is also a general principle of Community law, is now enshrined in Article 5 of the Treaty of Rome. This principle applies to all Community activity, including the implementation of Community competition policy. Article 5 provides:

In areas which do not fall within its exclusive competence, the Community shall take action, in accordance with the principle of subsidiarity, only if and insofar as the objectives of the proposed action cannot be sufficiently achieved by the Member States and can therefore, by reason of the scale or effects of the proposed action, be better achieved by the Community.

The Community competition rules apply only when there is an effect on trade between Members States or when the relevant transaction has a Community dimension. The rules thus incorporate the notion of subsidiarity. However, the Commission has recently suggested that the subsidiarity principle supports the need for greater enforcement of the competition rules at the national level.[49]

C. A NEW LEGAL ORDER OF INTERNATIONAL LAW

(i) DIRECT EFFECT

Although the European Communities are founded on international agreements, European Community law has developed to create its own unique legal system, with its own institutions and extremely effective enforcement mechanisms.

International law and international treaties traditionally impose obligations only on States and do not impose obligations or confer rights on private individuals. It might perhaps have been assumed that Community law would merely create obligations between Member States. The Treaty specifically sets out a mechanism for both the European Commission and Member States to enforce Treaty obligations against recalcitrant Member States (see, in particular, Articles 226–228). However, very early in the Community's development

---

[47] See, e.g. Case 5/88, *Wachauf* v. *Federal Republic of Germany* [1989] ECR 2609, [1990] 1 CMLR 328; Case C–260/89 *Ellinki Radiophonia Tileorassi—Anonimi Etairia (ERT-AE)* v. *Dimotiki Etairia Pliroforissis (DEP)* [1991] ECR I–2925, [1994] 4 CMLR 540.

[48] See *infra* Chap. 14.

[49] See the Notice on Co-operation between National Competition Authorities and the Commission [1997] OJ C313/1; Notice on Co-operation between National Courts and the Commission [1993] OJ C39/5; Commission White Paper on Modernisation of the Rules Implementing Art. 85 and 86 [now 81 and 82] of the EC Treaty [1999] OJ C132/1, [1999] 5 CMLR 208.

the ECJ ruled that this would not be the limit of Community law. Rather, it has become clear that the rights and obligations created by European Community law are enforceable by and against private individuals and not just the Member States. In *Van Gend en Loos* v. *Nederlandse Administratie der Belastingen*[50] the ECJ ruled that individuals are entitled to rely on rights that they derive from Community measures (such as the Treaty competition rules) before national courts even if those measures have not been implemented by national legislation.[51] In addition, the rights conferred by Treaty Articles and regulations can be relied upon against a Member State or a state entity *and* against another individual or private party (they impose obligations on private entities and are capable of 'horizontal direct effect'[52]). The only requirement is that the Community measure is *capable of direct effect*. The provision relied upon must be sufficiently precise and unconditional.

The question whether the Treaty competition rules have direct effect is dealt with below and also in other parts of this book. The broad position is, however, that the main prohibitions set out in the Treaty are directly effective and can be relied upon by or against private individuals.[53]

(ii) SUPREMACY

Where there is a conflict between a directly effective Community provision and national law, the former must prevail.[54] The principle of supremacy ensures the full effectiveness and uniform application of directly effective Community law.[55]

The doctrine of supremacy does not ordinarily mean that national competition legislation cannot be applied where Community competition rules apply.[56] It does mean, however, that where there is a conflict between national and Community law, the latter must prevail.[57]

---

[50] Case 26/62, *Van Gend en Loos* v. *Nederlandse Administratie der Belastingen* [1963] ECR 1, 12, [1963] CMLR 105, 129.

[51] European Communities Act 1972, s. 2(1) obliges English courts to recognize and enforce directly effective Community law.

[52] Dirs. are not directly effective against private parties but only against the State and emanations of the State (they are capable only of 'vertical direct effect': see Case 152/84, *Marshall* v. *Southampton and South-West Hampshire Area Health Authority (Teaching)* [1986] ECR 723, [1986] 1 CMLR 688 and Case C–91/92, *Faccini Dori* v. *Recreb* [1994] ECR I–3325, [1995] 1 CMLR 665). The ECJ has given a wide interpretation to the term State: see Case C–188/89, *Foster* v. *British Gas plc* [1990] ECR I–3313, [1990] 2 CMLR 833. Even if a provision is not directly effective, however, a national court still has an obligation to interpret, in so far as it is possible, provisions of national law in conformity with that Community law (indirect effect): see e.g. Case 14/83, *Von Colson and Kamann* v. *Land Nordrhein-Westfalen* [1984] ECR 1891, [1986] 2 CMLR 430 and Case C–106/89, *Marleasing SA* v. *La Comercial Internacional de Alimentacion SA* [1990] ECR I–4135, [1992] 1 CMLR 305. Further, a Member State may be liable for any loss caused by its failure to implement a directive or its failure to implement it correctly.

[53] Art. 81(1), Art. 81(2), Art. 82, and Art. 86 are directly effective. Art. 81(3) is not, however, currently directly effective, see in particular the discussion *infra* in Chap. 16.

[54] Case 6/64, *Costa* v. *ENEL* [1964] ECR 585, 593–4, [1964] CMLR 425, 456.

[55] A national court faced with national rules or legislation that conflict with Community law has an obligation to give immediate precedence to the Community provisions. If necessary it must refuse to apply the provisions of national legislation even if subsequently adopted: see Case 106/77, *Amministrazione delle Finanze dello Stato* v. *Simmenthal SpA* [1978] ECR 629, [1978] 3 CMLR 263, para. 24.

[56] But see the provisions dealing with mergers, *infra* Chap. 12.

[57] See discussion *infra* in Chap. 14. But the Commission's proposal for a new reg. implementing Arts. 81 and 82, COM (2000) 582, Art. 3, says that where there is an effect on trade between Member States Community Competition Law shall apply to the exclusion of national competition laws.

(iii) ARTICLE 234 (EX ARTICLE 177) OF THE EC TREATY

It is Article 234 of the EC Treaty which has enabled the enforcement of the Community rules at the national level through the principles of direct effect and supremacy without compromising the uniformity of Community law. It enables, and in some circumstances requires, national courts or tribunals to refer questions to the ECJ concerning, for example, the interpretation of the Treaty and Community acts where necessary to enable the national court to give judgment. The ECJ then gives preliminary rulings on those questions. This procedure has been 'essential for the preservation of the Community character of the law established by the Treaty and has the object of ensuring that in all circumstances the law is the same in all states of the Community'.[58]

2. THE COMPETITION PROVISIONS

A. GENERAL

(i) ARTICLE 3(1)(g) OF THE TREATY

The tasks and activities of the Community and the foundations of all Community policies are set out in Articles 2, 3, and 4 of the Treaty.[59] Article 3(1)(g) (ex Article 3(f)) provides that the activities of the Community shall include 'a system ensuring that competition in the internal market is not distorted'. This aim is crucial when interpreting the Treaty provisions which set out the common competition rules in greater detail. In *Continental Can*[60] the ECJ stated:

Article [82] is part of the chapter devoted to the common rules on the Community's policy in the field of competition. This policy is based on Article [3(1)(g)] of the Treaty according to which the Community's activity shall include the institution of a system ensuring that competition in the Common Market is not distorted. The applicants' argument that this provision merely contains a general programme devoid of legal effect, ignores the fact that Article 3 considers the pursuit of the objectives which it lays down to be indispensable for the achievement of the Community's tasks. As regards in particular the aim mentioned in Article [3(1)(g)], the Treaty in several provisions contains more detailed regulations for the interpretation of which this aim is decisive.

---

[58] Case 166/73, *Rheinmühlen-Düsseldorf v. Einfuhr und Vorratsstelle für Getreide und Futtermittel* [1974] ECR 33, [1974] 1 CMLR 523.

[59] See *supra* Chap. 1.

[60] Case 6/72, *Europemballage Corporation and Continental Can Co Inc* v. *Commission* [1973] ECR 215, [1973] CMLR 199, para. 23. For greater discussion of this case see Chap. 5. See also Case C–68/94, *French Republic* v. *Commission* [1998] ECR I–1375, [1998] 4 CMLR 829.

(ii) THE MAIN TREATY PROVISIONS AND THE MERGER REGULATION

The main competition rules are contained in Chapter 1 of Title VI of the Treaty. Section 1 (Articles 81–86) deals with rules applying to undertakings.[61] Section 2 (Articles 87–89) deals with State Aids. The regulation of State Aids granted by Member States to industry is outside the scope of this book.[62] Article 31 deals with state monopolies of a commercial character. It is situated in Title I but the Commission treats it as part of the competition rules.[63] A general power to control mergers is not expressly contained in the Treaty.[64] Provision for merger control is, however, now set out in Council Regulation 4064/89.[65]

(iii) SPECIAL SECTORS

The competition rules cover all areas of the economy. However, a few comments should be made about the special position of certain sectors.

First, the coal and steel industries are currently dealt with by the European Coal and Steel Community.[66] The competition provisions set out in this Treaty are very similar to those of the EC Treaty but have important differences.[67] Secondly, Regulation 26[68] modified the competition rules in respect of agriculture, and there is some tension between the objectives of the common agricultural policy[69] and competition policy. Nevertheless, where there is still space for competition between undertakings in the agricultural sector, or where the products concerned are not 'agricultural products' within Annex II of the EC Treaty the competition rules will be applied.[70] Thirdly, the rules have been applied to the transport sector by separate implementing legislation.[71] Fourthly, the Community has embarked on programmes of liberalization and/or harmonization of the utilities, telecommunications, broadcasting, and financial services sectors with the aim of opening them up to greater

---

[61] Broadly, any entity engaged in commercial activities: see *infra* Chap. 3.

[62] But see P. Craig and G. de Búrca, *EU Law: Text, Cases and Materials* (2nd edn, Oxford University Press, 1998), 1075–1102.

[63] See the 'Laws and Procedures' section of the Mission Statement on DG Competition's homepage (http://europa.eu.int/pol/comp/info_en.htm), and the Commission's Annual Reports on Competition Policy, which cover Art. 31 (ex Art. 37).

[64] Although in Case 6/72, *Europemballage Corporation and Continental Can Co Inc* v. *Commission* [1973] ECR 215, [1973] CMLR 199, the ECJ held that Art. 82 did prohibit some mergers conducted by dominant undertakings: see *infra* Chaps. 5 and 12.

[65] [1989] OJ L395/1, as amended by Council Reg. 1310/97 [1997] OJ L180/1.

[66] The ECSC Treaty was concluded for a finite period and expires on 23 July 2002. The tasks of the ECSC can be taken over by the EC so the ECSC Treaty will not be extended: see Resolution of the Council and the representatives of the Member States' governments meeting within the Council, 21 June 1999, [1999] OJ C190/1.

[67] E.g., the ECSC Arts. do not have direct effect: Case C–128/92, *H. J. Banks* v. *British Coal Corporation* [1994] ECR I–1209, [1994] 5 CMLR 30.

[68] [1959–62] OJ Spec. Ed. 129.

[69] Art. 33 (ex Art. 39).

[70] See e.g. Case 61/80, *Coöperative Stremsel- en Kleurselfabriek* v. *Commission* [1981] ECR 851, [1982] 1 CMLR 240; Case 71/74, *FRUBO* v. *Commission* [1975] ECR 563, [1975] 2 CMLR 123, Case 40–48, 50, 54–56, 111, 113 and 114/73, *Suiker Unie* v. *EC Commission* [1975] ECR 1663, [1976] 1 CMLR 295.

[71] See *infra* n. 80.

competition.[72] There has been very little sympathy for the claims that these sectors should receive favourable treatment and should be protected from the competitive process. The Commission has recognized, however, that the full rigour of the competition rules might have to be tempered within the sphere of sport. Competition law is applied to the commercial aspects of sport.[73] Nevertheless, the regulatory powers of sports organizations in respect of the non-economic aspects linked to the specific nature of sport, and the rules of sports organizations which uphold matters such as the integrity and functioning of competitions, are not in principle caught.[74] Finally, Article 296(1)(b) (ex Article 223(1)(b)) provides that the Treaty provisions shall not preclude any Member State from taking 'such measures as it considers necessary for the protection of the essential interests of its security which are connected with the production of or trade in arms, munitions and war material'. This provision has, for example, been used by Member States to retain jurisdiction over mergers with a military significance.[75]

B. THE SUBSTANTIVE PROVISIONS OF THE TREATY

The substantive competition provisions of the Treaty are summarized here. The provisions are dealt with more fully in later chapters.

(i) ARTICLE 81 (EX ARTICLE 85)

Article 81 is in three parts: Article 81(1) prohibits agreements, decisions of associations of undertakings and concerted practices which have as their object or effect the prevention, restriction or distortion of competition and which may affect trade between Member States. Article 81(2) says that such agreements are void. But Article 81(3) provides, however, that Article 81(1) may be 'declared inapplicable' in respect of agreements, decisions, or concerted practices or of categories of such agreements which are on balance beneficial since they satisfy the criteria set out in that provision. Exemptions are thus granted individually by Commission decision to agreements and by regulations (block exemptions) to certain types of agreements.

The wording in Article 81(3) that Article 81(1) 'may . . . be declared inapplicable' to certain agreements left open, deliberately perhaps,[76] the question of how and by whom this declaration was to be made. The Council in 1962 conferred exclusive power on the Commission to exempt agreements from the prohibition of Article 81(1).[77] The Commission has,

---

[72] See P. Freeman and R. Whish (eds.), *Butterworths Competition Law* (Butterworths, looseleaf), Div IX.

[73] See, e.g., the application of Art. 82 to the ticketing arrangements for the 1998 World Cup in *1998 Football World Cup* [2000] OJ L5/55, [2000] 4 CMLR 963.

[74] The Commission published an Art. 19(3) Notice under Reg. 17 (see Chaps. 4 and 14) setting out its initial view that a UEFA rule precluding more than one club belonging to the same owner from taking part in the same competition did not fall within the competition rules: *UEFA* [1999] OJ C363/2. For the Commission's policy on the competition rules and sport generally see Mario Monti, *Sport and Competition*, speech given at a Commission-organized conference on sports, Brussels, 17 Apr. 2000.

[75] See *infra* Chap. 12.

[76] See *infra* Chap. 16.

[77] Reg. 17 [1959–1962] OJ Spec. Ed. 87, Art. 9.

however, now stated in its White Paper on modernization[78] that this system should be abandoned. Instead it has proposed that Article 81(3) should be applied directly by the Commission, national courts, and national competition authorities as an exception to the Article 81(1) prohibition (i.e. it should have direct effect).

(ii) ARTICLE 82 (EX ARTICLE 86)

Article 82 prohibits an undertaking which holds a dominant position in the common market, or a substantial part of it, from abusing that position in so far as it may affect inter-Member State trade. It contains no provision for exemption.

(iii) ARTICLES 86 AND 31 (EX ARTICLES 90 AND 37)

Article 86 deals with the application of the competition rules (and other rules of the Treaty) to public undertakings and those given special or exclusive rights by Member States. It contains a limited exemption (Article 86(2)) from the Treaty rules for such undertakings. That limitation has, however, been construed narrowly.

Article 31 is situated in the part of the Treaty concerned with the free movement of goods. It requires Member States which have state monopolies of a commercial character to eliminate discrimination between nationals of Member States regarding the conditions under which goods are procured and marketed.

C. THE PROCEDURAL PROVISIONS

(i) ARTICLE 83 (EX ARTICLE 87)

Article 83 confers a general power on the Council to adopt secondary legislation to give effect to the principles laid down in Articles 81 and 82. It provides:[79]

1. The appropriate regulations or directives to give effect to the principles set out in Articles 81 and 82 shall be laid down by the Council, acting by a qualified majority on a proposal from the Commission and after consulting the European Parliament.
2. The regulations or directives referred to in paragraph 1 shall be designed, in particular:
    (a) to ensure compliance with the prohibitions laid down in Article 81(1) and in Article 82 by making provision for fines and periodic penalty payments;
    (b) to lay down detailed rules for the application of Article 81(3), taking into account the need to ensure effective supervision on the one hand, and to simplify administration to the greatest possible extent on the other;
    (c) to define, if need be, in the various branches of the economy, the scope of the provisions of Articles 81 and 82;

---

[78] Commission White Paper on Modernisation of the Rules Implementing Articles 85 and 86, [now 81 and 82] of the EC Treaty [1999] OJ C132/1, [1999] 5 CMLR 208, paras. 11–13. See *infra* Chap. 16. The Commission has adopted a proposal for a Council reg. to render Art. 81(3) directly applicable, COM (2000) 582.

[79] Art. 83, formerly Art. 87, was slightly amended by the Treaty of Amsterdam. It previously provided that the appropriate regs. or dirs. should be laid down 'within three years of the entry into force of this Treaty'. This requirement has been removed to make it clear that the Council has an ongoing power to adopt secondary legislation which gives effect to Arts. 81 and 82.

(d) to define the respective functions of the Commission and of the Court of Justice in applying the provisions laid down in this paragraph;

(e) to determine the relationship between national laws and the provisions contained in this Section or adopted pursuant to this Article.

a. IMPLEMENTING LEGISLATION

The Council has adopted regulations pursuant to Article 83 implementing Articles 81 and 82. The most important of these regulations is Regulation 17. Regulation 17 confers power on the Commission to enforce the competition rules in most sectors. Other regulations confer the requisite power in certain transport sectors.[80]

b. THE MERGER REGULATION

The Merger Regulation, Regulation 4064/89, was adopted by the Council pursuant to Article 83 and Article 308 (ex Article 235) of the Treaty.[81]

c. BLOCK EXEMPTIONS

The Council has adopted regulations declaring Article 81(1) to be inapplicable to categories of agreements pursuant to Article 81(3). Further, it has also adopted regulations delegating power to the Commission itself to adopt regulations granting block exemptions to specified types of agreements.[82] The Commission has issued a number of block exemptions under these delegated powers. Some of these are general (such as those on vertical restraints[83] and technology transfer licences[84]) and some relate only to special sectors (such as motor vehicle distribution[85] or insurance[86]).

d. OTHER REGULATIONS ADOPTED BY THE COMMISSION

The Commission has also adopted secondary legislation which implements Council Regulation 17. For example, Regulation 2842/98[87] governs hearings that Regulation 17 requires the Commission to carry out and Regulation 3385/94[88] deals with the form, content, and other details of applications and notifications provided for in Regulation 17.

---

[80] Council Reg. 17 [1959–62] OJ Spec. Ed. 87. The Commission has proposed the modernisation of Reg. 17, see *infra* Chap. 16. Reg. 141 [1959–62] OJ Spec. Ed. 291 retrospectively withdrew transport from the application of Reg. 17. The regs. applying the competition rules in the transport sector are now Council Reg. 1017/68 [1968] OJ Spec. Ed. 302, as regards land and inland waterways, Council Reg. 4056/86 [1986] OJ L378/4, as regards maritime transport, and Council Reg. 3975/87 [1987] OJ L374/1, in the aviation sector.

[81] Art. 308 contains a residual legislative power, the exercise of which requires unanimous voting in the Council. It was used as one of the bases for the Merger Reg., 4064/89 as it was thought that, on its own, Art. 83 was an inadequate basis: see *infra* Chap. 12.

[82] See Chap. 4.

[83] Commission Reg. 2790/99 [1999] OJ L336/21.

[84] Commission Reg. 240/96 [1996] OJ L31/2.

[85] Commission Reg. 1475/95 [1995] OJ L145/25.

[86] See Commission Reg. 3932/92 [1991] OJ L143/1, made pursuant to Council Reg. 1534/91 [1991] OJ L143/1, empowering the Commission to issue block exemptions for certain types of agreements in the insurance sector.

[87] This reg., [1998] OJ L354/18, replaces Commission Reg. 99/63 [1963] OJ Spec. Ed. 47.

[88] Commission Reg. 2843/98 [1998] OJ L354/22 is the equivalent in the transport sector.

The Commission has also issued a number of notices.[89] These notices do not have the force of law but set out guidance on the interpretation of the Community competition law provisions. They are important statements of how the Commission will deal with certain matters and help undertakings build an understanding of how the competition rules will be applied in practice. In many cases these notices are crucial to complete an overall picture of a particular competition rule.

(ii) ARTICLE 84 (EX ARTICLE 88)

Article 84 enables Member States to apply Articles 81 and 82 in certain circumstances:

Until the entry into force of the provisions adopted in pursuance of Article 83, the authorities in Member States shall rule on the admissibility of agreements, decisions and concerted practices and on abuse of a dominant position in the common market in accordance with the law of their country and with the provisions of Article 81, in particular paragraph 3, and of Article 82.

This Article confers power on 'authorities in Member States' to apply the competition rules prior to the Council's adoption of implementing rules. In *Nouvelles Frontières*[90] the ECJ held that the term authorities 'refers to either the administrative authorities entrusted, in most Member States, with the task of applying domestic legislation on competition subject to the review of legality carried out by competent courts, or else the courts to which, in other Member States, the task has been especially entrusted'. In the UK the Secretary of State for Trade and Industry and the Director General of Fair Trading (who heads the Office of Fair Trading (OFT)) are the competent authorities. This provision does not, however, apply to an ordinary national court before which the direct effect of an EC competition provision is pleaded.[91]

Article 84 appears to have been designed as a transitional provision. It has, however, remained significant in conferring power on the national competition authorities to act whenever EC implementing legislation does not apply.[92] Further, the powers of the national competition authorities to act under this Article were extended by Article 9(3) of Regulation 17 to permit 'competent authorities' to act in all situations in which the Commission has not instituted proceedings. The Commission is seeking to encourage a greater participation by national authorities in the application of the Community competition rules.[93]

(iii) ARTICLE 85

Article 85 imposes a general duty on the Commission to ensure compliance with the competition rules:

---

[89] See *infra* Chap. 3.

[90] Cases 209–213/84, *Ministère Public* v. *Lucas Asjes (Nouvelles Frontières)* [1986] ECR 1425, [1986] 3 CMLR 173, para. 55.

[91] Case 127/73, *BRT* v. *SABAM* [1974] ECR 51, [1974] 2 CMLR 23; see *infra*, 79–80.

[92] The UK authorities asserted jurisdiction over the proposed alliance between British Airways and American Airlines. In this case no EC implementing provision conferred jurisdiction on the Commission: see *infra* 75. The UK had to adopt regs. to enable the competition authorities to act: see EC Competition Law (Art. 88 and 89) Enforcement Regulations (SI 1996 No 2199).

[93] See *infra* 84.

1. Without prejudice to Article 84, the Commission shall ensure the application of the principles laid down in Articles 81 and 82. On application by a Member State or on its own initiative, and in co-operation with the competent authorities in the Member States, who shall give it their assistance, the Commission shall investigate cases of suspected infringement of these principles. If it finds that there has been an infringement, it shall propose appropriate measures to bring it to an end.

2. If the infringement is not brought to an end, the Commission shall record such infringement of the principles in a reasoned decision. The Commission may publish its decision and authorise Member States to take the measures, the conditions and details of which it shall determine, needed to remedy the situation.

Article 85, (ex Article 89) was amended by the Treaty of Amsterdam. Previously it included the words 'as soon as it takes up its duties' between the words 'shall' and 'ensure' in the first line. This suggested that it was merely a transitional provision enabling the Commission to enforce Articles 81 and 82 prior to the adoption of implementing legislation. The change of wording recognizes that Article 85 is not a temporary measure, but in fact confers on the Commission an important and permanent residual power to intervene[94] which did not become redundant upon the adoption of Regulation 17. Implementing rules governing the transport sector were introduced only gradually,[95] and are not all-embracing. If the Commission wishes to intervene in a transport case which is not covered by these regulations it must rely on its powers under Article 85. For example, the air transport Regulation, 3975/87, applies only to 'air transport between Community airports'[96] and not to air transport between a Community airport and a non-Member State. As a result of this the Commission was forced to assert jurisdiction under Article 85 when concerned about a proposed alliance between British Airways and American Airlines.[97] Similarly, the maritime transport Regulation, 4056/86, does not apply to maritime transport in a single Member State, between two or more non-EC ports, or to transport involving tramp vessel services.

D. OTHER RELEVANT TREATY PROVISIONS

Other provisions of the Treaty may interact with the competition provisions. For example, the Treaty provisions relating to the free movement of goods, Articles 28–30, and relating to the free movement of services, Articles 49–55, are important when dealing with intellectual property rights.[98] Articles 94 and 95 permit the Community institutions to adopt measures to achieve the approximation of national rules which affect the establishment and functioning of an internal market. Articles 96 and 97 also enable the Community institutions to act where measures in Member States are distorting competition in the common market. These latter two Articles have, however, rarely been used.[99]

---

[94] See C. Kerse, 'Enforcing Community Competition Policy under Articles 88 and 89 of the EC Treaty—New Powers for UK Competition Authorities' [1997] 1 *ECLR* 17.

[95] See *supra* n. 80.

[96] Reg. 3975/87 [1987] OJ L374/1, Art. 1(2).

[97] Commission Notice concerning the Alliance Agreement between British Airways and American Airlines [1996] OJ C288/4; see *supra* n. 92.

[98] See *infra* Chap. 10.

[99] See P. J. G. Kapteyn and P. VerLoren van Themaat, *Introduction to the Law of the European Communities* (3rd edn. by L. R. Gormley, Kluwer, Deventer, 1998), 802–10.

3. THE COMPETITION RULES AND THE EUROPEAN ECONOMIC AREA

The agreement establishing the European Economic Area (EEA) came into force on 1 January 1994. The EEA creates a free trade area between the EC and the EFTA countries with the exception of Switzerland.[100] The competition rules in the EEA are modelled on those in the Treaty. References to trade between the contracting parties, however, replace references to trade between Member States. The agreement effectively extends to the territory of the relevant EFTA States the EC competition rules and all the rules governing the internal market, including intellectual property.

Article 53 EEA is modelled on Article 81 of the EC Treaty, Article 54 EEA is modelled on Article 82, Article 59 EEA is modelled on Article 86, and Article 57 EEA effectively applies the rules set out in the EC Merger Regulation, 4064/89, to the EEA.

The EFTA Surveillance Authority (ESA) is entrusted, together with the Commission, with the enforcement of the EEA competition rules. The EEA Agreement sets out when the ESA or the Commission has jurisdiction over a particular case. Essentially the ESA has jurisdiction where:

i. only trade between the EFTA states is affected; or

ii. trade between one or more EFTA states and the EC is affected and the turnover of the undertakings concerned in the EFTA states is one third or more of the total turnover of those undertakings in the EEA as a whole.[101]

Where, however, trade in the EC is affected to an appreciable extent the Commission and not the ESA has jurisdiction.[102]

The Commission has jurisdiction in all other cases.

The EEA Agreement also established an EFTA Court. This court has jurisdiction in competition matters to deal with appeals from the ESA, infringement actions bought by the ESA against EFTA States, and the settlement of disputes between two or more EFTA States.[103]

---

[100] Switzerland did not join the EEA after membership was rejected in a referendum. As Austria, Finland, and Sweden joined the EU on 1 Jan. 1995, the only States which are in the EEA and not also in the EU are Liechtenstein, Iceland, and Norway.

[101] EEA Agreement, Art. 56(1)(a) and (b).

[102] EEA Agreement, Art. 56(1)(c) and (3).

[103] EEA Agreement, Art. 108(2).

4. THE ENFORCEMENT AND APPLICATION OF EC COMPETITION LAW

A. GENERAL

A more detailed discussion relating to the enforcement and application of the EC competition rules is found in Chapters 14 and 15. An introduction is set out here however, as it is necessary to an understanding of the development of the substantive law and the impact of that law on the undertakings subject to it.

The Commission has, so far, played the central role in the enforcement of the law.[104] Both the national courts (through the doctrine of direct effect) and the national competition authorities (through Article 84), to a lesser extent, have also played a part. Further, the Court has the over-arching responsibility for ensuring that 'in the application and interpretation of this Treaty the law is observed'.[105] It will be seen in later chapters, however, that the Commission, although wishing to retain control over competition policy, wishes to hand greater responsibility for the enforcement of Articles 81 and 82 to national entities. In April 1999 the Commission published a White Paper on the modernization of the rules implementing Articles 81 and 82[106] which would give a greater role to national courts and competition authorities and relieve the Commission of some of the burdens currently incumbent upon it. The sections that follow describe the present system and the Commission's proposals are noted at the end.

B. ENFORCEMENT BY THE COMMISSION

(i) BASIS OF THE COMMISSION'S POWERS OF ENFORCEMENT

Article 85 grants the Commission power to enforce the competition rules in the absence of implementing legislation provided for in Article 83. However, in most spheres the Commission's powers are set out in the implementing Regulation 17.[107]

This Chapter discusses the procedures set out in, and the powers conferred upon the Commission by, Regulation 17 unless otherwise indicated.

(ii) NOTIFICATIONS

Parties to an agreement who are afraid that their agreement might infringe Article 81(1) may apply to the Commission for 'negative clearance'[108] (a decision confirming that the

---

[104] See *infra* Chap. 15.

[105] EC Treaty, Art. 220 (ex Art. 164).

[106] Commission White Paper on Modernisation of the Rules Implementing Articles 85 and 86 [now 81 and 82] of the EC Treaty [1999] OJ C132/1, [1999] 5 CMLR 208.

[107] For the implementing Regs in the transport sector see n. 80.

[108] Reg. 17, Art. 2. Negative clearance can in theory also be sought in respect of Art. 82.

agreement does not infringe Article 81(1) at all) and/or notify requesting the grant of an exemption pursuant to Article 81(3). Regulation 17 sets out when notification should occur[109] and what advantages result to the parties from notification. Article 9(1) of Regulation 17 sets up a centralized system conferring the exclusive power on the Commission to declare Article 81(1) inapplicable under Article 81(3).[110]

(iii) INVESTIGATIONS AND FINDINGS OF INFRINGEMENTS

The Commission has power to investigate, and to take action against, those it suspects of infringing the competition rules.[111] The Commission also has power to penalize those infringing the competition rules by imposing fines.[112] Article 17 of Regulation 17 confers 'unlimited jurisdiction' on the Court in review proceedings to cancel, reduce, or increase fines imposed by the Commission.[113]

Regulation 17 confers extensive powers of investigation on the Commission. These are principally contained in Articles 11 and 14. Of particular importance is the power in Article 14(3) for the Commission to conduct a 'dawn raid'. This entitles the Commission to arrive unannounced at an undertaking's premises and to carry out investigations.

Many of the Commission's investigations and findings of infringement have been instigated as a result of a complaint to the Commission lodged by a third party, for example, an aggrieved competitor, customer, or an injured third party. The Commission is not obliged, however, to investigate every complaint that it receives, but can set its own priorities and focus on cases which raise points of particular Community interest.[114] In cases which do not raise such a point the Commission would prefer to see enforcement at the national level.[115]

(iv) THE MERGER RULES

Regulation 4064/89[116] applies to 'concentrations' with a 'Community dimension'. Broadly, with certain limited exceptions, concentrations with a Community dimension must be notified to the Commission and are assessed under the provisions of the Merger Regulation.[117] The Commission must then determine whether or not the concentration falls within the scope of the Merger Regulation and, if it does, whether it is compatible with the

---

[109] See, in particular, Reg. 17, Art. 4(1) and (2) and discussion of the notification system *infra* in Chap. 4. Reg. 3385/94 [1994] OJ L377/94, sets out rules governing the form, content and other details of applications and notifications.

[110] See *infra* Chap. 4.

[111] Reg. 17, Art. 3(1) and (2): see *infra* Chap 14.

[112] Reg. 17, Art. 15(2).

[113] There are similar provisions in the implementing reg. in the transport sector, Reg. 1017/68 [1968] OJ Spec. Ed. 302, Art. 22 and 23; Reg. 4056/86 [1986] OJ, L378/4 19 Art 19 and 20; Reg. 3975/87 [1987] OJ L374/1, Art. 12 and 13.

[114] Case T–24/90, *Automec v. Commission (No 2)* [1992] ECR II–2223, [1992] 5 CMLR 431. The Commission does, however, owe some obligations to a complainant: see *infra* Chap. 15.

[115] See *infra* Chaps. 15 and 16.

[116] [1989] OJ L395/1, as amended by Council Reg. 1310/97 [1997] OJ L180/1.

[117] See *infra* Chap. 12. In contrast, concentrations which do not have a Community dimension are assessed under any applicable national competition rules.

common market. As a general rule the Commission's decision is decisive and no other rule of national or Community competition law applies.[118] The basic scheme is that concentrations with a Community dimension benefit from a 'one stop shop' and are not subject to assessment under the competition rules of the Member States.

C. ENFORCEMENT BY NATIONAL COURTS

(i) DIRECT EFFECT

The Court of Justice held in *BRT* v. *SABAM* that both Article 81(1) and Article 82 have direct effect. The national courts are obliged to protect rights conferred under directly effective Community provisions.

Case 127/73, *BRT* v. *SABAM* [1974] ECR 51, [1974] 2 CMLR 238

SABAM was a copyright collecting society in Belgium and the parties were in dispute about whether its statutes and standard contractual terms infringed Article 82. This matter fell to be decided by the Belgian courts. Meanwhile, the Commission had also instituted proceeding against SABAM over the same issue. SABAM claimed that the Belgian courts could not hear the case in these circumstances. Once the Commission institutes proceedings the courts, being 'authorities of Member States', could no longer act and should stay proceedings.

Court of Justice

10. It has been maintained that the Court is not obliged to reply to the questions referred by the Tribunal of Brussels since the Commission has initiated, of its own motion, a procedure in respect of SABAM in pursuance of Article 3 of Regulation No. 17.

11. According to SABAM, as the civil courts must be considered to be 'authorities of the Member States' within the meaning of Article 9(3) of the said Regulation, the Tribunal of Brussels ought to have stayed the proceedings as from 8 June until the Commission has given its decision.

12. Under Article 9(3) 'as long as the Commission has not initiated any procedure under Articles 2, 3 or 6, the authorities of the Member States shall remain competent to apply Article [81(1)] and Article [82] in accordance with Article [84] of the Treaty'.

13. Consequently, as soon as the Commission has initiated such a procedure the authorities of the Member States cease to be competent to proceed against the same practices or agreements under the said provisions.

14. It must thus be examined whether the national courts, before which the prohibitions contained in Articles [81] and [82] are invoked in a dispute governed by private law, must be considered as 'authorities of the Member States'.

15. The competence of those courts to apply the provisions of Community law, particularly in the case of such disputes, derives from the direct effect of those provisions.

---

[118] Subject of course to the right of those with *locus standi* to bring judicial review proceedings. A Member State may, however, have jurisdiction over various aspects of concentrations with a Community dimension: see Arts 9, 21(3), 223 EC and the discussion *infra* in Chap. 12.

16. As the prohibitions of Articles [81(1)] and [82] tend by their very nature to produce direct effects in relations between individuals these Articles create direct rights in respect of the individuals concerned which the national courts must safeguard.

17. To deny, by virtue of the aforementioned Article 9, the national courts' jurisdiction to afford this safeguard, would mean depriving individuals of rights which they hold under the Treaty itself.

18. The fact that Article 9(3) refers to 'the authorities of the Member States' competent to apply the provisions of Articles [81(1)] and [82] 'in accordance with Article [84]' indicates that it refers solely to those national authorities whose competence derives from Article [84].

19. Under that Article the authorities of the Member States—including in certain Member States courts especially entrusted with the task of applying domestic legislation on competition or that of ensuring the legality of that application by the administrative authorities—are also rendered competent to apply the provisions of Articles [81] and [82] of the Treaty.

20. The fact that the expression 'authorities of the Member States' appearing in Article 9(3) of Regulation No.17 covers such courts cannot exempt a court before which the direct effect of Article [82] is pleaded from giving judgment.

21. Nevertheless, if the Commission initiates a procedure in application of Article 3 of Regulation No.17 such a court may, if it considers it necessary for reasons of legal certainty, stay the proceedings before it while awaiting the outcome of the Commission's action.

The ECJ thus clearly stated that Articles 81(1) and 82 have direct effect and must be applied by national courts in the course of national proceedings. The direct effect of Article 81 is not straightforward however. Currently the exclusive power to confer exemptions pursuant to Article 81(3) is conferred upon the Commission so this provision does not have direct effect.[119]

The ECJ also made it clear that courts acting as 'ordinary' courts are able to apply Articles 81(1) and 82 even where the Commission is itself investigating the matter before the national court. The national courts have a duty, however, to avoid giving judgments which would conflict with a Commission decision or Court judgment. A national court would, therefore, be advised to stay proceedings and/or to adopt interim measures where this is a possibility.[120]

Article 86 has direct effect.[121] Regulations and decisions also produce direct effects, in accordance with normal Community law principles.

(ii) REMEDIES IN NATIONAL COURTS FOR BREACH OF THE EC COMPETITION RULES

Because Article 81 and 82 are directly effective a national court may have to consider arguments raising the compatibility of agreements or conduct with those rules.

a. THE ENFORCEABILITY OF AGREEMENTS

It is fairly common for a party to an agreement to raise a 'Euro-defence' to a contractual

---

[119] Case C–234/89, *Delimitis* v. *Henninger Bräu* [1991] ECR 1–935, [1992] 5 CMLR 210, paras. 44–46.
[120] Case C–234/89, *Delimitis* v. *Henninger Bräu* [1991] ECR 1–935, [1992] 5 CMLR 210; see *infra* Chap. 15.
[121] See *infra* Chap. 8.

claim arguing that it is not bound by the agreement, or a provision within it, since it infringes Article 81(1) and is void. The national court will, therefore, have to determine whether or not the agreement or any provisions within it does in fact infringe Article 81(1) and if so whether or not the agreement is or may be exempted from the prohibition.

b. ACTIONS BY THIRD PARTIES

In many cases a claimant may seek a remedy in respect of another's breach of the Community competition provisions. For example, a purchaser from a cartel concluded in breach of Article 81(1) may claim damages in respect of loss it has suffered as a result of its having had to pay a high purchase price fixed by the cartel's members. A national court will then have to determine whether or not a breach of the rules has been established and whether the claimant should be entitled to damages (or any other remedy requested) to compensate it in respect of its loss.

The starting point is that the national court should determine the success of any claim raising a breach of the Community rules in accordance with its own national rules (the principle of 'national procedural autonomy'[122]). As a matter of English law it has still yet to be resolved whether or not damages are available to compensate an individual which has suffered loss as a result of another's breach of the EC competition rules.

A more interesting and extremely important question, however, is whether or not Community law actually requires a national court to ensure that a specific remedy is available to an individual suffering or who has suffered as a result of another's breach of the competition rules. The answer to this question is considered in Chapter 15.

c. THE ENCOURAGEMENT OF GREATER PROCEEDINGS AT THE NATIONAL LEVEL

The Commission is extremely keen to encourage greater enforcement of the competition rules by national courts, both as a matter of principle and on pragmatic grounds.

As a matter of principle greater national enforcement would bring the enforcement of the law nearer to the citizen, and thus conform with the Community principle of subsidiarity. Further, it would lead to greater incorporation of the national courts within the Community judicial system and would demonstrate to individuals that the competition rules affect undertakings and individuals in their relations *inter se* and not merely *vis-à-vis* an administrative authority. More pragmatically, greater decentralization is essential to ensure that the Commission' resources are available to bring proceedings in cases of particular importance from a Community perspective.

If the Commission's far-reaching proposals to 'modernize' the implementation of the competition rules by decentralization are implemented the national courts will play a fuller role in the enforcement of competition law.

---

[122] Case 33/76, *Rewe-Zentral Finanz eG and Rewe-Zentral AG* v. *Landeswirtschaftskammer für das Saarland* [1976] ECR 1989, [1997] 1 CMLR 533, para. 5, discussed in Chap. 15.

D. ENFORCEMENT BY NATIONAL AUTHORITIES

The combination of Article 84 of the Treaty and Article 9(3) of Regulation 17 means that national authorities empowered to do so by national rules[123] may apply Article 81(1) and Article 82 unless and until the Commission has itself instituted proceedings. However, those provisions confer the sole right to grant exemptions on the Commission.

In practice national authorities have not played a major role in the enforcement of the competition rules.[124] In eight of the fifteen Member States the national competition authorities are not actually empowered by their own national legislation to do so.[125] Even those which are empowered to act have been slow to make use of their powers. This is largely because: (1) they cannot give Article 81(3) exemptions; (2) their proceedings will be terminated if the Commission instigates proceedings (Regulation 17, Article 9(3)); and (3) Community law confers no right on them to impose fines. One of the officials of the German *Bundeskartellamt*, which is competent to apply Articles 81 and 82, summed up the difficulties in the extract below.

H. P. von Stoephasius, 'Enforcement of EC Competition Law by National Authorities' in P. J. Slot and A. MacDonnell (eds), *Procedure and Enforcement in EC and US Competition Law* (Proceedings of the Leiden Europa Institut Seminar on User-friendly Competition Law, Sweet and Maxwell, 1993), 34

Under paragraph 47 GWB [the German Antitrust Act], the FCO [Federal Cartel Office, the Bundeskartellamt] is now competent to exercise responsibilities based on Articles [84] and [85 EC]. The originally unlimited competence of Member States was reduced the moment that all the necessary regulations in favour of the Commission's competence were issued, as intended, *e.g.* Regulation 17 and Regulation 1017/68. These provisions still correspond to Article [84 EC]. According to the Council regulations mentioned above, national authorities remain competent as far as application of Articles [81(1)] and [82] is concerned, in principle, but only as long as the Commission itself has not initiated proceedings. . . .

What appears reasonable in terms of avoiding loopholes turns out to be a real obstacle. What national authority willing to deal with a European case wants to face the fact that this legal action may be cut off by the Commission at any time by the Commission opening its own proceedings?

---

[123] See *infra* n. 125.

[124] National authorities are, however, involved in the enforcement of the competition rules *by the Commission*: see *infra* Chap. 14.

[125] They are not empowered to do so in Austria, Denmark, Finland, Ireland, Luxembourg, Sweden, or the UK (Commission's website on 1 May 2000). They are empowered to do so in Belgium, France, Germany, Greece, Italy, the Netherlands, Portugal, and Spain. In the UK, however, the EC Competition Law (Articles 88 & 89) Enforcement Regulations 1996, SI 1996/2199, allow the UK authorities to deal with matters which are not covered by implementing legislation. The Secretary of State may request the Director General of Fair Trading to carry out an investigation and, following the investigation, refer the matter to the Competition Commission (formerly the Monopolies and Mergers Commission). If the Competition Commission decides there is an infringement the Secretary of State may take remedial action. The regs. were introduced as a response to the dispute over the BA/American Airlines alliance in order to give the UK authorities competence to deal with such issues if they wished: see *supra* n. 92.

A further obstacle to national application of European competition rules is the exclusive power of the Commission to grant individual exemptions under Article [81(3)]. Realistically, is it not a waste of time if the FCO finds a violation of Article [81(1)], and at once, before the national procedure is concluded, the companies concerned turn to Brussels, and apply for an exemption under Article 81(3)? Most probably, such a notification to the Commission will be put in much earlier—and it will have the same effect: to put a stop to every national action based on European competition law.

The third obstacle for the FCO is the lack of a right to impose fines under E.C. law. One can discuss whether this is another exclusive power of the Commission (because this sector is not mentioned in Article [84] at all); in any case, so far there has been no national provision for imposing fines for a violation of E.C. competition rules.

It follows that, to the extent the FCO is competent to apply European competition law,

—such application may be interrupted or terminated at any time by the Commission itself initiating proceedings, and

—no pressure can be brought to bear in applying European competition law, *e.g.* by imposing fines.

Under these circumstances, what impetus is there for a national authority to exercise its rights to apply European competition rules directly? On the contrary, it is clear that there is no motivation for applying these rules.

If the Commission is going to encourage greater decentralized enforcement of the competition law it will have to encourage national authorities to play a greater role. Such a move would again be in accordance with the spirit of subsidiarity. The advantage of the national competition authorities being able to act from the Commission's point of view is that, unlike the national courts, the authorities can actually initiate proceedings and bring infringement proceedings. Proceedings before the national courts, in contrast, are entirely dependent upon individual undertakings commencing proceedings.[126]

In 1997 the Commission published a Notice on co-operation between national competition authorities and the Commission.[127] The Notice points out the advantages which result from the application of the rules by national authorities but fails to deal with the fundamental problem that those authorities cannot grant exemptions. There has, over the years, been debate whether the Commission should relinquish its monopoly over the grant of exemptions and share this responsibility with the national competition authorities. The Commission has been reluctant to do so, largely because it has feared that those authorities would give divergent decisions and that Article 81(3) would, consequently, be applied inconsistently. Further, if exemptions were limited to the territory of the Member State in which they were granted they would be of limited value to undertakings.[128] In its White Paper on modernization, however, the Commission has finally made a much more revolutionary proposal which it hopes will secure greater enforcement of the competition rules at the national level.

---

[126] In the 1997 Notice on agreements of minor importance, for example, the Commission has stated that in cases involving, *inter alia*, price fixing or market sharing where the applicability of Art. 81(1) cannot be ruled out even below the threshold, the Commission will not normally intervene but will leave it for the authorities and courts of the Member States to take action, [1997] OJ C372/13, para. 11. See *infra* Chaps. 3 and 4.

[127] [1997] OJ C313/1.

[128] See Dr A. Schaub, Director-General of Competition, in an address entitled *EC Competition System—Proposals for Reform*, delivered on 22 October 1998 to the 25th Annual Conference on International Antitrust Law and Policy at the Fordham Corporate Law Institute, published on the Competition DG's homepage, http://europa.eu.int/comm/dg04/speech/eight/en.

5. THE COMMISSION'S WHITE PAPER ON THE MODERNIZATION OF THE RULES IMPLEMENTING ARTICLES 81 AND 82

The Commission's White Paper on modernization was published on 28 April 1999.[129] The Commission has been aware for a long time of the need to change the current mechanisms for the enforcement of the competition rules. It is unable to detect and to pursue all serious infringements of the competition rules and needs greater support from the authorities at the national level. The timing of the White Paper was perhaps provoked by a number of factors likely to exacerbate the current position, in particular: the possibility of enlargement of the Community; economic and monetary union (which may encourage economic operators to turn to protectionist measures rather than face the new competitive environment);[130] and increasing globalization of the economy (which may lead firms to attempt to erect artificial barriers between regions).[131]

The Commission has been promoting greater enforcement through the national courts and competition authorities for some time, but little has been happening. The Commission has thus set out proposals in the White Paper to deal with this problem which are radical. The Commission has proposed the abolition of the notification and authorization system set out in Regulation 17 and its sole power to grant exemptions pursuant to Article 81(3). Instead, it has suggested a fully directly applicable system which would allow the Commission, the national courts, and the national competition authorities to apply Article 81 in full.

The proposals in the White Paper on modernization, which have led to the adoption by the Commission of a proposal for a Regulation to replace Regulation 17, are discussed in greater detail in later chapters of this book.[132]

6. FURTHER READING

A. BOOKS

Craig P., and Burca G., *EU Law: Text, Cases and Materials* (2nd edn., Oxford University Press, 1998).

Hartley T.C., *The Foundations of European Community Law* (4th edn., Oxford University Press, 1998).

Slot P.J., and, McDonnell, A., (eds.), *Procedure and Enforcement in EC and US Competition Law* (Sweet and Maxwell, 1993)

---

[129] Commission White Paper on modernisation of the rules implementing Art. 85 and 86 [now 81 and 82] of the EC Treaty [1999] OJ C132/1, [1999] 5 CMLR 208.

[130] *Ibid*, para. 6.

[131] *Ibid*, para. 8.

[132] See in particular *infra* Chap. 16.

3

ARTICLE 81 (FORMERLY ARTICLE 85): THE ELEMENTS

1. INTRODUCTION

The purpose of Article 81 EC (ex Article 85) is to preclude restrictive agreements between independent market operators, whether 'horizontal' (between parties operating at the same level of the economy) or 'vertical'[1] (between parties operating at different levels).

Whether or not an agreement is considered to be restrictive of competition and to contravene the Article will depend, of course, upon the policy objectives being pursued in the enforcement of the rules. In many cases it appears that Article 81 has been used to prohibit agreements which affect competition adversely. In others, it appears that the Community authorities have relied, not on economic analysis and the economic view of the impact of the agreement on competition but on the formal provisions of the agreement. In particular, the Commission has been eager to prevent agreements which might be used to divide up the common market and thwart the single market project. The aims of Article 81 and the policy pursued in its enforcement will be discussed in greater detail in Chapter 4 below.[2]

2. THE TEXT OF ARTICLE 81

Article 81 provides:

(1) The following shall be prohibited as incompatible with the common market: all agreements between undertakings, decisions by associations of undertakings and concerted practices which may affect trade between Member States and which have as their object or effect the prevention, restriction or distortion of competition within the common market, and in particular those which:

    (a) directly or indirectly fix purchase or selling prices or any other trading conditions;

    (b) limit or control production, markets, technical development, or investment;

    (c) share markets or sources of supply;

    (d) apply dissimilar conditions to equivalent transactions with other trading parties, thereby placing them at a competitive disadvantage;

---

[1] See Cases 56 & 58/64, *Etablissements Consten SA & Grundig-Verkaufs-GmbH* v. *Commission* [1966] ECR 299, [1966] CMLR 418 and *infra* 107–109.

[2] See also *supra* Chap. 1.

(e) make the conclusion of contracts subject to acceptance by the other parties of supplementary obligations which, by their nature or according to commercial usage, have no
connection with the subject of such contracts.

(2) Any agreements or decisions prohibited pursuant to this Article shall be automatically void.

(3) The provisions of paragraph 1 may, however, be declared inapplicable in the cases of:

—any agreement or category of agreements between undertakings;
—any decision or category of decisions by associations of undertakings;
—any concerted practice or category of concerted practices,

which contributes to improving the production or distribution of goods or to promoting
technical or economic progress, while allowing consumers a fair share of the resulting benefit,
and which does not:

(a) impose on the undertakings concerned restrictions which are not indispensable to the
attainment of these objectives;

(b) afford such undertakings the possibility of eliminating competition in respect of a substantial part of the products in question.

3. THE SCHEME OF ARTICLE 81

A. THE THREE PARAGRAPHS

It can be seen from the text that Article 81 is in three parts.

(i) THE PROHIBITION

Article 81(1) sets out the prohibition. It prohibits collusion between undertakings which has
as its object or effect the prevention, restriction, or distortion of competition within the
common market and which may affect trade between Member States. It sets out examples of
such preventions, restrictions, or distortions. The list is illustrative, not exhaustive. For the
prohibition in Article 81(1) to apply the following must be established:

• The existence of undertakings;
• Collusion (an agreement, decision or concerted practice) between those under-
takings;
• Collusion which has as its object or effect the prevention, restriction, or distortion of
competition;
• An effect on trade between Member States; and
• An appreciable effect on both competition and trade.[3]

---

[3] Art. 81 does not provide that the effect on competition and trade must be an appreciable one. The Court
of Justice (ECJ) has, however, held that an agreement falls outside the prohibition if its effect on the market is
insignificant, see *infra* 127 ff.

(ii) NULLITY

Although Article 81(2) specifically states that an agreement, decision, or concerted practice prohibited by Article 81(1) is automatically void, the ECJ has held that the nullity affects *only* the clauses in the agreement prohibited by the provision.[4] The agreement as a whole is void only if the prohibited clauses cannot be severed from the remaining terms of the agreement. The nullity is automatic and is not dependent upon any prior decision to that effect.[5]

(iii) EXEMPTION

Agreements, decisions, and concerted practices may be exempted from the prohibition of Article 81(1) under Article 81(3). Exemption may be granted to an agreement etc.[6] which fulfils the four criteria (two positive and two negative) set out in Article 81(3) (broadly where the beneficial aspects of the agreement outweigh its restrictive effect). Exemptions are granted either to individual agreements or to categories of agreements by way of block exemptions. The Commission currently has sole power to declare Article 81(1) inapplicable pursuant to Article 81(3).[7] The Commission has, however, proposed significant changes to the exemption procedure.[8]

B. THE CONSEQUENCES OF INFRINGEMENT

Severe consequences may result for parties to an agreement that contravenes Article 81(1) but which does not benefit from an exemption under Article 81(3).

(i) NULLITY AND PRIVATE PROCEEDINGS BETWEEN THE PARTIES TO A CONTRACT

Provisions in an agreement that contravene Article 81(1) are automatically void. Article 81(2) may, therefore, render carefully negotiated clauses in an agreement void and unenforceable.[9] Further, if the remaining terms of the agreement are severable from the void provisions the parties may be bound to perform the remainder of the contract (one which

---

[4] Case 56/65 *Société La Technique Minière* v. *Maschinebau Ulm GmbH* [1966] ECR 234, [1966] CMLR 357. See *infra* 136.

[5] See Reg. 17 [1959–62] OJ Spec. Ed. 87, Art. 1.

[6] In this chap. unless the context otherwise requires or the discussion is specifically about one or other category of collusion the word 'agreement' is used as shorthand to cover agreements, decisions, and concerted practices.

[7] This monopoly was conferred on the Commission by the Council. The exclusive power is set out in Reg. 17 [1959–62] OJ Spec. Ed. 87, Art. 9(1), see *supra* Chap. 2 and *infra* Chap. 4.

[8] Commission White Paper on modernisation of the rules implementing Articles 85 and 86 [now 81 and 82] of the EC Treaty [1999] OJ C132/1, [1999] 5 CMLR 208 and proposal for a new Reg. implementing Arts. 81 and 82, COM (2000) 582, 27 Sept. 2000; see discussion *infra* Chaps. 4 and 16.

[9] These provisions are directly effective: see *supra* Chap. 2. The English CA (in *Passmore* v. *Morland plc* [1999] 3 All ER 1005, see *infra* 136) has held that the nullity is not absolute but is transient. Thus a void agreement or provision may become valid if the agreement ceases to restrict competition or to affect trade between Member States.

may differ significantly from that which was originally negotiated). The sanction of nullity may, consequently, have a devastating impact on parties to, for example, a joint venture or distribution agreement, and it may be that benefits (money, goods, or services) conferred under a void contractual provision will be irrecoverable.[10]

(ii) INVESTIGATION AND FINES

The sanction of nullity will not be much of a threat to some parties to a prohibited agreement. Members of a cartel, for example, are unlikely to be concerned about their inability to enforce the agreement in court (rather, they are likely to have their own mechanisms in place for enforcement of the cartel). Cartels may, however, be deterred by the risk of investigation by the Commission and the likelihood of a fine if a breach is detected. The Commission has power under Regulation 17 to investigate suspected infringements of Article 81, to order those found to have violated the provision to put an end to the breach, and to impose fines on undertakings that have committed a breach of the competition rules. Fines imposed may be of up to 10 per cent of an undertaking's turnover in the preceding year of business, and in cases of serious violations of the rules have tended to be large.[11]

(iii) THIRD PARTY ACTION

In addition, a third party injured by the action of a cartel or another prohibited agreement may bring tortious or other proceedings at the national level before a national court. In particular, damages in respect of any loss suffered in consequence of the prohibited contract might be sought.

4. THE INTERPRETATION AND APPLICATION OF ARTICLE 81(1)

A. GENERAL

(i) A NOTE ON INTERPRETATION

In Chapter 2 it was explained that the Court's method of statutory interpretation, although drawing on those of the national courts, is an individual one. In particular, it adopts a 'teleological' approach construing Community acts in accordance with the broad system of Treaty aims and objectives set out in Articles 2 and 3. When construing the elements of

---

[10] This has been the view taken by the English courts: see, e.g., *Gibbs Mew plc* v. *Gemmel* [1999] 1 EGLR 43 and discussion *infra* in Chap. 15.

[11] Reg. 17, Art. 15: see *infra* Chap. 14.

Article 81 the ECJ has, therefore, tended to adopt an interpretation which best reflects the Treaty's aims and principles.[12]

(ii) ECONOMICS AND ARTICLE 81

Article 81 is drafted in terms of economic concepts. Before it can be determined whether or not an agreement restricts competition or restricts competition and trade appreciably for the purposes of Article 81(1) or whether an agreement eliminates competition substantially for the purposes of Article 81(3) it would seem essential that the market the agreement affects is analysed. The definition of the relevant market is, or should be, of vital importance in determining the compatibility of agreements with Article 81.[13]

S. Bishop and M. Walker, *The Economics of EC Competition Law: Concepts, Application and Measurement* (Sweet & Maxwell, 1999)

4.45 Traditionally, the definition of the relevant market has not played a significant part in the competitive assessment in Article [81] decisions. While the Court of First Instance in its *Italian Flat Glass* . . . judgment argued that an analysis of the market, contrary to the Commission's view, would not have been superfluous, Article [81] decisions have to date tended to pay lip service to the relevant market concept and it is typically defined in an ad hoc fashion.

However, the definition of the relevant market potentially has a similarly important role to play in Article [81] decisions as it does in decisions taken under Article [82] or the Merger Regulation. Relevant market definitions when conducted properly helps to focus attention on the nature of the competitive constraints which exist between products and helps to understand the various ways in which products do—or might—compete with one another.

B. THE MEANING OF 'UNDERTAKING'

(i) EVERY ENTITY ENGAGED IN AN ECONOMIC ACTIVITY

The term 'undertaking' is not defined in the Treaty but has been widely construed by the European Court. It has the same meaning for the purposes of both Article 81 and Article 82.[14]

In *Polypropylene*[15] the Commission stated that '[t]he subjects of [EC] competition rules are undertakings, a concept which is not identical to the question of legal personality for the purposes of company law and fiscal law . . . It may, however, refer to any entity engaged in

---

[12] See, in particular, Case 56/65, *Société La Technique Minière* v. *Maschinenbau Ulm GmbH* [1966] ECR 234, [1966] 1 CMLR 357 (see *supra* n. 4 and accompanying text), and Cases 56 & 58, *Etablissements Consten SA & Grundig-Verkaufs-GmbH* v. *Commission* [1966] ECR 299, [1966] CMLR 418, *infra* 122.

[13] For the difficulties involved in market definition, see *supra* Chap. 1 and *infra* Chap. 6.

[14] See Cases T–68, 77 & 78/89, *Società Italiana Vetro* v. *Commission* [1992] ECR II–1403, [1992] 5 CMLR 302. Many of the cases discussed below concerned Art. 82 rather than Art. 81.

[15] [1986] OJ L230/1, [1988] 4 CMLR 347, para. 99.

commercial activities.' The ECJ has confirmed this broad interpretation. In *Höfner and Elser* v. *Macrotron* it stated that 'the concept of undertaking encompasses every entity engaged in an economic activity regardless of the legal status of the entity and the way in which it is financed'.[16]

(ii) THE LEGAL STATUS OR FORM OR THE ENTITY IS IMMATERIAL

Because the focus is on the activities or functions of the entity its legal personality is irrelevant. As well as companies and partnerships, therefore, individuals,[17] sporting bodies,[18] professional bodies (the fact that the business occupation of a body is viewed as a liberal profession is not inconsistent with the fact that it may be an undertaking or an association of undertakings engaged in an economic activity[19]), trade associations,[20] agricultural co-operatives[21] and P & I[22] have been held to be undertakings for the purposes of the rules. It is not the nature of the body but the nature of the activity it pursues which is important. This point is illustrated by a case concerning the 1990 World Cup. In this case the Commission held that sporting and other associations, the international football federation (FIFA), the Italian FA (FIGC), and the local organizing committee, which carried out economic activities, were undertakings within the meaning of Article 81(1).[23]

The Distribution of Package Tours During the 1990 World Cup [1992] OJ L326/31, [1994] 5 CMLR 253

FIFA appointed the Italian football federation (FICG) organiser of the 1990 Football World Cup, held in Italy in 1990 (Italia '90). A local organising committee was set up. This committee granted a joint venture, set up by two Italian travel agencies, exclusive worldwide rights for the sale of match tickets as part of package tours. Apart from this, tickets were sold through national football and other sports associations, the European Football Federation, the tournament sponsors and an Italian bank. The national associations and the bank were prohibited from selling their tickets to travel agents. As a consequence of these arrangements, travel agents outside the Italian joint venture could not put together package tours which included match tickets. Complaints were, therefore,

---

[16] See Case C–41/90, *Höfner and Elser* v. *Macroton* [1991] ECR I–1979, [1993] 4 CMLR 306, para. 21; Cases C–159–160/91 *Poucet and Pistre* v. *Assurances Générales de France* [1993] ECR I–637, para. 17; Case 364/92, *SAT Fluggesellschaft* v. *Eurocontrol* [1994] ECR I–43, [1994] 5 CMLR 208, para. 18.

[17] E.g., opera singers in *RAI/UNITEL* [1978] OJ L157/39 and individual inventors in *Reuter/BASF* [1976] OJ L254/40, [1976] 2 CMLR D44. See also Case 42/84, *Remia BV and Verenigde Bedrijven Nutricia* v. *Commission* [1985] ECR 2545, [1987] 1 CMLR 1; *Vaassen BV /Moris* [1979] OJ L19/32, [1979] 1 CMLR 511.

[18] *Distribution of Package Tours During the 1990 World Cup* [1992] OJ L326/31, [1994] 5 CMLR 253, paras. 43–58.

[19] *AICIA* v. *CNSD* [1993] OJ L203/27, [1995] 5 CMLR 495, para. 40.

[20] Case 96/82, *IAZ International Belgium NV* v. *Commission* [1983] ECR 3369, [1984] 3 CMLR 276.

[21] See Case C–250/92, *Gøttrup-Klim Grovvareforening and Others* v. *Dansk Landbrugs Grovvareselskab AmbA* [1994] ECR I–5641, [1996] 4 CMLR 191.

[22] *P&I Clubs* [1985] OJ L376/2, [1989] 4 CMLR 178.

[23] Note that the French organizers of the 1998 World Cup were also found to have infringed the competition rules. In this case it was found that they had abused their dominant position contrary to Art. 82 by discriminating on grounds of nationality: *1998 World Cup Finals* IP(99)541, [2000] OJ L5/55, [2000] 4 CMLR 963.

lodged with the Commission alleging that the arrangements were contrary to Article 81(1). One question which arose was whether or not the football authorities were 'undertakings' within the meaning of Article 81(1).

Commission

44. *Regarding the commercial nature of the World Cup*

The World Cup is indisputably a major sporting event. However, it also involves activities of an economic nature, notably as regards:

— the sale of 2,700,000 entrance tickets for matches, more than 20% of which are included in package tours comprising hotel accommodation, transport and sightseeing,

— the conclusion of contracts for advertising on panels within the grounds,

— the commercial exploitation of the FIFA emblems, the World Cup, the FIFA fair-play trophy and the World Cup mascot,

— the commercial exploitation by the local organizer of a specific emblem for the 1990 World Cup, and

— the conclusion of television broadcasting contracts.

45. The economic value of the World Cup is, moreover, acknowledged in Article 3.4 of the specifications and conditions laid down by FIFA for the organising federation.

46. The economic value of the World Cup was also acknowledged by FIFA representatives at the hearing (see page 126 of the hearing record).

47. *FIFA*

FIFA is a federation of sports associations and accordingly carries out sports activities. However, FIFA also carried out activities of an economic nature, notably as regards:

— the conclusion of advertising contracts,

— the commercial exploitation of the World Cup emblems, and

— the conclusion of contracts relating to television broadcasting rights.

48. In the case of the 1990 World Cup, the sale of advertising and television broadcasting rights by FIFA accounted for some 65% of total World Cup revenue, estimated at Sfr 220 million.

49. It must therefore be concluded that FIFA is an entity carrying on activities of an economic nature and constitutes an undertaking within the meaning of Article [81 EC].

50. The *Federazione Italiana Gioco Calcio (FIGC)* is the national Italian football association, appointed by FIFA to organize the 1990 World Cup.

51. The FIGC was accordingly responsible for the entire organization of the event in accordance with the provisions of the 1990 World Cup regulations and had in particular the task of ensuring that grounds were in order, press facilities provided, parking spaces laid out, etc.

52. For the purpose of financing such expenditure, the FIGC had a share in the net profits of the competition and was able to exploit commercially in Italy the 1990 World Cup emblem, which it had itself created.

53. The FIGC thus also carries on activities of an economic nature and is consequently an undertaking within the meaning of Article [81 EC].

54. *Local organizing committee*

The local organizing committee is a body set up jointly by FIFA and the FIGC for the purpose of carrying on all activities relating directly or indirectly to the technical and logistical organisation of the World Cup. The local organising committee's tasks included the establishment and implementation of the ticket distribution arrangements.

55. The local organising committee's revenue derived partly from television rights, advertising rights, the sale of tickets and the commercial exploitation in Italy of the World Cup emblem.

56. The exclusive rights granted to 90 Tour Italia resulted in remuneration for the local organising committee, in accordance with the provisions of Article 5 of the contract of 26 June 1987.

57. It must therefore be concluded that the local organising committee was a body carrying on activities of an economic nature and consequently constituted an undertaking within the meaning of Article [81].

58. *The Compagnia Italiana Tourismo SpA (CIT)* is an Italian company engaged in travel agency activities. It is therefore an undertaking within the meaning of Article [81].

59. Italia Tour SpA is a company carrying on an activity similar to that of CIT and is thus also an undertaking within the meaning of Article [81].

60. 90 Tour Italia SpA is a company established under Italian law by CIT and Italia Tour for the purpose of putting together and marketing package tours to the 1990 World Cup. It is therefore an undertaking within the meaning of Article [81].

(iii) PUBLIC BODIES AND BODIES PERFORMING PUBLIC FUNCTIONS

The conclusion that any entity which engages in commercial activities and provides a service, or product, on the market may be an undertaking means that the agreements and conduct of public bodies or corporations can be scrutinized for compatibility with the rules. An entity may be an undertaking even where it does not have an independent legal personality but forms part of a State's general administration.[24] It is irrelevant that the body is not profit-making,[25] or that is not set up for an economic purpose.[26] However, an entity, public or private, which performs tasks of a public nature will not be an undertaking, and so will be immune from the application of the rules.

The following public or quasi-public bodies have, applying these criteria, been found to be undertakings: a German state-run employment agency;[27] the European Broadcasting Union;[28] independent customs agents in Italy;[29] the association of public broadcasting institutions in Germany;[30] a voluntary old-age pension scheme for agricultural workers in France;[31] a sectoral pension fund to which workers were compulsorily affiliated by govern-

[24] *Spanish Courier Services* [1990] OJ L233/19, [1991] 3 CMLR 560; *Aluminium Products* [1985] OJ L92/1, [1987] 3 CMLR 813.

[25] Case 96/82, *IAZ International Belgium NV* v. *Commission* [1983] ECR 3369, [1984] 3 CMLR 276; Case C–67/96, *Albany International BV* v. *Stichting Bedrijfspensioenfonds Textielindustrie*, judgment of 21 Sept. 1999 discussed *infra* at 000–000.

[26] Case 155/73, *Sacchi* [1974] ECR 409, [1974] 2 CMLR 177.

[27] Case C–41/90, *Höfner and Elser* v. *Macrotron* [1991] ECR I–1979, [1993] 4 CMLR 306: see extract *infra* at 000.

[28] *EBU* [1993] OJ L179/23, [1995] 4 CMLR 56.

[29] Case C–35/96, *Italy* v. *Commission* [1998] ECR I–3851, [1998] 5 CMLR 889, paras 36–38.

[30] *Film Purchases by German Television Stations* [1989] OJ L284/96, [1990] 4 CMLR 841.

[31] Case C–244/94, *Fédération Française des Sociétés d'Assurance and Others* v. *Ministère de l'Agriculture et de la Pêche* [1995] ECR I–4013, [1996] 4 CMLR 536: see discussion *infra* 96 ff.

ment regulation;[32] the Spanish post office;[33] and public television broadcasting organizations.[34] In *Höfner and Elser* v. *Macrotron* the ECJ focused on the responsibilities of the relevant entity.

Case C–41/90, *Höfner and Elser* v. *Macrotron* [1991] ECR I–1979, [1993] 4 CMLR 306

Under German law on the promotion of employment (the AFG) the Bundesanstalt für Arbeit (Federal Office for Employment, the Bundesanstalt), a public agency, had a monopoly in employment recruitment. Nevertheless the Bundesanstalt tolerated private agencies dealing with the recruitment of business executives. This case concerned a dispute which arose in the German courts between a private recruitment agency and a company for which it had provided recruitment services in breach of the Bundesanstalt's exclusive right. The private agency sought to recover fees payable under the terms of the recruitment contract. The German courts took the view that the claim should fail on the grounds that the contract had been concluded in breach of German law and was void. The German Civil Code provides that any legal act which infringes a statutory prohibition is void (the prohibition applies to employment procurement activities carried out in breach of the AFG). The Oberlandesgericht München nevertheless considered that the outcome of the dispute might be dependent on Community law and referred a number of questions to the Court of Justice under Article 234. In particular, it asked whether the Bundesanstalt had committed an abuse of a dominant position.[35] This necessitated consideration of whether the Bundesanstalt was an undertaking for the purposes of the competition rules.

Court of Justice

21. It must be observed, in the context of competition law, first that the concept of an undertaking encompasses every entity engaged in an economic activity, regardless of the legal status of the entity and the way in which it is financed and, secondly, that employment procurement is an economic activity.

22. The fact that employment procurement activities are normally entrusted to public agencies cannot affect the economic nature of such activities. Employment procurement has not always been, and is not necessarily, carried out by public entities. That finding applies in particular to executive recruitment.

23. It follows that an entity such as a public employment agency engaged in the business of employment procurement may be classified as an undertaking for the purpose of applying the Community competition rules.

24. It must be pointed out that a public employment agency which is entrusted, under the legislation of a Member State, with the operation of services of general economic interest, such as those envisaged in Article 3 of the AFG, remains subject to the competition rules pursuant to Article [86(2) EC] unless and to the extent to which it is shown that their application is incompatible with the discharge of its duties: see Case 155/73, *Sacchi* [[1974] ECR 409].

In contrast, the following bodies have been found *not* to be undertakings and so not

---

[32] Case C–67/96 *Albany International BV* v. *Stichting Bedrijfspensioenfonds Textielindustrie* [2000] 4 CMLR 446: see discussion *infra* 96 ff. See also Cases (–180–184/98 *Parlou* v. *Stichting Pensioenfonds Medische Specialisten*, judgment of 12 Sept. 2000.

[33] *Spanish Courier Services* [1990] OJ L233/19, [1991] 4 CMLR 560.

[34] Case 155/73, *Sacchi* [1974] ECR 409, [1974] 2 CMLR 177.

[35] This aspect of the case is discussed in Chaps. 7 and 8.

subject to the prohibitions set out in Article 81 or Article 82: Eurocontrol;[36] a French body running a compulsory social security scheme;[37] a body governed by private law but entrusted by the public authorities with anti-pollution surveillance and control at the port of Genoa;[38] and French municipal authorities giving exclusive concessions in respect of funeral services.[39]

In the latter case, *Bodson*,[40] the competition rules were not applicable because the local authority was carrying out an administrative duty, granting concessions for funeral services. Similarly, in *Eurocontrol*, the European air traffic control organization, which performed tasks which were in the public interest (maintaining and improving air navigation safety), was found not to be an undertaking even though it collected route charges. The supervision of airspace was a duty typically reserved to public authorities.

Case C–364/92, *SAT Fluggesellschaft* v. *Eurocontrol* [1994] ECR I–43, [1994] 5 CMLR 208

Eurocontrol is an international organisation established to deal with matters of air navigation safety. At the time of the case nine of the (then) twelve EC Members States were members of Eurocontrol. However, because many of the States were reluctant to give up control of their respective air space, Eurocontrol attended to the common organisation of air navigation services only in respect to Northern Germany and the Benelux countries. A German airline, SAT, was in dispute with Eurocontrol about route charges. SAT refused to pay claiming that Eurocontrol was infringing Articles 82 and 86 EC. The Belgian Cour de Cassation made a reference to the Court of Justice asking whether Eurocontrol was an undertaking within the meaning of those Articles.

Court of Justice

19. In order to determine whether Eurocontrol's activities are those of an undertaking within the meaning of Articles [82] and [86] of the Treaty, it is necessary to establish the nature of those activities.

20. Under Article 1 of the Convention on International Civil Aviation, signed at Chicago on 7 December 1944. . . . [t]he Contracting States recognise that every State has complete and exclusive sovereignty over the air space above its territory. It is in the exercise of that sovereignty that the States ensure, subject to compliance with the provisions of the applicable international conventions, the supervision of their air space and the provision of air navigation control services.

21. According to the Convention establishing it, Eurocontrol is a regionally-oriented international organization, whose aim is to strengthen cooperation between the Contracting States in the field of air navigation and develop joint activities in this field, making due allowance for defence needs and providing maximum freedom for all space users consistent with the required level of safety. The organisation is to act in cooperation with the civil and military authorities of the Contracting States (Article 1 of the amended Convention).

22. Eurocontrol's tasks, as defined in Article 2 of the amended Convention, are concerned in the first place with research, planning, coordination of national policies and staff training.

---

[36] Case C–364/92, *SAT Fluggesellschaft* v. *Eurocontrol* [1994] ECR I–43, [1994] 5 CMLR 208.
[37] Case C–159/91, *Poucet et Pistre* v. *Assurances Générales de France* [1993] ECR I–637; see discussion *infra* at 96 ff.
[38] Case C–343/95, *Diego Cali* v. *SEPG* [1997] ECR I–1547, [1997] 5 CMLR 484.
[39] Case 30/87, *Bodson* v. *Pompes Funèbres des Régions Libérées* [1988] ECR 2479, [1989] 4 CMLR 984.
[40] *Ibid.*

23. Secondly, Eurocontrol is competent to establish and collect the route charges levied on users of air space. Eurocontrol settles, in accordance with the guidelines laid down by the International Civil Aviation Organisation, the common formula on the basis of which the route charges are calculated. That formula takes into account the weight of the aircraft and the distance travelled, to which a 'rate per unit' is applied. That rate is not fixed by Eurocontrol, but by each of the Contracting States for the use of its air space. A single charge, making up the sum of the charges payable, is calculated and collected by Eurocontrol for each flight. The charges are collected on behalf of the Contracting States to which they are paid over, after deduction of a proportion of the revenue corresponding to an 'administrative rate' intended to cover collection costs.

24. Finally, as the Protocol of 12 February 1981 expressly provides, the operational exercise of air navigation control is limited since Eurocontrol can only carry on that activity at the request of the Contracting States. In that connection, it is common ground that Eurocontrol confines itself to providing air space control for the Benelux countries and the northern part of the Federal Republic of Germany from its Maastricht centre. For the purposes of such control, Eurocontrol is vested with rights and powers of coercion which derogate from ordinary law and which affect users of air space. In exercising those particular powers, it must ensure compliance with international agreements and national rules concerning access, overflying and the territorial security of the Contracting States concerned.

25. So far as the last-mentioned activity is concerned, it may be noted that it has not been disputed that Eurocontrol is required to provide navigation control in that air space for the benefit of any aircraft travelling through it, even where the owner of the aircraft has not paid the route charges owed to Eurocontrol.

26. Finally, Eurocontrol's activities are financed by the contributions of the Contracting States.

27. Eurocontrol thus carries out, on behalf of the Contracting States, tasks in the public interest aimed at contributing to the maintenance and improvement of air navigation safety.

28. Contrary to SAT's contention, Eurocontrol's collection of route charges, which gave rise to the dispute in the main proceedings, cannot be separated from the organizations other activities. Those charges are merely the consideration, payable by users, for the obligatory and exclusive use of air navigation control facilities and services. As the Court has already held, specifically in connection with the interpretation of the abovementioned Convention of 27 September 1968, Eurocontrol must, in collecting the charges, be regarded as a public authority acting in the exercise of its powers . . .

29. Eurocontrol acts in that capacity on behalf of the Contracting States without really having any influence over the amount of the route charges. Responsibility for the fact, relied upon by SAT before the national court, that the amounts of the charges vary in time or with respect to the areas overflown, cannot be attributed to Eurocontrol, which merely establishes and applies a common formula in the circumstances set out above, but to the Contracting States which set the amount of the rates per unit.

30. Taken as a whole, Eurocontrol's activities, by their nature, their aim and the rules to which they are subject, are connected with the exercise of powers relating to the control and supervision of air space which are typically those of a public authority. They are not of an economic nature justifying the application of the Treaty rules of competition.

31. Accordingly, an international organization such as Eurocontrol does not constitute an undertaking subject to the provisions of Articles [82] and [86] of the Treaty.

32. On those grounds, the answer to the question submitted must be that Articles [82] and [86] of the Treaty are to be interpreted as meaning that an international organisation such as Eurocontrol does not constitute an undertaking within the meaning of those articles.

In *Diego Cali*,[41] the ECJ referred to *Eurocontrol* when dealing with a case in which the national port authority at Genoa entrusted anti-pollution surveillance and intervention to a *private* limited company. That company was found not to be an undertaking since it carried out services which were not of an economic nature but which were essential functions of the State.

Case C–343/95, *Diego Cali* v. *SEPG* [1997] ECR I–1547, [1997] 5 CMLR 484

Court of Justice

22. The anti-pollution surveillance for which SEPG was responsible in the oil port of Genoa is a task in the public interest which forms part of the essential functions of the State as regards protection of the environment in maritime areas.

23. Such surveillance is connected by its nature, its aim and the rules to which it is subject with the exercise of powers relating to the protection of the environment which are typically those of a public authority. It is not of an economic nature justifying the application of the Treaty rules on competition . . .

The outcome of *Höfner and Elser* v. *Macrotron*, *Eurocontrol*, and *Diego Cali* turned, therefore, upon the ECJ's assessment of whether or not the entity concerned was carrying out functions of a commercial/economic or public nature.

In a line of cases concerning pension funds and social security schemes the ECJ has drawn a distinction between entities which operate in the same way as, or in competition with, ordinary commercial enterprises in the same sector and entities which fulfil an exclusively social function. In *Poucet et Pistre*[42] it was held that a French body running a compulsory social security scheme was not an undertaking. In this case benefits received under the scheme were not proportionate to contributions and contributions made were proportionate to income (there was an element of cross-subsidy).

Case C–159/91, *Poucet et Pistre* v. *Assurances Générales de France* [1993] ECR I–637

Court of Justice

18. Sickness funds, and the organizations involved in the management of the public social security system, fulfil an exclusively social function. That activity is based on the principle of national solidarity and is entirely non-profit-making. The benefits paid are statutory benefits bearing no relation to the amount of contributions.

19. Accordingly, that activity is not an economic activity and, therefore, the organizations to which it is entrusted are not undertakings within the meaning of Articles [81] and [82] of the Treaty.

Conversely, in *Fédération Française des Sociétés d'Assurance*[43] a body operating a pension scheme was found to be an undertaking. Although it was non profit-making it operated in the same way as other insurance companies, the rules were like those of private schemes

---

[41] Case C–343/95, *Diego Cali* v. *SEPG* [1997] ECR I–1547, [1997] 5 CMLR 484.

[42] Case C–159/91 *Poucet et Pistre* v. *Assurances Générales de France* [1993] ECR I–637.

[43] Case C–244/94, *Fédération Française des Sociétés d'Assurance and Others* v. *Ministère de l'Agriculture et de la Pêche* [1995] ECR I–4013, [2000] 4 CMLR 446.

and there was no mutuality or cross-subsidy between the beneficiaries. The ECJ further considered these cases in *Albany*.

Case C–67/96, *Albany International BV* v. *Stichting Bedrijfspensioenfonds Textielindustrie,* ECJ, 21 September 1999, [2000] 4 CMLR 446

This case concerned a dispute between Albany International BV (hereinafter 'Albany') and Stichting Bedrijfspensioenfonds Textielindustrie (the Textile Industry Trade Fund, hereinafter 'the Fund'). Broadly, the Fund had been established following a collective agreement between organisations representing employers and workers in the Textile Industry sector. Such supplementary pensions were normally managed by collective schemes covering a sector of the economy, a profession or the employees of an undertaking by funds. In this case affiliation to the Fund has been made compulsory, by the Minister for Social Affairs and Employment on 4 December 1975 in accordance with the Wet van 17 maart 1949 houdende vaststelling van en regeling betreffende verplichte deelneming in een bedrijfspensioenfonds (Law of 17 March 1949 on compulsory affiliation to a sectoral pension fund, hereinafter the 'BPW')

Albany operated a textile business which had been affiliated to the Fund since 1975. Because the pension organised by the Fund was originally not very generous Albany, in 1981, concluded arrangements with an insurance company for a supplementary pension for its workers so that the total pension to which they would be entitled after 40 years' employment amounted to 70% of their last salary. In 1989 the Fund changed its pension scheme, also awarding workers an amount representing 70% of their final salary. After the changes Albany requested to be exempted from the affiliation, broadly on the grounds that it had concluded arrangements for a supplementary pension scheme for its staff several years earlier and the arrangements were similar to those introduced by the Fund. Nonetheless the Fund demanded payment of NLG 36 700.29, representing all statutory contributions payable since 1989 together with interest, collection charges, non-judicial expenses and legal aid costs. Albany challenged that demand before the Kantongerecht, Arnhem. It contended amongst other points that the system of compulsory affiliation to the Fund was contrary to Article 3(1)(g) of the Treaty and Articles 81, 82 and 86 EC. The Kantongerecht, Arnhem, stayed proceedings and requested a preliminary ruling from the Court of Justice. One of the questions asked was whether a sectoral pension fund within the meaning of Article 1(1)(b) of the BPW was an undertaking within the meaning of Articles 81, 82 or 86 of the EC Treaty.[44]

Court of Justice

71. By its first question, the national court seeks essentially to ascertain whether a pension fund responsible for managing a supplementary pension scheme set up by a collective agreement concluded between organisations representing employers and workers in a given sector and to which affiliation has been made compulsory by the public authorities for all workers in that sector is an undertaking within the meaning of Article [81] et seq. of the Treaty.

72. According to the Fund and the governments which have intervened, such a fund does not constitute an undertaking within the meaning of Article [81] et seq. of the Treaty. They describe the various characteristics of the sectoral pension fund and of the supplementary pension scheme which it manages.

73. First, compulsory affiliation of all workers in a given sector to a supplementary pension scheme pursues an essential social function within the pension system applicable in the Netherlands because of the extremely limited amount of the statutory pension calculated on the basis of the minimum

---

[44] But see also *infra* n. 46 and accompanying text and discussion of the case *infra* 110.

statutory wage. Provided that a supplementary pension scheme has been established by a collective agreement within a framework laid down by law and affiliation to that scheme has been made compulsory by the public authorities, it constitutes an element of the Netherlands system of social protection and the sectoral pension fund responsible for management of it must be regarded as contributing to the management of the public social security service.

74. Second, the sectoral pension fund is non-profit-making. It is managed jointly by both sides of the industry, who are equally represented on its management committee. The sectoral pension fund collects an average contribution fixed by that committee which strikes a balance, collectively, between the amount of the premiums, the value of the benefits and the extent of the risks. Moreover, the contributions may not fall below a certain level, so as to establish adequate reserves, and may not, in order to preserve its non-profit-making status, exceed an upper limit, observance of which is ensured by management and labour and by the Insurance Board. Even though the contributions levied are invested on a capitalisation basis, the investments are made under the supervision of the Insurance Board and in accordance with the provisions of the PSW and the statutes of the sectoral pension fund.

75. Third, operation of the sectoral pension fund is based on the principle of solidarity. Such solidarity is reflected by the obligation to accept all workers without a prior medical examination, the continuing accrual of pension rights despite exemption from contributions in the event of incapacity for work, the discharge by the fund of arrears of contributions due from an employer in the event of the latter's insolvency and by the indexing of the amount of the pensions in order to maintain their value. The principle of solidarity is also apparent from the absence of any equivalence, for individuals, between the contribution paid, which is an average contribution not linked to risks, and pension rights, which are determined by reference to an average salary. Such solidarity makes compulsory affiliation to the supplementary pension scheme essential. Otherwise, if 'good' risks left the scheme, the ensuing downward spiral would jeopardise its financial equilibrium.

76. On that basis, the Fund and the intervening governments consider that the sectoral pension fund is an organisation charged with the management of social security schemes of the kind referred to in the judgment in Joined Cases C–159/91 and C–160/91 *Poucet and Pistre* [1993] ECR I–637, and is unlike the organisation at issue in Case C–244/94 *Fédération Française des Sociétés d'Assurance and Others* v. *Ministère de l'Agriculture et de la Pêche* [1995] ECR I–4013, which was regarded as an undertaking within the meaning of Article [81] et seq. of the Treaty.

77. It should be borne in mind that, in the context of competition law, the Court has held that the concept of an undertaking encompasses every entity engaged in an economic activity, regardless of the legal status of the entity and the way in which it is financed (see, in particular, Case C–41/90 *Höfner and Elser* [1991] ECR I–1979, paragraph 21; *Poucet and Pistre*, cited above, paragraph 17; and *Fédération Française des Sociétés d'Assurance*, cited above, paragraph 14).

78. Moreover, in *Poucet and Pistre*, cited above, the Court held that that concept did not encompass organisations charged with the management of certain compulsory social security schemes, based on the principle of solidarity. Under the sickness and maternity scheme forming part of the system in question, the benefits were the same for all beneficiaries, even though contributions were proportional to income; under the pension scheme, retirement pensions were funded by workers in employment; furthermore, the statutory pension entitlements were not proportional to the contributions paid into the pension scheme; finally, schemes with a surplus contributed to the financing of those with structural financial difficulties. That solidarity made it necessary for the various schemes to be managed by a single organisation and for affiliation to the schemes to be compulsory.

79. In contrast, in *Fédération Française des Sociétés d'Assurance*, cited above, the Court held that a non-profit-making organisation which managed a pension scheme intended to supplement a basic compulsory scheme, established by law as an optional scheme and operating according to the prin-

ciple of capitalisation, was an undertaking within the meaning of Article [81] et seq. of the Treaty. Optional affiliation, application of the principle of capitalisation and the fact that benefits depended solely on the amount of the contributions paid by the beneficiaries and on the financial results of the investments made by the managing organisation implied that that organisation carried on an economic activity in competition with life assurance companies. Neither the social objective pursued, nor the fact that it was non-profit-making, nor the requirements of solidarity, nor the other rules concerning, in particular, the restrictions to which the managing organisation was subject in making investments altered the fact that the managing organisation was carrying on an economic activity.

80. The question whether the concept of an undertaking, within the meaning of Article [81] et seq. of the Treaty, extends to a body such as the sectoral pension fund at issue in the main proceedings must be considered in the light of those considerations.

81. The sectoral pension fund itself determines the amount of the contributions and benefits and that the Fund operates in accordance with the principle of capitalisation.

82. Accordingly, by contrast with the benefits provided by organisations charged with the management of compulsory social security schemes of the kind referred to in *Poucet and Pistre*, cited above, the amount of the benefits provided by the Fund depends on the financial results of the investments made by it, in respect of which it is subject, like an insurance company, to supervision by the Insurance Board.

83. In addition, as is apparent from Article 5 of the BPW and Articles 1 and 5 of the Guidelines for exemption from affiliation, a sectoral pension fund is required to grant exemption to an undertaking where the latter has already made available to its workers for at least six months before the request was lodged on the basis of which affiliation to the fund was made compulsory, a pension scheme granting them rights at least equivalent to those which they would acquire if affiliated to the fund. Moreover, under Article 1 of the abovementioned Guidelines, that fund is also entitled to grant exemption to an undertaking which provides its workers with a pension scheme granting them rights at least equivalent to those deriving from the fund, provided that, in the event of withdrawal from the fund, compensation considered reasonable by the Insurance Board is offered for any damage suffered by the fund, from the actuarial point of view, as a result of the withdrawal.

84. It follows that a sectoral pension fund of the kind at issue in the main proceedings engages in an economic activity in competition with insurance companies.

85. In those circumstances, the fact that the fund is non-profit-making and the manifestations of solidarity referred to by it and the intervening governments are not sufficient to deprive the sectoral pension fund of its status as an undertaking within the meaning of the competition rules of the Treaty.

86. Undoubtedly, the pursuit of a social objective, the abovementioned manifestations of solidarity and restrictions or controls on investments made by the sectoral pension fund may render the service provided by the fund less competitive than comparable services rendered by insurance companies. Although such constraints do not prevent the activity engaged in by the fund from being regarded as an economic activity, they might justify the exclusive right of such a body to manage a supplementary pension scheme.

87. The answer to the first question must therefore be that a pension fund charged with the management of a supplementary pension scheme set up by a collective agreement concluded between organisations representing employers and workers in a given sector, to which affiliation has been made compulsory by the public authorities for all workers in that sector, is an undertaking within the meaning of Article [81] et seq. of the Treaty.

The ECJ stressed the economic functions carried out by the pension fund. The fund was, therefore, found to be an undertaking even though affiliation to the scheme was compulsory; the supplementary pension scheme was designed to top up an extremely limited statutory pension; the sectoral pension fund was non-profit-making; and the pension fund was obliged to accept all workers without a medical examination. The ECJ accepted that the social objectives which the pension fund were required to pursue might make the service it provided less competitive than those offered by other insurance companies. These factors did not, however, detract from the fact that the activities it engaged in were economic ones. The pension fund determined the amount of contributions made and benefits received (the latter were dependent upon the results of the investments made by it) and it could, in certain circumstances, grant exemption from affiliation to the fund. The social objectives were relevant, however, to the ECJ's finding that the public authority could nonetheless confer on a pension fund the exclusive right to manage a supplementary pension scheme in a given sector.[45]

The distinctions set out in this series of cases are fine ones but turn on the *functions* performed by the bodies, *viz.* whether the entity performs tasks which are of a commercial character or which are essentially those which should be discharged by the State. This focus on the tasks carried out by the body involved may mean that that entity is characterized as an undertaking in respect of some of the functions it performs but not others. When carrying out public duties it may not be acting as an undertaking and so outside the ambit of the competition rules. However, when acting in a commercial context it will need to comply with the competition rules unless the conditions set out in Article 86(2) of the Treaty are satisfied.

(iv) PUBLIC UNDERTAKINGS AND ARTICLE 86 (EX ARTICLE 90)

Article 86 of the Treaty exempts some activities of public bodies or bodies entrusted with public services from the application of the competition rules even when the body is found to be an 'undertaking' within the meaning of Article 81 or Article 82. Broadly, Article 86(2) provides that undertakings entrusted with the operation of services of general economic interest or having the character of a revenue-producing monopoly are subject to the competition rules only in so far as the application of the rules does not obstruct the performance of the tasks assigned to them. Like all derogations from the main Treaty objectives, Article 86(2) has been construed narrowly.[46]

(v) EMPLOYEES AND TRADE UNIONS

It seems that employees acting as employees are not undertakings for the purposes of the competition rules (although in some circumstances the actions of the employee will, however, be attributable to the employer).[47] Rather employees in an employment relationship are incorporated within their employers and 'do not therefore in themselves constitute

---

[45] See *infra* n. 46 and accompanying text. See also and discussion of the case *infra* 110.

[46] In Case C–67/96, *Albany International BV* v. *Stichting Bedrijfspensioenfonds Textielindustrie* [2000] 4 CMLR 446, however, the ECJ accepted that the application of the competition rules would make it impossible for the pension fund to perform its tasks of an economic nature: see *infra* Chap. 8.

[47] See *infra* 117.

"undertakings" within the meaning of Community competition law'.[48] In *Albany* Advocate General Jacobs took the view that the competition rules were not designed to cover the activities of employees. They were not structured to be applicable to employees and employees did not perform the 'functions' of undertakings. In addition, trade unions would not be characterized as undertakings in so far as they acted as agent for their members (employees).

Case C–67/96, *Albany International BV* v. *Stichting Bedrijfspensioenfonds Textielindustrie* 28 January, 1999, [2000] 4 CMLR 446

Advocate General Jacobs

(a) *Employees*

. . .

211. Accordingly, the question arises how to classify the fact that employees offer labour against remuneration.

212. One could argue that it is an economic activity similar to the sale of goods or the provision of services. From an economic point of view, that may—arguably—be true. However, I do not think that, from a legal perspective, the assertion is correct.

213. First, it is difficult to see how the term 'undertaking' could be understood in the sense of 'employee'. To interpret the Treaty in a manner that would include the latter term in the former would, in my view, exceed the limits which its wording imposes.

214. Secondly, the functional interpretation of the term 'undertaking' which the Court has adopted in its case-law leads to the same result. With respect to public bodies the Court examines whether the activity in question is—at least potentially—performed by private entities engaged in the supply of goods or services. . . . Individuals, too, may be classified as undertakings . . . if they are independent economic actors on the markets for goods or services. The rationale underlying those cases is that the entities under scrutiny are fulfilling the 'function' of an undertaking. The application of Articles [81] and [82] is justified by the fact that those public bodies or individuals are operating on the same or similar markets and according to similar principles as 'normal' undertakings. . . .

215. Dependent labour is by its very nature the opposite of the independent exercise of an economic or commercial activity. Employees normally do not bear the direct commercial risk of a given transaction. They are subject to the orders of their employer. They do not offer services to different clients, but work for a single employer. For those reasons there is a significant functional difference between an employee and an undertaking providing services. That difference is reflected in their distinct legal status in various areas of Community . . . or national law.

216. Thirdly, the system of Community competition law is not tailored to be applicable to employees. The examples of anticompetitive practices in Articles [81(1)] and [82] or the conditions for exemption in Article [81(3)] are clearly drafted with regard to economic actors engaged in the supply of goods or services. Article [81(1)(a)] for example refers to 'purchase or selling prices' and to 'other trading conditions'. Employees, on the contrary, are concerned with 'wages' and 'working conditions'. To apply Article [81(1)] to employees would therefore necessitate the use of uneasy analogies between the markets for goods and services and labour markets.

---

[48] Case C–22/98 *Criminal proceedings against Becu*, judgment of 16 September, 1999, para. 26.

217. Accordingly, in my view, employees in principle fall outside the personal scope of the prohibition of Article [81(1)]. The future will probably show whether that principle applies also in certain borderline areas such as for example professional sport.

(b) *Trade unions*

218. Since employees cannot be qualified as undertakings for the purposes of Article [81], trade unions, or other associations representing employees, are not 'associations of undertakings'.

219. However, are trade unions themselves 'undertakings'?

220. The mere fact that a trade union is a non-profit-making body does not automatically deprive the activities which it carries on of their economic character . . .

221. A trade union is an association of employees. It is established that associations may also be regarded as 'undertakings' in so far as they themselves engage in an economic activity. . . .

222. It must be borne in mind that an association can act either in its own right, independent to a certain extent of the will of its members, or merely as an executive organ of an agreement between its members. In the former case its behaviour is attributable to the association itself, in the latter case the members are responsible for the activity.

223. With regard to ordinary trade associations, the result of that delimitation is often not important, since Article [81] applies in the same way to agreements between undertakings and to decisions by associations of undertakings. . . . It may be relevant when the Commission has to decide to whom to address its decision and whom to fine. . . .

224. However, in the case of trade unions that delimitation becomes decisive, since, if the trade union is merely acting as agent, it is solely an executive organ of an agreement between its members, who themselves—as seen above—are not addressees of the prohibition of Article [81(1)].

225. With regard to trade union activities one has therefore to proceed in two steps: first, one has to ask whether a certain activity is attributable to the trade union itself and if so, secondly, whether that activity is of an economic nature.

226. There are certainly circumstances where activities of trade unions fulfil both conditions. Some trade unions may for example run in their own right supermarkets, savings banks, travel agencies or other businesses. When they are acting in that capacity the competition rules apply.

227. However in the present cases the trade unions are engaged in collective bargaining with employers on pensions for employees of the sector. In that respect the trade unions are acting merely as agent for employees belonging to a certain sector and not in their own right. That alone suffices to show that in the present cases they are not acting as undertakings for the purposes of competition law.

The ECJ in *Albany* did not rule specifically on whether or not, or when, employees or trade unions qualify as undertakings for the purposes of the competition rules. On the facts of the case it held that collective agreements concluded between trade unions and employers relating to conditions of employment and working conditions fell outside Article 81(1) altogether. These agreements were concluded to fulfil important social objectives which should not be frustrated by the application of Article 81(1).[49]

---

[49] See *infra* 110.

(vi) SUCCESSION

Difficulties may arise where an undertaking responsible for an infringement of the competition rules does not exist (or does not exist in an identical form) at the date that enforcement proceedings are commenced or concluded. In each case, it must be determined who is the natural or legal person responsible for operating the undertaking at the time the infringement took place. That person must answer for the infringement.[50]

A successor which has acquired all the rights and liabilities of an undertaking involved in an infringement (which has ceased to exist) will be liable for the actions of the predecessor.[51] This may be a significant potential liability for a would-be acquirer of an undertaking. A change of the legal form and name of an undertaking does not create a new undertaking free of liability for the anti-competitive behaviour of its predecessor, when, from an economic point of view, the two are identical.[52] The determining factor is 'whether there is a functional and economic continuity between the original infringer and the undertaking into which it was merged'[53] ('undertaking identity'). However, where a company responsible for operating the undertaking involved in the infringement is still in existence, it may be liable under Article 81(1) even though it has disposed of the assets in the affected market.[54] Liability will be imposed only where there is no doubt about the identity of the entity which is the legal successor or about the reality of the continuations by that entity of the activity which gave rise to the proceedings. In *All Weather Sports Benelux BV* v. *European Commission*,[55] for example, the CFI considered that doubt did exist: although the undertaking imputed with liability had taken over the assets of the undertaking involved in the infringement, the latter undertaking still continued to exist (in a different name), albeit only for tax purposes.

(vii) SINGLE ECONOMIC ENTITY

a. WHAT IS A SINGLE ECONOMIC ENTITY?

Companies belonging to the same group and having the status of parent and subsidiary may have distinct legal personalities. However, 'if the undertakings form an economic unit within which the subsidiary has no real freedom to determine its course of action on the market'[56] they are treated, for the purpose of Article 81, as a single economic entity. The unified conduct on the market of the parent company and its subsidiaries takes precedence

---

[50] See Case T–9/89, *Enichem Anic SpA* v. *Commission* [1991] ECR II–1623 paras. 234–36. See generally, L. Garzamiti and G. Scassellati-Sforzolini, 'Liability of Successor Undertakings for Infringements of EC Competition Law Committed Prior to Corporate Reorganisations' (1995) ECLR 348.

[51] Cases 40–48, 50, 54–56, 111, 113–4/73, *Re the European Sugar Cartel; Coöperative Vereniging 'Suiker Unie' UA and others* v. *Commission* [1975] ECR 1663, [1976] 1 CMLR 295.

[52] Cases 29, 30/83, *Compagnie Royale Asturienne des Mines SA and Rheinzink GmbH* v. *Commission* [1984] ECR 1697, [1985] 1 CMLR 688, para. 9.

[53] *PVC* [1989] OJ L74/1, [1990] 4 CMLR 345, para. 42; see also *Peroxygen Products* [1985] OJ L35/1, [1985] 1 CMLR 481; *Polypropylene* [1986] OJ L230/1, [1988] 4 CMLR 347; *Welded Steel Mesh* [1989] OJ L 260/1, [1991] 4 CMLR 13, para. 194.

[54] Case T–9/89, *Enichem Anic SpA* v. *Commission* [1991] ECR 11–1623.

[55] Case T–38/92 [1994] ECR 11–211.

[56] Case 15/74, *Centrafarm BV and Adnaan De Peijper* v. *Sterling Drug Inc* [1974] ECR 1183, [1974] 2 CMLR 480, para. 41. See generally W. P. J. Wils, 'The Undertaking as Subject of E.C. Competition Law and the Imputation of Infringements to Natural or Legal Persons' (2000) 25 *ELRev.* 99.

over the formal separation between the companies resulting from their separate legal personalities. Whether or not a subsidiary does have sufficient freedom of action to be considered a separate entity will depend on a number of factors, for example, whether the parent has control of the board of directors, the amount of profit taken by the parent, and whether the subsidiary complies with directions given by the parent on matters such as marketing and investment. Where a parent has a majority shareholding, there is a presumption that the subsidiary is not independent.[57] In *Viho Europe BV v. Commission*,[58] the ECJ confirmed that the Commission had correctly found that a parent company and its 100 per cent owned subsidiaries were a single economic unit. Consequently, agreements between these companies were not caught by Article 81(1) as an agreement *between undertakings* did not exist.

Case C–73/95P, *Viho Europe BV* v. *Commission* [1996] ECR I–5457, [1997] 4 CMLR 419

Parker Pen Ltd is a company incorporated under English law which produces writing utensils. This case concerned a complaint made by a Dutch company, Viho, which marketed office equipment on a wholesale basis. Viho had been unable to obtain Parker products on conditions equivalent to those granted to Parker's subsidiaries and independent distributions. It complained to the Commission that Parker's distribution system (which prohibited exports between Member States, divided the common market into national markets, and maintained artificially high prices on those national markets) was in breach of Article 81(1). Parker sold its products in Europe through subsidiary companies in Germany, Belgium, France, Spain and the Netherlands of which it owned 100% of the shares. Sales and marketing of the products through the subsidiaries were controlled by an area team of three directors.

After an investigation the Commission informed Viho that it was rejecting the complaint. Parker's subsidiary companies were wholly dependent on it, enjoyed no real autonomy and the distribution system did not go beyond the normal allocation of tasks within a group of undertakings. Viho appealed against the Commission's rejection of the complaint to the Court of First Instance which upheld the decision (Case T–102/92 [1995] ECR II–17, [1995] 4 CMLR 299). Article 81(1) referred only to relations between economic entities which were capable of competing with one another. It did not cover agreements or concerted practices between entities belonging to the same group if they formed an economic unit. Viho appealed to the Court of Justice. That Court confirmed that the Commission and the Court of First Instance had correctly classified the Parker Group as one economic unit within which the subsidiaries did not enjoy real autonomy in determining their course of action in the market.

Court of Justice

13. The appellant claims that the fact that the conduct in question occurs within a group of companies does not preclude the application of Article [81(1)], since the division of responsibilities between the companies in the Parker group aims to maintain and partition national markets by means of absolute territorial protection. The evaluation of such conduct, which has harmful effects on competition, should not therefore depend on whether it takes place within a group or between Parker and its independent distributors. The appellant points out that such territorial protection prevents third parties such as itself from obtaining supplies freely within the Community from the

---

[57] See the Opinion of Warner AG in Cases 6, 7/73, *Istituto Chemioterapico Italiano Spa and Commercial Solvents Corp v. EC Commission* [1974] ECR 223, [1974] 1 CMLR 309 .

[58] Case C–73/95P, *Viho Europe BV v. Commission* [1996] ECR I–5457, [1997] 4 CMLR 419.

subsidiary which offers the best commercial terms, so as to be able to pass such benefits on to the customer.

14. Consequently, the appellant considers that Article [81(1)], interpreted in the light of Articles 2 and [3(1)(c) and (g)] . . . of the E.C. Treaty must apply, since the referral policy in question goes far beyond a mere internal allocation of tasks within the Parker group.

15. It should be noted, first of all, that it is established that Parker holds 100 per cent of the shares of its subsidiaries in Germany, Belgium, Spain, France and the Netherlands and that the sales and marketing activities of its subsidiaries are directed by an area team appointed by the parent company and which controls, in particular, sales targets, gross margins, sales costs, cash flow and stocks. The area team also lays down the range of products to be sold, monitors advertising and issues directives concerning prices and discounts.

16. Parker and its subsidiaries thus form a single economic unit within which the subsidiaries do not enjoy real autonomy in determining their course of action in the market, but carry out the instructions issued to them by the parent company controlling them (Case 48/69, *ICI* v. *E.C. Commission* . . .; Case 15/74, *Centrafarm* v. *Sterling Drug* . . .; Case 16/74, *Centrafarm* v. *Winthrop* . . .; Case 30/87, *Bodson* v. *Pompes Funebres* . . .; and Case 66/86, *Ahmed Saeed Flugreisen and Others* v. *Zentrale zur Bekämpfung Unlauteren Wettbewerbs* . . .).

17. In those circumstances, the fact that Parker's policy of referral, which consists essentially in dividing various national markets between its subsidiaries, might produce effects outside the ambit of the Parker group which are capable of affecting the competitive position of third parties cannot make Article [81(1)] applicable, even when it is read in conjunction with Article 2 and Article [3(1)(c)] and (g) of the Treaty. On the other hand, such unilateral conduct could fall under Article [82] of the Treaty if the conditions for its application, as laid down in that article were fulfilled.

18. The Court of First Instance was therefore fully entitled to base its decision solely on the existence of a single economic unit in order to rule out the application of Article [81(1)] to the Parker group.

This case establishes that truly unilateral behaviour of an undertaking, even a group of connected companies, will escape the ambit of the competition rules unless that undertaking holds a dominant position and commits an infringement of Article 82.[59] In contrast, distribution arrangements concluded between independent undertakings may be caught by Article 81(1). The complaints lodged by Viho about the arrangements between Parker and its *independent distributors* i.e. firms which were not connected to Parker by any type of ownership or control (and which were not part of the same economic unit) led to a Commission decision finding that the distribution arrangements were in breach of Article 81(1) and to the parties being fined.[60]

Whether or not an undertaking is independent or part of the same economic unit is a question of degree. In contrast to *Viho*, the Commission found in *Gosmé/Martell-DMP*,[61] that an agreement between a parent and its 50 per cent owned joint venture company fell within the scope of Article 81(1). The parent only jointly owned the company which was able to operate to a large extent autonomously of it.

---

[59] See Chap. 5, but see *infra* 114 ff.

[60] See the appeals to the CFI in Case T–66/92, *Herlitz AG* v. *Commission* [1994] ECR II–531, [1995] 5 CMLR 458 and Case T–77/92, *Parker Pen Ltd* v. *Commission* [1994] ECR II–549, [1995] 5 CMLR 435.

[61] [1991] OJ L185/23, [1992] 5 CMLR 586.

b. CONSEQENCES OF THE SINGLE ECONOMIC ENTITY DOCTRINE

It was seen from the case of *Viho Europe BV* v. *Commission* that one vital consequence of the doctrine is that arrangements between entities within an economic unit cannot amount to an agreement or concerted practice between undertakings[62] (although it is of course possible that the conduct of the undertaking is incompatible with Article 82[63]). Further, other consequences may flow from a finding that entities form a single economic unit.

First, such entities are counted as only one party to an agreement. This is vital to the application of some block exemptions which permit only 'bilateral' agreements.[64]

Secondly, companies can be held responsible for the acts of other entities, within the economic unit, such as subsidiaries found to be in breach of a Treaty provision. Consequently, both the parent company and the subsidiary may be liable for the breach of the competition rules. Where both are liable each can be fined under Council Regulation 17, Article 15, and they will be jointly and severally liable. In *Commercial Solvents*[65] the ECJ upheld the Commission's decision fining both a parent and its subsidiary for breach of the competition rules. The two undertakings were to be treated as one economic unit.[66] Further the Commission may impose fines 'from [Euro] 1,000 to 1,000,000 . . . or a sum in excess thereof but not exceeding 10 per cent of the turnover in the preceding business year of each of the undertakings participating in the infringement'. The reference is to 10 per cent of the infringing undertaking's turnover worldwide. This inevitably includes turnover of all the entities within the corporate group and is not restricted to the entity concerned or the turnover earned in the market in which the infringement was committed.[67]

Thirdly, the existence of other entities within the same economic unit may affect the application of some Community secondary legislation and Commission Notices. For example, some block exemptions, such as Regulation 2790/1999,[68] and the Commission's Notice on agreements of minor importance[69] apply only to undertakings which do not exceed certain specified market shares. These provisions make clear that, when calculating market shares, the shares of all entities closely connected to the body that actually entered

---

[62] See also Case 15/74, *Centrafarm BV and Adnaan De Peijper* v. *Sterling Drug Inc* [1974] ECR 1183, [1974] 2 CMLR 480.

[63] See generally *infra* Chap. 5.

[64] See the block exemption on technology transfer agreements, Reg. 240/96 [1996[OJ L31/2 (see also, for example, Reg. 1983/83 [1993] OJ L173/1 and Reg. 1984/83 [1983] OJ L173/7, which were replaced on 1 June 2000 by the new block exemption Reg. 2790/1999 [1999] OJ L336/21 applying to categories of vertical agreements and concerted practices: see *infra* Chap. 9) and Case 170/83, *Hydrotherm Gerätebau GmbH* v. *Compact de Dott Ing Mario Adredi & CSAS* [1984] ECR 2999, [1985] 3 CMLR 224.

[65] Cases 6, 7/73, *Istituto Chemioterapico Italiano Spa and Commercial Solvents Corp* v. *Commission* [1974] ECR 223, [1974] 1 CMLR 309.

[66] The parent may not, however, be liable where the subsidiary's conduct diverges from the instructions of the parent, as was the case with the imposition of the export ban in *BMW*, Cases 32/78, 32–82/78 *BMW Belgium* v. *Commission* [1979] ECR 2435, [1980] 1 CMLR 370.

[67] See Reg. 17 [1959–62] OJ Spec. Ed. 87, Art. 15(2) and discussion of fines and fining policy *infra* in Chap. 14.

[68] Reg. 2790/1999 [1999] OJ L336/21 on the application of Art. 81(3) of the Treaty to categories of vertical agreements or concerted practices, Art. 11.

[69] Commission Notice on agreements of minor importance which do not fall within the meaning of Article 85(1) [now Article 81(1)] of the Treaty establishing the European Community [1997] OJ C372/13, [1998] 4 CMLR 192, para. 12.

into the agreement must be taken into account.[70] Similarly, the activities of the whole group must be considered when determining whether or not the parties to the agreement are competing undertakings.[71]

Fourthly, the doctrine may be critical when considering the position of undertakings outside the EC's jurisdiction. In *ICI* v. *Commission (Dyestuffs)*,[72] the ECJ rejected the applicant's argument that the Commission was not empowered to impose fines on it in respect of actions taken outside the Community. By the use of its power to control its subsidiaries established in the Community, the applicant had been able to ensure that its decisions were implemented on that market. The subsidiary did not enjoy real autonomy in determining its course of actions in the market. Its action could, therefore, be attributed to the parent. In this way the single economic entity doctrine avoids many of the problems of the extraterritorial application of EC competition law. It enables the competition rules to be applied to companies outside the jurisdiction without recourse to the more controversial 'implementation' or 'effects' doctrines.[73]

C. THE MEANING OF 'AGREEMENT'

(i) HORIZONTAL AND VERTICAL AGREEMENTS

Article 81(1) applies to agreements concluded between two or more undertakings. It is not applicable, however, where agreements are concluded between companies forming part of a single economic entity or to genuine agency agreements.[74] In the course of argument in *Consten and Grundig* v. *Commission*[75] it was suggested that, similarly, Article 81(1) should not be applied to agreements concluded between undertakings operating at different levels of the economy. If a producer could restrict the actions of its commercial representative without triggering the operation of Article 81(1) it should also be able to restrict the action of independent distributors. Article 81 should not be concerned with agreements concluded between entities which were not competitors and which were not on an equal footing. Rather, any conduct considered to be restrictive of competition should be dealt with under Article 82. The ECJ rejected these arguments, holding that Article 81(1) could apply to vertical arrangements.[76] The wording of the provision did not suggest that a distinction between horizontal and vertical agreements should be drawn. The agreement had not been concluded between a manufacturer and an entity integrated within it but had been concluded between independent undertakings. Further, the fact that the agreement was not concluded between competitors

---

[70] The term participating or connected undertakings seeks to include all undertakings which form part of the same economic unit: see also the Notice on agreements of minor importance, para 12, *infra* 130 and Reg. 2790/1999 [1999] OJ L336/21, Art. 11.

[71] See Reg. 2790/1999, Arts 2(4) and 11.

[72] Cases 48, 49, 51–7/69 [1972] ECR 619, [1972] CMLR 557, paras 125–146.

[73] The extraterritorial application of the competition rules is discussed *infra* Chap. 17.

[74] Case C–73/95P, *Viho Europe BV* v. *Commission* [1996] ECR I–5457, [1997] 4 CMLR 419 and *infra* n. 167 and Chap. 9.

[75] Cases 56 & 58 *Etablissements Consten SA & Grundig-Verkaufs-GmbH* v. *Commission* [1966] ECR 299, [1966] CMLR 418.

[76] Distribution agreements are discussed *infra* in Chap. 9.

was immaterial. Article 81 applied to all agreements between undertakings which might distort competition within the common market.

Cases 56 & 58, *Etablissements Consten SA & Grundig-Verkaufs-GmbH* v. *Commission* [1966] ECR 299, 339–40 [1966] CMLR 418, 469–71

In 1957 Grundig, a German manufacturer of radios, tape recorders, dictaphones and televisions, appointed Consten as its exclusive agent for France. Consten agreed, amongst other things, not to handle any competing products, to order a minimum quantity of Grundig products, to stock accessories and spare parts and to provide after-sales services. In return, Grundig agreed not to deliver the product for sale in France and imposed export and re-export restrictions on all distributors in other Member States. The Grundig trade mark, Gint was registered in France in Consten's name. Under the agreements Consten, therefore, had absolute territorial protection. No-one else was entitled to sell Grundig products in France either actively or passively. In fact, UNEF, a Parisien company, started importing and selling Grundig products at more favourable prices in France. Consten commenced proceedings in the French courts contending that UNEF had failed to respect its contract with Grundig, that it was indulging in unfair competition and that it was infringing Consten's trade mark rights. It also brought proceedings against Leissner in Strasbourg which had also obtained Grundig products for resale in France. UNEF complained to the Commission and, in 1963, the agreement was notified to the Commission for examination. The French court adjourned its proceedings to await the Commission's decision.

   The Commission concluded that the agreements did infringe Article 81(1) and could not be exempted under Article 81(3). Consten and Grundig appealed to the Court of Justice. One of their pleas was that Article 81(1) applied only to 'horizontal' and not 'vertical' agreements. This argument was supported by the Italian government.

Court of Justice
The complaints concerning the applicability of Article [81(1)] to sole distributorship contracts.

The applicants submit that the prohibition in Article [81(1)] applies only to so-called horizontal agreements. The Italian Government submits furthermore that sole distributorship contracts do not constitute 'agreements between undertakings' within the meaning of that provision, since the parties are not on a footing of equality. With regard to these contracts, freedom of competition may only be protected by virtue of Article [82] of the Treaty.

Neither the wording of Article [81] nor that of Article [82] gives any ground for holding that distinct areas of application are to be assigned to each of the two Articles according to the level in the economy at which the contracting parties operate. Article [81] refers in a general way to all agreements which distort competition within the Common Market and does not lay down any distinction between those agreements based on whether they are made between competitors operating at the same level in the economic process or between non-competing persons operating at different levels. In principle, no distinction can be made where the Treaty does not make any distinction.

Furthermore, the possible application of Article [81] to a sole distributorship contract cannot be excluded merely because the grantor and the concessionnaire are not competitors inter se and not on a footing of equality. Competition may be distorted within the meaning of Article [81(1)] not only by agreements which limit competition which might take place between one of them and third parties. For this purpose, it is irrelevant whether the parties to the agreement are or are not on a footing of equality as regards their position and function in the economy. This applies all the more, since, by such an agreement, the parties might seek, by preventing or limiting the competition of third parties in respect of the products, to create or guarantee for their benefit an unjustified advantage at the expense of the consumer or user, contrary to the general aims of Article [81].

It is thus possible that, without involving an abuse of a dominant position, an agreement between economic operators at different levels may affect trade between Member States and at the same time have as its object or effect the prevention, restriction or distortion of competition, thus falling under the prohibition of Article [81(1)].

In addition, it is pointless to compare on the one hand the situation, to which Article [81] applies, of a producer bound by a sole distributorship agreement to the distributor of his products with on the other hand that of a producer who includes within his undertaking the distribution of his own products by some means, for example, by commercial representatives, to which Article [81] does not apply. These situations are distinct in law and, moreover, need to be assessed differently, since two marketing organizations, one of which is [i]ntegrated into the manufacturer's undertaking whilst the other is not, may not necessarily have the same efficiency. The wording of Article [81] causes the prohibition to apply, provided that the other conditions are met, to an agreement between several undertakings. Thus it does not apply where a sole undertaking integrates its own distribution network into its business organization. It does not thereby follow, however, that the contractual situation based on an agreement between a manufacturing and a distributing undertaking is rendered legally acceptable by a simple process of economic analogy—which is in any case incomplete and in contradiction with the said Article. Furthermore, although in the first case the Treaty intended in Article [81] to leave untouched the internal organization of an undertaking and to render it liable to be called in question, by means of Article [82], only in cases where it reaches such a degree of seriousness as to amount to an abuse of a dominant position, the same reservation could not apply when the impediments to competition result from agreement between two different undertakings which then as a general rule simply require to be prohibited.

Finally, an agreement between producer and distributor which might tend to restore the national divisions in trade between Member States might be such as to frustrate the most fundamental objections of the Community. The Treaty, whose preamble and content aim at abolishing the barriers between States, and which in several provisions gives evidence of a stern attitude with regard to their reappearance, could not allow undertakings to reconstruct such barriers. Article [81(1)] is designed to pursue this aim, even in the case of agreements between undertakings placed at different levels in the economic process.

The submissions set out above are consequently unfounded.

(ii) AGREEMENTS MAY BE CAUGHT WHATEVER THEIR FORM

The word 'agreement' has been given an extremely broad construction. It catches agreements whether or not they amount to a contract under national rules, whether or not they are intended to be legally binding, and whether they are in writing or oral. It covers so-called 'gentlemen's agreements'[77] standard conditions of sale,[78] trade association rules (which are treated as an agreement between the members to abide by the rules)[79] and agreements entered into to settle disputes, such as trade mark delimitation agreements.[80] It does not matter that no sanction is provided for breach of the agreement. Further, an agreement

---

[77] Case 41/69, *ACF Chemiefarma NV* v. *Commission* (the *Quinine Cartel*) [1970] ECR 661.
[78] Case C–277/87, *Sandoz Prodotti Farmaceutici Spa* v. *Commission* [1990] ECR I–45.
[79] *Nuovo Cegam* [1984] OJ L99/29, [1984] 2 CMLR 484.
[80] See *infra* Chapter 10.

which has been terminated may be caught by Article 81(1) in respect of the period after termination if the effects of the agreement continue to be felt.[81] Agreements may be caught even if they are encouraged or approved by national law[82] or entered into after consultation with the national authorities.[83]

Article 81(1) *does not*, however, apply to collective agreements between workers and employers intended to improve working conditions which belong to the realm of social policy. In *Albany International BV* v. *Stichting Bedrijfspensioenfonds Textielindustrie*[84] the ECJ held that agreements concluded by representative of employers and workers in a sector would not be caught by Article 81(1) in so far as those agreements related to the improvement of conditions of work and employment. Not only was it an objective of the Treaty to ensure that competition in the common market was not distorted, but one of the Treaties objectives was to achieve a high level of employment and social protection. The latter objective would be thwarted if Article 81(1) applied to agreements adopted by management and labour to improve conditions of work and employment. Consequently, such agreements fell outside the scope of Article 81(1) of the Treaty altogether.

Case C–67/96, *Albany International BV* v. *Stichting Bedrijfspensioenfonds Textielindustrie*, 21 September 1999, [2000] 4 CMLR 446

Court of Justice

46. By its second question, which it is appropriate to consider first, the national court seeks essentially to ascertain whether Article [3(1)(g)] of the Treaty, Article 5 of the EC Treaty (now Article 10 EC) and Article [81] of the Treaty prohibit a decision by the public authorities to make affiliation to a sectoral pension fund compulsory at the request of organisations representing employers and workers in a given sector.

47. Albany contends that the request by management and labour to make affiliation to a sectoral pension fund compulsory constitutes an agreement between the undertakings operating in the sector concerned, contrary to Article [81(1)] of the Treaty. . . .

52. It is necessary to consider first whether a decision taken by the organisations representing employers and workers in a given sector, in the context of a collective agreement, to set up in that sector a single pension fund responsible for managing a supplementary pension scheme and to request the public authorities to make affiliation to that fund compulsory for all workers in that sector is contrary to Article [81] of the Treaty.

53. It must be noted, first, that Article [81(1)] of the Treaty prohibits all agreements between

---

[81] Case T–7/89, *SA Hercules NV* v. *Commission* [1991] ECR II–1711, [1992] 4 CMLR 84. Whether or not an agreement has been terminated may be difficult to determine: see *Soda-ash—Solvay* [1991] OJ L152/1, [1994] 4 CMLR 645.

[82] See Cases 43 & 63/88, *VBVB & VBBB* v. *Commission* [1984] ECR 19, [1985] 1 CMLR 27; *Aluminium Imports from Eastern Europe* [1985] OJ L92/1, [1987] 3 CMLR 813; *AROW/BNIC* [1982] OJ L379/1, [1983] 2 CMLR 240.

[83] Cases 240/82 etc, *SSI* v. *Commission* [1985] ECR 3831, [1987] 3 CMLR 661. Where the State *requires* undertakings to enter into anti-competitive agreements, and the situation is created by the State, Art. 86 may be relevant, see *infra* in Chap. 8.

[84] Case C–67/96 *Albany International BV* v. *Stichting Bedrijfspensioenfonds Textielindustrie*, [2000] 4 CMLR 446.

undertakings, decisions by associations of undertakings and concerted practices which may affect trade between Member States and which have as their object or effect the prevention, restriction or distortion of competition within the common market. The importance of that rule prompted the authors of the Treaty to provide expressly in Article [81(2)] of the Treaty that any agreements or decisions prohibited pursuant to that article are to be automatically void.

54. Next, it is important to bear in mind that, under Article 3(g) and (i) of the EC Treaty (now, after amendment, Article 3(1)(g) and (j) EC), the activities of the Community are to include not only a 'system ensuring that competition in the internal market is not distorted' but also 'a policy in the social sphere'. Article 2 of the EC Treaty (now, after amendment, Article 2 EC) provides that a particular task of the Community is 'to promote throughout the Community a harmonious and balanced development of economic activities' and 'a high level of employment and of social protection'.

55. In that connection, Article 118 of the EC Treaty (Articles 117 to 120 of the EC Treaty have been replaced by Articles 136 EC to 143 EC) provides that the Commission is to promote close co-operation between Member States in the social field, particularly in matters relating to the right of association and collective bargaining between employers and workers.

56. Article 118b of the EC Treaty (Articles 117 to 120 of the EC Treaty having been replaced by Articles 136 EC to 143 EC) adds that the Commission is to endeavour to develop the dialogue between management and labour at European level which could, if the two sides consider it desirable, lead to relations based on agreement.

57. Moreover, Article 1 of the Agreement on social policy (OJ 1992 C 191, p. 91) states that the objectives to be pursued by the Community and the Member States include improved living and working conditions, proper social protection, dialogue between management and labour, the develop-ment of human resources with a view to lasting high employment and the combatting of exclusion.

58. Under Article 4(1) and (2) of the Agreement, the dialogue between management and labour at Community level may lead, if they so desire, to contractual relations, including agreements, which will be implemented either in accordance with the procedures and practices specific to management and labour of the Member States, or, at the joint request of the signatory parties, by a Council decision on a proposal from the Commission.

59. It is beyond question that certain restrictions of competition are inherent in collective agree-ments between organisations representing employers and workers. However, the social policy object-ives pursued by such agreements would be seriously undermined if management and labour were subject to Article [81(1)] of the Treaty when seeking jointly to adopt measures to improve conditions of work and employment.

60. It therefore follows from an interpretation of the provisions of the Treaty as a whole which is both effective and consistent that agreements concluded in the context of collective negotiations between management and labour in pursuit of such objectives must, by virtue of their nature and purpose, be regarded as falling outside the scope of Article [81(1)] of the Treaty.

61. The next question is therefore whether the nature and purpose of the agreement at issue in the main proceedings justify its exclusion from the scope of Article [81(1)] of the Treaty.

62. First, like the category of agreements referred to above which derive from social dialogue, the agreement at issue in the main proceedings was concluded in the form of a collective agreement and is the outcome of collective negotiations between organisations representing employers and workers.

63. Second, as far as its purpose is concerned, that agreement establishes, in a given sector, a supplementary pension scheme managed by a pension fund to which affiliation may be made compul-sory. Such a scheme seeks generally to guarantee a certain level of pension for all workers in that

sector and therefore contributes directly to improving one of their working conditions, namely their remuneration.

64. Consequently, the agreement at issue in the main proceedings does not, by reason of its nature and purpose, fall within the scope of Article [81(1)] of the Treaty.

(iii) COMPLEX ARRANGEMENTS

An agreement can consist of a whole complex of arrangements spread over a period of time. This was the case in *Polypropylene*.[85] This case concerned a cartel in the petrochemical industry which was found to have lasted for many years. Fifteen firms were held by the Commission to have infringed the competition rules by participating in a framework agreement to fix prices and sales volumes. The Commission considered that the cartel, which was based on a common and detailed plan, constituted a single continuing agreement for the purpose of Article 81(1). Some firms claimed they were not liable as they had not participated in all aspects of the arrangements. The CFI held that the Commission was justified in treating the entire course of the collusion as one single agreement. For there to be an 'agreement' for the purposes of Article 81(1) it was sufficient for the undertakings to have 'expressed their joint intention to conduct themselves on the market in a specific way'. In this case the undertakings had, throughout the whole course of the arrangements, pursued the single economic aim of distorting the polypropylene market.

Similarly, in *PVC*[86] a plan setting out a framework for regular meetings to operate a cartel fixing prices and imposing restrictions on sales in the PVC market was discovered at the premises of ICI in the course of the Commission's investigation into the polypropylene cartel. In its decision the Commission held that the undertakings had been party to collusive schemes, arrangements, and measures worked out within a framework of regular meetings which amounted to an agreement. Sufficient consensus had been reached on a plan which limited, or was likely to limit, the operators' commercial freedom on the market. It was not necessary that a legally binding agreement be shown to exist.

---

[85] *Polypropylene* [1986] OJ L230/1, [1988] 4 CMLR 84; on appeal Cases T–1/89, *Rhône-Poulenc* v. *Commission* [1991] ECR II–867; T–2/89, *Petrofina SA* v. *Commission* [1991] ECR II–1087; T–3/89 *Atochem* v. *Commission* [1991] ECR II–1177; T–6/89, *Enichem Anic SpA* v. *Commission* [1991] ECR II–1623; T–7/89, *SA Hercules NV* v. *Commission* [1991] ECR II–1711, [1992] 4 CMLR 84, etc. The appeals by the companies to the ECJ were broadly dismissed: Cases C–51/92P, *Hercules* v. *Commission* [1999] 5 CMLR 976; C–199/92P, *Hüls* v. *Commission* [1999] 5 CMLR 1016; C–200/92P, *ICI* v. *Commission* [1999] 5 CMLR 1110 etc., although the appeal by the Commission against the partial annulment of its Decision against Enichem was mainly successful: Case C–49/92P, *Commission* v. *Anic Partecipazioni*, judgment of 8 July 1999.

[86] [1994] OJ L239/3, upheld by the CFI on appeal in Cases T–305–307, 313–316, 318, 325, 328–329 & 335/94, *Limburgse Vinyl Maatschappij NV and others* v. *Commission* [1999] ECR 11–931, [1999] 5 CMLR 303 (*PVC Cartel II*). The 1994 decision replaced the original 1990 one [1989] OJ L 74/1, [1990] 4 CMLR 345, annulled on appeal by the ECJ on procedural grounds: Case C–137/92P *Commission* v. *BASF and others* [1994] ECR I–2555 setting aside the judgment of the CFI in Cases T–79/89 etc., *BASF and others* v. *Commission* [1992] ECR II–315, [1992] 4 CMLR 357 which had declared the decision non-existent. For this aspect of the case, see *infra* Chap. 14.

(iv) THE DISTINCTION BETWEEN AGREEMENT AND CONCERTED PRACTICE

Article 81(1) prohibits agreements, decisions by associations of undertakings, and concerted practices. Because of the broad definition adopted of the term agreement it may sometimes be difficult to determine whether or not informal contact between undertakings should be characterized as an 'agreement' or a 'concerted practice'. The term concerted practice[87] has also been construed broadly to catch all:

co-ordination between undertakings which, without having reached the stage where an agreement, properly so called, has been concluded, knowingly substitutes practical co-operation between them for the risks of competition.[88]

The purpose of the term is thus to catch undertakings which have not concluded an agreement to behave in a particular way but which determine their market policy in co-operation with other undertakings and not *independently*. Article 81(1) is aimed at explicit collusion whatever form it takes.

S. Bishop and M. Walker, *The Economics of EC Competition Law: Concepts, Application and Measurement* (Sweet & Maxwell, 1999), 79

4.06 In most markets firms recognise that the profitability of a given commercial strategy is dependent on the strategies pursued by competing firms. This raises the possibility that a firm can increase its profitability by co-ordinating with these rival firms. By not competing so vigorously, prices and hence profits can be increased to the detriment of consumers.

Such collusive behaviour is prohibited by the E.C. Treaty. Article [81(1)] makes reference to both agreements and to concerted practices . . . . The object of the Treaty in creating a separate concept of concerted practice is to prevent the possibility of undertakings evading the application of Article [81(1)] by colluding in a manner which does not involve an agreement *per se* but still has an adverse impact on the competitive process. For example, firms may collude by reaching an understanding to inform one another of the prices they intend to charge. This means that in general nothing turns in cartel cases on the precise form of the collusive arrangements.

At first sight, it therefore appears to be immaterial whether or not the parties involved have engaged in an agreement or a concerted practice. The purpose of the terms is to ensure that undertakings do not jointly resolve to co-ordinate their behaviour. There is a difference between the two concepts, however. If the Commission discovers an agreement, for example, to fix prices that will be sufficient to establish an infringement of the rules (assuming the other conditions of Article 81(1) are satisfied). In contrast, it is necessary to show both concertation *and* subsequent conduct on the market before a concerted practice can be established. There is, however, a presumption that the conduct will follow contact.[89] The concept of a concerted practice and the difficulty of distinguishing between collusion and non-collusive parallel behaviour are discussed in greater detail in Chapter 11 below.

---

[87] The definition of concerted practice is explored more fully in Chap. 11.

[88] Cases 48, 49, 51–7/69, *ICI* v. *Commission* [1972] ECR 619, [1972] CMLR 557, paras 64 and 65.

[89] Case C–199/92P, *Hüls* v. *Commission* [1999] 5 CMLR 1016.

(v) AGREEMENT AND UNILATERAL CONDUCT

It is clear that the term 'agreement' catches terms and conditions even if imposed by one party on another. If the terms are accepted the fact that one of the parties was unwilling to accept them does not prevent the agreement from being formed. In *BMW*[90] it was found that an agreement had been concluded which incorporated export bans imposed on reluctant BMW dealers. The Commission has, however, in some of its decisions reserved fines for the principal beneficiaries of activity prohibited by Article 81(1). It may, therefore, decline to impose a fine on a party that has acted unwillingly, against its own economic interest, or under duress.[91] The Commission clearly recognizes that in some instances a smaller undertaking may be oppressed in a bargain concluded with a larger and more powerful undertaking. The Commission is fully aware of the pressure that producers or suppliers, for instance, may apply over their dealers/ distributors.[92]

Further, and paradoxically perhaps, it also seems to be the case that conduct which appears to be purely unilateral may be found to form part of contractual relations between undertakings.

It is Article 82 which applies to unilateral acts of individual undertakings which have a dominant position (Article 82 prohibits abusive conduct, such as a refusal to supply or the imposition of unfair prices etc). At first sight it may appear, therefore, that a non-dominant firm could act unilaterally without the risk of infringing either Article 81 or Article 82.[93] The Commission has, however, sometimes characterized what appears to be unilateral behaviour as, in fact, being attributable to an underlying agreement or concerted practice between the parties. It has often done this when dealing with distribution agreements. Until *Bayer AG v. Commission*,[94] this approach had generally been endorsed by the Court.

Where, for example, a distribution agreement has been validly created in compliance with the competition rules, the Commission will not tolerate its being operated by one of the parties (a non-dominant undertaking) in a manner which is discriminatory or contrary to the goal of achieving a single market.[95] Such acts are considered to be an integral part of the distribution agreement, not unilateral actions, and are subject to Article 81(1). This is so whether or not they operate to the advantage of the other party to the contract. The operation of this principle is shown by the facts of *AEG*.

---

[90] Case 32/78, *BMW v. Commission* [1979] ECR 2435, [1980] 1 CMLR 370.

[91] The Commission may decline to fine a distributor which has acted against its own economic interests: see, e.g., *Volkswagen* [1998] OJ L124/60, [1998] 5 CMLR 33. See *infra* Chap. 14 for a discussion of the Commission's fining policy.

[92] Commission Regulation No 1475/95 on the application of Article 85(3) [now Article 81(3)] to motor vehicle distribution and servicing agreements [1995] OJ L145/25, for example, was intended amongst other things to take 'account of the need for a balance between the interests of the various parties involved' and to give dealers, the great majority of which are SMEs, greater commercial independence *vis-à-vis* manufacturers: see Commission communication of 23rd Feb. 1994 on the European automobile industry.

[93] See the discussion of Case C–73/95P. *Viho Europe BV v. Commission* [1996] ECR I–5457, [1997] 4 CMLR 419.

[94] Case T–41/96, judgment of 26 Oct. 2000, *infra* 117.

[95] See *infra* Chap. 9.

Case 107/82, *AEG-Telefunken* v. *Commission* [1983] ECR 3151, [1984] 3 CMLR 325

AEG-Telefunken (a developer and manufacturer of consumer electronic products) notified its select-ive distribution system to the Commission. The system provided that it would supply its products to all distributors/resellers that satisfied certain objective criteria (e.g. on the suitability of its staff and trading premises).[96] In this case, the Commission indicated to AEG that the system did not infringe Article 81(1). Subsequently, however, the Commission received numerous complaints alleging that AEG was not operating the scheme in the manner notified. AEG had refused to supply certain resellers which satisfied the stipulated objective criteria, but which would not adhere to a policy of charging minimum prices. Had the agreement contained a clause imposing resale price maintenance the agreement would have fallen within Article 81(1) and would have been unlikely to have received an exemption under Article 81(3).[97] AEG argued that the acts complained of were not part of its agreement with resellers, but were decisions that it had taken unilaterally. Article 81(1) did not apply, since it caught only agreements *between* undertakings. Both the Commission and the Court rejected this argument.

Court of Justice

31. AEG contends that the acts complained of in the contested decision, namely the failure to admit certain traders and steps taken to exert an influence on prices, are unilateral acts and do not therefore, as such, fall within Article [81(1)], which relates only to agreements between undertak-ings, decisions by associations of undertakings and concerted practices.

32. In order properly to appreciate that argument it is appropriate to consider the legal signifi-cance of selective distribution systems.

33. It is common ground that agreements constituting a selective system necessarily affect com-petition in the common market. However, it has always been recognized in the case-law of the Court that there are legitimate requirements, such as the maintenance of a specialist trade capable of providing specific services as regards high-quality and high-technology products, which may justify a reduction of price competition in favour of competition relating to factors other than price. Systems of selective distribution, in so far as they aim at the attainment of a legitimate goal capable of improving competition in relation to factors other than price, therefore constitute an element of competition which is in conformity with Article [81(1)].

34. The limitations inherent in a selective distribution system are however acceptable only on condition that their aim is in fact an improvement in competition in the sense above mentioned. Otherwise they would have no justification inasmuch as their sole effect would be to reduce price competition.

35. So as to guarantee that selective distribution systems may be based on that aim alone and cannot be set up and used with a view to the attainment of objectives which are not in con-formity with Community law, the Court specified in its judgment of 25 October 1977 (*Metro* v. *Commission*, [1977] ECR 1875) that such systems are permissible, provided that re-sellers are chosen on the basis of objective criteria of a qualitative nature relating to the technical quali-fications of the reseller and his staff and the suitability of his trading premises and that such conditions are laid down uniformly for all potential resellers and are not applied in a discriminatory fashion.

36. It follows that the operation of a selective distribution system based on criteria other than

---

[96] Selective distribution systems will be discussed *infra* in Chap. 9.

[97] See *infra* Chap. 4.

those mentioned above constitutes an infringement of Article [81(1)]. The position is the same where a system which is in principle in conformity with Community law is applied in practice in a manner incompatible therewith.

37. Such a practice must be considered unlawful where the manufacturer, with a view to maintaining a high level of prices or to excluding certain modern channels of distribution, refuses to approve distributors who satisfy the qualitative criteria of the system.

38. Such an attitude on the part of the manufacturer does not constitute, on the part of the undertaking, unilateral conduct which, as AEG claims, would be exempt from the prohibition contained in Article [81(1)] of the Treaty. On the contrary, it forms part of the contractual relations between the undertaking and resellers. Indeed, in the case of the admission of a distributor, approval is based on the acceptance, tacit or express, by the contracting parties of the policy pursued by AEG which requires *inter alia* the exclusion from the network of all distributors who are qualified for admission but are not prepared to adhere to that policy.

39. The view must therefore be taken that even refusals of approval are acts performed in the context of the contractual relations with authorized distributors inasmuch as their purpose is to guarantee observance of the agreements in restraint of competition which form the basis of contracts between manufacturers and approved distributors. Refusals to approve distributors who satisfy the qualitative criteria mentioned above therefore supply proof of an unlawful application of the system if their number is sufficient to preclude the possibility that they are isolated cases not forming part of systematic conduct.

The Court found that the systematic refusal by AEG to supply resellers not tolerating the pricing policy arose out of the agreement between AEG and its retailers. The latter had either expressly or tacitly accepted the policy which formed part of the contractual relations. The contract also, therefore, also included a provision imposing resale price maintenance on the retailers. It was understood that retailers which sold below recommended retail prices would not be supplied.

A similar approach has been adopted in other cases in which the Commission has dealt with distribution systems. In several cases the Commission has considered it clear from the unilateral behaviour of the producer of a product that its distributors are prohibited from exporting those products outside a specified territory. In *Ford*,[98] the Commission refused an exemption to a selective distribution for the distribution and sale of Ford products in Germany. Ford had stopped supplying right-hand drive cars to its German dealers in order to prevent those distributors from exporting those cars into the UK (where its car prices were higher). The Commission considered that Ford's act was an integral part of the agreements with its German dealers. This act was taken into account when determining whether or not Article 81(1) was infringed and whether the agreement should benefit from an exemption. The ECJ upheld the finding that the decision on the part of Ford formed part of the contractual relations between the undertakings and its dealers. Admission to the Ford AG dealer network implied acceptance by the contracting parties of the policy pursued by Ford with regard to the models delivered to the German market.

In *Ford* the ECJ accepted that unilateral conduct could be read into an agreement even though it clearly did not operate to the dealer's advantages. In contrast it is arguable that the resale price maintenance in *AEG* operated to the advantage of the AEG dealers which did

---

[98] Cases 228, 229/82, *Ford Werke AG and Ford of Europe Inc* v. *Commission* [1984] ECR 1129, [1984] 1 CMLR 649. See also Case 227/87, *Sandoz Prodotti Farmaceutici SpA v. Commission* [1990] ECR I–45 and Case C–279/87 Tipp-Ex v. Commission [1990] ECR 1–261.

not face price competition from other retailers of the products.[99] It has been seen that the Commission is likely to look favourably, when deciding to impose fines, on a party to a contract which has been persuaded to act against its own economic interests.[100] However, the finding that the unilateral conduct is part of the agreement still means that a distributor which has been persuaded to act against its own interests is labelled as a party to the contract and has committed a breach of Article 81(1). This may have important implications. That party could then become liable for damages to a third party which suffered loss in consequence of the infringement, for example. Further, an English court would currently deny the party any relief in respect of the contract on the grounds of its participation in an illegal or immoral agreement.[101]

The question whether unilateral refusals to supply should be construed as an integral part of an agreement has been raised again in *Bayer/ADALAT*. In this case[102] the Commission imposed a fine of ECU 3 million on Bayer AG for taking action to prevent parallel imports in the pharmaceutical market. In particular, Bayer had acted (by reducing volumes of the drug supplied) to prevent its distributors in France and Spain from exporting types of the drug ADALAT into the UK. The Commission found that the export ban was an integral element in the continuous commercial relations between Bayer and its wholesalers. The wholesalers were aware of the purposes of Bayer and regularly placed and renewed orders for the product and aligned their conduct to the ban. On appeal the CFI annulled the decision, holding that an agreement between Bayer and its wholesalers, designed to prevent or limit exports of Adalat had not been established. The concept of an agreement centred around the concurrence of wills between the parties. In this case it had not been shown that Bayer had sought to obtain agreement from its wholesalers to adhere to its policy or that the wholesalers had acquiesced explicitly or implicitly, in the policy.[104]

(vi) AGREEMENTS CONCLUDED BY EMPLOYEES

An agreement (or concerted practice) can arise from the actions of employees acting within the scope of their employment. EC law holds that the undertaking will be liable even if the employees were not authorized or instructed to act in that way by senior management. This is particularly relevant in situations where employees have entered into secret collusive conspiracies to rig markets. Undertakings should have in place, and should enforce, a compliance programme to prevent breaches of the competition rules.[105] The individual employees, however, cannot be fined or imprisoned.[106]

---

[99] If the distributors and the producer have met illicitly to discuss the fixing of prices or other prohibited conduct a concerted practice between the producer and distributors may be found: see the discussion of *Pioneer* [1980] OJ L60/1, [1980] 1 CMLR 457 *infra* 119.

[100] See *supra* n. 91.

[101] See *infra* Chap. 15.

[102] [1996] OJ L201/1, [1996] 5 CMLR 416.

[103] Case T–41/96, judgment of 26 Oct. 2000.

[104] Ibid, paras 66–185. In the context of a selective distribution system admission to the network may be based on acceptance by the distributors of the policy pursued by the producers, para 170.

[105] See further *infra* Chap. 14.

[106] Contrast the position in the USA where a breach of the competition rules is actually illegal. In the UK employees who obstruct the OFT in its investigations may be sent to prison: see Competition Act 1998, ss. 42–44.

(vii) RECOMMENDATIONS BY BODIES CONSTITUTED UNDER STATUTORY POWERS

Several cases have raised the question whether there is an 'agreement' where undertakings are represented on a body constituted under statutory powers to make recommendations in respect of a certain industry etc. The ECJ has held that there is not an agreement even when the trade representatives are in the majority on the committee, provided that the public authorities have not delegated their power of decision and that the matters to be fixed (e.g. tariffs) are fixed with due regard for public-interest criteria.[107]

D. DECISIONS BY ASSOCIATIONS OF UNDERTAKINGS

(i) WHAT IS AN ASSOCIATION OF UNDERTAKINGS?

Undertakings which operate on a particular market often belong to an industry-wide or some other trade association. The reference to associations in Article 81(1) is clearly designed to extend the prohibition to illegitimate collusion concluded within the framework of trade associations. The term 'association' is not, however, limited to trade associations. An 'association' includes other bodies such as an agricultural co-operative[108] or a body set up by statute and with public functions if they represent the trading interests of the members, even if there are some members appointed by the government or another public authority.[109]

(ii) DECISIONS BY ASSOCIATIONS

Trade and other associations of course perform functions which are legitimate and which promote the competitiveness of the industry as a whole. However, membership of an association, particularly a trade association, may also tempt the members of undertakings meeting within its auspices to collude together and to co-ordinate their action. Although such co-ordination may, in any event, be caught by the term 'agreement' or 'concerted practice', the provision prohibiting decisions of associations of undertakings which restrict competition may, in certain circumstances, facilitate the proof of such anti-competitive behaviour. It may be that the conduct adopted by the members of the association may be characterized alternatively as a decision or an agreement or a concerted practice. However, the conduct may be prohibited even if technically speaking no agreement or concerted practice has been concluded. The concept of a decision has been interpreted broadly to catch conduct designed to co-ordinate the conduct of the members contrary to Article 81(1),[110] whether engaged in through resolutions of the association, recommendations, the operation of certi-

---

[107] See e.g. Case C–96/94, *Centro Servizi Spediporto* v. *Spedizioni Maritima del Golfo srl* [1995] ECR I–2883, [1996] 4 CMLR 613; Case C–38/97, *Autotrasporti Librandi* v. *Cuttica Spedizioni* [1998] ECR I–5955, [1998] 5 CMLR 966.

[108] Case C–250/92, *Gøttrup-Klim Grovvareforening and Others* v. *Dansk Landbrugs Grovvaresel-skab AmbA* [1994] ECR I–5641, [1996] 4 CMLR 191.

[109] Case 123/83, *BNIC* v. *Clair* [1985] ECR 391, [1985] 2 CMLR 430.

[110] Case 96/82, *IAZ International Belgium NV* v. *Commission* [1983] ECR 3369, [1984] 3 CMLR 276.

fication schemes or through the association's constitution itself. The types of conduct which have been found to constitute a decision by an association of undertakings are discussed in Chapter 11.

E. CONCERTED PRACTICES

The definition of the term concerted practice and the distinction between a concerted practice and an agreement have been discussed above. The questions of how the existence of a concerted practice can be proved and whether evidence of parallel behaviour will furnish such proof will be examined in Chapter 11 below. It is worth pointing out, however, that a concerted practice may be operated horizontally between colluding competitors and vertically between a manufacturer and its distributors. In *Pioneer*,[111] for example, the Commission found that Pioneer and its European exclusive distributors had engaged in concerted practices to prevent the parallel import of Pioneer products from the UK and Germany into France.

F. OBJECT OR EFFECT THE PREVENTION, RESTRICTION OR DISTORTION OF COMPETITION

(i) INTRODUCTION

Whether or not an agreement has as its object or effect the prevention, restriction, or distortion of competition is the heart of Article 81(1). Agreements and other collusive practices are not prohibited unless they prevent, restrict, or distort competition within the meaning of Article 81(1). The way in which this phrase is interpreted determines the types of agreements which are prohibited and the scope of application of Article 81(1). Further, the way in which Article 81(1) is interpreted has a crucial impact on the role played and the interpretation of Article 81(3). Obviously there is a need to exempt only agreements which are prohibited under Article 81(1). So if Article 81(1) is interpreted broadly, many agreements will need to be exempted under Article 81(3). Conversely, if a narrow definition of the term is adopted, Article 81(3) will have a more limited role to play.

The relationship and interaction of these two paragraphs and the question of what issues should be considered under each Article has caused enormous controversy. The relationship of these two provisions is fully explored in Chapter 4 below. In this section we will confine ourselves to a few basic points.

---

[111] [1980] OJ L60/1, [1980] 1 CMLR 457. The finding that Pioneer had participated in the concerted practices was upheld on appeal: see Cases 100–103/80, *Musique Diffusion Française SA* v. *Commission* [1983] ECR 1825, [1983] 3 CMLR 528. See also Case 86/82, *Hasselblad (GB) Ltd* v. *Commission* [1984] ECR 883, [1984] 1 CMLR 559.

(ii) OBJECT OR EFFECT

Article 81(1) prohibits an agreement which has either as its object *or* its effect the prevention, restriction, or distortion of competition.[112] If, therefore, it is clear from the terms of the agreement that its object is to prevent, restrict or distort competition there is no need to examine its effects.[113] A cartel which has the object of restricting competition cannot be defended on the ground that it did not have this effect, perhaps because it did not work or because the parties (or one of the parties) had always intended to cheat on the agreement.[114] Where, however, the object of the agreement cannot be said to restrict competition an analysis of the effect of the agreement on the market is necessary before it can be determined whether the agreement infringes Article 81(1).[115]

(iii) THE PREVENTION, RESTRICTION, OR DISTORTION OF COMPETITION

The main difficulty is to determine which agreements have as their object the prevention, restriction, or distortion of competition and in what circumstances an agreement will be found to have the effect of preventing, restricting, or distorting competition within the meaning of Article 81. Broadly, the ECJ has ruled that certain provisions in an agreement constitute such serious restrictions that their object is to restrict competition: for example horizontal agreements containing price-fixing or market-sharing provisons or vertical agreements imposing resale prices or conferring absolute territorial protection on distributors.[116] In other cases, however, agreements must be assessed in their market context to determine whether the restrictions within them do in fact have as their effect the restriction of competition. The market on which the restriction of competition is to be assessed has to be defined. The Commission Notice sets out guidelines on how this is done.[117]

It will be seen in Chapter 4 that the Commission has, in the past, been criticized for adopting an overly formalistic approach to this question. It has been quick to find that restrictions on conduct amount to restrictions of competition and has adopted an excessively broad approach. At times, however, it is difficult, or impossible, to reconcile this approach with that adopted by the Court and the Commission has more recently been indicating that it now takes a more realistic approach when interpreting Article 81(1).

---

[112] Case 56/65, *Société Technique Minière* v. *Maschinebau Ulm GmbH* [1966] ECR 234, 249, [1966] CMLR 357. See also Case C–234/89, *Stergios Delimitis* v. *Henninger Bräu* [1991] ECR 1–935, [1992] 5 CMLR 210, para 13 and Cases T–374, 375, 384 & 388/94, *European Night Services* v. *Commission* [1998] ECR II–3141, [1998] 5 CMLR 718, para. 136, discussed *infra* in Chap. 4.

[113] Cases 56 & 58/64 *Etablissements Consten SA & Grundig-Verkaufs-GmbH* v. *Commission* [1966] ECR 299, [1966] CMLR 418.

[114] An analysis of the market may still be necessary if the parties consider that the agreement does not affect competition or trade to an *appreciable* extent: see *infra* 127 ff. The effect of the agreement may also be relevant to the amount of fine imposed: see *infra* Chap. 14.

[115] Case C–234/89, *Stergios Delimitis* v. *Henninger Bräu* [1991] ECR 1–935, [1992] 5 CMLR 210, para. 13 ff.

[116] See *infra* Chap. 4.

[117] Commission Notice on the definition of the relevant market, [1997] OJ C372/5: see *supra* Chap. 1 and *infra* Chap. 6.

G. EFFECT ON TRADE BETWEEN MEMBER STATES

(i) JURISDICTIONAL LIMIT

The concept of an agreement 'which may affect trade between Member States is intended to define, in the law governing cartels, the boundary between the areas respectively covered by Community law and national law'.[118] The requirement thus sets out a jurisdictional limit to the prohibition laid down in Article 81 (it is also a requirement that any abuse of a dominant position should affect trade for the purposes of Article 82).[119] Since the requirement is merely viewed as a jursidictional matter, it has been interpreted broadly. However, the Community accepts that it has no jurisdiction over cases in which the effects of an agreement, or conduct, are confined to one Member State.[120]

(ii) THE TESTS

An agreement will be found to 'affect trade' if it interferes with the pattern of trade between Member States.[121] An agreement may also be found to affect trade if it intereferes with the structure of competition in the common market. This latter structural test is more commonly used in the context of Article 82 than Article 81.[122]

(iii) PATTERN OF TRADE TEST

In *Société La Technique Minière* v. *Maschinenbau Ulm*, the ECJ set out a broad interpretation of the phrase, so the requirement that an agreement should affect trade is easily satisfied. All that is necessary is that 'it must be possible to foresee with a sufficient degree of probability on the basis of a set of objective factors of law or of fact that the agreement in question may have an influence, direct or indirect, actual or potential, on the pattern of trade between Member States . . .'.[123]

---

[118] Cases 56 & 58/64, *Etablissements Consten SA & Grundig-Verkaufs-GmbH* v. *Commission* [1966] ECR 299, [1966] CMLR 418.

[119] Although the application of Art. 81 to an agreement does not preclude the simultaneous application of national competition rules, national rules must not be applied in a manner that infringes the principle of supremacy of Community law: Case 106/77, *Amministrazione delle Finanze dello Stato* v. *Simmenthal SpA* [1978] ECR 629, [1978] 3 CMLR 263. In the case of a conflict between national and Community rules, the general rule is that Community law should prevail: Case 14/68, *Walt Wihelm* v. *Bundeskartellant* [1969] ECR 1, [1969] CMLR 100: see *infra* Chap. 15. The objective of these principles is to rule out any national measures which could jeopardize the full effectiveness of the provisions of Community law. A wide interpretation of an effect on inter-state trade enlarges the scope of EC competition law and diminishes the impact of the domestic competition law of the individual Member States.

[120] Case 22/78, *Hugin* v. *Commission* [1979] ECR 1869, [1970] 3 CMLR 345.

[121] Case 56/65, *Société La Technique Minière Ulm* v. *Maschinenbau* [1966] ECR 235, [1966] CMLR 357.

[122] See Cases 6–7/73, *Istituto Chemioterapico Italiano SpA and Commercial Solvents Corp* v. *Commission* [1974] ECR 223, [1974] 1 CMLR 309 and *infra* Chap. 5.

[123] Case 56/65, *Société La Technique Minière Ulm* v. *Maschinenbau* [1966] ECR 235, 249, [1966] CMLR 357, 375 and Case 5/69, *Völk* v. *Vervaecke* [1969] ECR 295, 302, [1969] CMLR 273, 282.

Agreements will, therefore, be caught even if it is only anticipated that they will affect the pattern of trade in the future. In *AEG* v. *Commission*,[124] the ECJ held that the fact that there was little inter-state trade did not mean that Article 81(1) was inapplicable if it could reasonably be expected that the patterns of trade in the future might change.

(iv) AN INCREASE IN TRADE

In *Consten and Grundig,* the parties argued before the ECJ that their distribution agreement did not produce an effect on trade within the meaning of Article 81(1) since it increased trade between Member States (in the absence of the agreement, Grundig products might not have been sold in France at all). This argument was partially supported by a textual analysis of the Treaty since, in at least one language (Italian), the text suggested that the effect on trade should be a harmful or prejudicial one. The ECJ[125] rejected this argument, ruling that 'the fact that an agreement encourages an increase, even a large one, in the volume of trade between states is not sufficient to exclude the possibility that the agreement may "affect" such trade. . . .'.[126] Rather, it examined the contract, which precluded anyone other than Consten from importing Grundig products into France, and prohibited Consten from re-exporting the products into other Member States, and concluded that it 'indisputably affects trade between Member States'. Instead of attempting to adopt a literal interpretation of the provision the ECJ adopted an interpretation which respected the aims and spirit of the Treaty. It was important that agreements such as the exclusive distribution agreement at issue in that case should be capable of being scrutinized under the provisions.[127] The aim of the Treaty was not to increase trade as an end in itself, but to create a system of undistorted competition. The ECJ concluded that Article 81 applied to any agreement which might threaten the freedom of trade between Member States in a manner which might harm the attainment of the single market.

Cases 56 & 58/64, *Etablissements Consten SA & Grundig-Verkaufs-GmbH* v. *Commission* [1966] ECR 299, 341 and [1966] CMLR 418, 471–472

Court of Justice

The complaints relating to the concept of 'agreements . . . which may affect trade between Member States'.

The applicants and the German Government maintain that the Commission has relied on a mistaken interpretation of the concept of an agreement which may affect trade between Member States and has not shown that such trade would have been greater without the agreement in dispute.

---

[124] Case 107/82 [1983] ECR 3151, [1984] 3 CMLR 325, para. 60; see also A *EI/Reyrolle Parsons re Vacuum Interrupters* [1977] OJ L48/32, [977] 1 CMLR D67, discussed *infra* in Chap. 13.

[125] The argument was, however, supported by Roemer AG. He took the view that the effect on trade would have to be an unfavourable one before the prohibition applied.

[126] Cases 56 & 58/64, *Etablissements Consten SA & Grundig-Verkaufs-GmbH* v. *Commission* [1966] ECR 299, 341, [1966] CMLR 418, 472.

[127] The agreement was capable of bringing about a partition of the market in certain products between Member States, rendering more difficult the interpenetration of trade which the Treaty was intended to create and impeding the goal of single market integration.

The defendant replies that this requirement in Article [81(1)] is fulfilled once trade between Member State develops, as a result of the agreement, differently from the way in which it would have done without the restriction resulting from the agreement, and once the influence of the agreement on market conditions reaches a certain degree. Such is the case here, according to the defendant, particularly in view of the impediments resulting within the Common Market from the disputed agreement as regards the exporting and importing of Grundig products to and from France.

The concept of an agreement 'which may affect trade between Member States' is intended to define, in the law governing cartels, the boundary between the areas respectively covered by Community law and national law. It is only to the extent to which the agreement may affect trade between Member States that the deterioration in competition caused by the agreement falls under the prohibition of Community law contained in Article [81; otherwise it escapes the prohibition.

In this connexion, what is particularly important is whether the agreement is capable of constituting a threat, either direct or indirect, actual or potential, to freedom of trade between Member States in a manner which might harm the attainment of the objectives of a single market between States. Thus the fact that an agreement encourages an increase, even a large one, in the volume of trade between States is not sufficient to exclude the possibility that the agreement may 'affect' such trade in the abovementioned manner. In the present case, the contract between Grundig and Consten, on the one hand by preventing undertakings other than Consten from importing Grundig products into France, and on the other hand by prohibiting Consten from re-exporting those products to other countries of the Common Market, indisputably affects trade between Member States. These limitations on the freedom of trade, as well as those which might ensure for third parties from the registration in France by Consten of the GINT trade mark, which Grundig places on all its products, are enough to satisy the requirement in question.

(v) PARTITIONING OF THE COMMON MARKET

Many vertical agreements are capable of an effect on trade between Member States because of their tendency to incorporate territorial restrictions and their ability to partition the common market. It was seen in the extract set out above that the ECJ in *Consten and Grundig* found that the nature of the territorial restrictions was to affect trade. Similarly, other agreements containing provisions sharing markets between a manufacturer and its distributor or between distributors *inter se* are capable of affecting trade between Member States.[128] Even an agreement preventing a distributor appointed for a territory outside the EU from making sales outside its contractual territory (and, consequently, into the Community) may appreciably affect the pattern of trade between Member States. Whether or not it does so will depend on factors such as the prices of the contractual products charged in the Community and those charged outside the Community, the level of customs duties, and transport costs.[129]

Further, it is possible that an agreement may have an effect on trade even if it does not appear to at first sight. The impact on inter-state trade may be revealed on a closer examination of the agreement. In *Delimitis* v. *Henninger Bräu*,[130] for example, a beer-supply agreement between a German brewer and a German café proprietor imposed an obligation on the

---

[128] Case 161/86, *Pronuptia de Paris* v. *Schillgalis* [1986] ECR 353, [1986] 1 CMLR 414, para. 27.

[129] Case C–306/96, *Javico International and Javico AF* v. *Yves Saint Laurent Parfums SA* [1998] ECR I–1983, [1998] 5 CMLR 172.

[130] Case C–234/89, [1991] ECR 1–935, [1992] 5 CMLR 210.

latter to purchase beer only from the brewer. In derogation from this obligation, however, it permitted the café proprietor to purchase competing beer from suppliers in other Member States. The ECJ ruled that the national court would have to examine the agreement in greater detail. It was critical to determine whether or not this 'access' clause was hypothetical or real. The contract obliged the café proprietor to purchase a specific quantity of the brewer's beer each year. It had to be determined, therefore, whether or not this clause stipulating the minimum quantity of the brewery's beer to be purchased in reality left the café proprietor with a real opportunity to purchase beer from brewers in other Member States. If it did not, the agreement would produce an effect on inter-state trade, despite the access clause. On the other hand, if the agreement left a real possibility for foreign brewers to supply the outlet, the agreement was not in principle capable of affecting trade between Member States.[131]

Case C–234/89, *Delimitis* v. *Henninger Bräu* [1991] ECR I–935, [1992] 5 CMLR 210

Court of Justice

The compatibility with Article [81(1)] of a beer supply agreement containing an access clause

28. A beer supply agreement containing an access clause differs from the other beer supply agreements normally entered into inasmuch as it authorizes the reseller to purchase beer from other Member States. Such access mitigates, in favour of the beers of other Member States, the scope of the prohibition on competition which in a classic beer supply agreement is coupled with the exclusive purchasing obligation. The scope of the access clause must be assessed in the light of its wording and its economic and legal context. . . .

30. As far as its economic and legal context is concerned, it should be pointed out that where, as in this case, one of the other clauses stipulates that a minimum quantity of the beers envisaged in the agreement must be purchased, it is necessary to examine what that quantity represents in relation to the sales of beer normally achieved in the public house in question. If it appears that the stipulated quantity is relatively large, the access clause ceases to have any economic significance and the prohibition on selling competing beers regains its full force, particularly when under the agreement the obligation to purchase minimum quantities is backed by penalties.

31. If the interpretation of the wording of the access clause or an examination of the specific effect of the contractual clauses as a whole in their economic and legal context shows that the limitation on the scope of the prohibition on competition is merely hypothetical or without economic significance, the agreement in question must be treated in the same way as a classic beer supply agreement. Accordingly, it must be assessed under Article [81(1)] of the Treaty in the same way as beer supply agreements in general.

32. The position is different where the access clause gives a national or foreign supplier of beers from other Member States a real possibility of supplying the sales outlet in question. An agreement containing such a clause is not in principle capable of affecting trade between Member States within the meaning of Article [81(1)], with the result that it escapes the prohibition laid down in that provision.

---

[131] Case C–234/89, [1991] ECR 1–935, [1992] 5 CMLR 210, paras 28–33.

(vi) AGREEMENTS OPERATING IN ONE MEMBER STATE

It tends to be assumed that an agreement between parties situated in different Member States affects trade between Member States. It can be seen from the *Delimitis* case (an agreement between a German brewer and a German café proprietor) that an agreement which operates in only one Member State is also quite capable of affecting trade between Member States.

Similarly, national cartels, especially those dominating the whole or a large part of a market, tend to reinforce compartmentalization and make it more difficult for undertakings from other Member States to penetrate the market.[132] The ECJ has consistently held the fact that a cartel relates only to the marketing of products in a single Member State is not sufficient to exclude the possibility that trade between member-States might be affected.[133] Indeed, the cartel is likely to be successful only if the members can defend themselves against foreign competition. The agreement in *BELASCO*,[134] for example, specifically provided for protective and defensive measures to be taken against foreign undertakings. Where the relevant product or service affected by the cartel is easily transmissible across borders it is likely that an effect on trade will be found. A Dutch cartel agreement which operated in order to restrict competition in the market for mobile cranes was held to have an effect on intra-Community trade. Since the cranes could travel at speeds of between 63 and 78 kph, the agreement was likely to affect German and Belgian firms operating near the Dutch border.[135]

(vii) RESTRICTIONS ON COMPETITION AND RESTRICTIONS ON TRADE

It is clear that so long as the agreement as a whole affects trade between Member States it is immaterial that the clause (or clauses) which restricts competition does not itself affect trade.[136]

(viii) A NEW JURISDICTIONAL TEST?

The broad interpretation which has been adopted in relation to Article 81(1) in general as well as to the jurisdictional criteria has, due to the enormous number of agreements potentially falling within the scope of Article 81(1), resulted in an excessive workload being imposed on the Commission. The limited resources of the Commission are inadequate to

---

[132] Case 8/72 *Vereeniging van Cementhandelaren* v. *Commission* [1972] ECR 997, [1973] CMLR 7. In Cases C–215/96 *Bagnasco* v. *Banca Popolare di Novarra (NPN) and Cassa di Risparmio di Genova e Imperia (Carige)* [1999] ECR I–135 [1999] 4 CMLR 624, paras. 38–53, however, the ECJ held that standard bank conditions relating to the provision of general guarantees required to secure the opening of current-account credit facilities in Italy did not have an appreciable effect on intra-Community trade within the meaning of Art. 81(1).

[133] Case 246/86, *BELASCO* v. *Commission* [1989] ECR 2117, [1991] 4 CMLR 96, para. 33.

[134] *Ibid*, paras. 35–38.

[135] *Stichting Certificatie Kraanberhuuvedrijf and the Federatie van Nederlandse Kraanverhuurvedrijven* [1995] OJ L312/79.

[136] See Case 193/83, *Windsurfing International Inc* v. *Commission* [1986] ECR 611, [1986] 3 CMLR 489. This case is discussed *infra* Chap. 10.

cope with the numerous cases falling within its jurisdiction. It will be seen in subsequent discussion in this book[137] that the Commission has been obliged to adopt a number of different techniques in order to try and mitigate this problem. For example, it has issued block exemptions and has issued a notice in an attempt to facilitate and encourage the application of the EC competition provisions (particularly Article 81) at a national level.[138] Further, it has indicated its intention to preserve its resources for cases with a particular political, economic or legal significance for the Community[139] and it has now issued a White Paper setting out further proposals for dealing with this problem.[140] It has also been argued that the burden on the Commission could be lessened by adopting a narrower jurisdictional test.

In *Papiers Peints*,[141] Advocate General Trabucchi suggested that in a unified multinational market a new interpretation could be matched to the new situation. He suggested shifting the emphasis from the objective of assisting in the dismantling of obstacles to trade between Member States to the aim of preventing restrictions of competition which would preclude the retention of competition in healthy terms in the common market. The development of a comprehensive system to regulate the market economy could replace the pattern of trade test. Agreements having a relatively large impact in the Community (even if concentrated in one Member State) would be caught, but minor agreements (even those that might affect trade patterns) would not (the concept would need to be developed alongside the *appreciability* doctrine discussed below).

Were such an approach adopted, sole jurisdiction could be allocated to the Community competition provisions where an effect on trade was found.[142] Currently, the applicability of Community law does not exclude the application of national competition law. National authorities have concurrent jurisdiction to apply their own provisions of national law so long as that application does not conflict with the Community principle of supremacy.[143] However, the approach adopted by Advocate General Trabucchi could be used to introduce the idea of a 'Community dimension' into Article 81, similar to that which has been utilized in the sphere of merger control.[144] Such an approach would resolve some of the difficulties arising where different decisions are taken, or different policies pursued, by national and Community competition authorities applying their national and Community competition laws respectively. It would also avoid the inconvenience for undertakings and the waste of resources that result in cases of multiple investigation.

The approach suggested by Advocate General Trabucchi was not taken up by the ECJ.

---

[137] See, in particular, *infra* Chap. 4.

[138] Commission Notice on cooperation between national courts and the Commission in applying Articles 85 and 86 [now 81 and 82] of the EEC [now EC] Treaty [1993] OJ C39/6.

[139] *Ibid.*

[140] See *infra* Chaps. 4 and 16.

[141] Case 73/74, *Papiers Peints de Belgique* v. *Commission* [1975] ECR 1491, [1976] 1 CMLR 589.

[142] At present this would leave the national authorities an extremely limited field in which to apply their competition laws. However, Italian antitrust legislation (introduced in 1990 and modelled on the EC Treaty), for example, grants jurisdiction only in respect of matters which do not fall within the scope of EC competition law.

[143] See *supra* n. 119.

[144] Broadly, merger cases with a Community dimension are under the sole jurisdiction of the Commission, *infra* Chap. 12.

The Commission has, however, now proposed in a draft Regulation that agreements that affect trade should be dealth with exclusively by Community Competition Law.[145] This proposal, combined with the extremely broad interpretation given to the term 'affect trade between Member States', would leave a very limited role for national law to play.

H. AN APPRECIABLE EFFECT ON COMPETITION AND TRADE

(i) *VÖLK* v. *VERVAECKE*

The text of Article 81(1) does not require that the effect on competition or trade should be appreciable. Nonetheless the case law of the ECJ has clearly established that 'in order to come within the prohibition imposed by Art. [81], the agreement must affect trade between Member States and the free play of competition to an appreciable extent'.[146] The concept of appreciability was first accepted by the ECJ in *Völk* v. *Vervaecke*.

Case 5/69, *Völk* v. *Vervaecke* [1969] ECR 295, 302, [1969] CMLR 273, 282

The case concerned an exclusive distribution agreement concluded between Mr Völk, the owner of a company, Erd & Co, which manufactured washing machines, and Vervaecke, a Belgian company which distributed household electrical appliances. Under the agreement, Vervaecke had the exclusive right to sell Völk's products in Belgium and Luxembourg. According to the Commission, Erd & Co had only 0.08% of the market for the production of washing machines Community wide, 0.2% of the market in Germany and 0.6% of the market in Belgium and Luxembourg. Following a dispute which raised the validity of the agreement before the German courts, the Oberlandesgericht in Munich made an Article 234 reference to the Community Court. In particular, it asked the Community Court whether, in considering if an agreement fell within Article 81(1), regard had to be had to the proportion of the market that the grantor had.

Court of Justice
If an agreement is to be capable of affecting trade between Member States it must be possible to foresee with a sufficient degree of probability on the basis of a set of objective factors of law or of fact that the agreement in question may have an influence, direct or indirect, actual or potential, on the pattern of trade between Member States in such a way that it might hinder the attainment of the objectives of a single market between States. Moreover the prohibition in Article [81(1)] is applicable only if the agreement in question also has as its object or effect the prevention,

---

[145] Proposal for a Reg. implementing Arts. 81 and 82 Com (2000) 582, Art. 3. See discussion of the proposals for modernizing the rules currently governing the implementation of Arts. 81 and 82, *infra* Chaps. 4, 15 and 16.

[146] Case 22/71, *Béguelin Import Company* v. *GL Import-Export SA* [1971] ECR 949, [1972] CMLR 81.

restriction or distortion of competition within the common market. Those conditions must be understood by reference to the actual circumstances of the agreement. Consequently an agreement falls outside the prohibition in Article [81] when it has only an insignificant effect on the markets, taking into account the weak position which the persons concerned have on the market of the product in question. Thus an exclusive dealing agreement, even with absolute territorial protection, may, having regard to the weak position of the persons concerned on the market in the products in question in the area covered by the absolute protection, escape the prohibition laid down in Article [81(1)].

This case thus makes it absolutely crystal clear that agreements concluded between parties that hold a weak position on the market are not caught by Article 81(1) on account of their insignificant effect on intra-community trade and/or on competition.

(ii) UNDERSTANDING THE REQUIREMENT OF APPRECIABILIY

In its judgment in *Völk* v. *Vervaecke* the ECJ unequivocally held that even agreements which have as their *object* the prevention, restriction, or distortion of competition may escape the prohibition of Article 81(1) on this ground.[147] In *Völk* itself the distributor had been granted absolute territorial protection.[148] It must be assumed, therefore, that similarly horizontal price-fixing or market-share agreements concluded between undertakings with a weak market position would also be considered to be insignificant.[149]

The concept of appreciability is thus completely distinct from the requirement that the agreement should restrict competition. Some agreements, even those containing the most pernicious provisions held automatically to restrict competition, may escape as a result of the minimal impact they will have on competition and/or trade. The insignificant position held by the undertakings causes the Community institutions to take the view that the agreement cannot possibly threaten the Community objectives. Rather, it is more appropriate that they should be examined, if at all, within the framework of national competition legislation.

In this sense the concept of appreciability undoubtedly has similarities to the view expounded by Advocate General Trabucchi in *Papiers Peints* that Community law should only be concerned with agreements which have a relatively large impact within the Community.

(iii) COMMISSION NOTICE ON AGREEMENTS OF MINOR IMPORTANCE

In *Völk* v. *Vervaecke* the undertakings involved had really very small shares of the markets potentially affected by the agreement.[150] Although the ECJ, in the Article 234 reference, was not at liberty to apply Community law to the facts at issue in that case, in interpreting Article 81(1) it clearly indicated that Article 81 would not in fact prohibit the agreement in

---

[147] Case 5/69, *Völk* v. *Vervaecke* [1969] ECR 295, 302, [1969] CMLR 273, 282.

[148] Case C–306/96, *Javico International and Javico AG* v. *Yves Saint Laurent Parfums SA* [1998] ECR I–1983, [1998] 5 CMLR 172, para. 17.

[149] See *infra* 131.

[150] The relevant geographical market in that case was not defined. It was unclear whether the relevant product market was divided on national, Community, or some other line.

question. In what other circumstances, however, might an agreement be considered to be insignificant on account of the weak position of the parties involved?

The concept of appreciability is obviously of huge practical importance to undertakings, particularly small and medium-sized ones. Because of this the Commission has, over the years, issued a series of notices indicating when, in its view, an agreement is likely to be considered to be of minor importance. Each notice has been intended to enable under-takings to be able to judge for themselves whether their agreements fall outside the Article 81(1) prohibition. Like all other Commission notices, however, the current notice sets out guidance only and is not legal binding on anyone, even the Commission.[151] The most recent notice was published on 9 December 1997 and replaces the notice published in 1986.[152]

Commission Notice on agreements of minor importance which do not fall within the meaning of Article 85(1) [now 81(1)] of the Treaty establishing the European Community [1997] OJ C372/13, [1998] 4 CMLR 192

2. Article [81(1)] prohibits agreements which may affect trade between Member States and which have as their object or effect the prevention, restriction or distortion of competition within the common market. The Court of Justice of the European Communities has clarified that this provision is not applicable where the impact of the agreement on intra-Community trade or on competition is not appreciable. Agreements which are not capable of significantly affecting trade between Member States are not caught by Article [81]. They should, therefore, be examined on the basis, and within the framework, of national legislation alone. This is also the case for agreements whose actual or potential effect remains limited to the territory of only one Member State or of one of more third countries. Likewise, agreements which do not have as their object or their effect an appreciable restriction of competition are not caught by the prohibition contained in Article [81(1)].

3. In this Notice the Commission, by setting quantitative criteria and by explaining their application, has given a sufficiently concrete meaning to the term 'appreciable' for undertakings to be able to judge for themselves whether their agreement does not fall within the prohibition pursuant to Article [81(1)] by virtue of their minor importance.

One criticism of the 1986 Notice was that it indicated that an agreement would be of minor importance only if the parties satisfied two distinct criteria. The first was that the parties did not have more than 5 per cent of the relevant market of the goods or services which were the subject of the agreement in the area of the common market affected by the agreement. The second was that the parties were required to show that the aggregate annual turnover of the participating undertakings did not exceed ECU 300 million.[153] The necessity of satisfying the turnover criterion was criticized on account of its irrelevance to the signifi-cance of the impact of the agreement on the market.

---

[151] See *infra* 134.

[152] Commission Notice on agreements of minor importance [1986] OJ C231/2. The first notice was published in 1970, [1970] OJ C64/1.

[153] See para. 7 of the 1986 Notice (the sum was increased from ECU 200 to 300 million by a Commission Notice of 23 Dec. 1994).

Taking heed of the criticism, the 1997 Notice[154] omitted any reference to turnover thresholds and defines the term 'appreciable effect' on competition by using only quantative criteria. Appreciability is determined by reference to market shares alone. Further, and in recognition of their differences, the notice makes a distinction between vertical and horizontal agreements. Horizontal agreements between undertakings engaged in the production or distribution of goods or in the provision of services do not fall under Article 81(1) where the aggregate market share held by all the participating undertakings does not exceed 5 per cent. Vertical agreements do not fall within Article 81(1) where the aggregate market share held by the participating undertakings does not exceed 10 per cent.

9. The Commission holds the view that agreements between undertakings engaged in the production or distribution of goods or in the provision of services do not fall under the prohibition in Article [81 (1)] if the aggregate market shares held by all of the participating undertakings do not exceed, on any of the relevant markets:

(a) the 5% threshold, where the agreement is made between undertakings operating at the same level of production or of marketing ('horizontal' agreement);

(b) the 10% threshold, where the agreement is made between undertakings operating at different economic levels ('vertical' agreement).

In the case of a mixed horizontal/vertical agreement or where it is difficult to classify the agreement as either horizontal or vertical, the 5% threshold is applicable.

10. The Commission also holds the view that the said agreements do not fall under the prohibition of Article [81(1)] if the market shares given at point 9 are exceeded by no more than one 10th during two successive financial years.

Participating undertakings covers not only those undertakings which are party to the agreement but all other entities which are closely connected to those parties:

12. For the purposes of this notice, 'participating undertakings' are:

    (a) undertakings being parties to the agreement;
    (b) undertakings in which a party to the agreement, directly or indirectly,

    —owns more than half of the capital or business assets, or
    —has the power to exercise more than half of the voting rights, or
    —has the power to appoint more than half of the members of the supervisory board, board of
       management or bodies legally representing the undertakings, or
    —has to the right to manage the undertaking's business;

(c) undertakings which directly or indirectly have over a party to the agreement the rights or powers listed in (b);

(d) undertakings over which an undertaking referred to in (c) has, directly or indirectly, the rights or powers listed in (b).

Undertakings over which several undertakings as referred to in (a) to (d) jointly have, directly or indirectly, the rights or powers set out in (b) shall also be considered to be participating undertakings.

---

[154] The notice was issued with the intention of enhancing legal clarity in the text, updating the text, making it more realistic, and avoiding unnecessary administrative burdens being imposed on undertakings whose agreements cannot exert any appreciable influence on intra-community trade or competition.

The important part played by market shares means, of course, that the relevant product and geographic markets must be defined in each case. This is an inherent (but inevitable) source of weakness of the Notice. Although the notice sets out guidance on defining the relevant market and makes reference to the Commission Notice on the definition of the relevant market for the purposes of Community competition law the definition of the market is uncertain.[155] In addition, the Commission further detracts from the certainty of the notice by stating, in paragraph 11, that the applicability of Article 81(1) cannot be ruled out even if the market shares are below these thresholds where: (a) a horizontal agreement has as its object the fixing of prices, limiting production or sales, or sharing market; or (b) where a vertical agreement has as its object the fixing of resale prices or confers territorial protection. At first sight this seems to be contrary to the clear view expressed by the ECJ in *Völk* v. *Vervaeke*.[156] However, it may simply indicate the Commission's view that where the agreement contains particularly serious restrictions of competition from a Community perspective the agreement will not be considered to be of minor importance unless the parties' market share is considerably lower than that set out in the notice.[157]

11. With regard to:

(a) horizontal agreements which have as their object

—to fix prices or to limit production or sales, or
—to share markets or sources of supply,

(b) vertical agreements which have as their object

—to fix resale prices, or
—to confer territorial protection on the participating undertakings or third undertakings,

the applicability of Article [81 (1)] cannot be ruled out even where the aggregate market shares held by all of the participating undertakings remain below the thresholds mentioned in points 9 and 10.

The Commission considers, however, that in the first instance it is for the authorities and courts of the Member States to take action on any agreements envisaged above in (a) and (b). Accordingly, it will only intervene in such cases when it considers that the interest of the Community so demands, and in particular if the agreements impair the proper functioning of the internal market.

Interestingly, the Notice comments that agreements between small and medium-sized undertakings are rarely capable of significantly affecting trade or competition within the common market.[158]

---

[155] Paras. 13–16 of the notice.
[156] Set out *supra* 127–128.
[157] This point is discussed more fully, *infra* in Chap. 4.
[158] But see *infra* n. 161.

Commission Notice on agreements of minor importance which do not fall within the meaning of Article 85(1) [now 81(1)] of the Treaty establishing the European Community [1997] OJ C372/13, [1998] 4 CMLR 192

19. Agreements between small and medium-sized undertakings, as defined in the Annex to Commission recommendation 96/280/EC are rarely capable of significantly affecting trade between Member States and competition within the common market. Consequently, as a general rule, they are not caught by the prohibition in Article [81 (1)]. In cases where such agreements exceptionally meet the conditions for the application of that provision, they will not be of sufficient Community interest to justify any intervention. This is why the Commission will not institute any proceedings, either on request or on its own initiative, to apply the provisions of Article [81 (1)] to such agreements, even if the thresholds set out in points 9 and 10 above are exceeded.

20. The Commission nevertheless reserves the right to intervene in such agreements:

(a) where they significantly impede competition in a substantial part of the relevant market,
(b) where, in the relevant market, competition is restricted by the cumulative effect of parallel networks of similar agreements made between several producers or dealers.

(iv) EFFECT OF THE NOTICE

The market shares set out in the Notice are useful in indicating the parties' position on the market but are not conclusive. Those shares merely provide useful guidance to undertakings: the Commission's notices are not legally binding on the Commission or the Courts. Agreements between parties with smaller market shares may produce a significant impact (although the Commission is unlikely to fine undertakings that have failed to notify their agreement).[159] Conversely, agreements between undertakings with greater shares of the market may produce insignificant results.[160]

The Commission should, therefore, where it takes the view that an agreement infringes Article 81(1), take care to define the relevant markets and to set out the parties' share of that market. Where the parties to an agreement only slightly exceed the market shares set out in the Notice the Commission must justify a finding that the agreement nonetheless has an appreciable effect on competition and trade. Where it fails to do so the Court may quash a decision holding that an agreement falls within Article 81(1).

Cases T–374, 375, 384 & 388/94, *European Night Services* v. *Commission* [1998] ECR II–3141, [1998] 5 CMLR 718

Court of First Instance

102. In any event, even if, as noted above, ENS's share of the tourist travel market was in fact likely to exceed 5% on certain routes, attaining 7% on the London-Amsterdam route and 6% on the London-Frankfurt/Dortmund route, . . . it must be borne in mind that, according to the case-law, an agreement may fall outside the prohibition in Article [81(1)] of the Treaty if it has only an insignificant effect on the market, taking into account the weak position which the parties concerned

---

[159] See para. 5 of the notice.
[160] See Art. 3 of the notice and, e.g., Case 319/82, *Société de Vente de Ciments et Bétons de l'Est SA* v. *Kerpen & Kerpen GmbH & Co KG* [1983] ECR, [1985] 1 CMLR 511, para. 8.

have on the product or service market in question (Case 5/69, *Völk* v. *Vervaecke* [1969] ECR 295 paragraph [7].). With regard to the quantitative effect on the market, the Commission has argued that, in accordance with its notice on agreements of minor importance, . . . Article [81(1)] applies to an agreement when the market share of the parties to the agreement amounts to 5%. However, the mere fact that that threshold may be reached and even exceeded does not make it possible to conclude with certainty that an agreement is caught by Article [81(1)] of the Treaty. Point 3 of that notice itself states that 'the quantitative definition of 'appreciable' given by the Commission is, however, no absolute yardstick and that 'in individual cases . . . agreements between undertakings which exceed these limits may . . . have only a negligible effect on trade between Member States or on competition, and are therefore not caught by Article [81(1)]' (see also *Langnese-Iglo* . . .). It is noteworthy, moreover, if only as an indication, that that analysis is corroborated by the Commission's 1997 notice on agreements of minor importance ([1997] OJ C372, p. 13.) replacing the notice of 3 September 1986, . . . according to which even agreements which are not of minor importance can escape the prohibition on agreements on account of their exclusively favourable impact on competition.

103. That being so, where, as in the present case, horizontal agreements between undertakings reach or only very slightly exceed the 5% threshold regarded by the Commission itself as critical and such as to justify application of Article [81(1)] of the Treaty, the Commission must provide an adequate statement of its reasons for considering such agreements to be caught by the prohibition in Article [81(1)] of the Treaty. Its obligation to do so is all the more imperative here, where, as the applicants stated in their notification, ENS has to operate on markets largely dominated by other modes of transport, such as air transport, and where, on the assumption of an increase in demand on the relevant markets and having regard to the limited possibilities for ENS to increase its capacity, its market shares will either fall or remain stable. In addition, such a statement of reasons is necessary in the present instance in view of the fact that, as the Court of Justice held at paragraph 86 of its judgment in *Musique Diffusion Française*, . . . an agreement is capable of exercising an appreciable influence on the pattern of trade between Member States even where the market shares of the undertakings concerned do not exceed 3%, provided that those market shares exceed those of most of their competitors.

104. There is, however, no such statement of reasons in the present case.

105. It must be concluded from the foregoing that the contested decision does not contain a sufficient statement of reasons to enable the Court to make a ruling on the shares held by ENS on the various relevant markets and, consequently, on whether the ENS agreements have an appreciable effect on trade between Member States, and the decision must therefore be annulled on that ground.

Where an agreement falls within the ambit of the notice, the Commission states that it will not, generally, institute proceedings or impose fines. However, parties to an agreement must still be wary of the possibility of proceedings where the agreement contains restrictions referred to in Article 11 of the notice or if the agreement nevertheless significantly restricts competition or where the relevant market is restricted by networks of agreements.[161] The

---

[161] See paras. 5, 11, and 20 of the notice. In *Greek Ferries* [1999] OJ L109/124 the Commission imposed fines on ferry operators it found to have colluded in the setting of fares for ferry services between Italy and Greece even though at least one, or probably two, of the undertakings involved were small and medium-sized enterprises (SMEs) (Commission's Recommendation 96/280/EC of 3 Apr. 1996). The Commission recognized that it had stated in its notice that agreements between SMEs are not, in general, caught by the prohibition in Art. 81(1). In this case, however, it took account of the fact that only two of the parties to the agreement could be described as SMEs and that the agreement undoubtedly significantly impeded competition in a substantial part of the relevant market.

parties cannot, however, be saved from the consequence of nullity in the event of the agreement being found to contravene Article 81(1). National courts are not bound by the notice. In practice, however, a national court would be likely to take it into account when assessing whether or not an agreement has an appreciable effect on competition and trade within the meaning of Article 81(1).

(v) OUTGROWING THE NOTICE

A possible difficulty is that parties may outgrow the notice by subsequently acquiring greater market shares or achieving increased turnovers. Paragraph 10 of the Notice[162] provides for some marginal relief.

(vi) NETWORKS OF AGREEMENTS

Paragraph 18 provides that the notice is not applicable where the relevant market is restricted by the cumulative effects of parallel networks of similar agreements established by several manufacturers or dealers. This paragraph will be of particular importance in the context of distribution agreements which compete with other similar networks of agreements. Thus, although, for example, in principle, the Community authorities would not be concerned with an exclusive purchasing agreement concluded between parties with only 2 per cent of the relevant market, the notice will not in fact apply where a competitor's access to the market is foreclosed by the existence of a network of similar agreements. On some markets, paragraph 18 deprives the notice of much of its utility.

It is possible, however, that, even where there is a network of agreements, an agreement concluded between undertakings which have a small market share will not restrict competition within the meaning of Article 81(1) at all. Rather, following *Delimitis* the agreement will be held to restrict competition only if it makes a significant contribution to the cumulative effect of the network. Both the market position of the parties and the duration of the agreement will, therefore, be relevant.[163]

I. COMMISSION NOTICES

In addition to the Notice on agreements of minor importance, the Commission has issued other notices which indicate that certain agreements may not infringe Article 81(1). The Commission started issuing notices in 1962 in order to clarify circumstances in which certain restrictive practices would fall outside Article 81(1). As in the case of the Notice on agreements of minor importance, these notices provide useful guidance for parties but are not binding on either the Commission or Courts. The following notices are of particular significance in determining the application of Article 81(1) to agreements:

---

[162] Set out *supra* 130.
[163] Case 234/89, *Delimitis* v. *Henninger Bräu* [1991] ECR 1–935, [1992] 5 CMLR 210, paras. 24–26. This aspect of the case is discussed *infra* Chap. 4.

- Commission Notice concerning agreements, decisions and concerted practices in the field of co-operation between enterprises;[164]
- Commission Notice concerning its assessment of certain subcontracting agreements in relation to Article 85(1) [now 81(1)] of the EEC [now EC] Treaty.[165]

Further, of particular importance are the Notices and draft guidelines which deal with the application of Community competition law to horizontal co-operation agreements[166] and the Commission's guidelines setting out when vertical restraints and agency agreements fall within the scope of Article 81(1). In respect of agency agreement, the guidelines replace an earlier Commission Notice on exclusive dealing arrangements with commercial agents.[167]

J. EXTRATERRITORIALITY

The question of when and in what circumstances the competition rules may be applied to the acts of overseas undertakings (which are not established in the EU) is a controversial one and a politically sensitive issue. The answer to this question does, of course, have an impact on the scope of Article 81(1). In particular, the Commission is concerned to ensure that Article 81 can be applied to all agreements which produce effects within the EU even if concluded outside of it.[168] It has been seen in *ICI* v. *Commission (Dyestuffs)*[169] that Article 81(1) will apply to an undertaking situated outside the Community which implements an agreement through a subsidiary (which forms part of the same economic unit) situated or present within it. The extraterritorial reach of Article 81(1) and the EC competition rules generally is dealt with in Chapter 17.

K. SUMMARY OF AGREEMENTS FALLING OUTSIDE ARTICLE 81(1)

The following list provides a checklist of agreements which fall outside Article 81(1) altogether:

1 Agreements between entities which are part of the same economic unit, for example, parent and subsidiary;

2 Agreements which do not have as their object or effect the prevention, restriction, or distortion of competition;

3 Agreements which do not affect trade between Member States;

---

[164] [1968] OJ C75/3.

[165] [1979] OJ C1/2.

[166] Chap. 12 and 13 will deal with these issues in more detail.

[167] The new Guidelines on Vertical Restraints [2000] OJ C291/1 replacing the Notice on exclusive dealing contracts with commercial agents [1962] OJ L39/2921.

[168] Although the EC competition authorities may claim jurisdiction in cases involving non-EC undertakings, enforcement of this jurisdiction may be more problematic.

[169] Cases 48, 49, 51–7/69 [1972] ECR 619, [1972] CMLR 557, paras. 125–146, see *supra* 107.

4   Agreements which do not affect trade between Member States and the free play of
    competition to an appreciable extent;

5   Agreements may also escape the ambit of Article 81(1) if the criteria of any of the
    Commission notices or guidelines are satisfied;

6   Agreements which are truly extra-territorial; and

7   Some full-function joint ventures within the meaning of the Merger Regulation.[170]

5. ARTICLE 81(2)

It has already been seen[171] that despite the clear wording of Article 81(2), the nullity
provided for in that provision applies only to individual *clauses* in the agreement affected by
the Article 81(1) prohibition. In *Société La Technique Minière* v. *Maschinenbau Ulm
GmbH*,[172] the ECJ held the the agreement as a whole is void only where those clauses are
not severable from the remaining terms of the agreement. It thus interpreted Article 81(2)
with reference only to its purpose in Community law and to ensure compliance with the
Treaty. It may also be the case that the nullity imposed by Article 81(2) is not absolute. The
English Court of Appeal has taken the view that the nullity has only the same temporaneous
or transient effect as the prohibition in Article 81(1) (an agreement will cease to be void if
the agreement itself ceases to restrict competition or to affect trade within the meaning of
Article 81(1)[173]).

The ECJ has held that the question whether any null clause or clauses in an agreement can
be severed from the rest of the agreement must be decided by national, not Community,
law.[174] Each national court will, therefore, have to apply its own national rules on severance
to determine the impact of Article 81(2) on the agreement before it.

6. FURTHER READING

ARTICLES

Faull, J., 'Effect on Trade between Member
States' [1991] *Fordham Corporate Law Institute* 485

Garzamiti, L., and Scassellati-Sforzolini,

G., 'Liability of Successor Undertakings for
Infringements of EC Competition Law
Committed Prior to Corporate Reorganisa-
tions' [1995] *ECLR* 348

---

[170] For discussion of the complicated question of which joint ventures fall to be assessed within the
procedure of the Merger Reg. Council Reg. 4064/89 [1989] OJ L395/1, as amended by Council Reg. 1310/97
[1997] OJ L180/1, and not under Art. 81 see *infra* Chaps. 12 and 13.

[171] See *supra* 87.

[172] Case 56/65 [1966] ECR 234, 250, [1966] CMLR 357.

[173] *Passmore* v. *Morland plc* [1999] 3 All ER 1005.

[174] See also Case 319/82, *Société de Vente de Ciments et Bétons de l'Est* v. *Kerpen & Kerpen GmbH & Co KG*
[1983] ECR 4173, [1985] 1 CMLR 511, para. 11. See *infra* Chap. 15.

4

THE RELATIONSHIP BETWEEN ARTICLE 81(1) AND ARTICLE 81(3) OF THE TREATY

1. INTRODUCTION

A. ARTICLE 81(1) AND ARTICLE 81(3)

It was seen in Chapter 3 that Article 81 provides for a two-tier analysis of agreements between undertakings. First, an agreement between undertakings must be scrutinized to see whether it infringes Article 81(1). If it does not that is the end of the story. If it does, however, it must, secondly, be determined whether or not it merits exemption. Any agreement within Article 81(1) which provides specified benefits (it improves the production or distribution of goods or promotes technical or economic progress) allows consumers a fair share of the benefit, does not contain any indispensable restrictions, and does not substantially eliminate competition may be exempted under Article 81(3).

Article 81 clearly aims to prevent the conclusion and operation of restrictive agreements. The key question which arises in the application of Article 81 is, therefore, whether or not an agreement has as its object or effect the prevention, restriction, or distortion of competition for the purposes of Article 81(1) and, where it does, in what circumstances it should nonetheless be exempted under Article 81(3). If many agreements are found to restrict competition (the words 'prevention, restriction, or distortion' are intended to cover any interference with competition and are synonymous[1] so the term 'restriction' will be used as shorthand in this text to cover all three) numerous agreements will be prohibited by Article 81(1) *unless* exempted. Consequently, the interpretation and application of Article 81(3) becomes of crucial importance since it becomes the main vehicle for authorizing agreements which are compatible with the common market and the Community objectives. If, however, a narrower interpretation is adopted when determining whether or not a contractual provision restricts competition and, consequently whether there has been an infringement of

---

[1] It is, therefore, unnecessary to decide whether competition is being restricted, prevented, or distorted.

Article 81(1), the role played by Article 81(3) becomes more limited. Finding the right balance between the application of Article 81(1) and Article 81(3) has proved to be an extremely difficult and tortuous one.

B. THE INTERPRETATION OF 'OBJECT OR EFFECT IS THE PREVENTION, RESTRICTION, OR DISTORTION OF COMPETITION'—THE BROAD APPROACH

One of the most strident criticisms made of the Commission's application of the competition rules has been its failure, in the past at least, to adopt a sufficiently realistic interpretation of Article 81(1), in particular, when determining whether or not an agreement restricts competition. The broad criticism has been that it has tended to take the view that a restriction on a party's conduct is tantamount to a restriction on competition. Further, that any restriction which might interfere with the single market objective amounts to a restriction of competition.[2] In short, the Commission has found that many agreements restrict competition. Numerous agreements have consequently, been caught within the widely cast net of Article 81(1) but then exempted. The Commission has conducted the analysis when scrutinizing an agreement for its compliance with the requirements set out in Article 81(3) which it could in fact have conducted earlier when determining whether or not the agreement restricts competition under Article 81(1).

C. THE DRAWBACKS OF A BROAD INTERPRETATION OF ARTICLE 81(1)

At first sight, it may appear immaterial whether or not the scrutiny of the pro- and anti-competitive aspects of the agreement is conducted under Article 81(1) or Article 81(3) if the outcome is the same—the parties may operate their agreement. This is not just an academic point, however. Severe negative consequences may result both to the parties to the agreement and the Commission from this approach so that the conclusion of agreements which are neutral from a competition perspective, or even pro-competitive, may be deterred.

A large number of fish are caught entirely unnecessarily within the net of European competition policy, and have to be returned to the sea at the expense of considerable effort and uncertainty.[3]

Firstly, businesses may find it hard to understand why their agreement is characterized as restrictive of competition. It may seem perverse to brand an agreement as 'anti-competitive' simply because it imposes 'restrictions' on the conduct of one or all of the parties, especially if, in subsequently exempting the agreement, the Commission is essentially accepting that the agreement is a pro-competitive one.

---

[2] See *supra* Chap. 1.
[3] D. Neven, P. Papandropoulos, and P. Seabright, *Trawling for Minnows: European Competition Policy and Agreements Between Firms* (Centre for Economic Policy Research, 1998), 37.

S. Bishop and M. Walker, *The Economics of EC Competition Law: Concepts, Application and Measurement* (Sweet & Maxwell, 1999)

4.04 Article [81] applies to all agreements which entail 'the prevention, restriction or distortion of competition'. This immediately raises the question of when competition can be said to be prevented, restricted or distorted. The current interpretation holds that very many agreements may be covered by Article [81(1)] regardless of the market position of the parties involved or of the economic impact of the agreement. In other words, the legal interpretation of what constitutes a prevention, distortion or restriction of competition is extremely wide. The result of such a wide interpretation not only has little to do with an analysis of competition and if taken literally would be nonsensical . . . but has caused an administrative log-jam.

. . . [A] definition of effective competition from a policy perspective depend[s] on market outcomes rather than form. Standard economic theory dictates that unless firms possess and exercise market power, they are unable to affect competition adversely. In other words, in the absence of market power, agreements between firms do not prevent, restrict or distort competition. This distinction explains why it is perfectly consistent for a given contract clause in one agreement to have benign outcomes while in others form the same clause to be prohibited as anti-competitive. Whether an agreement adversely affects competition depends not its form but its impact on the market. . . .

4.05 To illustrate this point, consider a shoe manufacturer who wishes to restrict the supply of its products only to those retailers who agree not to stock the products of other manufacturers. Is such an exclusivity agreement anti-competitive? The answer to this question depends on the facts of the particular case. For example, if the shoe manufacturer has a relatively small market share of retail sales of shoes—say 10 per cent—then it is unlikely that the exclusivity agreement would adversely affect competition since competing shoe manufacturers can easily gain access to other retail outlets not subject to such restrictions. . . . On the other hand, if the shoe manufacturer were able to sign up 90 per cent of the retail outlets the impact on competition might be different.

Although the interpretation of Article [81(1)] adopts a formalistic interpretation of when an agreement is said to affect competition, the assessment of the compatibility of agreements under Article [81(3)] tends to revert to a more economic view of the impact on competition. In one sense these views are inconsistent. Either an agreement is pro-competitive or it restricts competition. Under the current application of Article [81], many of the Commission's decisions appear to imply that both outcomes are possible. . . .

Apart from these conceptual difficulties, the decision to deal with the agreement under Article 81(3) rather than Article 81(1) imposes a huge cost on business. The process of gaining an exemption has, to put it mildly, by no means been straightforward.[4]

---

[4] 'In one sense, provided that a complete assessment of the economic impact of a particular agreement is made at some stage, it could be argued that the argument over the scope of Art. [81(1)] is academic. However, such a view ignores the huge burden placed not only on the Commission but also the companies involved. . . . It can also be argued that the current system is deficient because it leads to too few published decisions. This not only hinders transparency but also the development of a consistent policy approach, which can be contrasted with [the] Commission's approach to mergers where a decision is published following each notification whether or not a detailed investigation is required': S. Bishop and M. Walker, *The Economics of EC Competition Law: Concepts, Application and Measurement* (Sweet & Maxwell, London, 1999), para. 4.05.

The easiest and cheapest means of obtaining an exemption is for the parties to draft their agreement to fall within the terms of one of the Community regulations which grant block exemptions to categories of agreements (for example, to certain research and development or to certain technology transfer agreements). Where an agreement satisfies the requirements of such a block exemption notification to the Commission is unnecessary because the agreement is automatically exempted from the Article 81(1) prohibition.[5] Prior to 2000, however, the terms of these regulations have been strict[6] and it may not be beneficial to society for undertakings to have to mould and alter their pro-competitive agreements to squeeze them within the terms of such a regulation. Parties to an agreement may not wish to be confined to such a straight-jacket and/or may feel that it distorts their bargaining position or unduly interferes with their freedom of contract. In some cases they may simply be unable to bring their agreement within its terms.

Where parties to an agreement are unable to draft their agreement within the terms of a block exemption, they may wish[7] to notify the agreement to the Commission.[8] Notification is a time- and cost-consuming exercise but enables the parties to apply for a negative clearance (a decision stating that the agreement does not fall within Article 81(1) at all) and/ or to seek an individual exemption. In the past, many undertakings have felt compelled to notify since the Commission has sole power to issue decisions granting exemptions to individual agreements[9] and the general rule has been that exemptions can only be granted to notified agreements from the date of notification (the general rule does not however now apply to most verrical agreements).[10] The difficulty, however, is that the Commission does not generally grant more than twenty decisions in total each year.[11] The parties will, therefore, certainly face a delay. Further, even if the Commission takes the view that the agreement falls within Article 81(1) it will be only in exceptional circumstances that the agreement will be exempted by decision from the Article 81(1) prohibition (it does not have the resources to grant exemptions to all). In most cases parties to an agreement will have to be content with a 'comfort letter' instead. A comfort letter is not, however, a Commission decision. It is simply an informal letter stating the Commission's view on the compatibility of the agreement with Article 81 and is not binding on national courts (or even the Commission). Consequently, it leaves the parties in an uncomfortable state of legal limbo. There

[5] The sanction of nullity set out in Art. 81(2) does not therefore apply, see *infra* 216–217.

[6] But see, e.g., the new block exemption dealing with vertical agreements, Reg. 2790/99 [1999] OJ L336/21 (discussed *infra* in Chap. 9), which was enacted partly to prevent the straightjacketing effect which arose from its predecessors.

[7] But see the proposals contained in the Commission's White Paper on modernisation of the rules implementing Articles 85 and 86 [now 81 and 82] of the EC Treaty [1999] OJ C 132/1, [1999] 5 CMLR 208, discussed *infra* 219 ff. The Commission has proposed abolishing the entire notification procedure.

[8] Reg. 17 [1959–62] OJ Spec. Ed. 87, Art. 4(1). But see *infra* n. 10.

[9] Reg. 17 [1959–62] OJ Spec. Ed. 87, Art. 9(1).

[10] The category of agreements which do not have to be notified has now been expanded (see Reg. 17 [1959–62] OJ Spec. Ed. 87, Art. 4(2) as amended by Reg. 1216/99 [1999] OJ L148/5, and discussion *infra* 210–211). The practical advantage for agreements falling within this category is that exemptions can be granted retrospectively until the date the agreement was commenced. A failure to notify is not fatal to the validity of the agreement.

[11] This is to be contrasted with the 200 or so notifications that it receives each year. If it were not for the existence of a number of block exemptions and the doctrine of appreciability, the Commission would obviously receive many more notifications.

is no provisional validity for notified agreements[12] and restrictions in agreements contravening Article 81(1) are void and unenforceable unless exempted.[13]

Even if the Commission decides to proceed and to clear or exempt an agreement by formal decision, it may decide to do so only after the agreement has been altered. Regulation 17 specifically provides that exemptions may be granted subject to the fulfillment of certain stipulated conditions.[14] Again, this may interfere with and affect the bargaining position of the parties and the terms of the agreement.

Many of the practical consequences that have arisen from the Commission's practice are explained by Korah in the extract below.

V. Korah, 'EEC Competition Policy — Legal Form or Economic Efficiency?' [1986] *CLP* 85, 95–8

One consequence of the Commission's practice of not attempting a realistic economic analysis under Article [81(1)] has been unfortunate. It has the exclusive power to exempt, yet grants few exemptions: until 1983 only three in a good year, sometimes none; since then, only slightly more. It is short of staff. It finds the necessary analysis difficult and time-consuming. National judges asked to enforce such contracts may incline to follow Commission precedents . . .

The Commission's practice has led to a backlog of cases, since every agreement caught by Article [81(1)] requires exemption. It has reduced it by various devices. It has granted group exemptions for some common kinds of commercial transaction. . . .

Where it is vital that an agreement should be enforceable in the courts, the parties may distort their transaction to come within a group exemption. Contracts not brought within the straightjacket of any group exemption may be harder to enforce, which leads to other distortions, such as the desire to receive services or payments early before the other party repudiates the contract. . . .

Even if the agreement is notified to the Commission with a request for exemption, it is unlikely to receive one. The Commission may write a comfort letter. One of the sort sent in *Guérlain* . . . stating that the agreement does not infringe Article [81(1)] owing to the small market share of the participants is useful, since it should be taken into account by national courts enforcing the agreement. One, as in *Rovin*, . . . stating that the agreement merits exemption, has been described as a 'discomfort letter' . . . since it may imply that the agreement infringes Article [81(1)] and a national court cannot exempt.

The most recent attempt by the Commission to clear its backlog is the short form exemption. The Commission publishes in the Official Journal a notice . . . describing the particular agreement and a few facts about the industry, stating its intention to exempt it. This will have to be translated into all the Community languages. The Commission will add a statement in standard form that it has received no comments in answer to its notice and a very short legal appraisal granting the exemption. Only this last will require translation. The need for translations is one of the matters that has delayed the Commission's decisions in the past. . . .

The Commission may well impose conditions on an individual exemption years after the agreement was made, or refuse one unless some of the terms are modified. Even comfort letters may be sent only if the parties amend their agreements. This gives each party who can object to the modification a chance to renegotiate all its liabilities. . . . Fear of such opportunist renegotiation years later has deterred many large forms from notifying significant agreements to the Commission. They prefer to

---

[12] See *infra* 206.
[13] See *supra* Chap. 3 and *infra* Chap. 15.
[14] Reg. 17 [1959–62] OJ Spec. Ed. 87, Art. 8(1).

rely, if necessary on the argument that the agreement contains no more ancillary restrictions than are necessary to make the transaction viable and that it increases more competition than it reduces, or on the principle of honour between the thieves!

If the parties do not wish to notify and their agreement does not fall within one of the Community block exemptions then, unless their agreement is non-notifiable, they will have to take the risk that their agreement (or clauses in their agreement) may subsequently be found to be in contravention of Article 81(1).[15] Commercially, this may be an unappealing position to be in. In the event of a dispute arising between the parties to the agreement, the invalidity of the agreement, or some of its provisions, may be raised. An undertaking may then find that its agreement or certain provisions within it are void and unenforceable. If the agreement contains serious restrictions of competition the parties may be fined if the Commission decides to bring infringement proceedings.

Because of these conceptual and practical difficulties arising from a wide interpretation of Article 81(1) the Commission has been urged to take a more economically sophisticated approach in assessing whether or not an agreement restricts competition.[16] Article 81(1) should not be applied formalistically to an agreement (or provisions within it) which does not have an appreciable adverse effect on competition. As an alternative, it has been advocated that before it is decided whether or not the agreement restricts competition, a 'rule of reason' style analysis similar to that adopted in the USA should be conducted weighing the pro- and anti-competitive effects of the agreement.

D. THE RULE OF REASON

The phrase 'rule of reason'[17] derives from the case law of the US courts when interpreting section 1 of the Sherman Act 1890. This provision provides that '[e]very contract, combination in the form of a trust or otherwise, or conspiracy, in restraint of trade or commerce among the several States, or with foreign nations, is declared to be illegal . . .'.

Since the main objective of a contract is to restrain the conduct of the parties to it a literal interpretation of the section might result in all agreements being held to be illegal. The US courts have, however, construed the section to mean that contracts must not restrain competition unreasonably.[18] In determining whether or not an agreement does restrain competition unreasonably the courts adopt two separate approaches.

Some contracts are considered to be illegal *per se*. 'There are certain agreements or practices which because of their pernicious effect on competition and lack of any redeeming virtue are conclusively presumed to be unreasonable and therefore illegal without elaborate

---

[15] The contract or contractual provisions will be void, of course, only if the national court takes the view that the agreement restricts competition within the meaning of Art. 81(1) and cannot be exempted: see *supra* n. 10.

[16] See, e.g. I. Forrester and C. Norall, 'The Laïcization of Community Law: Self-help and the Rule of Reason: How Competition is and could be Applied' (1984) 21 *CMLRev.* 11, V. Korah, 'EEC Competition Policy-Legal Form or Economic Efficiency?' [1986] *CLP* 85, B.E. Hawk, 'System Failure: Vertical Restraints and EC Competition Law' (1995) 32 *CMLRev* 973.

[17] The term 'rule of reason' should not be confused with the use of the same term which has been adopted in connection with Art. 28 (ex Art. 30) EC on the free movement of goods.

[18] *Standard Oil Co of New Jersey* v. *US* 221 US 1 (1911); *US* v. *American Tobacco Co*, 221 US 106 (1911).

inquiries as to the prices, harm they have caused or the business excuse for their use.'[19] Thus some agreements, such as naked price-fixing among competitors,[20] are automatically held to restrain competition unreasonably. They are anti-competitive and the court will not waste time or resources hearing justifications for the agreement.

Although in the 1960s the US courts tended to take a formalistic approach to section 1 characterizing many contracts as illegal *per se*, the majority of agreements are now[21] appraised under the 'rule of reason'. Agreements are assessed in their legal and economic context to determine 'whether the restraint imposed is such as merely regulates and perhaps thereby promotes competition or whether it is such as may suppress or even destroy competition. To determine that question the court must ordinarily consider the facts peculiar to the business to which the restraint is applied; its condition before and after the restraint was imposed; the nature of the restraint and its effect, actual or probable.'[22]

In short, the pro- and anti-competitive aspects of the agreement are weighed in their legal and economic context before an agreement is condemned as illegal. The question thus arises whether or not a similar balancing act should be done in EC law when deciding whether a provision in an agreement is a restriction of competition within Article 81(1).

E. THE RULE OF REASON AND ARTICLE 81 OF THE TREATY

(i) THE POSSIBILITY OF EXEMPTION

A crucial difference between EC and US law is that there is no equivalent in the Sherman Act of Article 81(3). Because the Sherman Act provides no exemption for contracts found to be in restraint of trade it is of great importance that the provision is interpreted sensibly and reasonably. If an agreement is found to be in restraint of trade the agreement is illegal. There is no scope for the beneficial aspects of the agreement to be taken into account later. In contrast, Article 81(3) specifically provides for exemption of agreements that are restrictive of competition. A broad interpretation of Article 81(1) can, therefore, be adopted safe in the knowledge that the agreement can nonetheless be exempted. Indeed, the Commission has stated in the White Paper on modernisation[23] that it is Article 81(3), not Article 81(1), which contains all the elements of the rule of reason and which is ideally suited for the weighing of the pro- and anti-competitive aspects of the agreement. Further, it questions why Article 81(3) was included if a full analysis of the harmful and beneficial effects of agreement were intended to be made at the Article 81(1) stage. Such an approach would either render Article 81(3) virtually redundant or would cause it to be used to exempt agreements on broader, socio-political grounds.

---

[19] *Northern Pac R Co* v. *United States*, 356 US 1, 5 (1958).

[20] *US* v. *Trenton Potteries Co*, 273 US 392 (1927); *US* v. *Socony-Vaccuum Oil Co*, 310 US 150 (1940).

[21] There was a time when the US courts took the view that almost all restraints in vertical agreements were illegal *per se*: see *infra* Chap. 9.

[22] *Chicago Board of Trade* v. *US*, 246 US 231 (1918), *per* Brandeis J.

[23] White Paper on modernisation of the rules implementing Articles 85 and 86 [now 81 and 82] of the EC Treaty [1999] OJ C132/1, [1999] 5 CMLR 208. But see *infra* n. 96 and accompanying text.

White Paper on the Modernization of the Rules Implementing Articles 85 and 86 [now 81 and 82] of the EC Treaty [1999] OJ C132/1, [1999] 5 CMLR 208

56. . . . It would in a way mean interpreting Article [81(1)] as incorporating a 'rule of reason'. . . Such a system would ease the notification constraints imposed on undertakings, since they would not be required to notify agreements in order to obtain negative clearance.

57. The Commission has already adopted this approach to a limited extent and has carried out an assessment of the pro- and anti-competitive aspects of some restrictive practices under Article [81(1)]. This approach has been endorsed by the Court of Justice . . . However, the structure of Article [81] is such as to prevent greater use being made of this approach: if more systematic use were made under Article [81(1)] of an analysis of the pro- and anti-competitive aspects of a restrictive agreement, Article [81(3)] would be cast aside, whereas any such change could be made only through revision of the Treaty. It would at the very least be paradoxical to cast aside Article [81(3)] when that provision in fact contains all the elements of a 'rule of reason' . . . Lastly, this option would run the risk of diverting Article [81(3)] from its purpose, which is to provide a legal framework for the economic assessment of restrictive practices and not to allow application of the competition rules to be set aside because of political considerations.

(ii) THE ROLE OF ARTICLE 81(3)

It is true that, were a more realistic assessment to be conducted under Article 81(1), it might seem logical that Article 81(3) should be used to exempt restrictive agreements resulting in broader benefits, for example, from an economic, social, industrial, environmental, employment, and/or regional perspective. Whether or not these latter socio-political factors may, or should, be taken into account when making the assessment under Article 81(3) will be discussed in greater detail in the section below dealing with the interpretation of Article 81(3). Such an approach might be preferable to the taking of a formalistic view of Article 81(1) only to conduct economic analysis at the Article 81(3) stage.

(iii) THE COMMISSION'S MONOPOLY OVER EXEMPTION

The decision to take a broad view has had another added attraction for the Commission. The Commission has the exclusive power to grant exemptions.[24] An expansive interpretation of Article 81(1) has, therefore, meant that the Commission has the key role in the determination of whether an agreement can be operated and, if so, in what form. This has enabled the Commission to develop its own view of what goals EC Community competition law should serve. In particular it has used the competition rules as a tool in pursuit of the single market objective. Further, it has been more concerned than other competition authorities about restrictions on conduct which it believes restrict rivalry between undertakings operating on a market.[25]

---

[24] Reg. 17 [1959–62] OJ Spec. Ed. 87, Art. 9(1).

[25] See *supra* Chap. 1. These goals are different from those of its US counterparts: see e.g. the discussion of vertical restraints *infra*, at Chap. 9.

J. Faull and A. Nikpay (eds.), *The EC Law of Competition* (Oxford University Press, 1999)

2.73 This approach, which some have described as 'a rule of reason', has been regularly rejected by the Commission. The most recent exposition of this view came in the 1999 White Paper on Modernisation of the Rules Implementing Articles 85 and 86 [now Articles 81 and 82] of the EC Treaty . . .

2.74 Apart from the structure and wording of Article 81(1), the Commission's rejection of this approach is due to the assumptions it has made regarding the role of competition in the economy and the policy considerations which have underpinned its application of the rules.

2.75 The first, and perhaps most significant, assumption the Commission has made is that the process of competition itself, or, to be more precise, the process of rivalry between undertakings, produces the best results. For example, in its *Report on Competition Policy 1971* (Vol I), the Commission described competition as 'the best stimulant of economic activity'. It went on to argue that competition, '[t]hrough the interplay of decentralised decision-making machinery', enabled enterprises 'continuously to improve their efficiency which is the sine qua non for a steady improvement in living standards and employment prospects. From this point of view, competition policy is an essential means for satisfying to a great extent the individual and collective needs of our society.' Over a decade later, in its Fifteenth Report, the Commission described the role of competition, and thus of Article 81(1), as preserving 'the freedom and right of initiative of the individual economic operators' and fostering 'the spirit of enterprise'. Thus for the Commission the protection of rivalry has been an end in itself.

2.76 The Commission has found some support for its view in the European Court of Justice. . . .

2.77 In practice this philosophy has often led to an examination of the clauses in agreements to identify whether restraints have been placed on the commercial conduct of the parties or third parties.

In contrast, a different approach would have delegated more enforcement of agreements to the national level. Both the national and Community courts would, therefore, have played a greater role in development of competition policy and the interpretation of the competition rules, especially Article 81(1).[26] Further, if, initially, the national courts or national competition authorities had been given such a role,[27] the uniform application of Article 81(1) might have been compromised. National courts may have adopted divergent views on whether an agreement restricted competition within the meaning of Article 81 and applied Article 81 differently to identical agreements or problems. Although Article 234 of the Treaty sets out a procedure for national courts to refer questions relating to the interpretation of Community law to the ECJ that provision does not guarantee that references will be made. Only courts from which there is no appeal are obliged to make such a reference.[28]

(iv) CERTAINTY FOR BUSINESS

Article 81(1) is directly effective and it is not necessary to obtain a decision from the

---

[26] In addition, it has been questioned whether the national courts provide a suitable forum for making the analysis of agreements required by Art. 81(1): see the discussion of the enforcement of the competition rules before the national courts, *infra* Chap. 15.

[27] Art. 81(1) and (2) are directly effective and confer rights on individuals which the national courts are obliged to protect. Because, however, the Commission has the sole power to grant exemptions from Art. 81(3) it seems that this provision is not directly effective: see *supra* Chap. 2, and *infra* Chap. 16.

[28] See *supra* Chap. 2.

Commission holding that an agreement falls outside Article 81(1) altogether. Consequently, it is unnecessary to notify an agreement that does not appear to infringe Article 81(1). A more leading role for Article 81(1) would thus have been likely to mean less certainty for undertakings. In every case it would be necessary to assess an agreement to determine whether, in the legal and economic context in which it operates, it can be said to restrict competition. Further, it would only have been in exceptional circumstances that the parties would have received assurance that their agreement was compatible with the competition rules.[29]

F. THE NEED FOR CHANGE

The Commission is fully aware of the difficulties that have resulted from its broad interpretation of Article 81(1) and its monopoly over exemption. Consequently, the Commission has taken numerous steps to try and deal with this problem. For example, the Commission has introduced broad block exemptions and sought other ways to discourage notification. In its 1999 White Paper on modernisation the Commission reviews the steps taken and makes further proposals to deal with the problems resulting from the bifurcation of Article 81 and the notification and authorization system generally.[30] In particular, the Commission indicates in paragraph 78 of the Paper that it will adopt a more realistic approach when applying Article 81(1) and will seek to refrain from applying it to agreement concluded between undertakings that do not possess a degree of market power; that it should forgo its exclusive right to grant exemptions; and that, instead, Article 81 should be directly applicable.

2. AGREEMENTS WHICH HAVE AS THEIR OBJECT OR EFFECT THE PREVENTION, RESTRICTION OR DISTORTION OF COMPETITION

A. GENERAL

In section 1 above it was pointed out that, in the past, the Commission has been criticized for failing to take a sufficiently realistic view of whether or not an agreement restricts competition within the meaning of Article 81(1). Nonetheless some decisions and other initiatives of the Commission reflect a growing willingness to embark on an economic

---

[29] Business will have to live with greater uncertainty if the Commission's proposals set out in its White Paper on modernisation of the rules implementing Articles 85 and 86 [now 81 and 82] of the EC Treaty [1999] OJ C132/1, [1999] 5 CMLR 208 are adopted: see the discussion *infra* 219 ff.

[30] See discussion of the White Paper, *ibid.*, *infra* 219 ff and Chapter 16.

analysis and to grant negative clearances to agreements which it finds do not restrict competition for the purposes of Article 81. Further, it must not be forgotten that it is the ECJ which is responsible for the interpretation of the Treaty, not the Commission.[31] The case law of that Court suggests that in a majority of circumstances the Commission is required, as a matter of law, to take a more economic approach when assessing the compatibility of an agreement with Article 81(1).

B. OBJECT OR EFFECT

(i) ALTERNATIVE, NOT CUMULATIVE, REQUIREMENTS

The ECJ has held that the words 'object or effect' are to be read disjunctively. They are alternative, not cumulative, requirements. An agreement is caught if *either* its object *or* its effect is the restriction of competition.[32]

(ii) THE OBJECT OF THE AGREEMENT

a. THE IMPORTANCE OF THE TERMS OF THE AGREEMENT

In the first instance it is necessary to look at the terms of the agreement to determine its object. Where the object of the agreement is to restrict competition there is no need to look further and to prove that its effect is the restriction of competition. '[F]or the purposes of applying Article [81(1)], there is no need to take account of the concrete effects of an agreement once it appears that it has as its object the prevention, restriction or distortion of competition.'[33] To this extent, the jurisprudence of the Court does support a formalistic approach to Article 81(1). In a similar way to the US courts, the ECJ finds that some agreements or provisions in an agreement have so 'pernicious' an effect that they automatically restrict competition. In contrast to the position in the USA, however, any alleged pro-competitive aspects of the agreement may, in theory, be weighed against the restrictive elements at the Article 81(3) stage. Although in practice it is rare for parties to notify agreements containing these types of clauses, or for exemption to be granted to agreements containing such provisions on notification,[34] this possibility at least remains.

---

[31] Art. 220 of the EC Treaty.

[32] Case 56/65, *Société La Technique Minière* v. *Maschinebau Ulm GmbH* [1966] ECR 234, 249. See also Case C–234/89, *Delimitis* v. *Henninger Bräu* [1991] ECR 1–935, [1992] 5 CMLR 210, para. 13. See also Cases T–374, 375, 384 & 388/94, *European Night Services* v. *Commission* [1998] ECR II–3141 [1998] 5 CMLR 718, para. 136, discussed *infra*.

[33] Cases 56 & 58/64, *Etablissements Consten SA & Grundig-Verkaufs-GmbH* v. *Commission* [1966] ECR 299, [1966] CMLR 416.

[34] *Infra* 197–198. If the Commission discovers undertakings operating an agreement containing these types of clauses it is likely to impose a fine: see e.g., *Bayer* [1996] OJ L201/1, [1996] 5 CMLR 416 and *Volkswagen* [1998] OJ L124/60, [1998] 5 CMLR 33, on appeal Case T–62/98, *Volkswagen AG* v. *Commission* [2000] 5 CMLR 853.

P Freeman and R. Whish (eds.) *Butterworths Competition Law* (Butterworths, looseleaf, no date) Division I

(a) Per se rules

[185]

It is possible to discern a similarity between the classification of agreements as per se illegal under the Sherman Act and as having the object of restricting competition under Article 81(1). In each case it is unnecessary for the relevant competition authorities to prove that the agreement in question actually has an adverse effect on competition: it is insufficient to show simply that there is an agreement. . . However the parallel between per se rules in the US and the position under Article 81(1) should not be pursued further than this. . . First, under the Sherman Act an agreement which is caught per se cannot be vindicated or justified because it might have beneficial effects. Under EC law, even if an agreement falls per se within Article 81(1), it is always possible that it might qualify for an exemption under Article 81(3). . . Admittedly it is unlikely that horizontal price fixing would benefit from an exemption, but even this is not a total impossibility; in some cases in the services sector, and in particular, in banking, the Commission has permitted some restrictions of price competition. . . The structure of Article [81] is fundamentally different from that of s 1 of the Sherman Act and it would be misleading to assert that there is a total correspondence between the operation of these two provisions.

[186]

A second point is that agreements that have the object of restriction competition may, even so, fall outside Article 81(1) because they are of no economic importance or because they do not affect inter-state trade. The third point is that the competition authorities in the US and the EC perceive particular types of agreement differently: systems of competition law have different preoccupations, and this is reflected in the way the law develops. The category of agreements per se illegal under the Sherman Act is different from the class of agreements the object of which is held to be the restriction of competition under Article 81(1). Given these comments, it is questionable whether it is useful to adopt the language of per se illegality at all under EC competition law: it is preferable to avoid borrowing terminology from another system of law which may confuse more than it clarifies.

b. THE EFFECT ON TRADE AND THE CONCEPT OF APPRECIABILITY

Where the terms of the agreement are found to have as their object the prevention, restriction, or distortion of competition the effect of the agreement is irrelevant to the question whether the agreement restricts competition within the meaning of Article 81(1).[35] It will be remembered, however, that Article 81(1) also requires that the agreement should affect trade and that any restriction of competition or effect on trade should be appreciable. An analysis of the market will, therefore, be necessary to determine whether the agreement affects trade and whether the effect of the agreement on competition (and/or trade) is appreciable or insignificant.[36]

---

[35] It is irrelevant, therefore, that the objectives of the agreement have not been carried out. It is no defence, for example, that the cartel has been unsuccesful so that the agreement did not have the effect of restricting competition, see the *Polypropylene Cartel* [1986] OJ L230/1, [1988] 4 CMLR 347, discussed *supra* in Chap. 3.

[36] See *supra* Chap. 3 and the discussion *infra* 172 ff. The Commission may also take account of the effect of the agreement when determining the amount of the fine.

(iii) THE EFFECT OF THE AGREEMENT

If the object of the agreement cannot be said to restrict competition then, before it can be determined whether the agreement restricts competition, account must be taken of its effect. 'Where . . . an analysis of the said clauses does not reveal the effect on competition to be sufficiently deleterious, the consequence of the agreement should then be considered and for it to be caught by the prohibition it is then necessary to find that those factors are present that show that competition has in fact been prevented or restricted or distorted to an appreciable extent. The competition in question must be understood within the actual context in which it would occur in the absence of the agreement in dispute.'[37]

C. A RESTRICTION OF COMPETITION

The approach to the terms object or effect is clear enough. The real difficulty is, however, that before it can be determined whether or not the object or effect of an agreement is to restrict competition, it is necessary to define what is meant by a 'restriction of competition'. This is one of the most difficult problems for EC competition law.[38] Anyone who could define exactly what amounts to a restriction of competition would have achieved the competition law equivalent of finding the Holy Grail. The problem does not only plague EC competition law, for all systems of competition law are faced with the same intractable difficulty.

The problem arises because every contract restricts the conduct of the parties, but restrictions on *conduct* are not necessarily the same as restrictions on competition. Moreover even if an agreement *does* produce a restriction of competition in one respect, that restriction may be outweighed by the increase in competition it creates in other respects, so that on balance the agreement is pro- rather than anti-competitive.

The difficulties involved in making this assessment are illustrated by the facts of *Consten and Grundig*. It was seen in Chapter 3 that this case involved an agreement concluded between Grundig, a German manufacturer of radios, tape recorders, dictaphones, and televisions, and Consten, which it appointed exclusive distributor of its products in France. The salient facts of the case will be set out again here for the purposes of this discussion. The agreement undoubtedly restricted the conduct of the parties involved. For example, it obliged Consten not to handle competing products, to order a minimum quantity of Grundig products, to stock accessories and spare parts, to provide after-sales services, and not to sell Grundig products outside France. In return, Grundig agreed not to deliver the product for sale in France itself and to prohibit all other distributors from seeking sales, actively or passively, within France. To reinforce the territorial protection Grundig assigned to Consten the rights to the Grundig trade mark GINT, in France. This meant that Consten would be able to bring proceedings against any parallel importer of Grundig products for infringement of its trade mark.

---

[37] Case 56/65, *Société La Technique Minière* v. *Maschinebau Ulm GmbH* [1966] ECR 234, 249, [1966] 1 CMLR 357.

[38] But see also the difficulty of defining and identifying 'dominant' undertaking and 'abuses' of that dominant position for the purposes of Art. 82: see *infra* Chaps. 5–7.

Following proceedings brought by Consten in the French courts against a parallel trader[39] the compatibility of the agreement with Article 81(1) was raised. The parties notified the agreement to the Commission (the French courts adjourned proceedings) so this question fell to be decided, initially, by the Commission. The provisions in the agreement were intended to confer *absolute territorial protection* upon Consten and to prevent all parallel trade in Grundig products. Could it be said, however, that the restrictions on the conduct of the parties and/or the restriction on the sale of Grundig products by anyone else in France amounted to restrictions of competition?

The Commission issued a decision finding that the agreement was designed to restrict and distort competition. The exclusive contract and ancillary arrangements (in particular, in relation to the trade mark) had the object of relieving Consten of the competition of other undertakings in so far as it involved the import or wholesale trade in Grundig products in France. Further, an exemption was refused. The agreement created absolute territorial protection, prevented consumers obtaining a fair share of any of the benefits of the agreement, and contained restrictions which were not indispensable to the attainment of any benefit.

The parties appealed to the ECJ, challenging the Commission's decision on several grounds (one of the grounds being that Article 81(1) did not apply to vertical agreements at all[40]). In particular, it was complained that the Commission had erred in its application of Article 81(1) since it had failed to base itself on the 'rule of reason'. It had been wrong simply to conclude that the object of its agreement was to restrict competition without considering its effect. Broadly, the parties' argument hinged on the fact that the agreement had been essential to enable Grundig to penetrate the French market and could not, therefore, be said to restrict competition. The Commission had wrongly considered the transaction with hindsight, *ex post*, when matters had turned out well. If, however, it had taken account of the market at the time that the agreement was entered into, *ex ante*, when matters looked risky and uncertain, it would have been apparent that the distributor would not have proceeded without the territorial protection.[41]

In the absence of the promise of exclusivity, a distributor would not have been encouraged to take on the risky new venture and invest resources in promoting the new product on the French market. Such a distributor would have to persuade French consumers to purchase Grundig products instead of other competing brands of electrical products available and established on the French market. Although it is true that, had exclusivity not been promised, there might have been competition between different distributors of the Grundig products, that exclusivity was crucial to protect other distributors from taking a 'free ride'[42] on the distributor's promotional and investment efforts and activities. They would have been able to import the products more cheaply from Germany[43] (this is in fact exactly what UNEF, a Parisian company, and Leissner in Strasbourg had done).

---

[39] Consten sought to enforce its exclusive right of sale against other businesses which had started importing and selling Grundig products at more favourable prices in France. Those businesses claimed that the agreement was in contravention of Art. 81(1).

[40] See *supra* in Chap. 3.

[41] See e.g. V. Korah, *An Introductory Guide to EC Competition Law and Practice* (7th edn. Hart, 2000), sect. 2.4.

[42] For a greater discussion of the free rider arguments, see *infra* Chap. 9.

[43] The German distributors did not, consequently, have to engage in such high levels of promotion and investment.

The parties thus argued that despite the fact that the agreement resulted in the existence of only one distributor of Grundig products in France (there was a restriction of *intra-brand competition*), the agreement led to an increase in competition for electrical products in France (there was an increase in *inter-brand competition*). French consumers wishing to purchase such products now also had the option to purchase Grundig products in addition to those of the other manufacturers on the market. Consequently, the Commission had been wrong to focus solely on the restriction in intra-brand competition. It should instead have considered the effects of the disputed contract upon competition between Grundig and its competitors products.

V. Korah, *An Introductory Guide to EC Competition Law and Practice* (7th edn. Hart, 2000)

2.4.1 . . . Consten and Grundig asked the Court to quash the Commission's decision for not having made an analysis of the market for the kinds of equipment affected by the agreement; the Commission had not stated even that Grundig was an important brand name. . . .

In 1957, when Consten undertook to incur costs promoting the product, before the common market had removed quotas, it incurred significant risks. It might not be able to obtain import licences for many or even for any items of equipment. Even if Consten managed to obtain a licence, the expenditure would have to be spread over a limited number of items and would be wasted unless Consten were able to sell enough of the Grundig products. The costs were sunk—the investment had no value save for promoting the Grundig brand. Consequently, Consten would need to expect unusually high profit if it was to be successful.

A high margin would attract imports from Germany, where there was no need for an import licence and average costs and risk would be less. Such traders from Germany would take a free ride on Consten's investment in making the product acceptable. Unless Consten could be protected sufficiently from these parallel imports, it might well have found the risk unacceptable.

If Grundig could not have found someone to promote its product in the early days, Grundig products might have been less attractive to the parallel importers. The Commission never investigated how much protection was necessary to induce the optimal amount of investment in promotion. Nor was the question raised whether Grundig, which backed its judgement as to the amount of protection needed with its expectation of profit, was better able to judge than officials in the Commission.

Given these powerful arguments could the exclusivity provisions in the agreement really be said to restrict competition?

The notion that the Commission's decision should have been marked with greater market analysis was supported by Advocate General Roemer.[44] The Advocate General was highly critical of the Commission's approach. The Commission should have considered both whether the agreement was necessary for Grundig to penetrate the French market and whether or not there was vigorous competition between producers of competing products. Article 81(1) should not have been applied on the basis of purely theoretical considerations to a situation which might, upon closer inspection, reveal no appreciable adverse effects on competition. Article 81(1) required a consideration of the effects of the agreement on the market. This could not be established without looking at the market *in concreto* and without taking account of competition between similar products. In a case like this one, where the

---

[44] Cases 56, 58/64 *Etablissements Consten SA & Grundig-Verkaufs-GmbH* v. *Commission* [1966] ECR 299, [1966] CMLR 418.

agreement had already been implemented, the Commission should have made a comparison between two market situations: that after making the agreement and that which would have arisen had there been no agreement.[45] If Grundig would not have found an outlet for its products in the absence of supplying a sole concessionaire, the exclusive distribution agreement clearly promoted competition. It would have been necessary for Grundig to gain access to or penetrate the new market.

In his view, therefore, Article 81(1) should not be applied if, in the absence of the agreement appointing a single distributor exclusively in France, Grundig would not have found an outlet for its products.

Advocate General Roemer

(aa) *the criterion of adverse effect upon competition*

The statement of the reasons for the decision and the observations made during the proceedings show us that the Commission was content to find that the agreement in question *has as its object* an adverse effect upon competition, because it has the aim of freeing Consten from the competition of other wholesalers in the sale of *Grundig equipment*. The statement that the agreement has such an objective would suffice for the application of Article [81]; and it would not be necessary to take into consideration the concrete effects on the market.

I consider that there are several reasons why that point of view is invalid. . . .

I have already indicated in another case that American law (the 'White Motor Case' . . .) requires for situations of the type before us a comprehensive examination of their economic repercussions. Clearly I do not mean to say that we should imitate in all respects the principles of American procedure in the field of cartels. This would not in fact be justified by reason of the essential differences between the systems (prohibition *per se* in American law; possibility of exemption under [81(3)] of the [EC] Treaty). But such a reference is useful nevertheless in so far as it shows that in respect of Article [81(1)] also it is not possible to dispense with observing the market *in concreto*. It seems to me wrong to have regard to such observations only for the application of paragraph (3) of Article [81], because that paragraph requires an examination from other points of view which are special and different. But in particular . . . it would be artificial to apply Article [81(1)], on the basis of purely theoretical considerations, to situations which upon closer inspection would reveal no appreciable adverse effects on competition, in order then to grant exemption on the basis of Article [81(3)].

Properly understood, therefore, Article [81(1)] requires a comparison between two market situations: that which arises after the making of an agreement and that which would have arisen had there been no agreement. This concrete examination may show that it is not possible for a manufacturer to find an outlet in a particular part of the market unless he concentrates supply in the hands of a sole concessionnaire. That would signify that in a given situation an exclusive distributorship agreement has effects which are likely only to *promote* competition. Such a situation can in particular appear when what is at issue is gaining access to an[d] penetrating a market. It is clear that the Commission did not take considerations of this type into account as regards the relationship between Grundig and Consten; although they must have come to the fore as regards the problem of gaining access to the market, in view of the fact that the measures for liberalization of the French import trade were taken only during the years 1960–1961. The possibility cannot be excluded that such an examination of the market might have led to a finding that in the Grundig-Consten case the *suppression* of the sole distributorship might involve a noticeable reduction in the supply of Grundig products on the French market and consequently an unfavourable influence on the conditions of competition existing there.

---

[45] See the ECJ's judgment in Case 56/65 *Société La Technique Minière* v. *Maschinebau Ulm GmbH* [1966] ECR 234, [1966] 1 CMLR 357, discussed *infra* 162.

A second point is even more important. As we know, the Federal Government has above all insistently opposed the opinion that to be able to apply Article [81(1)] it suffices to find that the agreement excludes competition between various importers of *Grundig* products and that 'real possibilities of choice' exist for subsequent commercial stages only if there is internal competition among the Grundig products in the field of concessions. The Federal Government considers that, on the contrary, it is necessary to take account of the general situation of the market and also to take into account the competition between *similar* products of other manufacturers and importers.

This point of view is to be commended without reservation. . . . Doubtless it is undeniable that in a given market situation competition between several sellers of a single product can also take on great importance, that it may be indispensable for the normal play of competition on the market. But the Commission i[s] wrong in taking account of this last-mentioned internal competition exclusively and in neglecting completely in its considerations competition with similar products. In fact, it is perfectly possible that there exists between different products or rather between different producers such sharp competition that there remains no appreciable margin for what is called internal competition in a product (for example, in relation to price and servicing). The Commission considers that it does not have to take into consideration this competition between different manufacturers except for simple mass-produced articles. That does not seem to be correct, if it is desired to judge economic phenomena realistically. Even for very specialised instruments, like radio receivers, which are sold under a special mark and which are distinguished from one another by external and technical characteristics, genuine and perceptible competition is perfectly possible . . . The objection that in such a case the purchasers are not really able to judge and compare for lack of sufficient knowledge cannot have any bearing in this case, for the simple reason that here competition is to be judged at the wholesale level in the face of which there are technically competent retailers. So in reality it was necessary to require from the Commission a judgment on the whole of the competitive conditions, such as Section 18 of the German Law against Restraint of Competition also requires in a general way for sole distributorship contracts when it speaks of a considerable interference caused to competition on market of the *products in question or other products*. It is possible that such observation of the effects on the market (which, contrary to the opinion of Consten, need not necessarily be entrusted to an independent committee of experts under the Community law on cartels) would have led to a conclusion favourable to the appli[c]ants. It might have been so for example because of the fairly small share of the French market for tape-recorders and dictaphones held by Grundig (about 17%) (we know that the Commission did not make any inquiry in respect of other products) or because of the applicants' assertion that the market for television sets (in which for technical reasons there were no parallel imports of Grundig models) and the transistor market were subject to such strong competition from various producers (some of [which] were very powerful) in the Community and from third countries that the price of the Grundig models had to be reduced considerably several times.

Since an examination of the market of this kind did not take place because of the Commission's narrow view of the concept of 'restriction on competition', and as the Court of Justice cannot be required to carry out such an examination itself during the course of the proceedings, it only remains for me to say that the conclusions reached by the Commission in examining the criterion of 'adverse effect upon competition' must be considered as insufficiently based and consequently must be rejected.

In this case the ECJ did not agree with its Advocate General but took the view that the object of this agreement was to restrict competition so that an assessment of its effect was unnecessary. Despite the rigid approach in this particular case, it will become apparent from the discussion below that the jurisprudence of the Court does not generally support a formalistic interpretation of Article 81(1). Rather, ever since 1966 and its judgment in *Société La Technique Minière* v. *Maschinebau Ulm GmbH*, it has recognized that most agreements should be assessed in their market context.[46] This position has been reiterated on many occasions.

P. Freeman and R. Whish (eds.) *Butterworths Competition Law* (Butterworths, looseleaf), Division I

[189]

In a series of important judgments, the ECJ has held that restrictions on conduct do not necessarily amount to restrictions on competition; there have been several judgments of this kind in recent years, which has encouraged the view that the ECJ may be moving towards the adoption of rule-of-reason analysis under Article 81(1). The first case of note was as long ago as 1966. . . .

[190–200]

In these cases one sees the ECJ developing its notion of a restriction of competition, and generally its movement has been towards a narrower meaning of this term, thereby taking numerous agreements outside Article 81(1). In *European Night Services* . . . the CFI has taken a similar line, annulling the Commission's finding that the establishment of a joint venture by a number of railway undertakings had infringed Article [81(1)]. The important conceptual question is whether these judgments are symptomatic of an underlying trend towards the adoption of a US-style rule of reason. Close analysis of the ECJ's judgments would suggest that they are not. Rather, the ECJ has been developing its own jurisprudence on a case-by-case basis, and to attribute to the process the rule of reason label confuses more than it clarifies, by introducing into EC competition law the tensions of US antitrust generally and the problems of analysis under s1 of the Sherman Act in particular . . . US and EC competition law are materially different in numerous respects, and terminology should not be imported from US law that could blur this significant fact . . . The fact that the EC has handed down reasonable judgements does not mean that it had adopted the rule of reason. Various commentators have argued against incorporation into EC law of a rule of reason modeled upon US experience . . .

The ECJ has not, therefore, adopted a 'rule of reason' approach similar to that adopted by the US courts. It has, however, handed down 'reasonable' judgments which do not support the rigid view traditionally associated with that of the Commission. How the Court determines whether or not the object or effect of an agreement is to restrict competition depends upon a number of factors. There are several ways of looking at the Court's case law. One can consider it chronologically. One can distinguish between different type of cases, for example, those in which the Court has accepted that agreements may contain clauses which are objectively necessary for the performance of a specific type of agreement ('ancillary restraint' cases) and those in which the Court has accepted that specific clauses are necessary to induce a producer into a market (the 'commercial risk' cases).[47] Alternatively, one can look at different categories of agreement, considering first whether or not these agreements have as their object the restriction of competition and, secondly, how they will be assessed when they do not do so. In this section we begin with the latter approach and then look at the cases overall to see what themes can be discerned. We begin with vertical restraints and look first at the Court's judgment in *Consten and Grundig*.

---

[46] In Case 56/65 [1966] ECR 234, [1966] 1 CMLR 357, the ECJ held that a term conferring exclusivity on a distributor might not infringe Art. 81(1) where it was a vital element in its decision to market a supplier's goods at all: see *infra* 162.

[47] See P. Freeeman and R. Whish (eds.) *Butterworths Competition Law* (Butterworths, looseleaf), Div 1, paras. 201 and 205 and *infra* 186.

D. VERTICAL AGREEMENTS

(i) RESTRICTION BY OBJECT

The subject of vertical restraints, which is considered in Chapter 9 below, has caused as much controversy as, if not more than, any other area of EC competition law. Although many of the Commission's decisions taken under Article 82 have been controversial their impact on the commercial activities of undertakings as a whole has been less far-reaching. In contrast, every producer must distribute its products so that the policy in relation to vertical agreements has been far-reaching.

Partly because of the single market objective the Commission has adopted an inter-ventionist stance when dealing with vertical agreements. This approach has been subjected to consistent criticism and the reasons for this will be more fully rehearsed in the Chapter 9. Broadly, however, the arguments rest on the fact that since vertical agreements are not made between competitors they are *prima facie* less obviously anti-competitive than horizontal agreements. Rather, a manufacturer of a product when arranging for the distribution of its products will want to ensure that this is performed in the most efficient manner possible, so that its products compete more effectively with the products of his competitors. Further, that although vertical agreements may restrict *intra–brand competition*, by imposing restric-tions on distributors of the product regarding the way in which they may deal with it, they frequently encourage *inter–brand competition* between competitors and increase the range of products available to consumers. (see the discussion of *Consten and Grundig* above).[48] It may be thought, therefore, that in many cases vertical agreements would fall outside the scope of Article 81(1). Indeed, many other systems of competition law take a fairly relaxed or laissez-faire approach to vertical agreements.[49]

In *Société La Technique Minière* v. *Maschinebau Ulm GmbH* and *Consten & Grundig*, decided in 1966 within a fortnight of each other, the ECJ held that Article 81 applied to both horizontal and vertical agreements.[50] The Court has, however, held that only two types of provision in a distribution agreements will cause it to be found to have as its object the restriction of competition: those which grant a distributor absolute territorial protection and those which impose minimum resale prices on a distributor. In all other cases, an examination of the agreement's effects is necessary.

---

[48] This point is clearly illustrated by the arguments of the parties in Cases 56 & 58/64 *Consten and Grundig* [1966] ECR 299, [1966] CMLR 418 set out *supra* 149 ff.

[49] This has been the position in the UK both prior and subsequent to the Competition Act 1998. Vertical agreements were not in general caught by the Restrictive Trade Practices Act 1976 (R. Whish, *Competition Law* (3rd edn., Butterworths, 1993), Chap. 5), and vertical agreements (except for price-fixing agreements) have been excluded from the Competition Act 1998's Chapter I prohibition (the provision modelled on Art. 81); see s. 50 of the Act and the Competition Act 1998 (Land and Vertical Agreements Exclusion) Order 2000/310. See also the approach adopted in the USA, discussed *infra* in Chap. 9.

[50] In Cases 56 & 58/64, *Etablissements Consten SA & Grundig-Verkaufs-GmbH* v. *Commission* [1966] ECR 299, [1966] CMLR 418, the ECJ did not accept the argument that Art. 81 should have no application to vertical agreements at all because they are analogous to relationships between a parent and its commercial representative or subsidiary and should be controlled, if at all, under Art. 82: see *supra* Chap. 3.

a. AGREEMENTS GRANTING A DISTRIBUTOR ABSOLUTE TERRITORIAL PROTECTION

In *Consten and Grundig* the ECJ upheld the view of the Commission,[51] ruling that the agreement giving Consten a monopoly over the sale of Grundig products in France had as its object the restriction of competition.

Cases 56 & 58/64, *Etablissements Consten SA & Grundig-Verkaufs-GmbH* v. *Commission* [1966] ECR 299, 342–3 [1966] CMLR 418, 472–4

Court of Justice

The complaints concerning the criterion of restriction on competition.

The applicants and the German Government maintain that since the Commission restricted its examination solely to Grundig products the decision was based upon a false concept of competition and of the rules on prohibition contained in Article [81(1)], since this concept applies particularly to competition between similar products of different makes; the Commission, before declaring Article [81(1)] to be applicable, should, by basing itself upon the 'rule of reason', have considered the economic effects of the disputed contract upon competition between the different makes. There is a presumption that vertical sole distributorship agreements are not harmful to competition and in the present case there is nothing to invalidate that presumption. On the contrary, the contract in question has increased the competition between similar products of different makes.

The principle of freedom of competition concerns the various stages and manifestations of competition. Although competition between producers is generally more noticeable than that between distributors of products of the same make, it does not thereby follow that an agreement tending to restrict the latter kind of competition should escape the prohibition of Article [81(1)] merely because it might increase the former.

Besides, for the purpose of applying Article [81(1)], there is no need to take account of the concrete effects of an agreement once it appears that it has as its object the prevention, restriction or distortion of competition.

Therefore the absence in the contested decision of any analysis of the effects of the agreement on competition between similar products of different makes does not, of itself, constitute a defect in the decision.

It thus remains to consider whether the contested decision was right in founding the prohibition of the disputed agreement under Article [81(1)] on the restriction on competition created by the agreement in the sphere of the distribution of Grundig products alone. The infringement which was found to exist by the contested decision results from the absolute territorial protection created [by] the said contract in favour of Consten on the basis of French law. The applicants thus wished to eliminate any possibility of competition at the wholesale level in Grundig products in the territory specified in the contra[c]t essentially by two methods.

First, Grundig undertook not to deliver even indirectly to third parties products intended for the area covered by the contract. The restrictive nature of that undertaking is obvious if it is considered in the light of the prohibition on exporting which was imposed not only on Consten but also on all the other sole concessionaires of Grundig, as well as the German wholesalers. Secondly, the registration in

---

[51] See the discussion *supra* 150.

France by Consten of the GINT trade mark, which Grundig affixes to all its products, is intended to increase the protection inherent in the disputed agreement, against the risk of parallel imports into France of Grundig products, by adding the protection deriving from the law on industrial property rights. Thus no third party could import Grundig products from other Member States of the Community for resale in France without running serious risks.

The defendant properly took into account the whole distribution system thus set up by Grundig. In order to arrive at a true representation of the contractual position the contract must be placed in the economic and legal context in the light of which it was concluded by the parties. Such a procedure is not to be regarded as an unwarrantable interference in legal transactions or circumstances which were not the subject of the proceedings before the Commission.

The situation as ascertained above results in the isolation of the French market and makes it possible to charge for the products in question prices which are sheltered from all effective competition. In addition, the more producers succeed in their efforts to render their own makes of product individually distinct in the eyes of the consumer, the more the effectiveness of competition between producers tend to diminish. Because of the considerable impact of distribution costs on the aggregate cost price, it seems important that competition between dealers should also be stimulated. The efforts of the dealer are stimulated by competition between distributors of products of the same make. Since the agreement thus aims at isolating the French market for Grundig products and maintaining artificially, for products of a very well-known brand, separate national markets within the Community, it is therefore such as to distort competition in the Common Market.

It was therefore proper for the contested decision to hold that the agreement constitutes an infringement of Article [81(1)]. No further considerations, whether of economic data (price differences between France and Germany, representative character of the type of appliance considered, level of overheads borne by Consten) or of the corrections of the criteria upon which the Commission relied in its comparisons between the situations of the French and German markets, and no possible favourable effects of the agreement in other respects, can in any way lead, in the face of abovementioned restrictions, to a different solution under Article [81(1)].

The judgment in *Consten and Grundig* is one of the most important judgments of EC competition law. Apart from establishing that Article 81(1) applies to horizontal and vertical agreements, to all agreements which affect trade between Member States even if the effect on trade is not a prejudicial one,[52] and, potentially, to agreements relating to the licensing of intellectual property rights,[53] the ECJ clarified some other vital points relating to the application of Article 81(1). It held that Article 81(1) applied to an agreement which had as its object the restriction of competition irrespective of its alleged effects, thus even though the parties might be able to show that the agreement was necessary to ensure that a producer found an outlet for its products. In addition, although the ECJ recognized the importance of competition between producers it held that agreements which restricted competition between distributors could also restrict competition for the purposes of Article 81(1). It was important that competition between dealers should be stimulated and intra-brand as well as inter-brand competition maintained. In particular, restrictions on intra-brand competition

[52] The effect of the agreement in *Consten & Grundig* was that *more*, not less, of Grundig's products would flow from Germany to France and would compete there with other brands: see *supra* Chap. 3.

[53] The ECJ also went on to hold that the agreement relating to the GINT trade mark infringed Art. 81(1). Otherwise, Consten could have used the trade mark to achieve the objectives of the prohibited exclusive distribution agreement: see *infra* Chap. 10.

might facilitate brand differentiation and diminish competition between producers. In particular, the agreement in question eliminated any possibility of competition between distributors of Grundig products and led to the isolation of the French and so distorted competition on the market and infringed Article 81(1). The Commission had not, therefore, erred by failing to consider the effects of the agreement for the purposes of Article 81(1).

There seems little doubt that the Court's judgment in *Consten and Grundig* was influenced not so much by the pernicious effects of the agreement's provisions from a competition perspective but by the effects of the agreement from the single market perspective. Whatever the economic justifications for the agreement the affront to the single market goal in this case was too severe.[54] The *object* of the agreement was to grant absolute territorial protection and eliminated any possibility of competition at a wholesale level in Grundig products in the territory. The French market had been isolated and the French distributor sheltered from all effective competition. The Court sent out a clear message: agreements which divide up the common market and preclude all cross-border trade in the contract product will not be tolerated. Provisions providing for such protection in an agreement will automatically infringe Article 81(1).

G. Amato, *Antitrust and the Bounds of Power* (Hart Publishing, 1997), 48–9

In the leading case in this area, *Consten & Grundig*, of 1966, . . . the Commission challenged the exclusive agreement for France that Grundig had given to Consten and had strengthened by barring its wholesale distributors in Germany and other countries from selling to France, where the price of Grundig products was kept higher than elsewhere, net of French tax. The parties maintained, first before the Commission itself and then before the Court of Justice, that Article [81] referred primarily to inter-brand competition, and that as far as intra-brand restrictions went, one had to presume efficiency in promoting inter-brand competition failing proof of the contrary. This argument copied word-for-word approaches of the Chicago School, which in fact at the time the American courts themselves had rejected, in the name of protection (dropped later in the *Sylvania* case) for the right of each distributor or retailer to exercise freedom of trade without restraint.

Our court did not accept the arguments either, but for very different reasons. It accepted that inter-brand competition was the most relevant for the purposes of prohibition under Article [81], but added that this did not *a priori* exempt intra-brand restrictions, with the consequence-inconceivable today (and perhaps in earlier times too) for an American court-that the fact that the Commission was not concerned to ascertain the size of inter-brand competition was irrelevant. On this basis, the absolute territorial protection by which the exclusivity for France was guaranteed was illegitimate. It is indeed true, said the Court, that imports have an effect on the supply planning that Consten may engage in and on the organization of services it may offer customers. But a margin of risk is inherent in commercial activity, and in any case 'the more manufacturers isolate themselves from each other in consumers' eyes, the more competition among them is reduced. Moreover, competition among wholesale distributors of products of one and the same brand enlivens the downstream market of sales to final consumers'.

As we can see, these are very important assertions of principle that bring the decision close to the American ones of the 1960s. But there are two important differences, one explicit and the other implicit. The explicit one is that the need for intra-brand competition is based on protection not of an individual right (freedom of trade) but of a general and objective principle (competitiveness of the

---

[54] See *supra* Chap. 1.

market in all its segments). The implicit one is that such a pervasive and rigorous principle is asserted to the extent that it serves to protect another principle, a higher one in 1966, that of market integration. For the territory protected by Consten's rigid exclusivity coincided with that of the French State, and both the Commission and the Court saw this protection as persistence of the segmentation of economic activities along national frontiers, violating the 'Grundnorm' of the whole Community system.

The ECJ has reiterated this view that agreements which isolate national markets and preclude cross-border trade automatically offend Article 81(1).[55] To this limited extent the Court has, therefore, endorsed the Commission's view that distribution agreements pose a threat to the common market because of their ability to divide it.

The Community goal of integrating the single market has resulted in a preoccupation with 'restrictions' on cross-border trade, particularly when dealing with distribution agreements which have the ability and tendency to divide markets geographically. *Consten & Grundig* vividly illustrates how these restrictions may automatically be perceived as restrictions of competition. In this respect the single market objective has had a very special influence on the interpretation of what amounts to a restriction of competition for the purpose of Article 81(1).

b. AGREEMENTS IMPOSING MINIMUM RETAIL PRICES ON DISTRIBUTORS

The Commission undoubtedly takes the view that a provision setting out minimum retail prices to be charged by distributors has as its object the restriction of competition. It believes that the practice leads to the ossification of distribution networks.[56] This view is supported by the jurisprudence of the Court. In *Pronuptia de Paris* v. *Schillgalis* the ECJ, in setting out guidelines on the compatibility of distribution franchises with Article 81(1),[57] held that 'provisions which impair the franchisee's freedom to determine his own prices are restrictive of competition'.[58] In *Metro* v. *Commission (No 1)*, an appeal from a Commission decision authorizing the operation of a selective distribution system pursuant to Article 81, the Court stated that 'price competition is so important that it can never be eliminated'[59] and in *SA Binon & Cie* v. *SA Agence et Messageries de la Presse*[60] the Court specifically held that 'provisions which fix the prices to be observed in contracts with third parties constitute, of themselves, a restriction on competition within the meaning of Article [81(1)]'.

---

[55] See, e.g., Case C–234/89, *Delimitis* v. *Henninger Bräu* [1991] ECR 1–935, [1992] 5 CMLR 210; Case 161/84, *Pronuptia de Paris GmbH* v. *Pronuptia de Paris Irmgard Schillgallis* [1986] ECR 353, [1986] 1 CMLR 414; Case T–77/92, *Parker Pen* v. *Commission* [1994] ECR II–549, [1995] 5 CMLR 435.

[56] See the discussion of resale price maintenance (RPM), *infra* Chap. 9.

[57] See *infra* 163 ff and Chap. 9.

[58] Case 161/84, *Pronuptia de Paris GmbH* v. *Pronuptia de Paris Irmgard Schillgallis* [1986] ECR 353, [1986] 1 CMLR 414, para. 25.

[59] Case 26/76, *Metro-SB-Grossmärkte GmbH* v. *Commission (No 1)* [1977] ECR 1875, [1978] 2 CMLR 1, para. 21.

[60] Case 234/83 [1985] ECR 2015, para. 44

Case 243/85, *SA Binon & Cie* v. *SA Agence et Messageries de la Presse* [1985] ECR 2015

This case concerned proceedings between SA Binon & Cie and SA Agence et Messageries de la Presse (AMP) in the Belgian courts. Broadly, Binon had been refused, by AMP, the supply of newspapers magazines and periodicals for whose distribution it was responsible (close to 70% of Belgian newspapers and periodicals and virtually all newspapers and periodicals published abroad). AMP operated a selective distribution system for the supply of its newspapers and periodicals. One of the questions which arose before the Belgian court was whether a provision within the framework of a selective distribution system which required fixed prices to be observed was compatible with Article 81(1) of the Treaty.

Court of Justice

(E) The fixed prices

39. Finally, the third question is concerned with the problem whether the fact that, within the framework of a selective distribution system of newspapers and periodicals, fixed prices must be observed renders the system incompatible with the prohibition laid down in Article [81] of the [EC] Treaty.

40. AMP contends in that regard that the prices of newspapers and periodicals are fixed by the publishers and not, as the national court seems to think, by the distribution agency. Observance by retailers of the prices fixed by publishers arises from the aforementioned special characteristics of the distribution of newspapers and periodicals.

41. The Government of the Federal Republic of Germany, which took part in the proceedings solely in order to submit observations with regard to the third question, considers that the freedom of the press, as a fundamental right protected by the constitutional law of the Member States and by the Court's case-law, entails the freedom to contribute to the formation of public opinion. For that reason newspapers and periodicals as well as their distribution have special characteristics. The nature of newspapers and periodicals requires an extremely rapid system for their distribution in view of the very limited period during which they can be sold before they are out of date; at the end of that period, the length of which varies according to the specific publication in question, newspapers and periodicals have practically no value. To those factors must be added the heterogeneity of newspapers and periodicals and the lack of elasticity in demand since each newspaper or periodical has more or less its own body of customers.

42. The German Government concludes that, from the point of view of competition, the position of the market in newspapers and periodicals is so special that it is not possible to apply to it without modification principles which have been developed in completely different contexts. If the possibility of fixing prices for newspapers and periodicals is not accepted any effective distribution system for such products would be incompatible with the rules on competition and the effect on the diversity and freedom of the press would be disastrous. From that point of view it is not unimportant to note that systems of fixed prices in relation to the distribution of newspapers and periodicals are accepted under the legislation of most Member States or are operated without encountering any difficulties.

43. In the Commission's opinion any price-fixing agreement constitutes, of itself, a restriction on competition and is, as such, prohibited by Article [81(1)]. The Commission does not deny that newspapers and periodicals and the way they are distributed have special characteristics but considers that these cannot lead to an exclusion of such products and their distribution from the scope of Article [81(1)]. On the contrary, those characteristics should be put forward by the undertakings relying upon them in the context of an application for exemption under Article [81(3)].

44. It should be observed in the first place that provisions which fix the prices to be observed in

contracts with third parties constitute, of themselves, a restriction on competition within the meaning of Article [81(1)] which refers to agreements which fix selling prices as an example of an agreement prohibited by the treaty.

45. In those circumstances, where an agreement which establishes a selective distribution system and which affects trade between Member States includes such a provision, an exemption from the prohibition contained in Article [81(1)] of the [EC] Treaty may only be granted by means of a decision adopted by the Commission in the conditions laid down by Article [81(3)].

46. If, in so far as the distribution of newspapers and periodicals is concerned, the fixing of the retail price by publishers constitutes the sole means of supporting the financial burden resulting from the taking back of unsold copies and if the latter practice constitutes the sole method by which a wide selection of newspapers and periodicals can be made available to readers, the Commission must take account of those factors when examining an agreement for the purposes of Article [81(3)].

47. Consequently, the answer to the third question must be that the requirement, in the framework of a selective distribution system for newspapers and periodicals which affects trade between Member States, that fixed prices must be respected renders that system incompatible with Article [81(1)] of the Treaty. However, the Commission may, in considering an application for exemption under Article [81(3)] examine whether, in a particular case, such an element of a distribution system may be justified.

The cases establish that a provision fixing minimum resale prices to be charged by distributors will be held to have as its object the restriction of competition. Despite this strict approach it seems acceptable for a franchisor, and other producers, to provide 'franchisees with price-guidelines, so long as there is no concerted practice between the franchisor and the franchisees or between the franchisees themselves for the actual application of the prices'.[61] Further, a producer may operate a selective distribution system in which 'price competition is not generally emphasized either as an exclusive or indeed as a principal factor'. On the contrary, in *Metro* v. *Commission* the Court accepted that price competition 'does not constitute the only effective form of competition or that to which absolute priority must in all circumstances be afforded.'[62]

c. A CRITICISM?

The above restrictions are considered so serious that they are always viewed as restrictions of competition whatever the strength of the free rider argument, or other economic rationale. Economic or other justifications may only be considered within the context of Article 81(3).[63]

Despite the clear textual support for such an approach (Article 81(1) specifically prohibits agreements which have as their object *or* effect the restriction of competition) and the possibility of exemption some commentators regret the fact that the Court, and more frequently the Commission, have adopted this formalistic interpretation of a provision drafted in terms of economic concepts. 'One might have expected [it] to be applied only after a careful commercial and economic analysis of the market they affect . . . To see

---

[61] Case 161/84, *Pronuptia de Paris GmbH* v. *Pronuptia de Paris Irmgard Schillgallis* [1986] ECR 353, [1986] 1 CMLR 414, para. 25.

[62] Case 26/76, *Metro-SB-Grossmärkte GmbH* v. *Commission (No 1)* [1977] ECR 1875, [1978] 2 CMLR 1, para. 21.

[63] See extract from Case 243/85, *SA Binon & Cie* v. *SA agence et messageries de la presse* [1985] ECR 2015, *supra* 160.

whether an agreement restricts competition, it is not enough to examine its provisions. One needs to know about the market and the commercial reasons for inserting restrictive provisions.'[64]

Pragmatically, however, the finding that some contracts or contractual provisions have as their object the restriction of competition eradicates the need to prove, at the cost of time and money, the adverse consequences of such provisions in circumstances where they are unlikely to have any redeeming justification.[65]

(ii) RESTRICTION BY EFFECT

Where a vertical agreement admits the possibility of passive territorial sales and does not require the distributors to charge minimum retail prices, the Court does not take the view that the object of the agreement is to restrict competition. Rather, the ECJ has stressed that it is necessary to look to the effect of the agreement before it can be determined whether or not competition has been restricted.

a. EXCLUSIVE DISTRIBUTION AGREEMENTS

Consequently, in *Société La Technique Minière* v. *Maschinenbau Ulm GmbH* ('*STM*') the ECJ indicated that an exclusive distribution agreement would not restrict competition if the appointment of the exclusive distributor was necessary in order to enable a manufacturer to penetrate a new market. Before it could be determined whether the agreement may restrict competition, the agreement should be examined in the light of the competition which would occur *if the agreement in question were not or had not been made*. In contrast to the facts which occurred in *Consten and Grundig*, in *STM* the distributor had not been given a complete monopoly over the right to distribute in France. The contractual arrangements did admit the possibility of parallel imports from distributors in other Member States. In this case, therefore, the economic justifications for the agreement outweighed the territorial restrictions inherent in the agreement.

Case 56/65, *Société La Technique Minière* v. *Maschinenbau Ulm GmbH* [1966] ECR 234, 249–50, [1966] CMLR 357, 375–6

The parties entered into an agreement by which a French company was given exclusive rights to distribute in France the equipment (levelling machines) of a German manufacturer. The French company was free to re-export the equipment outside France. The parties fell out, and in litigation in the French courts the French company claimed that the agreement was void under Article 81(2) because it infringed Article 81(1). The Cour d'Appel Paris asked the Court of Justice on a preliminary reference how it should assess the compatibility of this type of agreement with Article 81(1).

Court of Justice

The effects of the agreement on competition

Finally, for the agreement at issue to be caught by the prohibition contained in Article [81(1)] it

---

[64] V. Korah, 'EEC Competition Policy—Legal Form or Economic Efficiency?' [1986] *CLP* 85, 92–3.

[65] See the discussion of *per se* prohibitions, *supra* 142–143.

must have as its 'object or effect the prevention, restriction or distortion of competition within the Common Market'.

The fact that these are not cumulative but alternative requirements indicated by the conjunction 'or', leads first to the need to consider the precise purpose of the agreement, in the economic context in which it is to be applied. This interference with competition referred to in Article [81(1)] must result from all or some of the clauses of the agreement itself. Where, however, an analysis of the said clauses does not reveal the effect on competition to be sufficiently deleterious, the consequences of the agreement should then be considered and for it to be caught by the prohibition it is then necessary to find that those factors are present which show that competition has in fact been prevented or restricted or distorted to an appreciable extent.

The competition in question must be understood within the actual context in which it would occur in the absence of the agreement in dispute. In particular it may be doubted whether there is an interference with competition if the said agreement seems really necessary for the penetration of a new area by an undertaking. Therefore, in order to decide whether an agreement containing a clause 'granting an exclusive right of sale' is to be considered as prohibited by reason of its object or of its effect, it is appropriate to take into account in particular the nature and quantity, limited or otherwise, of the products covered by the agreement, the position and importance of the grantor and the concessionnaire on the market for the products concerned, the isolated nature of the disputed agreement or, alternatively, its position in series of agreements, the severity of the clauses intended to protect the exclusive dealership or, alternatively, the opportunities allowed for other commercial competitors in the same products by way of parallel re-exportation and importation.

b. FRANCHISING AGREEMENTS

In *Pronuptia* the ECJ also rejected a formalistic approach when setting out guidelines for a national court ruling on the compatibility of a distribution franchising agreement with Article 81(1). Rather, it held that restrictions essential to the successful operation of a distribution franchise agreement would not restrict competition.

Case 161/84, *Pronuptia de Paris GmbH* v. *Pronuptia de Paris Irmgard Schillgallis* [1986] ECR 353, [1986] 1 CMLR 414

A franchise agreement had been concluded between Pronuptia de Paris and Mrs Schillgalis. The latter had the exclusive right to use the 'Pronuptia de Paris' trademark in specific territories. Pronuptia assisted Mrs Schillgalis with the commercial aspects of her business. In exchange Mrs Schillgalis had undertaken to equip her shop in accordance with the franchisor's instructions, not to move its location, to purchase 80% of her wedding dresses and accessories from the franchisor and to pay royalties etc. Following a dispute between the parties, the compatibility of the agreement with Article 81(1) was raised before the German courts. The Bundesgerichtshof, considering that the outcome of the case depended on the interpretation of Community law, made an Article 234 reference to the Court of Justice. The first question it asked was whether Article 81(1) was applicable to franchise agreements such as the contract between the parties.

Court of Justice
14. The compatibility of franchise agreements for the distribution of goods with Article [81(1)] cannot be assessed in abstracto but depends on the provisions contained in such agreements . . .

15. In a system of distribution franchises of that kind an undertaking which has established itself as a distributor on a given market and thus developed certain business methods grants independent traders, for a fee, the right to establish themselves in other markets using its business name and the business methods which have made it successful. Rather than a method of distribution, it is a way for an undertaking to derive financial benefit from its expertise without investing its own capital. Moreover, the system gives traders who do not have the necessary experience access to methods which they could not have learned without considerable effort and allows them to benefit from the reputation of the franchisor's business name. Franchise agreements for the distribution of goods differ in that regard from dealerships or contracts which incorporate approved retailers into a selective distribution system, which do not involve the use of a single business name, the application of uniform business methods or the payment of royalties in return for the benefits granted. Such a system, which allows the franchisor to profit from his success, does not in itself interfere with competition. In order for the system to work two conditions must be met.

16. First, the franchisor must be able to communicate his know-how to the franchisees and provide them with the necessary assistance in order to enable them to apply his methods, without running the risk that that know-how and assistance might benefit competitors, even indirectly. It follows that provisions which are essential in order to avoid that risk do not constitute restrictions on competition for the purpose of Article [81(1)]. That is also true of a clause prohibiting the franchisee, during the period of validity of the contract and for a reasonable period after its expiry, from opening a shop of the same or a similar nature in an area where he may compete with a member of the network. The same may be said of the franchisee's obligation not to transfer his shop to another party without the prior approval of the franchisor; that provision is intended to prevent competitors from indirectly benefiting from the know-how and assistance provided.

17. Secondly, the franchisor must be able to take the measures necessary for maintaining the identity and reputation of the network bearing his business name or symbol. It follows that provisions which establish the means of control necessary for that purpose do not constitute restrictions on competition for the purposes of Article [81(1)].

. . .

23. It must be emphasized on the other hand that, far from being necessary for the protection of the know-how provided or the maintenance of the network's identity and reputation, certain provisions restrict competition between the members of the network. That is true of provisions which share markets between the franchisor and franchisees or between franchisees or prevent franchisees from engaging in price competition with each other.

The Court held, therefore, that restrictions within the agreement would fall outside Article 81(1) if they were objectively necessary to the successful operation of the franchising transaction. Clauses essential to enable the franchisor to transfer know-how etc. without the risk of aiding competitors and to preserve its identity and reputation could not be characterized as restrictions of competition within the meaning of Article 81(1). However, clauses in the agreement which conferred territorial exclusivity upon Mrs Schillgalis were not essential to the functioning of the agreement and restricted competition. The combination of an exclusivity and location clause essentially gave the franchisees absolute territorial protection within their franchise area.[66]

---

[66] For franchise agreements generally, see *infra* Chap. 9.

G. Amato, *Antitrust and the Bounds of Power* (Hart Publishing, 1997), 50–1

In *Pronuptia* v. *Schillgallis*, . . . the Court was for the first time called on to speak on franchising contracts. It did so without going into the facts, since it was in a context of a preliminary ruling, that is, merely supplying the national judge dealing with the case with the interpretation of Community law he has asked for pursuant to Article [234] of the EC Treaty. The question it was answering was whether the vertical restrictions inherent in the franchising relationship are compatible with Article [81], knowing that in this specific case the franchising generated exclusivity concerning not a whole Member State, but the Paris region only.

The Court accepted that the good functioning of franchising (the commercial utility of which it stressed) might require clauses protecting against competitors the know-how the producer transfers to the retailer, making the retailer subject to requirements as to the location and decor of points of sale, and as to the selection of products to sell, and even publicity. If however the contract were to provide both for an obligation to sell only at the points of sale indicated by the manufacturer and for the retailer's right to absolute exclusiveness on a given territory, then, said the Court, this would entail a division of the market contrary to Article [81], as decided in *Consten & Grundig* . . . Moreover, no restraint should be imposed on the seller's freedom of pricing.

Pronuptia is a problematic decision, opening a sort of transition. The Court well understood that if it accepted the efficiency of franchising it would perforce have to accept also the restrictive clauses it requires, including exclusive agreements with territorial protection. Moreover, in the specific underlying case . . . there was no national segmentation at stake. On the other hand, *Consten & Grundig* was there, and had set a general principle. The Court then on the one hand reaffirmed it, thus apparently from this viewpoint renewing its strength in still more expansive terms; on the other, however, it continued to circumscribe its scope to cases involving established brands, and let it be understood that territorial exclusivity, without absolute territorial protection, might be allowed to pass.

c. SELECTIVE DISTRIBUTION SYSTEMS

In *Metro (No1)* the ECJ set out guidelines which could be used for determining the compatibility of selective distribution systems with Article 81(1).

Case 26/76, *Metro-SB-Grossmärkte GmbH v. Commission (No 1)* [1977] ECR 1875, [1978] 2 CMLR 1

SABA manufactured televisions, radios and tape-recorders, which it distributed through a selective distribution network (SDN), whereby only specialist dealers who met certain criteria sold the products.[67] The Commission held that some aspects of the SDN were outside Article 81(1). Other provisions it held to be within Article 81(1) but it granted an exemption. Metro was a self-service dealer who SABA refused to admit to the network because it did not fulfill all the criteria. It appealed to the Court of Justice under Article 230 against the grant of the exemption to SABA.[68]

Court of Justice

19. The applicant maintains that Article 2 of the contested decision is vitiated by misuse of powers inasmuch as the Commission has failed to recognise 'what is protected under Article [81]

---

[67] For selective distribution systems generally, see *infra* Chap. 9.
[68] For the *locus standi* under Art. 230 of an undertaking in Metro's position, see *infra* Chap. 14.

[namely] freedom of competition for the benefit of the consumer, not the coincident interests of a manufacturer and a given group of traders who wish to secure selling prices which are considered to be satisfactory by the latter'. Furthermore, if it were to be considered that an exemption from the prohibition might be granted in respect of the distribution system in dispute pursuant to Article [81(3)], the applicant maintains that the Commission has misapplied that provision by granting an exemption in respect of restrictions on competition which are not indispensable to the attainment of the objectives of improving production or distribution or promoting technical or economic progress and which lead to the elimination of competition from self-service wholesale traders.

A Misuse of powers

20. The requirement contained in Articles [3(1)] and [81] of the [EC] Treaty that competition shall not be distorted implies the existence on the market of workable competition, that is to say the degree of competition necessary to ensure the observance of the basic requirements and the attainment of the objectives of the Treaty, in particular the creation of a single market achieving conditions similar to those of a domestic market. In accordance with the requirement the nature and intensiveness of competition may vary to an extent dictated by the products or services in question and the economic structure of the relevant market sectors. In the sector covering the production of high quality and technically advanced consumer durables, where a relatively small number of large- and medium-scale producers offer a varied range of items which, or so consumers may consider, are readily interchangeable, the structure of the market does not preclude the existence of a variety of channels of distribution adapted to the peculiar characteristics of the various producers and to the requirements of the various categories of consumers. On this view the Commission was justified in recognising that selective distribution systems constituted, together with others, an aspect of competition which accords with Article [81(1)], provided that resellers are chosen on the basis of objective criteria of a qualitative nature relating to the technical qualifications of the reseller and his staff and the suitability of his trading premises and that such conditions are laid down uniformly for all potential resellers and are not applied in a discriminatory fashion.

21. It is true that in such systems of distribution price competition is not generally emphasised either as an exclusive or indeed as a principal factor. This is particularly so when, as in the present case, access to the distribution network is subject to conditions exceeding the requirements of an appropriate distribution of the products. However, although price competition is so important that it can never be eliminated, it does not constitute the only effective form of competition or that to which absolute priority must in all circumstances be accorded. The powers conferred upon the Commission under Article [81(3)] show that the requirements for the maintenance of workable competition may be reconciled with the safeguarding of objectives of a different nature and that to this end certain restrictions on competition are permissible, provided that they are essential to the attainment of those objectives and that they do not result in the elimination of competition for a substantial part of the Common Market. For specialist wholesalers and retailers the desire to maintain a certain price level, which corresponds to the desire to preserve, in the interests of consumers, the possibility of the continued existence of this channel of distribution in conjunction with new methods of distribution based on a different type of competition policy, forms one of the objectives which may be pursued without necessarily falling under the prohibition contained in Article [81(1)], and, if it does fall thereunder, either wholly or in part, coming within the framework of Article [81(3)]. This argument is strengthened if, in addition, such conditions promote improved competition inasmuch as it relates to factors other than prices.

The principles set out by the ECJ in *Metro (No 1)* relating to the compatibility of selective distribution networks with Article 81(1) are rather different from those adopted in relation to other vertical agreements, and as such should be considered *sui generis*.[69] The Court has developed a particular jurisprudence on this type of distribution which is at times hard to comprehend or rationalize fully.[70] Nonetheless, the judgment throws interesting light on the Court's thinking. It appears to say that certain restrictions in the selective distribution network are not caught by Article 81(1) because they are necessary in pursuance of a desirable end. Although realising that the provisions will lead to greater price rigidity the Court held that this rigidity may be outweighed by the benefits such a distribution would produce as a whole.

d. EXCLUSIVE PURCHASING AGREEMENTS

Over the years the Commission, the national courts, and the ECJ have had to consider the compatibility with Article 81(1) of beer supply agreements containing 'beer ties'. In many Member States brewers conclude agreements with outlets such as public houses, which, in return for certain benefits from the brewer, oblige the outlet to purchase beer (and perhaps other drinks) exclusively from the brewer (or another named supplier). This obligation is frequently accompanied by a non-compete provision preventing the sale of competing products from the outlet. In many Member States the problems associated with such agreements result from networks of similar agreements being operated by all brewers on the market. In practice, this may mean that it is extremely difficult for a new brewer to gain access to the market of for any brewer to increase its market share. Access to the retail outlets is foreclosed.

In *Brasserie de Haecht (No 1)*[71] the ECJ held, in the context of such an agreement, that in considering whether there was a restriction of competition within Article 81(1) it was necessary to take account of the whole economic context in which the agreement operated. This included the existence of other agreements. Thus even though the exclusive purchasing obligation did not of its nature fall within Article 81(1) the simultaneous existence of numerous similar agreements might mean that the agreement appreciably restricted competition.

In *Delimitis* v. *Henninger Bräu* the ECJ forcefully restated the necessity of appraising beer tie agreements within their legal and economic context before finding that they infringed Article 81(1). The object of a commitment to purchase beer and other drinks exclusively from named suppliers was not to restrict competition. On the contrary, the Court specifically referred to the benefits which flowed from such an agreement, for example: the guarantee for a supplier of an outlet for its product; the assurance that the retailer would concentrate its sales efforts on the distribution of the contract goods; the ability for the retailer to gain access to the market on favourable terms; and the guarantee for the retailer a supply of products. Since the object of the agreement was not to restrict competition the agreement would only be prohibited by Article 81(1) if this was its effect.

---

[69] P. Freeman and R. Whish (eds.) *Butterworths Competition Law* (Butterworth, London, no date), Div I, para. 205.

[70] See Case 75/84, *Metro-SB-Grossmärkte GmbH* v. *Commission (No.2)* [1986] ECR 3021, [1987] 1 CMLR 118; Case T–19/92 *Groupement d'Achat Edouard Leclerc* v. *Commission* [1996] ECR II–1851, [1997] 4 CMLR 968 and Chap. 9.

[71] Case 23/67, *Brasserie de Haecht SA* v. *Wilkin (No 1)* [1967] ECR 407, [1968] CMLR 26.

Case C–234/89, *Delimitis* v. *Henninger Bräu* [1991] ECR 1–935, [1992] 5 CMLR 210

Delimitis and a brewer concluded an agreement in which the brewer let a public house to Delimitis. In return, Delimitis undertook to obtain beer and soft drinks from the brewer or its subsidiaries. On the termination of the agreement a dispute arose as to the agreement's compatibility with Article 81. On a preliminary reference the Court of Justice set out guidelines in order to enable the national court to assess the compatibility of the agreement with Article 81. The extract below deals with Article 81(1).

Court of Justice
The compatibility of beer supply agreements with Article 81(1) of the Treaty

10. Under the terms of beer supply agreements, the supplier generally affords the reseller certain economic and financial benefits, such as the grant of loans on favourable terms, the letting of premises for the operation of a public house and the provision of technical installations, furniture and other equipment necessary for its operation. In consideration for those benefits, the reseller normally undertakes, for a predetermined period, to obtain supplies of the products covered by the contract only from the supplier. That exclusive purchasing obligation is generally backed by a prohibition on selling competing products in the public house let by the supplier.

11. Such contracts entail for the supplier the advantage of guaranteed outlets, since, as a result of his exclusive purchasing obligation and the prohibition on competition, the reseller concentrates his sales efforts on the distribution of the contract goods. The supply agreements, moreover, lead to co-operation with the reseller, allowing the supplier to plan his sales over the duration of the agreement and to organize production and distribution effectively.

12. Beer supply agreements also have advantages for the reseller, inasmuch as they enable him to gain access under favourable conditions and with the guarantee of supplies to the beer distribution market. The reseller's and supplier's shared interest in promoting sales of the contract goods likewise secures for the reseller the benefit of the supplier's assistance in guaranteeing product quality and customer service.

13. If such agreements do not have the object of restricting competition within the meaning of Article [81(1)], it is nevertheless necessary to ascertain whether they have the effect of preventing, restricting or distorting competition.

14. In its judgment in Case 23/67 *Brasserie De Haecht* v. *Wilkin* [1967] ECR 407, the Court held that the effects of such an agreement had to be assessed in the context in which they occur and where they might combine with others to have a cumulative effect on competition. It also follows from that judgment that the cumulative effect of several similar agreements constitutes one factor amongst others in ascertaining whether, by way of a possible alteration of competition, trade between Member States is capable of being affected.

15. Consequently, in the present case it is necessary to analyse the effects of a beer supply agreement, taken together with other contracts of the same type, on the opportunities of national competitors or those from other Member States, to gain access to the market for beer consumption or to increase their market share and, accordingly, the effects on the range of products offered to consumers.

16. In making that analysis, the relevant market must first be determined. The relevant market is

primarily defined on the basis of the nature of the economic activity in question, in this case the sale of beer. Beer is sold through both retail channels and premises for the sale and consumption of drinks. From the consumer's point of view, the latter sector, comprising in particular public houses and restaurants, may be distinguished from the retail sector on the grounds that the sale of beer in public houses does not solely consist of the purchase of a product but is also linked with the provision of services, and that beer consumption in public houses is not essentially dependent on economic considerations. The specific nature of the public house trade is borne out by the fact that the breweries organize specific distribution systems for this sector which require special installations, and that the prices charged in that sector are generally higher than retail prices.

17. It follows that in the present case the reference market is that for the distribution of beer in premises for the sale and consumption of drinks. That finding is not affected by the fact that there is a certain overlap between the two distribution networks, namely inasmuch as retail sales allow new competitors to make their brands known and to use their reputation in order to gain access to the market constituted by premises for the sale and consumption of drinks.

18. Secondly, the relevant market is delimited from a geographical point of view. It should be noted that most beer supply agreements are still entered into at a national level. It follows that, in applying the Community competition rules, account is to be taken of the national market for beer distribution in premises for the sale and consumption of drinks.

19. In order to assess whether the existence of several beer supply agreements impedes access to the market as so defined, it is further necessary to examine the nature and extent of those agreements in their totality, comprising all similar contracts tying a large number of points of sale to several national producers (judgment in Case 43/69 *Bilger* v. *Jehle* [1970] ECR 127). The effect of those networks of contracts on access to the market depends specifically on the number of outlets thus tied to national producers in relation to the number of public houses which are not so tied, the duration of the commitments entered into, the quantities of beer to which those commitments relate, and on the proportion between those quantities and the quantities sold by free distributors.

20. The existence of a bundle of similar contracts, even if it has a considerable effect on the opportunities for gaining access to the market, is not, however, sufficient in itself to support a finding that the relevant market is inaccessible, inasmuch as it is only one factor, amongst others, pertaining to the economic and legal context in which an agreement must be appraised (Case 23/67 *Brasserie De Haecht*, cited above). The other factors to be taken into account are, in the first instance, those also relating to opportunities for access.

21. In that connection it is necessary to examine whether there are real concrete possibilities for a new competitor to penetrate the bundle of contracts by acquiring a brewery already established on the market together with its network of sales outlets, or to circumvent the bundle of contracts by opening new public houses. For that purpose it is necessary to have regard to the legal rules and agreements on the acquisition of companies and the establishment of outlets, and to the minimum number of outlets necessary for the economic operation of a distribution system. The presence of beer wholesalers not tied to producers who are active on the market is also a factor capable of facilitating a new producer's access to that market since he can make use of those wholesalers' sales networks to distribute his own beer.

22. Secondly, account must be taken of the conditions under which competitive forces operate on the relevant market. In that connection it is necessary to know not only the number and the size of producers present on the market, but also the degree of saturation of that market and customer fidelity to existing brands, for it is generally more difficult to penetrate a saturated market in which customers are loyal to a small number of large producers than a market in full expansion in which a large number of small producers are operating without any strong brand names. The trend in beer sales in the retail trade provides useful information on the development of demand and thus an

indication of the degree of saturation of the beer market as a whole. The analysis of that trend is, moreover, of interest in evaluating brand loyalty. A steady increase in sales of beer under new brand names may confer on the owners of those brand names a reputation which they may turn to account in gaining access to the public-house market.

23. If an examination of all similar contracts entered into on the relevant market and the other factors relevant to the economic and legal context in which the contract must be examined shows that those agreements do not have the cumulative effect of denying access to that market to new national and foreign competitors, the individual agreements comprising the bundle of agreements cannot be held to restrict competition within the meaning of Article [81(1)] of the Treaty. They do not, therefore, fall under the prohibition laid down in that provision.

24. If, on the other hand, such examination reveals that it is difficult to gain access to the relevant market, it is necessary to assess the extent to which the agreements entered into by the brewery in question contribute to the cumulative effect produced in that respect by the totality of the similar contracts found on that market. Under the Community rules on competition, responsibility for such an effect of closing off the market must be attributed to the breweries which make an appreciable contribution thereto. Beer supply agreements entered into by breweries whose contribution to the cumulative effect is insignificant do not therefore fall under the prohibition under Article [81(1)].

25. In order to assess the extent of the contribution of the beer supply agreements entered into by a brewery to the cumulative sealing-off effect mentioned above, the market position of the contracting parties must be taken into consideration. That position is not determined solely by the market share held by the brewery and any group, to which it may belong, but also by the number of outlets tied to it or to its group, in relation to the total number of premises for the sale and consumption of drinks found in the relevant market.

26. The contribution of the individual contracts entered into by a brewery to the sealing-off of that market also depends on their duration. If the duration is manifestly excessive in relation to the average duration of beer supply agreements generally entered into on the relevant market, the individual contract falls under the prohibition under Article [81(1)]. A brewery with a relatively small market share which ties its sales outlets for many years may make a significant contribution to a sealing-off of the market as a brewery in a relatively strong market position which regularly releases sales outlets at shorter intervals.

27. The reply to be given to the first three questions is therefore that a beer supply agreement is prohibited by Article [81(1)] of the [EC] Treaty, if two cumulative conditions are met. The first is that, having regard to the economic and legal context of the agreement at issue, it is difficult for competitors who could enter the market or increase their market share to gain access to the national market for the distribution of beer in premises for the sales and consumption of drinks. The fact that, in that market, the agreement in issue is one of a number of similar agreements having a cumulative effect on competition constitutes only one factor amongst others in assessing whether access to that market is indeed difficult. The second condition is that the agreement in question must make a significant contribution to the sealing-off effect brought about by the totality of those agreements in their economic and legal context. The extent of the contribution made by the individual agreement depends on the position of the contracting parties in the relevant market and on the duration of the agreement.

The Court in *Delimitis* thus set out guidelines for application by the national court which had asked the Community Court how it should determine whether or not the beer-supply agreement containing an exclusive purchasing commitment was compatible with Article 81(1).[72] The Court indicated that it is first necessary to define the relevant market. It must

---

[72] These guidelines should also be applied by other bodies, the Commission, or a national competition authority, when determining whether or not a beer supply agreement infringes Art. 81(1).

then be determined whether there is a concrete possibility for new competitors to penetrate the market taking account of the number and size of producers operating on the market, the existence of networks of agreements, the saturation of the market, and brand loyalty etc. If analysis shows that there is no denial of access to the market, an agreement cannot be found to restrict competition. Conversely, if access is inhibited it must then be assessed whether the agreement in question (which is taken to mean the agreements of that particular producer or brewer) contributes appreciably to that situation.

e. THE COMMISSION'S APPROACH

Despite these clear statements of the ECJ set out in 1966, 1977, 1986, and 1991 the Commission had a tendency to take a hard-line approach, interpreting the Court's judgments broadly.[73] This approach was subject to overwhelming criticism and eventually the Commission, in 1996, instituted a review of its entire policy towards vertical restraints and, in January 1997, published a Green Paper on Vertical Restraints.[74] The Paper set out four options for changing the way in which it handled distribution agreements. Although not one of the suggested options, the advantages which would flow from the adoption of a rule-of-reason-style approach to Article 81(1) featured heavily in the debate that the Green Paper invited. Following this review, it does appear that the Commission has taken note of the criticism levelled at its strict approach to Article 81(1). Not only has the Commission adopted a wide block exemption applicable to all vertical agreements but it has indicated in its Guidelines on vertical restraints that it will take a more principled approach to vertical restraints when considering their compatibility with Article 81(1).[75] This view is supported by cases dealing with beer supply agreements in which the Commission has faithfully and carefully applied the Court's guidelines set out in *Delimitis* before ruling on their compatibility with Article 81(1). In *Scottish and Newcastle*[76] the Commission defined the relevant product and geographic market prior to determining whether or not the exclusive purchasing obligation in the agreement had a restrictive effect on retailers and suppliers in the relevant market. In that case an examination of all tying agreements and other factors relevant to the economic and legal context of the UK on-trade markets established that the tying agreements in the UK had the cumulative effect of considerably hindering access to that market for national and foreign competitors. Further, Scottish and Newcastle's

---

[73] It took the view that the ECJ's judgment in Cases 56 & 58/64, *Etablissements Consten SA & Grundig-Verkaufs-GmbH* v. *Commission* [1966] ECR 299, [1966] CMLR 418 licensed it to adopt a strict approach to distribution agreements incorporating territorial restraints. Similarly, on the basis of the Court's judgment in *Delimitis* the Commission adopted a strict attitude towards beer supply agreements. It considered that because of the 'network effect' they were generally caught by Art. 81(1) however insignificant an individual agreement might appear. Prior to June 2000 Commission Reg. 1984/83 [1983] OJ L173/7, Title II, set out a special block exemption for beer supply agreements (this block exemption has now been replaced by Reg. 2790/1999 [1999] OJ L336/21, which applies to all vertical agreements). For a more detailed discussion of the treatment of specific types of vertical agreements see *infra* Chap. 9.

[74] Green Paper on Vertical Restraints in Competition Policy, COM(96)721, final, 22 Jan. 1997 [1997] 4 CMLR 519, discussed in greater detail in Chap. 9 below.

[75] Guidelines on Vertical Restraints, [2000] OJ C 291/1 especially paras. 121–133. See also the Commission's White paper on Modernisation of the Rules, Implementing Articles 85 and 86 [now 81 and 82] of the EC Treaty [1999] OJ C132/1, [1999] 5 CMLR 208, para. 78. Vertical restraints are discussed *infra* in Chap. 9.

[76] [1999] OJ L186/28 , [1999] 5 CMLR 831. See also Bass [1999] OJ L186/1, [1999] 5 CMLR 782.

agreements significantly contributed to the cumulative effect produced.[77] The Commission has, however, taken the view that agreements concluded by small UK brewers do not significantly contribute to the cumulative foreclosure of the market and thus do not restrict competition for the purposes of Article 81(1) (see, for example, its rejection of a complaint levied against *Greene King*).[78]

(iii) VERTICAL AGREEMENTS WHICH APPRECIABLY RESTRICT COMPETITION

a. THE TEN PER CENT THRESHOLD

Before an agreement can be found to infringe Article 81(1) it is necessary to establish both that it restricts competition *and* that any restriction of competition, and/or effect on trade, is appreciable.[79] In its Notice on agreements of minor importance the Commission has stated its view that vertical agreements between undertakings whose aggregate market shares do not exceed 10 per cent of the relevant market do not appreciably restrict competition and do not, therefore, fall within Article 81(1).[80] Indeed, the 'mere fact that [the] threshold may be reached and even exceeded does not make it possible to conclude with certainty that an agreement is caught by Article [81(1)]'.[81] In some cases, therefore, an agreement concluded between undertakings with an aggregate share in excess of the 10 per cent threshold might also be held to have an insignificant impact on competition.

b. PROBLEMS WITH NETWORKS OF AGREEMENTS

The Commission states in the Notice on minor importance that the notice is not applicable where the relevant market is restricted by the cumulative effect of parallel networks of similar agreements. This may mean, in practice, that in many markets the utility of the notice is lost. It must be remembered, however, that although the notice may not apply, the agreement may not restrict competition at all (let alone restrict competition appreciably). In *Delimitis* v. *Henninger Bräu* the Court held that where a restriction of competition on a market is caused by a network of similar agreements, a producer's agreements will restrict competition only if that producer's agreements significantly contribute to the cumulative effect of the network.[82]

c. VERTICAL AGREEMENTS WITH PRICE OR TERRITORIAL RESTRAINTS

It is clear from the case law of the ECJ that even agreements which have as their object the prevention, restriction, or distortion of competition may escape the prohibition of Article

---

[77] The Commission went on, however, to grant the agreement an exemption pursuant to Art. 81(3).

[78] IP/98/967 and see Inntrepreneur and Spring [2000] 5 CMLR 948.

[79] See *supra* Chap. 3.

[80] Commission Notice on agreements of minor importance which do not fall within the meaning of Art. 85(1) [now 81(1)] of the Treaty establishing the European Community [1997] OJ C372/13, Art. 9. See the discussion *supra* Chap. 3. It seems likely that following the reform of the Commission's approach to both vertical and horizontal restraints that his Notice will be changed.

[81] Cases T–374, 375, 384 & 388/94, *European Night Services* v. *Commission* [1998] ECR II–3141, [1998] 5CMLR 718, para. 102.

[82] Case C–234/89 *Delimitis* v. *Henninger Bräu* [1991] ECR 1–935, [1992] 5 CMLR 210, *supra* 167 ff.

81(1) if that restriction and/or the effect on trade is not appreciable.[83] The Commission's Notice on agreements of minor importance states, however, that, although the aggregate market share of parties to a vertical agreement does not exceed 10 per cent, the applicability of Article 81(1) cannot be ruled out if the object of the agreement is to fix resale prices or to confer territorial protection on the distributor.

The Commission appears to have reconciled these two points of view by accepting that the effect of such serious restrictions may be found to be insignificant, but only where the parties' market shares are considerably below the 10 per cent threshold set out in the notice. In *Völk* v. *Vervaecke* the producer had an extremely small share of the relevant market, it seems considerably less than 1 per cent.[84] The Commission's view appears to be that undertakings with market shares which do not exceed 1 per cent are likely to escape the Article 81(1) prohibition altogether on account of the insignificant effect of their agreement on competition. However, where an agreement contains such severe restrictions of competition parties with market shares of between 1 and 10 per cent should not discount the possibility that Article 81(1) may still apply.

J. Faull and A. Nikpay (eds.), *The EC Law of Competition* (Oxford University Press, 1999)

Restriction by Object and Appreciability

2.66 An agreement which has as its object the restriction of competition can nevertheless escape the prohibition of Article 81(1). The *Völk* v. *Vervaecke* case, which concerned absolute territorial protection, established the principle that even in relation to restrictions by object it remains necessary to analyse the actual or potential effect of the agreement involved so as to rule out the possibility that it may only have an 'insignificant effect' . . . on the market or on trade . . .

2.67 However, in *Società Italiana Vetro, Fabbrica Pisana and PPG Vernante Pennitalia* v. *Commission*, the Commission sought to argue that the evidence of the agreements between the parties was so unambiguous and explicit that any investigation whatsoever into the structure of the market was entirely superfluous. While acknowledging that the Commission was not required to discuss in its decisions all the arguments raised by undertakings, the Court explicitly disagreed with the Commission's approach. It said that the Commission ought to have examined more fully the structure and the functioning of the market in order to show why the conclusions drawn by the applicants were groundless. . . . More recently, in *Javico*, the ECJ affirmed this position. It held that:

> anti-competitive conduct may not be struck down under Article 85(1) [now Article 81(1)] of the Treaty unless it is capable of affecting trade between Member States . . . Moreover, the effect must not be insignificant . . . Thus, even an agreement imposing absolute territorial protection may escape the prohibition laid down in Article [81] if it affects the market only insignificantly, regard being had to the weak position of the persons concerned on the market in the products in question. . . . [Case C–306/96 *Javico International* v. *Yves Saint Laurent Parfums* [1998] ECR I–1983, paras 15–17].

---

[83] Case 5/69, *Völk* v. *Vervaecke* [1969] ECR 295, 302.
[84] *Ibid.*, see *supra* Chap. 3.

This reference to 'affects the market' shows that this reasoning applies to the effect on competition as well as to effect on trade between Member States.

2.68 What is an '*insignificant effect*'? In its submission to the Court in *Völk* v. *Vervaecke*, the Commission stated that the production of washing machines by Mr Völk's company represented 0.08 per cent of the total production of the common market and 0.2 per cent of production in the Federal Republic of Germany. Its market share of sales in Belgium and Luxembourg, the territory of its exclusive distributor Vervaecke, was approximately 0.6 per cent. On the basis of these small market shares the Commission admitted that even an agreement guaranteeing strict 'territorial protection' did not appreciably restrict competition. Neither did the Commission believe that the 'may affect trade between Member States' criterion was fulfilled. On the other hand in *Miller*, which concerned a territorial restriction by object, the Court found that the company concerned, which had a market share of the German market in sound recordings which varied between 5 per cent and 6 per cent could not be compared with the undertakings in the *Völk* case and that Article 81(1) was infringed.

2.69 While market share is not the only criterion for assessing the impact of a vertical restraint, for restrictions by object it is suggested that below 1 per cent market share the effect on the market is likely to be insignificant and Article 81(1) is unlikely to apply, while above 5 per cent the effect is likely to be appreciable and Article 81(1) is likely to apply. Between 1 per cent and 5 per cent is best described as a grey area. This is reflected in the Commission's Notice on Agreement of Minor Importance (the so-called *de minimis* Notice), which offers little comfort to undertakings in this grey area. The current Notice states that the applicability of Article 81(1) cannot be ruled out below the *de minimis* threshold, defined solely in terms of market share, for 'horizontal agreements which has as their object to fix prices or to limit production or sales; or to share market or sources of supply' and for 'vertical agreements which have as their object to fix resale prices, or to confer territorial protection on the participating undertakings or third parties'. . . . Therefore, even companies with little market power who enter into restrictions by object run the risk of infringing Article 81(1).

2.70 Notwithstanding the terms of the current *de minimis* Notice, the Commission rarely challenges agreements, even those which are restrictive by object, below 5 per cent market share for horizontal restrictions or 10 per cent for vertical restrictions. In economic terms, the impact of most restrictive agreements would be muted at low market share levels and the allocation of resources to such cases would, it is submitted, be questionable. If the Commission did challenge such agreements, the most likely reason for doing so would be pedagogical—to help ensure that a 'competition culture' was developed or maintained in a particular sector of the economy.

E. HORIZONTAL AGREEMENTS

(i) RESTRICTION BY OBJECT

It is clear from the CFI's judgment in *European Night Services* v. *Commission*[85] that agreements contains obvious restrictions of competition will automatically be held to restrict competition within the meaning of Article 81(1). The CFI took the view that provisions fixing prices or sharing markets would be obvious restrictions of competition.

---

[85] Cases T–374, 375, 384 & 388/94 [1998] ECR II–3141, [1998] 5 CMLR 718, para 136 set out *infra* 176.

Thus competitors that agree or otherwise conspire to fix prices, share markets, or impose quotas etc. will almost certainty find that the object of their agreement is found to restrict competition. They will automatically infringe Article 81(1) and any claimed pro-competitive effect of such restrictions will only be considered, if at all, in the context of Article 81(3).

(ii) RESTRICTION BY EFFECT

a. JOINT VENTURE AGREEMENTS

In many cases parties operating at the same level of the economy may agree to establish a joint venture which does not have the sole purpose of co-ordinating the parties' market conduct. Rather, the parties may agree to pool their resources for a number of reasons: perhaps to facilitate or speed up new entry into a market, to share financial risks, to achieve cost savings or even to enable entry into a new market (each undertaking individually may not have the necessary skills or technology to make entry feasible).

In some circumstances, the establishment of a joint venture amounts to a concentration for the purposes of EC Merger Regulation.[86] In other cases the agreements fall to be assessed under Article 81 in order to determine whether they pose a risk to competition. Although collaboration between such undertakings may enhance the position of the competitors on the market and lead to advantages on that market which the competitors may be unable to achieve on their own, joint venture agreements may cause concern. In particular, a competition authority may fear that: a joint venture agreement will make it easier for the parties to collude (in particular, the collaboration may spill over outside the field of the agreement); the relevant market may become foreclosed to third parties; the agreement will be more restrictive than is necessary to achieve the objectives achieved; or there will be a loss of actual or potential competition between the competitors.[87]

In *European Night Services* v. *Commission* the CFI stressed that where an agreement does not contain obvious restrictions of competition, the actual conditions in which an agreement functions must be taken into account. In particular, account has to be taken of 'the economic context in which the undertakings operate, the products or services covered by the agreement and the actual structure of the market concerned'. In making such an assessment it was stressed that it is vital that the examination of the conditions of competition is based not only on existing competition between undertakings present on the relevant market but also on *potential* competition. This was necessary 'in order to ascertain whether, in the light of the structure of the market and the economic and legal context within which it functions, there are real concrete possibilities for the undertakings concerned to compete among themselves or for a new competitor to penetrate the relevant market and compete with the undertakings already established'.[88]

---

[86] Council Reg. 4064/89 [1989] OJ L395/1, as amended by Council Reg. 1310/97 [1997] OJ L 180/1.

[87] For joint ventures generally, see *infra* Chap. 13.

[88] Cases T–374, 375, 384 & 388/94, *European Night Services* v. *Commission* [1998] ECR II–3141, [1998] 5 CMLR 718, paras 136–137. For joint ventures generally, see *infra* Chap. 13.

Cases T–374, 375, 384 & 388/94, *European Night Services* v. *Commission* [1998] ECR II–3141, [1998] 5 CMLR 718

This case involved agreements notified to the Commission concerning the formation of European Night Services (ENS) by four undertakings, British Rail, Deutsche Bundesbahn, Nederlandse Spoorwegen and Société Nationale des Chemis de Fer Français. The purpose of ENS was to provide and operate overnight passenger rail services between the UK and the Continent through the Channel Tunnel. The Commission had only exempted the agreements from the application of Article 81(1) subject to the acceptance of stringent conditions. The applicants sought to have the decision annulled. On the facts the Court of First Instance annulled the Commission's decision. The decision had failed to give a sufficient statement of reasons as to how the ENS agreements could be said to restrict competition within the meaning of Article 81(1). It was not clear, consequently, that there was a need for exemption under Article 81(3).

Court of First Instance

135. According to the contested decision, the ENS agreements have effects restricting existing and potential competition (a) among the parent undertakings, (b) between the parent undertakings and ENS and (c) *vis-à-vis* third parties; furthermore (d), those restrictions are aggravated by the presence of a network of joint ventures set up by the parent undertakings.

136. Before any examination of the parties' arguments as to whether the Commission's analysis as regards restrictions of competition was correct, it must be borne in mind that in assessing an agreement under Article [81(1)] of the Treaty, account should be taken of the actual conditions in which it functions, in particular the economic context in which the undertakings operate, the products or services covered by the agreement and the actual structure of the market concerned (judgments in *Delimitis*, . . . *Gøttrup-Klim*, . . . Case C–399/93, *Oude Luttikhuis and Others* v. *Verenigde Coöperatieve Melkindustrie*, [1995] ECR I–1415 paragraph 10 and Case T–77/94, *VGB and Others* v. *Commission* [1997] ECR II–759, paragraph 140), unless it is an agreement containing obvious restrictions of competition such as price-fixing, market-sharing or the control of outlets (Case T–148/89, *Tréfilunion* v. *Commission* ([1995] ECR II–1063, paragraph, 109)). In the latter case, such restrictions may be weighed against their claimed pro-competitive effects only in the context of Article [81(3)] of the Treaty, with a view to granting an exemption from the prohibition in Article [81(1)].

137. It must also be stressed that the examination of conditions of competition is based not only on existing competition between undertakings already present on the relevant market but also on potential competition, in order to ascertain whether, in the light of the structure of the market and the economic and legal context within which it functions, there are real concrete possibilities for the undertakings concerned to compete among themselves or for a new competitor to penetrate the relevant market and compete with the undertakings already established (*Delimitis* . . . paragraph 21). Furthermore, according to the Commission notice of 1993 concerning the assessment of co-operative joint ventures pursuant to Article [81] of the Treaty: 'The assumption of potential competitive circumstances presupposes that each parent alone is in a position to fulfil the tasks assigned to the [joint venture] and that it does not forfeit its capabilities to do so by the creation of the [joint venture]. An economically realistic approach is necessary in the assessment of any particular case'.

138. It is in the light of those considerations, therefore, that it is necessary to examine whether the Commission's assessment of the restrictive effects of the ENS agreements was correct.

b. BUYING CO-OPERATIVES

In *Gøttrup-Klim Grovvareforening and Others* v. *Dansk Landbrugs Grovvareselskab AmbA*[89] the ECJ was asked by a Danish court whether a clause in the statutes of Dansk Landbrugs Grovvareselskab AmbA (a Danish co-operative association distributing farm supplies, 'DLG') restricted competition within the meaning of Article 81(1). The object of DLG was to provide its members with farm supplies (such as fertilizer) at the lowest possible prices and to offer its members other services, particularly in the area of finance. In 1988 the statutes of DLG were changed because of increasing competition from the claimants in this case. Essentially, the disputed clause precluded some of DLG's members from holding membership of, or any other kind of participation in, associations, societies, or other forms of co-operative organization in competition with DLG, with regard to the purchase and sale of fertilizers and plant protection products. The statutes provided that members which infringed this rule would be excluded from DLG (and some members were in fact excluded). DLG had notified the amendment to the Commission for negative clearance or exemption, but at the time of the proceedings before the ECJ had still not received an answer to the letter of notification. In the proceedings before the ECJ, however, the Commission stated in reply to a question from the Court that the amendment to the statutes did not infringe the Article 81(1) prohibition.

DLG contended that the aim of the clause was not to restrict competition. On the contrary it (1) enabled the members to stand up to a few very large multinational producers of fertilizers and plant protection products in order to obtain lower purchase prices for Danish farmers and, (2) secondarily, prevented competitors' representatives from taking part in the association's management bodies (shareholders' committee and board of directors) in which business secrets were discussed. The Danish authorities did not take the view that the statutes as amended infringed Danish competition law. Nonetheless, the claimants challenged the compatibility of the provision with Article 81 of the Treaty and sought compensation and damages in respect of the loss sustained from their exclusion from DLG. The Danish court referred the matter to the ECJ using the procedure set out in Article 234 of the Treaty. In particular it asked whether a provision in the statues of a commercial co-operative society which essentially excluded members which participated in a co-operative organization which competed with it was contrary to Article 81(1). The Court replied that it would not so long as the provision was restricted to what was necessary to ensure that the co-operative functioned properly and maintained its contractual power in relation to producers.

Case C–250/92, *Gøttrup-Klim Grovvareforening and Others* v. *Dansk Landbrugs Grovvareselskab AmbA* (DLG) [1994] ECR I–5641, [1996] 4 CMLR 191

18. In its order for reference, the Østre Landsret proceeds on the basis that DLG in essence sought to induce . . . members to stop purchasing fertilisers and plant protection products outside DLG, so that within the cooperative sector in Denmark there would be just one large association purchasing supplies on behalf of Danish farmers . . .

---

[89] Case C–250/92, *Gøttrup-Klim Grovvareforening and Others* v. *Dansk Landbrugs Grovvareselskab AmbA* [1994] ECR I–5641, [1996] 4 CMLR 191.

Restriction of competition

28. In the second set of questions, the national court seeks to ascertain whether a provision in the statutes of a cooperative purchasing association, the effect of which is to forbid its members to participate in other forms of organized cooperation which are in direct competition with it, is caught by the prohibition in Article [81(1)] of the Treaty.

29. The plaintiffs in the main proceedings claim that the object or effect of such an amendment to the statutes is to restrict competition, inasmuch as the objective pursued was to put an end to . . . members purchasing through LAG in competition with DLG, and thus to acquire a dominant position on the markets concerned.

30. A cooperative purchasing association is a voluntary association of persons established in order to pursue common commercial objectives.

31. The compatibility of the statutes of such an association with the Community rules on competition cannot be assessed in the abstract. It will depend on the particular clauses in the statutes and the economic conditions prevailing on the markets concerned.

32. In a market where product prices vary according to the volume of orders, the activities of co-operative purchasing associations may, depending on the size of their membership, constitute a significant counterweight to the contractual power of large producers and make way for more effective competition.

33. Where some members of two competing cooperative purchasing associations belong to both at the same time, the result is to make each association less capable of pursuing its objectives for the benefit of the rest of its members, especially where the members concerned, as in the case in point, are themselves cooperative associations with a large number of individual members.

34. It follows that such dual membership would jeopardize both the proper functioning of the co-operative and its contractual power in relation to producers. Prohibition of dual membership does not, therefore, necessarily constitute a restriction of competition within the meaning of Article [81(1)] of the Treaty and may even have beneficial effects on competition.

35. Nevertheless, a provision in the statutes of a cooperative purchasing association, restricting the opportunity for members to join other types of competing cooperatives and thus discouraging them from obtaining supplies elsewhere, may have adverse effects on competition. So, in order to escape the prohibition laid down in Article [81(1)] of the Treaty, the restrictions imposed on members by the statutes of cooperative purchasing associations must be limited to what is necessary to ensure that the cooperative functions properly and maintains its contractual power in relation to producers.

36. The particular features of the case at issue in the main proceedings, which are referred to in the questions submitted by the national court, must be assessed in the light of the foregoing considerations. In addition, it is necessary to establish whether the penalties for non-compliance with the statutes are disproportionate to the objective they pursue and whether the minimum period of membership is unreasonable.

37. First of all, the amendment of DLG's statutes is restricted so as to cover only fertilizers and plant protection products, the only farm supplies in respect of which a direct relationship exists between sales volume and price.

38. Furthermore, even after DLG has amended its statutes and excluded the plaintiffs, it is open to 'non-members' of the association, including the plaintiffs, to buy from it the whole range of products which it sells, including fertilizers and plant protection products, on the same commercial terms and at the same prices as members, except that 'non-members' are obviously not entitled to receive a yearly discount on the amount of the transactions carried out.

39. Finally, DLG's statutes authorize its members to buy fertilizers and plant protection products without using DLG as an intermediary, provided that such transactions are carried out otherwise than

through an organized consortium. In that context, each member acts individually or in association with others but, in the latter case, only in making a one-off common purchase of a particular consignment or shipload.

40. Taking all those factors into account, it would not seem that restrictions laid down in the statutes, of the kind imposed on DLG members, go beyond what is necessary to ensure that the co-operative functions properly and maintains its contractual power in relation to producers.

41. As regards the penalties imposed on the plaintiffs as a result of their exclusion for infringing DLG's rules, these would not appear to be disproportionate, since DLG has treated the plaintiffs as if they were members exercising their right to withdraw.

42. So far as concerns the membership period, this has been reduced from ten to five years, which does not seem unreasonable.

43. It is significant, in the last analysis, that after their exclusion, the plaintiffs succeeded, through LAG, in competing vigorously with DLG, with the result that in 1990 their market share was similar to DLG's.

44. The other matters mentioned in the second set of questions referred by the national court are not such as to affect the analysis of the problem.

45. The answer to the second set of questions referred by the national court must therefore be that a provision in the statutes of a cooperative purchasing association, forbidding its members to participate in other forms of organized cooperation which are in direct competition with it, is not caught by the prohibition in Article [81(1)] of the Treaty, so long as the abovementioned provision is restricted to what is necessary to ensure that the cooperative functions properly and maintains its contractual power in relation to producers.

c. SALE OF A BUSINESS

The ECJ has recognized that a non-compete clause on the sale of a business does not inevitably restrict competition within the meaning of Article 81(1). On the contrary, such a clause is likely to be an essential part of an agreement to sell a business. Viewed *ex post*, a non-compete clause may appear to restrict competition between the parties. However, when assessed *ex ante* it may become clear that competition is not restricted. No undertaking would be willing to purchase the business without an assurance from the vendor that it will not remain in business in such a way that it would still be able to exploit the goodwill and the customers of the business sold. Nonetheless the Court has held that the non-compete clause must be limited to what is necessary to make the transaction viable. It will be held to restrict competition if it is broader than required for the sale: for example, if it precludes the vendor from setting up any business within a wide geographic area for an indefinite period of time.

Case 42/84, *Remia BV and NV Verenigde Bedrijven Nutricia* v. *Commission* [1985] ECR 2545, [1987] 1 CMLR 1

This case concerned proceedings brought by Remia BV and NV Verenigde Bedrijven Nutricia (hereinafter referred to as 'Nutricia') under Article 230 of the EC Treaty for a declaration that a Commission decision[90] relating to an agreement between them was void. Broadly this case concerned

---

[90] [1983] OJ L376/22.

the sale by Nutricia (a manufacturer of health and baby foods) of two of its subsidiaries, Remia and Luycks. The sales agreements contained non-compete clauses designed to protect the purchasers from competition by the vendor on the same market for a period immediately after the transfer. Further, a provision in the sales agreements of Remia provided that neither Nutricia nor Luycks (engaged in the production of pickles and condiments) would engage directly or indirectly in the production of sale of sauces (Remia was principally engaged in sauce production,) on the Netherlands market. Further, Nutricia undertook to Luycks for a period of five years not to engage directly or indirectly in any production or sale of pickles or condiments in Europe. Campbell, the parent company of the undertaking purchasing Luycks considered that this clause infringed Article 81 of the Treaty and notified the two transfer agreements to the Commission requesting exemption. The Commission took the view that the duration and scope of the non-compete clauses were excessive and so restricted competition and were not eligible for exemption under Article 81(3). The applicants thus appealed to the Court of Justice seeking a declaration that the non-compete clause did not infringe Article 81(1) at all and in any case that the Commission had wrongly failed to apply Article 81(3).

Court of Justice

The application of Article [81 (1)] of the [EC] Treaty

17. It should be stated at the outset that the Commission has rightly submitted—and the applicants have not contradicted it on that point—that the fact that non-competition clauses are included in an agreement for the sale of an undertaking is not of itself sufficient to remove such clauses from the scope of Article [81 (1)] of the Treaty.

18. In order to determine whether or not such clauses come within the prohibition in Article [81 (1)], it is necessary to examine what would be the state of competition if those clauses did not exist.

19. If that were the case, and should the vendor and the purchaser remain competitors after the transfer, it is clear that the agreement for the transfer of the undertaking could not be given effect. The vendor, with his particularly detailed knowledge of the transferred undertaking, would still be in a position to win back his former customers immediately after the transfer and thereby drive the undertaking out of business. Against that background non-competition clauses incorporated in an agreement for the transfer of an undertaking in principle have the merit of ensuring that the transfer has the effect intended. By virtue of that very fact they contribute to the promotion of competition because they lead to an increase in the number of undertakings in the market in question.

20. Nevertheless, in order to have that beneficial effect on competition, such clauses must be necessary to the transfer of the undertaking concerned and their duration and scope must be strictly limited to that purpose. The Commission was therefore right in holding that where those conditions are satisfied such clauses are free of the prohibition laid down in Article [81(1)].

21. However, without denying the basic principle of that reasoning, the applicants challenge the way in which it has been applied to their case on the ground, first, that the non-competition clause contained in the sauce agreement does not affect trade between Member States within the meaning of Article [81 (1)] of the Treaty, and, secondly, that in view of the special circumstances surrounding the transfer at issue the Commission did not provide an adequate statement of the grounds for its decision and wrongly assessed the facts in limiting to four years the permissible duration of the non-competition clause included in the transfer agreement.

. . .

25. On the second point, namely the limitation of the non-competition clause to four years, the applicants contend first that the statement of the reasons for the contested decision is inadequate and secondly that it contains errors of fact and is based on an erroneous assessment of the facts of the case as a whole.

. . .

35. In this instance the applicants have confined themselves to contending that the limitation of the duration of the non-competition clause to four years is based on a number of incorrect findings of fact and, essentially, on the Commission's incorrect appraisal of the specific circumstances of the case.

36. It cannot be inferred either from the documents before the Court or from the oral argument presented to it that by setting at four years the period beyond which the non-competition clause contained in the sauce agreement came within the prohibition laid down in Article [81 (1)] of the [EC] Treaty, the Commission based its decision on incorrect findings of fact or committed a manifest error in its appraisal of the facts of the case as a whole.

d. THE COMMISSION'S APPROACH

Again, in the context of horizontal agreements, especially joint venture agreements, the Commission has been criticized for failing to make a realistic determination of whether or not an agreement restricts competition within the meaning of Article 81. The Commission has shown itself to be prepared to consider the effects of the agreement on the market under Article 81(1). In *ODIN*, for example, the Commission held that an agreement did not restrict competition so that the agreement was cleared rather than exempted under Article 81(3). This case concerned an agreement concluded between Elopak and Metal Box which established a jointly-owned company, 'ODIN', to carry out the research and development of a container with a carton base and separate closure that could be filled by an aseptic process with UHT processed foods. Article 81(1) was found not to apply because the parents, Elopak and Metal Box, were not actual or potential competitors in the relevant product market. Further, the Commission took account of the fact that, given the parties' technical expertise, it was highly unlikely that either party would develop the product alone, they were not competitors outside of the field and there was no risk of foreclosing the market from other potential competitors.

More often than not, however, the Commission has found that the agreement restricts competition and has completed its assessment under Article 81(3). The more rigorous scrutiny of the pro-competitive aspects of the agreement has been made at this stage rather than when determining whether or not the agreement can in fact be said to be restrictive of competition. In practice, there have been few appeals to the Community Courts on the legitimacy of this practice because once the exemption has been obtained the parties have not been minded to make an appeal from the decision.

The problems caused by this approach have been many. In particular, the current block exemptions in place for horizontal agreements, relating to research and development and specialization agreements respectively, have been much less useful than those applicable to distribution agreements. In practice, it has frequently been impossible for the parties to draft their agreement so that it falls within one of them. The Commission is proposing to replace these with two new block exemptions.[91]

In order that beneficial collaboration be encouraged, it has been urged that the Commission should undertake a more sophisticated analysis under Article 81(1). Recognizing the difficulties involved the Commission has attempted both to speed up its procedures when dealing with joint venture notifications under Article 81[92] *and* to adopt a more realistic

---

[91] [2000] OJ C118/4 and 10. See also the draft Commission Guidelines on Horizontal Co-operation *infra* n. 93 and *infra* Chap. 13.

[92] In contrast most joint ventures which fall to be assessed under the provisions of the Merger Reg. Reg. 4064/89 [1989] OJ L395/1, amended by Council Reg. 1310/97 [1997] OJ L180/1 are dealt with within a month of notification to the Commission: see *infra* Chap. 12.

assessment of joint ventures which fall to be assessed under Article 81. In its draft Guidelines on horizontal co-operation the Commission specifically recognizes that most horizontal co-operation agreements do not have as their object a restriction of competition and must, consequently, be analysed in their economic context to determine whether or not this is their effect.[93] This view seems to accord with that of the CFI set out in *European Night Services v. Commission*,[94] that a rigorous analysis will be necessary at the Article 81(1) level and that in the absence of a sufficiently reasoned decision the Commission risks its decision being quashed. The CFI clearly held that the Commission must make a correct and adequate assessment in its decision of the economic and legal context in which the relevant agreement was concluded and must give sufficient reasons justifying a finding that an agreement restricts competition.

It seems likely, therefore, that in the short-term at least,[95] we might expect to see more analysis of joint venture agreements completed at the Article 81(1) stage. The Commission's White Paper on modernisation indicates that it is keen to ensure that it no longer has to spend most of its time dealing with notifications. Indeed, in the Paper it states that 'in its handling of individual cases, the Commission will adopt a more economic approach to the application of Article [81(1)], which will limit the scope of its application to under-taking with a certain degree of market power'.[96] Arguably, it has already begun to adopt such an approach. It has already been seen that it has appeared more willing to do so when dealing with beer supply agreements and in 1999 in *Cégétel + 4*,[97] for example, it cleared rather than exempted a joint venture for the restructuring of Cégétel + 4. This company had been created by Compagnie générale des eaux SA (CGE, now named Vivendi) and was active in liberalized telecommunications markets, particularly in mobile telephony and paging. Broadly, the purpose of the restructuring was to enable Cégétel to become the second full service operator in France. This was to be achieved through the participa-tion of three other undertakings, British Telecommunications plc (BT), Mannesmann AG, and SBC International Inc (SBCI), in the agreement. The Commission found that neither the agreements relating to the restructuring of Cégétal nor the ancillary restric-tions relating to the agreements infringed Article 81(1) at all. Rather, the Commission concluded that:

Cégétel creates a more effective competition to the incumbent operator than the parent [co]m-panies would have been capable to create separately. Cégétel's restructuring does not restrict actual or potential competition on the French fixed voice telephony market (since the parties could not enter this market alone), [nor] on any other relevant segments of the telecommunications market (since Cégétel will be able to co[mpe]te strongly on these segments and since there are numerous other competitors), nor on the potential European market for mobile telecommunica-

---

[93] See especially paras. 23–25. The draft Guidelines [2000] OJ C118/14 are discussed *infra* in Chap. 13, the chap dealing with joint ventures and other beneficial horizontal agreements. See also the Commissions *XIIIth Report on Competition Policy* (Commission 1985), pt. 55.

[94] Cases T–374, 375, 384 & 388/94, *European Night Services v. Commission* [1998] ECR II–3141, [1998] 5 CMLR 718.

[95] In the medium term the Commission expects that all assessments of joint venture agreements will take place within the procedural framework of the Merger Reg.: see White Paper on modernisation of the rules implementing Art. 85 and 86 [now 81 and 82] of the EC Treaty [1999] OJ C132/1, [1999] 5 CMLR 208, para. 79.

[96] *Ibid.* para. 78 but see *supra* 143–144.

[97] *Re Cégétel: Vivendi/BT/Mannesmann/SBC International* [1999] OJ L218/14, [2000] 4 CMLR 106.

tions services. Therefore, Cégétel's restructuring falls outside the scope of Article 81(1) of the Treaty.[98]

(iii) HORIZONTAL AGREEMENTS WHICH DO NOT HAVE AN APPRECIABLE EFFECT ON COMPETITION AND TRADE

a. THE FIVE PER CENT THRESHOLD

Again it is necessary to show that the effect of the agreement on competition and trade is an appreciable one.[99] In its Notice on agreements of minor importance the Commission has stated its view that horizontal agreements between undertakings whose aggregate market shares do not exceed 5 per cent of the relevant market do not appreciably restrict competition and do not, therefore, fall within Article 81(1).[100] However, in *European Night Services* v. *Commission* the CFI indicated its willingness to quash a Commission decision which fails adequately to explain why the agreement in question restricts competition appreciably and so falls within the Article 81(1) prohibition.[101] Thus the 'mere fact that [the] threshold may be reached and even exceeded does not make it possible to conclude with certainty that an agreement is caught by Article [81(1)]'.[102]

b. HORIZONTAL PRICE-FIXING AND MARKET-SHARING AGREEMENTS

It follows from the Court's judgment in *Völk* v. *Vervaecke* that agreements containing the most serious of competition restrictions, such as horizontal price fixing and market-sharing provisions, may escape the impact of Article 81(1) on the grounds that the agreement does not have an appreciable effect on competition. Indeed, in *Flat Glass* the CFI held that 'the appropriate definition of the market in question is a necessary precondition of any judgment concerning allegedly anti-competitive behaviour'.[103] In the absence of a proper market definition, the Commission would be unable to determine whether or not the agreement between the undertakings in question had an appreciable impact on competition and trade.

F. INTELLECTUAL PROPERTY LICENSING AGREEMENTS

(i) RESTRICTION BY OBJECT

As in the case of vertical restraints, a strong argument may be presented to suggest that licences of intellectual property rights are not restrictive of competition at all and should

---

[98] *Ibid*, para. 46.

[99] See *supra* Chap. 3.

[100] Commission Notice on agreements of minor importance which do not fall within the meaning of Art. 85(1) [now Article 81(1)] of the Treaty establishing the European Community [1997] OJ C372/13, Art. 9. See the discussion *supra* at Chap. 3.

[101] See *supra* Chapter 3.

[102] Cases T–374, 375, 384 & 388/94, *European Night Services* v. *Commission* [1998] ECR II–3141, [1998] 5 CMLR 718, para. 102.

[103] Cases T–68/89, *Societa Italiano Vetro* v. *Commission*; T–77/89, *Fabbrica Pisana* v. *Commission*; T–78/89, *PPG Vernante Pennitalia* v. *Commission* [1992] ECR II–1403, [1992] 5 CMLR 302, para. 159.

not, therefore, be subjected to the control of Article 81(1). For example, the owner of a patent has the exclusive right to produce the patented product and to sell it at whatever price he wishes. The licensing of the right to exploit that patent in fact increases competition, in that a new licensee is introduced onto the market, and enables the new technology to be disseminated more widely. Further, like other vertical agreements, restrictive clauses, such as a clause giving the licensee territorial protection, may be necessary in order to persuade the licensee to enter into the agreement.

In accordance with its approach taken to vertical restraints, the ECJ generally takes the view that provisions in a licence which impose absolute territorial protection on the licensee have as their object the restriction of competition within the meaning of Article 81(1).[104] There is no need to consider the possible economic or other justification for such a provision.

(ii) RESTRICTION BY EFFECT

Where exclusivity provisions do not give the licensee absolute territorial protection, the ECJ recognizes that restrictions in a licensing agreement may not infringe Article 81(1) if necessary to protect the investment of the licensee. In *Nungesser* v. *Commission*,[105] the Court held that an open exclusive licence to produce maize seeds did not infringe Article 81(1). A licensee would not be prepared to take the licence and incur the risk/expense of producing the patented product without some protection from intra-brand competition. The Court developed this line of reasoning in *Erauw-Jacquéry Sprl* v. *La Hesbignonne Société Coopérative*.[106] In this case, it accepted that even export bans might, in certain circumstances, fall outside Article 81(1).

The Commission has, again, interpreted the Court's jurisprudence narrowly and tends to the view that many common clauses in licences infringe Article 81(1). Again the Commission is motivated by the fear that the agreements (particularly exclusivity clauses) will be used to compartmentalize the common market. It believes that, save in exceptional circumstances, licensing agreements fall within Article 81(1). It has thus been able to control the clauses inserted into such agreements by obliging parties to draft their agreements within the terms of a relevant block exemption.[107] or by vetting the clauses when deciding whether or not to grant an individual exemption. Again this approach has been subject to criticism. Not only does interference from the Commission undermine the sanctity of bargains but it may deter the conclusion of pro-competitive licensing agreements.

Licensing agreements are dealt with in greater detail in Chapter 10.

---

[104] Case 258/78, *Nungesser* v. *Commission* [1982] ECR 2015 but see n. 106 and accompanying text. *Cf.* the special position of copyright exploited by performance: see Case 62/79, *Coditel* v. *Ciné Vog Films* (*Coditel I*) [1980] ECR 881, [1981] 2 CMLR 362.

[105] Case 258/78 [1982] ECR 2015.

[106] Case 27/87 [1988] ECR 1999.

[107] See Reg. 240/96 [1996] OJ L31/2, replacing the patent and know-how Regs. (Regs. 2349/84 [1984] OJ L219/5 and 556/89 [1989] OJ L66/1.

G. JUDGMENTS BY CATEGORY

(i) GENERAL

It has been seen from the discussion above that the Court has adopted its own individual approach to the question whether or not an agreement restricts competition. Ever since 1966, however, it has been accepting of economic justifications and explanations for restraints contained in an agreement when determining whether they restrict competition within the meaning of Article 81(1). The Court has made it clear that, in the absence of serious territorial or price restraints, many agreements containing restraints on the parties' conduct fall outside Article 81(1). It has held that restraints in an agreement do not restrict competition if: necessary or ancillary to a pro-competitive agreement; essential to persuade a distributor to take on the risk of distributing a particular product in a particular market; necessary to the successful operation of a selective distribution system or where the agreement as a whole does not restrict inter-brand competition.

(ii) ANCILLARY RESTRAINTS OR OBJECTIVE NECESSITY

Some of the judgments of the Court suggest that restrictions on the conduct of the parties essential or ancillary to the operation of a pro-competitive agreement cannot be said to restrict competition. In *Remia and Nutricia* v. *Commission*,[108] for example, the Court accepted that a non-compete clause in an agreement for the sale of a business would ensure that the transfer had the intended effect. Without it, the vendor would be able to carry on its business as it had done previously and steal away the business of the transferee. The Court thus recognized the necessity of inserting such a clause into an agreement which would lead to an increase in competition on the market. Similarly, in *Pronuptia de Paris GmbH* v. *Pronuptia de Paris Irmgard Schillgallis*[109] the Court held that restrictions on a party's conduct necessary for the successful operation of any pro-competitive franchising distribution agreement did not infringe Article 81(1).

The doctrine has problems, however. In the first place it is necessary to identify what particular types of contract are sufficiently beneficial to merit clearance under Article 81(1). Secondly, it may still be difficult to identify whether or not a particular restraint is objectively necessary or ancillary to the operation of the particular agreement. In the absence of a large body of case law and guidelines applying to specific categories of agreements it may be difficult to apply in practice.

J. Faull and A. Nikpay (eds), *The EC Law of Competition* (Oxford University Press, 1999)

2.91 A more fundamental problem arises from the imprecise definition given to ancillary restraints under European competition law. Ancillary restraints are those which are 'directly related' to the agreement and objectively 'necessary for its existence'. However, they must

---

[108] [1985] ECR 2545, [1987] 1 CMLR 1.
[109] [1986] ECR 353, [1986] 1 CMLR 414.

also 'remain subordinate in importance to the main object' of the agreement . . . Thus for an R&D joint venture the 'main object' of the agreement would be the complete or partial integration of the R&D operations of the parties in a particular field of research. An obligation on the parties not to carry out research independently in this area for the lifetime of the joint venture could, if it were objectively 'necessary' for the implementation of the agreement, be described as a subordinate clause. On the other hand, it would be difficult to argue persuasively that a clause which prevented these parties from competing with each other in another, unrelated field is directly related to the agreement or objectively necessary for its existence.

2.92 It is clear that the concept begs more questions that it answers. It is very difficult, if not impossible, to identify in the abstract whether a particular restraint will be treated as ancillary to a particular type of agreement. Of course, similar problems exist when applying the concept of indispensability under Article 81(3) . . . However, in such cases, advisers can turn to the 'black lists' in the various block exemptions or the existing case law. Unfortunately, there is little case law under Article 81(1) . . . to guide companies and their advisers. The doctrine cannot therefore be applied with certainty by those who wish to argue that a particular restrictive clause in an agreement falls outside Article 81(1).

Thirdly, it appears that, because of the single market objective, the doctrine will not apply to territorial restraints. In *Pronuptia* the Court thus concluded that provisions in a franchising agreement which led to the sharing of markets between the franchisor and the franchisees or between franchisees would restrict competition for the purpose of Article 81(1).

(iii) COMMERCIAL RISK

Some judgments of the Court appear to recognize that particular restraints in an agreement will be necessary to persuade one of the parties to take on the commercial risk inherent in the agreement. A distributor of a product may be unwilling to take on the commercial risk of investing in the promotion and marketing of the contract product unless protected from the competition of other distributors of products. The restrictions imposed in the agreement to ensure such protection are not, therefore, restrictions of competition but are essential to induce the distributor actually to distribute the product. This doctrine has similarities to the ancillary restraints doctrine, since the protection afforded to the distributor is essential to induce the distributor to invest and to facilitate the producer's penetration of the market. In these cases, however, the focus is not so much on the type of pro-competitive agreement but on the risk faced by one of the parties to the agreement and the steps which must be taken to alleviate that risk.

The utility of this doctrine is also limited as a result of the Court's failure to push the argument to its logical conclusion and to accept that the protection of commercial risk may require that a distributor is given absolute territorial protection. In *STM* the Court was willing accept that a promise of exclusivity might be necessary to induce an undertaking to take on the responsibility of distribution. However, in *Consten and Grundig* the Court failed to accept that a distributor might only invest if intra-brand competition is completely eliminated within its territory.

P. Freeman and R. Whish (eds.), *Butterworths Competition Law* (Butterworths, looseleaf), Division I

[204]

It is questionable whether this aspect of the ECJ's case law is helpful. A common criticism of the application of Article 81(1) is that it causes delay and uncertainty: it is hard to see that greater certainty is provided by these cases which suggest that exclusivity may or may not infringe Article 81(1), depending on the extent of the commercial risk, the nature of the market, the novelty of a brand name or the technical characteristics of a particular product. It may be that the net effect of this reasoning is to take some agreements out of Article 81(1); in practical terms the important issue is whether it would be possible to say of any particular agreement whether it fell within the 'commercial risk' category. A further point about these cases is that the ECJ held in *Consten and Grundig* v. *Commission* . . . that it would not countenance absolute territorial protection for distributors: even when given an exclusive territory, there must always be the possibility of parallel imports . . .; the judgment in *Nungesser* v. *Commission*. . . adopted the same approach to absolute territorial protection for a licensee of plant breeders' rights. If the ECJ intended to embrace a totally economic approach to the application of Article 81(1) it could not adopt this formalistic rule: economically, absolute territorial protection might be commercially essential to a particular transaction. The ECJ's ultimate concern, however, is to ensure that private agreements do not compartmentalise the common market, and this issue will prevails over all others.

(iv) SELECTIVE DISTRIBUTION SYSTEMS

Selective distribution systems will be dealt with in greater detail in Chapter 9 below. It is important to point out at this stage, however, that the case law developed under Article 81 following *Metro (No1)* is different from that developed in relation to other vertical agreements. Both the Court and the Commission have accepted that selective distribution systems may fall outside Article 81(1) altogether. Nonetheless, the strict criteria which must be satisfied before an agreement can be held to escape Article 81(1) are hard to apply in practice and are difficult to explain on economic grounds.

(v) APPRAISAL OF AN AGREEMENT IN ITS LEGAL AND ECONOMIC CONTEXT: THE NEW ECONOMIC APPROACH

The ancillary restraints, commercial risk, and selective distribution cases show a willingness on the part of the Court to apply an economic approach when analysing agreements for their compatibility with Article 81.

J. Faull and A. Nikpay (eds.), *The EC Law of Competition* (Oxford University Press, 1999)

2.94 ... For example, in holding, in *Metro (No 1)*, that a particular type of distribution system which limited price competition could, in certain circumstances, fall outside the prohibition, the ECJ took into account the economic advantages of the system under Article 81(1). In doing so it implicitly balanced the potential pro- and anti-competitive effects of the system.

2.95 In fact, in a growing number of cases, the European Courts have looked beyond the negative elements of agreements in their analysis under Article 81(1) and have sought to determine what the actual or potential economic impact on the market of agreements hampering rivalry could be. For example, in *Breeders' rights—maize seed*, [[1978] OJ L286/23] the Commission had decided that by licensing a single undertaking to exploit a particular type of intellectual property in a given territory, the licensor had deprived itself for the duration of the contract of the ability to issue licences to other undertakings in the same territory, thereby eliminating them as competing suppliers. Further, by undertaking not to produce or market the product in the territory the licensor had likewise eliminated itself as a supplier in that territory. Applying its orthodox thinking, the Commission decided that competition was restricted by this agreement. This decision was challenged in *Nungesser* v. *Commission* . . . The Court adopted a different approach. While acknowledging that one form of competition might be restricted by such an agreement (ie that coming from other potential licensees or the licensor), the ECJ considered the overall impact of the agreement on competition. It found that an undertaking might be deterred from accepting the risk of entering the new market without the protection from competition offered by the exclusive territory, and found that 'such a result would be damaging to the dissemination of new technology and would prejudice competition in the Community between the new product and similar existing products' . . . It therefore held that an open exclusive licence of the sort under consideration did not fall within Article 81(1). In reaching this conclusion the Court was once again conducting a balancing exercise which has traditionally been undertaken under Article 81(3).

It was seen above that in *Delimitis* v. *Henninger Bräu* the ECJ expressly stated that before it could be determined whether or not the agreement restricted competition a full market analysis was necessary. The agreement had to be appraised in the legal and economic context within which it operated in order that it could be seen whether the retail outlets were foreclosed from a new entrant to the market or an incumbent undertaking wishing to expand its position on the market. Irrespective of the fact that the judgment in *Delimitis* dealt only with beer supply agreements it re-affirmed the need for an economic approach when determining the compatibility of an agreement with Article 81(1). The position adopted in this case by the Court thus reflects a very different philosophy from that underpinning its judgment in *Consten and Grundig* (also discussed above). Although the facts in *Delimitis* did not present such striking concerns from the single market perspective, the Court's focus shifted from restrictions on intra-brand competition to restrictions on interbrand competition. In the extract below Amato stresses the importance of this shift in emphasis when considering the compatibility of a distribution agreement with Article 81(1).

G. Amato, *Antitrust and the Bounds of Power* (Hart Publishing, 1997), 51–52

'[T]he court expressed itself in terms now almost the same as the American ones following *Sylvania* . . . It no longer made explicit reference to the need for intra-brand competition, and told the trial judge to verify carefully whether there was room for new entrants, bearing in mind that entry was harder in saturated markets in which, moreover, consumers were faithful to a limited number of big manufacturers. Attention was henceforth, as we see, entirely on inter-brand competition; it would seem to be the case that as long as it is there and in the absence of import bans, intra-brand restrictions are of much less interest.

There is, then, as in the USA, an evolutionary course. However, it is a different course, even though the outcome is similar. In Europe too the starting point was protection of intra-brand competition, but this was done, as we have noted, not in the name of individual freedom (the trader's), something always ignored with us, but to protect a principle, competitiveness in market integration, which with time would become increasingly less pressing and in any case generate a *per se* illegality, that of import restrictions. It was consequently not vertical agreements limiting intra-brand competition that were to be prohibited *per se* (except for price fixing, which was never to be permitted in this context), but only agreements containing that specific type of restriction.

Similarly, in the context of horizontal agreement the CFI in *European Night Services*[110] chastised the Commission for having failed to make an adequate assessment of the legal and economic context within which the agreements operated. It is arguable, therefore, that these two relatively recent cases are reflective of a new economic approach which requires a thorough examination of the agreement in its market context before it can be found to restrict competition within the meaning of Article 81(1).

J. Faull and A. Nikpay (eds.), *The EC Law of Competition* (Oxford University Press, 1999)

2.97 In *European Night Services* v. *Commission* . . . the undertakings concerned challenged a Commission decision grating them a conditional exemption for a limited period of time. The Court of First Instance annulled the Commission decision, finding that the Commission 'must be regarded as not having made a correct and adequate assessment in the contested decision of the economic and legal context in which the ENS agreements were concluded'. . . . During proceedings before the Court of First Instance, the applicants argued, inter alia, that as regards the overall assessment of the notified agreements:

> the Court of Justice has consistently held . . . that the pro-competitive effects of an agreement must be weighed up against its anti-competitive effects. If the pro-competitive effects outweigh the anti-competitive and the latter are necessary in order to implement the agreement, then the agreement cannot be regarded as having as its object or effect the prevention, restriction or distortion of competition within the common market within the meaning of Article 85(1) [now Article 81(1)] of the Treaty . . .

For its part the Commission challenged the argument that the case law cited by the applicants and the United Kingdom established that it was bound to apply a 'rule of reason' and to balance the competitive benefits and harms of an agreement under Article 81(1). The Commission argued that 'such an approach is required in the context of Article 85(3) [now Article 81(3)] of the Treaty but not in respect of the appraisal of restrictions of competition under Article [81(1)] . . .'.

2.98 In commenting on this issue the Court of First Instance chose its words very carefully, and appears to have left the door open for such a 'rule of reason' approach where restrictions by effect are involved. This, it is submitted, is because the Court in the last sentence of paragraph 136 of the judgment expressly excluded the weighing up of the pro-competitive effects of an agreement against its anti-competitive effects *only* where restrictions by object were involved.

If, as these cases suggest, a rigorous economic analysis is required under Article 81(1), the question arises, what is Article 81(3) for?

---

[110] Discussed *supra* at 175 ff.

3. ARTICLE 81(3) AND THE EXEMPTION PROCEDURE

A. GENERAL

(i) INDIVIDUAL AND GROUP EXEMPTIONS

The relationship between Article 81(1) and 81(3) has already been explained. Article 81(1) may be declared inapplicable to any agreement, decision of association of undertakings, or concerted practice, or to any category of them provided the criteria set out in Article 81(3) are satisfied. Exemptions can be granted *individually* (individual exemptions) or to *groups or categories* of agreements (block exemptions). Agreements which comply with the conditions set out in the Community block exemptions are automatically exempted from Article 81(1) without the need for notification.

An agreement which appears to infringe Article 81(1) and which does not fall within a block exemption must, as a general rule, be notified to the Commission before it can qualify for exemption. At present, the Commission alone has the right to grant exemption[111] and the general rule is that exemptions apply only from the date of notification. Certain 'non-notifiable' agreements may, however, be granted exemption retrospectively to the date that the agreement was concluded.[112]

The notification and exemption system has been unable to operate as originally envisaged in 1962 on the enactment of Regulation 17. The discussion in section 1 above set out how the Commission's broad interpretation of Article 81(1) has led to numerous notifications and an administrative log-jam. The volume of agreements potentially falling within Article 81(1) has forced the Commission to find ways of both discouraging notifications and dealing, other than by formal decision, with those notifications which it nonetheless receives. The difficulties still arising have finally prompted the Commission to propose modernizing the rules implementing Articles 81 and 82 by the complete abolition of the notification system and, to move instead to a fully directly applicable system.[113] This section describes the notification process as it exists at present. Section 4 below describes the Commission's proposals for reform.

(ii) ALL AGREEMENTS ARE ELIGIBLE FOR EXEMPTION

All agreements are, in theory, eligible for exemption under Article 81(3).[114] In practice, however, it will be rare for an agreement containing clauses which have as their object the restriction of competition to benefit from an exemption.[115]

---

[111] See *infra* 200.

[112] Reg. 17, [1959–62] OJ Spec. Ed. 87. Art. 4(2): see *infra* 210–211.

[113] White Paper on modernisation of the rules implementing Articles 85 and 86 [now 81 and 82] of the EC Treaty [1999] OJ C132/1, [1999] 5 CMLR 208: see *infra* 219 ff and Chap. 16. See also the Commission's proposal for a Reg. implementing Arts. 81 and 82 COM (2000) 582.

[114] Case T–17/93, *Matra Hachette v. Commission* [1994] ECR II–595.

[115] See *infra* 197.

B. THE INTERPRETATION AND APPLICATION OF ARTICLE 81(3)

(i) THE OBJECTIVES OF ARTICLE 81(3)

a. THE IMPACT OF ARTICLE 81(1)

The interpretation of the criteria set out in Article 81(3) of course relates to, and is affected by, the interpretation of the requirement in Article 81(1) that the agreement must restrict competition. In section 2 above it was seen that the bifurcation of Article 81 has had a profound effect on the interpretation of Article 81(1). The answer to the question 'what is Article 81(3) *for?*' is inevitably affected by the respondent's view of what Article 81(1) is for and which agreements it prohibits.

b. THE RULE OF REASON

In its White Paper the Commission states that Article 81(3) contains 'all the elements of a "rule of reason"'[116] and presents an ideal forum for the analysis of the pro- and anti-competitive aspects of an agreement.[117] The Commission's opinion is thus that Article 81(3) is intended 'to provide a legal framework for the economic assessment of restrictive practices and not to allow the application of the competition rules to be set aside because of political considerations'.[118]

c. SOCIO-POLITICAL FACTORS

If, however, it is correct that a vigorous economic assessment *is* required under Article 81(1) the Commission's view of Article 81(3) would leave it an extremely limited role. A question which consequently arises is whether Article 81(3) *may* or *should be* applied to exempt agreements on broader socio-political grounds. As the debate over the Commission's proposals in its White Paper develops, the answer to this question may come to be of critical importance. In particular, it may seem inappropriate to delegate the determination of socio-political issues to a multiplicity of different bodies, especially to national courts. Arguably, the balancing of the public and private interests and/or the conflicting Community policies required should be carried out by a public body (and with regard to the latter, a Community body), not a judicial one.

The suggestion that Article 81(3) should admit these types of factors is not of course welcomed by those who consider that economic efficiency should be the sole goal of competition rules.[119] A similar, ideological debate preceded the adoption of the EC Merger Regulation. Sir Leon Brittan the Commissioner for Competition at the time of the Merger Regulation's adoption was a strong proponent of the view that competition considerations

---

[116] White Paper on modernisation of the rules implementing Articles 85 and 86 [now 81 and 82] of the EC Treaty [1999] OJ C132/1, [1999] 5 CMLR 208, para. 57.

[117] See also discussion of the White Paper, *ibid.*, *infra* 219 ff.

[118] *Ibid.*, para. 56.

[119] See *supra* Chap. 1.

alone should affect the determination of whether or not a concentration should be permitted or prohibited. In the end this view appeared to prevail.[120]

However, the Court has been willing, when construing Treaty provisions, to adopt a teleological interpretation.[121] It is thus entirely conceivable that the four criteria set out in Article 81(3) might be interpreted broadly against the backdrop of the wider Community aims and objectives set out in Articles 2 and 3 of the Treaty to authorize agreements which provide benefits, for example, from a regional, social, environmental, cultural, and/or industrial perspective. In *Metro (No1)*,[122] for example, the ECJ seemed to affirm that employment was a relevant factor when assessing whether an agreement meets the criteria set out in Article 81(3).[123] Article 81(3) may, therefore, permit the admission of non-competition considerations.

Indeed, despite the Commission's robust view set out in the White Paper it will be seen from the discussion below there are a number of instances in which socio-political objectives appear to have impacted on decisions to exempt agreements pursuant to Article 81(3). The adherence by the Commission to the view set out in its White Paper that the purpose of Article 81(3) is only to provide a *rule of reason* may therefore seem difficult to reconcile with some of the decisions it has taken. The Commission's answer to this comment may be that non-competition issues are relevant only where an agreement in any event merits exemption from a competition perspective.[124] However, it may also be that the success of its proposals set out in the White Paper will be dependant on the assessment under Article 81(3) being confined to an examination of the agreement from an economic efficiency perspective. If Article 81(3) allows the weighing of broad socio-political issues the Member States may be reluctant to accept that this determination should be delegated to national authorities. Rather, it may be thought preferable that such a decision should be resolved centrally at the Community level.

(ii) SATISFACTION OF THE FOUR CRITERIA SET OUT IN ARTICLE 81(3)

Article 81(3) sets out four criteria, *all* of which must be satisfied if an exemption is to be granted.[125] The first two criteria are positive. The second two are negative. Whether or not 'non-competition' factors should intrude into the Article 81(3) analysis is of course dependent upon the interpretation of these four criteria.

---

[120] But see *infra* Chap. 12.

[121] See, e.g., Case 6/72, *Europemballage Corporation and Continental Can Co Inc* v. *Commission* [1973] ECR 215 (discussed *infra* Chap. 5) and Cases C–68/94 and 30/95, *France* v. *Commission* [1998] ECR I–1375, [1998] 4 CMLR 829 (discussed *infra* Chaps. 11 and 12).

[122] Case 26/76, *Metro-SB-Grossmärkte GmbH* v. *Commission (No 1)* [1977] ECR 1875, [1978] 2 CMLR 1, para. 43. See also, e.g., Case 42/84, *Remia and Nutricia* v. *Commission* [1985] ECR 2545, [1987] 1 CMLR 1, para. 42 and Case 136/86, *BNIC* v. *Yves Aubert* [1987] ECR 4789, [1988] 4 CMLR 331, paras. 20–21.

[123] See *infra* 193 ff.

[124] Case T–17/93, *Matra Hachette* v. *Commission* [1994] ECR II–595.

[125] Case T–528/93, *Métropole Télévision SA* v. *Commission* [1996] ECR II–649, [1996] 5 CMLR 386.

a. CRITERION 1: THE AGREEMENT MUST LEAD TO AN IMPROVEMENT IN THE PRODUCTION OR DISTRIBUTION OF GOODS OR THE PROMOTION OF TECHNICAL OR ECONOMIC PROGRESS

This provision is broad, enabling the Commission to authorize agreements which: (1) lead to an improvement in the production of goods or services;[126] (2) lead to an improvement in the distribution of goods or services; (3) promote technical progress; and/or (4) promote economic progress. The benefits referred to are not subjective ones that result to the parties to the agreement. Rather, the ECJ has stressed that the improvement must 'show appreciable objective advantages of such a character as to compensate for the disadvantages which they cause in the field of competition'.[127] Given the broad nature of these four categories, it is possible that more than one, and occasionally all, will be applicable in some cases.

It can be seen from these four categories that there should be little difficulty establishing that distribution and joint venture agreements satisfy this first criteria. Parties to research and development agreements, specialization agreements, and joint venture manufacturing agreements should be able establish that their agreement leads to the improvement in production of goods or services, for example by achieving efficiency, cost reduction, and/or improving the quality and choice of goods. These types of agreements will also frequently promote technical or economic progress by pooling skills and expertise, and/or by leading to rationalization, cost reduction, and/or by making the venture financially viable. In *Ford/Volkswagen*,[128] for example, the Commission held that the parties' creation of a joint venture company to develop and produce a multi-purpose vehicle ('MPV') in Portugal would improve the production of goods and promote technical development. It would rationalize product development and manufacturing and establish a new and modern manufacturing plant which would be using the latest production technology. In addition, the parties' pooling of technical knowledge would be converted into a significantly improved and innovative MPV. Similarly, many exclusive distribution, exclusive purchasing, franchising, selective distribution, and other distribution agreements will lead to improvements in the distribution of goods.

It also appears that the Commission has taken the view that certain industrial, social, and/or environmental factors may lead to an improvement in the production or distribution of goods or services and/or may contribute to technical and economic progress.

Social, Regional and Industrial Issues

In *Metro (No 1)* the ECJ took the view that employment was a matter which could be taken into account within the first criterion of Article 81(3). The agreement in question constituted 'a stabilizing factor with regard to the provision of employment which, since it improves the general conditions of production, especially when market conditions are unfavourable, comes within the framework of the objective to which reference may be had pursuant to Article [81(3)]'.[129]

---

[126] Although Art. 81(3) does not make specific reference to services, services are covered by analogy: see *P&I Clubs* [1985] OJ L376/2.

[127] Cases 56 & 58/64, *Etablissements Consten SA & Grundig-Verkaufs-GmbH* v. *Commission* [1966] ECR 299, 348 [1966] CMLR 418.

[128] [1993] OJ L20/14, [1993] 5 CMLR 617.

[129] Case 26/76 Metro-SB-Grossmärkte GmbH v Commission (No 1) [1977] ECR 1857, [1978] 2 CMLR 1, para. 43.

In a wider social context,[130] the Commission in *Ford/Volkswagen*[131] noted, in exempting the agreement, that the joint venture would lead to the creation of a number of jobs and substantial foreign investment in one of the poorest regions of the Community.[132]

36. In the assessment of this case, the Commission also takes note of the fact that the project constitutes the largest ever single foreign investment in Portugal. It is estimated to lead, *inter alia*, to the creation of about 5 000 jobs and indirectly create up to another 10 000 jobs, as well as attracting other investment in the supply industry. It therefore contributes to the promotion of the harmonious development of the Community and the reduction of regional disparities which is one of the basic aims of the Treaty. It also furthers European market integration by linking Portugal more closely to the Community through one of its important industries. This would not be enough to make an exemption possible unless the conditions of Article [81(3)] were fulfilled, but it is an element which the Commission has taken into account.

Although the Commission emphasized that these broader factors would not have caused the agreement to merit an exemption had the other conditions of Article 81(3) not been fulfilled,[133] the Competition Commissioner and other Commission officials subsequently admitted that these factors were relevant to its final decision.[134] Further, in an appeal from this decision the Commission argued that it was possible, when determining whether the agreement contributed to technical and economic progress,[135] to take into account factors such as the maintenance of employment.[136] Arguably, this decision is difficult to justify on pure efficiency grounds and it symbolizes the infiltrations of other policy objectives into EC competition law.[137]

In a series of decisions, the Commission has also exempted agreements concluded between competitors which seek to ensure an orderly reduction of capacity between the undertakings which were operating in an industry in crisis.[138] In *Synthetic Fibres*, for example, the Commission, in authorizing an agreement between competitors to reduce capacity, accepted that the decision to embark on an orderly reduction in output satisfied the first criteria of Article 81(3).[139]

In a free market economy it ought to be principally a matter for the individual undertaking to judge the point at which overcapacity becomes economically unsustainable and to take the necessary steps

---

[130] J. Faull and A. Nikpay (eds.), *The EC Law of Competition* (Oxford University Press, 1999), paras. 2.130–2.131.

[131] [1993] OJ L20/14, [1993] 5 CMLR 617.

[132] The Commission found that the agreement would promote harmonious development, reduce regional disparities, and contribute to the integration of the European market [1993] OJ L20/14, [1993] 5 CMLR 617, paras 23, 28, and 36; see also the Commission Press Release IP/92/1083 of 23 Dec. 1992.

[133] [1993] OJ L20/14, [1993] 5 CMLR 617, para. 36.

[134] See *supra* n. 132.

[135] See *supra* n. 129.

[136] Case T–17/93, *Matra Hachette v. Commission* [1994] ECR II–595, para. 96. The CFI considered that as the four criteria were fulfilled, apart from the 'exceptional circumstances' there was no defect in the Decision.

[137] See G. Amato, *Antitrust and the Bounds of Power* (Hart Publishing, Oxford, 1997), 58–63, and *infra* Chap. 13.

[138] Further, it is arguable that provisions in the Commission's specialization block exemption, which accept that production rationalization fulfils the Art. 81(3) criteria, reflect industrial policy rather than competition thinking: G. Amato, *Antitrust and the Bounds of Power* (Hart Publishing, 1997), 63–64. In the early days competition policy was influenced by industrial policy to a greater extent than it is now. Note that Art. 157 (ex Art. 130, introduced by the Maastricht Treaty) states that the Community's industrial policy is to be conducted 'in accordance with a system of open and competitive markets'.

[139] [1984] OJ L207/17, [1985] 1 CMLR 787, paras 30–31.

to reduce it . . . In the present case, however, market forces by themselves had failed to achieve the capacity reductions necessary to re-establish and maintain in the longer term an effective competitive structure within the common market. The producers concerned therefore agreed to organise for a limited period and collectively, the needed structural adjustment.

The Commission recognized that ordinarily individual undertakings should make their own decision about reduction in capacity. However, in this case market forces had not achieved the reductions necessary. The agreement would enable the establishment and maintenance in the long term of effective competitive structures and would improve technical efficiency by enabling the undertakings to specialize. The eventual result would be to raise profitability and restore competitiveness. The 'coordination of plant closures will also make it easier to cushion the social effects of the restructuring by making suitable arrangements for the retraining and redeployment of workers made redundant. It can be concluded then that the agreement contributes to improving production and promoting technical and economic progress'.[140]

Similarly, in *Stichting Baksteen*[141] the Commission, when exempting an agreement for the restructuring of the Dutch brick industry, took account of the fact that the agreement allowed the restructuring to be carried out in acceptable social conditions and in a way which would lead to the redeployment of employees. The Commission held that the social advantages resulting to employees would promote economic progress for the purposes of Article 81(3).[142]

Environmental issues

In *Exxon/Shell*[143] the Commission held that a reduction in pollution would lead to a technological improvement for the purposes of Article 81(3). Further, in *The European Council of Manufacturers of Domestic Appliances*[144] the Commission exempted an agreement concluded between 95 per cent of the producers and importers of washing machines on the EU market which restricted the freedom of these manufacturers and importers to manufacture or import the least energy-efficient washing machines. Although the Commission concluded that this agreement restricted competition under Article 81(1),[145] it considered that, on balance, the agreement would bring about important benefits and savings to the consumer, particularly with regard to the reduction of polluting emissions from electricity generation. Upon approval by the Commission the Competition Commissioner, Mario Monti declared:

When I took office as Commissioner responsible for Competition, I stressed before the European Parliament that environmental concerns are in no way contradictory with competition policy. This decision clearly illustrates this principle, enshrined in the Treaty, provided that *restrictions of competition are proportionate and necessary to achieving the environmental objectives aimed at*, to the benefit of current and future generations [emphasis added].[146]

---

[140] *Ibid*, paras. 37 and 38.
[141] [1994] OJ L131/15, [1995] 4 CMLR 646.
[142] *Ibid.*, paras 27–28.
[143] [1994] OJ L144/20
[144] IP/00/148. See also *EACEM* [1998] OJ C12/2. The Commission issued an Art. 19(3) Notice setting out its intention to take a favourable view under Art. 81 of a notified agreement concluded between certain members of EACEM, an organization representing the European consumer electronics industry.
[145] It would result in a reduction of choice for consumers since fewer, cheaper washing machines would be on the market.
[146] IP/00/148.

This decision thus reflects the sentiment expressed in the Commission's *XXVth Report on Competition Policy* (1995) that 'in its scrutiny of individual cases pursuant to Article [81(3)] ... it weighs up the restrictions on competition that result from the agreement and the environmental objectives to be attained'.[147] Indeed, the Treaty of Amsterdam has now increased the European's Union commitment to the environment.[148] It thus seems likely that environmental issues will, if anything, be given 'greater weight by the Commission when it considers the applicability of Article 81(3) to agreements with an impact on the environment'.[149]

Safety considerations

It also seems that the production of a product which increases safety for a consumer may constitute a technical improvement.[150]

b. CRITERION 2: ALLOWING CONSUMERS A FAIR SHARE OF THE RESULTING BENEFIT

The parties must also establish that the agreement allows consumers a fair share of the benefit. This criterion relates closely to both the first and the fourth criteria of Article 81(3). The benefit to the consumer referred to here is the same objective benefit which must be established to satisfy the first criterion (the improvement in production or distribution or the technical and economic progress).

Further, the more intense the competition the more willing the Commission is to conclude that the resulting benefits will accrue to the consumer. So long as the first and fourth criteria are satisfied, therefore, it is often assumed that this condition has been satisfied.

Consumer

Consumer is interpreted broadly to include not only final consumers but also intermediate consumers that purchase products in the course of their trade or business.[151]

Fair share

The Commission has not given a precise definition of when a consumer may be said to receive a 'fair share' of any resultant benefit. It instead retains a wide discretion to refuse an exemption where it appears that the consumer will not derive sufficient or any benefit from the agreement. Some agreements have been refused an exemption on the ground that consumers will not receive a fair share of the benefit. For example, in *VBBB and VBVB*[152] the Commission held that the consumers would not benefit from the parties' agreement to fix the retail prices of books. On the contrary, consumers would be forced to pay a higher price and would be deprived of the opportunity to pay lower prices.

---

[147] SEC(1997)628.

[148] EC Treaty, Art. 6.

[149] J. Faull and A. Nikpay (eds), *The EC Law of Competition* (Oxford University Press, 1999), 2.145.

[150] *BMW* [1978] OJ L46/33.

[151] *Kabel und Metallwerke Neumeyer AG and Etablissements Luchaire SA Agreement* [1975] OJ L222/34, [1975] CMLR D40.

[152] [1982] OJ L54/36, [1982] 2 CMLR 344, *aff'd.* in Cases 43, 63/82, *VBVB and VBBB* v. *Commission* [1984] ECR 19, [1985] 1 CMLR 27.

Similarly the Commission will refuse an exemption if the agreement is clearly designed to restrict competition and force consumers to pay a higher price for products in the absence of other compensating benefits. In *SPO and others* v. *Commission*,[153] for example, the CFI heard an appeal against the Commission's refusal of an exemption to a Dutch building association. The purpose of the agreement in question was to protect the members from ruinous competition. The Court upheld the Commission's decision stating that 'by taking action to counteract what they regard as ruinous competition, the applicants necessarily restrict competition and therefore deprive consumers of its benefits'.[154]

In contrast, however, to the decision it took in *SPO* the Commission in *Synthetic Fibres* concluded that consumers would benefit from an agreement between competitors on a market to reduce capacity. Although prices might rise initially, there was sufficient competition on the market and considerable countervailing purchasing power to limit these increases. Further, the agreement would result in a healthier more competitive industry in the long run.[155]

c. CRITERION 3: INDISPENSABLE RESTRICTIONS

An agreement which satisfies the first two positive criteria set out in Article 81(3) will not be exempted unless the restrictions contained within it are indispensable to the achievement of the benefits of the agreement. The Commission expends much effort ensuring that agreements are not more restrictive than they need to be to achieve their accepted benefits. This requirement thus has similarities to the ancillary restraints doctrine. Under that doctrine restraints which are essential to the operation of a particular pro-competitive agreement are held not to restrict competition at all. In this context, restrictions necessary to achieve the benefits of an agreement are 'indispensable' to its operation and so exempted from Article 81(1) pursuant to Article 81(3). Thus restrictive clauses in a franchise agreement will be accepted if necessary to encourage the franchisee to incur the expenditure involved in setting up the franchise.[156] Further, a joint venture agreement may be indispensable to the parties rapid and efficient entry to the market.[157]

It is rare, however, for provisions which are 'restrictive by object' or for hard-core restraints prohibited in the block exemptions to be held indispensable.

J. Faull and A. Nikpay (eds.), *The EC Law of Competition* (Oxford University Press, 1999)

2.167 As in many other areas of competition law, however, it is difficult, a priori, to determine whether a particular clause would be considered to be indispensable. Even the most restrictive provisions can, in the right circumstances, be indispensable. Two categories of restrictions will, almost invariably, fail to fulfil this criterion. The first are those which are restrictive by object. For example, absolute territorial protection will, almost certainly, not be considered indispensable, even if the parties were to bring forward convincing arguments

---

[153] Case T–29/92 [1992] ECR II–289.
[154] *Ibid*, para. 294.
[155] [1984] OJ L207/17, [1985] 1 CMLR 787, paras. 39–41.
[156] See *Computerland* [1987] OJ L222/12.
[157] See, e.g. *Ford/Volkswagen* [1993] OJ L20/14, [1993] 5 CMLR 617, and *infra* Chap. 13.

showing that major benefits would flow from the provision for the European economy. The single market imperative would trump such arguments. The second are clauses which appear on the black lists in the various block exemptions the Commission has adopted. Indeed, perusal of these black lists is often a good starting point for determining whether the Commission is likely to decide that a particular clause is indispensable.

The Commission[158] declined an exemption to the net book agreement concluded between members of the Publishers' Association partly on the ground that the restrictions involved in the collective agreement to fix prices were not indispensable to the operation of the agreement. In this case, however, the ECJ quashed the Commission's decision.[159] The Commission had failed to consider properly the argument of the applicants and to determine whether or not the restrictions were indispensable to the attainment of the objectives.

The Commission has, however, occasionally accepted that horizontal restrictions by object relating, for example, to capacity are indispensable to the successful operation of an agreement. In *Synthetic Fibres* the Commission insisted that the parties deleted all clauses restricting the parties' freedom to determine their output or deliveries. Having done this it was accepted that the clauses providing for the reduction of excess capacity over a limited period were indispensable to the achievement of the capacity cuts.

The black lists of the block exemptions provide useful guidance on the type of provisions that the Commission considers are dispensable and not essential to achieving the benefits produced by a particular type of agreement. For example, in the context of vertical agreements the Commission will not generally accept that a restriction on the distributor's freedom to determine prices is indispensable to the successful distribution system;[160] nor that the conferment of absolute territorial protection on a distributor is indispensable to the operation of, for example, an exclusive distribution agreement. However, it ordinarily permits a producer to protect an exclusive distributor within a territory from active selling by other distributors.[161] The Commission may not, therefore, allow a restriction which appears indispensable to achieving the benefits of the agreement if those benefits can be achieved through the adoption of less restrictive clauses. In *P&O Stena Line* the Commission granted an exemption to a joint venture which combined the parties' services on a particular ferry route. It accepted the argument that less restrictive alternatives, such as joint scheduling, or pooling, would not enable the parties to achieve the benefits, such as cost savings and increased frequency in service, of their joint venture.

d. CRITERION 4: THE AGREEMENT MUST NOT AFFORD THE PARTIES THE POSSIBILITY OF SUBSTANTIALLY ELIMINATING COMPETITION

The last requirement is that the agreement as a whole must not lead to the substantial elimination of competition. The agreement is likely to substantially eliminate competition if, as a result of the agreement, the parties will acquire market power.[162] A definition of the relevant market (product and geographic) will therefore be an essential prerequisite to a

---

[158] [1989] OJ L22/12.

[159] Case C–360/90P, *Publishers' Association* v. *Commission* [1995] ECR I–23, [1995] 5 CMLR 33.

[160] Reg. 2790/1999 [1990] OJ L336/21, Art. 4 (a).

[161] See Reg. 1983/83 [1983] OJ L173/1, Arts. 2 and 3 and Reg. 2790/1999, Arts 4 (b)–(d).

[162] The more restrictive the terms of the agreement between the parties the more eager the Commission is likely to be to see vigorous competition on the market as a whole.

determination under this fourth criterion.[163] Broadly, the larger the combined market share of the parties involved, the more likely that competition will be found to have been eliminated. Other factors, such as barriers to entry and the size and strength of competitors, will of course also be relevant to the assessment. In certain decisions relating to crisis cartels the Commission has, occasionally, exempted agreements concluded between undertakings with a large share of the relevant market.[164]

e. CONCLUSIONS

It appears from the decisions that the primary concern of the Commission in granting exemptions has been the impact of the agreement on competition in the relevant market. However, cases such as *Ford/Volkswagen* and *Synthetic Fibres* establish that the Commission's decision to exempt an agreement may in some circumstances be prompted or affected by the social and/or industrial benefits resulting from the agreement. Further, in some decisions the environmental benefits flowing from an agreement have caused the Commission to look favourably upon it.[165] There have also been a number of other instances in which sporting and cultural issues have been relevant to the Commission's assessment under Article 81(3). The Commission, when considering whether to exempt an agreement concerning the collective selling of broadcasting rights for football, may be willing to extend the analysis beyond 'simple economic considerations'. The agreement might lead to the redistribution of revenue which would 'promote sporting activities within the population, as well as providing for interesting sporting competitions . . . it must be stressed that these commendable aims, . . . would, under no circumstances, serves as a pretext, or as a justification, to prevent the a priori application of Community competition law'.[166] Further, in a case concerning fixed book prices between Germany and Austria Commissioner Monti announced that the solution reached was also fully supported by the Commissioner for Culture and Education 'with whom I have maintained regular contacts on this matter'.[167]

(iii) BURDEN OF PROOF

The onus is on the parties to prove that their agreement fulfils the criteria set out in Article 81(3).[168] The parties are, however, 'entitled to appropriate examination by the Commission

---

[163] See *supra* Chap. 1. A decision of the Commission is likely to be annulled if the market has not been defined adequately: see, e.g., Cases 19 & 20/74, *Kali und Salz AG* v. *Commission* [1975] ECR 499, [1975] 2 CMLR 154.

[164] See, e.g., *Synthetic Fibres* [1984] OJ L207/17, [1985] 1 CMLR 787 and *Bayer/ BP Chemicals* [1988] OJ L150/35, [1989] 4 CMLR 24.

[165] See *supra* 193 ff.

[166] See J.-F. Pons, 'Sport and European Competition Policy', 26th Fordham Corporate Law Institute, 14–15 Oct. 1999, 17. After proceedings in the UK's Restrictive Practices Court on the selling of broadcasting rights by the Premier League, *Re the Football Association Premier League Ltd* (28 July 1999) the Commission asked the parties to notify the agreements.

[167] IP/00/183 of 23 Feb. 2000. The German Government requested the Commission to consider cultural policy when assessing the compatibility of the resale price maintenance scheme for German-language books with the Treaty competition rules. The Council of Ministers has made the same point, see the Council Resolution on fixed book prices in homogeneous cross-border linguistic areas [1999] OJ C42/3.

[168] [1982] OJ L54/36, [1982] 2 CMLR 344, *aff'd.* Cases 43, 63/82, *VBVB and VBBB* v. *Commission* [1984] ECR 19, [1985] 1 CMLR 27.

of their requests for Article [81(3)] to be applied. For this purpose the Commission may not confine itself to requiring from undertakings proof of the fulfilment of the requirements for the grant of the exemption but must, as a matter of good administration, play its part, using the means available to it, in ascertaining the relevant facts and circumstances.'[169]

C. OBTAINING AN INDIVIDUAL EXEMPTION

(i) THE COMMISSION'S MONOPOLY OVER INDIVIDUAL EXEMPTIONS

Article 9(1) of Regulation 17[170] confers 'sole power' on the Commission 'to declare Article [81(1)] inapplicable pursuant to Article [81(3)] of the Treaty'.

(ii) THE NEED FOR NOTIFICATION

Article 4(1) of Regulation 17 provides that parties to an agreement seeking an exemption for their agreement must notify it to the Commission. Until they do so, no decision pursuant to Article 81(3) can be taken. The combination of Article 4(2) and Article 6(2), however, means that certain agreements, in particular, vertical agreements, can be exempted retrospectively to the date that the agreement was concluded irrespective of whether they have or have not been notified.[171] Agreements may also be notified for 'negative clearance' viz. a decision finding that an agreement does not infringe Article 81(1) at all.[172]

This centralized authorization system has meant that the Commission has had the opportunity to develop its own policy towards agreements.[173] However, it has also been the cause of the Commission's inundation with notifications. The Commission has not had the resources to deal formally with these. Further, the time devoted to notifications has meant that the Commission has been diverted from other more pressing concerns. We have already outlined some of the steps taken by the Commission in response to this problem.

An important response has been the adoption of a number of regulations or 'block exemptions' exempting certain categories of agreements from the application of Article 81(1).[174] Because agreements falling within the terms of a block exemption are exempted without any need for notification, these regulations have significantly reduced the number of notifications received by the Commission. The regulations have had considerable draw-

---

[169] Cases 56 & 58/64, *Etablissements Consten SA & Grundig-Verkaufs-GmbH* v. *Commission* [1966] ECR 299, [1966] CMLR 418.

[170] [1959–62] OJ Spec. Ed. 87.

[171] Non-notifiable agreements are defined in Reg. 17 [1959–62] OJ Spec. Ed. 87, Art. 4(2). This was initially a restricted category of agreements. However, in June 1999, as part of the reform of the policy towards vertical restraints, Art. 4(2) was amended by Reg. 1216/99 [1999] OJ 4148/5, and now covers all vertical agreements which 'relate to the conditions under which the parties may purchase, sell or resell certain goods or services': see *infra* 210–211 and Chap. 9.

[172] Reg 17, Art. 2. Negative clearance may also be sought in respect of Art. 82.

[173] See *supra* 143–145.

[174] Although some of these block exemptions are set out in Council Regs. the majority of the regs. have been adopted by the Commission once the Council has delegated authority to it to do so: see *infra* 214 ff.

backs, however. In particular, they have been criticized because of the limitations they have imposed on parties during the drafting of their agreements.

The Commission has also issued a number of notices and guidelines setting out when, in its view, agreements do not infringe Article 81(1) at all. These clarifications have been intended to provide guidance to undertakings and to encourage them to determine for themselves whether or not an agreement falls within Article 81(1). Again their objective has been to reduce the number of notifications that the Commission receives. The Commission's Notice on agreements of minor importance is discussed above and in Chapter 3.[175]

A third response has been to try and find a way to deal with the numerous notifications which are nonetheless made. In a majority of these cases the Commission does not proceed by formal decision.[176] Instead, it has had to resort to the issue of administrative letters, known as 'comfort' or 'discomfort' letters. The issue of a comfort letter does not require the Commission to comply with the lengthy procedures set out in Regulation 17 which must be followed prior to the issue of a formal decision. They can, consequently, be issued much more quickly. The drawback, however, is that since they are issued informally, the Commission does not rule formally on the compatibility of the agreement with Article 81 and the status of the agreement involved remains uncertain.[177]

(iii) NEGATIVE CLEARANCE

As well as notification for an exemption, parties to an agreement may 'apply' to the Commission for negative clearance. Application must be made in the format prescribed by Form A/B (described below). Article 2 of Regulation 17 provides:

Upon application by the undertakings or associations of undertakings concerned, the Commission may certify that, on the basis of the facts in its possession, there are no grounds under Article [81(1)] or Article [82] of the Treaty for action on its part in respect of an agreement, decision or practice.

The scope of the provision is limited, however. It simply authorizes the Commission to issue a decision stating its view that, on the facts before it, the agreement does not fall within Article 81(1) at all. It seems that this conclusion would not bind a national court which would remain free to adopt a different view of the facts. Further, the Commission itself might take a different view if the facts changed, for example, were a party to the agreement to conclude further transactions with third parties which changed the context in which the original agreement operated.[178]

One of the chief criticisms made of the Commission's approach to Article 81 has been its failure to take decisions granting negative clearance. However, a full negative clearance decision requires, in the same way as an exemption decision, the initiation of a formal procedure and adherence to the strict criteria set out in Regulation 17. In particular, the

---

[175] See *supra* Chap. 3 and the Notice on co-operation agreements [1968] OJ C75/3; the Notice on subcontracting agreements [1979] OJ C1/2: and the Notice on the assessment of co-operative joint ventures [1993] OJ C43/2. See also Guidelines on Vertical Restraints [2000] OJ C291/1 (discussed *infra* in Chap. 9) and the draft Guidelines on Horizontal Co-operation (discussed *infra* in Chap. 13).

[176] It proceeds to a formal decision in only approximately 10% of cases.

[177] See *infra* Chap. 14.

[178] See C. Kerse, *EC Antitrust Procedure* (4th edn.,) (Sweet & Maxwell, London, 1998), 2.05.

Commission must publish a notice in the Official Journal[179] and invite third parties to make observations. The fact that the Commission has restricted resources combined with the limited nature of a negative clearance has meant that it 'issues negative clearances only where an important problem of interpretation has to be solved'.[180] In other cases, it tends to send a comfort letter instead. A comfort letter stating the Commission's view that an agreement does not fall within Article 81(1) at all is, in practice, as valuable to the parties as a formal decision to this effect.[181]

Application for negative clearance, unlike notification for exemption, does not confer immunity from fines under Regulation 17, Article 15(5).

Negative clearance can also be applied for within the context of Article 82. However, such applications are rare, mainly because Article 82 contains no exemption procedure (in contrast, applications for negative clearance under Article 81 are almost invariably made in conjunction with, and as an alternative to, a notification for exemption under Article 81(3)).

(iv) NOTIFICATION FOR INDIVIDUAL EXEMPTION

a. GENERAL

When notifying an agreement it will be necessary for the parties and the Commission to comply with the requisite procedure. The procedures which are applicable are partly dependent, however, upon the sector within which the agreement operates. Council Regulation 17 is the regulation which has general application and which authorizes most of the Commission's enforcement activity. Regulation 3385/94 is the procedural regulation which sets out more specifically how notifications and/or applications for individual exemption and/or negative clearance should be made.[182] Another regulation governs notification in the sphere of transport.[183]

b. PRE-NOTIFICATION DISCUSSIONS

The Commission encourages undertakings contemplating notification of an agreement to have pre-notification discussions with it. The recitals to Regulation 3385/94 state that 'the Commission, in appropriate cases, will give the parties, if they so request, an opportunity before the application or notification to discuss the intended agreement, decision or practice informally and in strict confidence'.

c. FORM A/B

Notification for individual exemption is not obligatory, but a notification, if submitted, must be made in the format prescribed by Form A/B (within the sphere of transport the

---

[179] Reg. 17, Art. 19(3).

[180] Form A/B, para. A.II.I.

[181] See *infra* 212–213.

[182] Antitrust Procedure (Applications and Notifications) Reg. 3385/94 [1994] OJ L377/28, [1995] 5 CMLR 507, replacing Reg. 27/62 [1959–62] OJ Spec. Ed. 132 as amended.

[183] Reg 2843/98 [1998] OJ L354/22 which adopted a single form for notification of agreements within the transport sector.

form is Form TR[184]).[185] Use of the prescribed format is essential. The importance of notifying correctly is illustrated by *Distillers*.[186] In this case the ECJ declined to consider the merits of the undertaking's arguments in an appeal from a controversial Commission decision refusing an exemption. The ECJ upheld the Commission's view that there had been no valid notification because the undertaking had not used Form A/B to inform it of changes to an agreement which had already been notified. The submission of information, for example, in response to a Commission request for information[187] does not constitute notification.[188]

Form A/B is not actually a form which simply has to be 'filled in'.[189] It is a 'pattern', prescribing the information that has to be provided under set section and paragraph numbers. Section 2 requires information about the parties to the agreement:

2.1. State the name and address of the parties to the agreement being notified, and the country of their incorporation.

2.2. State the nature of the business of each of the parties to the agreement being notified.

2.3. For each of the parties to the agreement, give the name of a person that can be contacted, together with his or her name, address, telephone number, fax number and position held in the undertaking.

2.4. Identify the corporate groups to which the parties to the agreement being notified belong. State the sectors in which these groups are active, and the worldwide turnover of each group.

The form also requires extensive information about the agreement and the relevant markets (product and geographic) on which the agreement is to operate. Obviously this information is required in order to enable the Commission to determine whether or not the agreement infringes Article 81(1) and whether the four criteria in Article 81(3) are satisfied. It has been seen that the assessment under both Article 81(1) and Article 81(3) requires an appreciation of the legal and economic context of the agreement. Section 14 thus requests information about 'the position of competitors and customers on the relevant product market(s)':

14.1. Please identify the competitors of the parties on the relevant product market(s) that have a market share exceeding 10% in any EC Member State, EFTA State, in the territory of the EFTA States, in the EEA, or world-wide. Please identify the company and give your best estimate as to their market share in these geographic areas. Please also provide the address, telephone and fax numbers, and, where possible, the name of a contact person at each company identified.

14.2. Please describe the nature of demand on the relevant product market(s). For example, are there few or many purchasers, are there different categories of purchasers, are government agencies or departments important purchasers?

14.3. Please identify the five largest customers of each of the parties for each *relevant product*

---

[184] Reg. 2843/98. Form TR(B) applies to crisis cartels under Reg. 1017/68 [1968] OJ Spec. Ed. 302.

[185] Set out in Reg. 3385/94, *supra* n. 182.

[186] Case 30/78, *Distillers* v. *Commission* [1980] ECR 2229, [1980] 3 CMLR 121. See *infra* Chapter 9.

[187] Reg. 17, Art. 11: see *infra* Chap. 14.

[188] Cases 209–215 & 218/78, *Heintz van Landewyck* v. *Commission (Fedetab)* [1980] ECR 3125, [1981] 3 CMLR 134.

[189] Prior to the adoption of Reg. 3385/94 [1994] OJ L377/28, it was actually a form which had to be filled in, although after 1985 the form to be completed was quite short and the other documentation required had to be attached to it.

market(s). State company name, address, telephone and fax numbers, together with the name of a contact person.

If the notifying parties are unable to supply all the detailed information required, they must explain why this is so. They must not just ignore the question. Fines can be imposed pursuant to Article 15(2) of Regulation 17 where incorrect or misleading information has been provided on a notification. In addition, an exemption decision based on incorrect information may be revoked.[190] The Commission does, however, have a discretion to dispense with the obligation to provide any particular information.[191] Business secrets and other confidential information should be put 'in a separate annex with each page clearly marked "Business Secrets"'.[192] If a notification is made jointly the parties to the agreement can each put their confidential information in a separate annex.

The submitted notification has to contain on the first page the words 'Application for negative clearance/notification in accordance with Form A/B'. Seventeen copies,[193] including the latest (or final) version of all the agreements which are the subject of the notification, have to be submitted (one for the Commission, each of the Member States, and the EFTA Surveillance Authority). However, it is necessary to supply only three copies of certain supporting documentation such as the annual reports and accounts of all the parties for the last three years (Section 18).

d. NOTIFICATION BY PARTIES TO THE AGREEMENT

Only a party to an agreement may submit a notification.[194] If the notification is not submitted by all of the parties notice must be given to the others that notification is being made.[195] Article 2(4) of Regulation 3385/94 states that notification must be in one of the official languages of the Community. That language then becomes the language of the proceedings. Accompanying documentation must be in its original language and where that is not an official language, a translation into the language of the proceedings must be attached.

e. TIME LIMITS

There is no time limit within which the Commission must issue a decision following notification. This is striking, especially when the position is contrasted with the position of the Commission when dealing with notifications of 'concentrations' pursuant to the Merger Regulation. The Merger Regulation sets out an extremely strict timetable within which the Commission must deal with the notifications.[196] After this regulation came into force, the length of time which the Commission took in dealing with Article 81 notifications was highlighted. The difference in treatment has been particularly controversial within the con-

---

[190] Reg. 17, Art. 8(3

[191] Reg. 3385/94, Art. 3(3).

[192] Reg. 3385/94, Form A/B, Introduction Section I. See *infra* Chap. 14 for the protection of business secrets generally.

[193] *Ibid.*, Art. 2(1).

[194] Or applications for negative clearance.

[195] Reg. 3385/94, Art. 1. The Commission accepts in n. 1 to Chap. 1 of Form A/B that sometimes this may be impossible, for example where the notification of a standard form agreement is being notified.

[196] The only requirement under Reg. 17 is that the Commission must act within a reasonable time, Cases T–213195 and T–18/96, *SCK and FNK* v. *Commission*, para. 56, [1997] ECR II–1739, [1997] 4 CMLR 259 Reg. 4064/89 [1989] OJ L395/1. See *infra* Chap. 12.

text of joint venture agreements, some of which fall to be assessed within the framework of the Merger Regulation and some of which fall to be assessed within the framework of Article 81. In particular, it has been perceived that joint ventures falling to be assessed under the Merger Regulation (those characterized as 'concentrative') receive favourable treatment. One of the reasons for this is that most concentrations notified under the merger regime receive a formal decision within one month of notification (or within five months at the longest). In contrast, those which made notifications under Article 81 were likely to wait at least eighteen months just to receive a comfort letter.

The Commission has attempted to deal with some of the unsatisfactory distinctions by introducing a 'fast-track' procedure for the treatment of 'structural joint ventures' falling within Article 81. Broadly, since 1993 the Commission has promised[197] to inform the parties within *two months* of notification of the results of its initial analysis of the case. This time-limit is not binding, however, but is 'based entirely on the principle of self-discipline'.[198] Those who wish to take advantage of the accelerated procedure have to provide more extensive and detailed information on notification.[199] This procedure is now dealt with in Regulation 3385/94.

f. THE ADVANTAGES OF NOTIFICATION

Article 4(1) of Regulation 17 requires that, save where Article 4(2) applies, notification must occur prior to a decision in application of Article 81(3) being taken.[200] Article 15(5) of Regulation 17 provides those that notify with immunity from fines. The Commission can, however, lift immunity under Article 15(6) following a preliminary examination of the agreement by the Commission.

Paragraph 5 shall not have effect where the Commission has informed the undertakings concerned that after preliminary examination it is of the opinion that Article [81(1)] of the Treaty applies and that application of [Article 81(3)] is not justified.

A withdrawal of immunity from fines amounts to a *decision* because it changes the parties' legal position. Thus the ECJ held in *Cimenteries* that:[201]

[t]his measure deprived [the parties] of the advantages of a legal situation which Article 15(5) attached to the notification of the agreement, and exposed them to a grave financial risk. Thus the said measure affected the interests of the undertakings by bringing about a distinct change in their legal position. It is unequivocally a measure which produces legal effects touching the interests of the undertakings concerned and which is binding on them. It thus constitutes not a mere opinion but a decision.

Consequently, the Commission has to follow the procedures which are required prior to the adoption of a decision. For example, it must make its case known, issue a Statement of objections and give the parties a right to reply.[202] Although the Commission does not hold

---

[197] Reg. 3385/94, Form A/B, Introduction, Section D.

[198] Reg. 4064/89 sets out time limits which must be strictly adhered to. Since 1997 a wider category of joint ventures have been brought within the procedural framework of the Merger Reg.: see the amendments made by Reg. 1310/97 [1997] OJ L180/1, discussed *infra* in Chaps. 12 and 13. See *infra* Chap. 12.

[199] See Form A/B, Chap. III.

[200] See *supra* n. 171 and accompanying text.

[201] Cases 8–11/66 *Cimenteries* v. *Commission* [1967] ECR 75, [1967] CMLR 77, para. 4; see also Case 10/69, *Portelange SA* v. *Smith Corona Marchant International SA* [1969] ECR 309, [1974] 1 CMLR 397.

[202] For the right of the parties to know the case against them and to be heard, see *infra* Chap. 14.

an oral hearing prior to making such a decision, it is possible that the parties are entitled to one.[203] Article 15(6) decisions are rare, but were taken, for example, in *TACA*[204] and prior to the Commission's decision fining parties to a crane-hire cartel.[205]

There is no duty to notify only a duty not to infringe the rules.[206] It may be, therefore, that despite the possibility of an exemption and the immunity from fines parties to an agreement may take a commercial decision not to notify, for example, where the likelihood of litigation being commenced by one of the parties or a third party is perceived to be low.[207] The huge burden that the notification process involves, especially the completion of Form A/B, may make such a decision appealing, particularly as, having gone through the rigours of notification, the Commission may interfere with the parties' carefully negotiated agreement and is, in any event, unlikely to grant anything more than a comfort letter.

Where, however, the enforceability of the agreement is vital a party may not wish to take the risk that it may not be able to enforce its agreement or restrictions within it.[208]

g. NO PROVISIONAL VALIDITY

The general rule is that there is no 'provisional validity' for agreements which are notified. Thus if an agreement falls within Article 81(1) and the Commission declines it an exemption the position is that the agreement is void and has always been void *ab initio*. Further, in the case of notifiable agreements, where exemptions can generally be granted only back to the date of notification, the agreement will have been void, even if exempted, during the period prior to notification.

A limited exception to this rule applies to 'old' agreements (agreements concluded prior to the enactment of Regulation 17) and possibly also to agreements to which Article 81 applies by virtue of a State's accession to the Treaty. Old agreements, enjoy provisional validity and are valid until declared otherwise.[209]

h. PROCEDURE FOLLOWING NOTIFICATION

Where the Commission proceeds to a formal decision it must comply with the procedures laid down in Regulations 17 and 2842/98 (the Hearing Regulation).[210] For example, it must

---

[203] For a discussion of this, see C. Kerse, *EC Antitrust Procedure* (4th edn., Sweet & Maxwell, London, 1998) para. 6.15.

[204] It was challenged by the parties: see case T–395/94R, *Atlantic Container Liner AB v. Commission* [1995] ECR II–2893, and for the final decision, see *TACA (Transatlantic Conference Agreement)* [1998] OJ L95/1, [1999] 4 CMLR 1415.

[205] See *Crane-Hire Cartel* [1995] OJ L312/79, [1996] 4 CMLR 565, *aff'd.* in Cases T–213/95 and T–18/96, *Stichting Certificatie Kraanverhuurbedrijf (SCK) and Federatie Van Nederlandse Kraanverhuurbedrijven (FNK) v. Commission* [1997] ECR II–1739, [1998] 4 CMLR 259.

[206] Under in the Merger Reg. there is a *duty* to notify: see *infra* Chap. 12.

[207] See M. Siragusa, 'Notification of Agreements in the EEC—To Notify or Not to Notify' [1986] *Fordham Corp.L.Inst..* 243; also, A. Brown, 'Notification of Agreements to the EC Commission: Whether to Submit to a Flawed System' (1992), 17 *ELRev.* 323.

[208] In most cases this is likely to be more of a concern than the prospect of a fine.

[209] See C. Kerse, *EC Antitrust Procedure* (4th edn., Sweet & Maxwell, London, 1998), para. 10.07 and *infra* Chap. 15.

[210] Reg. 17 [1959–62] OJ Spec. Ed. 87; Reg. 2842/98 [1998] OJ L354/18.

make its case known to the undertakings concerned and allow them a right of reply. These matters are discussed in detail in Chapter 14, dealing with enforcement and procedure, but are also dealt with briefly below.

The Commission may enter into a dialogue with the parties and propose amendments to the notified agreement which would enable exemption to be given. Negative clearances and exemption decisions often result from such a process. The Commission can ask for further information and has powers under Regulation 17 (Article 11[211]) to that end. Before a final decision is taken the Commission is required to publish a summary of the application or notification and invite interested third parties to submit observations (an Article 19(3) notice[212]). The Commission may sometimes publish a preliminary notice asking for third party comments earlier in the proceedings. Although of course the parties themselves are seeking an exemption third parties may oppose it. Third parties with a 'sufficient interest'[213] are given an opportunity to be heard (the Commission is obliged to hear them) and can, if a decision exempting the agreement is granted, go on to challenge the legitimacy of the decision before the Court.[214]

Before the Commission takes a decision refusing exemption it must serve a Statement of Objections on the parties. The parties then have a specified period within which to make their views known and have a right to an oral hearing.[215] Third parties with a sufficient interest (other than complainants) may also be heard orally if the Commission thinks it appropriate.[216]

If the Commission refuses an exemption the decision applies retrospectively to the time the agreement was concluded. The general rule is that there is no 'provisional validity' for agreements.

i. THE OPPOSITION PROCEDURE

Some block exemptions contain an 'opposition procedure'. Essentially, this procedure enables agreements which do not, for specified reasons, fall precisely within the terms of that block exemption nonetheless to benefit from its protection. Where applicable, the parties must notify the agreement on Form A/B as usual but expressly claim the benefit of the opposition procedure. If the Commission does not 'oppose' exemption within a specified period (ordinarily six months, but four months in the case of Regulation 240/96 on

---

[211] See *infra* Chap. 14.

[212] Because it is published pursuant to Reg. 17, Art. 19(3).

[213] Reg. 17, Art. 19(2). There is little authority on what this means, for in practice the Commission does hear third parties, but it would appear to cover a legal or natural person whose interests may be detrimentally affected by the Commission's decision. A person who had a 'legitimate interest' to be accepted as a complainant under Reg. 17, Art. 3(2)(b) must also have a 'sufficient interest' under Art. 19(2) although Roemer AG suggested in Case 8/71, *Deutscher Komponistenverband v. Commission* [1971] ECR 705, [1973] CMLR 902 that 'sufficient interest' might require a lesser degree of interest than those that seek to establish a legitimate interest.

[214] See e.g. the *Metro/SABA* cases which involved an exemption given to a selective distribution network: Case 26/76, *Metro SB Grossmärkte v. Commission (SABA) (No. 1)* [1977] ECR 1875, [1978] 2 CMLR 1, and Case 75/84, *Metro v. Commission (No.2)* [1986] ECR 3021, [1987] 1 CMLR 118; see also Case T–528/93 *Métropole Télévision SA v. Commission* [1996] ECR II–649, [1996] 5 CMLR 386 (the first case in which a challenge by a third party succeeded before the Court).

[215] See *infra* Chap. 14.

[216] See Reg. 2842/98, Art. 9(2).

technology transfer agreements)[217] the agreement is protected by the block exemption which, in effect, is extended to cover the agreement. If the Commission does oppose, however, then the notification is treated in the ordinary way as an application for individual exemption. The Commission *must* oppose if requested to do so by a Member State (acting on competition considerations) within a specified period (three months or two months in the case of Regulation 240/96) of the notification being made.

(v) DECISIONS GRANTING EXEMPTION

a. EXEMPTIONS ARE ISSUED FOR A SPECIFIED PERIOD

A decision granting an individual exemption declares, pursuant to Article 81(3), that Article 81(1) shall not apply to the notified agreement. Regulation 17 stipulates that individual exemptions can be issued only for a specified period[218] (on the expiry of that period the parties can of course apply for it to be renewed[219]). Although Regulation 17 does not set out any minimum or maximum exemption period, it is important that the exemption period granted allows sufficient time for the beneficial objectives of the agreement to be achieved or carried out. In *European Night Services* v. *Commission*[220] four railway companies concluded a joint venture agreement to run overnight passenger rail services through the Channel Tunnel. The Commission exempted the agreement, but for a period of only eight years. The parties claimed that since a long-term investment was involved the return on the project was dependent on securing twenty-year financing. The CFI was not satisfied that the Commission had established that the agreement infringed Article 81(1) at all. However, even if it had been shown to do so, the Court made it clear that it would have annulled the decision exempting the agreement for lack of adequate reasons. The Commission had not clearly set out why the exemption had been confined to such a limited period relative to that sought by the parties.

Cases T–374, 375, 384 & 388/94, *European Night Services* v. *Commission* [1998] ECR II–3141 [1998] 5 CMLR 718

Court of First Instance

230. However, even if it is assumed that the Commission's assessment of the restrictions on competition in the contested decision was adequate and correct, the Court considers that the duration of an exemption granted under Article [81(3)] of the Treaty or, as here, Article 5 of Regulation No 1017/68 and Article 53(3) of the EEA Agreement must be sufficient to enable the beneficiaries to achieve the benefits justifying such exemption, namely, in the present case, the contribution to economic progress and the benefits to consumers provided by the introduction of new high-quality transport services, as stated in points 59 to 61 of the contested decision. Since, moreover, such progress and benefits cannot be achieved without considerable investment, the length of time required to ensure a proper return on that investment is necessarily an essential factor to be taken into account when determining the duration of an exemption, particularly in a case such as the present, where it is

---

[217] [1996] OJ L31/2.

[218] Reg. 17, Art. 8(1).

[219] *Ibid.*, Art. 8(2).

[220] Cases T–374, 375, 384 & 388/94, *European Night Services* v. *Commission* [1998] ECR II–3141 [1998] 5 CMLR 718.

undisputed that the services in question are completely new, involve major investments and substantial financial risks and require the pooling of know-how by the participating undertakings (see points 63, 64 and 75 of the decision).

231. The consideration set out in point 73 of the decision, that 'the duration of the exemption will therefore depend inter alia on the period for which it can reasonably be supposed that market conditions will remain substantially the same', cannot, therefore, be regarded as decisive, on its own, for determining the duration of the exemption, without also taking account of the length of time necessary to enable the parties to achieve a satisfactory return on their investment.

232. However, the contested decision does not contain any detailed assessment of the length of time required to achieve a return on the investments in question under conditions of legal certainty, in the light, in particular, of the fact that the parties have entered into financial commitments covering a period of 20 years for the purchase of the special rolling stock. The Commission's statement at point 76 of the decision that, in connection with the combined transport of goods, some railways had informed it that a period of five years was needed in order to set up the new services and ensure their viability is irrelevant since it concerns a joint venture operating . . . on a different market from that on which ENS operates.

233. As regards the Commission's conclusion at point 75 of the contested decision, that the scale of investment cannot be allowed to become a decisive factor in determining the duration of the exemption because there is no necessary link between the joint acquisition of 'plant and machinery' and the commercial use to which it is to be put, it must be held that there is nothing in the decision to explain why there is 'no necessary link' between the acquisition and the use of such equipment, given that the rolling stock in question was acquired, and the financial commitments relating thereto were entered into, exclusively in the context of the agreements notified. In any event, the Commission has not challenged the applicants' assertion that other possibilities for the use of the rolling stock in question are extremely limited.

234. Consequently, the Commission's decision to limit the duration of the exemption granted for the ENS agreements is in any event vitiated by an absence of reasoning.

b. CONDITIONS AND OBLIGATIONS

Exemptions may be granted subject to conditions and obligations (Regulation 17, Article 8(1)).[221] Where a condition is imposed the whole exemption procedure hinges upon it and a breach of a condition may lead to the entire decision being revoked. In contrast, an obligation is something added to a decision. A breach of the obligation is likely to result only in a fine.[222] The Court has, however, tended to use the two words interchangeably.[223]

The most common type of obligation is one to provide specified information to the Commission during the currency of the exemption, or to allow Commission officials access to business records. *European Night Services* v. *Commission* was a rare case in which the parties challenged a Commission decision exempting their agreement on the ground that

---

[221] The Commission must give the parties the opportunity to be heard if it is wishes to impose conditions: Case 17/74, *Transocean Marine Paint Association* v. *Commission* [1974] ECR 1063, [1974] 2 CMLR 459.

[222] Reg. 17, Art. 15(2). The fine can be as great as that imposed for substantive breaches of the rules, that is up to 10% of turnover. The Notice on the method of setting fines [1998] OJ C9/3, (see *infra* Chap. 14) does not deal with fines for breaches of obligations. For a more detailed discussion of the distinction between conditions and obligation see C. Kerse, *EC Antitrust Procedure* (4th edn., Sweet & Maxwell, London, 1998), paras. 6.32–6.34.

[223] E.g. in Cases T–374, 375, 384 & 388/94, *European Night Services* v. *Commission* [1998] ECR II–3141, [1998] 5 CMLR 718, para. 217.

they were unwilling to accept the stringent conditions imposed by the Commission. The exemption in this case was conditional on the parties supplying certain facilities and resources to third parties that wanted to compete with the joint venture. The CFI did not consider that the Commission had adequately explained why these were essential facilities which the parties should be required to allow others to use.[224] The result was that the Court annulled the *entire* decision. The Court did not consider that it had jurisdiction simply to annul the conditions imposed. Such a ruling would have required the Commission to grant the exemption without the conditions and the Court was not entitled to do this.[225]

c. EXEMPTIONS ARE GRANTED FROM DATE OF NOTIFICATION *OR* THE DATE THE AGREEMENT WAS CONCLUDED

The General Rule

The general rule set out in Article 6(1) of Regulation 17 is that exemption decisions must specify the date from which they run, but that *this cannot be earlier than the date of notification*. This means that an agreement which infringes Article 81(1) but which has not been notified is void pursuant to Article 81(2) even if, had it been notified, the agreement would have merited an exemption pursuant to Article 81(3). Such an agreement will not, therefore, be enforceable in a national court in respect of the period between the agreement coming into force and its notification. This, of course, has put a premium on timely notification in cases where there is concern about the applicability of Article 81(1)[226] and has, partly at least, contributed to the vast number of notifications which the Commission receives each year. Agreements falling within Article 4(2) of Regulation 17 may, however, be exempted *retrospectively* to the date that the agreement was concluded.[227]

Non-notifiable Agreements

Article 4(2) of Regulation 17 specifies four types of agreement which are exempt from the notification procedure as described above. This does *not* mean that they are exempt from Article 81(1) itself. What it does mean, however, is that should the compatibility of such an agreement with Article 81 ever arise, the Commission can examine the agreement and, where the Article 81(3) criteria are satisfied, grant it an exemption, retrospectively, to the date the agreement was concluded.

The purpose of including Article 4(2) within Regulation 17 was to avoid unnecessary notification of agreements considered to be 'less harmful'.[228] Parties do not, therefore, need to notify as a precaution, just in case the compatibility of the agreement is raised before a national court. Prior to Regulation 1216/99,[229] Article 4(2) was of comparatively little importance. It covered only a narrow range of transactions: specific types of intellectual

---

[224] Cases T–374, 375, 384 & 388/94, *European Night Services* v. *Commission* [1998] ECR II–3141, [1998] 5 CMLR 718, paras. 205–221. For the essential facilities doctrine, in the context of undertakings which hold a dominant position, see Chap. 7.

[225] *Ibid.*, para. 53.

[226] Unless, of course, the agreement falls within one of the Community block exemptions.

[227] Reg. 17, Art. 6(2).

[228] See the ECJ in Case 63/75, *Fonderie Roubaix-Wattrelos* v. *Fonderies A.Roux* [1976] ECR 111, [1976] 1 CMLR 538, para. 6.

[229] [1999] OJ L148/5.

property licences;[230] specific types of standardization; research and development, and specialization agreements;[231] and, agreements or concerted practices where:

the only parties thereto are undertakings from one Member State and the agreements, decisions, or practices do not relate either to imports or to exports between Member States.[232]

This latter category covers agreements which, while being confined to one Member State and not relating to imports or exports between Member States, do nevertheless have a possible effect on inter-Member State trade, perhaps because of a foreclosure effect arising from a network of similar agreements.[233] However, it does not include agreements which restrict competition to an extent which *is* harmful.[234] The limited nature of Article 4(2) and the uncertainty surrounding the question of what agreements were covered by it meant that the provision was difficult to rely on. However, the point is likely to be of much less interest since the adoption of Council Regulation 1216/99.[235] This amended Article 4(2) to cover almost all vertical agreements. Article 4(2)(2)(a) now covers cases where:

agreements or concerted practices are entered into by two or more undertakings, each operating, for the purposes of the agreement, at a different level of the production or distribution chain, and relate to the conditions under which the parties may purchase, sell or resell certain goods or services.

This widens the category of non-notifiable agreements to include most distribution and franchising agreements and makes the provision of much greater importance.

d. REVOCATION OF EXEMPTION

Article 8(3) of Regulation 17 provides that individual exemptions can be revoked or amended in certain specified circumstances. The Commission must make its case known to the parties and give them the opportunity to be heard.[236]

The Commission has, as yet, never exercised its power to withdraw an individual exemption. It has, however, withdrawn the benefit of a comfort letter.[237] The benefit of a block exemption may also be withdrawn from an agreement.[238]

---

[230] See Chap. 10.

[231] See Chap. 13.

[232] Art 4(2) (1).

[233] Case 43/69, *Bilger* v. *Jehle* [1970] ECR 127, [1974] 1 CMLR 382; Case 63/75, *Fonderie Roubaix-Wattrelos* v. *Fonderies A.Roux* [1976] ECR 111, [1976 1 CMLR 538; Case C–234/89, *Delimitis* v. *Henninger Bräu* [1991] ECR 1–935, [1992] 5 CMLR 210.

[234] Case 63/75, *Fonderie Roubaix-Wattrelos* v. *Fonderies A. Roux* [1976] ECR 111, [1976 1 CMLR 538, and Cases 96–102,104,105,108 & 110/82, *NV IAZ International Belgium SA* v. *Commission* [1983] ECR 3369, [1984] 3 CMLR 276.

[235] Enacted as part of the reform of the law on vertical restraints, discussed in greater detail *infra* in Chap. 9.

[236] *Infra* Chap. 14.

[237] *Langnese-Iglo* [1993] OJ L183/19, [1994] 4 CMLR 51; on appeal Cases T–7 & 9/93, *Langnese-Iglo & Schöller Lebensmittel* v. *Commission* [1995] ECR II–1533, [1995] 5 CMLR 602, upheld by the ECJ in Case C–279/95P, *Langnese-Iglo* v. *Commission* [1998] ECR I–5609, [1998] 5 CMLR 933: see *infra* Chap. 9.

[238] See *infra* 218.

(vi) COMFORT LETTERS

The Commission cannot issue decisions granting an exemption or negative clearance to all of the agreements notified to it each year. It is severely under-resourced and grants a formal decision to only 10 per cent or so of the notifications that it receives each year.[239] It rarely grants more than twenty decisions (in total) a year. The number of individual exemptions granted each year is even lower. The remainder are dealt with informally by administrative letter, a 'comfort letter'. In 1998, for example, the Commission received 216 notifications. Although it issued more decisions than normal that year, forty-two, none of these were exemption decisions. In contrast, it granted 152 Article 81 comfort letters.[240] The comfort letter has thus enabled the Commission to deal with the numerous notifications that it receives whilst at the same time allowing the Commission to give greater priority to cases which raise greater concern from the Community perspective.

On notification the notifying parties are asked 'Would you be satisfied with a comfort letter?' (Form A/B Section 3.3). This, in the classicist's terms, clearly anticipates the answer yes, as it continues 'If you consider that it would be inappropriate to deal with the notified agreement in this manner, please explain the reasons for this view'.

A comfort letter may take one of several forms. It may state the Commission's view that: (1) the agreement does not fall within Article 81(1) at all (a 'negative clearance comfort letter'); (2) the agreement is covered by a block exemption or by a Commission Notice; or (3) that the agreement is eligible for an Article 81(3) exemption.[241] In the first two cases the parties are likely to feel fairly contented with the letter. However, the procedure is less satisfactory from the legal perspective where it states that the agreement infringes Article 81(1) but in the Commission's view would be likely to benefit from an exemption. According to Article 81(2) an agreement which falls within Article 81(1) is void unless exempted and in these circumstances no exemption has been granted. This type of comfort letter is thus the least comforting of the three. Although assuring the parties that the Commission will not pursue the matter further, the letter is *not* a decision which can be applied by the national courts and consequently does not give the parties the same degree of legal certainty which results from a decision. The letter is not binding on the national courts (or the European courts or, for that matter, the European Commission). In practice, however, parties accept comfort letters as a matter of expediency. Further, if the question of the validity of the agreement is ever raised in national proceedings, the national court would be likely to

---

[239] The Commission states in its White Paper on modernisation of the rules implementing Articles 85 and 86 [now 81 and 82] of the EC Treaty [1999] OJ C132/1, [1999] 5 CMLR 208, para. 34, that 91% of cases (150–200 letters per year) are settled informally. Of course the problems will be exacerbated when more States join the EU and EC.

[240] Commission's *XXVIIIth Report on Completion Policy* (Commission, 1998). The Commission has usually taken only between one and two dozen substantive decisions a year which include infringement proceedings and rejection of complaints, as well as granting exemptions and negative clearances. In contrast it receives 200 to 300 notifications. The figures speak for themselves. There were 221 notifications in 1997. The Commission also takes procedural decisions ordering investigations under Reg. 17, Arts. 11 and 14 etc.

[241] In 1998 75 of the 152 comfort letters were such 'Art. 81(3)' comfort letters (the other 77 were Art. 81(1) ones).

stay proceedings and ask the Commission to take a decision on the compatibility of the agreement with Article 81(1).[242]

Some administrative letters issued by the Commission are better described as 'discomfort letters'. These letters inform the parties that although the Commission is not intending to take a formal decision it considers that the notified agreement infringes the rules, and does not merit exemption.

In the *XIth Report on Competition Policy* the Commission announced its intention to 'increase the legal value of these letters'. In some cases the Commission does this by publishing a notice in the Official Journal announcing its intention of issuing a comfort letter and giving third parties an opportunity to comment.[243] Since then a number of cases have been dealt with in this way.

Comfort letters may be limited in time, and may be withdrawn. In *Langnese-Iglo*,[244] which concerned agreements for the supply of ice-cream, the Commission sent the undertaking's lawyer a comfort letter in 1985, the relevant parts of which read:

> Schöller's 'ice-cream supply agreements' which were notified are therefore compatible with the competition rules of the [EC] Treaty. It is therefore unnecessary for the Commission to take action regarding the agreements notified by your client.

> The Commission nevertheless reserves the right to re-open the procedure if there is any appreciable change affecting certain matters of law or of fact on which the present assessment is based.

Nearly seven years later the Commission, following the receipt of a complaint, issued a decision which effectively withdrew the comfort letter. The undertakings concerned claimed that this was a breach of the principle of legitimate expectations. Both the CFI and the ECJ upheld the Commission's view that it was entitled to act as it had. The market had changed since the letter was sent, the letter had been based only on a provisional analysis of the market, and the Commission had only later become aware of the additional barriers which existed to entry on the market.[245]

(vii) HOSTILITY TO THE PROCEDURE

The adverse consequences resulting from the notification and authorization system have already been rehearsed above.[246] In particular, the difficulties involved in securing an

---

[242] A national court asked to rule on the validity of the agreement will thus be confronted with an agreement which appears to infringe Art. 81(1), which has not been exempted pursuant to Art. 81(3) and which, consequently, appears to be void (Art 81(2)). A national court in such a position should not, however, enter a judgment which would risk conflicting with a subsequent Commission decision: Case C–234/89, *Delimitis* v. *Henniger Bräu* [1991] ECR I–935, [1992] 5 CMLR 210. A national court should, therefore, stay the national proceedings or take interim measures and request the Commission to proceed to a formal decision. The status of comfort letters in national proceedings and their effect on the validity of agreements are considered in Chap. 15 which deals with the enforcement of the competition rules before the national courts. The ECJ held in the *Perfume* cases that a comfort letter can terminate the provisional validity of an 'old' agreement: see Case 99/70, *Lancôme* v. *Etos* [1980] ECR 2511, [1981] 2 CMLR 164.

[243] (1991), point 15. This was followed by two notices in the OJ about this procedure: [1989] OJ C343/4 in relation to negative clearance-type letters and [1983] OJ C295/6 in relation to exemption-type letters.

[244] *Langnese-Iglo* [1993] OJ L183/19, [1994] 4 CMLR 51.

[245] Cases T–7 & 9/93, *Lagnese-Iglo & Schöller Lebensmittel* v. *Commission* [1995] ECR II–1533, [1995] 5 CMLR 602; Case C–279/95P, *Langnese-Iglo* v. *Commission* [1998] ECR I–5609, [1998] 5 CMLR 933.

[246] See e.g. *supra* section 1.

individual exemption have led to dissatisfaction. The key complaints are founded on: the cost and delay involved in securing an individual exemption; the fact that any exemption granted will be for only a limited period; the fact that any exemption granted may be subject to conditions and obligations being imposed on the parties;[247] the fact that an individual exemption is unlikely and that the parties will have to make do with a comfort letter instead; and the fact that the parties are likely to have to amend and alter their agreement in order to secure an exemption or even a comfort letter.

(viii) JUDICIAL REVIEW

The parties to an agreement may appeal to the CFI against a Commission decision refusing, or even granting,[248] an individual exemption using the judicial review procedure set out in the Treaty. Article 230 specifically provides that individuals may bring judicial review proceedings to challenge decisions addressed to them. Further, an undertaking may appeal against a Commission decision to grant an exemption to an agreement concluded by other undertakings, where that decision is of direct and individual concern to that third party.[249] The appeal procedure and grounds for annulment are described in Chapter 14 below. However, it should be noted that the CFI (and the ECJ) have not taken a particularly interventionist stance when dealing with appeals against decisions taken under Article 81(3). In recognition of the complex economic assessments involved in decisions taken under Article 81(3) the Court confines itself to a review of the facts and the legal conclusions drawn from those facts.[250] Where, however, the Commission has clearly failed to explain why an agreement does not meet the criteria set out in Article 81(3),[251] why conditions have been imposed[252] or even where the Commission has failed adequately to explain why an agreement infringes Article 81(1) (so that an exemption is necessary)[253] the Court will not hesitate to quash the Commission's decision.

D. BLOCK EXEMPTIONS

(i) GENERAL

A number of Community regulations grant exemption to categories of agreements. A majority of these regulations are Commission regulations adopted following authorization from the Council. There are, however, two block exemptions which have been adopted

---

[247] Reg. 17, Art. 8(1).

[248] See Cases T–374, 375, 384 & 388/94, *European Night Services* v. *Commission* [1998] ECR II–3141 [1998] 5 CMLR 718.

[249] Case 26/76, *Metro-SB-Grossmärkte GmbH* v. *Commission (No 1)* [1977] ECR 1875, [1978] 2 CMLR 1.

[250] Cases 56 & 58/64, *Etablissements Consten SA & Grundig-Verkaufs-GmbH* v. *Commission* [1966] ECR 299, [1966] CMLR 418. The position may change if the Commission's proposal to make Art. 81(3) directly applicable comes to fruition, *infra* 219 ff and Chap. 16.

[251] Case C–360/92 *Publishers' Association* v. *Commission* [1995] ECR I–23.

[252] Cases T–374, 375, 384 & 388/94, *European Night Services* v. *Commission* [1998] ECR II–3141, [1998] 5 CMLR 718.

[253] *Ibid.*

directly by the Council. The current block exemptions and the legislation which authorized the adoption of the Regulation are described below.

(ii) CURRENT BLOCK EXEMPTIONS

a. BLOCK EXEMPTIONS ADOPTED BY THE COUNCIL

The Council has adopted two Regulations granting exemption to (1) agreements in road and inland waterway sectors and (2) liner conferences in the maritime transport sector. These are set out in Council Regulations 1017/68 and 4056/88 respectively.[254]

b. BLOCK EXEMPTIONS ADOPTED BY THE COMMISSION

Over the years the Commission has adopted a number of block exemptions which have applied to vertical, horizontal, technology transfer, and other particular agreements.

Table 4.1 Block Exemptions adopted by the Commission currently in force

Regulation	Categories of Agreements Covered	Enabling Legislation
Regulation 2790/1999	Vertical agreements. Replacing: Exclusive distribution, Exclusive purchasing and Franchising regulations	Council Regulation 19/65 (amended by Council Regulation 1215/99)
Regulation 1475/95	Distribution agreements for motor cars	Council Regulation 19/65
Regulation 240/96	Technology transfer agreements. Replacing: Patent licensing and know-how regulations	Council Regulation 19/65
Regulation 417/85	Specialization agreements	Council Regulation 2821/75
Regulation 418/95	Research and development agreements	Council Regulation 2821/75
Regulation 1617/93	Passenger transit consultations and slot allocations at airports etc	Council Regulation 1976/87
Regulation 3652/93	Agreements relating to computerised reservation systems	Council Regulation 3976/87
Regulation 3932/92	Agreements in the insurance sector	Council Regulation 1534/91
Regulation 823/2000	Liner shipping consortia	Council Regulation 479/92

A number of block exemptions which applied to exclusive distribution,[255] exclusive purchasing,[256] and franchising agreements[257] respectively were replaced on 1 June 2000 by a single block exemption applying more generally to vertical agreements.[258] This block exemption does not, however, replace the block exemption applying to motor car vehicle

---

[254] Reg. 1017/68 [1968] OJ Spec. Ed. 302; Reg. 4056/86 [1986] OJ L378/14.
[255] Reg. 1983/83 [1983] OJ L173/1.
[256] Reg. 1984/83 [1983] OJ L173/5.
[257] Reg. 4087/88 [1988] OJ L359/46.
[258] Reg. 2790/1999 [1999] OJ L336/21.

distribution agreements set out in Regulation 1475/95[259] or to technology transfer agreements set out in Regulation 240/96.[260]

There are currently two block exemptions which apply to horizontal agreements. Regulation 417/85[261] which applies to specialisation agreements and Regulation 418/95[262] which applies to research and development agreements. The Commission has adopted two draft block exemptions to replace these.[263]

The Commission has also adopted regulations which apply in the air transport and insurance sectors and to liner shipping consortia.

c. THE FORMAT OF A BLOCK EXEMPTION

Block exemptions typically commence with recitals explaining why the type of agreement covered by the block exemption merits exemption. These recitals may be relevant to the interpretation of the main body of the Regulation.

Until the adoption of Regulation 2790/1999[264] the Regulations have tended to adopt the following format: a list of restrictions which it is permissible for the agreement to contain ('white list') and a list of prohibited restrictions ('black list'). The Regulation may include a list of clauses which, although probably not restrictive of competition at all, are specifically authorized for the sake of clarity. The new block exemption relating to vertical agreements has, however, moved away from this format in an attempt to prevent the severe strait-jacketing and limitations on the parties' autonomy which result from this formula. This Regulation lists only restrictions which may *not* be included within the agreement and allows the parties the freedom to determine what other provisions the agreement should include.

The regulations also contain a number of miscellaneous provisions dealing with, for example, commencement and expiry dates of the regulation, withdrawal of the block exemption, and what entities are considered to be 'connected' to the agreements signatories (and so also in effect parties to the agreement).

(iii) BLOCK EXEMPTIONS ARE DIRECTLY APPLICABLE

Parties to an agreement which falls within the ambit of one of the block exemptions do not need to notify the agreement to the Commission. The agreement automatically merits exemption and the national courts are free to apply the terms of the block exemption (so long as they are sufficiently precise and unconditional) should the validity of the agreement be raised before such a court. Article 249 (ex Article 189) of the Treaty specifically provides that regulations are directly applicable.

If an agreement does not fall precisely within the scope of a block exemption the national court may not extend it to cover the agreement. If the conditions of the block exemption are

---

[259] Reg. 1475/958 [1995] OJ L145/25.
[260] Reg. 240/96 [1996] OJ L31/2.
[261] Reg. 417/85 [1985] OJ L53/1.
[262] Reg. 418/85 [1985] OJ L53/5.
[263] [2000] OJ C118/4 and 10.
[264] [1999] OJ L336/21. See *infra* Chap. 9.

not met the regulation ceases to apply in its entirety. The contract will be void, of course, only if provisions in the agreement restrict competition for the purposes of Article 81(1) and are not severable from the agreement itself. Moreover, parties which do not satisfy the conditions of a block exemption are free to request the Commission to grant an individual exemption. An agreement which contains clauses specifically prohibited by a regulation is, however, unlikely to merit individual exemption.[265] The 'black list' or prohibited clauses indicate the types of clauses which are not considered to be indispensable to the successful operation of the agreement.

(iv) SMALL AND MEDIUM-SIZED UNDERTAKINGS

Some of the block exemptions contain provisions which favour agreements concluded between undertakings with combined turnovers which are below a specified threshold.[266] The later block exemptions have, however, tended to place greater emphasis on market shares than turnover requirements. For example, Regulation 2790/1999 relating to vertical agreements applies only where the relevant undertakings' market share is below 30 per cent. Undertakings with lower market shares are not of course always small and medium-sized undertakings (and vice versa).

(v) OPPOSITION PROCEDURE

It has already been seen that some block exemptions contain an opposition procedure[267] which, in certain circumstances, enables undertakings whose agreements fall outside the terms of the block exemption to notify the agreement and to expect exemption unless the Commission opposes it within a specified period of time.[268]

The opposition procedure in Regulation 240/96 on technology transfer agreements applies where an agreement contains restrictions of competition which are neither expressly permitted nor expressly prohibited by the terms of the block exemption. Regulation 240/96 actually mentions certain provisions which do not fall either within the 'white' list or the 'black' list which the Commission considers to be suitable to be dealt with under the opposition procedure.[269]

The use of the opposition procedure has never been popular and the new block exemption on vertical restraints, Regulation 2790/99, does not contain such a procedure. This is presumably partly because it does not follow the traditional white and black list approach adopted in previous block exemptions. Rather, it simply lists clauses which preclude the application of the block exemption or which cannot themselves benefit from the block

---

[265] See Case C–234/89, *Delimitis* v. *Henninger Bräu* [1991] ECR 1–935, [1992] 5 CMLR 210, paras. 38–42.

[266] E.g., Reg. 1983/83 [1983] OJ L173/1 (which expired on 31 May 2000) permitted the conclusion of a non-reciprocal distribution agreement between competitors where one of the undertakings involved had a market share below ECU 100 million. See also Reg. 2790/1999, Art. 2(4)(a).

[267] See Reg. 417/85, Art. 4; Reg. 418/85, Art. 7; Reg. 4087/88, Art. 6; and Reg. 240/96, Art. 4.

[268] See *supra* 207–208.

[269] See *infra* Chap. 10. In the block exemption on specialization agreements, Reg. 417/85, the opposition procedure applies to agreements which are outside the block exemption because its threshold limits are exceeded.

exemption. It could, however, have been of use, for example, to parties which marginally exceeded the market share threshold of 30 per cent.[270]

(vi) WITHDRAWAL OF BLOCK EXEMPTIONS

Block exemptions invariably contain a provision permitting withdrawal of the block exemption where the parties fall within it but the Commission considers that, notwithstanding this formal compliance, competition is restricted or the parties are engaging in particular anti-competitive practices. Regulation 240/96 on technology transfer agreements, for example, provides that the Commission may withdraw the benefit from a licensing agreement where the licensee has a market share of more than 40 per cent.[271] Withdrawal has been threatened on several occasions[272] and finally occurred in *Langnese-Iglo*,[273] although the Court held that the benefit of the block exemption (in that case Regulation 1984/83 applying to exclusive purchasing agreements) could not be withheld in advance from *future* agreements.[274]

In a new departure Regulation 2790/99 on vertical restraints provides that the benefit of that block exemption may be withdrawn not only by the Commission but by a competent authority of a Member State 'in respect of that territory'.[275] This provision appears to be a manifestation of the Commission's policy aimed at encouraging greater enforcement of the competition rules at the national level.

E. UNILATERAL ACTION AND EXEMPTIONS

The Commission takes the view that the unilateral conduct of one party to a contract may form part of the contractual arrangements between it and a co-contractor. Thus where a distributor knows that if it, for example, sells a producer's product at prices below those recommended by the producer or outside a specified territory it will be refused supply, a contractual provision fixing minimum prices of sale of banning exports may be read into the contract. What appears at first sight to be a unilateral decision of the producer is instead characterized as an integral part of an underlying agreement or concerted practice between the parties. In many cases the Commission has relied on such behaviour to find a breach of Article 81(1) and to fine the parties to the prohibited contract (frequently the Commission has reserved fines for the party to the breach, the producer).[276] Similarly, in *Ford Werke AG v. Commission* the Commission relied both on the terms of the agreement and on the way in which it was operated by Ford when it issued a decision refusing Ford an exemption

---

[270] This was done in Reg. 417/85. Reg. 2790/99 replaces two block exemptions which did not contain an opposition procedure, Regs. 1983/83 and 1984/83 on exclusive distribution and exclusive purchasing, and one which did, Reg. 4087/88 on franchising.

[271] See *infra* Chap. 10.

[272] See e.g. *Tetra Pak/BTG* [1988] OJ L272/27, [1990] 4 CMLR 47.

[273] *Langnese-Iglo* [1993] OJ L183/19, [1994] 4 CMLR 51.

[274] Case C–279/95P, *Langnese-Iglo* v. *Commission* [1998] ECR I-5609, [1998] 5 CMLR 933, paras. 207–209.

[275] Reg. 2790/1999 [1999] OJ L336/21, Art. 7. This provision could be enacted only after Reg. 19/65 [1965–66] OJ Spec. Ed. 35, Art. 7 was amended to allow this by Reg. 1215/99 [1999] OJ L148/1.

[276] See *supra* Chap. 3, 114 ff.

for its selective distribution system. The ECJ held that the Commission was entitled when considering the terms of the agreement to take account not only of the written terms of the agreement but also the way the agreement was operated. In this case Ford had essentially refused to supply right-hand drive cars to its German dealers in order to protect the higher prices which the distributors charged in the UK. That unilateral decision formed part of the contractual arrangements since admission to the network involved implicit acceptance by the dealers of the terms imposed by Ford.

F. THE RELATIONSHIP BETWEEN ARTICLE 81(3) AND ARTICLE 82

The fact that an agreement has been exempted from the application of Article 81(1) under Article 81(3) does not mean that such conduct does not constitute an abuse of a dominant position for the purposes of Article 82. There is no provision for exempting abusive conduct under Article 82. The relationship between Article 81 and 83 is discussed in Chapter 5 below.

4. THE COMMISSION'S PROPOSALS FOR MODERNIZATION

A. GENERAL

Regulation 17[277] both confers the exclusive power to grant exemptions on the Commission and sets out the general rule that agreements have to be notified if exemption is to be possible. The discussion in this Chapter has established that the system set up in 1962 has not worked. It has imposed a great burden on both business and the Commission and has been operated in a significantly different fashion from that which was envisaged at the time of its creation. Although we have seen in this chapter that the Commission has taken steps to alleviate the burden resulting from the notification system (for example, the issue of Notices setting out guidance on agreements that fall outside Article 81(1); the adoption of block exemptions; and the adoption of procedures for faster and informal settlement of cases (in particular through the issues of 'comfort letters')) these steps have been insufficient to deal with the problems which the system presents.

In its White Paper on Modernisation of the Rules Implementing Articles 85 and 86 [now 81 and 82],[278] the Commission recognizes this fact and that a centralized prior

---

[277] [1959–62] OJ Spec. Ed. 87.
[278] [1999] OJ C132/1, [1999] 5 CMLR 208.

authorization system in Brussels is no longer possible.[279] On the contrary, the Commission indicates that the workload imposed on it by the notification system has precluded it from performing more important tasks, such as the active enforcement of the competition rules more generally.[280] The Commission has to date been unable to encourage much enforcement of the competition rules at the national level and to achieve greater decentralization.[281] It thus proposes steps to make this possible.

B. THE PROPOSAL FOR A DIRECTLY APPLICABLE EXCEPTION SYSTEM

The simplicity of the solution offered by the White Paper is striking. The suggestion is just to remove the cause of the difficulties. Rather than tinkering with the existing system,[282] the Commission has proposed that: (1) the notification and authorization should be abolished; and (2) the Commission's monopoly over the application of Article 81(3) be relinquished. These two steps would then leave the way open for the national authorities (both the national courts and the national competition authorities) to apply and enforce Article 81 in its entirety (Article 81(3) as well as Article 81(1) and (2)). The current system would be replaced by a fully directly applicable system within which national courts and national competition authorities would be free to apply the four criteria set out in Article 81(3).

C. THE IMPLICATIONS FOR BUSINESS

The Commission's view is that it is time for undertakings to become more 'self-reliant' and to 'make their own assessment of the compatibility of their restrictive practices with Community law, in the light of the legislation in force and the case-law'. Its point is that although the notification and authorization system was important whilst the interpretation of Article 81 and in particular of paragraph 3 was uncertain there is now sufficient jurisprudence of the Court, decisions and notices of the Commission, and block exemptions to guide

---

[279] White Paper on modernisation of the rules implementing Articles 85 and 86 [now 81 and 82] of the EC Treaty [1999] OJ C132/1, [1999] 5 CMLR 208, para. 40.

[280] *Ibid.*, para. 8.

[281] Although the Commission has issued a Notice to give impetus and to encourage increased enforcement of the competition rules by national courts and national competition authorities respectively (Commission Notice on co-operation between national courts and the Commission applying Articles 85 and 86 [now 81 and 82] of the EEC [now EC] Treaty [1993] OJ C39/6; Commission Notice on cooperation between the national competition authorities and the Commission in handling cases falling within the scope of Articles 85 and 86 [now 81 and 82] of the EC Treaty [1997] OJ C313/3, see *infra* Chap. 15) the Commission accepts that these Notices 'have now reached their limits within the existing legal framework' *ibid.*, para. 39.

[282] The Commission considered two separate means of moving forward, improving the current system (Option A) or moving to a directly applicable system (Option B). It did not find Option A appealing. Consequently, it advocated Option B. The Commission discussed but rejected the possibility of taking steps to ameliorate the current system.

undertakings and their advisers in the way that Article 81 is interpreted and applied.[283] The greater clarity in the interpretation of the elements of Article 81 means that the notification system, and the workload and expense which it generates, are not longer justified.[284] Instead, the Commission suggests a system of *ex post* control and proposes measures to ensure consistent and uniform application of Article 81 at the Community and national level.

White Paper on Modernisation of the Rules Implementing Articles 85 and 86 [now 81 and 82] of the EC Treaty [1999] OJ C132/1, [1999] 5 CMLR 208

70. The adoption of such a system in Community law is now possible because of the changes and developments that have occurred in Community competition law since 1962. The legislative framework in the competition policy area has been considerably strengthened, and the reforms currently under way on vertical restrictions and horizontal co-operation agreements will help to simplify and clarify it further. While there were legitimate doubts in 1960 as to the scope of the conditions for exemption under Article [81], the Commission's decision-making practice, the case-law of the Court of Justice and the Court of First Instance and the various block exemption regulations and general notices have made the conditions governing exemption much clearer. Furthermore, the national authorities and courts, undertakings and their legal advisers have progressively gained a better knowledge of Community competition law. These changes now make it possible to overcome obstacles which, at the time when Regulation No 17 was adopted, prevented the establishment of a system of *ex post* control and stemmed essentially from uncertainties as to the precise scope of the exemption conditions provided for in Article [81(3)].

. . .

76. The notification system established by Regulation No 17 has enabled the Commission to build up a coherent body of precedent cases, and to ensure that the competition rules are applied consistently throughout the Member States of the Community. But it has several disadvantages that make it questionable today. The requirement that an undertaking wishing to invoke Article [81(3)] must notify their restrictive practices to the Commission acts as a curb on their commercial strategy and represents a considerable cost. The drafting of notifications, and collection of the necessary information imposes a heavy burden of work and expense on undertakings, whether they carry out the task in-house or entrust it to outside legal advisers. In a directly applicable exception system they would be freed from this obligation to notify, and their position would be strengthened if they had to seek the enforcement of their restrictive practices in the courts, as they would now be able to plead that their restrictive practices were covered by Article [81(3)].

77. The notification system proved useful as long as the interpretation of Article [81] and in particular of paragraph 3 was uncertain; but it no longer makes it possible to detect the most serious infringements of the competition rules, and thus to ensure 'effective supervision' within the meaning of Article [83]. As evidence of this, it is only extremely rarely that notifications lead to prohibition decisions . . . and the Commission has made only exceptional use of Article 15(6) which empowers it to withdraw notifying undertakings' immunity from fines. In a system of *ex post* control, undertakings

---

[283] Para. 51 refers to 'a set of clear legal rules that have been developed and refined through more than 30 years of Commission decision-making practice and Court of Justice case-law and by the many different kinds of general instruments that have been adopted (block exemptions, notices and guidelines)'.

[284] White Paper on modernisation of the rules implementing Articles 85 and 86 [now 81 and 82] of the EC Treaty [1999] OJ C132/1, [1999] 5 CMLR 208, para. 76.

would have to make their own assessment of the compatibility of their restrictive practices with Community law, in the light of the legislation in force and the case-law; this would certainly lighten the administrative burden weighing on them, but it would also require them to take on added responsibility.

These proposals will, however, have a huge impact on undertakings which have become accustomed to receiving assurance that their agreements comply with the competition rules where the interpretation of Article 81 is uncertain and legal certainty is vital. In cases of uncertainty, the inability to obtain clarification may discourage the conclusion of agreements involving considerable investment, particularly where that investment must be made early on in the course of the agreement. To a certain extent the Commission has been understanding of these difficulties. It has thus proposed[285] the maintenance of a prior, but mandatory, authorization system in respect of partial-function joint ventures within the framework of the Merger Regulation.[286] It accepts that for some transactions prior authorization may be essential and that 'operations of this kind generally require substantial investment and far-reaching integration of operations which makes it difficult for them to unravel afterwards at the behest of a competition authority'.[287]

There are currently about 200 notifications each year. Notifications are generally made only where the risk assumed by the parties is great. It should be asked, therefore, whether the proposed arrangements will be satisfactory to undertakings concluding these types of agreements. If they are not, it should then be considered whether or not the advantages resulting to these undertakings in allowing notification would outweigh the cost. Although the Commission anticipates taking positive decisions 'in the general interest,'[288] in cases where a 'new' question is raised or market guidance is necessary there is no suggestion that such decisions will be taken in cases where the point is of interest only to the individual parties involved. In order to give parties greater certainty prior to their conclusion of an agreement, however, the Commission envisages giving 'opinions' on the compatibility of agreements with the competition rules.[289] The Commission will, as part of its *ex post* control, continue to take prohibition decisions in individual cases. Indeed, it anticipates that the number of these will increase.[290]

It should also be remembered that in the White Paper the Commission makes the highly significant statement that in future, in its handling of individual cases, the Commission will adopt a more economic approach to the application of Article 81(1), limiting the scope of its application to undertakings with a degree of market power.[291]

---

[285] White Paper on modernisation of the rules implementing Articles 85 and 86 [now 81 and 82] of the EC Treaty [1999] OJ C132/1, [1999] 5 CMLR 208, para. 79.

[286] Council Reg. 4064/89 [1989] OJ L395/1, as amended by Council Reg. 1310/97 OJ L180/1. See *infra* Chaps.12, 13, and 16.

[287] White Paper on Modernisation, *supra* n. 285, para. 79.

[288] White Paper on Modernisation, *supra* n. 285, para. 88. Proposal for a Reg. implementing Arts. 81 and 82, Art. 10, recital 13, COM (2000) 582.

[289] This process would be similar to the system in the USA in which the Federal Trade Commission or the Department of Justice issues Business Review Letters. These letters may state that on the basis of the information revealed to the authorities by the parties, they do not intend to take action. The effect of such a letter is similar to that of a comfort letters under the present system.

[290] White Paper on Modernisation, *supra* n. 285 para. 87.

[291] *Ibid.*, para. 78 and *supra* s.2.

D. PROPOSAL FOR A NEW REGULATION

On 27 September 2000 the Commission adopted a draft Regulation which, if adopted by the Council, would replace Regulation 17.[292] The draft Regulation proposes that Article 81 should be directly applicable in its entirety[293] and that both the national competition authorities and national courts should participate more fully in the enforcement of Articles 81 and 82.[294] The Regulation also contains provisions which would facilitate the Commission in detecting and deterring more serious infringements of these rules.[295]

5. FURTHER READING

A. BOOKS

AMATO, G., *Antitrust and the Bounds of Power* (Hart Publishing, 1997) Chapter 4

BUTTERWORTHS, *Competition Law* (eds. P. Freeman and R. Whish) (Butterworths, looseleaf), Division I, paras. 185–205

KERSE, C. S., *EC Antitrust Procedure* (4th edn., Sweet & Maxwell, 1998), Chapter 2

NEALE, A. D., and GOYDER, D. G., *The Antitrust Laws of the United States* (3rd edn., Cambridge University Press, 1981)

B. ARTICLES

BROWN, A., 'Notification of Agreements to the EC Commission: Whether to Submit to a Flawed System' (1992) 17 *ELRev.* 323

FORRESTER, I., and NORALL, C., 'The Laicization of Community Law: Self-help and the Rule of Reason: How Competition Law is and could be Applied' (1984) 21 *CMLRev.* 11

HAWK, B. E., 'System Failure: Vertical Restraints and EC Competition Law' (1995) 32 *CMLRev.* 973

KORAH, V., 'EEC Competition Policy—Legal Form or Economic Efficiency' [1986] *Current Legal Problems* 85

SIRAGUSA, M., 'Notification of Agreements in the EEC—To Notify or Not to Notify?' [1986] *Fordham Corporate Law Institute* 243

WHISH, R., and SUFRIN, B., 'Article 85 and the Rule of Reason' [1987] *YEL* 1

---

[292] COM (2000) 582.

[293] *Ibid*, Art. 1.

[294] *Ibid.*, e.g. Arts. 4–6, 11–16.

[295] *Ibid.*, e.g. Arts. 7, 19–20. It is also includes other provisions that the Commission considers will improve on the current system.

5

ARTICLE 82 (FORMERLY ARTICLE 86): THE ELEMENTS

1. INTRODUCTION

Article 82 is designed to deal with monopoly and market power. It focuses not on agreements *between* undertakings (as Article 81 does) but on undertakings which hold a 'dominant position'. It constrains the behaviour of undertakings which are not restrained by other competitors operating on the market by prohibiting the 'abuse' of a dominant position.

The application of Article 82 by the Commission and the Court has often been highly controversial. This has sometimes been due to a questionable finding that an undertaking is dominant for the purposes of the Article. It has also partly been due to the failure at times of the authorities to address the policy objectives being pursued in the enforcement of the prohibition. As in the case of Article 81, the objectives pursued have a huge impact on the interpretation of the provision,[1] in particular whether or not behaviour is characterized as abusive.

As we saw in Chapter 1,[2] a monopolist is able to restrict output and increase prices without losing sales to competitors. It can reap monopoly profits. Article 82 prohibits an undertaking with a dominant position from exploiting that position, for example by charging unfair prices, by limiting production, or by refusing to innovate to the prejudice of the consumer.[3] In addition, it is clear from the case law of the ECJ that the provision also prohibits dominant undertakings from engaging in anti-competitive conduct which reinforces their position and excludes actual or potential competitors from the market.[4] There is a fear that dominant undertakings will erect artificial barriers denying competitors the opportunity to compete. Article 82 therefore regulates the behaviour of dominant undertakings which weaken the already weak competitive structure of the market.

There have been decisions taken under Article 82 which suggest that the Commission has acted not to protect the competitive process but to protect a competitor or a smaller undertaking operating on the market.[5] In the extract below Korah suggests that this approach

---

[1] See *supra* Chap. 4.

[2] See *supra* Chap. 1.

[3] See *infra* Chap. 7.

[4] See Case 6/72, *Europemballage Corp and Continental Can Co Inc v. Commission* [1973] ECR 215, [1973] CMLR 199 and Chap. 7 *passim*.

[5] See e.g. Cases 6 and 7/73, *Istituto Chemioterapico Italiano SpA and Commercial Solvents Corp v. Commission* [1974] ECR 223, [1974] 1 CMLR 309; Case 22/78, *Hugin Kassaregister AB and Hugin Cash Registers Ltd v. Commission* [1979] ECR 1869, [1979] 3 CMLR 345.

penalizes competitors winning the competitive process on account of their superior efficiency.

V. Korah, *An Introductory Guide to EC Competition Law and Practice* (7ᵗʰ edn., Hart Publishing, 2000), paragraph 3.1

In the E.C., however, there is concern . . . that large firms may make it hard for smaller firms to compete, even if the latter are less efficient . . . The preamble to the treaty refers to many factors other than efficiency, such as social policy, fair competition, small and medium-sized undertakings, peace and liberty. To protect small firms that are less efficient, it may be necessary to control the conduct of firms that have no power over price. To serve these objectives, which may detract from efficiency, entry barriers may be perceived as pervasive including all the investments to be made by the new entrant, even if the incumbent had to make similar investments.

Further, some cases decided under Article 82 appear to have been motivated by a desire to prevent an undertaking from engaging in behaviour which divides up the market on territorial grounds, contrary to the goal of market integration. In *United Brands*, for example, the Commission particularly objected to UBC's policy of charging different prices for its bananas on different national markets.[6]

2.   THE TEXT OF ARTICLE 82

Article 82 provides:

Any abuse by one or more undertakings of a dominant position within the common market or in a substantial part of it shall be prohibited as incompatible with the common market insofar as it may affect trade between Member States.

Such abuse may, in particular, consist in:

(a) directly or indirectly imposing unfair purchase or selling prices or other unfair trading conditions;

(b) limiting production, markets or technical development to the prejudice of consumers;

(c) applying dissimilar conditions to equivalent transactions with other trading parties, thereby placing them at a competitive disadvantage;

(d) making the conclusion of contracts subject to acceptance by the other parties of supplementary obligations which, by their nature or according to commercial usage, have no connection with the subject of such contracts.

---

[6] Case 27/76, *United Brands Co and United Brands Continental BV* v. *Commission* [1978] ECR 207, [1978] 1 CMLR 429.

3. THE SCHEME OF ARTICLE 82

A. THE PROHIBITION

Article 82 prohibits undertakings from committing an abuse of a dominant position held within a substantial part of the common market where that abuse has an effect on trade between Member States. Although sub-paragraphs (a) to (d) set out examples of abuses, they are illustrative only and do not provide an exhaustive list.[7] The essential elements of Article 82 are set out in its first sentence.

Article 82 thus prohibits dominant undertakings from engaging in certain conduct. The provision does not set out a procedure for declaring an undertaking to be dominant and so subject to Article 82. An undertaking is dominant simply when it satisfies the definition set out by the ECJ.[8] Its conduct then, automatically, becomes subject to the prohibition.

Article 82 contains no exemption provision equivalent to that in Article 81(3).[9] It is, however, always open to a dominant undertaking to plead that its conduct is 'objectively justified' by legitimate commercial reasons.[10] Further, although it must be established that the dominant position is held 'in a substantial part of the common market', there is no *de minimis* rule equivalent to that adopted by the ECJ in relation to Article 81(1).[11]

It can be seen from the text of Article 82 that five essential elements must be established before the prohibition applies. The five elements are:

    (a) one or more undertakings;

    (b) a dominant position;

    (c) the dominant position must be held within the common market or a substantial part of it;

    (d) an abuse; and

    (e) an effect on inter-state trade.

It is extremely difficult to determine whether or not these criteria have been satisfied, in particular whether an undertaking holds a 'dominant position' and/or whether it has committed an 'abuse' of that dominant position.

The question whether an undertaking is dominant, for example, requires the market on which the undertaking is alleged to be dominant to be defined, and the problems of market definitions are notorious. The undertaking's position on the market must then be assessed. This depends primarily upon the complex question whether barriers to entry exist which

---

  [7] See Case 6/72, *Europemballage Corp and Continental Can Co Inc* v. *Commission* [1973] ECR 215, [1973] CMLR 199. See the discussion *infra*, 241–244.

  [8] See *infra*, 234.

  [9] Although it is possible to apply for a negative clearance, see Reg. 17, Art. 2 (JO 204/62, (1959–1962) OJ Spec. Ed. 87).

  [10] See *infra* 251 ff.

  [11] See Chap. 3. It could be argued, however, that the ECJ applied a type of *de minimis* rule in Case 22/78, *Hugin Kassaregister AB and Hugin Cash Registers Ltd* v. *Commission* [1979] ECR 1869, [1979] 3 CMLR 345, see *infra* 255–256.

prevent other undertakings from entering that market. It is crucial that these definitions and assessments are made properly. Although it is not an offence to hold a dominant position (Article 82 does not prohibit the holding of a dominant position *per se* but only an abuse of that dominant position), it is clear that some behaviour which may be competitive or at least neutral from a competition perspective when engaged in by an undertaking which does not have market power may have serious effects on competition and be prohibited when engaged in by a dominant undertaking.[12] An incorrect finding of dominance may consequently lead to a ruling that an undertaking's ordinary competitive behaviour is abusive conduct prohibited by Article 82. In addition, if the concept of an abuse is found to encompass a wide spectrum of behaviour, Article 82 may come perilously close to forbidding the dominance itself.

The question of what amounts to an 'abuse' is also a vexed one. It requires a determination of what conduct can and what conduct cannot legitimately be carried out by a dominant undertaking. This, of course, depends partly upon the purposes of the whole provision. As stated above, it has not always been entirely clear what objectives have been pursued in the enforcement of Article 82.[13]

Another important point is that the jurisprudence of the Court establishes that in some circumstances the abuse may be committed on a different market from that on which the dominant position is held. Thus an undertaking may be dominant on one market and abuse that dominant position by engaging in conduct on another.[14]

This chapter, after setting out the consequences of infringing Article 82, considers the five elements of Article 82 in turn and deals with general issues concerning their scope, interpretation, and application. Chapters 6 and 7 consider in greater detail (1) how it is ascertained whether an undertaking holds a dominant position and (2) what conduct constitutes an abuse of a dominant position. It is important to realise, however, that the different elements of Article 82 cannot always be considered separately from one another. In particular, the cases establish that the questions whether an undertaking is in a dominant position and whether it has committed an abuse may be interrelated and intertwined.

B. CONSEQUENCES OF INFRINGEMENT

(i) INVESTIGATION, FINES AND OTHER REMEDIES

The Commission may investigate undertakings it believes to have committed a breach of Article 82. Where it finds that a violation of Article 82 has been committed, the Commission can issue a decision ordering the undertaking to put an end to the abuse (by positive or negative conduct).[15] Further, it can impose fines on the undertaking of up to 10 per cent of its turnover in the preceding year of business. The Commission has imposed substantial

---

[12] See *infra* 239 ff.

[13] See *infra* Chap. 7.

[14] See Case C–333/94P, *Tetra Pak International SA v. Commission* [1996] ECR I–5951, [1997] 4 CMLR 662.

[15] See *infra* Chap. 14 particularly 892–896. The Commission proposes in the draft for a new Reg. implementing Arts. 81 and 82 that it should have the power to impose remedies of a structural nature: COM (2000) 582, Art. 7.

fines on undertakings found to have committed a breach of Article 82. In *Tetra Pak II*[16] the Commission imposed a fine of ECU 75 million on a single undertaking and in *TACA*[17] it imposed a total fine of ECU 273 million on undertakings found to have committed an abuse of a collective dominant position.

The difficulties involved in determining whether or not an infringement of Article 82 has been committed and the controversy surrounding many of the Commission's decisions taken under Article 82 has rendered the Commission's willingness to impose heavy fines in respect of breaches of the Article extremely contentious.

(ii) PRIVATE ACTION

Article 82, like Article 81(1), is directly effective.[18] It is possible, therefore, that an entity injured by a breach of Article 82 may bring proceedings before a national court seeking an injunction or damages in respect of loss resulting from the breach.[19]

Further, a party to a contract concluded with a dominant undertaking may claim that clauses within it are prohibited by Article 82 and consequently void or unenforceable. That party may also bring proceedings to recover benefits conferred under a prohibited provision.[20]

4. THE INTERPRETATION AND APPLICATION OF ARTICLE 82

A. THE MEANING OF ONE OR MORE UNDERTAKINGS

(i) GENERAL

'Undertaking' is interpreted in the same way for the purpose of Article 82 as it is in the context of Article 81. It has been construed broadly and 'encompasses every entity engaged

---

[16] [1992] OJ L72/1, [1992] 4 CMLR 551; on appeal Case T–83/91, *Tetra Pak International SA* v. *Commission* [1994] ECR II–755, [1997] 4 CMLR 726 (CFI) and Case C–333/94P, *Tetra Pak International SA* v. *Commission* [1996] ECR I–5951, [1997] 4 CMLR 662 (ECJ).

[17] *Re The Transatlantic Conference Agreement* [1999] OJ L95/1, [1999] 4 CMLR 1415.

[18] See Case 127/73, *Belgische Radio en Televisie and Société belge des auteurs, compositeurs et editeurs* v. *SV SABAM and NV Fonior* [1974] ECR 313, [1974] 2 CMLR 238. The equivalent Art. of the ECSC Treaty, Art. 66(7), does not have direct effect because it confers sole jurisdiction on the Commission; see Case C–128/92 *HJ Banks & Co Ltd* v. *British Coal Corp* [1994] ECR I–1209, [1994] 5 CMLR 30, paras. 18–19.

[19] Whether or not it will be able to do so will be dependent upon (a) whether there is a Community right to damages where undertakings have committed breaches of the Community competition rules and/or (b) the relevant national rules. It seems probable that a party injured by an undertaking's breach of Art. 82 would be able to recover damages before an English court on account of the undertaking's breach of statutory duty: see *infra* Chap. 15.

[20] See *infra* Chap. 15.

in an economic activity'.[21] Two points of particular importance arise when considering the meaning of the term 'undertaking' within the context of Article 82. First, since state regulation is a frequent source of an entity's market power, it is crucial to know to what extent public bodies or bodies with a special connection with the state will be characterized as undertakings and so potentially subject to Article 82. Secondly, it must be considered what is meant by 'one or more undertakings' in Article 82. So far, reference has been made to the problems caused by monopoly and market power held by an individual undertaking. It is clearly envisaged, however, that Article 82 should apply to the conduct of more than one undertaking. Is Article 82 confined to the conduct of undertakings which are part of the same single economic entity (in which a united policy may be pursued) or does Article 82 go further and prohibit the conduct of one or more independent undertakings?

(ii) PUBLIC BODIES AND BODIES PERFORMING PUBLIC FUNCTIONS

The term 'undertaking' applies to any entity engaged in commercial activities whether or not it is a state entity, even if it has no identity separate from that of the State.[22] Further, it is clear from Articles 10 and 86(1) of the Treaty that the State itself cannot confer immunity upon undertakings from the application of those rules. The fact that an undertaking's market power has been created by state action is no defence to an action based on Article 82 unless the narrow exception set out in Article 86(2) applies. This provision states that '[u]ndertakings entrusted with the operation of services of general economic interest or having the character of a revenue-producing monopoly' are subject to the competition rules unless those rules 'obstruct the performance, in law or in fact, of the particular tasks assigned to them'. The net result of the broad interpretation of the term 'undertaking' and the narrow interpretation of Article 86(2) mean that few entities escape on these grounds the prohibition set out in Article 82. This topic is discussed in Chapter 8.

(iii) ONE OR MORE UNDERTAKINGS—COLLECTIVE DOMINANCE

a. SINGLE ECONOMIC ENTITY

Initially it was believed that the term 'one or more undertakings' referred only to bodies which were part of the same economic entity. The purpose of the term was to ensure that the conduct of all bodies within the corporate group was taken into account when assessing whether or not a breach of Article 82 had occurred. Thus circumstances such as those which arose in *Continental Can* and *Commercial Solvents* would be caught. In *Continental Can*,[23] for example, a US company held an 85.8 per cent share in a German company (SLW). It formed a wholly owned Belgian subsidiary through which it acquired a Dutch company which was a competitor of SLW. The Commission held that the American parent had,

---

[21] See *supra* Chap. 3.

[22] See *supra* Chap. 3.

[23] Case 6/72, *Europemballage Corp and Continental Can Co Inc* v. *Commission* [1973] ECR 215, [1973] CMLR 199, see discussion of this case *infra* at 241 ff.

through SLW, a dominant position in a substantial part of the common market and that an abuse of the dominant position was committed when it used its Belgian subsidiary to take over the Dutch company.[24] Similarly, in *Commercial Solvents*[25] a US parent and its 51per cent owned Italian subsidiary were involved in a refusal to supply a third party in Italy with a raw material produced by the parent. The subsidiary followed the policy laid down by the parent and both were held to have abused a dominant position. This belief that Article 82 might be confined to bodies forming part of the same economic unit or the same corporate group found support from a statement of the ECJ in *Hoffmann La-Roche*[26].

Such an interpretation would, however, have meant that the term 'undertaking' in the context of Article 82 had a different meaning from that which it had in relation to Article 81. In Chapter 3 it was explained that the term 'undertaking' itself applied to all bodies which formed part of the same economic entity. Bodies within the same corporate group are treated as a single undertaking if those bodies 'form an economic unit within which the subsidiary has no real freedom to determine its course of action on the market, and if the agreements or practices are concerned merely with the internal allocation of tasks as between the undertakings'.[27] If interpreted in the same way, Article 82 would have applied to the behaviour of all bodies which formed an economic unit even if the Article had referred only to an abuse by *an* undertaking of a dominant position. So *what* interpretation should be given to the phrase 'one or more undertakings'?

b. ONE OR MORE INDEPENDENT UNDERTAKINGS

In *Flat Glass* the CFI confirmed that the term 'undertaking' had the same meaning within the context of both Articles 82 and 81.

It has consistently been held . . . that the concept of agreement or concerted practice between undertakings does not cover agreements or concerted practices among undertakings belonging to the same group if the undertakings form an economic unit . . . The Court considers that there is no legal or economic reason to suppose that the term 'undertaking' in Article [82] has a different meaning from the one given to it in the context of Article [81].[28]

The Court went on to say that Article 82 could apply to the conduct of two or more independent economic entities which were 'united by such economic links that, by virtue of

---

[24] *Re Continental Can Co Inc* [1972] JO L7/25, [1972] CMLR D11. The ECJ annulled the Commission's decision on the ground of an erroneous definition of the market (see *infra* Chap. 6) but the point about the aggregation of the activities of the group was not doubted.

[25] Cases 6 and 7/73, *Istituto Chemioterapico Italiano SpA and Commercial Solvents Corp* v. *Commission* [1974] ECR 223, [1974] 1 CMLR 309.

[26] Case 85/76, *Hoffmann-La Roche & Co AG* v. *Commission* [1979] ECR 461, [1979] 3 CMLR 211, para. 39.

[27] Case 15/74, *Centrafarm BV and Adriaan De Peijper* v. *Sterling Drug Inc* [1974] ECR 1147, [1974] 2 CMLR 480, para. 41, repeated in Case 30/87, *Bodson* v. *Pompes funèbres des régions libérées SA* [1988] ECR 2479, [1989] 4 CMLR 984, para. 19. See the discussion *supra* at Chap. 3. This seems to be a two-pronged test, but in Case C–73/95P *Viho Europe BV* v. *Commission* [1996] ECR I–5457, [1997] 4 CMLR 419, para. 16, the ECJ concentrated on the lack of freedom aspect. 'Parker and its subsidiaries thus form a single economic unit within which the subsidiaries do not enjoy real autonomy in determining their course of action in the market, but carry out the instructions issued to them by the parent company controlling them.' See further Cases C–395 & 396/96P *Compagnie Maritime Belge Transports SA* v. *Commission*, [2000] 4 CMLR 1076 Opinion of Fennelly AG para. 24.

[28] Cases T–68, 77 & 78/89, *Società Italiano Vetro SpA* v. *Commission* [1992] ECR II–1403, [1992] 5 CMLR 302, paras. 357–358.

that fact, together they hold a dominant position'. This is known as 'collective', 'joint' or 'oligopolistic' dominance. Immediately following *Flat Glass* there was much speculation about what the Court had meant when it referred to economic links. It was uncertain what types of links would have to be found between the entities before they could be held to be sufficiently united. It seemed clear that Article 82 would apply where the entities were united by structural links, such as contractual ones, but there was disagreement about when else it would apply. Would it, for example, apply where the only link between the parties was the economic interdependence which independent undertakings have with each other on an oligopolistic market? In *Compagnie Maritime Belge Transports SA v. Commission*, the ECJ held that contractual or other links in law are not essential to a finding of collective dominance. On the contrary, such a finding could be based on 'other connecting factors and would depend on an economic assessment and, in particular, on an assessment of the structure of the market in question'.[29] This appears to confirm the ruling of the CFI in *Gencor v. Commission*, a case dealing with the concept of collective dominance for the purposes of the Merger Regulation. In that case the Court held that a collective dominant position can be found where the economic links between the undertakings are formed only by 'the relationship of interdependence existing between the parties to a tight oligopoly within which, in a market with the appropriate characteristics, in particular in terms of market concentration, transparency and product homogeneity, those parties are in a position to anticipate one another's behaviour and are therefore strongly encouraged to align their conduct in the market'.[30] Although in this case the Court was not dealing with the meaning of collective dominance within the context of Article 82 it did refer to, and rely on, dicta of the CFI in *Flat Glass*. This and other cases[31] suggest that the Court will adopt a similar test when determining whether or not a collective dominant position exists for the purposes of both the Merger Regulation and Article 82. The extent to which Article 82 and the Merger Regulation apply to positions of collective dominance will be discussed in greater detail in Chapters 11 and 12 respectively.

B. DOMINANT POSITION

(i) WHAT IS MEANT BY A 'DOMINANT POSITION'?

Whether or not an undertaking holds a 'dominant position' is of central importance to Article 82. Clearly the phrase is not intended only to refer to monopolists (the sole undertaking on a relevant market). It is also intended to control the behaviour of undertakings which have market power.[32] The difficulty is to determine what degree of market power is necessary before Article 82 applies.

---

[29] Cases C–395 & 396/96P, *Compagnie Maritime Belge Transports SA v. Commission*, [2000] 4 CMLR 1076, para. 45.

[30] Case T–102/96, *Gencor Ltd v. Commission* [1999] ECR II–753, [1999] 4 CMLR 971, para. 276.

[31] See Case T–228/97, *Irish Sugar plc v. Commission* [1999] 5 CMLR 1300, and Cases C–395 & 396/96P, *Compagnie Maritime Belge Transports SA v. Commission*, [2000] 4 CMLR 1076, para. 41.

[32] Although the words 'monopoly' and 'monopolist' are sometimes used as a shorthand to cover both situations.

Perfect competition is rarely encountered outside textbooks, almost all firms have some market power, though most have very little. Accordingly, the relevant question in antitrust cases is not whether market power is present, but whether it is important. [33]

An initial problem for Article 82 is, therefore, to identify with sufficient clarity the point at which an undertaking becomes, and can know it becomes, dominant and so subject to the prohibition. This point is likely to be defined by reference to political considerations as much as scientific ones. The authorities identify the point on the spectrum of market power at which they wish to be able to control the activities of an undertaking.

In the extract below, Hawk suggests that the point at which undertakings are found to become subject to competition rules aimed at controlling the behaviour of firms with market power may, or may not, coincide with an economist's view:

B.E. Hawk, *United States, Common Market and International Antitrust: A Comparative Guide* (2nd edn., Aspen Law & Business, 1990), ii, 788–789

Economics provides a variety of tools to measure degrees of market power. Market power is the power to raise prices by restricting output without a significant loss of sales—i.e., the power to fix prices or exclude competition. Any firm facing an inelastic demand or downward-sloping demand curve has some market power in an economic sense. But economics does not define—except at the extreme—at what point that market power becomes 'monopoly power' . . . Thus, economics does not provide the means to resolve the essentially legal question whether the market power of a firm is sufficiently great to constitute a 'dominant position' or 'monopoly power.' Like relevant market definition, 'dominant position' and 'monopoly power' are legal constructs based on policy considerations which suggest where the line should be drawn between acceptable market power and suspect monopoly power. For example, there could be an inverse sliding scale between the degree of power required and the invidiousness of the abusive or monopolizing conduct. Or broad definitions of what constitute abusive conduct might prompt a higher threshold of market power, particularly where broad definitions of abuse capture competitively ambiguous conduct and run the risk of inhibiting desirable competitive conduct (such as price reductions).

Obviously the definition of the term 'dominant position' should relate to the adverse consequences which result when an undertaking has market power. The traditional objection to an undertaking with market power is, of course, its inefficiency. Allocative inefficiency results from its ability to increase price and productive inefficiency is likely to result from the ability to lead a quiet life. These problems will not arise if consumers have an alternative choice of products/services or suppliers. The increase in price or poor quality of the product or service will prompt consumers to look elsewhere. An undertaking should be found to be dominant, therefore, only if its conduct is not constrained by the existence of competitors producing competing products and services.

[33] R. Schmalensee, 'Another Look at Market Power' (1981–82) 95 *Harvard LR* 1789, 1790.

V. Korah, 'Concept of a Dominant Position Within the Meaning of Article 86' (1980) 17 *CMLRev.* 395, 395–6

The objection to market power expressed by classical economists is the ability of the monopolist to pursue goals other than production and distribution of goods and services that customers are prepared to pay for with a minimum of resources. Their emphasis was on efficiency, both in the use of existing resources. . . and in increasing output with existing or new investment when and where demand is buoyant and more than a normal return on capital may be expected. . .

The functions of prices in competitive markets include matching supply and demand in the short and long terms. Prices act as signals. If demand exceeds supply, prices rise and in the short term ration the use of scarce resources through high prices that deter those whose demand is least strong. In the longer term, prices that yield high profits encourage new suppliers to enter a market or existing firms to expand production, thereby increasing supply to the benefit of customers. Where supply exceeds demand, prices that yield low profits have the opposite effects. If competitive pressures from existing or new firms are allowed to operate freely, this ensures that those firms that use existing resources inefficiently, or enter markets where demand is insufficient should earn lower profits and be unable to expand as much as those making products for which customers are prepared to pay a price yielding higher profits. Where markets are less competitive, however, existing firms have greater freedom of action in their pricing and other marketing strategies and the risk of new competition materialising is less. Existing firms may be able to survive and expand even if they operate inefficiently. Like their predecessors, modern economists focus their interest on the discretionary power of the monopolist both in marketing and production, unconstrained towards efficiency judged in terms of customer demand rather than profits for shareholders or employees.

Monopoly may be defined either in terms of freedom of action for the monopolist or absence of risk. Many firms have enough market power to adopt a marketing strategy—most well-advertised brands sell at higher prices than unbranded substitutes and trade mark holders can choose whether to advertise more or cut prices. In a competitive market, however, price differences maintained by advertising become eroded by retailers' house brands and monopoly pricing of manufacturers' brands becomes eroded by competition from other brands. Only a monopoly can exercise a marketing strategy without exposing himself to considerable risks if he makes the wrong decision.

There is no sharp division between monopoly and competition: market power is a matter of degree. Considerable market power over a period of time presupposes the absence of substitutes to which customers could turn at lower prices and the existence of barriers to entry preventing new competition from materialising, even when supply is profitable. The absence of new competition does not demonstrate market power. Even a sole supplier may be constrained by fear of entry and charge only competitive prices where barriers to entry are not high; in which case, the market is already operating competitively. There will be market power only if entry is not attracted when prices and other market policies are such that an efficient existing firm can earn abnormal profits on the capital invested therein. It is, however, difficult to judge whether the existing firm is earning high profits . . .

In this extract it is suggested that dominance can be defined in terms either of freedom of action or of absence from risk. Further, the importance of identifying both the products/ services and firms (existing or potential) whose presence constrains the price-setting behaviour of the firm in question is stressed. In determining whether or not an undertaking is dominant the authorities should, therefore, seek to identify whether there are any competitors capable of constraining the undertaking's behaviour and preventing it from behaving independently of effective competitive pressure.

(ii) THE LEGAL DEFINITION

Both the Commission and the Court have concentrated on the ability of a dominant under-taking to act independently on a market and, consequently, their freedom of action. In *Continental Can* the Commission described market power in terms of independence and power over price.

Undertakings are in a dominant position when they have the power to behave independently, which puts them in a position to act without taking into account their competitors, purchasers or suppliers. That is the position when, because of their share of the market, or of their share of the market combined with the availability of technical knowledge, raw materials or capital, they have the power to determine prices or to control production or distribution for a significant part of the products in question. This power does not necessarily have to derive from an absolute domination permitting the undertakings which hold it to eliminate all will on the part of their economic partners, but it is enough that they be strong enough as a whole to ensure to those undertakings an overall independence of behaviour, even if there are differences in intensity in their influence on the different partial markets.[34]

In *United Brands* the ECJ set out a definition of 'dominant position' which it has fre-quently relied upon. It held that an undertaking would hold a dominant position where it could prevent effective competition being maintained by virtue of its ability to behave independently of the usual competitive constraints facing an entity operating on a market.

The dominant position referred to in this article relates to a position of economic strength enjoyed by an undertaking which enables it to prevent effective competition being maintained on the relevant market by giving it the power to behave to an appreciable extent independently of its competitors, customers and ultimately of its consumers.[35]

In *Hoffmann-La Roche* the ECJ elaborated on this definition. It emphasized that a position of dominance did not preclude some competition and particularly focused on the ability of the undertaking to influence the conditions of competition occurring on the market:

38. The dominant position thus referred to relates to a position of economic strength enjoyed by an undertaking which enables it to prevent effective competition being maintained on the relevant market by affording it the power to behave to an appreciable extent independently of its competitors, its customers and ultimately of its consumers.

39. Such a position does not preclude some competition, which it does where there is a monopoly or quasi-monopoly, but enables the undertaking which profits by it, if not to determine, at least to have an appreciable influence on the conditions under which that competition will develop, and in any case to act largely in disregard of it so long as such conduct does not operate to its detriment.[36]

Commentators have questioned whether the reference both to the ability of the undertaking

---

[34] *Re Continental Can Co Inc* [1972] JO L7/25, [1972] CMLR D11, para. 3. In the appeal, Case 6/72, *Europemballage Corp and Continental Can Co Inc v. Commission* [1973] ECR 215, [1973] CMLR 199 the ECJ did not expressly comment on the Commission's formulation of dominance, but it was approved by Roemer A-G at [1973] ECR 215, 257, [1973] CMLR 199, 209–10 and implicitly by the Court.

[35] Case 27/76, *United Brands Co and United Brands Continental BV v. Commission* [1978] ECR 207, [1978] 1 CMLR 429, para. 65.

[36] Case 85/76, *Hoffmann-La Roche & Co AG v. Commission* [1979] ECR 461, [1979] 3 CMLR 211.

to impede effective competition—which means the power to exclude competition—and to behave independently are different tests or part of the same test.[37]

V. Korah, *An Introductory Guide to EC Competition Law and Practice* (7th edn., Hart Publishing, 2000), section 3.2.

The power to behave independently sounds like the economists' concept of power over price. A monopolist, unconstrained by competitive pressures, enjoys a discretion in its pricing and other market decisions. The application of competition policy to the conduct of such a firm may protect those with whom it deals. The concept of 'economic strength . . . which enables a firm to impede effective competition', however, may indicate a different idea: the ability to foreclose and keep other firms out of the market. Such strategic behaviour may be restrained by the Commission to help a firm's competitors. Such strength does not always imply power over price.

The better view is that the requirement that the undertaking should be able to exclude competition is descriptive. It describes the ability of a dominant undertaking to act independently on the market by engaging in anti-competitive conduct and excluding competition from the market.

The freedom of action normally considered by economists to be the hallmark of monopoly-type power is power over price: the ability of a firm to raise price above the competitive level without attracting new entrants and without losing sales to competitors so rapidly that the price increase is unprofitable and must be rescinded.[38] In US law, monopoly power for the purposes of section 2 of the Sherman Act has been defined as the power to control prices or to exclude competition.[39] The difference between that and the EC test is therefore that the latter uses a wider concept of 'independence' rather than expressing it as the power to control prices. The EC test is more nebulous, and, in conjunction with finding that the independence has to exist only 'to an appreciable extent', arguably brings inherent uncertainty to the operation of Article 82.

(iii) SUPER-DOMINANCE

It seems that a new concept of 'super-dominance'[40] is emerging.[41] Such a concept may mean that there is an important relationship between the degree of market power and the types of behaviour characterized as abusive. A wider spectrum of conduct may be found to be abusive the closer the undertaking's position approximates to that of a monopolist.[42]

---

[37] See, e.g., R. Joliet, *Monoplization and Abuse of Dominant Position* (Nijhoff, Dordredit, 1970), 75–7, J. Temple Lang, 'Abuse of Dominant Positions in European Community Law, Present and Future: Some Aspects [1978] Fordham Corp. L Inst. 25, 34–5; V. Korah, *An Introductory Guide to EC Competition Law and Practice* (7th edn. Hart Publishing, 2000), para. 3.2; B.E. Hawk, *United States, Common Market and International Antitrust: A Comparative Guide* (2nd edn. Aspen Law and Business, 1990) II, 796–9.

[38] See W. Landes and R. Posner, 'Market Power in Antitrust Cases' (1980–81) 94 *Harvard, LR* 937.

[39] See *Standard Oil Co of New Jersey* v. *United States*, 221 US 1 (1911); *United States* v. *E I du Pont de Nemours & Co*, 351 U.S. 377 (1956); *United States* v. *Grinnell Corp*, 384 US 563 (1966).

[40] Super-dominance will be discussed in greater detail in Chaps. 6 and 7 *infra*.

[41] See, e.g., *1998 Football World Cup* [2000] OJ L5/55, [2000] 4 CMLR 963, para. 86; Cases C–395 & 396/96P, *Compagnie Maritime Belge Transports SA* v. *Commission* [2000] 4 CMLR 1076, paras. 113–121, and Opinion of Fennelly AG, and para. 136.

[42] See Chaps. 6 and 7.

(iv) ASSESSING DOMINANCE

It is clear from this discussion of dominance and market power that neither concept exists in abstract. Rather, a dominant position exists in relation to a market. In *Continental Can* the ECJ stated that 'the definition of the relevant market is of essential significance'[43] and has stressed this consistently ever since. It will quash the Commission's decision where it fails adequately to define the market.[44]

The relevant market has three aspects, product (or service), geographic, and, in some cases, temporal, although the temporal aspect is sometimes a part of the product dimension.[45] The practice of the Commission, endorsed by the Court, has been first to identify the relevant market and then to assess the undertaking's position on that market. The Community authorities usually assess the power of the undertaking by looking at its market share and then at other factors which may indicate that an undertaking is dominant.

In some cases it may be difficult to separate these two stages in the process.[46] The two issues may be intertwined. Further to complicate matters, the question whether an undertaking is dominant may be affected by its allegedly abusive conduct.[47]

In Chapter 6 we set out how the Community authorities have defined the market and assessed market power. In many of the cases the findings of both the Court and the Commission have been controversial. The authorities have been criticized for defining markets too narrowly and for being too ready to find that an undertaking is dominant on a particular market, usually because they have not taken a realistic view of what amounts to a barrier to entry but have seen barriers as pervasive. This approach, coupled with the wide interpretation that has been adopted in relation to the term 'abuse',[48] means that the EC competition authorities have played an interventionist, regulatory role. The Commission has been much more interventionist than the US antitrust authorities, for example, when applying the US counterpart, section 2 of the Sherman Act.[49]

The concept of a 'dominant position' is also a term employed within the Merger Regulation.[50] The Commission has relied on the definition of dominance set out in Article 82 cases when dealing with mergers. It thus appears that the concept of a dominant position is interpreted in the same way for the purposes of both Article 82 and the Merger Regulation. An important point, however, is that the concept is 'necessarily applied from different perspectives'.[51] In the context of Article 82 a retrospective analysis is necessary (did the

---

[43] Case 6/72, *Europemballage Corp and Continental Can Co Inc* v. *Commission* [1973] ECR 215, [1973] CMLR 199, para. 42.

[44] In Case 6/72, *Europemballage Corp and Continental Can Co Inc* v. *Commission* [1973] ECR 215, [1973] CMLR 199, the ECJ quashed the Commission's decision on account of its failure to define adequately the market from the supply side.

[45] See *infra* Chap. 6.

[46] See *ibid.*

[47] See *ibid.*

[48] See *infra* Chaps. 6 and 7.

[49] See, e.g., P. Jebsen and R. Stevens, 'Assumptions, Goals and Dominant Undertakings: The Reg. of Competition Under Art 86 of the European Union' (1995–96) 64 *Antitrust Law Journal* 443, *infra* 248.

[50] Council Reg. 4046/89 [1989] OJ L395/1, as amended by Council Reg. 1310/97 [1997] OJ L180/1. See *infra* Chap. 12.

[51] J. Faull and A. Nikpay (eds.), *The EC Law of Competition* (Oxford University Press, Oxford 1999), para. 3.32.

undertaking have a dominant position and did it abuse that position?). In contrast, a prospective analysis is usually[52] necessary for the purposes of the Merger Regulation (will this concentration lead to the creation or strengthening of a dominant position?).[53]

C. A DOMINANT POSITION WITHIN A SUBSTANTIAL PART OF THE COMMON MARKET

(i) PURPOSE OF THE REQUIREMENT

The dominant position of the undertaking must be held within the common market or within a substantial part of it. The purpose of this requirement is to exclude from the Article's scope purely localized monopoly situations in which there is no Community interest. Together with the necessity that the abuse of a dominant position has an effect on trade between Member States,[54] the requirement determines the limit of the Community jurisdiction.

(ii) MEANING OF A SUBSTANTIAL PART OF THE COMMON MARKET

A 'substantial part' does not simply mean substantial in geographic terms. It is not a matter of counting hectares. In *Suiker Unie* the ECJ stated that:

[f]or the purpose of determining whether a specific territory is large enough to amount to a 'substantial part of the common market' within the meaning of Article [82] of the Treaty the pattern and volume of the production and consumption of the said product as well as the habits and economic opportunities of vendors and purchasers must be considered.[55]

(iii) RELEVANCE OF VOLUME OF PRODUCTION

In *Suiker Unie* the ECJ compared the volume of sugar production in Belgium, Luxembourg, and southern Germany to that of Community production overall. It held that each of those markets was a substantial part of the common market. The ECJ has never specified whether there is a particular percentage of the Community market which could automatically be said to satisfy the 'substantial' criterion. However, Advocate General Warner, in his Opinion in the *ABG Oil* case,[56] considered that the Dutch petrol market, which was approximately 4.6 per cent of the overall Community market, was substantial. He stated that:

---

[52] It is only very occasionally that the Commission has to assess the compatibility with the merger rules of a concentration which has already been completed: see *infra* Chap. 12.

[53] The SSNIP test, employed in the determination of the relevant market, is more likely to be accurate where a prospective analysis is carried out than when a retrospective analysis is carried out. See the discussion of the SSNIP test and the *Cellophane* fallacy, *supra* Chap. 1.

[54] See *infra* 255 ff.

[55] Cases 40–48, 50, 54–56, 111, 113 and 114/73, *Coöperatieve Vereniging 'Suiker Unie' UA* v. *Commission* [1975] ECR 1663, [1976] 1 CMLR 295, para. 371.

[56] Case 77/77, *Benzine en Petroleum Handelsmaatschappij BV* v. *Commission* [1978] ECR 1513, [1978] 3 CMLR 174.

[t]here is . . . in my opinion, in this kind of field, a danger in focusing attention exclusively on percentages. The opposite of 'substantial' is 'negligible', and what may seem negligible when looked at in the terms of a percentage may seem otherwise when looked at in absolute terms. The population of Luxembourg is, I believe, about 0.23% of the population of the whole Community. I would however shrink from saying that one who had a monopoly, or near monopoly, of the Luxembourg market for a particular product was exempt from the application of Article [82].[57]

(iv) A MEMBER STATE IS LIKELY TO BE A SUBSTANTIAL PART OF THE COMMON MARKET

In a number of cases individual Member States have been held to be a 'substantial part'[58] of the common market as have parts of Member States.[59] It has been suggested[60] that as the EU is enlarged the concept of what is a 'substantial part' of it will alter, with previously substantial parts becoming more insignificant so that older cases on this point may no longer be a reliable guide. It is difficult to imagine, however, that the ECJ would find that a single Member State does not constitute a substantial part of the common market even in an EU of twenty or more Member States. This attitude is reflected in the opinion of Advocate General Warner set out above (although at the time there were only nine Member States). As the process of European integration proceeds, however, the delineation of geographic markets is likely to become broader and it will become rarer for a position of dominance to be found to exist in a single Member State.

(v) TRANSPORT CASES

What constitutes a 'substantial part' of the common market may depend on the nature of the market in issue. For example, there have been a number of transport cases in which very small areas have been found to be substantial. In both *Sealink/B&I Holyhead: Interim Measures*[61] and *Sea Containers Ltd* v. *Stena Sealink Ports*[62] Holyhead Harbour was held to be a substantial part of the common market. In the former case the Commission stated:

40. . . . The port of Holyhead constitutes a substantial part of the Common Market because it is a port providing one of the main links between two member-States; more especially, it provides the direct link between Great Britain and the capital city of Ireland. It should also be noted that this is, at least for passengers and cars, the most popular ferry route between Ireland and Great Britain.

---

[57] [1978] ECR 1513, 1537, [1978] 3 CMLR 174, 184.The ECJ held that the undertaking's conduct could not constitute an abuse and did not address the dominance issue: see further Chaps. 6 and 7.

[58] The UK was held to be a substantial part of the common market in Case 226/84, *British Leyland plc* v. *Commission* [1986] ECR 3363, [1987] 1 CMLR 185, as was Belgium in Case 127/73, *Belgische Radio en Televisie and Société belge des auteurs, compositeurs et editeurs* v. *SV SABAM and NV Fonior* [1974] ECR 313, [1974] 2 CMLR 238 and Case 26/75, *General Motors Continental NV* v. *Commission* [1975] ECR 1367, [1976] 1 CMLR 95.

[59] E.g., the south-east of England in Case 22/78, *Hugin Kassaregister AB and Hugin Cash Registers Ltd* v. *Commission* [1979] ECR 1869, [1979] 3 CMLR 345.

[60] See, e.g., M. Furse, *Competition Law of the UK & EC* (2nd edn., Blackstone Press, 2000), 200–201.

[61] [1992] 5 CMLR 255, Commission's, *XXIInd Annual Report on Competition Policy* (Commission, 1992), point 219.

[62] [1994] OJ L15/8, [1995] 4 CMLR 84.

In *Port of Roscoff*[63] the Commission emphasized the importance that might be played by the catchment area served by the port.

58. The market for the supply of port services does not exist in isolation. If there was no demand from consumers for transport services, there would be no demand for port services from ferry operators. The market for transport services between Ireland and Brittany must therefore be taken into account. The port services in Brittany are essential for the operation of ferry services between a Member State, Ireland, to which can be added part of another Member State, Northern Ireland (around five million inhabitants in total), and an important region of another Member State, Brittany (around three million inhabitants). These three regions form a substantial part of the common market. For Ireland, also, the port of Roscoff is an important entry point to the continent and the rest of the Community. It is already used by 25 per cent of ferry passengers between Ireland and France each year.

In *Merci convenzionali* the Court looked to the volume of traffic handled by the port of Genoa. After stressing its importance in relation to the overall volume of imports and exports by sea to and from Italy the Court held that the *market* 'may be regarded as constituting a substantial part of the common market'.[64] The Commission has also found the activities at the port of Rødby[65] and various airports to involve substantial parts of the common market.[66]

The transport cases suggest, therefore, that, once it has been established that the routes or traffic concerned are significant in anything other than a purely domestic context, the 'substantial part' criterion will be satisfied.[67] Indeed, the full application of Article 82 to maritime and air transport would be impossible in the absence of such an interpretation.

D. THE MEANING OF ABUSE

(i) INTRODUCTION

It has already been pointed out that Article 82 does not forbid the holding of a dominant position *per se* but only an abuse of it. The meaning of 'abuse' is, therefore, of vital importance. Although the term is not defined, Article 82 itself sets out an illustrative list of examples.[68]

---

[63] Reported as *Irish Continental Group* v. *CCI Morlaix* [1995] 5 CMLR 177.

[64] Case C–179/90, *Merci Convenzionali Porto di Genova SpA* v. *Siderurgica Gabrielli SpA* [1991] ECR I–5889, [1994] 4 CMLR 422, para. 15; see also Case C–266/96, *Corsica Ferries France SA* v. *Gruppo Antichi Ormeggiatori del Porto di Genova Coop arl* [1998] ECR I–3949, [1998] 5 CMLR 402, para. 38.

[65] *Port of Rødby* [1994] OJ L55/52, [1994] 5 CMLR 457.

[66] E.g., *FAG-Flughafen Frankfurt/Main AG* [1998] OJ L72/30, [1998] 4 CMLR 779, *Alpha Flight Services/ Aéroports de Paris* [1998] OJ L230/ 10, [1998] 5 CMLR 611.

[67] See Case 66/86, *Ahmed Saeed Flugreisen and Silver Line Reisebüro GmbH* v. *Zentrale zur Bekämpfung unlauteren Wettbewerbs eV* [1989] ECR 803, [1990] 4 CMLR 102; *British Midland* v. *Aer Lingus* [1992] OJ L96/ 34, [1993] 4 CMLR 596.

[68] See *supra* 226.

(ii) EXPLOITATIVE AND ANTI-COMPETITIVE ABUSES

The obvious objection to an undertaking with market power is its ability to 'exploit' its position in a way which would be impossible for an undertaking operating on a competitive market.[69] It is clearly the purpose of Article 82 to prevent such conduct and Article 82(a) and (b) refer specifically to ways in which market power may be exploited to the detriment of *consumers* (for example, by the dominant undertaking's imposition of unfair prices). It was questioned initially whether or not Article 82 went any further than this. In particular, the text of Article 82 in some language versions suggested that the Article was intended to forbid *only* the *exploitation* and *use of* the dominant position in certain ways. For example the French and German texts state that there should be an 'abusive exploitation'.[70]

Relying partly on the textual support, some commentators in the early days of EC competition law argued that Article 82 should be interpreted to catch only exploitative behaviour which harms consumers and should not prohibit conduct which has *structural* effects, perhaps because it excludes or disadvantages other *competitors*. René Joliet, later a judge at the ECJ, argued that the prohibition of conduct because of its structural effects would be tantamount to the prohibition of the dominant position itself, which was not the purpose of Article 82.

R. Joliet, *Monopolization and Abuse of Dominant Position* (Nijhoff, 1970), 250–2

Under a second abuse theory—which in our view is the theory applicable to Article [82]—the test of legality is not the interference with other firms' freedom to compete and the use of 'exclusionary' practices to achieve and hold power, but *rather whether there is monopolistic exploitation of the market—however market domination has been achieved and maintained.* Under this approach a dominant firm has no interest in consolidating its position by resorting to exclusionary practices. For if it does, it will not be in a position to exploit its power and to gain advantages which would have been impossible in the face of effective competition, since it can be subject to direct price and output regulation. *Its power can be neutralized.* In a way this approach is more hostile to a free enterprise system: a dominant firm can be subject to direct price control, although it has achieved and held its position by mere virtue of its superior performance. *Where the test of abuse is monopolistic exploitation of the market, through unduly high prices for instance, remedies must clearly involve the possibility of establishing direct price and output control as is shown by the example of Article 66(7) of the ECSC Treaty.* There is thus a necessary link between the offense and the possible remedies. If the offense lies in monopolistic performance as demonstrated by Article [82](a) and (b), the remedies can only consist of injunctions specifying performance. If the offense is unduly high prices, the only possible remedy is direct price control. *Thus the remedies consist of regulating market power and not of restoring workable competitive conditions through structural reorganization of the industry or through injunctions directed against exclusionary practices which are the cause of power.* It could be asserted of course that coercive practices designed to destroy competition such as predatory price cutting can only be indulged in by dominant firms. Market power alone would make them possible, and thus they would also have to be considered as abusive under Article [82] . . . But this would be

---

[69] See *supra* 224.
[70] '. . . d'exploiter de façon abusive' in French, '*mißbräuchliche Ausnutzung*' in German.

only a superficial analysis. Although it is clear that 'if a firm can coerce rivals, suppliers, or customers, there must be some reservoir of force on which it draws that accounts for the acquiescence of the coerced party' . . ., and that coercive practices may always indicate some degree of market power, such power does not necessarily amount to market domination. . .

Regulation of market power or preservation of the competitive processes: these are two possible ways to deal with market domination. Each of them corresponds to a certain choice of economic policy. Both systems have to be clearly distinguished.

It is of course possible to conceive a third alternative which would be a mixture of the preceding ones. This is for instance the position in the United Kingdom. Practices which are the result of monopoly power as well as those which are designed to consolidate this position can be subject to corrective orders. Furthermore although it is based on a test of performance, British law has given the Board of Trade, subject to Parliamentary control, the power to order 'monopoly' firms to divest themselves of certain assets or stocks. This possibility of administering structural remedies has not been regarded as incompatible with the neutral and uncommitted approach taken by the law toward monopolies.

In conclusion, contrary to the suggestions of the [EC] Commission and of certain legal writers such as Mestmäcker, we feel that Article [82] does not cover the unilateral practices of independently acting single-firm monopolies which are designed to entrench such firms' hold over the market. According to the unanimous view of legal writers and of the [EC] Commission, a market dominant position is always beyond attack. . . . But if Article [82] were to be applied to policies erecting barriers to entry and *consolidating* market domination, it is difficult to perceive why in such a case the market dominant position itself should not be dismantled, a consequence which is rejected by all. It is also difficult to understand why the manner in which market domination has been *orginally secured* could not constitute an abusive practice. In fact to apply the Commission's theory in all its consequences would transform Article [82] into the exact equivalent of Section 2 of the Sherman Act.

Joliet took the view, therefore, that Article 82 was intended to prohibit only conduct which exploited a dominant position. It was not intended to prohibit conduct which affected the structure of the market.

The Commission did not agree with this view and believed that Article 82 could be applied broadly to prohibit conduct affecting the structure of the market.[71] In conformity with this view in 1972 it issued its decision in *Continental Can*, finding that an undertaking which had merged with another had committed an abuse of a dominant position.[72] In the subsequent appeal the ECJ confirmed this broad view of what may constitute an abuse for the purposes of Article 82.[73] The ECJ's judgment in this case is of great importance.

---

[71] *Le Problème de la Concentration dans le Marché Commun*, Etudes CEE, Série Concurrence No 3, 1966, particularly paras. 25–7.

[72] *Re Continental Can Co Inc* [1972] JO L7/25, [1972] CMLR D11. The Treaty of Rome contains no provisions which expressly enable the Commission to exercise merger control; for a full discussion of the current position in respect of EC merger control, see *infra* Chap. 12.

[73] Case 6/72, *Europemballage Corp and Continental Can Co Inc v. Commission* [1973] ECR 215, [1973] CMLR 199.

Case 6/72, *Europemballage Corp and Continental Can Co Inc* v. *Commission* [1973] ECR 215, [1973] CMLR 199

Continental Can Co Inc was an American company which manufactured metal packaging. It acquired an 85.8% share in a German metal can manufacturer, SLW. It then set about forming under Belgian law a wholly owned subsidiary, Europemballage, through which it planned to acquire a controlling interest in various other European can manufacturers. Only one of these transactions finally proceeded, the acquisition of a Dutch company, TDV. The Commission adopted a decision[74] holding that this was contrary to Article 82 on the grounds that through SLW Continental Can held a dominant position in a substantial part of the Common Market in the markets for light packaging for preserved meat, fish and crustacea and for metal caps for glass jars, and that by Europemballage's purchase of a majority shareholding in TDV Continental Can had abused this dominant position by practically eliminating competition in the relevant market.

On appeal the Court of Justice annulled the decision on the grounds that the Commission had wrongly defined the relevant market because it had failed properly to take into account supply side substitutability.[75] Nevertheless, and contrary to the Opinion of Advocate General Roemer, the Court held that where there *was* a dominant position it was possible for a merger to amount to an abuse within Article 82.

Court of justice

19. The applicants maintain that the Commission by its decision, based on an erroneous interpretation of Article [82] of the [EC] Treaty, is trying to introduce a control of mergers of undertakings, thus exceeding its powers. Such an attempt runs contrary to the intention of the authors of the Treaty, which is clearly seen not only from a literal interpretation of Article [82], but also from a comparison of the [EC] Treaty and the national legal provisions of the Member States. The examples given in Article [82] of abuse of a dominant position confirm this conclusion, for they show that the Treaty refers only to practices which have effects on the market and are to the detriment of consumers or trade partners. Further, Article [82] reveals that the use of economic power linked with a dominant position can be regarded as an abuse of this position only if it constitutes the means through which the abuse is effected. But structural measures of undertakings—such as strengthening a dominant position by way of merger—do not amount to abuse of this position within the meaning of Article [82] of the Treaty. The decision contested is, therefore, said to be void as lacking the required legal basis.

20. Article [82] (1) of the Treaty says 'Any abuse by one or more undertakings of a dominant position within the common market or in a substantial part of it shall be prohibited as incompatible with the common market in so far as it may affect trade between Member States'. The question is whether the word 'abuse' in Article [82] refers only to practices of undertakings which may directly affect the market and are detrimental to production or sales, to purchasers or consumers, or whether this word refers also to changes in the structure of an undertaking, which lead to competition being seriously disturbed in a substantial part of the Common Market.

21. The distinction between measures which concern the structure of the undertaking and practices which affect the market cannot be decisive, for any structural measure may influence market conditions, if it increases the size and the economic power of the undertaking.

---

[74] *Re Continental Can Co Inc* [1972] JO L7/25, [1972] CMLR D11.
[75] See *infra* Chap. 6.

22. In order to answer this question, one has to go back to the spirit, general scheme and wording of Article [82], as well as to the system and objectives of the Treaty. These problems thus cannot be solved by comparing this Article with certain provisions of the ECSC Treaty.

23. Article [82] is part of the chapter devoted to the common rules on the Community's policy in the field of competition. This policy is based on Article [3(1)(g)] of the Treaty according to which the Community's activity shall include the institution of a system ensuring that competition in the Common Market is not distorted. The applicants' argument that this provision merely contains a general programme devoid of legal effect, ignores the fact that Article 3 considers the pursuit of the objectives which it lays down to be indispensable for the achievement of the Community's tasks. As regards in particular the aim mentioned in [3 (1)(g)], the Treaty in several provisions contains more detailed regulations for the interpretation of which this aim is decisive.

24. But if Article [3(1)(g)] provides for the institution of a system ensuring that competition in the Common Market is not distorted, then it requires a fortiori that competition must not be eliminated. This requirement is so essential that without it numerous provisions of the Treaty would be pointless. Moreover, it corresponds to the precept of Article 2 of the Treaty according to which one of the tasks of the Community is 'to promote throughout the Community a harmonious development of economic activities'. Thus the restraints on competition which the Treaty allows under certain conditions because of the need to harmonize the various objectives of the Treaty, are limited by the requirements of Articles 2 and 3. Going beyond this limit involves the risk that the weakening of competition would conflict with the aims of the Common Market.

25. With a view to safeguarding the principles and attaining the objectives set out in Articles 2 and 3 of the Treaty, Articles [81] to [86] have laid down general rules applicable to undertakings. Article [81] concerns agreements between undertakings, decisions of associations of undertakings and concerted practices, while Article [82] concerns unilateral activity of one or more undertakings. Articles [81] and [82] seek to achieve the same aim on different levels, *viz.* the maintenance of effective competition within the Common Market. The restraint of competition which is prohibited if it is the result of behaviour falling under Article [81], cannot become permissible by the fact that such behaviour succeeds under the influence of a dominant undertaking and results in the merger of the undertakings concerned. In the absence of explicit provisions one cannot assume that the Treaty, which prohibits in Article [81] certain decisions of ordinary associations of undertakings restricting competition without eliminating it, permits in Article [82] that undertakings, after merging into an organic unity, should reach such a dominant position that any serious chance of competition is practically rendered impossible. Such a diverse legal treatment would make a breach in the entire competition law which could jeopardize the proper functioning of the Common Market. If, in order to avoid the prohibitions in Article [81], it sufficed to establish such close connections between the undertakings that they escaped the prohibition of Article [81] without coming within the scope of that of Article [82], then, in contradiction to the basic principles of the Common Market, the partitioning of a substantial part of this market would be allowed. The endeavour of the authors of the Treaty to maintain in the market real or potential competition even in cases in which restraints on competition are permitted, was explicitly laid down in Article [81 (3) (b)] of the Treaty. Article [82] does not contain the same explicit provisions, but this can be explained by the fact that the system fixed there for dominant positions, unlike Article [81 (3)], does not recognize any exemption from the prohibition. With such a system the obligation to observe the basic objectives of the Treaty, in particular that of Article [3 (1)(g)], results from the obligatory force of these objectives. In any case Articles [81] and [82] cannot be interpreted in such a way that they contradict each other, because they serve to achieve the same aim.

26. It is in the light of these considerations that the condition imposed by Article [82] is to be interpreted whereby in order to come within the prohibition a dominant position must have been abused. The provision states a certain number of abusive practices which it prohibits. The list merely

gives examples, not an exhaustive enumeration of the sort of abuses of a dominant position prohibited by the Treaty. As may further be seen from letters (c) and (d) of Article [82] (2), the provision is not only aimed at practices which may cause damage to consumers directly, but also at those which are detrimental to them through their impact on an effective competition structure, such as is mentioned in Article [3 (1)(g)] of the Treaty. Abuse may therefore occur if an undertaking in a dominant position strengthens such position in such a way that the degree of dominance reached substantially fetters competition, i.e. that only undertakings remain in the market whose behaviour depends on the dominant one.

27. Such being the meaning and the scope of Article [82] of the [EC] Treaty, the question of the link of causality raised by the applicants which in their opinion has to exist between the dominant position and its abuse, is of no consequence, for the strengthening of the position of an undertaking may be an abuse and prohibited under Article [82] of the Treaty, regardless of the means and procedure by which it is achieved, if it has the effects mentioned above.

The judgment in *Continental Can* is a seminal one for EC competition law. First, it clarified that Article 82 did not set out an exhaustive list of prohibited conduct and, on the contrary, it could prohibit a dominant undertaking from merging with another. The finding that the provision might prohibit mergers was crucial to the Commission since it had no direct means of controlling mergers until 1990.[76]

Secondly, the ECJ established that the conduct was prohibited irrespective of the fact that the dominant undertaking had not exploited, or otherwise used, its market power in concluding the merger transaction. Thus anti-competitive conduct which excludes competitors, strengthens the dominant position and weakens competition on the market *is* within the prohibition. The ECJ held that the object of Article 82 is not just to protect the dominant undertaking's customers from the exploitation of its market power, but to protect the competitive process itself. Conduct is prohibited if it threatens to weaken further the competitive structure of the market. In this case the ECJ accepted that a dominant undertaking could strengthen its position and eliminate competition by taking over its rival.[77]

Thirdly, the *way* in which it interpreted Article 82 is of both interest and importance. In determining the scope of the rule the Court looked to the basic objectives of the Community and construed Article 82 as a specific application of Article 3(1)(g). This 'teleological' reasoning was an early indication of how the Treaty and other Community rules, particularly the competition rules, would be interpreted in the future.[78] The Court has frequently referred to the broad Treaty aims and objectives. For example in *Commercial Solvents* the ECJ held that:

[t]he prohibitions of Articles [81] and [82] must in fact be interpreted and applied in the light of

---

[76] See *infra* Chap. 12.

[77] On the facts, however, the ECJ quashed the Commission's decision because it had failed adequately to define the market and, consequently, to show that the undertaking was dominant.

[78] See *supra* Chap. 2. For another striking example in the competition field, see the interpretation of 'dominant position' in Art. 2 of the Merger Reg. Council Reg. 4046/89 [1989] OJ L395/1, as amended by Council Reg. 1310/97 [1997] OJ L180/1, to encompass a collective dominant position in Cases C–68/94 & C–30/95, *France* v. *Commission* [1998] ECR I–1375, [1998] 4 CMLR 829, and Case T–102/96 *Gencor* v. *Commission* [2000] ECR II–753 [1999] 4 CMLR 971.

Article [3(1)(g)] of the Treaty, which provides that the activities of the Community shall include the institution of a system ensuring that competition in the Common Market is not distorted, and Article 2 of the Treaty, which gives the Community the task of promoting 'throughout the Community harmonious development of economic activities'. By prohibiting the abuse of a dominant position within the market in so far as it may affect trade between Member States, Article [82] therefore covers abuse which may directly prejudice consumers as well as abuse which indirectly prejudices them by impairing the effective competitive structure as envisaged by Article [3 (1)(g)] of the Treaty.[79]

Since *Continental Can* the Commission and the Court have confirmed on numerous occasions that Article 82 may apply not only to exploitative behaviour but also to anti-competitive conduct which weakens competition on a dominated market. In *Hoffmann La-Roche* the ECJ stated:[80]

For the purpose of rejecting the finding that there has been an abuse of a dominant position the interpretation suggested by the applicant that an abuse implies that the use of the economic power bestowed by a dominant position is the means whereby the abuse has been brought about cannot be accepted.

The concept of abuse is an objective concept relating to the behaviour of an undertaking in a dominant position which is such as to influence the structure of a market where, as a result of the very presence of the undertaking in question, the degree of competition is weakened and which, through recourse to methods different from those which condition normal competition in products or services on the basis of the transactions of commercial operators, has the effect of hindering the maintenance of the degree of competition still existing in the market or the growth of that competition.

Similarly, in *Michelin* the Court stressed 'that in prohibiting any abuse of a dominant position on the market . . . Article [82] covers practices which are likely to affect the structure of a market where, as a direct result of the presence of the undertaking in question, competition has already been weakened and which, through recourse to methods different from those governing normal competition in products or services based on traders' performance, have the effect of hindering the maintenance or development of the level of competition still existing on the market'.[81] It should be noted that the definitions given in these cases describe *only* anti-competitive abuses. There have, in fact, been few cases in which an undertaking's exploitation of its dominant position has been prohibited.[82]

It is true that the prohibition of anti-competitive conduct may benefit consumers by protecting the competitive structure. However, such a prohibition also *directly* benefits competitors.[83] It prevents their exclusion from the market. It is possible that the prohibition of anti-competitive conduct might, therefore, in some circumstances encourage the competition authorities to go beyond the objective of protecting the competitive process. Indeed it has been questioned whether in some cases the Commission acted with the purpose of

---

[79] Cases 6 and 7/73, *Istituto Chemioterapico Italiano SpA and Commercial Solvents Corp* v. *Commission* [1974] ECR 223, [1974] 1 CMLR 309, para. 32.

[80] Case 85/76, *Hoffmann-La Roche & Co AG* v. *Commission* [1979] ECR 461, [1979] 3 CMLR 211, para. 91.

[81] Case 322/81, *NV Nederlandsche Banden-Industrie Michelin* v. *Commission* [1983] ECR 3461, [1985] 1 CMLR 282, para. 70.

[82] See *infra* Chap. 7.

[83] Clearly the prohibition of the exploitation of market power protects those with whom the monopolist or dominant undertaking deals, such as consumers. The objection to monopoly is based on its being less desirable for society as a whole than a more competitive market. See *supra* Chap. 1.

protecting a *competitor* and not *competition* and whether or not the action, preventing the exclusion of a competitor, did in fact benefit consumers.[84] This raises again the question of what are and what should be the objectives of competition law.[85]

(iii) CATEGORIES OF ABUSE ARE NOT MUTUALLY EXCLUSIVE

It is clear that it is possible to classify abuses as 'exploitative' or 'anti-competitive'. It has been suggested that there is also a third category, 'reprisal' abuses. These are abuses which are specifically aimed at another undertaking and are made in response to behaviour of that other. The breadth of the concept of abuse subsequent to *Continental Can* and *Hoffmann-La Roche*[86] was analysed by a Commission lawyer in 1979:

J. Temple Lang, 'Monopolisation and the Definition of "Abuse" of a Dominant Position under Article 86 EEC Treaty' (1979) 16 *CMLRev.* 345, 363–4

A dominant enterprise may act contrary to Article [82] for any of the following reasons:

(1) if its behaviour takes advantage of economic power to obtain benefits or to impose burdens not obtainable or imposable in conditions of normal and reasonably effective competition, at the expense of the interests of customers or consumers (or, in the case of a dominant buyer, of suppliers). These are 'exploitative' abuses.

(2) if its behaviour significantly restricts intra-brand or inter-brand competition, or alters the market in such a way that competition is likely to be significantly reduced, or increases or reinforces the dominant firm's economic power. However, normal and legitimate competition is lawful, even if it increases the market share or economic power of the dominant enterprise. These are 'anti-competitive' abuses.

(3) if its behaviour is calculated to damage or seriously interfere with the business of another enterprise. If these abuses are to be regarded as a separate category, they can be called 'reprisal' abuses.

The types of infringement are not mutually exclusive. A dominant enterprise could take advantage of the absence of effective competition to restrict competition further for its own benefit, thereby committing both an 'exploitation' and an 'anti-competitive' abuse. A reprisal can be carried out in circumstances in which it substantially restricts competition.

In general, exploitative behaviour can *only* be committed by dominant enterprises, because it can be committed (or at least can be committed successfully) only in the absence of effective competition. On the other hand, anti-competitive abuses may consist of types of behaviour (*e.g.* total requirements contracts) which can be engaged in by enterprises with relatively little market power, but which have serious effects on competition when dominant firms engage in them. Exploitative and reprisal abuses are prohibited even though they do not necessarily have any adverse effect on competition.

---

[84] See, e.g., Cases 6 and 7/73, *Istituto Chemioterapico Italiano SpA and Commercial Solvents Corp* v. *Commission* [1974] ECR 223, [1974] 1 CMLR 309; Case 22/78, *Hugin Kassaregister AB and Hugin Cash Registers Ltd* v. *Commission* [1979] ECR 1869, [1979] 3 CMLR 345, discussed *infra* Chap. 7.

[85] See *supra* Chap. 1.

[86] The abuse aspects of *Hoffmann-La Roche* are discussed *infra* in Chap. 7.

If this is the law, Article [82] is an important and effective weapon for the protection of competition and the protection of consumers and enterprises against exploitation. Also, Article [82] is much more like section 2 of the U.S. Sherman Act than has hitherto been believed.

It must be emphasized that these categories of abuse—exploitative, anti-competitive and reprisal (if a separate category)—are not mutually exclusive. For example, the same conduct may be both exploitative *and* make it more difficult for a competitor to gain access to the market. This might be the case where, for example, a firm charges discriminatory prices (prohibited by Article 82(c)). Those discriminatory prices might exploit one set of customers and exclude competitors by charging lower prices to customers which might otherwise purchase from the competitor.[87] Similarly, it seems that reprisal abuses are really a sub-category of anti-competitive and/or exploitative abuses. In most cases they will exclude competitors from the market. They have an added element however, since, as described above, they are 'calculated' to damage. It may, therefore, be possible to classify predatory pricing as a reprisal abuse where it is intended to punish a competitor.[88] However, it is also anti-competitive since it is calculated to drive a competitor out of a market or to deter and prevent competitors from gaining access to the market.

(iv) THE BROAD NATURE OF THE CONCEPT

a. ABUSE NEED NOT BE CAUSALLY CONNECTED TO THE DOMINANT POSITION

It has been seen in *Continental Can* that the Court adopted a broad view of what conduct may amount to an abuse of a dominant position for the purposes of Article 82. Further, it is clear from that judgment[89] and the extracts from the judgments in *Hoffmann-La Roche* and *Michelin* set out above that there is no need for a causal link to be established between the dominant position and the abuse. It is necessary only that the conduct strengthens the undertaking's dominant position and fetters competition on the market.

Since a dominant undertaking may be prohibited from some conduct even though it is not actually *using* its market power, some strategies possible for, and permitted to, non-dominant firms will be prohibited. This is because a dominant undertaking has a special responsibility on the market which it dominates. It may abuse its position by engaging in conduct which is acceptable when carried out by its competitors and irrespective of any intention to commit an abuse.

b. THE SPECIAL RESPONSIBILITY OF DOMINANT UNDERTAKINGS

The issue of what conduct amounts to an abuse is governed by the fact that the ECJ has consistently stressed that dominant firms have a 'special responsibility' towards the

---

[87] This can be seen from para. 26 of the *Continental Can* judgment (Case 6/72 *Europemballage Corp. and Continental Can Co. Inc.* v. *Commission* [1973] ECR 215, [1973] CMLR 199) itself, where the conduct towards customers in headings (c) and (d) of Art 82 (discriminatory pricing and enforcing a tie) is described as having an impact on an effective competitive structure.

[88] See Case C–62/86, *AKZO Chemie BV* v. *Commission* [1991] ECR I–3359, [1993] 5 CMLR 215, discussed *infra* Chap. 7.

[89] Case 6/72, *Europemballage Corp and Continental Can Co Inc* v. *Commission* [1973] ECR 215, [1973] CMLR 199, particularly paras 26–27.

competitive process and, implicitly, its competitors. This idea was first expressed by the Court in *Michelin*:

It is not possible to uphold the objections made against those arguments by Michelin NV, supported on this point by the French Government, that Michelin NV is thus penalized for the quality of its products and services. A finding that an undertaking has a dominant position is not in itself a recrimination but simply means that, irrespective of the reasons for which it has such a dominant position, the undertaking concerned has a special responsibility not to allow its conduct to impair genuine undistorted competition on the common market.[90]

This 'special responsibility' means that conduct which may at first sight look like ordinary business behaviour (such as in *Michelin* itself[91]) may be condemned as abusive. Article 82 thus prohibits what might otherwise be considered as normal methods of competition. The special responsibility arises 'irrespective of the reasons for which it has such a dominant position'.

The development of the concept of 'super-dominance'[92] makes it likely that the undertaking's special responsibility will become greater where the undertaking 'enjoys a position of dominance approaching a monopoly'.[93] This clearly appeared to be the view of the Advocate General in *Compagnie Maritime Belge* v. *Commission*. Although the ECJ did not expressly endorse this view it did state that the scope of the special responsibility was affected by the circumstances of the case and the competition existing on the market. It indicated that an undertaking with a very large market share and only one competitor would be more likely to be found to have abused its dominant position than a dominant undertaking with a lesser degree of market power.[94]

This concept of 'special responsibility' and the Commission's readiness to intervene means that the EC competition regime has been more regulatory than the US regime under section 2 of the Sherman Act. The breadth with which Article 82 has been applied has caused many commentators to be critical:[95]

P. Jebsen and R. Stevens, 'Assumptions, Goals and Dominant Undertakings: The Regulation of Competition Under Article 86 of the European Union' (1995–96) 64 *Antitrust Law Journal* 443, 487–91

Nothing distinguishes the U.S. and EU approaches more clearly than what transpires following the decision that an undertaking has monopoly power or a dominant position. Superficially, the United States and the European Union impose somewhat similar restraints upon the exercise of monopoly power; for instance, both prohibit predatory pricing or tie-ins. They diverge strikingly, however, in the standard of behavior that must be met before they will impose sanctions. The United States is much

---

[90] Case 322/81, *NV Nederlandsche Banden-Industrie Michelin* v. *Commission* [1983] ECR 3461, [1985] 1 CMLR 282, para. 57; see also Case T–228/97, *Irish Sugar plc* v. *Commission* [1999] 5 CMLR 1300, para. 112.

[91] For the conduct found abusive in *Michelin*, see *infra* Chap. 7.

[92] See the discussion of super-dominance *supra* 235 and *infra* in Chaps. 6 and 7.

[93] Cases C–395 & 396/96P, *Compagnie Maritime Belge Transports SA* v. *Commission*, [2000] 4 CMLR 1076, Opinion of Fennelly AG, para. 136.

[94] Cases C–395 & 396/96P, *Compagnie Maritime Belge Transports SA* v. *Commission*, [2000] 4 CMLR 1076, paras 112–119, discussed *infra* Chap. 7.

[95] This is discussed in the context of particular types of conduct held to be abusive; see *infra* Chap. 7. Note that the Sherman Act prohibits monopolization and attempts to monopolize.

more reluctant to restrict what some perceive as monopoly power abuses; the European Union, with its *dirigiste* tradition, states that dominant undertakings bear a 'special responsibility' towards their competitors and must act accordingly. With such different philosophies it is not surprising that the two systems differ significantly in substance. A business that might continue to flourish under the U.S. approach may wither under the EU regime.

In *United States* v. *Grinnell Corp* . . . the Supreme Court stated that the 'offense of monopoly under § 2 of the Sherman Act has two elements: (1) the possession of monopoly power in the relevant market and (2) the willful acquisition or maintenance of that power as distinguished from growth or development as a consequence of a superior product, business acumen, or historic accident.' . . . The Court's inclusion of the qualifying phrase 'superior product, business acumen, or historic accident' captures the difference in tone and substance of the American approach. As stated by Judge Learned Hand in *United States* v. *Aluminum Co. of America* . . . 'the successful competitor, having been urged to compete, must not be turned upon when he wins.' This concern animates many of the U.S. decisions.

In fact, the U.S. opinions take pains to resist condemning monopoly power per se. The American courts—at least in recent years—have not condemned the possession of monopoly power when it arises 'unexpectedly or unavoidably.' . . . In *United States* v. *United Shoe Machinery Corp* . . . the court emphasized that a monopolist is immune from statutory liability where:

> it owes its monopoly solely to superior skill, superior products, natural advantages (including accessibility to raw materials or markets), economic or technological efficiency (including scientific research), low margins of profit maintained permanently and without discrimination, or licenses conferred by, and used within, the limits of law (including patents of one's own inventions, or franchises granted directly to the enterprise by a public authority).

Businesses with monopoly positions may therefore pursue competitive advantage. In *Berkey Photo* . . . for instance, the court explained:

> [A] large firm does not violate § 2 simply by reaping the competitive rewards attributable to its efficient size, nor does an integrated business offend the Sherman Act whenever one of its departments benefits from association with a division possessing a monopoly in its own market. So long as we allow a firm to compete in several fields, we must expect it to seek the competitive advantages of its broad-based activity—more efficient production, greater ability to develop complementary products, reduced transaction costs, and so forth. These are gains that accrue to any integrated firm, regardless of its market share, and they cannot by themselves be considered uses of monopoly power . . .

The EU approach presents a stark contrast. Reaping competitive rewards may give rise to an Article [82] violation. Moreover, in the European Union the decisions stress a form of strict liability—that an abuse of monopoly power may arise without there having been any intent to commit an abuse. . . The notion is alleged to be 'objective'. In *Hoffmann-La Roche* . . . the Court of Justice asserted:

> The concept of abuse is an *objective* concept relating to the behavior of an undertaking in a dominant position which is such as to influence the structure of a market where, as a result of the very presence of the undertaking in question, the degree of competition is weakened and which, through recourse to methods different from those that condition normal competition in products or services on the basis of the transactions of commercial operators, has the effect of hindering the maintenance of the degree of competition still existing in the market or the growth of that competition . . .

. . .

The notion of 'special responsibility' has taken on many manifestations and lies at the core of the EU authorities' attitudes towards a dominant entity's behaviour . . .

The imposition of special responsibility notions in the area of monopoly power, and the willingness of the authorities to take actions beyond those which might be called for in situations of 'normal' competition, permit the EU competition regime to be regulatory in a fashion that the United States is not. Moreover, the notion applies not only in cases of pure monopoly, but also in oligopoly situations. . . The EU authorities are granted the power and ability to regulate competition without effective constraint in statute or precedent, since the standards by which these authorities implicitly regulate are nowhere laid down any more than they are readily deducible from the jurisprudence.

c. ABUSE AS AN OBJECTIVE CONCEPT

In *Hoffmann-La Roche*[96] the ECJ stressed that the notion of an abuse is an 'objective concept'. Although the Court has not elaborated on this statement it appears to reinforce the fact that it is not essential to a finding of an abuse that the dominant undertaking has used its dominant position.[97] Further, it may also mean that the characterization of a dominant undertaking's conduct as abusive does not depend on the undertaking's subjective intent to exclude competitors or weaken competition. The competition authorities look to the effect of the conduct, not the reasons for it. If this is so, an important *caveat* must be entered. Although there are many cases in which an abuse has been found to have been committed without an investigation into the motives of the undertaking, there are some cases in which the undertaking's intent is of relevance. In particular, the ECJ has held that a dominant undertaking which prices its product between average variable and average total cost will be found to have engaged in predatory pricing and to have committed an abuse of Article 82 only if this level of pricing was adopted as part of a plan to eliminate competitors.[98] Further, the intent of the dominant undertaking may be crucial in some cases involving refusal to supply. Although a dominant undertaking does not always have a duty to supply,[99] a refusal to supply may be found to be an abuse where it was carried out, for example, to discipline a customer,[100] or to compete with a customer downstream.[101]

d. DISTINGUISHING COMPETITION ON THE MERITS FROM ANTI-COMPETITIVE BEHAVIOUR

The finding that a dominant undertaking has a special responsibility to the competitive process and that any conduct which strengthens the dominant position/further weakens the competitive structure may be an abuse potentially brings within the prohibition an indefinite spectrum of conduct. The parameters of that spectrum have been the subject of judgments by the Court and decisions of the Commission (many of them highly controversial) ever since *Continental Can*. The difficulty is that anything done by a dominant undertaking

---

[96] See *supra* 245.

[97] See Kirschner AG in Case T–51/89, *Tetra Pak Rausing SA* v. *Commission* [1990] ECR II–309, [1991] 4 CMLR 334, para. 64.

[98] See Case C–62/86 *AKZO Chemie BV* v. *Commission* [1991] ECR I–3359, [1993] 5 CMLR 215, discussed *infra* in Chap. 7.

[99] For a discussion of this question see *infra* Chap. 7.

[100] See Case 27/76, *United Brands Co and United Brands Continental BV* v. *Commission* [1978] ECR 207, [1978] 1 CMLR 429; *BBI/Boosey & Hawkes: Interim Measures* [1987] OJ L286/36 [1988] 4 CMLR 67.

[101] See Cases 6 and 7/73, *Istituto Chemioterapico Italiano SpA and Commercial Solvents Corp* v. *Commission* [1974] ECR 223, [1974] 1 CMLR 309; Case 22/78, *Hugin Kassaregister AB and Hugin Cash Registers Ltd* v. *Commission* [1979] ECR 1869, [1979] 3 CMLR 345.

may improve its market position in comparison to those of its competitors. New and attractive products, better quality, better service, good advertising, low prices may all attract custom from the competitors. Should improving market share as a result of the dominant undertaking's increased efficiency and unbeatable performance be forbidden? Obviously such a finding would be absurd.

The key to answering this question lies in the extracts of the judgments in *Hoffmann-La Roche* and *Michelin*, quoted above.[102] In these cases the Court speaks respectively of 'recourse to methods different from those which condition normal competition in products or services on the basis of the transactions of commercial operators' and 'recourse to methods different from those governing normal competition in products or services based on traders' performance'. The Court thus appears to distinguish between anti-competitive behaviour and 'competition on the merits' or 'competition on the basis of performance'.[103] A dominant undertaking providing a superior product at a low price which reflects its costs is competing on the merits. Its conduct is not prohibited even though its competitors, producing inferior products at less attractive prices, lose customers. This is the natural operation of the market. In contrast, a dominant undertaking which almost gives away its products in order to attract customers from its competitors and to drive them out of business is not competing on the merits but acting anti-competitively. Often, however, the situation is not so clear-cut. The enduring difficulty with Article 82 is where the Court and the Commission draw the line between anti-competitive conduct and competition on the merits.

e. OBJECTIVE JUSTIFICATION, PROPORTIONALITY, AND THE RIGHT OF DOMINANT UNDERTAKINGS TO DEFEND THEIR COMMERCIAL INTERESTS

The Court and Commission have also developed the concept of 'objective justification' in order to distinguish between abusive conduct and conduct which is pursued for legitimate commercial reasons. If conduct is objectively justified or 'objectively necessary' it is outside Article 82. A dominant producer may, therefore, legitimately tie the sale of nails to the sale of its nail-guns if necessary for safety reasons.[104] Further, it may cut off supplies to a bad debtor,[105] or offer quantity discounts to customers where those discounts reflect costs savings.[106] It does not, however, allow a dominant undertaking to cease to supply a customer with whom the dominant producer wishes to compete downstream[107] or who goes into competition with the producer,[108] or to discipline a distributor where the circumstances do not warrant it.[109]

---

[102] See *supra* 245.

[103] See Korah, *An Introductory Guide to EC Competition Law and Practice* (7th edn) (Hart Publishing, 2000), para. 3.3.

[104] See *Eurofix-Bauco* v. *Hilti* [1988] OJ L65/19, [1989] 4 CMLR 677.

[105] See *BBI/Boosey & Hawkes* [1987] OJ L286/36, [1988] 4 CMLR 67.

[106] See *BPB Industries plc* [1989] OJ L10/50, [1990] 4 CMLR 464.

[107] See Cases 6 and 7/73, *Istituto Chemioterapico Italiano SpA and Commercial Solvents Corp* v. *Commission* [1974] ECR 223, [1974] 1 CMLR 309.

[108] See *BBI/Boosey & Hawkes* [1987] OJ L286/36 [1988] 4 CMLR 67.

[109] See Case 27/76, *United Brands Co and United Brands Continental BV* v. *Commission* [1978] ECR 207, [1978] 1 CMLR 429.

Case 27/76 *United Brands Co and United Brands Continental BV* v. *Commission* [1978] ECR 207, [1978] 1 CMLR 429

United Brands (UBC) was an undertaking found to be dominant in the market for bananas in several Member States.[110] One of the abuses UBC was found by the Commission to have committed was its decision to cut off supplies of its branded 'Chiquita' bananas to Oelsen. Oelsen was one of its ripener/distributors in Denmark. The distributor had, however, taken part in the advertising and promotion campaign of a rival producer's bananas, Dole. UBC claimed that it was justified in defending itself against attack from its main competitor. The Court of Justice, however, upheld the Commission's finding of abuse.

Court of justice

189. Although it is true, as the applicant points out, that the fact that an undertaking is in a dominant position cannot disentitle it from protecting its own commercial interests if they are attacked, and that such an undertaking must be conceded the right to take such reasonable steps as it deems appropriate to protect its said interests, such behaviour cannot be countenanced if its actual purpose is to strengthen this dominant position and abuse it.

190. Even if the possibility of a counter-attack is acceptable that attack must still be proportionate to the threat taking into account the economic strength of the undertakings confronting each other.

It is clear from this extract that, in addition to being objectively justified, the conduct must be proportionate. The principle of proportionality is an established general principle of Community law, based on the German principle, *Verhältnismässigkeit*. It has been developed by the ECJ to judge both the validity of the actions of Community institutions (it is now embodied in Article 5[111] of the EC Treaty) and, in some contexts, the actions of Member States.[112] The problems in its application are well known and its use to judge the legitimacy of a dominant undertaking's behaviour is equally problematic. Broadly, however, it involves the court weighing up the relationship between means and ends. When this is done in the context of the conduct of dominant undertakings it does not provide a definitive answer to the question 'is this an abuse?' because the relationship of means to ends is inherent in the concept of abuse as formulated by the Court. The application of proportionality to the facts of any given case does not help to predict the outcome.

The Court and Commission often use the language of objective justification and proportionality when judging a dominant firm's claim that its allegedly abusive conduct was merely the protection of its own commercial interests.

BBI/Boosey & Hawkes: Interim Measures [1987] OJ L282/36, [1988] 4 CMLR 67

This Commission decision concerned interim measures ordering the musical instrument manufacturer Boosey & Hawkes to recommence supplies to two of its erstwhile distributors and repairers. Boosey & Hawkes stopped supplying them when they went into business together manufacturing instruments

---

[110] See *infra* Chap. 6.

[111] Formerly, Art. 3b. This Art. was incorporated in to the EC Treaty by the TEU (the Maastricht Treaty).

[112] See *supra* Chap. 2, and P. Craig and G. de Búrca, *EU Law: Text, Cases and Materials* (2nd edn., Oxford University Press, Oxford 1998), 349–357; T.C. Hartley, *The Foundations of European Community Law* (4th edn., Oxford University Press, Oxford 1998), 148–9.

in competition with it. As in *United Brands* the dominant firm pleaded that it was only taking reasonable steps to protect itself. The Commission disagreed.

Commission

19. A dominant undertaking may always take reasonable steps to protect its commercial interests, but such measures must be fair and proportional to the threat. The fact that a customer of a dominant producer becomes associated with a competitior or a potential competitor of that manufacturer does not normally entitle the dominant producer to withdraw all supplies immediately or to take reprisals against that customer.

There is no obligation placed on a dominant producer to subsidize competition to itself. In the case where a customer transfers its central activity to the promotion of a competing brand it may be that even a dominant producer is entitled to review its commercial relations with that customer and on giving adequate notice terminate any special relationship. However, the refusal of all supplies to GHH and RCN, and the other actions B&H has taken against them as part of its reaction to the perceived threat of BBI, would appear in the circumstances of the present case to go beyond the legitimate defence of B&H's commercial interests.

In this case it seems to have been the undertaking's *immediate* withdrawal of supplies which was unacceptable. It was not *proportional* to the threat faced by Boosey & Hawkes. As in *United Brands* the dominant undertaking was held to have gone too far in the defence of its interests.

This requirement that any objective justification be proportionate is crucial when assessing the compatibility with Article 82 of conduct which looks like 'normal' competitive behaviour. The actions of the dominant undertaking may be aimed not at extending its power, but at maintaining its market share in the face of aggressive competition—'meeting' competition rather than 'beating' it. A dominant undertaking which responds to competition by, for example, lowering its prices may be met with an accusation of abuse, but if it does nothing it will lose business. The question of what was meant by proportional in this context was explored by Advocate General Kirschner in *Tetra Pak I*.

Case T–51/89 *Tetra Pak Rausing SA* v. *Commission* [1990] ECR II–309, [1991] 4 CMLR 334

This case involved an appeal against a Commission decision finding that Tetra Pak's acquisition of a exclusive patent licence constituted an abuse. The judgment on this point (which did not review the proportionality issue) is discussed in Chapter 10.

Advocate General Kirschner

67. [Article 82] ... contains four examples of abuses of a dominant position. The first two examples are concerned primarily about protecting parties to contracts with undertakings in dominant positions and consumers against exploitation of their dependence on the dominant undertaking, whilst the prohibition in subparagraph (d) on making the conclusion of contracts subject to the acceptance of supplementary obligations is clearly aimed at protecting competitors as well as contracting parties and example (c) prohibits discrimination as between the trading partners of the undertaking in a dominant position which would have an adverse impact on competition. The common feature shared by the first three examples is that the conduct to which they refer pursues the legitimate end of making profits through disproportionate means. Cases of abuse not expressly mentioned can be inferred from those examples. They point to limits which the undertaking in the

dominant position must respect even in the case of activities which fall outside the examples, . . . namely the principle of proportionality . . . and the prohibition of discrimination.

68. In this case, the principle of proportionality is of primary importance, since the complaint relating to the acquisition of the exclusive licence (and only the exclusive licence) implies a complaint of disproportionate conduct. Applied to the conduct of an undertaking in a dominant position, that principle has the following meaning: the undertaking in a dominant position may act in a profit-oriented way, strive through its efforts to improve its market position and pursue its legitimate interests. But in so doing it may employ only such methods as are necessary to pursue those legitimate aims. In particular it may not act in a way which, foreseeably, will limit competition more than is necessary.

69. The Court of Justice has assessed the conduct of undertakings in a dominant position in terms of the principle of proportionality in this way in a series of decisions.

In *Compagnie Maritime Belge*[113] the CFI upheld the Commission's finding that the association's use of fighting ships to counter a new competitor was an abuse.[114] Although the Court dismissed the appellants' reasons for the conduct as not proven, it held that, even if they *were* proved, 'those circumstances could not render the response put into effect by the members of Cewal reasonable and proportionate'. On appeal, the Advocate General seemed to consider that what might be proportional behaviour for a dominant undertaking or undertakings might not be proportionate when carried out by a super-dominant undertaking. Such undertakings' 'special responsibility' to the competitive process was a particularly onerous one.[115] The Advocate General stated:[116]

137. In all these circumstances, the Court of First Instance committed no error of law in finding that the response of Cewal members to the entrance of G & C was not 'reasonable and proportionate' . . . To my mind, Article [82] cannot be interpreted as permitting monopolists or quasi-monopolists to exploit the very significant market power which their superdominance confers so as to preclude the emergence either of a new or additional competitor. Where an undertaking, or group of undertakings whose conduct must be assessed collectively, enjoys a position of such overwhelming dominance verging on monopoly, comparable to that which existed in the present case at the moment when G & C entered the relevant market, it would not be consonant with the particularly onerous special obligation affecting such a dominant undertaking not to impair further the structure of the feeble existing competition for them to react, even to aggressive price competition from a new entrant, with a policy of targeted, selective price cuts designed to eliminate that competitor.

The ECJ dismissed the parties' appeal on this point. The judgment did not expressly address the 'proportionality' point but did tie its condemnation of the undertakings' behaviour to their very strong dominant position.[117]

---

[113] Cases T–24–26 & 28/93, *Compagnie Maritime Belge Transports SA* v. *Commission* [1996] ECR II–1201, [1997] 4 CMLR 273.

[114] See *infra* Chap. 7. This point was not pursued on appeal: Cases 395 & 396/96P *Compagnie Maritime Belge Transports SA* v. *Commission*, [2000] 4 CMLR 1076.

[115] For the emerging concept of super-dominance, see *supra* 235.

[116] Cases C–395 & 396/96P, *Compagnie Maritime Transports Belge SA* v. *Commission* [2000] 4 CMLR 1076, Opinion of Fennelly AG.

[117] See Cases 395 & 396/96P, *Compagnie Maritime Belge Transports SA* v. *Commission*, ECJ, 16 Mar. 2000, paras. 112–119, reproduced *infra* in Chap. 7.

The Court and the Commission have thus accepted that dominant undertakings do have the right to defend their commercial interests, but the action of such undertakings is severely restricted. The judgments have not clearly distinguished between maintaining the dominant position and strengthening it.[118] Further, the permissible level of action appears to be related to the strength of the dominant position. It must be remembered that the existence of a dominant position indicates that the market is not competitive. The Commission does not therefore view sympathetically action taken to prolong that undesirable state of affairs. This issue is discussed further in Chapter 7.

E. AN EFFECT ON TRADE BETWEEN MEMBER STATES

Article 82 applies only if the abuse of a dominant position affects trade between Member States. As in the context of Article 81, this requirement marks the jurisdictional divide between Community and national law. The concept of an effect on trade is interpreted in the same way under the two articles.[119] Thus an agreement or conduct will affect trade if it interferes with the pattern of trade between Member State or if it interferes with the structure of competition on the common market (even if there is no alteration to the flow of goods or services between Member States).[120] The latter test is more commonly utilized in Article 82 cases and was first adopted by the Court in an Article 82 case, *Commercial Solvents*.[121] This approach is particularly germane to Article 82 cases in which abusive conduct might result in a competitor leaving the market.[122]

In *Hugin*,[123] however, it was shown that not all abusive conduct in the common market affects trade. This case concerned the supply of cash register spare parts by a Swedish undertaking to a servicing and repair firm in south-east England at a time prior to Sweden joining the EU. The servicing firm's activities were confined to the London area and there was no inter-State trade in the spare parts. The ECJ quashed the Commission's decision on the ground that there was not an effect on trade between Member States. The alteration in the competitive structure if the firm went out of business would not be felt outside one part of the UK. The ECJ stated:

17. . . . The interpretation and application of the condition relating to effects on trade between Member States contained in Articles [81] and [82] of the Treaty must be based on the purpose of that condition which is to define, in the context of the law governing competition, the boundary between the areas respectively covered by Community law and the law of the Member States. Thus Community law covers any agreement or any practice which is capable of constituting a threat to freedom of trade between Member States in a manner which might harm the attainment of the objectives of a single market between the Member States, in particular by partitioning the national markets or by affecting the structure of competition within the common market. On the other hand

---

[118] See also Case T–228/97, *Irish Sugar plc* v. *Commission* [1999] 5 CMLR 1300.

[119] See *supra* Chap. 3.

[120] See *ibid.*

[121] Cases 6 and 7/73, *Istituto Chemioterapico Italiano SpA and Commercial Solvents Corp* v. *Commission* [1974] ECR 223, [1974] 1 CMLR 309.

[122] *Ibid.*

[123] Case 22/78, *Hugin Kassaregister AB and Hugin Cash Registers Ltd* v. *Commission* [1979] ECR 1869, [1979] 3 CMLR 345.

conduct the effects of which are confined to the territory of a single Member State is governed by the national legal order.

This cases establishes, therefore, that before trade between Member States will be affected the alteration in the competitive structure has to have some repercussion beyond the borders of a single Member State.

5. THE RELATIONSHIP BETWEEN ARTICLE 82 AND ARTICLE 81

Articles 81 and 82 are not mutually exclusive. In *Hoffmann-La Roche*[124] the ECJ confirmed that both Articles 81 and 82 may apply to the same contractual arrangements. When dealing with an exclusive requirements contract concluded by a dominant undertaking the Commission was, therefore, at liberty to proceed under either Article 81 or Article 82. The ECJ held that:

the question might be asked whether the conduct in question does not fall within Article [81] of the Treaty and possibly within its paragraph (3) thereof.

However, the fact that agreements of this kind might fall within Article [81] and in particular within paragraph (3) thereof does not preclude the application of Article [82], since this latter article is expressly aimed in fact at situations which clearly originate in contractual relations so that in such cases the Commission is entitled, taking into account the nature of the reciprocal undertakings entered into and to the competitive position of the various contracting parties on the market or markets in which they operate to proceed on the basis of Article [81] or Article [82].[125]

The fact that an agreement is eligible for exemption, or has in fact been exempted, from the application of Article 81(1) under Article 81(3) does not necessarily mean, therefore, that the performance of the agreement will not constitute an abuse of a dominant position for the purposes of Article 82. There is no provision for exempting abusive conduct under Article 82.

In practice, the Commission is, of course, unlikely to grant a dominant undertaking an individual exemption in respect of an agreement the operation of which is likely to constitute an abuse of a dominant position. It is likely to take these aspects into account before granting an exemption.[126] An agreement concluded by a dominant undertaking may, however, benefit from a block exemption which does not restrict its ambit to undertakings with market shares below a specified threshold. In these circumstances the Commission will almost certainly have power to withdraw the benefit of the exemption if it wishes. It is

[124] Case 85/76, *Hoffmann-La Roche & Co AG* v. *Commission* [1979] ECR 461, [1979] 3 CMLR 211.

[125] *Ibid.* para. 116.

[126] Under Art. 8(3), Reg. 17 [1959–62] OJ Spec. Ed. 87, an individual decision may be revoked, *inter alia*, where it is based on incorrect information or induced by deceit, or where the facts basic to the decision have changed. (Note that in Case C–279/95P, *Langnese-Iglo GmbH* v. *Commission* [1998] ECR I–5609, [1998] 5 CMLR 933, the ECJ held that the Commission could 'revoke' a comfort letter because of a factual situation which had existed at the time the letter was sent but of which the Commission was unaware until later.) Where there are no Art. 8(3) grounds for revocation the Commission must take account of its earlier findings.

possible, nonetheless, that even prior to the benefit of the block exemption being withdrawn a dominant undertaking may be found to have committed an abuse of a dominant position.

In *Tetra Pak I*[127] the Commission found that Tetra Pak had committed an abuse of a dominant position when it acquired an undertaking which held an exclusive patent licence. That patent licence was exempted under a block exemption. The CFI[128] affirmed that an undertaking could commit an abuse of a dominant position by operating an agreement which was exempted under a block exemption even if the benefit of the block exemption had not been withdrawn. Otherwise an exemption under Article 81(3) would also operate as an exemption from Article 82.

Case T–51/89 *Tetra Pak Rausing SA* v. *Commission (Tetra Pak I)* [1990] ECR II–309, [1991] 4 CMLR 334

Court of First Instance

25. In these circumstances, this Court holds that in the scheme for the protection of competition established by the Treaty the grant of exemption, whether individual or block exemption, under Article [81(3)] cannot be such as to render inapplicable the prohibition set out in Article [82]. This principle follows both from the wording of Article [81(3)] which permits derogation, through a declaration of inapplicability, only from the prohibition of agreements, decisions and concerted practices set out in Article [81(1)], and also from the general scheme of Articles [81] and [82] which, as noted above, are independent and complementary provisions designed, in general, to regulate distinct situations by different rules. Application of Article [81] involves two stages: a finding that Article [81(1)] has been infringed followed, where appropriate, by exemption from that prohibition if the agreement, decision or concerted practice in question satisfies the conditions laid down in Article [81(3)]. Article [82], on the other hand, by reason of its very subject-matter (abuse), precludes any possible exception to the prohibition it lays down. . . If the Commission were required in every case to take a decision withdrawing exemption before applying Article [82], this would be tantamount, in view of the non-retroactive nature of the withdrawal of exemption, to accepting that an exemption under Article [81(3)] operates in reality as a concurrent exemption from the prohibition of abuse of a dominant position. For the reasons just given, that would not be consistent with the very nature of the infringement prohibited by Article [82]. Moreover, in view of the principles governing the hierarchical relationship of legal rules, grant of exemption under secondary legislation could not, in the absence of any enabling provision in the Treaty, derogate from a provision of the Treaty, in this case Article [82].

26. Having established that, in principle, the grant of exemption cannot preclude application of Article [82], the question remains whether, in practice, findings made with a view to the grant of exemption under Article [81(3)] preclude application of Article [82].

27. Under Article [81(3)] the prohibition laid down in Article [81(1)] may be declared inapplicable to agreements, decisions or concerted practices, or to categories thereof, which fulfil the conditions set out in Article [81(3)]. Article [81(3)] provides *inter alia* that the agreement must not afford the undertakings the possibility of eliminating competition in respect of a substantial part of the products in questions.

28. The way in which the question of exemption arises may in practice be different depending on whether an individual or block exemption is involved. The grant of individual exemption presupposes

---

[127] [1988] OJ L272/27, [1990] 4 CMLR 47.
[128] Case T–51/89, *Tetra Pak Rausing SA* v. *Commission* [1990] ECR II–309, [1991] 4 CMLR 334.

that the Commission has found that the agreement in question complies with the conditions set out in Article [81(3)]. So, where an individual exemption decision has been taken, characteristics of the agreement which would also be relevant in applying Article [82] may be taken to have been established. Consequently, in applying Article [82], the Commission must take account, unless the factual and legal circumstances have altered, of the earlier findings made when exemption was granted under Article [81(3)].

29. Now it is true that regulations granting block exemption, like individual exemption decisions, apply only to agreements which, in principle, satisfy the conditions set out in Article [81(3)]. But unlike individual exemptions, block exemptions are, by definition, not dependent on a case-by-case examination to establish that the conditions for exemption laid down in the Treaty are in fact satisfied. In order to qualify for a block exemption, an agreement has only to satisfy the criteria laid down in the relevant block-exemption regulation. The agreement itself is not subject to any positive assessment with regard to the conditions set out in Article [81(3)]. So a block exemption cannot, generally speaking, be construed as having effects similar to negative clearance in relation to Article [82]. The result is that, where agreements to which undertakings in a dominant position are parties fall within the scope of a block-exemption regulation (that is, where the regulation is unlimited in scope), the effects of block exemption on the applicability of Article [82] must be assessed solely in the context of the scheme of Article [82].

30. Lastly, the possibility of applying Article [82] to an agreement covered by a block exemption is confirmed by analysis of the scheme of the block-exemption regulations. First, those regulations do not, in principle, exclude undertakings in a dominant position from qualifying the exemption and therefore do not take account of the position on the relevant markets of the parties to any given agreement. That is particularly so in the case of Regulation 2349/84 on exemptions in respect of patent licensing agreements . . . which is relevant in this case. Second, the possibility of applying Article [81(3)] and Article [82] concurrently is expressly confirmed by certain of the block-exemption regulations where it is provided that enjoyment of block exemption does not preclude application of Article [82]—in particular, the three block-exemption regulations in the field of air transport adopted by the Commission on 26 July 1988, each of which states expressly in the preamble that group exemption does not preclude the application of Article [82]. (The relevant regulations are Regulations (EEC) No 2671/88 on the application of Article [81(3)] of the Treaty to certain categories of agreements between undertakings, decisions of associations of undertakings and concerted practices concerning joint planning and co-ordination of capacity, sharing of revenue and consultations on tariffs on scheduled air services and slot allocation at airports, Regulation (EEC) No 2672/88 on the application of Article [81(3)] of the Treaty to certain categories of agreements between undertakings relating to computer reservation systems for air transport services and Regulation (EEC) No 2673/88 on the application of Article [81(3)] of the Treaty to certain categories of agreements between undertakings, decisions of associations of undertakings and concerted practices concerning ground handling services (Official Journal 1988, pp. 9, 13 and 17, respectively).) Similarly, Article 8(1) of Council Regulation 4056/86, cited above, states expressly that abuse of a dominant position within the meaning of Article [82] is prohibited, no prior decision to that effect being required.

31. It follows from all the foregoing considerations that the first head of argument in support of the sole ground of action, based on a schematic analysis of Article [81(3)] and Article [82], is unfounded.

The relationship between Article 81 and 82 has also become acute in the context of undertakings found to be 'collectively dominant' for the purposes of Article 82 by virtue of the contractual links between the parties. It is possible in such cases that the agreement between the parties will infringe Article 81 and that the behaviour conducted in consequence of the agreement will amount to an abuse of a collective dominant position.[129]

6. CONCLUSIONS

Article 82 is a powerful regulatory tool. Undertakings held to be 'dominant'—itself an uncertain concept—are debarred from an open-ended range of conduct which goes beyond the bounds of 'normal competition'. Heavy fines may be levied on those found to have infringed the prohibition even though the Commission may have sought, in intervening, to promote a goal other than the pursuit of economic efficiency. The following chapters describe how dominance is ascertained, how abuse is identified and what policies have been pursued in the interpretation and application of Article 82.

7. FURTHER READING

A. BOOKS

JOLIET R., *Monoplization and Abuse of Dominant Position* (Nijhoff, 1970)

B. ARTICLES

JEBSEN P., and STEVENS, R., '*Assumptions, Goals and Dominant Undertakings: The Regulation of Competition under Article 86 of the European Union*' (1996) 64 *Antitrust LJ* 443

TEMPLE LANG, J., '*Monopolization and the Definition of "Abuse" of a Dominant Position under Article 86 EEC Treaty*' (1979) 19 *CML-Rev* 345

---

[129] See *infra* Chap. 11.

6

ARTICLE 82:
ESTABLISHING DOMINANCE

1. INTRODUCTION

In Chapter 5 it was seen that the Court, has, in defining dominance, focussed on the ability of a dominant undertaking to act independently of its competitors, customers, and consumers and to prevent effective competition. In *Hoffmann-La Roche*[1] the Court stated:

38. The dominant position thus referred to relates to a position of economic strength enjoyed by an undertaking which enables it to prevent effective competition being maintained on the relevant market by affording it the power to behave to an appreciable extent independently of its competitors, its customers and ultimately of its consumers.

39. Such a position does not preclude some competition, which it does where there is a monopoly or quasi-monopoly, but enables the undertaking which profits by it, if not to determine, at least to have an appreciable influence on the conditions under which that competition will develop, and in any case to act largely in disregard of it so long as such conduct does not operate to its detriment.

In this chapter we consider how the existence of a 'dominant position' is actually established, that is, how it is decided whether or not a particular undertaking is dominant. It will be seen that the criteria the Commission employs, and the way it applies them, have not always met with the approval of commentators or the approbation of economists. On the contrary, the Commission is often criticized for finding that an undertaking occupies a 'dominant position' where, in reality, it has little market power.

In *Continental Can*[2] the ECJ stressed that dominance, or market power, exists only in relation to a particular market and not in the abstract. It held that 'the definition of the relevant market is of essential significance'[3] to the determination of whether or not an undertaking is dominant. In accordance with this judgment the practice of the Commission in ascertaining dominance is, first to identify the relevant market and then to assess the undertaking's position or power on that market. The position on the market is generally

---

[1] Case 85/76, *Hoffmann-La Roche & Co AG v. Commission* [1979] ECR 461, [1979] 3 CMLR 211.

[2] Case 6/72, *Europemballage Corp and Continental Can Co Inc v. Commission* [1973] ECR 215, [1973] CMLR 199.

[3] *Ibid.*, para. 32.

determined by looking at the market share of the undertaking concerned and at 'other factors indicating dominance'.

This two-stage procedure may, at times, be problematic. Not only are markets notoriously difficult to define,[4] but the process of market definition may be hard to separate from what is supposed to be the second step, assessing the undertaking's power on that market. It can be difficult to determine which factors should be taken into account when defining markets and which factors should be taken into account when considering the undertaking's position on the market.[5] For example, it may not be easy to decide whether account should be taken of the presence of a producer which can switch its production to making a particular product when defining the market or when assessing the competitive constraints that the allegedly dominant undertaking faces on a particular market. Similarly, where a product has two distinct uses it may be difficult to determine whether the relevant market is for the product as a whole or whether there are two distinct markets, both of which are affected by competition on the other market.[6] In addition, the question whether a particular undertaking is dominant can be hard to disentangle from the question whether or not it has committed an abuse of its dominant position.[7]

Whatever the complexities involved, it is essential to define the market before it can be ascertained whether or not an undertaking holds a dominant position. When doing so it is important to remember that market definition is not an end in itself. Rather, it is a preliminary step and a tool necessary to answer the real question: does this firm have sufficient market power to occupy a dominant position for the purposes of Article 82?

2. MARKET DEFINITION

A. GENERAL

It was seen in Chapter 1 that the purpose of defining the relevant market is to identify those products and services that are such close substitutes for one another that they operate as a competitive constraint on the behaviour of the suppliers of those respective products and services. The relevant market has both a product aspect and a geographical aspect. The difficult question of how the relevant market is defined was discussed in the first chapter because it is central to all areas of competition law. Not only is it an essential component to a

---

[4] See *supra* Chap. 1.

[5] In *BPB Industries* [1989] OJ L10/50, [1990] 4 CMLR 464, for example, a question which arose was whether plasterboard and wet plastering formed part of the same market or whether there was a separate market for plasterboard alone. If the answer was the latter it was clear that the presence of undertakings operating on the market for wet plastering had to be taken into account when assessing an undertaking's position on the plasterboard market. The Commission found that there was a distinct plasterboard market: see para. 108. See also the discussion of supply side substitutability, *infra* 284 and *supra* in Chap. 1.

[6] See the Notice on the definition of the relevant market for the purposes of Community competition law [1997] OJ C372/5, discussed *supra* in Chap. 1.

[7] In some cases it has been indicated that the undertaking must be dominant, since if it was not it could not possibly have engaged in the conduct concerned: see *infra* 315–316.

finding of dominance for the purposes of Article 82 but it has already been seen that market definition plays an important role in the context of Article 81: the determination of the market is ordinarily necessary before it can be determined whether or not an agreement has as its effect the prevention, restriction, or distortion of competition; it is essential to the determination of whether or not an agreement *appreciably* restricts competition or trade and is essential to the determination of whether or not an agreement substantially eliminates competition in the common market for the purposes of Article 81(3). The relevant market also has a crucial role to play in the application of the Merger Regulation, Regulation 4064/89.[8] Broadly, a merger's compatibility with the common market is dependent upon whether or not the merger leads to the creation or strengthening of a dominant position.[9]

In this chapter the discussion is generally confined to how the Commission and the Court have defined the relevant markets in Article 82 cases. In most such cases an undertaking concerned will argue that the market is a wide one (for example, all fruit, rather than just bananas). The broader the market, the less likely the finding of dominance.[10] In contrast, the Commission has often been criticized for adopting too narrow a market definition.[11] In many instances this practice has made a finding of dominance inevitable. The assessment of the relevant market is therefore crucial. If defined too narrowly, an undertaking's position will be exaggerated and a finding of dominance made more likely.[12]

It was seen in Chapter 1 that in its Notice on market definition the Commission identifies three main competitive constraints that firms are subject to: demand substitutability, supply substitutability and potential competition.[13] Demand and, to a more limited extent, supply substitutability are relevant to the determination of the market. Although potential competition may be relevant when considering supply substitutability it will more usually be relevant only when considering the allegedly dominant undertaking's position on the relevant market once defined.

---

[8] [1989] OJ C395/1, as amended by Council Reg. 1310/97 [1997] OJ L180/1.

[9] Art. 2(2) and (3) of the Merger Reg.. See *infra* Chap. 12.

[10] Occasionally the undertaking argues for a narrow definition: e.g. in Case C–62/86, *AKZO Chemie BV* v. *Commission* [1991] ECR I–3359, [1993] 5 CMLR 215, the undertaking argued for a narrow market definition as in the narrow niche market it was relatively weak, but in the wider market as a whole it had a large market share. See *infra* 277.

[11] In merger cases the Commission has perhaps tended to be more objective in its definition of the market. In contrast, in Art. 82 cases, the Commission is investigating what it considers to be a breach of Art 82 and perhaps sometimes begins its case with a predisposition to a finding of dominance. This may encourage a narrow market definition.

[12] If defined too widely the undertaking's position will, of course, be under-estimated. Narrow market definitions do not, however, give cause for concern where it is recognized that the undertaking may suffer competitive restraints from outside the market. This is important in the case of complementary products (such as cartons and machines for packaging products in cartons) where the markets are interlinked.

[13] Commission Notice on the definition of the relevant market for the purposes of Community competition law [1997] OJ C372/5, [1998] 4 CMLR 177, para. 13.

B. THE PRODUCT MARKET

(i) DEMAND SUBSTITUTION

a. INTERCHANGEABILITY

When identifying the relevant market the ECJ has stressed the importance of the notion of *interchangeability*.[14] Effective competition operates between products which are interchangeable with one another. In *Hoffmann–La Roche*, for example, the ECJ held that:

The concept of the relevant market in fact implies that there can be effective competition between the products which form part of it and this presupposes that there is a sufficient degree of interchangeability between all the products forming part of the same market insofar as a specific use of such products is concerned.[15]

It is clear, therefore, that all products that have 'a sufficient degree of interchangeability'[16] form part of the same market. The problems that such an identification process poses is illustrated by two of the most notorious and important Article 82 cases, *United Brands* and *Michelin*.[17]

The United Brands *case*

In *United Brands* the ECJ had to consider why people eat bananas and whether or not they are treated by consumers as reasonably interchangeable with other kinds of fresh fruit.[18]

Case 27/76, *United Brands & Co and United Brands Continental BV* v. *Commission* [1978] ECR 207, [1978] 1 CMLR 429

United Brands Company was a US company which produced bananas. Its European subsidiary was United Brands Continental B.V. The Commission found that United Brands had abused its dominant position on the banana market in a number of different ways, in particular by engaging in excessive and discriminatory pricing and refusal to supply. United Brands challenged the Commission's decision. One of the arguments raised was that the Commission had been wrong to find that there was a separate market for bananas. It claimed that, on the contrary, bananas formed part of a wider fresh fruit market. Bananas were reasonably interchangeable with other kinds of fresh fruit such as apples, oranges, grapes, peaches, and strawberries. The Commission contended that bananas were a separate market because of their unique physical, functional and economic characteristics and because Food and Agriculture Organization studies had demonstrated only low cross-elasticity between bananas and other fruit.

---

[14] See *supra* Chap. 1.

[15] Case 85/76, *Hoffmann-La Roche & Co AG* v. *Commission* [1979] ECR 461, [1979] 3 CMLR 211, para. 28.

[16] Or 'substitutability'.

[17] Case 322/81, *NV Nederlandsche Banden-Industrie Michelin* v. *Commission* [1983] ECR 3461, [1985] 1 CMLR 282.

[18] Mayras AG confidently declared: 'As far as eating habits are concerned there is no doubt that a mother who gives her young child a fruit yoghurt will not give him a banana as well . . .' [1978] ECR 207, 312.

Court of Justice

12. As far as the product market is concerned it is first of all necessary to ascertain whether, as the applicant maintains, bananas are an integral part of the fresh fruit market, because they are reasonably interchangeable by consumers with other kinds of fresh fruit such as apples, oranges, grapes, peaches, strawberries, etc. or whether the relevant market consists solely of the banana and is a market sufficiently homogeneous and distinct from the market of other fresh fruit.

13. The applicant submits in support of its argument that bananas compete with other fresh fruit in the same shops, on the same shelves, at prices which can be compared, satisfying the same needs: consumption as a dessert or between meals.

14. The statistics produced show that consumer expenditure on the purchase of bananas is at its lowest between June and December when there is a plentiful supply of domestic fresh fruit on the market.

15. Studies carried out by the Food and Agriculture Organization (FAO) (especially in 1975) confirm that banana prices are relatively weak during the summer months and that the price of apples for example has a statistically appreciable impact on the consumption of bananas in the Federal Republic of Germany.

16. Again according to these studies some easing of prices is noticeable at the end of the year during the 'orange season'.

17. The seasonal peak periods when there is a plentiful supply of other fresh fruit exert an influence not only on the prices but also on the volume of sales of bananas and consequently on the volume of imports thereof.

18. The applicant concludes from these findings that bananas and other fresh fruit form only one market and that UBC's operations should have been examined in this context for the purpose of any application of Article [82] of the Treaty.

19. The Commission maintains that there is a demand for bananas which is distinct from the demand for other fresh fruit especially as the banana is a very important part of the diet of certain sections of the community.

20. The specific qualities of the banana influence customer preference and induce him not to readily accept other fruits as a substitute.

21. The Commission draws the conclusion from the studies quoted by the applicant that the influence of the prices and availability of other types of fruit on the prices and availability of bananas on the relevant market is very ineffective and that these effects are too brief and too spasmodic for such other fruit to be regarded as forming part of the same market as bananas or as a substitute therefor.

22. For the banana to be regarded as forming a market which is sufficiently differentiated from other fruit markets it must be possible for it to be singled out by such special features distinguishing it from other fruits that it is only to a limited extent interchangeable with them and is only exposed to their competition in a way that is hardly perceptible.

23. The ripening of bananas takes place the whole year round without any season having to be taken into account.

24. Throughout the year production exceeds demand and can satisfy it at any time.

25. Owing to this particular feature the banana is a privileged fruit and its production and marketing can be adapted to the seasonal fluctuations of other fresh fruit which are known and can be computed.

26. There is no unavoidable seasonal substitution since the consumer can obtain this fruit all the year round.

27. Since the banana is a fruit which is always available in sufficient quantities the question whether it can be replaced by other fruits must be determined over the whole of the year for the purpose of ascertaining the degree of competition between it and other fresh fruit.

28. The studies of the banana market on the Court's file show that on the latter market there is no significant long term cross-elasticity any more than—as has been mentioned—there is any seasonal substitutability in general between the banana and all the seasonal fruits, as this only exists between the banana and two fruits (peaches and table grapes) in one of the countries (West Germany) of the relevant geographic market.

29. As far as concerns the two fruits available throughout the year (oranges and apples) the first are not interchangeable and in the case of the second there is only a relative degree of substitutability.

30. This small degree of substitutability is accounted for by the specific features of the banana and all the factors which influence consumer choice.

31. The banana has certain characteristics, appearance, taste, softness, seedlessness, easy handling, a constant level of production which enable it to satisfy the constant needs of an important section of the population consisting of the very young, the old and the sick.

32. As far as prices are concerned two FAO studies show that the banana is only affected by the prices—falling prices—of other fruits (and only of peaches and table grapes) during the summer months and mainly in July and then by an amount not exceeding 20%.

33. Although it cannot be denied that during these months and some weeks at the end of the year this product is exposed to competition from other fruits, the flexible way in which the volume of imports and their marketing on the relevant geographic market is adjusted means that the conditions of competition are extremely limited and that its price adapts without any serious difficulties to this situation where supplies of fruit are plentiful.

34. It follows from all these considerations that a very large number of consumers having a constant need for bananas are not noticeably or even appreciably enticed away from the consumption of this product by the arrival of other fresh fruit on the market and that even the personal peak periods only affect it for a limited period of time and to a very limited extent from the point of view of substitutability.

35. Consequently, the banana market is a market which is sufficiently distinct from the other fresh fruit markets.

The ECJ upheld the Commission's finding that there was a separate market for bananas. In particular, the ECJ stressed that bananas are uniquely suitable for certain consumers, the very young, the old, and the sick (they can be mashed up for babies, are easily digestible, are easy to handle, and can be eaten by people with no teeth). This justification led, however, to wide-spread criticism of the judgment.

The fact that the product satisfies a unique need of a particular class of customers does not mean that bananas constitute a separate market if other customers (the majority) are not so limited in their choice of fruit and can respond to a price rise in bananas by buying other fruit. Although it may be possible at point of sale to discriminate *in favour* of certain customers (such as students or old age pensioners) by charging them less than the standard price on production of identification, it is generally not possible to discriminate in the same way against individuals, for example, pensioners and to charge them a *higher* price. If it is impossible to discriminate against the young, old, and sick (or those buying to feed them) by charging them a higher price then the behaviour of marginal customers (who *are* able to switch) must be taken into account. It is the marginal customers who affect a supplier's pricing decisions and whose behaviour is, consequently, crucial in the determination of the market. One group of customers who have a particular need for the product is difficult to exploit *unless* it can somehow be kept separate from other customers and if those other customers can be prevented from making sales on to the special class.

In its Notice on market definition the Commission recognizes that a distinct group of customers will be relevant to market definition only where they, themselves, constitute a separate market and price discrimination between the different groups of customers is possible:

43. The extent of the product market might be narrowed in the presence of distinct groups of customers. A distinct group of customers for the relevant product may constitute a narrower, distinct market when such a group could be subject to price discrimination. This will usually be the case when two conditions are met: (a) it is possible to identify clearly which group an individual customer belongs to at the moment of selling the relevant products to him, and (b) trade among customers or arbitrage by third parties should not be feasible.

The Michelin *case*

In *Michelin* the Commission found that Michelin had committed an abuse of a dominant position on the market for new replacement tyres for lorries, buses, and similar vehicles. Michelin claimed, *inter alia*, that the Commission's definition of the market was narrow and arbitrary and that Michelin did not hold a dominant position on the wider tyre market.[19] The ECJ had to determine whether or not the Commission had correctly defined the market. In considering this question a number of facts had to be taken into account: that lorries and buses need larger tyres than cars and vans; that there are different sizes of lorry and bus tyres; that tyre manufacturers supply their tyres separately to new lorry and bus manufacturers *and* to dealers who fit tyres on lorries and buses as replacements; and that tyre dealers also fit retreaded or remoulded tyres to vehicles whose owners do not want new replacement tyres. Which, if any, of these tyres were substitutes for each other so that they formed part of the same product market?

Case 322/81, *Nederlandsche Banden-Industrie Michelin v. Commission* [1983] ECR 3461, [1985] 1 CMLR 282

Court of Justice

(aa) The market in replacement tyres for heavy vehicles

35. The applicant claims that the definition of the relevant market on which the Commission based its decision is too wide, inasmuch as in the eyes of the consumer different types and sizes of tyres for heavy vehicles are not interchangeable, and at the same time too narrow inasmuch as car and van tyres are excluded from it although they occupy similar positions on the market. It further argues that the Commission's reasoning in its decision is contradictory in so far as it puts itself alternately in the shoes of the ultimate consumer and in those of the dealer. However, at the level of dealers' total sales,

---

[19] Michelin also challenged the definition of the geographic market as being the Netherlands. See *infra* 288–289.

the average proportion of sales of Michelin heavy-vehicle tyres represents only 12 to 18%, which rules out the existence of any dominant position.

36. The Commission defends the definition of the relevant product market used in its decision by pointing out that with a technically homogeneous product it is not possible to distinguish different markets depending on the dimensions, size or specific types of products: in that connection the elasticity of supply between different types and dimensions of tyre must be taken into account. On the other hand the criteria of interchangeability and elasticity of demand allow a distinction to be drawn between the market in tyres for heavy vehicles and the market in car tyres owing to the particular structure of demand, which, in the case of tyres for heavy vehicles, is characterized by the presence above all of experienced trade buyers.

37. As the Court has repeatedly emphasized, most recently in its judgment of 11 December 1980 in Case 31/90 *NV L'Oreal and SA L'Oreal v PVBA De Nieuwe AMCK* [1980] ECR 3775, for the purposes of investigating the possibly dominant position of an undertaking on a given market, the possibilities of competition must be judged in the context of the market comprising the totality of the products which, with respect to their characteristics, are particularly suitable for satisfying constant needs and are only to a limited extent interchangeable with other products. However, it must be noted that the determination of the relevant market is useful in assessing whether the undertaking concerned is in a position to prevent effective competition from being maintained and behave to an appreciable extent independently of its competitors and customers and consumers. For this purpose, therefore, an examination limited to the objective characteristics only of the relevant products cannot be sufficient: the competitive conditions and the structure of supply and demand on the market must also be taken into consideration.

38. Moreover, it was for that reason that the Commission and Michelin NV agreed that new, original-equipment tyres should not be taken into consideration in the assessment of market shares. Owing to the particular structure of demand for such tyres characterized by direct orders from car manufacturers, competition in this sphere is in fact governed by completely different factors and rules.

39. As far as replacement tyres are concerned, the first point which must be made is that at the user level there is no interchangeability between car and van tyres on the one hand and heavy-vehicle tyres on the other. Car and van tyres therefore have no influence at all on competition on the market in heavy-vehicle tyres.

40. Furthermore, the structure of demand for each of those groups of products is different. Most buyers of heavy-vehicle tyres are trade users, particularly haulage undertakings, for whom, as the Commission explained, the purchase of replacement tyres represents an item of considerable expenditure and who constantly ask their tyre dealers for advice and long-term specialized services adapted to their specific needs. On the other hand, for the average buyer of car or van tyres the purchase of tyres is an occasional event and even if the buyer operates a business he does not expect such specialized advice and service adapted to specific needs. Hence the sale of heavy-vehicle tyres requires a particularly specialized distribution network which is not the case with the distribution of car and van tyres.

. . .

42. The Commission rightly examined the structure of the market and demand primarily at the level of dealers to whom Michelin NV applied the practice in question. Michelin NV has itself stated, although in another context, that it was compelled to change its discount system to take account of the tendency towards specialization amongst its dealers, some of whom, such as garage owners, no longer sold tyres for heavy vehicles and vans. This confirms the differences existing in the structure of

demand between different groups of dealers. Nor has Michelin NV disputed that the distinction drawn between tyres for heavy vehicles, vans and cars is also applied by all its competitors, especially as regards discount terms, even if in the case of certain types of tyre the distinctions drawn by different manufacturers may vary in detail.

43. Nevertheless, it cannot be deduced from the fact that the conduct to which exception is taken in this case affects dealers that Michelin NV's position ought to be assessed on the basis of the proportion of Michelin heavy-vehicle tyres in the dealers' total turnover. Since it is a question of investigating whether Michelin NV holds a dominant position in the case of certain products, it is unimportant that the dealers also deal in other products if there is not competition between those products and the products in question.

44. On the other hand, in deciding whether a dominant position exists, neither the absence of elasticity of supply between different types and dimensions of tyres for heavy vehicles, which is due to differences in the conditions of production, nor the absence of interchangeability and elasticity of demand between those types and dimensions of tyre from the point of view of the specific needs of the user allow a number of smaller markets, reflecting those types and dimensions, to be distinguished, as Michelin NV suggests. Those differences between different types and dimensions of tyre are not vitally important for dealers, who must meet demand from customers for the whole range of heavy-vehicle tyres. Furthermore, in the absence of any specialization on the part of the undertakings concerned, such differences in the type and dimensions of a product are not a crucial factor in the assessment of an undertaking's market position because in view of their similarity and the manner in which they complement one another at the technical level, the conditions of competition on the market are the same for all the types and dimensions of the product.

45. In establishing that Michelin NV has a dominant position the Commission was therefore right to assess its market share with reference to replacement tyres for lorries, buses and similar vehicles and to exclude consideration of car and van tyres.

(bb) The taking into consideration of competition from retreads

46. In order to prove that its market share is less than the Commission claims the applicant also contends that the Commission arbitrarily excluded retreads from the relevant market; in the applicant's view these offer consumers a genuine alternative as regards both quality and price. To support that argument Michelin NV produces a number of calculations intended to show the competitiveness of retreads compared with new tyres.

47. In the Commission's view retreads must be excluded from the relevant market because they cannot replace new tyres. This, it argues, is first of all because consumers consider them inferior in terms of safety; secondly most retreads are produced to order for the transport undertakings themselves so that the market in question is one for the supply of services; lastly, since retreads are a secondary product as compared with new tyres, which are, as it were, the raw material for retreading, which largely prevents them from being replaced by retreads, competition must be assessed on the primary market, which is the key to the whole market.

48. In this regard it must first be recalled that although the existence of a competitive relationship between two products does not presuppose complete interchangeability for a specific purpose, it is not a pre-condition for a finding that a dominant position exists in the case of a given product that there should be a complete absence of competition from other partially interchangeable products as long as such competition does not affect the undertaking's ability to influence appreciably the conditions in which that competition may be exerted or at any rate to conduct itself to a large extent without having to take account of that competition and without suffering any adverse effects as a result of its attitude.

49. It is clear from the facts, as established from the parties' statements and those made by the witnesses examined at the hearing during the administrative procedure, that it cannot be denied that new tyres and retreads are interchangeable to some degree but only to a limited extent and not for all purposes. Although Michelin NV has produced calculations to show that the price and quality of retreads are comparable to those of new tyres and that a number of users do in fact consider the two groups of products interchangeable for their purposes, it has nevertheless admitted that in terms of safety and reliability a retread's value may be less than that of new tyre and, what is more, the Commission has shown that a number of users have certain reservations, which may or may not be justified, regarding the use of a retread, particularly on a vehicle's front axle.

50. In order to assess the effect of this limited competition from retreads on Michelin NV's market position it must be borne in mind that at least some retreads are not put on sale but are produced to order for the user as some transport undertakings attach importance to having their own tyre carcasses retreaded in order to be sure of not receiving damaged carcasses. It must be acknowledged that there has been no agreement between the parties as regards the percentage of tyres retreaded in this way as a form of service; the Commission has estimated it at 80% to 95% of retreads whereas Michelin NV maintains that it is only 15 to 20% and that in most cases the order is placed in the name of the dealer and not that of the user. Despite that disagreement between the parties it may said that a proportion of retreads reaching the consumer stage are not in competition with new tyres because they involve a service provided directly by the retreading firms to the users.

51. Furthermore, in assessing the size of Michelin NV's market share in relation to its competitors' it must not be overlooked that the market in renovated tyres is a secondary market which depends on supply and prices on the market in new tyres since every retread is made from a tyre which was originally a new tyre and there is a limit to the number of occasions on which a tyre may be retreaded. Consequently a considerable proportion of demand will inevitably always be satisfied by new tyres. In such circumstances the possession by an undertaking of a dominant position in new tyres gives it a privileged position as regards competition from retreading undertakings and this enables it to conduct itself with greater independence on the market than would be possible for a retreading undertaking.

52. It is clear from the considerations set out above that the partial competition to which manufacturers of new tyres are exposed from retreading undertakings is not sufficient to deprive a manufacturer of new tyres of the economic power which he possesses by virtue of his dominant position on the market in new tyres. In assessing Michelin NV's position in relation to the strength and number of its competitors the Commission was therefore right to take into consideration a market share to 57 to 65% on the market in new replacement tyres for heavy vehicles. Compared with the market shares of Michelin NV's main competitors amounting to 4 to 8%, that market share constitutes a valid indication of Michelin NV's preponderant strength in relation to its competitors, even when allowance is made for some competition from retreads.

The ECJ thus upheld the Commission's decision in *Michelin*.[20] The Commission's decision itself was trenchantly criticized in an article by Korah. In the extract of that article set out below it is considered whether it was right to exclude retreads or remoulds from the relevant market.

---

[20] [1981] OJ L353/33, [1982] 1 CMLR 643.

V. Korah, 'The Michelin Decision of the Commission' (1982) 7 *ELRev.* 130, 130–1

In order to decide whether a firm enjoys market power, it is necessary to analyse the market to see what competitive pressures constrain the ability of the firm to exploit it suppliers, customers or consumers. The Court has held in *Continental Can* that the Commission should define the relevant market and give reasons for its definition. In *Michelin* it was defined (para. 31) as new replacement tyres for trucks, buses and similar vehicles. The Commission excludes remoulds, as these are not adequate substitutes. Some users of heavy vehicles doubt the reliability of remoulds, and tend not to site them on the front, or driven axle for long distance transport or for the transport of rapidly perishable goods (para. 5). Moreover, most heavy vehicle users will use as remoulds only tyres that they themselves have used and which they know are not based on defective casings, so few buy these from dealers. Most have their own used tyres remoulded by specialists. Remoulds sell at a discount of at least 40 per cent of the price of new replacement tyres (we are not told what price—the retail price, the base price of the manufacturers or the net price paid by retailers after discount). At that relative price, contrary to the Commission's view, they must be substitutes for many vehicle users. Competitive pressures on market decisions may come from the supply of goods that are not identical, even if some customers would not switch. The possibility of losing the custom of those who would have their tyres remoulded must constrain Michelin Netherlands's pricing decisions. . . . One of its reasons for excluding remoulds would be right, although it is not spelled out, but it is submitted that the other is wrong. The Commission limits its consideration of the relevant market to the 'level of the retailer' (para. 31). It seems that it is concerned with the retailer of replacement tyres being able to obtain adequate supplies. If one is concerned only with the welfare of retailers, the remoulders must by definition be excluded; but why should the inquiry be so limited? The interests of the remoulders is equally important, and to the extent that vehicle users prefer to have their tyres remoulded at a lower charge, the public interest in the efficient and competitive supply of usable tyres embraces both forms of supply.

b. THE SSNIP TEST

Although it is clear that all products that have 'a sufficient degree of interchangeability'[21] form part of the same market these cases illustrate the difficulties involved in determining whether or not products are in fact interchangeable with one another.

In its 1997 Notice on market definition[22] the Commission states the importance of the SSNIP test in measuring interchangeability or substitutability. It will be remembered that the SSNIP test essentially asks whether a small (5–10 per cent) but non-transitory increase in price of one product (product A) will cause purchasers to purchase sufficient of another product instead (product B).[23] If it does, then the test indicates that both A and B form part of the same product market.[24]

In the extract below Bishop, an economist, explains the significance and advantages of the Commission's use of the SSNIP test when defining markets:

---

[21] Case 85/76, *Hoffmann-La Roche & Co AG* v. *Commission* [1979] ECR 461, [1979] 3 CMLR 211, para. 28.

[22] Commission Notice on the definition of the relevant market for the purposes of Community competition law [1997] OJ C372/5, [1998] 4 CMLR 177, see *supra* Chap. 1.

[23] *Supra* Chap. 1.

[24] Or whether a small non-transitory increase in the price of a product in Member State A will cause a purchaser to purchase the product from another producer in Member State B. If it does, then the test indicates that Member State A and B form part of the same geographic market.

W. Bishop, 'Editorial: The Modernization of DGIV' [1997] *ECLR* 481[25]

The success of the SSNIP is no accident. The question that it asks goes to the core of why we care about market definition in the first place. We can only answer the question of whether, for instance, a 70 per cent share of a 'market' is likely to give a company market power if that 'market' is an economically meaningful market. The key question is whether substitution to other products or other geographic regions is a substantial, or only a trivial, limitation on the conduct of the parties offering those products. We want to include within the market everything that offers substitution to the products at issue for significant numbers of consumers and to exclude from the market all those things that are not realistic substitutes. The SSNIP test is a convenient way of doing this.

When looking at the Article 82 cases in this chapter it will be seen that, at times, the Commission's decisions and the case law of the Court diverge significantly from the approach espoused in the Notice on market definition. The adoption of the SSNIP test in the Notice signals a more recently adopted 'quantitative' approach to market definition which is less intuitive than that which is manifest in many of the Article 82 cases. The approach reflects the increased experience which the Commission has acquired in market definition as a result of carrying out its obligations under the Merger Regulation. In some cases, however, it will not be possible to determine scientifically whether or not certain products are interchangeable. Further, it must never be forgotten that the Commission's Notice on market definition is simply that, a notice with no binding legal force, and that it is the ECJ which interprets Article 82. The definition of the relevant market must therefore be guided not only by the Commission's practice as described in its notice, but by the case law of the Court. The case law of the Court and the practice of the Commission have indicated the importance of looking at a number of other factors when defining markets.

The Commission and the Court have, however, been criticized in respect of the attention focussed on many of these other factors. If too much attention is placed on factors which in reality tell us little about a relevant market then decisions are of course likely to be arbitrary.[26] In particular, if the market cannot be determined scientifically, reference to factors such as product characteristics, intended use, and consumer preference may mean that too much subjectivity is introduced into the determination. In many circumstances this may result in the adoption of too narrow a market definition.

c. PRODUCT CHARACTERISTICS, PRICE, AND INTENDED USE

The SSNIP test measures interchangeability and customer preferences by considering the impact on the market of an increase in price of a product. Whether or not such an increase in price will cause a consumer to substitute another product will be dependent upon a number of different factors. In the past, however, both the ECJ and the Commission have placed importance on the characteristics and intended use of the product when considering their substitutability from a consumer's point of view. The extracts set out above show the

---

[25] This was written when the Notice was in draft form. The final version, however, did not differ in any material respect relevant here.

[26] See e.g. S. Bishop and M. Walker, *The Economics of EC Competition Law: Concepts, Application and Measurement* (Sweet & Maxwell, London, 1999), chap. 3.

importance that these factors played in both *United Brands* and *Michelin*.[27] In particular, in *United Brands* the ECJ considered the small degree of substitutability between bananas and other fruit to be partly to do with the unique appearance, taste, softness, seedlessness, and easy handling nature of the banana. The judgment does not make it clear why these distinctive characteristics should impact on the determination of the product market.

In many cases, however, characteristics and intended use will not be particularly useful to the determination of the relevant market. They will not shed light when trying to determine, for example, whether or not sparkling mineral water is in the same market as still mineral water, tap water, orange juice, or tonic water. All of these products have similar characteristics and uses.

S. Bishop and M. Walker, *The Economics of EC Competition Law: Concepts, Application and Measurement* (Sweet & Maxwell, 1999)

3.27 . . . On occasions firms under investigation will appeal to the commonality of physical characteristics or intended use in making representations to the Commission. For example, in *Nestlé/Perrier* [OJ [1992] L 356/1, [1993] 4 CMLR M17[28]], the parties initially argued that, in addition to bottled waters, the relevant product market included all non-alcoholic beverages on the basis that all products in this market had the same base function: namely, quenching consumers' thirst. However, the Commission itself showed exactly how arbitrary such appeals can be. The Commission states in reply that, when purchasing bottled water, consumers were not simply seeking to quench their thirst but were seeking to do so with liquid from a healthy (unsweetened) source. On this basis, soft-drinks were excluded. However, on this definition the market seemed to include purified tap-water (which meant that Coca-Cola would have been a potential entrant as all Coca-Cola bottlers are required to start with purified tap water before adding the Coca-Cola syrup and bubbles). To eliminate this possibility the Commission added that consumers were seeking to quench their thirst with liquid from a *healthy, natural source that provided minerals*.

3.28 As a further example of where this sort of reasoning can lead, consider that some consumers regard sparkling water as a substitute for still water while others do not. Should it be concluded that because, to some consumer, the two types of water are not considered to be substitutes, they lie in separate markets? Or should it be concluded that the existence of those consumers who would switch points to the two products properly being in the same market? The example could clearly be extended further by asking whether, since they are all fizzy, soft drinks are in the same market as sparkling mineral waters.

There is a similarity between these sorts of arguments and the process of narrowing market definitions by simply adding more and more adjectives. This process is totally arbitrary and any

---

[27] See also *BBI/Boosey & Hawkes: Interim Measures* [1987] OJ L286/36, [1988] 4 CMLR 67 (brass instruments for British-style brass bands); *Decca Navigator System (Racal)* [1989] OJ L43/27, [1990] 4 CMLR 627 (no substitute for a radio transmission service of technical superiority); *Spanish Courier Services* [1990] OJ L233/19, [1991] 4 CMLR 560 (basic postal service and express postal service are separate markets). In Cases T–69–70/89, 76/89, *Television Listings/Magill RTE, ITP, BBC* v. *Commission* [1991] ECR II–485, [1991] 4 CMLR 586, confirmed by the ECJ, Cases C–241–241/91 P, *RTE & ITP* v. *Commission* [1995] ECR I–743, [1995] 4 CMLR 718, the CFI held that the market for weekly TV listings magazines was distinct from that of daily listings as they were only to a limited extent interchangeable, as daily listings do not allow viewers to plan their leisure activities for the week ahead.

[28] For a discussion of this case see *infra* Chap. 12.

market definition can be advanced simply by *selectively* appealing to product characteristics and intended end use. Too much importance is laid on physical difference since such a focus does not answer the main question—what is the extent of lost sales following a price rise?

3.29 This point is demonstrated clearly in the *United Brands* case . . . In *United Brands* the European Court of Justice found that the banana market had certain special features that were sufficiently distinctive for it to be regarded as representing a distinct relevant product market—year round availability, the ability to satisfy the constant needs of an important part of the population and the limited effect of competition from other fresh fruits at the banana's peak periods. This conclusion appears to have been made on the basis of very limited empirical evidence, and there appears to have been no attempt to determine whether these differences were meaningful in that they imply that the bananas are a product worth monopolising. It will always be possible to construct a list of differences. But the real question is whether or not these differences are meaningful—an issue that need to be settled by having recourse to empirical observation.

In paragraph 36 of its Notice on market definition the Commission recognizes the limited usefulness of looking at the characteristics and intended use of a product when defining the market. The notice indicates, however, that their consideration may be useful as a preliminary step when considering the possible substitutes for a product.

36. An analysis of the product characteristics and its intended use allows the Commission, in a first step, to limit the field of investigation of possible substitutes. However, product characteristics and intended use are insufficient to conclude whether two products are demand substitutes. Functional interchangeability or similarity in characteristics may not provide in themselves sufficient criteria because the responsiveness of customers to relative price changes may be determined by other considerations also. For example, there may be different competitive constraints in the original equipment market for car components and in spare parts, thereby leading to a distinction of two relevant markets. Conversely, differences in product characteristics are not in themselves sufficient to exclude demand substitutability, since this will depend to a large extent on how customers value different characteristics.

As indicated above, it must be recognized that the notice cannot affect the interpretation of Article 82 adopted by the Court. It cannot be concluded, therefore, that the importance of looking at the characteristics and intended use of a product can be confined to the first step taken in market definition. Indeed, in 1998 in *Oscar Bronner*[29] the ECJ reiterated the importance that its case law has attached to these factors:

It is settled case-law that, for the purpose of applying Article [82] of the Treaty, the market for the product or service in question comprises all the products or services which in view of their characteristics are particularly suited to satisfy constant needs and are only to a limited extent interchangeable with other products or services.

The Commission itself has in fact continued in some cases to use characteristics, price, and intended use as criteria in market definition. For example, in *Van den Bergh Foods Ltd*[30] the Commission held that impulse ice-cream cream (bought as individual portions in shops for immediate consumption) and take-home ice-cream[31] (multi-packs of single items designed

---

[29] Case C–7/97, *Oscar Bronner GmbH & Co KG* v. *Mediaprint* [1998] ECR I–7791, [1999] 4 CMLR 112, para. 33.

[30] [1998] OJ L246/1, [1998] 5 CMLR 530, particularly paras. 130–138.

[31] It also distinguished catering ice-cream (sold in bulk to catering establishments) from impulse and take-home ice-cream.

for storage and consumption at home) were in different markets. This was partly because the 'distinction on the basis of the consumer's intended purpose in purchasing the ice cream in turn determines the differences in characteristics and price between impulse and take-home products'.[32]

d. THE STRUCTURE OF SUPPLY AND DEMAND

The structure of supply and demand may be important in determining the relevant market and may cause identical products to fall into different markets. The structure of supply and demand was relevant to the determination of the market in *Michelin*. It is seen from the extract set out above[33] that the ECJ upheld the Commission finding that identical new heavy vehicle tyres and retreads formed two separate product markets. The market for the supply of heavy vehicle tyres to vehicle manufacturers as original equipment was distinct from the market for the supply to dealers to be fitted as replacements. In these two types of cases the Court stressed the difference in the dynamics of the transactions.[34] Conversely, the ECJ accepted (in paragraph 44) that different types of heavy vehicle tyres, although *not* substitutes for each other, *were* in the same market. This was because dealers[35] had to stock all tyres and the conditions of competition were the same for all types and dimensions.

Similarly, in *Van den Bergh Foods* the Commission placed emphasis on the structure of supply and demand in finding that the markets for single wrapped individual ice cream and individual portions of soft ice cream were distinct. Although the consumer might perceive the two-types of ice-cream to be reasonably interchangeable, the competitive conditions under which they were offered to the retail trade were different and distinct. Soft ice cream had, for example, to be processed by the retailer and so required the installation of special processing and dispensing machines; it was not self-service and was not normally branded.

The consumer's point of view is, . . . not in every instance the sole criterion in the determination of a product market; nor is an examination limited only to the objective characteristics of the products in question sufficient. The competitive conditions and the structure of supply and demand on the market must also be taken into consideration.[36]

e. MARKETS CREATED BY STATE REGULATION

A relevant market may be affected by state regulation. Legislation may, for example, define a statutory market. Such regulation may mean that no substitutes are permitted for a particular product or service.

In *General Motors*[37] and *British Leyland*[38] national regulations required conformity or type-approval certificates from importers of motor vehicles and provided that they could

---

[32] *Ibid.*, para. 132. It also distinguished between the markets for industrial (produced for wide-scale distribution) and 'artisan' (produced, distributed and consumed locally on a small scale) ice-cream.

[33] *Supra* 266.

[34] See also Case C–333/94P, *Tetra Pak International SA* v. *Commission* [1996] ECR I–5951, [1997] 4 CMLR 662, para. 13.

[35] For the abuse issues in *Michelin* see *infra* Chap. 7.

[36] [1998] OJ L246/1, [1998] 5 CMLR 530, para. 133.

[37] Case 26/75, *General Motors* v. *Commission* [1975] ECR 1367, [1976] 1 CMLR 95.

[38] Case 226/84, *British Leyland* v. *Commission* [1986] ECR 3323, [1987] 1 CMLR 185.

only be issued by the vehicle manufacturer. In both cases the ECJ held that the provision of the certificates was a separate market and not part of the motor car market.

f. CHAINS OF SUBSTITUTION

There can also be a chain of substitution, where B is a substitute for A and C is a substitute for B etc. Particular problems of market definition arise where a product has more than one use, and there are substitutes for one use and not for others, or different substitutes for different uses.

The difficulties emerging when a product has multiple applications arose in *Hoffmann-La Roche*.[39] In this case Hoffmann-La Roche (HLR) challenged the Commission's finding that it had committed a number of abuses of dominant positions held on several separate vitamin markets. Two of the vitamins concerned, C and E, had two distinct uses. In each case the vitamin had a bio-nutritive use for which there were no substitutes, and an anti-oxidant use. Both vitamins C and E and other products could be used for the anti-oxidant use. Hoffmann-La Roche claimed that the two vitamins were in the same market for anti-oxidants together with these other products. The ECJ, concentrating on the bio-nutritive use, upheld the Commission's finding that the vitamins each constituted a separate market. The reasoning was not, however, entirely satisfactory. In particular, the judgment is criticized for the Court's failure to take account of the two distinct uses. If HLR could not profitably increase the price to customers in the bio-nutritive market without also losing customers in the anti-oxidant market, then arguably they should have been found to form part of the same market.[40]

Case 85/76, *Hoffmann-La Roche & Co AG v. Commission* [1979] ECR 461, [1979] 3 CMLR 211

Court of Justice

28. If a product could be used for different purposes and if these different uses are in accordance with economic needs, which are themselves also different, there are good grounds for accepting that this product may, according to the circumstances, belong to separate markets which may present specific features which differ from the standpoint both of the structure and of the conditions of competition. However this finding does not justify the conclusion that such a product together with all the other products which can replace it as far as concerns the various uses to which it may be put and with which it may compete, forms one single market. The concept of the relevant market in fact implies that there can be effective competition between the products which form part of it and this presupposes that there is a sufficient degree of interchangeability between all the products forming part of the same market in so far as a specific use of such products is concerned. There was no such interchangeability, at any rate during the period under consideration, between all the vitamins of each of the groups C and E and all the products which, according to the circumstances, may be substituted for one or other of these groups of vitamins for technological uses which are themselves extremely varied.

29. On the other hand there may be some doubt whether, for the purpose of delimiting the respective markets of the C and E groups of vitamins, it is necessary to include all the vitamins of each of

---

[39] Case 85/76, *Hoffmann-La Roche & Co AG v. Commission* [1979] ECR 461, [1979] 3 CMLR 211.
[40] See the discussion *supra* 270–271.

these groups in a market corresponding to that group, or whether, on the contrary, each of these groups must be placed in a separate market, one comprising vitamins for bio-nutritive use and the other vitamins for technological purposes.

30.   However, in order to calculate the market shares of Roche and its competitors correctly this question did not have to be answered because, as the Commission has rightly pointed out, if it had been necessary to draw this distinction, it would have to be drawn for Roche's competitors as well as for Roche itself, and—in the absence of any indication to the contrary by the applicant—in similar proportions with the result that the market shares in percentages would remain unchanged. Finally Roche, in answer to a question put to it by the Court, has stated that all the vitamins of each group, irrespective of the ultimate intended use of the product, were subject to the same price system so that they could not be split up into specific markets. It follows from the foregoing that the Commission has correctly delimited the relevant markets in its contested decision.

The narrow definition adopted by the Commission and upheld by the Court in *Hoffmann-La Roche* is less troubling if it is remembered that market definition is not an end in itself, but a step towards assessing market power. As long as it is recognized that markets are not impermeable and may be subject to competitive pressures from *outside* the market, a narrow market definition is not serious. This point is made by Baden Fuller[41] in the extract below.

C.W. Baden Fuller, 'Article 86: Economic Analysis of the Existence of a Dominant Position' (1979) 4 *ELRev.* 423, 425

The Court has said that it is necessary to define a market: economists would agree—for to point out dominance, one must say upon what market a firm is dominant. In *Roche* (paragraph 28) and *UBC* (paragraph 22), the Court defined the extent of a market by reference to the existence of substitutes on the demand side and in *Continental Can Company* to substitute on the supply side . . . For example, in *Roche* the defendants disputed whether Vitamins C and E should each be considered as part of one market. According to the Court (paragraphs 28 and 29), Vitamins C and E had two usages, one as additives to foodstuffs (called the bio-nutritive use), and the other as anti-oxydants, fermentation agents and additives (called the technological usage); in their first usage, C and E performed different functions and in this usage neither could be substituted for the other, and there was no other product which could perform as substitutes for either; in their second usage, C and E were not only inter-changeable with each other, but there was a variety of other products which could also be inter-changed with them. The notable aspect of the case was that it was not always possible for Roche to distinguish between customers who wanted Vitamins C and E for the different uses, because some buyers who used C or E in foodstuffs also required anti-oxydants for which C and E could be used interchangeably. An economist would argue that there were three markets defined from the demand side: the two separate bio-nutritive usage markets of C and E, and the technological usage market which included C, E and other anti-oxydants. It is obvious that a change in price of (say) Vitamin C would have little effect on the quantity of E sold for its bio-nutritive use. Economists would say that there is a low cross elasticity between C and E, and that these products were not substitutes (*i.e* they were in different markets). But a change in price of C would have a substantial effect on the quantity of E sold for its technological use, indicating a high cross elasticity, and that these products were substitutes (*i.e* in the same market). The Court ruled that Vitamins C and E were separate markets

---

[41] See e.g. V. Korah, 'Concept of a Dominant Position within the Meaning of Art 86' (1980) 17 *CMLRev.* 395.

stressing their bio-nutritive uses. Here economists would agree with the Court, but would note that any analysis of these markets must also consider the technological market . . .

A narrower market definition may, however, be more likely to result in a finding of dominance.[42]

The Commission Notice on market definition recognizes that where chains of substitution are possible practical problems may arise in determining both the geographic and the product market.

57. In certain cases, the existence of chains of substitution might lead to the definition of a relevant market where products or areas at the extreme of the market are not directly substitutable. An example might be provided by the geographic dimension of a product with significant transport costs. In such cases, deliveries from a given plant are limited to a certain area around each plant by the impact of transport costs. In principle, such an area could constitute the relevant geographic market. However, if the distribution of plants is such that there are considerable overlaps between the areas around different plants, it is possible that the pricing of those products will be constrained by a chain substitution effect, and lead to the definition of a broader geographic market. The same reasoning may apply if product B is a demand substitute for products A and C. Even if products A and C are not direct demand substitutes, they might be found to be in the same relevant product market since their respective pricing might be constrained by substitution to B.

58. From a practical perspective, the concept of chains of substitution has to be corroborated by actual evidence, for instance related to price inter-dependence at the extremes of the chains of substitution, in order to lead to an extension of the relevant market in an individual case. Price levels at the extremes of the chains would have to be of the same magnitude as well.

At the end of paragraph 57 the Commission stresses that the real question is how far the existence of substitutes has a constraining influence on an undertaking's pricing policy.

In *AKZO*[43] AKZO Chemie was found to be dominant on the market for organic peroxides which had multiple uses. The case shows how each of these situations has to be examined in the light of the particular circumstances.[44] Organic peroxides are used in polymer manufacture, where in some fields of application they have limited substitutes. The main organic peroxide, benzoyl peroxide, can also be used as a bleaching agent in flour-milling in the UK and Ireland. AKZO argued that the relevant market should be considered as that for flour additives (where it did not have a high market share). The Commission found that the relevant market was the organic peroxides market as a whole. Since AKZO concentrated its production on the polymer sector its share of the whole peroxides market was 50 per cent. The ECJ upheld the Commission's definition of the market because AKZO's conduct—lowering its prices in the flour-milling sector in order to protect its position in the polymer sector—as well as its internal documentation, showed that the undertaking itself treated the market as a single one.

g. RAW MATERIALS

A raw material may constitute a separate product market even though the derivative product made from it forms part of a wide product market which has a number of substitutes. In

---

[42] The higher the undertaking's market share, the more likely a finding of dominance: see *infra* 298 ff.

[43] Case C–62/86, *AKZO Chemie BV* v. *Commission* [1991] ECR I–3359, [1993] 5 CMLR 215.

[44] *Ibid.*, para. 38.

Commercial Solvents, for example, it was held that a raw material, aminobutanol, used to produce ethambutol, an anti-TB drug, constituted a product market of its own.[45] In this case Zoja manufactured ethambutol from aminobutanol which had been manufactured by Commercial Solvents Corporation. Other anti-TB drugs existed on the market, which were not ethambutol based. The ECJ held that the relevant market was not the market for the derivatives, the drug, but the market for the raw material. There may have been substitute drugs which could be used to combat TB but a manufacturer of ethambutol, such as Zoja, could not operate without aminobutanol.[46]

Commercial Solvents was the first case to deal with the problems posed by derivative or ancillary markets. The concept developed in this case, that such markets can be distinguished from those for the primary product, has proved of great importance in the Article 82 jurisprudence, as the following sections show.

h. AFTERMARKETS

'Aftermarkets' is the expression used to describe markets which consist of a product or service which is complementary to another. Many durable goods, such as cars, need compatible spare parts, and some, such as vacuum cleaners or photocopiers, also need a constant supply of 'consumables' in order to operate: some cleaners need bags, photocopiers need toner cartridges and suitable paper. All these durables, and many others, may need to be serviced and repaired. The customer may be 'locked in'—the owner of a Ford Fiesta needs spare parts which fit a Ford Fiesta, not those which fit a Nissan Micra—and competition issues can arise when the supplier of the original product or equipment also supplies the product or service in the aftermarket. If competition authorities take the view that there is one market, consisting of the original equipment together with its spare parts/consumables/servicing needs, then Article 82 will apply only if the supplier is dominant in that market as a whole, which will usually turn on the question whether he is dominant in the supply of the original equipment. However, since the judgment in *Commercial Solvents*, in which the raw material market was distinguished from the ancillary market for the derivative product, the Commission has defined markets narrowly, finding that spare parts and consumables form part of a separate market from the original equipment supplied. The justification for this approach is that the original equipment and its spare parts or consumables are not substitutes for one another. The net result of such a division is that an undertaking with a small share of the original equipment market may be found to be dominant in the aftermarket and to have committed an abuse of its dominant position in that market.

Spare parts

A spare part in this context is a replacement for an integral part of the original product, produced by the supplier of that product, although it may be produced by independent manufacturers as well. Car tyres, for example, are not described as spare parts as they are not manufactured by the car makers. The question whether the market for spare parts of a product might constitute a separate market for the purposes of EC competition law first

---

[45] Cases 6 and 7/73, *Istituto Chemioterapico Italiano SpA and Commercial Solvents Corp* v. *Commission* [1974] ECR 223, [1974] 1 CMLR 309.

[46] Other possible ways of producing ethambutol, using thiophenol or butatone, were dismissed by the ECJ as they were uncertain and experimental and had not been used on an industrial scale.

arose in *Hugin*. This case concerned a refusal to supply by Hugin, a Swedish firm which produced and sold cash registers and their spare parts. It had approximately 12 per cent of the Community cash register market. After-sales, maintenance, and repair services of Hugin machines were conducted by local subsidiaries, agents, and distributors in, *inter alia*, all the Member States. From October 1972 Hugin decided no longer to supply machines or their spare parts to Liptons, a small firm in south-east England which sold, leased, repaired, serviced, and reconditioned cash registers, including Hugin machines. Without the spare parts Liptons could not continue servicing and repairing etc. Hugin machines. Liptons complained to the Commission and the Commission issued a decision holding that Hugin had committed an abuse of its dominant position on the spare parts market.[47] The ECJ held that the relevant market in this case was a narrow one. It was constituted only by Hugin spare parts which were required by independent undertakings that maintained and repaired Higin cash registers. Since Hugin was the sole supplier of those spare parts it was held to be dominant on that market.[48]

Case 22/78, *Hugin Kassaregister AB and Hugin Cash Registers Ltd* v. *Commission* [1979] ECR 1869, [1979] 3 CMLR 345[49]

Court of Justice

5. To resolve the dispute it is necessary, first, to determine the relevant market. In this respect account must be taken of the fact that the conduct alleged against Hugin consists in the refusal to supply spare parts to Liptons and, generally, to any independent undertaking outside its distribution network. The question is, therefore, whether the supply of spare parts constitutes a specific market or whether it forms part of a wider market. To answer that question it is necessary to determine the category of clients who require such parts.

6. In this respect it is established, on the one hand, that registers are of such a technical nature that the user cannot fit the spare parts into the machine but requires the services of a specialized technician and, on the other, that the value of the spare parts is of little significance in relation to the cost of maintenance and repairs. That being the case, users of cash registers do not operate on the market as purchasers of spare parts, however they have their machines maintained and repaired. Whether they avail themselves of Hugin's after-sales service or whether they rely on independent undertakings engaged in maintenance and repair work, their spare part requirements are not manifested directly and independently on the market. While there certainly exists amongst users a market for maintenance and repairs which is distinct from the market in new cash registers, it is essentially a market for the provision of services and not for the sale of a product such as spare parts, the refusal to supply which forms the subject matter of the Commission's decision.

7. On the other hand, there exists a separate market for Hugin spare parts at another level, namely that of independent undertakings which specialize in the maintenance and repair of cash registers, in the reconditioning of used machines and in the sale of used machines and the renting out of machines. The role of those undertakings on the market is that of a business which require spare parts for their

---

[47] See *infra* Chap. 7.

[48] See *infra* 316 ff.

[49] The Commission Decision is reported at [1978] OJ L22/23, [1978] CMLR D19. The ECJ quashed the Commission's decision on the basis that it had not been established that there was an effect on inter-Member State trade: see *supra* Chap. 5.

various activities. They need such parts in order to provide services for cash register users in the form of maintenance and repairs and for the reconditioning of used machines intended for re-sale or renting out. Finally, they require spare parts for the maintenance and repair of new or used machines belonging to them which are rented out to their clients. It is, moreover, established that there is a specific demand for Hugin spare parts, since those parts are not interchangeable with spare parts for cash registers of other makes.

Consequently the market thus constituted by Hugin spare parts required by independent undertakings must be regarded as the relevant market for the purposes of the application of Article [82] to the facts of the case. It is in fact the market on which the alleged abuse was committed.

8. It is necessary to examine next whether Hugin occupies a dominant position on that market. In this respect Hugin admits that it has a monopoly in new spare parts. For commercial reasons any competing production of spare parts which could be used in Hugin cash registers is not conceivable in practice. Hugin argues nevertheless that another source of supply does exist, namely the purchase and dismantling of used machines. The value of that source of supply is disputed by the parties. Although the file appears to show that the practice of dismantling used machines is current in the cash register sector it cannot be regarded as constituting a sufficient alternative source of supply. Indeed the figures relating to Liptons' turnover during the years that Hugin refused to sell spare parts to it show that Liptons' business in the selling, renting out and repairing of Hugin machines diminished considerably, not only when expressed in absolute terms but even more so in real terms, taking inflation into account.

9. On the market for its own spare parts, therefore, Hugin is in a position which enables it to determine its conduct without taking account of competing sources of supply. There is therefore nothing to invalidate the conclusion that it occupies, on that market, a dominant position within the meaning of Article [82].

The ECJ's finding that the market was defined not as the market for spare parts needed by the owners of Hugin machines, but by general repairers and servicers of the machines has been criticized.

C.W. Baden Fuller, 'Article 86: Economic Analysis of the Existence of a Dominant Position' (1979) 4 *ELRev.* 423, 426

In *Hugin* . . . , the Court defined the relevant market as Hugin spare parts required by independent undertakings. This definition of the market is conceptually different from that used in Roche and UBC. First, the Court defined the relevant market with respect to a brand, not a product. This is a minor point. Economists would have noted that spare parts could be made by independent concerns to fit Hugin machines. The Court . . . says that this was not the case, nor could ever be the case.

Second, the Court defined the relevant market without discussing the existence of possible substitutes on the demand side for independent undertakings. This is not a minor point. Consider those independent undertakings in the business of repairing, maintaining or refurbishing (but not renting or leasing) cash registers for independent customers. They often dealt in more than one brand of machine. Their engineers could, and did, repair more than one brand. In this respect, substitutes did exist on the demand side from the point of view of independent undertakings. The Court never discussed whether this substitution was easy, that is, whether the cross-elasticity was high or low. Hugin, in refusing to supply Liptons, apparently forced the latter to turn to servicing other machines. Liptons had said this shift was costly. . . . The Commission in its Decision (paragraphs 27 and 28) did not show a proper analysis of this cost. Moreover, it did not even give figures on sales, costs or profits for Lipton's servicing business for outside customers separated from its other activities such as renting and leasing.

Without such an analysis it is not clear that the shift was so costly or difficult that it is reasonable to consider each brand of spare parts as forming a separate market. To me, the only sensible definitions of the relevant market are those which make specific reference to the owners of the machines. I believe the Court should have defined the market as: 'Spare parts required by those who are owners of Hugin machines.' One such owner would have been Liptons which owned machines as part of its business of renting and leasing and whose users were its customers. These spare parts could be obtained only from Hugin directly or indirectly by means of maintenance contracts. A rise in the price of Hugin maintenance contracts (of which the costs of spare parts are but one component) does not lead to an easy substitution of any other spare parts for reasons noted. It is also unlikely to lead to a widescale scrapping of Hugin machines (incidentally, it is irrelevant but possibly correct to argue that increasing the price of such spare parts is likely to have adverse effects on Hugin's sales of new machines and hence Hugin's overall profits).

Despite this criticism, *Hugin* provides authority for the proposition that one brand of spare parts can constitute a separate product market for the purposes of Article 82. This principle has been applied and relied upon in a number of cases, in particular in two cases involving the motor industry, namely *Volvo*[50] and *Renault*.[51] In these cases it was held that spare parts for cars constitute a separate market from the cars themselves. A manufacturer of a car with a low market share may therefore find that it is dominant on the market for the supply of its spare parts. The *Volvo* and *Renault* cases are discussed in Chapter 10 below.

Consumables

The *Hugin* principle has also been applied to consumables. A consumable is something which is used when operating the original product and which needs constant replenishing, for example, an ink cartridge used for a printer. Consumables are frequently produced by the manufacturer of the original product. In many cases the manufacturer will wish to present itself as supplying an indivisible 'system' consisting of the durable, an on-going supply of the consumable, and, also, perhaps, a maintenance and repair service. It is likely to try to ensure that the purchaser of the original product also buys the goods and services in the aftermarket from it.

The Commission first had to deal with these difficulties in *Hilti*. Hilti made nail guns which were a technologically-advanced way of making secure fastenings in the construction industry. The guns were used together with cartridges in cartridge strips and nails. The cartridges provided the explosive power, which enabled the gun to fire the nails into different materials as required. Nails compatible with Hilti guns were made not only by Hilti but by a number of independent firms. These firms complained that Hilti was indulging in practices designed to ensure that purchasers of the guns bought only Hilti's own nails. The Commission held that these practices constituted an abuse.[52] Hilti argued that its nail gun and consumables formed a powder–actuated fastening system which was in competition with, and in the same market as, other forms of construction fastening system. Since the nail guns, cartridges, and nails were not in separate markets but formed one indivisible product,

---

[50] Case 238/87, *AB Volvo v. Erik Veng* [1988] ECR 6211, [1989] 4 CMLR 122.
[51] Case 53/87, *CICCRA v. Renault* [1988] ECR 6039, [1990] 4 CMLR 265.
[52] *Eurofix-Bauco/Hilti* [1988] OJ L65/19, [1989] 4 CMLR 677. For the abuse issue, see Chap. 7.

its conduct in 'tying' the sales together could not constitute an abuse. These arguments were rejected both by the CFI and the ECJ. The CFI set out its reasoning more fully:[53]

Case T–30/89, *Hilti AG* v. *Commission* [1991] ECR II–1439, [1992] 4 CMLR 16

Court of First Instance

64. It should be observed at the outset that in order to assess Hilti's market position it is first necessary to define the relevant market, since the possibilities of competition can only be judged in relation to those characteristics of the products in question by virtue of which those products are particularly apt to satisfy an inelastic need and are only to a limited extent interchangeable with other products. . . .

65. In order to determine, therefore, whether Hilti, as a supplier of nail guns and of consumables designed for them, enjoys such power over the relevant product market as to give it a dominant position within the meaning of Article [82], the first question to be answered is whether the relevant market is the market for all construction fastening systems or whether the relevant markets are those for PAF tools and the consumables designed for them, namely cartridge strips and nails.

66. The Court takes the view that nail guns, cartridge strips and nails constitute three specific markets. Since cartridge strips and nails are specifically manufactured, and purchased by users, for a single brand of gun, it must be concluded that there are separate markets for Hilti-compatible cartridge strips and nails, as the Commission found in its decision (paragraph 55).

67. With particular regard to the nails whose use in Hilti tools is an essential element of the dispute, it is common ground that since the 1960s there have been independent producers, including the interveners, making nails intended for use in nail guns. Some of those producers are specialised and produce only nails, and indeed some make only nails specifically designed for Hilti tools. That fact in itself is sound evidence that there is a specific market for Hilti-compatible nails.

68. Hilti's contention that guns, cartridge strips and nails should be regarded as forming an indivisible whole, 'a powder-actuated fastening system' is in practice tantamount to permitting producers of nail guns to exclude the use of consumables other than their own branded products in their tools. However, in the absence of general and binding statements or rules, any independent producer is quite free, as far as Community competition law is concerned, to manufacture consumables intended for use in equipment manufactured by others, unless in doing so it infringes a patent or some other industrial or intellectual property right. Even on the assumption that, as the applicant has argued, components of different makes cannot be interchanged without the system characteristics being influenced, the solution should lie in the adoption of appropriate laws and regulations, not in unilateral measures taken by nail gun producers which have the effect of preventing independent producers from pursuing the bulk of their business.

77.The conclusion must be that the relevant product market in relation to which Hilti's market position must be appraised is the market for nails designed for Hilti nail guns.

---

[53] ECJ in Case C–53/92, *P. Hilti* v. *Commission* [1994] ECR I–666, [1994] 4 CMLR 614, confirmed the reasoning of the CFI.

78. That finding is corroborated by the abovementioned letter of 23 March 1983 from Hilti to the Commission, in which the opinion was expressed that there were separate markets for guns, cartridge strips and nails. Although that did not, at the time, represent an interpretation of the term 'relevant market' for the purposes of Article [82] [EC], the content of the letter is nevertheless quite revealing as to Hilti's own commercial view of the markets in which it operated at the time. Hilti has explained that the letter was therefore drafted by persons who may be assumed to have had a sound knowledge of the undertaking and its business.

In paragraph 68 the Court states that independent producers are free, as far as Community competition law is concerned, to manufacture consumables. This statement is revealing of the policy behind the narrow market definition adopted in some of the cases. It is not, as the wording rather strangely suggests,[54] that Community competition law *allows* independents to manufacture but that Article 82 may preclude the producer of the original equipment from preventing others' access to the market. This prohibition is imposed in order to increase competition.[55]

The consumable issue also arose in *Tetra Pak II*,[56] one of the most complex Article 82 cases on market definition (an extract of the case is set out below[57]). Essentially in this case the Commission and the Court refused to accept that Tetra Pak operated on a market for systems in packaging liquid food. Rather it was found that it operated on four separate product markets: the market in machinery for the aseptic packaging of liquid foods in cartons and the corresponding market for cartons, and the market in machinery for the non-aseptic packaging of liquid foods in cartons and the corresponding market in cartons.

In *Info-Lab/Ricoch*,[58] however, the Commission declined to accept that there was a separate market for empty toner cartridges compatible with a specific (Ricoch) photocopy machine. This case concerned a complaint lodged by Info-Lab which made toner for photocopiers. It alleged that Ricoch, a manufacturer of photocopiers, was abusing its dominant position by refusing to supply Info-Lab with empty toner cartridges for Ricoch machines which Info-Lab could then fill with toner. Info-Lab could not make the cartridges itself without infringing Ricoch's intellectual property rights. It thus alleged that the empty cartridges, which could be filled with toner and sold to customers, constituted a separate product market and that Ricoch had abused its dominant position on this market. The Commission rejected the complaint, holding that the market identified by the complainant was not a separate product market. No producer or dealer produced or sold empty toner cartridges. There was no consumer demand for such a product. Rather, cartridge and powder were always sold together as a single product. The Commission went on to hold that Ricoch could not be forced to supply Info-Lab with empty cartridges.[59]

[54] The language of the case was English.

[55] See *infra* Chap. 7.

[56] *Elopak Italia/Tetra Pak* [1991] OJ L72/1, [1992] 4 CMLR 551, on appeal Case T–83/91, *Tetra Pak International SA v. Commission* [1994] ECR II–755, [1997] 4 CMLR 726, on appeal Case C–333/94P, *Tetra Pak International SA v. Commission* [1996] ECR I–5951, [1997] 4 CMLR 662. For all the market definition issues involved in this case, see *infra* 291.

[57] *Infra* 291 ff.

[58] Case IV/36431, rejection of a complaint by decision: see *Competition Policy Newsletter* 1999, No. 1, 35.

[59] See *infra* 319–320 and Chap. 7.

Servicing and maintenance

Servicing and maintenance may constitute an aftermarket. In *Digital*[60] the Commission took the view that there was a market for the maintenance services for Digital computer systems, separate from that for the computer systems themselves. Moreover, it considered that the maintenance services themselves fell into two separate markets: the market for hardware maintenance and the market for software maintenance services. The two services were not interchangeable with each other.

Aftermarkets generally

The Commission refers in its Notice on market definition to the difficulties in defining the market where aftermarkets are involved.

56. There are certain areas where the application of the principles above has to be undertaken with care. This is the case when considering primary and secondary markets, in particular, when the behaviour of undertakings at a point in time has to be analysed pursuant to Article [82]. The method of defining markets in these cases is the same, i.e. assessing the responses of customers based on their purchasing decisions to relative price changes, but taking into account as well, constraints on substitution imposed by conditions in the connected markets. A narrow definition of market for secondary products, for instance, spare parts, may result when compatibility with the primary product is important. Problems of finding compatible secondary products together with the existence of high prices and a long lifetime of the primary products may render relative price increases of secondary products profitable. A different market definition may result if significant substitution between secondary products is possible or if the characteristics of the primary products make quick and direct consumer responses to relative price increases of the secondary products feasible.

These narrow market definitions may perhaps seem alarming. However, the narrow definitions are not important if a realistic assessment is made when determining whether or not an undertaking operating on that market has market power. It will be seen in the discussion below that it will be rarely that even a monopolist operating on a narrowly defined aftermarket can be said to have market power. In many cases such a monopolist will not be able to exploit his position on the aftermarket or secondary market (or act with the 'independence' which the ECJ considers to be the mark of a dominant position) without compromising his position on the primary market. The need for compatible products or services may 'lock in' the purchaser of the original product but the supplier will ordinarily be constrained from exploiting this dependence. The question of market power in aftermarkets is discussed below.[61]

(ii) SUPPLY SUBSTITUTION

In *Continental Can*,[62] the ECJ held that the market must be defined not only from the demand side but from the supply side. In that case the Commission found three separate markets consisting of different types of metal containers for food packaging. The ECJ held

---

[60] Commission Press Release IP/97/868. The Commission terminated its investigation following the acceptance of undertakings.

[61] See *infra* 316 ff.

[62] Case 6 & 7/72, *Europemballage Corp and Continental Can Co Inc* v. *Commission* [1973] ECR 215, [1973] CMLR 199.

that the Commission had not explained why these products were in separate markets and were not all part of a larger light metal container market. In particular, it had not set out why competitors could not enter the identified markets by a simple adaptation of their production facilities.

Case 6/72, *Europemballage Corp & Continental Can Co Inc v. EC Commission* [1973] ECR 215 [1973] CMLR 199

Court of Justice

32. For the appraisal of SLW's dominant position and the consequences of the disputed merger, the definition of the relevant market is of essential significance, for the possibilities of competition can only be judged in relation to those characteristics of the products in question by virtue of which those products are particularly apt to satisfy an inelastic need and are only to a limited extent interchangeable with other products.

33. In this context recitals Nos 5 to 7 of the second part of the decision deal in turn with a 'market for light containers for canned meat products', a 'market for light containers for canned seafood', and a 'market for metal closures for the food packing industry, other than crown corks', all allegedly dominated by SLW and in which the disputed merger threatens to eliminate competition. The decision does not, however, give any details of how these three markets differ from each other, and must therefore be considered separately. Similarly, nothing is said about how these three markets differ from the general market for light metal containers, namely the market for metal containers for fruit and vegetables, condensed milk, olive oil, fruit juices and chemico-technical products. In order to be regarded as constituting a distinct market, the products in question must be individualized, not only by the mere fact that they are used for packing certain products, but by particular characteristics of production which make them specifically suitable for that purpose. Consequently, a dominant position on the market for light metal containers for meat and fish cannot be decisive, as long as it has not been proved that competitors from other sectors of the market for light metal containers are not in a position to enter this market, by a simple adaption, with sufficient strength to create a serious counterweight.

The ECJ also held that the Commission should not have dismissed the possibility of the customers themselves commencing manufacture of their own cans.[63]

In cases subsequent to *Continental Can* the possibility of supply-side substitution has been considered. In *Michelin*[64] the ECJ held that there was no elasticity of supply between tyres for heavy vehicles and car tyres 'owing to significant differences in production techniques and in the plant and tools needed for their manufacture. The fact that time and considerable investment are required in order to modify production plant for the manufacture of light-vehicle tyres or vice versa means that there is no discernible relationship between the two categories of tyre enabling production to be adapted to demand on the market'. Similarly, in *Tetra Pak I*[65] the Commission dismissed the feasibility of supply-side

---

[63] *Ibid.*, para. 36.

[64] Case 322/81, *NV Nederlandsche Banden-Industrie Michelin* v. *Commission* [1983] ECR 3461, [1985] 1 CMLR 282, para. 41. The issue of supply substitutability was not addressed by the Commission in its decision, *Bandengroothandel Frieschebebrug BV /Nederlandsche Banden-Michelin NV* [1981] OJ L353/33, [1982] 1 CMLR 643.

[65] Commission decision in *TetraPak (BTG Licence)* [1988] OJ L272/27, [1988] 4 CMLR 881, paras 36–38, upheld by the CFI Case T–51/89, *Tetra Pak Rausing SA* v. *Commission* [1990] ECR II–309,[1991] 4 CMLR 334 where the market definition was not challenged.

substitution. Manufacturers of other types of milk–packaging machinery were not readily able to switch to producing aseptic packaging machinery and cartons.

The difficulty when considering supply–side substitution is to distinguish undertakings that are able easily to switch production to produce another product from potential competitors. When is a potential competitor capable of switching production to be considered at the stage of market definition and when at the stage of assessing market power on the defined market?[66] In Chapter 1 it was seen that the Commission stipulates in its Notice on market definition, at paragraphs 20–23, that potential competition is relevant to market definition only when a supplier is able to switch production in the short term without incurring significant additional costs or risks. Only where the impact is effective and immediate is it equivalent to the demand substitution effect.

These difficulties once more illustrate how difficult it may be to divide market definition from the assessment of market power. Although it could be argued that it does not matter *when* the possibility of other producers switching is considered so long as it *is* considered, the extract from Bishop and Walker set out below indicates that a more rigorous approach to supply side substitutability is desirable. Not only would it encourage less narrow market definitions to be adopted but it would make it less likely that wrong characterizations of dominance are made.

S. Bishop and M. Walker, *The Economics of EC Competition Law: Concepts, Application and Measurement* (Sweet & Maxwell, 1999)

3.36 It appears that the Commission's assessment of relevant product markets focuses, almost completely, on demand-side factors. In general, a failure to consider supply-side issues will lead to overly narrow relevant product markets. It may be that the Commission believes that it is following the lead of the U.S. Department of Justice (DoJ) and Federal Trade Commission (FTC) which also consider only demand-side responses when determining the relevant market. However, the DoJ and FTC do consider supply-side responses in some detail at later stages of its assessment, both in calculating market shares and in its assessment of competition. It does not matter whether supply-side responses are taken into account at the market definition stage or at the latter stage of interpreting the market shares—provided that the pressures from supply-side responses are taken into account at *some* stage it should not matter precisely when. It is, however, important that a consistent approach is adopted.

An approach in which supply-side substitution is taken into account at the market definition stage has much to recommend it. First, supply-side considerations can be an important determinant of the elasticity of demand for a product. Secondly, since ease of understanding is important, concluding that a firm with a market share of 70 per cent has no market power is a difficult concept for many to understand. Thirdly, and above all, since the supply-side is important, it would force the Commission to take account of the supply-side in a more systematic manner.

---

[66] See the problem in *BPB Industries, supra* n. 5.

C. THE GEOGRAPHIC MARKET

We saw in Chapter 1 that the relevant market has a geographic as well as a product dimension. Obviously an undertaking will not be able to raise price above the competitive level if consumers are willing and able to purchase a substitute from another area. The Commission Notice on market definition explains at length how the geographic market is determined.[67] The breadth of the geographic market will depend on a number of factors, especially transport. Where products are valuable in relation to their transport costs, as with microchips or diamonds, the geographic market will tend to be wide. Conversely, where the cost of a product is low in relation to its transport cost, as in the case of bricks or roofing tiles, the geographic market is likely to be narrower.

The case law of the Court indicates that the geographic market will encompass all areas in which the conditions of competition are sufficiently homogenous. In *United Brands*[68] the ECJ held that '[t]he opportunities for competition under Art, [82] of the Treaty must be considered . . . with reference to a clearly defined geographic area in which it is marketed and where the conditions of competition are sufficiently homogenous for the effect of the economic power of the undertaking concerned to be able to be evaluated'. Thus 'the objective conditions of competition applying to the product in question must be the same for all traders'. In that case France, Italy, and the UK were excluded from the consideration of the banana market because they had special arrangements with their former colonies. In *Deutsche Bahn*[69] the CFI held that 'the definition of the geographical market does not require the objective conditions of competition between traders to be perfectly homogenous. It is sufficient if they are "similar" or "sufficiently homogenous" and accordingly, only areas in which the objective conditions of competition are "heterogenous" may not be considered to constitute a uniform market'.

Although the Court has thus stressed the need for sufficiently homogenous conditions of competition this requirement is not stressed in the Commission's Notice on market definition. Rather the Commission appears to recognize that the behaviour of undertakings may be constrained by imports from areas where the conditions of competition are not the same.[70]

It is clear from the case law that legal regulation may create national markets, as in the type–approval certificate cases.[71] Similarly, in *British Telecommunications*[72] BT was found to have a statutory monopoly and in *AKZO*[73] the geographic market was confined by the fact that the UK and Ireland were the only Member States which permitted the use of bleaching agents in flour. With barriers to trade between Member States being further reduced as the

---

[67] See *supra* Chap. 1.

[68] Case 27/76, *United Brands Co and United Brands Continental BV* v. *Commission* [1978] ECR 207, [1978] 1 CMLR 429, paras. 11 and 44.

[69] Case T–229/94, *Deutsche Bahn AG* v. *Commission* [1998] 4 CMLR 220, para. 92; see also Case T–51/89, *Tetra Pak Rausing SA* v. *Commission* [1990] ECR II–309, 1991] 4 CMLR 334, paras. 91 and 92.

[70] See V. Korah, *An Introductory Guide to EC Competition Law and Practice* (7th edn., Hart Publishing, 2000) 3.2.1.2.

[71] Case 26/75, *General Motors* v. *EC Commission* [1975] ECR 1367, [1976] 1 CMLR 95; Case 226/84, *British Leyland* v. *EC Commission* [1986] ECR 3323, [1987] 1 CMLR 185; see *infra* 000.

[72] [1982] OJ L360/36, [1983] 1 CMLR 457.

[73] Case C–62/86, *AKZO Chemie BV* v. *Commission* [1991] ECR I–3359, [1993] 5 CMLR 215.

internal market is completed, markets may be expected to become broader and to be EU–
wide at least. However, narrower markets may be created through Community regulation
(as is the case with sugar[74]), as a result of high transport costs, or as a result of consumer
preference. The market may then be confined to a number of Member States,[75] to a single
Member State, or to part of a Member State. In *Nestlé/Perrier*,[76] (a decision taken under the
Merger Regulation, not Article 82), for example, the Commission found that the relevant
geographic market for mineral water was limited to France. Irrespective of the integration of
Europe, French consumers obstinately continued to choose local products.

In cases involving the transport sector narrow geographic markets have been defined (in
these cases the geographic and product markets may in effect be the same). The Commission has, for example, defined as separate markets the air route between Dublin and Heathrow,[77] the air route between Brussels and Luton,[78] and in *Sealink/B&I Holyhead: Interim
Measures* the ferry route between Holyhead and Dun Laoghaire.[79] In the latter decision the
Commission distinguished the 'northern', 'southern', and 'central' corridor routes between
Great Britain and Ireland. Further, within the 'central corridor' it distinguished the Liverpool and Holyhead routes, concluding that 'potential competition from Liverpool does not
constrain the market power of Sealink at Holyhead'.

One of the most criticized cases on the geographic market is *Michelin*.[80] In this case the
ECJ upheld the Commission's finding that there was a separate market for heavy vehicle new
replacement tyres in the Netherlands.

Case 322/81, *Nederlandsche Banden-Industrie Michelin* v. *Commission* [1983] ECR 3461 [1985] 1 CMLR 282

Court of Justice

23. The applicant's first submission under this head challenges the Commission's finding that the
substantial part of the common market on which it holds a dominant position is the Netherlands.
Michelin NV maintains that this geographical definition of the market is too narrow. It is contradicted by the fact that the Commission itself based its decision on factors concerning the Michelin
group as a whole such as its technological lead and financial strength which, in the applicant's view,
relate to a much wider market or even the world market. The activities of Michelin NV's main
competitors are world-wide too.

24. The Commission maintains that this objection concerns less the definition of the market than
the criteria used to establish the existence of a dominant position. Since tyre manufacturers have on
the whole chosen to sell their products on the various national markets through the intermediary of
national subsidiaries, the competition faced by Michelin NV is on the Netherlands market.

---

[74] See *Napier Brown–British Sugar* [1988] OJ L284/41, [1990] 4 CMLR 196; *Irish Sugar* [1997] OJ L258/1,
[1997] 5 CMLR 666.

[75] Case 27/76, *United Brands Co and United Brands Continental BV* v. *Commission* [1978] ECR 207, [1978]
1 CMLR 429; see *infra*.

[76] *Nestlé/Perrier* [1992] OJ L356/1, [1993] 4 CMLR M17. See *infra* Chap. 12.

[77] *British Midland* v. *Aer Lingus* [1992] OJ L96/34, [1993] 4 CMLR 596.

[78] *London European-Sabena* [1988] OJ L31/47, [1989] 4 CMLR 662.

[79] [1992] 5 CMLR 255.

[80] Case 322/81, *NV Nederlandsche Banden-Industrie Michelin* v. *Commission* [1983] ECR 3461, [1985] 1
CMLR 282.

25. The point to be made in this regard is that the Commission addressed its decision not to the Michelin group as a whole but only to its Netherlands subsidiary whose activities are concentrated on the Netherlands market. It has not been disputed that Michelin NV's main competitors also carry on their activities in the Netherlands through subsidiaries of their respective groups.

26. The Commission's allegation concerns Michelin NV's conduct towards tyre dealers and more particularly its discount policy. In this regard the commercial policy of the various subsidiaries of the groups competing at the European or even the world level is generally adapted to the specific conditions existing on each market. In practice dealers established in the Netherlands obtain their supplies only from suppliers operating in the Netherlands. The Commission was therefore right to take the view that the competition facing Michelin NV is mainly on the Netherlands market and that it is at that level that the objective conditions of competition are alike for traders.

27. This finding is not related to the question whether in such circumstances factors relating to the position of the Michelin group and its competitors as a whole and to a much wider market may enter into consideration in the adoption of a decision as to whether a dominant position exists on the relevant product market.

28. Hence the relevant substantial part of the common market in this case is the Netherlands and it is at the level of the Netherlands that Michelin NV's position must be assessed.

In this case it was not asked whether or not customers could easily have bought Michelin or other tyres outside the Netherlands. Rather, the geographic market appears to have been confined to the area in which the Commission found that the abuse had been committed.[81] The Commission's reasoning was criticized, *inter alia*, by Korah:[82]

The Commission defines the relevant geographic market as being the Netherlands, on the ground that this is where Michelin Netherlands operated and where the practice took place. Yet, that company would have no market power if the Dutch market could be flooded from Denmark, Germany or Belgium. The Commission merely states that dealers can obtain Michelin tyres only from retailers in the other Member States, and cannot obtain reliable and continuous supplies. Yet, were the Dutch subsidiary to attempt to exploit the Dutch dealers, the latter would not be able to pass the onus on to their customers if their customers could buy abroad directly, and so retailers would not agree to being exploited. If necessary, they would turn to selling other brands, or leave the market and sell completely different products. In that case, Michelin would not enjoy market power. The writer would have thought that many users of heavy vehicles must be well informed and able to shop around for new tyres in other Member States. In the U.S.A., Mr Baxter, currently in charge of antitrust in the Department of Justice, stated in his address to the Antitrust section of the A.B.A. in April 1981 that he treats a small percentage of imports as a welcome sign that the cost of transport is not too high to prevent a flood of imports if the local manufacturers restricted production to raise price. In *Bayer/Gist* . . . the Commission, quite rightly, relied on world statistics in order to assess the effect of the agreement on competition within the Common Market.

In some cases the ECJ has been more sceptical about narrowly drawn markets. In *Alsatel v. Novasam*,[83] for example, it did not accept that the evidence established that a particular region of France, rather than the country as a whole, was the geographic market for

[81] S. Bishop and M. Walker, *The Economics of EC Competition Law: Concepts, Application and Measurement* (Sweet & Maxwell, London, 1999), para. 3.48.

[82] V. Korah, 'The Michelin Decision of the Commission' (1982) 7 *ELRev.* 130, 131.

[83] Case 247/86 [1988] ECR 5987, [1990] 4 CMLR 434.

telephonic installations. In *BPB*,[84] however, a national market was found despite the existence of pressure from imports from elsewhere. The market was defined as being just the UK and Ireland.

Again the difficulty involved in defining the geographic market, as is the case when defining product markets, can be tempered if competition from outside the market is taken into account when assessing market power. If that is done, over-narrow market definitions and the rather artificial distinction between market definition and market power assessment are not so misleading.

D. THE TEMPORAL MARKET

The temporal dimension of the market is often ignored and the Commission Notice does not refer to it. Many markets do not have a temporal dimension. It can, however, be relevant, for example when considering transport markets.[85] In such markets the temporal dimension may in fact be an inherent part of the definition of the product market.

In *United Brands*[86] there was evidence that the demand for bananas fluctuated from season to season depending on the availability of other fruits. This suggested that there were different seasonal markets and that in the summer at least bananas were part of a wider fruit market. The Commission disregarded this evidence and defined a single year-round market consisting only of bananas. The ECJ did not pursue the issue. In *ABG Oil*[87] the Commission looked at the oil market just in the period of the OPEC crisis in the 1970s.

---

[84] *BPB Industries* [1989] OJ L10/50, [1990] 4 CMLR 464, upheld in Case T–65/89 *BPB Industries and British Gypsum Ltd* v. *Commission* [1993] ECR II–389, [1993] 5 CMLR 32, and Case C–310/93P, *BPB Industries PLC and British Gypsum Ltd* v *Commission* [1995] ECR I–865 [1997] 4 CMLR 238.

[85] In Cases T–374–375, 384 & 388/94 *European Night Services* v. *Commission* [1998] ECR II–3141, [1998] 5 CMLR 718, where the CFI annulled an Art. 81 Commission decision on a joint venture, the Commission raised during the appeal the matter of confining the business transport market to early morning and late evening rather than all round the clock.

[86] Case 27/76, *United Brands Co and United Brands Continental BV* v. *Commission* [1978] ECR 207, [1978] 1 CMLR 429.

[87] [1977] OJ L117/1, [1977] 2 CMLR D1 (the decision was annulled on appeal but on abuse, not dominance, grounds: Case 77/77, *Benzine Petroleum Handelsmaatschappij BV* v. *Commission* [1978] ECR 1513, [1978] 3 CMLR 174, see *infra* Chap. 7).

E. THE *TETRA PAK II* CASE

The difficulties and complexities of market definition are illustrated by *Tetra Pak II*.[88] This case raised acute problems of demand substitutability and of aftermarkets. The CFI judgment was confirmed by the ECJ, but the arguments are more fully set out by the CFI.[89]

Case T–83/91, *Tetra Pak Rausing* v. *Commission* [1994] ECR II–755, [1997] 4 CMLR 726

Tetra Pak produced aseptic cartons for packaging ultra-heat treated milk and the machines for processing the milk and filling the cartons. It also produced non-aseptic cartons for pasteurised (non-aseptic) milk and the machines for pasteurising the milk and filling those cartons. The Courts confirmed the Commission's finding that there were four product markets concerned: aseptic packaging machines, aseptic cartons, non-aseptic machines and non-aseptic cartons

Court of First Instance

60. Before considering whether the definition of the four aseptic and non-aseptic markets given in the Decision is valid, the exact content of that definition in the aseptic sector must be determined.

61. Contrary to the applicant's arguments, the Decision seeks to encompass in the two aseptic markets, mentioned above, all aseptic machinery and cartons, whether used for the packaging of UHT milk or for the packaging under aseptic conditions of liquid foods not needing UHT treatment, such as fruit juice. The aseptic markets are expressly defined in paragraph 11 of the Decision as '(a) the market for machinary incorporating technology for the sterilization of cartons and the packaging in those cartons, under aseptic conditions, of UHT-treated liquid foods; and (b) the corresponding market for packaging cartons'. It is clear from this that those markets are determined exclusively by reference to the technological characteristics of machinery and cartons for packaging UHT-treated products. That interpretation is confirmed by Article 1 of the Decision, which simply finds the existence of a dominant position on the 'so-called aseptic markets in machines and cartons intended for the packaging of liquid foods', without making any reference to the use to which that equipment is put.

62. It is therefore for the Court to consider whether the four markets so defined by the Decision were indeed markets distinct from other sectors of the general market in systems for packaging liquid food products.

63. A preliminary point to note is that, according to settled case law, the definition of the market in the relevant products must take account of the overall economic context, so as to be able to assess the actual economic power of the undertaking in question. In order to assess whether an undertaking is in a position to behave to an appreciable extent independently of its competitors and customers and consumers, it is necessary first to define the products which, although not capable of being substituted for other products, are sufficiently interchangeable with its products, not only in terms of the objective characteristics of those products, by virtue of which they are particularly suitable for

---

[88] *Elopak Italia/Tetra Pak* [1991] OJ L72/1, [1992] 4 CMLR 551, confirmed by the CFI, Case T–83/91, *Tetra Pak International SA* v *Commission* [1994] ECR II–755, [1997] 4 CMLR 726, confirmed by the ECJ, Case C–333/94P, *Tetra Pak International SA* v *Commission* [1996] ECR I–5951, [1997] 4 CMLR 662. The case is trenchantly criticised by V. Korah, 'The Paucity of Economic Analysis in the EEC Decisions on Competition—Tetra Pak II' [1993] *Current Legal Problems* 148.

[89] The abuse issues in the case are dealt with in Chap. 7.

satisfying constant needs, but also in terms of the market: see Case 322/81, *Michelin v EC Commission* . . .

64. In this case, the 'interchangeability' of aseptic packaging systems with non-aseptic systems and of systems using cartons with those using other materials must be assessed in the light of all the competitive conditions on the general market in systems for packaging liquid food products. Accordingly, in the specific context of this case, the applicant's approach of dividing that general market into differentiated sub-markets depending on whether the packaging systems are used for packaging milk, dairy products other than milk or non-dairy products by virtue of the specific characteristics of the packaging of those different categories of products, in which the possibility exists that various kinds of substitutable equipment may be used, would lead to a compartmentalization of the market which would not reflect economic reality. There is a comparable structure of supply and demand for both aseptic and non-aseptic machinery and cartons, however they are used, since all belong to one sector, the packaging of liquid food products. Whether they are used for packaging milk or other products, aseptic and non-aseptic machinery and cartons not only share the same characteristics of production but also satisfy identical economic needs. In addition, a not insignificant proportion of Tetra's Pak's customers operate in both the milk sector and the fruit juice sector, as the applicant has admitted. In all those respects, therefore, this case is distinguishable from the situation contemplated in Case 85/76, *Hoffmann-La Roche v EC Commission* . . ., relied on by the applicant, in which the Court of Justice had first considered the possibility of finding that there were two separate markets for one product which, unlike in this case, was used in two ways in wholly distinct sectors, one 'bio-nutritive' and the other 'technological' . . . . Furthermore, as both parties have submitted, Tetra Pak machinery and cartons of the same type were uniformly priced whether they were intended for packaging milk or other products, which confirms that they belong to a single product market. There is accordingly no need, contrary to the applicant's arguments, to find that there are differentiated sub-markets for packaging systems of the same type depending on whether they are used for packaging a particular category of products.

65. Accordingly, in order to ascertain whether the four markets defined in the Decision were indeed separate markets during the period in question, it is necessary — as the Commission submits — to determine in particular which products were sufficiently interchangeable with aseptic and non-aseptic machinery and cartons in the predominant milk sector. To the extent that the carton-packaging systems were used primarily for packaging milk, a dominant position in that sector was sufficient evidence, if relevant, or a dominant position on the market as a whole. Any such dominant position could not be called in question by the existence of substitutable equipment, alleged by the applicant, in the non-milk product packaging sector, since such equipment accounted for only a very small proportion of all products packaged in cartons during the period covered by the Decision. The predominance of the milk-packaging sector is clearly demonstrated by data given in the Decision (recital 6) and not disputed by the applicant, according to which 72 per cent in 1987 of carton systems were used for packaging milk and only 7 per cent for packaging other milk products. According to the same source, in 1983 90 per cent of those systems were used for packaging milk and other diary products. That pattern was even more marked in the case of the systems marketed by Tetra Pak. Tables produced by Tetra Pak in reply to a written question from the Court show that in the Community 96 per cent of the aseptic systems manufactured by it were used for packaging milk in 1976, 81 per cent in 1981, 70 per cent in 1987 and 67 per cent in 1991. Those figures indicate that, notwithstanding a decrease, the majority of Tetra Pak aseptic cartons were used for packaging milk during the period in question. As for non-aseptic cartons, 100 per cent were used for packaging milk until 1980 and 99 per cent thereafter, according to the same source. For all those reasons, the Commission was entitled to take the view that it was not necessary to carry out a separate analysis of the non-milk-packaging sector.

66. In the milk-packaging sector, the Commission correctly based itself, in this case on the test of sufficient substitutability of the different systems for packaging liquid foods, as laid down by the Court of Justice: see in particular Case 6/72, *Europemballage and Continental Can v EC Commission* . . . and Case 85/76 *Hoffmann La Roche v EC Commission* . . . It is also in accordance with case law (see Joined Cases 6 & 7/73, *Commercial Solvents v EC Commission)* that the Commission applied the test of sufficient substitutability of products at the stage of the packaging systems themselves, which constitute the market in intermediate products on which Tetra Pak's position must be assessed, and not at the stage of the finished products, in this case the packaged liquid food products.

67. In order to assess the interchangeability for packers of the packaging systems, the Commission necessarily had to take account of the repercussions of the final consumers' demand on the packers' intermediate demand. It found that the packers could influence consumer habits in the choice of types of product packaging only by promotion and publicity in a long and costly process, extending over several years, as Tetra Pak had expressly acknowledged in its reply to the statement of objections. In those circumstances, the various types of packaging could not be considered to be sufficiently interchangeable for packers, whatever their bargaining power, referred to by the applicant.

68. It is therefore exclusively to assess the effect of final demand on the packers' intermediate demand that the Commission referred to the lack of perfect substitutability, which concerned only the package products and not the packaging systems. In particular, the Commission correctly considered that, because of the small proportion of the retail price of milk accounted for by the cost of its packaging, 'small but significant changes in the relative price of the different packages would not be sufficient to trigger off shifts between the different types of milk with which they are associated because the substitution of different milks is less than perfect' (decision in *Tetra Pak I* . . .). The applicant's complaints that the Commission based itself on the model of perfect competition and defined the relevant markets solely by reference to consumer demand must accordingly be rejected.

69. The Court of First Instance therefore holds first that the Commission was entitled to find that during the period in question there was not sufficient interchangeability between machinery for aseptic packaging in cartons and machinery for non-aseptic packaging whatever the material used. At the level of demand, aseptic systems are distinguished by their inherent characteristics, satisfying specific consumer needs and preferences in relation to the duration and quality of conservation and to taste. Moreover, to move from packaging UHT milk to packaging fresh milk requires the setting up of a distribution system which ensures that the milk is continuously kept in a refrigerated environment. Furthermore, at the level of supply, the manufacture of machinery for the aseptic packaging of UHT milk in cartons requires complex technology, which only Tetra Pak and its competitor PKL have succeeded in developing and making operational during the period considered in the Decision. Manufacturers of non-aseptic machinery using cartons, operating on the market closest to the market in the aseptic machinery in question, were therefore not in a position to enter the latter market by modifying their machinery in certain respects for the market in aseptic machinery.

70. As for aseptic cartons, they also constituted a market distinct from that in non-aseptic packaging. At the level of the packers' intermediate demand, aseptic cartons were not sufficiently interchangeable with non-aseptic packages, including cartons, for the same reasons as those already set out in the preceding paragraph in relation to machinery. At the level of supply, the documents before the Court indicate that notwithstanding the absence of insurmountable technical problems, manufacturers of non-aseptic cartons were not in a position in the circumstances in question to adapt to the manufacture of aseptic cartons. The fact that on that market there was only one competitor of Tetra Pak, namely PKL, with only 10 per cent of the market in aseptic cartons during the period in

question, demonstrates that the conditions of competition were such that in practice there was no possibility for manufacturers of non-aseptic cartons to enter the market in aseptic cartons, in particular given the lack of aseptic filling machines.

71. Secondly, the Court holds that, during the period in question, aseptic machinery and cartons were not sufficiently interchangeable with aseptic packaging systems using other materials. According to the data provided in the documents before the Court, which are not disputed by the applicant, no such substitutable equipment existed, with the exception of the arrival on the market towards the end of the relevant period of systems for aseptic packaging in plastic bottles, returnable glass bottles and pouches in France, Germany and Spain respectively. However, each of those new products was introduced in only one country and, what is more, accounted for only a marginal share of the UHT-milk-packaging market. According to information provided by the applicant, that share has been only 5 per cent of the market in France since 1987. In the Community as a whole, in 1976, all UHT milk was packaged in cartons. The observations submitted by the applicant in response to the statement of objections indicate that in 1987 approximately 97.7 per cent of UHT milk was packaged in cartons. At the end of the period in question, that is 1991, cartons still accounted for 97 per cent of the UHT-milk-packaging market, the remaining 3 per cent being held by plastic containers, as the applicant indicated in answer to a written question from the Court. The marginal share of the market thus held by aseptic containers cannot be considered, even during the last years of the period covered by the Decision, as products which are sufficiently interchangeable with aseptic systems using cartons (see *Commercial Solvents v EC Commission . . .*).

72. Thirdly, the Court finds that non-aseptic machinery and cartons constituted markets which were distinct from those in non-aseptic packaging systems using materials other than cartons. It has already been shown . . . that because of the marginal proportion of the price of milk attributable to packaging costs, packers would have been led to consider that containers—in this case cartons, glass or plastic bottles and non-aseptic pouches—were easily interchangeable for only if there had been an almost perfect substitutability of final consumer demand. In the light of their very different physical characteristics and the system of doorstep delivery of pasteurized milk in glass bottles in the UK, that form of packaging was not interchangeable for consumers with packaging in cartons. Moreover, the fact that environmental factors led some consumers to prefer certain types of packaging, such as returnable glass bottles, did not promote the substitutability of those containers with cartons. Consumers who were aware of those factors did not consider those containers to be interchangeable with cartons. The same applies to consumers who, conversely, were attracted to a certain convenience in using products packaged in cartons. As for plastic bottles and plastic pouches, they were on the market only in countries where consumers accepted that type of packaging, in particular, according to information in the Decision which is not disputed by the applicant, Germany or France. Furthermore, according to the same source, that packaging was used for only approximately one-third of pasteurised milk in France and 20 per cent in Germany. It follows that those products were not in practice sufficiently interchangeable with non-aseptic cartons throughout the Community during the period covered by the Decision.

73. Analysis of the markets in the milk-packaging sector thus shows that the four markets concerned, defined in the Decision, were indeed separate markets.

74. Moreover and in any event, the Court finds that an examination of the substitutability of the various packaging systems in the fruit-juice sector, fruit juices being the largest category of liquid foods other than milk, shows that in that sector also there was no sufficient interchangeability either between aseptic and non-aseptic systems or between systems using cartons and systems using other materials.

75. The market in the carton packaging of fruit juices was held mainly by aseptic systems during the period in question. In 1987, 91 per cent of cartons used for packaging fruit juice were aseptic. That proportion remained stable until 1991, when 93 per cent of all cartons were aseptic according to Tetra Pak's reply to a written question from the Court. The marginal share held by non-aseptic cartons for packaging fruit juice, which continued for several years as has been shown, demonstrates that in practice they were barely interchangeable with aseptic cartons.

76. Nor were aseptic machinery and cartons sufficiently interchangeable with equipment using other materials for packaging fruit juice. The tables provided by Tetra Pak in answer to a written question from the Court show that during the period in question the two major rival types of packaging in the fruit-juice sector were glass bottles and cartons. In particular, the tables indicate that in 1976 in the Community more than 76 per cent of fruit-juice (by volume) was packaged in glass bottles, 9 per cent in cartons and 6 per cent in plastic bottles. The share held by cartons reached approximately 50 per cent of the market in 1987 and 46 per cent in 1991. The share held by glass bottles increased from 30 to 39 per cent between those dates and the share held by plastic bottles remained negligible, decreasing from approximately 13 per cent to 11 per cent.

77. Taking into account their very different characteristics, concerning both price and presentation, weight and the way in which they are stored, cartons and glass bottles could not be considered to be sufficiently interchangeable. In relation particularly to comparative prices, both parties' answers to a written question from the Court show that the total cost to the packer of packaging fruit juice in non-returnable glass bottles is significantly higher by approximately 75 per cent than that of packaging in aseptic cartons.

78. It follows from all the above considerations that the Commission has established to the requisite legal standard that the markets in aseptic machinery and cartons and those in non-aseptic machinery and cartons were insulated from the general market in systems for packaging liquid foods.

2. The machinery and carton markets cannot be separated

Summary of the arguments of the parties

79. The applicant states that the relevant market must be defined as the integrated packaging-systems market, comprising machines for packaging liquid foods and the packaging itself. It argues that there is a natural and commercial link of the type referred to in Article 82(d) of the Treaty between machines and the cartons. In particular, segregating aseptic filling machines and aseptic cartons may involve grave risks for public health and serious consequences for Tetra Pak's customers.

80. The applicant considers that the Commission took no account of the submissions of Tetra Pak's competitors, which support Tetra Pak's arguments, and adduced no evidence that the separate provision of machines and cartons reflected either the wishes of packers for independent suppliers of cartons or the wishes of the carton suppliers themselves.

81. The Commission disputes the link alleged by the applicant between machinery and cartons. Its submits that Article 82 of the Treaty precludes the manufacturer of a complex product from hindering production by a third party of consumable products intended for use in its systems.

Assessment by the Court

82. First, and contrary to the arguments of the applicant, consideration of commercial usage does not support the conclusion that the machinery for packaging a product is indivisible from the cartons.

For a considerable time there have been independent manufacturers who specialise in the manufacture of non-aseptic cartons designed for the use in machines manufactured by other concerns and who do not manufacture machinery themselves. It is apparent in particular from the Decision, . . . and not disputed by the applicant, that, until 1987, Elopak, which was set up in 1957, manufactured only cartons and accessory equipment, for example handling equipment. Moreover, also according to the Decision . . . and not contested by the applicant, approximately 12 per cent of the non-aseptic carton sector was shared in 1985 between three companies manufacturing their own cartons, generally under licence and acting, for machinery, only as distributors. In those circumstances, tied sales of machinery and cartons cannot be considered to be in accordance with commercial usage, given that such sales were not the general rule of the non-aseptic sector and that there were only two manufacturers in the aseptic sector, Tetra Pak and PKL.

83. Furthermore, the applicants argument as to the requirements for the protection of public health and its interests and those of its customers cannot be accepted. It is not for the manufacturers of complete systems to decide that, in order to satisfy requirements in the public interest, consumable products such as cartons constitute, with the machines with which they are intended to be used, an inseparable integrated system. According to settled case law, in the absence of general and binding standards or rules, any independent producer is quite free, as far as Community competition law is concerned, to manufacture consumables intended for use in equipment manufactured by others, unless in doing so it infringes a competitor's intellectual property right: see Case T–30/89, *Hilti v EC Commission* . . . and Case C–53/92P, *Hilti v EC Commission* . . .

84. In those circumstances, whatever the complexity in this case of aseptic filling processes, the protection of public health may be guaranteed by other means, in particular by notifying machine users of the technical specifications with which cartons must comply in order to be compatible with those machines, without infringing manufacturers' intellectual property rights. Moreover, even on the assumption, shared by the applicant, that machinery and cartons from various sources cannot be used together without the characteristics of the system being affected thereby, the remedy must lie in appropriate legislation or regulations, and not in rules adopted unilaterally by manufacturers, which would amount to prohibiting independent manufacturers from conducting the essential part of their business.

85. It follows that the applicant's argument that the markets in machinery for packaging a product and those in packaging cartons are inseparable cannot be accepted.

3. ASSESSING MARKET POWER

A. GENERAL[90]

Once the market has been defined the power which the undertaking has on that market must be assessed in order to determine whether the undertaking is 'dominant'.

If legal regulation causes the undertaking concerned to have 100 per cent of the market

---

[90] See D. Landes and R. A. Posner, 'Market Power in Antitrust Cases' (1981) 94 *Harvard LR* 937, R. Schmalensee, 'Another Look at Market Power' (1982) 95 *Harvard LR* 1789.

and no competitors can enter the market, for example where a statutory monopoly over the market has been conferred upon it, then it may be a true monopoly. In other situations the matter will not be so clear.

It is possible, in the absence of a statutory monopoly, for an undertaking to have 100 per cent of a market. It was seen in Chapter 1, however, that even an undertaking which has a 100 per cent share of the market does not, in the theory of industrial economics, necessarily occupy a dominant position or possess market power. Market shares do not indicate why that undertaking has 100 per cent of the market or tell us about potential competition. They do not explain, for example, whether the undertaking has a high market share because it produces the best products, most cheaply and most efficiently, or because the minimum efficient scale of production means that it is a 'natural' monopoly,[91] or whether that undertaking is vulnerable to market entry and to potential competition, or whether it is shielded from competition by barriers to entry. Whether or not an undertaking is vulnerable to such competition will be dependent upon whether or not there are 'barriers to entry' to the market. This is why the definition of a barrier to entry, discussed in Chapter 1, is such a central concept.

We saw in Chapter 1 that there is an on-going debate about what constitutes a barrier to entry, and even about how the term should be defined. It should also be noted that there is an argument that the disciplining effect of potential, as distinct from existing, competitors can be exaggerated.[92] A major belief of the Chicago school,[93] however, is that there are few barriers to entry. Markets do not therefore need to be policed by competition authorities but will rectify themselves. Monopolies will endure only through superior efficiency. An extract from Bork's book sets out these arguments:

R. Bork, *The Antitrust Paradox: A Policy at War With Itself* (Basic Books, 1978), 195–196

The basic ambiguity of this concept has led to its misuse in antitrust analysis. If everything that makes entry more difficult is viewed as a barrier, and if barriers are bad, then efficiency is an evil. That conclusion is inconsistent with consumer-oriented policy. What must be proved to exist, therefore, is a class of barriers that do not reflect superior efficiency and can be erected by firms to inhibit rivals. I think it clear that no such class of artificial barriers exists. It is the same phenomenon as Judge Wyzanski's 'intermediate cases'—practices that are neither deliberately predatory nor efficiency creating, but are nevertheless somehow exclusionary. The idea is so transparent, so obviously lacking in substance, that one suspects it would never have been devised but for the desperate need to shore up a crumbling theory that markets allow unwarranted market shares to persist. Stigler states: 'Barriers to entry arise because of economies of scale, or differences in productive factors, or legal control of entry.' . . . None of these, of course, is properly subject to attack by antitrust. There is in the list no 'artificial barrier' other than legal control of entry by government, and since we want the more efficient firm to have the extra share of the market its efficiency commands, there is no reason for concern over the other barriers.

---

[91] See *supra* Chap. 1. [1981] *GVL* OJ L370/49, [1982] 1 CMLR 221 is an example of a monopoly which was in neither of those categories.

[92] See E.M. Fox and L.A. Sullivan, 'Antitrust—Retrospective and Prospective: Where Are We Coming From? Where Are we Going?' (1987) 62 *New York Univ. LR* 936, 975: 'Potential competition is not an existing alternative source of supply; it does not satisfy buyers' desires for choice or the opportunity for buyers to play one seller against another; and it is normally an inconsequential source of pressure to innovate'.

[93] See *supra* Chap. 1.

Bork concludes that all the other 'artificial barriers' with which competition law is concerned are, in fact, activities that create efficiency.

Neither the Court nor the Commission appears to have followed any particular school of economic thought, and they certainly do not adhere to the Chicago view. In the past, a very wide variety of factors have been found to be barriers to entry or, in the terminology the Court, 'other factors indicating dominance'.[94] In addition a shorter time-frame has been habitually used than that which would be used by an economist. Factors which might hinder immediate entry but which would not hinder it long-term have been found to constitute a barrier to entry.[95] The use of the term 'other factors indicating dominance' may indeed be a recognition that not all the difficulties facing competitors entering a market can be described as barriers to entry under any definition. This eclectic approach means that in trying to ascertain whether an undertaking is likely to be held dominant for the purposes of Article 82 it is necessary carefully to study the case law of the Court and the Commission. It will be seen that this body of reasoning should perhaps be regarded as *sui generis*, rather than economic theory.

The sections below set out the approach of the Community authorities when determining whether or not an undertaking is dominant on a particular market. It will be seen that the authorities place emphasis both on the market shares of the undertaking concerned and 'other factors indicating dominance'. Throughout these sections it will be seen that a severe criticism of the case law and decisions taken under Article 82 is their tendency to place too great an emphasis on market shares and the failure, at least in the past, to display rigorous economic analysis when dealing with barriers to entry. On the contrary, barriers to entry have often been seen as pervasive. When combined with the tendency to define markets narrowly, the importance attached to market shares and the broad approach to 'other factors indicating dominance' means that an undertaking's market power may be considerably exaggerated. Undertakings which do not in reality have market power may, therefore, be precluded or deterred from engaging in conduct which is pro-competitive or at least neutral from a competition perspective. Competition law may then have the perverse effect of inhibiting the competitive process on the market.

B. MARKET SHARE

If an undertaking has a statutory monopoly over a relevant market, that is the end of the matter. It is in a dominant position. In the absence of statutory monopoly the Court and Commission begin the assessment of market power by looking at market shares.

The calculation of market shares is dealt with in the Commission's Notice on market definition which explains that in some industries sales figures may not be the most appropriate basis for the calculation:

---

[94] 'Other' meaning factors other than market share.

[95] See V. Korah, *An Introductory Guide to EC Competition Law and Practice* (7th edn) (Hart Publishing, 2000), 3.2.1.3 and 3.2.4.1.

Commission Notice on the definition of the relevant market for the purposes of Community competition law [1997] OJ C372/5, [1998] 4 CMLR 177

53. The definition of the relevant market in both its product and geographic dimensions allows the identification of the suppliers and the customers/consumers active on that market. On that basis, a total market size and market share for each supplier can be calculated on the basis of their sales of the relevant products in the relevant area. In practice, the total market size and market shares are often available from market sources, i.e. companies' estimates, studies commissioned from industry consultants and/or trade associations. When this is not the case, or when available estimates are not reliable, the Commission will usually ask each supplier in the relevant market to provide its own sales in order to calculate total market size and market shares.

54. If sales are usually the reference to calculate market shares, there are nevertheless other indications that, depending on the specific products or industry in question, can offer useful information such as, in particular, capacity, the number of players in bidding markets, units of fleet in aerospace, or the reserves held in the case of sectors such as mining.

55. As a rule of thumb, both volume sales and value sales provide useful information. In cases of differentiated products, sales in value and their associated market share will usually be considered to better reflect the relative position and strength of each supplier.

Although, as explained above, economic theory holds that in the absence of barriers to entry high market shares are not themselves indicative of dominance the Court has placed great emphasis on market share. The higher the market share the more likely a finding of dominance. In *Hoffmann-La Roche*[96] the Court held that 'very large shares' are in themselves indicative of dominance unless there are 'exceptional circumstances'. The Court did, however, hold that the shares should be held 'for some time'. This appears therefore to recognize that time-scale *is* a factor and that dominance requires power over time.

41. Furthermore although the importance of the market shares may vary from one market to another the view may legitimately be taken that very large shares are in themselves, and save in exceptional circumstances, evidence of the existence of a dominant position. An undertaking which has a very large market share and holds it for some time, by means of the volume of production and the scale of the supply which it stands for—without those having much smaller market shares being able to meet rapidly the demand from those who would like to break away from the undertaking which has the largest market share—is by virtue of that share in a position of strength which makes it an unavoidable trading partner and which already because of this secures for it, at the very least during relatively long periods, that freedom of action which is the special feature of a dominant position.

In *Hoffmann-La Roche* itself the Court considered market shares, expressed both by value and quantity, over a three-year period. In respect of the various separate vitamin markets, market shares of:
- 75–87 per cent were found to be 'so large that they are in themselves evidence of a dominant position';[97]

---

[96] Case 85/76, [1979] ECR 461, [1979] 3 CMLR 211, para. 41.
[97] *Ibid.*, paras. 53–56 (Vitamin B2).

- 84–90 per cent were 'so large that they prove the existence of a dominant position';[98] and
- '93–100 per cent had the result that it in fact has a monopoly'.[99]

In none of these instances did the Court look beyond the market shares figures.

Where the market share figures were lower in *Hoffmann-La Roche* (47 per cent,[100] 63–66 per cent[101] and 54 per cent[102]) dominance was also found, but after only after looking at other factors, particularly the market shares of the undertaking's competitors. The Court annulled the Commission's finding in respect of the Vitamin B3 market where in the three-year period only the share by value (51 per cent) in the last year had exceeded 42 per cent, saying:[103]

... the Commission, in the case of this particular market, has not indicated what the additional factors would be, which, together with the market share as corrected, nevertheless would be of such a kind as to admit of the existence of a dominant position.

These findings lead to the conclusion that, as far as concerns Vitamin B3, there is insufficient evidence of the existence of a dominant position held by Roche for the period under consideration.

The approach indicated in this case, therefore, is that where an undertaking has 'very high market shares' there is a presumption of dominance. In other cases, dominance is only found after a consideration of other factors indicating dominance.

In *Hilti*[104] and *Tetra Pak II*[105] the CFI held, citing *Hoffmann-La Roche*, that market shares respectively of 70–80 per cent and 90 per cent were in themselves evidence of a dominant position. In both case, however, the Court also stated briefly that barriers to entry were high. Further, and much more controversially, in *AKZO* the ECJ held that a share of 50 per cent of the market was a 'very high market share' within the meaning of the test set out in *Hoffmann-La Roche*:

With regard to market shares the Court has held that very large shares are in themselves, and save in exceptional circumstances, evidence of the existence of a dominant position: Case 85/76 *Hoffmann-La Roche v EC Commission*. That is the situation where there is a market share of 50 per cent. such as that found to exist in this case.[106]

In *AKZO* the Court added that the Commission had 'rightly pointed out that other factors confirmed AKZO's predominance in the market'. Nonetheless the significance of this case is enormous: once the market share is above 50 per cent there is, essentially, a presumption of dominance. An undertaking is, of course, free to adduce evidence establishing that despite is high market share it has no market power. However, this will be a heavy burden to discharge.

---

[98] *Ibid.*, paras. 59–60 (Vitamin B6).

[99] *Ibid.*, para. 67 (Vitamin H).

[100] *Ibid.*, paras. 50–52 (Vitamin A).

[101] *Ibid.*, paras. 61–63 (Vitamin C).

[102] *Ibid.*, paras. 64–66 (Vitamin E).

[103] *Ibid.*, para. 58.

[104] Case T–30/89, *Hilti v. Commission* [1991] ECR II–1439, [1992] 4 CMLR 16, paras. 91–94, upheld by the ECJ, Case C–53/92 P, *Hilti v. Commission* [1994] ECR I–666, [1994] 4 CMLR 614.

[105] Case T–83/91, *Tetra Pak International SA v. Commission* [1994] ECR II–755, [1997] 4 CMLR 726, paras. 109–110, upheld by the ECJ, Case C–333/94P, *Tetra Pak International SA v. Commission* [1996] ECR I–5951, [1997] 4 CMLR 662.

[106] Case C–62/86, *AKZO Chemie BV v. Commission* [1991] ECR I–3359, [1993] 5 CMLR 215.

When considering market shares of the undertaking concerned it is also important to consider the market shares of competitors. The market power of an undertaking with a market share of 51 per cent will be considerably different depending on whether, for example, it simply has one competitor with a 49 per cent share of the market, three competitors which have 16, 16, and 17 per cent of the market respectively or forty-nine competitors each with 1 per cent of the market. The differentials in market share are extremely important. A market where there are two undertakings, A with 51 per cent and B with 49 per cent, is an oligopoly. It is not dominated by A.

In *United Brands*[107] UBC was held to be dominant even though it had a market share of only 45 per cent. This share however was almost twice as large as that of its nearest competitor. In *Michelin*[108] Michelin was found to hold a share of 57–65 per cent of the relevant market but the remainder of the market was fragmented, the competitors each having only 4–8 per cent of the market. Once an undertaking has a market share as large as 70 per cent its share is bound to be at least twice the share of its nearest competitor. In these circumstances it will be very difficult indeed, given the attitude of the Court and Commission towards barriers to entry, for it to preclude a finding of dominance. There is no case where an undertaking with such a high market share has been held not to be dominant. It will therefore be appreciated why narrow market definitions may be fatal for undertakings and how important it is to make a realistic determination of the market.

It is important to know the minimum market share at which an undertaking is likely to be found to be dominant. The crucial range is 40–50 per cent. There is no case in which an undertaking has been found to be dominant with a market share of less than 40 per cent. Although the Commission has not ruled out such a possibility,[109] it is only generally when an undertaking has such a share that the Commission is worried about the impact of that undertaking's existence on the competitive process.[110] When an undertaking has a share which exceeds 50 per cent there is a presumption of dominance. Between 40 and 50 per cent the other factors indicating dominance will be of great significance.

[107] Case 27/76, *United Brands Co and United Brands Continental BV* v. *Commission* [1978] ECR 207, [1978] 1 CMLR 429.

[108] Case 322/81, *Nederlandsche Banden-Industrie Michelin* v. *Commission* [1983] ECR 3461, [1985] 1 CMLR 282.

[109] See Commission's *Xth Report on Competition Policy* (Commission, 1981) pt. 150. However, the Merger Reg. 4064/89 [1989] OJ L257/14, recital 15, states a presumption that there will not be a dominant position where the merging undertakings' aggregate market shares are less than 25%. The UK Fair Trading Act 1973 provides a 25% market share threshold for monopoly investigations, but this is in the context of an investigatory system rather than a prohibition and sanction system as provided by Art. 82.

[110] This is the figure of the licensee's share of the market at which the Commission may withdraw the block exemption, Reg. 240/96 [1996] OJ L31/2, from a patent/know-how licence on the ground that the licensed products are not exposed to effective competition: Art. 7(1). See further *infra* Chap. 10. However, the verticals block exemption, Reg. 2790/1999 [1999] OJ L336/21, does not apply above 30% because of concerns about market power. See *infra* Chap. 9.

C. OTHER FACTORS INDICATING DOMINANCE

(i) GENERAL

As explained above, a wide range of matters have been held by the Court and the Commission to constitute 'other factors indicating dominance'. In *United Brands* the ECJ held that a dominant position derives from a combination of several factors which, taken separately, are not necessarily determinative.[111] The way in which dominance is derived from a combination of these factors in addition to market share is illustrated by some of the leading cases on Article 82.

(ii) SOME LEADING CASES

a. *UNITED BRANDS*

Case 27/76, *United Brands Co and United Brands Continental BV v. Commission* [1978] ECR 207 [1978] 1 CMLR 429

The issues in *United Brands* were firstly whether bananas were a separate relevant market from other fruit (see above in the discussion on market definition) and if so, whether, secondly, United Brands was dominant on it.

Court of Justice

67. In order to find out whether UBC is an undertaking in a dominant position on the relevant market it is necessary first of all to examine its structure and then the situation on the said market as far as competition is concerned.

68. In doing so it may be advisable to take account if need be of the facts put forward as acts amounting to abuses without necessarily having to acknowledge that they are abuses.

. . . . . *The structure of UBC*

69. It is advisable to examine in turn UBC's resources for and methods of producing, packaging, transporting, selling and displaying its product.

70. UBC is an undertaking vertically integrated to a high degree.

71. This integration is evident at each of the stages from the plantation to the loading on wagons or lorries in the ports of delivery and after those stages, as far as ripening and sale prices are concerned, UBC even extends its control to ripener/distributors and wholesalers by setting up a complete network of agents.

72. At the production stage UBC owns large plantations in Central and South America.

73. In so far as UBC's own production does not meet its requirements it can obtain supplies without any difficulty from independent planters since it is an established fact that unless circumstances are exceptional there is a production surplus.

74. Furthermore several independent producers have links with UBC through contracts for the

---

[111] Case 27/76, *United Brands Co and United Brands Continental BV* v. *Commission* [1978] ECR 207, [1978] 1 CMLR 429, para. 66.

growing of bananas which have caused them to grow the varieties of bananas which UBC has advised them to adopt.

75. The effects of natural disasters which could jeopardize supplies are greatly reduced by the fact that the plantations are spread over a wide geographic area and by the selection of varieties not very susceptible to diseases.

76. This situation was born out by the way in which UBC was able to react to the consequences of hurricane 'Fifi' in 1974.

77. At the production stage UBC therefore knows that it can comply with all the requests which it receives.

78. At the stage of packaging and presentation on its premises UBC has at its disposal factories, manpower, plant and material which enable it to handle the goods independently.

79. The bananas are carried from the place of production to the port of shipment by its own means of transport including railways.

80. At the carriage by sea stage it has been acknowledged that UBC is the only undertaking of its kind which is capable of carrying two thirds of its exports by means of its own banana fleet.

81. Thus UBC knows that it is able to transport regularly, without running the risk of its own ships not being used and whatever the market situation may be, two thirds of its average volume of sales and is alone able to ensure that three regular consignments reach Europe each week, and all this guarantees it commercial stability and well being.

82. In the field of technical knowledge and as a result of continual research UBC keeps on improving the productivity and yield of its plantations by improving the draining system, making good soil deficiencies and combating effectively plant disease.

83. It has perfected new ripening methods in which its technicians instruct the distributor/ripeners of the Chiquita banana.

84. That is another factor to be borne in mind when considering UBC's position since competing firms cannot develop research at a comparable level and are in this respect at a disadvantage compared with the applicant.

85. It is acknowledged that at the stage where the goods are given the final finish and undergo quality control UBC not only controls the distributor/ripeners which are direct customers but also those who work for the account of its important customers such as the Scipio group.

86. Even if the object of the clause prohibiting the sale of green bananas was only strict quality control, it in fact gives UBC absolute control of all trade in its goods so long as they are marketable wholesale, that is to say before the ripening process begins which makes an immediate sale unavoidable.

87. This general quality control of a homogeneous product makes the advertizing of the brand name effective.

88. Since 1967 UBC has based its general policy in the relevant market on the quality of its Chiquita brand banana.

89. There is no doubt that this policy gives UBC control over the transformation of the product into bananas for consumption even though most of this product no longer belongs to it.

90. This policy has been based on a thorough reorganization of the arrangements for production, packaging, carriage, ripening (new plant with ventilation and a cooling system) and sale (a network of agents).

91. UBC has made this product distinctive by large-scale repeated advertizing and promotion campaigns which have induced the consumer to show a preference for it in spite of the difference between the price of labelled and unlabelled bananas (in the region of 30 to 40%) and also of Chiquita bananas and those which have been labelled with another brand name (in the region of 7 to 10%).

92. It was the first to take full advantage of the opportunities presented by labelling in the tropics for the purpose of large-scale advertizing and this, to use UBC's own words, has 'revolutionized the commercial exploitation of the banana' (Annex II to the application, p.10).

93. It has thus attained a privileged position by making Chiquita the premier banana brand name on the relevant market with the result that the distributor cannot afford not to offer it to the consumer.

94. At the selling stage this distinguishing factor—justified by the unchanging quality of the banana bearing this label—ensures that it has regular customers and consolidates its economic strength.

95. The effect of its sales networks only covering a limited number of customers, large groups or distributor/ripeners, is a simplification of its supply policy and economics of scale.

96. Since UBC's supply policy consists—in spite of the production surplus—in only meeting the requests for Chiquita bananas parsimoniously and sometimes incompletely UBC is in a position of strength at the selling stage.

. . .

121. UBC's economic strength has thus enabled it to adopt a flexible overall strategy directed against new competitors establishing themselves on the whole of the relevant market.

122. The particular barriers to competitors entering the market are the exceptionally large capital investments required for the creation and running of banana plantations, the need to increase sources of supply in order to avoid the effects of fruit diseases and bad weather (hurricanes, floods), the introduction of an essential system of logistics which the distribution of a very perishable product makes necessary, economics of scale from which newcomers to the market cannot derive any immediate benefit and the actual cost of entry made up *inter alia* of all the general expenses incurred in penetrating the market such as the setting up of an adequate commercial network, the mounting of very large-scale advertizing campaigns, all those financial risks, the costs of which are irrecoverable if the attempt fails.

123. Thus, although, as UBC has pointed out, it is true that competitors are able to use the same methods of production and distribution as the applicant they come up against almost insuperable practical and financial obstacles.

124. This is another factor peculiar to a dominant position.

125. However UBC takes into account the losses which its banana division made from 1971 to 1976—whereas during this period its competitors made profits—for the purpose of inferring that, since dominance is in essence the power to fix prices, making losses is inconsistent with the existence of a dominant position.

126. An undertaking's economic strength is not measured by its profitability; a reduced profit margin or even losses for a time are not incompatible with a dominant position, just as large profits may be compatible with a situation where there is effective competition.

127. The fact that UBC's profitability is for a time moderate or non-existent must be considered in the light of the whole of its operations.

128. The finding that, whatever losses UBC may make, the customers continue to buy more goods from UBC which is the dearest vendor, is more significant and this fact is a particular feature of the dominant position and its verification is determinative in this case.

129. The cumulative effect of all the advantages enjoyed by UBC thus ensures that is has a dominant position on the relevant market

b. *HOFFMAN-LA ROCHE*

Case 85/76, *Hoffmann-La Roche & Co AG* v. *Commission* [1979] ECR 461, [1979] 3 CMLR 211

The case concerned Hoffmann-La Roche's practices on various vitamin markets.

Court of Justice

48. . . . the relationship between the market shares of the undertaking concerned and of its competitors, especially those of the next largest, the technological lead of an undertaking over its competitors, the existence of a highly developed sales network and the absence of potential competition are relevant factors, the first because it enables the competitive strength of the undertaking in question to be assessed, the second and third because they represent in themselves technical and commercial advantages and the fourth because it is the consequence of the existence of obstacles preventing new competitors from having access to the market. As far as the existence or non-existence of potential competition is concerned it must, however, be observed that, although it is true—and this applies to all the groups of vitamins in question—that because of the amount of capital investment required the capacity of the factories is determined according to the anticipated growth over a long period so that access to the market by new producers is not easy, account must also be taken of the fact that the existence of considerable unused manufacturing capacity creates potential competition between established manufacturers. Nevertheless Roche is in this respect in a privileged position because, as it admits itself, its own manufacturing capacity was, during the period covered by the contested decision, in itself sufficient to meet world demand without this surplus manufacturing capacity placing it in a difficult economic or financial situation.

49. It is in the light of the preceding considerations that Roche's shares of each of the relevant markets, complemented by those factors which in conjunction with the market shares make it possible to show that there may be a dominant position, must be evaluated. Finally, it will also be necessary to consider whether Roche's submissions relating to the implication of its conduct on the market, mainly as far as concerns prices, are of such a kind as to alter the findings to which the examination of the market shares and the other factors taken into account might lead.

c. MICHELIN

Case 322/81, *Nederlandsche Banden-Industrie Michelin* v. *Commission* [1983] ECR 3461, [1985] 1 CMLR 282

As discussed above in relation to market definition, this case concerned Michelin's position on the tyre market. The Commission's definition of the market as being that for new replacement lorry and bus tyres was upheld. The alleged abuse concerned the terms Michelin offered its dealers. This part of the judgment deals with the assessment of dominance.

Court of Justice

53. The applicant challenges next the relevance of the other criteria and evidence used by the Commission to prove that a dominant position exists. It claims that it is not the only undertaking to have commercial representatives, that the numbers employed by its main competitors are even larger in relative terms and that its wide range of products is not a competitive advantage because the different types of tyre are not interchangeable and it does not require dealers to purchase its whole range of tyres.

54. It also claims that the Commission took no account of a number of evidential factors which were incompatible with the existence of a dominant position. For instance, dealers' net margins on Michelin tyres and competing tyres are comparable and the cost per mile of Michelin tyres is the most favourable for users. Since 1979 Michelin NV has made a loss. As its production capacity is insufficient, its competitors, which are also financially stronger and more diversified than the Michelin groups, can at any moment replace the quantities which it supplies. Lastly, because users of heavy-vehicle tyres are experienced trade buyers they have the ability to act as a counterpoise to the tyre manufacturers.

55. In reply to those arguments it should first be observed that in order to assess the relative economic strength of Michelin NV and its competitors on the Netherlands market the advantages which those undertakings may derive from belonging to groups of undertakings operating throughout Europe or even the world must be taken into consideration. Amongst those advantages, the lead which the Michelin group has over its competitors in the matters of investment and research and the special extent of its range of products, to which the Commission referred in its decision, have not been denied. In fact in the case of certain types of tyres the Michelin group is the only supplier on the market to offer them in its range.

56. That situation ensures that on the Netherlands market a large number of users of heavy-vehicle tyres have a strong preference for Michelin tyres. As the purchase of tyres represents a considerable investment for a transport undertaking and since much time is required in order to ascertain in practice the cost-effectiveness of a type or brand of tyre, Michelin NV therefore enjoys a position which renders it largely immune to competition. As a result, a dealer established in the Netherlands normally cannot afford not to sell Michelin tyres.

57. It is not possible to uphold the objections made against those arguments by Michelin NV, supported on this point by the French Government, that Michelin NV is thus penalized for the quality of its products and services. A finding that an undertaking has a dominant position is not in itself a recrimination but simply means that, irrespective of the reasons for which it has such a dominant position, the undertaking concerned has a special responsibility not to allow its conduct to impair genuine undistorted competition on the common market.

58. Due weight must also be attached to the importance of Michelin NV's network of commercial representatives, which gives it direct access to tyre users at all times. Michelin NV has not disputed the fact that in absolute terms its network is considerably larger than those of its competitors or challenged the description, in the decision at issue, of the services performed by its network whose efficiency and quality of service are unquestioned. The direct access to users and the standard of service which the network can give them enables Michelin NV to maintain and strengthen its position on the market and to protect itself more effectively against competition.

59. As regards the additional criteria and evidence to which Michelin NV refers in order to disprove the existence of a dominant position, it must be observed that temporary unprofitability or even losses are not inconsistent with the existence of a dominant position. By the same token, the fact that the prices charged by Michelin NV do not constitute an abuse and are not even particularly high does not justify the conclusion that a dominant position does not exist. Finally, neither the size, financial strength and degree of diversification of Michelin NV's competitors at the world level nor

the counterpoise arising from the fact that buyers of heavy-vehicle tyres are experienced trade users are such as to deprive Michelin NV of its privileged position on the Netherlands market.

60. It must therefore be concluded that the other criteria and evidence relevant in this case in determining whether a dominant position exists confirm that Michelin NV has such a position.

61. Michelin NV's submissions disputing that it has a dominant position on a substantial part of the common market are therefore unfounded.

d. EUROFIX-BAUCO/HILTI

Eurofix-Bauco/Hilti [1988] OJ L65/19, [1989] 4 CMLR 677[112]

For the market definition aspects of this case see the section on market definition above.[113] The case concerned the consumables (nails and cartridges) for Hilti's nail-guns.

Commission

69. In addition to the strength derived from its market share and the relative weakness of its competitors, Hilti has other advantages that help reinforce and maintain its position in the nail gun market:

—its biggest selling nail gun, the DX 450, has certain novel technically advantageous features which are still protected by patents,
—Hilti has an extremely strong research and development position and is one of the leading companies worldwide not only in nail guns but also other fastening technologies
—Hilti has a strong and well-organized distribution system—in the EEC it has subsidiaries and independent dealers integrated into its selling network who deal mostly direct with customers, and
—the market for nail guns is relatively mature, which may discourage new entrants since sales or market shares can only be obtained at the expense of existing competitors in the market for replacements.

70. The foregoing considerations lead to the conclusion that Hilti holds a dominant position in the EEC for nail guns, as well as the markets for Hilti-compatible nails and cartridge strips. These are the relevant markets for the purposes of this Decision. It should be stressed that, in this particular case, the relevant markets for Hilti compatible nails and cartridge strips are important because of Hilti's large share of sales of nail guns. Because of this large share, independent manufacturers of nails and cartridge strips must manufacture nails and/or cartridge strips which can be used in Hilti tools if they are to produce for more than a small segment of the market thus achieving the economies of scale necessary to be both competitive and profitable.

71. Hilti's market power and dominance stem principally from its large share of the sales of nail guns coupled with the patent protection for its cartridge strips. The economic position it enjoys is such that it enables it to prevent effective competition being maintained on the relevant markets for Hilti-compatible nails and cartridge strips. In fact Hilti's commercial behaviour, which has been described above and is analysed below, is witness to its ability to act independently of, and without due regard to, either competitors or customers on the relevant markets in question. In addition, Hilti's

---

[112] The appeals, Case T–30/89, *Hilti* v. *Commission* [1991] ECR II–1439, [1992] 4 CMLR 16 and Case C–53/92P, *Hilti* v. *Commission* [1994] ECR I–666, [1994] 4 CMLR 614, confirmed the Commission.
[113] *Supra* 281 ff.

pricing policy also described above reflects its ability to determine, or at least to have an appreciable influence on the conditions under which competition will develop. This behaviour and its economic consequences would not normally be seen where a company was facing real competitive pressure. Therefore the Commission considers that Hilti holds a dominant position in the two separate relevant markets for Hilti-compatible nails and cartridge strips.

e. SODA ASH/SOLVAY

Soda-Ash-Solvay [1991] OJ L152/21, [1994] 4 CMLR 645[114]

The case concerned the soda-ash market.

Commission

1.   To assess market power for the purposes of the present case, the Commission takes into account all the relevant economic evidence, including the following elements:

    (i)   Solvay's position as the only soda-ash producer operating throughout the Community (with the exception of the United Kingdom and Ireland);

    (ii)   Solvay's manufacturing strength with plant in Belgium, France, Germany, Italy, Spain and Portugal;

    (iii)   Solvay's 'upstream' integration in raw materials as the largest producer of salt in the Community;

    (iv)   The absence of any competition from ICI, the only other Community producer of comparable market strength to Solvay;

    (v)   Solvay's high market share in the Benelux countries, France and Germany and its monopoly or near-monopoly position in Italy, Spain and Portugal;

    (vi)   Solvay's excellent 'market coverage' as the exclusive or near-exclusive supplier to almost all the major customers in the Community;

    (vii)   The improbability of any new producer of synthetic ash entering the market and setting up manufacturing facilities in the Community;

    (viii) The protection against non-Community producers afforded by the anti-dumping duties;

    (ix)   Solvay's traditional role of price leader;

    (x)   The perception of Solvay by other Community producers as the dominant producer and their reluctance to compete aggressively for Solvay's traditional customers.

(iii) SUMMARY OF 'OTHER FACTORS INDICATING DOMINANCE'

It is possible from looking at the cases set out above and others to describe the main factors which the Court and the Commission do or do not consider indicate dominance.

a. STATUTORY MONOPOLY, LEGAL REGULATION, INTELLECTUAL PROPERTY RIGHTS

State or regulatory measures which grant to a particular undertaking a statutory monopoly, an exclusive concession (such as in the provision of undertaking services in *Bodson v*

---

[114] This decision was annulled on appeal by the CFI on procedural grounds: Cases T–30/91 etc., *Solvay SA v. Commission* [1995] ECR II–1775, [1996] 5 CMLR 57 (see *infra* Chap. 14), but that does not affect the Commission's assessment of dominance.

Pompes Funèbres[115]) or exclusive access to finite resources (such as radio frequencies in *Decca Navigator*[116] or airport slots in *British Midland–Aer Lingus* [117]) are obvious barriers to entry. Even economists of the Chicago school recognise that governmental restrictions may operate as a barrier to entry. Most legal and regulatory barriers to entry would come under the heading of absolute cost advantages in the classification discussed in Chapter 1.[118] The Court and Commission have frequently held such measures to be factors indicating dominance and many cases on Article 82 concern statutory monopolists.[119]

Intellectual property rights are a particular type of legal right granted by national (or Community[120]) law. The ECJ has consistently held that the ownership of intellectual property rights does not necessarily mean that the owner has a dominant position.[121] The legal monopoly may not equate to an economic monopoly if the relevant market is wider than the protected product. However, the fact that access to a market is protected by intellectual property rights may be relevant as a factor indicating dominance. This was found to be the case in *Hugin*,[122] (where the Court of Justice seemed to accept the argument that the spare parts were protected by the UK's Design Copyright Act 1968), *Eurofix-Bauco (Hilti)*[123] (above), and *Tetra Pak II*[124]. Again, economists classify intellectual property rights as absolute cost advantages.

b. SUPERIOR TECHNOLOGY AND EFFICIENCY

The superior technology of an undertaking has often been found to be a factor indicating dominance. This can be seen from the extracts set out from *United Brands, Hoffmann-La Roche, Michelin, Eurofix-Bauco (Hilti)*, and *Tetra Pak* above. It is, however, questionable from an economic point of view to hold that an undertaking's technological superiority operates as a barrier to entry *per se*. It is true that expenditure on technological development can be a sunk cost of entry but it is also true that a new entrant on to the market may not have to spend the same resources on research and development as the incumbent on the market:

[115] Case 30/87 *Bodson* v. *Pompes Funèbres des Régions Libérées* [1988] ECR 2479, [1989] 4 CMLR 984.

[116] [1989] OJ L43/27, [1990] 4 CMLR 627.

[117] [1992] OJ L96/34, [1993] 4 CMLR 596.

[118] See the article by D. Harbord and T. Hoehn, 'Barriers to Entry and Exit in European Competition Policy' (1994) 14 *Int. Rev. of L and Econ.* 411 and the extract from the OFT report *supra* Chap. 1.

[119] E.g. Case 311/84, *Centre Belge d'Etudes du Marché-Télémarketing* v. *Compagnie Luxembourgeoise de Télédiffusion SA and Information Publicité Benelux SA* [1985] ECR 3261, [1986] 2 CMLR 558; Cases C241–242/91 P, *RTE & ITP* v. *Commission (Magill)* [1995] ECR I–743, [1995] 4 CMLR 718; Case 226/84, *British Leyland* v. *Commission* [1986] ECR 3323, [1987] 1 CMLR 185; *Sealink/B&I Holyhead: Interim Measures* [1992] 5 CMLR 255, and other transport cases.

[120] As with the Community Trade Mark (1994) and the Community Plant Variety Right (1996). The Community Patent Convention (1975) is not yet in force. There is a regional trade mark regime covering the Benelux countries.

[121] Case 24/67, *Parke Davis* v. *Probel* [1968] ECR 55, [1969] CMLR 47; Cases C–241–241/91 P, *RTE & ITP* v. *Commission (Magill)* [1995] ECR I–743,[1995] 4 CMLR 718.

[122] Case 22/78, *Hugin Kassaregister AB and Hugin Cash Registers Ltd* v. *EC Commission* [1979] ECR 1869, [1979] 3 CMLR 345.

[123] [1988] OJ L65/19, [1989] 4 CMLR 677.

[124] Case C–333/94P, *Tetra Pak International SA* v. *Commission* [1996] ECR I–5951, [1997] 4 CMLR 662.

there is no need to reinvent the wheel.[125] Superior technology could not operate as a barrier to entry according to Stigler since it does not represent a cost to the new entrant which was not borne by the incumbent.[126]

The Court and the Commission have held in several cases that the overall efficacy of the undertaking's commercial arrangements contributed to and enhanced its dominant position. This is particularly marked in *United Brands* (above, paras 75–95 of the judgment), in *Michelin* (above, paragraph 58) and in *Eurofix-Bauco* (above, paragraph 69) where the Court and Commission took into account the effectiveness of the undertakings' distribution networks. These judgments may, therefore, be criticized for failing to explain sufficiently *why* a new entrant could not replicate these arrangements. Otherwise, the authorities appear simply to be penalising an the undertaking in respect of their efficiency.[127]

c. VERTICAL INTEGRATION

The Court and Commission have also found that vertical integration is a factor indicating dominance. Again this appears to condemn an undertaking in respect of its efficiency (see also (b) above). Further, economists generally argue that when vertical integration takes place the barriers to entry are only added up and are not multiplied. Vertical integration may therefore accompany monopoly but is not an indicator of it.[128] Nonetheless in *United Brands* UBC's vertical integration was an important factor for the Court in the finding of dominance. Clearly in the context of the growing and marketing of bananas, a highly perishable product, this vertical integration played an important part in UBC's ability to get its bananas across the world and into the hands of European distributors as quickly as possible. It is quite another thing, however, to hold that this vertical integration constituted a barrier to entry. There was no explanation in the case of why, or even if, the vertical integration was to be regarded as a barrier to entry.

d. ECONOMIES OF SCALE

In *United Brands* (above, paragraph 122) the ECJ recognised that economies of scale operate as a barrier to entry. It was seen in Chapter 1 that, according to the definition of barriers set out by Stigler, economies of scale do not operate as a barrier to entry. It was also explained, however, in the extract from the OFT Report,[129] that under modern industrial organization theory, economies of scale can operate as strategic entry barriers: these stem from first-mover advantages. According to this theory, economies of scale combined with large sunk

---

[125] See V. Korah, 'Concept of a Dominant Position Within The Meaning of Art. 86' (1980) 17 *CMLRev.* 395, 408 and 410; D. Harbord and T. Hoehn, 'Barriers to Entry and Exit in European Competition Policy' (1994) 14 *International Review of Law and Economics* 411, 419; C. Baden Fuller, 'Article 86 EEC: Economic Analysis of the Existence of a Dominant Position' (1979) 4 *ELRev.* 423, 437.

[126] See *supra* Chap. 1.

[127] Despite the ECJ's protestations in, *inter alia, Michelin* (para. 57) that finding an undertaking has a dominant position is not a reproach, the consequences are such that it is invariably to the undertaking's disadvantage.

[128] See C. Baden Fuller, 'Art. 86 EEC: Economic Analysis of the Existence of a Dominant Position' (1979) 4 *ELRev.* 423, 440 and the economic literature cited there; Harbord and Hoehn, *supra* n. 125, 419; V. Korah, 'Concept of a Dominant Position Within The Meaning of Art. 86' (1980) 17 *CMLRev.* 395, 408.

[129] OFT Research Paper 2, 'Barriers to Entry and Exit in Competition Policy (OFT, 1994). See *supra* Chap. 1.

costs can be a serious deterrent to market entry. In *United Brands*, the ECJ did refer to sunk costs when it spoke of 'costs which are irrecoverable if the attempt fails'.[130] It is also argued in the OFT Report that economies of scale would deter entry if they cause tougher price competition. Thus it seems that economies of scale will sometimes create a barrier to entry. Baden Fuller, for example, takes the view that the crucial impact of economies of scale is on the probability of lack of profits. Usually profits are unlikely to be high for a small entrant where the minimum efficient scale of production is high in relation to the market.[131]

The main criticism of the cases is that they do not explain why economies of scale are considered to be a barrier to entry in the particular situation under consideration. In *BPB*, for example, the Commission merely stated that 'BPB enjoys substantial economies in producing on a large scale in integrated industrial complexes, extracting gypsum and producing plaster then plasterboard'.[132]

e. ACCESS TO FINANCIAL RESOURCES AND THE NEED FOR INVESTMENT

In *United Brands*[133] and *Hoffmann-La Roche*[134] the ECJ considered that the need for large-scale capital investment constituted a barrier to entry. In *Continental Can*[135] the Commission also appeared to consider that the undertaking's access to international capital markets was an indicator of its dominance. Bain considered that capital requirements could give rise to barriers to entry because of the amount a new entrant would need to enter the market at an efficient scale.[136] Whether or not this is correct however is extremely controversial. In Bork's view:[137]

Capital requirements exist and certainly inhibit entry—just as talent requirements for playing professional football exist and inhibit entry. Neither barrier is in any sense artificial or the proper subject of special concern for antitrust policy.

In EC case law, again, the reasons the capital requirements have been seen as an indicator of the incumbent undertaking's dominance have not been elaborated upon.

f. ACCESS TO KEY INPUTS

New entrants may be unable to enter the market because of lack of access to key inputs. This can cover items such as airport slots or things which are covered by intellectual property

---

[130] Case 27/76, *United Brands Co and United Brands Continental BV* v. *Commission* [1978] ECR 207, [1978] 1 CMLR 429, para. 122.

[131] C. Baden Fuller, 'Article 86 EEC: Economic Analysis of the Existence of a Dominant Position' (1979) 4 *ELRev.* 423, 429–33 and see also Korah, *supra* n. 125, 407.

[132] *BPB Industries* [1989] OJ L10/50, [1990] 4 CMLR 464, para. 116. The issue of dominance was not addressed in the appeals: Case T–65/89, *BPB Industries and British Gypsum Ltd* v. *Commission* [1993] ECR II–389, [1993] 5 CMLR 32; Case C–310/93P, *BPB Industries and British Gypsum Ltd* v. *Commission* [1995] ECR I–865, [1997] 4 CMLR 238.

[133] Case 27/76, *United Brands Co and United Brands Continental BV* v. *Commission* [1978] ECR 207, [1978] 1 CMLR 429, para 122.

[134] *Ibid.*, para. 49.

[135] *Re Continental Can Co* [1972] JO L7/25, [1972] CMLR D11, para. 13.

[136] J.S. Bain, *Barriers to New Competition* (Harvard University Press, Cambridge Mass., 1956) where he reported on a survey of 20 US industries. Capital requirements are therefore linked to economies of scale. See *supra* Chap. 1.

[137] R.H. Bork, *The Antitrust Paradox* (Basic Books, 1978), 320.

rights (see (a) above) but may also mean there is no access to raw materials. In *BPB*[138] a new entrant to the market would have needed access to the raw material, gypsum. There was no access to this in the UK without opening new mines. The only alternative was thus to import it. This would incur cost and risk and therefore relates to access to financial resources as discussed in (e) above. Where key inputs are unavailable to new entrants, refusals to supply can amount to strategic entry-deterring behaviour by the incumbent undertaking[139] and may amount to an abuse: see *Commercial Solvents*.[140]

g. ADVERTIZING, REPUTATION, PRODUCT DIFFERENTIATION

There is a large economics literature about the extent to which advertizing, reputation, and goodwill, may operate as barriers to entry. There can be economies of scale in advertizing and advertizing expenditures will usually be sunk costs.[141] Bain considered advertizing a barrier to entry.[142] Advertising builds up goodwill and reputation, and the first brand in the market may enjoy a classic first-mover advantage which will operate as a barrier to entry to later entrants.[143]

These potential barriers have not been much discussed in the EC cases. However, in *United Brands* the ECJ considered that advertizing and promotion had enhanced United Brands' large market share, because it had 'induced the customer to show a preference for' branded Chiquita bananas despite a large price differential with unlabelled and differently labelled bananas.[144] United Brands had 'thus attained a privileged position by making Chiquita the premier banana brand name'.[145] The Court did not appear to contemplate the possibility that consumers might have been swayed by the quality of the product rather than by advertizing. The ECJ concluded that among the barriers faced by new competitors would be 'the mounting of very large-scale advertising campaigns'.[146] Similarly, in the merger case of *Nestlé/Perrier*[147] the Commission considered it relevant to the existence of a dominant position that any new entrant to the market would face formidable advertising and promotion requirements. In *BBI/Boosey & Hawkes*[148] the Commission relied on the goodwill and

---

[138] *BPB Industries* [1989] OJ L10/50,[1990] 4 CMLR 464, para. 120.

[139] See the discussion of conduct as a barrier to entry, *infra* 316.

[140] Cases 6 and7/73, *Istituto Chemioterapico Italiano SpA and Commercial Solvents Corp* v. *Commission* [1974] ECR 223, [1974] 1 CMLR 309. See also the concept of refusal to supply as an abuse and the essential facilities doctrine discussed *infra* in Chap. 7.

[141] Although a brand image built up by advertizing might be deployable in a separate market, e.g. the name Virgin is applied to vastly different products and services. The Commission described advertizing and promotion as sunk costs in the merger decision *Nestlé/Perrier* [1992] OJ L356/1, [1993] 4 CMLR M17, para. 97.

[142] J. S. Bain, *Barriers to New Competition* (1956, Harvard University Press). See also M. Spence, 'Notes on Advertising, Economies of Scale and Entry Barriers' (1980) 95 *Quarterly Journal of Economics* 493; J. Sutton, *Sunk Costs and Market Structure: Price Competition, Advertising, and the Evolution of Concentration* (MIT Press).

[143] See R. Schmalensee, 'Entry Deterrence in the Ready-to-eat Breakfast Cereal Industry' (1978) 9 *Bell Journal of Economics* 305.

[144] Case 27/76, *United Brands Co and United Brands Continental BV* v. *Commission* [1978] ECR 207, [1978] 1 CMLR 429, para. 91.

[145] *Ibid.*, para. 92.

[146] *Ibid.*, para. 122.

[147] [1992] OJ L356/1, [1993] 4 CMLR M17 at recital 97. See *infra* Chap. 12.

[148] *BBI/Boosey & Hawkes* [1987] OJ L286/36, [1988] 4 CMLR 67, para. 18, where the product concerned was brass band instruments.

reputation enjoyed by Boosey and Hawkes, listing among 'other factors which tend . . . to support a preliminary finding of dominance' the 'strong buyer preference for B&H instruments' and 'its close identification with the brass band movement'.

There is also a significant literature on brand proliferation and product differentiation as barriers to entry,[149] but the issue has not specifically arisen in Article 82 cases before the Court or Commission. In the *Nestlé/Perrier* merger decision, however, the Commission did consider the difficulty of access to distribution outlets in a brand-crowded market and referred to the problem of shelf-space in retail stores.

h. OVERALL SIZE AND STRENGTH AND RANGE OF PRODUCTS

In its decision in *Hoffmann-La Roche* the Commission took into account the undertaking's position as the world's largest vitamin producer and leading pharmaceuticals producer and the wide range of vitamins it manufactured. The ECJ rejected the assertion that these factors were indicators of dominance, saying:[150]

45. The fact that Roche produces a far wider range of vitamins than its competitors must similarly be rejected as being immaterial. The Commission regards this as a factor establishing a dominant position and asserts that 'since the requirements of many users extend to several groups of vitamins, Roche is able to employ a sales and pricing strategy which is far less dependent than that of the other manufacturers on the conditions of competition in each market.'

46. However, the Commission has itself found that each group of vitamins constitutes a specific market and is not, or at least not to any significant extent, interchangeable with any other group or with any other products (Recital 20 to the decision) so that the vitamins belonging to the various groups are as between themselves products just as different as the vitamins compared with other products of the pharmeceutical and food sector. Moreover, it is not disputed that Roche's competitors, in particular those in the chemical industry, market besides the vitamins which they manufacture themselves, other products which purchasers of vitamins also want, so that the fact that Roche is in a position to offer several groups of vitamins does not in itself give it any advantage over its competitors, who can offer, in addition to a less or much less wide range of vitamins, other products which are also required by the purchasers of these vitamins.

47. Similar considerations lead also to the rejection as a relevant factor of the circumstance that Roche is the world's largest vitamin manufacturer, that its turnover exceeds that of all the other manufacturers and that it is at the head of the largest pharmaceuticals group in the world. In the view of the Commission these three considerations together are a factor showing that there is a dominant position, because 'it follows that the applicant occupies a preponderant position not only within the Common Market but also on the world market; it therefore enjoys very considerable freedom of action, since its position enables it to adapt itself easily to the developments of the different regional markets. An undertaking operating throughout the markets of the world and having a market share which leaves all its competitors far behind it does not have to concern itself unduly about any competitors within the Common Market.' Such reasoning based on the benefits reaped from economics of scale and on the possibility of adopting a strategy which varies according to different regional markets is not

---

[149] See Bain, *supra* n. 134; R. Schmalensee, 'Product Differentiation Advantages of Pioneering Brands' (1981) 72 *American Economic Review* 349. See also *infra* Chap. 12.

[150] [1976] OJ L223/27, [1976] 2 CMLR D25 at recitals 5, 6, and 21. On appeal case 85/76, *Hoffmann La Roche & Co AG v. Commission* [1979] ECR 461, [1979] 3 CMLR 211.

conclusive, seeing that it is accepted that each group of vitamins constitutes a group of separate products which require their own particular plant and form a separate market, in that the volume of the overall production of products which are different as between themselves does not give Roche a competitive advantage over its competitors, especially over those in the chemical industry, who manufacture on a world scale other products as well as vitamins and have in principle the same opportunities to set off one market against the other as are offered by a large overall production of products which differ from each other as much as the various groups of vitamins do.

Although size is not therefore *per se* an indicator of dominance on a particular market, the authorities have found it to be relevant in some situations. In *Michelin* the ECJ took into account the advantages Michelin NV derived from belonging to a group of undertakings which operated throughout Europe and the world.[151] In *Soda Ash-Solvay*[152] the Commission considered Solvay's manufacturing strength with plant in six other Member States to be part of the 'relevant economic evidence' to be taken into account in assessing dominance. The geographical spread of the undertaking's operations has also held to be an advantage where it makes it less vulnerable to natural disasters[153] and/or other fluctuations.[154]

It can be seen above that in *Hoffmann-La Roche* the ECJ overturned the Commission's finding that the wide range of vitamins produced by the undertaking was an indication of dominance because each vitamin was a separate market. It is otherwise if the undertaking benefits from the diversity of products. In *Tetra Pak II*[155] the Commission held that the diversity 'allows it, if necessary, to make financial sacrifices on one or other of its products without affecting the overall profitability of its operations'. This is a polite way of saying that a 'deep pocket' can facilitate practices such as predatory pricing.[156]

i. PROFITS

Since a monopolist can reap the benefits of its market power by earning monopoly profits, it is possible that these profits can be used as a means of identifying market power. However, it may be difficult to determine whether or not an undertaking is in fact earning monopoly profits. In practice therefore this is not likely to be a particularly helpful means of determining dominance.[157] Indeed the Community authorities have held that the fact that an undertaking is not earning profits at all, or a *lack* of profits, is not necessarily a contra-indication of dominance. In *United Brands*[158] and *Michelin*[159] the ECJ held that an undertaking's economic strength is not measured by profitability alone. Losses, at least if

---

[151] Although without specifying what these were: Case 322/81, *Nederlandsche Banden-Industrie Michelin* v. *Commission* [1983] ECR 3461, [1985] 1 CMLR 282, para. 55.

[152] [1991] OJ L152/21, para. 45.

[153] As with the banana plantations in *United Brands* [1978] ECR 207, [1978] 1 CMLR 429, para. 75.

[154] See *Elopak Italia/Tetra Pak* [1991] OJ L72/1, [1992] 4 CMLR 551, para. 101.

[155] *Ibid.*

[156] One of the abuses which was found in *Tetra Pak II*: see *infra* Chap. 7.

[157] Further economists generally prefer to determine the existence of market power by considering whether or not the undertaking is able to raise prices without losing part of its market share to competitors and, as we have seen, it is the latter which is employed by the ECJ in its definition of dominance *supra*, Chap. 5.

[158] Case 27/76, *United Brands Co and United Brands Continental BV* v. *Commission* [1978] ECR 207, [1978] 1 CMLR 429, paras. 126–128.

[159] Case 322/81, *NV Nederlandsche Banden-Industrie Michelin* v. *Commission* [1983] ECR 3461, [1985] 1 CMLR 282, para. 59.

temporary, may demonstrate the economic strength of the undertaking which has the ability to absorb them.

j. PERFORMANCE INDICATORS

The undertaking's economic performance has sometimes been held to be an indicator of dominance. In *Hoffmann-La Roche*[160] the ECJ took spare manufacturing capacity into account as a factor indicating dominance, although it did not distinguish between idle and excess capacity. Capacity is idle when its use would not be profitable because the market price is less than the cost of its use. It is found on both competitive and non-competitive markets. Excess capacity means that the undertaking is producing less output than the optimal output the plant is designed to produce, so that it could increase its output without its unit costs increasing. Excess capacity is a feature of monopolized markets.

The ability of an undertaking to obtain premium prices was relevant in *United Brands*[161] and in *BBI/Boosey & Hawkes.*[162]

k. OPPORTUNITY COSTS

Opportunity costs are the value of something which must be given up in order to achieve or acquire something else and can be classified as an absolute cost advantage for the incumbent undertaking. In *British Midland–Aer Lingus*[163] the Commission considered as a barrier to entry to the Heathrow-Dublin air route the opportunity costs involved in an airline having to divert its Heathrow airport slots, currently employed for other (profitable) routes, to service the less profitable Irish destination.

l. THE UNDERTAKING'S OWN ASSESSMENT OF ITS POSITION

The Court and the Commission have sometimes relied on an undertaking's own internal documentation as indicating its dominance. Such evidence was referred to in *BBI/Boosey & Hawkes* ('"automatic first choice" of all the top brass bands'[164]), *AKZO* ('AKZO regards itself as the world leader in the peroxides market'[165]), and the *Soda Ash* decisions ('ICI's own documentation recognizes that it holds a dominant position in the UK'[166]). The opinions of managers, however, are not incontrovertible evidence of their truth. Managers may try to 'talk up' the undertaking's position to convince themselves, others, or both.[167]

m. CONDUCT

The undertaking's conduct may be taken as an indicator of dominance. In *United Brands* the

---

[160] Case 85/76, *Hoffmann-La Roche & Co AG* v. *Commission* [1979] ECR 461, [1979] 3 CMLR 211, para. 48.

[161] Case 27/76, *United Brands Co and United Brands Continental BV* v. *Commission* [1978] ECR 207, [1978] 1 CMLR 429, para. 91.

[162] *BBI/Boosey & Hawkes* [1987] OJ L286/36 [1988] 4 CMLR 67, para. 18.

[163] *British Midland–Aer Lingus* [1992] OJ L96/34, [1993] 4 CMLR 596.

[164] *BBI/Boosey & Hawkes* [1987] OJ L286/36, [1988] 4 CMLR 67, para. 18.

[165] Case C–62/86, *AKZO Chemie BV* v. *Commission* [1991] ECR I–3359, [1993] 5 CMLR 215, para. 61.

[166] *Soda Ash-ICI* [1991] OJ L152/40, para. 47.

[167] The same problem of taking account of internal documentation arises when it is used to show that an abuse has been committed: see *infra* Chap. 7.

Commission considered that the undertaking's geographical price-discrimination and export bans were evidence of its dominance and the ECJ said that its economic strength had 'enabled it to adopt a flexible overall strategy directed against new competitors'.[168] In *Eurofix-Bauco* the Commission said that the undertaking's behaviour was 'witness to its ability to act independently of, and without due regard to, either competitors or customers ... This behaviour and its economic consequences would not normally be seen where a company was facing real competitive pressure'.[169]

This reasoning causes concern, however, on account of its circularity: the conduct leads to finding dominance which leads to finding the conduct is an abuse because the undertaking is dominant. It is justified, however, in some circumstances so long as caution is exercised. First, some conduct *is* impossible without market power. Secondly, some conduct may operate as a strategic entry barrier, as is discussed in the extracts from Harbord and Hoehn and the OFT Report.[170] If the conditions of post-entry competition are an important factor in undertakings' decisions about entering markets, predatory behaviour may deter entry, and exclusive dealing, tying, and similar practices may foreclose markets to new entrants.[171] Modern industrial organization theory, by emphasizing the analysis of strategic competition, makes the incumbent undertakings' conduct a major consideration in assessing dominance. Giving a prime place to conduct in the assessment of market power is the major reason why the issue of ascertaining whether an undertaking is dominant, and the issue of deciding whether it has abused that position, cannot be neatly separated.

D. POWER OVER LOCKED-IN CUSTOMERS AND ON AFTERMARKETS

It was seen above[172] that in *Hugin*,[173] *Hilti*,[174] *Volvo*,[175] *Renault*,[176] and *Tetra Pak II*[177] it was held that aftermarkets may be part of a separate product market from the primary product. These cases recognize that customers may, having made a choice of product on a primary market, subsequently be 'locked in' on the secondary market and obliged to purchase compatible goods and services. Thus even though a primary market may be competitive (as in *Hugin*, *Volvo*, and *Renault*, for example) the Court and Commission have held that the undertaking which is the sole producer of the products on the aftermarket has a dominant position on that market. The question whether, and if so when, undertakings really *do* have market power on aftermarkets or over locked-in customers is, however, controversial.

---

[168] Case 27/76, *United Brands* v. *Commission* [1978] ECR 207, [1978] 1 CMLR 429, para. 121.

[169] [1988] OJ L65/19, [1989] 4 CMLR 677 at recital 71. See similarly *ECS/AKZO* [1985] OJ L374/1, [1986] 3 CMLR 273 at recital 56, upheld in Case C–62/86, *AKZO Chemie BV* v. *Commission* [1991] ECR I–3359, [1993] 5 CMLR 215, para. 61.

[170] See *supra* Chap. 1.

[171] For a discussion of these practices as abuses under Art. 82 see Chap. 7.

[172] *Supra* 278 ff.

[173] Case 22/78, *Hugin Kassaregister AB and Hugin Cash Registers Ltd* v. *EC Commission* [1979] ECR 1869, [1979] 3 CMLR 345.

[174] Case C–53/92P, *Hilti* v. *Commission* [1994] ECR I–666, [1994] 4 CMLR 614.

[175] Case 238/87, *AB Volvo* v. *Erik Veng* [1988] ECR 6211, [1989] 4 CMLR 122.

[176] Case 53/87, *CICCRA* v. *Renault* [1988] ECR 6039, [1990] 4 CMLR 265.

[177] Case C–333/94P, *Tetra Pak International SA* v. *Commission* [1996] ECRI–5951, [1997] 4 CMLR 662.

Arguably, an undertaking cannot exploit its position over customers in a secondary market by raising prices if the primary market is competitive. This is due to the fact that:

(i)   a customer who has been exploited on an aftermarket will go elsewhere when the primary product (or 'installed base') needs replacing;

(ii) a customer may prefer to purchase another brand of product on the primary market rather than suffer continued exploitation on the aftermarket; and

(iii) when a customer decides, originally, to purchase the product in the primary product market its decision will be affected partly by the prices and conditions existing in the aftermarket. In some markets the costs in the aftermarket over the lifetime of the primary product may exceed the price of the primary product. Customers choosing the original product will be sensitive to the 'lifetime cost' and make decisions accordingly. Undertakings may therefore only be able to exploit the aftermarket if the latter is not transparent and the costs there can be hidden at the time of the primary product purchase.[178]

Before it is determined whether or not an undertaking has market power on the aftermarket it should therefore be considered (1) whether customers can easily switch to a competing product in the primary market; and (2) what information is available to customers when making their initial decision to purchase the product in the primary market.

In earlier cases such as *Hugin, Volvo,* and *Renault* the Commission was criticized for having failed to take account of these factors. In *Pelikan* v. *Kyocera*,[179] however, the Commission took a more realistic view. This case concerned a complaint about the conduct of a Japanese manufacturer of printers. It was alleged that the manufacturer was abusing its dominant position on the market for the supply of toner cartridges for its printers. In its *XXVth Report on Competition Policy* (1995) the Commission discussed the issue of secondary markets and set out how it had dealt with this case.

Commission's *XXVth Report on Competition Policy* (Commission, 1995)

86. Several complaints which the Commission received concern the alleged abuse of a dominant position in secondary product markets such as spare parts, consumables or maintenance services. These products are used in conjunction with a primary product and have to be technically compatible with it (e.g. software or hardware peripheral equipment for a computer). Thus, for these secondary products there may be no or few substitutes other than parts or services supplied by the primary product supplier. This prompts the question whether a non-dominant manufacturer of primary products can be dominant with respect to a rather small secondary product market, i.e. secondary products compatible with a certain type of that manufacturer's primary products.

The question raises many complex issues. Producers of primary equipment argue that there cannot be dominance in secondary products if there is lack of dominance in the primary product market because potential buyers would simply stop buying the primary products if the

---

[178] M. Williams, 'Sega, Nintendo and Aftermarket Power: The Monopolies and Mergers Commission Report on Video Games' (1995) 5 *ECLR* 310 discusses these arguments in the context of a UK Monopolies and Mergers Commission report.

[179] *Commission's XXVth Report on Competition Policy* (Commission, 1995), point 87.

prices for parts or services were raised. This theory implies a timely reaction on the primary product market due to consumers' ability to calculate the overall life-time costs of the primary product including all spare parts, consumables, upgrades, services, etc. It furthermore implies that price discrimination is not possible between potentially new customers and 'old' captive customers or that switching costs for the latter are low. On the other hand, complainants who produce consumables or maintenance services assume dominance in the secondary product market if market shares are high in this market, i.e. this approach focuses only on the second-ary products without analysing possible effects emanating from the primary product market.

In the Commission's view, neither of these approaches reflects reality sufficiently. Dominance has always been defined by the Commission as the ability to act to an appreciable extent independently of competitors and consumers. Therefore, an in-depth fact-finding exercise and analysis on a case-by-case basis are required. In order to assess dominance in this context the Commission will take into account all important factors such as the price and life-time of the primary product, transparency of prices of secondary products, prices of secondary products as a proportion of the primary product value, information costs and other issues partly men-tioned above. A similar approach was taken by the US Supreme Court in its 1992 Kodak decision.

Pelikan/Kyocera

87. The Commission took this approach when it rejected in 1995 the complaint of Pelikan, a German manufacturer of toner cartridges for printers, against Kyocera, a Japanese manu-facturer of computer printers including toner cartridges for those printers. Pelikan's com-plaint alleged a number of practices by Kyocera to drive Pelikan out of the toner market and accused Kyocera, among others, of abusing its dominant position in the secondary market although Kyocera was clearly not dominant in the primary market. Apart from the fact that there was no evidence of behaviour that could be considered abusive, neither did the Commis-sion find that Kyocera enjoyed a dominant position in the market for consumables. This was due to the particular features of the primary and secondary markets. Thus, purchasers were well informed about the price charged for consumables and appeared to take this into account in their decision to buy a printer. 'Total cost per page' was one of the criteria most commonly used by customers when choosing a printer. This was due to the fact that life-cycle costs of consumables (mainly toner cartridges) represented a very high proportion of the value of a printer. Therefore, if the prices of consumables of a particular brand were raised, consumables would have a strong incentive to buy another printer brand. In addition, there was no evidence of possibilities for price discrimination between 'old'/captive and new customers.

The *Kodak* case referred to by the Commission is *Eastman Kodak Co* v. *Image Technical Services Inc*[180] in which, after much economic argument, the US Supreme Court ruled that it *was* possible for a manufacturer to have monopoly power over the spare parts for its equip-ment even if it did not have market power in the original market for that equipment. The Court held that although competition in the primary market *could* restrain power in the aftermarket there was no rule of law to that effect. Existing customers could be bound to the primary product supplier because it was too expensive to switch and there might not be sufficient transparency to give new customers enough information about the future costs in the aftermarket when making the original purchase. The *Kodak* case was controversial and

---

[180] 504 US 451, 112 S.Ct 2072 (1992).

has been argued to signify a shift in the Supreme Court's policy in antitrust matters.[181] Consequently, the Commission's action in *Pelikan/Kyocera* has been favourably compared to the *Kodak* judgment.[182] However, in *Digital*[183] the Commission considered that Digital was dominant in the software and hardware services market in its own systems despite the fact that the primary market for computer systems was intensely competitive. The Commission's Competition Policy Report for 1997 is not explicit about the reasons for the finding of market power[184] but the Commission's position is discussed by an official of the Competition Directorate in a Competition Policy Newsletter.[185] He gives four reasons why the Commission adopted a different position in *Digital* to that which was adopted in *Kyocera*:

(i) Digital had a large base of captive customers who could not easily replace their installed system with another brand;

(ii) It did not seem that Digital's customers usually based their decision about the purchase of the primary system on the total lifetime costs partly because evaluating those costs was difficult and there was a lack of transparency in the aftermarket;

(iii) The costs in the aftermarket were not large enough to influence the customer's choice in the primary market (unlike Kyocera where toner cartridges were a major expense);

(iv) The nature of the product meant that Digital had the possibility of offering well-informed new customers individual servicing conditions.

The Digital case did not proceed to a formal decision, but was settled. The Commission's views were not therefore set out in a decision or reviewed by the Court. The message from *Pelikan/Kyocera* and *Digital* seems to be, however, that dominance in aftermarkets will not be assumed but that the individual circumstances of each case will be subjected to a full economic analysis.[186] This view is affirmed by the Commission's decision rejecting a complaint, in *Info-Lab/Ricoh*,[187] that Ricoch had abused its dominant position by refusing to supply it with empty toner cartridges compatible for its photocopy machines.[188] The Commission concluded that even if there was a separate market for Ricoch toner cartridges, Ricoch did not have a dominant position on that market. Although it was the only supplier of the cartridges for Ricoch photocopiers it could not act independently in setting prices. The upstream photocopier market was competitive and, in accordance with the principles set out in *Pelikan/Kyocera*, this was a market in which the consumer was *able* to make an

---

[181] See e.g. C. Shapiro, 'Aftermarkets and Consumer Welfare: Making Sense of Kodak' (1995) 63 *Antitrust Law Journal* 483. In his book Bork warns that the judgement 'may be as ominous a harbinger as *Sylvania* was a hopeful one': R.H. Bork, *The Antitrust Paradox: A Policy at War with Itself* (Basic Books, 1978, reprinted with a new Introduction and Epilogue, 1993), 430. See his discussion of the case at 436–9.

[182] D. Muldoom, 'The Kodak Case: Power in Aftermarkets' (1996) 8 *ECLR* 473.

[183] Commission Press Release IP/97/868 of 10 Oct. 1997.

[184] Commission's *XXVIIth Report* (Commission, 1997) point 69 and 153.

[185] P. Chevalier, 'Dominance sur un marché de produits secondaires', Commission's Competition Policy Newsletter 1998/1, 26.

[186] See also M. Dolmans and V. Pickering, 'The 1997 Digital Undertaking' [1998] *ECLR* 108; P. Andrews, 'Aftermarket Power in the Computer Services Market' [1998] *ECLR* 176; B. Bishop and C. Caffarra, 'Editorial, Dynamic Competition and Aftermarkets' [1998] ECLR 265 discuss the issue but mainly from the perspective of merger control.

[187] Case IV/36431, rejection of a complaint by decision, see Competition Policy Newsletter 1999, Number 1, 35.

[188] For the market definition aspect of this case, see *supra* 283.

informed choice, appreciating the lifetime costs in the aftermarket; it was a market in which the consumer was *likely* to make an informed choice; potential new customers (of which there were a considerable number because of the short life-span of photocopiers) would be deterred by the exploitation of existing customers; and new customers could adapt their purchasing pattern within a reasonable span of time.

4. CONCLUSION

The Article 82 case law on the ascertainment of dominance is often criticized for defining markets arbitrarily and too narrowly, over-estimating undertakings' market power and lacking sophisticated economic analysis. The Court and Commission are said to identify as factors indicating dominance things which should not be considered barriers to entry whatever school of economic theory is being followed. Much of this argument is about time-scale: the Commission looks at a shorter time-scale than most economists would. Dominance denotes power over time, but the question is how much time. Economists talk about the time-scale of competition as 'dynamic competition' and recognize that temporary market power is in some industries, such as technologically innovative ones, inevitable.

Competition policy, however, needs to ensure that entry into the market remains open. The EC cases take account of factors which can be described as *impediments*, rather than barriers, to entry.[189] The Commission tends to act against undertakings which are in a position to act anti-competitively and to the detriment of consumers *now* and in the medium term, although they may well be subject to competition from new entrants in the longer term. As Hovenkamp has succinctly put it:[190]

The importance of time in antitrust analysis results from the fact that the policy maker is necessarily concerned with *short*-run dislocations in the market. We could presume that all markets will eventually become competitive, but antitrust is concerned with ensuring that this occurs sooner rather than later. The concern is not unique to antitrust . . . in the long run all of us will be dead. But that fact does not undermine the state's concern to protect us from murderers or see to it that we are provided with nutrition and health care.

---

[189] See R. Schmalensee, 'Ease of Entry: Has the Concept Been Applied too Readily' (1987) 56 *Antitrust Law Journal* 41.

[190] H. Hovenkamp, *Federal Antitrust Policy: The Law of Competition and its Practice* (West Publishing Co, St. Paul, Minn., 1994), 7.

5. FURTHER READING

A. BOOKS

BAIN, J.S., *Barriers to New Competition* (Harvard University Press, 1956)

SCHERER, F.M., and Ross, D., *Industrial Market Structure and Economic Performance* (3rd edn.) Houghton Mifflin, 1990, Chapters 4 and 16

SUTTON, J., *Sunk Costs and Market Structure: Price Competition, Advertising, and the Evolution of Concentration* (MIT Press, 1991)

B. ARTICLES

BADEN FULLER, C.W., 'Article 86 EEC: Economic Analysis of the Existence of a Dominant Position' (1979) 4 *ELRev.* 423

BISHOP, W., 'Editorial: The Modernisation of DGIV' [1997] *ECLR* 481

—— and CAFFARRA, C., 'Editorial, Dynamic Competition and Aftermarkets' [1998] *ECLR* 265

FOX, E.M., and SULLIVAN, L.A., 'Antitrust—Retrospective and Prospective: Where Are We Coming From? Where Are We Going?' (1987) 62 *New York Univ.* 936

GYSELEN, L., and KYRIAKIS, N., 'Article 86 EEC: The Monopoly Power Issue Revisited' (1986) 11 *ELRev.* 134

HARBORD, D., and HOEHN, T., 'Barriers to Entry and Exit in European Competition Policy' (1994) 14 *Int'l Rev. L & Econ.* 411

KORAH, V., 'Concept of a Dominant Position within the Meaning of Article 86' (1980) 17 *CMLRev.* 395

—— 'The Michelin Decision of the Commission' (1982) 7 *ELRev.* 13

—— 'The Paucity of Economic Analysis in the EEC Decisions on Competition—Tetra Pak II' [1993] *Current Legal Problems* 148

LANDES, D., and POSNER, R.A., 'Market Power in Antitrust Cases' (1981) 94 *Harv. LR* 937

MULDOOM, D., 'The Kodak Case: Power in Aftermarkets' [1996] *ECLR* 473

SCHMALENSEE, R., 'Entry Deterrence in the Ready-to-eat Breakfast Cereal Industry' (1978) 9 *Bell Journal of Economics* 305

—— 'Another Look at Market Power' (1981–82) 95 *Harv. LR* 1789

—— 'Product Differentiation Advantages of Pioneering Brands' (1981) 72 *Am. Ec. Rev.* 349

—— 'Ease of Entry: Has the Concept Been Applied too Readily' (1987) 56 *Antitrust LJ* 41

SHAPIRO, C., 'Aftermarkets and Consumer Welfare: Making Sense of Kodak' (1995) 63 *Antitrust LJ* 483

SPENCE, M., 'Notes on Advertising, Economies of Scale and Entry Barriers' (1980) 95 *Quart of Econ.* 493

7

CONDUCT WHICH CAN BE AN ABUSE

1. INTRODUCTION

In Chapter 5 it was seen that the concept of 'abuse' in Article 82 has been widely interpreted. The definition of abuse often repeated by the Court and the Commission is that set out, *inter alia*, in *Michelin*:[1]

Article [82] covers practices which are likely to affect the structure of a market where, as a direct result of the presence of the undertaking in question, competition has already been weakened and which, through recourse to methods different from those governing normal competition in products or services based on traders' performance, have the effect of hindering the maintenance or development of the level of competition still existing on the market.

It was also noted that, although this definition describes only anti-competitive abuses, Article 82 also prohibits, of course, exploitative abuses.

In this chapter we describe the types of conduct which have been held to constitute an abuse of a dominant position within the meaning of Article 82. It will be seen, however, that abuses cannot be pigeon-holed and do not fit into neat categories.

The key concern of the Commission is with conduct which excludes competitors from the market. Conduct so aimed, or having such an effect, is likely to be condemned as an abuse, whatever form it takes. As the ECJ first said in *Michelin*,[2] dominant firms have a 'special responsibility' towards the competitive process. Many of the cases also reflect the Commission's concern with *leverage*, which means the dominant undertaking's use of its market power in one market to affect competition in another.

It is not always clear, however, whether the competition authorities in applying Article 82 are concerned with the exclusion only of *equally* efficient firms from the market or also of *less* efficient ones, whether they want competition to be *fair* as well as free, and whether they want as many firms as possible in the market regardless of efficiencies. These questions should be borne in mind when reading the cases and decisions. Above all one must reflect on the Court's idea, in the definition of dominance quoted above, that an abuse is conduct which does not constitute 'normal competition'.

---

[1] Case 322/81, *Nederlandsche Banden-Industrie Michelin* v. *Commission* [1983] ECR 3461, [1985] 1 CMLR 282, para. 70; Case 85/76, *Hoffmann-La Roche* v. *Commission* [1979] ECR 461, [1979] 3 CMLR 211, para. 91.

[2] Case 322/81, *Nederlandsche Banden-Industrie Michelin* v. *Commission* [1983] ECR 3461, [1985] 1 CMLR 282, para. 57.

2. ABUSE AND THE DEGREE OF DOMINANCE

In Chapter 5 it was noted that a concept of 'super-dominance' appears to be emerging. In several recent cases the Court, Advocate General, and Commission have variously alluded to the position of undertakings which are not merely dominant (within the usual *United Brands/ Hoffmann-La Roche* test) but which have a position of actual or quasi-monopoly. Advocate General Fennelly used the term 'super-dominant' in his opinion in *Compagnie Maritime Belge*.[3] Where an undertaking is in such a position it appears that its 'special responsibility' towards the competitive process is particularly onerous, and its conduct therefore more likely to be categorized as an abuse. When considering the types of conduct which can be abusive, therefore, it may be necessary to take account of the degree of dominance of the undertaking concerned.[4]

3. DOMINANCE AND ABUSE ON DIFFERENT MARKETS

In *Tetra Pak II*[5] the ECJ held that in some circumstances the abuse can be committed on a different market from that on which the undertaking holds a dominant position. An undertaking can therefore have a dominant position on one market and infringe Article 82 by its conduct on another. In earlier cases this idea was applied to situations in which the abuse took place on a market *ancillary to* the dominated one or where there was a clear connection between the dominant position and the conduct on the non-dominated market.[6] Indeed, the prevention of leverage on ancillary markets has been a major theme in the application of Article 82. For example, in *Elliniki Radiophonia*[7] the Court held that it was contrary to Article 82 for a television monopoly to pursue a discriminatory broadcasting policy which favoured its own programmes.

Télémarketing was a highly significant case in the development of the application of

---

[3] Cases C–395 and 396/96P, *Compagnie Maritime Belge and others v. Commission* [2000] 4 CMLR 1076, para. 137 of the Opinion.

[4] See Case C–333/94P, *Tetra Pak International SA v. Commission* [1996] ECR I–5951, [1997] 4 CMLR 662; Cases C–395 and 396/96P, *Compagnie Maritime Belge and others v. Commission*, [2000] 4 CMLR 1076: Case T–228/97, *Irish Sugar plc v. Commission* [1999] 5 CMLR 1300; *Football World Cup 1998* [2000] OJ L5/55, [2000] 4 CMLR 963, paras. 85–86.

[5] Case C–333/94P, *Tetra Pak International SA v. Commission* [1996] ECR I–5951, [1997] 4 CMLR 662, paras. 24–32.

[6] Such as Cases 6, 7/73, *Istituto Chemioterapico Italiano Spa and Commercial Solvents Corp. v. EC Commission* [1974] ECR 223, [1974] 1 CMLR 309 and Case T–65/89, *BPB Industries and British Gypsum Ltd v. Commission* [1993] ECR II–389, [1993] 5 CMLR 32. The Court's interpretation of these precedents as having already in effect established the position reached in *Tetra Pak II* is criticized by V. Korah, '*Tetra Pak II*—Lack of Reasoning in the Court's Judgment' [1997] 2 *ECLR* 98, 100 and N. Levy: '*Tetra Pak II*: Stretching the Limits of Art. 86' [1995] 2 *ECLR* 104, 106–7.

[7] Case C–260/89, *Elliniki Radiophonia Tileorasi (ERT) v. DEP* [1991] ECR I–2925, paras. 37–38: the case also raised Art. 86 issues which are discussed *infra* Chap. 8.

Article 82 to abuses committed on ancillary markets. This case has frequently been relied on by the Court and the Commission in subsequent cases.[8]

Case 311/84 *Centre Belge d'Etudes du Marché-Télémarketing* v. *Compagnie Luxembourgeoise de Télédiffusion SA and Information Publicité Benelux SA* [1985] ECR 3261, [1986] 2 CMLR 558

In 'tele-sales' or 'telemarketing' television advertisements carry a telephone number which viewers ring to order the goods or services or obtain further information. Luxembourg Television (CLT) stopped accepting advertisements on its television station unless the phone number used was that of its own subsidiary. Centre Belge, an independent company who ran a telesales operation could not therefore use its own number. It challenged CLT's behaviour in the Belgian courts and the Commercial Court made a reference for a preliminary ruling. CLT was a statutory monopolist and dominated the market in television advertising aimed at French-speaking viewers in Belgium as in Belgium itself there was at the time no advertising on national television stations.

Court of Justice

19. The second question asks whether an undertaking holding a dominant position on a particular market, by reserving to itself or to an undertaking belonging to the same group, to the exclusion of any other undertaking, an ancillary activity which could be carried out by another undertaking as part of its activities on a neighbouring but separate market, abuses its dominant position within the meaning of Article [82].

. . .

23. The Commission infers from the judgment of the Court of 6 March 1974 in Joined Cases 6 and 7/73 (*Commercial Solvents and Others* v. *Commission* [1974] ECR 223) that there is an abuse of a dominant position for the purposes of Article [82] where an undertaking which occupies a dominant position on a market and which is thus able to control the activities of other undertakings on a neighbouring market decides to establish itself on the second market and for no good reason refuses to supply the product or service in question on the market where it already occupies a dominant position to the undertakings whose activities are centred on the market which it is penetrating.

24. Even if the conduct in issue in the main proceedings were to be regarded not as a refusal to supply but as the imposition of a contractual condition, it would, in the Commission's view, be contrary to Article [82]. First, Information publicité, as a seller of television time, imposes on all other undertakings for telemarketing operations a condition which it does not impose on itself for the same operations, namely the condition that it must not use its own telephone number; that is an unfair trading condition within the meaning of Article [82(a)]. Secondly, Information publicité subjects the conclusion of contracts to the acceptance of supplementary obligations which have no connection with the subject of the contracts, and that is contrary to Article [82(d)].

25. In order to answer the national court's second question, reference must first be made to the aforesaid judgment of 6 March 1974 (*Commercial Solvents*), in which the Court held that an undertaking which holds a dominant position on a market in raw materials and which, with the object of reserving those materials for its own production of derivatives, refuses to supply a customer who also produces those derivatives, with the possibility of eliminating all competition from that customer, is abusing its dominant position within the meaning of Article [82].

---

[8] Case 311/84, *Centre Belge d'Etudes du Marché-Télémarketing* v. *Compagnie Luxembourgeoise de Télédiffusion SA and Information Publicité Benelux SA* [1985] ECR 3261, [1986] 2 CMLR 558.

26. That ruling also applies to the case of an undertaking holding a dominant position on the market in a service which is indispensable for the activities of another undertaking on another market. If, as the national court has already held in its order for reference, telemarketing activities constitute a separate market from that of the chosen advertising medium, although closely associated with it, and if those activities mainly consist in making available to advertisers the telephone lines and team of telephonists of the telemarketing undertaking, to subject the sale of broadcasting time to the condition that the telephone lines of an advertising agent belonging to the same group as the television station should be used amounts in practice to a refusal to supply the services of that station to any other telemarketing undertaking. If, further, that refusal is not justified by technical or commercial requirements relating to the nature of the television, but is intended to reserve to the agent any telemarketing operation broadcast by the said station, with the possibility of eliminating all competition from another undertaking, such conduct amounts to an abuse prohibited by Article [82], provided that the other conditions of that article are satisfied.

27. It must therefore be held in answer to the second question that an abuse within the meaning of Article [82] is committed where, without any objective necessity, an undertaking holding a dominant position on a particular market reserves to itself or to an undertaking belonging to the same group an ancillary activity which might be carried out by another undertaking as part of its activities on a neighbouring but separate market, with the possibility of eliminating all competition from such undertaking.

Another important case, *Tetra Pak II*, built upon the principle set out in *Télémarketing*. It applied the principle to abuses committed on a market which was not ancillary to the dominated one. The case involved two carton markets: aseptic and non-aseptic. They were held to be separate, distinct markets. Neither was ancillary to the other.[9] The Commission held that Tetra Pak was dominant on the aseptic market but made no finding of dominance with regard to the non-aseptic market. It held, however, that Tetra Pak had abused its dominant position on the aseptic market by its conduct on the non-aseptic market. The Commission's decision was upheld by the Court of First Instance,[10] which was approved by the Court of Justice.

Case C–333/94P, *Tetra Pak International SA* v. *Commission* [1996] ECR I–5951, [1997] 4 CMLR 662

Court of Justice

24. It must first be stressed that there can be no question of challenging the Court of First Instance's assessment, at paragraph 113 of its judgment, that Article [82] gives no explicit guidance as to the requirements relating to where on the product market the abuse took place. That Court was therefore correct in stating, at paragraph 115, that the actual scope of the special responsibility imposed on a dominant undertaking must be considered in the light of the specific circumstances of each case which show a weakened competitive situation.

25. In that regard, the case-law cited by the Court of First Instance is relevant. Joined Cases 6/73 and 7/73 *Commercial Solvents* v. *Commission* [1974] ECR 223 and Case 311/84 *CBEM* v. *CLT and IPB* [1985] ECR 3261 provide examples of abuses having effects on markets other than the dominated markets. In Case C–62/86 *AKZO* v Commission [1991] ECR I–3359 and Case T–65/89 *BPB*

---

[9] For market definition in *Tetra Pak II*, see *supra* Chap. 6.
[10] Case T–83/91, *Tetra Pak Rausing* v. *Commission* [1994] ECR II–755, [1997] 4 CMLR 726.

Industries and British Gypsum v. *Commission* [1993] ECR II–389, the Community judicature found certain conduct on markets other than the dominated markets and having effects on the dominated markets to be abusive. The Court of First Instance was therefore right in concluding from that case-law, at paragraph 116 of the judgment under appeal, that it must reject the applicant's arguments to the effect that the Community judicature had ruled out any possibility of Article [82] applying to an act committed by an undertaking in a dominant position on a market distinct from the dominated market.

26. Nor, for the reasons set out by the Advocate General at point 61 of his Opinion, can Tetra Pak derive any support from the judgments in Case 85/76 *Hoffmann-La Roche* v. *Commission* [1979] ECR 461 or *Michelin* v. *Commission*, cited above.

27. It is true that application of Article [82] presupposes a link between the dominant position and the alleged abusive conduct, which is normally not present where conduct on a market distinct from the dominated market produces effects on that distinct market. In the case of distinct, but associated, markets, as in the present case, application of Article [82] to conduct found on the associated, non-dominated market and having effects on that associated market can only be justified by special circumstances.

28. In that regard, the Court of First Instance first considered, at paragraph 118 of its judgment, that it was relevant that Tetra Pak held 78% of the overall market in packaging in both aseptic and non-aseptic cartons, that is to say seven times more than its closest competitor. At paragraph 119, it stressed Tetra Pak's leading position in the non-aseptic sector. Then, in paragraph 121, it found that Tetra Pak's position on the aseptic markets, of which it held nearly a 90% share, was quasi-monopolistic. It noted that that position also made Tetra Pak a favoured supplier of non-aseptic systems. Finally, at paragraph 122, it concluded that, in the circumstances of the case, application of Article [82] was justified by the situation on the different markets and the close associative links between them.

29. The relevance of the associative links which the Court of First Instance thus took into account cannot be denied. The fact that the various materials involved are used for packaging the same basic liquid products shows that Tetra Pak's customers in one sector are also potential customers in the other. That possibility is borne out by statistics showing that in 1987 approximately 35% of Tetra Pak's customers bought both aseptic and non-aseptic systems. It is also relevant to note that Tetra Pak and its most important competitor, PKL, were present on all four markets. Given its almost complete domination of the aseptic markets, Tetra Pak could also count on a favoured status on the non-aseptic markets. Thanks to its position on the former markets, it could concentrate its efforts on the latter by acting independently of the other economic operators.

30. The circumstances thus described, taken together and not separately, justified the Court of First Instance, without any need to show that the undertaking was dominant on the non-aseptic markets, in finding that Tetra Pak enjoyed freedom of conduct compared with the other economic operators on those market.

31. Accordingly, the Court of First Instance was right to accept the application of Article [82] of the Treaty in this case, given that the quasi-monopoly enjoyed by Tetra Pak on the aseptic markets and its leading position on the distinct, though closely associated, non-aseptic markets placed it in a situation comparable to that of holding a dominant position on the markets in question as a whole.

32. An undertaking in such a situation must necessarily be able to foresee that its conduct may be caught by Article [82] of the Treaty. Thus, contrary to the appellant's argument, the requirements of legal certainty are observed.

The Court stated in paragraph 27 that Article 82 can be applied to conduct by a dominant undertaking on a distinct, non-dominated market only where it is justified by 'special circumstances'. The special circumstances in this case were the 'close associative links' between the two markets, and the quasi-monopolistic position held by Tetra Pak on the dominated market, where it had a 90 per cent market share. Both types of carton were used for packaging the same basic liquid, and many customers bought on both markets. Its powerful position on the dominated market therefore meant that Tetra Pak could concentrate its efforts on the associated market where it enjoyed a greater freedom of action than its competitors. It was thus in a position comparable to that of holding a dominant position on the two markets as a whole (paragraph 31). *Tetra Pak II*, therefore, does *not* mean that dominance on one market can always be abused by conduct on another, distinct, market. It *does* mean that it is a possibility where the markets are associated and there are particular circumstances pertaining which mean that the undertaking's dominance gives it significant advantages on the second market.

What amounts to 'special circumstances' will vary from case to case. The importance accorded in *Tetra Pak II* to the quasi-monopolistic position should, however, be noted. This reflects the added responsibility of undertakings which enjoy a position of 'super-dominance'.

4. PRICING POLICIES

A. GENERAL

Many of the cases and decisions on Article 82 concern the pricing policies of dominant firms. One of the most serious consequences of being found in a dominant position is that a firm's pricing policies may be condemned as abusive. Although some condemned forms of pricing, such as excessive pricing and predatory pricing, are impossible or at least unlikely in the absence of market power, others, such as discriminatory pricing in the form of discount and rebate schemes, can be practised by any firm, and in non-dominated markets may be applauded as lively competition. Abusive pricing policies cannot really be separated from other forms of abuse, such as tying policies, since, as becomes apparent later in this section, the former are often pursued in furtherance of the latter.

B. UNFAIRLY HIGH OR LOW PRICING

(i) EXCESSIVE PRICES ON THE SUPPLY SIDE

Article 82 (a) specifically prohibits the imposition of 'unfair purchase or selling prices'. On the selling side 'unfair' prices can be equated with 'excessive' prices.[11] Excessive pricing is the

---

[11] In Case 78/70 *Deutsche Grammophon* v. *Metro* [1971] ECR 487, [1971] CMLR 631, the Court spoke of prices which were 'excessive and consequently unfair'.

most obvious way in which a monopolist can exploit its position. Economic theory demonstrates[12] that monopoly prices are likely to be higher than those in competitive markets and excessive prices match the popular conception of the evils of monopoly. However, excessive prices may be pro- rather than anti-competitive because high prices and profits may act as a signal to attract new competitors on to the market. Where this cannot happen because barriers to entry are high the spectre of competition authorities acting as price regulators arises. Price regulation, however, is the antithesis of the free market and the Commission has not much concerned itself with excessive prices,[13] appearing to agree with the view that interference with high prices and profits *per se* is a disincentive to innovation and investment. Price regulation is better restricted to situations of natural or legal monopoly.[14] It may be preferable to solve the problem of excessive pricing in other situations by taking vigorous action against anti-competitive conduct whereby dominant firms seek to preserve their dominance. The Commission explained this in its 1994 Competition Report:[15]

The existence of a dominant position is not itself against the rules of competition. Consumers can suffer from a dominant company exploiting this position, the most likely way being through prices higher than would be found if the market were subject to effective competition. However, the Commission in its decision—making practice does not normally control or condemn the high level of prices as such. Rather it examines the behaviour of the dominant company designed to preserve its dominance, usually directed against competitors or new entrants who would normally bring about effective competition and the price level associated with it.

It is, in any case, difficult to decide what constitutes an excessive price. Ascertaining what the price might have been in a more competitive market is rarely possible in practice, so what other yardstick can be used? In *United Brands* the Commission condemned UBC for charging excessive prices for Chiquita bananas in Germany, Denmark, and Benelux. It compared the prices with those for unbranded bananas, competitors' bananas, and with the price of Chiquitas in Ireland, and it said that the prices were 'excessive in relation to the economic value of the product supplied'. The Court annulled the Commission's decision that unfair prices had been charged.

---

[12] See *supra* Chap. 1.

[13] Although there are instances in the special sector of telecommunications. For example, the investigation into prices in mobile telephone services in the EC (Press Releases IP/98/141, IP 98/707, IP (98) 1036). It found 14 cases of discrimination and high prices but closed its files when prices were reduced or there was action by the domestic regulator. In 1997 the Commission took a decision to initiate proceedings against Deutsche Telekom, but the undertaking agreed to reduce certain tariffs and the matter went no further (Commission's XXVIIth Report on Competition Policy (Commission, 1997), pt 7).

[14] For the position of public undertakings and other statutory monopolists, see *infra* Chap. 8. For example, in Cases C–147–148/97, *Deutsche Post AG* v. *Gesellschaft für Zahlungssysteme mbH (GZS) and Citicorp Kartenservice GmbH* [2000] 4 CMLR 838, an Art. 234 reference concerning the German postal monopoly, the ECJ said that the monopolist would commit an abuse if it charged the full internal rate for forwarding international mail without offsetting the 'terminal dues' to which it was entitled.

[15] XXIVth Report on Competition Policy (Commission, 1994), pt 207.

Case 27/76 *United Brands* v. *Commission* [1978] ECR 207, [1978] 1 CMLR 429

Court of Justice

248. The imposition by an undertaking in a dominant position directly or indirectly of unfair purchase or selling prices is an abuse to which exception can be taken under Article [82] of the Treaty.

249. It is advisable therefore to ascertain whether the dominant undertaking has made use of the opportunities arising out of its dominant position in such a way as to reap trading benefits which it would not have reaped if there had been normal and sufficiently effective competition.

250. In this case charging a price which is excessive because it has no reasonable relation to the economic value of the product supplied would be such an abuse.

251. This excess could, *inter alia*, be determined objectively if it were possible for it to be calculated by making a comparison between the selling price of the product in question and its cost of production, which would disclose the amount of the profit margin; however the Commission has not done this since it has not analysed UBC's costs structure.

252. The questions therefore to be determined are whether the difference between the costs actually incurred and the price actually charged is excessive, and, if the answer to this question is in the affirmative, whether a price has been imposed which is either unfair in itself or when compared to competing products.

253. Other ways may be devised—and economic theorists have not failed to think up several—of selecting the rules for determining whether the price of a product is unfair.

254. While appreciating the considerable and at times very great difficulties in working out production costs which may sometimes include a discretionary apportionment of indirect costs and general expenditure and which may vary significantly according to the size of the undertaking, its object, the complex nature of its set up, its territorial area of operations, whether it manufactures one or several products, the number of its subsidiaries and their relationship with each other, the production costs of the banana do not seem to present any insuperable problems.

. . .

258. The Commission bases its view that prices are excessive on an analysis of the differences—in its view excessive—between the prices charged in the different Member States and on the policy of discriminatory prices which has been considered above.

. . .

260. Having found that the prices charged to ripeners of the other Member States were considerably higher, sometimes by as much as 100%, than the prices charged to customers in Ireland it concluded that UBC was making a very substantial profit.

. . .

264. However unreliable the particulars supplied by UBC may be . . . the fact remains that it is for the Commission to prove that the applicant charged unfair prices.

265. UBC's retraction, which the Commission has not effectively refuted, establishes beyond doubt that the basis for the calculation adopted by the latter to prove the UBC's prices are excessive is open to criticism and on this particular point there is doubt which must benefit the applicant, especially as for nearly 20 years banana prices, in real terms, have not risen on the relevant market.

266. Although it is also true that the price of Chiquita bananas and those of its principal competitors is different, that difference is about 7%, a percentage which has not been challenged and which cannot automatically be regarded as excessive and consequently unfair.

267. In these circumstances it appears that the Commission has not adduced adequate legal proof of the facts and evaluations which formed the foundation of its finding that UBC had infringed Article [82] of the Treaty by directly and indirectly imposing unfair selling prices for bananas.

268. Article 1 (c) of the decision must therefore be annulled.

The Commission's decision on excessive pricing was thus quashed because the Commission had failed to do its homework properly. It had not presented sufficient evidence and had not analysed UBC's costs. The Court accepted that excessive prices can constitute an abuse and that charging a price which has no relation to the product's 'economic value' would be excessive (paragraph 250). But what is the economic value of a banana other than what a customer is prepared to pay for it? The Court thought the excess could be determined by comparing the selling and production costs, which would disclose the profit margin (paragraph 251), but it did not suggest the level at which the profit would become excessive, and hence abusive. If undertakings' profit margins are attacked under Article 82 then undertakings may be discouraged from costs savings. Further, high profits may be necessary to provide a fair return on the costs of innovation, or to act as a spur to further innovation in a dynamic market. It is unsatisfactory to leave undertakings without guidance on what levels of profitability are acceptable in a competition law regime like Article 82 in which past conduct is penalized.[16]

The notion that the price charged should relate to the 'economic value' of the product or service was first discussed by the ECJ in *General Motors*.[17] In this case a car company was charging a high price for the production of documentation without which car owners could not bring their cars into Belgium. The documentation was obviously cheap to produce, but in fact the 'value' to the customers was great since without the certificate the car could not be imported. On the facts the Court accepted that no abuse had been committed[18] and so the meaning of 'economic value' or excessive prices did not need to be more specifically defined. After *United Brands*, a similar case arose. In *British Leyland*[19] the manufacturer demanded a high price for type-approval certificates as a way of discouraging individuals

---

[16] In the UK a considerable number of Monopolies and Mergers Commission reports under the Fair Trading Act 1973 have dealt with high prices, but most of these have concerned 'complex monopolies' (oligopolies). The MMC (now the Competition Commission) has used criteria such as ROCE (return on capital employed) and CCA (Current Cost Accounting) in determining profit levels. It is possible to compare the Certainty Equivalent Accounting Rate of Return (CARR) over a number of years with the risk-free rate of interest. These methods of estimating the rate of supra—normal profitability are discussed in the Office of Fair Trading's Research Paper No 10 (OFT, 1997). Under the Fair Trading Act 1973 the procedure, however, is an investigatory one and penalties are not imposed for past conduct. The FTA procedure survived the reform of UK law which, by the Competition Act 1998, also introduced a prohibition system (the 'Chapter II prohibition') modelled on Art. 82. The OFT Guideline, *Assessment of Individual Agreements and Conduct* (OFT 414), which explains how the prohibitions in the Act may be expected to operate, contains an interesting discussion (2.1–2.29) of the assessment of excessive prices. The Guideline (paragraph 2.19) says that the Director General will not normally be concerned by periods of *transiently* high prices.

[17] Case 26/75, *General Motors* v. *Commission* [1975] ECR 1367, [1976] 1 CMLR 95.

[18] Because the high price had been a temporary blip while national procedures were changed.

[19] Case 226/84, British Leyland v. *EC Commission [1986] ECR 3323, [1987] 1 CMLR 185.*

from importing cars from Member States where they were cheaper. The price was con-demned as 'excessive and discriminatory' but viewed by the Court as a part of a policy of maintaining price differentials and compartmentalizing the common market rather than as a simple garnering of monopoly profits.

In *United Brands* the Court referred to other ways economists have devised for identify-ing unfair prices (paragraph 253) but did not identify them. It did however consider that a comparison with the price of other products (paragraph 252) or other areas was valid—it dismissed the comparison with Ireland for lack of proper analysis, not because it rejected the comparison as a technique. In *Bodson* v. *Pompes Funèbres des Régions Libéréés*,[20] which concerned funeral services in areas of France where there were monopoly concessions granted by local authorities, the Court talked of whether the price was 'fair' in comparison with prices in areas where there were no such concessions. In *Ministère Public* v. *Tournier*[21] it said in the context of a complaint about the high charges imposed by the French copyright collecting society, SACEM, that:

38. When an undertaking holding a dominant position imposes scales of fees for its services which are appreciably higher than those charged in other member-States and where a comparison of the fee levels has been made on a consistent basis, that difference must be regarded as indicative of an abuse of a dominant position. In such a case it is for the undertaking in question to justify the difference by reference to objective dissimilarities between the situation in the member-State concerned and the situation prevailing in all the other member-States.

This suggests that once it is shown that there is an appreciable price differential between Member States the burden of proof is on the dominant undertaking to justify its higher price.[22]

In *Deutsche Grammophon*[23] the Court said that the fact that the price of the product in one Member State was different from that when re-imported from another did not necessar-ily constitute an abuse, but it would be a determining factor if the difference was very marked and unjustified by any objective criteria. *Deutsche Grammophon, Bodson,* and *Tournier* were all Article 234 references where the Court was merely giving guidance to the national court. This was also the case in *Alsatel* v. *Novasam*[24] where the Court said that a rental increase of 25 per cent for telephone installations might 'constitute unfair trading conditions'. The Court has also considered excessive pricing in references concerning intel-lectual property rights. In *Parke, Davis*[25] it said that the higher price of a patented compared with a non-patented product did not necessarily mean that an abuse had been committed. In *Renault*,[26] however, it suggested that a car manufacturer which refused to license its intellectual property rights in respect of its spare parts to other manufacturers might com-mit an abuse if it charged 'unfair prices' for its own parts. The idea that intellectual property rights owners are not entitled to extract the maximum return from their monopoly position,

[20] Case 30/87 [1988] ECR 2479, [1989] 4 CMLR 984, para. 31.

[21] Case 395/87, *Ministère Public* v. *Tournier* [1989] ECR 2521, [1991] 4 CMLR 248, para. 38.

[22] If different prices are charged in different Member States by the *same* dominant undertaking for the same product that may amount to an infringement of Art. 82 on grounds of geographical price discrimin-ation: see *infra* 000.

[23] Case 78/70, *Deutsche Grammophon* v. *Metro* [1971] ECR 487, [1971] CMLR 631.

[24] Case 247/86, *Alsatel* v. *Novasam* [1988] ECR 5987, [1990] 4 CMLR 434.

[25] Case 24/67, *Parke, Davis & Co* v. *Probel* [1968] ECR 55, [1968] CMLR 47.

[26] Case 53/87 *CICCRA* v. *Renault* [1988] ECR 6039, [1990] 4 CMLR 265, para. 16.

however, raises serious questions about the value of such rights, If the competition authorities are to look at a cost-price comparison in order to detect excessive pricing they will need to consider the undertaking's past research costs, including research costs which do not result in commercially exploitable products.

The case law therefore reveals neither a clear consistent test for excessive pricing nor any enthusiasm for price regulation.

(ii) LOW PRICES ON THE BUYING SIDE

Although there is as yet little case law on it, it is possible that unfairly low purchase prices may constitute an abuse where the dominant position is on the buying side. *CICCE v. Commission*[27] concerned a complaint about the allegedly low prices paid as licence fees for the showing of films on French television. The Commission dismissed the complaint on the ground that the complainant had produced insufficient evidence but did not deny that low prices *could* constitute an abuse. This may become more of an issue in future, as in several Member States (including the UK) there is disquiet about the power of large retail groups.[28]

C. PREDATORY PRICING

(i) GENERAL

Predatory pricing is the practice whereby an undertaking prices its product so low that competitors cannot live with the price and are driven from the market. Once the competitors are excluded from the market the undertaking is able to increase prices to monopoly levels and recoup its losses. It is objectionable because, although it means low prices in the short term, its effects are to strengthen the power of the dominant undertaking. Competition policy should not be concerned with the exclusion of *less* efficient competitors from the market but the problem with predatory pricing is that it can exclude firms which are *equally efficient* to the predator.

The intractable problem for competition authorities is to identify where robust price competition ends and predatory pricing begins. As one American commentator has stated: '[p]redatory pricing is one of the most daunting subjects confronting nations with competition policies'.[29]

There are different opinions about how often predatory pricing actually occurs. The strategy of the predator is to sacrifice profit-maximization in the short term in order to reap monopoly profits in the long term. Some economists have argued that it is hardly ever a rational business strategy and that it is very, very rare. This view was famously adopted by

---

[27] Case 298/83, *CICCE v. Commission* [1985] ECR 1105, [1986] 1 CMLR 486, upholding the Commission.

[28] The Commission noted the matter in its *XVIth Report on Competition Policy* (Commission, 1986), pts 345–348. And see the report *Buyer Power and its Impact on Competition in the Food Retail Distribution Sector of the European Union*, produced by Dobson Consulting for the Commission, 13 Oct. 1999, and published on the Commission's website.

[29] E. Fox, 'Price Predation—US and EEC: Economics and Values' [1989] *Fordham Corporate Law Institute* 687, 687.

Bork: '[i]t seems unwise . . . to construct rules about a phenomenon that probably does not exist or which, should it exist in very rare cases, the courts would have grave difficulty in distinguishing from competitive price behavior'.[30] Most economists do not take this extreme position and consider that predatory pricing can be a rational strategy where the conditions are right. The conditions are neatly summed up in the following passage.

R.T. Rapp, *Predatory Pricing and Entry Deterring Strategies: the Economics of AKZO* [1986] ECLR 233 pp 234–235.

The right conclusion to draw from the economics of predatory pricing is not that it never happens, but rather that conditions have to be right for it to happen. The true contribution of the sceptics is that they have forced a close examination of the necessary conditions for successful predation.

For an economist to find predatory behaviour, the following elements must be present:

(1) *Evidence of dominant position* Mere market power is not enough. The predator's sales must account for a sizeable fraction of market sales. If not, loss-making prices attract sales from the entire market which makes the strategy unworkably expensive. What is more, eliminating only one of many rivals leads to insufficient gains. All the incumbents stand to benefit from that turn of events and the prior investment by any one of them in loss-making prices never pays off.

The investigation of dominance begins with and depends crucially on a correct definition of the market. Properly defined, a relevant market includes within it all the firms whose production capacity meaningfully constrain the power of the defendant to raise the market price as a monopolist.

(2) *Evidence that recoupment is possible* Generally this means a finding that the conditions of entry in the relevant market are sufficiently unfavourable to allow the predator a period in which to enjoy the fruits of dominant position after the victim has been driven off. If entry is easy, predatory pricing will never pay off and no rational firm will attempt it.

(3) *Evidence of investment in the destruction of a rival* predatory pricing, as we have noted, involves suffering losses in the present where the compensating benefits lie in the destruction of a competitor. *When pricing is the issue the tell-take is charging a price lower than the lowest profitable price a non-predatory, rational firm would charge in competition. . . .*

Each element is a necessary condition of a finding of abuse of a dominant position by predatory behaviour; without all three conditions being met, predation makes no sense. Together the three are sufficient evidence for an economic analyst to draw the conclusion that predation has occurred.

Rapp suggests that for predatory pricing to occur the predator should hold a position of 'super-dominance' in the sense of a very high market share.[31] Another condition is the

---

[30] R. Bork, *The Antitrust Paradox* (Basic Books 1978, reprinted with new introduction and epilogue, Free Press, Macmillan, 1993), 154. This conclusion was based, *inter alia*, on a study in the USA by J. McGee, 'Predatory Price Cutting; The Standard Oil (New Jersey) Case' (1958)1 *Journal of Law and Economics* 137 , described by R.T. Rapp, 'Predatory Pricing and Entry Deterring Strategies: the Economics of AKZO' [1986] *ECLR* 233, n. 1 as 'a work combining exceptionally bad economics and equally bad history' and its influence on US courts as showing 'that bad economic history can have a long, happy life'. For the influence on US courts see *Matsushita Elec. Indust.Co.Ltd* v. *Zenith Radio Corp.*, 475 US 574 (1986), where the Sup. C., having quoted Bork, McGee, and others, said 'for this reason, there is a consensus among commentators that predatory pricing schemes are rarely tried, and even more rarely successful', before rejecting claims of predatory pricing by a cartel.

[31] See also H.Hovenkamp, *Federal Antitrust Policy* (West Publishing, St. Paul, Minn., 1994), 308. For the developing concept of 'super-dominance' in EC law see *supra* Chap. 5 and 323.

existence of barriers to entry. Predatory pricing may, however, itself *constitute* a barrier to entry. Industrial organization theory[32] suggests that the conditions of post-entry competition are a major factor in decisions about market entry and that the presence of a known predator on the market is a disincentive to entry. In this way predatory pricing not only drives out existing competitors, but also repels potential competition. This point should always be borne in mind. It may be easier to deter potential competitors through predatory pricing than to expel existing ones, as incumbents may have incurred sunk costs and have an incentive to remain on the market.

(ii) COST LEVELS

If it is accepted that predatory pricing *does* occur the problem is to identify it. Most predatory pricing theory centres around costs levels. The basic concept of predatory pricing is that a dominant firm prices below cost. The difficulty with this is that a firm's costs are usually difficult to compute and so is the relationship between its costs and prices. Particular problems arise where a firm uses the same production capacity to make different products.

The terminology used is as follows:[33]

Total cost	The total costs of production
Average Total Cost (ATC)	The total costs involved in the production of one unit of output (i.e. total cost divided by the number of units produced)

Total costs are of two kinds:

Fixed costs	Those which do not change with output over a given time period
Variable costs	Those which do change with output
Average Variable Cost	(AVC)The variable costs involved in the production of one unit (i.e. the variable costs added up and divided by the number of units produced)
Marginal cost	The increase in total costs of a firm caused by increasing its output by one extra unit
Short–run Marginal Cost (SRMC)	The marginal cost based on a firm's existing plant and equipment, not on that which would be the most efficient.

Average variable cost is always lower than average total cost.

(iii) THE AREEDA–TURNER TEST

In a seminal *Harvard Law Review* article Areeda and Turner put forward a test for identifying predatory pricing.[34] Under this test a price lower than reasonably anticipated short-run

---

[32] See *supra* Chap.1

[33] See also *supra* Chap. 1 and the Glossary.

[34] P. Areeda and D. Turner, 'Predatory Pricing and Related Practices Under Section 2 of the Sherman Act' (1975) 88 *Harv. L Rev.* 697.

marginal cost is predatory, whilst a price equal to or higher than reasonably anticipated short-run marginal cost is not predatory. 'Reasonably anticipated' means that a firm's conduct is not judged *ex post facto*. The marginal cost is judged by what seemed reasonable at the time. If the SMRC turned out higher than anticipated the firm should not be condemned for predatory pricing.

SRMC is, however, almost impossible to compute in practice, as it is a question of looking back to determine what the firm's marginal cost was during a past period of time. The Areeda–Turner test therefore uses average variable cost (AVC) as a surrogate for SRMC. The test is stated as follows:

A price at or above reasonably anticipated AVC should be conclusively presumed lawful.

A price below reasonably anticipated AVC should be conclusively presumed unlawful.

(iv) PROBLEMS WITH THE AREEDA–TURNER TEST

The formulation of the Areeda–Turner test provoked a lively debate amongst lawyers and economists, especially in the US.[35] Particular criticisms of the test which have been made are:

- SRMC is not the right level from which to measure predatory pricing as some above SRMC -level pricing may also be predatory. One argument is that the test does not accommodate 'limit pricing'[36] where pricing is geared to potential entrants rather than existing competitors;
- AVC is an unsatisfactory substitute for SRMC, because the AVC cost curve tends to be U-shaped and gives the undertaking a lot of room for manœuvre. Marginal cost rises and falls more dramatically than AVC because AVC averages out the cost of one additional unit over the entire output being produced;
- It is difficult to draw a rigid demarcation line between fixed and variable categories (as was demonstrated in the leading EC case, *AKZO*[37]). Classification is dependent upon the industry and the time period in issue. Areeda and Turner recognized this problem and proposed[38] that certain costs should always be considered fixed (interest on debt, depreciation, taxes which do not vary with output);
- In certain markets where AVC (or SRMC) may be minimal (such as intellectual property markets) the test does not work.

Despite the perceived flaws in the test it has been highly influential in antitrust thinking and some version of it is commonly used in US antitrust cases. It formed the basis for the discussion in *AKZO*.

---

[35] See the summary in J. Brodley and D. Hay, 'Predatory Pricing: Competing Economic Theories and the Evolution of Legal Standards' (1981) 66 *Cornell L Rev.* 738.

[36] See *infra* 349.

[37] Case C–62/86 *AKZO Chemie BV* v. *Commission* [1991] ECR I–3359, [1993] 5 CMLR 215, discussed *infra* 336.

[38] P. Areeda and D. Turner: *Antitrust Law* (Little Brown, 1978) para. 715c.

(v) THE *AKZO* CASE

The Commission first considered predatory pricing in *AKZO*.[39]

ECS was a small UK firm based in Epsom and Gloucester which produced benzoyl peroxide. Benzoyl peroxide is used as a catalyst in plastics production and also (in the UK and Ireland) as a bleaching agent in flour-milling. ECS concentrated on the flour sector, where its major customer was Allied Mills. AKZO, a multinational chemicals company also produced benzoyl peroxide but concentrated on the plastics sector. The facts as found by the Commission were that ECS decided to expand its operations in the plastics sector (capturing one of AKZO's largest customers), whereupon AKZO retaliated by threatening to attack ECS's business in the UK flour sector by reducing prices. It then set about supplying benzoyl peroxide to the UK flour sector at low prices, offering large discounts to ECS's best customers. ECS originally obtained an interim injunction in the High Court in London to prevent AKZO from implementing its threats, and those proceedings were terminated by agreement. ECS then complained to the Commission, which first granted interim relief[40] and subsequently adopted a final decision[41] holding that AKZO had abused a dominant position contrary to Article 82.

The Commission found that AKZO was dominant in the organic peroxides market as a whole[42] and had infringed Article 82 by pursuing a course of predation against ECS designed to drive it from the the plastics sector. It fined AKZO ECU 10 million and ordered it to terminate the infringement. The order required AKZO to refrain from offering or applying prices which would result in customers in respect of whose business it was competing with ECS paying prices dissimilar to those applied to comparable customers. The Commission decision finding predation focussed on AKZO's threats[43] and its eliminatory intent. The decision did not lay down specific rules about the point at which low prices become predatory, and abusive.

ECS/AKZO [1985] OJ L374/1, [1986] 3 CMLR 273

Commission

77. The Commission does not accept the argument that the incidence of Article [82] depends entirely on the mechanical application of a *per se* test based on marginal or variable cost. The standard proposed by AKZO based on a static and short-term conception of 'efficiently' takes no account of the broad objectives of EEC competition rules set out in Art 3[(1)(g)] and particularly the need to guard against the impairment of an effective structure of competition in the Common Market. It also fails to take account of the longer-term strategic considerations which may underlie sustained price cutting and which are particularly apparent in the present case. Further it ignores the fundamental importance of the element of discrimination in seeming to permit a dominant manufacturer to recover its full costs from its regular customers while tempting a rival's customers at lower prices. Yet even if the underlying policy considerations of Article [81] and [82] were limited (as

---

[39] *ECS/AKZO* [1985] OJ L374/1, [1986] 3 CMLR 273; on appeal Case C–62/86, *AKZO Chemie BV* v. *Commission* [1991] ECR I–3359, [1993] 5 CMLR 215.

[40] [1983] OJ L252/13, [1983] 3 CMLR 694.

[41] [1985] OJ L374/1, [1986] 3 CMLR 273.

[42] See *supra* Chap. 6 for the market definition aspects of the case.

[43] It uncovered the evidence of these to support ECS's contentions when it conducted a Reg. 17, Art. 14 (3) investigation on AKZO's premises (for Commission investigations, see *infra* Chap. 14).

AKZO argues) to the achievement of short-term efficiency, it is not only the 'less efficient' firms which will be harmed if a dominant firm sells below its total cost but above variable cost. If prices are taken to a level where a business does not cover its total costs, smaller but possibly more efficient firms will eventually be eliminated and the larger firm with the greater economic resources—including the possibility of cross-subsidisation—will survive.

. . .

79. Indeed it is not necessary, in order to achieve the desired long-term goal behind a price cutting campaign, for a dominant firm to go beneath its own total average costs . . . The important element is the rival's assessment of the aggressor's determination to frustrate its expectations, for example as to rate of growth or attainable profit margins, rather than whether or not the dominant firm covers its own costs. There can thus be an anticompetitive object in price cutting whether or not the aggressor sets its prices above or below its own costs (in one or other meaning of the term).

80. The pursuance by a dominant firm of a strategy of eliminating competitors or potential competitors by unfair means differing from normal competition would in principle fall under Article [82] whatever the detailed mode of implementation. It could be manifested not only in pricing policies but also in exclusionary commercial practices such as exclusive requirements contracts or loyalty rebates. A detailed analysis of the alleged aggressor's costs may however be of considerable importance in establishing the reasonableness or otherwise of its pricing conduct as well as the underlying purpose thereof.

There may be circumstances where the exclusionary consequences of a price cutting campaign by a dominant producer are so self-evident that no evidence of intention to eliminate a competitor is necessary. On the other hand, where low pricing could be susceptible of several explanations, evidence of an intention to eliminate a competitor or restrict competition might also be required to prove an infringement. Such evidence may exist in the form of internal documentation of the dominant company pointing to a scheme to damage competitors. In the absence however of direct documentary evidence an exclusionary intention might be inferred from all the circumstances of the case

AKZO appealed to the Court. It argued that it could not be guilty of an abuse since it had not reduced its prices below AVC, and that under the Areeda–Turner test its prices were therefore not predatory. The Court confirmed the Commission's definition of the market and the finding of dominance. It did accept AKZO's arguments that some costs which the Commission had classified as variable were, in this case, fixed. The Court confirmed that AKZO had been guilty of predatory pricing,[44] but set out a more structured, costs-based test for identifying it.

Case C–62/86, *AKZO Chemie BV* v. *Commission* [1991] ECR I–3359, [1993] 5 CMLR 215

The Court of Justice

66. AKZO disputes the relevance of the criterion of lawfulness adopted by the Commission, which it regards as nebulous or at least inapplicable. It maintains that the Commission should have adopted an objective criterion based on its costs.

67. In that respect, it states that the question of the lawfulness of a particular level of prices cannot be separated from the specific market situation in which the prices were fixed. There is no

---

[44] It annulled the Commission's decision in respect of offers made to one particular customer and reduced the fine to ECUs 7.5 million.

abuse if the dominant undertaking endeavours to obtain a optimum selling-price and a positive coverage margin. A price is optimum if the undertaking may reasonably expect that the offer of another price or the absence of a price would produce a less favourable operating profit in the short term. Furthermore, coverage margin is positive if the value of the order exceeds the sum of the variable costs.

68. According to AKZO, a criterion based on an endeavour to obtain an optimal price in the short term cannot be rejected on the grounds that it would jeopardise the viability of the undertaking in the long term. It is only after a certain time that the undertaking in the question could take measures to eliminate the losses or withdraw from a loss-making branch of business. In the meantime the undertaking would have to accept 'optimum orders' in order to reduce its deficit and to ensure continuity of operation.

69. It should be observed that, as the Court held in Case 85/76, *Hoffmann-la Roche* v. *E.C.Commission* [1979] ECR 461, paragraph 91, the concept of abuse is an objective concept relating to the behaviour of an undertaking in a dominant position which is such as to influence the structure of a market where, as a result of the very presence of the undertaking in question, the degree of competition is weakened and through recourse to methods which, different from those which condition normal competition in products or services on the basis of the transactions of commercial operations, has the effect of hindering the maintenance of the degree of competition still existing in the market or the growth of that competition.

70. It follows that Article [82] prohibits a dominant undertaking from eliminating a competitor and thereby strengthening its position by using methods other than those which come within the scope of competition on the basis of quality. From that point of view, however, not all competition by means of price can be regarded as legitimate.

71. Prices below average variable costs (that is to say, those which vary depending on the quantities produced) by means of which a dominant undertaking seeks to eliminate a competitor must be regarded as abusive. A dominant undertaking has no interest in applying such prices except that of eliminating competitors so as to enable it subsequently to raise its prices by taking advantage of its monopolistic position, since each sale generates a loss, namely the total amount of the fixed costs (that is to say, those which remain constant regardless of the quantities produced) and, at least, part of the variable costs relating to the unit produced.

72. Moreover, prices below average total costs, that is to say, fixed costs plus variable costs, but above average variable costs, must be regarded as abusive if they are determined as part of a plan for eliminating a competitor. Such prices can drive from the market undertakings which are perhaps as efficient as the dominant undertakings but which, because of their smaller financial resources, are incapable of withstanding the competition waged against them.

73. These are the criteria that must be applied to the situation in the present case.

74. Since the criterion of legitimacy to be adopted is a criterion based on the costs and strategy of the dominant undertaking itself, AKZO's allegation concerning the inadequacy of the Commission's investigation with regard to the cost structure and the pricing policy of its competitors must be rejected at the outset.

It can be seen from the Court's judgment that the costs-based test it adopted differs significantly from the Areeda–Turner test. The test set out in AKZO states that prices below AVC 'must be regarded as abusive' because there is no profit-maximizing reason for them. The only explanation for them is that they are directed at eliminating competitors. This appears to set out a *presumption*, albeit a very strong one, that pricing below AVC is abusive.[45] The Court went on to hold that above AVC but below ATC prices can also be abusive if they are part of a plan to eliminate competitors (under the Areeda–Turner test there is no predation where prices are above AVC). There appears to be no presumption as to the undertaking's intention, so the onus is on the Commission to prove it.[46] Eliminatory intent was found in *AKZO* from the direct threats and from the price cuts the dominant firm introduced.

The Court did not expressly deal with the situation where prices are at or above ATC. Nor did it say anything *expressly* about the dominant undertaking's possibility of recouping its losses, although it can be argued that it is implicit in paragraph 71.[47]

(vi) PROBLEMS WITH THE CRITERIA LAID DOWN IN AKZO

The test laid down in *AKZO* raises some problems. For example:

- As noted above, when discussing the Areeda–Turner test, costs–based criteria are inherently problematic. It was noted there that AVC is in any case an inadequate substitute for SRMC and that classification of costs can be difficult. In *AKZO* itself the parties submitted to the Court very different calculations of AKZO's costs. The Court stated that 'an item of cost is not fixed or variable by nature' and overruled the Commission's classification of the labour costs as variable rather than fixed. In this case there was no direct correlation between labour costs and quantities produced.[48] The Court gave no guidance on how costs are to be allocated in multi-product firms,[49] nor did it address known problems such as stepwise or semi-variable costs.
- There *are* sometimes rational, non-predatory reasons for pricing under AVC: for example the launch of new lines, obsolete stock clearance, and using continuous production facilities. It may be better for an undertaking to sell temporarily at a loss and make *some* return, than to make none at all. If paragraph 71 of the Court's judgment *does* only set out a presumption then circumstances such as these could be recognized and the presumption rebutted.
- Under the *AKZO* test the intention of the undertaking becomes the crucial factor when prices are in the 'grey' area between AVC and ATC. This part of the test accepts that pricing at that level can be a rational, non-predatory strategy in certain circumstances because the undertaking will be covering the variable costs and at least some part of the fixed costs on every unit sold. However, reliance on intention is problematic, as in one sense all undertakings might be said to intend to eliminate their competitors by the very fact that they are participating in the struggle for custom in the market place. The Court presumably means intending to eliminate competitors by competition which is not on the basis of performance (a better widget, better

---

[45] Although see Case C–333/94P, *Tetra Pak International SA v. Commission* [1996] ECR I–5951, [1997] 4 CMLR 662, discussed *infra* 341–343, where the language of the Court is arguably more absolute.

[46] But see the Commission's attitude in the *Digital Undertaking* (Commission Press Release IP/97/868), *infra* 343.

[47] Fennelly AG argued this in his opinion in *Compagnie Maritime Belge*, see *infra* 343.

[48] Case C–62/86, *AKZO Chemie BV v. Commission* [1991] ECR I–3359, [1993] 5 CMLR 215, para. 90.

[49] In the USA the standard of average incremental cost (where it is assumed that all other products would be produced anyway and account is only taken of the cost added by the product in question) has been used: see *MCI v. AT & T*, 708 F 2d 1081 (7th Circ., 1983).

service etc.), and therefore not, in the words of *Hoffmann-La Roche*, 'normal' competition,[50] but the distinction between 'normal' price competition and predatory pricing is the very thing this test is trying to identify. The formulation 'determined as part of a plan' seems to denote some degree of systematic and deliberate strategy. In *AKZO* the anti-competitive intentions were derived from company documentation, but words may be open to different interpretations and what seemed like an exhortationary address to the troops in the sales department at the time may read like threats of ruthless predatory intent months or years afterwards.[51] *AKZO* itself may make proving intent more difficult as undertakings are now advised to be more careful in what they record.

- The emphasis in *AKZO* is placed on intention, not on effect. It can be argued, however, that the firm which embarks on a process of price-cutting to exclude its rivals *and does not succeed* benefits its customers and harms only itself. In *AKZO* the customers were presumably happy to have the lack of price competition between AKZO and ECS in the flour sector replaced with some robust soliciting of their custom. On the other hand it is not sensible for competition authorities (and courts) to stand back and refuse interim relief while a firm is driven from the market by anti-competitive conduct and, in driving prices below costs, the dominant undertaking may cause harm to competitors short of elimination and cause other distortions in the market which may affect third parties.[52] At the end of the day it is the effect of the predator's behaviour, rather than the intention, which should be the decisive matter.

- The ECJ in *AKZO* did not expressly address the issue of recoupment. The rationality of predatory pricing hinges on the possibility that the predator can recoup its losses i.e. that short-term loss of profitability is more than compensated for by long-run profitability when, after the competitor's exit, the undertaking can raise prices to monopoly level. If there are no barriers to entry to the market the undertaking will not be able to recoup if it is continually having to price low in order to fight off new competitors (although one must remember that predation may constitute a barrier to entry). The Court did not expressly consider whether predation was a plausible strategy for AKZO.[53]

- The rules may need to be different in certain industries. In network industries, common and joint costs are large and cost structures are not the same as in other industries. The Commission accepted this in its Notice on the Application of the Competition Rules to Access Agreements in the Telecommunications Sector, where it said that in the case of telecommunications variable cost may be substantially lower than the price the operator needs to cover the cost of providing the service. The Commission therefore contemplates using long-run average incremental cost (the

---

[50] See the definition of 'abuse' in Case 85/76, *Hoffmann-La Roche* v. *Commission* [1979] ECR 461, [1979] 3 CMLR 211, para. 91; see *supra* Chap. 5.

[51] See e.g. *Napier Brown/British Sugar* [1988] OJ L284/41, [1990] 4 CMLR 196 where an internal memo which said '[i]f we are to succeed in seeing off the Whitworths threat, we MUST attack on all fronts. It is time to get nasty!' did not go down well with the Commission.

[52] See H. Hovenkamp, *Federal Antitrust Policy* (West Publishing, 1998), Chap. 8.

[53] But see Case C–333/94P, *Tetra Pak International SA* v. *Commission* [1996] ECR I–5951, [1997] 4 CMLR 662, *infra* p. 341–343.

cost of each increment of output) as the cost floor for examining predatory pricing in this sector.[54] A Commission official has said that in some high-technology indus-tries the variable cost is near-zero and that the test for predation should therefore be:

whether a company charges a price for goods or services which, although above the average variable cost of providing the specific goods or services for which the price in question is paid, is so low that its overall revenues for all the goods or services in question would be less than its average variable cost of providing them if it sold the same proportion of its output at the same price on a continuing basis, even where no intent to exclude a competitor is proved.[55]

(vii) THE *TETRA PAK II* CASE

The principles laid down in *AKZO* were confirmed and developed in *Tetra Pak II*.[56] *Tetra Pak II* was the case in which the ECJ confirmed that an undertaking could be in a dominant position in one market and in 'special circumstances' abuse that position in another if the markets had 'close associative links'.[57] This idea is particularly relevant to predatory pricing where an undertaking may be able to 'cross-subsidize'—use excess profits from a monopol-ized market to pursue a predatory pricing strategy on a more competitive one. Predatory pricing is usually considered only to be feasible for undertakings which have a higher market share than that required for a mere finding of dominance.[58] Tetra Pak's share of the domin-ated market (aseptic cartons) was over 90 per cent. Cross-subsidization is a complex issue and *Tetra Pak II* barely began to explore it.

In *Tetra Pak II* the Commission imposed a fine of ECU 75 million in respect of various abuses found to have been committed. One of the abuses was that Tetra Pak had engaged in predatory pricing in the non-aseptic carton market. On appeal Tetra Pak argued before the Court that economic theory says predatory pricing is plausible only if losses can be recouped after the competitor's exit. The Commission had not found that it did have a reasonable chance of recoupment: *ergo* it could not be guilty of predation. The Court said that the possibility of recoupment was not a necessary element.

Case C–333/94P, *Tetra Pak International SA* v. *Commission* [1996] ECR I–5951, [1997] 4 CMLR 662

Court of Justice

39. In its fourth plea, Tetra Pak submits that the Court of First Instance erred in law when, at paragraph 150 of the judgment under appeal, it characterised Tetra Pak's prices in the non-aseptic sector as predatory without accepting that it was necessary for that purpose to establish that it had a reasonable prospect of recouping the losses so incurred.

40. Tetra Pak considers that the possibility of recouping the losses incurred as a result of

[54] [1998] OJ C265/2, paras. 114 and 115.

[55] J. Temple Lang (speaking in a personal capacity), 'European Community Antitrust Law: Innovation Markets and High Technology Industries', [1996] *Fordham Corporate Law Institute* 519, 575 n.117.

[56] Case C–333/94P, *Tetra Pak International SA* v. *Commission* [1996] ECR I–5951, [1997] 4 CMLR 662 , confirming Case T–83/91 *Tetra Pak Rausing* v. *Commission* [1994 ECR II–755, [1997] 4 CMLR 726, and Commission decision [1991] OJ L72/1, [1992] 4 CMLR 551.

[57] See *supra* 325–327.

[58] See the extract from Rapp, *supra* 333 for why this is so.

predatory sales is a constitutive element in the notion of predatory pricing. That is clear, it claims, from paragraph 71 of the AKZO judgment. Since, however, both the Commission and the Court of First Instance accept that sales below cost took place only on the non-aseptic markets, on which Tetra Pak was not found to hold a dominant position, it had no realistic chance of recouping its losses later.

41. In AKZO this Court did indeed sanction the existence of two different methods of analysis for determining whether an undertaking has practised predatory pricing. First, prices below average variable costs must always be considered abusive. In such a case, there is no conceivable economic purpose other than the elimination of a competitor, since each item produced and sold entails a loss for the undertaking. Secondly, prices below average total costs but above average variable costs are only to be considered abusive if an intention to eliminate can be shown.

42. At paragraph 150 of the judgment under appeal, the Court of First Instance carried out the same examination as did this Court in AKZO. For sales of non-aseptic cartons in Italy between 1976 and 1981, it found that prices were considerably lower than average variable costs. Proof of intention to eliminate competitors was therefore not necessary. In 1982, prices for those cartons lay between average variable costs and average total costs. For that reason, in paragraph 151 of its judgment, the Court of First Instance was at pains to establish—and the appellant has not criticized it in that regard—that Tetra Pak intended to eliminate a competitor.

43. The Court of First Instance was also right, at paragraphs 189 to 191 of the judgment under appeal, to apply exactly the same reasoning to sales of non-aseptic machines in the United Kingdom between 1981 and 1984.

44. Furthermore, it would not be appropriate, in the circumstances of the present case, to require in addition proof that Tetra Pak had a realistic chance of recouping its losses. It must be possible to penalize predatory pricing whenever there is a risk that competitors will be eliminated. The Court of First Instance found, at paragraphs 151 and 191 of its judgment, that there was a such a risk in this case. The aim pursued, which is to maintain undistorted competition, rules out waiting until such a strategy leads to the actual elimination of competitors.

In paragraph 44 the Court stressed that the important factor in the determination of predation is the risk that competitors will be eliminated. This could be shorthand for saying that once that happened Tetra Pak would be able to raise prices. Economic theory, however, suggests that the possibility of recoupment can only be judged after a thorough analysis of the structure of the market and other factors. In fact, the Court does not say in paragraph 44 that it would *never* be necessary to show the feasibility of recoupment, but only that it would not be appropriate *in the circumstances of the present case*. Those circumstances included the fact that Tetra Pak had a quasi-monopoly and that the alleged predation was on a market distinct from the dominated one. Both factors may have been relevant. The importance of a proper structural analysis where abuse and dominance are on the same market was recognized by a Commission official:[59]

Under a first possibility, the alleged predatory pricing is effected in one single product market by a firm mainly active in that market. In such cases, the analysis of the objection structural conditions under which the predator would be likely to recoup short-term losses over time seem necessary as a

[59] See M. Martinez, 'Some Views on Pricing and EC Competition Policy' at 'Legal Challenges of Pricing' Conference, Norton Rose, London, 7 Dec. 1998, available on the Competition DG's homepage.

supplement to cost-based analysis, whatever the benchmark used (MC, AVC, ATC). The Commission has not had so far the opportunity to have this approach confirmed by the CFI or the Court.

In his Opinion in *Compagnie Maritime Belge* Advocate General Fennelly considered that the possibility of recoupment should be an essential part of the test for predatory pricing.[60] He thought it was implicit in paragraph 71 of the Court's judgment in *AKZO*.[61] In *Compagnie Maritime Belge*, however, the Court did not deal with the point.[62]

(viii) THE *DIGITAL UNDERTAKING*

In *Digital Undertaking*[63] the Commission accepted undertakings from a company alleged to be dominant in the software support services market for its own computer systems. It supplied a 'package' consisting of software support and hardware maintenance together.[64] In the undertakings given by Digital to settle the proceedings it undertook, *inter alia*, to ensure a non-discriminatory and transparent discount policy and that 'all discounted prices will remain above average total costs'. Digital reserved the right to grant non-standard price reductions to meet competition but undertook that they would be proportionate and not foreclose or distort competition. It expressly acknowledged that the Commission could initiate proceedings if in specific cases allowances resulted in service prices below its average total costs. This case shows that the Commission recognizes that even dominant firms must be allowed to 'meet' competition.[65] However, the suggestion that the Commission might initiate proceedings if prices were below ATC does not seem to reflect the Court's judgment in *AKZO*. There was nothing in the undertaking about below ATC prices having to be part of a plan to eliminate competition. The answer may that the Commission was concerned about *selective* price-cutting and that this *would* be practised in order to exclude competitors.[66] Selective price cutting is dealt with further in the following sections.

(ix) SELECTIVE LOW PRICING

As can be seen from *AKZO*, predatory pricing may involve not just across-the-board low prices but price discrimination[67]—targeting the low prices on certain customers so that they are charged less than others for the same product. The cases indicate that in some situations the EC authorities are concerned with low prices which are *not* below cost but which are part of a deliberate plan to eliminate competitors through selective price-cutting. One question is whether it is possible to identify when selective price-cutting constitutes an abuse. The point is important because it affects the extent to which dominant undertakings may *defend* themselves against competition rather than act to *increase* their dominance.

---

[60] Para. 136 of his Opinion in Cases C–395 and 396/96P, *Compagnie Maritime Belge and others* v. *Commission* [2000] 4 CMLR 1076.

[61] See *supra* 338.

[62] Cases C–395 and 396/96P, *Compagnie Maritime Belge and others* v. *Commission* [2000] 4 CMLR 1076.

[63] Commission Press Release IP/97/868; see *supra* Chap. 6.

[64] For the tying aspects of the case see *infra* 373.

[65] See *infra* 343 *et seq.*

[66] As indeed it was in *AKZO* itself. See further, P.Andrews, 'Aftermarket Power in the Computer Services Market: The Digital Undertaking' [1998] *ECLR* 176, 180.

[67] For price discrimination generally, see *infra* 349.

The first relevant case is *Eurofix –Bauco*.[68] In this case the Commission found that the dominant undertaking, Hilti, had lowered its prices in order to tie customers for its nail-guns into buying its consumables also.[69]

Commission

80. The evidence presented shows that Hilti has a policy designed illegally to limit the entry into the market of competitors producing Hilti-compatible nails. On several occasions Hilti singled out some of the main customers of these competitors and offered them especially favourable conditions in order to attract their loyalty, going in certain cases so far as to give away products free of charge. These conditions were selective and discriminatory in that other customers of Hilti buying similar or equivalent quantities did not benefit from these special conditions. The customers of Hilti who did not receive these special offers are discriminated against and effectively bear the cost of the lower prices to other customers. These special offers were not a direct defensive reaction to competitors, but reflected Hilti's pre-established policy of attempting to limit their entry into the market for Hilti-compatible nails. Only a dominant undertaking such as Hilti could carry out such a strategy because it is able, through its market power, to maintain prices to all its other customers unaffected by its selectively discriminatory discounts.

81. An alternative strategy devised by Hilti to illegally limit its competitors' sales is through its carefully orchestrated policy to damage seriously or even eliminate certain of these competitors' main customers. Internal Hilti documentation fully supports Firth's views that its business was singled out in this way, on the one hand by creating difficulties in supplying Firth and by reducing its discount to uneconomic levels, and on the other hand applying the above described favourable and selective discrimination to Firth's customers.

Application of such a policy not only damages the business of Hilti's competitors and their customers directly, but also has a disciplinary and anticompetitive effect on other potential customers for the independents' nails, in that they can be threatened with similar policies which would then discourage them from buying non-Hilti nails.

An aggressive price rivalry is an essential competitive instrument. However, a selectively discriminatory pricing policy by a dominant firm designed purely to damage the business of, or deter market entry by, its competitors, whilst maintaining higher prices for the bulk of its customers, is both exploitive of these other customers and destructive of competition. As such it constitutes abusive conduct by which a dominant firm can reinforce its already preponderant market position. The abuse in this case does not hinge on whether the prices were below costs (however defined—and in any case certain products were given away free). Rather it depends on the fact that, because of its dominance, Hilti was able to offer special discriminatory prices to its competitors' customers with a view to damaging their business, whilst maintaining higher prices to its own equivalent customers.

In this case the Commission was not concerned with the relationship between the under-taking's prices and its costs.[70]

---

[68] *Eurofix-Bauco* [1988] OJ L65/19, [1989] 4 CMLR 677, on appeal (on the dominance issue only) Case T–30/89 *Hilti* v. *Commission* [1991] ECR II–1439, [1992] 4 CMLR 16 and Case C–53/92 P, *Hilti* v. *Commission* [1994] ECR I–666, [1994] 4 CMLR 614.

[69] See *infra* 370.

[70] Although Hilti sought annulment of the Commission decision, this point was not raised in those proceedings (Case T–30/89, *Hilti* v. *Commission* [1991] ECR II–1439, [1992] 4 CMLR 16; Case C–53/92 P *Hilti* v. *Commission* [1994] ECR I–666, [1994] 4 CMLR 614).

In *CEWAL*[71] the Commission found that undertakings in a collective dominant position had engaged in predatory conduct through selective low pricing targeted at a competitor's customers. The undertakings in this case were parties to a liner conference[72] (CEWAL) which was confronted with competition from an independent shipping line (G & C). Among the practices it adopted to counter this threat was the use of so-called 'fighting ships', which were specially designated CEWAL vessels whose sailing dates were close to those of G & C ships. CEWAL dropped the rates on fighting ships to match those of G & C. The Commission condemned this conduct as an abuse of CEWAL's collective dominant position[73] without an analysis of CEWAL's costs. The prices caused the members of CEWAL some revenue losses, but did not appear to have been below their total costs. The shipping lines appealed, *inter alia*, on the grounds that their prices were not an abuse as they were not predatory within the *AKZO* test.

The Commission decision was upheld by the CFI, focussing on CEWAL's intent to eliminate G & C and the possible effect of its actions.[74] The CFI rejected the argument that CEWAL was merely trying to *meet* rather than *beat* the competition and said that its response to the threat from G & C was not reasonable and proportionate.[75] The Commission was therefore justified in holding that the response by CEWAL's members was an abuse of their collective dominant position. In the appeal to the ECJ the shipping lines argued that the CFI 'erred in law in refusing to recognise that a dominant undertaking may, in reaction to price competition from a new undertaking wishing to penetrate the market, devise a plan designed to eliminate that undertaking by using selective price-cutting, so long as the prices it quotes are not abusive, within the definition given by the ECJ in . . . *AKZO* . . . the mere fact that the aim of that price competition was to drive a competitor from the market cannot render legitimate competition lawful'.[76]

Advocate General Fennelly took the view that this was a case of a 'super-dominant' entity setting out to exclude a competitor. In such a situation targeted, selective price cuts designed to eliminate would be an abuse regardless of the relationship of the prices to costs.

[71] *CEWAL* [1993] OJ L34/20, [1995] 5 CMLR 198.

[72] A 'liner conference', according to the UNCTAD Liner Code, is a group of two or more vessel—operators providing international liner services for carrying cargo on a particular route or routes within specified geographical limits, which has an agreement or arrangement within the framework of which they operate under uniform or common freight rates and other agreed conditions. Council Reg. 4056/86, [1986] OJ L378/4, provides a block exemption for liner conferences which, *inter alia*, allows horizontal price-fixing between the members of the conference. As Faull and Nikpay say, 'This is without question the most generous exemption which exists in Community competition law especially as it is unlimited in time and is granted regardless of market shares', (*The EC Law of Competition* (Oxford University Press, 1999), 12.108). Art. 8 of the Reg. provides that an abuse of a dominant position within Art. 82 is prohibited and that the Commission has power to withdraw the benefit of the exemption if the exemption brings about effects which are incompatible with Art. 82. This provision was referred to by the CFI in Cases T–68/89 etc. *Società Italiana Vetro Spa* v. *EC Commission* [1992] ECR II–1403, [1992] 5 CMLR 302, para. 359, as support for interpreting Art. 82 as applying to collective dominance.

[73] For the collective dominance aspects of this case, see *infra* Chap. 11.

[74] Case T–24/93 etc *Compagnie Maritime Belge Transports* v. *Commission* [1996] ECR II–1201, [1997] 4 CMLR 273.

[75] *Ibid.*, para. 148, and see the discussion *supra* in Chap. 5.

[76] Cases C–395 and 396/96P, *Compagnie Maritime Belge and others* v. *Commission*, [2000] 4 CMLR 1076, paras. 96–97.

Cases C–395 and 396/96P, *Compagnie Maritime Belge* v. *Commission* [2000] 4 CMLR 1076

Advocate General Fennelly

137. In all these circumstances, the Court of First Instance committed no error of law in finding that the response of Cewal members to the entrance of G & C was not 'reasonable and proportionate'. To my mind, Article [82] cannot be interpreted as permitting monopolists or quasi-monopolists to exploit the very significant market power which their superdominance confers so as to preclude the emergence either of a new or additional competitor. Where an undertaking, or group of undertakings whose conduct must be assessed collectively, enjoys a position of such overwhelming dominance verging on monopoly, comparable to that which existed in the present case at the moment when G & C entered the relevant market, it would not be consonant with the particularly onerous special obligation affecting such a dominant undertaking not to impair further the structure of the feeble existing competition for them to react, even to aggressive price competition from a new entrant, with a policy of targeted, selective price cuts designed to eliminate that competitor. Contrary to the assertion of the appellants, the mere fact that such prices are not pitched at a level that is actually (or can be shown to be) below total average (or long-run marginal) costs does not, to my mind, render legitimate the application of such a pricing policy.

The ECJ also held that the prices charged were abusive,[77] but its judgment was couched in narrower terms than the wide sweep of the Advocate General's Opinion. It concentrated on the actual situation, i.e. that this was the conduct of a liner conference.

Cases C–395 and 396/96P, *Compagnie Maritime Belge and others* v. *Commission*, judgment 16 March 2000, [2000] 4 CMLR 1076

Court of Justice

111. The third ground of appeal concerns the question whether the alleged abuse, as defined in the contested Decision and the defence, can properly be so characterised.

112. It is settled case-law that the list of abusive practices contained in Article [82] of the Treaty is not an exhaustive enumeration of the abuses of a dominant position prohibited by the Treaty (Case 6/72 *Europemballage and Continental Can* v. *Commission* . . . paragraph 26).

113. It is, moreover, established that, in certain circumstances, abuse may occur if an undertaking in a dominant position strengthens that position in such a way that the degree of dominance reached substantially fetters competition (*Europemballage and Continental Can*, paragraph 26).

114. Furthermore, the actual scope of the special responsibility imposed on a dominant undertaking must be considered in the light of the specific circumstances of each case which show that competition has been weakened (Case C–333/94 P *Tetra Pak* v. *Commission* . . . , paragraph 24).

115. The maritime transport market is a very specialised sector. It is because of the specificity of that market that the Council established, in Regulation No 4056/86,a set of competition rules different from that which applies to other economic sectors. The authorisation granted for an

---

[77] The fines on the shipping lines were, however, annulled for procedural reasons as the Commission had not stated in its Statement of Objections that it intended to impose fines on the individual members: see *infra* Chap. 14.

unlimited period to liner conferences to co-operate in fixing rates for maritime transport is exceptional in light of the relevant regulations and competition policy.

116. It is clear from the eighth recital in the preamble to Regulation No 4056/86 that the authorisation to fix rates was granted to liner conferences because of their stabilising effect and their contribution to providing adequate efficient scheduled maritime transport services. The result may be that, where a single liner conference has a dominant position on a particular market, the user of those services would have little interest in resorting to an independent competitor, unless the competitor were able to offer prices lower than those of the liner conference.

117. It follows that, where a liner conference in a dominant position selectively cuts its prices in order deliberately to match those of a competitor, it derives a dual benefit. First, it eliminates the principal, and possibly the only, means of competition open to the competing undertaking. Secondly, it can continue to require its users to pay higher prices for the services which are not threatened by that competition.

118. It is not necessary, in the present case, to rule generally on the circumstances in which a liner conference may legitimately, on a case by case basis, adopt lower prices than those of its advertised tariff in order to compete with a competitor who quotes lower prices, or to decide on the exact scope of the expression 'uniform or common freight rates' in Article 1 (3) (b) of Regulation No 4056/86.

119. It is sufficient to recall that the conduct at issue here is that of a conference having a share of over 90% of the market in question and only one competitor. The appellants have, moreover, never seriously disputed, and indeed admitted at the hearing, that the purpose of the conduct complained of was to eliminate G & C from the market.

120. The Court of First Instance did not, therefore, err in law, in holding that the Commission's objections to the effect that the practice known as 'fighting ships', as applied against G & C, constituted an abuse of a dominant position were justified. It should also be noted that there is no question at all in this case of there having been a new definition of an abusive practice.

121. The grounds of appeal concerning fighting ships must therefore be rejected as inadmissible or unfounded.

The Court stated that the 'special responsibility' of dominant undertakings has to be considered in the light of the circumstances in each case (paragraph 114) citing *Tetra Pak II* . However, it confined its remarks thereafter to the facts of the case and stressed the specialized nature of the maritime transport sector (paragraph 115).[78] In that context selective price-cutting deliberately made in order to meet the prices of the only competitor was an abuse. The Court expressly declined to say (paragraph 118) when a liner conference *could* legitimately drop its prices from its advertised tariff in order to compete with a competitor, let alone to say when this is *generally* permissible. The general question posed by the case, i.e. when is above-cost price competition, designed to eliminate a new competitor, illegitimate, remains unanswered. However, it should be noted that in paragraph 119 the Court remarked that the conference had over 90 per cent of the market, and its comments about liner conferences in paragraphs 116–117, read with the reference to *Tetra Pak II*, confirm that undertakings in a monopolistic or quasi–monopolistic position do have a particularly heavy responsibility towards the competitive process.

---

[78] And thus the liner conference had already been given a lot of leeway by the competition rules in the shape of Reg. 4056/86, [1986] OJ L378/4.

Selective price cutting arose again in the Commission decision, *Irish Sugar*.[79] Irish Sugar was the sole producer of sugar beet in Ireland and Northern Ireland. It reacted to increasing imports from other Member States by a variety of pricing practices.[80] In particular it dropped its prices to customers identified as most vulnerable to the imports although the reductions do not seem to have taken prices below total cost. As in *CEWAL* the Commission held that the conduct was abusive because of the intent to exclude competition (shown by company documents) and the selective, targeted nature of the price cuts. Again, the undertaking appealed to the CFI on the grounds that it was only defending its position as it was entitled to do, and that its pricing policy could not be considered an abuse.

Case T–228/97, *Irish Sugar plc* v. *Commission*, judgment 7 October 1999 [1999] 5 CMLR 1300

Court of First Instance

111. The case law shows that an 'abuse' is an objective concept referring to the behaviour of an undertaking in a dominant position which is such as to influence the structure of a market where, as a result of the very presence of the undertaking in question, the degree of competition is already weakened and which, through recourse to methods different from those governing normal competition in products or services on the basis of the transactions of commercial operators, has the effect of hindering the maintenance of the degree of competition still existing in the market or the growth of that competition (*Hoffman-La Roche*, paragraph 91 . . .) It follows that Article [82] of the Treaty prohibits a dominant undertaking from eliminating a competitor and thereby reinforcing its position by having recourse to means other than those within the scope of competition on the merits. From that point of view, not all competition on price can be regarded as legitimate (*AKZO*, paragraph 70 . . .). The prohibition laid down in Article [82] is also justified by the consideration that harm should not be caused to consumers (*Continental Can*, paragraph 26; *Suiker Unie*, paragraphs 526 and 527 . . .).

112. Therefore, whilst the finding that a dominant position exists does not in itself imply any reproach to the undertaking concerned, it has a special responsibility, irrespective of the causes of that position, not to allow its conduct to impair genuine undistorted competition on the Common Market (*Michelin* paragraph 57 . . .). Similarly, whilst the fact that an undertaking is in a dominant position cannot deprive it of its entitlement to protect its own commercial interests when they are attacked, and whilst such an undertaking must be allowed the right to take such reasonable steps as it deems appropriate to protect those interests, such behaviour cannot be allowed if its purpose is to strengthen that dominant position and thereby abuse it (*United Brands*, paragraph 189; *BPB Industries*, paragraph 69; Case 83/91 *Tetra Pak II*, paragraph 147; Case T–24/93 *CMB*, paragraph 107 . . .).

. . .

189. Thus, even if the existence of a dominant position does not deprive an undertaking placed in that position of the right to protect its own commercial interests when they are threatened (see paragraph 112 above), the protection of the commercial position of an undertaking in a dominant position with the characteristics of that of the applicant at the time in question must, at the very least, in order to be lawful, be based on criteria of economic efficiency and consistent with the

---

[79] [1997] OJ L258/1, [1997] 5 CMLR 666 .

[80] See further in the discussion of discriminatory pricing and rebates and discounts, *infra* 356.

interests of consumers. In this case, the applicant has not shown that those conditions were fulfilled.

It should be noted that this case concerned, once again, an undertaking with a very high market share. In paragraph 189 the CFI specifically refers to an undertaking 'with the characteristics of that of the applicant at the time in question' and relates the abuse to that. It is clear from this judgment at least that the ability of 'super-dominant' undertakings to react to encroachments on their market position is limited, and that they have to act in a way 'based on criteria of economic efficiency' and consistent with consumers' interests.

(x) LIMIT PRICING

There is as yet no Community jurisprudence on what is known as 'limit pricing'. Neither the Areeda–Turner test nor the *AKZO* test makes any reference to limit pricing, which is a form of strategic entry deterrence aimed at potential entrants rather than existing competitors. It can occur when the dominant undertaking creates excess capacity and uses this to deter entrants without ever lowering its price below ATC, for if entry is attempted the dominant firm can increase its production and lower its price without going below cost.[81]

(xi) TRANSFORMATION COSTS AND 'PRICE SQUEEZING'

Where an undertaking operates in both upstream and downstream markets it should not charge prices in the upstream market which mean that its competitors are unable to operate profitably downstream. It is a matter of looking at the margin between the two prices. In *Napier Brown-British Sugar*[82] the Commission held that British Sugar abused its dominant position in the upstream, industrial sugar, market. British Sugar also operated in the downstream, retail sugar, market but the margin between its two prices was below its own repackaging and selling costs. Its competitor in the retail market, Napier Brown, which was dependant on British Sugar for its supplies, could not therefore viably operate. The Commission considered this part of a deliberate strategy to force Napier Brown out of the market.

D. PRICE DISCRIMINATION

(i) GENERAL[83]

Price discrimination occurs where the same commodity is sold at different prices to different customers[84] despite identical costs, i.e. the sales have different ratios of price to marginal cost. It also covers sales at the same price despite different costs. Price discrimination covers

---

[81] For the economics of this, see F M Scherer and D. Ross, *Industrial Market Structure and Economic Performance* (3rd edn., Houghton & Mifflin, 1993), Chap. 4.

[82] [1988] OJ L284/41, [1990] 4 CMLR 196.

[83] See Scherer and Ross, *supra* n. 81, Chap. 13; L. Phlips, *The Economics of Price Discrimination* (Cambridge University Press, 1983).

[84] See Phlips, n. 83, 5.

a wide range of practices. As seen above, excessive pricing and predatory pricing may involve price discrimination.

Price discrimination is described as persistent when a supplier maintains a policy of obtaining a higher rate of return from some customers than from others. The ability to practise persistent price discrimination is a characteristic of market power. In a competitive market the customers who are 'disfavoured', i.e. charged the higher price, will be able to take their custom elsewhere. The fact that an undertaking can persistently discriminate against some customers shows that it is difficult or impossible for them to change suppliers. Price discrimination occurs in competitive markets too, as suppliers respond to events in the market, but it is only *sporadic*, i.e. it changes frequently and customers may be in a favoured group today and a disfavoured one tomorrow.

All customers have a 'reservation' 'price', the maximum price they will pay for the product.[85] In *perfect price discrimination* the dominant supplier would charge each customer his reservation price. In the real world this can rarely happen. The supplier can only practise *imperfect* price discrimination whereby he identifies different *groups* of customers with similar reservation prices and charges each group differently.

Price discrimination works only if arbitrage is not possible or feasible. Arbitrage is where the customers trade amongst themselves, which means the customers charged the lowest prices selling on to those charged more. There will be no incentive to do this if the difference in prices charged is not sufficient to recompense the selling customer for the transport, administrative, or other costs involved in selling on. In some cases arbitrage is not possible. In *United Brands*,[86] for example, it was difficult to transport bananas, a highly delicate and perishable product, between Member States.

Article 82 expressly refers to discriminatory pricing, as an example of an abuse in Article 82 (c):

applying dissimilar conditions to equivalent transactions with other trading parties, thereby placing them at a competitive disadvantage.

'Equivalent transactions' refers to the idea that price discrimination involves different prices for the same thing. However, the elements which make up a transaction may be complex and identifying equivalence can be difficult. Is the sale of a train ticket for a journey during the weekday rush-hour equivalent to the sale of a ticket for the same journey on a Sunday morning? The Court and Commission have often assumed that transactions are equivalent without a great deal of analysis.[87]

Price discrimination may involve primary line or secondary line injury. Primary line injury prejudices the supplier's competitors. Secondary line injury causes distortions in competition in downstream markets, between the supplier's customers or third parties *inter se*. The EC cases have concentrated on primary line injury, although there are some examples where the Commission has intervened to protect customers from the actions of a statutory monopolist as those who were charged higher prices suffered a competitive

---

[85] See *supra* Chap. 1.

[86] Case 27/76, *United Brands* v. *Commission* [1978] ECR 207, [1978] 1 CMLR 429; see *infra* 352.

[87] E.g., railway traffic via German ports and via Belgian and Dutch ones (Case T–229/94 *Deutsche Bahn AG* v. *Commission* [1997] ECR II–1689, [1998] 4 CMLR 220, upheld on appeal, Case C–436/97 *Deutsche Bahn AG* v. *Commission* [1999] 5 CMLR 776) and transactions with exclusive and non-exclusive customers (in the loyalty rebate cases, see *infra* 358).

disadvantage.[88] It seems from the case law, however, that discriminatory pricing may be found to constitute an abuse even if nobody is put at a competitive disadvantage: in *United Brands*, where the customers did not compete with one another, the Court paid no attention to this issue. This is unfortunate, as economic theory suggests that price discrimination can be welfare-enhancing. Simply to condemn it as 'unfair' is simplistic, as Bishop explains below:

W. Bishop, 'Price Discrimination under Article 86: Political Economy in the European Court' (1981) 44 *MLR* 282, 286–8

Economists judge efficiency or economic welfare primarily against the standard of perfect competition. Under certain stringent conditions, production by competing firms will lead to an allocation of society's productive resources to various productive activities in a way that is 'optimal.' . . . Just the 'right' amount of each good will be produced in the sense that any different arrangement would leave some people worse off. When production in one industry is monopolistic then the monopolist will seek to maximise his profits by charging a higher price than perfect competitors could charge. At this higher price his customers will buy less and so the monopolist produces less than the combined production of the perfectly competitive firms.

Both the neoclassical economist and the plain man condemn monopoly, but their reasons differ sharply. The plain man is likely to object to monopoly for two reasons. First, the monopolist's customers pay higher prices. Secondly, some people who would be buyers at competitive prices do not buy under monopoly because the price is too high, and hence monopoly output is lower than perfectly competitive output. Here there is cleavage between standards of the plain man and those of the economist. The economist agrees only with the second of the plain man's reasons: that output is lower. He reasons that resources which could and should be used to produce this good are under monopoly directed elsewhere, even though some customers would be willing to 'hire' those resources if a perfectly competitive price prevailed. The plain man's first reason, higher price, does not in itself attract criticism from the economist. Customers pay higher prices, but that is merely a wealth transfer from the customer to employees or shareholders of the firm. It is a loss to customers but a gain to employees or shareholders, and economists as social scientists have no ground for preferring one group to the other. By contrast where output is reduced below the optional point this deprives some potential customers of the benefit of the good, but this happens without any compensating gain to anyone. So long as more goods are better than fewer, this is an unambiguously bad result for society. The economist can safely condemn it as inefficient and still preserve his impartiality. . . .

This difference between the standards of the plain man and those of the economist is critical for assessing the effect of price discrimination on economic efficiency. Since the economist is indifferent to wealth transfers he need ask only about the effect on output of a monopolist's practising of price discrimination. If a monopolist were able to charge each customer exactly that customer's maximum price, then the monopolist would realise very large profits, but output would be identical to that under perfect competition with not a single sale being sacrificed because of higher price. This is called perfectly discriminating monopoly and is very rare, perhaps non-existent.

Much more important is imperfect price discrimination—different prices in a number of different markets or for different classes of customers. It is very common. British Rail for example

---

[88] As in *Deutsche Bahn supra* n. 87, and in *Alpha Flight Services* v. *Aéroports de Paris* [1998] OJ L 230/10, [1998] 5 CMLR 611, where the airport authority at Orly and Charles de Gaulle in Paris charged different levels of fees without objective justification to companies it licensed to provide groundhandling services, so handicapping the company which had to pay the higher fees.

discriminates by offering special discounts to students for no reason other than that most of them would not travel by train otherwise, and a little more revenue is better than none at all when it costs virtually nothing to carry an extra passenger outside peak hours.

In *United Brands* the court condemned imperfect price discrimination when practised on a regional basis so as to divide the common market into a number of sub-markets with different, discriminatory prices. However it is not at all clear that imperfect price discrimination generally reduces output below the level that would prevail under simple monopoly. Whether output under imperfectly discriminatory monopoly is nearer the perfectly competitive or further from it will depend upon the facts of each case. Unfortunately in any real case the relevant facts are extremely difficult to ferret out—in practice usually impossible to ascertain at all.

Moreover, as several economists have demonstrated, it is conceivable that price discrimination in practice may reduce economic efficiency, *i.e.* increase the misallocation of money and resources, even if it increases output as compared with output in the absence of discrimination. . . . Probably the best we can do is to adopt one general rule on price discrimination. Many economists guess that price discrimination is probably on balance efficient, assuming there will be monopoly pricing anyway. . . . Certainly there is no reason to suppose that a rule prohibiting it will promote more efficient allocation of resources. Furthermore it is clear that enforcing the prohibition will lead both enforcers and defendants to incur costs that consume real social resources. In the absence of any empirical evidence on the actual effects of price discrimination a rational, efficiency based system of competition law would not adopt the general rule in *United Brands*. So efficiency cannot be the justification for the decision.

Price discrimination by dominant undertakings has been held to infringe Article 82 in many cases. *United Brands*, to which Bishop refers, dealt with geographical price discrimination, as we see in the next section.

(ii) GEOGRAPHICAL PRICE DISCRIMINATION

Geographical price discrimination means charging different prices for the same products or services in different geographical territories. It is more of an issue in EC competition law than in national systems because its most obvious form—different prices in different Member States—may be contrary to the objectives of market integration and not just a competition issue. Artificial price differences across the Community should be eliminated or reduced by arbitrage and parallel trade, but this may be impeded by other factors. If these factors are measures taken by the dominant undertaking to buttress the pricing policy the prices will be an abuse in themselves and the buttressing measures are also likely to infringe Article 82. In both leading cases on geographical price discrimination, *United Brands*[89] and *Tetra Pak II*,[90] the dominant undertaking was found to have taken measures to prevent parallel trade.

Case 27/76, *United Brands* v. *Commission* [1978] ECR 207, [1978] 1 CMLR 429

United Brands shipped its bananas across the Atlantic and unloaded them at Rotterdam and Bremerhaven. At those ports it sold them to its approved ripener/distributors from various Member States at different prices. The prices reflected the different prices in the retail markets in the Member States. The contractual conditions under which the bananas were sold contained a prohibition on the

[89] Case 27/76, United Brands v. *Commission* [1978] ECR 207, [1978] 1 CMLR 429.
[90] Case C–333/94P, *Tetra Pak International SA* v. *Commission* [1996] ECR I–5951, [1997] 4 CMLR 662.

distributors reselling the bananas while they were still green (the 'green banana' clause). The Commission concluded that this clause was simply a tactic to reinforce the price differences because once the bananas had started to turn yellow they were so perishable that it was not possible to export them to other Member States. The Commission also found that United Brands' practice of supplying the distributors with less than they ordered made them sell locally instead of in other markets. The Commission held that these practices infringed Article 82. United Brands appealed.[91]

Court of Justice

204. All the bananas marketed by UBC under the brand name 'Chiquita' on the relevant market have the same geographic origin, belong to the same variety (Cavendish Valery) and are of almost the same quality.

205. They are unloaded in two ports, Rotterdam and Bremerhaven, where unloading costs only differ by a few cents in the dollar per box of 20 kilogrammes, and are resold, except to Scipio and in Ireland, subject to the same conditions of sale and terms of payment after they have been loaded on the buyer's wagons or lorries, the price of a box amounting on average to between 3 and 4 dollars and going up to 5 dollars in 1974.

206. The costs of carriage from the unloading ports to the ripening installations and the amount of any duty payable under the Common Customs Tariff are borne by the purchaser except in Ireland.

207. This being so all those customers going to Rotterdam and Bremerhaven to obtain their supplies might be expected to find that UBC offers them all the same selling price for 'Chiquita' bananas.

208. The Commission blames the applicant for charging each week for the sale of its branded bananas—without objective justification—a selling price which differs appreciably according to the Member State where its customers are established.

209. This policy of charging differing prices according to the Member States for which bananas are intended has been applied at least since 1971 in the case of customers of the Federal Republic of Germany, the Netherlands and the BLEU and was extended in January 1973 to customers in Denmark and in November 1973 to customers in Ireland.

. . .

227. Although the responsibility for establishing the single banana market does not lie with the applicant, it can only endeavour to take 'what the market can bear' provided that it complies with the rules for the regulation and co-ordination of the market laid down by the Treaty.

228. Once it can be grasped that differences in transport costs, taxation, customs duties, the wages of the labour force, the conditions of marketing, the differences in the parity of currencies, the density of competition may eventually culminate in different retail selling price levels according to the Member States, then it follows those differences are factors which UBC only has to take into account to a limited extent since it sells a product which is always the same and at the same place to ripener/distributors who—alone—bear the risks of the consumer's market.

229. The interplay of supply and demand should, owing to its nature, only be applied to each stage where it is really manifest.

230. The mechanisms of the market are adversely affected if the price is calculated by leaving out one stage of the market and taking into account the law of supply and demand as between the vendor

---

[91] United Brands also appealed against the finding that the relevant market was bananas and that it was dominant in the Member States in issue. See *supra* Chap. 6.

and the ultimate consumer and not as between the vendor (UBC) and the purchaser (the ripener/distributor).

231. Thus, by reason of its dominant position UBC, fed with information by its local representatives, was in fact able to impose its selling price on the intermediate purchaser. This price and also the 'weekly quota allocated' is only fixed and notified to the customer four days before the vessel carrying the bananas berths.

232. These discriminatory prices, which varied according to the circumstances of the Member States, were just so many obstacles to the free movement of goods and their effect was intensified by the clause forbidding the resale of bananas while still green and by reducing the deliveries of the quantities ordered.

233. A rigid partitioning of national markets was thus created at price levels, which were artificially different, placing certain distributor/ripeners at a competitive disadvantage, since compared with what it should have been competition had thereby been distorted.

234. Consequently the policy of differing prices enabling UBC to apply dissimilar conditions to equivalent transactions with other trading parties, thereby placing them at a competitive disadvantage, was an abuse of a dominant position.

This part of the *United Brands* judgment contains some unconvincing reasoning which has been savagely criticized.

W. Bishop, 'Price Discrimination under Article 86: Political Economy in the European Court' (1981) 44 *MLR* 282 at 284–286[92]

Supply and demand

The 'law of supply and demand' referred to in [229] is a 'law' of economics in the sense that the fundamental theorem of micro-economics is that price is determined by supply of and demand for a good. This theorem has been empirically confirmed as having considerable predictive power. It is a descriptive law and not a prescriptive or normative one. What can be meant by the statement that firms in setting prices should only 'apply' the law 'to each stage where it is really manifest'? To speak of applying a descriptive law is odd. Surely the court has not made the elementary blunder of confusing descriptive and prescriptive concepts of law?

The court seems to have thought that when a producer faces separate regional markets, and consumer demand is stronger in one than in the other, then this demand is 'really manifest' only in the retail market and not in the wholesale market. But this is in fact wrong. Demand in the retail market will be transmitted by retailers through implicit or explicit bids for various price and quantity combination in the wholesale and ripener-distributor markets. It truly will be, 'really manifest' in those markets.

The court might have meant by this strange language to say that a firm should set its prices at the same level as it would if it faced keen competition. Alternatively the court might have meant to say that a producer should behave as if there were one market where no price discrimination is possible. If the court intended either of these it should have said so clearly. To call either 'applying the law of supply and demand' is a travesty of language and is pregnant with confusion for the future.

---

[92] See also L. Zanon, 'Price Discrimination under Art. 82 of the EEC Treaty: A Comment on the UBC Case' (1982) 31 *ICLQ* 36; M. Siragusa, 'The Application of Art. 86 to the Pricing Policy of Dominant Companies: Discriminatory and Unfair Prices' (1979) 16 *CMLRev.* 179.

Bearing risks

The court said that in setting prices the firm should take into account different retail demand conditions in different markets to only a 'limited extent,' since UBC did not 'bear the risks of the consumers' market.' This reasoning is wholly novel and wholly bad. The test of 'bearing risks' is misconceived in principle, undesirable in its consequences and misapplied on the facts before the court.

The existence of risk in retailing may lead to a level of normal profit to each retailer that is higher or lower than in other industries, because risk is different. This may happen if investors are risk averse over the relevant range . . . The court seems to regard monopoly profit as a reward of risk. That is an error. Many risky industries are competitive and many non-risk ones are monopolistic.

Confusion is bad enough. Worse follows from use of the 'bearing the risks' criterion. Why should a firm be allowed to consider demand conditions if it is a retailer, or combines both manufacturing and retaining, but not if it is only manufacturer? Apparently a vertically integrated firm can use differential pricing because its wholesaling or retailing division 'bears risks'. This creates an incentive for a manufacturer to integrate an industry vertically. This is an artificial incentive that will have costly effects and consume resources. It will be attractive to firms intent on harvesting some part of those monopoly profits, derived from discrimination, of which the *United Brands* judgment seeks to deprive them. In future a manufacturer may find it profitable to undertake local distribution himself so that he can claim to be 'bearing risks'—even if the net cost of distributing himself is higher than selling to local distributors. This is inefficiency created solely by legal decision. Furthermore no one, neither consumers nor anyone else, benefits. It is pure waste.

Even if the consideration of 'bearing risks' were not irrelevant or undesirable, the criterion was misapplied by the court. On the facts UBC probably did bear all the risks of changes in demand in consumer markets. It did not sell to ripeners at prices and quantities fixed long in advance, but announced weekly prices a few days before the ships were due. Even if UBC had wished to shift to its dealers all the risks from time of shipment it would probably have been unable to sell such long term forward contracts profitably, because ripeners are probably not as well placed as UBC to assess changes in retail market conditions and would therefore have to be given price inducements to enter long term contracts. Also ripeners were probably less liquid and more risk averse than UBC. Ripeners bore risks only for a very short period and even then UBC may have been the real risk bearer. For if a contract of sale turned out badly for a ripener, UBC would probably find it too costly to hold a ripener to that contract since his bankruptcy would deprive UBC of continuity of outlet. . . .

The real Community objection to the price discrimination in *United Brands* was of course that it offended against the concept of the single market.

In *Tetra Pak II* the Commission found wide disparities in the prices that Tetra Pak charged for its milk packaging machinery and cartons in different Member States despite the fact that the geographical market was Community-wide. It held these prices differences to be due to artificial partitioning of the market and not to objective market conditions.[93] The decision was upheld by the CFI, which found that 'those disparities in price could not be attributed to objective market conditions'.[94]

Whether or not geographical price discrimination is an abuse in the absence of measures

---

[93] E.g., customers for the machines could purchase cartons only from Tetra Pak itself or a company designated by it, and so customers in high price countries were not free to purchase from third parties in lower price areas.

[94] Case T–83/91 *Tetra Pak Rausing* v. *Commission* [1994] ECR II–755, [1997] 4 CMLR 726, para. 170. Tetra Pak did not appeal the geographical price discrimination point to the ECJ.

taken by the dominant undertaking to partition the separate geographical areas is less clear. In *Tetra Pak II* the CFI reiterated that setting different prices could be justified by local conditions. In *United Brands*, however, local conditions did not justify variations in retail prices. This suggests that once the Member States are held to be in the same geographic market and costs are the same, objective justification for price discrimination between them will be hard to prove.[95]

What has been described as a 'peculiar form of geographical price discrimination'[96] was condemned in *Irish Sugar*.[97] The dominant undertaking operated a system of 'sugar export rebates', granted on sales of industrial sugar to companies exporting to other Member States. The Commission found that this practice discriminated against customers of industrial sugar supplying the domestic Irish market. The CFI upheld the Commission's finding that this was an abuse, holding that market mechanisms were distorted by pricing according to the location of the customers' buyers. It did not accept that the non-export customers were not put at a competitive disadvantage.[98]

(iii) DISCOUNT AND REBATE SCHEMES[99]

a. GENERAL DISTINCTION BETWEEN NON-ABUSIVE AND ABUSIVE DISCOUNTS

The granting of discounts and rebates (the terms are used synonymously) is a common fact of commercial life and a major way in which suppliers compete on price and try to attract customers to themselves and away from competitors. The ability to grant discounts is not a characteristic of market power, but the case law on Article 82 establishes that where undertakings *are* dominant their discounting policies will be severely constrained. This is a classic case of the difficult line between 'normal' competition and abusive conduct.

The concern of the Commission and the Court over discount policies has concentrated on the primary line injury they are perceived to cause. Such policies have been held to foreclose the market and make it more difficult for smaller competitors to compete. The basic distinction made in the cases is between discounts relating to objective amounts (such as ten widgets for the price of nine) offered on equal terms to all customers without discrimination, and other types of discount. In the *Tetra Pak II*[100] decision the Commission ordered Tetra Pak not to practise predatory or discriminatory prices:. '[t]hus, discounts on cartons should be granted solely according to the quantity of each order'. In *Irish Sugar* the CFI summed up the approach of EC competition law to pricing policies:[101]

the case law shows that, in determining whether a pricing policy is abusive, it is necessary to consider all the circumstances, particularly the criteria and rules governing the grant of the discount, and to investigate whether, in providing an advantage not based on any economic service justifying it, the

---

[95] See J. Faull and A. Nikpay, (eds.), *The EC Law of Competition* (Oxford University Press, 1999) para. 3.329.

[96] *Ibid.*, para. 3.331.

[97] [1997] OJ L258/1, [1997] 5 CMLR 666.

[98] Case T–228/97, *Irish Sugar plc* v. *Commission* [1999] 5 CMLR 1300, paras. 140–149.

[99] See M. Waelbroeck, 'Price Discrimination and Rebate Policies under EU Competition Law' [1995] *Fordham Corporate Law Institute*, 147.

[100] *Elopak Italia/Tetra Pak* [1991] OJ L72/1, [1992] 4 CMLR 55.

[101] Case T–228/97, *Irish Sugar plc* v. *Commission* [1999] 5 CMLR 1300, para. 114.

discount tends to remove or restrict the buyer's freedom to choose his sources of supply, to bar competitors from access to the market, to apply dissimilar conditions to equivalent transaction with other trading parties or to strengthen the dominant position by distorting competition (*Hoffman-La Roche*, paragraph 90; *Michelin*, paragraph 73). The distortion of competition arises from the fact that a financial advantage granted by the undertaking in a dominant position is not based on any economic consideration justifying it, but tends to prevent the customers of that dominant undertaking from obtaining their supplies from competitors (*Michelin*, paragraph 71). One of the circumstances may therefore consist in the fact that the practice in question takes place in the context of a plan by the dominant undertaking aimed at eliminating a competitor (*AKZO*, paragraph 72, Case T–24/93 *Compagnie Maritime Belge*, paragraphs 147 and 148).

b. QUANTITY DISCOUNTS

The usual justification for quantity discounts is that they reflect the supplier's costs savings. In *Irish Sugar*[102] the Commission described quantity discounts as 'normally unobjectionable' and said they are 'normally paid in respect of individual orders (i.e. unrelated to the customer's purchases over a period of time) and in return for costs savings achieved by the supplier'. The question of costs savings arose in *BPB Industries*.[103] BPB, through its subsidiary British Gypsum (BG), supplied plasterboard in the UK and Ireland. From 1982 onwards it faced increasing competition from imports from France and Spain and the importers complained to the Commission about the pricing practices BG adopted. The Commission held that BPB/BG was dominant in the plasterboard market in the UK and Ireland. One of the practices it considered was BG's introduction of a 'Super Schedule A' discount whereby all customers (builders merchants) in Hampshire and Dorset were offered special discounts for plasterboard delivered in particularly large lorry loads. The discount was greater than the costs savings actually made.

BPB Industries [1989] OJ L10/50, [1990] 4 CMLR 464

Commission

131. From August 1984 to April 1987, BG operated a scheme of discounts for merchants buying in large loads, in a limited geographical area, the counties of Hampshire and Dorset, where BG was facing particular price competition from Lafarge. Though initially designed, at least in part, as a test exercise to gain experience in the delivery of larger loads than previously, the scheme was subsequently maintained as a competitive measure. Only a part of the price reduction by BG was offset by the cost savings which were actually made. Another part of the price reduction corresponded to additional savings which might have been made had the scheme been operated nationally. This part may therefore be regarded as objectively justified during the initial experimental phase.

132. In any event, the part of the price reduction which was not objectively justified, whether in the initial phase or later, amounted to a small price reduction. Furthermore, the offer was open to all customers albeit, in a fairly limited geographical area. In the area, BPB was facing competition from relatively lower zone prices charged by Lafarge or low prices charged by Lafarge to certain large customers.

133. There has been no suggestion that the Super Schedule A prices were in themselves predatory,

---

102 [1997] OJ L258/1, [1997] 5 CMLR 666 at para. 153.
103 *BPB Industries* [1989] OJ L10/50, [1990] 4 CMLR 464.

nor that they were part of any scheme of systematic alignment. There was a single price reduction to a level broadly equivalent to or slightly below those of Lafarge until April 1985, when Lafarge increased its prices.

134. On the basis of the matters stated above and the arguments presented by BG during the procedure on these points, the Commission concludes that BG's geographically selective Super Schedule A prices in Hampshire and Dorset did not constitute an abuse of BG's dominant position.

It is notable here that the part of the price reduction which was *not* objectively justified was not, on the facts, held to be an abuse, although the reasons for this are unclear.[104] This should be regarded as exceptional: the Commission will usually expect costs savings before it finds that the discount does not infringe Article 82.[105]

c. LOYALTY (FIDELITY) REBATES

Loyalty (or fidelity) rebates are discounts given to a customer as a reward for loyalty to the supplier. They are given not because the customer has bought a certain objective *amount* from the supplier but because he has not bought from others. Dominant undertakings which grant loyalty rebates will infringe Article 82 because they are considered unjustifiably to tie the customer to the dominant undertaking and so have an exclusionary effect on competitors. They are also discriminatory and cause secondary line injury in that customers buying the same amounts from the dominant supplier pay different prices. The Court and Commission have concentrated on the former objection and stressed the exclusionary effect of loyalty rebates. In *Hoffmann-La Roche*[106] the Court upheld the Commission's decision without considering whether the customers were put at a competitive disadvantage by the discounting practice. Nor did it consider whether transactions with exclusive customers and non-exclusive customers really are 'equivalent' to one another.

Loyalty rebates may be given in return for a contractual obligation on the part of the customer to buy all its requirements of the product from the dominant undertaking. Such an exclusive supply obligation will in itself normally infringe Article 82.[107] They may also be given as a carrot to induce customers to stay loyal even though the supplier is under no contractual obligation to do so. In either case they will infringe Article 82. It makes no difference if the arrangements were requested by the customer rather than imposed by the supplier, or if they are common practice within the industry concerned.[108] Loyalty rebates will be an abuse if they relate to a certain proportion of the customer's requirements, at least if it is a substantial proportion: if the customer is rewarded by an extra discount on *all* his purchases for buying more than, say, 75 per cent of his requirements from X, a competitor will have to offer a price low enough to compensate the customer for the lost discount on the total.

---

[104] See M. Waelbroeck 'Price Discrimination and Rebate Policies under EU Competition Law' [1995] *Fordham Corporate Law Institute* 147, 159.

[105] And see J. Faull and A. Nikpay (eds.), *The EC Law of Competition* (Oxford University Press, 1999), para. 3.246.

[106] Case 85/76, *Hoffmann-La Roche* v. *Commission* [1979] ECR 461, [1979] 3 CMLR 211.

[107] See *infra* 366.

[108] *BPB Industries* [1989] OJ L 10/50, [1990] 4 CMLR 464.

Loyalty rebates were first considered contrary to Article 82 in the *European Sugar Cartel*.[109] This was confirmed in the leading case, *Hoffmann-La Roche*:

Case 85/76, *Hoffmann-La Roche* v. *Commission* [1979] ECR 461, [1979] 3 CMLR 211

Hoffmann-La Roche (HLR) supplied a number of vitamins. The Commission held that it was in a dominant position[110] and had abused its position by giving loyalty rebates to 22 large customers. HLR appealed. The Court dealt with three arguments on the question of the loyalty rebates: whether such rebates are an abuse, what was the nature of the rebates in this case, and whether they were saved from infringing Article [82] by the presence in the contracts of an 'English clause'.[111]

Court of Justice

89. An undertaking which is in a dominant position on the market and ties purchasers—even if it does so at their request—by an obligation or promise on their part to obtain all or most of their requirements exclusively from the said undertaking abuses its dominant position within the meaning of Article [82] of the Treaty, whether the obligation in question is stipulated without further qualification or whether it is undertaken in consideration of the grant of a rebate. The same applies if the said undertaking, without tying the purchasers by a formal obligation, applies, either under the terms of agreements concluded with these purchasers or unilaterally, a system of fidelity rebates, that is to say discounts conditional on the customer's obtaining all or most of its requirements— whether the quantity of its purchases be large or small—from the undertaking in a dominant position.

90. Obligations of this kind to obtain supplies exclusively from a particular undertaking, whether or not they are in consideration of rebates or of the granting of fidelity rebates intended to give the purchaser an incentive to obtain his supplies exclusively from the undertaking in a dominant position, are incompatible with the objective of undistorted competition within the Common Market, because—unless there are exceptional circumstances which may make an agreement between undertakings in the context of Article [81] and in particular of paragraph (3) of that Article, permissible—they are not based on an economic transaction which justifies this burden or benefit but are designed to deprive the purchaser of or restrict his possible choice of sources of supply and to deny other producers access to the market. The fidelity rebate, unlike quantity rebates exclusively linked with the volume of purchases from the producer concerned, is designed through the grant of a financial advantage to prevent customers from obtaining their supplies from competing producers. Furthermore, the effect of fidelity rebates is to apply dissimilar conditions to equivalent transactions with other trading parties in that two purchasers pay a different price for the same quantity of the same product depending on whether they obtain their supplies exclusively from the undertaking in a dominant position or have several sources of supply. Finally, these practices by an undertaking in a dominant position and especially on an expanding market tend to consolidate this position by means of a form of competition which is not based on the transactions effected and is therefore distorted.

Any discount or rebate scheme which has the effect of rewarding loyalty, whatever form it takes, will be treated with hostility by the Court and Commission. In *British Plasterboard*

---

[109] Cases 40/73 etc., *Suiker Unie* v. *EC Commission* [1975] ECR 1663, [1976] 1 CMLR 295.

[110] For the dominance aspects of this case see *supra* Chap. 6.

[111] For 'English clauses' see *infra* 367.

Industries,[112] BG, the dominant supplier, was faced with competition from importers,[113] and the managing director asked the marketing director how the company could 'reward the loyalty of merchants who remained exclusively with us'.[114] The company then devised a system of payments for promotional and advertising expenses to customers who bought exclusively from it. These were condemned for infringing Article 82, as was the scheme put in place in Northern Ireland for offering rebates to those buying exclusively from BG and not dealing with the importers.[115] The Commission's decision was upheld by the CFI and ECJ. BG argued that the promotional payments were normal commercial practice, made in response to growing buyer power, and that BG was entitled to take steps to protect its legitimate commercial interests.

Case T–65/89, *BPB Industries and British Gypsum Ltd* v. *Commission* [1993] ECR II–389, [1993] 5 CMLR 32

Court of First Instance[116]

65. The Court considers, *in limine,* that the applicants are correct in their view that the making of promotional payments to buyers is a standard practice forming part of commercial co-operation between a supplier and its distributors. In a normal competitive market situation, such contracts are entered into in the interest of both parties. The supplier thereby seeks to secure its sales by ensuring loyalty of demand, whereas the distributor, for his part, can rely on security of supply and related commercial facilities.

66. It is not unusual for commercial co-operation of that kind to involve, in return, an exclusive purchasing commitment given by the recipient of such payments or facilities to his supplier. Such exclusive purchasing commitments cannot, as a matter of principle, be prohibited. As the Court of First Instance stated in Case T–61/89, *Dansk Pelsdyravlerforening* v. *E.C. Commission,* . . . appraisal of the effects of such commitments on the functioning of the market concerned depends on the characteristics of that market. As the ECJ held in Case C–234/89, *Delimitis v. Henninger Brau,* . . . it is necessary, in principle, to examine the effects of such commitments on the market in their specific context.

67. But those considerations, which apply in a normal competitive market situation, cannot be unreservedly accepted in the case of a market where, precisely because of the dominant position of one of the economic operators, competition is already restricted. An undertaking in a dominant position has a special responsibility not to allow its conduct to impair genuine undistorted competition in the common Market (Case 322/81 *Michelin* v. *Commission,* paragraph 57 . . .).

68. As regards the nature of the contested obligation, the Court observes that, as the ECJ has held, an undertaking which is in a dominant position in a market and ties purchasers—even if it does so at their request—by an obligation or promise on their part to obtain all or most of their requirements exclusively from the said undertaking abuses it dominant position within the meaning of Article [82] . . . , whether the obligation in question is stipulated without further

---

[112] Case C–310/93P, *BPB Industries and British Gypsum Ltd* v. *Commission* [1995 ECR I–865, [1997] 4 CMLR 238, on appeal from Case T–65/89 *BPB Industries and British Gypsum Ltd* v. *Commission* [1993] ECR II–389, [1993] 5 CMLR 32, on appeal from *BPB Industries* [1989] OJ L10/50, [1990] 4 CMLR 464.

[113] See *supra* 357.

[114] [1989] OJ L10/50, [1990] 4 CMLR 464, para. 58.

[115] The company also put in place a system of priority deliveries for loyal customers.

[116] The judgment of the ECJ merely confirms that of the CFI.

qualification or whether it is undertaken in consideration of the grant of a rebate (Case 85/76 *Hoffman-La Roche* v. *Commission*, paragraph 89 . . . , Case C–62/86 *AZKO* v. *Commission*, paragraph 149. .). That solution is justified by the fact that where, as in the present case, an economic operator holds a strong position in the market, the conclusion of exclusive supply contracts in respect of a substantial proportion of purchases constitutes an unacceptable obstacle to entry to that market. The fact—even if it were established—that the promotional payments represented a response to requests and to the growing buying power of merchants does not, in any case, justify the inclusion in the supply contracts in question of an exclusivity clause. Consequently, the applicants cannot maintain that the Commission has not established the abusive nature of the practice at issue, and it is unnecessary to give a decision on the dispute between the parties as to the meaning of exclusivity in regard to purchasing since it is in any event clear from the documents before the Court that the contractual condition at issue related to all or nearly all the customers' purchases.

69. Whilst the fact that an undertaking is in a dominant position cannot disentitle it from protecting its own commercial interests if they are attacked and whilst such an undertaking must be conceded the right to take such reasonable steps as it deems appropriate to protect its said interests, such behaviour cannot be countenanced if its actual purpose is to strengthen this dominant position and abuse it (Case 27/76 *United Brands* v. *Commission* . . .). It follows that neither the argument that BG was under a duty to ensure continuity and reliability of supplies nor the argument relating to Iberian's commercial practices can be upheld (Case T–30/89 *Hilti* v. *Commission*, paragraph 118 . . ., Case 226/84 *British Leyland* v. *Commission* . . .).

70. The Court further observes that the concept of abuse is an objective one (Case 85/76 *Hoffman-La Roche* v. *Commission*, paragraph 91 . . .) and that, accordingly, the conduct of an undertaking in a dominant position may be regarded as abusive within the meaning of Article [82]. even in the absence of any fault. Consequently, the applicants' argument according to which BG never had any intention to discourage or weaken Iberian has no bearing on the legal classification of the facts.

71. Even if it is conceded that one of the aims of that system might, as maintained by the applicants, have been to promote plaster products in general, it must nevertheless be stated that it leads to the grant of payments which are strictly conditional upon exclusive loyalty to BG and are therefore abusive, irrespective of the merits of the argument that brand loyalty is lacking.

72. Similarly, the applicants' reference to their competitors' supply difficulties cannot justify the exclusive supply arrangements which they brought into being, since they cannot reasonably contend that their customers were not in a position to adjust their marketing policy to take account of those difficulties.

73. The argument that the merchants were entitled to discontinue their contractual relations with BG at any time has no forcé since the right to terminate a contract in no way prevents its actual application until such time as the right to terminate it has been exercised. It should be observed that an undertaking in a dominant position is powerful enough to require its customers not only to enter into such contracts but also to maintain them, with the result that the legal possibility of termination is in fact rendered illusory

In the *Soda Ash* cases[117] the Commission condemned a pricing structure based on 'top

---

[117] *Soda Ash—ICI* and *Soda Ash—Solvay* [1991] OJ L152/40 and 152/21, [1994] 4 CMLR 645; annulled for procedural reasons, Cases T–30/91 etc *Solvay* v. *Commission* [1995] ECR II–1775, [1996] 5 CMLR 57 and 91 and Cases C–286–288/96P, *Commission* v. *Solvay*, judgments of 6 Apr. 2000.

slice' rebates, whereby customers got the basic tonnage, which would have been bought from the dominant undertaking anyway, at the normal price, but were offered substantial discounts on extra amounts above that. This amounted to a loyalty rebate and was discriminatory also in that the basic tonnage was set at a different figure for each customer.

d. TARGET DISCOUNTS

Target discounts are discounts awarded when customers reach targets in their purchases from the supplier. The customer receives a discount on all his purchases if he buys more than a certain amount in a certain period. Like pure loyalty rebates they put pressure on the customer to stay with the supplier in order in order to ensure that the discount at the end of the reference period is obtained. They will be discriminatory if, as is usually the case, customers are given different targets to reach in order to obtain the discount. The target may be set by reference to the customer's perceived capacity to absorb the goods, and often requires the customer to buy a certain amount in excess of his purchases in the past.

Target discounts given by a dominant supplier are likely to infringe Article 82. They were first considered, and held to be an abuse, in the *Michelin* case:

Case 322/81, *Nederlandsche Banden-Industrie Michelin* v. *Commission* [1983] ECR 3461, [1985] 1 CMLR 282

Michelin supplied heavy vehicle new replacement tyres to tyre dealers who sold both Michelin tyres and competing brands. It ran a fixed invoice discount and a cash discount for early payment, which were the same for all dealers. These were not found to infringe Article 82. Michelin also offered a discount linked to an annual sales target which was personal to each dealer. A proportion of this variable discount was paid in advance, initially every month and then every four months as an advance on the annual sum. The full sum became payable only if the dealer attained a pre-determined sales target. The target was fixed for each dealer by a Michelin sales representative at the beginning of each year. The discount was basically geared to turnover and to the proportion of Michelin tyres sold and the aim was to ensure that the dealer sold more Michelin tyres than he had in the year before although if times were hard it might be sufficient to equal the previous year. Towards the end of each sales year Michelin's sales representative would urge the dealer to place an order big enough to obtain the full discount. The Commission held that the scheme infringed Article 82. This finding was upheld by the Court of Justice.

Court of Justice

73. In deciding whether Michelin NV abused its dominant position in applying its discount system it is therefore necessary to consider all the circumstances, particularly the criteria and rules for the grant of the discount, and to investigate whether, in providing an advantage not based on any economic service justifying it, the discounts tends to remove or restrict the buyer's freedom to choose his sources of supply, to bar competitors from access to the market, to apply dissimilar conditions to equivalent transactions with other trading parties or to strengthen the dominant position by distorting competition.

74. It is in the light of those considerations that the submissions put forward by the applicant in answer to the two objections raised in the contested decision to the discounted system in general, namely that Michelin NV bound tyre dealers in the Netherlands to itself and that it applied to them dissimilar conditions in respect of equivalent transactions, must be examined.

. . .

81. The discount system in question was based on an annual reference period. However, any system under which discounts are granted according to the quantities sold during a relatively long reference period has the inherent effect, at the end of that period, of increasing pressure on the buyer to reach the purchase figure needed to obtain the discount or to avoid suffering the expected loss for the entire period. In this case the variations in the rate of discount over a year as a result of one last order, even a small one, affected the dealer's margin of profit on the whole year's sales of Michelin heavy-vehicle tyres. In such circumstances, even quite slight variations might put dealers under appreciable pressure.

82. That effect was accentuated still further by the wide divergence between Michelin NV's market share and those of its main competitors. If a competitor wished to offer a dealer a competitive inducement for placing an order, especially at the end of the year, it had to take into account the absolute value of Michelin NV's annual target discount and fix is own discount at a percentage which, when related to the dealer's lesser quantity of purchases from that competitor, was very high. Despite the apparently low percentage of Michelin NV's discount, it was therefore very difficult for its competitors to offset the benefits or losses resulting for dealers from attaining or failing to attain Michelin NV's targets as the case might be.

83. Furthermore, the lack of transparency of Michelin NV's entire discount system, whose rules moreover changed on several occasions during the relevant period, together with the fact that neither the scale of discounts nor the sales targets or discounts relating to them were communicated in writing to dealers meant that they were left in uncertainty and on the whole could not predict with any confidence the effect of attaining their targets or failing to do so.

84. All those factors were instrumental in creating for dealers a situation in which they were under considerable pressure, especially towards the end of a year, to attain Michelin NV's sales targets if they did not wish to run the risk of losses which its competitors could not easily make good by means of the discounts which they themselves were able to offer. Its network of commercial representatives enabled Michelin NV to remind dealers of this situation at any time so as to induce them to place orders with it.

85. Such a situation is calculated to prevent dealers from being able to select freely at any time in the light of the market situation the most favourable of the offers made by the various competitors and to change supplier without suffering any appreciable economic disadvantage. It thus limits the dealers' choice of supplier and makes access to the market more difficult for competitors. Neither the wish to sell more nor the wish to spread production more evenly can justify such a restriction of the customer's freedom of choice and independence. The position of dependence in which dealers find themselves and which is created by the discount system in question, is not therefore based on any countervailing advantage which may be economically justified.

86. It must therefore be concluded that by binding dealers in the Netherlands to itself by means of the discount system described above Michelin NV committed an abuse, within the meaning of Article [82] of the Treaty, of its dominant position in the market for new replacement tyres for heavy vehicles. The submission put forward by the applicant to refute that finding in the contested decision must therefore be rejected.

The particular objections to the *Michelin* scheme were therefore that it required the customer to purchase more than in the preceding period, it set a different target for each customer based on exceeding the previous purchases, it had a long reference period (a year), and it was not transparent. A more transparent scheme, with a short reference period and less discriminatory targets, might on this basis be less likely to infringe Article

82. However, in *Irish Sugar*[118] (where the main reference period was twenty-six weeks and the calculation was based on average weekly sales) the Commission unequivocally condemned discount schemes which are conditional on the customer buying more than in a previous period because they tie the customers to the supplier and foreclose the market to competitors. Although it found that the lack of transparency in Irish Sugar's entire rebate scheme was in itself an abuse (paragraph 150 of the decision) it is clear from *Irish Sugar* that there are fundamental objections to this type of target. The Commission rejected the contention that they are a species of quantity discount. The CFI upheld the Commission's decision, taking the view that the discount could only be 'intended to tie the customers to which it is granted and place competitors in an unfavourable competitive position'.[119]

The message from these cases is that target rebates will be objectionable if they have any appreciable tying effect on customers.[120] In *Coca Cola*,[121] the Commission dealt with the distribution arrangements of Coca Cola's Italian subsidiary. The Commission settled the proceedings by taking undertakings by which the company undertook not to include in agreements concluded with distributors in Member States 'clauses which make the granting of rebates subject to the joint contracting party's purchasing quantities of "Coca-Cola" set individually during a period of more than three consecutive months'. Individually set targets of less than three months were accepted because the Commission considered that the new scheme did not substantially impede the customers from switching suppliers.[122]

The Commission first held target discounts to be an abuse of a dominant position in the services sector in *BA/Virgin*.[123] BA was fined EURO 6.8 million for offering travel agents commission schemes which included extra payments in return for meeting or exceeding their previous year's sales of BA tickets. At the same time the Commission issued a public announcement setting out the principles it considers apply to such practices by airlines: target discounts (or commissions) and indeed any discounts not reflecting costs savings or differences in value, are not allowed.[124]

e. AGGREGATED REBATES

Schemes in which discounts are given on aggregated purchases of products belonging to different product markets have been found to infringe Article 82. The objection to this practice is that the scheme acts as a tie-in. If the dominant supplier of widgets also supplies blodgets, and offers a discount scheme whereby purchases of blodgets (for which the customer is not dependent on the supplier) are aggregated with those of widgets for discount purposes, the customer will have an incentive to buy the blodgets from the dominant widget

---

[118] [1997] OJ L258/1, [1997] 5 CMLR 666.

[119] Case T–228/97, *Irish Sugar plc* v. *Commission* [1999] 5 CMLR 1300, para. 213.

[120] See J. Faull and A. Nikpay, (eds.), *The EC Law of Competition* (Oxford University Press, 1999), para. 3.255.

[121] *XIXth Report on Competition Policy* (Commission, 1989) pt 50.

[122] The Commission's clearance in 1997 of the *Coca Cola/Amalgamated Beverages* merger [1997] OJ L218/15 was on the basis that Coca-Cola undertook to adopt the 1989 undertakings (para. 212 of the decision).

[123] [2000] OJ L30/1, [2000] 4 CMLR 999.

[124] Principles concerning travel agents' commissions: Press Release IP/99/504, 14 July 1999.

supplier. Aggregated rebates were condemned in *Hoffmann-La Roche*[125] and *Tetra Pak II*.[126] Tie-ins are discussed below.[127]

(iv) DELIVERED PRICING

Delivered pricing is a method of pricing where the supplier quotes a price for the product which includes delivery and does not offer an *ex works* or *ex factory* price which allows the customer the choice of making its own transport arrangements. The Commission has condemned it as an infringement of Article 82 because it distorts competition on the downstream market in transport and means that the dominant undertaking is using its position in one market to strengthen its position in another.[128] It is therefore an example of leverage.[129] Delivered pricing may however be *uniform*, which means that all customers are charged the same delivered price irrespective of their distance from the place from which they are being supplied. It is discriminatory as the same price is being charged for transactions which entail different costs: the proximate customers subsidize those which are far off and competition on the downstream market between the customers is thereby distorted. This is a classic case of putting a trading party at a competitive disadvantage contrary to Article 82 (c).

(v) LEGITIMATE REASONS FOR DIFFERENT PRICES

The case law indicates that discriminatory pricing may be abusive even where trading parties are not being put at a competitive disadvantage. In *United Brands*[130] the discrimination neither put parties at a disadvantage nor excluded competitors from the market. It simply offended the concept of the single market. In other cases the assumption is made that discrimination is not efficiency-enhancing and prejudices actual or potential competitors of the dominant undertaking. Non-discriminatory quantity discounts escape being abusive where they are costs saving, but any other discount scheme is likely to be considered to tie customers to the dominant supplier. Differential prices will be legitimate only if they are objectively justified. Situations in which there may be objective justification are described by Waelbroeck in the following comments.

M. Waelbroeck, 'Price Discrimination and Rebate Policies under EU Competition Law', in B.Hawk (ed), [1995] *Fordham Corporate Law Institute* 147, 152–153

Differentiation criteria that do not raise problems

1. *Cost differences*—Two transactions cannot be considered as 'equivalent' if their costs for the seller are different. Thus, the Commission does not object to the grant of quantity discounts, when such discounts are justified by cost reductions. In the *HOV-SVZ/MCN* case the German

---

[125] Case 85/76, *Hoffmann-La Roche v. Commission* [1979] ECR 461, [1979] 3 CMLR 211.
[126] *Elopak Italia/Tetra Pak* [1991] OJ L72/1, [1992] 4 CMLR 551.
[127] See *infra* 368.
[128] *Napier Brown-British Sugar* [1988] OJ L284/41, [19990] 4 CMLR 196.
[129] See *infra* 377.
[130] See *supra* 352–354.

railroad company Deutsche Bundesbahn claimed that the fact that its tariffs for carriage towards Dutch and Belgian ports were higher than those charged for carriage to ports in Northern Germany could be explained by differences in costs. The Commission did not question the validity of this argument, but rejected it on the facts. . . .[131]

2. *Cash discounts*—The Commission has never questioned the practice of granting cash discounts or discounts for prompt payment. Receiving prompt payment clearly constitutes a benefit for the supplier. Therefore, to the extent that amount of the discount is in proportion with the importance of such benefit, it does not constitute unjustified unequal treatment.

3. *Services rendered*—The same consideration explains why the Commission has never objected to discounts that correspond to a service actually rendered by the purchaser. Indeed, to that extent too, the supplier is receiving something of value in exchange for the discount, so that the grant of the discount is justified by an objective consideration. This applies, among other things, to 'functional discounts,' i.e. discounts given to a wholesaler as opposed to a retailer or a final purchaser.

4. *Customer complaints*—If a customer complains that the goods or services he purchased were not of the quality specified in the contract, the supplier will often agree to offer him a reduction in the price. To the extent such reduction does not exceed the value of the quality defect, it does not constitute discriminatory treatment: indeed, a defective transaction is clearly not 'equivalent' to an up-to-standard transaction.

5. *The time factor*—Very often, the price of goods or services fluctuates over time. Thus, the fact that there exists a difference in the prices charged for two transactions that occurred at different points in time does not mean that such prices are discriminatory. However, if large differences exist between the prices of transactions that were entered into at approximately the same time and in the same market environment, there will be a presumption of discriminatory pricing unless the supplier can provide a convincing explanation for such differences. . . .

6. *Intellectual property rights*—It is legitimate for the holder of an intellectual property right to limit the number of acts of exploitation of the right which he authorizes third parties to accomplish. . . . Although this prerogative may be used to charge the different licensees amounts that vary in accordance with the intensity with which they use the licensed process, this does not amount to discrimination so long as all licensees are being charged the same royalty for each use.

5. EXCLUSIVE CONTRACTS

A. GENERAL

Discount schemes such as loyalty rebates[132] are concerned with actions which are aimed at ensuring that customers buy from the dominant undertaking and not from its competitors. They are particular instances of arrangements seeking to ensure exclusive purchasing by customers.

---

[131] This decision ([1994] OJ L104/34) was upheld, see Case C–436/97, *Deutsche Bahn AG* v. *Commission* [1999] 5 CMLR 776.

[132] *Supra* p. 358.

It can be seen from the approach of the Court and Commission to loyalty rebates that contractual provisions which encourage the customer to buy only from the dominant undertaking by offering incentives will infringe Article 82. Exclusive purchasing agreements may also be caught by Article 81[133] but Articles 81 and 82 apply concurrently. The fact that an agreement is block exempted does not preclude the application of Article 82.[134] Prior to 1 June 2000, block exemption Regulation 1984/83[135] applied to exclusive purchasing agreements for goods for resale regardless of the market share of the supplier, but this did not prevent the agreement infringing Article 82. Regulation 2790/1999 on vertical agreements applies only to cases in which the supplier has a market share of less than 30 per cent.[136]

It should be noted that the abusive nature of exclusive contracts and loyalty rebates is not removed by the presence of an 'English clause'. This is a clause in a supply contract whereby the customer is allowed to switch suppliers without penalty if the dominant undertaking cannot or will not match more favourable terms offered by another supplier. In *Hoffmann-La Roche*[137] the dominant firm argued that the English clause denuded the loyalty rebate provision of its anti-competitive effect so that there was no abuse. The Court held, on the contrary, that the clause exacerbated the abuse by enabling Hoffman-La Roche to learn of its competitors' offers.[138] The Commission considers that not only do these clauses create transparency in the market, which could be exploited by the players on highly concentrated markets, but they impede other suppliers from attracting customers.[139]

In *Hoffmann-La Roche*[140] Article 82 was infringed by exclusive purchasing induced by loyalty rebates. In *BPB Industries* the incentives to exclusivity were not only loyalty rebates[141] but also priority deliveries at times of shortage. The Commission's condemnation of this as an abuse[142] was upheld by the CFI.

Case T–65/89 *BPB Industries and British Gypsum Ltd* v. *Commission* [1993] ECR II–389, [1993] 5 CMLR 32

Court of First Instance

94. As regards the abusive nature of the practice in question, the Court observes that, whilst, as the applicants maintain, it is open to an undertaking in a dominant position and is also a matter of normal commercial policy, in times of shortage, to lay down criteria for according priority in meeting orders, those criteria must be objective and must not be discriminatory in any way. They must be objectively justified and observe the rules governing fair competition between economic

---

[133] See *supra* Chap. 3 and 9.

[134] See *supra* Chap. 5

[135] [1983] OJ L173/5.

[136] [1999] OJ L336/21. See *infra* Chap. 9.

[137] Case 85/76, *Hoffmann-La Roche* v. *Commission* [1979] ECR 461, [1979] 3 CMLR 211.

[138] *Ibid.*, paras. 107–108.

[139] See J. Faull and A. Nikpay, (eds.), *The EC Law of Competition* (Oxford University Press, 1999) para. 3.192–3.193; the Commission objected to an English clause in *IRI/Nielsen*, XXXVIth Report on Competition Policy (1996) pt 64.

[140] Case 85/76, *Hoffmann-La Roche* v. *Commission* [1979] ECR 461, [1979] 3 CMLR 211.

[141] See *supra* 360.

[142] *BPB Industries* [1989] OJ L 10/50, [1990] 4 CMLR 464, paras. 141–147.

operators. Article [82] . . . prohibits a dominant undertaking from strengthening its position by having recourse to means other than those falling within competition based on merits. . . . That requirement is not met by the criterion adopted in this case by BG, which was based on a distinction between, on the one hand, customers who marketed plasterboard imported and produced by certain of its competitors and, on the other, 'loyal' customers who obtained their supplies from BG. Such a criterion, which results in the provision of equivalent services on unequal terms, is in itself anti-competitive by reason of the discriminatory purpose which it pursues and the exclusionary effect which may result from it.

The main objection to exclusive contracts is that they foreclose the market to other competitors. Any means which a dominant undertaking uses to achieve exclusivity in its dealings with customers is therefore also likely to infringe Article 82. Exclusivity arrangements will escape only if they can be objectively justified because 'the anti-competitive effects are kept to the minimum necessary for the attainment of some economic advantage' as, for example, where they provide the customer with the benefit of security of supply.[143]

Two particular types of arrangement which have excited the interest of the Commission are worthy of special mention however: tying arrangements and freezer exclusivity.

B. TYING

(i) GENERAL

Article 82 (d) specifically lists as an example of abuse:

making the conclusion of contracts subject to acceptance by the other parties of supplementary obligations which, by their nature or according to commercial usage, have no connection with the subject of such contracts.

This describes tying, the practice of supplying something on condition that the customer obtains something else from the supplier as well.[144] Suppose X makes both widgets and blodgets. X is the monopoly supplier of widgets but the blodget market is competitive. Customers for widgets need to buy blodgets as well. If X refuses to supply widgets unless the customers buy its blodgets as well the other manufacturers of blodgets may be squeezed out of the market. Tying can apply to both products and services and the tying of services to products has become a particular problem for competition law.

Competition policy is concerned with tying because it involves leverage which, as we have seen before, means an undertaking which is dominant on one market using that position to interfere with competition on another market, strengthening its position there, and creating barriers to entry. Tying can work because the supplier is dominant in the market for the *tying* product, so the customer has difficulty going elsewhere for it and therefore does not shop around for the *tied* product. Competition authorities fear that the dominant supplier

---

[143] J. Faull and A. Nikpay (eds.), *The EC Law of Competition* (Oxford, 1999), para. 3.188.

[144] Tying can arise as an issue in distribution arrangements which do not involve dominant firms (see *infra* Chap. 9) and in technology transfer agreements, such as patent licensing (see *infra* Chap. 10).

can extract two monopoly prices: one from the tying and one from the tied product.[145] The Chicago school has argued that this is not possible, but economists have demonstrated that it *is* possible unless the two products are used in fixed proportions and the market for the tied good would be competitive if it were not for the tying.[146] Where the dominant under-taking will not supply the tying product without the tied product this may be seen as constituting an infringement of Article 82 as a *refusal to supply*. It can also be a form of price discrimination.

Tying can be economic as well as contractual. Instead of providing that the customer must obtain the tied product from him in order to be supplied with the tying product the supplier may offer a deal which induces the customer to obtain both. Such offers will usually amount to discriminatory pricing. If the normal unit price for widgets is £10 and the competitive unit price for blodgets is £5 the supplier may offer widgets for £8 if both are bought from him. Competitors on the blodget market will have to reduce the price to £3 per unit in order to compete. Where services are tied to products the supplier may quote a price for the product which includes the service (repair and maintenance for example). If the customer does not want the service he will still have to pay the full price, or be offered only a reduction which does not reflect the cost of the service element. In either case he has an incentive to obtain the service from the supplier of the product rather than from an independent service provider. The inducements offered may be non-financial, such as refusing to honour guarantees on the tying product[147] or offering priority delivery to customers who take both products.

(ii) COMMERCIAL REASONS FOR TYING

Tying is a strategy which may make good commercial sense for reasons which are not necessarily anticompetitive. It can be used as a method for obtaining royalties or fees for the use of a process or product. A good example is the patent licensing case *Vaassen/Moris*[148] where the inventor of a device for filling *saucissons de Boulogne* supplied it royalty free but on the condition that customers bought their sausage skins from him. This was an easy way of monitoring, and charging for, the use of the device. Tying can also allow the supplier to achieve economies of scale which are then reflected in the price reduction offered to customers, or to 'spread the risk' when trying to penetrate a new market.[149] Suppliers may also tie products or services together in order to ensure their optimal performance and maintain the supplier's reputation, or to ensure safety, although the Court and Commission have not proved receptive to this justification for tying.[150]

---

[145] The Commission considered in *Eurofix-Bauco* [1988] OJ L65/19, [1989] 4 CMLR 677, that Hilti was trying to raise prices in the market for the consumables (the nails).

[146] For the economics of this, see S. Bishop and M. Walker, *The Economics of EC Competition Law* (Sweet and Maxwell, 1999), paras. 5.13–5.22.

[147] See *Eurofix-Bauco* v. *Hilti* [1988] OJ L65/19, [1989] 4 CMLR 677, para. 44.

[148] [1979] OJ L19/32, [1979] 1 CMLR 511. The tie was condemned by the Commission as contrary to Art. 85(1): see *infra* Chap. 10.

[149] See N. Green and A. Robertson *Commercial Agreements and Competition Law* (2nd edn., Kluwer, Deventer, 1997) paras. 11.227 (e).

[150] See the *Hilti* and *Tetra Pak II* cases (*infra*).

(iii) MARKET DEFINITION, ANCILLARY MARKETS, CONSUMABLES AND AFTERMARKETS

Where an undertaking dominant in one market ties in a product or service in another market it is an instance of a practice which the Court and Commission have repeatedly held to infringe Article 82—leverage, the projection of dominance from one market to another. The *Télémarketing* case,[151] where the television company tied the use of its own sales agents to the sale of its advertising slots, is a clear example of this. The delivered pricing policy in *Napier Brown/British Sugar*[152] was condemned as an abuse because, by providing the product and the delivery together, the dominant undertaking was excluding competition on the separate although ancillary market. However, the whole concept of tying presupposes that different products or services are being tied together. If what is supplied consists of one product there cannot be a tie as one cannot tie something to itself. Whether products or services are components of a single product or service or are in distinct markets is a difficult issue, and one that goes back to questions of market definition.[153] As seen in Chapter 6, the tendency of the Court and Commission is to separate products and services into different markets and then to condemn the supplier's attempts to ensure that the customer buys them all as a package. Even if the products are in different markets it should be noted that Article 82 (d) specifically refers to supplementary obligations which 'by their nature or according to commercial usage, have no connection with the subject of such contracts' which suggests that ties will be permitted if there is an inherent or customary link between the products.

The approach of EC competition law towards ties in shown by two leading cases, *Hilti*[154] and *Tetra Pak II*, in which the Court upheld the Commission's finding that a dominant undertaking had committed an abuse by tying the supply of consumables to the primary product:

Case T–30/89, *Hilti* v. *Commission* [1991] ECR II–1439, [1992] 4 CMLR 16[155]

Hilti was dominant in the supply of nail guns, the biggest selling models of which were protected by patents. It supplied the cartridge strips which were also protected by patents. The nails which were fired out of the cartridge strips in the guns were not, however, covered by patents and there were some small, independent manufacturers of Hilti-compatible nails. Hilti followed a number of practices to ensure that customers who bought its cartridges also bought its nails and did not buy nails from the independent suppliers: i) making the sale of patented cartridge strips conditional upon taking a corresponding complement of nails; ii) reducing discounts on cartridges where the customer did not order nails as well; iii) inducing its distributors not to supply certain customers so that the independent nail producers could not get hold of Hilti cartridges; iv) refusing supplies of cartridges to long-standing customers who might resell to independent nail producers; v) frustrating or delaying applications for licences of right of the cartridge strip technology so that the independent producers could

---

[151] See *supra* 324. The Court treated this as a refusal to supply scenario: see *infra* 377.

[152] [1988] OJ L284/41, [19990] 4 CMLR 196.

[153] It was the issue at the heart of the *Microsoft* litigation in the USA which culminated in the final order of 3 Apr. 2000.

[154] See R. Downing, 'Hilti: The Final Nail' [1995] 1 *ECLR* 53.

[155] The appeal to the ECJ, Case C–53/92 P *Hilti* v. *Commission* [1994] ECR I–666, [1994] 4 CMLR 614, was on the market definition point only, not on the abuse. This aspect of the case is dealt with *supra* in Chap. 6.

not obtain non-Hilti cartridges; vi) refusing to honour guarantees on nail guns if non-Hilti nails had been used with them.

The Commission held[156] that the nail-guns, cartridges and nails each constituted a separate relevant product market and that Hilti was dominant in the EEC in all of them. It held that Hilti had infringed Article 82 by the practices above which were designed to tie the nails to the cartridges and thus to prevent or limit the entry of independent producers of Hilti-compatible consumables into the markets. Hilti claimed that the practices were objectively justified because it was necessary for safety reasons to ensure that Hilti guns were only used with Hilti consumables and that the nails produced by the independents were sub-standard. The Commission rejected this, pointing out that Hilti had never communicated its safety concerns to the independents or taken steps to alert the UK Trading Standards Departments or the Health and Safety Executive about any danger and that there had never been any report of safety difficulties stemming from the use of non-Hilti nails. Hilti appealed to the Court of First Instance both on the issue of market definition[157] and on the finding of abuse.

Court of First Instance

115. It is common ground that at no time during the period in question did Hilti approach the competent United Kingdom authorities for a ruling that the use of the interveners' nails in Hilti tools was dangerous.

116. The only explanation put forward by Hilti for its failure to do so is that recourse to judicial or administrative channels would have caused greater harm to the interests of Bauco and Eurofix than the conduct which it in fact pursued.

117. That argument cannot be accepted. If Hilti had made use of the possibilities available to it under the relevant United Kingdom legislation, the legitimate rights of the interveners would in no way have been impaired had the United Kingdom authorities acceded to Hilti's request for a ban on the use in its tools of nails produced by the interveners and, where appropriate, on all misleading advertisements issued by them. If on the other hand the authorities had dismissed those requests, Hilti would have had great difficulty in persisting in its allegations against Profix and Bauco.

118. As the Commission has established, there are laws in the United Kingdom attaching penalties to the sale of dangerous products and to the use of misleading claims as to the characteristics of any product. There are also authorities vested with powers to enforce those laws. In those circumstances it is clearly not the task of an undertaking in a dominant position to take steps on its own initiative to eliminate products which, rightly or wrongly, it regards as dangerous or at least as inferior in quality to its own products.

119. It must further be held in this connection that the effectiveness of the Community rules on competition would be jeopardised if the interpretation by an undertaking of the laws of the various member-States regarding product liability were to take precedence over those rules. Hilti's argument based on its alleged duty of care cannot therefore be upheld.

The facts of *Tetra Pak II* have already been described.[158] The Commission held that aseptic packaging machines, aseptic cartons, non-aseptic machines, and non-aseptic cartons were four separate relevant markets, and that Tetra Pak was dominant on the markets for aseptic machines and cartons and had committed abuses on the associated non-aseptic

---

[156] *Eurofix-Bauco* [1988] OJ L65/19, [1989] 4 CMLR 677.

[157] See *supra* Chap. 6.

[158] See *infra* Chap. 6 and *supra* 325.

markets.[159] One of the ways the Commission held that Tetra Pak had infringed Article 82[160] was by tying the supply of its non-aseptic packaging machines to the supply of cartons which the machines filled. Tetra Pak either sold or leased the machines and imposed a contractual condition on its customers that obliged them to purchase only Tetra Pak cartons. The contract also obliged customers to obtain the cartons only from Tetra Pak itself or from a company it designated (although as there were no independent distributors the Commission pointed out that this clause was superfluous). Customers were obliged to obtain all maintenance and repair services and the supplies of spare parts from Tetra Pak. Tetra Pak claimed that the machines and the cartons formed 'integrated distribution systems' and that in any event the tie was justified for technical reasons, considerations of public liability and health, and by the need to protect its reputation. The Commission's rejection of these arguments was upheld by the CFI.

Tetra Pak appealed to the ECJ, claiming that the CFI erred in law in holding that the tied sales of cartons and filling machines were contrary to Article 82. In particular, it said that Article 82 (d) prohibited tying only where the supplementary obligations imposed had by their nature, or according to commercial usage, no connection with the subject of the contract. The ECJ confirmed the CFI's judgment. It held that the reasoning of the CFI, holding that there was no natural link, was correct. It also held that, as the examples in Article 82 are not exhaustive, a tie may constitute an abuse even if there *is* a natural link or the tied sale is in accordance with commercial usage.

Case C–333/94P, *Tetra Pak International SA* v. *Commission* [1996] ECR I–5951, [1997] 4 CMLR 662

Court of Justice

34. In its third plea, Tetra Pak submits that the Court of First Instance erred in law in holding that the tied sales of cartons and filling machines were contrary to Article [82] in circumstances where there was a natural link between the two and tied sales were in accordance with commercial usage.

35. Tetra Pak interprets Article [82] (d) of the Treaty as prohibiting only the practice of making the conclusion of contracts dependent on acceptance of additional services which, by nature or according to commercial usage, have no link with the subject-matter of the contracts.

36. It must be noted, first, that the Court of First Instance explicitly rejected the argument put forward by Tetra Pak to show the existence of a natural link between the machines and the cartons. In paragraph [82] of the judgment under appeal, it found: 'consideration of commercial usage does not support the conclusion that the machinery for packaging a product is indivisible from the cartons. For a considerable time there have been independent manufacturers who specialise in the manufacture of non-aseptic cartons designed for use in machines manufactured by other concerns and who do not manufacture machinery themselves'. That assessment, itself based on commercial usage, rules out the existence of the natural link claimed by Tetra Pak by stating that other manufacturers can produced cartons for use in Tetra Pak's machines. With regard to aseptic cartons, the Court of First Instance found, at paragraph [83] of its judgment, that 'any independent producer is quite free, as far as Community competition law is concerned, to manufacture consumables intended

---

[159] For a discussion of the issue of the dominant position and the abuse being on different markets see *supra* 325.

[160] *Elopak Italia/Tetra Pak* [1991] OJ L72/1, [1992] 4 CMLR 551.

for use in equipment manufactured by others, unless in doing so it infringes a competitor's intellectual property right'. It also noted, at paragraph [138], rejecting the argument based on the alleged natural link, that it was not for Tetra Pak to impose certain measures on its own initiative on the basis of technical considerations or considerations relating to product liability, protection of public health and protection of its reputation. Those factors, taken as a whole, show that the Court of First Instance considered that Tetra Pak was not alone in being able to manufacture cartons for use in its machines.

37. It must, moreover, be stressed that the list of abusive practices set out in the second paragraph of Article [82] of the Treaty is not exhaustive. Consequently, even where tied sales of two products are in accordance with commercial usage or there is a natural link between the two products in question, such sales may still constitute abuse within the meaning of Article [82] unless they are objectively justified. The reasoning of the Court of First Instance in paragraph [137] of its judgement is not therefore in any way defective.

(iv) TYING IN AFTERMARKETS WHERE THE PRIMARY MARKET IS COMPETITIVE

It was seen in Chapter 6 that, even if aftermarkets are defined as separate markets from those for the primary products, it is doubtful whether power can be exercised on an aftermarket in the absence of dominance on the primary product market. In both *Hilti* and *Tetra Pak II* the consumable related to a primary product over which the supplier *was* dominant. However, the Commission suggested in *Hilti* that its decision would have been the same even if Hilti had not been dominant in the nail-gun market.[161]

In a controversial US case in 1992, *Eastman Kodak* v. *Image Technical Services*,[162] the Supreme Court held that it was possible for a firm which tied spare parts to the sale of the primary product to contravene the Sherman Act even where the primary market was competitive. The Commission dealt with the issue in the *Digital Undertaking*,[163] where the primary product market of computer systems was competitive and the aftermarket consisted of both hardware maintenance services and software support services for Digital systems. The Commission alleged that Digital had abused its dominant position on the software support market for Digital systems by offering customers a 'package' of software support plus hardware maintenance. The Commission considered that the price of the software support alone was high, but the price was 'considerably more attractive when included in a hardware and software package than when sold on a stand-alone basis'. This meant it was uneconomic for customers to buy the hardware from a third party, so companies in the hardware maintenance market were excluded from servicing Digital systems. The Commission issued a Statement of Objections and following negotiations Digital undertook:[164]

---

[161] *Eurofix-Bauco* [1988] OJ L65/19, [1989] 4 CMLR 677, para. 72.

[162] 112 S Ct 2072 (1992).

[163] Commission Press Release IP/97/868. Cf the *Pelikan/Kyocera* case, *XXVth Report on Competition Policy* (Commission, 1995) pt 87: see *supra* Chap. 6. See also D. Maldoom: 'The Kodka Case: Power in Aftermarkets' [1996] *ECLR* 473; M. Dolmans and V. Pickering: 'The 1997 Digital Undertaking' [1998] 2 *ECLR* 108; P. Andrews, 'Aftermarket Power in the Computer Services Market: The Digital Undertaking' [1998] 3 *ECLR* 176.

[164] Commission Press Release IP/97/868.

to offer hardware maintenance services for Digital systems on a stand-alone basis and to implement a pricing policy for its software support services based on a single flat fee per Central Processing Unit. Whereas it will continue to offer a software and hardware service package (so-called 'DSS' package), the price of the DSS package will not be less than 90 per cent of the sum of the list prices of the individual component services; the difference of up to 10 per cent allows costs savings or other benefits to be passed on to system users while ensuring the maintenance of effective competition in the supply of hardware services. In addition, Digital will introduce a new software service package consisting of software support and license [sic] update services.

Digital will make its price list publicly available and will include in all customer quotations for Digital's DSS package separate quotations for each of the individual components thereof.

Digital undertakes to ensure a transparent and non-discriminatory discount policy and to publish or otherwise make known the eligibility provisions for all discount programs. When offering a discount for its DSS package, it will also offer the same discount on the component services of the package if taken separately. All discounted prices will remain above average total costs.[165]

    The terms of the undertaking show that the Commission will allow a dominant undertaking to pass on costs savings stemming from the efficient packaging together of different products or services. However, it also shows that the Commission will in some circumstances interfere in an undertaking's activities on the aftermarket of its own product even if that primary product market is intensely competitive. Moreover, the discount on a package of products and/or services is liable to infringe Article 82 whenever an undertaking is dominant over one of the elements of the package and it is uneconomical for customers to go to third parties for any of the elements as a result of the discount, unless the discount can be objectively justified on costs savings grounds.

(v) CONCLUSIONS

It is clear from *Tetra Pak II* that, once it is shown that the products or services tied together are in different markets, a dominant undertaking cannot rely on the words about nature and commercial usage in Article 82 (d). 'Commercial usage' may merely have been established by the dominant undertaking itself[166] and the Court has stressed the non-exhaustive character of the particular examples listed in the Article, thereby emasculating the conditions in that sub-paragraph. EC law on tying is driven by concerns about the structure of the market, not about the extraction of monopoly profits or the protection of consumers. In *Tetra Pak II* the monopoly profit could have been extracted from the tying product (the machines), had Tetra Pak wished.[167] The economics of ties and monopoly profits are complex[168] and neither the Commission nor the Court has addressed the issue. Their concern has been with the ability of smaller firms to compete. This is a matter of policy and is summed up in paragraph 36 of the *Tetra Pak II* judgment, quoting the CFI, where the ECJ says 'any independent producer is quite free, as far as Community competition law is concerned, to

---

[165] For the predatory pricing aspects of these proceedings, see *supra* 343.

[166] See V. Korah, 'The Paucity of Economic Analysis in the EEC Decisions on Competition: Tetra Pak II' [1993] *CLP* 150.

[167] See *ibid.*

[168] See F. M. Scherer and D. Ross, *Industrial Market Structure and Economic Performance* (3rd Ed) (Houghton and Mifflin, 1990) pp 565–9; S. Bishop and M. Walker, *The Economics of EC Competition Law* (Sweet and Maxwell, 1999) paras. 5.13–5.69.

manufacture consumables intended for use in equipment manufactured by others.' This is rather strange wording but means not so much that independents are *free* to manufacture but that Community competition law will positively *help* them to do so by constraining the conduct of dominant undertakings for whose equipment they wish to provide products or services. The Commission and Court have been dismissive of arguments about systems and quality. This is sometimes a policy not so much about efficiency and free competition as the protection of small firms and competitors.

C. FREEZER EXCLUSIVITY

A particular type of exclusivity provision which has recently provoked a great deal of attention is the practice of freezer exclusivity.[169] This is the practice whereby frozen goods suppliers (often ice cream manufacturers) provide retail outlets with freezers but stipulate that no other supplier's brand can be stored there.[170] It can be argued that this creates a strategic barrier to the entry of new competition and reduces the intensity of competition between incumbent firms, because in practice it is impractical for a retailer to make room for a second freezer and he has no incentive to do so.[171] The Commission dealt with the practice in *Van den Bergh Foods*.[172] HB Ice Cream Ltd (which in the course of the proceedings became Van den Bergh Foods) entered into distribution agreements for its impulse ice cream with retailers. Under the terms of the agreement a freezer cabinet was made available to the retailer for the storage and display of HB's ice cream at the point of sale. The cabinet was either loaned with no direct charge or leased for a nominal sum which was not collected, and the maintenance and repair of the cabinet was done by HB. The cabinet had to be used exclusively for HB's products. These agreements were found by the Commission to infringe Article 81 and not to satisfy the criteria for exemption in Article 81 (3).[173] The Commission also found that HB held a dominant position in the Irish impulse ice cream market (its market share was 75 per cent) and that its distribution arrangements infringed Article 82.

---

[169] Considered in the UK under the Fair Trade Act 1973 by the MMC in its report, *Ice Cream: A report on the Supply in the UK of Ice Cream for Immediate Consumption*, Cm. 2524 (TSO, 1994), and by the Competition Commission in its report, *The Supply of Impulse Ice Cream* Cm 4510 (TSO, 2000). In the latter, but not the former, the practice was held to operate against the public interest.

[170] The issue relates to 'impulse ice cream', that is ice cream sold in individual wrapped portions for immediate consumption, not ice cream bought in multi-packs from supermarkets.

[171] See A. Robertson and M. Williams, 'The Law and Economics of Freezer Exclusivity' [1995] 1 *ECLR* 7 (written after the MMC report) but cf. W. Sibree 'Ice Cream War: In Defence of the MMC' [1995] *ECLR* 203.

[172] Decision of 11 Mar. 1998, [1998] OJ L246/1, [1998] 5 CMLR 530. The decision was suspended by Order of the President of the CFI pending the appeal, on 7 July 1998; Case 65/98R [1998] 5 CMLR 475. The Commission had originally addressed a Statement of Objections to HB, the ice cream supplier, in July 1993 in which it considered that HB's distribution system infringed both Art. 82 and 81. HB therefore modified its distribution system and the Commission was for a time satisfied (see [1995] OJ C211/4). In 1997 the Commission decided that the distribution system still raised competition problems and it addressed a new Statement of Objections to HB on 22 Jan. 1997, which in due course led to the Mar. 1998 Decision. In the meantime proceedings initiated in the Irish High Court by Mars, which was a competitor of HB on the Irish ice cream market, asking for a declaration that HB's cabinet exclusivity agreements breached Arts. 81 and 82, reached the Irish Supreme Court, which on 10 June 1998 decided to refer the issue to the Court under Art. 234.

[173] See paras. 130–254 of the decision.

HB put forward certain arguments which were equally relevant to both Article 81 and Article 82. It argued that the application of Article 81 to the exclusivity provisions in the freezer agreements would be tantamount to interference with its property rights, contrary to Article 295 (ex Article 222) of the EC Treaty, in that it would permit other manufacturers' products to be stored in its property. The Commission replied[174] that, although the Community legal order recognizes the right to property in Article 295,[175] it is recognized in the constitutions of all Member States that the exercise, as distinct from the essence, of property rights may be restricted in the public interest to the necessary extent. This distinction between the existence and exercise of property rights is a familiar one in EC jurisprudence,[176] particularly in the field of intellectual property rights.[177] It sounds plausible, but the distinction is not theoretically convincing and is difficult to apply in practice. In *Van den Bergh* the Commission said that its condemnation of exclusivity could not be construed as an interference with HB's property rights. In essence, the retailer was paying for the freezer as part of the ice cream price and yet the exclusivity was for HB's benefit.

6. REFUSALS TO SUPPLY

A. GENERAL

A number of cases on Article 82 have concerned a dominant undertaking's refusal to supply its products or services or to grant access to its facilities. The CFI said in *Bayer*:[178]

. . . under Article [82] refusal to supply, even where it is total, is prohibited only if it constitutes an abuse. The case-law of the Court of Justice indireclty recognises the importance of safe-guarding free enterprise when applying the competition rules of the Treaty where it expressly acknowledges that even an undertaking in a dominant position may, in certain cases, refuse to sell . . .

The Court, therefore, has never said that all dominant undertakings have an absolute duty to supply all those who request them to do so. However, where *existing* customers are concerned it can be stated as a general proposition that a dominant undertaking will bear the burden of proving that the refusal to supply has some objective justification. Where *new* customers are concerned the position is more complex and it is necessary to distinguish

---

[174] Para. 212.

[175] Art. 295 EC says '[t]his Treaty shall in no way prejudice the rules in Member States governing the system of property ownership'.

[176] See Case 44/79 *Hauer* v. *Land Rheinland Pfalz* [1979] ECR 3727, [1980] 3 CMLR 42.

[177] See *infra* Chap. 10.

[178] Case T–41/96, *Bayer A.G.* v. *Commission*, Judgment 26 October 2000. See also *XIIIth Report on Competition Policy* (Commision, 1983), pt 157 in the context of the *Polaroid/SSI* investigation where Polaroid was alleged to have refused to supply a customer with the quantities ordered because of concerns that SSI intended to export some of the products. Polaroid agreed to supply the full amount and the Commission closed its file.

between products and facilities. Unsurprisingly, refusals to supply based on grounds of nationality have been held to infringe Article 82.[179]

The idea that a dominant undertaking has a duty to supply, in that a refusal to do so will be an abuse, is contrary to deep-seated notions of freedom of contract which decree that one should be free to deal with whom one chooses. The Court and Commission have developed their notions of when and why, in the name of competition, that freedom should be limited through a steady stream of decisions and judgments since *Commercial Solvents*[180] in 1973. The theme which pervades much Article 82 jurisprudence, that firms dominant in one market should not extend their dominance to ancillary markets,[181] has been prominent in this case law. It has made it difficult for undertakings wishing to integrate vertically or to operate downstream, and it has laid the foundations for the 'essential facilities' doctrine.

The Commission indicated in its 1983 Report that refusal to supply includes making supplies conditional on control over further processing or marketing and 'refusal to supply' includes supplying only on discriminatory and unfair conditions, or 'constructive refusals' where the offer is such that the supplier knows it is unacceptable. Conduct which can be described under some other heading of abuse, such as tying, can also be seen as a refusal to supply. In *Télémarketing*[182] the condition that advertisers could buy advertising time on television only if they used the television company's own telesales agency was both a refusal to supply and a tie, and so was the delivered pricing policy in *Napier Brown/British Sugar*.[183]

The cases show how difficult it is for a dominant undertaking to prove that a refusal to supply an existing customer is objectively justified. The defence did succeed, however, in *BP v. Commission*[184] where, during the OPEC oil boycott in 1973, an oil supplier dealt with the shortage by supplying its regular, long-term rather than occasional customers. The Commission found that the refusal to deal with occasional customers on the basis of what they ordered in a previous period was an abuse.[185] However, the Court held that the supply strategy was reasonable in the circumstances and that the refusal to supply ABG was justified.

A finding that a refusal to supply is an abuse raises the question of what is the appropriate remedy. Article 3 of Regulation 17[186] states that where the Commission finds an infringement of Article 82 'it may by decision require the undertakings . . . concerned to bring such infringement to an end'. In *Commercial Solvents* the Court established that this does not restrict the Commission to prohibiting actions or practices which are contrary to the Treaty.

---

[179] Case 7/82, *GVL v. Commission* [1983] ECR 483, [1983] 3 CMLR 645, which concerned the German collecting society's refusal to offer its services to artists established outside Germany unless they were of German nationality.

[180] Cases 6, 7/73, *Istituto Chemioterapico Italiano SpA and Commercial Solvents Corp. v. EC Commission* [1974] ECR 223, [1974] 1 CMLR 309.

[181] See Case 311/84, *Centre Belge d'Etudes du Marché-Télémarketing v. Compagnie Luxembourgeoise de Télédiffusion SA and Information Publicité Benelux SA* [1985] ECR 3261, [1986] 2 CMLR 558 .

[182] *Ibid.* See *supra* 324.

[183] *Napier Brown British Sugar* [1988] OJ L284/41, [1990] 4 CMLR 196: see *supra* 365.

[184] Case 77/77, *BP v. Commission* [1978] ECR 1513, [1978] 3 CMLR 174.

[185] *ABG Oil* [1977] OJ L117/1, [1977] 2 CMLR D1. The Commission held that for the duration of the crisis each supplier was in a dominant position in respect of its former customers, a point on which it was upheld by the Court.

[186] See *infra* Chap. 14.

It allows it to order an undertaking positively to do certain acts or to provide certain advantages which have been wrongfully withheld, including making specific orders about what exactly the dominant undertaking should supply to whom.

B. THE *COMMERCIAL SOLVENTS* CASE: REFUSAL TO SUPPLY IN ORDER TO EXCLUDE COMPETITORS FROM ANCILLARY MARKETS

Commercial Solvents was the first case in which a refusal to supply was held to be capable of infringing Article 82.

Cases 6, 7/73, *Istituto Chemioterapico Italiano Spa and Commercial Solvents Corp.* v. *Commission* [1974] ECR 223, [1974] 1 CMLR 309

Commercial Solvents (CSC) supplied aminobutanol, a raw material from which a derivative, ethambutaol, could be produced. CSC had an Italian subsidiary, Istituto, which resold aminobutanol in Italy to Zoja, an Italian pharmaceuticals company which used it to make ethambutol based anti-TB drugs. In 1970 Zoja cancelled its orders for aminobutanol from Istituto as independent distributors were supplying it cheaper. When these alternative supplies proved unsatisfactory Zoja placed new orders with Istituto. However, CSC had decided no longer to supply aminobutanol to the EEC but only an upgraded product, dextroaminobutanol, which Istituto would convert into ethambutol itself, manufacturing its own ethambutol based drugs. Zoja was therefore refused supplies. Zoja found it impossible to obtain supplies on the world market as all its searches led back to CSC. Zoja complained to the Commission. The Commission held that CSC was dominant in the market for aminobutanol and had abused its position by refusing to supply it to Zoja, a refusal which would lead to the elimination of one of the principal manufacturers of ethambutol in the common market. CSC appealed to the Court, which upheld the finding of dominance on the raw material market[187] and the finding of abuse.[188]

Court of Justice

23. The applicants state that they ought not to be held responsible for stopping supplies of aminobutanol to Zoja for this was due to the fact that in the spring of 1970 Zoja itself informed Istituto that it was cancelling the purchase of large quantities of aminobutanol which had been provided for in a contract then in force between Istituto and Zoja. When at the end of 1970 Zoja again contacted Istituto to obtain this product, the latter was obliged to reply, after consulting CSC, that in the meantime CSC had changed its commercial policy and that the product was no longer available. The change of policy by CSC was, they claim, inspired by a legitimate consideration of the advantage that would accrue to it of expanding its production to include the manufacture of finished products and not limiting itself to that of raw material or intermediate products. In pursuance of this policy it decided to improve its product and

---

[187] See *supra* Chap. 6.

[188] It also upheld the finding that there was an effect on inter-Member State trade on the basis that although few of Zoja's ethambutol-based drugs were exported to other Member States the elimination of Zoja as a competitor would affect the competitive structure of the common market: see *supra* Chap. 5.

no longer to supply aminobutanol save in respect of commitments already entered into by its distributors.

24. It appears from the documents and from the hearing that the suppliers of raw material are limited, as regards the EEC, to Istituto, which, as stated in the claim by CSC, started in 1968 to develop its own specialities based on ethambutol, and in November 1969 obtained the approval of the Italian government necessary for the manufacture and in 1970 started manufacturing its own specialities. When Zoja sought to obtain further supplies of aminobutanol, it received a negative reply. CSC had decided to limit, if not completely to cease, the supply of nitropropane and aminobutanol to certain parties in order to facilitate its own access to the market for the derivatives.

25. However, an undertaking being in a dominant position as regards the production of raw material and therefore able to control the supply to manufacturers of derivatives, cannot, just because it decides to start manufacturing these derivatives (in competition with its former customers) act in such a way as to eliminate their competition which in the case in question, would amount to eliminating one of the principal manufacturers of ethambutol in the Common Market. Since such conduct is contrary to the objectives expressed in Article [3 (1) (g)] of the Treaty and set out in greater detail in Articles [81] and [82], it follows that an undertaking which has a dominant position in the market in raw materials and which, with the object of reserving such raw materials for manufacturing its own derivatives, refuses to supply a customer, which is itself a manufacturer of these derivatives, and therefore risks eliminating all competition on the part of this customer, is abusing its dominant position within the meaning of Article [82]. In this context it does not matter that the undertaking ceased to supply in the spring of 1970 because of the cancellation of the purchases by Zoja, because it appears from the applicants' own statement that, when the supplies provided for in the contract had been completed, the sale of aminobutanol would have stopped in any case.

26. It is also unnecessary to examine, as the applicants have asked, whether Zoja had an urgent need for aminobutanol in 1970 and 1971 or whether this company still had large quantities of this product which would enable it to reorganize its production in good time, since that question is not relevant to the consideration of the conduct of the applicants.

27. Finally CSC states that its production of nitropropane and aminobutanol ought to be considered in the context of nitration of paraffin, of which nitropropane is only one of the derivatives, and that similarly aminobutanol is only one of the derivatives of nitropropane. Therefore the possibilities of producing the two products in question are not unlimited but depend in part on the possible sales outlets of the other derivatives.

28. However the applicants do not seriously dispute the statement in the Decision in question to the effect that 'in view of the production capacity of the CSC plant it can be confirmed that CSC can satisfy Zoja's needs, since Zoja represents a very small percentage (approximately 5–6 per cent) of CSC's global production of nitropropane'. It must be concluded that the Commission was justified in considering that such statements could not be taken into account.

29. These submissions must therefore be rejected.

According to paragraph 25, the factors leading to the finding of abuse were that CSC was using its dominant position on the raw material market to affect competition on the derivatives market, that it refused to supply an existing customer[189] because it wanted to compete

---

[189] It was not material that Zoja had previously cancelled its purchases from Istituto (see para. 25, last sentence).

with it downstream, and that the refusal risked eliminating the customer from the downstream market.

CSC had, in effect, decided to integrate vertically. The Court did not consider, however, whether this strategy might produce efficiencies, and there is no discussion in the judgment about the possible benefits to the end user, the consumer. It appears to be an instance of the competition authorities protecting the situation of the 'small' competitor and it may have been significant that Zoja was a small *Italian* competitor suffering at the hands of an American multinational.

C. REFUSAL TO SUPPLY IN RESPONSE TO AN ATTACK ON THE DOMINANT UNDERTAKING'S COMMERCIAL INTERESTS

It has been held that a dominant undertaking may infringe Article 82 by refusing to supply as a response to a perceived threat to its commercial interests. In *United Brands*[190] the Commission held that UBC had abused its dominant position on the banana market by refusing to continue supplying its Chiquita bananas to its Danish ripener/distributor, Oelsen. The refusal was made in response to Oelsen taking part in an advertising and promotion campaign for a rival brand, Standard Fruit's 'Dole' bananas. Oelsen was not under an exclusive purchasing obligation but UBC argued that Oelsen had sold fewer and fewer Chiquitas in comparison to Doles, and had taken less trouble in ripening them. Without gainsaying UBC's allegations, the Court upheld the Commission's finding that there was no objective justification for the refusal to supply and that it infringed Article 82.

Case 27/76, *United Brands* v. *Commission* [1978] ECR 207, [1978] 1 CMLR 429

Court of Justice

182. . . . [i]t is advisable to assert positively from the outset that an undertaking in a dominant position for the purpose of marketing a product—which cashes in on the reputation of a brand name known to and valued by the consumers—cannot stop supplying a long standing customer who abides by regular commercial practice, if the orders placed by that customer are in no way but of the ordinary.

183. Such conduct is inconsistent with the objectives laid down in Article [3(1)(g)] of the Treaty, which are set out in detail in Article [82], especially in paragraphs (b) and (c), since the refusal to sell would limit markets to the prejudice of consumers and would amount to discrimination which might in the end eliminate a trading party from the relevant market.

. . .

189. Although it is true, as the applicant points out, that the fact that an undertaking is in a dominant position cannot disentitle it from protecting its own commercial interests if they are attacked, and that such an undertaking must be conceded the right to take such reasonable steps as it deems appropriate to protect its said interests, such behaviour cannot be countenanced if its actual purpose is to strengthen this dominant position and abuse it.

---

[190] [1976] OJ L95/1, [1976] 1 CMLR D28.

190. Even if the possibility of a counter-attack is acceptable that attack must still be proportionate to the threat taking into account the economic strength of the undertakings confronting each other.

191. The sanction consisting of a refusal to supply by an undertaking in a dominant position was in excess of what might, if such a situation were to arise, reasonably be contemplated as a sanction for conduct similar to that for which UBC blamed Olesen.

192. In fact UBC could not be unaware of that fact that by acting in this way it would discourage its other ripener/distributors from supporting the advertising of other brand names and that the deterrent effect of the sanction imposed upon one of them would make its position of strength on the relevant market that much more effective.

193. Such a course of conduct amounts therefore to a serious interference with the independence of small and medium sized firms in their commercial relations with the undertaking in a dominant position and this independence implies the right to give preference to competitors' goods.

194. In this case the adoption of such a course of conduct is designed to have a serious adverse effect on competition on the relevant banana market by only allowing firms dependant upon the dominant undertaking to stay in business.

195. The applicant's argument that in its view the 40 per cent fall in the price of bananas on the Danish market shows that competition has not been affected by the refusal to supply Olesen cannot be upheld.

196. In fact this fall in prices was only due to the very lively competition—called at the time the 'banana war'—in which the two transnational companies UBC and Castle and Cooke engaged.

This is a prime example of the objective justification issue in the context of Article 82. Whilst affirming that dominant undertakings are justified in acting to prevent attacks on their commercial interests, the Court nevertheless judged UBC's response here to be disproportionate. It reached this conclusion despite recognizing that the company was in the midst of a 'banana war'.[191] It is not clear, given Oelsen's conduct, what the Court meant when it stated, in paragraph 182, that a dominant undertaking could not stop supplying a regular customer who 'abides by regular commercial practice'. Jebsen and Stevens argue[192] that 'the Court of Justice inferred an anti-competitive motive on United Brands' part, without, as far as one can see, a scintilla of evidence, and then condemned United Brands for having had this improper motive'. In their view the case results in the Court effectively precluding dominant undertakings 'from refusing to supply customers who either directly or indirectly wage an assault on their businesses'.

A similar situation arose in *Boosey & Hawkes*[193] where B&H, which the Commission held to be dominant in the narrowly defined British-style brass band instrument market, refused to have further dealings with two firms, one a distributor of its instruments and the other a

---

[191] In para. 196. As discussed *supra* in Chap. 6, UBC was found dominant with 45% of a narrowly drawn market (bananas rather than fruit) despite evidence of what the Court itself here calls 'very lively competition'.

[192] P. Jebsen and R. Stevens, 'Assumptions, Goals, and Dominant Undertakings: The Reg. of Competition Under Art. 86 of the European Union' (1996) 64 Antitrust L-J. 443, 510–11.

[193] *BBI/Boosey & Hawkes* [1987] OJ L 286/36, [1988] 4 CMLR 67. There were other alleged abuses by B&H, such as engaging in vexatious litigation (see *infra* 423).

repairer, who formed a company to manufacture and market instruments which competed with B&H's. The Commission took interim measures, ordering B&H to recommence supplies to its two customers. Again, the Commission recognized the right of dominant undertakings to protect their interests when attacked but refused to accept the conduct here was justified and proportionate.

BBI/Boosey & Hawkes: Interim Measures [1987] OJ L286/36, [1988] 4 CMLR 67

Commission

19. A course of conduct adopted by a dominant undertaking with a view to excluding a competitor from the market by means of other than legitimate competition on the merits may constitute an infringement of Article [82].

In the present case the documentary evidence indicates that B&H embarked on a course of conduct intended to remove the competitive threat from BBI, and that its withdrawal of supplies from GHH and RCN was part of that plan.

It is well established that refusal of supplies by a dominant producer to an established customer without objective justification may constitute an abuse under Article [82] (Case 27/76 *United Brands v. Commission*; Cases 6/73 and 7/73 *Commercial Solvents . . .*).

On the facts of the present case, the dependence of GHH and RCN on B&H products is such that there was a substantial likelihood of their going out of business as a result of the withholding of supplies.

The injury to competition would be aggravated where (as is alleged here) the stated purpose of the action is indirectly to prevent the entry into the market of a potential competitor to the dominant producer.

A dominant undertaking may always take reasonable steps to protect its commercial interests, but such measures must be fair and proportional to the threat. The fact that a customer of a dominant producer becomes associated with a competitor or a potential competitor of that manufacturer does not normally entitle the dominant producer to withdraw all supplies immediately or to take reprisals against that customer.

There is no obligation placed on a dominant producer to subsidize competition to itself. In the case where a customer transfers its central activity to the promotion of a competing brand it may be that even a dominant producer is entitled to review its commercial relations with that customers and on giving adequate notice terminate any special relationship. However, the refusal of all supplies to GHH and RCN, and the other actions B&H has taken against them as part of its reaction to the perceived threat of BBI, would appear in the circumstances of the present case to go beyond the legitimate defence of B&H's commercial interests.

B&H took the measures it did to retaliate against its customers for entering into competition with it. Had the new company been successful it could have seriously threatened B&H's position in a highly specialized, narrowly-defined market. The Commission saw here a dominant undertaking trying to exclude others from the market and seems only reluctantly to admit that in the circumstances which arose in this case 'even a dominant producer is entitled to review its commercial relations.' It shows, like *United Brands*, how seriously a finding of dominance limits an undertaking's conduct.

D. THE REFUSAL TO SUPPLY SPARE PARTS

A firm which refuses to supply spare parts may infringe Article 82 even though it is not dominant in the primary product market, but only in the market for its own spare parts. This was established in *Hugin*.

Hugin AB was a Swedish manufacturer of cash registers. Hugin's share of the cash register market was 12–14 per cent. Liptons was a UK firm which had been Hugin's exclusive distributor in the UK and had built up a business of servicing and repairing Hugin machines and renting them out, for which it required a constant supply of Hugin spare parts. Hugin supplied Liptons with spare parts until 1972 when it established a UK subsidiary to deal with its products in the UK and ceased to supply Liptons with spare parts. Liptons said that it was likely to go out of business as a result. The Commission held that in refusing to carry on supplying Liptons Hugin had abused its dominant position in the market for its own spare parts.[194] The Court annulled the decision, ruling that there was no effect on inter-Member State trade, but it confirmed the finding of dominance.[195] The Court did not rule on the finding of abuse but in the light of other developments in the cases on refusal to supply the reasoning in the Commission's decision is significant.

Liptons Cash Registers/ Hugin [1978] OJ L22/23, [1978] 1 CMLR D19

Commission

63. In cases in which an undertaking holding a dominant position within the Common Market or in a substantial part of it for the supply of certain products, and in particular where the dominant position is a monopoly:

(a) refused without objective justification to supply those products to existing substantial customers for and users of the products, and the refusal to supply seriously injures the latter in their business by interfering with and ultimately preventing them from continuing to offer a service or to carry on a line of business, thereby ultimately eliminating all competitors independent of the dominant undertaking from the market for that service or that line of business; and

(b) prohibits its subsidiaries and dealers from supplying those products outside its own distribution network and in particular to buyers in other member-States, thereby making the refusal to supply more effective by denying those products to the customers and users in question.

such conduct amounts to an abuse of a dominant position, where it causes competition to be substantially restricted and trade between member-States to be affected appreciably.

64. Hugin AB, both directly and through its subsidiaries, has abused its dominant position in the Common Market in each of the ways described above in a manner likely to strengthen and consolidate its dominant position.

65. (a) The stated policy of Hugin AB is that spare parts for Hugin cash registers are only delivered to its own subsidiaries and its own authorised dealers for their own use and are not for resale. From the moment, therefore, that a cash register user purchases a Hugin cash register, the

---

[194] For the dominant position aspect of this case, see *supra* Chap. 6.
[195] See *supra* Chap. 6.

result of Hugin's refusal to supply is to make the user in question totally dependent on Hugin AB for the supply of spare parts and in effect, for the maintenance and repair of that machine. Purchasers and users are thereby prevented from purchasing such spare parts from any other source and are in addition thereby also deprived of their freedom to choose where they will obtain the maintenance and repair of their machines.

66. Liptons allege, and Hugin AB does not dispute this, that the maintenance and repair of Hugin cash registers is within the competence of anyone having the skill to maintain and repair competitive cash registers and provided that they have experience and training in the repair of such machines. No other justification has been offered for the refusal to supply spare parts. There is therefore no valid objective reason for depriving companies such as Liptons, which have the requisite skills and training, from competing with Hugin AB, its subsidiaries and authorised dealers in the maintenance and repair of Hugin cash registers nor for depriving the owners and users of such machines from having access to such independent sources of maintenance and repair. Such refusal throughout the Common Market therefore constitutes an abuse of Hugin AB's dominant position in that it restricts effective competition. The refusal to supply also restricts trade in reconditioned Hugin cash registers which compete with new Hugin cash registers.

67. (b) With regard to Liptons the conduct of Hugin AB and Hugin UK is an abuse in that Liptons was in 1972 a principal customer for spare parts and had been a customer for spare parts for over 12 years and that the refusal to supply amounted to a withdrawal of supplies which had the result of removing a major competitor in the matter of service, maintenance, repair and the supply of reconditioned machines from a substantial part of the Common Market. Not only had Liptons been the main distributor for Hugin GB in England, Scotland and Wales, but it had started a substantial business in its own right of renting out of Hugin cash registers in which it had invested a considerable sum of money. Liptons was also qualified to service, maintain and repair such machines, and this business as it relates to new machines has ceased as a result of Hugin's refusal to supply spare parts. Liptons is now no longer in a position to buy the necessary spare parts for the maintenance and repair of Hugin cash registers for customers requiring that service, nor to undertake that service in respect of new machines it might wish to rent to its customers, nor, to a large extent, to meet its commitments to existing customers. In addition Liptons is severely restrained in the business it had carried on for over 12 years in reconditioning Hugin cash registers for resale.

68. Liptons has accordingly been forced gradually to withdraw from these businesses in which it had invested time and money and had established a strong basis for profitable expansion. Without a supply of spare parts Liptons will eventually be eliminated as a competitor in all these lines of business. The fact that Liptons has ceased to be a distributor of Hugin cash registers does not in the circumstances amount to a valid objective reason for refusing to supply spare parts as the business created by the 'main agency' agreement is separate from the other business of servicing, maintaining, repairing, renting out and reconditioning Hugin cash registers which Liptons undertook in its own right both before, during and to some extent, at least until supplies of spare parts ceased, after the agreement was in force.

69. (c) As a result of its policy of not supplying spare parts outside its own network, Hugin AB also abused its dominant position by prohibiting its subsidiaries in France, Belgium, Germany and the United Kingdom, and its independent distributors in Ireland, Italy and the Netherlands from supplying spare parts outside the Hugin distribution network. The letters from these companies clearly establish that such a prohibition was in force at the time Liptons endeavoured to obtain spare parts from Hugin AB itself and from the subsidiaries and the distributors referred to above. Such conduct shelters Hugin AB from all effective competition in the matter of service, maintenance and repair of

Hugin cash registers and from competition from reconditioning and rented Hugin cash registers throughout the Common Market.

70. The reasons given by Hugin for its refusal to supply Liptons are not objectively sufficient to justify such refusal. Even if it were correct that a Hugin cash register was a product of such complexity as to require special training beyond that required for any other mechanical, electro-mechanical or electronic product of a similar kind which, in view of the evidence available, the Commission does not accept, it would still not justify Hugin from withdrawing supplies of spare parts from Liptons at a time when it clearly was in possession of the necessary skills. Hugin cannot, therefore, rely on the fact that because of the lapse of time since the refusal to supply Liptons may have lost those skills if such loss is the result of the deliberate act of Hugin AB. Neither can the argument that there is no market for spare parts be accepted since Liptons was supplied with such spare parts for a period in excess of 12 years at the time when the supply of spare parts was withdrawn by Hugin. Liptons has spent more than five years seeking to obtain such spare parts from Hugin UK, Hugin AB and the other Hugin companies and distributors throughout the Common Market.

The definition of the market in *Hugin* as consisting solely of Hugin's own spare parts has been much criticized[196] but the entire case remains controversial. Hugin was not dominant on the cash register market, and the case raises the issues of power in aftermarkets and tying in aftermarkets which are discussed above.[197] Hugin, like Commercial Solvents, wanted to integrate vertically. The Commission rejected its claim of objective justification and (at paragraph 63 (a)) said that the refusal to supply was an abuse because it would lead to an existing customer being unable to carry out a particular line of business. As in *Commercial Solvents* the Commission did not consider questions of efficiencies or the advantages to owners of Hugin machines of the vertical integration but looked at the situation from the perspective of Liptons. It seems that the Commission's objective was Lipton's continued presence on the market: the protection of competitors rather than competition.

The Court did deal, obliquely, with the refusal to supply spare parts in two Article 234 references concerning the licensing of intellectual property rights covering car parts, *Renault*[198] and *Volvo*.[199] In *Volvo* the Court held that a refusal by the car manufacturer to license did not necessarily constitute an abuse, but would do so if it gave rise to 'certain abusive conduct ... such as the arbitrary refusal to deliver spare parts to independent repairers'.[200]

---

[196] See *supra* Chap. 6.
[197] See *supra* Chap. 6 and *supra*, 373.
[198] Case 53/87, *CICCRA* v. *Renault* [1988] ECR 6039, [1990] 4 CMLR 265.
[199] Case 238/87, *AB Volvo* v. *Erik Veng* [1988] ECR 6211, [1989] 4 CMLR 122.
[200] Case 53/87, *CICCRA* v. *Renault. supra* n. 198, para. 16. The case is considered further *infra*, 341.

E. REFUSAL TO SUPPLY AND THE EXCLUSION OF COMPETITORS FROM DOWNSTREAM MARKETS: THE APPLICATION OF THE *COMMERCIAL SOLVENTS AND TELEMARKETING PRINCIPLES*

(i) GENERAL

In *Commercial Solvents* and *Télémarketing* it was found that an outright refusal to supply, or a refusal to supply unless tied products or services were accepted, constituted an abuse. In both cases the refusal interfered with competition on a downstream market. The principle in those cases has been expanded upon and applied subsequently. A good example of a refusal to supply as a deliberate move to remove a competitor from a downstream market is *Napier Brown/British Sugar*,[201] where the dominant supplier of industrial sugar, which itself produced the derivative retail sugar, refused to supply industrial sugar to a competitor on the downstream market who was an existing customer.

(ii) ACCESS TO FACILITIES AND RESOURCES

A number of Commission decisions concerning refusal to supply have led to the development in EC law of what is called an 'essential facilities doctrine'. These decisions have concerned not the supply of products but the grant of access to some kind of facility or resource controlled by the dominant undertaking.[202] One of these decisions was *London-European Sabena*.[203] In this case the Belgian airline Sabena was dominant in Belgium in the computer reservation services market. It refused to give London-European, a competing airline, access to the system (although it had spare capacity). The Commission found that the refusal, which was to pressurize London-European either to withdraw from the London-Brussels route or to raise prices and also to punish London-European for its failure to use Sabena's ground-handling services, was an abuse. The Commission said that Sabena's conduct could equally be seen as a desire to limit production, markets, or technical development to the prejudice of consumers, contrary to Article 82 (b), and as enforcing a tie contrary to Article 82 (d). In this case, therefore, the Commission required a dominant undertaking to share its facilities with a competitor. As is seen below, in many of the cases where access to facilities or resources has been denied the undertaking refusing access has been dominant in consequence of a legal or statutory monopoly. The issue has particularly arisen in the transport sector, but it is also very important in the liberalization of sectors such as telecommunications.[204]

---

[201] *Napier Brown British Sugar* [1988] OJ L284/41, [19990] 4 CMLR 196.
[202] This is one reason why it is sometimes preferable to use the expression 'refusal to deal', rather than 'refusal to supply'.
[203] [1988] OJ l317/47, [1989] 4 CMLR 662.
[204] See *infra* 418.

(iii) THE DEVELOPMENT OF THE 'ESSENTIAL FACILITIES' DOCTRINE IN EC LAW

a. GENERAL

The definition of an 'essential facility' is fraught with difficulty. However, the central idea is that it is something owned or controlled by a dominant undertaking to which other undertakings need access in order to provide products or services to customers. It is sometimes called a 'bottleneck monopoly'. A refusal to grant access to an essential facility may be a breach of the competition rules.

The essential facilities doctrine originates in US law. Section 2 of the Sherman Act prohibits the acquisition or maintenance of monopoly power. In *United States* v. *Colgate & Co*,[205] however, the Supreme Court said that in the absence of any purpose to create or maintain a monopoly a private trader may freely 'exercise his own independent discretion as to parties with whom he may deal' and the US courts have consequently been generally reluctant to condemn refusals to deal. However, they have held that such refusals do come within section 2, by way of exception to the *Colgate* principle, where they are intended to eliminate competition in the monopolized market without a 'business justification' or where, according to some cases, they are an attempt at leverage, i.e. to gain a competitive advantage in a vertically related market. The US courts have also been willing to intervene where an 'essential facility' is in issue.[206] This has become known as the 'essential facilities doctrine'. There is a controversy in US antitrust law whether the doctrine is really part of the two recognized exceptions to the *Colgate* principle, or whether it is a separate principle.[207] In any event, many American commentators are highly critical of the application of the doctrine in US law. Hovenkamp says the 'so-called essential facilities doctrine is one of the most troublesome, incoherent and unmanageable bases for Sherman section 2 liability. The antitrust world would almost certainly be a better place if it were jettisoned, with a little fine tuning of the general doctrine of the monopolist's duty to deal to fill in the resulting gaps'.[208]

b. THE COMMISSION DECISIONS ON ESSENTIAL FACILITIES

The Commission did not use the expression 'essential facility' until *Sealink/B&I Holyhead*[209] in 1992. It is possible, however, particularly with hindsight, to see that the doctrine

---

[205] 250 US 300, 39 S Ct. 465 (1919).

[206] See *United States* v. *Terminal Railroad Association* 224 US 383 (1912); *Associated Press* v. *US*, 326 US 1 (1945); *Otter Tail Power Co.* v. *US*, 410 US 366 (1973); *Aspen Skiing Co.* v. *Aspen Highlands Skiing Corp.* 472 US 585 (1985): *MCI Communications Corp & MCI Telecommunications Corp* v. *American Telephone and Telegraph Company* 708 F 2d 1081 (1983) and P. Areeda: 'Essential Facilities: An Epithet in Need of Limiting Principles' (1990) 58 Antitrust LJ 841, which discusses the American cases: note that the expression 'essential facilities' was not used in the older ones.

[207] See L. Hancher, Case note on *Oscar Bronner* (1999) 36 CMLRev 1289; H. Hovenkamp, *Federal Antitrust Policy* (West Publishing, 1994) chap. 7; P. Areeda, Essential Facilities: An Epithet in Need of Limiting Principles [1990] *Antitrust LJ* 841.

[208] Hovenkamp, *supra* n. 207 273; see also Areeda, *supra* n. 207 a passage from which is reproduced *infra* at 397. Jacobs AG, reviewing the US position in Case C–7/97, *Oscar Bronner GmbH & Co. KG* v. *Mediaprint* [1998] ECR I–7791, [1999] 4 CMLR at 112, para. 46 of his Opinion, pointed out that s.2 of the Sherman Act and Art. 82 protect competition in different ways. The Sherman Act prohibits the acquisition or maintenance of monopoly power, whereas Art. 82 regulates the actions of companies in dominant positions.

[209] *Sealink/B&I Holyhead: Interim Measures* [1992] 5 CMLR 255.

manifested itself in earlier cases discussed above and in the Commission decision *British-Midland/Aer Lingus.*[210]

British Midland/Aer Lingus [1992] OJ L96/34, [1993] 4 CMLR 596

Interlining is a standard practice in the air transport industry, operated by IATA through a multi-lateral agreement to which interested airlines become parties, whereby airlines are authorised to sell each other's services. As a result a single ticket can be issued which comprises segments to be performed by different airlines. The issuing airline collects the price for all segments from the passenger and pays the fare due to the carrying line. The system enables a passenger to use a ticket issued by one airline for a return journey on another. Aer Lingus, which was held by the Commission to be in a dominant position on the London (Heathrow)–Dublin air-route, withdrew from its interlining arrangements with British Midland when British Midland started to operate a Heathrow–Dublin service. In a press statement at the time Aer Ligus said 'We have established ourselves as the dominant carrier on the routes between the two capitals, and intend to remain so . . . , British Midland does not have the resources to offer a similar frequency or service, so they want us to provide product for them via an interline agreement'.[211] The Commission held that the refusal to interline was an abuse of Aer Lingus's dominant position, fined it ECU 750,000 and ordered it to interline with British Midland on the Heathrow–Dublin route for two years.

Commission

24. Abusive conduct is defined as 'practices which are likely to affect the structure of a market where, as a result of the presence of the undertaking in question, competition has already been weakened and which, through recourse to methods differing from those governing normal competition in goods or services based on traders' performance, have the effect of hindering the maintenance or development of the level of competition existing on the market' (Case 85/76, *Hoffmann-La Roche* v. *E.C.Commission . . .*).

25. Refusing to interline is not normal competition on the merits. Interlining has for many years been accepted industry practice, with widely acknowledged benefits for both airlines and passengers. A refusal to interline for reasons other than problems with currency convertibility or doubts about the creditworthiness of the beneficiary airline is a highly unusual step and has up to now not been considered by the European airline industry as a normal competitive strategy. Aer Lingus itself has maintained interline agreements with the other airlines competing with it on London-Dublin services, British Airways and Dan Air.

Aer Lingus has argued that, whereas interlining in most circumstances is beneficial to all partici-pating airlines, it would suffer from interlining with British Midland by losing several points of market share to the new entrant. Even if this could be demonstrated, the argument that interlining would result in a loss of revenue would not in itself make the refusal legitimate. Aer Lingus has not argued that interlining with British Midland would have a significant effect on its own costs, whereas there is evidence that a refusal to interline would impose a significant handicap on British Midland.

26. Both a refusal to grant new interline facilities and the withdrawal of existing interline facilities may, depending on the circumstances, hinder the maintenance or development of competition.

---

[210] See J. Temple Lang, 'Defining Legitimate Competition: Companies' Duties to Supply Competitors and Access to Essential Facilities' (1994) 18 *Fordham International LJ* 437 and the Commission's citation of cases in *Sealink/B&I.*

[211] Para. 7.

Whether a duty to interline arises depends on the effects on competition of the refusal to interline; it would exist in particular when the refusal or withdrawal of interline facilities by a dominant airline is objectively likely to have a significant impact on the other airline's ability to start a new service or sustain an existing service on account of its effects on the other airline's costs and revenue in respect of the service in question, and when the dominant airline cannot give any objective commercial reason for its refusal (such as concerns about creditworthiness) other than its wish to avoid helping this particular competitor. It is unlikely that there is such justification when the dominant airline singles out an airline with which it previously interlined, after that airline starts competing on an important route, but continues to interline with other competitors.

27. When an airline commences a new service, it will normally expect to incur some losses during an initial period, during which it will have to organise economic operation of its service and to attract sufficient interest from the travel trade and from travellers. It cannot expect to attain the load factors and the revenue necessary to ensure profitable operations from the beginning of the service. Therefore new entry will always be difficult.

Denying interline facilities is likely to increase that difficulty. A new entrant without interlining facilities is likely to be considered in this respect as a second-rate airline by travel agents and by travellers alike, which will make it more difficult to attain the commercial standing required to operate profitably. Travel agents wish to avoid the loss of time, the extra work and the potential loss of revenue caused by issuing tickets for transport on an airline without interline facilities. Furthermore a significant number of passengers consider the possibility to change tickets and to organise complex journeys on a single ticket as necessary; a refusal to interline will have the effect of diverting many of these passengers away from the new entrant airline. In this respect, a refusal to interline affects in particular the well-informed business travellers who require fully flexible tickets and who make a disproportionately large contribution to the revenue of the new entrant; significantly reducing this revenue will have a serious affect on the economics of the new entrant's operations . . .

28. A refusal to interline also hinders the maintenance or development of competition when it imposes a significant cost on competitors. . . .

29. It is true that Aer Lingus' strategy in the event has not resulted in British Midland's departure from the route, and that British Midland has succeeded in building up a reasonable schedule and in obtaining a significant market share . . .

The fact that British Midland has been able to continue operations notwithstanding the handicap imposed on it by Aer Lingus, is due in the first place to British Midland's determination to succeed in the face of unusual difficulties; it does not mean that the refusal had no effect on competition. There is no doubt that at the time the practice was implemented, the refusal to interline was intended and was likely to hinder the development of competition. The lawfulness of the refusal at the time when it occurred cannot depend on whether the competitor was later willing and able to remain on the route in spite of the disadvantages imposed on it.

30. Consequently, Aer Lingus has pursued a strategy which (even if not wholly effective) is both selective and exclusionary and restricts the development of competition on the London (Heathrow)–Dublin route.

The refusal to interline in this case essentially consists in the imposition, contrary to normal industry practice, of a significant handicap on a competitor by raising its costs and depriving it of revenue. Aer Lingus has not been able to point to efficiencies created by a refusal to interline nor to advance any other persuasive and legitimate business justification for its conduct. Its desire to avoid loss of market share, the circumstance that this a route of vital importance to the company and that its operating margin in under pressure do not make this a legitimate response to new entry.

In this case the refusal to supply affected competition on the market on which the dominant position existed, and not on a downstream market. The Commission did not condemn refusals to interline *per se* but only where they have significant effects on competition (paragraph 26) and are not objectively justified. In this case, in fact, Aer Lingus's strategy had *not* resulted in British Midland's departure from the route, and it is difficult to see that the interlining could be classified as an essential facility. It was not *essential* to the competitor's operations.[212] However, the mode of reasoning is similar both to the American cases and to the Commission decisions which succeeded it. It was a case of a clear intention of refusing to supply in order to exclude a competitor, although Aer Lingus was dominant only because of the narrowly defined market and no more than a minnow in the wider European airline market.[213] The case well illustrates the point that it does not matter if the new competitor is a powerful player on *another* market (a similar situation arose in *Irish Sugar*[214] where the undertaking dominant in Ireland was trying to exclude the dominant French supplier from the Irish market). *British-Midland* needs to be seen in context, however, as part of the Commission's drive to liberalize the European air transport sector. The Commission said of the case in its 1992 *Report on Competition Policy*:

218. This decision is evidence of the Commission's determination to act against airlines holding dominant positions, if they attempt to prevent the development or maintenance of competition. At a time when the European air transport industry is being liberalized, airlines making use of the new opportunities for competition should be given a fair chance to develop and sustain their challenge to established carriers.

Airlines holding dominant positions should not penalize this competition. They should not withold facilities which the industry traditionally provides to all other airlines, and they should take care to compete strictly on the merits of their own services.

The first express reference to the essential facilities doctrine in EC law was made in *B&I/Sealink*:

Sealink/B&I Holyhead: Interim Measures [1992] 5 CMLR 255

Sealink Harbours was the owner and operator of the port at Holyhead, in Wales, and as such was held by the Commission to be in a dominant position on the market on the British side for port facilities for ferry services on the 'central corridor' route between Wales and Ireland (i.e. Holyhead to Dublin and Dun Laoghaire). It ran ferries on that route. B&I also ran ferries from the port. B&I used a particular berth, the Admiralty Pier, and the limitations of the harbour were such that whenever Sealink's ferries passed the berth the drawing away of water and turbulence meant that B&I had to cease all loading and unloading activity. B&I complained that Sealink intended to introduce a new timetable which would cause greater disruption to B&I's schedules in this way. The Commission adopted a decision providing for interim measures, ordering Sealink to return to its previous timetable. The matter never went to a final decision as the dispute was settled.

---

[212] It would not fulfill the criteria laid down by the ECJ in Case C–7/97 *Oscar Bronner GmbH & Co. KG* v. *Mediaprint* [1998] ECR I–7791, [1999] 4 CMLR 112, discussed *infra* at 412.

[213] A point which was made in a question about the decision put to the Competition Commissioner by an Irish MEP: E.P. Deb. 3–418/222 (13 May 1992), question no. H–0464/92, [1992] 5 CMLR 209.

[214] Case T–228/97, *Irish Sugar plc* v. *Commission* [1999] 5 CMLR 1 300.

Commission

41. A dominant undertaking which both owns or controls and itself uses an essential facility i.e. a facility or infrastructure without access to which competitors cannot provide services to their customers, and which refuses its competitors access to that facility or grants access to competitors only on terms less favourable than those which it gives its own services, thereby placing the competitors at a competitive disadvantage, infringes Article [82], if the other conditions of that Article are met. . . .[215] A company in a dominant position may not discriminate in favour of its own activities in a related market (Case C–260/89 *Elliniki Radiophonia*, paragraphs 37–38) ... The owner of an essential facility which uses its power in one market in order to strengthen its position in another related market, in particular, by granting its competitor access to that related market on less favourable terms than those of its own services, infringes Article [82] where a competitive disadvantage is imposed upon its competitor without objective justification. . . . .

42. The owner of the essential facility, which also uses the essential facility, may not impose a competitive disadvantage on its competitor, also a user of the essential facility, by altering its own schedule to the detriment of the competitor's service, where, as in this case, the construction or the features of the facility are such that it is not possible to alter one competitor's service in the way chosen without harming the other's. Specifically, where, as in this case, the competitor is already subject to a certain level of disruption from the dominant undertaking's activities, there is a duty to the dominant undertaking not to take any action which will result in further disruption. That is so even if the latter's actions make, or are primarily intended to make its operations more efficient. Subject to any objective elements outside its control, such an undertaking is under a duty not to impose a competitive disadvantage upon its competitor in the use of the shared facility without objective justification, as seemed to be accepted by S H L in 1989.

In the first sentence of paragraph 41 the Commission laid down the basic principle that an owner of an essential facility may have to provide non-discriminatory access to it to a competitor. The Commission developed the theme in three further decisions concerning ports, *Sea Containers Ltd* v. *Stena*,[216] *Port of Rødby (Euro-port)* v. *Denmark*,[217] and *Morlaix (Port of Roscoff)*.[218]

Sea Containers Ltd /Stena Sealink [1994] OJ L15/8, [1995] 4 CMLR 84

Stena Sealink was the owner and operator of the port of Holyhead in Wales and ran ferries to and from Ireland. Before 16 November the company was called Sealink Harbours Ltd and as such was

---

[215] The Commission here cited Cases 6, 7/73 *Istituto Chemioterapico Italiano Spa and Commercial Solvents Corp.* v. *EC Commission* [1974] ECR 223, [1974] 1 CMLR 309; Case 311/84, *Centre Belge d'Etudes du Marché-Télémarketing* v. *Compagnie Luxembourgeoise de Télédiffusion SA and Information Publicité Benelux SA* [1985] ECR 3261, [1986] 2 CMLR 558; Case 53/87 *CICCRA* v. *Renault* [1988] ECR 6039, [1990] 4 CMLR 265; Case 238/87, *AB Volvo* v. *Erik Veng* [1988] ECR 6211, [1989] 4 CMLR 122; Case C–260/89, *Elliniki Radiophonia Tileorasi (ERT)* v. *DEP* [1991] ECR I–2925; Cases T–69–70/89, *Television Listings/Magill RTE, ITP, BBC* v. *EC Commission* [1991] ECR II–485, [1991] 4 CMLR 586, (the ECJ judgment had not yet been given); Case C–18/88 *RTT* v. *GB-INNO-BM SA* [1991] ECR I–5941; and the Commission decisions *National Carbonising* [1976] OJ L35/6, [1976] 1 CMLR D82; *London-European/Sabena* [1988] OJ l317/47, [1989] 4 CMLR 662.; *British Midland/Aer Lingus* [1992] OJ L 96/34, [1993] 4 CMLR 596.

[216] *Sea Containers Ltd /Stena Sealink* [1994] OJ L15/8, [1995] 4 CMLR 84.

[217] [1994] OJ L55/52, [1994] 5 CMLR 457.

[218] [1995] 5 CMLR 177 .

the company involved in the previous decision, *B&I/Sealink*. Sea Containers (SC) was a company operating ferries which wanted to operate a fast ferry service on the central corridor route by lightweight SeaCat catamaran. There was a series of negotiations between the two companies but Sealink would not agree to the access which Sea Containers wanted. Sea Containers complained to the Commission. However, the parties came to an agreement, with Sealink offering access on terms which the Commission considered to be reasonable and non-discriminatory, before the Commission had made any order. Nevertheless, the Commission went ahead and adopted a formal decision with regard to the position before the agreement 'in order to clarify the legal position for the benefit of the companies and other interested parties'.[219] It held, as before, that Sealink was in a dominant position as the port authority on the British side of the central corridor and that there was 'a sufficient prima facie case of a pattern of behaviour constituting abuse under Article [82] to order interim measures'. In fact it did not order the measures because of the developments which had occurred in the meantime.

Commission

66. An undertaking which occupies a dominant position in the provision of an essential facility and itself uses that facility (*i.e.* a facility or infrastructure, without access to which competitors cannot provide services to their customers), and which refuses other companies access to that facility without objective justification or grants access to competitors only on terms less favourable than those which it gives its own services, infringes Article [82] if the other conditions of that Article are met. An undertaking in a dominant position may not discriminate in favour of its own activities in a related market. The owner of an essential facility which uses its power in one market in order to protect or strengthen its position in another related market, in particular, by refusing to grant access to a competitor, or by granting access on less favourable terms than those of its own services, and thus imposing a competitive disadvantage on its competitor, infringes Article [82].

67. This principle applies when the competitor seeking access to the essential facilities is a new entrant into the relevant market. . .

. . .

75. It is the Commission's view that in the circumstances of the present case an independent harbour authority, which would of course have had an interest in increasing revenue at the port, would at least have considered whether the interests of existing and proposed users of the port could best be reconciled by a solution involving modest changes in the allocated slot times or in any plans for the development of the harbour. In situations such as the present one, unless a solution is considered fully and discussed with all the interests involved, it is likely that a port authority which is not independent will prefer an arrangement which minimises inconvenience to itself (especially in relation to its own operations as a user) but which does not necessarily provide non-discriminatory access to the new entrant. If Sealink, in drawing up the various versions of its redevelopment plan for the east side, had always duly consulted SC (and B & I), it might have been possible to avoid the difficulty of reconciling the plan with SC's wish for temporary facilities there

In its 1993 *Report on Competition Policy* the Commission said in respect of this case:

The Commission believes that, when a company is in a position such as that of Sealink in this case, it cannot normally expect to fulfil satisfactorily its duty to provide non-discriminatory access and to resolve its conflicts of interest unless it takes steps to separate its management of the essential facility from its use of it. This could involve, for example, having different employees responsible for the management of the port than for the management of the ferry service, the establishment of a non-

---

[219] Commission's *XXIII Report on Competition Policy* (Commission, 1993) pt 234.

discriminatory code of practice, a consultation procedure involving other port users, and arrangements for independent arbitration in the event of disputes.

The *Sea Containers/Stena* decision made it clear that the duty to supply essential facilities set out in *Sealink/B&I* applies to *new* as well as to existing customers. This was shown in another decision taken on the same day, *Port of Rødby*. In this case the Commission held that Denmark had infringed Article 86 (1) in conjunction with Article 82.[220]

Port of Rødby [1994] OJ L55/52, [1994] 5 CMLR 457

The port of Rødby in Denmark was owned and managed by a publicly owned port authority (DSB) which operated the only ferry between there and Puttgarden in Germany jointly with German national railways (DB). Two other companies, Euro-Port and Scan-Port wanted to run a ferry on the same route. The Danish Government refused either to grant them access to the port or to grant permission to build another terminal on the immediate vicinity. The Commission held that DSB was a public undertaking in a dominant position on the market for the organisation of port services in Denmark for ferries on the Rødby—Puttgarden route and that the double refusal had the effect of eliminating a potential competitor and infringed Article [82].

Commission

12. The refusal to allow 'Euro-Port A/S', a subsidiary of the Swedish group 'Stena Rederi AB' (Stena) to operate from Rødby has the effect of eliminating a potential competitor on the Rødby-Puttgarden route and hence of strengthening the joint dominant position of DSB and DB on that route.

According to the case law of the Court, an abuse within the meaning of Article [82] is committed in cases, where, without any objective necessity, an undertaking holding a dominant position on a particular market reserves to itself an ancillary activity which might be carried out by another undertaking as part of its activities on a neighbouring but separate market, with the possibility of eliminating all competition from such undertaking: Case 311/84, *CBEM* v. *CLT and IPB* . . .

Thus, an undertaking that owns or manages and uses itself an essential facility, *i.e* a facility or infrastructure without which its competitors are unable to offer their services to customers, and refuses to grant them access to such facility is abusing its dominant position.

Consequently, an undertaking that owns or manages an essential port facility from which it provides a maritime transport service may not, without objective justification, refuse to grant a shipowner wishing to operate on the same maritime route access to that facility without infringing Article [82].

The decision in *Morlaix (Port of Roscoff)* dealt with a slightly, though significantly, different situation. Irish Continental Group (ICG) wanted to run a ferry service from Ireland to Brittany and needed access to the port of Roscoff, which was managed by CCI Morlaix, a French administrative body granted a concession by the State for that purpose. CCI Morlaix did *not* run ferries itself, although it did have a shareholding of about 5 per cent in Brittany Ferries, which at the time operated the only ferry running from Ireland to Brittany. The

---

[220] For Art. 86, which deals with the application of the competition rules to public undertakings, see *infra* Chap. 8.

Commission found that CCI Morlaix's difficult behaviour over the negotiations for access amounted to a refusal to supply and that the refusal would have been an abuse *even if the authority had had no interest in Brittany Ferries.*

Morlaix (Port of Roscoff) [1995] 5 CMLR 177

Commission

59. CCI Morlaix occupies a dominant position in the provision of an essential facility (*i.e.* a facility or infrastructure, without access to which competitors cannot provide services to their customers). Its refusal, without objective justification, to grant access to these facilities to a company wishing to compete with a company active in a secondary market constitutes an abuse of its dominant position, even leaving aside any economic interest held by CCI Morlaix in Brittany Ferries.

60. This conclusion is not invalidated by the fact that the competitor seeking access to the essential facilities is a new entrant into the relevant market. In Case 85/76, Hoffmann-la Roche v. *E.C. Commission . . . the Court said:*

> The concept of abuse is an objective concept relating to the behaviour of an undertaking in a dominant position which is such as to influence the structure of a market . . . and which, through recourse to methods different from those which condition normal competition in products or services on the basis of the transactions of commercial operators, has the effect of hindering the maintenance of the degree of competition still existing in the market *or the growth of that competition.*

. . .

66. A company in a dominant position which sells services must have a valid reason for refusing to sell them to a willing buyer, in particular where the company in a dominant position controls access to an essential facility. The Commission considers that the unjustified behaviour of CCI Morlaix, in particular its lack of will concerning the continuation of negotiations and the weakness of the arguments advanced by it after 4 January, amounts to a refusal to sell, which is aimed at exercising its power as a port authority to go back on its agreement in principle of 16 December, without objective justification. This behaviour is not consistent with the obligations on an undertaking which enjoys a dominant position in relation to an essential facility

As in *Port of Rødby* the Commission cited and relied upon the passage from *Hoffmann-La Roche* which states that an abuse may occur where recourse is had to methods different from those which condition normal competition, stressing the Court's reference to behaviour which hinders *the growth* of competition.[221] The decision in *Morlaix (Port of Roscoff)* showed in paragraph 59 that the Commission would not just apply the essential facilities doctrine where a dominant undertaking interfered with competition on a secondary market which it competed on itself. Rather, it sets out more broadly how an undertaking with a statutory monopoly must conduct itself. Ironically it seems from the Commission's comment on the *Sea Containers/Stena* case that a dominant undertaking which *does* compete downstream is supposed to behave on the dominated market as though it were, in effect, a disinterested public authority.

---

[221] At para. 60.

c. ISSUES IN THE ESSENTIAL FACILITIES DOCTRINE

The recognition of the concept of essential facilities is just the beginning. Once the doctrine is accepted many questions follow which have to be answered: what exactly constitutes an essential facility? when does access have to be given? to whom does it have to be given? on what terms must it be given?

In *B&I/Sealink* essential facilities were defined as 'a facility or infrastructure without access to which competitors cannot provide services to their customers'. This definition provides only a starting point. The definition should, however, be narrowly confined, since a finding that an undertaking is dominant over essential facilities may result in that undertaking being forced to share its facilities or assets with its competitors. This represents a severe interference with an undertaking's rights which can only be justified where there would otherwise be a serious effect on competition which cannot be remedied by less intrusive measures.

There has to be some way of identifying assets to which access by competitors is truly 'essential' rather than merely desirable. Even when these are identified there may be practical problems about access or sharing. Some facilities (ports for example) have limited physical capacity, and the question arises *which* competitors should be given access. There is also the matter of the *terms* on which access is given. If the parties are left to settle their own terms the owner of the facility may be able to impose a price which is prohibitively high.[222] If the terms are to be set by an authority such as the Commission, however, the authority ends up acting as a price regulator.

It will be noted that the Commission decisions mentioned above concern the transport sector. The development of the essential facilities doctrine in EC law has been closely bound up with liberalization in that sector. This is no coincidence. The Commission has used the doctrine to encourage competition where there had previously been monopoly. The essential facilities doctrine has a particular relevance to liberalization in transport and in the utilities sectors,[223] which across the Community are being opened up to competition. Competition will, however, be possible only if new competitors are granted access to existing facilities, such as networks, which cannot feasibly be replicated and which may originally have been developed with public money. Even where replication is possible it may be against the public interest on other grounds, such as environmental considerations. On the other hand, an over-enthusiastic approach to essential facilities may result in undertakings having to share with competitors assets which they have developed over many years at great expense. Robbing firms of the fruits of their endeavours may be injurious to the public interest as it removes incentives to innovation.

These issues and the difficulties inherent in the recognition of the essential facilities doctrine are discussed in the following extracts. The first author is an economist, the second was an eminent American commentator, and the third is a Commission official who at the time of writing was concerned with opening up the air transport sector to competition.

---

[222] See Case C–242/95, *GT–Link A/S v. De Danske Statsbaner (DSB)* [1997] ECR I–4449, [1997] 5 CMLR 601, where the ECJ held that excessive duties levied by a public undertaking on a ferry company in breach of Art. 86, in conjunction with Art. 82, must be repaid.

[223] See the Notice on the Application to Access Agreements in the Telecommunications Sector [1998] OJ C265/2.

D.Ridyard: 'Essential Facilities and the Obligation to Supply Competitors' [1996] *ECLR* 438 at 447–8, 450, 451

Identifying the Essential Facility

Essential facilities cases invariably originate from a complaint by a firm that feels disadvantaged by a competitor's position. Unless a complete revolution in competition policy enforcement is envisaged, however, it does not make sense to treat 'disadvantage to a competitor' as a sufficient condition for the existence of an essential facility. This would lead to intervention as soon as any firm gained a competitive advantage that its rivals envied.

Equally, 'disadvantage to consumers' is likely to be a poor or unworkable criterion despite its superficial appeal. The tension between static and dynamic incentives for efficiency within a market economy will always entail unrealised potential consumer gains remaining untapped at any point in time if the market is working effectively. Any competition policy action that focuses exclusively on the immediate short-term impact on consumers, whether in essential facility or other circumstances, stands to do considerable economic damage . . .

To gain a proper perspective, it is necessary to stand back from specific concerns of consumers and competitors, and instead to ask where essential facilities issues fit into the general objective of competition rules to protect effective competition. This suggests that the key to the problem is to assess whether the owner of the allegedly essential facility is subject to effective competitive pressure, either in the form of existing assets also competing at the up-stream level, or in the form of potential assets that other firms might create. Any rational standard of effective or workable competition must acknowledge that some competitive activity will be very highly rewarded, so assets created through the competitive process will be highly sought after by others. But it is only where competition has seriously broken down or cannot be expected to operate that a case for compulsion arises.

In the great majority of cases, this approach will confine the existence of essential facilities to natural monopoly activities that, quite apart from it being commercially infeasible, one would not even want competitors to replicate. . . .

The identification of an essential facility using this test has important consequences that must be acknowledged in full if a rational policy is to emerge. Once it is acknowledged that it is neither feasible nor even desirable for competitors to replicate the asset concerned, it follows that the essential facility is a monopoly asset, and that if the competition rules are used to impose a duty on the owner to share the asset with competitors, these powers must also be used to regulate the terms on which that access is granted.

This need for the regulator to enter into price decisions does imply an unattractive degree of intervention in the market, but one that logically must be unavoidable once it is decided that an essential facility must be shared. A recognition of the difficulties that the competition body must resolve once it has identified the essential facility should serve to provide a sharp reminder not to take up essential facilities cases too readily.

Negotiation between the owner of the essential facility and the complainant

Free negotiation cannot be expected to provide a satisfactory solution. If the essential facility is indeed a monopoly, the outcome of free negotiation between a monopoly asset owner and a competitive complainant must also be unsatisfactory. Indeed, refusal to supply or deal is itself equivalent to the asset owner setting an access price that is prohibitively high, and any asset owner subject to free negotiation will be able to replicate this outcome by quoting a sufficiently high price.

There are several reasons why it may be pro-competitive and welfare enhancing for an asset owner to retain joint control of both up-stream and down-stream activities, and thus impose access terms that are prohibitive. Reasons include the possible existence of scope economics, and adverse effects on the asset owner's reputation if a third party fails to meet the same standards as the in-house operator.

. . .

Optimal access pricing requires the competition authority or regulator to reach a view on the appropriate asset value for the essential facility. That appropriate value will correspond to the value the asset would command if it were subject to effective competition from rival assets. If the asset in question is indeed an essential facility, the appropriate asset value will always be less than the value of the essential facility if the owner is free to exploit the asset to maximise profits without regulatory constraint. The difference between the appropriate and the unconstrained asset values will be the excess profit or monopoly component of the property right that is being confiscated by the competition policy intervention.

Access pricing to the essential facility should be set such as to provide a revenue stream (including both in-house and third party use of the asset) that will remunerate the appropriate value of the asset, but no more.

When the problem is put in these terms it is easy to see why competition authorities choose to evade the question of access prices. Even for a relatively stable essential facility such as BG's [British Gas] UK network of gas pipes, reasonable people can and do hold widely divergent views on the appropriate asset value. In cases where the existence of the essential facility is more contentious, and where the value of the asset in question is more susceptible to shifts in market circumstances, the scope for varying outcomes is even wider.

However, evading the problem does not make it disappear. It simply makes the solutions adopted more difficult to interpret and less likely to form part of a rational and consistent response to the essential facilities problem.

Ridyard discusses several fundamental points here. He stresses that access to a facility should be required only where competition in the downstream market has seriously broken down, that the concept of an 'essential facility' should be very narrowly defined, that there are difficult problems of access pricing to be faced, and that competition authorities may as a result of the doctrine end up as price regulators.

The next comment is the conclusion from Areeda's critical survey of the essential facilities doctrine in US law. He considers it a concept which should be treated with the greatest circumspection, in particular because it is a dangerous disincentive to innovation. Obviously, his remarks describe the doctrine as it is applied in US law.

P. Areeda 'Essential Facilities: An Epithet in Need of Limiting Principles', (1990) 58 *Antitrust LJ*, 841 at 852–3

I conclude by offering six principles that should limit application of the essential facilities concept.

(1) There is no general duty to share. Compulsory access, if it exists at all, is and should be very exceptional. . . .

(2) A single firm's facility, as distinct from that of a combination, is 'essential' only when it is both critical to the plaintiff's competitive vitality and the plaintiff is essential for competition in the marketplace. 'Critical to the plaintiff's competitive vitality' means that the plaintiff cannot compete effectively without it and that duplication or practical alternatives are not available.

(3) No one should be forced to deal unless doing so is likely substantially to improve competition in the marketplace by reducing price or by increasing output or innovation. Such an improvement is

unlikely (a) when it would chill desirable activity; (b) the plaintiff is not an actual or potential competitor; (c) when the plaintiff merely substitutes itself for the monopolist or shares the monopolist's gains; or (d) when the monopolist already has the usual privilege of charging the monopoly price for its resources. . . .

(4) Even when all these conditions are satisfied, denial of access is never per se unlawful; legitimate business purpose always saves the defendant. What constitutes legitimacy is a question of law for the courts. Although the defendant bears the burden of coming forward with a legitimate business purpose, the plaintiff bears the burden of persuading the tribunal that any such claim is unjustified.

(5) The defendant's intention is seldom illuminating, because every firm that denies its facilities to rivals does so to limit competition with itself and increase its profits. Any instruction on intention must ask whether the defendant had an intention to exclude by *improper* means. To get ahead in the marketplace is not, itself the kind of intention that contaminates conduct. . . .

(6) No court should impose a duty to deal that it cannot explain or adequately and reasonably supervise. The problem should be deemed irremedial by antitrust law when compulsory access requires the court to assume the day-to-day controls characteristic of a regulatory agency. Remedies may be practical (a) when admission to a consortium is at stake, especially at the outset, (b) when divestiture is otherwise appropriate and effective, or (c) when, as in *Otter Tail*, a regulatory agency already exists to control the terms of dealing. However, the availability of a remedy is not reason to grant one. Compulsory sharing should remain exceptional.

The sceptical tenor of the above passage is in contrast to the comments below. In this extract Temple Lang takes a much more enthusiastic view of the essential facilities doctrine and the part it can play in promoting competitive markets. The writer addresses some of the practical problems which may actually arise following a requirement of access.

J. Temple Lang 'Defining Legitimate Competition: Companies' Duties to Supply Competitors and Access to Essential Facilities' (1994) 18 *Fordham International* 437, 475–6, 478–83

A company whose business is the sale of goods or services must have a reason if it refuses to sell them to a willing buyer. It might wish to use the goods or service in its own operations, or to distribute them itself. In the absence of some legitimate business explanation, a refusal to supply is not what the Court calls 'normal competition.' A refusal to supply a customer that is not a competitor of any part of the dominant supplier's activities has anticompetitive effects only if it is an effort, directly or indirectly, to get the customer to buy exclusively from the dominant company. The *United Brands* . . . case presents an example of this situation.

When the customer is also a competitor of the dominant company in some market, usually downstream from the point at which the refusal to supply occurs, the effect on competition largely depends on three factors: (1) whether the buyer can obtain the goods or service elsewhere; (2) whether there are other downstream competitors; and (3) how important the goods or services are to the buyer's business. If the buyer has another satisfactory source of supply, if the goods or services are not essential, or if one more competitor will not add significantly to competition, antitrust law should not oblige the dominant company to supply. . . . If however, in practice, the refusal by the dominant company to supply means that one of the very few competitors is forced out of the market, EC antitrust law requires the dominant company to supply.

The EC case law does not suggest that a refusal to supply by a dominant enterprise is always regarded as having an effect on competition. Such a strict view would probably be incorrect. There would be no basis in antitrust law for a rule requiring a dominant enterprise to supply even if a refusal caused no effect on competition. However, if the consequence of a refusal by a dominant enterprise to supply is that all or most of its competitors are excluded from the market, only strong business reasons can justify the refusal. In brief, access to a facility is 'essential' when refusal would exclude all or most competitors from the market. . . .

Apart from the question of whether the company in question is dominant in the upstream market, several kinds of questions arise:

— what are the dominant company's duties to grant is competitors access to facilities that it owns or operates and that its competitors need to carry on their business and to compete with it?
— what are the dominant company's duties to grant licenses of intellectual property rights to its competitors to enable them to make products that compete with some of its products?
— what are the dominant company's duties to enable its competitors to adapt their products to make them compatible with the dominant company's new or altered products?

Although the company's market power in the downstream market may be relevant, the company need not be dominant on both markets for these questions to arise. Such issues may arise if the company is dominant on the market for the supply of the essential goods or the services provided by giving access to the essential facility. In practice, in most cases the dominance will be largely due to owning or controlling the essential facility. If the company is also dominant in the downstream market, so that a duty to provide access to the essential facility is required for competition in that market, the arguments for a duty to give access are much stronger.

These problems also raise a number of related difficulties. There is a conflict between the fact that it is, in general, pro-competitive to allow a company to retain for its own exclusive use advantages it has legitimately obtained, and the fact that access to certain facilities may be so essential to competitors that ownership of those facilities may give a company the power to exclude competitors entirely from a market, without having any justification other than its ownership for doing so. The dominant company has a conflict of interest between its interest as a competitor (to keep the benefits of ownership or control to itself) and its interest as owner (to maximize the profits from its ownership or the ownership of those on whose behalf it acts). This gives rise to the question of distinguishing between legitimately obtained and legitimately used competitive advantages, which a dominant company may exclusively enjoy, and advantages that are, in some sense, unfair or improper or otherwise contrary to Article [82] to use exclusively, or which competition law should not allow to be used exclusively.

Another difficulty is that, in most essential facility cases, the dominant company has denied competitors satisfactory access to a facility that it uses, without thereby improving the services offered. A dominant owner of a facility is not entitled to improve its service to recipients if there is a corresponding reduction in the quality of the service offered by its downstream competitors. . . . More difficult questions would arise if, for example, the dominant company is able to show that all the available capacity should be used by only one company to optimize the service to consumers. Therefore, one question can be whether the advantage to consumers outweighs the harm done to competition. A marginal benefit to consumers would not outweigh the exclusion of competitors from the market. If only one user can be efficient, the right to use might have to be auctioned at intervals.

It is also important to note that any legal principle that obliges a dominant company to make a contract with a competitor involves administrative costs for the companies and for authorities responsible for enforcing the principle. This burden is significant for the EC Commission, which is already short-staffed in relation to its responsibilities.

When a dominant company owns or controls a facility access that is essential for its competitors, it has a conflict of interest that would not arise if the facility were owned by an independent public utility, which would have a duty of impartiality, or by a separate owner, which, even if dominant, would be entitled to protect its interests as owner. The dominant company's duty is to operate the facility in such a way that the goods and services offered by its downstream competitors are not made less satisfactory or less readily available unless there is some sufficient overriding benefit to consumers or some reason based on the dominant company's objective interests as the owner of the essential facility, but not merely those of its own downstream operation. The dominant company may always make its own goods or services better for consumers, but may not take steps that merely make its competitors' worse or discriminate against its downstream competitor. . . .

A dominant company is always allowed to behave as would a separate and independent owner, or an impartial independent public authority. A standard of impartiality appropriate to an independent owner, or the still higher standard appropriate to a public authority, may seem strict, in relation to a company that is not exercising authority on behalf of the state. However, where one rule applies, it is not easy to see how any standard lower than that of an independent owner could be justified or formulated satisfactorily. Further, the duty of nondiscrimination applies only if the facility is genuinely essential. . . . The case law of the ECJ on the duties of state enterprises with regulatory powers, another situation involving conflicts of interest, is therefore relevant. . . .

While the essential legal principle is that the dominant company must not discriminate, the *National Carbonising* . . . case shows that other principles can be involved. For example, it would also be illegal for the dominant company to charge a combination of prices for access to the essential facility and for its downstream products or services, such that no reasonably efficient downstream competitor could make a reasonable return on capital on that basis. . . . This would imply, unless the dominant company's downstream operations could be shown to be abnormally efficient, that it was subsidizing them in some concealed way, such as by not requiring dividends to be paid or a reasonable return on capital to be made. A dominant company could also act contrary to Article [82] by charging 'unfairly' high prices for access to the essential facility. If the competitor is seeking shared access to the facility, it should act reasonably and co-operate with the dominant company and other users to seek solutions maximizing the overall benefits offered to their customers, to solve whatever difficulty it is encountering, and to negotiate the terms of the contract for use of the facility.

Where the duty to provide nondiscriminatory access to an essential facility applies, denial of access and discrimination are in themselves unlawful. Except in the case of intellectual property rights, the duty to provide access is not merely a remedy to be imposed if and when some other kind of abuse occurs. Whether the dominant company's activities are separately incorporated or not is irrelevant. A dominant company cannot avoid its duty to contract, or justify discrimination in favor of its own operation, by having a branch rather than a subsidiary.

(vi) REFUSAL TO SUPPLY AND INTELLECTUAL PROPERTY RIGHTS

a. GENERAL

The question whether it is an abuse to refuse to supply others with intellectual property rights has become intertwined with the debate about essential facilities. Neither the Court nor Commission has applied the phrase 'essential facilities' to intellectual property rights[224] but the leading case on intellectual property rights, *Magill*[225] featured significantly in *Oscar*

---

[224] The ECJ (as distinct from the CFI) has never used the expression at all.

[225] Cases C–241–241/91 P, *RTE & ITP* v. *Commission* [1995] ECR I–743, [1995] 4 CMLR 718, on appeal from Cases T–69–70/89, 76/89, *RTE, ITP, BBC* v. *EC Commission* [1991] ECR II–485, [1991] 4 CMLR 586.

Bronner,[226] the leading ECJ judgment on essential facilities. The CFI has also obliquely addressed the issue in a case on intellectual property rights.[227] It is therefore impossible to discuss essential facilities further without considering the application of Article 82 to refusals to supply intellectual property rights.[228]

b. BEFORE *MAGILL*—THE CAR PARTS CASES

It is obvious that the existence of intellectual property rights will prevent undertakings competing on certain markets. Although the Court has held that the ownership of intellectual property rights does not necessarily mean that an undertaking holds a dominant position,[229] some rights can nonetheless constitute a barrier to entry under any conception of that term.[230] Another undertaking cannot usually produce something which is protected by intellectual property rights without the consent of the rights holder. Intellectual property rights owners often *do* license their rights to others and Chapter 10 deals with the application of Article 81 to such agreements. Article 82 may be relevant, however, when the rights holder *is* in a dominant position and refuses to give licences to those wanting them.

The matter first came before the ECJ in two Article 234 references, *AB Volvo* v. *Erik Veng*[231] and *CICCRA* v. *Renault*[232] which were decided on the same day. The specific questions asked by the national courts were formulated differently, but amounted in essence to the same thing: is it an abuse for a car manufacturer to refuse to license the design rights on its car parts to third parties wishing to manufacture and sell such parts? The cases arose as the Court in *Hugin* had confirmed that an undertaking may be dominant on the market for its own spare parts even if the primary product market is competitive.[233]

The Court held that a refusal to license was not *per se* an abuse, but might become so in certain circumstances.

Case 238/87, *AB Volvo* v. *Erik Veng* [1988] ECR 6211, [1989] 4 CMLR 122

Court of Justice

8. It must also be emphasized that the right of the proprietor of a protected design to prevent third parties from manufacturing and selling or importing, without its consent, products incorporating the design constitutes the very subject-matter of his exclusive right. It follows that an obligation imposed upon the proprietor of a protected design to grant to third parties, even in return for a reasonable royalty, a licence for the supply of products incorporating the design would lead to the proprietor thereof being deprived of the substance of his exclusive right, and that a refusal to grant such a licence cannot in itself constitute an abuse of a dominant position.

---

[226] Case C–7/97 *Oscar Bronner GmbH & Co. KG* v. *Mediaprint* [1999] 4 CMLR 112; see *infra* 412.

[227] Case T–504/93 *Tiercé Ladbrooke SA* v. *Commission* [1997] 5 CMLR 309.

[228] The issue of intellectual property rights and competition law is dealt with more fully *infra* in Chap. 10.

[229] See *supra* Chap. 6 and *infra* Chap. 10.

[230] See *supra* Chap. 1.

[231] Case 238/87, *AB Volvo* v. *Erik Veng* [1988] ECR 6211, [1989] 4 CMLR 122.

[232] Case 53/87, *CICCRA and Maxicar* v. *Renault* [1988] ECR 6039, [1990] 4 CMLR 265.

[233] Case 22/78, *Hugin Kassaregister AB* v. *EC Commission* [1979] ECR 1869 [1979] 3 CMLR 345; see *supra* Chap. 6.

9. [234] It must however be noted that the exercise of an exclusive right by the proprietor of a registered design in respect of car body panels may be prohibited by Article [82] if it involves, on the part of an undertaking holding a dominant position, certain abusive conduct such as the arbitrary refusal to supply spare parts to independent repairers, the fixing of prices for spare parts at an unfair level or a decision no longer to produce spare parts for a particular model even though many cars of that model are still in circulation, provided that such conduct is liable to affect trade between Member States.

The references in the judgments to the 'very subject-matter of the exclusive right' and the 'exercise of an exclusive right' are to concepts which the Court had already developed to deal with the tension between intellectual property rights and Community law, mainly in the area of the free movement of goods and services. They are discussed further in Chapter 10. The outcome of their application in *Volvo* and *Renault* was that the Court held that a refusal to grant licences would be an abuse only if it involved or gave rise to 'certain abusive conduct'. In effect the car makers were given a choice: either they could license third parties, or they could retain their monopoly and ensure *inter alia* that they did not arbitrarily refuse to supply independent repairers, did not charge unfairly and continued to supply parts for old models. These examples of abusive conduct give rise to difficulties, however.

First, to be an abuse the refusal to supply independents would have to be 'arbitrary'. What constitutes arbitrariness? Does it mean the same as not objectively justified? The concern of the Court here was really to ensure that no distortions of competition in the car servicing market arose. Korah asks:[235]

Is a refusal to supply body panels to an independent repairer arbitrary if it is costly to test his ability to fit the parts properly, and the car producer wants to maintain the reputation of his brand without incurring that cost by supplying only his franchised dealers whose skills and stock of tools and parts he controls? Is it more arbitrary if the brand owner wants to ensure sufficient turnover for his network of appointed dealers in order to persuade them to make the necessary investment in personnel, equipment and spares? He may even have promised his dealers to supply only them in an area.

The striking thing about categorizing the refusal to supply spare parts to independent repairers as an abuse is that it involves the supply of *products* to *new*, rather than existing, customers.

Secondly, with regard to the unfair prices, the Court stated in *Renault*:

17. With reference more particularly to the difference in prices between components sold by the manufacturer and those sold by the independent producers, it should be noted that the Court has held (Case 24/67, *Parke Davis*) . . . that a higher price for the former than for the latter does not necessarily constitute an abuse, since the proprietor of protective rights in respect of an ornamental design may lawfully call for a return on the amounts which he has invested in order to perfect the protected design.

The Court recognized here that the holder of an intellectual property right is entitled to

---

[234] Para. 9, with only insignificant changes in wording, was repeated in the *Renault* judgment at para. 16.
[235] V. Korah 'No Duty to License Independent Repairers to Made Spare Parts: The Renault, Volvo and Bayer and Hennecke Cases' [1988] *EIPR* 381 at 382 (the *Bayer-Hennecke* case was about no challenge clauses in licence agreements (see *infra* Chap. 10) and is not relevant here).

charge in a way that recompenses him for his development efforts. In his Opinion in the case Advocate General Mischo considered that the car producer should be able to allocate his costs between the whole car and the individual parts, as all are protected.[236] The whole point of granting protection to a design or patent is to reward innovation and provide incentives and it is difficult to determine what is an 'unfair' price for the protected product.[237] The difficulties of determining at what level a price becomes 'unfair' are discussed above.[238] Further, the extent to which a car manufacturer has power to charge excessively in the aftermarket for spare parts without affecting sales in the competitive foremarket is questionable.[239]

The third example, prematurely terminating the production of spare parts, may or may not be a real problem. It can be argued that if the car maker itself is not interested in further production it will not object to a third party manufacturing the parts and may be happy to profit through licensing: on the other hand the car maker may have an interest in obsolescence and not want old models to be repairable.[240] In any event, the yardstick 'many cars still in production' is too vague to provide a properly applicable criterion.

c. THE *MAGILL* CASE

Magill[241] concerned copyright in 'television listings' (television programme schedules). Under UK and Irish law copyright protects not only literary works which result from creative or intellectual endeavour but also compilations of information resulting from 'skill, judgment and labour' or the 'sweat of the brow', including listings of programmes to be broadcast.[242] Such compilations are not protected by intellectual property laws in the other Member States of the EU, where copyright covers only the fruits of creative or intellectual effort. The EU has not (yet) harmonized the copyright laws of the Member States[243] but the Court has said on several occasions that where intellectual property laws are not harmonized Community law recognizes the *existence* of rights granted by the Member States.

In 1985 RTE had a statutory monopoly over television broadcasting in Ireland and the BBC and IBA had a statutory duopoly in the UK (including Northern Ireland). Most television viewers in Ireland and Northern Ireland could receive the channels of all three

---

[236] At para. 31.

[237] See I. Govaere, *The Use and Abuse of Intellectual Property Rights in EC Law* (Sweet & Maxwell, 1996), paras. 8.55–8.56.

[238] *Supra* 327.

[239] See *supra* Chap. 6.

[240] Korah, *supra* n. 235., cf Govaere, *supra* at n. 237, 8.57–8.59.

[241] Cases C–241–241/91 P, *RTE & ITP* v. *Commission* [1995] ECR I–743, [1995] 4 CMLR 718 on appeal from Cases T–69–70/89, 76/89, *RTE, ITP, BBC* v. *EC Commission* [1991] ECR II–485,[1991] 4 CMLR 586, on appeal from *Magill TV Guide* [1989] OJ L78/43, [1989] 4 CMLR 757.

[242] The relevant UK law is now the Copyright Designs and Patents Act 1988 s. 3 (1), although at the time of the *Magill* decision it was still the Copyright Act 1956. The protection of programme listings by copyright in the UK was confirmed by *Independent Television Publications* v. *Time Out* [1984] FSR 64. The Broadcasting Act 1990 s. 176 specifically provides that persons broadcasting television and radio programmes in the UK have to make information about the programme schedules available to any person in the UK who wants to publish it: the actual dispute in *Magill* therefore became a dead issue as regards the UK during the course of the case, which is why the BBC was not party to the appeal to the ECJ.

[243] See *infra* Chap. 10.

television authorities. RTE and the BBC owned the copyright in the programme listings for their respective channels and Independent Television Publications (ITP) owned the copyright in the programme listings of the IBA franchised channels. RTE, the BBC, and ITP each published a weekly TV guide containing only their own individual weekly programme listings. They also gave listings information to the press to be published according to strictly enforced licensing conditions. An Irish publisher, Magill, started to publish a comprehensive weekly TV guide giving details of all programmes available to viewers in Ireland and Northern Ireland, but the television companies obtained injunctions against it in national legal proceedings. Magill complained to the Commission that the television companies, by refusing to give out reliable advance listings information and protecting their listings by enforcing their copyright, were infringing Article 82.

Nowhere else in the Community but the UK and Ireland did copyright laws protect TV listings, and in the rest of the Community comprehensive composite TV guides were a popular commonplace. These facts seem to have influenced the approach of the Court and Commission to the case.[244] The case became perceived as a battle between the protection of national intellectual property rights and competition law, for if the TV companies' refusal to deal with Magill *was* an abuse the only remedy was, in effect, to order them to give the publisher a licence of their copyrights. This raised the spectre of compulsory licensing of intellectual property rights more generally. If the Commission found an abuse, did this mean that in future pharmaceutical companies holding a dominant position on a particular market might have to license their patents to third parties wanting to use them to manufacture?[245] If so, the risk of removing incentives for innovation, discussed by Areeda and Ridyard (in the passages reproduced above), which intellectual property rights are particularly designed to protect, would be acute.

The Commission did hold that the television companies had infringed Article 82. It held that the companies were each dominant in the market for their weekly listings and that their policies in restricting the availability of the information were driven by a desire to protect their own individual weekly guides. The Commission's decision was upheld by the CFI, which related its discussion of Article 82 to the case law of the Court on intellectual property rights in the context of the free movement of goods and services.[246] RTE and ITP appealed to the ECJ. The ECJ confirmed the finding of abuse but its judgment is strikingly narrow. It concentrates on the specific scenario in issue and eschews extended discussion about the nature of intellectual property rights and their relationship to the competition rules.[247] The ECJ treated the matter as a straightforward refusal to supply and applied the principles laid down in previous Article 82 case law.

---

[244] See particularly the Commission's submissions to the CFI, [1991] ECR II–485, summarized in paras. 43–59 of the judgment, culminating in the Commission's statement in para. 59 that 'copyright should not subsist in compilations of such banal information'.

[245] Compulsory licensing of patents is provided for in the patent legislation, but only in clearly defined circumstances: see *infra* Chap. 10.

[246] There were three separate judgments, but the crucial paras. are the same in all three: see *RTE* v. *Commission* para. 71, *BBC* v. *Commission* para. 58, *ITP* v. *Commission*, para. 56. The CFI judgment is discussed *infra* in Chap. 10.

[247] See particularly para. 58 of the judgment. The Court did not follow the opinion of Gulmann AG, who recommended setting aside the CFI judgment, primarily to uphold the inviolability of intellectual property rights.

Cases C–241–241/91 P, *RTE & ITP* v. *Commission* [1995] ECR I–743, [1995] 4 CMLR 718

Court of Justice

(a) *Existence of a dominant position*

46. So far as dominant position is concerned, it is to be remembered at the outset that mere ownership of an intellectual property right cannot confer such a position.

47. However, the basic information as to the channel, day, time and title of programmes is the necessary result of programming by television stations, which are thus the only source of such information for an undertaking, like Magill, which wishes to publish it together with commentaries or pictures. By force of circumstance, RTE and ITP, as the agent of ITV, enjoy, along with the BBC, a *de facto* monopoly over the information used to compile listings for the television programmes received in most households in Ireland and 30–40 per cent. of households in Northern Ireland. The appellants are thus in a position to prevent effective competition on the market in weekly television magazines. The CFI was therefore right in confirming the Commission's assessment that the appellants occupied a dominant position (*Michelin, paragraph 30*)

(b) *Existence of abuse*

48. With regard to the issue of abuse, the arguments of the appellants and IPO wrongly presuppose that where the conduct of an undertaking in a dominant position consists of the exercise of a right classified by national law as 'copyright', such conduct can never be reviewed in relation to Article [82] of the Treaty.

49. Admittedly, in the absence of Community standardisation or harmonisation of laws, determination of the conditions and procedures for granting protection of an intellectual property right is a matter for national rules. Further, the exclusive right of reproduction forms part of the author's rights, so that refusal to grant a licence, even if it is the act of an undertaking holding a dominant position, cannot in itself constitute abuse of a dominant position (*Volvo* v. *Veng*, paragraphs 7 and 8.).

50. However, it is also clear from that judgment (paragraph 9.) that the exercise of an exclusive right by the proprietor may, in exceptional circumstances, involve abusive conduct.

51. In the present case, the conduct objected to is the appellants' reliance on copyright conferred by national legislation so as to prevent Magill—or any other undertaking having the same intention—from publishing on a weekly basis information (channel, day, time and title of programmes) together with commentaries and pictures obtained independently of the appellants.

52. Among the circumstances taken into account by the CFI in concluding that such conduct was abusive was, first, the fact that there was, according to the findings of the Court of First Instance, no actual or potential substitute for a weekly television guide offering information on the programmes for the week ahead. On this point, the CFI confirmed the Commission's finding that the complete lists of programmes for a 24-hour period—and for a 48-hour period at weekends and before public holidays—published in certain daily and Sunday newspapers, and the television sections of certain magazines covering, in addition, 'highlights' of the week's programmes, were only to a limited extent substitutable for advance information to viewers on all the week's programmes. Only weekly television guides containing comprehensive listings for the week ahead would enable users to decide in advance which programmes they wished to follow and arrange their leisure activities for the week accordingly. The CFI also established that there was a specific, constant and regular potential

demand on the part of consumers (see the *RTE* judgment, paragraph 62, and the *ITP* judgment, paragraph 48).

53. Thus the appellants—who were, by force of circumstance, the only sources of the basic information on programme scheduling which is the indispensable raw material for compiling a weekly television guide—gave viewers wishing to obtain information on the choice of programmes for the week ahead no choice but to buy the weekly guides for each station and draw from each of them the information they needed to make comparisons.

54. The appellants' refusal to provide basic information by relying on national copyright provisions thus prevented the appearance of a new product, a comprehensive weekly guide to television programmes, which the appellants did not offer and for which there was a potential consumer demand. Such refusal constitutes an abuse under heading (b) of the second paragraph of Article [82] of the Treaty.

55. Second, there was no justification for such refusal either in the activity of television broadcasting or in that of publishing television magazines (*RTE* judgment, paragraph 73, and *ITP* judgment, paragraph 58).

56. Third, and finally, as the CFI also held, the appellants, by their conduct, reserved to themselves the secondary market of weekly television guides by excluding competition on that market (*Commercial Solvents*, paragraph 25) since they denied access to the basic information which is the raw material indispensable for the compilation of such a guide.

57. In the light of all those circumstances, the CFI did not err in law in holding that the appellants' conduct was an abuse of a dominant position within the meaning of Article [82] of the Treaty.

58. It follows that the plea in law alleging misapplication by the CFI of the concept of abuse of a dominant position must be dismissed as unfounded. It is therefore unnecessary to examine the reasoning of the contested judgments in so far as it is based on Article [30] of the Treaty.

The following points should particularly be noted:

- The ECJ based its finding of dominance on the fact that theTV companies had a *de facto* monopoly over the listings, i.e. they were responsible for producing the TV schedules and were the only source of advance information about them (paragraph 47). The Commission (paragraph 22) based the finding of dominance on both the *de facto* monopoly and the legal monopoly stemming from the copyright. The CFI based it on the legal monopoly (paragraph 63 of the *RTE* judgment). The ECJ did not even *mention* the existence of the intellectual property rights in its discussion of dominance in paragraph 47.
- The ECJ said (paragraph 48) that while it is not true that the exercise of intellectual property rights can *never* be reviewed under Article 82, a refusal to grant a licence to reproduce cannot *in itself* constitute an abuse of a dominant position (paragraph 49). It cited *Volvo* as establishing, however, that a refusal might constitute an abuse in exceptional circumstances. In this case the exceptional circumstances were:

  —there was no substitute for a composite weekly television guide, for which there was a specific, constant and regular potential demand on the part of consumers;
  —the appellants' refusal to supply prevented the appearance of a new product for

which there was a potential consumer demand[248] (this constituted an abuse under Article 82 (b));

—there was no justification for such refusal;

—the appellants were reserving to themselves the secondary market of weekly television guides by excluding all competition on the market.

It is not altogether clear from this judgment whether the hindrance of a new product is a separate and sufficient ground for holding the refusal to supply to be abusive. If the television companies had already produced their *own* composite guides by cross-licensing each other, the composite guide of a third party would not have been a new product, but the undertakings would still have reserved for themselves a special position on the secondary market. The fact that a refusal to supply might deprive consumers of a new product has been referred to in subsequent cases (see *Tiercé Ladbrooke* and *Oscar Bronner*, below). However, in the extract from his article, above,[249] Ridyard takes issue with the idea that competition authorities should intervene just because there are unrealized potential consumer gains. He argues that such intervention will cause economic damage because it upsets the tension between static and dynamic incentives for efficiency.

- The ECJ (paragraphs 53 and 56) described the companies' conduct in terms of refusal to supply a raw material. It did not use essential facilities terminology.
- The Court referred back to the early case of *Commercial Solvents* (paragraph 56) seeing the present case as an example of the established abuse of an undertaking dominant on one market trying to exclude competition on an ancillary market.
- Unlike the car makers in *Volvo* and *Renault* the television companies were not given a choice of how they could avoid committing an abuse. Although the judgment did not mention compulsory licensing there was only one way in which the abuse could be remedied.[250]

The narrow terms in which this judgment was couched did not indicate that the Court was likely to embark on wholesale condemnation of refusals to license patents. It established that the norm, as exemplified in *Volvo* and *Renault*, was that refusal to license is *not* generally an abuse. The judgment was less of an assault on intellectual property rights than it was on the exploitation of compilations of information gained as a by-product of an undertaking's main business. The case is thus of a piece with all the previous cases on interference with ancillary markets: a significant difference between *Magill* and the car parts cases is that in the latter the would-be licensee wished to compete with the dominant undertaking in the core area of its business. In contrast, the television companies were not set up to publish magazines. It is true that *British Midland* also concerned competition with the dominant undertaking's core business, but that case did not involve intellectual property rights and was bound up with the liberalization of the air transport market.

---

[248] The AG on the other hand (paras. 93–102 of the Opinion) thought that the fact that the product Magill wanted to produce was new and would compete with the right holders' own products was a reason to find that the refusal to supply was *not* abusive.

[249] D. Ridyard, 'Essential Facilities and the Obligation to Supply Competitors' [1996] *ECLR* 438, 447; see *supra* 396.

[250] The existence of the Copyright Tribunal in the UK meant that the Commission itself did not have to become involved in price-setting.

It is possible to see *Magill* as a limitation of the power wielded by statutory monopolists. The power of the television companies in respect of the TV guides arose as a result of their privileged position on the broadcasting market. In a market which had more numerous television channels they would probably have been glad to provide their programme details to composite magazines: although consumers may buy two or three guides, they will not buy fifty, and television companies *need* to advertise their programme schedules.

c. REFUSAL TO SUPPLY INTELLECTUAL PROPERTY RIGHTS AFTER *MAGILL*—THE *LADBROOKE* CASE

In the next case concerning a refusal to license intellectual property rights, *Tiercé Ladbrooke*, the CFI's judgment was couched in an essential facilities type of terminology. The Court appeared to be limiting the application of that doctrine.

Case T–504/93, *Tiercé Ladbrooke SA* v. *Commission* [1997] ECR II–923, [1997] 5 CMLR 309

Ladbrooke ran betting shops in Belgium taking bets on horse races run abroad, including France. The French race course societies (sociétés de course) and their associated companies (PMU and PMI) had exclusive responsibility for organising off-course betting in France, taking bets abroad on French races, taking bets in France on races run abroad and exploiting outside France televised pictures of, and information about, French horse races. PMI granted exclusive rights to show televised broadcasts of French horse races in Germany and Austria to DSV. PMI and PMU refused to supply broadcasts to Ladbrooke's outlets in Belgium and DSV refused to retransmit to them. Ladbrookes complained to the Commission that this was an infringement of Article 82 (and Article 81) but the Commission rejected the complaint. Ladbrooke challenged the decision rejecting the complaint before the Court of First Instance. The CFI held that the geographic market was Belgium alone, and not a wider area including at least Belgium, France and Germany. It continued:

Court of First Instance

123. The applicant's argument that the *sociétés de courses* abused their joint dominant position is based on a definition of the geographical market which includes at least Belgium, France and Germany. However, for the reasons already given, . . . the relevant market, namely the Belgian market in sound and pictures, is a national one.

124. It is common ground that the *sociétés de courses* have not granted any licence for the territory of Belgium to date. Accordingly, their refusal to grant a licence to Ladbroke does not constitute discrimination as between operators on the Belgian market. The mere fact that, according to the applicant, the *sociétés de courses* have offered to supply French sound and pictures to Belgian outlets does not suffice, for the purposes of Article [82] of the Treaty, for them to be treated as having already exploited their intellectual property rights, in respect of races organised by them, in a discriminatory manner in Belgium. Finally, the *sociétés de courses* likewise cannot be regarded as being present in the Belgian market through their subsidiary PMB, given that the applicant does not deny that the latter company, although actually set up under Belgian law by PMI, has never engaged in any commercial activity in Belgium. . . .

125. Furthermore, since, on the basis of its structure, which is determined according to criteria relating to the conditions of competition and, in particular, the pattern of demand on the market in the sound and pictures of races in general, the geographical market is divided into distinct national markets, there is no basis for the applicant's allegation that there is a

partitioning of the Common Market resulting from the licensing policy of the *sociétés de courses*.

126. As regards, finally, the allegedly arbitrary nature of the refusal of the *sociétés de courses* to supply French sound and pictures to the applicant, the Court considers that, since the markets are on a national scale, the arbitrariness or otherwise of the refusal by the *sociétés de courses* to exploit their intellectual property rights in Belgium cannot be assessed in the light of the policy followed by the *sociétés de courses* on other, geographically distinct markets. The fact that the applicant is prepared, as it states, to pay an appropriate fee for a licence to transmit French races does not constitute sufficient evidence of an abuse in the absence of discrimination against it by the *sociétés de courses* in the relevant geographical market.

127. The applicant maintains that, even assuming that the relevant geographical market is Belgium, the refusal by the *sociétés de courses* to grant it a transmission licence is arbitrary because they have granted licences to economic operators established in neighbouring countries.

128. It must be pointed out, however, that, if the refusal to supply the applicant with French sound and pictures in Belgium does not constitute an abuse because, as the Court has just found, it involves no discrimination as between operators on the Belgian market, that refusal likewise cannot be held to be an abuse merely because outlets operating on the German market have French sound and pictures available to them. There is no competition between betting outlets operating in Belgium and those operating in Germany.

129. Moreover, neither the absence of technical barriers to the transmission of French sound and pictures in Belgium nor the fact that the applicant might be regarded, from an overall perspective, as a potential competitor of the *sociétés de courses* is sufficient for the refusal to supply sound and pictures to be regarded as constituting an abuse of a dominant position since the *sociétés de courses themselves are not present in the separate geographical market on which the applicant operates and, secondly, they have not granted any licence to other operators on that market.*

130. The applicant cannot rely on the *Magill* judgment to demonstrate the existence of the alleged abuse, since that decision is not in point. In contrast to the position in *Magill*, where the refusal to grant a licence to the applicant prevented it from entering the market in comprehensive television guides, in this case the application is not only present in, but has the largest share of, the main betting market on which the product in question, namely sound and pictures, is offered to consumers whilst the *sociétés de courses*, the owners of the intellectual property rights, are not present on that market. Accordingly, in the absence of direct or indirect exploitation by the *sociétés de courses* of their intellectual property rights on the Belgian market, their refusal to supply cannot be regarded as involving any restriction of competition on the Belgian market.

131. Even if it were assumed that the presence of the *sociétés de courses* on the Belgian market in sound and pictures were not, in this case, a decisive factor for the purposes of applying Article [82] of the Treaty, that provision would not be applicable in this case. The refusal to supply the applicant could not fall within the prohibition laid down by Article [82] unless it concerned a product or service which was either essential for the exercise of the activity in question, in that there were no real or potential substitute, or was a new product whose introduction might be prevented, despite specific, constant and regular potential demand on the part of consumers (see in that connection Joined Cases C–241–242/91P, *RTE and ITP* v. *E.C.Commission* . . .

132. In this case, as moreover the Commission and the interveners have pointed out, the televised broadcasting of horse races, although constituting an additional, and indeed suitable, service for

bettors, it is not in itself indispensable for the exercise of bookmakers' main activity, namely the taking of bets, as is evidenced by the fact that the applicant is present on the Belgian betting market and occupies a significant position as regards bets on French races. Moreover, transmission is not indispensable, since it takes place after bets are placed, with the result that its absence does not in itself affect the choices made by bettors and, accordingly, cannot prevent bookmakers from pursuing their business.

133. For the same reasons, the applicant likewise cannot rely on the *London European* v. *Sabena* decision and the *ICI and Commercial Solvents* v. *E.C.Commission* and *CBEM* judgments. . . . In the *London European* v. *Sabena* decision, the action taken to exclude a competitor related to a market in which both Sabena and that competitor, London European, were operating, whereas in this case the *sociétés de courses* are not present on the Belgian market. The same applies to the two judgments relied upon. In *ICI and Commercial Solvents* v. *E.C.Commission*, the abuse consisted in the refusal by a company occupying a dominant position on the market in raw materials to provide those materials to a customer producing derivatives in order to keep those raw materials for its own production of derivatives, and so the company in a dominant position, like its customers, was present on the downstream market, namely the market in derivatives. In contrast, in this case the *sociétés de courses* are not present on the Belgian market in French sound and pictures. In the *CBEM* judgment, the ECJ held that an undertaking abuses a dominant position where, without any objective necessity, it reserves to itself or to an undertaking belonging to the same group an ancillary activity which might be carried out by another undertaking as part of its activities on a neighbouring but separate market. However, in this case the *sociétés de courses* have not reserved the Belgian market in French sound and pictures to themselves and have not granted access to that market to a third-party undertaking or to an undertaking belonging to them.

134. It follows from the whole of the foregoing that the applicant's plea alleging abuse of a dominant position by the *sociétés de courses* must be rejected.

In this case the CFI distinguished the situation before it from that in *Magill*. The *sociétés de courses* did not operate betting shops in Belgium, so the ancillary market issue did not arise. Showing films of the races was not essential to providing services in betting shops. The copyright owners were not discriminating in that they did not supply *anybody* with licences in the relevant market (Belgium). The refusal to supply could constitute an abuse only if *either* the product or service was essential to the activity in question *or* the introduction of a new product demanded by consumers was being prevented. The Court thus considered, following *Magill*, that a refusal to supply which precluded the introduction of a new product might constitute an abuse. This suggestion means that Article 82 is being employed to enable assumed consumer demand to be satisfied: this is refusal to supply characterized as an exploitative abuse capable of harming consumers directly, by depriving them of things they want.

The concern about the essential facilities doctrine detectable in *Tiercé Ladbrooke* was expressly addressed by the ECJ in *Oscar Bronner* (below).

(vii) REFUSAL TO SUPPLY AND ESSENTIAL FACILITIES IN THE *EUROPEAN NIGHT SERVICES* AND *OSCAR BRONNER* CASES

a. *EUROPEAN NIGHT SERVICES*

The Commission decision in *European Night Services*,[251] was taken under Article 81 of the

---

[251] [1994] OJ L259/20, [1995] 5 CMLR 76.

Treaty. It raised similar issues to the Article 82 cases although the *Commission* did not actually use the expression 'essential facilities'. Railway undertakings in the UK, France, Germany, and the Netherlands formed a joint venture (ENS) to provide overnight passenger rail services between the UK and the Continent via the Channel Tunnel. The Commission granted an exemption on condition that the parent companies should provide locomotives, train crews and train paths to any other undertaking wishing to compete in the running of a similar service, on the same terms as they gave to the joint venture. The CFI annulled the decision on various grounds.[252] The condition as regards the locomotives and train crews was quashed because the Commission had not properly analysed why the requirement to supply was appropriate and had not supplied adequate reasoning for imposing this condition. In this case the CFI expressly referred to essential facilities. It stressed that a facility can be essential only if there are no substitutes. Mere advantage to the competitor is not enough.

Cases T–374–375, 384 & 388/94 *European Night Services* v. *Commission* [1998] ECR II–3141 [1998] 5 CMLR 718[253]

Court of First Instance

215. As the applicants have argued, the contested decision does not contain any analysis demonstrating that the locomotives in question are necessary or essential. More specifically, it is not possible to conclude from reading the contested decision that third parties cannot obtain them either directly from manufacturers or indirectly by renting them from other undertakings. Nor has any correspondence between the Commission and third parties, demonstrating that the locomotives in question cannot be obtained on the market, been produced before the Court. As the applicants have stated, any undertaking wishing to operate the same rail services as ENS through the Channel Tunnel may freely purchase or rent the locomotives in question on the market. It is clear, moreover, from the papers before the Court that the contracts for the supply of locomotives entered into between the notifying undertakings and ENS do not involve any exclusively in favour of ENS, and that each of the notifying undertakings is thus free to supply the same locomotives to third parties and not only to ENS.

216. It must further be pointed out in that regard that the Commission has not denied that third parties may freely purchase or rent the locomotives in question on the market; it has merely asserted that the possibility is in fact purely theoretical and that only the notifying undertakings actually possess such locomotives. That argument cannot, however, be accepted. The fact that the notifying undertakings have been the first to acquire the locomotives in question on the market does not mean that they are alone in being able to do so.

217. Consequently, the Commission's assessment of the necessary or essential nature of the special locomotives designed for the Channel Tunnel and, thus, the obligation imposed on the parent undertakings to supply such locomotives to third parties are vitiated by an absence or, at the very least, an insufficiency of reasoning.

. . .

221. As regards the supply to ENS of special locomotives and crew for the Channel Tunnel, the

---

[252] Cases T–374–375, 384 & 388/94, *European Night Services* v. *Commission* [1998] ECR T–3141, [1998] 5 CMLR 718. Other aspects of this case are dealt with in Chaps. 3, 4 and 13. The requirement that train paths should be provided was quashed because it was based on false premises to do with the relevant transport dir. (91/440 [1991] OJ L237–25).

[253] The judgment was delivered after the opinion of Jacobs AG in Case C–797, *Oscar Bronner GMBH & Co. KG* v. *Mediaprint* [1998] ECR I–7791, [1999] 4 CMLR 112.

mere fact of its benefiting from such a service could impede access by third parties to the downstream market only if such locomotives and crew were to be regarded as essential facilities. Since, for the reasons set out above, . . . they cannot be categorized as such, the fact that they are to be supplied to ENS under the operating agreements for night rail services cannot be regarded as restricting competition *vis-à-vis* third parties. That aspect of the Commission's analysis of restrictions *vis-à-vis* third parties is therefore also unfounded.

Again, this judgment shows a disinclination to apply the essential facilities concept too widely.

b. THE *OSCAR BRONNER* CASE

Oscar Bronner, like *Volvo* and *Renault*, arose before the ECJ on an Article 234 reference. It is notable for a thoughtful opinion in which Advocate General Jacobs discussed the necessity of confining the essential facilities concept within strict limits.

Case C–7/97 *Oscar Bronner GmbH & Co. KG* v. *Mediaprint* [1998] ECR I–7791, [1999] 4 CMLR 112

Bronner published a newspaper, *Der Standard* which had approximately 3.6 per cent of the daily newspaper market in Austria in terms of circulation and 6 per cent in terms of advertising revenue. Mediaprint published two daily newsapapers in Austria, *Neue Kronen Zeitung* and *Kurier* which together had a combined market share of 46.8 per cent of circulation and 42 per cent of advertising revenues. For the distribution of its newspapers Mediaprint had established a nationwide home-delivery scheme. Bronner wanted Mediaprint to include *Der Standard* in its delivery scheme but Mediaprint refused. Mediaprint did include another newspaper it did not publish in its scheme but it did the whole of the printing and distribution in respect of that paper. Bronner sought an order from the Austrian courts requiring Mediaprint to cease abusing its alleged dominant position on the home-delivery market and requiring it to include *Der Standard* in its home-delivery service in return for reasonable remuneration. It claimed that other methods of sale, such as postal delivery, were less advantageous than home-delivery and that given the small circulation of *Der Standard* it would be entirely unprofitable for it to organise its own home-delivery service. The Austrian court referred to the ECJ two questions as to whether the conduct in issue amounted to an abuse of a dominant position. Although the situation related only to trade inside Austria, the Austrian court asked for the reference because it wished to avoid a conflict between the interpretation of domestic and EC law. The ECJ held that the reference was admissible.

Advocate General Jacobs

56. First, it is apparent that the right to choose one's trading partners and freely to dispose of one's property are generally recognized principles in the laws of the Member States, in some cases with constitutional status. Incursions on those rights require careful justification.

57. Secondly, the justification in terms of competition policy for interfering with a dominant undertaking's freedom to contract often requires a careful balancing of conflicting considerations. In the long term it is generally pro-competitive and in the interest of consumers to allow a company to retain for its own use facilities which it has developed for the purpose of its business. For example, if access to a production, purchasing or distribution facility were allowed too easily there would be no incentive for a competitor to develop competing facilities. Thus while competition was increased in the short term it would be reduced in the long term. Moreover, the incentive for a dominant undertaking to invest in efficient facilities would be reduced if its competitors were, upon request, able to share the benefits. Thus the mere fact that by retaining a facility for its own use a dominant undertaking retains an advantage over a competitor cannot justify requiring access to it.

58. Thirdly, in assessing this issue it is important not to lose sight of the fact that the primary purpose of Article [82] is to prevent distortion of competition—and in particular to safeguard the interests of consumers—rather than to protect the position of particular competitors. It may therefore, for example, be unsatisfactory, in a case in which a competitor demands access to a raw material in order to be able to compete with the dominant undertaking on a downstream market in a final product, to focus solely on the latter's market power on the upstream market and conclude that its conduct in reserving to itself the downstream market is automatically an abuse. Such conduct will not have an adverse impact on consumers unless the dominant undertaking's final product is sufficiently insulated from competition to give it market power.

. . .

61. It is on the other hand clear that refusal of access may in some cases entail elimination or substantial reduction of competition to the detriment of consumers in both the short and long term. That will be so where access to a facility is a precondition for competition on a related market for goods or services for which there is a limited degree of interchangeability.

62. In assessing such conflicting interests particular care is required where the goods or services or facilities to which access is demanded represent the fruit of substantial investment. That may be true in particular in relation to refusal to license intellectual property rights. Where such exclusive rights are granted for a limited period, that in itself involves a balancing of the interest in free competition with that of providing an incentive for research and development and for creativity. It is therefore with good reason that the Court has held that the refusal to license does not of itself, in the absence of other factors, constitute an abuses.

63. The ruling in *Magill* can in my view be explained by the special circumstances of that case which swung the balance in favour of an obligation to license. First, the existing products, namely individual weekly guides for each station, were inadequate, particularly when compared with the guides available to viewers in other countries. The exercise of the copyright therefore prevented a much needed new product from coming on the market. Secondly, the provision of copyright protection for programme listings was difficult to justify in terms of rewarding or providing an incentive for creative effort. Thirdly, since the useful life of programme guides is relatively short, the exercise of the copyright provided a permanent barrier to the entry of the new product on the market. It may incidentally be noted that national rules on intellectual property themselves impose limits in certain circumstances through rules on compulsory licensing.

64. While generally the exercise of intellectual property rights will restrict competition for a limited period only, a dominant undertaking's monopoly over a product, service or facility may in certain cases lead to permanent exclusion of competition on a related market. In such cases competition can be achieved only by requiring a dominant undertaking to supply the product or service or allow access to the facility. If it is so required the undertaking must however in my view be fully compensated by allowing it to allocate an appropriate proportion of its investment costs to the supply and to make an appropriate return on its investment having regard to the level of risk involved. I leave open the question whether it might in some cases be appropriate to allow the undertaking to retain its monopoly for a limited period.

65. It seems to me that intervention of that kind, whether understood as an application of the essential facilities doctrine or, more traditionally, as a response to a refusal to supply goods or services, can be justified in terms of competition policy only in cases in which the dominant undertaking has a genuine stranglehold on the related market. That might be the case for example where duplication of the facility is impossible or extremely difficult owing to physical, geographical or legal

constraints or is highly undesirable for reasons of public policy. It is not sufficient that the undertaking's control over a facility should give it a competitive advantage.

66. I do not rule out the possibility that the cost of duplicating a facility might alone constitute an insuperable barrier to entry. That might be so particularly in cases in which the creation of the facility took place under non-competitive conditions, for example, partly through public funding. However, the test in my view must be an objective one: in other words, in order for refusal of access to amount to an abuse, it must be extremely difficult not merely for the undertaking demanding access but for any other undertaking to compete. Thus, if the cost of duplicating the facility alone is the barrier to entry, it must be such as to deter any prudent undertaking from entering the market. In that regard it seems to me that it will be necessary to consider all the circumstances, including the extent to which the dominant undertaking, having regard to the degree of amortisation of its investment and the cost of upkeep, must pass on investment or maintenance costs in the prices charged on the related market (bearing in mind that the competitor, who having duplicated the facility must compete on the related market, will have high initial amortisation costs but possibly low maintenance costs).

67. It is in my view clear that in the present case there can be no obligation on Mediaprint to allow Bronner access to its nation-wide home-delivery network. Although Bronner itself may be unable to duplicate Mediaprint's network, it has numerous alternative—albeit less convenient—means of distribution open to it.

That conclusion is borne out by the claims made in *Der Standard* itself that 'the 'Standard' is enjoying spectacular growth in terms of both new subscriptions (an increase of 15 per cent) and placement of advertisements (an increase of 30 per cent by comparison with last year)'. . . . Such a claim hardly seems consistent with the view that Mediaprint's home-delivery system is essential for it to compete on the newspaper market.

68. Moreover, it would be necessary to establish that the level of investment required to set up a nation-wide home distribution system would be such as to deter an enterprising publisher who was convinced that there was a market for another large daily newspaper from entering the market. It may well be uneconomic, as Bronner suggests, to establish a nation-wide system for a newspaper with a low circulation. In the short term, therefore, losses might be anticipated, requiring a certain level of investment. But the purpose of establishing a competing nation-wide network would be to allow it to compete on equal terms with Mediaprint's newspapers and substantially to increase geographical coverage and circulation.

69. To accept Bronner's contention would be to lead the Community and national authorities and courts into detailed regulation of the Community markets, entailing the fixing of prices and conditions for supply in large sectors of the economy. Intervention on that scale would not only be unworkable but would also be anti-competitive in the longer term and indeed would scarcely be compatible with a free market economy.

70. It seems to me therefore that the present case falls well short of the type of situation in which it might be appropriate to impose an obligation on a dominant undertaking to allow access to a facility which it has developed for its own use.

Court of Justice

38. Although in *Commercial Solvents* v. *Commission and CBEM*, cited above, the ECJ held the refusal by an undertaking holding a dominant position in a given market to supply an undertaking with which it was in competition in a neighbouring market with raw materials (*Commercial Solvents* v. *Commission*, paragraph 25) and services (*CBEM*, paragraph 26) respectively, which were indispensable to carrying on the rival's business, to constitute an abuse, it should be noted, first, that

the Court did so to the extent that the conduct in question was likely to eliminate all competition on the part of that undertaking.

39. Secondly, in *Magill*, at paragraphs 49 and 50, the Court held that refusal by the owner of an intellectual property right to grant a licence, even if it is the act of an undertaking holding a dominant position, cannot in itself constitute abuse of a dominant position, but that the exercise of an exclusive right by the proprietor may, in exceptional circumstances, involve an abuse.

40. In *Magill*, the Court found such exceptional circumstances in the fact that the refusal in question concerned a product (information on the weekly schedules of certain television channels) the supply of which was indispensable for carrying on the business in question (the publishing of a general television guide), in that, without that information, the person wishing to produce such a guide would find it impossible to publish it and offer it for sale (paragraph 53), the fact that such refusal prevented the appearance of a new product for which there was a potential consumer demand (paragraph 54), the fact that it was not justified by objective considerations (paragraph 55), and that it was likely to exclude all competition in the secondary market of television guides (paragraph 56).

41. Therefore, even if that case-law on the exercise of an intellectual property right were applicable to the exercise of any property right whatever, it would still be necessary, for the *Magill* judgment to be effectively relied upon in order to plead the existence of an abuse within the meaning of Article [82] of the Treaty in a situation such as that which forms the subject-matter of the first questions, not only that the refusal of the service comprised in home delivery be likely to eliminate all competition in the daily newspaper market on the part of the person requesting the service and that such refusal be incapable of being objectively justified, but also that the service in itself be indispensable to carrying on that person's business, inasmuch as there is no actual or potential substitute in existence for that home-delivery scheme.

42. That is certainly not the case even if, as in the case which is the subject of the main proceedings, there is only one nationwide home-delivery scheme in the territory of a Member State and, moreover, the owner of that scheme holds a dominant position in the market for services constituted by that scheme or of which it forms part.

43. In the first place, it is undisputed that other methods of distributing daily newspapers, such as by post and through sale in shops and at kiosks, even though they may be less advantageous for the distribution of certain newspapers, exist and are used by the publishers of those daily newspapers.

44. Moreover, it does not appear that there are any technical, legal or even economic obstacles capable of making it impossible, or even unreasonably difficult, for any other publisher of daily newspapers to establish, alone or in co-operation with other publishers, its own nationwide home-delivery scheme and use it to distribute its own daily newspapers.

45. It should be emphasised in that respect that, in order to demonstrate that the creation of such a system is not a realistic potential alternative and that access to the existing system is therefore indispensable, it is not enough to argue that it is not economically viable by reason of the small circulation of the daily newspaper or newspapers to be distributed.

46. For such access to be capable of being regarded as indispensable, it would be necessary at the very least to establish, as the Advocate General has pointed out at point 68 of his Opinion, that it is not economically viable to create a second home-delivery scheme for the distribution of daily newspapers with a circulation comparable to that of the daily newspapers distributed by the existing scheme.

47. In the light of the foregoing considerations, the answer to the first question must be that the refusal by a press undertaking which holds a very large share of the daily newspaper market in a Member State and operates the only nationwide newspaper home-delivery scheme in that Member State to allow the publisher of a rival newspaper, which by reason of its small circulation is unable either alone or in co-operation with other publishers to set up and operate its own home-delivery scheme in economically reasonable conditions, to have access to that scheme for appropriate remuneration does not constitute abuse of a dominant position within the meaning of Article [82] of the Treaty.

It is significant that in this judgment the ECJ continued to avoid using the term 'essential facilities'. It approached the reference question as being one about refusal to supply. In paragraph 41 the ECJ listed four factors which would have to be present before the refusal could be an abuse. First, the refusal would have to be likely to eliminate all competition in the downstream market from the person requesting access; secondly, the refusal must be incapable of objective justification; thirdly, the access must be indispensable to carrying on the other person's business; and, fourthly, there must be no actual or potential substitute for it. These criteria were patently not fulfilled in *Bronner*.

In *Bronner* the Court took a restrictive view of the obligation to grant access to facilities. It stressed that the refusal must be likely to *eliminate* all competition from the undertaking requesting access. It was not sufficient that the refusal would just make it harder for it to compete. Access must also be *indispensable*, not desirable or convenient, since there must be no actual or potential substitute for the requesting undertaking. The conditions for indispensability are problematic, however. In paragraphs 45–46 the Court held that in the case before it access could have been indispensable only if it was not economically viable to create a home-delivery system for a newspaper *with a comparable circulation to the dominant firm's*. It was not enough to show it was not viable for a small-circulation paper. The Chief Economist in the Swedish Competition Authority takes issue with that point in this extract from the ECLR. He considers that the Court may have been too restrictive on this point and that the requirement may restrict the application of the essential facilities doctrine to markets which are natural monopolies.

M.A. Bergman, 'Editorial: The Bronner Case—A Turning Point for the Essential Facilities Doctrine? [2000] *ECLR* 59, 60–2

There are alternative interpretations of this second criterion for when the essential facilities doctrine is applicable. Obviously, it is extremely rare that duplication is impossible in an absolute sense. For example, even under geologically unfavourable conditions, a new harbour could in principle be built close to any existing harbour, although costs might be astronomical. Whether a facility is duplicable or not is always, or almost always, determined by economic considerations, rather than by, *e.g.* the laws of nature. This insight is reflected in the language used in earlier cases, *e.g.* that the competing firm 'lacks the ability to duplicate the facility', rather than that it would be 'impossible'. . . . That a firm 'lacks the ability' is not a very precise statement; in *Bronner* the Court has chosen to clarify that statement. However, at least two alternative interpretations are possible.

First, the formulation used can be given the interpretation that a competing publisher must lack the ability to duplicate the home-delivery scheme even if it reaches a market *share* comparable to that of Mediaprint, *i.e.* approximately half of the market. Alternatively, the formulation can be given the interpretation that a competing publisher must lack the ability to arrange home deliveries even if it reaches the same *circulation* as Mediaprint, which could imply that, first, the market must grow to twice its current size and, second, the competitor must attain half of the redoubled market. In economic terms, the criterion set up by the Court can be interpreted as a requirement that the market must be such that only *one* firm is economically viable and, hence, that it is impossible for two firms to operate simultaneously in the market unless at least one of them is unprofitable. This criterion has sometimes been used to define the concept 'natural monopoly'. (Nowadays, in the economics literature, the definition normally used is that over the relevant range of production, a lower level of cost should always be attainable if only one firm produces, compared to a situation when production is divided between two or more firms.). This would have to be true for a market of the same size as the affected market with the first interpretation above, and for a market of up to twice the size of the affected market with the second interpretation. It appears likely that the Court was thinking primarily along the lines of the first interpretation.

A More Restrictive View

If the new criterion set out in the *Bronner* case were to be used in other cases, without consideration of the specific circumstances, a Catch-22 situation may result. The criterion does not explicitly take into consideration that it may be impossible for the competitor to *attain* a market share of 50 per cent, even if in principle it would be possible to create and operate the required facility once that market share is reached. Furthermore, if this new criterion is applied generally, this will severely restrict the applicability of the essential facilities doctrine, *i.e.* to markets where only one firm has the possibility to be viable.

With such an interpretation, the essential facilities doctrine cannot be used to facilitate entry into markets with limited competition, as entry is only possible if more than one firm is expected to be economically viable in the long run. Instead, the doctrine will only be applicable to markets in which two or more firms can never be economically viable on their own *unless* the essential facilities doctrine is applied. Such markets are sometimes referred to as natural monopolies, although a more correct denomination may be 'inevitable monopolies'. In such markets, a second firm can only thrive on an artificial habitat created by the application of the doctrine. The effect of the doctrine is hence to serve as an instrument for indirect price regulation of markets that are 'inevitable monopolies'. In particular, the doctrine *cannot* create or preserve a market structure that will in turn stimulate competition and efficiency. The price-regulatory effect will follow because competitors will be granted access to the facility at non-discriminatory terms, which in turn will limit the dominant firm's ability to exploit customers on the related market. To favour the method of indirect price regulation over the method of creating structural conditions for competition stands in stark contrast to predominant views on competition policy. Normally, measures that prevent a firm from strengthening its dominance, *e.g.* by eliminating its rivals with predatory measures, are preferred over measures that prevent a firm from exploiting its customers, *e.g.* by abusively high prices.

Bergman thus considers that the criteria set out by the Court in *Bronner* appear to depart from those in previous cases. This view is shared by Hancher,[254] who argues in particular that the Commission decisions in *British Midland/Aer Lingus*[255] and *London European/Sabena*[256] would not have passed the Court's more stringent test. Hancher also expresses concern that the *Bronner* judgment does not really address the vexed question of what essential facilities are. Is there any scope for the concept outside cases of monopoly leveraging, i.e. where a monopolist on one market projects its dominance on to an ancillary

---

[254] L. Hancher, 'Case Note on Oscar Bronner' (1999) 36 CMLRev. 1289, 1306–1307.
[255] See *supra* 388.
[256] See *supra* 386.

market? Or does it also apply to the actions of a non-integrated or single monopolist who has no rivals to exclude from either its own or a related market (which is how the Commission applied it in the *Morlaix* decision)?

Bronner is obviously not the last word on essential facilities. It did not address the problems about pricing, for example, or how the facility owner should deal with competing claims for access, or the role of competition authorities in essential facilities scenarios. The judgment itself rather coyly (paragraph 41) side-stepped the question whether the case law on intellectual property rights (i.e. *Magill*), is applicable to other property rights. It did, however, make quite clear that an obligation to grant access to a facility will arise only in exceptional circumstances. *Bronner*, of course, was an easy case for the Court. It concerned a facility built up by a private undertaking with its own resources and a situation in which the other undertaking was operating satisfactorily on the downstream market without access to it. If the Court had considered that it was a situation suitable for the application of the essential facilities doctrine then all dominant firms owning or controlling a facility someone else might have found useful should have been worried, and incentives to innovation would have been seriously undermined. As it is, it seems clear that facilities are not lightly to be termed 'essential' or access lightly required. The questions left unanswered by *Bronner* will have to be answered in the end. In the meantime the essential facilities doctrine has been reined in by the Court.

The Commission recognized the Court's restrictive approach to the issue in the *Info-Lab* decision.[257] A producer of toner for photocopiers complained to the Commission that Ricoh, a photocopier manufacturer, refused to supply it with empty cartridges compatible with Ricoh machines so that it could fill them with toner and compete with Ricoh in the market for filled toner cartridges. Ricoh did not make empty cartridges. The Commission held that Ricoh did not have a dominant position[258] but considered that even if it had, in the light of *Bronner* such forced co-operation could be envisaged only under exceptional circumstances which did not pertain here.

The most likely markets for the application of the essential facilities doctrine remain transport infrastructures and/or infrastructures originally developed with public money. The Commission decisions discussed above demonstrate how the essential facilities concept is used to open up transport markets. In some cases, where competition is being brought on to markets which have previously been statutory monopolies, duplication of facilities, such as networks, is not feasible in the real world. Liberalization therefore cannot take place unless the new competitors are given access to the established facilities. The Commission has dealt specifically with access agreements in the telecommunications sector,[259] and it also intervened in the financial services sector, and issued a notice on cross-border credit transfers, because it considered that access to payment systems is vital if banks are to compete on relevant markets.[260] In special sectors, therefore, the Commission applies the concept of an essential facility through regulation.

---

[257] Case IV/36431, see Competition Policy Newsletter, 1999, No. 1, 35
[258] See *supra* Chap. 6.
[259] Commission notice on access agreements in the telecommunications sector [1998] OJ C265/2.
[260] [1995] OJ C251/3.

7. INFORMATION TECHNOLOGY COMPANIES

The Commission has settled proceedings involving information technology companies on a number of occasions. The 1997 *Digital Undertaking* is dealt with above.[261] In 1984 the Commission settled proceedings with IBM.[262] The Commission was concerned about a number of practices including tying, discrimination, and refusal to supply.

Commission's *XIVth Report on Competition Policy* (Commission, 1984)

94. . . . IBM was alleged to have abused [its] dominant position:

    (i) by failing to supply other manufacturers in sufficient time with the technical information needed to permit competitive products to be used with System/370 ('interface information');

    (ii) by not offering System/370 central processing units ('CPUs') without a capacity of main memory included in the price ('memory bundling');

    (iii) by not offering System/370 CPUs without the basic software included in the price ('software bundling');and

    (iv) by discriminating between users of IBM software, i.e. refusing to supply certain software installation services ('installation productivity options' = IPOs) to users of non-IBM CPUs.

95. While not admitting the existence of a dominant position nor any abuse thereof, IBM has now undertaken to offer its System/370 CUPs in the EEC either without main memory or with only such capacity as is strictly required for testing, and to disclose, in a timely manner, sufficient interface information to enable competing companies in the EEC to attach both hardware and software products of their design to System/370. IBM will also disclose adequate and timely information to competitors to enable them to interconnect their systems or networks with IBM's System/370 using Systems Network Architecture. For interfaces to hardware products, information will be made available by IBM within 4 Months of the date of announcement of the product concerned or at the general availability of the product if earlier. For interfaces between software products the information will now be made available as soon as the interface is reasonably stable but no later than general availability.

These undertakings do not extend to interfaces between two specific products of a subsystem, which are those most likely to reveal product design. This exception will not, however, exclude competition from suppliers who themselves offer both products as a subsystem.

The duration of the undertaking is for an indefinite period, but IBM has reserved the right to terminate its engagement on giving one year's notice, which cannot take effect before 1 January 1990.

The undertaking will have the effect of substantially improving the position of both users and competitors in the markets for System/370 products in the EEC. As a result, competition in

---

[261] Commission Press Release IP/97/868; see *supra* 374.
[262] See *XIVth Report on Competition Policy* (Commission, 1984) pts 94–95.

> the common market can be expected to be strengthened and made more effective. Users will now be given the possibility of a choice between different suppliers at an earlier time. They may also be free to choose from a wider selection of products because other manufacturers will now have the incentive to develop new products in the knowledge that the essential interface information will be made available.

The issue of access to interface information which arose in *IBM* is one of increasing importance in the information technology industry and is considered further in Chapter 10.

In 1994 the Commission launched an investigation into Microsoft's licensing practices. In particular it was concerned that Microsoft's standard agreements for licensing software to PC manufacturers excluded competitors from selling their products. For example, Microsoft: (a) used 'per processor' and 'per system' licences which required payment of royalties on every computer made by a PC manufacturer either containing a particular processor type or belonging to a particular model series, whether or not the computer was shipped with Microsoft software pre-installed; (b) used 'minimum commitment' clauses which required licensees to pay for a minimum number of copies of a product regardless of actual use; and (c) had excessively long licence agreements. The Commission (and the US Department of Justice) reached a settlement with Microsoft.[263] Microsoft undertook not to enter licence contracts of more than one year's duration, not to impose minimum commitments, and not to use per processor clauses: per system clauses would be allowed if the licensees were given flexibility not to buy Microsoft products and not to have to pay for what they did not buy.

8. IMPOSING UNFAIR OR DISCRIMINATORY TRADING CONDITIONS AND ENTERING INTO RESTRICTIVE AGREEMENTS

A wide variety of provisions imposed by dominant undertakings on their customers have been condemned as abuses because they were unfair or discriminatory, and some of these have been dealt with above under other heads of abuse. Article 82 (a) expressly condemns unfair conditions as well as prices, as does Article 82 (c) with regard to conditions. In *Tetra Pak II*[264] the terms on which the dominant undertaking dealt with its customers (in fact in pursuance of a marketing policy which aimed to restrict supply and compartmentalize national markets) were found by the Commission to be unfairly onerous. The conditions included placing limitations on the purchasers' use of the machines, binding purchasers to Tetra Pak's repair and maintenance services, and reserving to Tetra Pak the right to make surprise inspections. The Commission held that these conditions deprived the purchaser of certain aspects of its property rights. Although it accepted that stipulations in the terms upon which the supplier *leased* machines, such as prohibitions on modifying or moving the equipment, were not *in themselves* abusive, it held they were in this case. The rental pay-

---

[263] *Microsoft*, IP (94)653 of 17 July 1994, [1994] 5 CMLR 143. The US Federal Trade Commission was investigating similar concerns over Microsoft at the same time.

[264] *Elopak Italia/Tetra Pak* [1991] OJ L72/1, [1992] 4 CMLR 551.

ments were so high in comparison to sale prices that the supplier had to be taken to have relinquished its property rights to the hirer. Lease terms which exceeded the technological (though not the physical) life of the machine were abusive. Further, clauses imposing penalties for breach of any of the terms of the agreements at Tetra Pak's discretion also infringed Article 82, as these were aimed at ensuring the customers complied with terms of the agreements which were in themselves abuses.

In a number of cases concerning performing rights societies the Commission has found the society to have committed abuses by virtue of the terms on which the society did business. For example, in *GEMA*[265] the society wished to prevent members leaving it and entering into direct relationships with undertakings such as record companies. Its rules took the rights to works even after the member's resignation, provided for long periods of withdrawal and made payments to the social fund payable only to members of twenty years' standing.

GEMA also discriminated on grounds of nationality, always a heinous offence in EC law.[266] Discriminatory treatment of other trading parties on *any* grounds without objective justification is expressly prohibited by Article 82 (c) and is a policy which the dominant undertaking is likely to have adopted in pursuance of some other abusive practice. Discriminatory pricing is dealt with above.[267] In *BPB Industries*[268] the company gave priority of delivery of *plaster* to certain customers. The favoured customers were those who were 'loyal' to BPB and did not buy imported *plasterboard*. The purpose of the provision was to ensure exclusive purchasing of plasterboard by the customers and to make it more difficult for the competitors to penetrate the market. The CFI recognized that in times of shortage it is a matter of normal commercial policy to lay down criteria for meeting orders. The criterion in this case was not, however, acceptable. In its appeal to the ECJ BPB claimed that it could not have infringed Article 82 in this way since the discrimination took place on the plaster market where it was not dominant. The answer to this was that the plaster and plasterboard markets were connected and that the company had applied dissimilar conditions to equivalent transactions on one market in order to strengthen its dominance on the other.[269]

When a dominant undertaking enters into restrictive agreements it may be caught by both Article 81 and Article 82. In *Ahmed Saeed*[270] the Court, in the context of an agreement fixing air tariffs, said that what appeared to be an agreement could really be the imposition on the other party of the dominant undertaking's will, the agreement simply constituting 'the formal measure setting the seal on an economic reality characterised by the fact that an

---

[265] [1971] OJ L134/15, [1971] CMLR D35.

[266] Which is of course contrary to Art. 12 EC where it relates to citizens of the Union; see also Case 7/82, *GVL v. Commission* [1983] ECR 483, [1983] 3 CMLR 645. See also *1998 Football World Cup* [2000] OJ L5/55, [2000] 4 CMLR 963.

[267] See *supra* 349.

[268] Case T–65/89, *BPB Industries and British Gypsum Ltd v. Commission* [1993] ECR II–389, [1993] 5 CMLR 32; on appeal Case C–310/93P, *BPB Industries PLC and British Gypsum Ltd v. Commission* [1995] ECR I–865, [1997] 4 CMLR 238.

[269] On this point (which applies the same principle as Case C–62/86 *AKZO Chemie BV v. Commission* [1991] ECR I–3359, [1993] 5 CMLR 215 and foreshadows Case C–333/94P *Tetra Pak International SA v. Commission* [1996] ECR I–5951, [1997] 4 CMLR 662) the Court (paragraph 11) simply adopted the reasoning of Léger AG, paras. 70–86.

[270] Case 66/86, *Ahmed Saeed Flugreisen and Silver Line Reisebüro GmbH v. Zentrale zur Bëkämpfung Unlauteren Wettbewerbs eV* [1989] ECR 803, [1990] 4 CMLR 102.

undertaking in a dominant position has succeeded in having the tariffs in question applied by other undertakings'.

9. EXPORT BANS

Any type of conduct dividing markets or hindering exports and imports in the EC will be abusive not just on competition grounds but also as it is contrary to single market integration.[271] The excessive prices charged for the type approval certificates in *British Leyland*[272] were held to be an abuse because they both hindered parallel imports and exploited consumers. In *United Brands*[273] UBC imposed on its ripener/distributors the obligation not to resell the bananas while they were still green. This was treated by the Court and Commission as tantamount to an export ban (as bananas once yellow were so perishable that exporting them was not feasible) which reinforced UBC's policy of geographical price discrimination.[274] UBC claimed throughout that the 'green banana clause' was only a necessary measure of quality control and had never been understood, applied, or enforced as an export ban, but it was nevertheless held to infringe Article 82.

10. THE ACQUISITION OF INTELLECTUAL PROPERTY RIGHTS

It was seen in Chapter 5 that in *Tetra Pak I*[275] the acquisition by a dominant undertaking of an exclusive patent licence was held to be an abuse even though the licence agreement did not infringe Article 81 as it fell within the block exemption regulation.[276] The CFI said that although the acquisition of an exclusive licence by a dominant undertaking is not an abuse *per se*, it may be so, and was on the facts of this case. The principle in *Tetra Pak I*, which is a striking example of the onerous nature of the 'special responsibility' towards the competitive process imposed on dominant firms, is further discussed in Chapter 10.[277]

---

[271] See e.g. Case 40/73, *Suiker Unie* v. *EC Commission* [1975] ECR 1663, [1976] 1 CMLR 295, *Eurofix-Bauco* [1988] OJ L65/19, [1989] 4 CMLR 677 ; Case C–333/94P *Tetra Pak International SA* v. *Commission* [1996] ECR I–5951, [1997] 4 CMLR 662; Case C–310/93P, *BPB Industries PLC and British Gypsum Ltd* v. *Commission* [1995] ECR I–865, [1997] 4 CMLR 238; Case T–228/97, *Irish Sugar plc* v. *Commission* [1999] 5 CMLR 1300.

[272] Case 226/84, British Leyland v. *EC Commission* [1986] ECR 3323, [1987] 1 CMLR 185.

[273] Case 27/76, *United Brands* v. *Commission* [1978] ECR 207, [1978] 1 CMLR 429.

[274] See *supra* 352.

[275] Case T–51/89 *Tetra Pak Rausing* v. *Commission* [1990] ECR II–309, [1991] 4 CMLR 334.

[276] Reg. 2349/84, [1984] OJ L219/15, on patent licensing agreements (replaced by 240/96, [1996] OJ L31/2, on Technology Transfer Agreements (see *infra* Chap. 10)).

[277] The principle has been applied subsequently in cases which were settled informally to the Commission's satisfaction: *Carlsberg/Interbrew*, XXIVth Report on Competition Policy (Commission, 1994), pts 209 and 213; *Svenska Tobaks*, XXVIIth Report on Competition Policy (Commission, 1997), pt 66. See J. Faull and A. Nikpay (eds), *The EC Law of Competition* (Oxford University Press, 1999) paras. 3.288–3.289.

11. VERTICAL AND HORIZONTAL INTEGRATION

Although it is not an infringement of Article 82 for a dominant undertaking to integrate vertically, it has been seen that actions taken in pursuit of a policy of vertical integration may infringe. Many cases finding a refusal to supply[278] or tying[279] to infringe Article 82 involved actions taken by a dominant undertaking which would enable it to integrate vertically.

In *Continental Can*[280] it was established that Article 82 could apply to mergers whereby an undertaking strengthened its dominant position. Since the Merger Regulation 4064/89 has come into force, however, the general rule is that the Regulation alone applies to mergers falling within its scope.[281]

12. PURSUIT OF LEGAL PROCEEDINGS AND VEXATIOUS LITIGATION

It may be an infringement of Article 82 for a dominant undertaking to pursue legal proceedings against a competitor. This was suggested by *BBI/Boosey & Hawkes*[282] where it was alleged that Boosey & Hawkes had pursued unjustified breach of copyright actions in the UK and actions for 'slavish copying' in the German courts against a new competitor it was trying to exclude from the market. The Commission did not pursue these allegations but concentrated its decision on the refusal to supply aspect.[283] The matter arose again in *ITT Promedia v. Commission*.[284] Promedia, which was engaged in a dispute with Belgacom, the dominant supplier of voice telephony services in Belgium, about the publication of telephone directories complained to the Commission that Belgacom was abusing its dominant position by entering into national litigation against it. The Commission rejected the complaint as it considered that the conduct of litigation by a dominant firm could be abusive only if two cumulative criteria were met, and that these criteria had not been met in this case. Promedia appealed to the CFI. The judgment of the CFI is unsatisfactory in some respects because Promedia alleged that the Commission had *applied the criteria incorrectly* but did not challenge the *criteria themselves*. The CFI expressly said that it was not necessary

---

[278] Such as Cases 6, 7/73, *Istituto Chemioterapico Italiano Spa and Commercial Solvents Corp. v. EC Commission* [1974] ECR 223, [1974] 1 CMLR 309 and Case 22/78, *Hugin Kassaregister AB v. EC Commission* [1979] ECR 1869, [1979] 3 CMLR 345

[279] e.g. the *Digital Undertaking*, Commission Press Release IP/97/868; see *supra* 373.

[280] Case 6/72, *Europemballage Corp. & Continental Can Co Inc v. EC Commission* [1973] ECR 215, [1973] CMLR 199; see Chaps. 5 and 12.

[281] For a discussion of this, see *infra* Chap. 12.

[282] *BBI/Boosey & Hawkes* [1987] OJ L286/36, [1988] 4 CMLR 67.

[283] See *supra* 382.

[284] Case T–111/96 *ITT Promedia NV v. Commission* [1998] ECR II–2937, [1998] 5 CMLR 491.

for it to rule on the correctness of the criteria[285] and confined itself to holding that they had been properly applied. The implication of the CFI judgment, however, is that the criteria themselves are correct.

Case T–111/96, *ITT Promedia* v. *EC Commission* [1998] ECR II– 2937, [1998] 5 CMLR 491

Court of First Instance

60. . . . [a]s the Commission has rightly emphasised, the ability to assert one's rights through the courts and the judicial control which that entails, constitute the expression of a general principle of law which underlies the constitutional traditions common to the Member States and which is also laid down in Articles 6 and 13 of the European Convention for the Protection of Human Rights and Fundamental Freedoms of 4 November 1950 (see Case 222/84, *Johnson v. Chief Constable of the Royal Ulster Constabulary . . .*). As access to the Court is a fundamental right and a general principle ensuring the rule of law, it is only in wholly exceptional circumstances that the fact that legal proceedings are brought is capable of constituting an abuse of a dominant position within the meaning of Article [82] of the Treaty.

61. Second, since the two cumulative criteria constitute an exception to the general principle of access to the courts, which ensures the rule of law, they must be construed and applied strictly, in the manner which does not defeat the application of the general rule (see, *inter alia*, Case T–105/95, *WWF UK v. E.C.Commission . . .*).

. . .

72. According to the first of the two cumulative criteria set out by the Commission in the contested decision, legal proceedings can be characterised as an abuse, within the meaning of Article [82] of the Treaty, only if they cannot reasonably be considered to be an attempt to assert the rights of the undertaking concerned and can therefore only serve to harass the opposing party. It is therefore, the situation existing when the action in question is brought which must be taken into account in order to determine whether that criterion is satisfied.

73. Furthermore, when applying that criterion, it is not a question of determining whether the rights which the undertaking concerned was asserting when it brought its action actually existed or whether that action was well founded, but rather of determining whether such an action was intended to assert what that undertaking could, at that moment, reasonably consider to be its rights. According to the second part of that criterion, as worded, it is satisfied solely when the action did not have that aim, that being the sole case in which it may be assumed that such action could only serve to harass the opposing party.

The Commission based its criteria on human rights—the rights of access to the courts. The test is not whether the right claimed exists, but whether the dominant undertaking may reasonably consider that it does. The CFI judgment confirms that vexatious litigation *can* be an abuse, but only in limited circumstances. Moreover, the CFI held that Belgacom was entitled to rely on its rights under national law unless and until the Court ruled that the national law had been invalidated:

93. The purpose of Belagcom's first two actions must therefore be regarded as the assertion of what Belagacom, at the moment when it brought those two actions, could reasonably consider, on the basis of the Belgian provisions governing the publishing of telephone directories, to be its rights. Consequently, the first of the Commissions two cumulative criteria was not satisfied.

[285] *Ibid.*, at para. 57.

94. In such circumstances, an examination of the question whether the relevant Belgian provisions governing the publishing of telephone directories were compatible with Community law could not have shown that the objective of Belgacom's first two actions was not to assert what Belgacom, at the moment when it brought those actions, could reasonably consider to be its rights under those provisions and that the two actions therefore served only to harass the applicant. Consequently, that question fell to be considered in the examination of the merits, which was a matter for the national court hearing Belgacom's first two actions.

95. In that context, the Court rejects the applicant's argument that the Commission should have examined whether the relevant Belgian provisions were, at least apparently, compatible with Community law. Such an interpretation of the first of the two cumulative criteria would make it practically impossible for undertakings in a dominant position to have access to the courts. In order to avoid the risk of infringing Article [82] of the Treaty solely because they had brought an action before the courts, those undertakings would have to ensure beforehand that the relevant provisions on which they based their rights were compatible with Community Law.

The CFI also held that a dominant undertaking which sought performance of a contract would commit an abuse only if the claim went beyond what it could reasonably expect from the contract.[286]

13. OTHER EXCLUSIONARY PRACTICES

A. GENERAL

It is clear that any conduct which is intended to exclude competitors from the market, or which has that effect, may constitute an abuse, whatever form that conduct takes. The 'special responsibility' of dominant undertaking towards the competitive process must always be remembered. Miscellaneous exclusionary conduct which has come before the Court or Commission includes alleging to third parties that a competitor is a bad debtor,[287] buying up a competitor's machines,[288] and monopolizing the specialist advertising media.[289] In *Irish Sugar*[290] the dominant undertaking in the Irish sugar market persuaded certain wholesalers and retailers to swap the sugar they had bought from a competitor for its own. This conduct was found to be an abuse. Irish Sugar also put pressure on a shipping line to stop carrying the competitor's product by threatening to withdraw its own custom if this continued. The Commission commented that '[p]utting pressure on a carrier to prevent him from transporting competing goods cannot be considered to constitute a normal business practice'.[291]

---

[286] *Ibid.*, para. 129.
[287] *BBI/Boosey & Hawkes* [1987] OJ L286/36, [1988] 4 CMLR 67.
[288] *Elopak Italia/Tetra Pak* [1991] OJ L72/1, [1992] 4 CMLR 551, para. 165.
[289] *Ibid.*
[290] Case T–228/97, *Irish Sugar plc* v. *Commission* [1999] 5 CMLR 1300.
[291] Commission Decision, [1997] OJ L258/1, [1997] 5 CMLR 666, paras. 120–122.

B. STRATEGIC ENTRY DETERRENCE AND RAISING RIVALS' COSTS

Exclusionary behaviour is often described, particularly in the USA, as 'strategic entry deterrence'. This can be used to cover practices such as tying on which, as is seen above, there is considerable EC case law. There is as yet no EC jurisprudence on what is called predatory product or process innovation. This occurs when a dominant undertaking introduces a product or process which appears to present no technological, æsthetic, or other improvement, but is introduced merely to exclude existing competitors, for example where a product is redesigned with the purpose of making it incompatible with a complementary product offered by a competitor. Nor is there as yet specific case law on other practices much discussed in economics literature, such as predatory advertising and excessive product differentiation. This type of practice may particularly deter new entrants and operate as a barrier to entry. Existing competitors may fight to stay in the market because they have incurred sunk costs. Many types of abusive conduct which have arisen in the EC case law and which are discussed in this chapter can be classed as behaviour which 'raises rivals' costs'. Practices such as tying, refusals to deal,[292] exclusive dealing, discriminatory pricing, and vexatious litigation may all raise the competitor's costs relative to those of the dominant undertaking and result in inefficiencies for the competitor. The essence of raising rivals' costs is that the dominant undertaking raises the competitor's costs relative to its own, resulting in inefficiencies for the competitor. In 'non-price predation' the line between normal competition and abusive conduct is difficult to draw. As Rapp says:[293]

Non-price predation is said to take a variety of different forms whose common characteristics is that they raise costs for rivals. Excessive advertising and building excess capacity (with its implied threat that the dominant firm will flood the market in response to the entry or expansion of smaller firms) are two of the forms most often discussed. Even partisans for the theory of non-price predation admit that the line between normal competitive behaviour and anti-competitive action is so hard to distinguish in most cases that the risk of harm from enforcement often may outweigh the possible benefits to competition.

14. INEFFICIENCY

Article 82 (b) prohibits 'limiting production, markets, or technical development to the prejudice of consumers'. This has been applied to dominant undertakings operating inefficiently and unable to meet demand, particularly public undertakings with statutory monopolies where Article 82 has applied in conjunction with Article 86.[294] In *Port of Genoa*[295]

---

[292] For example, in *British Midland/Aer Lingus* [1992] OJ L96/34, [1993] 4 CMLR 596, para. 30, the Commission described the refusal to interline as raising the competitor's costs.

[293] R. Rapp: 'Predatory Pricing and Entry Deterring Strategies: the Economics of AKZO' [1986] *ECLR* 233. See also J. Faull and A. Nikpay (eds), *The EC Law of Competition* (Oxford University Press, 1999), paras. 3.262–3.271.

[294] See further Chap. 8.

[295] Case C–179/90, *Merci Convenzionali Porto di Genova* v. *Siderurigica Gabrielle* [1991] ECR I–5889, [1994] 4 CMLR 422.

the Court held that an undertaking with the exclusive right to organize dock work at Genoa, which refused to use modern technology and thus raised costs and caused delays, was in breach of Article 82. In *Höfner* v. *Macroton*[296] the Court held that a state employment agency which was unable to meet the demand for its services would infringe Article 82. This type of abuse can, however, also be committed by private undertakings. In *P and I Clubs*,[297] which concerned associations providing marine insurance, the Commission stated that it would intervene in situations only where there is 'clear and uncontroversial evidence that a very substantial share of the demand is being deprived of a service that it manifestly needs'.[298]

15. ABUSE AND COLLECTIVE DOMINANCE

It was explained in Chapter 5 that a 'dominant position' may be held by a single undertaking or by one or more independent undertakings which hold a collective dominant position. This concept and its application are explored below in Chapter 11, in the context of cartels and oligopolies, and in Chapter 12 in the context of mergers. In some of the cases discussed in this chapter, the dominant position being abused was a collective one.[299] It should be noted here, however, that in *Irish Sugar* the CFI said that it was not necessary for the collective dominant position to be *abused* collectively. It is possible therefore that an undertaking may individually commit an abuse of a dominant position held collectively with other undertakings.[300]

16. FURTHER READING

A. BOOKS

BORK, R., *The Antitrust Paradox* (Basic Books, 1978, reprinted with a new Introduction and Epilogue, 1993), Chapter 7

HOVENKAMP, H., *Federal Antitrust Policy* (West Publishing Co., 1994), Chapters 6, 7, 8, and 10

GOVAERE, I., *The Use and Abuse of Intellectual Property Rights in EC Law* (Sweet & Maxwell, 1996)

PHLIPS, L., *The Economics of Price Discrimination* (Cambridge University Press, 1983)

SCHERER, F. M., and Ross, D., *Industrial Market Structure and Economic Performance* (3rd edn. Houghton Mifflin, 1990), Chapters 13 and 16

---

[296] Case C–41/90, *Höfner* v. *Macroton* [1991] ECR I–1979, [1993] 4 CMLR 306; Case C–55/96, *Job Centre Co-op.arl* [1998] 4 CMLR 708 was a similar case from Italy.

[297] [1999] OJ L125/12.

[298] *Ibid.*, para. 128. The Commission's Statement of Objections stated that the undertaking had abused its (collective) dominant position by offering only a single insurance product. The undertaking amended its arrangements and the Decision found that there was no longer any question of an infringement of Art. 82.

[299] Cases C–395 and 396/96P, *Compagnie Maritime Belge and others* v. *Commission* [2000] 4 CMLR 1076, e.g.

[300] Case T–228/97, *Irish Sugar plc* v. *Commission* [1999] 5 CMLR 1300, para. 66.

B. ARTICLES

Andrews, P., 'Aftermarket Power in the Computer Services Market: The Digital Undertaking' [1998] *ECLR* 176

Areeda, P., 'Essential Facilities: An Epithet in Need of Limiting Principles' (1990) 58 *Antitrust LJ* 841

—— and Turner, D., 'Predatory Pricing and Related Practices under Section 2 of the Sherman Act' (1975) 88 *Harv LR* 697

Bergman, M. A., 'Editorial: The Bronner case—A Turning Point for Essential Facilities' [2000] *ECLR* 59

Bishop, W., 'Price Discrimination under Article 86: Political Economy in the European Court' (1981) 66 *MLR* 282

Brodley, J., and Hay, D., 'Predatory Pricing: Competing Economic Theories and the Evolution of Legal standards' (1981) 66 *Cornell LR* 738

Dolmans, M., and Pickering, V., 'The 1997 Digital Undertaking' [1998] *ECLR* 108

Downing, R., 'Hilti: The Final Nail' [1995] *ECLR* 53

Fox, E., 'Price Predation—US and EEC: Economics and Values' [1989] *Fordham Corporate Law Institute* 687

Hancher, P., 'Case Note on Oscar Bronner' (1999) 36 *CMLRev* 1289

Jones, A., 'Distinguishing Predatory Prices from Competitive Ones' [1995] *EIPR* 252

Korah, V., 'The Paucity of Economic Analysis in the EEC Decisions on Competition: Tetra Pak II' [1993] *Current Legal Problems* 150

McGee, J., 'Predatory Price Cutting: The Standard Oil (New Jersey) Case' (1958) 1 *J Law and Econ.* 137

Maldoom, D., 'The Kodak Case: Power in Aftermarkets' [1996] *ECLR* 473

Rapp, R. T., 'Predatory Pricing and Entry Deterring Strategies: The Economics of AKZO' [1986] *ECLR* 233

Ridyard, D., 'Essential Facilities and the Obligation to Supply Competitiors' [1996] *ECLR* 438

Robertson, A., and Williams, M., 'The Law and Economics of Freezer Exclusivity' [1995] *ECLR* 7

Sibree, W., 'Ice Cream War: In Defence of the MMC' [1995] *ECLR* 203

Siragusa, M., 'The Application of Article 86 to the Pricing Policies of Dominant Companies' (1979) 16 *CMLrev.* 179

Temple Lang, J., 'Defining Legitimate Competition: Companies' Duties to Supply Competitors and Access to Essential Facilities' (1994) 18 *Fordham Int'l LJ* 437

Waelbroeck, M., 'Price Discrimination and Rebate Policies under EU Competition Law' [1995] *Fordham Corporate Law Institute* 147

Zanon, L., 'Price Discrimination under Article 86 of the EEC Treaty: A Comment on the UBC Case' (1982) 31 *ICLQ* 36

8

COMPETITION, THE STATE, AND PUBLIC UNDERTAKINGS: ARTICLE 86 (EX ARTICLE 90)

1. INTRODUCTION[1]

In this chapter we consider how competition law applies to the actions of the State when it intervenes in the market through undertakings which it controls or owns or which it places in a privileged position. We do not deal with the subject of state aids, which is outside the scope of this book.[2]

A competition policy which did not deal with the State in the market place would be incomplete and would disadvantage other undertakings. The State plays some part in the market place, directly or indirectly, in all the Member States, although the means and extent of this varies. The means and extent have also changed over time since the inception of the European Community. In 1957 there was still a fashion for nationalization, and it will be remembered that the leading case on the supremacy of Community law, *Costa* v. *ENEL*,[3] concerned the nationalization of the Italian electricity industry. More recently there has been a move in Europe away from nationalization. This is due not only to shifts in ideology but also to technological and economic advances which have meant that the arguments for publicly-owned monopolies in sectors such as telecommunications and electricity generation have diminished.[4] As well as nationalization, however, distortions to the competitive structure may be caused by monopolies created by privatization and by other undertakings which, although not in public ownership, are given an exclusive or protected position. Here again, new technology has eroded many of the arguments for maintaining such arrangements. One problem with national monopolies is that they maintain the compartmentalization of

---

[1] For an analysis of the development of the law in this area, see L.Hancher, 'Community, State and Market' in P. Craig and G. de Búrca (eds.), *The Evolution of EU Law* (Oxford University Press, Oxford, 1999), 721. And see generally J. Faull and A. Nikpay (eds.), *The EC Law of Competition* (Oxford University Press, Oxford, 1999), chap. 5; J.L. Buenida Sierra, *Exclusive Rights and State Monopolies in EC Law* (Oxford University Press, Oxford, 1999).

[2] But see P. Craig and G. de Búrca, *EU Law: Text, Cases and Materials* (2nd edn., Oxford University Press, Oxford, 1998), 1077–1102.

[3] Case 6/64, *Flaminio Costa* v. *ENEL* [1964] ECR 585, [1964] CMLR 425.

[4] See G. Amato, *Antitrust and the Bounds of Power: The Dilemma of Liberal Democracy in the History of the Market* (Hart Publishing, 1997), 88–9.

the common market. The programme of liberalization upon which the Community has embarked in the telecommunications sector, for example, is inspired as much by the desire to increase the integration of the market as that of increasing competition.[5]

The original version of the Treaty of Rome was neutral as between public and private ownership. Article 295 (ex Article 222) states that the Treaty in no way prejudices the rules in Member States governing the system of property ownership. That Article, which has been important in the formulation of Community law on intellectual property rights,[6] is unchanged, but it is arguable that the insertion by the Treaty of European Union of what is now Article 4 of the EC Treaty,[7] represents a shift in policy which favours private over public ownership. Article 4 says that the activities of the Member States and the Community shall be conducted 'in accordance with the principle of an open market economy with free competition'. Article 4, in contrast to Article 295, is among the 'Principles' set out in Part One of the EC Treaty. Article 4 is elaborated upon in Article 157 which provides that the 'Community and Member States shall ensure that the conditions necessary for the competitiveness of the Community's industry exist' and that their action in this respect which should be aimed, *inter alia*, at encouraging an environment favourable to initiative and the development of small and medium-sized undertakings, should be in accordance 'with a system of open and competitive markets'. It is essential to remember at the outset, however, that the competition rules do not apply to the *non-economic* activities of the States, such as compulsory education and social security, or to the prerogatives of the States such as security or the administration of justice.[8]

The Court's case law on Article 86 (ex Article 90), which is discussed in the following sections, shows some hostility towards the consequences of statutory monopoly and, as we shall see, has sometimes called into question the legitimacy of statutory monopoly itself. The debate about competition and the public services led to the introduction into the Treaty of Rome by the Treaty of Amsterdam of what is now Article 16,[9] which trumpets the value and importance of 'services of general economic interest'. This is discussed below.[10]

2. ARTICLE 86 (EX ARTICLE 90)

The application of Community rules to public undertakings and those granted special or exclusive rights is dealt with in Article 86 (ex Article 90). Article 86 states:

1.   In the case of public undertakings and undertakings to which Member States grant special or exclusive rights, Member States shall neither enact nor maintain in force any measure

---

[5] See principally Commission Dir. 90/388 [1990] OJ L192/10, Commission Dir. 94/46 [1994] OJ L268/15, Commission Dir. 96/2 [1996] OJ L20/59, Commission Dir. 95/51 [1995] OJ L256/49; Commission Dir. 96/19 [1996] OJ L74/13; and Hancher, *supra* n. 1, 722.

[6] See *infra* Chap. 10.

[7] Ex Art. 3a(2).

[8] Acknowledged by the Commission in its Notice on Services of General Interest in Europe, [1996] OJ C281/03, para. 18.

[9] Ex Art. 7d.

[10] See *infra* p. 476.

contrary to the rules contained in this Treaty, in particular to those rules provided for in Article 12 and Articles 81 to 89.

2. Undertakings entrusted with the operation of services of general economic interest or having the character of a revenue producing monopoly shall be subject to the rules contained in this Treaty, in particular to the rules on competition, insofar as the application of such rules does not obstruct the performance, in law or in fact, of the particular tasks assigned to them. The development of trade must not be affected to such an extent as would be contrary to the interests of the Community.

3. The Commission shall ensure the application of the provisions of this Article and shall, where necessary, address appropriate directives or decisions to Member States.

A. THE OBJECTIVES OF ARTICLE 86

As will be appreciated from its wording, Article 86 is normally applied in conjunction with another Article of the Treaty, since its function is to limit the ways in which State measures protecting certain undertakings hinder the operation of the Treaty. Thus Article 86 does not deal only with competition, despite its position in the Treaty. It deals rather with the application of *all* the rules in the EC Treaty, although it mentions in particular the competition rules (Articles 81–89) and the prohibition on discrimination on the grounds of nationality (Article 12, ex Article 6). Apart from those, the rules most likely to be concerned are those on free movement and state monopolies.[11] Article 86 does, however, have particular relevance to the competition provisions and especially Article 82, because public undertakings and undertakings granted special or exclusive rights frequently hold a dominant position.[12]

Article 86 is a specific manifestation of the duty of Community loyalty contained in Article 10 (ex Article 5) which requires Member States to take all appropriate measures to ensure fulfilment of their Treaty obligations, facilitate the achievement of the Community's tasks and abstain from measures which could jeopardize the attainment of the Treaty's objectives. The Court held in *INNO* v. *ATAB*, and has consistently stated ever since, that the Treaty imposes a duty on Member States not to adopt or maintain in force measures which could deprive the competition provisions of their effectiveness. It is an infringement of Articles 10 and 81, for example, for a Member State to require or favour the adoption of agreements, decisions or concerted practices contrary to Article 81, or to reinforce their effect.[13]

---

[11] See *Spanish Transport Fares to the Balearic and Canary Islands* [1987] OJ L194/28; *Flemish Television Advertising* [1997] OJ L244/18; Case C–260/89, *Elliniki Radiophonia Tileorasi (ERT)* v. *DEP* [1991] ECR I–2925, [1994] 4 CMLR 540.

[12] But not inevitably: the usual criteria of dominance apply, and the exclusive right has to be over a relevant market: see Case 30/87, *Bodson* v. *Pompes Funèbres des Régions Libérées* [1988] ECR 2479, [1989] 4 CMLR 984, paras. 26–29.

[13] Case 267/86, *Van Eycke* v. *ASPA NV* [1988] ECR 4769, [1990] 4 CMLR 330, para. 16; Cases C–140–142/94, *DIP and others* v. *Commune di Bassano del Grappa and Commune di Chioggia* [1995] ECR I–3257, [1996] 4 CMLR 157, para. 15.

Case 13/77, *NV GB-INNO-BM* v. *ATAB* [1977] ECR 2115

The Court was asked by the Belgian Court of Cassation about the compatibility with Community law of Belgian rules prohibiting the sale of tobocco at less than the price fixed by the manufacturers or importers.

Court of Justice

28. First, the single market system which the Treaty seeks to create excludes any national system of regulation hindering directly or indirectly, actually or potentially, trade within the Community.

29. Secondly, the general objective set out in Article [3(1)(g)] is made specific in several Treaty provisions concerning the rules on competition, including Article [82], which states that any abuse by one of more undertakings of a dominant position shall be prohibited as incompatible with the Common Market in so far as it may affect trade between Member States.

30. The second paragraph of Article [10] of the Treaty provides that Member States shall abstain from any measure which could jeopardize the attainment of the objectives of the Treaty.

31. Accordingly, while it is true that Article [82] is directed at undertakings, nonetheless it is also true that the Treaty imposes a duty on Member States not to adopt or maintain in force any measure which could deprive that provision of its effectiveness.

32. Thus Article [86] provides that, in the case of public undertakings and undertakings to which Member States grant special or exclusive rights, Member States shall neither enact nor maintain in force any measure contrary *inter alia* to the rules provided for in Articles [81] to [89].

33. Likewise, Member States may not enact measures enabling private undertakings to escape from the constraints imposed by Articles [81] to [89] of the Treaty.

34. At all events, Article [82] prohibits any abuse by one or more undertakings of a dominant position, even if such abuse is encouraged by a national legislative provision.

35. In any case, a national measure which has the effect of facilitating the abuse of a dominant position capable of affecting trade between Member States will generally be incompatible with Articles [28] and [29], which prohibits quantitative restrictions on imports and exports and all measures having equivalent effect.

B. THE FORMAT OF ARTICLE 86

Article 86 contains three interrelated provisions.

(i) ARTICLE 86(1): PROHIBITION ADDRESSED TO MEMBER STATES

The prohibition in Article 86(1) is addressed to Member States, not to undertakings. It prohibits Member States from enacting or maintaining in force any measures in relation to public undertakings and undertakings to which they have granted special or exclusive rights which are contrary to the rules of the Treaty. It is designed to prevent Member States from depriving the Treaty rules of their effectiveness through the measures they adopt in respect of public undertakings or through measures which enable private undertakings to escape the constraints of the competition provisions.

(ii) ARTICLE 86(2): PROVISION ADDRESSED TO UNDERTAKINGS PROVIDING FOR LIMITED IMMUNITY FROM THE TREATY RULES

Article 86(2) is addressed to the undertakings themselves. It gives a limited derogation from the Treaty rules to ' undertakings entrusted with the operation of services of general economic interest or having the character of a revenue producing monopoly' in so far as that is necessary for the carrying out of their tasks. Despite being addressed to undertakings, Article 86(2) can be invoked by Member States in relation to exclusive rights they have granted.[14]

(iii) ARTICLE 86(3): POLICING AND LEGISLATIVE POWERS OF THE COMMISSION

Article 86(3) provides that the Commission may address decisions to Member States to ensure the observance of Article 86. This is an expedited enforcement mechanism which does not have to comply with the procedures of the general enforcement provision, Article 226 (ex Article 169), which provides for infraction proceedings brought by the Commission against Member States.

It also gives the Commission power to issue directives to Member States to ensure the application of the Article. This power does not have to be exercised within the detailed procedural framework ordinarily applicable to the adoption of directives, which involves other Community institutions and is set down in Articles 250 to 252 (ex Articles 189a, b, and c).

The Commission's exercise of these special powers under Article 86(3) has sometimes led to challenges by Member States claiming that the situation concerned was not one to which Article 86(3) applied, that the Commission was acting *ultra vires* and/or that some other legislative base should have been used.[15]

C. ARTICLE 86(1)

(i) DEFINITIONS

When considering Article 86(1) it is first necessary to determine the meaning of the concepts it employs, in particular the terms 'public undertakings', 'granted special or exclusive rights', and 'measures'.

---

[14] See *infra* 456 ff.

[15] Cases 188–190/88, *France, Italy and the UK* v. *Commission* [1982] ECR 2545 (the *Transparency Dir.* case); Cases C–271, 281 & 289/90, *Spain, Belgium & Italy* v. *Commission* [1992] ECR I–5833 (The *Telecommunications Services* case); Case C–202/88, *France* v. *Commission* [1991] ECR I–1223 (the *Telecommunications Equipment* case).

a. 'PUBLIC UNDERTAKINGS'

Determining the meaning of 'public undertakings' is a two-step procedure. First, one must ask whether a particular body is an 'undertaking' and secondly, if it is, whether it is a 'public undertaking'.

The answer to the first question, what constitutes an undertaking, has already been considered in the context of Articles 81 and 82.[16] It will be recalled that 'undertaking' is a Community concept and that it is immaterial how the entity is regarded in national law. The fundamental question is whether it carries out commercial activities and not whether it is governed by public law or is non-profit-making. The Court held in *Höfner* v. *Macrotron* that in regard to competition law 'the concept of an undertaking encompasses every entity engaged in an economic activity, regardless of the legal status of the entity and the way it is financed'.[17] In that case the fact that employment procurement was normally entrusted to public agencies could not affect the economic nature of the activity the entity carried out. It was not always an activity carried out by public entities and it followed that a public employment agency could be classified as an undertaking.[18]

The second question is whether an undertaking is a 'public' undertaking. Again, this is a Community concept[19] because Article 86(1) would be deprived of its effect if Member States were free to choose their own conception of 'public undertaking'. State participation in the ownership or running of undertakings comes in an almost indefinite range of guises and the Community concept must embrace them all.

The concept of a 'public undertaking' was clarified by the Court in the *Transparency Directive* case.[20] This case arose as a result of a directive issued by the Commission pursuant to Article 86(3) aimed at creating greater transparency in the financial relationship between the Member States and public undertakings.[21] Article 2 defined 'public undertaking' as:

undertakings over which public authorities may exercise, directly or indirectly, a dominant influence by virtue of their ownership of it, their financial participation therein or the rules which govern it. A dominant influence is to be presumed when the public authority holds the major part of the undertaking's subscribed capital, controls the majority of votes attached to the shares issued or can appoint more than half of the members of the undertaking's administrative, managerial or supervisory body.

Various Member States challenged the directive, *inter alia* on the ground that the Commission was not entitled to amplify the concept of public undertaking contained in Article 86(1). The Court upheld the definition set out in the directive.[22]

---

[16] *Supra* Chaps. 3 and 5; and see Case 82/71, *Pubblico Ministero della Repubblica Italiana* v. *Società Agricola Industria Latte (SAIL)* [1972] ECR 119; Case 155/73, *Sacchi* [1974] ECR 409, [1974] 2 CMLR 177; Case 52/76, *Benedetti* v. *Munari F.illi* [1977] ECR 163; Case 123/83 *BNIC* v. *Clair* [1985] ECR 391; *European Broadcasting Union* [1993] OJ L179/23, [1995] 4 CMLR 56; Case C–364/92, *SAT Fluggesellschaft* v. *Eurocontrol* [1994] ECR I–43, [1994] 5 CMLR 208; Case C–159/91 etc *Poucet* [1993] ECR I–637; Case C–343/95, *Diego Cali* v. *Servizi Ecologici Porto di Genova* [1997] ECR I–1547, [1997] 5 CMLR 484.

[17] Case C–41/90, *Höfner* v. *Macrotron* [1991] ECR I–1979, [1993] 4 CMLR 306, para. 21.

[18] *Ibid.*, paras. 22–23.

[19] See the Opinion of Reischl AG in Cases 188–190/88, *France, Italy and the UK* v. *Commission* [1982] ECR 2545, para. 9 (the *Transparency Dir.* case).

[20] Cases 188–190/88, *France, Italy and the UK* v. *Commission* [1982] ECR 2545.

[21] Commission Dir. 80/723 [1980] OJ L195/35, amended by Commission Dir. 85/413. [1985] OJ L229/20.

[22] For Art. 86(3) see the discussion *infra* 471 ff.

The key to the concept is therefore control by the State. This can be through ownership or through some contractual, financial, or structural connection between the State and the undertaking.

b. UNDERTAKINGS GRANTED SPECIAL OR EXCLUSIVE RIGHTS

Special or exclusive rights may be granted in the whole of a national territory or in only part of it.[23] Undertaking is defined as discussed above and in Chapters 3 and 5, but difficulties have arisen over the definition of 'special and exclusive rights'. Two categories are involved here: 'special' and 'exclusive' are not synonymous. Entities with such rights may or may not be public undertakings.

Exclusive rights are the most easily identified. They exist where a monopoly has been granted by the State to one entity to engage in a particular economic activity on an exclusive basis. They have been held to have been conferred, for example, upon broadcasting monopolies,[24] and upon undertakings granted the sole right to operate employment recruitment services,[25] the sole right to operate on a particular air route,[26] the sole right to supply unloading services at a port,[27] and the sole right to provide bovine insemination services.[28] Rights of this type granted to more than one undertaking have been designated as 'special or exclusive' as, for example, the television duopoly in the Greek television case, *ERT*.[29] It is important to note that the grant of intellectual property rights does not entail the granting of exclusive rights for the purposes of Article 86(1) because it involves laws which lay down criteria which any undertaking is free to satisfy: there is no question of a closed class.

What amounts to 'special rights' has been determined by the Court as a result of a series of challenges brought by Member States to directives issued by the Commission under Article 86(3) in pursuance of its objective to liberalize the telecommunications market. This liberalization inevitably meant ensuring the removal of the protection hitherto given by Member States to national telecommunications operators.

The *Telecommunications Equipment Case*[30] concerned the challenge by France to Directive 88/301 on competition in the markets in telecommunications terminal equipment.[31] According to Article 2, Member States which had granted special or exclusive rights to undertakings for the importation, marketing, connection, bringing into service of

---

[23] e.g. Case 30/87, *Bodson v. Pompes Funèbres des Régions Libérées* [1988] ECR 2479, [1989] 4 CMLR 984 (funeral services in particular French communes); Case C–179/90, *Merci Convenzionali v. Porto di Genova* [1991] ECR I–5009, [1994] 4 CMLR 422 (unloading services in the port of Genoa); Case C–323/93, *Société Civile Agricole du Centre d'Insémination de la Crespelle v. Coopérative d'Elevage et d'Insémination Artificielle du Département de la Mayenne* [1994] ECR I–5077 (exclusive rights to provide bovine insemination services in defined areas of France).

[24] Case 155/73, *Sacchi* [1974] ECR 409, [1974] 2 CMLR 177.

[25] Case C–41/90, *Höfner v. Macrotron* [1991] ECR I–1979, [1993] 4 CMLR 306.

[26] Case 66/86, *Ahmed Saeed Flugreisen and Silver Line Reisebüro GmbH v. Zentrale zur Bëkampfung Unlauteren Wettwerbs eV* [1989] ECR 803, [1990] 4 CMLR 102; *Sterling Airways/SAS Denmark, Commission's* X[th] *Report on Competition Policy* (Commission, 1980) pts. 136–138.

[27] Case C–179/90, *Merci Convenzionali v. Porto di Genova* [1991] ECR I–5009, [1994] 4 CMLR 422.

[28] Case C–323/93, *Société Civile Agricole du Centre d'Insémination de la Crespelle* [1994] ECR I–5077.

[29] Case C–260/89, *Elliniki Radiophonia Tileorasi (ERT) v. DEP* [1991] ECR I–2925, [1994] 4 CMLR 540.

[30] Case C–202/88, *France v. Commission* [1991] ECR I–1223.

[31] [1988] OJ L131/73.

telecommunications terminal equipment and/or maintenance of such equipment were to ensure that those rights were withdrawn. The Court held that Article 2 was void in so far as it concerned the withdrawal of *special* rights because:

45. . . . . neither the provisions of the directive nor the preamble thereto specify the type of rights which are actually involved and in what respect the existence of such rights is contrary to the various provisions of the Treaty.

46. It follows that the Commission has failed to justify the obligation to withdraw special rights regarding the importation, marketing, connection, bringing into service and/or maintenance of tele-communications equipment.

The *Telecommunications Services*[32] case concerned a similar challenge by Spain, Belgium, and Italy to Directive 90/388 on competition in the markets for telecommunications ser-vices.[33] Again the Court annulled the provisions concerning the requirement to withdraw all special rights. In this directive the Commission had defined 'special or exclusive rights' in Article 1 as being 'rights granted by a Member State or a public authority to one or more private or public bodies through any legal, regulatory or administrative instrument reserv-ing them the right to provide a service or undertake an activity'. The Court held that this was inadequate as it did not make it possible 'to determine the type of special rights with which the directive is concerned or in what respect the existence of those rights is contrary to the various provisions of the Treaty'.[34]

As a result of these cases, the Commission set out an extended definition of the meaning of 'special rights' in the field of telecommunications in the Preamble to Directive 94/46[35] stating that special rights (in field of telecommunication services) are:

rights that are granted by a Member State to a limited number of undertakings through any legisla-tive, regulatory or administrative instruments which, within a given geographical area, limits to two or more, otherwise than according to objective, proportional and non-discriminatory criteria, the num-ber of undertakings which are authorised to provide any such service, or designates, otherwise than according to such criteria, several competing undertakings, as those which are authorised to provide any such service, or confers on any undertaking or undertakings otherwise than according to such criteria, legal or regulatory advantages which substantially affect the ability of any other undertaking to provide that same service in the same geographical area under substantially equivalent conditions.

Although this definition is set out in a directive relating to telecommunications there is no reason to suppose that it is not also applicable in other fields. What it does is to identify as 'special rights' those which are given by the State to a limited number of undertakings chosen in a subjective and discretionary manner.[36] This is borne out by the contrast with those cases in which it has been held that special or exclusive rights do not exist. So in *NV-GB-INNO* v. *ATAB* the Court doubted whether special or exclusive rights could result from allowing manufacturers and importers of a particular product to impose resale price main-

---

[32] Cases C–271, 281 & 289/90, *Spain, Belgium & Italy* v. *Commission* [1992] ECR I–5833.

[33] [1990] OJ L192/10.

[34] [1992] ECR I–5833, para. 31.

[35] Dir. amending Dir. 88/301 and 90/388 in particular with regard to satellite communications, [1994] OJ L268/15.

[36] See also the Commission's statement at the hearing in the *Telecommunications Services* case, Cases C–271, 281 & 289/90, *Spain, Belgium & Italy* v. *Commission* [1992] ECR I–5833, quoted by Jacobs AG at para. 50 of his Opinion.

tenance.[37] In *Banchero*[38] it held that Italian laws on the distribution of tobacco did not entail special or exclusive rights as, although they governed access to the market, all undertakings were treated in the same way. Further, in *GEMA*[39] the Commission held that an authors' rights society did not enjoy special or exclusive rights even though legislation required authors to exercise their rights through such a society, because there was no limit on the number of rights societies which could exist. As with exclusive rights, special rights involve the creation of some sort of limited, closed class.

c. 'MEASURES'

The word 'measures' also appears in Article 10 (ex Article 5) which obliges Member States to fulfill their Treaty obligations and not to jeopardize Treaty objectives, and in Article 28 (ex Article30) which prohibits, *inter alia*, measures having an equivalent effect to quantitative restrictions on imports between Member States. In Directive 70/50[40] the Commission defined measures as 'laws, regulations, administrative provisions, administrative practices, and all instruments issued from a public authority, including recommendations' and both Articles 10 and 28 have been interpreted to give a very wide interpretation to the word. The best illustration of this point is provided by the *Buy Irish* case[41] in which a number of steps taken by the Irish Government to encourage the public to buy home-produced goods were condemned as contrary to Article 28. The Court held that 'measures' do not have to have a binding effect.[42] 'Measures' does not, however, cover the actions of private undertakings rather than the State actions which allow or authorize them, so that anti-competitive conduct engaged in by undertakings on their own initiative must be dealt with by Articles 81 and 82.[43]

(ii) MEASURES WHICH ARE FORBIDDEN BY ARTICLE 86(1)

There is some uncertainty about what measures violate Article 86(1). In some cases there is clearly a violation in that some aspect of the State's arrangements inherently infringes a Treaty rule in itself. A good example, which does not involve the competition rules, is *Merci Convenzionali*,[44] where Italian laws reserved the loading and unloading of ships at an Italian port to certain dock-work companies whose worker-members had to be of Italian nationality. This infringed Article 39 (ex Article 48) on the free movement of workers, which specifically applies Article 12 forbidding nationality discrimination in situations governed by Community law.[45] In other cases the measures taken by the Member State *result in*

---

[37] Case 13/77 [1977] ECR 2115, [1978] 1 CMLR 283: the point did not actually have to be answered because of the reply given to an earlier question.

[38] Case C–387/93, *Banchero* [1995] ECR I–1085.

[39] [1971] OJ L134/15, [1971] CMLR D35.

[40] On the abolition of measures which have an effect equivalent to quantitative restrictions on imports and are not covered by other provisions [1970] OJ Spec. Ed. 17.

[41] Case 249/81, *Commission v. Ireland* [1982] ECR 4005, [1983] 2 CMLR 104.

[42] *Ibid.*, para. 28.

[43] Case C–202/88, *France v. Commission* [1991] ECR I–1223, para. 55.

[44] Case C–179/90, *Merci Convenzionali Porto di Genova v. Siderurgica Gabrielli SpA* [1991] ECR I–5009, [1994] 4 CMLR 422.

[45] *Ibid.*, paras. 10–13.

violations of the Treaty. The problem is that where the measures result in violations of the competition rules there are suggestions in some cases that the *very fact of granting monopoly rights* may itself be a violation. If this is so, the neutrality as to the organization of economic activities within the Member States discussed at the beginning of the Chapter is truly eroded and the right of Member States to make certain economic choices is limited.

It has been clear since the *Telecommunications Equipment* case in 1991 that Member States do not have unassailable rights to create legal monopolies under any conditions they choose:

Case C–202/88 *France v Commission* [1991] ECR I–1223

France challenged the Telecommunications Terminal Equipment Directive, 88/301, inter alia on the grounds that the Commission had no competence to adopt it on the basis of Article 86(3)(ex Article 90(3)). France claimed that Article 86 did not allow the Commission to interfere with the granting of special or exclusive rights by Member States because Article 86(1) presupposed the existence of special or exclusive rights so the granting of such rights could not itself constitute a 'measure' within the Article.

Court of Justice

21. . . . . it must be held in the first place that the supervisory power conferred on the Commission includes the possibility of specifying, pursuant to Article [86(3)], obligations arising under the Treaty. The extent of that power therefore depends on the scope of the rules with which compliance is to be ensured.

22. Next, it should be noted that even though that article presupposes the existence of undertakings which have certain special or exclusive rights, it does not follow that all the special or exclusive rights are necessarily compatible with the Treaty. That depends on different rules, to which Article [86(1)] refers.

As Edward and Hoskins say:[46]

It follows from *France v Commission* that Member States have not retained complete sovereignty in relation to the creation of legal monopolies. Rather, the creation of such monopolies must be balanced with the principle of free competition. However, the precise point at which the balance is to be struck is less clear.

It is therefore important to look at the cases to try to determine the point at which that balance is to be struck. Guidance can be derived in particular from *Höfner* v. *Macrotron, Merci Convenzionali, ERT, RTT, Corbeau,* and *La Crespelle.*

Case C–41/90, *Höfner* v. *Macrotron* [1991] ECR–I–1979, [1993] 4 CMLR 306

A dispute arose in a German court, the Oberlandsgericht München, between a company and the recruitment consultants it had employed to find it a sales director. In a dispute about fees the company claimed that the contract between the parties was void as it infringed the German law on the promotion of employment, the Arbeitsförderungsgesetz (the AFG). The AFG conferred on the Bundesanstalt, the Federal Office for Employment, the exclusive right to put prospective employees

---

[46] D. Edward and M. Hoskins, 'Art. 90: Deregulation and EC Law. Reflections Arising from the XVI FIDE Conference' (1995) 32 *CMLRev.* 157, 160.

and employers in contact with one another. Nevertheless, to some extent the Budesanstalt tolerated the existence and activities of independent recruitment consultants and it appeared that the Bundesanstalt was unable, on its own, to meet the demand for executive recruitment. The questions referred by the Oberlandsgericht raised the issue of whether there was an abuse of a dominant involved and whether Article 86(1) was infringed by the exclusive rights. The Court first held that the Bundesanstalt was an undertaking for the purposes of Articles 82 and 86.[47] It then considered the possible infringements.

Court of Justice

24. It must be pointed out that a public employment agency which is entrusted, under the legislation of a Member State, with the operation of services of general economic interest, such as those envisaged in Article 3 of the AFG, remains subject to the competition rules pursuant to Article [86(2)] of the Treaty unless and to the extent to which it is shown that their application is incompatible with the discharge of its duties (see judgment in Case 155/73 *Sacchi* . . . .).

25. As regards the manner in which a public employment agency enjoying an exclusive right of employment procurement conducts itself in relation to executive recruitment undertaken by private recruitment consultancy companies, it must be stated that the application of Article [82] of the Treaty cannot obstruct the performance of the particular task assigned to that agency in so far as the latter is manifestly not in a position to satisfy demand in that area of the market and in fact allows its exclusive rights to be encroached on by those companies.

26. Whilst it is true that Article [82] concerns undertakings and may be applied within the limits laid down by Article [86(2)] to public undertakings or undertakings vested with exclusive rights, or specific rights, the fact nevertheless remains that the Treaty requires the Member States not to take or maintain in force measures which could destroy the effectiveness of that provision (see judgment in Case 13/77 *Inno* . . . paragraphs 31 and 32). Article [86(1)] in fact provides that the Member States are not to enact or maintain in force, in the case of public undertakings and the undertakings to which they grant special or exclusive rights, any measure contrary to the rules contained in the Treaty, in particular those provided for in Articles [81] to [89].

27. Consequently, any measure adopted by a Member State which maintains in force a statutory provision that creates a situation in which a public employment agency cannot avoid infringing Article [82] is incompatible with the rules of the Treaty.

28. It must be remembered, first, that an undertaking vested with a legal monopoly may be regarded as occupying a dominant position within the meaning of Article [82] of the Treaty (see judgment in Case 311/84 *CBEM*, [1985] ECR 3261) and that the territory of a Member State, to which that monopoly extends, may constitute a substantial part of the common market (judgment in Case C 322/81 *Michelin* . . . , paragraph 28).

29. Secondly, the simple fact of creating a dominant position of that kind by granting an exclusive right within the meaning of Article [86(1)] is not as such incompatible with Article [82] of the Treaty (see Case 311/84 *CBEM*, above, paragraph 17). A Member State is in breach of the prohibition contained in those two provisions only if the undertaking in question, merely by exercising the exclusive right granted to it, cannot avoid abusing its dominant position.

30. Pursuant to Article [82(b)], such an abuse may in particular consist in limiting the provision of a service, to the prejudice of those seeking to avail themselves of it.

31. A Member State creates a situation in which the provision of a service is limited when the

[47] See *supra* Chap. 3.

undertaking to which it grants an exclusive right extending to executive recruitment activities is manifestly not in a position to satisfy the demand prevailing on the market for activities of that kind and when the effective pursuit of such activities by private companies is rendered impossible by the maintenance in force of a statutory provision under which such activities are prohibited and non-observance of that prohibition renders the contracts concerned void.

32. It must be observed, thirdly, that the responsibility imposed on a Member State by virtue of Articles [82] and [86(1)] of the Treaty is engaged only if the abusive conduct on the part of the agency concerned is liable to affect trade between Member States. That does not mean that the abusive conduct in question must actually have affected such trade. It is sufficient to establish that the conduct is capable of having such an effect (see Case 322/81 *Michelin*, above, paragraph 104).

33. A potential effect of that kind on trade between Member States arises in particular where executive recruitment by private companies may extend to the nationals or to the territory of other Member States.

34. In view of the foregoing considerations, it must be stated in reply to the fourth question that a public employment agency engaged in employment procurement activities is subject to the prohibition contained in Article [82] of the Treaty, so long as the application of that provision does not obstruct the performance of the particular task assigned to it. A Member State which has conferred an exclusive right to carry on that activity upon the public employment agency is in breach of Article [86(1)] of the Treaty where it creates a situation in which that agency cannot avoid infringing Article [82] of the Treaty. That is the case, in particular, where the following conditions are satisfied.

— the exclusive right extends to executive recruitment activities;

— the public employment agency is manifestly incapable of satisfying demand prevailing on the market for such activities;

— the actual pursuit of those activities by private recruitment consultants is rendered impossible by the maintenance in force of a statutory provision under which such activities are prohibited and non-observance of that prohibition renders the contracts concerned void;

— the activities in question may extend to the nationals or to the territory of other Member States.

In *Höfner* v. *Macrotron* the Court reiterated (at paragraph 29) that the fact of creating a dominant position by granting exclusive rights is not *as such* incompatible with the Treaty. However, a Member State *will* infringe the Treaty if the undertaking in question, merely by exercising the exclusive right granted to it, *cannot avoid* abusing its dominant position. In this case the criterion was fulfilled as German law had given the undertaking a monopoly over executive recruitment services, the demand for which it was incapable of satisfying. Such limitation of the service offered to customers constituted an abuse under Article 82(b), and so the Member State had created a situation in which the agency could not avoid infringing the Article.[48]

In *ERT*, the Court took a slightly different approach:

---

[48] See para. 27 of the judgment. See also the similar judgment of the Court in respect of the public placement office monopoly in Italy, Case C–55/96, *Job Centre Coop. arl* [1997] ECR II–7119, [1998] 4 CMLR 708. The Commission came to a similar conclusion in *Spanish Courier Services* [1990] OJ L233/19 (courier services reserved to Post Office which could not offer complete services). For inefficiency and the limitation of production and services as an abuse, see *supra* Chap. 7.

Case C–260/89, *Elliniki Radiophonia Tileorassi Anonimi Etaira (ERT)* v. *Dimotiki Etairia Pliroforissis (DEP)* [1991] ECR I–2925, [1994] 4 CMLR 540

The Thessaloniki Regional Court referred to the Court under Article 234 various questions concerning the position of the Greek radio and television undertaking (ERT) to which the Greek government had granted exclusive rights in regard to the original broadcasting and retransmitting of programmes in Greece. Greek law prohibited any person from engaging in activities for which ERT had an exclusive right without ERT's authorisation. The Mayor of Thessaloniki and a municipal company, DEP, set up a television station and began to broadcast television programmes. ERT sought an injunction and the seizure of the new station's technical equipment.

Court of Justice

10. In Case C–155/73 *Sacchi* . . . , paragraph 14, the Court held that nothing in the Treaty prevents Member States, for considerations of a non-economic nature relating to the public interest, from removing radio and television broadcasts from the field of competition by conferring on one or more establishments an exclusive right to carry them out.

11. Nevertheless, it follows from Article [86(1) and (2)] of the Treaty that the manner in which the monopoly is organized or exercised may infringe the rules of the Treaty, in particular those relating to the free movement of goods, the freedom to provide services and the rules on competition.

12. The reply to the national court must therefore be that Community law does not prevent the granting of a television monopoly for considerations of a non-economic nature relating to the public interest. However, the manner in which such a monopoly is organized and exercised must not infringe the provisions of the Treaty on the free movement of goods and services or the rules on competition.

. . .

27. As a preliminary point, it should be observed that Article [3(1)(g)] of the Treaty states only one objective for the Community which is given specific expression in several provisions of the Treaty relating to the rules on competition, including in particular Articles [81],[82] and [86].

28. The independent conduct of an undertaking must be considered with regard to the provisions of the Treaty applicable to undertakings, such as, in particular, Articles [81],[82] and [86(2)].

29. As regards Article [81], it is sufficient to observe that it applies, according to its own terms, to agreements 'between undertakings'. There is nothing in the judgment making the reference to suggest the existence of any agreement between undertakings. There is therefore no need to interpret that provision.

30. Article [82] declares that any abuse of a dominant position within the common market or in any substantial part of it is prohibited as incompatible with the common market in so far as it may affect trade between Member States.

31. In that respect it should be borne in mind that an undertaking which has a statutory monopoly may be regarded as having a dominant position within the meaning of Article [82] of the Treaty (see the judgment in Case C–311/84 *CBEM v CLT and IBP* . . . , paragraph 16) and that the territory of a Member State over which the monopoly extends may constitute a substantial part of the common market (see the judgment in Case C–322/81 *Michelin v Commission* . . . , paragraph 28).

32. Although Article [82] of the Treaty does not prohibit monopolies as such, it nevertheless prohibits their abuse. For that purpose Article [82] lists a number of abusive practices by way of example.

33. In that regard it should be observed that, according to Article [86(2)] of the Treaty, undertakings entrusted with the operation of services of general economic interest are subject to the rules on competition so long as it is not shown that the application of those rules is incompatible with the performance of their particular task (see in particular, the judgment in *Sacchi*, cited above, paragraph 15).

34. Accordingly it is for the national court to determine whether the practices of such an undertaking are compatible with Article [82] and to verify whether those practices, if they are contrary to that provision, may be justified by the needs of the particular task with which the undertaking may have been entrusted.

35. As regards State measures, and more specifically the grant of exclusive rights, it should be pointed out that while Articles [81] and [82] are directed exclusively to undertakings, the Treaty none the less requires the Member States not to adopt or maintain in force any measure which could deprive those provisions of their effectiveness (see the judgment in Case C–13/77 *INNO v ATAB* ..., paragraphs 31 and 32).

36. Article [86(1)] thus provides that, in the case of undertakings to which Member States grant special or exclusive rights, Member States are neither to enact nor to maintain in force any measure contrary to the rules contained in the Treaty.

37. In that respect it should be observed that Article [86(1)] of the Treaty prohibits the granting of an exclusive right to retransmit television broadcasts to an undertaking which has an exclusive right to transmit broadcasts, where those rights are liable to create a situation in which that undertaking is led to infringe Article [82] of the Treaty by virtue of a discriminatory broadcasting policy which favours its own programmes.

38. The reply to the national court must therefore be that Article [86(1)] of the Treaty prohibits the granting of an exclusive right to transmit and an exclusive right to retransmit television broadcasts to a single undertaking, where those rights are liable to create a situation in which that undertaking is led to infringe Article [82] by virtue of a discriminatory broadcasting policy which favours its own programmes, unless the application of Article [82] obstructs the performance of the particular tasks entrusted to it.

In *ERT* the Court said that the Treaty does not prevent the granting of a monopoly (*in casu* a television monopoly) but stressed, as it had in *INNO v. ATAB*, that the Treaty prohibits Member States from adopting measures which deprive the competition rules of their effectiveness. This means that the *manner in which the monopoly is organized* may infringe the rules of the Treaty (paragraph 11). The Court therefore concluded that the Treaty prohibits the granting of an exclusive right to retransmit TV broadcasts to an undertaking which has exclusive rights to transmit broadcasts *where those rights are liable to create a situation in which that undertaking is led to infringe Article 82* by virtue of a discriminatory broadcasting policy which favours its own programmes (paragraphs 37 and 38). This is different from the situation in *Höfner*, where the infringement was unavoidable because the State had given monopoly rights to a body manifestly unable to deal with the demand for its services. In *ERT* the cumulation of rights in the hands of the monopolist did not result in an *unavoidable* infringement of Article 82 but to a situation where the monopolist was *led to* infringe the Article because it would inevitably discriminate in favour of retransmitting its own programmes rather than anyone else's.

The theme of the monopolist being led to an infringement was taken up in the next case, *Merci Convenzionali*:

Case C–179/90, *Merci Convenzionali Porto di Genova* v. *Siderurgica Gabrielli SpA* [1991] ECR I–5009, [1994] 4 CMLR 422

By Italian law Merci had the exclusive right to organize the loading, unloading and other handling of goods within the Port of Genoa through a dock-work company.[49] There was a delay in unloading Siderurgica's ship, caused in particular by the dock-work company's workers being on strike. The exclusive rights meant that the vessel's crew were not able to do the work themselves. Siderurgica demanded compensation for the damage it suffered due to the delay and the reimbursement of the charges it had paid to Merci, which it claimed were unfair given the service it had received, or rather, not received. The Tribunale di Genoa made an Article 234 reference, asking inter alia[50] whether Article [86(1)] in conjunction with Article 82 precluded the Italian rules. The Court confirmed in paragraph 14 that an undertaking with a statutory monopoly over a substantial part of the Common Market[51] could be regarded as having a dominant position within Article 82.

Court of Justice

16. It should next be stated that the simple fact of creating a dominant position by granting exclusive rights within the meaning of Article [86(1)] of the Treaty is not as such incompatible with Article [82].

17. However, the Court has had occasion to state, in this respect, that a Member State is in breach of the prohibitions contained in those two provisions if the undertaking in question, merely by exercising the exclusive rights granted to it, cannot avoid abusing its dominant position (see the judgment in Case C–41/90 *Höfner*, cited above, paragraph 29) or when such rights are liable to create a situation in which that undertaking is induced to commit such abuses (see the judgment in Case C–260/89 *ERT*, cited above, paragraph 37).

18. According to subparagraphs (a), (b) and (c) of the second paragraph of Article [82] of the Treaty, such abuse may in particular consist in imposing on the persons requiring the services in question unfair purchase prices or other unfair trading conditions, in limiting technical development, to the prejudice of consumers, or in the application of dissimilar conditions to equivalent transactions with other trading parties.

19. In that respect it appears from the circumstances described by the national court and discussed before the Court of Justice that the undertakings enjoying exclusive rights in accordance with the procedures laid down by the national rules in question are, as a result, induced either to demand payment for services which have not been requested, to charge disproportionate prices, to refuse to have recourse to modern technology, which involves an increase in the cost of the operations and a prolongation of the time required for their performance, or to grant price reductions to certain consumers and at the same time to offset such reductions by an increase in the charges to other consumers.

---

[49] For another case involving Italian law on dock-work companies, see Case C–163/96, *Silvano Raso* [1998] 4 CMLR 737.

[50] For the nationality discrimination issue, see *supra* p. 437.

[51] The Court held (para. 15) that the Port of Genoa was a substantial part: for this aspect of Art. 82 see *supra* Chap. 3.

20. In these circumstances it must be held that a Member State creates a situation contrary to Article [82] of the Treaty where it adopts rules of such a kind as those at issue before the national court, which are capable of affecting trade between Member States as in the case of the main proceedings, regard being had to the factors mentioned in paragraph 15 of this judgment relating to the importance of traffic in the Port of Genoa.

In this judgment the Court quoted *Höfner* and *ERT* and cited the latter for the proposition that a Member State infringes Article 82 where it grants rights which are liable to *induce* the undertaking to commit abuses (paragraphs 17 and 19). So we reach the position that although, as the Court said in *Merci* (paragraph 16), the simple fact of creating a dominant position by granting exclusive rights is not incompatible with Article 86 the granting of rights which induce or lead to the undertakings committing abuses *is* incompatible.[52] The question then is: what rights induce abuses? The problem is that any dominant position enables the undertaking to conduct itself in ways which would not be feasible on a more competitive market, but the existence of a statutory monopoly puts an undertaking in an even stronger position.[53] A statutory monopolist does not have to worry, for example, that excessive or discriminatory pricing may ultimately attract new entrants into the market, for the barriers to entry are absolute. Can we not argue, therefore, that *all* undertakings with exclusive rights are being led or induced by their special position to commit abuses since they are safe from competition?

ERT (above) was less to do with the *fact* of abusive conduct than with the *possibility* of it. This is also shown in *RTT* below. Both *ERT* and *RTT* involved the culmination of rights, a matter of particular concern.

Case C–18/88, *RTT* v. *GB-INNO-BM SA* [1991] ECR I–5973

Under Belgian law RRT held a monopoly over the establishment and operation of the public telephone system. The law also provided that only equipment supplied by RTT or approved by it could be connected to its network. GB-INNO sold in its shops telephones which had not been approved by RTT. RTT brought proceedings in the Commercial Court for an order that GB-INNO should not sell telephones without informing the purchasers that they were not approved. The Commercial Court asked the Court, inter alia, whether Articles 3(1)(g), 82 and 86 precluded a Member State from granting to the company operating the public telephone network the power to lay down the standards for telephone equipment and to check that economic operators meet those standards when it is competing with those operators on the market for terminals.

Court of Justice

15. Under Belgian law, the RTT holds a monopoly for the establishment and operation of the public telecommunications network. Moreover, only equipment supplied by the RTT or approved by it can be connected to the network. The RTT thus has the power to grant or withhold authorization to connect telephone equipment to the network, the power to lay down the technical standards to be met by that equipment, and the power to check whether the equipment not produced by it is in conformity with the specifications that it has laid down.

---

[52] See also Case C–18/93, *Corsica Ferries Italia Srl* v. *Corpo dei Piloti del Porto di Genovo* [1994] ECR I–1783.

[53] See the discussion in Craig and de Búrca: *EU Law: Text Cases and Materials* (2nd ed.), Oxford University Press (1998) 5, 1069.

16. At the present stage of development of the Community, that monopoly, which is intended to make a public telephone network available to users, constitutes a service of general economic interest within the meaning of Article [86(2)] of the Treaty.

17. The Court has consistently held that an undertaking vested with a legal monopoly may be regarded as occupying a dominant position within the meaning of Article [82] of the Treaty and that the territory of a Member State to which that monopoly extends may constitute a substantial part of the common market (judgments in Case C–41/90 *Höfner* . . . , paragraph 28, and in Case C–260/89 *ERT* . . . , paragraph 31).

18. The Court has also held that an abuse within the meaning of Article [82] is committed where, without any objective necessity, an undertaking holding a dominant position on a particular market reserves to itself an ancillary activity which might be carried out by another undertaking as part of its activities on a neighbouring but separate market, with the possibility of eliminating all competition from such undertaking (judgment in Case 311/84 *CBEM* . . .).

19. Therefore the fact that an undertaking holding a monopoly in the market for the establishment and operation of the network, without any objective necessity, reserves to itself a neighbouring but separate market, in this case the market for the importation, marketing, connection, commissioning and maintenance of equipment for connection to the said network, thereby eliminating all competition from other undertakings, constitutes an infringement of Article [82] of the Treaty.

20. However, Article [82] applies only to anti-competitive conduct engaged in by undertakings on their own initiative (see judgement in Case C–202/88 *France v Commission* 'Telecommunications terminals', . . .), not to measures adopted by States. As regards measures adopted by States, it is Article [86(1)] that applies. Under that provision, Member States must not, by laws, regulations or administrative measures, put public undertakings and undertakings to which they grant special or exclusive rights in a position which the said undertakings could not themselves attain by their own conduct without infringing Article [82].

21. Accordingly, where the extension of the dominant position of a public undertaking or undertaking to which the State has granted special or exclusive rights results from a State measure, such a measure constitutes an infringement of Article [86] in conjunction with Article [82] of the Treaty.

22. The exclusion or the restriction of competition on the market in telephone equipment cannot be regarded as justified by a task of a public service of general economic interest within the meaning of Article [86(2)] of the Treaty. The production and sale of terminals, and in particular of telephones, is an activity that should be open to any undertaking. In order to ensure that the equipment meets the essential requirements of, in particular, the safety of users, the safety of those operating the network and the protection of public telecommunications networks against damage of any kind, it is sufficient to lay down specifications which the said equipment must meet and to establish a procedure for type-approval to check whether those specifications are met.

23. According to the RTT, there could be a finding of an infringement of Article [86(1)] of the Treaty only if the Member State had favoured an abuse that the RTT itself had in fact committed, for example by applying the provisions on type-approval in a discriminatory manner. It emphasizes, however, that the order for reference does not state that any abuse has actually taken place, and that the mere possibility of discriminatory application of those provisions by reason of the fact that the RTT is designated as the authority for granting approval and is competing with the undertakings that apply for approval cannot in itself amount to an abuse within the meaning of Article [82] of the . . . Treaty.

24. That argument cannot be accepted. It is sufficient to point out in this regard that it is the extension of the monopoly in the establishment and operation of the telephone network to the market in telephone equipment, without any objective justification, which is prohibited as such by Article [82], or by Article [86(1)] in conjunction with Article [82], where that extension results from a measure adopted by a State. As competition may not be eliminated in that manner, it may not be distorted either.

25. A system of undistorted competition, as laid down in the Treaty, can be guaranteed only if equality of opportunity is secured as between the various economic operators. To entrust an undertaking which markets terminal equipment with the task of drawing up the specifications for such equipment, monitoring their application and granting type-approval in respect thereof is tantamount to conferring upon it the power to determine at will which terminal equipment may be connected to the public network, and thereby placing that undertaking at an obvious advantage over its competitors (judgment in Case C–202/88, paragraph 51).

26. In those circumstances, the maintenance of effective competition and the guaranteeing of transparency require that the drawing up of technical specifications, the monitoring of their application, and the granting of type-approval must be carried out by a body which is independent of public or private undertakings offering competing goods or services in the telecommunications sector (judgment in Case C–202/88, paragraph 52).

27. Moreover, the provisions of the national regulations at issue in the main action may influence the imports of telephone equipment from other Member States, and hence may affect trade between Member States within the meaning of Article [82] of the Treaty.

28. Accordingly, it must first be stated, in reply to the national court's questions, that Articles [3(1)(g)], [86] and [82] of the . . . Treaty preclude a Member State from granting to the undertaking which operates the public telecommunications network the power to lay down standards for telephone equipment and to check that economic operators meet those standards when it is itself competing with those operators on the market for that equipment.

It will be noticed here that there was no allegation that RTT had actually behaved improperly in its authorization of equipment. The objection was that the state measures in effect extended the monopoly position from one market to another, a situation which, if brought about by the conduct of an undertaking rather than by state measures, would have constituted an abuse, as the Court pointed out at paragraphs 18–20.[54] The rights conferred on the undertakings in both *ERT* and *RTT* were found to be contrary to Article 86 since they created a conflict of interest.[55] State measures cannot 'bundle' regulatory functions and commercial activities together.

In the case of *Corbeau*, however, the Court appeared to go further and suggest that the very granting of special or exclusive rights, even where the elements in the cases discussed above are not present, might be contrary to Article 86(1):

---

[54] See Case 311/84, *Centre Belge d'Etudes du Marché—Télémarketing* v. *Compagnie Luxembourgeoise de Télédiffusion SA and Information Publicité Benelux SA* [1985] ECR 3261, [1986] 2 CMLR 558 (quoted in para. 18 of the *RTT* judgment) and the cases discussed *supra* in Chap. 7.

[55] See also Case C–163/96, *Silvano Raso* [1998] ECR I–533, [1998] 4 CMLR 737, where an Italian law, which gave the exclusive right to supply temporary labour to other dock-work companies operating in a port to an undertaking which was also authorized to carry out dock-work itself, was held to infringe Art. 86(1).

Case C–320/91, *Corbeau* [1993] ECR I–1477, [1995] 4 CMLR 621

Belgian law conferred a monopoly on the Belgian Post Office, the Regie des Postes, in respect of the collection, transporting and delivery throughout the Kingdom of various forms of correspondence. Criminal sanctions were imposed for infringing the monopoly. Corbeau set up his own postal service in the Liège area, whereby personal collection would be made from the sender's premises and delivery made before noon next day in the same area, although deliveries outside the area were made by putting the items in the ordinary post. Corbeau was prosecuted for infringing the Post Office's monopoly. The Liège court referred questions to the Court concerning the compatibility of the post office monopoly with Articles 81, 82 and 86, whether the monopoly should be modified to comply with Article 86(1), the application of Article 86(2) and whether the post office was in a dominant position. (The part of the judgment concerning Article 86(2) is reproduced later).

Court of Justice

7. With regard to the facts in the main proceedings, the questions referred to the Court must be understood as meaning that the national court is substantially concerned with the question whether Article [86] of the Treaty must be interpreted as meaning that it is contrary to that article for the legislation of a Member State which confers on a body such as the Régie des Postes the exclusive right to collect, carry and distribute mail to prohibit an economic operator established in that State from offering, under threat of criminal penalties, certain specific services on that market.

8. To reply to that question, as thus reformulated, it should first be pointed out that a body such as the Régie des Postes, which has been granted exclusive rights as regards the collection, carriage and distribution of mail, must be regarded as an undertaking to which the Member State concerned has granted exclusive rights within the meaning of Article [86(1)] of the Treaty.

9. Next it should be recalled that the Court has consistently held that an undertaking having a statutory monopoly over a substantial part of the common market may be regarded as having a dominant position within the meaning of Article [82] of the Treaty (see the judgments in Case C–179/90 *Merci Convenzionali Porto di Genova* . . . , paragraph 14 and in Case C–18/88 *RTT v GB–Inno–BM* . . . , paragraph 17).

10. However, Article [82] applies only to anti-competitive conduct engaged in by undertakings on their own initiative, not to measures adopted by States (see the *RTT v GB–Inno–BM* judgment, cited above, paragraph 20).

11. The Court has had occasion to state in this respect that although the mere fact that a Member State has created a dominant position by the grant of exclusive rights is not as such incompatible with Article [82], the Treaty none the less requires the Member States not to adopt or maintain in force any measure which might deprive those provisions of their effectiveness (see the judgment in Case C–260/89 *ERT* . . . , paragraph 35).

12. Thus Article [86(1)] provides that in the case of public undertakings to which Member States grant special or exclusive rights, they are neither to enact nor to maintain in force any measure contrary to the rules contained in the Treaty with regard to competition.

13. That provision must be read in conjunction with Article [86(2)] which provides that undertakings entrusted with the operation of services of general economic interest are to be subject to the rules on competition in so far as the application of such rules does not obstruct the performance, in law, or in fact, of the particular tasks assigned to them.

14. That latter provision thus permits the Member States to confer on undertakings to which they entrust the operation of services of general economic interest, exclusive rights which may hinder the application of the rules of the Treaty on competition in so far as restrictions on competition, or even the exclusion of all competition, by other economic operators are necessary to ensure the performance of the particular tasks assigned to the undertakings possessed of the exclusive rights.

There was no suggestion in *Corbeau* that the Régie des Postes had acted abusively. The challenge raised by Corbeau's defence to the criminal charges was to the monopoly itself. The Court answered this in paragraphs 7–12 of the judgment. It repeated there (paragraph 11) its usual mantra about the mere grant of exclusive rights not in itself being incompatible with the Treaty but said that Member States are not to adopt or maintain provisions which may deprive the provisions of their effectiveness. It then quoted Article 86(1). It never clearly identified which, if any, features of the Belgian legislation were contrary to Article 86(1) and Article 82.[56] This case did not concern an undertaking accused of acting abusively, the extension of the monopoly into a neighbouring market, a conflict of interest or the bundling of regulatory functions with entrepreneurial activities. It did however, as Hancher notes,[57] appear to suggest that, in order to ensure the *effet utile* or effectiveness of Articles 86(1) and 82 and, despite the Court's statement to the contrary at paragraph 11, the very existence of national rules conferring a dominant position on an undertaking is unacceptable unless the rights at issue can be justified under Article 86(2) (see paragraphs 13 and 14). In effect, it reversed the burden of proof: exclusive rights are not *prima facie* legal, but *prima facie* illegal unless they are objectively justified or fulfill the Article 86(2) criteria.[58]

Edward and Hoskins argue that it is a question whether the Court chooses to take a 'limited sovereignty' or 'limited competition' approach. Under the limited sovereignty approach, the Member States are free to grant legal monopolies provided that the operation of the monopoly does not have the *necessary* consequence of contravening the competition rules of the Treaty. This is illustrated by *Höfner* v. *Macroton* and by the post-*Corbeau* case, *La Crespelle* (below). Under the Limited Competition approach, however:[59]

. . . . the creation of a legal monopoly must: (a) be justified by a legitimate national objective and (b) satisfy the principle of proportionality, that is, the consequent restriction of competition must not exceed what is necessary in order to attain the objective.. The underlying rationale for this approach is that the creation of a legal monopoly will necessarily produce restrictive effects on competition so such monopolies should be permitted only where there is a particular justification for their existence . . .

The Limited Competition approach starts from the presumption that the restriction of competition inherent in legal monopolies is illegal. The *onus* is placed squarely on the Member State to prove that the existence of a particular legal monopoly is justified and that the consequent restriction of competition is limited to what is necessary to achieve the relevant objective.

If we accept that legal monopolies by definition hinder free competition since they prevent other

---

[56] As Jacobs AG pointed out in his Opinion in Joined Cases C–67/96, 115–117/97 and 219/97, *Albany International BV* v. *Stichting Bedrijfspensioenfonds Textielindustrie* [2000] 4 CMLR 466, para. 417.

[57] See L. Hancher, Casenote on *Corbeau* (1994) 31 *CMLRev.* 105, 111.

[58] See J. Faull and A. Nikpay (eds.), *The EC Law of Competition* (Oxford University Press, 1999), para. 5.76.

[59] D. Edward and M. Hoskins 'Art. 90: Deregulation and EC Law. Reflections Arising from the XVI FIDE Conference' (1995) 32 *CMLRev.* 157, 164 and 167.

undertakings from entering the reserved market, and that Member States may choose to create or maintain such monopolies for reasons such as bare protectionism, the Limited Competition approach would appear to be more in keeping with the purpose and aims of the EC Treaty.

Both these authors and Hancher in the extract below argue that one way of looking at the dilemma about the status of legal monopoly itself is to take the time factor into account. Market conditions change and therefore Member States have an obligation to keep legal monopolies under review.[60]

L. Hancher, Casenote on *Corbeau* (1994) 31 *CMLRev.* 105 at 115–16

Before jumping to the conclusion that all state measures conferring exclusive rights or creating national monopolies must now be considered as prima facie illegal, an assertion which would conflict with the first sentence of Article [86(1)], one should bear in mind certain aspects of the market for postal services. As the Advocate General had pointed out in his Opinion, this market has been the subject of quite recent development in the sense that demand for 'added-value' services by certain types of consumer, including personal collection, tracing and tracking services has grown rapidly. At the time when the monopoly to provide postal services was conferred on national postal administrations in the majority of the Member States demand for this sort of service simply did not exist. The relevant question was then whether the initial grant of general monopoly rights to the national postal administrations could be legitimately interpreted as covering these new added value services as well as the more traditional basic services. From this perspective, neither the Member State nor the postal monopoly had actively abused a dominant position, for example by illegally extending an existing monopoly into new markets or through the accumulation of additional exclusive rights. The essence of the problem was whether the original monopoly should now be redefined and circumscribed to take account of the changing nature of demand for postal services. . . .

In addressing this issue, the Advocate General took the Court's ruling in Case C–18/88, *RTT*, as his point of departure. This case, it will be recalled, dealt with the active extension of one monopoly right into a related market. Advocate General Tesauro argued that the same reasoning should apply to measures which create a monopoly (para 14)—measures actively extending the scope of the exclusivity are no different from those which institute that exclusivity in the first place. Either way then, the effectiveness of the Treaty rules on competition would be limited. The relevant question was whether the scope of the original monopoly could be said to meet objective justifications given the current nature of the market.

The Advocate General's reasoning has been dealt with at some length because it helps to cast some light on the novelty of the case before the Court in *Corbeau*. The Court was effectively being asked to rule upon the compatibility with Community competition rules of a measure which had conferred an exclusive right in general terms on an undertaking, almost forty years previously to a market situation which had altered fundamentally with the passage of time. The abuse, if any, lay in the failure on the part of the Member State to respond to such changes, by refining the scope of the initial right. Thus inaction could be considered a violation of Article [86(1)]. This was obviously the essence of the second question referred by the national court. If this interpretation is correct, then the first part of the *Corbeau* ruling represents a significant extension of the Court's jurisprudence on the **effet utile** of the Treaty's competition rules to situations where the development of competition is restricted because the market itself has changed, and not necessarily as a result of any independent action on

[60] *Ibid.*, at 167–8.

the part of either the Member State or the statutory monopoly. The first part of the Court's reasoning in *Corbeau* suggests that failure to redefine a right conferring a wide-ranging exclusivity can indeed amount to a breach of Articles [86(1)] and [82], unless there are objective justifications for maintaining a monopoly of this scope. These justifications are to be sought in Article [86(2)].

The Court subsequently retreated from the position it adopted in *Corbeau*. In *La Crespelle* it again held that a Member State contravenes the Treaty only if, in merely exercising the exclusive right granted to it, the undertaking cannot avoid abusing its dominant position:[61] it is not possible automatically to impute the abuse to the existence of the right. In this case, where the exclusive right concerned bovine insemination centres, there was nothing in the grant of exclusive rights which made an abuse (excessive pricing) unavoidable.

Case C–323/93, *Société Civile Agricole du Centre d'Insémination de la Crespelle* v. *Coopérative d'Elevage et d'Insemination Artificielle du Département de la Mayenne* [1994] ECR I–5077

French law conferred on certain bovine insemination centres the exclusive right to provide insemination services over a particular geographical area. It was alleged that the centres charged excessively for their services.

Court of Justice

15. So far as concerns the relevant provisions of the Treaty, Article 10 requires Member States to carry out their Community obligations in good faith. However, the Court has consistently held that that provision cannot be applied independently when the situation concerned is governed by a specific provision of the Treaty, as in the present case (see the judgment in Joined Cases C–78/90 to C–83/90 *Compagnie Commerciale de l'Ouest and Others* [1992] ECR I–1847, paragraph 19). The question must therefore be considered in the light of Articles [86(1)] and [82] of the Treaty.

16. Article [86(1)] of the Treaty provides that, in the case of public undertakings and undertakings to which Member States grant special or exclusive rights, Member States may neither enact nor maintain in force any measure contrary to the rules contained in the Treaty, in particular to those rules provided for in Article [12] and Articles [81] to [89].

17. In this case, by making the operation of the insemination centres subject to authorization and providing that each centre should have the exclusive rights to serve a defined area, the national legislation granted those centres exclusive rights. By thus establishing, in favour of those undertakings, a contiguous series of monopolies territorially limited but together covering the entire territory of a member State, those national provisions create a dominant position, within the meaning of Article [82] of the Treaty, in a substantial part of the common market.

18. The mere creation of such a dominant position by the granting of an exclusive right within the meaning of Article [86(1)] is not as such incompatible with Article [82] of the Treaty. A Member State contravenes the prohibitions contained in those two provisions only if, in merely exercising the exclusive right granted to it, the undertaking in question cannot avoid abusing its dominant position (see the judgments in Case C–41/90 *Höfner and Elser* . . . , paragraph 29, and most recently, in Case C–179/90 *Merci Convenzionali Porto di Genova* . . . , paragraph 17).

---

[61] See also Case C–387/93, *Banchero* [1995] ECR I–4663.

19. The alleged abuse in the present case consists in the charging of exorbitant prices by the insemination centres.

20. The question to be examined is therefore whether such a practice constituting the alleged abuse is the direct consequence of the national Law. It should be noted in this regard that the Law merely allows insemination centres to require breeders who request the centres to provide them with semen from other production centres to pay the additional costs entailed by that choice.

21. Although it leaves to the insemination centres the task of calculating those costs, such a provision does not lead the centres to charge disproportionate costs and thereby abuse their dominant position.

22. The answer to this part of the question must therefore be that Articles [86(1)] and [82] of the Treaty do not preclude a Member State from granting to approved bovine insemination centres certain exclusive rights within the defined area.

The same approach can be seen in *Corsica Ferries*,[62] where the Court held that the grant of the exclusive right to offer compulsory piloting services in a port was not in itself an infringement of Article 86(1) but the approval of the discriminatory tariffs, which were contrary to Article 82(c), *was* an infringement.

In *Corsica Ferries France*,[63] *Albany*,[64] and *Deutsche Post*[65] the ECJ again linked Article 86(1) to Article 86(2). *Albany* concerned the Dutch regime of compulsory affiliation to sectoral pension funds:

Case C–67/96, *Albany International BV* v. *Stichting Bedrijfspensioenfonds Textielindustrie*, judgment 21 September 1999, [2000] 4 CMLR 446

Under Dutch law pension provision included a system whereby, at the request of the representatives of employers and employees in a particular sector of the economy, affiliation to a sectoral pension fund was made compulsory for all undertakings in that sector. This was to provide a pension supplementary to the basic state pension. Various undertakings brought proceedings in the Dutch courts challenging the compulsory affiliation regime on the grounds that they provided equivalent supplementary pension schemes themselves. The Dutch courts referred to the Court of Justice the question, inter alia, whether the exclusive rights conferred on the sectoral pension funds infringed the Treaty.[66]

Court of Justice

90. It must be observed at the outset that the decision of the public authorities to make affiliation to a sectoral pension fund compulsory, as in this case, necessarily implies granting to

---

[62] Case C–18/93, *Corsica Ferries Italia Srl* v. *Corpo dei Piloti del Porto di Genova* [1994] ECR I–1783.

[63] Case C–266/74, *Corsica Ferries France SA* v. *Gruppo Artichi Ormeggiatori del Porto di Genovo Coop and Others* [1998] ECR I–3949, [1998] 5 CMLR 402; see *infra* p. 464.

[64] Case C–67/96, *Albany International BV* v. *Stichting Bedrijfspensioenfonds Textielindustrie* [2000] 4 CMLR 446.

[65] Cases C–147–148/97, *Deutsche Post AG* v. *Gesellschaft für Zahlungssysteme mbH (GZS) and Citicorp Kartenservice GmbH* [2000] 4 CMLR 838.

[66] See also Cases C–115–117/97, *Brentjens' Handelsonderneming BV* v. *Stichting Bedrijfspensioenfonds voor de Handel in Bouwmaterialen* [2000] 4 CMLR 566 and Case C–219/97, *Maatschappij Drijvende Bokken BV* v. *Stichting Pensioenfonds voor de Vervoer-en Havenbedrijven* [2000] 4 CMLR 599, which raised the same issue. The cases also raised questions about the application of the Treaty rules to collective agreements between employers and employees. For these aspects, see *supra* Chap. 3.

that fund an exclusive right to collect and administer the contributions paid with a view to accruing pension rights. Such a fund must therefore be regarded as an undertaking to which exclusive rights have been granted by the public authorities, of the kind referred to in Article [86(1)] of the Treaty.

91. Next, it should be noted that according to settled case-law an undertaking which has a legal monopoly in a substantial part of the common market may be regarded as occupying a dominant position within the meaning of Article [82] of the Treaty (see Case C–179/90 *Merci Convenzional Porto di Genova* [1991] ECR I–5889, paragraph 14, and Case C–18/88 *GB-Inno-BM* [1991] ECR I–5941, paragraph 17).

92. A sectoral pension fund of the kind at issue in the main proceedings, which has an exclusive right to manage a supplementary pension scheme in an industrial sector in a Member State and, therefore, in a substantial part of the common market, may therefore be regarded as occupying a dominant position within the meaning of Article [82] of the Treaty.

93. It must not be forgotten, however, that merely creating a dominant position by granting exclusive rights within the meaning of Article [86(1)] of the Treaty is not in itself incompatible with Article [82] of the Treaty. A Member State is in breach of the prohibitions contained in those two provisions only if the undertaking in question, merely by exercising the exclusive rights granted to it, is led to abuse its dominant position or when such rights are liable to create a situation in which that undertaking is led to commit such abuses (*Höfner and Elser*, cited above, paragraph 29; Case C–260/89 *ERT* [1991] ECR I–2925, paragraph 37; *Merci Convenzionali Porto di Genova*, cited above, paragraphs 16 and 17; Case C–323/93 *Centre d'Insémination de la Crespelle* . . . , paragraph 18; and Case C–163/96 *Raso and Others* . . . , paragraph 27).

94. Albany contends in that connection that the system of compulsory affiliation to the supplementary pension scheme managed by the Fund is contrary to the combined provisions of Articles [82] and [86] of the Treaty. The pension benefits available from the Fund do not, or no longer, match the needs of the undertakings. The benefits are too low, are not linked to wages and, consequently, are generally inadequate. Employers have therefore to make other pension arrangements. The system of compulsory affiliation deprives those employers of any opportunity of arranging for comprehensive pension cover from an insurance company. Pension arrangements spread over a number of insurers would increase administrative costs and reduce efficiency.

95. It should be remembered that, in *Höfner and Elser*, cited above, paragraph 34, the Court held that a Member State which conferred on a public employment agency an exclusive right of recruitment was in breach of Article [86(1)] of the Treaty where it created a situation in which that office could not avoid infringing Article [82] of the Treaty, in particular because it was manifestly incapable of satisfying the demand prevailing on the market for such activities.

96. In the present case, it is important to note that the supplementary pension scheme offered by the Fund is based on the present norm in the Netherlands, namely that every worker who has paid contributions to that scheme for the maximum period of affiliation receives a pension, including the State pension under the AOW, equal to 70% of his final salary.

97. Doubtless, some undertakings in the sector might wish to provide their workers with a pension scheme superior to the one offered by the Fund. However, the fact that such undertakings are unable to entrust the management of such a pension scheme to a single insurer and the resulting restriction of competition derive directly from the exclusive right conferred on the sectoral pension fund.

98. It is therefore necessary to consider whether, as contended by the Fund, the Netherlands

Government and the Commission, the exclusive right of the sectoral pension fund to manage supplementary pensions in a given sector and the resultant restriction of competition may be justified under Article [86(2)] of the Treaty as a measure necessary for the performance of a particular social task of general interest with which that fund has been charged.

The Court then went on to consider whether the exclusive right and the restriction of competition could indeed be justified under Article 86(2). This part of the judgment is reproduced below.[67]

It can be seen from the above extract that the Court said once again that the granting of exclusive rights is not contrary to the Treaty unless merely by exercising the right the undertaking is led to commit an abuse (paragraph 93) or unless an abuse is unavoidable (paragraph 95). It cited its previous case law, but not *Corbeau*. The Court did not proceed to consider whether the undertaking here was put in such a position, but instead turned to see whether the justification under Article 86(2) applied.

However, in *Deutsche Post* the ECJ cited its judgment in *Corbeau*. The case concerned the German post office, Deutsche Post (a state monopoly with the exclusive right to collect, carry, and deliver mail in Germany) and the obligations flowing from the Universal Postal Convention (UPC).

Joined Cases C–147–148/97, *Deutsche Post AG* v. *Gesellschaft für Zahlungssysteme mbH (GZS) and Citicorp Kartenservice GmbH*, judgment 10 February 2000, [2000] 4 CMLR 838

Under the Universal Postal Convention 1989 the contracting states are obliged to forward and deliver international mail addressed to persons resident in their country which is passed to them by the postal services of other contracting parties. The Convention provides for the receiving state to charge a fixed fee for the costs of delivering the mail (terminal dues). The Convention also provides *inter alia* that where senders resident in country A cause mail addressed to addressees in country A to be posted in bulk in country B, country A is entitled to either charge its full internal rate for the items or to return them to their origin (Article 25). Various credit-card companies based in Germany electronically transmitted the data for their customers' bills to processing centres outside Germany which prepared the German customers' bills and posted them back to Germany. In one case this resulted in the bills being posted in Denmark, where the rate for international mail is lower than the internal rate in Germany. Deutsche Post was merely paid the terminal dues. It demanded the full internal rate. The credit companies refused to pay. In the course of the subsequent litigation the German courts referred to the Court questions about whether it was contrary to Article 86 and Article 82 (and Article 49, which was also relevant since the situation involved the freedom to provide services) for Deutsche Post to exercise its rights under Article 25 of the Convention to charge the internal postage rate.

Court of Justice

36. ... the national court is to be understood in the first three questions as essentially asking whether it is contrary to Article [86] of the Treaty, read in conjunction with Articles [82] and [49] thereof, for a body such as Deutsche Post to exercise the right provided for by Article 25(3) of the UPC to charge, in the cases referred to in the second sentence of Article 25(1)and Article 25(2), internal postage on items of mail posted in large quantities with the postal services of a Member State other than the Member State to which that body belongs.

[67] See *infra* p. 467.

37. To reply to that question, as reformulated, it should first be noted that a body such as Deutsche Post, which has been granted exclusive rights as regards the collection, carriage and delivery of mail, must be regarded as an undertaking to which the Member State concerned has granted exclusive rights within the meaning of Article [86(1)] of the Treaty (Case C–320/91 *Corbeau* . . . , paragraph 8).

38. Also, it is settled case-law that an undertaking having a statutory monopoly over a substantial part of the common market may be regarded as holding a dominant position within the meaning of Article [82] of the Treaty (see Case C–179/90 *Merci Convenzionali Porto di Genova v Siderurgica Gabrielli* . . . , paragraph 14, Case C–18/88 *RTT v GB-Inno-BM* . . . , paragraph 17, and *Corbeau*, cited above, paragraph 9).

39. The Court has had occasion to state in this respect that although the mere fact that a Member State has created a dominant position by the grant of exclusive rights is not as such incompatible with Article [82], the Treaty none the less requires the Member States not to adopt or maintain in force any measure which might deprive that provision of its effectiveness (see Case C–260/89 *ERT* [1991] ECR I–2925, paragraph 35, and *Corbeau*, cited above, paragraph 11).

40. Article [86(1)] of the Treaty thus provides that in the case of undertakings to which Member States grant special or exclusive rights, they are neither to enact nor to maintain in force any measure contrary, in particular, to the rules contained in the Treaty with regard to competition (see *Corbeau*, paragraph 12).

41. That provision must be read in conjunction with Article [86(2)] which provides that undertakings entrusted with the operation of services of general economic interest are to be subject to the rules contained in the Treaty in so far as the application of such rules does not obstruct the performance, in law or in fact, of the particular tasks assigned to them.

42. A final point to note is that the UPC proceeds on the basis of a market in letter-post where the postal services of the various Contracting States of the Universal Postal Union are not in competition.

43. In that context, the UPC is designed to establish rules ensuring that international items of mail addressed to residents of a Contracting State and passed on by the postal services of other Contracting States are forwarded and delivered. One of the fundamental principles of the UPC, set out in Article 1 thereof, is the obligation of the postal administration of the Contracting State to which international mail is sent to forward and deliver it to addressees resident in its territory using the most rapid means of its letter post. In that regard, the States which have adopted the Convention of the Universal Postal Union constitute a single postal territory, in which the freedom of transit of reciprocal international mail is in principle guaranteed.

44. For the postal services of the Member States, performance of the obligations flowing from the UPC is thus in itself a service of general economic interest within the meaning of Article [86(2)] of the Treaty.

45. In the present case, German legislation assigns the operation of that service to Deutsche Post.

46. As has been noted in paragraph 5 of this judgment, postal services initially delivered international mail without being paid for that task. However, when it became apparent that the flows of postal traffic between two Contracting States frequently did not balance out, so that the postal services of the various Contracting States had to process quantities of international mail which differed greatly, specific provisions were laid down in that regard, one of which is Article 25 of the UPC.

47. Under Article 25(3) of the UPC, the postal services of the Contracting States may in particu-

lar, in the cases referred to in Article 25(1) and (2), charge postage on items of mail at their internal rates.

48. The grant to a body such as Deutsche Post of the right to treat international items of mail as internal post in such cases creates a situation where that body may be led, to the detriment of users of postal services, to abuse its dominant position resulting from the exclusive right granted to it to forward and deliver those items to the relevant addressees.

49. It is accordingly necessary to examine the extent to which exercise of such a right is necessary to enable a body of that kind to perform its task of general interest pursuant to the obligations flowing from the UPC and, in particular, to operate under economically acceptable conditions.

50. If a body such as Deutsche Post were obliged to forward and deliver to addressees resident in Germany mail posted in large quantities by senders resident in Germany using postal services of other Member States, without any provision allowing it to be financially compensated for all the costs occasioned by that obligation, the performance, in economically balanced conditions, of that task of general interest would be jeopardised.

51. The postal services of a Member State cannot simultaneously bear the costs entailed in the performance of the service of general economic interest of forwarding and delivering international items of mail, which is their responsibility by virtue of the UPC, and the loss of income resulting from the fact that bulk mailings are no longer posted with the postal services of the Member State in which the addressees are resident but with those of other Member States.

52. In such a case, it must be regarded as justified, for the purposes of the performance, in economically balanced conditions, of the task of general interest entrusted to Deutsche Post by the UPC, to treat cross-border mail as internal mail and, consequently, to charge internal postage.

. . .

54. Article [86(2)] of the Treaty therefore justifies, in the absence of an agreement between the postal services of the Member States concerned fixing terminal dues in relation to the actual costs of processing and delivering incoming trans-border mail, the grant by a Member State to its postal services of the statutory right to charge internal postage on items of mail where senders resident in that State post items, or cause them to be posted, in large quantities with the postal services of another Member State in order to send them to the first Member State.

. . .

56. On the other hand, in so far as part of the forwarding and delivery costs is offset by terminal dues paid by the postal services of other Member States, it is not necessary, in order for a body such as Deutsche Post to fulfil the obligations flowing from the UPC, that postage be charged at the full internal rate on items posted in large quantities with those services.

57. It is to be remembered that a body such as Deutsche Post which has a statutory monopoly over a substantial part of the common market may be regarded as holding a dominant position within the meaning of Article [82] of the Treaty.

58. Thus, the exercise by such a body of the right to demand the full amount of the internal postage, where the costs relating to the forwarding and delivery of mail posted in large quantities with the postal services of a Member State other than the State in which both the senders and the addressees of that mail are resident are not offset by the terminal dues paid by those services, may be regarded as an abuse of a dominant position within the meaning of Article [82] of the Treaty.

59. In order to prevent a body such as Deutsche Post from exercising its right, provided for by Article 25(3) of the UPC, to return items of mail to origin, the senders of those items have no choice but to pay the full amount of the internal postage.

60. As the Court has stated in relation to a refusal to sell on the part of an undertaking holding a dominant position within the meaning of Article [82] of the Treaty, such action would be inconsistent with the objective laid down by Article [3(1)(g)] of the EC Treaty] . . ., as explained in Article [82], in particular in subparagraphs (b) and (c) of its second paragraph (Case 27/76 *United Brands v Commission* [1978] ECR 207, paragraph 183).

In this judgment the Court said that Deutsche Post had been granted exclusive rights within the meaning of Article 86(1), and that Article 86(1) had to be read in conjunction with Article 86(2). In saying this (paragraphs 40–41), the Court repeated the wording in paragraphs 12–13 of the *Corbeau* judgment. The performance of the obligations of the UPC was a service of general economic interest within the meaning of Article 86(2) (paragraph 44). The Court held that granting Deutsche Post the right under the UPC to treat international mail as internal mail *did* create a situation where 'it may be led, to the detriment of users of postal services, to abuse its dominant position' (paragraph 48). The Court therefore said it was necessary to examine whether the exercise of the right was necessary to perform its task of general interest 'under economically acceptable conditions' (paragraph 49). It concluded that it *was* necessary, because of the financial loss Deutsche Post would otherwise incur. On the other hand, it would be an abuse of a dominant position if Deutsche Post were to charge the full internal postage without offsetting the terminal dues against the money demanded from the senders.

Albany and *Deutsche Post*, therefore, both say that the grant of exclusive rights is contrary to Article 86(1) only where it leads to the undertaking committing an abuse, or makes it unavoidable. Where that is so, however, the rights can be justified only under Article 86(2).

D. ARTICLE 86(2)

(i) THE PURPOSE OF ARTICLE 86(2)

Article 86(2) provides a limited derogation from the rules of the Treaty in order to deal with the activities of undertakings entrusted by the State with certain tasks. It provides that the Treaty rules shall apply to two sorts of undertaking—revenue-producing monopolies and those entrusted with services of general economic interest—only in so far as that does not obstruct the performance of their tasks. It is subject to the proviso that the exception should not affect trade to an extent contrary to the interests of the Community. Unlike Article 86(1), Article 86(2) is addressed to undertakings themselves and not to Member States, although Member States may rely on Article 86(2)[68] and, as we have seen above, the two provisions may be applied together. As with Article 86(1), the competition rules are singled out for special mention and Article 86(2) is particularly important in relation to the application of Article 82, to which no other exemption or derogation applies.[69] Article 86(2) is therefore the only defence to an Article 82 abuse.

---

[68] See e.g. Case C–203/96, *Chemische Afvalstoffen Dusseldorp BV v. Minister van Volkshuisvesting, Ruimtelijke Ordening en Milieubeheer* [1998] ECR I–4075, [1998] 3 CMLR 873.

[69] Unlike Art. 81, which contains exemption provisions in Art. 81(3) and the free movement provisions which are subject to the mandatory requirements doctrine and to the exceptions in Arts. 30 (ex Art. 36), 39(3) (ex Art. 48(3), 45 (ex Art. 55) and 46 (ex Art.56).

The Treaty does not say in Article 86(2) what value is to be accorded to services of general economic interest and in particular does not say that 'universal service' should be protected or promoted.[70] In the past the Court tended to construe the provision narrowly (as with other derogations from the Treaty) and so preserve the widest possible application of the competition rules.[71] Nevertheless, from the case of *Corbeau* in 1993 onwards, the Court has been more willing to accept that providers of public services may need to be protected from the full rigours of competition and has become more flexible in the way in which it applies the criteria in Article 86(2).

(ii) UNDERTAKINGS HAVING THE CHARACTER OF A REVENUE PRODUCING MONOPOLY

This is a reference to undertakings which exploit their exclusive rights to raise revenue for the State. They may well constitute commercial monopolies and so be subject to the rules laid down in Article 31 of the EC Treaty. Article 31 appears among the free movement provisions, but the Court has said that it aims to eliminate distortions in competition in the common market as well as discrimination against the products and trade of other Member States.[72]

(iii) UNDERTAKINGS ENTRUSTED WITH THE OPERATION OF SERVICES OF GENERAL ECONOMIC INTEREST

a. 'UNDERTAKINGS ENTRUSTED WITH . . .'

'Undertaking' has the meaning previously discussed.[73] The legal status of the undertaking in national law is immaterial. It can be a public or private undertaking, but the important thing is that the State has assigned it certain tasks by a positive act conferring on it certain functions or by granting it a concession. Merely tolerating, approving or endorsing its activities is insufficient. So according to the Commission the Member States' approval of the Eurocheque system did not mean that Article 86(2) applied to the banks concerned,[74] and an authors' rights society was not within the provision merely because it was subject to obligations imposed on all monopolies by national law.[75] In *Dusseldorp* the Advocate General said that an undertaking is 'entrusted with' a service where 'certain obligations are imposed on it by the State in the general economic interest'.[76]

---

[70] See M. Ross, 'Art. 16 EC and Services of General Interest: From Derogation to Obligation?' (2000) 25 *ELRev.* 22, 24. 'Universal service' is discussed *infra* at 461.

[71] See Case 127/73, *BRT* v. *SABAM* [1974] ECR 313, [1974] 2 CMLR 238.

[72] There is a cogent argument that, except in the case of new Member States, Art. 31 as an independent provision is obsolete: see G. Tesauro, 'The Community's Internal Market in the Light of the Recent Case—law of the Court of Justice', (1995) 15 *YEL* 1, and the discussion in S. Weatherill and P. Beaumont, *EU Law* (3rd edn. Penguin, 1999), 1017–8.

[73] See *supra* 434 and Chaps. 3 and 5.

[74] *Uniform Eurocheques* [1985] OJ L35/43, [1985] 3 CMLR 434.

[75] *GEMA* [1971] OJ L134/15.

[76] Opinion of Jacobs AG, para. 103, in Case C–203/96, *Chemische Afvalstoffen Dusseldorp BV* v. *Minister van Volkshuisvesting, Ruimtelijke Ordening en Milieubeheer* [1998] ECR I–4075, [1998] 3 CMLR 873.

b. OPERATION OF SERVICES OF GENERAL ECONOMIC INTEREST

Not surprisingly, the Court has held that 'services of general economic interest' is a Community concept, and must be uniformly applied by the Member States.[77] The word 'services' is construed to cover the widest spectrum of activities and is not limited to the meaning of the term as used in Title III, Chapter 3, of the Treaty on free movement. 'Services of general economic interest' denotes activities that need to be carried out in the public interest. As the Advocate General said in *Dusseldorp*:[78]

The reason for the assignment of particular tasks to undertakings is often that the tasks need to be undertaken in the public interest but might not be undertaken, usually for economic reasons, if the service were to be left to the private sector.

In the Telecommunications Equipment case the Court explained that Article 86(2) reconciles the interests of Member States and Community:[79]

In allowing derogations to be made from the general rules of the Treaty on certain conditions, that provision seeks to reconcile the Member States' interest in using certain undertakings, in particular in the public sector, as an instrument of economic or fiscal policy with the Community's interest in ensuring compliance with the rules on competition and the preservation of the unity of the common market.

Further, this passage refers to undertakings which are used as instruments of economic or fiscal policy. In *Albany International* the Court applied the same principle to social policy.[80] The most obvious candidates for recognition as services of general economic interest on this basis are the utilities, as the Commission stated in its *XXth Report on Competition Policy*.[81] In its Notice on Services of General Interest in Europe[82] the Commission said that the term used in Article 86 refers to 'market services which the Member States subject to specific public service obligations by virtue of a general interest criterion. This would tend to cover such things as transport networks, energy and communications'. These services often involve obligations of 'universal service', which means the obligation to ensure 'that everyone has access to certain essential services of high quality at prices they can afford'.[83] The Court has accepted as services of general economic interest the administration of major waterways;[84] the operation of non-economically viable air routes;[85] the operation of the electricity supply network;[86] the operation of the basic, as distinct from

---

[77] Case 10/71, *Ministère Public of Luxembourg* v. *Muller* [1971] ECR 723, paras. 14–15.

[78] Opinion of Jacobs AG in Case C–203/96, *Chemische Afvalstoffen Dusseldorp BV* v. *Minister van Volkshuisvesting, Ruimtelijke Ordening en Milieubeheer* [1998] ECR I–4075, [1998] 3 CMLR 873, para. 105.

[79] Case C–202/88, *France* v. *Commission* [1991] ECR I–1223 (the *Telecommunications Equipment* case), para. 12; see also Case C–157/94, *Commission* v. *Netherlands (Re Electricity Imports)* [1997] ECR I–5699, para. 39.

[80] Case C–67/96, *Albany International BV* v. *Stichting Bedrijfspensioenfonds Textielindustrie* [2000] 4 CMLR 446, paras. 103–105.

[81] (Commission, 1990), Introduction, 12.

[82] [1996] OJ C281/3. See *infra* 474.

[83] *Ibid.* and see Case C–320/91, *Corbeau* [1993] ECR I–1477, [1995] 4 CMLR 621.

[84] Case 10/71, *Ministère Public of Luxembourg* v. *Muller* [1971] ECR 723.

[85] Case 66/86, *Ahmed Saeed Flugreisen and Silver Line Reisebüro GmbH* v. *Zentrale zur Bëkampfung Unlauteren Wettwerbs eV* [1989] ECR 803, [1990] 4 CMLR 102.

[86] Case C–393/94, *Gemeente Almelo* [1994] ECR I–1477; in Case 157/94, *Commission* v. *Netherlands (Re Electricity Imports)* [1997] ECR I–5699 the Commission did not contest that the monopoly electricity distributor in the Netherlands provided a services of general economic interest.

extra 'added-value', postal service;[87] mooring services in ports;[88] sectoral supplementary pension funds;[89] and the performance of obligations flowing from the Universal Postal Convention.[90] It has not accepted that commercial port operations are services of general economic interest[91] and it has sometimes left open the status of the services provided, and said that even if they were of general economic interest the other criteria in Article 86(2) were not fulfilled.[92] Extracts from the judgments in the leading cases on what amounts to a service of general economic interest are set out in the section below as they usually deal also with the question of whether non-compliance with the Treaty rules is essential to the fulfilment of the entrusted tasks. The status of services of general economic interest in Community law has been given a new dimension by the new Article 16 added to the EC Treaty by the Treaty of Amsterdam.[93]

c. OBSTRUCT THE PERFORMANCE OF THE PARTICULAR TASKS ASSIGNED TO THEM

Even if an activity is accepted as a service of general economic interest it still has to be shown that compliance with the Treaty rules would 'obstruct the performance' of the particular tasks assigned to the undertaking. As Article 86(2) is a derogation from the normal rules it is for those claiming its benefit to show that its terms are satisfied.

In *Corbeau*[94] the Court said that the question is:

16. . . . the extent to which a restriction on competition or even the exclusion of all competition from other economic operators is necessary in order to allow the holder of the exclusive right to perform its task of general interest and in particular to have the benefit of economically acceptable conditions.

The Court elaborated on this ruling in *Commission* v. *Netherlands*:[95]

52. . . . it is not necessary, in order for the conditions for the application of Article [86(2)] to be fulfilled, that the financial balance or economic viability of the undertaking entrusted with the operation of a service of general economic interest should be threatened. It is sufficient that, in the absence of the rights at issue, it would not be possible for the undertaking to perform the particular tasks entrusted to it, defined by reference to the obligations and constraints to which it is subject.

---

[87] *Dutch Courier Services* [1990] OJ L10/47, [1990] 4 CMLR 947; *Spanish Courier Services* [1990] OJ L233/19, [1991] 4 CMLR 560; Case C–320/91, *Corbeau* [1993] ECR I–1477, [1995] 4 CMLR 621.

[88] Case C–266/96, *Corsica Ferries France SA* v. *Gruppo Antichi Ormeggiatori del Porto di Genova* [1998] ECR I–3949, [1998] 5 CMLR 402.

[89] Case C–67/96, *Albany International BV* v. *Stichting Bedrijfspensioenfonds Textielindustrie* [2000] 4 CMLR 466.

[90] Joined Cases C–147–148/97 *Deutsche Post AG* v. *Gesellschaft für Zahlungssysteme mbH (GZS) and Citicorp Kartenservice GmbH* [2000] 4 CMLR 838.

[91] Case C–179/90, *Merci Convenzionali Porto di Genova* v. *Siderurigica Gabrielle* [1991] ECR I–5009, [1994] 4 CMLR 422; Case C–242/95, *GT—Link* v. *De Danske Statsbaner (DSB)* [1997] ECR I– 4449, [1997] 5 CMLR 601.

[92] Case C–203/96, *Chemische Afvalstoffen Dusseldorp BV* v. *Minister van Volkshuisvesting, Ruimtelijke Ordening en Milieubeheer* [1998] ECR I–4075, [1998] 3 CMLR 873.

[93] Discussed *infra* at 473.

[94] Case C–320/91, *Corbeau* [1993] ECR I–1477, [1995] 4 CMLR 621, para. 16.

[95] Case 157/94, *Commission* v. *Netherlands (Re Electricity Imports)* [1997] ECR I–5699.

53. Moreover, it follows from the *Corbeau* judgment . . . , that the conditions for the application of Article [86(2)] are fulfilled in particular if maintenance of those rights is necessary to enable the holder of them to perform the tasks of general economic interest assigned to it under economically acceptable conditions.

. . .

58. Whilst it is true that it is incumbent upon a Member State which invokes Article [86(2)] to demonstrate that the conditions laid down by that provision are met, that burden of proof cannot be so extensive as to require the Member State, when setting out in detail the reasons for which, in the event of elimination of the contested measures, the performance, under economically acceptable conditions, of the tasks of general economic interest which it has entrusted to an undertaking would, in its view, be jeopardized, to go even further and prove, positively, that no other conceivable measure, which by definition would be hypothetical, could enable those tasks to be performed under the same conditions.

The Court has been slow to accept that compliance with the Treaty rules, particularly the competition rules, is incompatible with the tasks assigned to the undertaking. Thus in *Höfner* v. *Macrotron*[96] the Court accepted that the Bundesanstalt had been entrusted with services of general economic interest but not that it had to abuse its dominant position to order to carry them out; in *Merci Convenzionali*[97] it said that even if services of general economic interest had been involved it would not have been necessary for the undertaking to infringe the Treaty rules; in *British Telecom*[98] it said that Italy had failed to establish that compliance by BT with the competition rules would obstruct it in carrying out its tasks; and in *RTT*[99] it did not accept that the undertaking entrusted with the public telephone network also needed power to lay down the standards for telephone equipment and to check rival equipment suppliers' compliance with them.[100]

Article 86(2) contains what is in effect a proportionality requirement. The first time the Court recognized that this was satisfied was in *Corbeau*,[101] the facts of which are given above. It will be recalled that the Court considered both Article 86(1) and Article 86(2) and seemed to say that Member States may grant special or exclusive rights only in so far as they entrust undertakings with services of general economic interest and the criteria in Article 86(2) are fulfilled.[102] The Court went on to consider the application of Article 86(2):

Case C–320/91, *Corbeau* [1993] ECR I–1477, [1995] 4 CMLR 621

Court of Justice

15. As regards the services at issue in the main proceedings, it cannot be disputed that the Régie des Postes is entrusted with a service of general economic interest consisting in the obligation to

---

[96] Case C–41/90, *Höfner* v. *Macroton* [1991] ECR I–1979, [1993] 4 CMLR 306.

[97] Case C–179/90, *Merci Convenzionali Porto di Genova* v. *Siderurigica Gabrielle* [1991] ECR I–5009, [1994] 4 CMLR 422.

[98] Case 41/83, *Italy* v. *Commission* [1985] ECR 873, [1985] 2 CMLR 368.

[99] Case C–18/88, *RTT* v. *GB-INNO-BM SA* [1991] ECR I–5973.

[100] See also Case 66/86, *Ahmed Saeed Flugreisen and Silver Line Reisebüro GmbH* v. *Zentrale zur Bëkampf Unlauteren Wettwerbs eV* [1989] ECR 803, [1990] 4 CMLR 102; Commission Decision, *Dutch Courier Services* [1990] OJ L10/47, [1990] 4 CMLR 947.

[101] Case C–320/91, *Corbeau* [1993] ECR I–1477, [1995] 4 CMLR 621.

[102] *Ibid.*, para. 14: see *supra* 448.

collect, carry and distribute mail on behalf of all users throughout the territory of the Member State concerned, at uniform tariffs and on similar quality conditions, irrespective of the specific situations or the degree of economic profitability of each individual operation.

16. The question which falls to be considered is therefore the extent to which a restriction on competition or even the exclusion of all competition from other economic operators is necessary in order to allow the holder of the exclusive right to perform its task of general interest and in particular to have the benefit of economically acceptable conditions.

17. The starting point of such an examination must be the premise that the obligation on the part of the undertaking entrusted with that task to perform its services in conditions of economic equilibrium presupposes that it will be possible to offset less profitable sectors against the profitable sectors and hence justifies a restriction of competition from individual undertakings where the economically profitable sectors are concerned.

18. Indeed, to authorize individual undertakings to compete with the holder of the exclusive rights in the sectors of their choice corresponding to those rights would make it possible for them to concentrate on the economically profitable operations and to offer more advantageous tariffs than those adopted by the holders of the exclusive rights since, unlike the latter, they are not bound for economic reasons to offset losses in the unprofitable sectors against profits in the more profitable sectors.

19. However, the exclusion of competition is not justified as regards specific services dissociable from the service of general interest which meet special needs of economic operators and which call for certain additional services not offered by the traditional postal service, such as collection from the senders' address, greater speed or reliability of distribution or the possibility of changing the destination in the course of transit, in so far as such specific services, by their nature and the conditions in which they are offered, such as the geographical area in which they are provided, do not compromise the economic equilibrium of the service of general economic interest performed by the holder of the exclusive right.

20. It is for the national court to consider whether the services at issue in the dispute before it meet those criteria.

21. The answer to the questions referred to the Court by the Tribunal Correctionnel de Liége should therefore be that it is contrary to Article [86] of the EEC Treaty for legislation of a Member State which confers on a body such as the Régie des Postes the exclusive right to collect, carry and distribute mail, to prohibit, under threat of criminal penalties, an economic operator established in that State from offering certain specific services dissociable from the service of general interest which meet the special needs of economic operators and call for certain additional services not offered by the traditional postal service, in so far as those services do not compromise the economic equilibrium of the service of general economic interest performed by the holder of the exclusive right. It is for the national court to consider whether the services in question in the main proceedings meet those criteria.

In this judgment the Court recognized that the operation of a basic postal system providing a universal service is a service of general economic interest and that the normal principles of competition law will not apply to the extent necessary to preserve it through cross-subsidy. If competitors are allowed to come in and 'cherry-pick' or 'cream-skim' the most profitable parts of the system the holder of the exclusive right required to operate the universal service cannot operate under economically acceptable conditions. The Court said, however, in paragraph 19 that this does not justify the exclusion of competition from additional services, separable from the basic public service, if these could be offered by other undertakings without compromising the economic viability of the latter. The Court did not consider whether the universal service provision could be achieved by a less extreme measure than granting a monopoly. Universal service and cross-subsidization are not inseparable: it is possible for the State to subsidize the universal service, for example.

It will be noted that it was left (paragraph 21) to the national court actually to determine whether or not the additional services *were* severable and able to be operated by other undertakings without prejudicing the economic equilibrium of the traditional postal service. This left the national court with a difficult task involving extensive economic analysis. It had to decide the extent of the cross-subsidization, and how far this was necessary to maintain the 'economic equilibrium'.[103] Cross-subsidization is a problematic issue, particularly in respect of network monopolies.

Edward and M. Hoskins, 'Article 90: Deregulation and EC Law. Reflections Arising from the XVI FIDE Conference' (1995) 32 *CMLRev.* 157, 179–81[104]

In *Corbeau*, the Court of Justice assumed that the *Régie des postes* should be permitted to use profitable activities to subsidize less profitable activities. However, in future cases, it will be necessary to examine further the situations in which cross-subsidization is incompatible with EC competition law.

The Commission has defined cross-subsidization as meaning 'that an undertaking allocates all or part of the costs of its activity in one product or geographic market to its activity in another product or geographic market' (Commission's Guidelines on the Application of EEC Competition Rules in the Telecommunications Sector at paragraph 102 (O.J. 1991 C 233/3). Thus, cross-subsidization may lead to a distortion in competition as it enables an undertaking to provide goods or services at a price lower than their true market price or even lower than their production cost.

The issues raised by cross-subsidization in the context of universal providers and legal monopolies are complex. As a starting point, if a particular undertaking has an obligation to provide a universal service *at a standard price* to all consumers, then it necessarily follows that geographical cross-subsidization must be permitted. Consumers in profitable urban areas will be obliged to subsidize consumers in unprofitable rural areas.

This assumption was confirmed by the Commission in its Telecommunications Guidelines: . . .

'Cross-subsidization does not lead to predatory pricing and does not restrict competition when it is the costs of reserved activities which are subsidized by the revenue generated by other reserved activities. This form of subsidization is even necessary, as it enables the TOs [Telecommunications Organizations] holders of exclusive rights to perform their obligation to provide a public service universally and on the same conditions to everybody. For instance, telephone provision in unprofitable rural areas is subsidized through revenues from telephone provision in profitable urban areas or long-distance calls.'

The Commission stated that the same reasoning could be applied to the subsidizing of reserved

---

[103] See L. Hancher, 'Casenote on *Corbeau*' (1994) 31 *CMLRev.* 105 at 119–20. For the issue of the direct effect of Art. 86, see *infra* 469.

[104] See also L. Hancher and J.L. Buendia Sierra, 'Cross-subsidization and EC Law' (1998) 35 *CMLRev.* 901.

services by means of activities which are subject to competition. However, it is very important to ensure that third party value-added service providers have access to the network on equitable terms, since there will be an incentive for the universal provider to try to improve its competitive position in the market for value-added services by imposing detrimental conditions of access to the network on its competitors.

The Commission also considered that subsidization of activities which are subject to competition by activities which are subject to a monopoly is likely to distort competition in violation of Article [82]. However, there is a strong argument that Article [82] should not be applied inflexibly to such cross-subsidization. Certainly, legal monopolies should not be permitted to use such cross-subsidization to finance predatory pricing in competitive markets. But it would be inefficient to prevent legal monopolies from using their resources to enter other, competitive markets under any circumstances.

A final point to note is that it is often very difficult to identify whether there has in fact been any cross-subsidization. This is because subsidies can be provided in a number of ways. For example, in setting the price to be charged to customers for a non-reserved value-added service, the universal provider may not take full account of the actual cost of access to the network involved in providing that service. Any shortfall can be absorbed by increasing the price of monopoly services. Furthermore, a universal provider may be able to obtain loan capital at a lower rate than normal private undertakings due to the financial security which it enjoys as a result of its legal monopoly. If such capital is then used to subsidize activities which are not covered by its legal monopoly, this may give the universal provider an unfair advantage over its competitors, for whom borrowing money is more expensive.

The existence of cross-subsidization can be controlled to a certain extent by ensuring that universal providers use transport accounting techniques which take full account of true cost allocations. The judgment of the Court of Justice in Case 66/86 *Ahmed Saeed* (. . .) recognizes the need for transparency in order to ensure the effective application of the competition rules. However, detailed rules (for example, in relation to accountancy practices to be followed) can be introduced only through legislation.

Issues similar to those in *Corbeau* arose in *Almelo* where the Court dealt with a preliminary reference from a Dutch court seised of litigation between regional and local electricity distributors concerning, *inter alia*, the legality of an exclusive purchasing clause:

Case C–393/94, *Gemeente Almelo and Others* v. *Energiebedrijf Ijsselmij NV* [1994] ECR I–1477

Court of Justice

46. Article [86(2)] of the Treaty provides that undertakings entrusted with the operation of services of general economic interest may be exempted from the application of the competition rules contained in the Treaty in so far as it is necessary to impose restrictions on competition, or even to exclude all competition, from other economic operators in order to ensure the performance of the particular tasks assigned to them (see the judgment in Case C–320/91 *Corbeau* . . . , paragraph 14).

47. As regards the question whether an undertaking such as IJM has been entrusted with the operation of services of general interest, it should be borne in mind that it has been given the task, through the grant of a non-exclusive concession governed by public law, of ensuring the supply of electricity in part of the national territory.

48. Such an undertaking must ensure that throughout the territory in respect of which the

concession is granted, all consumers, whether local distributors or end-users, receive uninterrupted supplies of electricity in sufficient quantities to meet demand at any given time, at uniform tariff rates and on terms which may not vary save in accordance with objective criteria applicable to all customers.

49. Restrictions on competition from other economic operators must be allowed so far as they are necessary in order to enable the undertaking entrusted with such a task of general interest to perform it. In that regard, it is necessary to take into consideration the economic conditions in which the undertaking operates, in particular the costs which it has to bear and the legislation, particularly concerning the environment, to which it is subject.

50. It is for the national court to consider whether an exclusive purchasing clause prohibiting local distributors from importing electricity is necessary in order to enable the regional distributor to perform its task of general interest.

Here again, the Court accepted that the undertaking provided a service of general economic interest and that Article 86(2) allows the restrictions of competition necessary for the performance of its universal service obligations (although it was for the national court to make the decision whether the actual restriction at issue in the case was necessary for that purpose). Ross comments that *Almelo*, reinforcing *Corbeau*, was a movement towards recognizing the value of public service independently of its economic viability because 'it clearly indicated that the availability of the derogation was to be measured by a balancing exercise based upon competing priorities rather than inhibiting that choice by insisting upon narrow economic tests to be satisfied before the normal market rules can be disapplied'.[105]

In *Dusseldorp*,[106] however, where the Court was dealing with an undertaking with a monopoly over certain waste incineration, it was less flexible and reverted to a previous, more stringent approach. It said that even if the task could constitute a task of general economic interest it was for the Dutch Government to show to the satisfaction of the national court that the objective could not be equally achieved by other means, and that Article 86(2) could apply only if it shown that without the contested measure the undertaking could not carry out its entrusted task.[107]

In some cases, unlike *Corbeau* and *Almelo*, the Court has not left the decision to the national court but has actually decided that the conditions in Article 86(2) were satisfied. This can be seen in *Corsica Ferries France*, *Albany*, and *Deutsche Post*:

Case C–266/96, *Corsica Ferries France SA* v. *Gruppo Antichi Ormeggiatori del Poro di Genovo Coop. and Others* [1998] ECR I–3949, [1998] 5 CMLR 402

Under Italian law ships from other Member States were required to use the services of local mooring companies who held exclusive concessions in each port. Corsica Ferries claimed that the Genoa and La Spezia mooring groups were abusing their dominant positions by preventing shipping companies

---

[105] M. Ross, 'Art. 16 EC and Services of General Interest: From Derogation to Obligation' (2000) 25 *ELRev.* 22, 24.

[106] Case C–203/96, *Chemische Afvalstoffen Dusseldorp BV* v. *Minister van Volkshuisvesting, Ruimtelijke Ordening en Milieubeheer* [1998] ECR I–4075, [1998] 3 CMLR 873.

[107] *Ibid.*, para. 67.

using their own staff to carry out mooring operations, in the excessive nature of the price of the service which bore no relation to the actual cost of the service provided, and in fixing tariffs that varied from port to port for equivalent services. The Italian court asked, inter alia, whether the Treaty prohibited national measures which put the mooring companies in the position to act in this way.

Court of Justice

36. The national court asks whether there is an abuse, on the part of the Genoa and La Spezia mooring groups, of their dominant position on a substantial part of the Common Market by virtue of the exclusive rights conferred upon them by the Italian public authorities.

37. There are three aspects of the abuse alleged in this case. It is said to reside in the grant of exclusive rights to local mooring groups, preventing shipping companies from using their own staff to carry out mooring operations, in the excessive nature of the price of the service, which bears no relation to the actual cost of the service provided, and in the fixing of tariffs that vary from port to port for equivalent services.

38. As regards the definition of the market in question, it appears from the order for reference that it consists in the performance on behalf of third persons of mooring services relating to container freight in the ports of Genoa and La Spezia. Having regard *inter alia* to the volume of traffic in those ports and their importance in intra-Community trade, those markets may be regarded as constituting a substantial part of the Common Market (Case C–179/90, *Merci Convenzionali Porto di Genova* . . . And Case C–163/96, *Raso and Others* . . . .

39. As far as the existence of exclusive rights is concerned, it is settled law that an undertaking having a statutory monopoly in a substantial part of the Common Market may be regarded as having a dominant position within the meaning of Article [82] of the Treaty (Case C–41/90, *Höfner and Elser v. Macrotron* . . . , Case C–260/89, *ERT v. DEP* . . . , *Merci Convenzionali Porto di Genova* . . . and *Raso and Others* . . . .

40. Next, it should be pointed out that although merely creating a dominant position by granting exclusive rights within the meaning of Article [86(1)] of the Treaty is not in itself incompatible with Article [82], a Member State is in breach of the prohibitions contained in those two provisions if the undertaking in question, merely by exercising the exclusive rights granted to it, is led to abuse its dominant position or if such rights are liable to create a situation in which that undertaking is led to commit such abuses (Case C–41/90, *Höfner and Elser v. Macrotron* . . . ; Case C–260/89, *ERT v. DEP* . . . ; *Merci Convenzionali Porto di Genova* . . . ; Case C–323/93, *Centre d'Insemination de la Crespelle* . . . ; *Raso and others* . . .).

41. It follows that a Member State may, without infringing Article [82] of the Treaty, grant exclusive rights for the supply of mooring services in its ports to local mooring groups provided those groups do not abuse their dominant position or are not led necessarily to commit such an abuse.

42. In order to rebut the existence of such abuse, the Genoa and La Spezia mooring groups rely on Article [86(2)] of the Treaty, which provides that undertakings entrusted with the operation of services of general economic interest are to be subject to the competition rules contained in the Treaty only in so far as their application does not obstruct the performance, in law or in fact, of the particular tasks assigned to them. Article [86(2)] of the Treaty further provides that, in order for it to apply, the development of trade must not be affected to such an extent as would be contrary to the interests of the Community.

43. They maintain that the tariffs applied are indispensable if a universal mooring service is to be maintained. On the one hand, the tariffs include a component corresponding to the additional cost of providing a universal mooring service. On the other hand, the difference in the tariffs from one port to

another, which, according to the file, result from account being taken, when the tariffs are calculated, of corrective factors reflecting the influence of local circumstances—which would tend to indicate that the services provided are not equivalent—are justified by the characteristics of the service and the need to ensure universal coverage.

44. It must therefore be considered whether the derogation from the rules of the Treaty provided for in Article [86(2)] of the Treaty may fall to be applied. To that end, it must be determined whether the mooring service can be regarded as a service of general economic interest within the meaning of that provision and, if so, first, whether performance of the particular tasks assigned to it can be achieved only through services for which the charge is higher than their actual cost, and secondly, whether the development of trade is not affected to such an extent as would be contrary to the interests of the Community (see, to that effect, Case C–157/94, *E.C. Commission v. Netherlands* . . .).

45. It is evident from the file on the case in the main proceedings that mooring operations are of general economic interest, such interest having special characteristics, in relation to those of other economic activities, which is capable of bringing them within the scope of Article [86(2)] of the Treaty. Mooring groups are obliged to provide at any time and to any user a universal mooring service, for reasons of safety in port waters. At all events, Italy could properly have considered that it was necessary, on grounds of public security, to confer on local groups of operators the exclusive right to provide a universal mooring service.

46. In those circumstances it is not incompatible with Articles [82] and [86(1)] of the Treaty to include in the price of the service a component designed to cover the cost of maintaining the universal mooring service, inasmuch as it corresponds to the supplementary cost occasioned by the special characteristics of that service, and to lay down for that service different tariffs on the basis of the particular characteristics of each port.

47. Consequently, since the mooring groups have in fact been entrusted by the Member State with managing a service of general economic interest within the meaning of Article [86(2)] of the Treaty, and the other conditions for applying the derogation from application of the Treaty rules which is laid down in that provision are satisfied, legislation such as that at issue does not constitute an infringement of Article [82] of the Treaty, read in conjunction with Article [86(1)].

As in *Corbeau*, the Court considered that the exclusive rights could escape the prohibition in Article 86(1) if they satisfied Article 86(2). However, the Court did not leave this determination to the national court, but said that the mooring operations were services of general economic interest provided on a universal basis and that it was, in the circumstances, not incompatible with the Treaty to include supplementary costs related to the running of that service and to charge varying tariffs (paragraph 46). Therefore there was no infringement of Article 86(1). There is no explanation of how the Court reached its conclusions in paragraph 46, or of how the supplementary costs arose or what cross-subsidization was taking place.

The ECJ also made a clear decision on the application of Article 86(2) in *Albany*. It will be remembered from the discussion of Article 86(1) above[108] that the case concerned the Dutch regime of compulsory affiliation to sectoral pension schemes. The Court considered whether the derogation in Article 86(2) applied, and held that it did because the scheme involved a service of general economic interest which had to operate under 'economically acceptable conditions'.

---

[108] *Supra* 451.

Case C–67/96, *Albany International BV* v. *Stichting Bedrijfspensioenfonds Textielindustrie*, judgment 21 September 1999, [2000] 4 CMLR 446

Court of Justice

102. It is important to bear in mind first of all that, under Article [86(2)] of the Treaty, undertakings entrusted with the operation of services of general economic interest are subject to the rules on competition in so far as the application of such rules does not obstruct the performance, in law or in fact, of the particular tasks assigned to them.

103. In allowing, in certain circumstances, derogations from the general rules of the Treaty, Article [86(2)] of the Treaty seeks to reconcile the Member States' interest in using certain undertakings, in particular in the public sector, as an instrument of economic or fiscal policy with the Community's interest in ensuring compliance with the rules on competition and preservation of the unity of the common market (Case C–202/88 *France v Commission* . . . , paragraph 12, and Case C–157/94 *Commission v Netherlands* . . . , paragraph 39).

104. In view of the interest of the Member States thus defined they cannot be precluded, when determining what services of general economic interest they entrust to certain undertakings, from taking account of objectives pertaining to their national policy or from endeavouring to attain them by means of obligations and constraints which they impose on such undertakings (*Commission v Netherlands*, cited above, paragraph 40).

105. The supplementary pension scheme at issue in the main proceedings fulfils an essential social function within the Netherlands pensions system by reason of the limited amount of the statutory pension, which is calculated on the basis of the minimum statutory wage.

106. Moreover, the importance of the social function attributed to supplementary pensions has recently been recognised by the Community legislature's adoption of Council Directive 98/49/EC of 29 June 1998 on safeguarding the supplementary pension rights of employed and self-employed persons moving within the Community (OJ 1998 L 209, p. 46).

107. Next, it is not necessary, in order for the conditions for the application of Article [86(2)] of the Treaty to be fulfilled, that the financial balance or economic viability of the undertaking entrusted with the operation of a service of general economic interest should be threatened. It is sufficient that, in the absence of the rights at issue, it would not be possible for the undertaking to perform the particular tasks entrusted to it, defined by reference to the obligations and constraints to which it is subject (*Commission v Netherlands*, cited above, paragraph 52) or that maintenance of those rights is necessary to enable the holder of them to perform tasks of general economic interest which have been assigned to it under economically acceptable conditions (Case C–320/91 *Corbeau* [1993] ECR I–2533, paragraphs 14 to 16, and *Commission v Netherlands*, cited above, paragraph 53).

108. If the exclusive right of the fund to manage the supplementary pension scheme for all workers in a given sector were removed, undertakings with young employees in good health engaged in non-dangerous activities would seek more advantageous insurance terms from private insurers. The progressive departure of 'good' risks would leave the sectoral pension fund with responsibility for an increasing share of 'bad' risks, thereby increasing the cost of pensions for workers, particularly those in small and medium-sized undertakings with older employees engaged in dangerous activities, to which the fund could no longer offer pensions at an acceptable cost.

109. Such a situation would arise particularly in a case where, as in the main proceedings, the supplementary pension scheme managed exclusively by the Fund displays a high level of solidarity resulting, in particular, from the fact that contributions do not reflect the risk, from the obligation to

accept all workers without a prior medical examination, the continuing accrual of pension rights despite exemption from the payment of contributions in the event of incapacity for work, the discharge by the Fund of arrears of contributions due from an employer in the event of insolvency and the indexing of the amount of pensions in order to maintain their value.

110. Such constraints, which render the service provided by the Fund less competitive than a comparable service provided by insurance companies, go towards justifying the exclusive right of the Fund to manage the supplementary pension scheme.

111. It follows that the removal of the exclusive right conferred on the Fund might make it impossible for it to perform the tasks of general economic interest entrusted to it under economically acceptable conditions and threaten its financial equilibrium.

. . .

123. The answer to the third question must therefore be that Articles [82] and [86] of the Treaty do not preclude the public authorities from conferring on a pension fund the exclusive right to manage a supplementary pension scheme in a given sector.

It is important to note that in paragraph 107 the Court did not demand that the economic viability of the entrusted undertaking should be threatened without the exclusive right. Article 86(2) can apply where it is necessary to provide economically acceptable conditions. Here again this meant preventing 'cherry-picking': without the exclusive rights other insurers would be able to offer a better deal to companies with predominantly young, healthy workforces.

The cross-subsidy argument did not succeed, however, in *Air Inter*[109] where the proportionality requirement was not satisfied. There the Commission challenged the granting of exclusive rights on two internal French air routes to Air Inter. The undertaking claimed that domestic air transport in France was based on cross-subsidy between profitable and unprofitable routes, but the Commission and the CFI were not convinced:

138. The application of those articles could, however, be excluded only in as much as they 'obstructed' performance of the tasks entrusted to the applicant. Since that condition must be interpreted strictly, it was not sufficient for such performance to be simply hindered or made more difficult. Furthermore, it was for the applicant to establish any obstruction of its task (see, to that effect, Case 155/73, *Sacchi* . . .).

139. In that regard, the applicant merely asserts that the organisation of domestic air transport was based on a system of cross-subsidy between profitable routes and unprofitable routes and that the exclusivity which had been granted to it on the Orly-Marseille and Orly-Toulouse routes was justified by its obligation to operate the unprofitable routes regularly and at tariffs that were not prohibitive, in order to contribute to regional development. It does not put a figure on the probable loss of revenue if other air carriers are allowed to compete with it on the two routes in question. Nor has it shown that that loss of income will be so great that it will be forced to abandon certain routes forming part of its network.

140. In any event, the domestic air network system combined with the internal cross-subsidy system to which the applicant refers in support of its case did not constitute an aim in themselves, but were the means chosen by the French public authorities for developing the French regions. The applicant has not argued and still less established that, following the entry into force of Regulation

---

[109] Case T–260/94, *Air Inter* v. *Commission* [1997] ECR II–997, [1997] 5 CMLR 851.

2408/92, there was no appropriate alternative system capable of ensuring that regional development and in particular or ensuring that loss-making routes continue to be financed (see also the order of the President of the Court in Case C–174/94 R, *France v E.C.Commission* . . .).

141. Consequently, the applicant has not shown that the contested decision would obstruct the performance in law or in fact of the particular task assigned to it. It follows that the plea of infringement of Article [86(2)] of the Treaty cannot be accepted either.

In *Deutsche Post*,[110] the facts of which are given above,[111] the ECJ had to consider a statutory monopolist's exercise of a right (charging for international mail as though it were internal mail) stemming from an international convention. It held that the German Post Office was justified in doing this. Fulfilling the obligations under the UPC was a service of general economic interest and the Court simply stated without further explanation that levying the charges in issue was necessary to the performance of the task in economically balanced conditions. Otherwise the task would be jeopardized.[112]

(iv) NO EFFECT ON TRADE CONTRARY TO THE INTERESTS OF THE COMMUNITY

Article 86(2) contains the proviso that 'the development of trade must not be affected to such an extent as would be contrary to the interests of the Community'. This is similar to the proviso in Article 30 (ex Article 36) that the derogation from the free movement provisions should not be 'a means of arbitrary discrimination or a disguised restriction on trade between Member States'. Unlike that proviso the tailpiece to Article 86(2) has not so far been of importance, not least because the other conditions of Article 86(2) have rarely been fulfilled. It was pleaded by the Commission in the electricity cases[113] but the Court held that the Commission had provided no explanation to demonstrate such an effect on trade. The proviso must denote something more than the phrase 'affect trade between Member States' in Articles 81 and 82 because without such an effect on trade those Articles cannot apply at all. It may, however, simply be a further proportionality requirement.

E. THE DIRECT EFFECT OF ARTICLE 86(1) AND (2)

(i) ARTICLE 86(1)

As Article 86(1) prohibits Member States from enacting or maintaining measures contrary to rules contained in the Treaty it applies, as we have seen, only in conjunction with some

---

[110] Cases C–147–148/97, *Deutsche Post AG v. Gesellschaft für Zahlungssysteme mbH (GZS) and Citicorp Kartenservice GmbH* [2000] 4 CMLR 838.

[111] *Supra* p. 453.

[112] Cases C–147–148/97, *Deutsche Post AG v. Gesellschaft für Zahlungssysteme mbH (GZS) and Citicorp Kartenservice GmbH* [2000] 4 CMLR 838, para. 50.

[113] Case 157/94, *Commission v. Netherlands (Re Electricity Imports)* [1997] ECR I–5699, paras. 66–72; Case C–159/94, *Commission v. France (Re Electricity and Gas Imports)* [1997] ECR I–5815, paras. 109–16.

other rule. Whether or not individuals may invoke Article 86(1) before a national court, i.e. whether Article 86(1) is directly effective, therefore depends on whether the rule infringed by the Member State is itself directly effective. In *Höfner* v. *Macrotron*, for example, the litigant was able to claim in the German court that the German laws breached Article 86(1) because they led to an infringement of Article 82, which is directly effective. The litigant was therefore able to rely on the Articles in conjunction with one another.

(ii) ARTICLE 86(2)

There are four questions raised by Article 86(2): is the undertaking 'entrusted' with a task; is that task a 'service of general economic interest'; would the task be obstructed by complying with the Treaty rules; and would a derogation from the Treaty rules have an effect on trade contrary to the interests of the Community.

As far as the first two questions are concerned, the Court confirmed long ago that Article 86(2) is directly effective in that a national court may decide whether or not an undertaking has been entrusted with a service of general economic interest.[114]

As for the third question, whether the task would be obstructed, for a long time it appeared from the judgment in *Muller*[115] that the national courts were not competent to answer it and that only the Community institutions could decide the point in favour of the undertaking. However, the position has changed and the Court expressly said at paragraph 34 of the *ERT* judgment[116] that it is for the national court to verify whether the application of the competition rules would obstruct the undertaking's task. As can be seen above, the Court also left this determination to the national court in *Corbeau* and *Almelo*.

The fourth question is more problematic as it requires an assessment of whether the *interests of the Community* would be adversely affected. At first sight the issue seems more suited to a decision by the Commission than to a judgment by a national court. However, it may be that this is not an additional requirement at all, but part of the overall proportionality requirement to which the first sentence is subject.[117] If this is so Article 86(2) as a whole has direct effect. There is as yet no definitive Court ruling on the point.

---

[114] Case 127/73, *BRT* v. *SABAM* [1974] ECR 313, [1974] 2 CMLR 238.

[115] Case 10/71, *Ministère Public of Luxembourg* v. *Muller* [1971] ECR 723; see also Case 155/73, *Sacchi* [1974] ECR 409, Case 172/82, *Syndicat National des Fabricants Raffineurs d'Huile de Graissage* v. *Inter Huiles* [1983] ECR 555; Guidelines on the Application of EC Competition Rules in the Telecommunications Sector [1991] OJ C233/2, para. 23.

[116] Case C–260/89, *Elliniki Radiophonia Tileorasi (ERT)* v. *DEP* [1991] ECR I–2925; see *supra* p. 442; see also Case 66/86, *Ahmed Saeed Flugreisen and Silver Line Reisebüro GmbH* v. *Zentrale zur Bëkampf Unlauteren Wettwerbs eV* [1989] ECR 803, [1990] 4 CMLR 102, paras. 55–57.

[117] See J. Faull and A. Nikpay (eds.), *The EC Law of Competition* (Oxford University Press, 1999) paras. 5.148–5.149.

F. ARTICLE 86(3)

(i) THE AMBIT OF THE PROVISION

Article 86(3) provides that the Commission shall ensure the application of the Article[118] and gives it the supervisory and policing powers with which to do this. These powers are in addition to the general powers conferred upon the Commission elsewhere in the Treaty. Under Article 86(3) the Commission can adopt two types of measure, decisions addressed to Member States (not to the undertakings themselves, in respect of whom the Commission must use its powers under Regulation 17) and directives. The Commission may use these powers either to deal with some existing infringement of the Treaty rules or to take steps to prevent future infringements. The adoption of directives to deal with the latter has proved particularly contentious.

(ii) DECISIONS

The power to issue decisions addressed to Member States provides the Commission with an enforcement mechanism in respect of infringements of the Treaty in addition to the general power in Article 226.[119] However, the Commission still has to comply with the general principles of Community law, such as giving reasons and allowing the addressee to be heard, and failure to do so means that the decision can be quashed.[120] The Commission has adopted Article 86(3) decisions in several of the cases mentioned in the sections above, such as *Spanish Courier Services*[121] and *ANA*.[122] The essential facilities case, *Port of Rødby*,[123] where the Commission condemned the refusal of access to a port, also involved an Article 86(3) decision.

(iii) DIRECTIVES

The reason that the adoption of directives under Article 86(3) is so contentious is that the Commission can thereby legislate alone, without going through any of the usual legislative procedures laid down in Articles 249 to 252 involving other Community institutions. The Member States do not therefore have any opportunity to vote against the measures in the Council, and the Commission can act where there is no political consensus. This has become an issue with regard to liberalization where there is a thin line to be drawn between harmonization under Articles 94 and 95 (ex Articles 100 and 100a) and preventing infringements of the competition rules under Article 86(3). Directives adopted under Article 86(3) have been challenged by Member States claiming that the wrong legal base was used for their adoption.

---

[118] This is a specific manifestation of the Commission's general duty of enforcement and supervision under Art. 211 (ex Art. 155).

[119] Cases C–48 & 66/90, *Netherlands and Koninklijke PTT Netherland v. Commission and PIT Post BIV v. Commission* [1992] ECR I–565.

[120] *Ibid.*

[121] [1990] OJ L233/19.

[122] [1999] OJ L69/31, [1999] 5 CMLR 103, which concerned discriminatory landing charges at Portugese airports.

[123] [1994] 5 CMLR 457, discussed *supra* in Chap. 7.

The Commission used its Article 86(3) powers for the first time in adopting the Transparency Directive[124] which was challenged by France, Italy, and the UK. The Court confirmed that the Commission was entitled to proceed under Article 86(3) in adopting the Directive, a preventive measure which was aimed at creating greater transparency in the financial relationship between Member States and public undertakings, as it was necessary to its duty of surveillance under the Article.[125]

The Commission used Article 86(3) as the legal basis for two directives in the telecommunications sector, on telecommunications equipment[126] and telecommunications services,[127] both of which were challenged by Member States.[128] In the *Telecommunications Equipment* case the Court held that Article 86(3) does not give the Commission a general legislative power, but a specific one to deal with state measures concerning legal monopolies:

Case C–202/88, *France* v. *Commission (Telecommunications Equipment)* [1991] ECR I–1223, [1992]

Court of Justice

23. As regards the allegation that the Commission has encroached on the powers conferred on the Council by Articles [83] and [95] of the Treaty, those provisions have to be compared with Article [86], taking into account their respective subject-matter and purpose.

24. Article [95] is concerned with the adoption of measures for the approximation of the provisions laid down by law, regulation or administrative action in Member States which have as their object the establishment and functioning of the internal market. Article [83] is concerned with the adoption of any appropriate regulations or directives to give effect to the principles set out in Articles [81] and [82], that is to say the competition rules applicable to all undertakings. As for Article [86], it is concerned with measures adopted by the Member States in relation to undertakings with which they have specific links referred to in the provisions of that article. It is only with regard to such measures that Article [86] imposes on the Commission a duty of supervision which may, where necessary, be exercised through the adoption of directives and decisions addressed to the Member States.

25. It must therefore be held that the subject-matter of the power conferred on the Commission by Article [86(3)] is different from, and more specific than, that of the powers conferred on the Council by either Article [95] or Article [83].

26. It should also be noted that, as the Court held in Joined Cases 188 to 190/80 (*France, Italy and United Kingdom* v *Commission* . . . paragraph 14), the possibility that rules containing provisions which impinge upon the specific sphere of Article [86] might be laid down by the Council by virtue of its general power under other articles of the Treaty does not preclude the exercise of the power which Article [86] confers on the Commission.

27. The plea in law alleging lack of powers on the part of the Commission must therefore be rejected.

In this case, although the Court upheld the Commission's power to legislate over tele-

---

[124] 80/723/EEC [1980] OJ L195/35 as amended [1985] OJ L229/20.
[125] *Ibid.*, para. 14.
[126] Dir. 88/301/EEC [1988] OJ L131/73.
[127] Dir. 90/388 [1990] OJ L192/10.
[128] For other aspects of the litigation, see *supra* 435.

communications equipment it did annul Article 7 of the Directive, which required Member States to ensure the telecommunications monopolies did not enter into certain types of long-term contracts. The Court said that 'anti-competitive conduct engaged in by undertakings on their own initiative' could be dealt with only by individual decisions adopted under Articles 81 and 82 and that Article 86(3) was not an appropriate basis. Likewise in the *Telecommunications Services* case[129] the Court upheld the Commission's right to use Article 86(3) for measures which were necessary for its surveillance function.[130]

The Member States look jealously at the Commission's use of its Article 86(3) powers and the Commission strives to distinguish its surveillance and supervisory powers from other measures. The Open Network Provision Directive,[131] to which the Services Directive was an accompaniment, was adopted under Article 95 (ex Article 100a), because it was a harmonization measure, dealing with the conditions for access to, and use of, public networks and services.

3. ARTICLE 16 EC: SERVICES OF GENERAL ECONOMIC INTEREST AND THE TREATY OF AMSTERDAM

A. THE BACKGROUND TO ARTICLE 16 AND THE COMMISSION'S NOTICE

It will be apparent from the above that much of the case law on Article 86(2) is inconsistent. That may be inevitable. Although it accepts that the (Community) goals of free markets and unrestricted competition may have to give way to the imperative of the (Member States') delivery of public services, Article 86(2) gives little guidance on how the balance is to be struck. This is not, however, an area where the Commission and the Member States line up against each other, for the Member States differ among themselves. Some States (such as France) have different values and priorities from others (such as the UK under the Thatcher and Major governments), and in modern economies the divide between public and private has become increasingly blurred.[132] Ultimately the whole issue comes down to one question: when do non-market considerations trump market concerns?

There was a lively debate in the European Union about liberalization, how public services

---

[129] Cases C–271, 281 & 289/90, *Spain, Belgium & Italy* v. *Commission* [1992] ECR I–5833, [1993] 4 CMLR 110.

[130] Although Art. 8 was annulled on the same grounds as Art. 7 of the Equipment Dir., Dir. 88/301/EEC [1988] OJ L131/73 and the provisions on special rights were annulled for inadequacy of reasons; for this aspect see *supra* 436.

[131] Council Dir. 90/387/EEC [1990] OJ L192/2.

[132] See E.M. Garcia, 'Public Service, Public Services, Public Functions, and Guarantees of the Rights of Citizens: Unchanging Needs in a Changed Context' in M. Freedland and S. Sciarra (eds), *Public Services and Citizenship in European Law* (Clarendon, Oxford, 1998).

should be delivered, and how far competition principles should be modified as regards public services, in the period leading up to the Intergovernmental Conference in 1996. France was in favour of amending Article 86 to remove public services from the competition rules altogether. In September 1996 the Commission produced a paper, *Services of General Interest in Europe,*[133] stressing the importance of services of general interest to the European citizen and the role which they play in promoting social and economic cohesion. Part of the Notice reads:[134]

5. The Community's involvement with services of general interest is within the context of an open economy which is based on a commitment to mutual assistance ('solidarity' for short), social cohesion and market mechanisms.

A. Serving the public

1. Shared values

6. European societies are committed to the general interest services they have created which meet basic needs. These services play an important role as social cement over and above simple practical considerations. They also have a symbolic value, reflecting a sense of community that people can identify with. They form part of the cultural identity of everyday life in all European countries.

7. The roles assigned to general interest services and the special rights which may ensue reflect considerations inherent in the concept of serving the public, such as ensuring that needs are met, protecting the environment, economic and social cohesion, land-use planning and promotion of consumer interests. The particular concern of consumers is to obtain high-quality services at prices they can afford. The sector-specific economic characteristics of the activities they cover also enter into the equation, since they have considerable knock-on effects for the economy and society as a whole and may require the use of scarce resources or large-scale long-term investment. This implies certain basic operating principles: continuity, equal access, universality and openness.

8. Central to all these issues are the interest of the public, which in our societies involves guaranteed access to essential services, and the pursuit of priority objectives.

    . . .

13. The context in which general interest services are provided has changed enormously over recent years and differs in important respects from the context in which they were originally introduced. The major developments are as follows:

    — consumers are becoming increasingly assertive in exercising their rights and desires as users of general interest services, including at European level, and are more demanding in terms of choice, quality and price,

    — worldwide competition is forcing companies using services to seek out better price deals comparable to those enjoyed by their competitors,

    — in contrast to the years immediately following the Second World War, it would now seem that private funding for maintaining and developing infrastructure networks is not as difficult to raise as public resources,

    — new technologies are changing the economic profile of sectors traditionally operated as

---

[133] [1996] OJ C281/3.

[134] There are sections in the Notice relating to specific sectors such as telecommunications, postal services, transport, electricity, and broadcasting (paras. 33–53).

monopolies, such as telecommunications, television and transport, paving the way for new services,

— in certain countries and sectors modernization has been slow to get off the ground, leaving little scope for change.

14. The creation of the single market and the introduction of greater competition requires providers of general interest services to meet the challenge of these developments and turn them to good account by improving range and quality and by lowering prices. This shift goes hand in hand with the implementation of an economic and social cohesion policy. The Community is also helping the modernisation of general interest services to ensure that essential needs continue to be met and to improve performance. This dynamism is the life blood of the European model of society, without which European citizenship will never become a reality.

B. *General interest and the single European market: working for each other*

15. Market forces produce a better allocation of resources and greater effectiveness in the supply of services, the principal beneficiary being the consumer, who gets better quality at a lower price. However, these mechanisms sometimes have their limits; as a result the potential benefits might not extend to the entire population and the objective of promoting social and territorial cohesion may not be attained. The public authority must then ensure that the general interest is taken into account. This is the reason for the Commission's action on the following fronts.

1. *Respecting diversity*

16. The Community's commitment to the European model of society is based on respect for the diversity of the organization of general interest services in Europe, which is underpinned by two basic principles:

 • neutrality as regards the public or private status of companies and their employees, as guaranteed by Article [295] of the Treaty. The Community has nothing to say on whether companies responsible for providing general interest services should be public or private and is not, therefore, requiring privatization. Moreover, the Community will continue to clamp down on unfair practices, regardless of whether the operators concerned are private or public;

 • Member States' freedom to define what are general interest services, to grant the special or exclusive rights that are necessary to the companies responsible for providing them, regulate their management and, where appropriate, fund them, in conformity with Article [86] of the Treaty.

The Commission explained how it defined 'universal service', which it claimed is a European concept ('originated by the Commission'[135]):

28. The basic concept of universal service is to ensure the provision of high-quality service to all at prices everyone can afford. Universal service is defined in terms of principles: equality, universality, continuity and adaptability; and in terms of sound practices: openness in management, price-setting and funding and scrutiny by bodies independent of those operating the services. These criteria are not always all met at national level, but where they have been introduced using the concept of European universal service, there have been positive effects for the development of general interest services.

The Commission concluded that the provision of public interest services is central to the values on which the European model of society is based.[136] The Notice elevates general

---

[135] *Ibid.*, para. 27.
[136] *Ibid*, para. 70.

interest services from merely a ground of derogation to a core element of European culture and a factor promoting European cohesion and solidarity. The Commission suggested (paragraphs 71–74) that a new paragraph should be inserted into Article 3 of the EC Treaty, adding 'a contribution to the promotion of services of general interest' to the activities of the Community.

B. ARTICLE 16

(i) ARTICLE 16 AND ITS PLACE IN THE TREATY

In the event the Commission's suggested amendment was not taken up. Instead, the Treaty of Amsterdam added a new 'Principle', now Article 16, to the EC Treaty:

Without prejudice to Articles 73, 86 and 87,[137] and given the place occupied by services of general economic interest in the shared values of the Union as well as their role in promoting social and territorial cohesion, the Community and the Member States, each within their respective powers and within the scope of application of this Treaty, shall take care that such services operate on the basis of principles and conditions which enable them to fulfil their missions.

The Article is accompanied by a Declaration:

The provisions of Article [16][138] of the Treaty establishing the European Community on public services shall be implemented with full respect for the jurisprudence of the Court of Justice, inter alia as regards the principles of equality of treatment, quality and continuity of such services.

The Treaty of Amsterdam also added a Protocol dealing with public broadcasting to the EC Treaty:[139]

The provisions of the Treaty establishing the European Community shall be without prejudice to the competence of Member States to provide for the funding of public service broadcasting insofar as such funding is granted to broadcasting organisations for the fulfilment of the public service remit as conferred, defined and organised by each Member State, and insofar as such funding does not affect trading conditions and competition in the Community to an extent which would be contrary to the common interest, while the realisation of the remit of that public service shall be taken into account.

(ii) THE INTERPRETATION AND MEANING OF ARTICLE 16

Article 16 has been described as initially appearing 'a triumph for ambiguous drafting and diplomacy insofar as it appears to support any interpretation along a spectrum running from defensive protection by Member States of their existing national public sector influence to the creation of a new *communautaire* concept of public service capable of horizontal application throughout Community law and policy'.[140]

---

[137] Art. 73 concerns transport policy, Art. 87 concerns state aids.

[138] Art. 7D before the renumbering took effect.

[139] In addition a Declaration on public credit institutions in Germany was adopted, and one by Austria and Luxembourg on credit institutions was annexed to the Final Act.

[140] M. Ross, 'Article 16 EC and Services of General Interest: From Derogation to Obligation', (2000) 25 ELRev. 22, 22.

The first thing to notice is that it is placed in the Treaty among the fundamental principles of the Community and so cannot be dismissed as an insignificant side-show. This can be contrasted with the rather confused placing of Article 86 which, as we saw at the beginning of this chapter, appears among the competition provisions despite being expressed to apply to all the rules of the Treaty. It can also be contrasted with Article 295, on national rules of property ownership, which languishes among the 'general and final provisions'. Whatever Article 16 means, the governments of the Member States have accorded it prominence.

The second thing to remark is that it assumes an existing state of affairs. It says '*given* the place occupied by services of general economic interest in the shared values of the Union as well as their role in promoting social and territorial cohesion' (emphasis added), thus accepting as a fact the vision described by the Commission in the Notice.

One interpretation of Article 16 is that, despite its place in the Treaty, it is ultimately no more than political window-dressing, changing nothing of substance. The Article says that it is 'without prejudice' to the existing case law and the annexed Declaration says it must be implemented with 'full respect' for the Court's jurisprudence. However, as we have noted above, the existing case law is far from clear, although the recent trend, seen in *Corbeau*, *Almelo*, and *Albany*,[141] is to interpret the derogation generously. Article 16 could be interpreted as simply giving Member States and entrusted undertakings more ammunition for justifying the latters' privileges and sending a message to the Court to continue on its present path. The Commission's view was that Article 16 reinforced the existing position:[142]

The new Treaty, while retaining the provisions of Article [86], thus reinforces the principle whereby a balance must be struck between the competition rules and the fulfilment of the public services' missions . . .

Regarding competition policy, a new legitimacy has thus been conferred on the main institutional and legal balances in the Treaty of Rome by the provisions contained in the Treaty of Amsterdam, particularly those of the new Article [16].

A further examination of the wording of Article 16, however, reveals that there is a crucial difference from Article 86(2). The latter Article is a derogation, whereas Article 16 puts a positive obligation on both Member States and the Community to ensure that entrusted undertakings are enabled to fulfill their missions by the principles and conditions under which they operate. Ross argues[143] that, although on one level Article 16 may simply be a 'seal of approval' for the existing law on Article 86(2), it may also represent a step forward. In elevating the support of services of general interest to an obligation owed by both the Community institutions and the Member States in the interests of solidarity and social

---

[141] And see also Case C–70/95, *Sodemare* v. *Regione Lombardia* [1997] ECR I–3395, [1998] 4 CMLR 667, where the Court said that Italian rules which provided that only non-profit-making private undertakings could be reimbursed by public authorities for running old people's homes were not against the competition rules.

[142] Commission's *XXVIIth Report on Competition Policy* (Commission, 1997), pts 97 and 100.

[143] M. Ross, 'Article 16 EC and Services of General Interest: From Derogation to Obligation' (2000) 25 ELRev. 22, 31–4.

cohesion, it realigns the Community's priorities and values. It is also been suggested that the values of universal service can provide a basis for conceptualizing the idea of Union citizenship.[144]

4. FURTHER READING

A. BOOKS

BUENIDA SIERRA, J.L., *Exclusive Rights and State Monopolies in EC Law* (Oxford University Press, 1999)

CRAIG, P., and DE BÚRCA, G., *EU Law: Text, Cases and Materials* (2nd edn., Oxford University Press, 1998), Chapter 25

B. ARTICLES

EDWARD, D., and HOSKINS, M., 'Article 90: Deregulation and EC Law. Reflections Arising from the XVI FIDE Conference' (1995) 32 *CMLRev.* 157

GARCIA, E.M., 'Public Service, Public Services, Public Functions, and Guarantees of the Rights of Citizens: Unchanging Needs in a Changed Context' in M. Freedland and S. Sciarra (eds.), *Public Services and Citizenship in European Law* (Clarendon, 1998)

HANCHER, L., 'Casenote on *Corbeau*' (1994) 31 *CMLRev.* 105

—— 'Community, State and Market' in P. Craig and G. de Búrca (eds.), *The Evolution of EU Law* (Oxford, 1999), 721

—— and BUENDIA SIERRA, J.L., 'Cross-Subsidization and EC Law' (1998) 35 *CMLRev.* 901

ROSS, M., 'Article 16 EC and Services of General Interest: From Derogation to Obligation?' (2000) 25 *ELRev.* 22

SAUTER, W., 'Universal Service Obligations and the Emergence of Citizens' Rights in European Telecommunications Liberalization' in M. Freedland and S. Sciarra (eds.), *Public Services and Citizenship in European Law* (Clarendon, 1998)

TESAURO, G., 'The Community's Internal Market in the Light of the Recent Case-law of the Court of Justice' (1995) 15 *YEL* 1

---

[144] *Ibid.*, 34–8; see also W. Sauter, 'Universal Service Obligations and the Emergence of Citizens' Rights in European Telecommunications Liberalization' in M. Freedland and S. Sciarra (eds), *Public Services and Citizenship in European Law* (Clarendon, 1998), 117.

9

DISTRIBUTION AGREEMENTS

1. INTRODUCTION

A. GENERAL

A manufacturer of a product is not solely concerned with manufacturing. It must also plan for the distribution of its products. Generally, the manufacturer will wish to minimize the costs of distribution and to ensure that its products are distributed in the most efficient manner. Broadly, this may be achieved either by doing it itself or by delegating the task to a third party. Similarly, a supplier of a service will need to decide how best to distribute its services.

This Chapter will outline the choices available to a supplier when deciding how best to market and sell its products or services to customers. It will, however, focus on distribution agreements and the competition law problems that such agreements raise.

It has already been mentioned in earlier Chapters of this book that the Commission's approach to vertical distribution agreements has sparked huge controversy and intense debate over the years. The Commission has taken an extremely strict approach to vertical agreements. One of the main reasons for this hostility has been the tendency of such agreements to incorporate territorial restraints and to interfere with the fundamental objective of the Community, the creation of a single market.[1] The extract below from the Commission's Green Paper on Vertical Restraints[2] explains that the Commission has been unwilling to allow private agreements to re-erect the barriers to trade between Member States that it has worked so hard to dismantle.

Green paper on vertical restraints in competition policy, COM(96) 721

70. The ongoing integration process of the Single Market adds an extra dimension to the analysis of vertical restraints. The 1992 programme was the result of a widely held conviction that the failure to achieve a single market has been costing European industry millions in unnecessary costs and lost opportunities. The exact title of the Cecchini Report, 'The cost of Non-Europe' . . . is a clear reflection of this. The efforts made since the entry into force of the EEC Treaty in 1958 had not exhausted

---

[1] See *supra* Chap. 2.
[2] European Commission, Green Paper on Vertical Restraints in EC Competition Policy, COM(96)721.

by the mid-1980's all the potential gains to be expected from the full economic integration of the economies of the Member States. Now that more steps have been taken to eliminate the remaining obstacles to the free movement of goods, services and factors of production, it is still apparent that further efforts are necessary to achieve the maximum possible level of integration. . . .

. . .

78. The EC experience shows that the removal of non-tariff barriers is not sufficient for the full development of parallel trade, arbitrage and changes in distribution across Europe. For the complete success of economic integration it is necessary that producers, distributors and consumers, find it profitable to move towards the new market situation and do not take actions to avoid or counteract the effects of the Single Market measures. The elimination of barriers to trade may not achieve its objectives if producers and/or distributors introduce practices contrary to integration. Unfortunately in many cases it is likely that they have strong incentives to do so.

The relentless stream of criticism that the Commission's approach to vertical restraints generally has provoked, charging it with a failure to take a sufficiently economic approach when dealing with vertical restraints and stultifying innovation in the distribution process, has eventually led the Commission to introduce changes. Of enormous importance has been its adoption of a block exemption on vertical restraints, Regulation 2790/1999 (the 'Verticals Regulation') which applies to all vertical agreements that meet its criteria.[3] The Commission's analysis of vertical restraints and agency agreements is elaborated upon in its *Guidelines on Vertical Restraints* (the 'Guidelines').[4] The enactment of this block exemption and the accompanying Guidelines heralds a new, more economic, approach to vertical agreements generally.

B. METHODS OF DISTRIBUTION

(i) FACTORS AFFECTING CHOICE

The method of distribution selected by a supplier is likely to be determined after consideration of a wide range of factors. In particular, the nature of the product or service, the nature of the market, the size and resources of the supplier, and any tax or legal implications will be relevant to the assessment. In addition, the decision may be affected by competition rules. This is possible where the rules are applied more stringently to some forms of distribution than to others.

(ii) VERTICAL INTEGRATION

A supplier which wishes to retain maximum control over distribution may take charge of it itself. This may be appealing to a manufacturer with considerable resources seeking to sell a highly complex product or to a manufacturer seeking to sell a high volume of low-margin products.[5] The manufacturer may set up a distribution arm (internal growth) or may acquire an undertaking that is already in the distribution business (external growth).

---

[3] [1999] OJ L336/21, [2000] 4 CMLR 398.

[4] [2000] OJ C291/1.

[5] This mode of distribution may become an increasingly popular option if the Internet takes off as a successful method of distribution.

A decision to move into distribution may, however, be impractical and an inefficient use of a firm's resources.

Retailers commonly secure economies of scope by offering the consumer under one roof dozens or even thousands of products, often gathered together from a diversity of manufacturers. It would be prohibitively costly for the manufacturer of paper towels, crescent wrenches, or anti-biotics to establish its own retail distribution facilities in order to control the conditions under which its product is resold to consumers. And even when there is a reasonably close fit between manufacturer product line and retail outlets' scope, as automobiles, major appliances, or photo supplies, the two stages require quite different skills, attitudes, and spans of managerial focus, and the advantages of specialization typically require that retailers be kept separate organizationally from their primary suppliers.[6]

In many cases a supplier will, therefore, consider it preferable to leave distribution to entities that are experienced in retailing and which know more about the markets and customers to be targeted. In particular, local distributors may be able to penetrate foreign markets more quickly and effectively.

(iii) AGENCY

Whether or not a supplier decides to appoint an agent or an independent distributor will be dependent mainly on the independence it wishes the third party to be given, the risk it wishes to bear, and the responsibilities of the supplier on the termination of the relationship. Ordinarily, the functions of an agent are restricted and limited to finding customers and negotiating sales with them on behalf of the principal. In its *Guidelines on Vertical Restraints* the Commission has defined agency agreements to cover:[7]

[T]he situation in which a legal or physical person (the agent) is vested with the power to negotiate and/or conclude contracts on behalf of another person (the principal), either in the agent's own name or in the name of the principal, for the:

— purchase of goods or services by the principal, or
— sale of goods or services supplied by the principal.

Commercial agents in the Community must be compensated on termination of the agency.[8]

(iv) DISTRIBUTION THROUGH INDEPENDENT DISTRIBUTORS

Alternatively, distribution may be left to a distributor that will itself sell or use the goods or supply the services.[9] A distribution agreement will be necessary. A supplier may simply

---

[6] F.M. Scherer and D. Ross, *Industrial Market Structure and Economic Performance* (3rd edn., Houghton Mifflin, Boston, Mass., 1990), 542.

[7] *Guidelines on Vertical Restraints*, [2000] OJ C291/1, para. 12.

[8] Council Dir. 86/653 on the co-ordination of the laws of the Member States relating to self-employed commercial agents [1986] OJ L382/17. See also the UK implementing legislation, the Commercial Agents (Council Directive) Reg. 1993, SI 1993/3053.

[9] In some cases the dealer will not just resell the product supplied but may use a raw material or component to produce another product.

wish to ensure that its products or services are distributed through as many outlets as possible. Alternatively or additionally restrictions and obligations limiting the number or type of distributors or restricting the conduct of the distributors may be considered necessary to make the distribution agreement commercially viable and/or acceptable.[10] For example:

- the area within which the distributor can resell may be *restricted (territorial restrictions)*;
- the distributor may be precluded from manufacturing, buying, marketing and/or selling competing products or services (*non-compete obligations*) or required to purchase a specific percentage or a specific amount of its requirements of a type of product from a supplier (*quantity forcing*);[11]
- the distributor may be obliged or have incentives to purchase a specific brand of product exclusively from the supplier (in the *Guidelines on Vertical Restraints* the Commission describes this kind of obligation as an *exclusive purchasing commitment*. The exclusive purchasing commitment does not preclude the distributor from purchasing competing goods or services from another supplier (non-compete provisions as described above[12]));
- the minimum price at which the products are to be resold may be fixed (*resale price maintenance*);
- a distributor may be granted an exclusive territory in which to sell the product or provide the service (*exclusive distribution*);
- the type or number of outlets in which the manufacturer's products are sold may be limited (*selective distribution*);
- distributors may be required to make specific services available to customers or engage in active promotion of the products (common where selective distribution, exclusive distribution or resale price arrangements are adopted);
- distributors may be required not to open a competing business for a certain period after the distribution agreement has been terminated. Such an obligation may be of particular importance in a *franchising agreement* where a supplier, a franchisor, grants the right to a dealer, a franchisee, to exploit a franchise and to set up a business marketing specified goods or services as part of a uniform business network established by the franchisor. The franchising agreement will ordinarily authorize the use of intellectual and industrial property rights, such as trade marks and know-how, to enable and to aid the franchisee to resell the goods and services.

---

[10] For the positive effects and the justifications for imposing vertical restraints, see *infra* 485 ff.

[11] See the definition of non-compete obligation in Reg 2790/1999, Art 1(b), set out *infra* 534.

[12] The Commission describes 'exclusive purchasing agreements' in its *Guidelines on Vertical Restraints* as 'where an obligation or incentive scheme agreed between the supplier and the buyer makes the latter purchase it requirements for a particular product, for instance beer of brand X, exclusively from the designated supplier'. The exclusive purchasing obligation may leave the buyer free to purchase competing products, for instance competing brands of beer, but is frequently backed by a non-compete obligation, a prohibition on selling competing products: see e.g. Case C–234/89, *Delimitis v. Henninger Bräu* [1991] ECR I–935, [1992] 5 CMLR 210, para. 10.

C. COMPETITION RULES AND DISTRIBUTION

(i) THE IMPACT OF THE COMPETITION RULES ON METHODS OF DISTRIBUTION

It will be seen from the discussion below that a decision to distribute products through an independent distributor raises the most significant problems from a competition law perspective in the European Community.

(ii) VERTICAL INTEGRATION

A producer that decides to set up its own distribution arm is unlikely to encounter difficulties with EC competition law. Agreements concluded between it and an entity forming part of the same economic unit are not caught by Article 81. Only if the undertaking is dominant may the distribution arrangements attract the attention of the EC authorities.[13] Further, integration through external growth will rarely cause competition law difficulties. Although 'vertical' mergers between undertakings may be notifiable to the European Commission the Commission is not ordinarily concerned with such mergers unless they have serious foreclosure effects.[14]

(iii) AGENCY

a. GENUINE AND NON-GENUINE AGENCY AGREEMENTS

In the *Guidelines on Vertical Restraints* the Commission recognizes that, in certain circumstances, agents may play an auxiliary function similar to that played by an employee. The selling or purchasing function of an agent may form 'part of the principal's activities, despite the fact that the agent is a separate undertaking'.[15] The Guidelines distinguish between 'genuine' and 'non-genuine' agency agreements.

Where the agency is 'genuine' the agency agreement, and all obligations imposed on the agent (including territorial, customer, and price restraints), falls outside Article 81(1)[16] unless the agreement contains a non-compete provision which leads to foreclosure on the relevant market or:

facilitates collusion. This could for instance be the case when a number of principals use the same agents while collectively excluding others from using these agents, or when they use the agents to collude on marketing strategy or to exchange sensitive market information between the principals.[17]

In contrast, where the agency is 'non-genuine' the agent is treated as an independent dealer, free to determine his own strategy to recoup investment costs. In such cases Article 81 may

---

[13] See discussion of the single economic entity doctrine, *supra* in Chap. 3.

[14] Concentrations with a Community dimension must be notified to the Commission. See the discussion of mergers, *infra* in Chap. 12.

[15] *Guidelines on Vertical Restraints*, [2000] OJ C291/1, para. 15.

[16] *Ibid.*, para. 18–19.

[17] *Ibid.*, para. 20.

apply to the agreements in the same way as it applies to other distribution agreements. Article 81(1) may be of relevance where an agency agreement contains provisions preventing the agent from acting for an undertaking which competes with the principal (non-compete provisions). The Commission indicates, however, that a provision preventing the principal from appointing other agents in respect of a given type of transaction, customer, or territory (exclusive agency provisions) will in general not have anti-competitive effects since they affect only intra-brand competition.[18] Agency agreements which fall within Article 81(1) may benefit from the Verticals Regulation, Regulation 2790/1999,[19] if the conditions set out in that regulation are met.[20]

The Commission's Guidelines (paragraphs 12–20) set out guidance on how to distinguish between 'genuine' and 'non-genuine' agency agreements. These Guidelines replace[21] the Commission's 1962 Notice on exclusive dealing contracts with commercial agents.[22]

b. THE DETERMINING FACTOR—RISK

The determining factor in assessing whether an agency agreement is 'genuine' is 'the financial or commercial risk borne by the agent in relation to the activities for which he has been appointed as an agent by the principal.'[23] The importance of risk in making this assessment has been stressed by the ECJ.[24] The agency will be genuine where the agent does not bear any or only insignificant risk, and non-genuine where he does accept the risk. Two types of risk are material in the determination:

First there are the risks which are directly related to the contracts concluded and/or negotiated by the agent on behalf of the principal, such as financing of stocks. Secondly, there are the risks related to market-specific investments. These are investments specifically required for the type of activity for which the agent has been appointed by the principal, i.e. which are required to enable the agent to conclude and/or negotiate this type of contract. Such investments are usually sunk, if upon leaving that particular field of activity the investment cannot be used for other activities or sold other than at a significant loss.[25]

Risks connected with agency income are not relevant. Risk must be assessed on a case-by-case basis. The Commission looks to the economic reality, not the form of the agency.

c. THE PASSING OF PROPERTY AND THE SUPPLY OF SERVICES

Article 81(1) is unlikely to apply where, subject to certain conditions, the property in the contract goods bought or sold on behalf of the principal does not vest in the agent or the contract services are not supplied by the agent. A non-exhaustive list of factors[26] indicating

---

[18] See *infra* 485 ff.

[19] [1999] OJ L336/21.

[20] For a discussion of the regulation see *infra* 532 ff.

[21] *Guidelines on Vertical Restraints,* [2000] OJ C291/1, n. 7.

[22] Notice on exclusive dealing contracts with commercial agents [1962] JO L39/2921.

[23] *Guidelines on Vertical Restraints, supra* n. 4, para. 13.

[24] In Case C–266/93, *Bundeskartellamt v. Volkswagen & VAG Leasing* [1996] ECR I–3477, [1996] 4 CMLR 505, para. 45 the Court held that risk was crucial in the determination of whether or not an agent should be characterized as an independent trader or as an entity operating as an auxiliary organ forming an integral part of the principal's undertaking.

[25] *Guidelines on Vertical Restraints,* [2000] OJ C291/1, para. 14.

[26] *Ibid.,* para. 17.

that such an agreement is a genuine agency is set out in paragraph 16. It may be important, for example, that the agent does not incur the costs relating to the supply/purchase of the contract goods or services (such as transport), does not invest in sales promotion, does not maintain its own cost or risk contract goods, does not create or operate an after-sales service, does not make market-specific investments, does not incur product liability, and does not take responsibility for the customers' non-performance of the contract.

(iii) DISTRIBUTION AGREEMENTS

a. RESTRAINTS ON CONDUCT AND RESTRICTIONS OF COMPETITION— THE PROBLEM

Distribution agreements concluded between producers and independent distributors generally contain restraints on the conduct of one or more of the parties. A key question arising is whether or not these restraints on conduct should be characterized as restrictions of competition for the purposes of Article 81(1) or, indeed, whether or not vertical agreements should fall within that provision at all.[27] Although economic theory supports a suspicion of horizontal agreements '[e]conomists are much more equivocal about vertical agreements, between firms at different stages of the value-added chain'.[28]

b. THE POSITIVE AND NEGATIVE EFFECTS OF VERTICAL RESTRAINTS

From the late 1960s lawyers and economists in the Chicago school argued that competition law should rarely, if at all, be troubled by vertical restraints which lead to increased sales and to the minimization of distribution costs. They propounded the view that a manufacturer will impose vertical restraints on *intra-brand* competition (competition between distributors of the supplier's product or service) only where necessary to enhance sales of its product and to encourage *inter-brand* competition (competition between the manufacturer and producers of competing products).

One of the main arguments is that vertical restraints are frequently necessary to enable a supplier to protect its distributors from *free riders*. Vertical agreements imposing resale price maintenance, awarding a distributor an exclusive distribution territory, or restricting supplies to selected retailers may be essential to encourage distributors to provide additional services necessary to boost sales and to persuade consumers to purchase more of the manufacturer's product. In the absence of such restraints,[29] distributors will be unwilling to incur the cost of providing additional services since other distributors will be able to take a 'free ride' on their investment.

Bork went further, arguing that not only was the rationale for the imposition of vertical restraints obvious, but their implication for economic efficiency was clear. A manufacturer would only ever impose vertical restraints in order to achieve distributive efficiency.[30] If the manufacturer wrongly required distributors to provide services that customers did not want, or did not consider to be worth the increase in price, those consumers would purchase

---

[27] See *supra* Chap. 4 and *infra* 503 ff.

[28] F. Fishwick, *Making Sense of Competition Policy* (Kogan Page, 1993), 56.

[29] Such as the grant of an exclusive distribution territory or the imposition of resale price maintenance.

[30] See *infra* 486.

rival products instead. The market itself would provide retribution for a manufacturer's mistaken belief that a vertical restraint was desirable.

The extract below from an article by Comanor explains these free-rider and distributive efficiency arguments more fully.

W. S. Comanor, 'Vertical price-fixing, vertical market restrictions, and the new antitrust policy' (1985) 98 *Harv, Rev.* 983, 986–90

Building on earlier studies . . . Lester Telser offered a detailed explanation of why manufacturers benefit from resale price maintenance [L. Telser, 'Why Should Manufacturers Want Fair Trade?, 3 *J.L. & E.* 86 (1960)] As he observed, because the quantity sold of a manufacturer's product depends on the final price paid by consumers, the manufacturer normally stands to gain from competition among dealers that limits the distribution margin. Only if other factors intervene can the manufacturer benefit from restraints on competition among his dealers . . .

Telser's primary explanation centered on the distributor's role in furnishing 'services' along with the manufactured product. By 'services,' Telser referred not only to delivery, credit, and repair, but also to selling, advertising, and promotional activities. . . In short . . . all factors supplied by the distributor that may influence demand for the manufacturer's product. The provision of these services benefits the manufacturer as long as the positive effect on demand outweighs the depressing effect of the accompanying rise in price.

The manufacturer, however, can influence the level of services furnished only by limiting competition among his distributors. He cannot simply lower his price in the hope that distributors will use their increased revenues to finance the appropriate services. Even if some distributors will do so— recognizing that greater sales result from providing services jointly with the product—others will not, and might compete by setting a lower price. The result is the classic 'free rider' problem:

> Sales are diverted from the retailers who do provide the special services at the higher price to the retailers who do not provide the special services and offer to sell the product at the lower price. The mechanism is simple. A customer, because of the special services provided by one retailer, is persuaded to buy the product. But he purchases the product from another paying the latter a lower price. In this way the retailers who do not provide the special services get a free ride at the expense of those who have convinced consumers to buy the product . . .

In order to remain competitive with free riders, other distributors will cease to provide the requisite services . . . Thus, fewer services will be offered and total sales of the product will be lower than they would be otherwise . . . The solution, according to Telser, is for manufacturers to establish minimum retail prices, forcing retailers 'to compete by providing special services,' . . . and thereby eliminating the free-rider problem . . .

Telser's analysis explains why manufacturers would wish to impose vertical restraints. What it does not do, nor claim to do, is answer the question whether dealers' provision of additional services is efficient—that is, whether the additional services justify the higher price charged for the product . . .

Judge Bork wrote the first article directly addressing the implications of vertical restraints for economic efficiency [R.H. Bork, *The Rule of Reason and the per se* Concept: Price Fixing and Market Division (pt. 2) 75 *Yale LJ*, 373 (1966)]. His test was simple: restrictions on output are anticompetitive, and increases in output are procompetitive. Using this criterion, Bork concluded that all restraints imposed by manufacturers *must* be efficiency-enhancing and procompetitive . . .

According to Bork, because a manufacturer will impose vertical restraints only if they lead to increased output and, in turn, to increased profits, such restraints must be procompetitive . . . his position assumes that the interests of manufacturers and consumers fully coincide.

The reasoning behind Bork's theory, which appears to have gained acceptance among both lawyers and economists, is that manufacturers will not find it profitable to impose vertical restraints when customers do not find the value of the new services exceeds their incremental cost. Otherwise a rival manufacturer would surely offer the product without the additional services and lure customers away.

The government's . . . brief in *Spray-Rite* adopts precisely this position. Monsanto, the manufacturer whose products were distributed by Spray-Rite, believed that demand for its products was unnecessarily low because many potential customers understood neither which Monsanto herbicides were appropriate for particular farming needs, nor the proper method of applying the products.' To spur the dissemination of information and avoid free-rider problems, the company initiated a policy of vertical restraints. The government argued that the restraints were pro-competitive:

> [A]lthough vertical restrictions increase both dealer costs and price, such restrictions will be unprofitable for the manufacturer unless they also increase the quantities of product that dealers sell. This is the critical, pro-competitive respect in which such vertical restrictions differ from a mere widening of dealer margins, which would increase price but *reduce* quantities of product sold. Indeed, the manufacturer usually will anticipate that its marketing program will enable its dealers to increase their prices, precisely so that they can recover their added costs. That is true whether the manufacturer uses restricted sales territories, location clauses, exclusive dealing arrangements, or some other vertical restriction. [Brief for the United States as Amicus Curiae in Support of Petitioner, *Spray-Rite* (No. 82–914)]

This extract stresses the positive effects that may result from vertical restraints, even price restraints imposing resale price maintenance. The imposition of resale prices may be necessary to encourage retailers to compete on non-price criteria, such as service and promotion, to protect a retailer's reputation for providing high-quality services and stocking high-quality products and to facilitate market entry by a new competitor or an undertaking producing a new product. In each case the imposition of resale prices prevents other retailers from free riding on the retailer's efforts.

The Commission in its *Guidelines on Vertical Restraints* shows that it is fully aware of the benefits that vertical restraints may bring, recognizing that '[w]hen a company has no market power, it can only try to increase its profits by optimising its manufacturing or distribution processes'.[31] Consequently, it accepts that vertical restraints may be essential to the realization of efficiencies and the development of new markets. In paragraphs 115–118 it summarizes the positive effects that vertical restraints may bring, especially the promotion of non-price competition and the improved quality of service.

In paragraph 116 a number of justifications for the imposition of certain vertical restraints are listed. In particular, it is recognized that vertical restraints may be essential:

(i) to prevent free riding on pre-sales services, for example by the allocation of an exclusive territory to a distributor, or the imposition of a non-compete obligation;

(ii) to induce a distributor to engage in sufficient investment to enable a manufacturer to enter a new geographic market, for example, by the allocation of an exclusive territory to a distributor;

(iii) to introduce a new product on a market, for example, by appointing an exclusive distributor or establishing a selective distribution system;

(iv) to encourage client-specific investment;

[31] *Guidelines on Vertical Restraints*, [2000] OJ C291/1, para. 115.

(v)   to protect know-how transferred under a distribution agreement, for example, by the imposition of non-compete restrictions;

(vi)   to enable a manufacturer to exploit economies of scale and to realize lower prices, for example, by using exclusive or selective distribution systems or quantity forcing provisions;

(vii)   to provide security in respect of loans made in the terms of the agreement, for example, through the use of exclusivity provisions; and/ or

(viii) to increase sales by creating a brand image and increasing the attractiveness of a product to the final consumer, for example, through the use of selective distribution or franchising agreements.

It should be added that vertical restraints may enable a manufacturer to distribute its product in a way which minimizes transaction costs[32] and/or which ensures the distributor's commitment to the sale of its products.[33]

The fact that vertical restraints might provide positive effects does not, however, mean that all commentators take the view that the imposition of vertical restraints is always justified and that such restraints will inevitably result in distributive efficiency.[34]

[E]conomists are becoming more cautious in their assessment of vertical restraints with respect to competition policy and less willing to make sweeping generalisations, and vertical restraints cannot all be regarded as *per se* beneficial for competition.[35]

Comanor, for example, criticized the assumption that restraints would always lead to the most efficient result. The theory failed to attach sufficient importance to the different preferences of consumers for extra dealer-provided services and to distinguish between marginal and infra-marginal consumers.

The 'marginal consumer' is one whose valuation of the product approximates to its current price. This consumer is, therefore, sensitive to improvements leading to an increase in the market price of a product. He will purchase more of the product only if he considers that the improvement in service or quality of the product is worth the increase in its price. If he does not he will generally purchase less. In contrast 'infra-marginal consumers' are consumers that place a value on the product substantially higher than the original price. Such consumers are relatively insensitive to increases in price. They will,

---

[32] The appointment of a single distributor may minimize distribution costs: see *infra* 506–507.

[33] Obligations requiring a dealer to purchase all of its requirements of a product from the supplier (an exclusive purchasing commitment) and not to handle competing goods (a non-compete obligation) encourage distributors to promote the supplier's product actively.

[34] 'As on several other fronts, the debate over vertical restraints can be characterized with only mild imprecision as a contest between the University of Chicago . . . and the rest of the world. And as in other areas, the 'Chicago school' has through superior organization, fervor, . . . and timing, if not superior access to revealed truth, sent the rest of the world reeling. But as competing in the marketplace of ideas continued, serious weaknesses in the Chicago position materialized': F. M. Scherer and D. Ross, *Industrial Market Structure and Economic Performance* (3rd edn., Houghton Mifflin, 1990), 541.

[35] European Commission, Green Paper on Vertical Restraints in EC Competition Policy, COM(96)721, para. 54. See, e.g. W.S. Comanor, *Vertical Price-Fixing, Vertical Market Restrictions, and the New Antitrust Policy* (1984–1985) 98 Harv. Law Rev 983 and J.J. Flynn, *The 'Is' and 'Ought' of Vertical Restraints After Monsanto Co. v. Spray-Rite Service Corp.*, (1985–1986) 71 *Cornell L. Rev.* 1095.

therefore, not refrain from purchasing the product on an increase in price even if, in their view, the improvement in the quality of the products did not merit that increase in price.[36]

In the view of Comanor 'societal gains or losses from changes in the product depend on the preferences of *all* consumers, not merely those at the margin. To the extent that such alterations fail to reflect the preferences of infra-marginal consumers, the interests of consumers in general may not be served'.[37]

W. S. Comanor, *Vertical price-fixing, vertical market restrictions, and the new antitrust policy* [1985] 98 *Harv. Law Rev.* 983, 992–9

Suppose, for example, that the service in question is the provision of information about how to use a product. Consumers who are 'ignorant' about the product value this information and are willing to pay more for it. For 'knowledgeable' consumers—those already familiar with the product—the opposite is true: this class of consumers is unwilling to pay the increased price for the product necessary to fund the information services.

Assume further that a large number of infra-marginal consumers are 'knowledgeable.' Many of the consumers in this class may be previous customers who originally learned about the product from outside sources of from advertising provided directly by the manufacturer. The 'ignorant' consumers, we may assume, are largely marginal. Perhaps they value the product less than 'knowledgeable' consumers do simply because they are uncertain of its merits.

Because marginal consumers desire the information services, the manufacturer will impose vertical restraints. But this action may not lead to an efficient result: the interests of 'knowledgeable' infra-marginal consumers must also be taken into account. If they are great in number, the harm caused by making them pay for unwanted services may exceed the benefit derived by marginal consumers. Thus, the mere fact that the services are profitable for the manufacturer is not sufficient evidence that all—or even most—consumers benefit from their supply . . . In short, these services may be oversupplied in relation to the consumer optimum . . .

Economic theory alone cannot predict whether the imposition of vertical restraints—and dealers' provision of additional services—will benefit consumers and enhance efficiency. Whether consumers benefit depends on whether gains to marginal consumers outweigh losses to their infra-marginal counterparts. Because such losses may predominate—particularly when the restraints are used to support services for established products—consumer harm may result.'

In this extract Commanor stresses therefore that vertical restraints which are profitable to a manufacturer may not always achieve economic efficiency. They may lead to a reduction in consumer welfare as a whole. In particular, vertical restraints imposed to promote the sale of established products may induce distributors to supply an excessive level of information services. In contrast, where consumers must be persuaded to purchase new products vertical restraints are less likely to harm consumer welfare. Consumers will require more information to entice them to purchase the products.

---

[36] W.S. Comanor, *Vertical Price-Fixing, Vertical Market Restrictions, and the New Antitrust Policy* (1984–1985) 98 Harv. Law Rev 983, 991.

[37] *Ibid.*

Several other concerns also cause scepticism about the necessity or legitimacy in all cases of vertical restraints, even those that limit only intra-brand competition.[38]

In the Community, there is a unique concern that agreements which impose territorial restrictions on dealers whilst restricting only intra-brand competition lead to the division of markets on national lines in contravention of the single market objective. This is an extremely important point, since this factor has affected the Community institution's approach to vertical restraints when applying Article 81(1), (3), and Article 82.

Further, and more generally, it is feared that restrictions on intra-brand competition may reinforce horizontal agreements, push up prices, and weaken inter-brand competition.

The imposition of resale prices, for example, may reinforce horizontal agreements, at either the manufacturers' or distributors' level. They may preclude distributors from pushing manufacturers for lower prices and provide a simple way for suppliers to prevent cheating on a cartel. Alternatively, they may be imposed as a result of colluding retailers cajoling or coercing suppliers.[39] There has also been concern that the free rider argument, used to justify many vertical restraints on intra-brand competition, especially resale price maintenance, exclusive distribution and selective distribution, is frequently exaggerated and in fact applies to only relatively few products.[40] In addition, if practices such as resale price maintenance and selective distribution are widespread, retailers engaging in significant price discounts will be eliminated from the market. Consumers may be deprived of innovative retailing and price discounting and prices may increase.[41]

Vertical agreements can also be used as a way of softening price competition between manufacturers. It is frequently alleged by consumer bodies that this is the intended effect of selective distribution. The argument is that selective distribution can be used by the manufacturer to increase his prices by reducing intra-brand competition. His increased prices may then encourage rival manufacturers to

---

[38] 'When the market is concentrated and manufacturers or distributors have market power, vertical restraints may be used to exploit consumers directly, or to put costs on competitors or raise barriers to entry, thus creating market power and inducing exploitation. The manufacturer may use the distributor to help it exploit the customer, and the manufacturer and distributor may share the extra gains': G. A. Bermann, R. J. Goebel, W. J. Davey, and E. M. Fox, *Cases and Materials on European Community Law* (West Publishing Company, 1993), 720.

[39] F. M. Scherer and D. Ross, *Industrial Market Structure and Economic Performance* (3rd edn.,) (Houghton Mifflin, 1990), 550.

[40] It applies only to pre-sales services (not post-sales services). Pre-sales services are unnecessary where the consumer knows what he wants to buy (see the extract from W. S. Comanor, 'Vertical Price-Fixing, Vertical Market Restrictions, and the New Antitrust Policy' (1984–1985) 98 *Harv. Rev.* 983 set out *supra*) and the free-rider argument is justified only in purchases of relatively high value. 'The consumer who secures from her friendly local hardware store a ten-minute demonstration of a $1.79 potato peeler's merits and then makes a special trip to the discount house to buy one is a candidate for something other than center stage in the economic theory of shopping behaviour', F. M. Scherer and D. Ross, *Industrial Market Structure and Economic Performance* (3rd edn.,) (Houghton Mifflin, 1990), 552.

[41] T. R. Overstreet, *Resale Price Maintenance: Economic Theories and Empirical Evidence* (Federal Trade Commission Bureau of Economics staff report, Nov. 1983). This report indicated that the more widespread practice of resale price maintenance in Europe delayed the arrival of supermarkets. Many cases involving selective distribution arise as a result of complaints or action by consumers or retailers that have been refused supply; e.g., in the UK the Director General of Fair Trading referred the issue of perfumes to the then Monopolies and Mergers Commission, as a result of complaints that chains such as Superdrug had been refused supply by the main perfume houses. The Monopolies and Mergers Commission, however, concluded that the complex monopoly situation did not operate against the public interest: see its *Report on Fine Fragrances*, Cm 2380, (TSO, 1993).

increase their prices (*i.e.* a reduction in inter-brand competition). On this view, selective distribution by a group of rival manufacturers is akin to tacit collusion. Exclusive distribution may have a similar effect as it also reduces intra-brand competition. Exclusive dealership where a manufacturer sells his products in outlets that stock only his products ie non-compete obligations has a more direct effect on inter-brand competition by removing other brands from the outlet. Again, if all manufacturers used exclusive dealership, this might be considered akin to collusion. Resale price maintenance (RPM) is another vertical restraint that can be akin to collusion. RPM directly reduces both intra-brand and inter-brand competition.[42]

Another vital concern is that vertical restraints may actually affect and stifle inter-brand competition. Obligations requiring dealers not to handle competing goods may foreclose the market to competitors.[43] Some writers have suggested that the foreclosure resulting from the imposition of vertical restraints should be the sole concern for competition authorities:

> Overall, the contribution of the economic literature on vertical restraints has been to establish that there should be no competition policy intervention, except where they are used strategically by the incumbent to foreclose the market to a new entrant, essentially by reducing rival manufacturers' access to downstream distributors.[44]

The Commission indicates in the Guidelines that its anxieties about vertical restraints are relatively broad. In particular, it fears that vertical restraints may foreclose the market, reduce rivalry and facilitate collusion between undertakings operating on the market, reduce intra-brand competition, and create obstacles to the single market.

103. The negative effects on the market that may result from vertical restraints which EC competition law aims at preventing are the following:

    (i)   Foreclosure of other suppliers or other buyers by raising barriers to entry;

    (ii) Reduction of inter-brand competition between the companies operating on a market, including facilitation of collusion amongst suppliers or buyers . . .;

    (iii) Reduction of intra-brand competition between distributors of the same brand;

    (iv) The creation of obstacles to market integration, including, above all, limitations on the freedom of consumers to purchase goods or services in any Member State they may choose.

104. Such negative effects may result from various vertical restraints. Agreements which are different in form may have the same substantive impact on competition. To analyse these possible negative effects, it is appropriate to divide vertical restraints into four groups: a single branding group, a limited distribution group, a resale price maintenance group and a market partitioning group. . . .

In order to assess the effects of vertical restraints the Commission thus divides distribution agreements into four different categories that include similar types of restraints, single branding, limited distribution, resale price maintenance, and market partitioning groups, and analyses the competition problems that each type of agreement may pose.

The Commission describes *single branding* agreements as those in which a buyer is

---

[42] S. Bishop and M. Walker, *The Economics of EC Competition Law: Concepts, Application and Measurement* (Sweet & Maxwell, 1999), para. 4.35.

[43] Provisions in a contract which require a distributor to purchase a product only from the supplier and not to purchase for resale competing goods, or other similar tying and requirements contracts, may preclude competitors from gaining access to retail outlets. Similarly exclusive supply contracts may preclude the buyer's competitors from gaining access to an essential source of supply.

[44] London Economics, *Competition in Retailing* (OFT Research Paper No 13, 1997).

induced to concentrate orders for a type of product with one supplier. This category includes agreements containing clauses that result in a buyer purchasing products or their substitutes only from one supplier such as non-compete or quantity forcing provisions. The Commission is concerned that these agreements may foreclose the market to competitors, make market shares more rigid, facilitate collusion between suppliers, limit in-store inter-brand competition, and lead to higher prices for buyers.

107. There are four main negative effects on competition: (1) other suppliers in that market cannot sell to the particular buyers and this may lead to foreclosure of the market or, in the case of tying, to foreclosure of the market for the tied product; (2) it makes market shares more rigid and this may help collusion when applied by several suppliers; (3) as far as the distribution of final goods is concerned, the particular retailers will only sell one brand and there will therefore be no inter-brand competition in their shops (no in-store competition); and (4) in the case of tying, the buyer may pay a higher price for the tied product than he would otherwise do. All these effects may lead to a reduction in inter-brand competition.

108. The reduction in inter-brand competition may be mitigated by strong initial competition between suppliers to obtain the single branding contracts, but the longer the duration of the non-compete obligation, the more likely it will be that this effect will not be strong enough to compensate for the reduction in inter-brand competition.

Limited distribution agreements are those in which the producer sells to only one or a limited number of buyers, for example, exclusive distribution, exclusive supply (where an obligation or incentive scheme makes the supplier sell only or mainly to one buyer), or selective distribution arrangements. The Commission notes that these agreements may foreclose the purchase market, may facilitate collusion between suppliers or distributors and, by severely limiting intra-brand competition, weaken inter-brand competition.

110. There are three main negative effects on competition: (1) certain buyers within that market can no longer buy from that particular supplier, and this may lead in particular in the case of exclusive supply, to foreclosure of the purchase market, (2) when most or all of the competing suppliers limit the number of retailers, this may facilitate collusion, either at the distributor's level or at the supplier's level, and (3) since fewer distributors will offer the product it will also lead to a reduction of intra-brand competition. In the case of wide exclusive territories or exclusive customer allocation the result may be total elimination of intra-brand competition. This reduction of intra-brand competition can in turn lead to a weakening of inter-brand competition.

The Commission also considers that agreements obliging or inducing a buyer not to sell below a certain price, at a certain price or not above a certain price, the *resale price maintenance* group, will both reduce intra-brand competition and lead to increased transparency on prices. These factors may make horizontal collusion between manufacturers or distributors easier, especially in concentrated markets.

112. There are two main negative effects of RPM on competition: (1) a reduction in intra-brand price competition, and (2) increased transparency on prices. In the case of fixed or minimum RPM, distributors can no longer compete on price for that brand, leading to a total elimination of intra-brand price competition. A maximum or recommended price may work as a focal point for resellers, leading to a more or less uniform application of that price level. Increased transparency on price and responsibility for price changes makes horizontal collusion between manufacturers or distributors easier, at least in concentrated markets. The

reduction in intra-brand competition may, as it leads to less downward pressure on the price for the particular goods, have as an indirect effect a reduction of inter-brand competition.

Finally, the Commission expresses the belief that agreements within the *market partitioning* groups, in which the buyer is restricted in where it either sources[45] or resells[46] a particular product, may reduce intra-brand competition and help the supplier to partition the market and to hinder market integration. Further, the limitation of sourcing or resale possibilities of buyers may facilitate collusion at both the distributors' and suppliers' level.

114. The main negative effect on competition is a reduction of intra-brand competition that may help the supplier to partition the market and thus hinder market integration. This may facilitate price discrimination. When most or all of the competing suppliers limit the sourcing or resale possibilities of their buyers this may facilitate collusion, either at the distributors' level or at the suppliers' level.

In this section we have seen that vertical restraints enable efficiencies to be achieved but may also result in an anti-competitive outcome. These pro- and anti-competitive effects have caused many competition lawyers and economists to disagree violently about when vertical restraints cause anti-competitive harm and as to how any such harm should be reconciled with the efficiencies that vertical restraints may generate.

Before we summarize the Community approach to vertical restraints a brief look at the experience in the USA is helpful. The approach of the US authorities has provoked and reflected much of the economic debate concerning the legitimacy of vertical restraints.

c. *PER SE* ILLEGALITY AND THE RULE OF REASON——THE APPROACH IN THE US

In the USA, as in the European Community, the analysis of vertical restraints has been the subject of excited debate.

US law on the permissibility of vertical restraints has had an unusually tumultuous history, marked by abrupt changes in legislated policy and judicial interpretations. Paralleling these changes, and sometimes influencing them, have been sharply conflicting interpretations of the economic motivations for, and consequences of, vertical restraints. Since the 1960s, few questions in the field of industrial organization economics have been debated more heatedly.[47]

Between 1967 and 1977 the Supreme Court took the position that the imposition of *any* vertical restraint would amount to a *per se* infringement of section 1 of the Sherman Act 1890.[48] Resale price maintenance has been illegal *per se* since 1911 and the Supreme Court's ruling in *Dr Miles Medical Co v. John D Park & Sons Co.*[49] In that case Justice Hughes stated:

---

[45] The Commission places 'exclusive purchasing agreements' within the 'market partitioning' group.

[46] E.g. where an agreement includes 'territorial resale restrictions, the allocation of an area of primary responsibility, restrictions on the location of a distributor and customer resale restrictions': *Guidelines on Vertical Restraints, supra* n. 4, para. 113.

[47] F.M. Scherer and D. Ross, *Industrial Market Structure and Economic Performance* (3rd edn.,) (Houghton Mifflin, 1990), 541.

[48] For a discussion of *per se* illegality and the rule of reason in relation to the Sherman Act see *supra* Chap. 4.

[49] 220 US 373 (1911). Under the 'Colgate' doctrine (*US v. Colgate & Co*, 250 US 300 (1919)) a producer may recommend prices and refuse to deal with those who do not adhere to the recommended prices if it acts *unilaterally* (see the discussion of selective distribution systems and refusal to supply, *infra* 514). Further, in many States resale price maintenance has been permitted at various periods since 1931. In 1937 (Miller–Tydings Act) and 1952 (McGuire Act) Congress passed legislation approving the practice of resale price maintenance. However, in 1975 the legislation was repealed so that, effectively, the ruling of *Dr Miles* was restored.

If there be an advantage to the manufacturer in the maintenance of fixed prices, the question remains whether it is one which he is entitled to secure by agreements restricting the freedom of trade on the part of dealers who own what they sell. As to this, the complainant can fare no better with its plan of identical contracts than could the dealers themselves if they formed a combination and endeavored to establish the same restrictions, and thus to achieve the same result, by agreement with each other. If the immediate advantage they would obtain would not be sufficient to sustain a direct agreement, the asserted ulterior benefit to the complainant cannot be regarded as sufficient to support its system.[50]

In 1967, in *United States v. Arnold Schwinn & Co*,[51] the Supreme Court extended the *per se* rule to other vertical restraints:

Under the Sherman Act, it is unreasonable without more for a manufacturer to seek to restrict and confine areas or persons with whom an article may be traded after the manufacturer has parted with dominion over it . . . Such restraints are so obviously destructive of competition that their mere existence is enough.

It has been seen that commentators, particularly those from the Chicago school, stressed the benefits for competition that result from vertical restraints. The decisions in *Dr Miles* and *Schwinn* were, therefore, subjected to fervent criticism. Indeed, Bork described Justice Hughes' decision to equate horizontal cartel behaviour with vertical price fixing as 'one decisive misstep that has controlled a whole body of law'. A manufacturer would not have the same motives in imposing resale price maintenance as distributors would in forming a cartel. The consequences for consumers were not the same. A manufacturer would have no interest in creating a monopoly profit for its distributors. A rule of *per se* illegality had, therefore, been created on an 'erroneous economic assumption'.[52]

R.H. Bork, *The Antitrust Paradox: A Policy at War with Itself* (Basic Books, 1978, reprinted with a new Introduction and Epilogue, 1993), 289–90

Vertical restraint law has reached its present unhappy state because the Supreme Court is struggling with the logical results of an incorrect premise laid down sixty years ago by Justice Hughes in the *Dr. Miles* opinion. That premise . . . holds that there is no more reason to permit a manufacturer to eliminate rivalry among his retailers than there is to permit the retailers to eliminate rivalry by agreement among themselves. The premise is wrong. Retailers who agree to a horizontal restraint that the manufacturer does not desire are almost certainly attempting to restrict output for the sake of monopoly gains. If such a restraint would increase efficiency, the manufacturer would not only favor it but would impose it himself. When a manufacturer wishes to impose resale price maintenance or vertical division of reseller markets, or any other restraint upon the rivalry of resellers, his motive cannot be the restriction of output and, therefore, can only be the creation of distributive efficiency. That motive should be respected by the law. . . .

Schwinn's vertical price fixing . . . and vertical market division did not eliminate the rivalry of any other bicycle manufacturer with itself. These vertical restraints could not, therefore, create any additional power in Shwinn to restrict output. This would be true whether Schwinn had 1 or 100

---

[50] 220 US 373 (1911), 407–8 *per* Justice Hughes.

[51] 388 US 365.

[52] R.H. Bork, *The Antitrust Paradox: A Policy at War with Itself* (Basic Books, 1978, reprinted with a new Introduction and Epilogue, 1993), 32–33.

percent of the bicycle market. If it had any power to restrict output, it would exercise that power directly and take the monopoly profits itself. There is no need for vertical restraints on retailers or wholesalers. The vertical restraint could not be anticompetitive for any effect they might have on the manufacturer's level of the industry

But by maintaining its retailers' prices and dividing its wholesalers' markets, did Schwinn simply give retailers and wholesalers the power to restrict output? That is so unlikely as not to be worth consideration. No manufacturer or supplier will ever use either resale price maintenance or reseller market division for the purpose of giving the resellers a greater-than-competitive return. The extra return would be money out of his pocket for no good reason, and we may safely assume that manufacturers are not moved to engage in that peculiar form of philanthropy. The manufacturer shares with the consumer the desire to have distribution done at the lowest possible cost consistent with effectiveness. That is why courts need never weigh the opposing forces of lessened intrabrand and heightened interbrand competition. When the manufacturer chooses, he chooses on criteria that also control consumer welfare. No court is likely to make a more accurate assessment than does a businessman with both superior information and the depth of insight that only self-interest can supply.

Since vertical restraints are not means of creating restriction of output, we must assume that they are means of creating efficiencies, and it is perfectly clear that they are. The Court in *Schwinn* admitted as much. The most obvious efficiency is the purchase of increased sales and service efforts by the reseller. A retailer whose price is controlled will have to vie for business by sales and service effort. In the absence of resale price maintenance, the problem of the free ride may arise ... Customers will be able to go to the retailer who offers a display of the full line, explanation of the product, and so forth, and then purchase from the retailer who offers none of these things but gives a lower price. The result will be a diminution in the amount of sale and service effort by all retailers. When this is to the manfuacturer's disadvantage, he may wish to employ either resale price maintenance or vertical division of territories to get the performance he wants.

The decision in *Schwinn* 'marked the apex of the trend toward prohibiting vertical restraints ... Since that time, however, the law has moved in the opposite direction.'[53] In 1977 in *Continental TV Inc v. GTE Slyvania Inc*,[54] the Supreme Court, recognizing that vertical restraints, especially those restricting only intra-brand competition, might promote inter-brand competition, overruled *Schwinn*. Instead, the Court ruled that the scope of *per se* illegality should be narrow in the context of vertical restraints. A rule of reason approach should be adopted in relation to vertical non-price restraints.

[T]he market impact of vertical restrictions is complex because of their potential for a simultaneous reduction of intrabrand competition [rivalry between sellers of the same brand] and stimulation of interbrand competition [rivalry with sellers of other brands] ... vertical restrictions promote interbrand competition by allowing the manufacturer to achieve certain efficiencies in the distribution of his products.[55]

The Court's ruling did not affect the *per se* illegality for vertical price fixing set out in *Dr Miles*. In maintaining a distinction between price and non-price restrictions the judgment

---

[53] W.S. Comanor *Vertical Price-Fixing, Vertical Market Restrictions, and the New Antitrust Policy* (1984–1985) 98 Harv. Law Rev 983, 985.

[54] 433 US 36 (1977).

[55] The Supreme Court upheld the validity of a location clause precluding the franchisee of a manufacturer of colour television sets, Sylvania, from selling the television sets from a new location.

did not go as far as some commentators would have liked.[56] Nevertheless, the judgment was welcomed, in particular, for the high degree of economic sophistication it displayed.

E. Gellhorn and W.E. Kovacic, *Antitrust Law and Economics* (4th edn., West Publishing Co.) 312–5

The decision in continental TV, Inc v. GTE Sylvania Inc., 433 U.S. 36 (1977) is the most important antitrust case since *Socony* and *Alcoa* in the 1940's . . .

In holding that vertically imposed nonprice territorial restraints should be tested under a reasonableness standard, the Court's new analysis emphasized the arrangement's redeeming purposes and possible benefits. Sylvania was allowed to seek more efficient distribution methods because *inter*-brand rivalry—competition among different television manufacturers-would thereby enhanced. And, as long as there was competition at the *inter*brand level, these benefits would probably outweigh the necessarily less significant limitation of *intra*brand rivalry-rivalry among dealers of Slyvania television sets.

The Court relied on economic theory to demonstrate that the location clause would increase Sylvania's ability to compete against other television manufacturers. Assuring dealers of Sylvania sets some insulation from other Sylvania dealers would elicit aggressive dealer efforts to advertise the product and provide customer services; the location clauses protected dealers from 'free-riding' retailers who might seek to reap benefits of these activities-and thereby discourage the initial dealer's effort to advance Sylnvania's product. Furthermore, the Court argued that consumers will be protected from excessive prices or service by competition from non-Sylvania television set sellers and because each manufacturer has an independent interest in maintaining as much intrabrand competition as is consistent with efficient distribution. Thus the Court concluded that, on balance, non-price distribution restraints yield sufficient economic benefits to warrant a rule of reason analysis. The Court did 'not foreclose the possibility that particular applications of vertical restrictions might justify *per se* prohibition,' but it emphasized that any 'departure from the rules of reason standard must be based upon demonstrable economic effect rather than-as in *Schwinn*-upon formalistic line drawing.'

Sylvania is important because it reversed a major legal doctrine and explicitly adopted price theory as the basis for the Court's decision.

Subsequently, the courts, in applying the rule of reason, recognized that violations of the Act[57] would be unlikely in the absence of market power.[58] They thus tended to decline to

---

[56] The Court did, however, provide a justification for the difference in treatment. In particular, it considered there to be support for the view that vertical price restraints would reduce *inter*-brand competition because they would facilitate cartelizing. In contrast support for the cartel-facilitating effect of non-price restraints was lacking, 433 US 36, 52 at n 18 quoting R. Posner, 'Antitrust Policy and the Supreme Court: An Analysis of the Restricted Distribution, Horizontal Merger and Potential Competition Decisions' (1975) 75 Colum L Rev 282, 294. However, Justice White recognized that, given that price restraints might be used to achieve the same result as non-price restraints, the logical conclusion of the ruling might be that price restraints should also be subject to the rule of reason. 'The effect, if not the intention, of the Court's opinion is necessarily to call into question the firmly established *per se* rule against price restraints': 433 US 36 (1977), 69–70 *per* Justice White (concurring in the judgment).

[57] The move from *per se* illegality to rule of reason analysis of course led to uncertainty and left, and still leaves, open difficult questions. In particular, how the rule of reason is to be applied and where the burden of proof lies.

[58] Since market power cannot easily be measured by the methods of litigation, it is normally inferred from possession of a substantial percentage of the sales in the relevant product or geographic market: see *infra* n. 59.

find an infringement unless the manufacturer imposing the restraint had substantial market share. In *Valley Liquors Inc v. Renfield Importers Ltd*,[59] for example, Judge Posner stated:

The plaintiff in restricted distribution cases must show that the restriction he is complaining of was unreasonable because, weighing effects on both intrabrand and interbrand competition, it made consumers worse off.

Admittedly, this test of illegality is easier to state than to apply, the effects to be weighed being so difficult to measure or even estimate by the methods of litigation. The courts have therefore looked for shortcuts. A popular one is to say that the balance tips in the defendant's favor if the plaintiff fails to show that the defendant has significant market power (that is, power to raise prices significantly above the competitive level without losing all of one's business) . . .

A firm that has no market power is unlikely to adopt policies that disserve its consumers; it cannot afford to. And if it blunders and does adopt such a policy, market retribution will be swift. Thus its mistakes do not seriously threaten consumer welfare . . . Even if there is some possibility that the distribution practices of a powerless firm will have a substantial anticompetitive effect, it is too small a possibility to warrant trundling out the great machinery of antitrust enforcement.

The emphasis on the distribution efficiencies brought about by vertical restraints prompted an almost complete U-turn in the attitude of the judicial and enforcement authorities to vertical restraints. 'By the early 1980's the position had swung from regarding them as suspect for competition, to a generalised perception that they were innocuous for competition (the Chicago school).'[60] In the 1980s the Department of Justice was rarely interested in vertical restraints, even price restraints.[61] The anecdote set out below emphasizes the striking nature of this change in policy:

I am . . . struck by an anecdote told by Mr Schroeter, the draftsman of the [EC] Regulations dealing with vertical restraints. When discussing the first Community Regulation for vertical restraints (67/ 67) with American friends in the FTC and the D of J he was severely criticised in that by exempting non-absolute territorial exclusivity and other vertical restraints he was permitting pernicious anti-competitive practices. Fifteen years later when drafting the renewal Regulation . . . he was also criticised from Washington for bothering at all with vertical restraints as clearly they were all pro-competitive. These criticisms referred to the same restraints and a very similar policy approach adopted by the Commission.[62]

Recognizing the validity of many of the criticisms of the Chicago school, the current authorities do not display quite such ambivalence to vertical restraints. In particular it seems that the federal enforcement agencies will take action against resale price maintenance agreements where no business justification is offered in support of the practice. Although it seems that the main focus of enforcement actions is vertical price restraints the authorities

---

[59] 678 F.2d 742 (7th Cir. 1982), 745. The shift from *per se* rules meant that the courts had, in order to minimize the complexity and the costs of litigation and to try and ensure legal certainty, to adopt a truncated rule of reason. This led effectively to a rule of *per se* legality for non-price vertical restraints.

[60] European Commission Green Paper on Vertical Restraints in EC Competition Policy, COM(96)721, 17.

[61] See its non-price vertical restraint guidelines published in 1985 Fed. Reg. 6263 (1985) (these guidelines are no longer in force). The Guidelines declared certain vertical agreements, such as selective distribution agreements, to be *per se* lawful. See also the *amicus curiae* brief filed by the Department of Justice in *Monsanto Co. v. Spray-Rite Service Corp*, 104 S Ct. 1464 (1984), *supra* 487. In the 1980s there was almost no federal enforcement action in the area of vertical restraints. These views no longer reflect current policy, however, see *infra* n. 63 and accompanying text.

[62] D. Deacon, 'Vertical Restraints under EU Competition Law: New Directions' [1995] *Fordham Corp. Law Inst.* 307, para. 8.

are also concerned that non-price vertical restraints may be anti-competitive if used to raise rivals' costs, to exclude (foreclose) competitors or where they facilitate tacit collusion between competitors.[63]

d. THE COMMUNITY APPROACH—AN OVERVIEW

The single market project and restrictions on economic freedom

The Commission policy, in contrast, has not generally been so willing to recognize the distribution efficiencies resulting from vertical restraints. Rather, the Commission has adopted a strict and extremely interventionist approach when dealing with vertical restraints. It has already been explained that one of the key causes of the Commission's pre-occupation with vertical restraints has been that they often demarcate territories between distributors, isolate national markets, erect barriers to trade and maintain price differences between Member States. The Commission has intervened to prevent agreements that thwart the single market objective and has tried to ensure in so far as is possible that agreements admit the possibility of *some* parallel trade.

The often bitter debate on vertical restraints has an added dimension in the Community because competition policy not only has a goal of undistorted competition but also market integration. This has led to a two-way tug on policy makers. On the one hand vertical restraints including territorial exclusivity were recognised as necessary to give both producers and distributors the protection and certainty needed for them to make the investments to launch new products or launch their products on the markets of other Member States outside their home markets. The pro-competitive arguments in favour of such restrictions are well rehearsed. On the other hand territorial exclusivity in particular was considered as contrary to one of the fundamental aims of the Community- the creation of real internal/single market. Such restrictions appeared to contribute both to the continued division of the market along national lines and the maintenance of price differences between Member States.[64]

Even where a distribution agreement does not impact on the single market project the Commission has shown considerable concern about agreements which restrain the parties' economic freedom. It has sought to encourage and to nurture the process of rivalry between undertakings and to foster the freedom and right of initiative of the individual economic operator and the spirit of enterprise.[65]

Article 81 and vertical restraints

Article 81, in contrast to section 1 of the Sherman Act, is divided into two parts. It requires, first, a determination of whether or not the agreement restricts competition and trade between Member States to an appreciable extent (Article 81(1)[66]) and, where it does, a determination of whether or not the agreement nonetheless merits exemption (Article 81(3)[67]).

---

[63] See, e.g., the speeches of Commissioners, Federal Trade Commission, at the ALI–ABA Annual Advanced Course on Product Distribution and Marketing: S.F. Anthony, *Vertical Issues in Federal Antitrust Law*, 19 Mar. 1998 and C.A. Varney, *Vertical Restraints Enforcement at the FTC*, 16 Jan. 1996.

[64] D. Deacon, 'Vertical Restraints under EU Competition Law: New Directions' [1995] *Fordham Corp. Law Inst.* 307, para. 8.

[65] See *supra* Chap. 4.

[66] See *supra* Chap. 4 and *infra* 503 ff.

[67] See *supra* Chap. 4 and *infra* 526 ff.

The Commission's obsession with vertical restraints has lead to two different results when interpreting Article 81. First, it has encouraged the Commission to take a broad view of what constitutes a restriction of competition within the meaning of Article 81(1). Secondly, it has led the Commission to adopt a very strict approach when exempting vertical agreements from the Article 81(1) prohibition under Article 81(3).

Article 81(1)[68]

The chief criticism made of the Commission in its approach to vertical restraints has been that it has failed to take a sufficiently realistic view of whether an agreement restricts competition for the purposes of Article 81(1). Although the Commission has been willing to exempt many agreements under Article 81(3), it has adhered to the view that all restrictions interfering with the single market objective and many restrictions on conduct are tantamount to restrictions of competition:

Vertical restraints are more strictly treated under EC competition law than is the case in most other jurisdictions. This strictness is a product of extreme hostility toward restrictions that threaten to interfere with trade between Member States. The strictness also results from a concern with restraints on so-called 'economic freedom' where the restraints frequently have no harmful effect on consumer welfare and may even promote consumer welfare through enhancing economic efficiency.[69]

It has taken the view, often without serious analysis of the effect of the agreement on the competitive process, that most restrictions on parties' freedom of action amount to restrictions of competition.[70] Not only is this approach difficult conceptually, the main objective of an agreement being to bind the parties and to restrict their freedom of action,[71] but the approach has caused the Commission to deal with agreements by category applying certain rules to one type of agreement and different rules to others. This has led to confusion and has inhibited flexibility in distribution.

Article 81(3)[72]

The broad view of Article 81(1) has meant, with the host of accompanying drawbacks, that businesses have felt the need to secure exemptions for their distribution agreements.[73] This has imposed an enormous and, arguably, unnecessary burden on firms wishing to conclude distribution agreements. The Commission cannot possibly exempt all distribution agreements falling within the prohibition of Article 81(1). On the contrary, exemptions are rarely

---

[68] See *supra* Chaps. 3 and 4.

[69] B.E. Hawk, 'System Failure: Vertical Restraints and EC Competition Law' (1995) 32 *CMLRev.* 973, 973.

[70] D. Deacon, 'Vertical Restraints under EU Competition Law: New Directions' [1995] *Fordham Corp. Law Inst.* 307, para. 9.

[71] 'There can be no doubt that the challenged practices of the NCAA constitute a 'restraint of trade' in the sense that they limit members' freedom to negotiate and enter into their own television contracts. In that sense, however, every contract is in restraint of trade, and . . . the Sherman Act was intended to prohibit only unreasonable restraints of trade': *National Collegiate Athletic Ass'n v. Board of Regents of University of Oklahoma*, 468 US 85, 98 (1984).

[72] See *supra* Chap. 4.

[73] 'A broad definition of restriction of competition under Art. [81(1)] shifts most of the inquiry over to Art. [81(3)] where only the Commission has the power to grant exemptions, thus requiring notification and excluding the national courts from the more important part of the anti-trust analysis': B.E. Hawk, 'The American (Anti-Trust) Revolution: Lessons for the EEC' [1988] *ECLR* 53, 65.

granted to vertical agreements,[74] and even comfort letters take approximately eighteen months from receipt of notification, and there is no provisional validity for notified agreements. Consequently, the Commission has, as well as developing the doctrine of appreciability within the context of Article 81(1), introduced block exemptions to exempt distribution agreements from the prohibition of Article 81(3). The old block exemptions, which applied until 31 May 2000, restricted the type of distribution agreement which parties could conclude and imposed severe limitations on the types of clauses that could be contained within them.

Where no block exemption applies the parties have had either to notify their agreement to the Commission and wait for a comfort letter or, in rare cases, an individual exemption, or to risk a finding that their agreement infringes Article 81(1). Even where an individual exemption or comfort letter has been granted the Commission has adopted an interventionist approach limiting the restrictions that they may contain.

The new block exemption and reform

The Commission has recognized the problems that its approach to vertical agreements has caused in the past and has taken heed of strident criticism that the system was failing.[75] In 1996 it issued a Green Paper on Vertical Restraints in EC Competition Policy in which it discussed possible ways for developing and ameliorating its approach to vertical restraints. The Paper canvassed and sought opinion upon four possible options for reform: maintaining the existing system; maintaining the system but making the, then, existing block exemptions more flexible; limiting the existing block exemption to agreements concluded between undertakings with a share of less than 40 per cent of the market; introducing an assumption that agreements concluded between undertakings with less than 20 per cent of the market do not infringe Article 81(1); and making changes to the existing block exemptions.

A fifth option, to adopt a more realistic approach when assessing the agreement's compatibility with Article 81(1), was not discussed within the Paper but provoked much attention in the discussion that the Paper provoked.

Following the introduction of that Paper a follow-up document to the Green Paper was published and several changes have been introduced, or promised, to the way in which vertical restraints are, or will be, dealt with under Article 81 of the Treaty. These can be summarized as follows:

A more realistic approach to Article 81(1)

The Commission has indicated in its *Guidelines on Vertical Restraints* that it will adopt a realistic approach when assessing an agreement's compatibility with Article 81(1). It states that it 'will adopt an economic approach in the application of Article 81 to vertical restraints' and that the scope of Article 81 will be limited 'to undertakings holding a certain degree of market power where inter-brand competition may be insufficient'.[76] In particular, it recognises that even agreements concluded between undertakings with more than 30 per cent of the relevant market may not fall within Article 81(1).

---

[74] 'Only a limited number of formal decisions can be rendered each year for cases under Articles [81] and [82]. . . . In most cases of application for negative clearance or individual exemption, the Commission declares by simple letter known as a "comfort letter"': European Commission Green Paper on Vertical Restraints COM(96) 721, 30.

[75] See B.E. Hawk, 'System Failure: Vertical Restraints and EC Competition Law' (1995) *CMLRev.* 973, discussed *infra*.

[76] *Guidelines on Vertical Restraints*, [2000] OJ C291/1, para. 102.

Agreements of minor importance[77]

In 1997 the Commission introduced a new Notice on agreements of minor importance which establishes that the Commission will rarely be interested in vertical agreements concluded between participating undertakings which do not have more than a 10 per cent[78] share of the relevant market. The authorities take the view that such vertical agreements will not appreciably impact on trade or competition within the Community, save where they contain hardcore restrictions or where there are cumulative effects.

Although the enactment of the 1997 Notice was not specifically stated to be part of the Commission's review of its policy towards vertical agreements it represented a major change to the Commission's treatment of vertical agreements. The previous notice[79] stipulated that an agreement would be of minor importance only where the parties did not have a share greater than 5 per cent of the relevant market *and* where the aggregate turnover of the undertakings did not exceed ECU 300 million. The distinction drawn in the 1997 Notice between horizontal and vertical agreements (the 5 per cent threshold is retained for the former) reflects the Commission's awareness that vertical agreements generally present fewer concerns from a competition perspective. Further, the deletion of the turnover requirement reflected a recognition that this requirement was irrelevant to the assessment of the impact that the agreement would have on the market.

Regulation 2790/1999—a new style block exemption

For those agreements falling within Article 81(1) the Commission has adopted a new block exemption, Regulation 2790/1999 (the Verticals Regulation),[80] which adopts a more flexible approach than that which has previously been displayed.

In order for the Commission to be able to adopt this regulation a new Council Regulation was required extending the Commission's *vires* to grant block exemption to vertical agreements. The previous Council Regulation, Regulation 19/65,[81] conferring such authority had its limitations. Regulation 1215/99[82] thus extended the legislative power of the Commission and conferred authority on the Commission to adopt a much broader exemption.

The Verticals Regulation replaces three regulations that exempted certain exclusive distribution, exclusive purchasing, and franchising agreements respectively. Primarily, it seeks to avoid the straight-jacketing that resulted from those regulations and to apply more broadly to *all* vertical agreements that satisfy the requirements set out in the regulation.

Retrospective exemptions[83]

Another extremely important change has been the adoption of Council Regulation 1216/99[84] which has ameliorated the position of undertakings whose agreements may infringe

---

[77] See *supra* Chaps. 3 and 4.

[78] The Notice recognizes that even where market shares are higher than this the agreement may produce only insignificant effects. Conversely, agreements between parties with a small market share may be held to have a significant impact on competition and trade between Member States. Although in the latter case the parties will be protected from fines, such an agreement will still be void until it has been exempted from the prohibition in Art. 81(1).

[79] See discussion *supra* Chap. 3.

[80] [1999] OJ L336/21.

[81] [1965–66] OJ Spec. Ed. 85.

[82] [1999] OJ L148/1.

[83] See *supra* Chap. 4.

[84] [1999] OJ L148/1.

Article 81(1) and do not benefit from a block exemption. In such cases it would previously have been necessary either to make prior notification to the Commission requesting negative clearance or exemption or to risk nullity. Regulation 1216/99 extends the category of non-notifiable agreements set out in Article 4(2) of Regulation 17[85] so that vertical agreements do not need to have been notified for an exemption to be granted. Rather, when it becomes important for the parties to know whether or not the agreement is compatible with Article 81 they may notify it to the Commission which may, where appropriate to do so, grant an exemption, with *retroactive* effect to the date that the agreement was concluded.

In practice this should mean that the Commission is deluged with fewer precautionary notifications. Further the alteration may deter artificial litigation before national courts and strengthen the civil enforceability of agreements.[86] In practice, parties to vertical agreements may nonetheless wish to notify in order to receive peace of mind and an assurance that their agreement is compatible with the competition rules.

Regulation 1216/99 does not stipulate whether or not the benefit of Article 4(2), as extended, applies only to agreements concluded after its adoption on 12 June 1999 or whether it applies to all vertical agreements concluded after to the adoption of Regulation 17. Arguably, since the policy of the Regulation is to limit the number of notifications and to prevent spurious claims being raised before national courts the amendment should apply retrospectively and be read as an integral part of Regulation 17.[87]

Modernization[88]

The Commission's White Paper on Modernisation indicates that the reform process is not over. In the Paper the Commission states that a centralized enforcement system requiring a decision by the Commission exempting agreements that infringe Article 81(1) is no longer possible.[89] The Commission has proposed that the whole notification and exemption system should be abolished. Instead, the Commission should forgo its monopoly over the grant of Article 81(3) exemptions and Article 81(3) should be applied by the Commission, the national competition authorities and the national courts.

If these proposals are implemented,[90] vertical agreements that are not exempted by the Verticals Regulation or another block exemption will not be able to benefit from an individual exemption. The undertakings themselves will have to make their own determination whether or not the agreement infringes Article 81(1) at all and, if it does, whether or not it merits exemption in accordance with the criteria set out in Article 81(3). Should the agreement's compatibility with Article 81 arise, however, the assessment could be made by a national court, a national competition authority or the Commission.

---

[85] See discussion *supra* in Chap. 4 and *infra* in Chap. 15.

[86] See *Guidelines on Vertical Restraints, supra* n. 4, paras 63–65 and *infra* Chap. 15, particularly the discussion of disputes between co-contractors.

[87] See R. Whish, 'Regulation 2790/1999: The Commission's "New Style" Block Exemption for Vertical Agreements' (2000) *CMLRev.*

[88] [1999] OJ C132/1, [1999] 5 CMLR 208. The White Paper is discussed *supra* in Chap. 4 and *infra* in Chap. 16.

[89] The Commission will then be freed to deal with serious competition infringement and individuals will be encouraged to enforce the competition rules at the national level. See B.E. Hawk, 'System Failure: Vertical Restraints and EC Competition Law' (1995) *CML Rev.* 973 set out *infra* at 000 ff.

[90] See the Commission's proposal for a Reg. implementing Arts. 81 and 82, COM (2000) 582, 27 Sept. 2000. For a discussion of the White Paper and the problems that it raises, see *infra* Chap. 16.

2. DISTRIBUTION AGREEMENTS AND ARTICLE 81(1) OF THE TREATY

A. GENERAL

Article 81(1) applies to agreements concluded between undertakings which have as their object or effect the prevention, restriction, or distortion of competition, which affect trade between Member States, and which affect competition and trade to an appreciable extent. In Chapters 3 and 4 a number of points relevant to the impact of Article 81(1) on vertical agreements were discussed.

B. VERTICAL AGREEMENTS AND SINGLE ECONOMIC ENTITIES

Article 81(1) does not apply to distribution arrangements concluded between a producer and its distributor subsidiary.[91] Nonetheless, it has been clear since *STM* and *Consten and Grundig* that it does apply to vertical agreements concluded between a producer and an *independent* distributor. In the latter case[92] the Court unequivocally rejected the applicants' argument that Article 81(1) applied only to 'so-called' horizontal agreements.

C. AN EFFECT ON TRADE

Because of the broad interpretation adopted of the term 'an effect on trade between Member States'[93] most vertical agreements affect trade within the meaning of that Article. An agreement concluded between parties situated in different Member States or even within a single Member State[94] and an agreement containing territorial restrictions may affect trade even where its effect is to *increase* (rather than decrease) trade between Member States.[95] Even a provision prohibiting a distributor appointed to resell in non-EU countries from re-importing into the EU may affect trade between Member States.[96]

---

[91] Case 15/74, *Centrafarm BV and Adnaan De Peijper v. Sterling Drug Inc* [1974] ECR 1183, [1974] 2 CMLR 480. See also discussion of agency, *supra* 483–485.

[92] Cases 56, 58/64, *Establissements Consten and Grundig v. Commission* [1966] ECR 299, 339–40, [1966] CMLR 418, 469–71.

[93] See Case 56/65, *Société La Technique Minière v. Maschinenbau Ulm* [1966] ECR 235, 249, [1966] CMLR 357, 375.

[94] Case C–234/89 *Delimitis v. Henninger Bräu* [1991] ECR I-935, [1992] 5 CMLR 210.

[95] Cases 56, 58/64 *Establissements Consten and Grundig v. Commission* [1966] ECR 299, 341–2, [1996] CMLR 418, 471–2.

[96] See Case C–306/96, *Javico v. Yves Saint Laurent* [1998] ECR I–1983, [1998] 5 CMLR 172.

D. OBJECT OR EFFECT THE RESTRICTION, PREVENTION, OR DISTORTION OF COMPETITION[97]

(i) THE OBJECT OR EFFECT

The most controversial question arising in the application of Article 81(1) to vertical agreements has been whether restraints imposed in distribution agreements have as their object or effect the prevention, restriction, or distortion of competition within the meaning of Article 81(1). The Court has persistently held that where the object of the agreement cannot be said to be the prevention, restriction, or distortion of competition it is necessary to look at its effect.

Where . . . an analysis of the said clauses does not reveal the effect on competition to be sufficiently deleterious, the consequence of the agreement should then be considered and for it to be caught by the prohibition it is then necessary to find that those factors are present that show that competition has in fact been prevented or restricted or distorted to an appreciable extent.[98]

In the absence of certain serious restraints the Court has been prepared to accept that many restrictions on conduct do not have as their effect the restriction of competition for the purposes of Article 81(1).[99] Many of the cases illustrating this point are set out and analysed in Chapter 4. Several cases dealt with there are discussed again here because of their importance to the question of whether and when Article 81(1) applies to distribution agreements. The full extracts of the cases which are set out in that Chapter should, however, be read again on account of their critical importance to this discussion.

(ii) AGREEMENTS WHICH HAVE AS THEIR OBJECT THE PREVENTION, RESTRICTION, OR DISTORTION OF COMPETITION

a. ABSOLUTE TERRITORIAL PROTECTION AND EXPORT BANS

The ECJ has, when dealing with distribution agreements, held that two types of clauses have as their object the restriction of competition. In particular, in *Consten and Grundig*[100] the Court held that clauses resulting in the isolation of a national market and/or maintaining separate national markets distorted competition and constituted an infringement of Article 81(1). The ECJ did not accept the view of its Advocate General[101] that Article 81(1)

---

[97] See the detailed discussion *supra* in Chap. 4.

[98] See Case 56/65, *Société La Technique Minière v. Maschinenbau Ulm* [1966] ECR 235, 249, [1966] CMLR 357, 375.

[99] e.g. restraints necessary or ancillary to the operation of a pro-competitive agreement or essential to persuade a distributor to take on the risk of distribution or necessary to the operation of a selective distribution agreement or which do not restrict inter-brand competition, *supra* Chap. 4.

[100] Cases 56 & 58/64, *Etablissements Consten SA & Grundig-Verkaufs-GmbH v. Commission* [1966] ECR 299 [1966] CMLR 418 (see extract set out in Chap. 4). See also, for example, Case T-77/92 *Parker Pen v. Commission* [1994] ECR II-559, [1995] 5 CMLR 435. But see, e.g. Case 262/81, *Coditel II* [1982] ECR 3382, [1983] 1 CMLR 49, and *infra* Chap. 10.

[101] See extract set out in Chap. 4.

required, in all cases, an examination of the market to determine whether or not the agreement was likely to promote or restrict competition. In that case the object of an agreement was the restriction of competition since it sheltered the distributor from all intra-brand competition and led to the division of national markets.

The Commission, seemingly supported by the Court, has maintained a strict policy against any measure inserted in an agreement, or imposed unilaterally by the producer,[102] which is designed to divide the EU market on territorial lines and to prevent parallel imports. An agreement which does not explicitly contain an export ban or confer absolute territorial protection on a distributor will nonetheless be found to restrict competition if this is its purpose,[103] for example:[104] where circulars are sent discouraging export;[105] where export is permitted but only if the consent of the producer is obtained;[106] where goods are supplied to distributors but the invoice for supply bears the words 'export prohibited';[107] where insufficient quantities of goods are supplied with the objective of precluding export;[108] where exported products are bought back by the manufacturer;[109] where products supplied are marked so that parallel importers can be identified;[110] where guarantees are limited to the Member State in which the product was purchased;[111] where discriminatory prices are charged to discourage export;[112] where an agreement requires a distributor to pass on any customer enquiries coming from outside the contract territory to the producer;[113] or where a producer threatens to terminate or actually terminates contractual arrangements with distributors or dealers which sell outside of their allotted territory.[114]

b. RESALE PRICE MAINTENANCE

The Court has also confirmed that the object of provisions setting out minimum retail prices to be charged by distributors is to restrict competition for the purposes of Article 81(1).[115] In contrast, the provision of price guidelines[116] or the operation of a selective

---

[102] See *supra* Chap. 3. But see, in particular, Case T–41/96, *Bayer AG v. Commission*, judgment of 26 Oct. 2000.

[103] An export ban will be prohibited even if it is stipulated to be applicable only 'unless prohibited by law', *Novalliance/Systemform* [1997] OJ L47/11, [1997] 4 CMLR 876.

[104] See also the discussion of hardcore restraints prohibited by the Verticals Reg., *infra* at 541 ff.

[105] *Konica* [1988] OJ L78/34, [1988] 4 CMLR 848.

[106] Case T–77/92, *Parker Pen v. Commission* [1994] ECR II–559, [1995] 5 CMLR 435; Case 19/77, *Miller v. Commission* [1978] ECR 131, [1978] 2 CMLR 334.

[107] Case C–227/87, *Sandoz Prodotti Farmaceutici SpA v. Commission* [1990] ECR I–45, [1990] 4 CMLR 242.

[108] See *infra* n. 102 and *Volkswagen* [1998] OJ L124/60, [1998] 5 CMLR 33, on appeal Case T–62/98 *Volkswagen AG v. Commission* [2000] 5 CMLR 853.

[109] Cases T–38 & 43/92, *Dunlop Slazenger v. Commission* [1994] ECR II–441, [1993] 5 CMLR 352.

[110] *Tretorn* [1994] OJ L378/45.

[111] *Zanussi* [1978] OJ L322/26, [1979] 1 CMLR 81; Case 31/85, *ETA Fabriques d'Ebauches v. DK Investments SA* [1985] ECR 3933, [1986] 2 CMLR 674.

[112] *The Distillers Company Limited* [1978] OJ L50/16, [1978] 1 CMLR 400; on appeal Case 30/78, *Distillers Company v.* Commission [1980] ECR 2229, [1980] 3 CMLR 121; and see *Distillers Company plc (Red label)* [1983] OJ C245/3, [1983] 3 CMLR 173; *Newitt/Dunlop Slazenger International* [1992] OJ L131/32; on appeal Cases T–38 & 43/92, *Dunlop Slazenger v. Commission* [1994] ECR II–441, [1993] 5 CMLR 352.

[113] Cases T–175/95, *BASF Coating AG v. Commission* [2000] 4 CMLR 33.

[114] *Volkswagen* [1998] OJ L124/60, [1998] 5 CMLR 33, on appeal Case T–62/98 *Volkswagen AG v. Commission* [2000] 5 CMLR 853.

[115] Case 243/85, *SA Binon & Cie v. SA Agence et Messageries de la Presse* [1985] ECR 2015, [1985] 3 CMLR 800.

[116] See, in particular, Case 161/84, *Pronuptia de Paris GmbH v. Pronuptia de Paris Irmgard Schillgallis* [1986] ECR 353, [1986] 1 CMLR 414.

distribution system that tends to limit price competition on a market,[117] may be compatible with Article 81(1) so long as it is not operated in a way which precludes price discounting.[118]

C. THE IRRELEVANCE OF THE EFFECT ON COMPETITION

It can be seen from the discussion in the introductory section above that a supplier or distributor may perceive territorial or price restraints such as those discussed above to be essential to the operation of a distribution agreements. In particular, both territorial restraints and resale price maintenance restrict only *intra-brand* competition and may be considered essential to induce a dealer to invest in pre-sales services, marketing, and advertising and to prevent free-riding on those investments and/or to enable a supplier to penetrate a market and to increase *inter-brand* competition on a market.

It has also been seen that the Community is acutely concerned with territorial restraints that preclude any cross-border sales since these provisions interfere with the Community single market programme. Further, many economists take the view that resale price maintenance is rarely justifiable given its tendency to reinforce cartels and to preclude innovation and discounting at the retail level.[119] It appears that for these reasons the Court adheres to the view that the objectives of the single market and the pernicious effects of resale price maintenance must trump any economic-driven justification for the agreement. These restrictions are so serious that they will be found to restrict competition for the purposes of Article 81(1)[120] whatever the reason for their imposition. Any economic justification explaining the need for the provision can, however, always be relied upon when seeking to persuade the Commission that the agreement merits exemption in accordance with the criteria set out in Article 81(3). These types of provisions have not, however, been permitted in the block exemptions[121] and have ordinarily caused the Commission to refuse an individual exemption or comfort letter.[122]

(iii) AGREEMENTS WHICH HAVE AS THEIR EFFECT THE PREVENTION, RESTRICTION OR DISTORTION OF COMPETITION

a. EXCLUSIVE DISTRIBUTION AGREEMENTS AND *STM*

In all other cases, i.e. where the agreement does not contain clauses imposing severe territorial or price restraints, the Court has been clear, since 1966 and its judgment in *Société La*

---

[117] See *infra* 509 ff.

[118] Case 107/82, *AEG-Telefunken v. Commission* [1983] ECR 3151, [1984] 3 CMLR 325.

[119] Bishop and Walker, e.g., state that although there are occasions where RPM can be efficiency enhancing these are rare: S. Bishop and M. Walker, *The Economics of EC Competition Law: Concepts, Application and Measurement* (Sweet & Maxwell, 1999), para. 4.35, n. 57.

[120] It is a separate question whether the restriction of competition is an appreciable one.

[121] See especially *infra* 526 ff.

[122] See *infra* 549 ff and, in particular, Case 243/85, *SA Binon & Cie v. SA Agence et Messageries de la Presse* [1985] ECR 2015, [1985] 3 CMLR 800; *Distillers Company plc (Red Label)* [1983] OJ C245/3, [1983] 3 CMLR 489; and *The Distillers Company Limited* [1978] OJ L50/16, [1978] 1 CMLR 400, on appeal Case 30/78, *Distillers Company v. Commission* [1980] ECR 2229, [1980] 3 CMLR 121, especially the opinion of the AG. See also Case 161/84, *Pronuptia de Paris GmbH v. Pronuptia de Paris Irmgard Schillgallis* [1986] ECR 353, [1986] 1 CMLR 414.

Technique Minière v. Maschinenbau Ulm GmbH,[123] that it is necessary to look at the *effect* of the agreement. Only then can it be determined whether or not competition has in fact been restricted.

In the introduction set out above it was seen that vertical restraints are imposed for a number of justifiable reasons. Exclusive distribution agreements, in which a manufacturer appoints a sole distributor for a particular area, have a number of positive effects and may consequently stimulate the competitive process. For example, efficiencies flow from the manufacturer's decision to deal only with one distributor in a particular territory. Transaction costs are saved and customer feedback may be more easily obtained. Further, such an agreement may be essential to solve a free-rider problem. If the distributor is sheltered from intra-brand competition it will be encouraged to incur expenditure promoting and advertising the product, safe in the knowledge that other distributors will not be able to take a 'free ride' on that expenditure.[124]

The case law of the ECJ clearly recognizes the benefits for the competitive process that potentially flow from exclusive distribution agreements. In *Société La Technique Minière v. Maschinenbau Ulm GmbH*[125] the ECJ held that exclusive distribution agreements will not restrict competition if the appointment of the exclusive distributor is necessary to enable the manufacturer to penetrate a new market. The Court thus accepted that a restraint necessary to persuade the distributor to take on the commercial risk inherent in the agreement would not constitute a restriction of competition within the meaning of Article 81(1).

In drawing up an exclusive distribution agreement varying degrees of immunity from intra-brand competition can be granted. The manufacturer may agree only to refrain from distributing the product itself within the distributor's territory. Additionally or alternatively, protection may be given from the selling efforts of other distributors. Distributors may be prohibited from actively seeking sales outside their own territory (qualified territorial protection) or from making any sales outside their territories at all (absolute territorial protection[126]). *Consten and Grundig* makes it clear that where the territorial protection granted to the distributor is absolute the affront to the single market objective is too severe. In consequence, the agreement will be found to have as its object the restriction of competition.

To encourage concentration of selling efforts exclusive distribution agreements are often combined with a commitment on the part of the distributor not to purchase the products of competitors for resale.[127]

b. FRANCHISING AGREEMENTS AND *PRONUPTIA DE PARIS*

Franchising arrangements in which a franchisee, or franchisees, is appointed and established as part of a uniform business network, may also have a positive impact on competition on a market. Franchise arrangements assist the entry of new competitors to a market and lead to an increase in inter-brand competition. They enable a franchisor to expand its reputation and network without engaging in substantial investment. A franchisee is also enabled to set

---

[123] Case 56/65 [1966] ECR 234, [1966] CMLR 357.

[124] See *supra* 485 ff.

[125] Case 56/65 [1966] ECR 234, [1966] CMLR 357. See extract set out in Chap. 4.

[126] Absolute territorial protection may be reinforced by the grant of intellectual property rights: see e.g. Cases 56 & 58, *Etablissements Consten SA & Grundig-Verkaufs-GmbH v. Commission* [1966] ECR 299, [1966] CMLR 418.

[127] See *infra* 517–518.

up and to enter a market with the assistance of an entrepreneur whose business has already been tried and tested on the market.

In *Pronuptia de Paris GmbH v. Pronuptia de Paris Irmgard Schillgallis*[128] the ECJ held that two categories of clauses essential to the successful operation of distribution *franchise agreements* did not constitute restrictions of competition for the purposes of Article 81(1):

First, the franchisor must be able to communicate his know-how to the franchisees and provide them with the necessary assistance in order to enable them to apply his methods, without running the risk that know-how and assistance might benefit competitors, even indirectly . . .

Secondly, the franchisor must be able to take the measures necessary for maintaining the identity and reputation of the network bearing his business name of symbol.[129]

The Court thus held that a restriction on the ability of a franchisee:

(1) to open a shop of a similar nature during the period of the contract and for a reasonable period thereafter; and
(2) to sell the shop without the franchisor's consent

will not restrict competition where essential to protect the know-how and assistance provided under the terms of the contract. Similarly, clauses requiring the franchisee:

(1) to apply and to use the franchisor's business methods and know how;
(2) to locate, lay out and decorate the sales premises according to the franchisor's instructions;
(3) to gain the franchisor's approval prior to an assignment of the franchise;
(4) to sell only products supplied by the franchisor; and
(5) to gain the franchisor's approval for all advertising

may also be essential to preserve the identity and the reputation of the network and so fall outside Article 81(1).[130]

The Court did not, however, totally embrace an economic approach to franchise agreements.[131] It would not accept that: (1) clauses effecting a division of territories between the franchisor and franchisees or between the franchisees *inter se*,[132] or (2) preventing price competition between them, were essential to the operation of the franchise agreement. These are the types of clauses, discussed above, which automatically restrict competition. Arguments raised justifying their imposition can be considered only when determining their compatibility with Article 81(3).

Case 161/84, *Pronuptia de Paris GmbH v. Pronuptia de Paris Irmgard Schillgallis* [1986] ECR 353, [1986] 1 CMLR 414

The facts of this case are set out in Chapter 4. Broadly, however, this case concerned a dispute that arose before the German courts between Pronuptia de Paris and Mrs Schillgallis. The German court

---

[128] Case 161/84, *Pronuptia de Paris GmbH v. Pronuptia de Paris Irmgard Schillgallis* [1986] ECR 353, [1986] 1 CMLR 414.

[129] *Ibid.*, paras 16–17.

[130] See paras. 16–22.

[131] See *supra* Chap. 4.

[132] This has created difficulties since many franchisees are not willing to make the requisite investment without such protection.

sought guidance from the Court of Justice as to how it could determine whether or not a franchising agreement was compatible with Article 81(1).

Court of Justice

23. It must be emphasized on the other hand that, far from being necessary for the protection of the know-how provided or the maintenance of the network's identity and reputation, certain provisions restrict competition between the members of the network. That is true of provisions which share markets between the franchisor and franchisees or between franchisees or prevent franchisees from engaging in price competition with each other.

24. In that regard, the attention of the national court should be drawn to the provision which obliges the franchisee to sell goods covered by the contract only in the premises specified therein. That provision prohibits the franchisee from opening a second shop. Its real effect becomes clear if it is examined in conjunction with the franchisor's undertaking to ensure that the franchisee has the exclusive use of his business name or symbol in a given territory. In order to comply with that undertaking the franchisor must not only refrain from establishing himself within that territory but also require other franchisess to give an undertaking not to open a second shop outside their own territory. A combination of provisions of that kind results in a sharing of markets between the franchisor and the franchisees or between franchisees and thus restricts competition within the network. As is clear from the judgment of 13 July 1966 (Joined Cases 56 and 58/64 *Consten and Grundig v. Commission* [1966] ECR 299), a restriction of that kind constitutes a limitation of competition for the purposes of Article [81(1)] if it concerns a business name of symbol which is already well-known. It is of course possible that a prospective franchisee would not take the risk of becoming part of the chain, investing his own money, paying a relatively high entry fee and undertaking to pay a substantial annual royalty, unless he could hope, thanks to a degree or protection against competition on the part of the franchisor and other franchisees, that his business would be profitable. That consideration, however, is relevant only to an examination of the agreement in the light of the conditions laid down in Article [81(3)].

25. Although provisions which impair the franchisee's freedom to determine his own prices are restrictive of competition, that is not the case where the franchisor simply provides franchisees with price guidelines, so long as there is no concerted practice between the franchisor and the franchisees or between the franchises themselves in the actual application of such prices.

c. SELECTIVE DISTRIBUTION AGREEMENTS AND *METRO*

A supplier wishing to project an image for its goods and/or to ensure that sales are accompanied by the provision of specific services may decide to establish a selective distribution system. Under such a system the supplier will select its retailers, perhaps by number but, more frequently, by reference to quality or location of the distributor. Where the supplier wishes to portray and enhance a luxury image and to capitalize on consumers' desires to purchase a luxury product it may restrict supplies to retailers selling from a high quality location. Alternatively, a supplier may agree only to supply retailers that will comply with certain obligations as to service, sales promotion or regular ordering. It may wish to ensure that consumers purchasing its product receive a minimum level of pre-sales services and are fully informed about the product's qualities and capabilities. If such a system is to be effective both the supplier and the distributors will wish to ensure that non-authorized retailers, which will detract from the image they are attempting to create or which will free-ride on the pre-sales services provided, are not supplied.

A prohibition on the supply of retailers that have not been authorized to sell the products impacts on *intra-brand* competition and may be aimed at promoting inter-brand competition. In an ideal world a consumer who does not value the luxury image or the additional services imposed will purchase other competing products instead. Nonetheless it has been seen that there the justifications for a selective distribution system may not be as strong as the supplier suggests and that, especially where networks of similar agreements are operated, the practice may in fact weaken inter-brand competition, facilitate horizontal co-ordination, and lead to higher prices.[133]

Despite the similarities between franchising agreements and selective distribution systems[134] they have been afforded quite different treatment under EC law. In *Pronuptia* the Court accepted that many clauses essential to the operation of a franchising agreement do not infringe Article 81(1). Further, Regulation 4087/88[135] (which has now expired) provided, from 1988, a block exemption for those franchising agreements that did infringe Article 81(1). In contrast, until 1 June 2000 there was no Community block exemption for selective distribution systems. The question whether or not selective distribution systems infringe Article 81(1) has therefore been of extreme importance. Although the ECJ has recognized that certain selective distribution systems may escape the Article 81(1) prohibition, the Community authorities have been less willing than they have in the context of franchising agreements to accept that clauses do not fall within Article 81(1).[136]

In *Metro-SB-Grossmärkte GmbH v. Commission (No 1)*[137] the ECJ recognized that a simple *selective distribution system* is compatible with Article 81(1). Although recognising that selective distribution limits price competition it accepted that price competition does not necessarily constitute the only form of competition.[138] It is clear, however, from the Court's judgments[139] that Article 81(1) is only inapplicable if certain conditions are satisfied:

(i)   the characteristics of the product in question merit a selective distribution system;

(ii) the distributors are chosen by reference to objective criteria of a qualitative nature which are set out uniformly and are not used arbitrarily to discriminate against certain retailers;

(iii) the system seeks to enhance competition and to counterbalance the restriction of

---

[133] See *supra* 488–493.

[134] In each case the producer wishes to project a certain image for its product or to ensure that specific services are provided by the distributor. It may therefore wish to control the dealers operating within the system and the location and/or the get-up of the premises. In each case the assignment of intellectual property rights might be essential to the successful operation of the agreement

[135] [1988] OJ L35/46, see *infra* 530–531.

[136] 'The Commission (and the Court) generally accord more favourable treatment to restrictive clauses in franchising agreements as compared to distributions agreements... For example, dealer location clauses, minimum purchasing obligations and stocking requirements in franchise agreement do not even fall within Art. [81(1)], while in selective distribution agreements the same clauses not only fall within Art. [81(1)] but might also be denied an exemption under Art. [81(3)]. This is problematic: many distribution agreements have elements that are characteristic of franchises, ... i.e. the transfer of commercial know-how to independent parties operating under the supplier's trademark and not dealing in certain competing goods.' B.E. Hawk, *System Failure: Vertical Restraints and EC Competition Law* [1995] 32 *CML Rev.* 973, 985.

[137] Case 26/76 [1977] ECR 1875, [1978] 2 CMLR 1; see *supra* Chap. 4. The Court's judgment was given soon after the US Supreme Court's judgment in *Sylvania* which overruled *Schwinn*: see *supra* 493–498.

[138] Case 26/76, *Metro-SB-Grossmärkte GmbH v. Commission (No 1)* [1977] ECR 1875, [1978] 2 CMLR 1, para. 21 set out *supra* in Chap. 4.

[139] *Ibid.*, paras 20, 33–34 and Case T–19/92 *Groupement d'Achat Edouard Leclerc v. Commission* [1994] ECR II–441, [1997] 4 CMLR 995, para. 112.

competition inherent in selective distribution systems, in particular as regards price; and

(iv) the criteria set out do not go beyond what is necessary for the product in question.[140]

Even a system complying with the requirements set out above may infringe Article 81(1) if the market is tied up with a network of similar agreements.[141]

The nature of the product

In *Metro*[142] the Court stated that the operation of a selective distribution system was justified in 'the sector covering the production of high quality and technically advanced consumer durables'. It is accepted that two categories of products justify a selective distribution system: technically complex products and luxury or branded products.

In the context of technically complex products it is necessary to determine whether or not the technology involved is so complex as to justify a distribution network involving specialized wholesalers and retailers.[143] In the case of luxury products it is necessary to assess the need for the producer to preserve its prestige brand image and the need to safeguard, in the mind of the consumer, the aura of exclusivity and prestige of the product. In such cases appropriate marketing and a setting and presentation in line with the luxurious and exclusive nature and brand image of the product is essential.[144]

It has been found that the following products justify such a system: televisions,[145] hi-fis,[146] cameras,[147] personal computers,[148] clocks and watches,[149] high-quality gold and silver products,[150] perfumes,[151] dinner services,[152] and cars[153] (a specific block exemption applies for motor vehicle distribution agreements). It has been doubted whether plumbing fittings are technically advanced products that necessitate a selective distribution system.[154]

---

[140] Case 31/80, *L'Oréal NV aud L'Oréal SA v. De Nieuwe AMCK Puba* [1980] ECR 3775, [1981] 2 CMLR 235. The restrictions must be objectively necessary to protect the quality of the products in question: see e.g. *Grohe* [1985] OJ L19/17, [1988] 4 CMLR 612.

[141] See Case 75/84, *Metro v. Commission (No 2)* [1986] ECR 3021, [1987] 1 CMLR 118, discussed *infra* at XXX.

[142] Case 26/76, *Metro-SB-Grossmärkte GmbH v. Commission (No 1)* [1977] ECR 1875, [1978] 2 CMLR 1.

[143] Case 75/84, *Metro v. Commission (No 2)* [1986] ECR 3021, [1987] 1 CMLR 118.

[144] Case T–19/92, *Groupement d'Achat Edouard Leclerc v. Commission* [1994] ECR II–441, [1997] 4 CMLR 995, para. 116.

[145] Case 75/84, *Metro v. Commission (No 2)* [1986] ECR 3021, [1987] 1 CMLR 118.

[146] *Grundig* [1985] OJ L233/1, renewed [1994] OJ L20/15, [1995] 4 CMLR 658.

[147] *Hasselblad* [1982] OJ L161/18, [1982] 2 CMLR 233.

[148] *IBM* [1984] OJ L118/24, [1984] 2 CMLR 342.

[149] *Junghans* [1977] OJ L30/10, [1977] 1 CMLR D 82; *cf* Case 31/85, *ETA Fabriques d'Ebauches v. DK Investments SA* [1985] ECR 3933, [1986] 2 CMLR 674.

[150] *Murat* [1983] OJ L348/20, [1984] 1 CMLR 219.

[151] *Parfums Givenchy* [1992] OJ L236/11, [1993] 5 CMLR 579; *Yves St Laurent* [1992] OJ L12/24, [1993] 4 CMLR 120, on appeal Case T–19/92, *Groupement d'Achat Edouard Leclerc v. Commission* [1994] ECR II–441, [1997] 4 CMLR 995.

[152] *Villeroy & Bosch* [1985] OJ L376/15, [1998] 4 CMLR 461.

[153] *BMW* [1975] OJ L29/1, [1975] 1 CMLR D44.

[154] *Grohe* [1985] OJ L19/17, [1988] 4 CMLR 612.

It also seems that 'selective distribution systems which are justified by the specific nature of the products or the requirements for their distribution may be established in other economic sectors'.[155] In *SA Binon & Cie v. SA Agence et Messageries de la Presse*,[156] for example, it was accepted that newspapers and periodicals would constitute a suitable product for selective distribution, partly because of the limited shelf life which each had:

> Such a system may be established for the distribution of newspapers and periodicals, without infringing the prohibition in Article [81(1)], given the special nature of those products as regards their distribution. As AMP rightly pointed out, newspapers and periodicals can, as a general rule, only be sold by retailers during an extremely limited period of time whereas the public expects each distributor to be able to offer a representative selection of press publications, in particular those of the national press. For their part, publishers undertake to take back unsold copies and this gives rise to a continuous exchange of products between publishers and distributors.

It may be hard to persuade the Commission or a court that a product merits a selective distribution system if such a system if not operated in all jurisdictions.

Qualitative not quantitative criteria applied uniformly

The Court in *Metro* stated clearly that a selective distribution system in which 'resellers are chosen on the basis of objective criteria of a qualitative nature relating to the technical qualifications of the reseller and his staff and the suitability of his trading premises and that such conditions are laid down uniformly for all potential resellers and are not applied in a discriminatory fashion'[157] would accord with Article 81.

An immediate problem is to determine whether or not criteria are qualitative or quantitative in nature. The distinction is a difficult one since qualitative restrictions inevitably lead to restrictions on the number of resellers selected. It seems however that '[t]hese criteria may be defined as criteria aimed to select dealers in view of their objective suitability to distribute a particular kind of good'.[158] The Court's judgments and Commission's decisions indicate the types of restrictions likely to be held to be qualitative and the types of restrictions likely to be found to be quantitative. Unfortunately, the cases are not always entirely consistent.

It is clear from *Metro* itself that criteria relating to the technical qualification of the reseller and its staff and suitability of trading premises are of a qualitative nature. Further, it seems that obligations precluding the sale of goods that would detract from the product's brand image[159] and requiring dealers to provide after-sales services[160] are qualitative and compatible with Article 81(1). In some cases the Commission has found an obligation requiring a dealer to stock a wide or an entire range of products to be qualitative and in

---

[155] Case T–19/92, *Groupement d'Achat Edouard Leclerc v. Commission* [1994] ECR II–441, [1997] 4 CMLR 995, para. 113.

[156] Case 234/83 [1985] ECR 2015, para. 32.

[157] Case 26/76, *Metro-SB-Grossmärkte GmbH v. Commission (No 1)* [1977] ECR 1875, [1978] 2 CMLR 1, para. 20.

[158] J. Faull and A. Nikpay (eds.), *The EC Law of Competition* (Oxford University Press, 1999), para. 7.192.

[159] *Parfums Givenchy* [1992] OJ L236/11, [1993] 5 CMLR 579.

[160] *Grundig* [1985] OJ L233/1, renewed [1994] OJ L20/15, [1995] 4 CMLR 658; *Villeroy & Bosch* [1985] OJ L376/15, [1998] 4 CMLR 461.

others it has found them to be quantitative. It seems that the classification of the obligation as qualitative or quantitative may turn upon the nature of the product involved.[161]

An obligation precluding members of the system from supplying unauthorized retailers does not infringe Article 81(1) since it is the corollary of the essential system of selective distribution.[162] Further a provision precluding wholesalers from supplying private customers does not infringe Article 81(1).[163]

Other restrictions

In contrast, quantitative restrictions will infringe Article 81(1). Although the exact meaning of the term quantitative is elusive, the purpose appears to be to catch all provisions that protect approved network members from the competition of other retailers meeting the qualitative criteria. It is thus broader than where a simple numerical limit is placed on the number of dealers in a particular area, although a clause fixing the number of dealers for a specific area[164] is of course prohibited. The following have also been held to be quantitative restrictions which infringe Article 81(1):[165] clauses restricting sales to specific types of stores;[166] or clauses requiring dealers to maintain specific amounts of stocks,[167] to promote the manufacturers product, to stock an entire range of products,[168] or to have a minimum annual turnover.[169]

Further, provisions directly or indirectly aimed at resale price maintenance[170] or

---

[161] In *Grundig* OJ [1985] L 233/1, renewed [1994] OJ L20/15, [1995] 4 CMLR 658 the Commission found a requirement that retailers had to carry and stock a whole range of products went beyond what was necessary for the distribution of products and was an impediment to competition. In contrast, in *Villeroy & Bosch* [1985] OJ L376/15, [1998] 4 CMLR 461, the requirement that the retailer had to display and stock a sufficiently wide and varied range of products did not infringe Art. 81(1) and the system was granted negative clearance. In this case sales targets were not imposed, the requirement did not prevent retailers stocking competing products and inter-brand competition was high. In the *Guidelines on Vertical Restraints*, [2000] OJ C291/1, para. 185, the Commission states that an obligation requiring dealers to sell a certain range of the products is purely of a qualitative nature.

[162] Case 26/76, *Metro-SB-Grossmärkte GmbH v. Commission (No 1)* [1977] ECR 1875, [1978] 2 CMLR 1, para. 27.

[163] Case 26/76, *Metro-SB-Grossmärkte GmbH v. Commission (No 1)* [1977] ECR 1875, [1978] 2 CMLR 1.

[164] In *Hasselblad* [1982] OJ L161/18, [1982] 2 CMLR 233, e.g. the supplier supplied only a few of those dealers which satisfied the criteria set out.

[165] Such clauses may also limit the freedom of a dealer to purchase other supplier's products.

[166] Case T-19/92, *Groupement d'Achat Edouard Leclerc v. Commission* [1994] ECR II-441, [1997] 4 CMLR 995 (it is not justifiable to have a provision precluding supermarkets or hypermarkets becoming part of the network). See also *Vichy* [1991] OJ L75/57.

[167] Case 26/76, *Metro-SB-Grossmärkte GmbH v. Commission (No 1)* [1977] ECR 1875, [1978] 2 CMLR 1.

[168] See *supra* n. 161.

[169] *Parfums Givenchy* [1992] OJ L236/11, [1993] 5 CMLR 579, *Yves St Laurent* [1992] OJ L12/24. [1993] 4 CMLR 120; on appeal Case T-19/92, *Groupement d'Achat Edouard Leclerc v. Commission* [1994] ECR II-441, [1997] 4 CMLR 995.

[170] Case 243/85, *SA Binon & Cie v. SA Agence et Messageries de la Presse* [1985] ECR 2015, [1985] 3 CMLR 800 and Case 107/82, *AEG-Telefunken v. Commission* [1983] ECR 3151, [1984] 3 CMLR 325.

preventing retailers from selling to each other (bans on cross-suppliers)[171] or to consumers in other Member States[172] will infringe Article 81(1).

Provisions setting out a difficult or lengthy procedure for retailers to join the network may also infringe Article 81(1).[173]

Discriminatory application of the criteria and refusal to supply

Article 81(1) will apply if the supplier precludes network members from supplying other members of the system[174] or if the supplier itself, acting in agreement with its dealers (and not unilaterally), refuses to supply retailers which meet its requirements. A breach of Article 81 will therefore be committed if a supplier refuses to supply dealers known, for example, to sell at prices below those recommended by the supplier or outside their territory. Dealers which are part of the network but which understand that they will not be supplied if they do not adhere to the manufacturer's policy may be taken to have agreed, explicitly or implicitly, to these terms.[175]

Where a supplier is found to be operating a selective distribution system in a discriminatory manner in breach of Article 81(1) it appears that the Commission may not make an order for supply. In *Automec v. Commission (No 2)* the CFI indicated that the Commission did not have power to order supply[176] and to insist on contractual arrangements when other suitable means were available to ensure that the infringement was terminated.[177] The Commission[178] may declare that the relevant agreement infringes Article 81(1), consider whether or not the agreement merits exemption (where the system is being operated so as to deter dealers from selling outside their territory or to interfere with their freedom to set resale prices an exemption will also almost certainly be refused) and, where appropriate, fine

---

[171] *Hasselblad* [1982] OJ L161/18, [1982] 2 CMLR 233.

[172] See Cases 228, 229/82, *Ford Werke AG and Ford of Europe Inc. v. Commission* [1984] ECR 1129, [1984] 1 CMLR 649; Case 32/78, *BMW v. Commission* [1979] ECR 2435, [1980] 1 CMLR 370; *Kodak* [1970] JO L142/24, [1970] CMLR D19. Guarantees granted on sale in one Member State must be honoured by dealers in other Member States: Case 31/85, *ETA Fabriques d'Ebauches v. DK Investments SA* [1985] ECR 3933, [1986] 2 CMLR 674.

[173] *Parfums Givenchy* [1992] OJ L236/11, [1993] 5 CMLR 579; *Yves St Laurent* [1992] OJ L12/24. [1993] 4 CMLR 120; on appeal Case T–19/92 *Groupement d'Achat Edouard Leclerc v. Commission* [1994] ECR II–441, [1997] 4 CMLR 995.

[174] See *supra.*

[175] See Case 107/82, *AEG-Telefunken v. Commission* [1983] ECR 3151, [1984] 3 CMLR 325; Cases 228, 229/82, *Ford Werke AG and Ford of Europe Inc. v. Commission* [1984] ECR 1129, [1984] 1 CMLR 649 and Case T–41/96 *Bayer AG v. Commission*, judgment of 26 Oct. 2000. Only truly unilateral behaviour escapes the Art. 81(1) prohibition: see discussion of unilateral conduct and agreements, *supra* at Chap. 3.

[176] See *supra* Chap. 7.

[177] Case T–24/90 [1992] ECR II–2223, [1992] 5 CMLR 431, para. 51. This aspect of *Automec II* is discussed in Chaps. 14 and 15.

[178] If an action is commenced privately by an undertaking, the national court can declare that the agreement infringes Art. 81(1) and is void (a national court cannot, of course, exempt the agreement). If the agreement has been notified to the Commission or is a non-notifiable agreement (as most vertical agreements are) the national court may have to stay proceedings or take interim measures pending a decision by the Commission on the compatibility of the agreement with Art. 81(3): see *infra* Chap. 15.

the parties in breach.[179] If the supplier is dominant it is possible that a refusal to supply may constitute an abuse of a dominant position and that an order for supply will be made.[180]

Difficulties in applying the metro criteria and article 81(3)

Although a welcome recognition that selective distribution systems may enhance inter-brand competition the judgment in *Metro* is frustrating. First, the requirement that the product should fall within one of two categories that the Commission and/or the Court has ruled should be able to benefit from such a system may seem inappropriate. Although it may be true that the need for a selective distribution system has sometimes been exaggerated, a producer operating on a competitive market will be punished by consumers if they do not believe that the product in question merits the system.

Secondly, the requirement that retailers should be selected by reference only to *qualitative* criteria makes no economic sense. If a retailer has to comply with stringent qualitative criteria this may involve considerable expense which may demand that a quantitative limit on dealers is imposed. Apart from being economically indefensible it has been seen that the requirement has proved difficult to apply in practice and that identical restrictions have been labelled as qualitative in some cases and quantitative in others.[181]

The Court's view that some restrictions of conduct imposed on dealers do not restrict competition is welcome, but the narrowness of the tests is regretted. The rules are nonsense commercially and economically speaking. It is very difficult for the holder of a prestigious brand to become master of its retail outlets. The rules encourage a firm that is concerned about the services offered by retailers to integrate forward and sell as far down the distribution chain as it can manage. This policy does not increase competition and may well reduce inefficiency. Moreover, it cannot be adopted by small firms.[182]

The net outcome has been that the authorities have not, in the context of Article 81(1) adequately assessed whether or not a selective distribution system has led to an anti-competitive outcome on the market.[183] In a majority of cases a producer wishing to operate a selective distribution system had had to apply to the Commission for a negative clearance or an exemption. In practice the Commission has been willing to exempt many quantitative restrictions, for example, an obligation to engage in sales promotions.[184] The Commission will almost certainly refuse exemption however, where resale prices are fixed or restrictions on parallel imports are imposed.[185]

---

[179] See *infra* Chap. 14.

[180] See *supra* Chap. 7. In Case 75/84, *Metro v. Commission (No 2)* [1986] ECR 3021, [1987] 1 CMLR 118) the argument that SABA was dominant was rejected. The market for TVs and other such goods was competitive and SABA's market share was less than 10 per cent.

[181] Although the Commission has nonetheless exempted many quantitative restrictions in decisions issued under Art. 81(3) an exemption can only be obtained at great cost to business; *supra* Chap. 4.

[182] V. Korah, *An Introductory Guide to EC Competition Law and Practice* (7th edn.,) (Hart Publishing, 2000), para. 8.4.

[183] But see Case 75/84, *Metro v. Commission (No 2)* [1986] ECR 3021, [1987] 1 CMLR 118.

[184] See Case 26/76, *Metro-SB-Grossmärkte GmbH v. Commission (No 1)* [1977] ECR 1875, [1978] 2 CMLR 1; *Grundig* [1985] OJ L233/1, renewed OJ [1994] L 20/15, [1995] 4 CMLR 658; *Parfums Givenchy* [1992] OJ L236/11, [1993] 5 CMLR 579.

[185] See also *infra* 526 ff.

Networks of agreements

It has been clear since *Metro (No 2)* that even a simple selective distribution system will fall within Article 81(1) where a network of similar agreements exist which tie up the market and leave no room for other methods of distribution.

Case 75/84, *Metro-SB-Grossmärkte GmbH & Co.KG v. Commission (No 2)* [1986] ECR 3021, [1987] 1 CMLR 118

Following the expiry of its exemption, SABA applied for its renewal. Metro again objected, this time asserting that market conditions had changed significantly since the grant of the last exemption. It pointed out that many other electronics companies now operated selective distribution systems and that the market had become much more rigid. Although the Court accepted that it is necessary to determine whether or not the existence of other systems lead to rigidity in the market it agreed with the Commission that the systems in issue had not led to rigidity in price structures.

Court of Justice

40 It must be borne in mind that, although the Court has held in previous decisions that 'simple' selective distribution systems are capable of constituting an aspect of competition compatible with Article [81(1)], there may nevertheless be a restriction or elimination of competition where the existence of a certain number of such systems does not leave any room for other forms of distribution based on a different type of competition policy or results in a rigidity in price structure which is not counterbalanced by other aspects of competition between products of the same brand and by the existence of effective competition between different brands.

41. Consequently, the existence of a large number of selective distribution systems for a particular product does not in itself permit the conclusion that competition is restricted or distorted. Nor is the existence of such systems decisive as regards the granting or refusal of an exemption under Article [81(3)], since the only factor to be taken into consideration in that regard is the effect which such systems actually have on the competitive situation. Therefore the coverage ratio of selective distribution systems for colour television sets, to which Metro refers, cannot in itself be regarded as a factor preventing an exemption from being granted.

42. It follows that an increase in the number of 'simple' selective distribution systems after an exemption has been granted must be taken into consideration, when an application for renewal of that exemption is being considered, only in the special situation in which the relevant market was already so rigid and structured that the element of competition inherent in 'simple' systems is not sufficient to maintain workable competition. Metro has not been able to show that a special situation of that kind exists in the present case.

. . .

46. Therefore Metro's submission based on the growth of selective distribution systems in the consumer electronics sector must be rejected.

It is possible therefore that a simple selective distribution system may fall within Article 81(1) and be refused an exemption where the existence of networks of other similar agreements leads to excessive rigidity on the market.

Although it is true that, especially where selective distribution systems are commonplace throughout a market, they may lead to an increase in consumer prices[186] and the judgment

---

[186] See *supra* 488–493. Although dealers still compete on the basis of enhanced services there are fears that the operation of selective distribution systems throughout a market will lead to tacit or explicit co-ordination of suppliers' or distributors' behaviour, higher consumer prices, and limited discounting on the market.

displays a willingness to embark on economic analysis, the case has raised several practical difficulties.[187] In particular, given the Court's unwillingness to embrace a realistic economic analysis to selective distribution systems in *Metro (No 1)*, it seems peculiar to add an economic layer later, the effect of which is to bring more agreements within the net of Article 81(1). The usual argument advanced is that a more realistic approach should be adopted to ensure that more agreements fall outside of Article 81(1) altogether.

R. Whish, *Competition Law* (3rd edn., Butterworths, 1993), 594

At one level this judgment might be welcomed, in that it requires economic analysis in deciding upon the application of Article [81]. On the other hand its practical application seems rife with difficulty. It requires a producer or its legal adviser to undertake an extensive analysis of the market in order to decide whether the *Metro* doctrine applies. A further problem is that it would seem that either the creation of one further selective distribution system takes it, though not the existing ones, within Article [81(1)], which seems unfair to the last one to be established; or that the creation of the last system falls within Article [81(1)] and brings the previous ones within it as well, which is manifestly unfair to them. Either way the legal uncertainty coupled with the element of unfairness makes the concept unappealing. Furthermore if one is to argue after *Metro (No 2)* that the economic context in some circumstances brings a selective distribution system within Article [81(1)], even though the criteria are qualitative, one might just as well argue the matter the other way around and contend that, because of the economic context, even criteria of a quantitative nature fall outside Article [81(1)]. If one is to inject more economic analysis into Article [81(1)], there seems little logic in applying it to catch agreements but not to exclude them.

d. BEER SUPPLY AGREEMENTS AND *DELIMITIS*

The most important of all of the Court's judgments in the context of distribution agreements is *Delimitis v. Henninger Bräu*.[188] In this case the Court had to give guidance to a national court asked to rule on the compatibility of a beer supply agreement with Article 81(1). It will be remembered that the contract obliged the café proprietor to obtain his beer requirements from the brewer, Henninger Bräu (although once a fixed quantity had been bought Delimitis was free to purchase beer from other Member States). Agreements such as this which oblige a buyer to obtain all, most, or a certain percentage or amount of its requirements from a named supplier frequently lead to efficiencies in distribution. A supplier is enabled to plan the number of sales it will make with greater precision, and distributors are encouraged actively to promote the supplier's product. Further, suppliers often confer reciprocal benefits (such as loans at below market rates, training, business and financial advice) on distributors which agree not to purchase a competitor's products. Obviously the supplier will wish to ensure that these benefits are not used to assist sales of competitors' products.

Since, however, these non-compete or quantity forcing agreements prohibit or deter distributors from handling competitors' products, there is clearly a concern that that these agreements, or networks of similar agreements, might tie up outlets and preclude competitors from gaining access to the retail market. This worry is particularly acute in markets

---

[187] See e.g. R.J. Goebel, 'Metro II's Confirmation of the Selective Distribution Rules: Is This the End of the Road?' (1987) *CMLRev.* 605.

[188] Case C–234/89, *Delimitis v. Henninger Bräu* [1991] ECR I–935, [1992] 5 CMLR 210.

where access to the market is not easy on account of the existence of barriers to entry, such as planning restrictions or licensing requirements.[189]

In *Delimitis*[190] the ECJ recognized that an obligation imposed on the café proprietor to purchase most of its beer requirements from the brewer entailed advantages for both the supplier and the reseller. It set out guidelines for the national court to determine whether or not the effect of such an agreement foreclosed access to the market and so prevented, restricted, or distorted competition. This could be determined by, first, defining the relevant market and considering whether or not that market was foreclosed to other competitors or precluded expansion by existing competitors. If it was, secondly, it had to be determined whether or not the agreement in question restricted competition. It would only do so if the agreements concluded by that producer appreciably contributed to the foreclosure effect.

This case clearly demonstrates that in the absence of territorial exclusivity or resale price maintenance a careful analysis of the impact of the agreement on the market should be made. The Court focussed its enquiry on the important question whether or not the agreement, alone or in conjunction with a network of similar agreements, would lead to a restriction of inter-brand competition. The Court considered that only where an agreement contributes to the foreclosure of the market and to a restriction of inter-brand competition will it be found to restrict competition within the meaning of Article 81(1).

Similarly, in *Langnese-Iglo GmbH v. Commission*, an appeal from a Commission decision finding that an agreement providing for the exclusive sale of ice creams for impulse purchase in retail outlets infringed Article 81(1) and could not be exempted under Article 81(3),[191] the CFI recognized that a clause:

whereby the retailer undertakes to sell through its sales outlet only products purchased directly from the applicant contains both an exclusive purchasing obligation and a prohibition of competition, which are capable of giving rise to a restriction of competition within the meaning of Article [81(1)] of the Treaty both between products of the same brand and between products of different brands. In those circumstances, the Court must consider whether the Commission has established to the requisite factual and legal standard that the contested supply agreements has, at it contends, an appreciable effect on competition in the common market.[192]

The Court stressed, however, that consideration of the effects of an exclusive agreement required regard to be had to the economic and legal context of the agreement, in which it might combine with others to have a cumulative effect on competition.

As regards the impact of networks of exclusive agreements on access to the market, it is also apparent from the case law of the Court of Justice, first, that it depends in particular on the number of sales outlet tied to the producers in relation to the number of retailers not so tied, on the quantities to which those commitments related and on the proportion between those quantities and those which are sold through retailers that are not tied. Furthermore, the extent of the tying-in brought about by a network of exclusive purchasing agreements, although of some importance in assessing the partitioning of the market, is only one factor amongst others pertaining to the economic and legal context in which the agreement, or as in this case, a network of agreements must be assessed (*Delimitis*) . . .[193]

---

[189] See *supra* 491–492.

[190] The relevant paras. of the judgment are set out *supra* in Chap. 4.

[191] *Langnese-Iglo GmbH* [1993] OJ L183/19, [1994] 4 CMLR 51. See also the Commission's decision in *Schöller Lebensmittel GmbH & Co KG* [1993] OJ L183/1, [1994] 4 CMLR 51.

[192] Case T–7/93 [1995] ECR II-1583, [1995] 5 CMLR 602, paras. 94–95.

[193] Case T–7/93 [1995] ECR II–1583, [1995] 5 CMLR 602, para. 101.

(iv) CONFUSION AND THE COMMISSION'S VIEW

Despite the clear view expounded by the Court in the series of cases set out above, it was seen in Chapter 4 that the Commission has been rebuked for its hard-line approach to vertical agreements. The Commission's tendency has, in the past, been to adopt a narrow interpretation of the case law or to distinguish it completely.[194] Although of course it is the Court and not the Commission that is entrusted with the interpretation of the Treaty the different approaches of the two have led to confusion and to a perception that distribution agreements generally require exemption from the prohibition set out in Article 81(1).[195]

The Commission has taken the view that many distribution agreements infringe Article 81(1). The fact that it felt a need to adopt regulations exempting categories of exclusive distribution,[196] exclusive purchasing,[197] franchising,[198] and motor vehicle distribution agreements[199] reflects its view that these types of agreement restrict competition and, consequently, require exemption under Article 81(3). Although the Commission recognizes the benefits resulting from these types of agreements it has tended to rehearse those advantages in the context of Article 81(3)[200] rather that in its analysis of agreements under Article 81(1).

It has been seen that this narrow view of Article 81(1) has been caused by a suspicion of both restrictions on trade between Member States and restrictions imposed on the parties' economic freedom.

Although the strict treatment of agreements containing territorial restraints has been criticized, the Commission has at least sought to reconcile consumer welfare and efficiency considerations with market integration goals.[201] In contrast, the most strident criticism has been that the equation of restraints on conduct with restrictions of competition is wrong in law,[202] has 'emasculated' economic analysis, has generated uncertainty and led to arbitrary division in treatment of distribution agreements by category,[203] and has meant that no account is taken of the structure of the market and the impact of the relevant agreement on that market. The approach focuses on the clauses of the agreement rather than the effect of

---

[194] See, e.g. the Commission's decision in *Langnese-Iglo GmbH* [1993] OJ L183/19, [1994] 4 CMLR 51 and *Schöller Lebensmittel GmbH & Co KG* [1993] OJ L183/1, [1994] 4 CMLR 51, in which the Commission appeared to adopt an extremely narrow construction of the Court's judgment in Case C–234/89, *Delimitis v. Henninger Bräu* [1991] ECR I-935, [1992] 5 CMLR 210.

[195] For the view of the ECJ, see *supra* 506–518.

[196] Reg. 1983/83, [1983] OJ L173/1 the successor to Reg. 67/67 [1967] OJ Spec. Ed. 10.

[197] Reg 1984/83, [1983] OJ L173/7 the successor to Reg. 67/67.

[198] Reg. 4087/88 [1988] OJ L359/46.

[199] Reg. 1475/95 [1995] OJ L178/1.

[200] See, e.g. Reg. 1983/83, [1983] OJ L173/1, recitals 5 and 6.

[201] See B.E. Hawk, 'System Failure: Vertical Restraints and EC Competition Law' (1995) 32 *CML Rev.* 973, 981. The approach to territorial restraints also gains support from the Court. It is arguable that market integration will more quickly be realized by allowing undertakings to pursue distributive efficiency.

[202] The reasoning of the Community Courts 'does not leave room for the theory which equates a restriction of competition with a restriction of freedom of action . . . . the application by the Court of restriction of freedom of action being caught *per se* by Art. [81(1)] only applies to absolute territorial protection. All other restrictions of freedom require a market analysis': D. Deacon, 'Vertical Restraints under EU Competition Law: New Directions' [1995] *Fordham Corp. Law Inst.* 307, paras. 16 and 18.

[203] Restrictions on conduct have been categorized as restrictions within the meaning of Art. 81(1) in some cases and as restrictions falling outside Art. 81(1) in others with no adequate justification or explanation for the difference in treatment.

the agreement on the competitive process. Innocuous agreements are brought within Article 81(1) and, in the absence of an exemption, condemned.

The Commission's tenacious adherence to such a broad interpretation of Article 81(1), and its reluctance to follow the case law of the ECJ have been very much tied to the issue of sovereignty. The broad application of Article 81(1) has meant that the Commission has sole control to exempt and authorize distribution agreements under Article 81(3). This has enabled it to regulate the types of restrictions (especially territorial ones) included in the agreements and to mould EC competition policy in relation to vertical restraints. In particular, to ensure that distribution agreements do not distort competition within the common market, are not 'used to prevent outsiders from entering a market, and to perpetuate the compartmentalization of the Community'[204] and do not discourage rivalry and interfere with the freedom and right of initiative of economic operators.[205] Further, in some instances it appears to have attempted to protect small and medium-sized undertakings (usually distributors) from the more aggressive tactics and stronger bargaining position of larger undertakings (usually manufacturers).[206]

In the extract from the article below Hawk fiercely criticizes this approach of the Commission, especially its broad and inconsistent application of Article 81(1). In his view the approach had caused the whole notification system to fail. It had led to legal uncertainty, proliferation of block exemptions, and, consequently, to rigid analysis of agreements by category rather than by economic effect.

B.E. Hawk, 'System Failure: Vertical Restraints and EC Competition Law' (1995) 32 *CMLRev.* 973, 974–86

2. System failure

The Commission's approach to vertical restraints evidences more fundamental institutional issues. Bluntly put, the notification system set up in 1962 in Regulation 17 has failed. The following flow-chart illustrates this system failure:

Step A   Overly broad application of Article [81(1)] (incoherent rationale, inconsistency with Court judgments and inadequate economic analysis)

↓

Step B   Generation of Extraordinary Legal Uncertainty

↓

Step C   Proliferation of Block Exemptions to Attempt to Reduce Legal Uncertainty

↓

Step D   Legal Formalisms and 'Analysis' by Categories

↓

Step E   De-emphasis on or Lack of Substantive (Economic) Analysis

---

[204] European Commission Green Paper, *supra* n. 2, 35.

[205] See J. Faull and A. Nikpay *The EC Law of Competition* (Oxford University Press, 1999), paras. 2.73–2.77, set out *supra* in Chap. 4.

[206] See, e.g. the discussion of the motor vehicle distribution block exemption *infra* 531–532.

2.1 Overbroad application of Article [81(1)]

The most fundamental, and most trenchant, criticism is that the Commission too broadly applies Article [81(1)] to agreements having little or no anticompetitive effects. This criticism rests on three pillars: 1) an inadequate economic analysis under Article [81(1)]; 2) an unpersuasive rationale for this overbroad application of [81(1)], notably the 'economic freedom' notion; and 3) the Commission's historical and continuing resistance to Court judgments evidencing a more nuanced economics-based interpretation of [81(1)].

2.1.1 Inadequate analysis under [81(1)]

The majority of the Commission decisions fail adequately to consider whether the restraint at issue harms competition in the consumer welfare sense of economics, i.e. effect on price or output. Concomitantly, market power, which should be the threshold issue, frequently is hardly examined (let alone given a central role) or is simply found to exist in a conclusory fashion under the rubric of 'appreciability.'

Market power is perhaps the most fundamental factor in a competition analysis. Market power is just as important under Article [81] as it is under Article [82]. The fact that the *legal* thresholds for the requisite degree of market power differ under Article [81] and [82] should not obscure that fact. There are no separate economics for Article [81(1)], (3) and [82].

It is essential to emphasize that a more rigorous economic analysis under [81(1)], does not mean that there must be only a 'rule of reason' under Article [81(1)]. There is room for both a *per se* rule and a rule of reason under Article [81(1)] . . .

The anaemic nature of the economic analysis under [81(1)] . . . can be seen in . . . examples . . .

Perhaps the most striking example is the Commission's (almost) automatic placement of *exclusive distributorships* or *exclusive supply obligations* under [81(1)] without any inquiry into actual anticompetitive effects or market power. But exclusive distributorships ordinarily pose no risk of anticompetitive effects where interbrand competition is healthy (i.e. the supplier lacks significant market power) and distributors and consumers have a range of similar products from which to choose. This automatic condemnation is particularly troublesome given the broad variety of efficiencies that can result from exclusive distribution.

A second example of anaemic economic analysis under Article [81] concerns *selective distribution*. Specific provision appear to be simply catalogued under [81(1)] or [81(3)] with little economic basis or analysis. There are exceptions, notably the Commission's decision in *Villeroy & Boch* [[1985] OJ L 376/15]. The Community Courts have engaged in a more economic analysis of selective distribution, an irony to some given that the Courts are intended to provide judicial review of an administrative body enjoying special antitrust expertise and experience.

A third example can be seen in the stark contrast between the Court of Justice's insistence on foreclosure and entry barrier analysis in examining *exclusive purchasing* and the Commission's begrudging and narrow use of foreclosure analysis . . .

Economic analysis of vertical arrangements in the United States has profoundly affected legal attitudes towards vertical arrangements. Vertical restraints are no longer viewed with suspicion. The most important threshold issue is the existence of market power: in most instances, the absence of market power means that competition is effective, that consumers have adequate choices available to them and that the market will correct temporary deficiencies far more efficiently than the law. Also, the existence of procompetitive or legitimate business justifications may validate a restraint even where there is market power.

. . .

2.1.2 The Commission's rationale under [81(1)] is unpersuasive

The first explanation for the inadequate economic analysis under [81(1)] lies in the Commission's stubborn (in the face of Court judgments) adherence to the definition of a restriction on competition as a restriction on the 'economic freedom' of operators in the marketplace. The principal weaknesses of the Freiburg School notion of restriction on economic freedom are (1) its failure to generate precise operable legal rules (i.e. failure to provide an analytical framework); (2) its distance from and tension with (micro) economics which does provide an analytical framework; (3) its tendency to favour traders/ competitors over consumers and consumer welfare (efficiency) and (4) its capture under Article [81(1)] of totally innocuous contract provisions having no anticompetitive effects in an economic sense.

The restriction on economic freedom notion could literally cover most if not all contractual agreements on the reasoning that the contract contains provisions which limit or 'restrict' the freedom of the parties as it existed prior to the contract . . .

Under U.S. law, an effect on competition is necessary; harm to the plaintiff or to a particular trader is not sufficient. This is clearly accepted. . . .

The economic freedom notion also fails to provide operable criteria to determine which agreements restrict competition. This is reflected in the handful of Court and Commission decisions finding that certain 'restrictions' do not fall within Article [81(1)] despite the fact that they clearly limit 'economic freedom.' These decisions do not provide a clear, consistent rationale to distinguish the 'exceptions' from the vast majority of 'restrictions' which have been held to fall within Article [81(1)]. . .

The breadth of coverage resulting from the economic freedom concept effectively shifts the analysis from [81(1)] to [81(3)] whenever notification of the agreement is required as a condition for the granting of an individual exemption. The Commission may find this shift of analysis and the resultant notification attractive because it appears to offer greater Commission surveillance and control.

Although the Court decisions are not entirely clear or consistent, it is fair to conclude that the Court has not accepted unequivocally the Commission's economic freedom definition.

Criticism of the Commission's overreaching under Article [81(1)] also comes from the highly interesting perspective of competition authority officials charged with enforcing mini-Article [81]s that have been exported to them. The head of the Venezuelan Authority stated that the Authority found the Article [81] bifurcation artificial and the consequent notification system infeasible. Despite the statutory language, Venezuela has gone to a unitary substantive analysis under their mini-[81]. Ferenc Vissi, head of the Hungarian competition authority, asked the following (rhetorical) question: does it make more sense to condemn all vertical restrains and then (block) exempt 90% à la Brussels, or to accept 90% and condemn only 10 per cent (à la Budapest).

These reactions suggest that the export of Article [81] is not carrying with it the Commission's interpretation of Article [81(1)].

The appreciability doctrine tempers this approach to some degree and could provide the doctrinal vehicle for a fuller economic analysis under [81(1)]. The Court of Justice has long recognised that an agreement may not have an appreciable effect on competition, and therefore not fall within Article [81(1)], because of the extremely small size of the supplier or the overall economic context . . .

A second explanation for the frequently sparce economic analysis under Article [81] (both (1) and (3)) derives form the market integration goal which impels both the Commission and the Community courts, according to the critics, to emasculate the economic analysis by rejecting in principle efficiency arguments/ justifications and by favouring intrabrand competition over interbrand competition. This criticism is most relevant with respect to territorial restraints. I shall limit myself here to only one comment. The economic freedom notion above and the market integration goal raise very different issues. The former effectively eliminates economics and should be discarded; the latter requires a more sophisticated economic analysis whose task is to reconcile the consumer welfare (efficiency) considerations with the market integration goal (e.g. an assessment of distributional (in the economic sense) variance among the different Member States).

A third possible explanation for some of the anaemic economics under Article [81] is a Commission desire to protect small and medium firms. For example, the treatment of exclusive distributorships, exclusive purchasing and intellectual property licensing appears partially motivated by a desire to protect smaller resellers and licensees from larger suppliers and licensors . . .

The protection of small and medium firms if often justified on the assumption that this promotes competition in the long run. Although this assumption might often be true, it should be put to the test with economic analysis in individual cases. Does a vertical restriction that would threaten the survival of certain small firms (a) harm competition by preventing them from becoming more formidable competitors in the future or (b) promote competition by exposing them to legitimate market forces?

A final explanation asserted by some critics of the Commission's overbroad [81(1)] approach is that it furthers the Commission's institutional interests; more specifically, it reinforces its monopoly to grant [81(3)] exemptions. If an economic analysis were made under Article [81(1)], far fewer vertical arrangements would be subject to the Commission's exclusive jurisdiction to grant individual exemption under Article [81(3)]. Economic analysis also would be within the competence of national courts when applying Article [81(1)].

2.1.3 Commission refusal to follow Community Courts

The Court of Justice and Court of First Instance have taken a more nuanced approach toward vertical arrangements under Article [81(1)]. The Courts have increasingly required an economic analysis of economic effects, particularly the possibility of foreclosure. This approach has largely been ignored or distinguished by the Commission, which adheres to its non-economics based application of Article [81(1)], i.e. restriction on economic freedom.

. . .

2.2 Step B—Generation of Extraordinary legal uncertainty

The overbroad application of Article [81(1)] generates extraordinary legal uncertainty about common contractual provisions that frequently raise little or no risk of anticompetitive effect in an economics sense, i.e. no effect on harm to consumer welfare in terms of price or output effects. The practical consequences cannot be exaggerated. Counsel's analysis of nonterritorial vertical arrangements under Article [81] is largely a matter of identifying for each party the clauses it may have difficulty enforcing, weighing the business interests involved and considering, on purely formalistic grounds, alternative that may fit more neatly within the Commission's maze of rules. This alters the content of agreements, upsets the bargain struck by agreements and undermines incentives necessary either to enter arrangements in the first place or to induce more specific forms of investment in distribution.

The Commission's fining policy also is important in this regard. Many agreements fall within Article [81(1)] and the parties are unable to obtain greater certainty without notifying the agreement to the Commission. If fines are unlikely, the decision largely comes down to an assessment of the timing and enforceability risks for each party with respect to each suspect clause. This situation is very common because significant fines are typically reserved for territorial restrictions, horizontal cartels and Article [82] cases.

2.3 Step C—Proliferation of block exemptions

The Commission has attempted to reduce the legal uncertainty generated by its overbroad application of [81(1)] by resorting to block exemptions . . .

2.4 Step D—Legal formalisms and 'analysis' by pigeonholing

The Commission largely applies Article [81(1)] to distribution arrangements according to formal legal categories. One set of rules applies to exclusive distribution, another to selective distribution, another to franchising, and a chaotic array of considerations apply to distribution arrangements that are not neatly pigeonholed. . . .

2.5 Lack of substantive analysis

The legal formalisms described above ultimately eliminate what should be the heart of the matter: and antitrust (i.e. economics/law) substantive analysis of a particular agreement or practice, i.e. its competitive harms and benefits. Competition law is economic law, and economics must play a predominant (if not exclusive) role in the examination of particular agreements. That is why the Commission's frequent inattention to market power and eeffects on price and output is so sorely criticized.

The legal formalisms under Article [81] contrast starkly with U.S. antitrust counselling practice. When dealing with non-territorial restraints under EC law, lawyers spend the great majority of their time in pigeonholing exercises and in textual exegesis of block exemptions and interpretative guidelines. It is shocking how little time is devoted to assessing the competitive risks and benefits for the vertical restraints at issue. The practice under the Sherman Act is exactly the opposite. It is difficult to believe that EC competition policy is furthered where there is far more attention and intellectual resources devoted to doctrinal fomalisms than to substantive analysis

(v) A NEW APPROACH TO ARTICLE 81(1) EMERGING?

Despite the strict approach taken by the Commission initially it appears more recently, particularly in the context of beer supply agreements, to have adopted an approach more reminiscent of that adopted by the Court. Further, there are clear indications in both the White Paper on Modernisation[207] and, more specifically, in the Guidelines on vertical restraints that the Commission might, in the future, adopt a more principled economic approach to vertical restraints.

In paragraphs 100–229 of the *Guidelines on Vertical Restraints* the Commission sets out its enforcement policy in relation to vertical agreements in individual cases (i.e. in relation to those agreements which will not benefit from the new Verticals Regulation). In this section the Commission explicitly recognizes that '[v]ertical restraints are generally less harmful than horizontal restraints'[208] and states that it will adopt an economic approach in its application of Article 81. It has already been seen[209] that the Commission rehearses in the Guidelines the *positive* effects of vertical restraints. It accepts that restraints may be essential to the realization of efficiencies and the development of new markets by, for example, solving a 'free rider' problem and opening up or facilitating entry to new markets and that, where there is sufficient inter-brand competition and there are no cumulative effects, vertical restraints are unlikely to cause competition concerns. Further, vertical restraints restricting inter-brand competition are more harmful than vertical restraints that reduce intra-brand competition.[210] The Commission concedes that vertical restraints may be warranted and essential to achieve efficiency, particularly where the restraints are 'of a limited duration which help the introduction of new complex products or protect relationship-specific investments'. The Commission also recognizes however that '[a] vertical restraint is sometimes necessary for as long as the supplier sells its product to the buyer'.[211]

---

[207] White Paper on Modernisation of the Rules Implementing Arts. 85 and 86 [now 81 and 82] of the EC Treaty [1999] OJ C132/1, [1999] 5 CMLR 208, para. 78.

[208] *Guidelines on Vertical Restraints*, [2000] OJ C291/1, para. 100.

[209] *Supra* 487–488. See also Inntrepreneur and Spring [2000] 5 CMLR 948.

[210] *Ibid.*, para. 119, sets out general rules for the evaluation of vertical restraints. The hardcore restraints prohibited by the Verticals Reg., however, all focus on restrictions on intra-brand competition.

[211] *Guidelines on Vertical Restraints*, [2000] OJ C291/1, para. 117.

In paragraphs 121–133 the Commission sets out the factors it considers to be most important when assessing whether or not an agreement appreciably restricts competition under Article 81(1). The central enquiry focuses on the market power of the undertakings concerned:

> 121. ... The following factors are the most important to establish whether a vertical agreement brings about an appreciable restriction of competition under Article 81(1):
>
> a) market position of the supplier;
> b) market position of competitors;
> c) market position of the buyer;
> d) entry barriers;
> e) maturity of the market;
> f) level of trade;
> g) nature of the product;
> h) other factors;
>
> 122. The importance of individual factors may vary from cases to case and depends on all other factors. For instance, a high market share of the supplier is usually a good indicator of market power, but in the case of low entry barriers it may not indicate market power. It is therefore not possible to provide strict rules on the importance of the individual factors.

It has also been seen,[212] however, that the Commission is concerned about the negative consequences that may flow from restrictions of both intra- and inter-brand competition.[213] Despite the promise of a more realistic approach these concerns may mean that the Commission continues to find many agreements infringe Article 81(1) and require exemption. Save where the agreement does not have an appreciable impact on competition or trade it may be desirable for undertakings, where possible, to draft their agreement so that it benefits from one of the Community block exemptions.

E. AN APPRECIABLE IMPACT ON COMPETITION AND TRADE

Article 81(1) does not apply to agreements which do not 'affect trade between Member States and the free play of competition to an appreciable extent.'[214] This appreciability requirement is totally distinct from the requirement that an agreement should restrict competition or affect competition. Thus even an agreement which has as its object the prevention, restriction, or distortion of competition will escape the Article 81(1) prohibition if the impact on competition and trade is minimal.

---

[212] See *supra* 491–493.

[213] The prevention of free riders may not always achieve economic efficiency: see, in particular, the view of W.S. Comanor, 'Vertical Price-Fixing, Vertical Market Restrictions, and the New Antitrust Policy' (1984–1985) 98 *Harv. Law Rev* 983 and discussion *supra* 488–493.

[214] Case 22/71, *Béguelin Import Company v. GL Import-Export SA* [1971] ECR 949, [1972] CMLR 81. See *supra* 501 and more detailed discussion *supra* at Chaps. 3 and 4.

3. ARTICLE 81(3)——EXEMPTIONS

A. GENERAL

The broad view taken of Article 81(1) has meant that many agreements infringe, or have been perceived to infringe, that provision. In a great number of cases parties to such an agreement have thus sought to ensure that their agreement is exempted under Article 81(3).

Most parties to an agreement are usually unwilling to expend the time, effort, and cost required to secure an individual decision exempting an agreement from the application of Article 81(1) (or more likely a comfort letter).[215] Further, the Commission does not have the resources to deal with the number of notifications which the broad interpretation of Article 81(1) makes likely. The Commission has consequently sought to stem the flow of notifications. It has done this in two main ways: first by clarifying when distribution agreements will be considered to be of minor importance,[216] and, secondly, by adopting block exemptions. In practice, businesses whose agreements may infringe Article 81(1) have preferred, or have been advised, to draft their agreements, if at all possible, to fall within one of the block exemptions. These at least carry the advantage of legal certainty. Agreements falling within them are automatically exempted from the application of Article 81(1) without the need for notification.

B. THE OLD BLOCK EXEMPTIONS AND THE MOTOR VEHICLE DISTRIBUTION BLOCK EXEMPTION

(i) EXCLUSIVE DISTRIBUTION, EXCLUSIVE PURCHASING, FRANCHISING AND MOTOR VEHICLE DISTRIBUTION AGREEMENTS

The adoption of block exemptions has saved the Commission from the fate of having to deal with an insurmountable mound of notifications. Prior to the adoption of Regulation 2790/1999[217] four block exemptions applied to four different categories of distribution agreement:

- Regulation 1983/83[218] applied to exclusive distribution agreements;
- Regulation 1984/83 applied to exclusive purchasing agreements (the regulation contained special provisions for beer supply and petrol agreements);[219]
- Regulation 4087/88[220] applied to franchising agreements; and

---

[215] See *supra* Chap. 4.
[216] See more detailed discussion *supra* in Chaps. 3 and 4.
[217] [1999] OJ L336/21.
[218] [1988] OJ L173/1.
[219] Regs. 1983/83 [1983] OJ L173/1 and 1984/83 [1983] OJ L173/7 were the successors of Reg. 67/67 [1967] OJ Spec. Ed. 10.
[220] [1988] OJ L359/46.

- Regulation 1475/95[221] applied (and still applies) to motor vehicle distribution agreements.

These Regulations have formed a vital part of the Commission's policy towards distribution agreements and through them the Commission has been able to mould and influence the content of distribution agreements.

(ii) THE STRAIGHT-JACKETING EFFECT OF THE BLOCK EXEMPTIONS

Although the exclusive distribution, exclusive purchasing, and franchising block exemptions (the 'old block exemptions') were, in contrast to those available to horizontal agreements,[222] moderately successful (although there was no block exemption for selective distribution agreements), that success has been at cost. Distribution agreements do not always fit neatly within one of these categories which the Commission, not business, has identified (for example, distribution will often accompany a licence of intellectual property rights) or within the mould that the Commission set out within those regulations. In practice, however, adhering to the terms of a block exemption has often been the only practical way to ensure the validity of an agreement.

The old block exemptions restricted the type of arrangement that parties to a distribution agreement could make. This structure (is this an exclusive distribution, exclusive purchasing, or franchise agreement?) did not cater for the variety of arrangements that suppliers sought to use to distribute their products or services. In particular, the regulations did not apply at all to selective distribution arrangements, even though they were very similar in effect and in their impact on competition to franchising agreements. The ECJ upheld the view that the block exemptions must be strictly construed and that an agreement that is, for example, primarily a franchising one cannot be drafted to fall within the terms of the block exemption exempting categories of exclusive distribution or exclusive purchasing agreements.[223] This approach has stultified the diversity of distribution arrangements within the European Union.

Further, even within the confines of one of these types of agreements, the parties' freedom of contract was curtailed. Each block exemption set out categories of clauses that were permissible and categories of clauses that were not. Any restriction on conduct not specifically exempted by the regulation would compromise and risk the validity of the agreement. The bargaining ability of the parties was thus constrained and, instead, distribution agreements tended to be drafted in similar, if not identical, ways.

The outline of the block exemptions set out below illustrates some of the limitations which those drafting distribution agreements faced. Although, apart from the motor vehicle distribution regulation, these regulations are no longer in force, some knowledge of them is important to understanding (a) why a new block exemption was thought necessary and (b) how the Verticals Regulation has altered and improved the current position.

---

[221] [1995] OJ L145/25.

[222] See *infra* Chap. 13.

[223] Case 161/84, *Pronuptia de Paris GmbH v. Pronuptia de Paris Irmgard Schillgallis* [1986] ECR 353, [1986] 1 CMLR 414.

(iii) REGULATION 1983/83—THE *EXCLUSIVE DISTRIBUTION* BLOCK EXEMPTION

a. THE REGULATION APPLIED ONLY TO BILATERAL EXCLUSIVE DISTRI-BUTION AGREEMENTS RELATING TO THE SUPPLY OF GOODS FOR RESALE

Article 1 of Regulation 1983/83 set out the type of agreement it exempted from the prohibition of Article 81(1). It stated that:

Article [81(1)] of the Treaty shall not apply to agreements to which only two undertakings are party and whereby one party agrees with the other to supply certain goods for resale within the whole or a defined area of the common market only to that other.

It can be seen immediately from this provision that the scope of the Regulation was limited. First, it applied only to *exclusive* arrangements, where one distributor was granted an exclusive territory (which could be the whole or a defined area of the common market) within which to sell the supplier's products. It did not apply if two distributors were appointed to a particular territory. Nor did it apply if a distributor was given the exclusive right to supply specific customers rather to supply all customers within a specific territory.

Secondly, it applied only where the agreement was to supply *goods for resale*. It did not apply to agreements relating to services or intermediate goods that the exclusive distributor had to finish or prepare for resale.[224] Thirdly, Article 1 limited the exemption to *bilateral agreements* concluded between two undertakings.

b. AGREEMENT NOT TO BE BETWEEN COMPETITORS

Article 3 set out a 'black' list of prohibited clauses. Article 3(a) and (b) of Regulation 1983/83 stipulated that the block exemption was not applicable to exclusive distribution agreements concluded between manufacturers of identical or equivalent goods.[225] The only exception was if the agreement was non-reciprocal and one of the parties had an annual turnover of less than ECUs 100 million.

c. PERMISSIBLE RESTRICTIONS OF COMPETITION

Article 2 set out restrictions which could be imposed on the supplier and the distributor respectively without jeopardizing the effect of the block exemption.

Article 2(1) established that, apart from the obligation on the supplier to supply only the exclusive distributor in the defined territory, the sole restriction of competition that could be imposed on the supplier was an obligation not itself to supply the contract goods to users in the distributor's territory.

Article 2

1. Apart from the obligation referred to in Article 1 no restriction on competition shall be imposed

---

[224] A Commission notice, [1984] OJ C101/2, set out the main considerations which would influence the Commission's view on whether or not an exclusive distribution or exclusive purchasing agreement was covered by Regs. 1983/83 and 1984/83 respectively.

[225] To 'manufacturers of identical goods or of goods which are considered by users as equivalent in view of their characteristics, price and intended use', Reg. 1983/83, Art. 3(a).

on the supplier other than the obligation not to supply the contract goods to users in the contract territory.

Article 2(2) set out three restrictions which could be imposed upon the exclusive distributor: an obligation not to handle competing goods, an obligation to obtain the contract goods only from the supplier, and an obligation not actively to seek customers outside the contract territory:

2. No restriction on competition shall be imposed on the exclusive distributor other than:

  (a) the obligation not to manufacture or distribute goods which compete with the contract goods;

  (b) the obligation to obtain the contract goods for resale only from the other party;

  (c) the obligation to refrain, outside the contract territory and in relation to the contract goods, from seeking customers, from establishing any branch and from maintaining any distribution depot.

This latter obligation, when read in conjunction with Article 3(c) and (d), made it clear that although some territorial protection could be afforded to the exclusive distributor that protection could *not* be absolute. The exclusive distributor could not be precluded from making passive sales outside its allotted territory.

The benefits of an exclusive distribution agreement are achieved by allowing the dealer to concentrate on his contract territory. The ban on active sales outside the contract territory is sufficient for this purpose. To impose in addition a ban on passive sales outside the territory is unnecessary since passive sales do not involve particular sales or advertising efforts and thus do not prevent the dealer from concentrating his sales efforts on the contract territory.[226]

Article 2(3) made it clear, for the sake of clarity, that the benefit of the block exemption would not be lost if certain obligations were imposed on the exclusive distributor.[227] It was therefore permissible, for example, to require the exclusive distributor to purchase a complete range of goods, to sell goods as specified by the supplier, and to take measure to promote sales.

d. NO OTHER RESTRICTIONS OF COMPETITION WERE ALLOWED

If the agreement contained any other clause that constituted a restriction of competition within the meaning of Article 81(1) the benefit of the block exemption would be lost. Thus even though Article 3 did not, for example, specifically provide that the Regulation would not apply if the agreement contained a clause imposing resale prices on the distributor the insertion of such a clause would mean that the regulation did not apply.[228] This meant that, in practice, parties to an agreement would attempt to limit the restrictions on conduct and obligations imposed to the clauses explicitly permitted by Article 2. Of course, this imposed a significant constraint on the clauses that the parties could include in the agreement, especially as the Regulation did not incorporate an opposition procedure[229] for agreements

---

[226] *BASF Lacke & Farben* [1995] OJ L272/16, [1996] 4 CMLR 811, para. 98.

[227] Even though these obligations probably would not amount to a restriction of competition for the purposes of Art. 81(1).

[228] *Novalliance/Systemform* [1997] OJ L47/11, [1997] 4 CMLR 876, para. 69.

[229] See *supra* Chap.4.

including a restriction not exempted by Article 1 or 2 but not specifically prohibited by Article 3.

(iv) REGULATION 1984/83—THE EXCLUSIVE PURCHASING BLOCK EXEMPTION

Regulation 1984/83 imposed similar constraints on parties wishing to conclude an exclusive purchasing agreement. The Regulation applied to agreements by which a reseller agreed to purchase goods for resale only from the supplier, a connected undertaking, or another specified supplier. Again this Regulation applied only to bilateral agreements relating to goods for resale that were not concluded between competitors (except for non-reciprocal agreements where one of the undertakings had a turnover which did not exceed ECUs 100 million).[230] Further, it did not apply if the exclusive obligation covered more than one type of goods or if the agreement was concluded for a period in excess of five years. In a similar way to Regulation 1983/83, this Regulation also listed restrictions that could be imposed on the supplier and the reseller respectively. The Regulation did not contain an opposition procedure.

Title II of the Regulation contained special provisions for beer supply agreements. Title III contained special provisions for service station agreements. Special provisions for these sectors have not been retained within the Verticals Regulation.

(v) REGULATION 4087/88—THE FRANCHISING BLOCK EXEMPTION

Regulation 4087/88 was more complex than the exclusive distribution and exclusive purchasing Regulations, reflecting the more involved nature of franchising agreements.

Broadly, the Regulation applied to bilateral franchising agreements, whereby a franchisor granted a franchisee, in exchange for direct or indirect financial consideration, the right to exploit a franchise for the purpose of marketing specified goods or services. A franchise was defined as 'a package of industrial or intellectual property rights relating to trade marks, trade names, shop signs, utility models, designs, copyrights, know-how or patents, to be exploited for the resale of goods or the provision of services to end users'.[231] The agreement had to include obligations relating to the use of a common name or shop sign and a uniform presentation, the communication of know-how by the franchisor to the franchisee, and the continuing provision by the franchisor to the franchisee of commercial or technical assistance during the life of the agreement.

Article 2 stipulated that the block exemption would apply to agreements containing certain specified restrictions imposed on the franchisor or franchisee. For example, it was possible to impose a restriction on the franchisor not to grant a franchise to a third party, to exploit a franchise itself, or to sell to customers within the contract territory, an obligation on the franchisee only to exploit the franchise from specified premises, not to seek customers outside the contract territory, and not to deal in competing goods.

Article 3 provided that the block exemption would apply notwithstanding the presence of

---

[230] Reg. 1984/83, Art. 1.
[231] Reg. 4087/88 [1988] OJ L359/46, Art. 1(3)(a).

certain restrictions or obligations that were in fact unlikely to fall within Article 81(1) at all. Article 3(1) dealt with clauses that were cleared in so far as they were necessary to protect the franchisor's industrial or intellectual property rights or to maintain a common identity and reputation of the franchised network. Article 3(2) exempted other obligations without condition, for example, an obligation on the franchisee not to disclose know-how provided by the franchisor to third parties both during and after the termination of the agreement, or to use it for purposes other than exploitation of the franchise; and obligations requiring the franchisee to use commercial methods required by the franchisor, to comply with the franchisor's standards, and not to change location of premises or to assign the franchise without the franchisor's consent.

Article 4 stipulated that the Regulation would not apply unless: the franchisee could obtain the contract goods not only from the franchisor but from other franchisees or distributors; guarantees (where applicable) were honoured by a franchisee in respect of a good supplied by any member of the network; and the franchisee indicated its independent status.

Article 5 listed the circumstances in which the regulation would not apply, for example, where the agreement was concluded between competitors.

Article 6 set out an opposition procedure for agreements (i) meeting the requirements of Article 4 but (ii) but containing restrictions not specifically authorized by Article 2 or 3 but which were not prohibited by Article 5.

(vi) REGULATION 1475/95—THE MOTOR VEHICLE DISTRIBUTION BLOCK EXEMPTION

Regulation 1475/95[232] applies specifically to motor vehicle distribution agreements and has not been replaced by the Verticals Regulation.[233] It will continue until its expiry date, 30 September 2002. Essentially this block exemption exempts bilateral agreements in which a supplier agrees to supply, in a specific territory, certain new motor vehicles for resale only to the other party, or to the other party and a specified number of other undertakings.

Controversy has surrounded the application of this Regulation since many believe it to be too lenient. For example, the UK Competition Commission's report on new cars published in April 2000 suggested that the block exemption is responsible, partly at least, for the high car prices in the UK. Following this report, the UK's Secretary of State for Trade and Industry negotiated with the Commission for drastic measures to be taken. In the meantime an Order has been made under national law.[234]

The Commission is considering whether to retain special provisions for motor vehicle

---

[232] [1995] OJ L145/25.

[233] [1999] OJ L336/21.

[234] The Competition Commission suggested in its report, *New Cars: A Report on Supply of New Motor Cars within the UK*, Cm 4660 (TSO, 2000) that both selective and exclusive distribution agreements should be prohibited in the car sector. The UK authorities have taken steps to bring about greater competition in the supply and selling cars, lower prices and increased sales: see SI 2000/2088. The British Consumers' Association in particular adopted the view that British car buyers were being ripped off in comparison to their European counterparts. The association forwarded 20,000 protest notes to Mario Monti, the Commissioner for Competition: see M. Monti, *Who Will be in the Driver's Seat*, Forum Europe Conference, Brussels, 11 May 2000.

distribution agreements when the exemption expires. The Directorate General for Competition has prepared an evaluation report on the block exemption. A preliminary evaluation of those findings[235] may suggest that some change at least, and possibly radical change, is likely.

M. Monti, *Who will be in the Driver's Seat?* Forum Europe Conference, Brussels, 11 May 2000

If I may return to the picture I introduced at the beginning of my presentation when I compared the motor vehicle Block Exemption Regulation to a 'highway code'.

- Based on the work undertaken by my Department, it would seem that the assumptions on which this 'highway code' is based are at least questionable. As regards the objectives pursued by the Regulation, it seems that most of them have not been achieved. In particular, it seems that the main driver of the distribution process is still the manufacturer and that dealers do not have much freedom as regards the way in which motor vehicles are distributed. Moreover, the code has not contributed to integrate the national markets and, more regrettably it has not been properly implemented by many manufacturers, as the procedures against manufacturers for infringements of the Regulation show.

- If I may come back to the subject of this conference: 'Who is in the driver's seat?', the following picture probably best describes the current situation with only a little exaggeration:

- The manufacturer is in the back seat of the car and gives instructions to his chauffeur, the dealer, on how to drive down the distribution highway to the consumer, who buys the car. The manufacturer finally manages to bring the car down to the consumer, but not always, it seems, in the fastest, most economic and smoothest way possible: moreover, all too often the manufacturer appears to instruct the dealer, who should really be the one responsible for driving the car, to do things which are outside the 'highway code'. In addition, according to consumers' expectations, the European 'highway code' seems not in all respects the best-possible solution to bring a new car to the consumer.

C. THE VERTICALS REGULATION–REGULATION 2790/1999[236]

(i) THE BACKGROUND

The background to the adoption of this new block exemption has already been discussed.[237] The Commission's treatment of vertical agreements had attracted so much criticism that the Commission adopted a Green Paper promising reform. The changes culminating from that

---

[235] *Ibid.* Report on the evaluation of Regulation (EC) No 1475/95 COM (2000) 743.
[236] *Guidelines on Vertical Restraints,* [2000] OJ C291/1, paras. 21–70 deal with the application of the block exemption reg.
[237] See *supra.*

Paper have already been outlined. A most significant change has been the recognition that the existing block exemptions were not working and the consequent adoption of the Verticals Regulation, which seeks to provide an umbrella block exemption applying to vertical agreements generally. The Regulation provides a safe harbour, or presumption of legality, for distribution agreements, whether for goods or services, where a market share threshold of 30 per cent is not exceeded. Not surprisingly, the Regulation reflects the old concerns manifest from the practice of the Commission, the case law of the Court, and the old block exemptions. Clauses conferring territorial protection or imposing resale prices may therefore prevent the block exemption from applying

The new Regulation came into force on 1 January 2000 and has applied since 1 June 2000.[238] It replaced the block exemptions dealing with exclusive distribution, exclusive purchasing, and franchising agreements but does not replace the motor vehicle distribution block exemption which applies until the end of September 2002.[239] Guidelines adopted on 24 May 2000 outline the enforcement policy of the Commission to vertical agreements generally. The purpose of the Guidelines is to enable undertakings to make their own assessment of the compatibility of their agreement with Article 81.

The commentary below sets out and explains the main provisions of the block exemption.

(ii) THE RECITALS

The block exemption contains seventeen recitals that set out the background to the Regulation. Of particular importance is the Commission's recognition in the recitals that vertical agreements 'can improve economic efficiency in a chain of production or distribution' and that the 'likelihood that such efficiency-enhancing will outweigh any anti-competitive effects due to restrictions contained in vertical agreement depends on the degree of market power of the undertakings concerned'.[240]

(iii) ARTICLE 1—DEFINITIONS

Article 1 defines concepts relevant to the remainder of the block exemption: competing undertakings, non-compete obligation, exclusive supply obligation, selective distribution system, intellectual property rights, know-how, and buyer. Surprisingly the regulation sets out no definition of franchising agreements.

Article 1

For the purposes of this Regulation:

(a) 'competing undertakings' means actual or potential suppliers in the same product market; the product market includes goods or services which are regarded by the buyer as interchangeable with or substitutable for the contract goods or services, by reason of the products' characteristics, their prices and their intended use;

---

[238] Art. 13, *infra* 549.
[239] See *supra* 531.
[240] Verticals Reg., recitals 6 and 7.

(b) 'non-compete obligation' means any direct or indirect obligation causing the buyer not to manufacture, purchase, sell or resell goods or services with compete with the contract goods or services, or any direct or indirect obligation on the buyer to purchase from the supplier or from another undertaking designated by the supplier more than 80% of the buyer's total purchases of the contract goods or services and their substitutes on the relevant market, calculated on the basis of the value of its purchases in the preceding calendar year;

(c) 'exclusive supply obligation' means any direct or indirect obligation causing the supplier to sell the goods or services specified in the agreement only to one buyer inside the Community for the purposes of a specific use or for resale;

(d) 'Selective distribution system' means a distribution system where the supplier undertakes to sell the contract goods or services, either directly or indirectly, only to distributors selected on the basis of specified criteria and where these distributors undertake not to sell such goods or services to unauthorised distributors;

(e) 'intellectual property rights' includes industrial property rights, copyright and neighbouring rights;

(f) 'know-how' means a package of non-patented practical information, resulting from experience and testing by the supplier, which is secret, substantial and identified: in this context, 'secret' means that the know-how, as a body or in the precise configuration and assembly of its components, is not generally known or easily accessible; 'substantial' means that the know-how includes information which is indispensable to the buyer for the use, sale or resale of the contract goods or services; 'identified' means that the know-how must be described in a sufficiently comprehensive manner so as to make it possible to verify that it fulfils the criteria of secrecy and substantiality;

(g) 'buyer' includes an undertaking which, under an agreement falling within Article 81(1) of the Treaty, sells goods or services on behalf of another undertaking.

Attention should be drawn to the definitions of non-compete obligations[241] and exclusive supply obligations set out in paragraphs (b) and (c) respectively.

The Commission is concerned that non-compete obligations restricting the ability of a distributor to handle competing goods and, consequently, inter-brand competition, should not be used to foreclose the market from competitors. Article 5 contains special provisions dealing with non-compete clauses. Even where the supplier does not have significant market power the Commission has stipulated in the Regulation that non-compete obligations should not be imposed for too long a period. The term non-compete includes both obligations not to purchase or manufacture the contract goods or services and their substitutes and obligations to purchase more than 80 per cent of requirements of contract goods and services and their substitutes from the supplier or other designated supplier.

The Regulation states that an exclusive supply obligation is imposed where only one distributor is appointed in the entire Community. The Commission fears that these agreements may foreclose other buyers from access to supply.

---

[241] Non-compete obligations are distinct from exclusive purchasing commitments, see *supra* n. 12.

(iv) ARTICLE 2—THE MAIN EXEMPTION

a. AN UMBRELLA EXEMPTION APPLYING TO ALL VERTICAL AGREEMENTS

Vertical agreements

The Regulation is much broader than the previous Regulations since it exempts *all* distribution agreements which meet its requirements whether for goods *or* services (it is not restricted to agreements relating to goods for resale[242]) and whatever their nature, whether their main objective is exclusive distribution, exclusive purchasing, franchising, selective distribution, *or* some other. The Regulation also applies to selective distribution systems which did not previously benefit from any Community block exemption. By providing an umbrella block exemption that is potentially applicable to all vertical restraints it seeks to answer the objection that the Commission's previous practice has resulted in bizarre and unjustified pigeon-holing and categorization of agreements. The Regulation contains some provisions that apply only to certain types of agreements. Some categorization thus seems inevitable, but the focus of the Regulation is more on the restrictive nature of the clause than the type of the agreement involved. The emphasis is on the substantive effect of the agreement and not its form.[243]

The key definition of vertical agreements is set out not in Article 1 but in Article 2. Article 2(1) states that Article 81(1)[244] shall not apply to:

agreements or concerted practices entered into between two or more undertakings each of which operates, for the purposes of the agreement, at a different level of the production or distribution chain, and relating to the conditions under which the parties may purchase, sell or resell certain goods or services.

Agreements between two or more undertakings

The exemption applies to agreements concluded between two or more undertakings[245] so long as each undertaking operates, for the purposes of the agreement,[246] at different levels of the production of distribution chain (for example, supplier, wholesaler, and retailer). Unlike its predecessors the regulation is not confined to bilateral agreements.

Agreements relating to the conditions under which the parties may purchase, sell or resell certain goods or services

The block exemption covers purchase and distribution agreements.

---

[242] Contrast the position in Reg. 1983/83.

[243] In the *Guidelines on Vertical Restraints*, [2000] OJ C291/1, the Commission states at para. 104 that agreements which are different in form may have the same substantive impact on competition.

[244] In so far as Art. 81(1) applies at all of course.

[245] The exemption applies therefore only where the agreement is concluded between undertakings (see discussion of that term, *supra* in Chap. 3). It is thus unlikely to apply to agreements concluded between a supplier and a final consumer which does not operate as an undertaking (of course such agreements would not be caught by Art. 81 at all which applies only to agreements between undertakings): see *Guidelines on Vertical Restraints*, [2000] OJ C291/1, para. 24.

[246] The general rule is that agreements concluded between competitors will not benefit from the block exemption.

These are agreements which concern the conditions for the purchase, sale or resale of the goods or services supplied by the supplier and/or which concern the conditions for the sale by the buyer of the goods or services which incorporate these goods or services. For the application of the BER both the goods or services supplied by the supplier and the resulting goods or services are considered to be contract goods or services. Vertical agreements relating to all final and intermediate goods and services are covered . . . the goods or services provided by the supplier may be resold by the buyer or may be used as an input by the buyer to produce its own goods or services.[247]

The regulation does not exempt agreements or restrictions or obligations that do *not* relate to the purchase, sale, or resale of goods or services, such as rent or leasing agreements or clauses preventing parties from carrying out independent research and development.

b. ASSOCIATION OF RETAILERS OF GOODS

Article 2(2) provides:

The exemption provided for in paragraph 1 shall apply to vertical agreements entered into between an association of undertakings and its members, or between such an association and its suppliers, only if all its members are retailers of goods and if no individual member of the association, together with its connected undertakings, has a total annual turnover exceeding EUR 50 million; vertical agreements entered into by such associations shall be covered by this Regulation without prejudice to the application of Article 81 to horizontal agreements concluded between the members of the association or decisions adopted by the association.

This provision permits vertical agreements concluded between an association of retailers[248] (no member of which, together with its connected undertakings, has a total turnover of more than Euro 50million) and its members or between an association and its supplier. Any horizontal agreements concluded between the members or any decisions adopted by the association must however be assessed separately for their compatibility with Article 81.

c. PROVISIONS RELATING TO THE ASSIGNMENT OF INTELLECTUAL PROPERTY RIGHTS (IPRs)

Article 2(3)[249]

Article 2(3) provides:

The exemption provided for in paragraph 1 shall apply to vertical agreements containing provisions which relate to the assignment to the buyer or use by the buyer of intellectual property rights, provided that those provisions do not constitute the primary object of such agreements and are directly related to the use, sale or resale of goods or services by the buyer or its customers. The exemption applies on condition that, in relation to the contract goods or services, those provisions do not contain restrictions of competition having the same object or effect as vertical restraints which are not exempted under this Regulation.

The assignment of IPRs, such as trade marks, copyright, or know-how, may be essential or extremely useful to the effective performance of a vertical agreement. The exemption therefore applies to vertical agreements containing ancillary provisions relating to the assignment

---

[247] *Guidelines on Vertical Restraints*, [2000] OJ C291/1, para. 24.
[248] *Ibid.* para. 28 the Commission states that retailers 'are distributors reselling goods to final consumers'.
[249] *Ibid.*, paras. 30–44.

or use of IPRs which are directly related to the use, sale, or resale of goods or services by the buyer or its customers. This provision is of importance to all vertical agreements but is particularly relevant to franchise agreements that ordinarily involve the assignment or licensing of intellectual property rights.

The five conditions

The Commission sets out the five conditions which must be fulfilled before the block exemption applies to vertical agreements containing IPR provisions in paragraph 30 of the Guidelines.

The BER applies to vertical agreements containing IPR provisions when five conditions are fulfilled:

— the IPR provisions must be part of a vertical agreement, i.e. an agreement with conditions under which the parties may purchase, sell or resell certain goods or services;
— the IPRs must be assigned to or for use by the buyer;
— the IPR provisions must not constitute the primary object of the agreement;
— the IPR provisions must be directly related to the use, sale or resale of goods or services by the buyer or his customers. In the case of franchising where marketing forms the object of the exploitation of the IPRs, the goods or services are distributed by the master franchisee or the franchisees;
— the IPR provisions, in relation to the contract goods or services, must not constrain restrictions of competition having the same object or effect as vertical restraints which are not exempted under the BER.

The block exemption will not therefore apply unless:

(i) the agreement is a vertical one and not, for example, an assignment of IPRs for the manufacture of goods or licensing agreements;[250]

(ii) the assignment of the IPRs is made by the supplier to the buyer and not vice versa;

(iii) the IPR provisions are *ancillary* to the implementation of the vertical agreement and not its primary object;

(iv) the IPR provisions are directly related to the use, sale, or resale of goods or services by the buyer or its customers, for example, where the licensing of a trade mark or know how is necessary for the marketing of a good.

It also essential that:

(v) the clauses relating to the IPRs must not have the same object or effect as restrictions that are not exempted under the regulation. For example, territorial exclusivity, which is prohibited by Article 4, cannot be circumvented by arrangements involving licensing or assignment of IPRs.[251]

Franchise agreements

Franchise agreements, which no longer benefit from their own independent regime, are dealt with in some detail in paragraphs 42–44 of the Guidelines. In particular, the Guidelines

---

[250] Reg. 240/96, [1996] OJ L31/2, which applies to technology transfer agreements may apply to such agreements; see *infra* Chap. 10.

[251] Reg. 2790/1999, Art. 2(3); see also Cases 56 & 58, *Etablissements Consten SA & Grundig-Verkaufs-GmbH v. Commission* [1966] ECR 299, [1966] CMLR 418, para. 48.

indicate that franchise agreements will ordinarily meet all five of the conditions set out in Article 2(3) as:

the franchisor provides goods and/or services, in particular commercial or technical assistance services, to the franchisee. The IPRs help the franchisee to resell the products supplied by the franchisor or by a supplier designated by the franchisor or to use these products and sell the resulting goods or services.[252]

Franchise agreements that do not fall within the block exemption on the ground that they principally concern the licensing of IPRs will be treated in a similar way to those dealt with under the block exemption.

Paragraph 44 of the Guidelines sets out the type of obligations related to IPRs which are likely to benefit from the block exemption:

44. The following IPR-related obligations are generally considered to be necessary to protect the franchisor's intellectual property rights and are, if these obligations fall under Article 81(1), also covered by the BER:

    (a) an obligation on the franchisee not to engage, directly or indirectly, in any similar business;

    (b) an obligation on the franchisee not to acquire financial interests in the capital of a competing undertaking such as would give the franchisee the power to influence the economic conduct of such undertaking;

    (c) an obligation on the franchisee not to disclose to third parties the know-how provided by the franchisor as long as this know-how is not in the public domain;

    (d) an obligation on the franchisee to communicate to the franchisor any experience gained in exploiting the franchise and to grant it, and other franchisees, a non-exclusive licence for the know-how resulting from that experience;

    (e) an obligation on the franchisee to inform the franchisor of infringements of licensed intellectual property rights, to take legal action against infringers or to assist the franchisor in any legal actions against infringers;

    (f) an obligation on the franchisee not to use know-how licensed by the franchisor for purposes other than the exploitation of the franchise;

    (g) an obligation on the franchisee not to assign the rights and obligations under the franchise agreement without the franchisor's consent.

d. AGREEMENTS BETWEEN COMPETING UNDERTAKINGS

Article 2(4) deals with agreements concluded between competing undertakings. Article 1 defines competing undertakings to mean actual or potential suppliers in the same product market, irrespective of whether or not they operate in the same geographic market.[253] A potential supplier is a supplier who could and would be likely to produce a competing product or service in response to a small and permanent increase in relative prices. The Commission promises in its guidelines that this assessment will be made on realistic grounds and that a theoretical possibility of entering a market is not enough. The supplier should be able to make the necessary investments and enter the market within a period of year.[254]

---

[252] *Guidelines on Vertical Restraints*, [2000] OJ C291/1, para. 43.

[253] See *infra* 540.

[254] *Guidelines on Vertical Restraints*, [2000] OJ C291/1, para. 26.

Article 2(4) states that the Regulation generally does not apply to agreements concluded between competing undertakings (even if operating for the purposes of the agreement at different levels of the production or distribution chain), *however:*

it shall apply where competing undertakings enter into a non-reciprocal vertical agreement and:

(a) the buyer has a total annual turnover not exceeding EUR 100 million,[255] or

(b) the supplier is a manufacturer and a distributor of goods, while the buyer is a distributor not manufacturing goods competing with the contract goods,[256] or

(c) the supplier is a provider of services at several levels of trade, while the buyer does not provide competing services at the level of trade where it purchases the contract services.

e. AGREEMENTS FALLING WITHIN THE SCOPE OF ANOTHER BLOCK EXEMPTION

Article 2(5) states that the Regulation does not apply to vertical agreements that fall within the scope of another block exemption. Agreements falling within the technology transfer Regulation[257] or the motor vehicle distribution Regulation[258] and vertical agreements concluded in connection with horizontal agreements benefiting from a block exemption[259] are, therefore, excluded.

(v) ARTICLE 3—THE MARKET SHARE CAP

a. THE 30 PER CENT THRESHOLD

A new feature introduced in the Verticals Regulation, not used in the old block exemptions (which applied, unless withdrawn, whatever the market shares of the parties), is the introduction of a market share cap of 30 per cent. Article 3(1) imposes the cap stipulating that the block exemption will not apply where the supplier's market share exceeds this amount:

Subject to paragraph 2 of this Article, the exemption provided for in Article 2 shall apply on condition that the market share held by the supplier does not exceed 30% of the relevant market on which it sells the contract goods or services.

This reflects the Commission's view that vertical restraints are unlikely, where inter-brand competition is strong and in the absence of hardcore restraints, to pose competition problems:

where the share of the relevant market accounted for by the supplier does not exceed 30 per cent, vertical agreements which do not contain certain types of severely anti-competitive restraints generally lead to an improvement in production or distribution and allow consumers a fair share of the resulting benefits.[260]

Where there is an exclusive supply obligation, a supplier agrees to supply only one buyer

---

255 See, e.g. Reg. 1983/83, Art. 3(b).
256 Dual distribution: *Guidelines on Vertical Restraints,* [2000] OJ C291/1, para. 27.
257 Reg. 240/96.
258 Reg. 1475/95.
259 See *infra* Chap. 13.
260 Verticals Reg., recital 8.

inside the Community,[261] the relevant market share is that of the buyer, not the supplier. The exemption applies only if the market share held by the buyer does not exceed 30 per cent of the market on which it purchases the goods or services (not the market on which the buyer sells the goods or services). Article 3(2) states:

In the case of vertical agreements containing exclusive supply obligations, the exemption provided for in Article 2 shall apply on condition that the market share held by the buyer does not exceed 30 per cent of the market on which it purchases the contract goods or services.

Where the vertical agreement is concluded between three parties each at different level of trade the market shares at both levels are relevant. Thus where, for example, an agreement is concluded between a supplier, a wholesaler (or an association of retailers), and retailers, the relevant market shares are those of both the manufacturer and the wholesaler.[262]

b. DEFINING THE MARKET

The Commission Notice on definition of the relevant market provides general guidance on market definition. Further, the Commission's decisions and Court judgments taken under Article 81, 82, and the Merger Regulation[263] provide useful guidance on how markets have been defined in the past. The Guidelines also set out information, on market definition and market share calculation issues, which is specifically focused on distribution cases.

The introduction of a market share test inevitably introduces an element of uncertainty into the block exemption which, arguably, is principally intended to provide legal certainty. The Commission was forced to abandon a proposal to incorporate a market share test within the Technology Transfer Regulation. However, the introduction of a market share test in that case may have created greater difficulties, given that it is frequently applicable in cases where new or emerging markets are involved.

Given the call for greater economic analysis in its approach to vertical restraints it is difficult to be too critical of the imposition of the market share cap. Many commentators would perhaps, however, have preferred to see the more economic approach manifested at the Article 81(1) stage of assessment, rather than when exempting the agreement under Article 81(3). The Regulation suggests that the main focus of the Commission's attention will remain the agreement's compatibility with Article 81(3).

c. EXCEEDING THE MARKET SHARES

Because of the inherent uncertainty which the market share tests set out in the Verticals Regulation brings, the Guidelines address at length what the Commission's enforcement policy will be in respect of individual agreements exceeding the 30 per cent threshold. In such cases there is no presumption that the agreement infringes Article 81(1). The block exemption will not, however, apply so the parties will have to make their own assessment of the agreement's compatibility with Article 81. The Commission sets out the factors that will be relevant to its assessment under Article 81(1) and 81(3) respectively and analyses in some detail several different types of vertical restraints.[264] The amendment made to Article 4(2)

---

[261] *Ibid.*, Art. 1(c), set out *supra* 534.
[262] *Guidelines on Vertical Restraints*, [2000] OJ C291/1, para. 93.
[263] Council Reg. 4064/89 [1989] OJ L395/1. As amended by Council Reg. 1310/97 [1997] OJ L180/1.
[264] *Guidelines on Vertical Restraints*, [2000] OJ C291/1, paras. 121–229.

of Regulation 17 means that it is not vital that, as a result of miscalculation of market shares or otherwise, prior notification is made to the Commission. An exemption can be granted to an agreement infringing Article 81(1) retrospectively to the date that the agreement was concluded.

Where an agreement has been operated in breach of Article 81 in consequence of an assumption, held in good faith, that the market share threshold was not exceeded, the Commission states in its Guidelines that fines will not be imposed.

d. PORTFOLIO OF PRODUCTS DISTRIBUTED THROUGH THE SAME DISTRIBUTION SYSTEM

Where the supplier uses the same distribution system to distribute several goods or services some of which are, and some of which are not, in view of the market share thresholds, covered by the block exemption the block exemption exempts only the former.[265]

(vi) ARTICLE 4—HARDCORE RESTRICTIONS[266]

a. THE BLOCK EXEMPTION IS NOT APPLICABLE TO VERTICAL AGREEMENTS CONTAINING HARDCORE RESTRAINTS

Article 4 sets out a list of 'prohibited' clauses, similar to the black list set out in the old block exemptions. The insertion of just one of these clauses precludes the entire vertical agreement from being exempted under the Regulation.[267]

The BER exempts vertical agreements on condition that no hardcore restriction, as set out in Article 4, is contained in or practised with the vertical agreement. If there are one or more hardcore restrictions, the benefit of the BER is lost for the entire vertical agreement. There is no severability for hardcore restrictions.[268]

Article 4 focuses on clauses, such as those imposing resale price maintenance or territorial restraints, which restrict intra-brand competition. It prohibits all clauses which, directly or indirectly, have as their object certain restrictions specified in paragraphs (a)–(e) of the Article.

Article 4

The exemption provided for in Article 2 shall not apply to vertical agreements which, directly or indirectly, in isolation or in combination with other factors under the control of the parties, have as their object:

  (a) the restriction of the buyer's ability to determine its sale price, without prejudice to the possibility of the supplier's imposing a maximum sale price or recommending a sale price, provided that they do not amount to a fixed or minimum sale price as a result of pressure from, or incentives offered by, any of the parties;

---

[265] *Ibid.*, para. 68.

[266] *Ibid.*, paras. 46–56 deals with hardcore restrictions under the block exemption.

[267] In contrast, clauses infringing Art. 5 are themselves prohibited, but the remainder of the agreement may benefit from the block exemption if the prohibited clauses are severable from the remaining terms of the agreement. See *infra* 546–547.

[268] *Guidelines on Vertical Restraints* [2000] OJ C291/1, para. 66.

(b)   the restriction of the territory into which, or of the customers to whom, the buyer may sell the contract good or services, except;

—the restriction of active sales into the exclusive territory or to an exclusive customer group reserved to the supplier or allocated by the supplier to another buyer, where such a restriction does not limit sales by the customers of the buyer,

—the restriction of sales to end users by a buyer operating at the wholesale level of trade,

—the restriction of sales to unauthorised distributors by the members of a selective distribution system, and

—the restriction of the buyer's ability to sell components, supplied for the purposes of incorporation, to customers who would use them to manufacture the same type of goods as those produced by the supplier;

(c)   the restriction of active or passive sales to end users by members of a selective distribution system operating at the retail level of trade, without prejudice to the possibility of prohibiting a member of the system from operating out of an unauthorised place of establishment;

(d)   the restriction of cross-supplies between distributors within a selective distribution system, including between distributors operating at different level of trade;

(e)   the restriction agreed between a supplier of components and a buyer who incorporates those components, which limits the supplier to selling the components as spare parts to end-users or to repairers or other service providers not entrusted by the buyer with the repair or servicing of its goods.

Unlike the earlier block exemptions the regulation does not contain a list of permissible restrictions. The straight-jacketing effect of the Regulation is therefore minimized. Vertical agreements may be exempted whatever restrictions or obligations they contain so long as they are not prohibited by Article 4.[269]

b. ARTICLE 4(a): FIXED OR MINIMUM SALES PRICES

Article 4(a) prohibits clauses resulting in the establishment of a fixed or minimum resale price or a fixed or minimum price level to be observed by the buyer. Recommended or maximum prices may be imposed so long as they do not amount to indirect means of achieving resale price maintenance.[270]

c. ARTICLE 4(b): RESTRICTIONS OF THE TERRITORY OR THE CUSTOMERS TO WHOM THE BUYER MAY SELL

Article 4(b) prohibits clauses that restrict the territories into which, or the customers to whom, the buyer can sell the contract goods or services. The provision prohibits both direct restrictions and provisions that, in practice, prevent or deter a distributor from making sales outside of specific territories or customer groups.[271]

---

[269] See also the discussion of Art. 5 *infra* 546–547.

[270] The Commission lists some means of indirectly imposing resale prices in the *Guidelines on Vertical Restraints*, [2000] OJ C291/1, para. 47 such as 'fixing the distribution margin, fixing the maximum level of discount the distributor can grant from a prescribed price level, making the grant of rebates or reimbursement of promotional costs by the supplier subject to the observance of a given price level, linking the prescribed resale price to the resale prices of competitors, threats, intimidation, warnings, penalties, delay or suspension of deliveries or contract terminations in relation to observance of a given price level'. The Guidelines note that recommended prices can frequently be an effective way of indirectly fixing prices.

[271] See the cases set out *supra* 504–505.

This hardcore restriction relates to market partitioning by territory or by customer. This may be the result of direct obligations, such as the obligation not to sell to certain customers or to customers in certain territories or the obligation to refer orders from these customers to other distributors. It may also result from indirect measures aimed at inducing the distributor not to sell to such customers, such as refusal or reduction of bonuses or discounts, refusal to supply, reduction of supplied volumes or limitation of supplied volumes to the demand within the allocated territory or customer group, threat of contract termination of profit pass-over obligations. It may further result from the supplier not providing a Community-wide guarantee service, whereby all distributors are obliged to provide the guarantee service and are reimbursed from this service by the supplier, even in relation to products sold by other distributors into their territory.[272]

Restrictions are not prohibited, however. if they relate to the display of the supplier's brand name or if there is *objective justification* for the provision that relates to the product. A ban on sales to certain customers could therefore be justified, for example, by health and safety considerations.[273]

Article 4 itself sets out four exceptions to the prohibition:

1) Restrictions on sales into exclusive territories or to an exclusive customer group reserved to another

The first exception allows a supplier to restrict active sales by a distributor into an exclusive territory or to an exclusive consumer group reserved either to itself or another buyer.

This provision is similar to the provisions in Regulation 1983/83 that authorized a supplier to prevent an exclusive distributor from seeking sales outside its territory.[274] It has a few important differences from that provision, however.

First, the Verticals Regulation allows a supplier to reserve both exclusive territories *and/or* exclusive customer groups to a distributor. Regulation 1983/83 authorized only the allocation of exclusive territories. In consequence, in contrast to the position under Regulation 1983/83, it is possible to appoint more than one distributor in a particular territory. A distributor can be appointed to supply a certain customer group in a certain territory and can be precluded from actively selling both into other territories reserved to another *and* to a customer group reserved to another within its territory.

Further, in contrast to Regulation 1983/83, the Verticals Regulation permits restrictions on active sales only to territories or customer groups that have actually been reserved to another. Regulation 1983/83 enabled the supplier to prohibit its exclusive distributors from making any active sales outside its territory. In practice, this is unlikely to be a material distinction, since if the supplier does not appoint a buyer for a particular area it can reserve it for itself.

In a similar way to Regulation 1983/83 the Regulation prohibits the buyer from making '*active*' sales to another's customers or customers in another's territory.[275] The Commission makes the corollary clear in the Guidelines, a prohibition on the making of '*passive*' sales into another's territory or to another's customer group is not permitted. The agreement

---

[272] *Guidelines on Vertical Restraints*, [2000] OJ C291/1, para. 49.

[273] *Ibid.*, para. 49.

[274] See *supra* 528–529.

[275] This is similar to Reg. 1983/83 which authorized an obligation on the exclusive distributor to refrain from 'seeking' customers, establishing a branch, or maintaining a distribution depot outside its allotted territory: see Art. 2(2)(c), *supra* 528–529.

must admit the possibility of some parallel trade in the goods or services. The distinction between active and passive sales is clearly very important, since it defines the border between what is and what is not permissible. The Guidelines explain that the prohibition on active sales is intended to prohibit a distributor from mailing, visiting, or targeting advertising on other customer groups or customers within another's territory or setting up a warehouse or distribution outlet in another's territory. No prohibition is permitted, however, on sales made in response to unsolicited orders.

A point which is of acute importance is whether or not distributors are entitled to advertise on the Internet—does this amount to active selling? It seems at first sight that this would amount to active selling by advertising to customers located in a different territory. The Commission, however, takes the opposite view. It states in its Guidelines that use of the Internet to advertise does not amount to active sales. On the contrary, it is a reasonable way to reach every customer, and the fact that it may have effects outside the distributor's own territory is a result of the technology. The sending of unsolicited e-mails to individual customers or to customer groups does, however, amount to active selling.

Guidelines on vertical restraints

50. . . .—'Active' sales mean actively approaching individual customers inside another distributor's exclusive territory or exclusive customer group by for instance direct mail or visits; or (2) actively approaching a specific customer group or customers in a specific territory allocated exclusively to another distributor through advertisement in media or other promotions specifically targeted at that customer group or targeted at customers in that territory; or establishing a warehouse or distribution outlet in another distributor's exclusive territory.

— 'Passive' sales mean responding to unsolicited requests from individual customers including delivery of goods or services to such customers. General advertising or promotion in media or on the Internet that reaches customers in other distributors' exclusive territories or customer groups but which is a reasonable way to reach customers outside those territories or customer groups, for instance to reach customers in non-exclusive territories or in one's own territory, are passive sales.

51. Every distributor must be free to use the Internet to advertise or to sell products. A restriction on the use of the Internet by distributors could only be compatible with the BER to the extent that promotion on the Internet or sales over the Internet would lead to active selling into other distributors' exclusive territories or customer groups. In general, the use of the Internet is not considered a form of active sales into such territories or customer groups, since it is a reasonable way to reach every customer. The fact that it may have effects outside one's own territory or customer group results from the technology, i.e. the easy access from everywhere. If a customer visits the web site of a distributor and contacts the distributor and if such contact leads to a sale, including delivery, then that is considered passive selling. The language used on the website or in the communication plays normally no role in that respect. Insofar as a web site is not specifically targeted at customers primarily inside the territory or customer group exclusively allocated to another distributor, for instance with the use of banners or links in pages of providers specifically available to these exclusively allocated customers, the website is not considered a form of active selling. However, unsolicited e-mails sent to individual customers or specific customer groups are considered active selling. The same considerations apply to selling by catalogue. Notwithstanding what has been said before, the supplier may require quality standards for the use of the Internet site to resell his goods, just as the supplier may require quality standards for a shop or for advertising and promotion in general. The latter may be relevant in particular for selective distribution. An outright ban on Internet or catalogue selling is only possible if there is an objec-

tive justification. In any case, the supplier cannot reserve to itself sales and/or advertising over the Internet.

2) Restrictions on wholesalers

The second exception permits a prohibition on a buyer at the wholesale level of trade from making active or passive sales to end users.

3) The restriction on sales to unauthorised distributors by the members of a select distribution system

This provision reiterates that where a selective distribution system is operated it is possible to prohibit members of the system from selling (actively or passively) to unauthorized distributors. In the absence of such a provision the system would obviously break down. The way in which the Verticals Regulation applies to selective distribution systems is discussed below.

4) Buyers of components

A supplier may preclude a buyer of components for incorporation into another product selling (actively or passively) to a customer who would use them to manufacture a product which competes with that produced by the supplier.

d. ARTICLE 4(c) AND (d): RESTRICTIONS IN SELECTIVE DISTRIBUTION SYSTEMS

Article 4(c) provides that members of a selective distribution system may not be precluded from making active or passive sales to end users and Article 4(d) provides that members of a system may not be precluded from making cross-supplies *inter se*.

It appears therefore that, in so far as a selective distribution system is caught by Article 81(1) at all, the main constraints on the operation of a selective distribution system are that: the parties do not exceed the 30 per cent market share threshold set out, resale price maintenance is not directly or indirectly imposed; and that members are not restrained from making sales to any end user or to another member of the network. The members may not, therefore, be required to purchase products only from the supplier but must be able to get them from other members of the network. Although an exclusive purchasing obligation is not permitted, Article 5 makes it clear that non-compete obligations are possible so long as they are not excessive in time and are not targeted at specific suppliers.[276]

Restraints can be imposed on the location and nature of the dealers' premises (this is ordinarily an essential feature of a selective distribution system)[277] and on sales being made to unauthorized distributors.[278] Further, in contrast to the position under Article 81(1) it is not necessary to establish that the products concerned merit selective distribution system nor that the members of the system are chosen only by reference to qualitative criteria. Quantitative criteria may be used to select distributors. The Guidelines make it clear that the supplier may decide to appoint only one or a few selected dealers that meet specific criteria in a particular territory.[279] In contrast to where an exclusive distribution system is set up,

---

[276] Verticals Reg., Art. 5(c).
[277] *Ibid.*, Art. 4(c).
[278] *Ibid.*, Art. 4(b).
[279] See also the position in Reg. 1475/95 on motor vehicle distribution, *supra* 531–532.

however, a single selected dealer must be able to make both passive and active sales to end users.[280]

e. ARTICLE 4(e): RESTRICTIONS ON SUPPLIERS OF COMPONENTS

Where a supplier supplies a buyer with components which the latter incorporates into its goods, a restriction may not be imposed which prevents the supplier from selling the components to customers or repairers which have not been authorized by the buyer to repair or service its goods.

(vii) ARTICLE 5—SEVERABLE, NON-EXEMPTED OBLIGATIONS

a. OBLIGATIONS WHICH ARE NOT EXEMPTED BUT WHICH ARE SEVERABLE

In contrast to the provision in Article 4 and to provisions in previous block exemptions, Article 5 provides that only the clauses prohibited by that provision are not exempted by the Regulation. The insertion of such a clause does not prevent the possibility of the remaining provisions of the agreement benefiting from the block exemption. They will not do so where the offensive clauses are severable from the remaining provisions of the agreement. It seems that whether or not the offending clauses can be severed is a question of national, not Community, law.[281]

Article 5, in comparison with Article 4, focuses on non-compete clauses[282] that are capable of foreclosing the market and restricting inter-brand competition.

Article 5

The exemption provided for in Article 2 shall not apply to any of the following obligations contained in vertical agreements;

(a) any direct or indirect non-compete obligation, the duration of which is indefinite or exceeds five years. A non-compete obligation which is tacitly renewable beyond a period of five years is to be deemed to have been concluded for an indefinite duration. However, the time limitation of five years shall not apply where the contract goods or services are sold by the buyer from premises and land owned by the supplier or leased by the supplier from third parties not connected with the buyer, provided that the duration of the non-compete obligation does not exceed the period of occupancy of the premises and land by the buyer;

(b) any direct or indirect obligation causing the buyer, after termination of the agreement, not to manufacture, purchase, sell or resell goods or services, unless such obligation:

—relates to goods or services which compete with the contract goods or services, and

—is limited to the premises and land from which the buyer has operated during the contract period, and

—is indispensable to protect know-how transferred by the supplier to the buyer.

and provided that the duration of such non-compete obligation is limited to a period of one year after

---

[280] *Guidelines on Vertical Restraints*, [2000] OJ C291/1, para. 53.
[281] See *supra* Chap. 3.
[282] See the definition of non-compete obligations in the Verticals Reg., Art. 1(b), set out *supra* 534.

termination of the agreement; this obligation is without prejudice to the possibility of imposing a restriction which is unlimited in time on the use and disclosure of know-how which has not entered the public domain;

(c) any direct or indirect obligation causing the members of a selective distribution system not to sell the brands of particular competing suppliers.

b. ARTICLE 5(a): NON-COMPETE OBLIGATIONS

Article 5(a) prohibits non-compete obligations imposed (or tacitly renewable) in excess of five years. An exception applies, however, where the buyer of the goods or services operates from premises owned by the supplier or leased by it from a third party not connected with the buyer. In this case the non-compete obligation can be imposed for the duration of the buyer's occupancy of the land. It thus seems, for example, that brewers leasing premises to a publican will be able to impose a non-compete obligation for the entire duration of the lease. The reason for this latter exception is that 'it is normally unreasonable to expect a supplier to allow competing products to be sold from premises and land owned by the supplier without its permission'. But '[a]rtifical ownership constructions intended to avoid the five-year duration limit cannot benefit from this exception'.[283]

c. ARTICLE 5(b): NON-COMPETE OBLIGATIONS AFTER THE TERMINATION OF THE AGREEMENT

Article 5(b) prevents obligations imposed on the buyer which prevents it from manufacturing, purchasing, or selling or reselling goods or services after the termination of the agreement *unless* the prohibition: relates to competing goods or services; is limited to the premises and land from which the buyer has operated during the agreement; is indispensable to protect know-how[284] transferred by the supplier under the agreement; and is limited to a period of one year. A restriction which is unlimited in time may be possible, however, where essential to prevent the use or disclosure of know-how which has not entered the public domain.

d. ARTICLE 5(c): NON-COMPETE OBLIGATIONS AND SELECTIVE DISTRIBUTION SYSTEMS

It can be seen from Article 5(a) above that the block exemption covers 'the combination of selective distribution with a non-compete obligation, obliging the dealer not to resell competing brands in general'. Article 5(c) does not, however, allow the supplier to prevent dealers from buying products for resale from *specific* competing suppliers.

The objective of the exclusion of this obligation is to avoid a situation whereby a number of suppliers using the same selective distribution outlets prevent one specific competitor or certain specific competitors from using these outlets to distribute their products (foreclosure of a competing supplier which would be a form of collective boycott).[285]

---

[283] *Guidelines on Vertical Restraints*, [2000] OJ C291/1, para. 59.
[284] Verticals Reg., Art. 1(f).
[285] *Guidelines on Vertical Restraints*, [2000] OJ C291/1, para. 61; see *Parfums Givenchy* [1992] OJ L236/11, [1993] 5 CMLR 579.

(viii) ARTICLE 6—WITHDRAWAL OF THE BLOCK EXEMPTION BY THE COMMISSION

Article 6 enables the Commission to withdraw the benefit of the block exemption where it considers that an *individual* agreement[286] is not in fact compatible with Article 81(3). In such cases the Commission will have to prove that the agreement infringes Article 81(1) and does not merit exemption.[287] The Regulation reserves, in particular, the right for the Commission to withdraw the benefit of a block exemption where foreclosure occurs, for example, as a result of parallel networks of vertical agreements. The Guidelines set out in greater detail the kind of factors likely to cause the Commission to withdraw the benefit of the block exemption.[288] A withdrawal does not apply retrospectively, so that the validity and enforceability of an agreement are not affected in the period prior to the withdrawal becoming effective.[289]

(ix) ARTICLE 7—WITHDRAWAL OF THE BLOCK EXEMPTION BY A NATIONAL COMPETITION AUTHORITY

Article 7 sets out a novel provision enabling the *authorities of a Member State*, authorized under national law to do so, to withdraw the benefit of the block exemption 'under the same conditions as provided in Article 6'.[290] It can do this in respect of vertical agreements where effects incompatible with Article 81(3) are felt in the territory of its State, or in part of it, 'which has all the characteristics of a distinct geographic market'. National decisions of withdrawal have effect only within the territory of that state. A national authority should not act where it would, by doing so, prejudice the uniform application of the competition rules and measures adopted in implementation of them.[291]

Where the geographical market is wider than the territory of a single Member State the Commission has the sole power to withdraw the benefit of the block exemption. Where the geographic market is confined to a single Member State, or a part thereof, the Commission and the national authorities have concurrent powers of withdrawal. In the latter case, and save in cases of particular Community interest, the national competition authority should act.[292]

(x) ARTICLE 8—REGULATIONS TO DEAL WITH NETWORKS OF AGREEMENTS

This Article also introduces a feature which is novel to block exemptions. It enables the Commission to declare by regulation that the exemption should not apply to agreements

---

[286] See Art. 8, discussed *infra*.

[287] *Guidelines on Vertical Restraints*, [2000] OJ C291/1, para. 72.

[288] *Ibid.*, paras. 71–75.

[289] *Ibid.*, para. 75.

[290] Presumably this means that the national authority may withdraw the benefit of the block exemption in the same sorts of circumstances as the Commission would withdraw the benefit of the block exemption, in particular where the market is foreclosed. See also the Commission's proposal for a Reg. implementing Arts. 81 and 92, COM (2000) 582, Art. 29(2).

[291] *Guidelines on Vertical Restraints*, *supra* n. 4, para. 78 and discussion of principle of the supremacy of Community law *infra* in Chap. 15.

[292] *Guidelines on Vertical Restraints*, [2000] OJ C291/1, para. 78. See also discussion of decentralized application of the competition rules, *infra* in Chap. 15.

containing specified restraints in cases where more than 50 per cent of the relevant market is covered by networks of similar vertical restraints.

(xi) ARTICLES 9, 10, AND 11—MARKET SHARE, TURNOVER, TRANSITIONAL PROVISIONS AND CONNECTED UNDERTAKINGS

Articles 9 and 10 contain provisions relating to the calculation of market share and turnover for the purposes of the Regulation. In particular, Article 9(2)(d) makes provision to exempt agreements for a period of one to three years which satisfy the 30 per cent threshold initially but subsequently exceed it.

Article 11 makes it clear that the terms undertaking, supplier, and buyer also include their respective connected undertakings. For the purposes of the regulation the turnover and market shares of these undertakings must, therefore, also be taken into account.

(xii) ARTICLE 12—THE OLD BLOCK EXEMPTIONS

Article 12 extended the application of the exclusive distribution, exclusive purchasing and franchising block exemptions until 31 May 2000. Further it provides transitional relief until 31 December 2001 to agreements concluded on or before 31 May 2000 which satisfy the conditions set out in one of those regulations.

(xiii) ARTICLE 13—COMMENCEMENT AND EXPIRY

Article 13 provides that the block exemption entered into force on 1 January 2000, applied from 1 June 2000,[293] and expires on 31 May 2010.

D. ARTICLE 81(3) AND INDIVIDUAL EXEMPTIONS

In some cases drafting within the confines of one of the block exemptions is not an appealing or possible option. Given the greater flexibility introduced in the new Verticals Regulation there should be fewer cases in which block exemption is not a realistic possibility. Where the parties will not or cannot ensure that their agreement benefits from either the Verticals Regulation (for example when the market share thresholds are exceeded) or the motor vehicle distribution block exemption and the risk of infringing Article 81(1) is real, it may still be important to secure an individual exemption for the agreement.

Prior to the amendment of Article 4(2) of Regulation 17,[294] parties seeking an *individual* exemption for their agreement had to notify it to the Commission. Exemptions could be granted only to the date of notification. It is now unnecessary to make prior notification to

---

[293] Except for the provision extending the application of the block exemption which has applied since 1 Jan. 2000.

[294] [1959–62] OJ Spec. Ed. 87, amended by Commission Reg. 1216/99 [1999] OJ L148/1.

the Commission for a vertical agreement to be exempted. In practice, however, many parties may wish to notify and to be certain that their agreement does not infringe Article 81.[295]

The Commission has granted individual exemptions to agreements in a number of cases, most notably in cases involving selective distribution systems.[296] When drafting agreements it is extremly important to look at the *Guidelines on Vertical Restraints* which set out how the Commission will enforce Article 81 in respect of agreements containing restraints such as, single branding; exclusive distribution and customer allocation; selective distribution; franchising; exclusive supply; and/or recommended and maximum prices; which do not fall within the confines of the block exemption. Further, Articles 4 and 5 of the Verticals Regulation indicate the types of clauses such as territorial and price restraints that are likely to cause the Commission to refuse an agreement an exemption.[297]

The Commission has therefore been unwilling to exempt agreements which confer absolute territorial protection on a distributor or which otherwise operate to prevent parallel imports (where the Commission discovers that such agreements are being operated in contravention of Article 81(3) it generally imposes large fines[298]). It will be remembered that in *Grundig*[299] it was the clauses resulting in Consten being granted the exclusive right to sell Grundig's products in France which caused the Commission both to find that the agreement infringed Article 81(1) and to refuse it an exemption under Article 81(3).[300] The Commission has not proved receptive to any argument that these types of clauses may be essential to prevent free-riding on the distributors' services or to ensure that a product is successfully launched in a new market.[301]

The events that occurred in *Distillers* illustrate the problems that this approach poses for undertakings, especially those wishing to sell a product in a new geographic market. In this case Distillers wished to promote certain of its product, in particular whisky, on a number of the European markets. Distributors in those countries would have to engage in considerable promotion to encourage local consumers to purchase whisky instead of other popular local products. Distillers wished to shelter local distributors from the competition of distributors in the UK, where whisky was already established on the market. These distributors did not consequently have to incur such heavy promotional expenses. The Commission issued a decision holding that provisions in Distillers agreements' with its UK distributors prohibiting export or imposing dual price terms (which allowed rebates etc. for home trade) infringed Article 81(1) and did not merit exemption under Article 81(3).[302] Distillers accepted that the prohibition on exports could not be exempted under Article 81(3), but argued that the dual price provisions were capable of enjoying exemption. Although

---

[295] See discussion of Reg. 17, Art. 4(2) *supra* 501–502. It is also possible to apply for negative clearance. Notification may not be possible much longer, *supra* 502.

[296] See *supra* 509 ff.

[297] All agreements are eligible for exemption, Case T–17/93, *Matra Hachette v. Commission* [1994] ECR II–595, discussed *supra* in Chap. 4.

[298] See *Volkswagen* [1998] OJ L124/60, [1998] 5 CMLR 33, on appeal Case T–62/98, *Volkswagen AG v. Commission* [2000] 5 CMLR 853.

[299] [1964] CMLR 489.

[300] See *supra* 504–505 and Chap. 4.

[301] See *supra* 504–505 and the opinion of AG in that case, set out *supra* in Chap. 4.

[302] *The Distillers Company Limited* [1978] OJ L50/16, [1978] 1 CMLR 400. The Commission considered that it did not have to rule on Art. 81(3) in respect of the latter since it had not been notified correctly in accordance with Reg. 17.

Distillers' view gained support from Advocate General Warner,[303] who accepted that dual pricing, which did not completely exclude the possibility of export, might be necessary to protect the promotional efforts of the Continental distributors, the Court rejected the plea. It found that notification had not been made in accordance with the provisions of Regulation 17 so that the agreement could not be exempted under Article 81(3).[304] The result was that Distillers was forced either to withdraw products it wished to promote on the Continent from the UK market or to raise the UK prices to such an extent that they almost ceased to sell. Consequently, different brands were sold in the UK and on the Continent and in '[t]he year after it split its brands, Distillers' turnover on the Continent for those brands, the price of which in England had not been raised and which ceased to be worth promoting on the continent, increased less than its turnover for those that suffered no parallel imports and whose price was higher'.[305]

In the end, Distillers was allowed a period of grace in which to launch one of its products on the Continental market. Distillers made a further notification seeking exemption for agreements providing for the institution of 'promotion equalization charge' (PEC) for its brand, Johnnie Walker Red Label. The PEC was an amount, calculated on the basis of the average expenditure by exclusive distributors in other Member States less an amount corresponding to the parallel trader's own marketing expenditure, which was to be levied on purchases of Red Label for export. The monies collected were to be spent on the promotion of Red Label in the EC, other than the UK. Because of the exceptional circumstances which existed (Red Label had been withdrawn from the UK market) the Commission stated that it would consider (no final decision was ever taken) granting an exemption which 'if given, would be conditional upon the progressive reduction of the PEC during the short period of time necessary to allow for the adaptation of marketing conditions for Red Label in the common market to the consequences of its large-scale re-introduction in one member-State'.[306] The Commission made it clear that no similar arrangements could be made in respect of other brands.

The Commission has also taken a rigid view of provisions imposing resale price maintenance. Thus despite any economic justifications which might be raised to justify the vertical price restraints, and which might be similar to those used to justify other non-price vertical restraints,[307] the Commission has found that such agreements infringe Article 81(1) and do not merit an exemption under Article 81(3).[308] Resale price maintenance is specifically prohibited by the Verticals Regulation.[309] The ECJ has recognized, however, in one case that

---

[303] Case 30/78, *Distillers Company* v. *Commission* [1980] ECR 2229, [1980] 3 CMLR 121, paras. 89–121.

[304] Case 30/78, *Distillers Company* v. *Commission* [1980] ECR 2229, [1980] 3 CMLR 121, para. 24. This aspect of the case is discussed *supra* in Chap. 4. At the time an exemption could be granted only if notification had been made to the Commission and in this case it had not, but now see Reg. 17, Art. 4(2).

[305] V. Korah, *An Introductory Guide to EC Competition Law and Practice* (7th edn.,) (Hart Publishing, 2000), para. 7.6.1.

[306] [1983] 3 CMLR 173, para. 12.

[307] See *supra* 485–488.

[308] The Commission states in its Green Paper on Vertical Restraints, COM (96) 721, para. 226 that resale price maintenance is unlikely to benefit from an exemption. See *Hennessy/Henkell* [1980] OJ L383/11, [1981] 1 CMLR 601; Case 161/84 *Pronuptia de Paris GmbH* v. *Pronuptia de Paris Irmgard Schillgallis* [1986] ECR 353, [1986] 1 CMLR 414; Cases 43 and 63/82, *VBBB and VBVB* v. *Commission* [1984] ECR 19, [1985] 1 CMLR 27; *cf.* Case C–360/92P, *Publishers' Association* v. *Commission* [1995] ECR I–23; [1995] 5 CMLR 33.

[309] *Infra* n. 303, Reg. 2790/1999, Art. 4(a).

an agreement imposing minimum resale prices might merit exemption by the Commission. In *Binon*, the ECJ indicated that the Commission might have to consider whether or not an agreement, where a publisher fixed the prices of its newspapers and periodicals, fulfilled the requirements for exemption.[310]

Case 243/85, *SA Binon & Cie* v. *SA Agence et Messageries de la Presse* [1985] ECR 2015, [1985] 3 CMLR 800

44. It should be observed in the first place that provisions which fix the prices to be observed in contracts with third parties constitute, of themselves, a restriction on competition within the meaning of Article [81(1)] . . .

45. In those circumstances, where an agreement which establishes a selective distribution system and which affects trade between Member States includes such a provision, an exemption from the prohibition contained in Article [81(1] of the [EC] Treaty may only be granted by means of a decision adopted by the Commission in the conditions laid down by Article [81(3)].

46. If, in so far as the distribution of newspapers and periodicals is concerned, the fixing of the retail price by publishers constitutes the sole means of supporting the financial burden resulting from the taking back of unsold copies and if the latter practice constitutes the sole method by which a wide selection of newspapers and periodicals can be made available to readers, the Commission must take account of those factors when examining an agreement for the purposes of Article [81(3)].

The net effect of the Commission's extremely strict approach to territorial and price restraints may mean, in some cases, that undertakings are encouraged to avoid distribution agreements and to seek other alternatives, perhaps vertical integration, instead. In the USA, the Supreme Court has recognized that 'the *per se* illegality of vertical restraints would create a perverse incentive for manufacturers to integrate vertically into distribution'.[311]

4. ARTICLE 82 AND DISTRIBUTION

Where the supplier has a large market share the possibility that its conduct may infringe Article 82 as well as Article 81 should be considered.

Article 82 may prohibit a number of clauses contained within a vertical agreement concluded by a dominant undertaking (for example, clauses imposing unfair or discriminatory selling prices, containing exclusive purchasing commitments or non-compete provisions, or granting discounts and rebates to purchasers[312]). Further, Article 82 applies more broadly to all individual acts of a dominant undertaking, including refusals to supply, as well as to agreements. Agreements or arrangements concluded between a dominant undertaking and entities within the same economic unit may also infringe Article 82.[313]

---

[310] In a subsequent notice the Commission did suggest, without giving reasons, that it might be willing to grant the agreement, including the resale maintenance provisions, an exemption under Art. 81(3): *Agence et Messageries de la Presse* [1987] OJ L164/2.

[311] *Business Electronics Corp v. Sharp Electronics Corp*, 485 US 717, 725, *per* Justice Scalia.

[312] See *supra* Chap. 7.

[313] See *supra* Chap. 3.

5. CONCLUSIONS AND THE FUTURE

The Commission has promised a new, more economic approach to vertical agreements. It is true that in the Verticals Regulation the Commission has set out a presumption that vertical agreements concluded between undertakings with a market share of less than 30 per cent of the market are compatible with Article 81. Problems still remain, however.

In particular, it seems clear that the main question for the Commission is still whether or not a vertical agreement or restraint is compatible with Article 81(3), not whether it is compatible with Article 81(1), i.e. whether it restricts competition within the meaning of that provision. For example, the Commission states in paragraph 120 of the Guidelines:

1) First, the undertakings involved need to define the relevant market in order to establish the market share of the supplier or the buyer, depending on the vertical restraint involved . . .

2) If the relevant market share does not exceed the 30 per cent threshold, the vertical agreement is covered by the BER, subject to the hardcore restrictions and conditions set out in that regulation.

3) If the relevant market share is above the 30 per cent threshold, it is necessary to assess whether the vertical agreement falls within Article 81(1).

4) If the vertical agreement falls within Article 81(1), it is necessary to examine whether it fulfils the conditions for exemption under Article 81(3).[314]

The Commission states that the first question to ask is whether or not the agreement falls within the block exemption, *not* whether the agreement actually falls within Article 81(1) and so requires exemption. Only once it appears that the agreement cannot benefit from the block exemption, on the ground that the market shares are exceeded, should it be asked whether or not the agreement actually infringes Article 81(1), and if so whether it fulfils the conditions set out in Article 81(3). Although this is clearly sensible, pragmatic advice it turns Article 81 on its head: no undertaking should feel the need to secure an exemption for an agreement which does not infringe Article 81(1).

The Guidelines do indicate that the Commission will take a more realistic approach at the Article 81(1) stage. In particular, the possibility that Article 81(1) does not apply cannot be ruled out even where the 30 per cent market share threshold is exceeded. However, if it is correct that a more economic approach will be taken at the *Article 81(1)* stage, no explanation is offered as to why such a broad overarching block exemption is necessary. The relationship between Article 81(1) and Article 81(3) has not therefore been cogently clarified in the context of vertical restraints, and the Commission has failed adequately to meet the criticism that it does not make a realistic economic assessment of agreements at the Article 81(1) stage.[315] The inevitable result will be that businesses will feel the need to comply, where possible, with the terms of the block exemption.

It is true that the Verticals Regulation does represent an improvement on the old block exemptions and should remove some of the arbitrary and unconvincing restrictions that

---

[314] *Guidelines on Vertical Restraints*, [2000] OJ C291/1, para. 120.

[315] Although the Commission states that agreements which are not capable of appreciably affecting competition or trade are not caught by Art. 81(1), this is an entirely separate issue from the question whether the agreement restricts competition: see *supra* Chap. 3.

those exemptions imposed on parties concluding vertical agreements. Nonetheless the complex nature of the hardcore and non-exemptable but severable restraints will no doubt provide pitfalls for undertakings when drafting their agreements. The hardcore restraints in particular reflect the Commission's old intolerance to agreements containing territorial and price restraints that impact, directly at least, only on intra-brand competition. Whatever the free rider or other rationale for these restraints, agreements containing such clauses, which affect competition and trade to an appreciable extent, are generally precluded.

Although no further changes to the Commission's approach to vertical restraints can be anticipated in the near future, subtle changes may result if the national courts and national competition authorities are given the opportunity to rule on an agreement's compatibility with the provisions of both Article 81(1) *and* Article 81(3). If the Commission's proposals for modernization set out in its White Paper and draft Regulation[316] become a reality, greater enforcement and litigation at the national level may be encouraged. Those authorities may be more willing to accept, in accordance with the Court's case law, that an agreement does not infringe Article 81(1) at all or that, in exceptional circumstances, agreements containing price[317] or territorial restraints satisfy the requirements of Article 81(3).

6. FURTHER READING

A. BOOKS

BORK R. H., *The Antitrust Paradox: A Policy at War with Itself* (Basic Books, 1978, reprinted with a new Introduction and Epilogue, 1993), Chapter 14

SCHERER, F. M., and ROSS, D., *Industrial Market Structure and Economic Performance* (3rd edn.,) (Houghton Mifflin, 1990), Chapter 15

B. ARTICLES

CHARD, J. S., 'The Economics of the Application of Article 85 to Selective Distribution Systems' (1982) 7 *ELRev*. 83

COMANOR, W. S., 'Vertical Price-Fixing, Vertical Market Restraints, and the New Antitrust Policy' (1984–1985) 98 *Harv. LR* 983

DEACON, D., 'Vertical Restraints under EU Competition Law: New Directions [1995] *Fordham Corp. L Inst.* 307

EASTERBROOK, F. H., 'Vertical Arrangements and the Rule of Reason' (1984) 53 *Antitrust LJ* 135

FLYNN, J. J., 'The "Is" and "Ought" of Vertical

Restraints After Monsanto Co. v. Sprayrite Service Corp'. (1985–1986) 1 *Cornell L Rev.* 1095

GOEBEL, R. J., 'Metro II's Confirmation of the Selective Distribution Rules: Is this the End of the Road?' (1987) 24 *CMLRev.* 605

GYSELEN, L., 'Vertical Restraints in the Distribution Process: Strengths and Weaknesses of the Free Rider Rationale under EEC Competition Law' (1984) 21 *CMLRev.* 647

HAWK, B. E., 'The American (Antitrust) Revolution: Lessons for the EEC' [1998] *ECLR* 53

---

[316] [1999] OJ C132/1, [1999] 5 CMLR 208 and COM (2000) 582.
[317] Although in most Member States resale price maintenance is not tolerated.

—— 'System Failure: Vertical Restraints and EC Competition Law' (1995) 32 *CMLRev.* 973

KORAH, V., 'Goodbye Red Label: Condemnation of Dual Pricing by Distillers' (1978) *El-Rev.* 62

—— 'Selective Distribution' [1994] *ECLR* 101

VENIT, J., 'Pronuptia: Ancillary restraints or Unholy Alliances?' (1986) 11 *ELRev* 213

WHISH, R., 'Regulation 2790/1999: the Commission's "New Style" Block Exemption for Vertical Agreements' (2000) 37 *CMLRev.* 887.

10

INTELLECTUAL PROPERTY RIGHTS

1. INTRODUCTION

Intellectual property rights are those rights which may be asserted in respect of the product of the human intellect. They are recognized and protected in some way in all developed countries and encompass a broad spectrum of different rights. For example, they safeguard the creators of æsthetic and artistic works from having their creations distorted and purloined by others, they provide an incentive for invention and innovation by enabling those who develop new products and processes to reap the financial rewards of their efforts, and they allow those who develop brand names to exploit the reputation attached to the brand. The value and importance of intellectual property rights in the modern commercial world is incontrovertible, but their interaction with Community law is complex. They raise problems not only for competition law but also for the free movement of goods and services and the operation of the single market. This is because:

a) Despite the introduction of some Community-wide rights[1] intellectual property rights are still typically granted by national laws and enforced on a national basis, conferring protection within national territories. This inevitably leads to a conflict with the Community provisions governing the free movement of goods and services;

b) Intellectual property rights may erect barriers to entry to a market and thus affect the determination of whether an undertaking is in a dominant position for the purposes of Article 82.[2] In addition, the use by a dominant undertaking of its intellectual property rights may constitute an abuse;

c) Transactions involving intellectual property rights may be agreements falling within Article 81. Holders of intellectual property rights often exploit them by licensing others to use them. The terms of such licences may involve restrictions of competition, including territorial restrictions which divide the common market.

---

[1] E.g., the Community Trade Mark, provided for by Council Reg. 40/94, [1994] OJ L11/1, and administered by the Office for Harmonization in the Internal Market (Trade Marks and Designs) in Alicante, Spain. The Community Patent Convention 1975 providing for a Community-wide patent, is not yet fully ratified, but see proposed Regulation on the Community Patent COM (2000) 412 final; the European Patent Convention, administered by the European Patent Office in Munich, enables a bundle of national patents to be granted on a single application.

[2] See *supra* Chap. 6.

2. TYPES OF INTELLECTUAL PROPERTY RIGHTS

Intellectual property rights give the holder an exclusionary, and sometimes exclusive, right to the exploitation of an emanation of the intellect. The nature of the right varies from one type of intellectual property to another. Intellectual property rights vary in duration. Some arise only upon registration, while others arise from the act of creation itself. In the absence of harmonization Community law does not regulate the conditions upon which national law grants intellectual property rights,[3] although it may curtail the *exercise* of them.[4] This section briefly describes the main types of intellectual property rights.

A. PATENTS

Patents relate to inventions. The grant of a patent confers on the holder (the patentee), for a maximum period of twenty years,[5] a monopoly to exploit a new and inventive product or process, and the right to prevent others from making, disposing of, using or importing a product which is the subject of the patent or derived from it, or from using the patented process itself. Patents protect applied technology, not abstract ideas. Patents are granted in respect of the product or process disclosed in the specification when the patent is applied for, and on the expiry of the patent anyone else in the world may use the information contained in the specification.

B. TRADE MARKS

A trade mark is a mark or sign used to identify and differentiate a product. Registration of a trade mark gives the holder an exclusive right to use it as such, although if it is a non-invented word it does not take the word out of general use, but only prevents its use by others as a trade mark.[6] Other parties remain free to offer competing goods and services under other marks and brand names. If renewal procedures are complied with trade mark registration can continue indefinitely. Trade mark law in the EU was harmonized by the First Trade Marks Directive of 21 December 1988.[7]

---

[3] See e.g. Case 144/81, *Keurkoop v. Nancy Kean Gifts* [1982] ECR 2653, [1983] 2 CMLR 47; Cases C241–241/91P, *RTE & ITP v. Commission* [1995] ECR I–743, [1995] 4 CMLR 718, para. 49.

[4] See *infra* 561–574.

[5] Patents Act 1977 ss. 25, 28, and 29. The maximum 20 year term is common throughout the EU. Council Reg. 1768/92, [1992] OJ L182/1, on the creation of supplementary protection certificates for medicinal products, enables a period not exceeding five years to be added to this in respect of the period between the date of filing the application and the grant.

[6] And the use of a *similar* mark or sign where there is a likelihood of confusion (Trade Marks Act 1994, s. 10).

[7] Dir. 89/104/EEC [1989] OJ L40/1, implemented in the UK by the Trade Marks Act 1994: the Dir. leaves to Member States the procedural details for applying for or revoking a mark or bringing infringement proceedings.

Marks and brand names which are not registered may also be protected by other means. In the UK this is by the law on passing-off, and in many other EU countries by laws on unfair competition.

C. COPYRIGHT

Copyright protects 'works' such as literary, dramatic, musical and artistic works, films, sound recordings, and broadcasts from unauthorized exploitation by third parties. Unlike a patent, copyright does not confer a monopoly because it prevents only *copying*: if a third party independently comes up with the same melody or words, he will not be liable for breach of copyright. Copyright does not depend on registration or formal procedures but arises automatically when the work is set down or recorded in some form. Copyright in the EU lasts for the lifetime of the author plus seventy years.[8]

There are greater differences between the laws of EU Member States in respect of copyright than there are with other forms of intellectual property. Common law notions of copyright emphasize the right of the author to prevent others exploiting his work for commercial gain whereas the civil law emphasizes the right of the creator of a work to be recognized as such and to be morally entitled to protect its integrity.[9] UK copyright law covers performers' rights, and similar rights but in most EU countries there is a distinction drawn between 'author's right' and 'neighbouring rights' (those accorded to sound recordings, broadcasts, and performers).Under UK law works created by the 'sweat of the brow', such as compilations of information, are accorded copyright protection, whereas civil law systems require a greater degree of creativity: this difference became an issue in the Article 82 case on television listings, *Magill*.[10] The Commission has proposed a Directive on Copyright and the Information Society which would harmonize various aspects of copyright.[11]

D. DESIGNS

Under the Berne Convention[12] countries are free to choose the way in which they protect industrial designs. In the UK designs which have features which in the finished article 'appeal to and are judged by the eye' can be registered.[13] Registration gives the proprietor a monopoly over its use for a maximum of twenty-five years, in respect of articles for

---

[8] Under Dir. 93/98 [1993] OJ L290/9, harmonizing the term of protection of copyright and related rights.

[9] The Copyright Designs and Patents Act 1988 ss. 77–85, introduced express 'moral rights' into UK law, partly to come into line with the Berne Convention for the Protection of Literary and Artistic Works, 1886.

[10] Cases C–241–241/91 P *RTE & ITP* v. *Commission* [1995] ECR I–743, [1995] 4 CMLR 718; see *infra* 627 and Chap.7. Specific protection is now accorded to databases under Dir. 96/9 [1996] OJ L77/20.

[11] The amended proposal, COM(1999)250 final [1999] OJ C180/6, was agreed to by the Council on 8 June 2000. The proposal is pursuant to the Commission's Green Paper, *Copyright in the Information Society* COM(95)382 final, 19 July 1995 and the *Follow-up to the Green Paper*, COM(96)568 final, 20 Nov. 1996. It is also driven by the need for the Community to ratify the WIPO (World Intellectual Property Organisation) Treaties jointly with the Member States.

[12] Berne Convention for the Protection of Literary and Artistic Works, 1886 (as subsequently revised).

[13] Registered Designs Act 1949 s. 1(3), as amended by the Copyright Designs and Patents Act 1988 s. 265.

which it has been registered. UK law also recognizes unregistered design rights in respect of the original design of any aspect of the shape or configuration of an article.[14] The right is analogous to copyright in that it arises automatically when the design is created, but it lasts for a maximum of fifteen years. Like copyright it protects the holder against *copying*, not against independent creation, whereas registered design right is like a patent in protecting against independent creation. The 1998 Directive on the legal protection of designs[15] dealt only with registered designs and is a partial harmonization measure only. Under the Directive protection is for twenty-five years and entitles the holder to prevent the making, offering, putting on the market, importing, exporting, and stocking of a product incorporating the design.

E. KNOW-HOW

Strictly speaking, know-how is not an intellectual property right, but it often features in commercial transactions such as licensing arrangements to which Article 81 applies. Know-how is confidential, technical, commercially valuable information which is not patented or registered in any way.[16] Know-how is defined in the block exemption on technology transfer agreements[17] and is protected by contractual provisions and breach of confidence laws.

F. MISCELLANEOUS

(i) PLANT BREEDERS' RIGHTS

Plant breeders' rights are given in respect of the creation of new plant varieties. They are similar to patents in that they confer a monopoly. Council Regulation 2100/94 on plant variety rights created a Community plant variety right which co-exists with national regimes.[18]

(ii) SEMI-CONDUCTOR TOPOGRAPHIES

The protection of the topography of semi-conductor chips was the subject of harmonization in Directive 87/54.[19]

---

[14] Copyright Designs and Patents Act 1988 s. 213. There are a number of exceptions: e.g., design right does not subsist in surface decoration, or features which enable the article to fit with or match another article.

[15] Dir. 98/71 of 13 Oct. 1998 [1998] OJ L289/28. The implementation date is 28 Oct. 2001.

[16] Usually because it does not fulfill the necessary criteria for patentability, but sometimes the creator chooses not to patent in order to keep the information out of the public domain.

[17] Reg. 240/96 [1996] OJ L31/2, Art. 10 (1)–(4); see *infra* 593.

[18] [1994] OJ L227/1.

[19] [1987] OJ L24/36. In the UK semiconductor topography is protected as an unregistered design. See the Design Right (Semi-conductor Topographies) Regulations 1989, SI 1989/1100.

(iii) DATABASES

Databases were the subject of specific harmonization in the 1996 Database Directive[20] which creates a *sui generis* right for their protection. Previously, Member States' copyright laws differed according to the extent of the protection that was afforded to databases.[21]

(iv) COMPUTER SOFTWARE

Before the implementation of the Software Directive[22] Member States varied in their ways of protecting software. The Directive requires them to do it by way of copyright as a literary work within the meaning of the Berne Convention. However, the Community has proposed that software programs should also qualify for patent protection in all Member States.[23]

3. THE RELEVANT PROVISIONS OF THE EC TREATY

Perhaps surprisingly for a document purporting to lay down the foundations for a single market, the EC Treaty itself contains very little about intellectual property. Article 295 (ex Article 222), however, contains a general rule about property rights:

This treaty shall in no way prejudice the rules in Member States governing the system of property ownership.

Community law therefore recognizes the existence and ownership of rights given by national law. Nevertheless, there is a fundamental conflict between this and the principle of the free movement of goods. Article 28 (ex Article 30), the basic provision on the free movement of goods, states:

Quantitative restrictions on imports and all measures having equivalent effect shall, without prejudice to the following provisions, be prohibited between Member States.

However, if widgets made in France by F cannot be imported into Germany because they would infringe G's German patent, the market is divided along national lines. Not only that, but G may wish to use its German patent to prevent its *own* widgets, which it has manufactured in the UK, from being imported into Germany by a parallel importer. In both these examples the free circulation of goods can be seriously impeded by national intellectual property rights.

Intellectual property rights are specifically dealt with in Article 30 (ex Article 36), which

---

[20] Dir. 96/9 on the legal protection of databases [1996] OJ L77/20.

[21] As illustrated in Cases C–241–241/91 P *RTE & ITP* v. *Commission* [1995] ECR I–743, [1995] 4 CMLR 718: see *infra* 627 and Chap. 7.

[22] Council Dir. 91/250 on the legal protection of computer programs, [1991] OJ L122/42.

[23] See Community Communication 'Promoting Innovation through Patents: the Follow-up to the Green Paper on the Community Patent System in Europe' COM(1999)42.

provides a derogation from Article 28. It is the only place in the Treaty where they are mentioned. Article 30 says:

The provisions of Articles 28 and 29 shall not preclude prohibitions or restrictions on imports, exports or goods in transit justified on grounds of public morality, public policy or public security; the protection of health and life of humans, animals or plants; the protection of national treasures possessing artistic, historic or archaeological value; or the protection of industrial and commercial property.[24] Such prohibition or restrictions shall not, however, constitute a means of arbitrary discrimination or a disguised restriction on trade between Member States.

Community law therefore accepts that restrictions on free movement may be justified to protect national intellectual property rights. However, Article 30 contains a final proviso in the last sentence. The restrictions are not to constitute 'a means of arbitrary discrimination or a disguised restriction' on inter-Member State trade. This has been described as the 'sting in the tail'[25] and used to justify many of the limitations which the ECJ has placed on the exercise of national intellectual property rights.

Intellectual property rights also affect the free movement of services. Article 49 (ex Article 59) is the basic provision on services:

Within the framework of the provisions set out below, restrictions on freedom to provide services within the Community shall be prohibited in respect of nationals of Member States who are established in a State of the Community other than that of the person for whom the services are intended.

Article 49 does not have a derogation equivalent to Article 30, but the ECJ has held that the principle in Article 30 should be applied to it by analogy.[26] Restrictions on the movement of services may therefore be justified by the need to protect intellectual property rights in the same way as they are justified in respect of the movement of goods.

4. THE CASE LAW OF THE COURT: EXISTENCE, EXERCISE AND THE EXHAUSTION OF RIGHTS

A. GENERAL

In its case law concerning both the free movement and the competition provisions the ECJ has attempted to reconcile the conflicting demands of the economic integration of the single

---

[24] It could be argued that the phrase 'industrial and commercial' property does not cover copyright, but the ECJ has held that it does: see Case 78/70, *Deutsche Grammophon* v. *Metro* [1971] ECR 487, [1971] CMLR 631 and Cases 55 & 57, *Musik-Vertrieb Membran* v. *GEMA* [1981] ECR 147, [1981] 2 CMLR 44. 'Intellectual property' is the generic phrase now used both at Community and international level.

[25] V. Korah, *An Introductory Guide to EC Competition Law and Practice* (7th edn. Hart Publishing, Oxford, 2000), 259.

[26] See Case 62/79, *Coditel* v. *Ciné Vog Films* [1980] ECR 881, [1982] 2 CMLR 362 (*Coditel I*); Case 262/81, *Coditel* v. *Ciné Vog Films* [1982] ECR 3381, [1983] 1 CMLR 49 (*Coditel II*).

market and the protection of intellectual property rights. It has developed a number of interlinking concepts by which to do this:

(a) it has drawn a dichotomy between the *existence* of intellectual property rights and their *exercise*: the existence of rights is unaffected by the EC Treaty but their exercise may be;

(b) it has developed the idea that there is a 'specific subject-matter' of each kind of right, the protection of which is justified even if it leads to restrictions on inter-Member State trade: the exercise of intellectual property rights which partitions the market will be allowed in so far as it is necessary to protect the 'specific subject matter';

(c) it has built up a jurisprudence on the 'exhaustion of rights'. Once a rights holder has consented to the marketing of the protected product within the Community,[27] the rights encompassed in the 'specific subject-matter' are exhausted and the holder cannot rely on national rights to prevent the movement of the goods between Member States.

The distinction between the existence and exercise of rights is not convincing. A property right which cannot be exercised has no value. Intellectual property rights are valuable because they enable the holder to exercise rights which prevent third parties from committing infringing acts. If Community law limits the holder's ability to control third parties then the value of the right is diminished, and the fact that the 'existence' of the right is untouched is of little comfort. Arguably the existence/exercise dichotomy is simply a flexible tool developed by the ECJ which enables it to make policy decisions under the guise of principle.

The distinction between existence and exercise was introduced in 1966 in *Consten & Grundig*.[28] It will be remembered that this was a case about an exclusive distribution agreement, which primarily concerned the competition rather than the free movement provisions. Grundig appointed Consten to be its exclusive distributor in France and allowed Consten to register its trade mark GINT in France. The provisions of the agreement and the registration of the trade mark conferred absolute territorial protection on Consten by enabling it to repel parallel imports of Grundig's products into France through proceedings for trade mark infringement. The Court held that the Commission's condemnation of these arrangements did not affect the grant of the trade mark rights but 'only limits their exercise'.

Cases 56 & 58, *Etablissements Consten SA & Grundig-Verkaufs-GmbH* v. *Commission* [1966] ECR 299, [1966] CMLR 418

Court of Justice

46. Consten's right under the contract to the exclusive user in France of the GINT trade mark, which may be used in a similar manner in other countries, is intended to make it possible to keep under surveillance and to place an obstacle in the way of parallel imports. Thus, the agreement by

---

[27] 'The Community' should be interpreted in this context to mean the whole EEA. The EEA (see *supra* Chap. 2) is the relevant area by virtue of Prot. 28 of the EEA Agreement, which provides for exhaustion throughout the EEA in accordance with the case law of the Court.

[28] Cases 56 & 58/64, *Consten & Grundig* v. *Commission* [1966] ECR 229, [1966] CMLR 418. The case is considered at length, *supra*, in Chaps. 3 and 4.

which Grundig, as the holder of the trade-mark by virtue of an international registration, authorized Consten to register it in France in its own name tends to restrict competition.

47. Although Consten is, by virtue of the registration of the GINT trade-mark, regarded under French law as the original holder of the rights relating to that trade-mark, the fact nevertheless remains that it was by virtue of an agreement with Grundig that it was able to effect the registration.

48. That agreement therefore is one which may be caught by the prohibition in Article [81(1)]. The prohibition would be ineffective if Consten could continue to use the trade-mark to achieve the same object as that pursued by the agreement which has been held to be unlawful.

49. Articles [30], [295] and [307] of the Treaty relied upon by the applicants do not exclude any influence whatever of Community law on the exercise of national industrial property rights.

50. Article [30], which limits the scope of the rules on the liberalization of trade contained in Title I, Chapter 2, of the Treaty, cannot limit the field of application of Article [81]. Article [295] confines itself to stating that the 'Treaty shall in no way prejudice the rules in Member States governing the system of property ownership'. The injunction contained in Article 3 of the operative part of the contested decision to refrain from using rights under national trade-mark law in order to set an obstacle in the way of parallel imports does not affect the grant of those rights but only limits their exercise to the extent necessary to give effect to the prohibition under Article [81(1)]. The power of the Commission to issue such an injunction for which provision is made in Article 3 of Regulation No 17/62 of the Council is in harmony with the nature of the Community rules on competition which have immediate effect and are directly binding on individuals.

51. Such a body of rules, by reason of its nature described above and its function, does not allow the improper use of rights under any national trade-mark law in order to frustrate the Community's law on cartels.

52. Article [307] which has the aim of protecting the rights of third countries is not applicable in the present instance.

This distinction drawn between the grant of rights and their exercise was elaborated in *Deutsche Grammophon.*

Case 78/70 *Deutsche Grammophon Gesellschaft* v. *Metro-SB-Großmärkte GmbH* [1971] ECR 487, [1971] CMLR 631

Deutsche Grammophon (DGG) marketed its records in France through its French subsidiary, Polydor, under the designation 'Polydor'. A quantity of records was pressed by DGG in Germany and supplied to Polydor in Paris. Polydor supplied them to an undertaking in a third country which resold them to a firm in Germany which resold them to Metro. Metro then marketed them in Germany, undercutting DGG's standard price for its records there. DGG sued Metro in the German courts for breach of its copyright. The Hamburg court made an Article 234 reference to the Court of Justice, asking whether the exercise of the intellectual property right infringed the Community provisions on free movement.

Court of Justice

4. It is clear from the facts recorded by the Hanseatisches Oberlandesgericht, Hamburg, that what it asks may be reduced in essentials to the question whether the exclusive right of distributing the protected articles which is conferred by a national law on the manufacturer of sound recordings

may, without infringing Community provisions, prevent the marketing on national territory of prod-ucts lawfully distributed by such manufacturer or with his consent on the territory of another Member State. The Court of Justice is asked to define the tenor and the scope of the relevant Community provisions, with particular reference to the second paragraph of Article [10] or Article [81(1)].

5. According to the second paragraph of Article [10] of the Treaty, Member States 'shall abstain from any measure which could jeopardize the attainment of the objective of this Treaty'. This provision lays down a general duty for the Member States, the actual tenor of which depends in each individual case on the provisions of the Treaty or on the rules derived from its general scheme.

6. According to Article [81(1)] of the Treaty 'The following shall be prohibited as incompatible with the common market: all agreements between undertakings, decisions by associations of under-takings and concerted practices which may affect trade between Member States and which have as their object or effect the prevention, restriction or distortion of competition within the Common Market'. The exercise of the exclusive right referred to in the question might fall under the prohibition set out by this provision each time it manifests itself as the subject, the means or the result of an agreement which, by preventing imports from other Member States of products lawfully distributed there, has as its effect the partitioning of the market.

7. If, however, the exercise of the right does not exhibit those elements of contract or concerted practice referred to in Article [81(1)] it is necessary, in order to answer the question referred, further to consider whether the exercise of the right in question is compatible with other provisions of the Treaty, in particular those relating to the free movement of goods.

8. The principles to be considered in the present case are those concerned with the attainment of a single market between the Member States, which are placed both in Part Two of the Treaty devoted to the foundations of the Community, under the free movement of goods, and in Article 3 [(1)(g)] of the Treaty which prescribes the institution of a system ensuring that competition in the common market is not distorted.

9. Moreover, where certain prohibitions or restrictions on trade between Member States are con-ceded in Article [30], the Treaty makes express reference to them, providing that such derogations shall not constitute 'a means of arbitrary discrimination or a disguised restriction on trade between Member States'.

10. It is thus in the light of those provisions, especially of Articles [28],[30], [81] and [82], that an appraisal should be made as to how far the exercise of a national right related to copyright may impede the marketing of products from another Member State.

11. Amongst the prohibitions or restrictions on the free movement of goods which it concedes Article [30] refers to industrial and commercial property. On the assumption that those provisions may be relevant to a right related to copyright, it is nevertheless clear from that article that, although the Treaty does not affect the existence of rights recognized by the legislation of a Member State with regard to industrial and commercial property, the exercise of such rights may nevertheless fall within the prohibitions laid down by the Treaty. Although it permits prohibitions or restrictions on the free movement of products, which are justified for the purpose of protecting industrial and commercial property, Article [30] only admits derogations from that freedom to the extent to which they are justified for the purpose of safeguarding rights which constitute the specific subject-matter of such property.

12. If a right related to copyright is relied upon to prevent the marketing in the Member State of products distributed by the holder of the right or with his consent on the territory of another Member

State on the sole ground that such distribution did not take place on the national territory, such a prohibition, which would legitimize the isolation of national markets, would be repugnant to the essential purpose of the Treaty, which is to unite national markets into a single market.

That purpose could not be attained if, under the various legal systems of the Member States, nationals of those States were able to partition the market and bring about arbitrary discrimination or disguised restrictions on trade between Member States.

13. Consequently, it would be in conflict with the provisions prescribing the free movement of products within the common market for a manufacturer of sound recordings to exercise the exclusive right to distribute the protected articles, conferred upon him by the legislation of a Member State, in such a way as to prohibit the sale in that State of products placed on the market by him or with his consent in another Member State solely because such distribution did not occur within the territory of the first Member State.

In this case, unlike *Consten & Grundig*, there was no agreement between any of the parties which could be caught by Article 81. The Court was thus faced with a stark conflict between the exercise of intellectual property rights and the free movement of goods in a situation where, in order to protect its higher price level in Germany, the holder was trying to use its German rights to prevent the import into Germany of its own records, which it had originally placed on the market itself. Like many of the cases in this area the scenario involved the activities of parallel importers. It can be seen from the judgment that the Court considered that the exercise of the right to prevent the imports in this situation would go beyond the protection of the 'specific subject-matter' of the right. Although *Deutsche Grammophon* did not expressly mention the principle of exhaustion of rights it is implicit in the judgment: DGG had exercised its German rights by putting the records on the market, and any further exercise of the rights was not permitted by Community law—its rights were exhausted. The Court did not explain what constituted the 'specific subject-matter' of the right in issue, but in subsequent cases it has defined the concept in relation to different rights and developed a complex case law on the exhaustion of rights.

B. PATENTS

The grant of a patent rewards invention and innovation. Many patented products and processes are the outcome of years of research and effort and the expenditure of large sums of money: the development of a new drug, for example, many involve the investment of many millions of pounds. Moreover, undertakings may invest such resources in research which never results in a marketable product, so that the profits of research which *does* come to fruition need to cover the costs of that which does not. The exclusive right to exploit an invention for a certain length of time provides the incentive for this investment and Community law fully recognizes the indispensability of the patent system to the economic well-being of Europe. The problems which have arisen in reconciling these exclusive rights with the single market have mainly concerned the attempts of holders of parallel patents[29] to seal

---

[29] Parallel intellectual property rights are where rights are held in the same (or virtually the same) subject matter under the laws of more than one Member State by the same person (including companies belonging to the same group), e.g. where an undertaking patents the same invention in several Member States.

off from one another the territories in which they hold those patents in order to frustrate the activities of parallel importers.

In *Centrafarm v. Sterling Drug*[30] the Court first defined the 'specific subject-matter' of a patent. A drug called 'Negram' was patented by Sterling Drug in the UK, the Netherlands, and Germany. In the UK the price of Negram was much lower than in the Netherlands. Centrafarm bought up supplies of Negram marketed by Sterling's subsidiaries in the UK and Germany, imported it into the Netherlands, and resold it at prices below those offered by Sterling. Sterling brought an action in the Dutch courts claiming that Centrafarm's actions infringed its Dutch patent. Under Dutch law an infringement action lay in these circumstances, so the question to be determined was whether the position was affected by Community law. The Court held that it was. It stated that the specific subject matter of a patent is:

the guarantee that the patentee, to reward the creative effort of the inventor, has the exclusive right to use an invention with a view to manufacturing industrial products and putting them into circulation for the first time, either directly or by the grant of licences to third parties, as well as the right to oppose infringements.[31]

The 'specific subject-matter' of a patent is therefore the right to put the patented product on the market *for the first time*. The exclusive right to do this is necessary to reward the inventor for its creative effort. Once it has placed the product on the market it has 'exhausted' the right and cannot prevent the product moving freely within the Community. The Court expressly denied the right of the patentee to take advantage of its product commanding higher prices in one Member State than in another.[32]

The exhaustion of rights doctrine has severely limited the ways in which the holders of parallel patents in different Member States may exploit their rights, and has had a particular effect on the trade in pharmaceuticals, where price differentials between Member States are common. In *Centrafarm v. Sterling Drug*, however, the Court accepted that a patentee *would* be allowed protection, despite the hindrance to inter—Member State trade, in two cases: first, where the imported product has been manufactured by a third party, without the consent of the patentee, in a Member State where it is not patentable; and, secondly, where the imported product has been manufactured by an independent third party in another Member State where the third party has the patent rights. In neither of these cases has the patentee in the Member State of import exhausted its rights because it has not already reaped the rewards of first marketing the imported product. In *Merck v. Stephar*[33] the ECJ had to consider a third scenario: the position where a parallel importer seeks to import products covered by a patent from a Member State where no patent protection for that product is available but where the patentee has marketed the products or consented to the marketing in that State. In the case Merck held patents for its drug 'Moduretic' in all Member States except Italy and Luxembourg. At the relevant time patent protection was not available in Italy for pharmaceuticals. Merck sold 'Moduretic' in Italy where a third party, Stephar, purchased stocks of it and imported them into the Netherlands. The price in Italy was much lower than in the Netherlands, so Stephar stood to profit considerably. Merck

---

[30] Case 15/74 [1974] ECR 1147, [1974] 2 CMLR 480.

[31] *Ibid.*, para. 9.

[32] *Ibid.*, paras. 22–25.

[33] Case 187/90, *Merck v. Stephar* [1981] ECR 2063, [1981] 3 CMLR 463.

tried to rely on its Dutch patent to exclude the imports. In *Merck* v. *Stephar* the argument turned on the question whether Merck should be protected from the Italian imports because it had had no chance of reaping a monopoly reward in Italy. The Court took the view that Merck had a free choice whether or not to sell in Italy, and in choosing to do so had to take the consequences of its actions.[34] It had consented to the marketing there, and the fact that there was no patent protection did not mean that it had not exhausted its rights. It repeated this ruling fifteen years later in *Merck* v. *Primecrown*[35] saying that this struck the correct balance between the principle of free movement of goods in the Community and the principle of protection of patentees' rights.

The exhaustion of rights doctrine is based on the idea of *consent*, i.e. if the patent holder has consented to the first marketing of the protected product in the Community it cannot prevent its circulation within the Community by relying on its national intellectual property rights. However, there is some doubt to what extent this doctrine applies to sales by a licensee. If a patent holder grants a licence to a licensee to make and sell the product in a particular territory, say France for example, what is the position if the licensee never puts the product on the market in France but sells it directly into another territory? It can be argued that such a sale was not with the patentee/licensor's *consent* and that in *Centrafarm* v. *Sterling Drug*[36] the ECJ formulated the exhaustion principle on the basis of *marketing* in the Member State from which the products have been imported. The Commission formerly took the view that the exhaustion principle did cover direct sales by licensees, but it appears from Article 2(1)(14) of the Transfer Technology block exemption, Regulation 240/96, that this is no longer so.[37]

The ECJ has held that there is no consent for the purposes of the exhaustion of rights where the patentee is legally bound to market the products in the exporting State[38] including where the patentee has been forced to give a compulsory licence by national law.[39]

C. TRADE MARKS

The worthiness of trade marks is not as immediately obvious as that of patents. Whereas patents protect innovators and inventors, trade marks reward the commercial acumen of those who have built up the reputation of the mark and the goodwill attaching to it. The ECJ used to be dismissive of trade marks. Its attitude was exemplified by its comments in 1971 in *Sirena* v. *Eda*, a case concerning the trade mark 'Prep Good Morning' for shaving cream, where it said that trade marks had become nothing more than an aid to advertising, and that 'the debt which society owes to the "inventor" of the name "Prep Good Morning" is

---

[34] *Ibid.*, para. 11.

[35] Cases C–267–268/95, *Merck* v. *Primecrown* [1996] ECR I–6285, [1997] 1 CMLR 83. A great deal of the argument in *Primecrown* centred on the judgment of the ECJ in a case after *Merck* v. *Stephar*, Case 156/86, *Warner Brothers* v. *Christiansen* [1988] ECR 2605, [1990] 3 CMLR 684, which concerned copyright; see *infra* 573. In his Opinion in *Primecrown* Fennelly AG advocated reversing the *Merck* v. *Stephar* rule: the Court did not follow him.

[36] [1974] ECR 1147, paras. 11 and 12.

[37] See *infra* 567 and 607.

[38] See Cases C–267–268/95, *Merck* v. *Primecrown* [1996] ECR I–6285, [1997] 1 CMLR 83 at paras. 49–50.

[39] Case 19/84, *Pharmon* v. *Hoechst* [1985] ECR 2281, [1985] 3 CMLR 775.

certainly not of the same nature, to say the least, as that which humanity owes to the discoverer of penicillin'.[40] Subsequently, however, the Court recognized the value of trade marks to the consumer.[41]

The Court first defined the specific subject-matter of a trade mark in *Centrafarm* v. *Winthrop*,[42] which concerned the same circumstances as the patent case Centrafarm v. *Sterling Drug*.[43] The Court stated that the specific subject-matter is:

the guarantee that the owner of the trade mark has the exclusive right to use that trade mark, for the purpose of putting products protected by the trade mark into circulation for the first time, and is therefore intended to protect him against competitors wishing to take advantage of the status and reputation of the trade mark by selling products illegally bearing that trade mark.[44]

The specific subject-matter of a mark is therefore formulated in terms analogous to the definition of the specific subject-matter of a patent. It is the right to first marketing. Once that has been done by, or with the consent of, the mark holder, any further use of the mark amounts to its *exercise* and may be affected by Community law. So the owner of a trade mark cannot exercise the right which it enjoys under the legislation of a Member State to prohibit the sale, in that State, of a product which has been marketed by it or with its consent under the trade mark in another Member State.[45]

Particular complications have arisen over the application of the consent and exhaustion principles to trade marks. The definition of the specific subject-matter of a trade mark in *Centrafarm* v. *Winthrop* is made from the point of view of the holder of the mark. Trade marks, however, also have a function from the consumer's point of view. They enable consumers to identify goods as being of a particular kind and originating from a particular manufacturer. The ECJ has come to recognize the valuable function which trade marks perform in this respect but not without some difficulties along the way. In 1974 the Court in the *Café Hag* (*HAG I*) case[46] laid down the so-called 'common origin' principle. Under this principle trade mark owners were prevented from bringing infringement proceedings against the goods of *other* manufacturers bearing the same mark if the marks once had a 'common origin'. This was a serious problem for trade mark owners,[47] particularly as trade marks can last indefinitely and marks registered in different Member States may come into the hands of different, independent parties. The point was illustrated by the facts of *HAG I*, where the ownership of the marks had been separated by government action: the rights to the 'HAG' trade mark in Belgium were sequestered in 1944 by the Custodian of Enemy Property and so came to be owned by a different company from that which owned the rights in Germany.

The common origin doctrine was highly controversial, for it was difficult to see what was

---

[40] Case 40/70, *Sirena* v. *Eda* [1971] ECR 69, [1971] CMLR 260, para. 17.

[41] See *infra* 569.

[42] Case 16/74, *Centrafarm BV* v. *Winthrop BV* [1974] ECR 1183, [1974] 2 CMLR 480.

[43] Case 15/74, *Centrafarm* v. *Sterling Drug* [1974] ECR 1147, [1974] 2 CMLR 480; see *supra* 566.

[44] *Ibid.*, para. 8.

[45] *Ibid.*, para. 12.

[46] Case 192/73, *Van Zuylen Frères* v. *Hag AG* [1974] ECR 731, [1974] CMLR 127.

[47] During the currency of the 'common origin' doctrine there was no case which raised the issue of its possible application to intellectual property rights other than trade marks. The Court further explained the thinking behind the common origin doctrine in Case 119/75, *Terrapin (Overseas) Ltd* v. *Terranova Industrie CA Kapferer & Co* [1976] ECR 1039, [1976] 2 CMLR 482, particularly at para. 6.

left of the 'specific subject-matter' of the mark if the holder could not use it against the same type of goods, identically marked, originating from a third party. Further, the Court failed to deal properly with the position of consumers who could be faced with identically marked products coming from different sources. *HAG I* showed a disregard of the value and function of trade marks, not just to the producer but also to the consumer. In 1990, the ECJ finally agreed that the common origin doctrine was unsupportable and in *CNL-SUCAL* v. *HAG GF AG* (*HAG II*),[48] took the (then) unprecedented step of overruling its previous decision. It held that a trade mark holder *could* rely on its national rights to exclude the products of a third party with which the trade mark holder had no economic links, even where the products bore a trade mark which had a 'common origin' with its own mark. In *Ideal Standard*[49] the Court confirmed that this applied even where the trade marks with a common origin had come into separate ownership through *voluntary* action, rather than by government intervention as in the *HAG* cases. It is now clear, therefore, that the notion of consent for the purpose of the exhaustion of rights does not cover marketing by an *assignee* of a trade mark: it seems that neither does it cover direct marketing by a licensee for another territory. The latter point is unclear, but although Article 2(1)(14) of the Technology Transfer block exemption, discussed below, would relate only to patents it appears to reflect the Commission's view generally.[50]

In *HAG II* the Court stressed the role which trade marks play *vis-à-vis* consumers, recognizing their *essential function* as a guarantee of the origin of the goods. The concept of the 'essential function' of trade marks was developed in cases raising another major problem which has arisen over trade marks: whether third parties may repackage and/or relabel (rebrand) goods without infringing trade mark rights. The extent to which the holder of a trade mark has exhausted its right by first putting the goods on the market, so that it cannot prevent third parties indulging in rebranding and repackaging activities, has been considered in a number of cases.[51] The position was fully set out as far as pharmaceuticals are concerned in *Bristol-Myers Squibb* v. *Paranova*.[52] The details of the issue is beyond the scope of this book, but what the Court has said about the 'essential function' of trade marks should be noted. In *Hoffmann-La Roche* v. *Centrafarm* it stated that the essential function:

is to guarantee to the identity of the origin of the trade-marked product to the consumer or ultimate user, by enabling him without any possibility of confusion to distinguish that product from products which have another origin. This guarantee of origin means that the consumer or ultimate user can be certain that a trade-marked product which is sold to him has not been subject at a previous stage of marketing to interference by a third person, without the authorisation of the proprietor of the trade mark, such as to affect the original condition of the product.[53]

---

[48] Case C–10/89, *CNL-SUCAL* v. *HAG GF AG* [1990] 1 ECR 3711, [1990] 3 CMLR 571.

[49] Case C–9/93, *IHT International Heiztechnik GmbH* v. *Ideal Standard GmbH* [1994] ECR I–2789, [1994] 3 CMLR 857.

[50] See *infra* 607 and Korah, n. 25, *supra* 264.

[51] See particularly Case 102/77, *Hoffmann-La Roche* v. *Centrafarm* [1978] ECR 1139, [1978] 3 CMLR 217; Case 3/78, *Centrafarm* v. *American Home Products* [1978] ECR 1823, [1979] 1 CMLR 326; Case 1/81, *Pfizer* v. *Eurim-Pharm* [1981] ECR 2913, [1982] 1 CMLR 406.

[52] Cases C–427, 429 and 436/93 etc. [1996] ECR I–3457, [1997] 1 CMLR 1151; see also Case C–379/97, *Pharmacia and Upjohn SA* v. *Paranova A/S* [2000] 1 CMLR 85. For non-pharmaceuticals, see Case C–349/95 *Frits Loendersloot* v. *George Ballantine & Son Ltd* [1997] ECR I–6227, [1998] 1 CMLR 1015; and Art. 7 of the First Trade Mark Dir., 89/104/EEC [1989] OJ L40/1.

[53] Case 102/77, *Hoffmann-La Roche* v. *Centrafarm* [1978] ECR 1139, [1978] 3 CMLR 217, para. 7.

The essential function of a trade mark as a guarantee of origin to the consumer was fundamental to the reasoning of the Court in *HAG II*:

Consequently, as the Court has ruled on numerous occasions, the specific subject-matter of trade marks is in particular to guarantee to the proprietor of the trade mark that he has the right to use that trade mark for the purpose of putting a product into circulation for the first time and therefore to protect him against competitors wishing to take advantage of the status and reputation of the trade mark by selling products illegally bearing that mark. In order to determine the exact scope of this right exclusively conferred on the owner of the trade mark, regard must be had to the essential function of the trade mark, which is to guarantee the identity of the origin of the marked product to the consumer or ultimate user by enabling him without any possibility of confusion to distinguish that product from products which have another origin (see, in particular, the judgments in Case 102/77 *Hoffmann-la Roche* v. *Centrafarm* . . . . , paragraph 7, and in Case 3/78 *Centrafarm* v. *American Home Products Corporation* [1978] ECR 1823, paragraphs 11 and 12).[54]

In *Silhouette*[55] the ECJ dealt with the question of exhaustion of rights where the trade marked goods are marketed *outside* the EEA. This turned on the interpretation of Article 7(1) of the First Council Trade Mark Directive[56]. The Court held that the Directive *does not permit* national laws to provide for international exhaustion, which means that all Member States must recognize the right of a trade mark proprietor to prohibit its use in relation to goods which it has first put on the market outside the EEA. In this case it meant that Silhouette could prevent the sale in Austria of the sunglasses it had marketed in Bulgaria.[57] The Court subsequently confirmed this ruling in *Sebago*.[58] The fact that a trade mark is not exhausted by putting the goods on the market outside the EEA means that trade mark owners can prevent Community consumers benefiting from lower priced parallel imports. Despite widespread criticism of the Court's rulings the Commission decided not to propose a change to the current exhaustion regime.[59] It is important to note that *Silhouette* did not consider any competition law aspects of the situation, although agreements with distributors outside the EEA not to import into the EEA *may* infringe Article 81(1).[60]

---

[54] Case C–10/89 *CNL-SUCAL* v. *HAG GF AG* [1990] 1 ECR 3711, [1990] 3 CMLR 571, para. 14.

[55] Case C–355/96, *Silhouette International Schmied GmbH & Co KG* v. *Hartlauer Handelsgesellschaft mbH* [1998] ECR I–4799, [1998] 2 CMLR 953.

[56] Dir. 89/104/EC on the approximation of the laws of the Member States relating to trade marks, [1989] OJ L40/1, as amended by the Agreement on the European Economic Area.

[57] Although it does not appear so from the judgment, the goods in *Silhouette* had in fact originally been put on the market *inside* the EEA, so they had been re-imported: T. Hays and P. Hansen, 'Silhouette is Not the Proper Case Upon Which to Decide the Parallel Importation Question' [1998] EIPR 277; See also F.M. Abbott and D.W. Feer Verkade, 'The Sihouette of a Trojan Horse' [998] JBL 413.

[58] Case C–173/98, *Sebago Inc and Ancienne Maison Dubois et Fils SA* v. *GB-Unic SA* [1999] 2 CMLR 1317. Note that the EFTA Court held in *Mag Instrument Inc* v. *California Trading Company* [1998] ETMR 85 that the EFTA members of the EEA *are* free to apply the principle of international exhaustion in their domestic law.

[59] The decision was made following a 1999 report from the NERA Institute in London, and reported to an Internal Market Council meeting on 25 May 2000. Several Member States opposed the Commission's view and advocated a change. Note also the disapproval of *Silhouette* in Laddie J's judgment in *Zino Davidoff SA* v. *A & G Imports Ltd* [1999] 2 CMLR 1056, where he made an Art. 234 reference to the ECJ, [2000] 2 CMLR 750.

[60] Case C–306/96, *Javico International and Javico AG* v. *Yves Saint Laurent Parfums SA* [1998] ECR I–1983, [1998] 5 CMLR 172.

D. COPYRIGHT

Copyright covers such a variety of different things that blanket definitions of its specific subject-matter are not appropriate. In *Coditel I* the Court recognized that a rule holding that a copyright owner exhausted its rights on the first marketing of a film would clearly be inappropriate to an industry where profits are made by charging each time a film is shown (and where distributors sometimes help to finance films).

Case 62/79 *SA Compagnie Générale pour la Diffusion de la Télévision, Coditel v. Ciné Vog Films (Coditel I)* [1980] ECR 881, [1981] 2 CMLR 362

Ciné Vog films acquired from Les Films de la Boétie an exclusive right to distribute Chabrol's film 'Le Boucher' in Belgium for seven years. The film was broadcast on German television and Coditel picked up the broadcast and relayed it through its cable channel to Belgium. Ciné Vog brought an action against Les Films de la Boétie for having set up a situation which did not observe its exclusive rights and against Coditel for having transmitted the film in infringement of its rights in Belgium. The Court of Justice held that these infringement actions were not barred by Article 49.[61]

Court of Justice

11. The second question raises the problem of whether Articles [49] and [50] of the Treaty prohibit an assignment, limited to the territory of a Member State, of the copyright in a film, in view of the fact that a series of such assignments might result in the partitioning of the Common Market as regards the undertaking of economic activity in the film industry.

12. A cinematographic film belongs to the category of literary and artistic works made available to the public by performances which may be infinitely repeated. In this respect the problems involved in the observance of copyright in relation to the requirements of the Treaty are not the same as those which arise in connexion with literary and artistic works the placing of which at the disposal of the public is inseparable from the circulation of the material form of the works, as in the case of books or records.

13. In these circumstances the owner of the copyright in a film and his assigns have a legitimate interest in calculating the fees due in respect of the authorization to exhibit the film on the basis of the actual or probable number of performances and in authorizing a television broadcast of the film only after it has been exhibited in cinemas for a certain period of time. It appears from the file on the present case that the contract made between Les Films la Boètie and Ciné Vog stipulated that the exclusive right which was assigned included the right to exhibit the film 'La Boucher' publicly in Belgium by way of projection in cinemas and on television but that the right to have the film diffused by Belgian television could not be exercised until 40 months after the first showing of the film in Belgium.

14. These facts are important in two regards. On the one hand, they highlight the fact that the right of a copyright owner and his assigns to require fees for any showing of a film is part of the essential function of copyright in this type of literary and artistic work. On the other hand, they demonstrate that the exploitation of copyright in films and the fees attaching thereto cannot

---

[61] In Community law the transmission of films is subject to Art. 49 (free movement of services) rather than Art. 28 (free movement of goods): see Case 52/79, *Procureur du Roi* v. *Debauve* [1980] ECR 833, [1981] 2 CMLR 362.

be regulated without regard being had to the possibility of television broadcasts of those films. The question whether an assignment of copyright limited to the territory of a Member State is capable of constituting a restriction on freedom to provide services must be examined in this context.

15. Whilst Article [49] of the Treaty prohibits restrictions upon freedom to provide services, it does not thereby encompass limits upon the exercise of certain economic activities which have their origin in the application of national legislation for the protection of intellectual property, save where such application constitutes a means of arbitrary discrimination or a disguised restriction on trade between Member States. Such would be the case if that application enabled parties to an assignment of copyright to create artificial barriers to trade between Member States.

16. The effect of this is that, whilst copyright entails the right to demand fees for any showing or performance, the rules of the Treaty cannot in principle constitute an obstacle to the geographical limits which the parties to a contract of assignment have agreed upon in order to protect the author and his assigns in this regard. The mere fact that those geographical limits may coincide with national frontiers does not point to a different solution in a situation where television is organized in the Member States largely on the basis of legal broadcasting monopolies, which indicates that a limitation other than the geographical field of application of an assignment is often impracticable.

17. The exclusive assignee of the performing right in a film for the whole of a Member State may therefore rely upon his right against cable television diffusion companies which have transmitted that film on their diffusion network having received it from a television broadcasting station established in another Member State, without thereby infringing Community law.

18. Consequently the answer to the second question referred to the Court by the Cour d'Appel, Brussels, should be that the provisions of the Treaty relating to the freedom to provide services do not preclude an assignee of the performing right in a cinematographic film in a Member State from relying upon his right to prohibit the exhibition of that film in that State, without his authority, by means of cable diffusion if the film so exhibited is picked up and transmitted after being broadcast in another Member State by a third party with the consent of the original owner of the right.

The position with regard to the protection of other forms of reproduction is more complex and the exhaustion of rights doctrine has had to accommodate considerable differences between national laws on copyright protection. In *Musik-Vertrieb Membran* v. *GEMA*[62] a question arose whether the principle of exhaustion of rights prevented the holder of the rights in a sound recording from obtaining the difference between the UK and German royalty rates when recordings first marketed in the UK were imported into Germany by a third party. The difference in the rates was caused by UK legislation on compulsory licensing. The German copyright management society claimed that the recordings could not be sold in Germany without its members receiving the extra payment. This raised a similar issue to that in *Merck* v. *Stephar*[63] viz. to what extent must the rights holder bear the consequences of a freely chosen marketing policy. The ECJ held that here, too, the holder could not prevent the free circulation of the goods as its rights were exhausted by the first marketing.

[62] Cases 55 & 57/80 [1981] ECR 147, [1981] 2 CMLR 44.
[63] See *supra* 566.

A different outcome, however, was reached in *Warner Bros* v. *Christiansen*.[64] There the Court held that consent to the marketing of a video for *sale* in the UK did not entail consent to marketing it for rental in Denmark which, unlike the UK, recognized a separate rental right. The distinction between *Musik-Vertrieb* and *Warner Brothers* v. *Christiansen* appears to be that in the former the same right was involved in both jurisdictions, whereas in the latter the Court was willing to hold that there were two rights concerned: the right to sell (distribute) and the right to hire. The exhaustion of the sale right did not exhaust the rental right because the essence of the latter was the right to authorize hiring operations, and if the owner could not do that the right was worthless. Moreover, if enforcement in Denmark of rental rights was not allowed in respect of videos imported from elsewhere in the Community where rental right did not exist, Danish law would be emasculated and reduced to the 'lowest common denominator' level of the protection allowed by UK law. The same point arose in *Electrola* v. *Patricia*.[65] In this case the ECJ upheld the copyright holder's right to prevent the importation of Cliff Richard records from Denmark, where copyright had expired, to Germany, where it had five years left to run. This situation did not fall within the *Musik-Vertrieb* principle because the sale in Denmark was not made with the consent of the copyright owner. Copyright no longer applied there, and there was therefore no exhaustion of rights. Again, a ruling to the contrary would have effectively harmonized the Member States' copyright laws to the level of the State which gave the least generous protection.[66]

All Member States are now obliged, since the enactment of the Rental Rights Directive, to recognize a separate rental right.[67]

E. DESIGNS

In the case of *Keurkoop* v. *Nancy Kean Gifts*[68] Nancy Kean had the exclusive right to market bags of a certain design in Benelux. Keurkoop sold in Benelux bags of the same design which had been imported from Germany. Nancy Kean sued for design infringement. The ECJ held that the action was not barred by Community law. Design law was not at the time harmonized so the conditions under which protection was given to designs were a matter for

---

[64] Case 156/86 [1988] ECR 2605, [1990] 3 CMLR 684. The videos concerned were of the James Bond film *Never Say Never Again*.

[65] Case 341/87, *EMI Electrola GmbH* v. *Patricia Im-nd Export* [1989] ECR 79, [1989] 2 CMLR 413.

[66] Community harmonization of copyright periods was instead effected by Council Dir. 93/98 [1993] OJ L290/9, harmonizing the term of protection of copyright and related rights at 70 years.

[67] Council Dir. 92/100 on rental right and lending right and on certain rights related to copyright in the field of intellectual property [1992] OJ L436/61. The UK implemented this by SI 1996/2967 which created a new s.18(a) of the Copyright Designs and Patents Act 1988. The validity of the Dir. was upheld by the Court in Case C–200/96, *Metronome Musik GmbH* v. *Musik Point Hokamp GmbH* [1998] ECR I–1953, [1998] 3 CMLR 919. The Court has held that consent to rental in one Member State does not denote consent to rental in another: Case C–61/97 *Foreningen af danske Videogramdistributører, acting for Egmont Films A/s a.o.* v. *Laserdisken, in the person of Hans Kristian Pedersen* [1998] ECR I–5171, [1999] 1 CMLR 1297. Note that a refusal to grant licences to hire out could amount to an abuse of a dominant position contrary to Art. 82 if circumstances were appropriate: see Tesauro AG. in *Metronome Musik* (*supra*) at para. 33 of his Opinion and N. Travers, Rental Rights and the Specific Subject-matter of Copyright in Community Law (1999) 24 *ELRev* 171.

[68] Case 44/81 [1982] ECR 2853, [1983] 2 CMLR 47.

national law, and there was no exhaustion of rights here through consent to marketing.[69] The ECJ reiterated this position in *Renault*,[70] a case which raised the question whether a refusal to license design rights was contrary to Article 82.[71] The Court explained in *Renault* what constitutes the specific subject matter of a design right:

> 10. It must first be stated that, as the Court held in is judgment of 14 September 1982 in Case 144/81 (*Keurkoop* v. *Nancy Kean Gifts* . . .), with respect to the protection of designs and models, in the present state of Community law and in the absence of Community standardization or harmonization of laws the determination of the conditions and procedures under which such protection is granted is a matter for national rules. It is for the national legislature to determine which products qualify for protection, even if they form part of a unit already protected as such.

> 11. It should then be noted that the authority of a proprietor of a protective right in respect of an ornamental model to oppose the manufacture by third parties, for the purposes of sale on the internal market or export, of products incorporating the design or to prevent the import of such products manufactured without its consent in other Member States constitutes the substance of his exclusive right. To prevent the application of the national legislation in such circumstances would therefore be tantamount to challenging the very existence of that right.

5. THE APPLICATION OF ARTICLE 81 TO INTELLECTUAL PROPERTY RIGHTS

A. GENERAL

Agreements concerning intellectual property rights are subject to the competition rules: *Consten & Grundig*[72] in 1966 put paid to any argument that such agreements are outside the prohibition in Article 81(1). The existence/exercise dichotomy discussed above has also been applied in the context of the competition rules: the position is that the existence of an intellectual property right does not infringe the competition rules but its exercise may.[73]

B. EXPLOITING INTELLECTUAL PROPERTY RIGHTS

The owner of an intellectual property right has a choice of ways in which to benefit from the right commercially. He may exploit it himself, assign it to a third party, or license it. The method chosen will depend on a number of factors. These include the resources available to

---

[69] The ECJ also considered the possible application of Art. 81.

[70] Case 53/87, *CICCRA* v. *Renault* [1988] ECR 6039, [1990] 4 CMLR 265.

[71] See *infra* 626 and *supra* Chap. 7.

[72] Cases 56 & 58/64, *Consten & Grundig* v. *Commission* [1966] ECR 229, [1966] CMLR 418.

[73] Case 24/67, *Parke Davis & Co* v. *Probel and Centrafarm* [1968] ECR 55, [1968] CMLR 47; Case 40/70, *Sirena* v. *Eda* [1971] ECR 69, [1971] CMLR 260.

the owner, the type of right concerned, the nature of the product and its life cycle, manu-facturing costs and complexity, the overall commercial strategy of the owner, local condi-tions in the territory in which the right is held, and taxation considerations. Some rights may be able to be carved up: for example the owner of copyright in a book may deal separately with the rights to make a television programme of it, the rights to film it, the rights to serialize it in a newspaper, and the rights to make an audio tape of it.

An *assignment* involves the outright transfer of the right to a third party. After transfer the original owner is excluded from using it without a licence from the new owner. An assignment may be gratuitous or by way of sale or swap. It may be made pursuant to a contract of employment when an employee assigns to the employer rights which he or she acquires in the course of employment. Rights are commonly sold on the transfer or take-over of a business, when they pass to the new owner along with the other assets.

A *licence* means that the owner confers upon another party permission to exploit the former's legally protected exclusive right. The advantages of licensing include:

(i)   the owner (the licensor) has continuing control of the use of the rights (in so far as this is not limited by competition law);
(ii) the ability to carve up the rights is normally greater with licensing than assignment;
(iii) the owner can obtain a continuing revenue stream from the exploitation and can benefit from the licensee's success;
(iv) the owner can continue to exploit the right himself.

An ordinary licence should be distinguished from a *subcontracting* agreement. In sub-contracting a manufacturer gives work to another party to do on its behalf. Subcontracting agreements between non-competitors which involve the transfer of know-how to the sub-contractor for the purposes of the agreement are the subject of a Commission Notice,[74] and are not normally within Article 81(1).[75]

C. ASSIGNMENTS

The question whether an assignment of intellectual property rights is caught by Article 81 arose in *Sirena* v. *Eda*.[76] An American company licensed a German company to use its trade mark for shaving cream 'Prep Good Morning' in Germany. It assigned its trade mark rights in Italy to an Italian company. When the German company sold its products in Italy the Italian company brought infringement proceedings.

---

[74] Commission Notice of 18 Dec. 1978 on Sub-Contracting Agreements, [1979] OJ C1/2.

[75] Sub-contracting agreements are usually vertical agreements, and may be covered by the block exemp-tion Reg., 2790/1999 [1999] OJ L336/21 (see *supra* Chap. 9). Where they are between competitors, however, they are horizontal agreements and are covered by the *Guidelines on Horizontal Co-operation* (draft published [2000] OJ C118/14, discussed *infra* Chap. 13).

[76] Case 40/70, *Sirena* v. *Eda* [1971] ECR 69, [1971] CMLR 260.

Case 40/70, *Sirena* v. *Eda* [1971] ECR 69, [1971] CMLR 260

Court of Justice

8. The request for interpretation is primarily directed to ascertaining in what circumstances the exercise of trade-mark rights may constitute infringement of the prohibition imposed by Article [81(1)].

9. By virtue of this provision, 'all agreements between undertakings, decisions by association of undertakings, and concerted practices' which may affect trade between Member States, and which have as their object or effect the distortion of competition, are prohibited as incompatible with the Common Market. A trade-mark right, as a legal entity, does not in itself possess those elements of contract or concerted practice referred to in Article [81(1)]. Nevertheless, the exercise of that right might fall within the ambit of the prohibitions contained in the Treaty each time it manifests itself as the subject, the means or the result of a restrictive practice. When a trade-mark right is exercised by virtue of assignments to users in one or more Member States, it is thus necessary to establish in each case whether such use leads to a situation falling under the prohibitions of Article [81].

10. Such situations may in particular arise from restrictive agreements between proprietors of trade-marks or their successors in title enabling them to prevent imports from other Member States. If the combination of assignments to different users of national trade-marks protecting the same product has the result of re-enacting impenetrable frontiers between the Member States, such practice may well affect trade between States, and distort competition in the Common Market. The matter would be different if, in order to avoid any partitioning of the market, the agreements concerning the use of national rights in respect of the same trade-mark were to be effected in such conditions as to make the general use of trade-mark rights as Community level compatible with the observance of the conditions of competition and unity of the market which are so essential to the Common Market that failure to observe them is penalized by Article [81] by a declaration that they are automatically void.

11. Article [81], therefore, is applicable to the extent to which trade-mark rights are invoked so as to prevent imports of products which originate in different Member States, which bear the same trade-mark by virtue of the fact that the proprietors have acquired it, or the right to use it, whether by agreements between themselves or by agreements with third parties. Article [81] is not precluded from applying merely because, under national legislation trade-mark rights may originate in legal or factual circumstances other than the abovementioned agreements, such as registration of the trade-mark, or its undisturbed use.

The issue rose again in *EMI* v. *CBS*:

Case 51/75, *EMI Records Ltd* v. *CBS UK Ltd* [1976] ECR 811, [1976] 2 CMLR 235

The 'Columbia' trade mark belonged to a US company which transferred the marks in Europe to its UK subsidiary in 1917. The UK company was sold in 1923. By the time of the case the mark was owned in the UK by EMI and in the US by CBS. CBS tried to market its products in the EEC under the Columbia mark. The Court of Justice held that the 'common origin' of trade marks doctrine laid down in *Hag I*[77] did not apply where the allegedly infringing goods came from outside the Community. On the question of whether the assignments were caught by Article 81:

---

[77] See *supra* 568.

Court of Justice

23. A trade-mark right, as a legal entity, does not possess those elements of contract or concerted practice referred to in Article [81(1)].

24. Nevertheless, the exercise of that right might fall within the ambit of the prohibitions contained in the Treaty if it were to manifest itself as the subject, the means, or the consequence of a restrictive practice.

25. A restrictive agreement between traders within the common market and competitors in third countries that would bring about an isolation of the common market as a whole which, in the territory of the Community, would reduce the supply of products originating in third countries and similar to those protected by a mark within the Community, might be of such a nature to affect adversely the conditions of competition within the common market.

26. In particular if the proprietor of the mark in dispute in the third country has within the Community various subsidiaries established in different Member States which are in a position to market the products at issue within the common market such isolation may also affect trade between Member States.

27. For Article [81] to apply to a case, such as the present one, of agreements which are no longer in force it is sufficient that such agreements continue to produce their effects after they have formally ceased to be in force.

28. An agreement is only regarded as continuing to produce its effects if from the behaviour of the persons concerned there may be inferred the existence of elements of concerted practice and of co-ordination peculiar to the agreement and producing the same result as that envisaged by the agreement.

29. This is not so when the said effects do not exceed those flowing from the mere exercise of the national trade-mark rights.

30. Furthermore it is clear from the file that the foreign trader can obtain access to the common market without availing himself of the mark in dispute.

In both *Sirena* v. *Eda* and *EMI* v. *CBS* the Court of Justice tackled the problem that once an assignment is completed the agreement to transfer is discharged. The Court therefore talked in terms of Article 81 catching acts which *continue* to have anti-competitive effects after they have formally ceased to be in force. The reference to concerted practices in paragraph 28 is rather strange, as indulging in a concerted practice would itself constitute an infringement without any prior assignment coming into the matter. It has been suggested[78] that the existence of the assignment might be relevant as making it easier to *prove* the existence of a concerted practice—a notoriously difficult matter.[79] It is now clear from the Court's ruling in *Ideal Standard*[80] that whether or not an assignment does have continuing anti-competitive effect is to be determined in the light of an economic assessment of the assignment's legal and economic context and not by the application of rigid rules:

---

[78] See P. Craig and G. de Búrca, *EU Law: Text, Cases and Materials* (2nd edn., Oxford University Press, Oxford, 1998) 1049–1050; D. Wyatt and A. Dashwood, *European Community Law* (4th edn. Sweet & Maxwell, London, 2000) 734.

[79] See *infra* Chap. 11.

[80] Case C–9/93, *IHT International Heiztechnik GmbH* v. *Ideal Standard GmbH* [1994] ECR I–2789, [1994] 3 CMLR 857.

59. It should be added that, where undertakings independent of each other make trade-mark assignments following a market-sharing agreement, the prohibition of anti-competitive agreements under Article 81 applies and assignments which give effect to that agreement are consequently void. However, as the United Kingdom rightly pointed out, that rule and the accompanying sanction cannot be applied mechanically to every assignment. Before a trade-mark assignment can be treated as giving effect to an agreement prohibited under Article [81], it is necessary to analyse the context, the commitments underlying the assignment, the intention of the parties and the consideration for the assignment.

D. DELIMITATION AGREEMENTS AND AGREEMENTS PUTTING AN END TO LITIGATION

Parties sometimes enter into agreements about the use of intellectual property rights in order to end a dispute between them concerning the rights. The most common are trade mark delimitation agreements where parties with similar trade marks agree to restrict their use in relation to certain products or certain territories. The fact that restrictions of competition appear in such agreements does not automatically take them outside Article 81(1). In *Bayer* v. *Süllhöfer*[81] the ECJ held that a no-challenge clause[82] was not outside Article 81(1) just because it was contained in an agreement settling litigation. Trade mark delimitation agreements are dealt with below.[83]

E. LICENSING

(i) COMMERCIAL CONSIDERATIONS IN LICENCES

A number of intellectual property rights may be licensed together, for example patents, know-how and trade marks. Whatever the licence consists of the licensor will normally be concerned with maximizing the financial return. The licensor may wish to incorporate in a licence agreement provisions about: safeguarding confidential information, ensuring quality control, supplying essential components or other goods to the licensee, ensuring (in the case of patents and know-how) that the licensor benefits from improvements made by the licensee, safeguarding the licensor from challenges by the licensee to the validity of the rights,[84] limiting what the licensee may do with the goods or services produced under the licence, ensuring that the licensee does not compete with the licensor, and providing for termination. Licensees will be concerned with the same issues but from the other side. How far such commercial requirements can be met will depend, in part, on competition law.

---

[81] Case 65/86, *Bayer AG and Maschinenfabrik Hennecke* v. *Heinz Süllhöfer* [1988] ECR 5249, [1990] 4 CMLR 182.

[82] For no-challenge clauses generally, see *infra* 606.

[83] See *infra* 615.

[84] With a patent, a licensee working it will be in the best position to identify the weaknesses in it.

(ii) EXCLUSIVE AND SOLE LICENCES

Licences can be exclusive, sole or non-exclusive.

A licence is said to be *exclusive* as regards a particular territory where it provides that the licensor will not grant further licences for that territory to other parties and will not itself exploit the licensed intellectual property rights in the territory. It means that only the licensee can exercise the licensed rights in the territory covered by the licence.

A *sole* licence is where the licensor undertakes not to grant other licences for the territory but remains free to exploit the rights there itself. The rights can therefore be exploited in the territory by the licensor, the licensee, and no-one else.

A *non-exclusive* licence is where the licensor remains free to grant other licences if it wishes and to exploit the licence in the territory itself.

Exclusive licences are a common phenomenon. Licensees will often be interested in taking a licence only if they are assured of exclusivity. An undertaking may be interested in taking a licence of X's French patent, for example, only if it can be certain that having invested large resources in tooling up to exploit the patented process it will not face competition from other licensees in France or from the licensor itself operating in France. It may also wish to be protected from competition from imports originating with undertakings which are granted licences in other territories. Clauses conferring such protection raise serious Community concerns since they compartmentalize the single market.

In EC law the term 'exclusive licence' is often used to cover both exclusive and sole licences.

(iii) DO LICENCES PREVENT, RESTRICT OR DISTORT COMPETITION?

The licensing of intellectual property rights helps to spread new technology, brings new competitors on to the market, and increases the rewards for innovation. Its effects are generally pro-competitive and beneficial to consumer welfare. It can be argued that since a licence of intellectual property rights allows a third party to exploit rights, allowing it to do what would otherwise be unlawful, the grant of a licence opens up markets and does not restrict competition. It should not therefore infringe Article 81(1).[85] However, licence agreements normally contain provisions which go beyond the bare permission for the licensee to exploit the right. Competition law has to decide whether, and in what circumstances, these further obligations have the effect of restricting competition.

A preliminary difficult question is whether manufacturing licences should be characterized as horizontal or vertical agreements.[86] In other jurisdictions, such as the USA and

---

[85] Cf. the approach of UK law to intellectual property licensing under the Restrictive Trade Practices Act 1976 where there was an argument that, even if licences *were* concerned with the supply of goods and services, the *Ravenseft* doctrine (*Ravenseft Properties Ltd's Application* [1978] QB 52, [1977] 1 All ER 47) meant that obligations in licences were not 'restrictions' within the meaning of the Act: see the Director General's 1976 *Annual Report* (HMSO, 1977) 36 and the DTI White Paper, *Opening Markets: New Policy on Restrictive Trade Practices* (1989) (Cm 727); N. Green and A. Robertson, *Commercial Agreements and Competition Law* (2nd edn. Kluwer, Deventer, 1997) 909: licences were, in any case, subject to exemption by Sched. 3 para. 5.

[86] Note that under the 1996 Notice on Agreements of Minor Importance [1997] OJ C372/13, the threshold is 5% market share for horizontal agreements and 10% for vertical. There is no indication in the Notice of how licences should be classified.

Germany, the matter turns upon whether *at the time of the transaction* the licensee could have entered the market or competed with the licensor without the licence:[87] if the answer is no, the agreement is vertical. In the 1960s the Commission appears to have viewed licences as a species of vertical agreement, but since the 1970s, at least until recently, it has tended to treat them as horizontal once the licensee began to manufacture similar products to the licensor. This led to a stricter line being taken[88] and an interventionist approach to licensing arrangements which may explain some of the blacklisting in the block exemption regulations on patents and know-how.[89]

If the Commission were to find that the application of Article 81 is dependent on the question whether the undertakings concerned were competitors or potential competitors at the outset a 'rule of reason' approach would be required. Each licence would have to be assessed in the light of the actual position of the parties on the market and analysed in its economic context. This is the approach of the US antitrust authorities.[90] The Commission, however, tends to look at the *form of the provisions in the agreement*. This is partly because of the bifurcated structure of Article 81 which enables restrictions to be exempted[91] and partly because of the EC preoccupation with territorial restraints hindering the single market. The result is that the emphasis in the application of EC competition law to licensing agreements is on what can be exempted pursuant to Article 81(3).[92]

(iv) THE DEVELOPMENT OF THE COMMISSION'S POLICY TOWARDS LICENSING AGREEMENTS

The Commission's early attitude was that even exclusive patent licensing agreements did not fall within Article 81(1) so long as the restrictions did not go beyond the 'scope of the patent'.[93] In its 1962 notice on patent licensing agreements (the so-called Christmas Message)[94] it stated:

I.   On the basis of the facts known at present, the Commission considers that the following clauses in patent licensing agreements are not caught by the prohibition laid down in Article 81(1) of the Treaty:

A.   Obligations imposed on the licensee which have as their object:

  1.   Limitation of the exploitation of the invention to certain of the forms which are provided for by patent law (manufacture, use, sale).

---

[87] Or a licence from another licensor.

[88] V. Korah, *Technology Transfer Agreements and the EC Competition Rules* (Clarendon, Oxford, 1996) 23–4; J. Venit, 'In the Wake of Windsurfing: Patent Licensing in the Common Market] [1986] *Fordham Corporate Law Institute* 521.

[89] Korah, *Technology Transfer Agreements and the EC Competition Rules*, (Clarendon, 1996), 23–4. Note that the new block exemption on vertical agreements, Commission Reg. 2790/1999 (discussed *supra* in Chap. 9) expressly excludes licensing agreements unless the licence is not the primary object of the agreement: see *infra* 591–592.

[90] *Guidelines for Licensing of Intellectual Property*, Department of Justice and Federal Trade Commission, 6 Apr. 1995, see (1995) 7 EIPR Supp. 3.

[91] See the discussion *supra* in Chap. 4.

[92] See further S. Anderman, *EC Competition Law and Intellectual Property Rights* (Clarendon, 1998), chap. 3 *passim*.

[93] See further *ibid.*, 53–54.

[94] 24 Dec. 1962 [1962–3] JO 2922/62, finally withdrawn in 1984 [1984] OJ C 220/14.

2. Limitation:
    (a) of the manufacture of the patented product,
    (b) of the use of the patented process, to certain technical applications;
3. Limitation of the quantity of productions to be manufactured or of the number of acts constituting exploitation.
4. Limitation of exploitation:
    (a) in time
         (a licence of shorter duration than the patent);
    (b) in space
         (a regional licence for part of the territory for which the patent is granted, or a licence limited to one place of exploitation or to a specific factory);
    (c) with regard to the person
         (limitation of the licensee's power of disposal, e.g., prohibiting him from assigning the licence or from granting sub-licences)

IV. The obligations listed at I(A) do not fall under the prohibition of Article 81(1) because they are covered by the patent. They entail only the partial maintenance of the right of prohibition contained in the patentee's exclusive right in relation to the licensee, who in other respects is authorized to exploit the invention. The list at 1(a) is not an exhaustive definition of the rights conferred by the patent.

The same approach can be seen in Article 4(2)(2)(b) of Regulation 17[95] which classes as non-notifiable agreements[96] those to which no more than two undertakings are party and which:

impose restrictions on the exercise of the rights of the assignee or user of industrial property rights — in particular patents, utility models, designs or trade marks — or of a person entitled under a contract to the assignment, or grant, of the right to use a method of manufacture or knowledge relating to the use and to the application of industrial processes . . .

Later, however, the Commission's attitude began to change and it moved towards the position that exclusive licences, unless *de minimis*, were always within Article 81 and that many common non-territorial restraints were also beyond the scope of the patent. The change was a result of the development of the exhaustion of rights doctrine and the elaboration of the existence/exercise dichotomy[97] as more and more intellectual property rights issues came before the Court and the Commission examined more notified agreements. The most significant event was the *Consten & Grundig* case[98] in which a trade mark licence was used to try to seal off Member States from one another and create absolute territorial protection. The Commission became acutely conscious of the potential of exclusive licensing agreements for isolating markets. It was also haunted by the idea that if the licensor had not given an *exclusive* licence he might have given a *non-exclusive* one, which would have led to competition between the different licensees in the same territory.

In its *First Report on Competition Policy* (Commission, 1971) the Commission said:

58. . . . It is also necessary to determine which clauses in agreements concerning industrial and commercial property rights are admissible under Article [81] of the EEC Treaty, bearing in mind the specific purpose of the protection rights and their function in a system

---

[95] [1959–62] OJ Spec. Ed. 87, as amended by Council Reg. 1216/1999 [1999] OJ L142/5.
[96] For non-notifiable agreements generally, see *supra* Chap. 4.
[97] See *supra* 561–574.
[98] See *supra* 562–563.

of competition and a unified market. While ensuring adequate remuneration for inventions and avoiding obstacles to the application of patented knowledge and to the communication of secret know-how, it is nevertheless necessary to establish a genuine common market for branded goods, either patented or incorporating secret know-how, without unjustifiably limiting the possibilities of competition and the free movement of goods among Member States.

. . .

78. It should be noted, however, that where the owner of a patent undertakes to restrict the exercise of his exclusive rights to a single enterprise in the assigned area, thus conferring upon that single enterprise the sole right to exploit the invention and to prevent other enterprises from exploiting it, he loses the freedom to enter into agreements with other applicants for licences. The exclusive character of such a licence may amount to a restriction of competition and thus fall within the category of prohibited agreements in so far that it has an appreciable effect on market conditions.

The argument in paragraph 78 is, however, specious. As suggested above,[99] in the real world licensees will frequently not entertain any licence but an exclusive (or at least a sole) one. The commercial risk is too great. The choice is therefore between an exclusive licence and no licence, not between an exclusive or a non-exclusive one. The question comes down, again, to whether the Commission is too prone to considering matters with hindsight, *ex post*, rather than *ex ante*, as the parties would have done, when the transaction might well have looked risky.[100] Nevertheless, throughout the 1970s the Commission held in a series of decisions that exclusive licences were restrictive of competition and so came within Article 81(1). However, so long as the parties were willing to modify the exclusivity clauses and other provisions held to be restrictions (such as tie-ins, no-challenge clauses and grant-backs of improvements), the Commission would exempt them under Article 81(3).[101]

In the Fourth Competition Policy Report (Commission, 1974) the Commission said:

20   On a legal plane, the Commission faces the problems of definition exposed by the Court of Justice in its distinction between the existence of nationally protected industrial property rights, which is not to be affected by Community law, and the exercise of these rights, which can be subject to the Treaty rules. Accordingly, any appraisal of particular patent licensing provisions requires prior differentiation between terms which are germane to the existence, and those which relate to the exercise, of patent rights, in order to establish upon which provisions the Commission may properly rule. While the differentiation remains to be more fully worked out by future decisions of the Court, it is clear that patent licensing agreements are not automatically within Article [81(1)] if the agreements simply confer rights to exploit patented inventions against payments of royalties, but that questions of applicability of Article [81(1)] arise if a grant is accompanied by terms which go beyond the need to ensure the existence of an industrial property right.

With the experience of handling these agreements the Commission set about adopting a

[99] *Supra* 579.

[100] See V. Korah, *Technology Transfer Agreements and the Competition Rules* (Clarendon, 1996), 23.

[101] *Re the Agreements of Davidson Rubber Co* [1972] OJ L143/31 [1972] CMLR D52; *Burroughs/Deplanque* [1972] OJ L13/50 [1972] CMLR 67; *Raymond/Nagoya* [1972] OJ L143/39, [1972] CMLR D45; *Bronbemaling* v. *Heidemaatschappij* [1975] OJ L249/27, [1975] 2 CMLR D67; *AOIP* v. *Beyrard* [1976] OJ L6/8, [1976] 1 CMLR D14.

block exemption regulation on patent licences. The first draft was produced in 1979 but there were lengthy negotiations with Member States, business, and other interested parties. The Commission also waited to take account of the ECJ's judgment in *Nungesser*, the appeal from its 1978 decision in *Maize Seeds*.[102] The block exemption was finally adopted in 1984.[103]

(v) EXCLUSIVITY AND TERRITORIAL RESTRICTIONS IN THE CASE LAW OF THE COURT

The ECJ took a different view of exclusivity from that adopted by the Commission,[104] as shown by its judgment in *Nungesser* (*Maize Seeds*), the first time since *Consten & Grundig* that it had to deal with an exclusive licence. The case concerned plant breeders' rights but the principles set out in the judgment are not limited to this type of right.[105]

Case 258/78 *Nungesser* v. *EC Commission* [1982] ECR 2015, [1983] 1 CMLR 278

INRA, a French state research institute, developed new strains of hybrid maize seed of great importance in European agriculture. Acting through FRAESMA, a French company set up to deal with INRA's seed varieties, it gave Kurt Eisele (later Nungesser KG) the exclusive right to produce and distribute INRA varieties in Germany. INRA agreed with Eisele not to import its seed into Germany itself and to prevent others from doing so. Eisele relied on the rights in Germany to prevent parallel importers from importing seed obtained from another source in France. One importer settled the action, but another complained to the Commission.

The Commission held that the exclusivity and territorial protection provisions were caught by Article [81(1)] and could not be exempted. Eisele/Nungesser appealed.

Court of Justice

41. Th[e] synopsis of the German legislation shows that seeds certified and approved for marketing are subject to quality control on the part of the public authorities and that that control extends to the stability of the variety. However, breeders' rights are not intended to substitute for controls carried out by the competent authorities, controls carried out by the owner of those rights, but to confer on the owner a kind of protection, the nature and effects of which all derive from private law. From that point of view the legal position of a breeder of seeds is not difficult from that of the owner of patent or trade mark rights over a product subject to strict control by the public authorities, as is the case with pharmaceutical products.

43. It is therefore not correct to consider that breeder's rights are a species of commercial or industrial property right with characteristics of so special a nature as to require, in relation to the competition rules, a different treatment from other commercial or industrial property rights. That conclusion does not affect the need to take into consideration, for the purposes of the rules on

---

[102] [1978] OJ L286/23, [1978] 3 CMLR 434.

[103] Commission Reg. 2349/84, [1984] OJ L219/15.

[104] For the differing views of the ECJ and the Commission to the question of exclusivity generally, see the discussion *supra* in Chap. 4.

[105] See *infra* 586–587. Plant breeders' rights were excluded from the scope of block exemption Reg. 2349/84 [1984] OJ L219/15 on patent licensing but are now covered by the block exemption on technology transfer agreements, Commission Reg. 240/96: [1996] OJ L31/2 see *infra* 593.

competition, the specific nature of the products which form the subject-matter of breeders' rights.

. . .

48 The statement of reasons on which the decision is based refers to two set of circumstances in order to justify the application of Article [81(1)] to the exclusive licence in question (II, No 3). The accuracy of the facts thus stated has not been challenged.

49. The first set of circumstances is described as follows . . .

> 'By licensing a single undertaking to exploit his breeders' rights in a given territory, the licensor deprives himself for the entire duration of the contract of the ability to issue licences to other undertakings in the same territory . . .'

> 'By undertaking not to produce or market the product himself in the territory covered by the contract the licensor likewise eliminates himself, as well as Frasema and its members, as suppliers in that territory.'

50. Corresponding to that part of the statement of reasons is Article 1 (b) of the decision, which in its first and second indents declares the exclusive nature of the licence granted by the 1965 contract to be contrary to Article [81(1)] of the Treaty in so far as it imposes:

An obligation upon INRA or those deriving rights through INRA to refrain from having the relevant seeds produced or sold by other licensees in German, and

An obligation upon INRA or those deriving rights through INRA to refrain from producing or selling the relevant seed in Germany themselves

51. The second set of circumstances referred to in the decision is described as follows:

> 'The fact that third parties may not import the same seed [namely the seed under licence] from other Community countries into Germany, or export from Germany to other Community countries, leads to market sharing and deprives German farmers of any real room for negotiation since seed is supplied by one supplier and one supplier only.'

52. That part of the statement of reasons is also reflected in Article 1 (b) of the decision, which in its third and fourth indents declares the exclusive nature of the licence granted by the 1965 contract to be contrary to Article [81(1)] of the Treaty in so far as it imposes:

An obligation upon INRA or those deriving rights through INRA to prevent third parties from exporting the relevant seeds to Germany without the licensee's authorization for use or sale there, and

Mr Eisele's concurrent use of his exclusive contractual rights and his own breeder's rights to prevent all imports into Germany or exports to other Member States of the relevant seeds.

53. It should be observed that those two sets of considerations relate to two legal situations which are not necessarily identical. The first case concerns a so-called open exclusive licence or assignment and the exclusivity of the licence relates solely to the contractual relationship between the owner of the right and the licensee, whereby the owner merely undertakes not to grant other licences in respect of the same territory and not to compete himself with the licensee on that territory. On the other hand, the second case involves an exclusive licence or assignment with absolute territorial protection, under which the parties to the contact propose, as regards the products and the territory in question, to eliminate all competition from third parties, such as parallel importers or licensees for other territories.

54. That point having been clarified, it is necessary to examine whether, in the present case, the exclusive nature of the licence, in so far as it is an open licence, has the effect of preventing or distorting competition with the meaning of Article [81(1)] of the Treaty.

55. In that respect the Government of the Federal Republic of Germany emphasized that the protection of agricultural innovations by means of breeders' rights constitutes a means of encouraging such innovations and the grant of exclusive rights for a limited period, is capable of providing a further incentive to innovative efforts.

From that it infers that a total prohibition of every exclusive licence, even an open one, would cause the interest of undertakings in licences to fall away, which would be prejudicial to the dissemination of knowledge and techniques in the Community.

56. The exclusive licence which forms the subject-matter of the contested decision concerns the cultivation and marketing of hybrid maize seeds which were developed by INRA after years of research and experimentation and were unknown to German farmers at the time when the co-operation between INRA and the applicants was taking shape. For that reason the concern shown by the interveners as regards the protection of new technology is justified.

57. In fact, in the case of a licence of breeders' rights over hybrid maize seeds newly developed in one Member State, an undertaking established in another Member State which was not certain that it would not encounter competition from other licensees for the territory granted to it, or from the owner of the right himself, might be deterred from accepting the risk of cultivating and market-ing that product; such a result would be damaging to the dissemination of a new technology and would prejudice competition in the Community between the new product and similar existing products.

58. Having regard to the specific nature of the products in question, the Court concludes that in a case such as the present, the grant of an open exclusive licence, that is to say a licence which does not affect the position of third parties such as parallel importers and licensees for other territories, is not in itself incompatible with Article [81(1)] of the Treaty.

59. Part B of the third submission is thus justified to the extent to which it concerns that aspect of the exclusive nature of the licence.

. . .

76. It must be remembered that under the terms of Article [81(3)] of the Treaty an exemption from the prohibition contained in Article [81(1)] may be granted in the case of any agreement between undertakings which contributes to improving the production or distribution of goods or to promoting technical progress, and which does not impose on the undertakings concerned restrictions which are not indispensable to the attainment of those objectives.

77. As it is a question of seeds intended to be used by a large number of farmers for the production of maize, which is an important product for human and animal foodstuffs, absolute territorial protection manifestly goes beyond what is indispensable for the improvement of produc-tion or distribution or the promotion of technical progress, as is demonstrated in particular in the present case by the prohibition, agreed to by both parties to the agreement of any parallel imports of INRA maize seeds into Germany even if those seeds were bred by INRA itself and marketed in France.

78. It follows that the absolute territorial protection conferred on the licensee, as established to exist by the contested decision, constituted a sufficient reason for refusing to grant an exemption under Article [81(3)] of the Treaty. It is therefore no longer necessary to examine the other grounds set out in the decision for refusing to grant such an exemption.

In this judgment the ECJ distinguished between 'open' and 'closed' exclusive licences (paragraph 53). On the one hand there is an 'open' licence which pertains only to the position between licensor and licensee. The licensor agrees not to grant further licences in the same territory and not to operate there itself. On the other hand there is a licence containing provisions which affect third parties and which create absolute territorial protection.

The distinction between 'open' licences and others is not completely clear as the Court did not expressly deal with a situation where the provisions fall short of granting absolute territorial protection, for example where restrictions on the licensee's activities outside the licensed territory are imposed. Presumably a provision whereby the licensee undertakes not to compete with the *licensor* in the latter's territory is covered by the 'open' designation, as it 'relates solely to the contractual relationship between the owner of the right and the licensee'. However, it appears that any further limitation on the licensee, other than an obligation not to *produce* outside its allocated territory, renders the licence closed rather than open.[106] The Commission held in *Boussois/Interpane*[107] that a licence which prohibited a licensee from selling outside its territory was closed.

As far as open licences are concerned, the Court in *Nungesser* adopted a 'rule of reason'— style approach.[108] Instead of concluding that the exclusivity provisions automatically infringed Article 81(1), as the Commission had done, the Court looked at the licence in its economic context: if the exclusivity provisions were necessary to induce the licensee to enter the transaction then competition was not restricted.

It should be noted that the Court's realistic approach was limited. In paragraphs 77 and 78 the Court condemned outright the clauses leading to the imposition of absolute territorial protection without considering their possible economic justifications.[109] Not only were these provisions automatically caught by Article 81(1), they did not qualify for exemption under Article 81(3).

The principles in *Nungesser* apply to other kinds of 'manufacturing' licences involving the licensing of patents and know-how, and not just to plant breeders' rights. The general applicability of *Nungesser* to such transactions is manifest from the Court's rationale for holding the open exclusive licence outside Article 81(1), i.e. the need to provide incentives for investment by the licensee. This can apply equally to other kinds of right. It is also shown by the recitals to the block exemptions on patent licensing, know-how licensing, and technology transfer agreements.[110]

However, it can be seen from paragraph 58 of *Nungesser* that, in deciding whether or not Article 81(1) applies, regard has to be had to the specific nature of the *products* in question. In the subsequent case of *Erauw-Jacquéry* the nature of the products concerned was crucial to the Court's finding that even an export ban could be outside Article 81(1). *Erauw-Jacquéry* concerned basic seed, which is seed which can lawfully be used to propagate further

---

[106] See M. Siragusa, 'EEC Technology Transfers—A Private View' [1982] *Fordham Corporate Law Institute* 95, 116–118.

[107] [1987] OJ L50/30, a know-how rather than a patent licence, but the difference does not appear to have been relevant.

[108] For a discussion of the rule of reason generally, see *supra* Chap. 4.

[109] See further the discussion of the application of Art. 81(3) generally, *supra* in Chaps. 3 and 4.

[110] See Reg. 2349/84 [1984] OJ L219/15, recital 11, Reg. 556/89, [1989] OJ L61/1, recital 6, Reg. 240/96 [1996] OJ L31/2, recital 10, discussed *infra* at 588.

seed, as distinct from the certified seed sold to produce crops. Plant breeders' rights in basic seeds are particularly vulnerable as they can easily be lost.[111]

Case 27/87 *Erauw-Jacquéry* v. *La Hesbignonne* [1988] ECR 1919, [1988] 4 CMLR 576

The owner of plant breeders' rights licensed them to a co-operative on the terms that the co-operative could propagate basic seed and sell seed of the first or second generation but could not sell or export basic seed. The Court of Justice recognised the need for quality control and for assuring the proper handling of the basic seed by those allowed to propagate it. Advocate General Mischo likened the situation to one of a franchise, where the franchisor is justified in preventing its know-how benefiting competitors.

Court of Justice

8. In the first place the national court seeks to ascertain whether the provision prohibiting the holder of the licence for propagating basic seed from selling, assigning or exporting that seed falls within Article [81(1)] of the Treaty.

9. The Commission and the breeder maintain that the provision prohibiting the sale and exportation of E2 basic seed, which is placed at the disposal of the growers only for the purposes of propagation, is not contrary to Article [81(1)] of the Treaty. Such a provision falls within the ambit of the plant breeder's rights.

10. In this respect, it must be pointed out that, as the Court acknowledged in its judgment of 8 June 1982 (in Case 258/78 *Nungesser v Commission* [1982] ECR 2015), the development of the basic lines may involve considerable financial commitment. Consequently, a person who has made considerable efforts to develop varieties of basic seed which may be the subject-matter of plant breeders' rights must be allowed to protect himself against any improper handling of those varieties of seed. To that end, the breeder must be entitled to restrict propagation to the growers which he has selected as licensees. To that extent, the provision prohibiting the licensee from selling and exporting basic seed falls outside the prohibition contained in Article [81(1)].

11. Therefore, the answer to the first part of the question referred by the national court must be that a provision of an agreement concerning the propagation and sale of seed, in respect of which one of the parties is the holder or the agent of the holder of certain plant breeders' rights, which prohibits the licensee from selling and exporting the basic seed is compatible with Article [81(1)] of the Treaty in so far as it is necessary in order to enable the breeder to select the growers who are to be licensees.

The Court in this case stressed the need to protect the licensor's investment. The Court recognized the particularly fragile nature of basic seed and was prepared to hold that in these special circumstances absolute territorial protection was not within Article 81(1). The Court referred to *Nungesser*, but in that case, where certified rather than basic seed was concerned, the absolute territorial protection caused the agreement both to infringe Article 81(1) and to be denied exemption pursuant to Article 81(3).[112]

---

[111] They are subject to cancellation if they cease to be stable or uniform. See in the UK the Plant Varieties and Seeds Act 1997 ss. 4(2) and 22 and, in respect of Community plant variety, Arts. 8, 9, and 21 of Reg. 2100/94 [1994] OJ L227/1.

[112] The Commission emphasized the special nature of basic seeds in its comment on the case in the XVIII *Report on Competition Policy Commission*, (1989) pt 103; in *Sicasov* [1999] OJ L4/27, [1999] 4 CMLR 192 the Commission applied *Erauw-Jacquery* to another licence of basic seed.

The position in respect of territorial exclusivity in trade mark and copyright licences is discussed below in the relevant sections.[113]

(vi) THE COMMISSION'S VIEW OF EXCLUSIVITY IN PATENT AND KNOW-HOW LICENCES AFTER THE *NUNGESSER* CASE

The Commission takes a restrictive view of *Nungesser*, which it has based on paragraphs 56 and 57 of the judgment where the ECJ explained why the exclusive licence did not infringe Article 81(1). The Court of Justice accepted that the technology, based on years of research and experimentation, was 'new' and unknown on the licensee's market when the transaction was being negotiated (paragraph 56), that the licensee might have been deterred from taking the licence without exclusivity, and that the absence of a licence might have damaged the dissemination of the new technology and prejudiced inter-brand competition (paragraph 58). The Commission has made it clear in the recitals to all the block exemptions on patents and know-how, of which the latest version is recital 10 of Regulation 240/96 on technology transfer agreements, that these criteria must be fulfilled if the open licence is to escape Article 81(1):[114]

Exclusive licensing agreements, i.e. agreements in which the licensor undertakes not to exploit the licensed technology in the licensed territory himself or to grant further licences there, may not be in themselves incompatible with Article [81(1)] where they are concerned with the introduction and protection of a new technology in the licensed territory, by reason of the scale of the research which has been undertaken, of the increase in the level of competition, in particular inter-brand competition, and of the competitiveness of the undertakings concerned resulting from the dissemination of innovation within the Community. In so far as agreements of this kind fall, in other circumstances, within the scope of Article [81(1)], it is appropriate to include them in Article 1 in order that they may also benefit from the exemption.

The Commission has narrowly interpreted the concept of 'new technology' for these purposes and it is clear that it is not the same as novelty in patent law. In *Velcro/Aplix*[115] the Commission held that the velcro fastening technology, on which the basic patents had expired in 1977, was not 'new' within the meaning of the *Nungesser* judgment. In *Rich Products/Jus Rol*[116], the Commission found that an exclusive know-how licence concerning frozen yeast dough was within Article 81(1) as other processes had been developed for freeezing yeast so the technology was not new. In *Delta Chemie/DDD Ltd*[117] there was insufficient 'newness' because the licensee had previously distributed the products in the licensed territory.

However, in *Sicasov*,[118] a decision on plant breeders' rights, the Commission applied the *Erauw-Jacquéry* judgment and held that Article 81 did not apply to provisions in a licence aimed solely at protecting the breeder's rights with regard to seeds which can lawfully be used to produce other seeds if such provisions are essential to protect the breeder's rights.

---

[113] See *infra* 610–611 and 616–619.
[114] [1996] OJ L31/2.
[115] [1985] OJ L233/22, [1989] 4 CMLR 157.
[116] [1988] OJ L69/21, [1988] 4 CMLR 527.
[117] [1988] OJ L309/34, [1989] 4 CMLR 535.
[118] [1999] OJ L4/27, [1999] 4 CMLR 192.

This covered a prohibition against multipliers selling or exporting seeds which did not belong to the last generation which could lawfully be reproduced and which had been made available to them solely for the purpose of multiplication, and a clause enabling the breeder to authorize and control any seed production act irrespective of the generation concerned. Article 81(1) *did* apply to a clause prohibiting exports of certified seeds for four years after registration in the Community's approved varieties catalogue. However, this was exempted under Article 81(3) for ten years taking into account criteria used in the Technology Transfer Regulation, 240/96.

Even after *Nungesser* therefore, few licences which affect inter-Member State trade and have an appreciable effect on competition and trade can in practice safely be taken to fall outside Article 81(1).[119]

(vii) NON-TERRITORIAL RESTRAINTS

The general approach of the Court and Commission to non-territorial restraints in patent licences was demonstrated by the *Windsurfing* case,[120] although the Commission's attitude to certain specific matters which arose there has undergone some revision since.[121]

Windsurfing International (WI), an American company founded by Hoyle Schweitzer, granted a number of non-exclusive licences of its German patent for windsurfing equipment to firms within the Community. Litigation was current in Germany over whether or not the patent covered both the rig and the board, but the Commission proceeded on the basis that it covered only the rig. The Commission found that the following provisions concerning quality control, tying, licensed-by notices, no-challenge clauses and royalty calculation, infringed Article 81(1):

(a) an obligation on the licensee to mount the patented rig only on boards approved by the licensor; the Commission rejected WI's contention that this was a permissible measure of quality control, as the controls did not relate to a product covered by the patent and were not laid down in advance on the basis of objectively verifiable criteria;

(b) an obligation on the licensee to sell the rigs only as part of a complete sailboard, and not separately; the Commission held that an obligation arbitrarily placed on a licensee to sell the patented product only in conjunction with a product outside the scope of the patent was not indispensable to the exploitation of the patent;

(c) an obligation on the licensee to pay royalties calculated on the net selling price of the whole sailboard and not just the rig; the Commission held that this method of calculation could be justified only where 'the number of items manufactured or consumed or their value are difficult to establish separately in a complex production process or . . . there is for the patented item on its own no separate demand which the licensee would be prevented from satisfying through such a method of calculation';

(d) an obligation on the licensee to affix to boards manufactured and marketed in

---

[119] See *supra* 579–580 on the question whether licences are horizontal or vertical agreements and so whether they have to fall below the 5% or 10% *de minimis* threshold. In any case, it is difficult to apply *de minimis* to technology licences because of problems of assessing market shares where new products are put onto the market.

[120] Case 193/83, *Windsurfing International v. EC Commission* [1986] ECR 611, [1986] 3 CMLR 489.

[121] See *infra* 598–608 for the clauses in the block exemption, Reg. 240/96 [1996] OJ L31/2.

Germany a notice saying 'licensed by Hoyle Schweitzer' or 'licensed by Windsurfing International'; the Commission said that this created the false impression that the board as well as the rig was covered by the patent;

(e)   an obligation on the licensees to acknowledge the word marks 'Windsurfer' and 'Windsurfing' as well as a design mark or logo as valid trade marks; the Commission considered this tantamount to a no-challenge clause to the validity of the trade mark, while WI claimed it was part of an attempt to stop its trade mark being used as a generic designation;

(f)   an obligation on the licensees to restrict production of the licensed product to specific manufacturing plant in Germany; the Commission rejected the plea that this was a measure of quality control and held that it limited freedom of competition by means of a clause which had nothing to do with the patent; neither the Commission nor the Court dealt with the position of a prohibition relating only to territories where there was patent protection; [122]

(g)   an obligation on the licensees not to challenge the validity of the licensed patents; the Commission had long held that no-challenge clauses restrict competition and that it is in the public interest that invalid patents should be challenged.

The ECJ, which agreed that the Commission was justified in treating the patent as covering only the rig, upheld all the Commission's findings except for (c), where it held that the global calculation of royalties on the complete sailboard was not a restriction of competition on the sale of separate *rigs*, although it was on the sale of *boards*. It took a highly formalistic approach and condemned the other provisions for going beyond the 'scope of the patent' and the 'specific subject-matter of the patent' without engaging in any economic analysis. As one critical commentator put it, the judgment as a whole is 'based on the assumptions that there is something inherently anticompetitive in the patent monopoly and that patent licenses [*sic*], even when arguably vertical in nature, differ fundamentally from distribution arrangements and warrant stricter treatment'.[123]

As the agreements were not notified and were not found to fall within Article 4(2)(2)(b) of Regulation 17[124] the ECJ did not have to decide whether any of the provisions could have been exempted under Article 81(3). The Commission had held that they could not have been. Between the date of the decision in *Windsurfing* and the judgment the Commission had adopted the block exemption Regulation on patent licensing agreements, 2349/84,[125] and both the decision and the judgment reflected the approach taken by the Commission in the block exemption. Block exemption Regulation 240/96[126] on technology transfer agreements has partly amended the black-listed clauses in Regulation 2349/84 and the Commission's current view of non-territorial restraints can be seen in that latest regulation, which is examined below.[127]

---

[122] For the Commission's attitude to 'site licences' generally, see *infra* 599–600.

[123] J. Venit, 'In the Wake of Windsurfing: Patent Licensing in the Common Market' [1986] *Fordham Corporate Law Institute* 517, 560–1.

[124] [1959–62] OJ Spec. Ed. 87. See *supra* 581.

[125] [1984] OJ L219/15

[126] [1996] OJ L31/2.

[127] See *supra* 592–608.

(viii) THE BLOCK EXEMPTIONS ON PATENT LICENSING AND KNOW-HOW LICENSING

The first block exemption in the field of intellectual property rights licensing was Regulation 2349/84[128] which applied to pure patent licensing agreements or to mixed patent and know-how licensing agreements where the patent was the predominant element. The second block exemption, Regulation 556/89,[129] applied to pure know-how licensing agreements and to mixed know-how and patent licensing agreements where know-how was the predominant element. Both exemptions applied only to agreements to which there were only two parties. The two Regulations were very similar: Article 1 set out the type of agreement covered and exempted certain restrictions of competition, mainly relating to exclusivity; Article 2 contained a 'white list' of provisions which did not normally restrict competition but were exempted just in case; Article 3 contained the 'black list' of provisions whose inclusion in an agreement took it outside the exemption; and Article 4 contained the opposition procedure.[130]

Patents and know-how are commonly licensed together and which element, if any, predominates depends on the precise terms of the agreement. Although they were very similar, there were material differences in the Regulations, some of which favoured the licensor and some the licensee. Lawyers could sometimes structure their clients' agreements to produce one sort of transaction rather than another in order to exploit these differences, and practitioners' books produced tables comparing each set of provisions. As Regulation 2349/84 reached its expiry date, 31 December 1994, the Commission decided that it was undesirable and unnecessary to have two different Regulations for transactions which essentially had the same economic effects. It therefore set about producing a single Regulation to replace both of them. The delay in adopting the new regulation meant that Regulation 2349/84 had to be renewed three times.

Under the transitional provisions in Article 11 of the new regulation, 240/96, any agreement in force on 31 March 1996 which fulfills the exemption requirements of Regulation 2349/84 or 556/89 remains exempted by those regulations for its lifetime. The old Regulations will therefore continue to be relevant for some years although Regulation 240/96 applies to all agreements concluded after 31 March 1996.

(ix) INTELLECTUAL PROPERTY RIGHTS AND THE BLOCK EXEMPTION ON VERTICAL RESTRAINTS

The umbrella block exemption on vertical restraints, Regulation 2790/1999, which came into force on 1 June 2000,[131] contains a provision on intellectual property rights. Article 1(3) provides:

This Regulation applies to provisions contained in vertical agreements concerning the assignment or use of intellectual property rights for the purpose of using or reselling the goods or services supplied, on condition that these provisions do not constitute the primary object of, but are directly necessary

---

[128] [1984] OJ L219/15; it came into force on 1 Jan. 1985.
[129] [1989] OJ L61/1; it came into force on 1 Apr. 1989.
[130] See *supra* Chap. 4.
[131] [1999] OJ L336/21. See *supra* Chap. 9.

for, the implementation of such agreements and do not contain restrictions of competition having the same object or effect as vertical restraints not exempted under the present Regulation.

This means that licences of intellectual property rights which are ancillary to vertical arrangements such as distribution agreements may be block exempted by Regulation 2790/1999. The provision is particularly relevant to franchise agreements. It is crucial that the dealings with the intellectual property rights are not the main object of the agreement[132] and that they do not involve restrictions of competition not covered by Regulation 2790/1999.

F. THE REGULATION ON TECHNOLOGY TRANSFER AGREEMENTS, 240/96[133]

(i) GENERAL

The delay in adopting a single replacement regulation for Regulations 2349/84 and 556/89 was a result of controversy over the proposed provisions of the regulation, mainly the Commission's proposal that the block exemption should not be available to undertakings with more than a certain share of the market (40 per cent was suggested). This would have meant the individual notification of many transactions, particularly given the difficulty in assessing market shares where new products or technology are put on the market.[134] In the end the market share threshold was dropped although the possibility of withdrawing the benefit of the exemption where the licensee's market share exceeds 40 per cent is specifically addressed in Article 7 of the Regulation.[135]

Regulation 240/96 is designated as being on technology transfer agreements, thereby denoting that it encompasses any transaction in which the predominate element is the licensing of patents or know-how. Compared to the previous Regulations it has a shortened 'black-list' of prohibited clauses and a longer 'white-list', reflecting the Commission's further experience of licensing arrangements and a more sophisticated view of what really restricts competition and cannot be exempted. More agreements fall within this exemption, therefore, than within the earlier regulations.

(ii) THE SCOPE OF REGULATION 240/96

a. TYPES OF AGREEMENT COVERED BY THE REGULATION

The Regulation applies to bilateral pure patent licensing agreements, pure know-how licensing agreements, and agreements which license patents and know-how together. 'Licence' is

---

[132] Since franchise agreements are intended to be covered by Reg. 2790/1999, the view of the ECJ in Case 161/84, *Pronuptia de Paris GmbH* v. *Pronuptia de Paris Irmgard Schillgallis* [1986] ECR 353, [1986] 1 CMLR 414 that franchises are really transactions with intellectual property rights appears to have to be overlooked in this context.

[133] [1996] OJ L31/2. For a detailed commentary on the reg. see *Butterworths Competition Law*, Division V, and Korah, *Technology Transfer Agreements and the EC Competition Rules* (Clarendon, Oxford, 1996).

[134] The Commission did not plan, however, to have more staff to deal with the anticipated increase in individual notifications.

[135] See *infra* 608–609.

not defined but Article 6(2) states that the Regulation also applies to 'assignments of know-how, patents or both where the risk associated with exploitation remains with the assignor.' This means that assignments made in return for royalty payments rather than for a lump sum will be treated as licences.

The Regulation also applies to patent, know-how and mixed agreements which also contain 'ancillary provisions relating to intellectual property rights other than patents'.[136] This means that the agreement may contain a licence of other intellectual property rights, '(in particular, trade marks, design rights and copyright, especially software protection), when such additional licensing contributes to the achievement of the objects of the licensed technology and contains only ancillary provisions'.[137] The requirement that the licensing of the extra rights be *ancillary* to the main provisions about patents and/or know-how is important: in *Moosehead/Whitbread*[138] a Canadian brewer granted to Whitbread an exclusive know-how and trade mark licence to produce, promote, market, and sell in the UK beer under the name 'Moosehead' using Moosehead's know-how. The Commission held that the agreement was not covered by Regulation 556/89 because the exploitation of the *trade mark* was the crucial element in the deal and it was therefore not ancillary to the know-how licence.[139] The clauses or agreement governing the ancillary rights must contain no restrictions of competition which are not also applied to the licensed patents or know-how and exempted by the Regulation.[140]

The Regulation *does* apply to certain things which are for the purpose of the Regulation deemed to be patents[141] including patent applications[142], utility models, applications for registrations of utility models, topographies of semiconductor products, supplementary protection certificates for medicinal products, and plant breeder's rights.

It does *not* apply to patent pools or reciprocal licences where there is territorial protection, or to licences between joint venturers above certain market shares.[143]

b. KNOW-HOW

The Regulation applies only to know-how as defined in Article 10(1), 'a body of technical information that is secret, substantial and identified in any appropriate form'.[144] These terms are defined in turn:

- *Secret*[145] means that the know-how 'as a body or in the precise configuration of its components is not generally known or easily accessible'. This seems to cover a situation where the components are known but the package as a whole is not. It is

---

[136] Reg. 240/96 Art. 1(1).

[137] *Ibid.*, recital 6.

[138] [1990] OJ L100/32, [1991] 4 CMLR 391.

[139] For trade mark licences see further *infra* 610–615.

[140] Reg. 240/96 Art. 10(15).

[141] *Ibid.*, Art. 8.

[142] It is not clear how agreements are to be treated if the application is rejected or not granted, although the application subsists but one possibility is to treat it as a know-how licence: see *Butterworths Competition Law*, Div. V, para 375.

[143] Reg. 240/96 Art. 5(1).

[144] Know-how is defined similarly, although more succinctly in Reg. 2790/1999, [1999] OJ L336/21, on vertical restraints, Art. 1(f).

[145] Reg. 240/96 Art. 10(2)

unclear whether the phrase 'generally known or easily accessible' refers to the world at large or insiders in the relevant industry.[146] It is the position at the time the licence is entered into which is relevant. Know-how may cease to be secret immediately when a product is first marketed because of reverse engineering and, if so, the agreement remains valid as far as the payment of royalties is concerned, although with a pure know-how agreement the exemption of territorial protection no longer applies.[147] The Regulation recognizes that part of the value of the know-how may be the lead time it gives the licensee.[148]

- *Substantial*[149] means that it includes information which is 'useful' i.e. it can improve the competitive position of the licensee. The old know-how block exemption expressed this as excluding know-how which was 'trivial', which seems to amount to the same thing. Licensees are, in any event, unlikely to pay for information either which can be described as trivial or which does nothing to improve their competitive position.

- *Identified*[150] means described or recorded in such a way as to ensure that the secret and substantial criteria are satisfied and that the licensee is not restricted in the exploitation of his own technology. Parties must be willing to record the secret information passing under the agreement in an adequate format, which might include diagrams, demonstrations,[151] or videos.

(iii) EXCLUSIVITY AND TERRITORIAL RESTRAINTS EXEMPTED BY ARTICLE 1

a. THE SCHEME OF THE PROVISIONS

Article 1 exempts some exclusivity provisions. Of course, the *Nungesser* case established that certain 'open' licences for new technology are not within Article 81(1) at all, but in recital 10 of the Regulation the Commission set out its narrow interpretation of that judgment,[152] and in so far as they *are* within Article 81(1) Article 1 of Regulation 240/96 exempts them.

Article 1 deals with two different matters, the relationship between licensor and licensee (Article (1)(1)(1)–(3)) and that between the licensees *inter se* (Article (1)(1)(4)–(6)). The Regulation allows greater territorial protection as between licensor and licensee than as between licensees. It is important for licensees to realize this. If a licensor holds patents in the UK, France, Germany, and Italy and grants a licence of the UK patent, France, Germany, and Italy will still be the 'licensor's territory', but if he gives a licence of his French patent France ceases to be the licensor's territory and becomes a licensee's territory.

Where patents are concerned territorial protection depends on there being *parallel patents* in existence i.e. parties are not allowed to protect territories in which they have no rights. If a

---

[146] See V. Korah, *Technology Transfer Agreements and the EC Competition Rules* (Clarendon, 1996), 129–31 *Boussois/Interpane* [1987] OJ L50/30, [1988] 4 CMLR 124 at para. 2.

[147] Reg. 240/96 Art. 1(3): see *infra* 596.

[148] *Ibid.*, Art. 10(2).

[149] *Ibid.*, Art. 10(3).

[150] *Ibid.*, Art. 10(4).

[151] See *Rich Products/Jus-Rol* [1988] OJ L69/21, [1988] 4 CMLR 527.

[152] *L.C. Nungesser RG and Kurt Eisele v. Commission.* See *supra* 588.

licensor has patents on the same technology in France and Germany the French licensee can be prohibited from using the technology to manufacture in Germany, but not from manufacturing in Spain, where the licensor has no patent.

The Regulation exempts exclusivity only for a certain time. In licences of patents the time limits normally relate to the life of the parallel patents in the protected territories. Know-how, however, can in theory last in perpetuity although in practice it usually gets into the public domain after a few years at most. As 'the point at which the know-how ceases to be secret can be difficult to determine'[153] the Regulation fixes a maximum length of time of ten years for exclusivity in pure know-how licences. The time (which is five years only where passive sales restrictions are concerned[154]) is measured from the date at which the licensed product is first put on the market within the common market by *one of the licensees*. This means that where licences are granted at different times only the first licensee can have the benefit of the full period and some licensees may have none at all. There is no definition of 'put on the market' in the Regulation, but it is generally thought to refer to commercial marketing and not to cover experimental sales for market research purposes.[155]

The exclusivity provisions of Regulation 240/96 are made unnecessarily difficult to read because the type of exclusivity exempted is in Article 1(1) while the permissible time limits on the exclusivity are in Article 1(2). It should be noted that references to 'within the common market' should be read as 'within the EEA' where the provisions of the EEA Agreement are relevant.

b. EXEMPTED EXCLUSIVITY AS BETWEEN LICENSOR AND LICENSEE: ARTICLE 1(1)(1)–(3)

Note that by Article 1(5) clauses which place obligations on the parties of the same type as those dealt with below, but which are *more limited* in scope, are also exempted.

• Restrictions on the licensor

By Article 1(1)(1) the licensor may agree not to license other undertakings to exploit the technology in the licensed territory. The licensee may thereby be given a territory in which he is the sole licensee.

By Article 1(1)(2) the licensor may agree not to exploit the licensed technology in the licensed territory himself. In conjunction with the previous provision this gives the licensee a licence which is not only sole, but exclusive.

In a pure patent licence these obligations are exempted for as long as the product is still protected by a parallel patent in the licensee's territory.[156] In a pure know-how licence the protection can last for ten years from the date the licensed product is first put on the market within the common market by one of the licensees, so long as the know-how remains secret and substantial.[157] It should be noted that the ten years runs from the first marketing by *any* licensee. In a mixed agreement exclusivity can last for as long as the licensed technology is

---

[153] Reg. 240/96 recital 13.

[154] See *infra* 597. The 5 year period even extends to pure patent agreements in the case of restrictions on passive sales.

[155] See N. Green and A. Robertson, *Commercial Agreements and Competition Law* (2nd edn., Kluwer, 1997) 847.

[156] Reg. 240/96 Art. 1(2).

[157] *Ibid.*, Art. 1(3).

protected by necessary patents in the licensee's territory *or* for ten years as in a pure know-how licence, whichever is the longer.[158] A 'necessary patent' is one which is necessary for putting the licensed technology into effect.[159] As the period of exemption for the exclusivity provisions of a know-how licence is only ten years, whereas the life of a patent is twenty, the object of this provision is to prevent the parties extending the period of exclusivity in a know-how licence by throwing in superfluous patents. A necessary patent is one without which the realization of the licensed technology would be impossible, less possible, more difficult, or more costly, i.e. it has to be of 'technical, legal or economic interest to the licensee'.[160]

'Exploit' is defined in Article 10(10) as any use of the licensed technology in particular the production, active or passive selling in a territory even if not coupled with manufacture in that territory, or leasing of the licensed products. The licensee can therefore be protected from the licensor's active *or passive* sales.

As a result of these two provisions the licensee is assured that he will not face direct competition from another licensee in the same territory or from the licensor. However, there is no protection from sales made by third parties who acquire the products after they have been marketed in the common market.

By Article 10(12) the 'licensed territory' means the territory covering all or part of the common market where the licensee is entitled to exploit the licensed technology.

- **Restrictions on the licensee**

By Article (1)(1)(3) the licensee may agree 'not to exploit the licensed technology within the territory of the licensor within the common market'. Such a provision protects the licensor against competition from his own licensee. The word 'exploit' has the same meaning as is explained above.

'The territory of the licensor' means, according to Article 10(12), territories in which the licensor has not granted any licences for the patents and/or know-how covered by the licensing agreement. In the equivalent provision in Regulation 2349/84 the licensee could be prohibited from exploitation in territories *reserved* to the licensor[161] and in Regulation 556/89 'territory of the licensor' covered only territories which the licensor *expressly* reserved for himself.[162] Regulation 240/96 has dropped this reference to reservation, which creates a problem. Know-how is information known to the licensor but, unlike a patent, it is not *registered* anywhere and does not have the same inherent territorial dimension as a patent. In a licence the licensee is allowed to use the know-how in a specified territory and it appears that everywhere else not licensed to other licensees is the 'licensor's territory'. Bearing in mind the difference in wording between Regulations 240/96 and 556/89, however, the parties are advised to stipulate expressly what is considered to be the licensor's territory.[163]

The time for which this provision may be exempted is the same as for the two earlier

---

[158] *Ibid.*, Art. 1(4).

[159] *Ibid.*, Art. 10(5).

[160] *Ibid.*

[161] Reg. 2349 184 [1984] OJ L219/15, Art. (1)(1)(3).

[162] Reg. 556/89 [1989] OJ L617/1, Art. 1(7)(12).

[163] See V. Korah, *Technology transfer Agreements and EC Competition Law* (Claradon, 1996), 141; S. Kinsella *EU Technology Licensing* (Palladian Law Publishing), 44–45.

provisions[164] except that it is existence of parallel patents in the *licensor's* territory which is relevant, because it is the licensor's territory, not the licensee's, which this provision protects.

c. EXEMPTED EXCLUSIVITY AS BETWEEN LICENSEES *INTER SE*

Article (1)(1)(4)–(6) do not use the word *exploit* but instead deals separately with restrictions on manufacture and those on sales.

By Article (1)(1)(4) the licensee may agree not to manufacture or use the licensed process in territories within the common market licensed to other licensees. The time limits for the exemption are the same as above, except that it is the continued existence of parallel patents in the territories of *other licensees* which is relevant.[165] This provision cannot prevent the licensee manufacturing outside his own territory in territories where there is no parallel patent.

By Article (1)(1)(5) the licensee may agree not to pursue an active sales policy in territories within the common market licensed to other licensees. A prohibition against active sales has long been familiar from the law on vertical restraints[166] and means the soliciting of sales from outside the allotted territory. The time limits are the same as for Article (1)(1)(4) above.

By Article 1(1)(6) the licensee may agree not to indulge in *passive* sales in territories within the common market licensed to other licensees. In accepting such a restriction the licensee agrees not to respond to would-be customers from outside his territory who approach him without being solicited. This is a great concession by the Commission, and differs from what is permitted in distribution agreements.[167] It is an appreciation of the degree of territorial protection that may be needed to induce licensees to take a licence by ensuring that they can, for example, recoup start-up costs. However, the passive sales prohibition can last for only a maximum of *five* years from the date that the licensed product is first put on the market within the common market by a licensee. In a pure patent agreement it is for five years or the remaining life of the parallel patents, *whichever is the shorter*, and, in a pure know-how agreement, for five years or the period for which the know-how remains secret and substantial, *whichever is the shorter*. In a mixed agreement it is for whichever is the longer of the life of the patent or the know-how remaining secret and substantial, subject to a maximum of five years. The fact that the time runs from the marketing by the first licensee, which while admittedly more generous than the time limit in Regulation 2349/84,[168] means that subsequent licensees may gain little from the provision. As explained above, as between licensor and licensee the protection from passive sales can last for longer periods.

Article 3(3)(a) blacklists a provision requiring licensees not to meet orders from customers *in* their territory who would market the products in other territories within the common market. Neither licensors nor licensees can therefore be protected from parallel imports and attempts to do so will take the agreement outside the block exemption.[169]

---

[164] Reg. 240/96 Art. 1(2)–(4).

[165] *Ibid.*, Art. 1(2).

[166] See Reg. 2790/1999 [1999] OJ L336/21, Art. 4(b), the block exemption on vertical restraints, and previously Reg.1983/83 [1983] OJ L173/1, the block exemption on distribution agreements, Art. 2(2)(c), discussed *supra* in Chap. 9.

[167] See Reg. 2790/1999, Art. 4(b), discussed *supra* in Chap. 9.

[168] [1984] OJ L219/15, Art. 1(1)(6) of which provided that the 5 years should run from the time that the *licensor or licensee* first put the product on the market within the common market.

[169] See Art. 3(3)(b).

It should be noted that Article 7[170] provides that one particular instance in which the block exemption might be withdrawn from a qualifying agreement is where a licensee refuses without objectively justifiable reason to meet unsolicited orders from users or resellers in the territories of other licensees. This is to cover the situation where the licensee's refusal to satisfy unsolicited customers, although not pursuant to an agreement, leads to an unacceptable degree of territorial protection and compartmentalisation of the market.[171]

(iv) NON-TERRITORIAL RESTRAINTS UNDER REGULATION 240/96

a. GENERAL

The non-territorial restraints found in technology transfer agreements are dealt with in one of four ways in Regulation 240/96:

First, there are two restrictions, concerning trade marks and quantities produced which are exempted in Article 1;[172] Article 1(5) applies to these provisions, so that more limited obligations of the same type are also exempted.

Second, there are a comparatively large number of clauses which are said in Article 2(1) (the 'white list') to be generally not restrictive of competition, but are exempted (by Article 2(2)) if they are. In many cases Article 2 applies only if the provisions are in a particular form or contain particular conditions, otherwise they may be 'black-listed' in Article 3, or not expressly dealt with in the Regulation at all. The clauses referred to in Article 2(1) are exempted if they fall within Article 81(1) even if they are not accompanied by any Article 1 restrictions, i.e. if they are in a non-exclusive licence.[173] Article 2(3) also exempts clauses of the type dealt with in Article 2(1) which are *more limited* in scope.

Third, there is a list of seven provisions in Article 3 (the 'black list') , the presence of any of which takes the agreement outside the exemption. In several cases these correspond to what *is* allowed by Article 2, so that a particular matter (for example, the grant of improvements) is allowed if it meets the criteria in Article 2 and not allowed if it is in the form prohibited by Article 3.

Fourth, Article 4 provides for an opposition procedure[174] in respect of restrictions of competition which are neither allowed by Article 1 or 2 nor disallowed by Article 3.

The following section deals with the matters in Articles 1, 2, and 3, putting together in each case what is and is not permitted in respect of each type of provision.

b. TRADE MARKS AND GET-UP

By Article (1)(1)(7) an obligation on the licensee to use the licensor's trade mark and get-up is considered as a restriction of competition but exempted provided the licensee can identify himself as the manufacturer. This exemption lasts for as long as the product is protected by parallel patents, or for the duration of an agreement concerning know-how provided the

---

[170] See *infra* 608.
[171] It may well be the result of concerted practices amongst the licensees.
[172] Art. (1)(1)(7) and (8).
[173] *Ibid.*, Art. 2(2).
[174] For the opposition procedure generally see Chap. 4.

know-how remains secret and substantial. An obligation on the licensee to mark the licensed product with an indication of the licensor's name or of the licensed patent is white listed by Article 2(1)(11). It should be remembered that in *Windsurfing*[175] (above) the ECJ held that an obligation on the licensee to identify part of his product (the board) as manufactured under licence when it was not covered by the licensed patent fell within Article 81(1).

c. QUANTITIES

The block exemption contains provisions about both minimum and maximum quantity stipulations.

As far as minimum quantities are concerned, Article 2(1)(9) states the basic principle, that the licensee can be required to produce minimum quantities of the licensed product, carry out a minimum number of operations using the licensed technology or pay a minimum royalty.[176] This is to ensure that the licensee sufficiently exploits the licensed technology and that the licensor is assured of a proper return. However, it *is* possible for a minimum quantity clause to be blacklisted if it places such a burden on the licensee that he cannot compete with the licensor within the terms of Article 3(2), which outlaws non-competition clauses.[177] Article 7(4) specifically allows the block exemption to be withdrawn from an agreement where the parties were competing manufacturers at the grant of the licence and minimum quantity obligations have the effect of preventing the licensee from using competing technologies.

As for maximum quantities, the basic principle is that such limitations are blacklisted by Article 3(5). However, there are exceptions to this. First, Article 2(1)(13) whitelists what is called 'second sourcing', where a licence is specifically granted in order to give a particular customer a second source of the product within the licensed territory and the licensee agrees just to supply a limited quantity to that customer (the licensee in such a case may be the customer himself, who wants to manufacture himself or through a sub-contractor). Secondly, Article 1(1)(8) exempts a restriction on quantities produced by the licensee in so far as it relates to quantities the licensee requires for his own use or for sale as part of his own products. This is a 'use' or 'production' licence and covers the situation where the licensee wants to make components or parts for his own complete product and is not going to market the licensed product as such. Article 1(1)(8) provides that the licensee must be able to determine freely the quantities he requires himself. The time limits on the exemption of this provision are the same as for Article (1)(1)(7), i.e. for as long as the product is protected by parallel patents or for the life of an agreement concerning know-how provided the know-how remains secret and substantial. Korah argues that a licence of this type is no different in effect from the arrangement condemned in *Windsurfing* whereby the licensee was allowed to sell only complete sailboards, with the patented rig attached to an approved board.[178]

d. SITE LICENCES

The prohibition in Article 3(5) on maximum quantities causes difficulties over what are known as 'site licences'. These are licences which limit the use of the technology to a

[175] Case 193/83, *Windsurfing International v. EC Commission* [1986] ECR 611, [1986] 3 CMLR 489.
[176] For further consideration of minimum royalty stipulations, see *infra* 601.
[177] See *infra* 601.
[178] V. Korah, *Technology Transfer Agreement and the Competition Rules* (Clarendon, 1996), 146–147.

particular location. They may involve quantity limits, either explicitly, in that a plant of a particular size is specified, or implicitly if expansion of the plant is not possible at the site. Two other provisions are relevant to this matter. First, Article 2(1)(12) whitelists an obligation not to use the licensor's technology to build facilities for third parties, although the licensee must be allowed to increase the capacity of his facilities or set up additional ones for his own use 'on normal commercial terms'. Secondly, Recital 24, explaining these provisions, says that quantity restrictions are blacklisted because they limit the extent to which the licensee can exploit the technology and may have the effect of an export ban but that:

This does not apply where a licence is granted for use of the technology in specific production facilities and where both a specific technology is communicated for the setting-up, operation and maintenance of these facilities and the licensee is allowed to increase the capacity of the facilities or to set up further facilities for its own use on normal commercial terms. On the other hand, the licensee may lawfully be prevented from using the transferred technology to set up facilities for third parties, since the purpose of the agreement is not to permit the licensee to give other producers access to the licensor's technology while it remains secret or protected by the patent (Article 2(1)(12).

Until 1997 the legality of site licences, which are widely used in certain large manufacturing sectors such as the chemical industry,[179] was not questioned.[180] Recital 24 was widely considered to look favourably on site licences. In April 1997, however, the Commission issued a Statement of Objections against ARCO Chemical, claiming that a 1986 agreement containing a site licence was caught by Article 81(1).[181] The Commission closed the case in July 1998 without any formal decision having been taken, leaving the status of such agreements uncertain.[182] The Commission's contention was that the 1986 agreement merely provided for the parties to negotiate mutually acceptable terms for an expanded licence but did not guarantee the licensee the right to build a new plant at another location on normal commercial terms. In effect the Commission wanted the original licence expressly to guarantee to the licensee the right to expand or build new plants. It took the view that silence equalled a contractual prohibition on doing so and that a provision that they would agree on terms at the time of any new licence was tantamount to the licensor having a veto. The heart of this matter is not how the wording of Recital 24 might or might not be deconstructed but whether site licence arrangements, which are essential to transactions concerning secret new technologies, can really be said to restrict competition.[183]

---

[179] They are common where a facility needs to be in a particular location because of environmental considerations or because access is required to certain inputs only available in certain places. They are often found in licences in the information technology industry, where the licensee may not transfer software from the licensed system to an unlicensed system.

[180] And see *Re the Agreement of Davide-Campari-Milano SpA* [1978] OJ L70/69, [1978] 2 CMLR 397, discussed below in the context of trade mark licences, where a restriction of the licence to those plants capable of guaranteeing the quality of the product was held to be outside Art. 81(1).

[181] *ARCO/Repsol*, Case E–2/36.233.

[182] The matter stirred up much disquiet and representatives of the chemical industry were invited to a meeting with DGIV in June 1998. The parties to the licence came to a settlement over the dispute which triggered the licensee's complaint to the Commission, but opposing views on the issues raised were expressed by the lawyers representing each side in articles in the *European Competition Law Review*: M. Dolmans and M. Odriozola, 'Site Licence, Right Licence? Site Licences under EC Competition Law' [1998] *ECLR* 493 and J.M. Townsend 'The Case For Site Licences' [1999] *ECLR* 169.

[183] For the arguments of the chemical industry at the June 1998 meeting with the Commission, see Townsend *supra* n. 182, 172–3.

e. PRICE RESTRICTIONS

There is no exemption for restrictions by which 'one party is restricted in the determination of prices, components of prices or discounts for the licensed products' (Article 3(1)). This applies to restrictions on both licensor and licensee although one would normally expect them to be on the latter. The prohibition does not cover mere *recommendations* on price, which have been held in other contexts to be outside Article 81(1) so long as there is no question of them being enforced.[184] Not only are price fixing clauses blacklisted in the block exemption, they are very unlikely ever to fulfill the criteria in Article 81(3).

f. NON-COMPETITION CLAUSES

The exclusivity clauses in Article 1(1), discussed above, allow for restrictions on competition between licensor and licensee in respect of the licensed products. Article 3(2), however, blacklists obligations which restrict the parties from competing within the common market with one another or with another undertaking in respect of competing products. Although an outright obligation not to exploit competing technology through research and development, production, use, or distribution is blacklisted, Article 2(1)(18) whitelists a reservation by the licensor to *terminate the exclusivity* under the agreement and stop licensing improvements if the licensee enters into competition with the licensor over competing products within the common market. This provision can be a serious deterrent to a licensee competing with the licensor, so it dilutes the effect of the Article 3(2) prohibition.

Article 3(2) is also without prejudice to Article 2(1)(17) which whitelists best endeavours clauses, i.e. 'the obligation on the licensee to use his best endeavours to manufacture and market the licensed products'. There is a conflict between the provisions as it is difficult to see how a licensee can be using his best endeavours to exploit one technology while exploiting a competing one, and it is suggested[185] that if the best endeavours obligation can be fulfilled only by the licensee refraining from competing activities, then he can be restrained from such activities. However, as noted above,[186] in Article 7(4) the Commission expressly states that it may withdraw the benefit of the block exemption where the parties were competing manufacturers at the time of the licence and either a minimum quantities or best endeavours clause bars a licensee from competing technologies.

g. FIELD OF USE RESTRICTIONS AND CUSTOMER ALLOCATION

Field of use restrictions are where the licensee is licensed to exploit the technology only within certain technical fields of application. Technology can often be used for several different things (for example, a patented chemical may be used to produce both fertilisers and pesticides) and the licensor may wish to grant a licence to exploit for only one or some of them, or to grant licences for different uses to different licensees. Field of use restrictions are whitelisted by Article 2(1)(8). However, if the parties were competing manufacturers before the grant of the licence, a restriction on which customers either party may supply (a

---

[184] See Case 161/84, *Pronuptia de Paris GmbH* v. *Pronuptia de Paris Irmgard Schillgallis* [1986] ECR 353, [1986] 1 CMLR 414, and *supra* Chaps. 4 and 9.

[185] See *Butterworths Competition Law*, Division V; see also V. Korah, *Technology Transfer Agreements and the EC Competition Rules* (Clarendon, 1996), 195–7.

[186] See *supra* 599.

customer allocation clause) is blacklisted by Article 3(4). The prohibition also covers provisions about the forms of distribution the parties may use, or (if the aim is to share customers) what types of packaging they can employ.[187] Field of use restrictions may be difficult to distinguish from customer allocation within the same field of use, as customers may well require the patented technology for different purposes and a field of use restriction may have the same effect as a customer allocation clause. The matter is exemplified by *French State/Suralmo*[188] where the Commission objected to the division between exploiting engine technology for use in military equipment and exploiting it in civilian equipment.

The prohibition on customer allocation is without prejudice to the 'second sourcing' permitted by Article 2(1)(13).[189] Where the parties are *not* competing manufacturers at the time of the grant of the licence a customer allocation is neither blacklisted nor whitelisted and Recital 23 says that the restriction 'remains subject to the opposition procedure'.[190]

h. IMPROVEMENTS

It is common for those using technology to discover improvements. The question then arises concerning what happens to them. Licensors will be keen to stipulate that licensees should assign (or 'grant-back') improvements to them. The Commission, however, blacklists such clauses in Article 3(6), possibly because it considers that such a restriction arises from unequal bargaining power between the parties,[191] as a licensee would have no interest in agreeing to it if he had a choice.

Although assignments back are prohibited, *licences* of improvements by licensee to licensor are whitelisted in Article 2(1)(4) so long as they meet certain criteria: the licensor must undertake to grant an exclusive or non-exclusive licence of *his* own improvements to the licensee, and in the case of severable improvements the licence must be non-exclusive.[192] There are obviously arrangements which can be made over improvements which do *not* fall within Article 2(1)(4) but which do *not* fall foul of Article 3(6). The opposition procedure can be used in respect of these.

The licensing of improvements can automatically extend the duration of the agreement. This is allowed by Article 8(3) provided that the licensee is free to refuse the improvements and each party is able to terminate the agreement when the initial term expires and at least every three years thereafter. However, this prolongation *cannot* extend the duration of the exclusivity permitted by Article 1 so further periods of exclusivity would need individual exemption.[193] If, however, the improvements result in 'innovations which are distinct from the licensed technology' the parties can conclude a fresh agreement which can benefit from the block exemption.[194]

---

[187] This is stated to be without prejudice to Art. (1)(1)(7) which exempts stipulations about using the licensor's get-up and trade marks.

[188] Commission's *IXth Report on Competition Policy* (Commission, 1979), pt 114.

[189] See *supra* 599.

[190] Provided for in Art. 4: see *infra* 608.

[191] See N. Green and A. Robertson *Commercial Agreements and Competition Law* (2nd edn., Kluwer, 1997), 856.

[192] Subject to the proviso that licences to third parties do not involve disclosing know-how which is still secret.

[193] Art. 3(7) and recital 14.

[194] Recital 14.

i. IMPEDING PARALLEL IMPORTS

Article 3(3) blacklists impeding or attempting to impede parallel imports. Article (3)(3)(a) deals with refusing to meet orders from would-be exporters inside the licensed territory.[195] Article 3(3)(b) covers situations where one or both of the parties are required without any objectively justified reason:

to make it difficult for users or resellers to obtain the products from other resellers within the common market, and in particular to exercise intellectual property rights or take measures so as to prevent users or resellers from obtaining outside, or from putting on the market in the licensed territory products which have been lawfully put on the market within the common market by the licensor or with his consent;

or where they do so as a result of a concerted practice between them. The phrase 'make it difficult for' is both vague and all-embracing, but the only example pertains to exercising intellectual property rights by trying to bring infringement actions where the rights have been exhausted under the exhaustion of rights principle.[196] However, although it does not say so, this provision must be without prejudice to any infringement action allowed by Article 2(14), discussed below.[197]

j. TIE-INS AND QUALITY CONTROLS

A tie-in is where the licensee is obliged as a condition of the licence to obtain certain goods or services from the licensor (or an undertaking designated by him). These are usually components, raw materials, etc. involved in the exploitation of the licensed technology. The Commission has a history of hostility to tie-ins on the basis that they bar other suppliers of the tied products from the licensee's custom even if they offer lower prices. Tie-ins are specifically mentioned in the list of restrictions of competition set out in Article 81(1)(e) and in the list of abuses in Article 82(d).[198]

The Commission's attitude to ties in patent licences was made manifest in its 1979 decision *Vaessen/Moris*.[199] Moris held a Belgian patent on a process and device used in manufacturing a Belgian speciality, *saucissons de Boulogne* (square horsemeat sausages), and controlled a company, ALMO, which made casings for these sausages. Moris licensed his patent to ALMO, which sub-licensed it to a number of Belgian sausage manufacturers free of charge on condition that they bought all the sausage casings used with the device from ALMO.[200] A rival manufacturer of sausage casings, Vaessen, complained to the Commission when it could not penetrate the *saucissons de Boulogne* casings market because the sausage makers were tied to ALMO. The Commission held that the tie infringed Article 81(1)[201] as it 'deprived the sublicensee of its business freedom to obtain supplies from other

---

[195] See *supra* 597.

[196] See *supra* 561–574.

[197] See *infra* 607.

[198] For the extensive attention which has been given to ties in the Art. 82 context, see Chap. 7. S. 44 of the Patents Act 1977, which prohibited ties in patent licences in UK law, was repealed by the Competition Act 1998.

[199] [1979] OJ L19/32, [1979] 1 CMLR 511.

[200] The economic value of the patent was primarily in the substantial labour savings that are available with the patented process, which enabled the number of workers to be reduced to one quarter: *ibid.*, para. 10.

[201] It did not consider the application of Art. 86 (now Art. 82).

undertakings, perhaps on more favourable terms as in the case of its purchases from Vaessen'.[202] It also refused exemption[203] on the ground that the tie was an impediment to the improvement in production, distribution, or technical or economic progress demanded by Article 81(3) and imposed a restriction 'which is not essential to the proper exploitation of the Moris patent, since it is proved that the casings supplied by Vaessen are perfectly adequate for use with the patented process and device'.[204] In this widely criticized finding the Commission seemed to ignore the realities of the situation, as Zanon explains:

L. Zanon, 'Ties in patent licensing agreements' (1980) 5 *ELRev* 391, at 392

ALMO's clients were not completely deprived of their freedom to choose, as they remained free to obtain casings from competitors when the patented process was not used. Their choice, therefore, was between using Mr Moris' process and ALMO's casings, or using cheaper casings without the benefit of Mr Moris' more efficient process. Secondly, the fact that Vaessen was able to offer casings at a price lower than the one charged by ALMO is not at all surprising, as it did not bear the costs of inventing and developing the device used to manufacture the sausages. In other words, the purchases of casings from ALMO and from Vaessen were only apparently identical, as in fact ALMO's clients obtained together with the casings also the right to use Mr Moris' process and device. The comparison between the prices charged for the casings is therefore irrelevant: it is the cost saving related to the use of ALMO's patent which should be compared with the cost saving derived from Vaessen's lower price. In this respect, it seems that the economic value of Mr Moris' invention was substantial, as it enabled manufacturers: (a) to use single-skin casings in the process, while previously only double-skin casings could be used, because of the pressure exerted on the casing by the filling process; and (b) to benefit from perceptible labour savings, as the number of workers employed in the process could be reduced to one quarter.

The amount of Vaessen's price advantage over ALMO is unknown, therefore any meaningful comparison is impossible; nevertheless, it seems unlikely that the cost savings connected to Vaessen's lower price would outweigh completely the benefits in efficiency deriving from the invention. This conclusion seems in accordance with the fact that most Belgian manufacturers of *saucissons de Boulogne* freely chose to remain faithful to ALMO, despite Vaessen's substantially lower price, and in the absence of any pressure deriving from a written agreement.

The Commission does however accept ties which are necessary to the technically satisfactory exploitation of the licensed technology (which was not the case in *Vaessen/Moris*). It could be argued that if the licensed technology will not work without the products stipulated to be bought from the licensor the tie is superfluous, but this overlooks the case of technology which *will* work but less satisfactorily and, as seen below, the licensor is able to impose quality standards. Moreover, licensors prefer an express tie to leaving it to the licensee to discover that other products are inadequate substitutes for theirs. In *Rich Products/JusRol*[205] the Commission accepted that a tie was necessary for the technically satisfactory exploitation and held it to be outside Article 81(1). This principle has been

---

[202] *Vaessen/Moris, supra* n.197, para. 15.

[203] The licensing agreements had not been notified but the Commission held that they were non-notifiable agreements within Art. (4)(2)(1) of Reg. 17 [1959–62] OJ Spec. Ed. 87.

[204] *Vaessen/Moris, supra* n. 197, para. 23.

[205] [1988] OJ L69/21, [1988] 4 CMLR 527.

stated many times[206] and is reflected in Article 2(1)(5) in the whitelist of the block exemption:

an obligation on the licensee to observe minimum quality specifications, including technical specifications, for the licensed product or to procure goods or services from the licensor or from an undertaking designated by the licensor, in so far as these quality specifications, products or services are necessary for:

(a) a technically proper exploitation of the licensed technology; or

(b) ensuring that the product of the licensee conforms to the minimum quality specifications that are applicable to the licensor and other licensees;

and to allow the licensor to carry out related checks.

'Necessary for a technically proper exploitation' is not defined but denotes something less than *essential*. In the old block exemptions[207] the phrase was 'technically *satisfactory* exploitation' and it is suggested[208] that 'proper' encompasses the licensee complying with the licensor's technology and processes even if they do not deliver a more 'satisfactory' result.

Article 2(1)(5) also allows the imposition of minimum quality standards if either they, too, are necessary for a technically proper exploitation *or* they are also applicable to the licensor and other licensees. The uniformity required by the latter provision excludes from the white list cases where different licensees are allowed to manufacture to different qualities, although there may be perfectly good commercial reasons for this.[209] Note that provisions allowing the licensor to carry out checks that his standards are being met are whitelisted by the tailpiece to the Article.

What happens to ties and quality specifications which are *not* necessary? The new block exemption departs from the old ones in its treatment of non-whitelisted provisions. They were previously blacklisted.[210] In Regulation 240/96 they are not blacklisted, but are specifically referred to in the Article 4 opposition procedure. Article 4(2)(a) says that the opposition procedure shall apply in particular to obligations on the licensee to accept quality specifications, further licences, or goods or services which are not necessary for the technically *satisfactory* exploitation or conformity with quality standards *respected* by the licensor and other licensees.[211] This does not mean that the Commission will exempt such provisions, but it does mean that they can be individually considered: for example, it would give the Commission the chance to accept that the *Vaessen/Moris* tie operated as a method of efficiently monitoring the use of the patent.

---

[206] See e.g. *Re the Agreement of Burroughs AG and Deplanque* [1972] OJ L13/50 [1972] CMLR 67; *Re the Agreement of Davide Campari-Milano SpA* [1978] OJ L70/69, [1978] 2 CMLR 397; Case 161/84, *Pronuptia de Paris GmbH* v. *Pronuptia de Paris Irmgard Schillgallis* [1986] ECR 353, [1986] 1 CMLR 414; Case 193/83, *Windsurfing International* v. *EC Commission* [1986] ECR 611, [1986] 3 CMLR 489.

[207] Reg. 2349/84 [1984] OJ L217/15, Art. 2(1), Reg. 556/89 [1989] OJ L61/1, Art. 2(5)(a).

[208] See *Butterworths Competition Law* (Butterworths, looseleaf), Division V.

[209] See V. Korah, *Technology Transfer Agreements and the EC Competition Rules* (Clarendon, 1196), 176 and 179–80.

[210] Reg. 2349/84, [1984] OJ L217/15, Art. 3(9), Reg. 556/89, [1989] OJ L61/1, Art. 3(3) (Reg. 2349/84 dealt only with technically satisfactory exploitation and not with quality specification).

[211] Note the slight difference in wording between this and the provision in Art. 2(5).

k. NO-CHALLENGE CLAUSES

No-challenge clauses prohibit the licensee from challenging the validity of the licensed patent or contesting the licensed know-how. The Commission had long disapproved of such provisions[212] and the ECJ upheld this in *Windsurfing*.[213] The argument about no-challenge clauses is that on the one hand competition is restricted if technology is treated as protected by intellectual property rights when it is not, but on the other hand rights holders may be reluctant to license if those most likely to challenge are free to do so. In the old block exemptions no-challenge clauses were blacklisted, although without prejudice to the licensor's right to terminate the licence in the event of a challenge.[214]

Later cases and decisions, however, have taken a less rigid attitude to no-challenge clauses. In *Bayer* v. *Süllhöfer*[215] the ECJ said that such clauses 'may, in the light of the economic context, restrict competition within the meaning of Article [81(1)] of the [EC] Treaty'[216] but that even if the national court decided that it did involve a 'limitation on the licensee's freedom of action' it would still have to verify whether competition was restricted to an appreciable extent.[217] In *Moosehead/Whitbread*[218] the Commission held that a no-challenge clause in a *trade mark* licence did not necessarily come within Article 81 and that prohibitions on challenging the *ownership* rather than the validity of marks never infringed Article 81(1).[219]

The position under the block exemption is that Article 2(1)(15) whitelists a reservation by the licensor of the right to terminate the licence in the event of a challenge to 'licensed patents within the common market belonging to the licensor or undertakings connected with him' or to the secret and substantial nature of the licensed know-how . Article 2(1)(16) whitelists a similar reservation in the event of a challenge to the *necessity* of the patent.[220] The change to the position under the old regulations is that an absolute prohibition on challenges is no longer blacklisted. Instead, no-challenge clauses which go further than a right to terminate are dealt with in Article 4(2)(a) which provides for them to be subject to the opposition procedure in Article 4(1):

Paragraph 1 shall apply, in particular, where:

(b) the licensee is prohibiting from contesting the secrecy or the substantiality of the licensed know-how or from challenging the validity of patents licensed within the common market belonging to the licensor or undertakings connected with him.

---

[212] See *Re the Agreements of Davidson Rubber Co* [1972] JO L 143/31, [1972] CMLR D 52; *AOIP* v. *Beyrard* [1976] OJ L6/8, [1976] 1 CMLR D14.

[213] Case 193/83 *Windsurfing International* v. *EC Commission* [1986] ECR 611, [1986] 3 CMLR 489; see *supra* 589–590.

[214] Reg. 2349/84, [1984] OJ L217/15, Art. 3(1), Reg. 556/89, [1989] OJ L61/1, Art. 3(4).

[215] Case 65/86, *Bayer AG and Maschinenfabrik Hennecke* v. *Heinz Süllhöfer* [1988] ECR 5249, [1990] 4 CMLR 182.

[216] *Ibid.*, para. 16.

[217] *Ibid.*, para. 19. The ECJ stated that a no-challenge clause in a royalty-free licence, or in a licence relating to outdated technology not used by the licensee, does not restrict competition: *ibid.*, paras 17 and 18.

[218] [1990] OJ L100/32, [1991] 4 CMLR 391.

[219] On the ground that the ability of other parties to compete is constrained whoever *owns* the trade mark: note that this reasoning applies equally to patents. For *Moosehead/Whitbread* see *infra* 614–615.

[220] Relevant in respect of the duration of the exemption of exclusivity provisions in mixed patent/know-how licences: see Art. 1(4) and *supra* 596.

Clauses containing other provisions, such as no-challenges to ancillary trade marks or to patents outside the common market, need individual notification in so far as they are within Article 81(1) in the first place.

l. RESERVATION OF RIGHT TO EXERCISE THE RIGHTS CONFERRED BY THE PATENT

Recital 10 is somewhat cryptic, stating that the exemption of export bans does not prejudice any developments in the case law of the Court and that '[t]his is also the case, in particular, regarding the prohibition on the licensee from selling the licensed product in territories granted to other licensees'. This is the basis for Article 2(1)(14), a rather curious provision whitelisting:

a reservation by the licensor of the right to exercise the rights conferred by a patent to oppose the exploitation of the technology by the licensee outside the licensed territory . . .

This provision did not appear in either of the old Regulations. It is worded as a reservation of the licensor's existing patent rights. It does not enable the licensor to do anything which he is prohibited from doing elsewhere. It would appear[221] that it means that the Commission has changed its mind about the ECJ's jurisprudence on the exhaustion of rights doctrine[222] and that it accepts that a patentee who grants a licence to a licensee to make and sell in a territory may be able to oppose *direct* sales on the part of the licensee from the licensed territory into other territories where there are parallel rights. The matter may one day be the subject of further clarification by the ECJ, as Recital 10 contemplates.

m. MOST-FAVOURED LICENSEE

Article 2(1)(10) whitelists 'most-favoured licensee' clauses, by which the licensor undertakes to grant to the licensee any more favourable terms that it grants to subsequent licensees. The provision does not, however, deal with clauses by which the licensor undertakes *not* to grant more favourable terms to subsequent licensees. In *Kabelmetal*[223] the Commission held such a clause to be outside Article 81(1) in the particular circumstances but stated this would not always be the case:

In specific cases, however, particularly where the market situation was such that the only way to find other licensees was to grant them more favourable terms than those granted to the first licensee, this obligation could be an obstacle to the granting of further licences and therefore constitute an appreciable restriction of competition.[224]

A clause of this type can be notified under the opposition procedure.

n. ROYALTIES

Article 2(1)(7)(a) whitelists an obligation on the licensee to continue paying royalties for the

---

[221] See V. Korah, *Technology Transfer Agreements and the EC Competition Rules* (Clarendon, 1996) 71–5, 205–6. See also J. Faull and A. Nikpay, (eds.), The EC Law of Competition (Oxford University Press, 1999) para 8.149.

[222] See *supra* 561–574.

[223] *Re the Agreement between Kabel- und Metalwerke Neumeyer AG and Etablissements Luchaire SA* [1975] OJ L222/34, [1975] 2 CMLR D40.

[224] *Ibid.*, para. 31(i).

use of the know-how for the duration of the agreement even if the know-how becomes publicly known, other than by the fault of the licensor. Once it is publicly known the licensee would be able to use it royalty-free like anyone else if he were not bound by this obligation. Article 2(1)(7)(b) allows royalty payments to extend beyond the duration of the patents, but only 'to facilitate' payment.[225]

o. OTHER CLAUSES WHITELISTED IN ARTICLE 2(1)

There are a number other clauses common in licensing transactions which are whitelisted by Article 2(1) as not causing competition problems:

Article 2(1)(1) covers confidentiality obligations, by which the licensee may not divulge the know-how communicated to him by the licensor even after the agreement has expired;

Article 2(1)(2) allows a prohibition on the licensee not to sub-licence or assign;

Article 2(1)(3) covers obligations on the licensee not to exploit the licensed patents or know-how after the agreement has ended in so far as the patents are still in force or the know-how is still secret;

Article 2(1)(6) covers obligations on the licensee to help the licensor maintain the licensed patents by informing him of any misappropriation or infringements and taking or assisting the licensor in infringement proceedings.

(v) THE OPPOSITION PROCEDURE[226]

The opposition procedure contained in Article 4 provides for agreements containing obligations restrictive of competition not covered by either Article 1, 2, or 3 to be notified to the Commission and to be covered by the block exemption unless the Commission opposes them within four months. Article 4(2) provides for this procedure to apply in particular to two types of clauses which were blacklisted in the old block exemptions: tying and quality specifications obligations where they are not necessary for technically satisfactory exploitation or uniformity with the licensor or other licensees, and absolute no-challenge provisions.[227]

(vi) THE COMMISSION'S POWER TO WITHDRAW THE BLOCK EXEMPTION

The Commission reserves the right to withdraw the benefit of the block exemption from any agreement which falls within it but which has effects incompatible with Article 81(3). It gives five particular instances of when it would be appropriate to do this. Three of these relate to territorial restrictions and restrictions which prevent parallel imports: not meeting unsolicited orders from customers in other territories (Article 7(2)), refusing to meet orders from customers in the territory who would export (Article 7(3)(a)), and making it difficult

---

[225] See recital 21 which accepts that the Commission does not need to protect the licensee against the consequences of a freely-entered into (bad) bargain.

[226] For the opposition procedure generally, see Chap. 4.

[227] Discussed above under (iv)(j) and (iv)(k).

for users or resellers to obtain the goods from other resellers (Article 7(3)(b)). These are discussed above.[228] Article 7(4) provides for withdrawal where a licence between competing manufacturers containing minimum quantity or best endeavours obligations prevents the licensee from using competing technologies.[229]

Article 7(1) provides for withdrawal if the licensed products are not exposed to effective competition from other goods or services, defined in terms of substitutes on the demand side.[230] The same provision appeared in the old block exemptions,[231] but here the Commission has added the phrase 'which may in particular occur where the licensee's market share exceeds 40%'. This is the residue of the Commission's widely deplored intention (originally) to make the new Regulation inapplicable to situations where there was market power[232] *at the time the licence was entered into*. 'Licensee's market share' is defined in Article 10(9) in terms of demand-side substitution. It is not certain either from Article 7(1), or from recital 26 which explains it, how the provision relates to a situation where the licensee's market share builds up to 40 per cent or beyond *during the currency of the agreement*, but it appears that the Regulation does contemplate withdrawal when that occurs. There are arguments, however, against such withdrawal, some of which are set out in the following extract:

V. Korah, *Technology Transfer Agreements and the EC Competition Rules* (Clarendon, 1996), 242

It is hoped that the exemption would not be withdrawn when the licensee was not competing with the licensor at the time of the licence, but later wins a high market share through the use of the technology. This is not so much a question of law, since the list is not exhaustive, but one of the Commission's policy.

I would be concerned about the basic concept of this provision if the Commission were to withdraw the exemption when the licensee achieves a high market share through use of the licensed technology. If the licensor has developed so good an idea that his licensees face no effective competition, should he not be encouraged and rewarded by being allowed to exploit the advantage as he thinks best?

Concern over subsequent market share would be based on static considerations; its underlying thought would be that, once the licensor has innovated and the licensee invested in production facilities and developing a market, it would be more competitive to have more firms in the market. Economists and businessmen, however, think *ex ante*. There must be incentives provided for the licensor to create the technology and for the licensees to invest. ... Either party might not be prepared to commit its capital and promise to make lump-sum payments or pay royalties unless protected from competition by other members of the network. To withdraw the benefit of the exemption from the big winners must reduce these incentives all round.

An innovator is under commercial pressure to think carefully before giving an exclusive territory to each licensee if it will not be exposed to effective inter-brand competition. If the licensor grants protection it must be because it considers it necessary to induce investment. Since the operation of

---

[228] See *supra* 597 and 603.

[229] See *supra* 601.

[230] Expressed in the usual formula of 'identical goods or services' or those 'considered by users as interchangeable or substitutable in view of their characteristics, price and intended use'.

[231] Reg. 2349/84, [1984] OJ L219/15, Art. 9(2), Reg. 556/89, [1989] OJ L61/1, Art. 7(2).

[232] On the part either of the licensee or of both parties: the various drafts differed.

article 7 is not automatic, these considerations may be argued should the Commission consider intervening.

The power to withdraw the benefit of the block exemption from particular agreements is common in block exemptions but is rarely exercised.[233] The Commission would, however, have withdrawn the benefit of Regulation 2349/84 from Tetra Pak if the company had not agreed to surrender the exclusivity.[234]

G. TRADE MARK LICENCES

(i) GENERAL

There is no block exemption on trade mark licences, although where the licence of a trade mark is ancillary to the licence of patents or know-how the block exemption on technology transfer will apply[235] and Article 1(1)(7) of Regulation 240/96 exempts a provision by which the licensee is obliged to use the licensor's trade mark or get-up.

Where trade marks in the context of distribution are concerned, it will be recalled that *Consten & Grundig*[236] found that an agreement seeking to confer absolute territorial protection on the licensee of a trade mark would infringe Article 81(1). Indeed, exclusivity in a trade mark licence will rarely fall outside Article 81(1) as a result of fulfilling the criteria in *Nungesser*.[237] According to that case[238] an 'open' exclusive licence would fall outside Article 81(1) if it were necessary for the dissemination of new technology in the licensed territory, and if without exclusivity the risk of exploitation would not be taken. The Commission's attitude to exclusivity in trade mark licences was demonstrated in *Moosehead/Whitbread*. The decision concerned the trade mark and know-how in respect of a Canadian brewer's lager which were licensed to a British brewer so that the lager could be produced in the UK. The Commission held that the agreement was caught by Article 81(1), as without the exclusivity any of the other five large brewers in the UK might have taken licences as well. Green and Robertson[239] point out that this bore 'no relation to the reality that no lager brewer would contemplate developing and marketing a new brand in competition with one of its rivals'. The conclusion to be drawn from the case, nevertheless, is that exclusive trade mark licences will invariably be caught by Article 81(1) unless they are *de minimis*.

[233] The first time was the withdrawal of Reg. 1984/83, [1983] OJ L173/1 on exclusive purchasing from agreements in the German ice cream market: *Langnese-Iglo GmbH* [1993] OJ L183/19, [1994] 4 CMLR 51, paras 115–148, confirmed in Case T–7/93, *Langnese-Iglo GmbH & Co KG* v. *Commission* [1995] ECR II–1533, [1995] 5 CMLR 602, confirmed in Case C–279/95P, *Langnese-Iglo GmbH & Co KG* v. *Commission* [1998] 5 CMLR 933.

[234] *Tetra Pak I (BTG Licence)* [1988] OJ L272/27, [1990] 4 CMLR 47: see *infra* 623 and *supra* Chap. 7.

[235] Reg. 240/96, [1996] OJ L31/2, Art. 6 and Art. (1)(1) and *Moosehead/Whitbread* [1990] OJ L100/32, [1991] 4 CMLR 391.

[236] Cases 56 & 58 164, *Etablissements Consten SA & Grundig-Verkaufs-GmbH* v. *Commission* [1966] ECR 299, [1966] CMLR 418: see *supra* 562–563.

[237] Case 258/78, *Nungesser* v. *EC Commission* [1982] ECR 2015, [1983] 1 CMLR 278.

[238] And note the interpretation by the Commission in recital 10 of Reg. 240/96 on technology transfer agreements: *supra* 588.

[239] N. Green and A. Robertson, *Commercial Agreements and Competition Law* (2nd edn., Kluwer, 1997), 931.

Trade mark licences may, however, be an important part of a franchise or distribution agreement. As noted above, the umbrella block exemption on vertical restraints, Regulation 2790/1999, which now covers distribution and franchising agreements,[240] also applies to licences of intellectual property rights which are contained in an agreement about the use or resale of goods and services and are not the primary object of the agreement.[241] So trade mark licences which are part of a franchise or distribution agreement may be block-exempted in this way.

The Commission has given two formal decisions on trade mark licences, *Campari*[242] and *Moosehead/Whitbread*,[243] which show that, exclusivity apart, the Commission applies broadly the same principles to trade mark licences as it does to patent and know-how licences. Where those decisions do not indicate a different treatment the relevant block exemptions, which now means Regulation 240/96, can be taken as a guide to what will be tolerated in trade mark licences, and it is usual for trade mark licences to be drawn up in the light of the provisions of the block exemption.

(ii) THE *CAMPARI* DECISION[244]

The *Campari* transaction is difficult to classify but the trade mark licence was a predominant element. The aperitifs Bitter Campari and Cordial Campari were made by mixing alcohol with a secret herbal concentrate. Campari-Milano set up a network of licensees to manufacture and sell its products in all Community countries except the UK and Ireland.[245] Under the agreements the licensees purchased the secret concentrate and colouring matter from the licensor and manufactured the drink in compliance with the licensor's instructions. The resulting bottles of aperitif were then sold under the licensor's Campari trade mark. The licences were exclusive, prevented the licensees from manufacturing or handling competing products or pursuing an active sales policy outside their territory, banned exports outside the common market and provided that only the original Italian product could be supplied to certain customers/outlets. There were also provisions about manufacture only at approved sites, confidentiality, advertising, and non-assignment. The Commission held that the following provisions were outside Article 81(1): the ban on exports outside the common market, as in the circumstances there was little chance of this indirectly affecting inter-Member State trade; the restriction of the licence to those plants capable of guaranteeing the quality of the product;[246] the obligation to follow the licensor's manufacturing instructions and to buy secret raw materials from the licensor, as this was central to the product being of proper 'Campari' quality;[247] the confidentiality of the know-how; the minimum advertising commitments and the prohibition on assignment.

---

[240] Franchising agreements were formerly dealt with in a specific block exemption, Reg. 4087/88 [1988] OJ L359/46: see *supra* Chap. 9.

[241] Reg. 2790/1999 [1999] OJ L336/21, Art. 2(3): see *supra* Chap. 9.

[242] *Re the Agreement of Davide Campari-Milano SpA* [1978] OJ L70/69, [1978] 2 CMLR 397.

[243] *Moosehead/Whitbread* [1990] OJ L100/32, [1991] 4 CMLR 391.

[244] *Re the Agreement of Davide-Campari-Milano SpA* [1978] OJ L70/69, [1978] 2 CMLR 397.

[245] The UK and Ireland were covered by a straightforward distribution agreement which fell within the block exemption then in force, Reg. 67/67 [1967] OJ Spec. Ed. 10.

[246] Note that so-called 'site licences' have since become more contentious: see *supra* 599–600.

[247] Certain other ingredients did not necessarily have to be bought from the licensor but had to be sourced on the basis of objective quality considerations.

Other clauses, including the exclusivity and the active sales ban, were held to infringe Article 81(1).

However, the Commission granted an exemption. This part of the decision is a particularly good illustration of how the four criteria in Article 81(3) are applied. Note that in paragraph 71 the Commission distinguishes between the effects of a non-competition clause in a trade mark licence and one in a patent licence.

Re the Agreement of Davide-Campari-Milano SpA [1978] OJ L70/69, [1978] 2 CMLR 397

Commission

68. 1. The exclusivity granted by Campari-Milano contributes to improving the production and distribution of the products. By giving each licensee a guarantee that no other undertaking will obtain a licence within its allocated territory, and that in this territory neither Campari-Milano nor any other licensee may manufacture products bearing the licensor's trade mark this commitment confers upon each licensee an advantage in its allotted territory. This territorial advantage is such as to permit a sufficient return on the investment made by each licensee for the purpose of manufacturing the product bearing the trade mark under conditions acceptable to the licensor and holder of the trade mark, and it enables the licensee to increase its production capacity and constantly to improve the already long-established distribution network.

69. In practice the exclusivity granted has allowed each licensee to improve its existing plant and to build new plant. It has also enabled each licensee to strengthen its efforts to promote the brand, doubling the total volume of sales in the Benelux countries and Germany over the last six years, and, by establishing a multistage distribution network, to secure a constantly increasing number of customers and thus to ensure supplies throughout the allotted territory.

70. 2. The ban on dealing in competing products also contributes to improving distribution of the licensed products by concentrating sales efforts, encouraging the build-up of stocks and shortening delivery times.

71. The restriction on the licensees' freedom to deal in other products at the same time as the products here in question prevents the licensees from neglecting Campari in the event of conflict between the promotion of Campari sales and possible interest in another product. Although a non-competition clause in a licensing agreement concerning industrial property rights based on the result of a creative activity, such as a patent, would constitute a barrier to technical and economic progress by preventing the licensees from taking an interest in other techniques and products, this is not the case with the licensing agreements under consideration here. The aim pursued by the parties, as is clear from the agreements taken as a whole, is to decentralise manufacture within the EEC and to rationalise the distribution system linked to it, and thus to promote the sale of Campari-Milano's Bitter, manufactured from the same concentrates provided by Campari-Milano, according to the same mixing process and using the same ingredients, and bearing the same trade mark, as that of the licensor.

72. The prohibition on dealing in competing products, therefore, makes for improved distribution of the relevant product in the same way as do exclusive dealing agreements containing a similar clause, which are automatically exempted by Regulation 67/67/EEC; a declaration that the prohibition in Article [81(1)] is inapplicable to this clause is accordingly justified.

73. 3. Distribution will also be improved by the prohibition against the parties engaging in an active sales policy outside their respective territories. This restriction on the licensees will help to

concentrate their sales efforts, and provide a better supply to consumers in their territories for which they have particular responsibility, without preventing buyers elsewhere in the Community from securing supplies freely from any of the licensees. Application of the same restriction to Campari-Milano encourages the efforts made by the each territory allotted; the licensees thus have the benefit of a certain protection relative to Campari-Milano's strong market position.

74. 4. The obligation on licensees to supply the original Italian product rather than that which they themselves manufacture, when selling to diplomatic corps, ships' victuallers, foreign armed forces and generally speaking all organisations with duty-free facilities, also helps to promote sales of Campari-Milano's Bitter. By restricting licensees' freedom to supply the products they manufacture themselves it makes sure that particular categories of consumers, who are deemed to be outside the licensee's territory and are usually required to move frequently from one territory to another, can always purchase the same original product with all its traditional features as regards both composition and outward appearance. Even though quality standards are observed, it is impossible in particular to avoid differences in taste between the products of the various manufacturers. This obligation is thus designed to prevent these consumers from turning to other competing products and to ensure that they continue to buy Bitter Campari, with the facility of being able to obtain stocks from their local dealer. Further, such consumers are not prevented from freely obtaining the licensees' own products even though any such purchase would be on the normal trading conditions applicable to non-duty free purchasers.

75. B. The licensing agreements have increased the quantities of Bitter Campari available to consumers and improve distribution, so that consumers benefit directly. There are other products of bitter on the market, and effective competition will be strengthened by the growing quantities produced by Campari-Milano's licensees, so that it can be assumed that the improvements resulting from the agreements and the benefits which the licensees obtain from them are shared by consumers.

76. As buyers may secure supplies of Bitter from other territories through unsolicited orders, they are in a position to exert pressure on the prices charged by the exclusive licensee in their territory if these should be too high.

77. C. The restrictions of competition imposed on the parties must be considered indispensable to the attainment of the benefits set out above. None of the restrictions could be omitted without endangering the parties' object of promoting sales of Bitter Campari by concentrating the activities of the licensees on this product and offering the same original product to certain customers. In particular, none of the licensees and in all probability no other undertaking in the spirituous liquors industry would have been prepared to make the investment necessary for a significant increase in sales of Bitter if it were not sure of being protected from competition from other licensees or Campari-Milano itself.

78. D. The licensing agreements which are the subject of this Decision do not give Campari-Milano or its licensees the possibility of eliminating competition in respect of a substantial part of the Bitter products in question. In the EEC there exists a fairly large number of other well-known brands of bitter, which are all able to compete against Bitter Campari. Campari-Milano's licensees and Campari-Milano itself are also free to sell the Campari products in question within the Common Market but outside their territory for which they have particular responsibility.

(iii) THE *MOOSEHEAD/WHITBREAD* DECISION[248]

This case concerned the manufacture in the UK of a lager produced by the Canadian brewer Mooosehead. According to the Commission, it had a taste typical of Canadian lagers.[249] Under the agreement Moosehead granted to the British brewer, Whitbread, the sole and exclusive right to produce and promote, market, and sell beer manufactured for sale under the name 'Moosehead' in the UK using Moosehead's secret know-how. Moosehead gave Whitbread an exclusive licence of its UK trade mark rights and agreed to provide it with all the relevant know-how (the know-how licence was non-exclusive) and to supply it with the necessary yeast. Whitbread agreed not to make active sales outside its territory, not to produce or promote any other beer identified as a Canadian beer, not to contest the ownership or validity of the trade mark, to comply with Moosehead's directions in relation to the know-how and to buy the yeast only from Moosehead or a designated third party.

The Commission held that the exclusivity provisions and the active sales ban in the trade mark licence were caught by Article 81(1). It did not consider the no-challenge clause to the *ownership* of the mark was caught because whoever's name it was registered in any parties would be prevented from using it. A no-challenge clause in respect of *validity*, however, was another matter. The Commission said that such clauses *may* infringe Article 81(1) but that it would depend on the circumstances. Here it did not infringe:

15. 4. In relation to the trade mark non-challenge clause:
(a) in general terms, a trade mark non-challenge clause can refer to the ownership and/or the validity of the trade mark:

— The ownership of a trade mark may, in particular, be challenged on grounds of the prior use or prior registration of an identical trade mark.
A clause in an exclusive trade mark licence agreement obliging the licensee not to challenge the ownership of a trade mark, as specified in the above paragraph, does not constitute a restriction of competition within the meaning of Article [81(1)]. Whether or not the licensor or licensee has the ownership of the trade mark, the use of it by any other party is prevented in any event, and competition would thus not be affected.
— The validity of a trade mark may be contested on any ground under national law, and in particular on the grounds that it is generic or descriptive in nature. In such an event, should the challenge be upheld, the trade mark may fall within the public domain and may thereafter be used without restriction by the licensee and any other party.

Such a clause may constitute a restriction of competition within the meaning of Article [81(1)], because it may contribute to the maintenance of a trade mark that would be an unjustified barrier to entry into a given market.

Moreover in order for any restriction of competition to fall under Article [81(1)], it mist be appreciable. The ownership of a trade mark only gives the holder the exclusive right to sell products under that name. Other parties are free to sell the product in question under a different trade mark or trade name. Only where the use of a well-known trade mark would be an important advantage to any company entering or competing in any given market and the absence of which therefore constitutes a significant barrier to entry, would this clause which impedes the licensee to challenge the validity of the trade mark, constitute an appreciable restriction of competition within the meaning of Article [81(1)].

---

[248] *Moosehead/Whitbread* [1990] OJ L100/32, [1991] 4 CMLR 391.
[249] *Ibid.*, para. 3.

(b) In the present case Whitbread is unable to challenge both the ownership and the validity of the trade mark.

As far as the validity of the trade mark is concerned it must be noted that the trade mark is comparatively new to the lager market in the territory. The maintenance of the 'Moosehead' trade mark will thus not constitute an appreciable barrier to entry for any other company entering or competing in the beer market in the United Kingdom. Accordingly, the Commission considers that the trade mark non-challenge clause included in the agreement, in so far as it concerns its validity (see the second indent of point 15.4 above), does not constitute an appreciable restriction of competition and does not fall under Article [81(1)].

This decision marked a change in the Commission's previously negative attitude to no-challenge clauses, which was ultimately reflected in the provisions of Regulation 240/96, discussed above.[250] The Commission granted an exemption to the agreement, holding that the exclusivity provisions, active sales ban, and non-competition clauses met the Article 81(3) criteria, particularly in view of the amount of inter—brand competition on the UK beer market.

H. TRADE MARK DELIMITATION AGREEMENTS

Trade mark delimitation agreements are entered into in order to settle disputes. They usually occur where one party opposes the other's application for, or use of, a mark on the ground that it is confusingly similar to one owned by the first party for similar products and the agreement may settle protracted litigation. The ECJ and Commission have made it clear that the provisions in such agreements may infringe Article 81(1) just like any others and that the context in which the agreement is made does not mean that it is immune from the application of Article 81(1).[251] Delimitation agreements may restrict the class of products for which a party may use the mark, or the territories in which he may use the mark, or a party may accept a no-challenge obligation in relation to certain products or territories. In *BAT* v. *Commission*[252] the Court took a more liberal attitude to delimitation agreements than the Commission had done previously. The position seems to be that an agreement will be outside Article 81(1) if there is a genuine risk of confusion between the parties and it is not just a guise for market-sharing, and if the agreement does not divide markets within the EC (at least unless there is no less restrictive means of dealing with the dispute).[253]

---

[250] See *supra* 606.

[251] See Case 65/86, *Bayer AG and Maschinenfabrik Hennecke* v. *Heinz Süllhöfer* [1988] ECR 5249, [1990] 4 CMLR 182 concerning a no-challenge clause.

[252] Case 35/83 *BAT* v. *Commission* [1985] ECR 363, [1985] 2 CMLR 470, the appeal from *Toltecs/Dorcet* [1982] OJ L379/19, [1983] 1 CMLR 412.

[253] See also *Sirdar/Phildar* [1976] 1 CMLR D93; *Hershey/Schiffers*, Commission Press Release IP(90)87; *Chiquita/Fyffes* Commission Press Release IP(92)461; *Synthex/Synthelabo* [1990] 4 CMLR 343.

I. COPYRIGHT LICENCES

(i) GENERAL

As with trade mark licences there is no specific block exemption covering copyright licences but where they are 'ancillary' to a licence of a patent and/or know-how they may be covered by Regulation 240/96. They may also be part of an agreement covered by the vertical restraints block exemption, Regulation 2790/1999.[254] As with trade marks, Regulation 240/96 and the cases and decisions on licences of other types of right can be used as guides, as there is little actual authority on copyright itself. There are some differences, however, in the way in which exclusivity is treated.

(ii) EXCLUSIVITY IN COPYRIGHT LICENCES

The way in which the competition rules apply to exclusivity in copyright licences varies according to the nature of the protected work. There is a distinction between works exploited by performance and those exploited in other ways. As regards the latter it seems that the principles in *Nungesser*[255] apply. In *Knoll/Hille-Form*,[256] a licence of various rights including copyright in respect of design furniture, the licensor undertook not to grant further licences in the allotted territory and not to exploit its rights there. The licensee was prohibited from selling in the rest of the common market where the licensor operated. As it says in the *Thirteenth Competition Policy Report*:

In investigating the case, the Commission had serious doubts whether the agreement met the conditions laid down by the Court of Justice in its Maize Seeds judgment as to when an exclusive licence will not be considered as incompatible with Article [81](1)—or whether any similar circumstances were present. Neither the 'newness' of the products concerned nor the amount of investment involved seemed to indicate that the exclusivity granted was indispensable to launching the products on the relevant market, at any rate not for the length of time originally envisaged (eight years).[257]

However, in the case of exploitation through performance, the ECJ held in *Coditel II*[258] that exclusivity (amounting in effect to absolute territorial protection) did not in itself infringe Article 81(1). This was because the Court recognized the special nature of the product and rights concerned. It will be recalled that in *Coditel I*[259] the Court considered the application of the exhaustion of rights doctrine to copyright in films and concluded that the owner's rights were not exhausted by the first showing of the film because the specific subject-matter was the entitlement of the owner to charge each time the film was shown.

---

[254] [1999] OJ L336/21, See *supra* 611.

[255] Case 258/78 *Nungesser* v. *EC Commission* [1982] ECR 2015, [1983] 1 CMLR 278: see *supra* 583–585.

[256] *XIIIth Report on Competition Policy* (Commission, 1983), pts 142–146.

[257] *Ibid.*, pt. 144. The Commission refused an exemption partly because of the significant market positions of both parties and the parties agreed to drop the export ban and to allow direct sales into each other's territory.

[258] Case 262/81, *Coditel* v. *SA Ciné Vog Films* (*Coditel II*) [1982] ECR 3381, [1983] 1 CMLR 49.

[259] Case 62/79, *SA Compagnie Générale pour la Diffusion de la Télévision, Coditel* v. *Ciné Vog Films* (*Coditel I*) [1980] ECR 881, [1981] 2 CMLR 362: see *supra* 571–572.

The same facts (a Belgian cable company relaying in Belgium the transmission of a film shown in Germany for which Ciné Vog had exclusive distribution rights in Belgium) gave rise to a second case in which the cable company claimed that the exclusive licence granted to Ciné Vog infringed Article 81(1).

Case 262/81 *Coditel* v. *SA Ciné Vog Films* (*Coditel II*) [1982] ECR 3381, [1983] 1 CMLR 49

Court of Justice

10. It should be noted, by way of a preliminary observation, that Article [30] permits prohibitions or restrictions on trade between Member States provided that they are justified on grounds *inter alia* of the protection of industrial and commercial property, a term which covers literary and artistic property, including copyright, whereas the main proceedings are concerned with the question of prohibitions or restrictions placed upon the free movement of services.

11. In this regard, as the Court held in its judgment of 18 March 1980 (*Coditel v Ciné-Vog Films* [1980] ECR 881), the problems involved in the observance of a film producer's rights in relation to the requirements of the Treaty are not the same as those of which arise in connection with literary and artistic works the placing of which at the disposal of the public is inseparable from the circulation of the material form of the works, as in the case of books or records, whereas the film belongs to the category of literary and artistic works made available to the public by performances which may be infinitely repeated and the commercial exploitation of which comes under the movement of services, no matter whether the means whereby it is shown to the public be the cinema or television.

12. In the same judgment the Court further held that the right of the owner of the copyright in a film and his assigns to require fees for any showing of that film is part of the essential function of copyright.

13. The distinction, implicit in Article [30], between the existence of a right conferred by the legislation of a Member State in regard to the protection of artistic and intellectual property, which cannot be affected by the provisions of the Treaty, and the exercise of such right, which might constitute a disguised restriction on trade between Member States, also applies where that right is exercised in the context of the movement of services.

14. Just as it is conceivable that certain aspects of the manner in which the right is exercised may prove to be incompatible with Articles [49] and [50] it is equally conceivable that some aspects may prove to be incompatible with Article [81] where they serve to give effect to an agreement, decision or concerted practice which may have as its object or effect the prevention, restriction or distortion of competition within the common market.

15. However, the mere fact that the owner of the copyright in a film has granted to a sole licensee the exclusive right to exhibit that film in the territory of a Member State and, consequently, to prohibit, during a specified period, its showing by others, is not sufficient to justify the finding that such a contract must be regarded as the purpose, the means or the result of an agreement, decision or concerted practice prohibited by the Treaty.

16. The characteristics of the cinematographic industry and of its markets in the Community, especially those relating to dubbing and subtitling for the benefit of different language groups, to the possibilities of television broadcasts, and to the system of financing cinematographic production in Europe serve to show that an exclusive exhibition licence is not, in itself, such as to prevent, restrict or distort competition.

17. Although copyright in a film and the right deriving from it, namely that of exhibiting the film, are not, therefore, as such subject to the prohibitions contained in Article 81, the exercise of those rights may, none the less, come within the said prohibitions where there are economic or legal circumstances the effect of which is to restrict film distribution to an appreciable degree or to distort competition on the cinematographic market, regard being had to the specific characteristics of that market.

18. Since neither the question referred to the Court nor the file on the case provides any information in this respect, it is for the national court to make such inquiries as may be necessary.

19. It must therefore be stated that it is for national courts, where appropriate, to make such inquiries and in particular to establish whether or not the exercise of the exclusive right to exhibit a cinematographic film creates barriers which are artificial and unjustifiable in terms of the needs of the cinematographic industry, or the possibility of charging fees which exceed a fair return on investment, or an exclusivity the duration of which is disproportionate to those requirements, and whether or not, from a general point of view, such exercise within a given geographic area is such as to prevent, restrict or distort competition within the common market.

20. Accordingly, the answer to be given to the question referred to the Court must be that a contract whereby the owner of the copyright in a film grants an exclusive right to exhibit that film for a specific period in the territory of a Member State is not, as such, subject to the prohibitions contained in Article [81] of the Treaty. It is, however, where appropriate, for the national court to ascertain whether, in a given case, the manner in which the exclusive right conferred by that contract is exercised is subject to a situation in the economic or legal sphere the object or effect of which is to prevent or restrict the distribution of films or to distort competition within the cinematographic market, regard being had to the specific characteristics of the market.

The Court therefore accepted that the absolute territorial protection given by the exclusive right was not *of itself* prohibited by Article 81(1), given the nature of the protected work and the characteristics of the film industry. It did not, nevertheless, rule out the possibility that in certain circumstances the exercise of the exclusive right might fall within Article 81(1). However, the criteria in the qualifications in paragraphs 17 and 19 as to when exclusivity *will* infringe the prohibition (the exclusivity might create artificial and unjustifiable barriers to trade, lead to excessive prices, or be for an excessive duration) are imprecise and uncertain.[260] Some indication of how the Commission will apply them was given in its decision in *Film Purchases by German Television Stations*.[261] In this case an exclusive broadcasting licence of MGM/UA films was granted to a group of German TV stations for fifteen years with a further 'selection period' which preceded this.[262] The Commission held that the agreement was within Article 81(1) because of the number of films covered by the transaction[263] and the long duration of the arrangements which excluded third parties for a length of time which was described as 'disproportionate within the *Coditel II* judgment of the

---

[260] Para. 19 mentions whether the rewards are excessive, although no indication is given of how the national court is to make such judgments in the context of the film industry.

[261] [1989] OJ L284/36.

[262] In fact the Commission left open whether the transaction amounted to a licence 'in the legal and technical sense' or an assignment of rights for a limited period and to a limited extent. In either case the Commission considered that there was a restriction of competition: *ibid.*, para. 41.

[263] And the fact that many of them were important or noteworthy or had 'particular mass appeal such as the James Bond films': *ibid.*, para. 43.

Court of Justice' and 'an artificial barrier to other undertakings'.[264] The agreement was exempted after provision was made for third-party broadcasters in Germany to apply for licences to show the films at times which did not clash with those of the licensees. The Commission held that Article 81(3) was satisfied because the arrangements as a whole allowed more films to be shown to German audiences and to be dubbed into German.

(ii) THE LIKELY TREATMENT OF OTHER TERMS IN COPYRIGHT LICENCES

Given the Commission's view of the similarity between copyright and patent licences it appears that the matters whitelisted in Regulation 240/96, such as minimum royalties and quantities, field of use restrictions, post-termination use, and sub-licensing prohibitions will escape Article 81(1) in copyright licences. In *Neilson-Hordell/Richmark*[265] the Commission closed its file after insisting on the removal from a copyright licence of a no-challenge clause, a non-competition clause, a clause requiring payment of royalties on products not protected by any copyright of the licensor, and a clause requiring the licensee to transfer to the licensor the licensee's copyright in improvements made to the licensed products. The Commission stressed the uniformity of its approach with that towards patents.[266]

J. SOFTWARE LICENCES

The main way in which software is protected, at least in the EU, is through copyright.[267] Council Directive 91/250 on the legal protection of computer programs[268] was adopted in order to harmonize the way in which Member States protect software. It stipulates that this should be done through copyright. Article 1(1) states:

Member States shall protect computer programs, by copyright, as literary works within the meaning of the Berne Convention for the Protection of Literary and Artistic Works.

Nevertheless, the application of copyright protection to software, and hence the application of competition law to the licensing of that copyright, does have some special features.[269] Although the details of software licensing will not be dealt with here[270] some general issues should be noted.

Software licensing is very common as software is usually licensed rather than sold. This is

---

[264] *Ibid.*, para. 44.

[265] Commissions *XIIth Report on Competition Policy* (Commission, 1982) pts 88–89.

[266] Presumably therefore the softening of its attitude to no-challenge clauses since this case, as shown in Reg. 240/96[1996] OJ L31/2, also applies in respect of copyright licences.

[267] Software 'as such' is not patentable (European Patent Convention Art. 52) but software which produces a technical effect is patentable. It is also possible for some forms of software such as source codes to constitute know-how.

[268] [1991] OJ L122/42.

[269] See generally, I. Forrester, 'Software Licensing in the Light of Current EC Competition Law Considerations' [1992] *ECLR* 5.

[270] Reference should be made to specialist and practitioner works, such as Butterworths Competition Law, Division V, Chap. 6, Section D.

because it is expensive to create software but easy and cheap to copy it. The author of the software therefore needs to control copying in order to obtain a proper financial return and tries to do this by only licensing its use and by hedging the use around with restrictions. Other features of software licensing are the speed of developments in the industry, so that the producer will be looking for a return in the short rather than the long term, and the fact that it is often necessary for the user (or a third party on its behalf) to modify the software for its own needs, in which case the producer may licence the software specifically for the licensee to modify it for particular purposes. There is a strong argument for copyright in software to be treated as a special case, and should the ECJ ever consider the matter it might well recognize its special nature in the same way as it recognised the particular character- istics of the film industry in the *Coditel* cases, and the particular need to protect seed in *Erauw-Jacquéry*.[271]

Another special feature of software licensing is the existence of Directive 91/250. Article 4 sets out what constitute the 'exclusive rights' of the rightholder, Article 5 provides for exceptions and Article 6 gives licensees a special right of decompilation.

Council directive 91/250 on the legal protection of computer programes [1991] OJ L122/42

Article 4

Restricted acts

Subject to the provisions of Articles 5 and 6, the exclusive rights of the rightholder within the meaning of Article 2, shall include the right to do or to authorize:

(a) the permanent or temporary reproduction of a computer program by any means and in any form, in part or in whole. Insofar as loading, displaying, running, transmission or storage of the computer program necessitate such reproduction, such acts shall be subject to author- ization by the rightholder;

(b) the translation, adaptation, arrangement and any other alternation of a computer program and the reproduction of the results thereof, without prejudice to the rights of the person who alters the program;

(c) any form of distribution to the public, including the rental, of the original computer pro- gram or of copies thereof. The first sale in the Community of a copy of a program by the rightholder or with his consent shall exhaust the distribution right within the Community of that copy, with the exception of the right to control further rental of the program or a copy thereof.

Article 5

Exceptions to the restricted acts

1. In the absence of specific contractual provisions, the acts referred to in Article 4 (a) and (b) shall not require authorization by the rightholder where they are necessary for the use of the computer program by the lawful acquirer in accordance with its intended purpose, including for error correction.

---

[271] See *supra* 587 and 617.

2. The making of a back-up copy by a person having a right to use the computer program may not be prevented by contract insofar as it is necessary for that use.

3. The person having a right to use a copy of a computer program shall be entitled, without the authorization of the rightholder, to observe, study or test the functioning of the program in order to determine the ideas and principles which underlie any element of the program if he does so while performing any of the acts of loading, displaying, running, transmitting or storing the program which he is entitled to do.

Article 6

Decompilation

1. The authorization of the rightholder shall not be required where reproduction of the code and translation of its form within the meaning of Article 4 (a) and (b) are indispensable to obtain the information necessary to achieve the interoperability of an independently created computer program with other programs, provided that the following conditions are met:

   (a) these acts are performed by the licensee or by another person having a right to use a copy of a program, or on their behalf by a person authorized to do so;

   (b) the information necessary to achieve interoperability has not previously been readily available to the persons referred to in subparagraph (a); and

   (c) these acts are confined to the parts of the original program which are necessary to achieve interoperability.

2. The provisions of paragraph 1 shall not permit the information obtained through its application:

   (a) to be used for goals other than to achieve the interoperability of the independently created computer program;

   (b) to be given to others, except when necessary for the interoperability of the independently created computer program; or

   (c) to be used for the development, production or marketing of a computer program substantially similar in its expression, or for any other act which infringes copyright.

Article 4 in effect sets out what comprises the 'specific subject-matter' of copyright in computer programs and it may reasonably be assumed that, although the Directive cannot actually affect the application of the competition rules, any clause in a licence safeguarding those rights would not fall foul of Article 81(1) unless it contradicted the exceptions in Articles 5 and 6. Article 6 is a crucial provision in that the licensee is given the right to decompile the licensed program (i.e. to run the program in order to reverse engineer and analyse how it functions) where it is necessary to achieve 'interoperability', i.e.to ensure that independently created programs can be used with 'other programs' (Article 6(1)). 'Other programs' covers not only the licensed program itself but also software which *competes* with the licensed program. Interoperability has become a major issue in the field of computer technology and the recitals to the Directive provide that its provisions are without prejudice to the application of Articles 81 and 82 if a dominant supplier refuses to make available information which is necessary for interoperability.[272]

One issue not dealt with in the Directive is that of 'site licences' and provisions which tie

---

[272] See further *supra* Chap. 7.

the licensed software to being used with only one computer. Site licences generally are discussed above[273] in the context of the Technology Transfer block exemption. Licences which tie the software to use with only the licensor's hardware will infringe Article 81(1)(e) and may also infringe Article 82.

6. THE APPLICATION OF ARTICLE 82 TO INTELLECTUAL PROPERTY RIGHTS

A. GENERAL

There are two facets to the relationship between Article 82 and intellectual property rights. First, there is the extent to which the ownership of intellectual property rights puts the holder in a dominant position. Secondly, there is the question whether the holding, acquisition, or exploitation of intellectual property rights can constitute an abuse of a dominant position, and if so in what circumstances.

The application of Article 82 to intellectual property rights is also dealt with in Chapters 6 and 7 because it is impossible to divorce these questions about intellectual property rights from the operation of Article 82 as a whole. Looking at them in isolation from other developments in Article 82 jurisprudence can lead to an incomplete and distorted picture. Reference should therefore be made to those chapters. Nevertheless there are some aspects of the topic which particularly relate to the nature of intellectual property and these are considered below.

B. INTELLECTUAL PROPERTY RIGHTS AND DOMINANCE

This is discussed in Chapter 6 and only summarized here.

The basic principle is that 'so far as a dominant position is concerned, it is to be remembered at the outset that mere ownership of an intellectual property right cannot confer such a position'.[274] Although it is common to talk of the 'monopoly' conferred by an intellectual property right such as a patent, this is not the same as a monopoly or dominant position in competition law. There is a difference between a legal and an economic monopoly. The latter depends on whether the product protected by the intellectual property right is co-extensive with a 'relevant market' in the competition sense. If the protected product is part of a wider market the intellectual property right will not in itself create dominance, but if the market is narrowed to comprise only the product covered by the intellectual property right then there

---

[273] See *supra* 599–600.
[274] Cases C–241–241/91 P, *RTE & ITP* v. *Commission* [1995] ECR I–743, [1995] 4 CMLR 718, para. 46: see also Case 78/70, *Deutsche Grammophon* v. *Metro* [1971] ECR 487, [1971] CMLR 631, para. 16.

will be a *de facto* monopoly, because the intellectual property right will constitute a barrier to entry preventing supply substitution or new entrants coming onto the market. The ECJ and the Commission have often defined very narrow markets, and in some cases the narrow market so defined has been completely covered by an undertaking's intellectual property rights. This leads inevitably to a finding of dominance. The definition of a single brand of spare parts or consumables as a relevant product market in *Hugin*,[275] *Hilti*,[276] *Volvo*[277] and *Renault*[278] illustrate this.

C. INTELLECTUAL PROPERTY RIGHTS AND ABUSE

(i) THE ACQUISITION OF AN EXCLUSIVE LICENCE

The CFI has held, upholding the Commission, that it can be an abuse for a dominant undertaking to acquire an exclusive patent licence.

Case T-51/89, *Tetra Pak Rausing* v. *Commission* [1990] ECR II–309, [1991] 4 CMLR 334[279]

Tetra Pak was held to be dominant in the market for aseptic liquid-food packaging. It took over another company, Liquipak, which was the exclusive licensee of a patent which was relevant to the manufacture of aseptic packaging. Tetra Pak thereby acquired the exclusive licence. A competitor of Tetra Pak, Elopak, complained to the Commission that this acquisition constituted an infringement of Article 82. After the Commission issued a Statement of Objections Tetra Pak abandoned all claims to exclusivity. Nevertheless the Commission proceeded to a formal Decision holding that Tetra Pak had infringed Article 82 as it wished to clarify the legal position. Tetra Pak appealed to the Court of First Instance. One issue in the case was whether a patent licence which complied with the block exemption on patent licensing agreements, 2349/84, could be the subject-matter of an Article 82 infringement. This aspect of the case on the relationship between Article [81] and Article 82 is dealt with in Chapter 5. The extract from the judgment below explains how and when the acquisition of an exclusive licence can constitute an abuse.

Court of First Instance

23. Turning to the specific nature of the conduct whose compatibility with Article [82] is considered in the Decision, this Court holds that the mere fact that an undertaking in a dominant position acquires an exclusive license does not *per se* constitute abuse within the meaning of Article [82]. For the purpose of applying Article [82], the circumstances surrounding the acquisition, and in particular its effects on the structure of competition in the relevant market, must be taken into account. This interpretation is borne out by the case law of the Court of Justice, in which the concept of abuse is defined as 'an objective concept relating to the behaviour of an

275 Case 22/78, *Hugin Kassaregister AB* v. *EC Commission* [1979] ECR 1869, [1979] 3 CMLR 345.

276 Case T–30/89, *Hilti* v. *Commission* [1991] ECR II–1439, [1992] 4 CMLR 16 and Case C–53/92 P *Hilti* v. *Commission* [1994] ECR I–666, [1994] 4 CMLR 614.

277 Case 238/87, AB Volvo v. *Erik Veng* [1988] ECR 6211, [1989] 4 CMLR 122.

278 Case 53/87, CICCRA v. *Renault* [1988] ECR 6039, [1990] 4 CMLR 265.

279 On appeal from *Tetra Pak* (*BTG Licence*) [1988] OJ L272/27, [1990] 4 CMLR 47: the case was not appealed from the CFI to the ECJ.

undertaking in a dominant position which is such as to influence the structure of a market where, as a result of the very presence of the undertaking in question, the degree of competition is weakened and which, through recourse to methods different from those which condition normal competition in products or services on the basis of the transactions of commercial operators, has the effect of hindering the maintenance of the degree of competition still existing in the market or the growth of that competition. ... So, here, the Commission was right not to put in issue the exclusive licence as such, but rather to object specifically under Article [82] to the anti-competitive effect of its being acquired by the applicant. It is plain from the reasoning and conclusions of the Decision that the infringement of Article [82] found by the Commission stemmed precisely from Tetra Pak's acquisition of the exclusive licence 'in the specific circumstances of this case'. The specific context to which the Commission refers is expressly characterised as being the fact that acquisition of the exclusivity of the licence not only 'strengthened Tetra's very considerable dominance but also had the effect of preventing, or at the very least considerably delaying, the entry of a new competitor into a market where very little if any competition is found' (paragraph 45 of the Decision; see also paragraph 60). The decisive factor in the finding that acquisition of the exclusive licence constituted an abuse therefore lay quite specifically in the applicant's position in the relevant market and in particular, as appears from the Decision (paragraph 27), in the fact that at the material time the right to use the process protected by the BTG licence was alone capable of giving an undertaking the means of competing effectively with the applicant in the field of the aseptic packaging of milk. The takeover of Liquipak was no more than the means—to which the Commission has attached no particular significance in applying Article [82]—by which the applicant acquired the exclusivity of the BTG licence, the effect of which was to deprive other undertakings of the means of competing with the applicant.

The acquisition of an exclusive licence by a dominant firm is not, therefore, necessarily an abuse. It will depend on the structure of competition in the market and the surrounding circumstances. In this instance Tetra Pak was in a very strong position on the market and the technology protected by the patent was the only existing process which gave another company the chance of effectively competing with it. The acquisition of exclusivity would have had serious effects on the structure of competition. The case is a paradigm example of an anti-competitive abuse.

(ii) THE EXPLOITATION OF RIGHTS GENERALLY

There are inherent problems in trying to reconcile the exploitation of intellectual property rights with the concept of abuse. First, there is the question of so-called 'exploitative' abuses, which include the charging of unfair or excessive prices.[280] Secondly, once abuse is defined to encompass 'anti-competitive' abuses, meaning conduct which goes beyond 'normal' competition and affects the structure of competition on already dominated markets,[281] there is the difficulty of distinguishing such conduct from the normal exploitation of intellectual property rights.

Before looking at the conflict—if such it is—between intellectual property rights and competition policy it is necessary to examine the object of intellectual property law. That body of law itself attempts to balance the need to give incentives for innovation with the interest of the public in having access to the products protected by the rights. Patent law is

[280] See *supra* Chap. 7.
[281] *Ibid.*

the clearest example of this balancing act: the grant of the patent gives the owner a twenty-year monopoly on exploitation, but at the price of having the details of the process made public, so that at the end of the twenty-year period everyone else has access to it. The owner's original monopoly enables him to reap the reward for the innovation and thereafter the public interest in access and dissemination takes over. The question is how far this inherent balancing act within intellectual property law between incentives and access makes interference by competition laws on monopolies superfluous. Is there any need for competition law to control the exploitation of the rights when intellectual property law has already taken care to strike a balance with the public interest? Govaere[282] argues that 'no additional restraints on intellectual property owners need to be introduced in order to safeguard competition; it suffices to reinforce the restrictions inherent in the different types of intellectual property rights'. In the extract below, however, Anderman argues that there *is* a role for competition law:

S. Anderman, EC *Competition Law and Intellectual Property Rights* (Clarendon, Oxford, 1998) 249–50[283]

. . . A case has sometimes been made that IPR legislation already incorporates its own form of self-regulation which balances access to markets with reward for invention. . . .

. . . it seems to be overly optimistic to expect that IPR legislation by itself can regulate the exercise of IPRs so comprehensively that it meets the objectives of public policy generally and competition policy in particular in relation to markets. The offer of an exclusive right to the undertaking or individual for a fixed period of time by IPR legislation is granted irrespective of the market power of the owner or the quality of the innovation, assuming that minimum standards of qualification are met. It entails no careful assessment of the balance between the social benefits of the reward and the social costs of the exclusive right in the case of any individual IPR. It provides, for the most part, a standard period of exclusivity for all IPRs which qualify. Suggestions that it would be more rational from an economic policy perspective to recognize this point by regulating IPRs by varying the length of protection depending on the balance between social benefit and social cost(. . .) have been acknowledged to be impractical. For pragmatic reasons, IPR legislation adopts a single period of time for exclusivity for all who meet the minimum requirements for validity.

The thinking underlying the grant of a fixed period of exclusivity is that market forces should determine the return to the inventor during that period. The reason for this is that it is difficult to place a value on an invention and it would not be appropriate to leave to a state agency the task of providing a reward based on industrial policy considerations.

However, the assumptions of IPR legislation that inventors are entitled to appropriate 'what the market can bear' presuppose that there is actually a market to regulate the return to the IPR owner. The theory is that there should be an appropriation of the value related to the invention, not the rewards of market power unrelated to the invention. Even under the assumptions of the IPR legislation, the return extracted can be excessive.

Whilst IPR legislation cannot be expected to assume the responsibilities of competition law to ensure that market forces actually operate in any one market, it can regulate the scope of IPR

[282] I. Govaere, *The Use and Abuse of Intellectual Property Rights in EC Law* (Sweet & Maxwell, London, 1996), 305.

[283] See also T.F. Cotter: 'Intellectual Property and the Essential Facilities Doctrine' [1999] *Antitrust Bulletin* 211.

protection to protect access to markets and innovation. IPR legislation such as patent laws build in certain safeguards to the scope of the exclusivity granted. Thus, a patent is granted only to a 'single invention' and a compulsory licence is available in cases where a licence or cross-licence is arbitrarily refused or the patent is not used. In the development of IPR legislation within the EC, moreover, there are signs that the issue of interoperability is modifying the contours of the grant of exclusivity. Possibly because the process of innovation is more complex today in an era of high technology, care is taken to ensure that the scope of intellectual property exclusivity does not extend to the access elements of an invention. Access information is sometimes required to be made available to competitors making related products, as if there is acceptance of a modern imperative that there must be certain safeguards for diffusion.

The concept of interoperability contained within the Computer Program Directive offers a good example of this policy. The presence of section 5 (protection of interfaces) indicates that access protocols and interfaces are regarded as not within the legitimate scope for exclusivity. Section 6 (permissibility of reverse analysis) suggests a concern to ensure that the innovation can be used as a platform for further innovation even during the period of exclusivity. Whether this policy offers an example of competition policy incorporated into intellectual property law or an acceptance of the principle of interoperability within IPR law itself is a debatable issue. What is undoubtedly the case is that interoperability has become an important issue on the overall agenda of legal and economic policy.

(iii) REFUSALS TO SUPPLY INTELLECTUAL PROPERTY RIGHTS

The main area of tension between intellectual property rights and Article 82 is whether it is an abuse for a dominant undertaking to refuse to allow others to use its rights. This matter is discussed in Chapter 7 as it is intertwined with the whole question of refusal to supply and the development of the 'essential facilities' doctrine. Reference should therefore be made to that chapter.

Refusal to supply intellectual property rights was always likely to be more of a problem with copyright and designs than with patents as the patent system itself provides for compulsory licensing in certain situations. In UK law, for example, compulsory licences are provided for in sections 48–50 of the Patents Act 1977 in situations where, *inter alia*, exports from the UK, the exploitation of other patents or the 'establishment or development of commerce or industrial activities in the UK' is being hindered or prejudiced.[284] The copyright system does not, however, have this system of 'checks and balances' built into it.

The ECJ first considered the issue in the cases on spare parts for cars, *Volvo*[285] and *Renault*.[286] It held that the right of the owner of a protected design to prevent third parties manufacturing, selling or importing, without its consent, products incorporating the design constitutes the very subject-matter of the exclusive right. As an obligation to license would therefore deprive it of the substance of its exclusive right, a refusal to license could not in itself constitute an abuse of a dominant position. The crucial phrase here was *in itself* because the Court went on to say that the *exercise* of the exclusive right may infringe Article 82 if it involves 'certain abusive conduct', such as the charging of high prices.[287]

---

[284] Patents Act 1977, s. 48(3)(d) and (e).
[285] Case 238/87, *AB Volvo v. Erik Veng* [1988] ECR 6211, [1989] 4 CMLR 122.
[286] Case 53/87, *CICCRA v. Renault* [1988] ECR 6039, [1990] 4 CMLR 265.
[287] See *supra* Chap. 7.

The issue next came before the Court in *Magill*[288] which concerned the refusal of various broadcasting authorities to allow a would-be publisher of a comprehensive television listings magazine to publish their programme schedules. The CFI upheld the Commission's condemnation of this refusal as an abuse. It based its judgment on the concepts developed in the case law on Articles 28 and 30 (ex Articles 30 and 36) and also relied on the ECJ judgments in *Volvo* and *Renault*, drawing an analogy between the refusal to license here and the arbitrary refusal to supply spare parts to independent repairers which was one of the examples the ECJ gave of conduct which would have constituted an abuse in the car parts scenario.

Cases T–69/70/89, 76/89, *RTE, ITP, BBC* v. *EC Commission* [1991] ECR II–485, [1991] 4 CMLR 586

Court of First Instance

70. It is common ground that in principle the protection of the specific subject-matter of a copyright entitles the copyright-holder to reserve the exclusive right to reproduce the protected work. The Court of Justice expressly recognised that in Case 158/86, *Warner Brothers v Christiansen*, cited above, in which it held that '[t]he two essential rights of the author, namely the exclusive right of performance and the exclusive right or reproduction, are not called in question by the rules of the Treaty. . . .

71. However, while it is plain that the exercise of the exclusive right to reproduce a protected work is not in itself an abuse, that does not apply when, in the light of the details of each individual case, it is apparent that that right is exercised in such ways and circumstances as in fact to pursue an aim manifestly contrary to the objectives of Article [82]. In that event, the copyright is no longer exercised in a manner which corresponds to its essential function, within the meaning of Article 36 of the Treaty, which is to protect the moral rights in the work and ensure a reward for the creative effort, while respecting the aims of, in particular, Article [81]. . . . In that case, the primacy of Community law, particularly as regards principles as fundamental as those of the free movement of goods and freedom of competition, prevails over any use of a rule of national intellectual property law in a manner contrary to those principles.

72. That analysis is borne out by the case law of the Court of Justice which in its abovementioned judgments— *Volvo v Veng*, on which the Commission relies, and *CICRA v Renault*—held that the exercise of an exclusive right which, in principle, corresponds to the substance of the relevant intellectual property right may nevertheless be prohibited by Article [82] if it involves, on the part of the undertaking holding a dominant position, certain abusive conduct. The questions referred to the Court in those two cases-both references for a preliminary ruling-turned on whether the conduct of two car manufacturers who reserved to themselves the exclusive right to manufacture and market spare parts for the vehicles which they produced, on the basis of their registered designs for those parts, was permissible. The Court cited, as examples of conduct constituting abuses within the meaning of Article [82], the arbitrary refusal to supply spare parts to independent repairers, the fixing of prices for spare parts at an unfair level or a decision no longer to produce spare parts for a particular model even though many cars of that model were still in circulation. . . .

73. In the present case, it must be noted that the applicant, by reserving the exclusive right to

---

[288] Cases C–241–241/91 P *RTE & ITP* v. *Commission* [1995] ECR I–743, [1995] 4 CMLR 718, on appeal from Cases T–69–70/89, 76/89, *RTE, ITP, BBC* v. *EC Commission* [1991] ECR II–485, [1991] 4 CMLR 586, on appeal from *Magill TV Guide* 1989 OJ L78/43, [1989] 4 CMLR 757.

publish its weekly television programme listings, was preventing the emergence on the market of a new product, namely a general television magazine likely to compete with its own magazine, the *RTE Guide*. The applicant was thus using its copyright in the programme listings which it produced as part of its broadcasting activity in order to secure a monopoly in the derivative market of weekly television guides. It appears significant, in that connection, that the applicant also authorised, free of charge, the publication of its daily listings and of highlights of its weekly programmes in the press in both Ireland and United Kingdom. Moreover, it authorised the publication of its weekly listings in other member-States, without charging royalties.

It will be noted that in paragraph 71 above the CFI introduced the concept of the 'essential function' of copyright 'within the meaning of Article [30]', using this as a means of determining whether the exercise of the rights falling within the specific subject-matter infringed Article 82.[289] On appeal, as explained in Chapter 7 where the relevant parts of the judgment are set out, the ECJ did not pursue this attempt to knit together Article 30 and Article 82. Indeed, it played down the intellectual property angle altogether, concentrating instead on the idea that the television companies were refusing to supply a *raw material*.

Nevertheless, the outcome of the ECJ's judgment in *Magill* was that competition law may, in exceptional circumstances, require dominant undertaking to license their rights. How exceptional those circumstances are is shown by the CFI judgment in *Tiercé Ladbrooke*.[290] The reining-in of the essential facilities doctrine in Community law by the ECJ in *Oscar Bronner*[291] also means that the obligation on dominant undertakings to license intellectual property rights is unlikely to be widely applied. Nevertheless, the CFI confirmed in *Micro Leader* that in exceptional circumstances enforcement of copyright could amount to an abuse.[292]

(iv) COMPULSORY LICENSING, INFORMATION TECHNOLOGY AND INTEROPERABILITY

A major question raised by *Magill* was how it could affect the information technology industry. The Commission had been concerned for some time that dominant undertakings should not hinder competitors from producing products and services which are compatible with those of the dominant undertaking. In the *IBM Settlement*[293] the Commission obtained from IBM an undertaking that it would reveal interface information on new IBM products at an earlier stage, thereby giving competitors more time to adapt to the IBM standard. This too could amount in effect to an obligation to license intellectual property rights.

As is seen above[294] the Commission has addressed the issue in the Software Directive, 91/250.[295] The directive enshrines the principle of interoperability, in that a licensee can

---

[289] See S. Anderman, *EC Competition Law and Intellectual Property Rights* (Clarendon, 1998), 207.

[290] Case T–504/93, *Tiercé Ladbrooke SA* v. *Commission* [1997] 5 CMLR 309: see *supra* Chap. 7.

[291] Case C–7/97 *Oscar Bronner GmbH & Co. KG* v. *Mediaprint* [1999] 4 CMLR 112: see Chap. 7.

[292] Case T–198/98, *Micro Leader* v. *Commission* [2000] 4 CMLR 886. The CFI annulled a Commission decision rejecting a complaint as there was enough evidence of the copyright owner (Microsoft) practising excessive pricing to have warranted the Commission examining that point.

[293] [1984] 3 CMLR 147; see *supra* Chap. 7.

[294] [1991] OJ L122/42; see *supra* 620–621.

[295] [1991] OJ L1227/42.

decompile a program in order to use it with other programs and can perform the acts permitted by Article 5 which would otherwise be within the exclusive rights of the licensor. The recitals to the Directive state that its terms are without prejudice to the application of Article 82 where a dominant supplier refuses to provide information necessary for the interoperability of the equipment.

The original draft of the Database Directive,[296] which creates a *sui generis* right for protecting databases, contained specific compulsory licensing provisions. These were excised from the final version, and the issue is simply mentioned in recital 47, which says:

Whereas, in the interests of competition between suppliers of information products and services, protection by the sui generis right must not be afforded in such a way as to facilitate abuses of a dominant position, in particular as regards the creation and distribution of new products and services which have an intellectual, documentary, technical, economic or commercial added value; whereas, therefore, the provisions of this Directive are without prejudice to the application of Community or national competition rules.

(v) COLLECTING SOCIETIES

Collecting societies, such as performers' rights societies, are organizations which collectively manage copyrights of behalf of rights holders. They exist because of the impracticality of performers, musicians, etc. individually giving permission for their work to be performed or collecting royalties. Performers' rights societies are usually organized on a national basis and often have a *de facto* monopoly. Their activities have often given rise to competition law problems, particularly in respect of Article 82, and these are dealt with in context in Chapters 6 and 7.

7. FURTHER READING

A. BOOKS

ANDERMAN, S., *EC Competition Law and Intellectual Property Rights* (Clarendon 1988)

CRAIG P. and DE BÚRCA, G., *EU Law: Text, Cases and Materials* (2nd edn., Oxford University Press 1998) 1049–1050

GOVAERE, I., *The Use and Abuse of Intellectual Property Rights in EC Law* (Sweet & Maxwell, 1996)

KINSELLA, S., *EU Technology Licensing* (Palladian Law Publishing, 1998)

Korah, V., *Technology Transfer Agreements and the EC Competition Rules* (Clarendon, 1996)

B. ARTICLES

COTTER, T. F., 'Intellectual Property and the Essential Facilities Doctrine' [1999] *Antitrust Bull.* 211

DOLMANS, M. and ODRIOZOLA, M., 'Site Licence, Right Licence? Site Licences under EC Competition Law' [1998] *ECLR* 493

---

[296] Dir. 96/9 1996] OJ L77/20.

FORRESTER, I., 'Software Licensing in the Light
of Current EC Competition Law Considerations' [1992] *ECLR* 5

SIRAGUSA, M., 'EEC Technology Transfers—A
Private View' [1982] *Fordham Corp. L. Inst.* 95

TOWNSEND, J.M., 'The Case For Site Licences'
[1999] *ECLR* 169

VENIT, J., 'In the Wake of Windsurfing: Patent
Licensing in the Common Market' [1986]
Fordham Corp. L Inst. 517

ZANON, L., 'Ties in Patent Licensing Agreements' (1980) 5 *ELRev.* 391

11

CARTELS AND OLIGOPOLY

1. INTRODUCTION

A. CARTELS AND OLIGOPOLY

It was seen in Chapter 1 that the objection to 'monopoly' is that the presence of a monopolist may lead to a reduction in economic efficiency and consumer welfare as a whole. Monopolists, having power over price, may charge a price higher than that charged in a competitive market by reducing output. Output is restricted to a level at which the monopolist's profits are maximized. Although a transfer of wealth from consumer to monopolist may be costless to society as a whole in economic terms, other costs arise. In particular, both allocative and productive inefficiency occur. The increase in cost of the product forces consumers to substitute products that cost relatively more to produce. Scarce resources are misallocated and the pressure on the monopolist to minimize its costs is relaxed since it is cushioned by the monopoly profits made.

Firms operating in an industry where there is not one but a number of producers may seek to emulate the economic effect of monopoly, realizing that this may increase their profitability. At one end of the spectrum, undertakings may decide to merge their businesses.[1] Alternatively, undertakings may agree, collectively, to exploit their joint economic power and to improve their profitability. Successful cartels raise the joint profits of all the firms in the industry and produce similar economic effects, and adverse consequences for society, as monopoly. Similarly, it seems that some undertakings, operating in an industry where there are only a few producers (an oligopolistic market), automatically emulate the economic effect of monopoly even in the absence of an agreement to do so. Market conditions dictate that the undertakings align their behaviour in a manner which maximizes the profits of the players involved.[2]

This chapter will consider the EC competition law applying both to undertakings operating cartels and undertakings operating on an oligopolistic market.

---

[1] See *infra* Chap. 12.
[2] See discussion *infra*, 635–636.

B. EXPLICIT AND TACIT COLLUSION

(i) EXPLICIT COLLUSION

In Chapter 13 it is seen that some co-operation between undertakings operating at the same level of the market may be highly beneficial to the competitive structure of that market. A joint venture agreement may seek to improve the parties' competitive position on a market by, for example, pooling resources and sharing the financial risk necessary to launch a new product on that market. However, some co-operation between producers may purely be intended to maximize the joint profits of the parties to the agreement. The objective of a cartel is to maintain the parties' respective positions on the market and to achieve pricing stability or an increase in prices. The parties thus deliberately set out to interfere with free competition (the best environment for ensuring the optimum allocation of resources and continuous economic progress) and to act instead to protect the prosperity of the industrial group as a whole.

In the 1940s the pioneering work of von Neumann and Morgenstern[3] laid the foundation for the development of a new branch of economics, 'game theory', which deals with the strategic interaction of firms and which is now highly developed. In particular, it has been used to address problems that may arise on an oligopolistic market.[4] The basic game model which can be applied to illustrate decision-making on a concentrated market is the 'prisoners' dilemma'.

The prisoners' dilemma explains the incentives that exist for firms operating on a concentrated market to agree to co-ordinate their behaviour and to charge prices which are higher than those which would occur on a competitive market. It also illustrates, however, the practical difficulties involved in operating such a cartel. The Nash non-co-operative equilibrium arises 'when, given the behaviour of all other firms in the market, no firm wishes to change its behaviour. Each firm maximises profit, taking as given the behaviour of all the other firms'.[5]

S. Bishop and M. Walker, *The Economics of EC Competition Law: Concepts, Application and Measurement* (Sweet & Maxwell, 1999), 23

2.21 The concept of a non-co-operative Nash equilibrium can be illustrated by reference to the following game, commonly known as the Prisoners' Dilemma . . . There are two firms, A and B, who must each decide whether to charge a high price or to charge a low price. The numbers in each box denote the profits resulting from the outcome of the two firms' decisions. The first number in each box shows the profits Firm A makes and the second the profits Firm B makes. For example, if both firms choose a low price, each firm makes profits of 4 (see bottom right quadrant).

---

[3] J. von Neumann and O. Morgenstern, *The Theory of Games and Economic Behaviour* (Princeton University Press, 1944).

[4] G. Stigler, 'A Theory of Oligopoly' (1964) 72 *J Pol. Econ.* 44.

[5] S. Bishop and M. Walker, *The Economics of EC Competition Law: Concepts, Application and Measurement* (Sweet & Maxwell, 1999), para. 2.20.

Fig. 2.3 Illustrating a Nash equilibrium

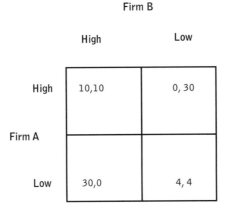

Considering the various outcomes, both firms would prefer an outcome in which both charged a high price to that in which they both charged a low price. In this case, Firm A would earn profits of 10 and so would Firm B (top left quadrant). But if firm A chooses a high price, what is the best action that Firm B can take? With Firm A choosing a high price, if Firm B also chooses a high price it earns profits of 10 (top left). But if Firm B chooses a low price, it earns profits of 30 (top right). Hence, given that Firm A chooses a high price, Firm B's best strategy is to charge a low price.

But if Firm B charges a low price, what is the best course of action for Firm A? With Firm B charging a low price, if Firm A charges a high price, it earns zero profits (top right) but if it charges a low price, Firm A earns profits of 4 (bottom right quadrant). This outcome . . . represents the *Nash equilibrium*: the best Firm A can do if Firm B charges a low price is also to choose a low price and vice versa.

This simple model shows that while both firms prefer a situation in which both firms charge a high price, the incentive to charge a low price while the rival firm charges a high price results in both firms charging a low price.

It is clear from this model that considerable advantages accrue to operators on a market that get together and agree to fix high prices. As Adam Smith noted in *The Wealth of Nations*:

people of the same trade seldom meet together, even for merriment and diversion, but the conversation ends in a conspiracy against the public, or in some contrivance to raise prices.

The game also illustrates, however, the strong temptation that exists for parties to an agreement to renege upon it. Both A and B can increase their own individual profit by violating the agreement, provided that the other does not also violate it. (If both cheat then a competitive outcome will result because both firms will charge a low price. This is the Nash Equilibrium.) This means that there will always be a temptation for an individual firm to cheat on a cartel agreement and indicates that a cartel will be successful only if the members can find a mechanism for enforcing the agreement, a method of detecting any cheating on the cartel provisions, and a method of punishing those that do cheat on the agreement. The operation of such internal enforcement mechanisms is inevitably time-consuming and expensive and on some markets may be impossible. The difficulties of enforcement and monitoring compliance with the agreement will become more acute the larger the number of participants and the greater the differentiation in their products.[6] Further, the more elaborate the

---

[6] See discussion of the types of market which particularly lend themselves to collusion, *infra* 636 *ff.*

monitoring and enforcement devices, the more vulnerable the cartel is to detection by competition authorities.

It is arguable that in the long run most cartels will break down without the intervention of any competition authorities. The Commission has, however, uncovered a number of cartels that have been operated successfully over long periods of time: for example, the market sharing agreement in *Soda Ash*[7] was thought to have been in operation since the nineteenth century and the cartel in *Peroxygen Products*[8] for a period of at least twenty years. In the meantime loss to society as a whole is suffered. It is thus widely accepted that cartels should be deterred.[9] Of all agreements, cartels most contradict the principles of the free market economy as the operators specifically attempt to eliminate or limit the free play of competition. Cartels have, therefore, provoked strong and hostile reactions from competition enforcement authorities.

In the USA, Richard Posner has commented that '[t]he elimination of the formal cartel from ... industries is an impressive, and remains the major, achievement of American antitrust law'.[10] In the UK, the elimination of the cartel is a major preoccupation of the competition authorities.[11] If the European Commission once felt inhibited against acting against national champions and industrial giants engaged in the operation of cartels, this can no longer be said to be the case. In its annual competition reports it has indicated that it is determined to take vigorous action against cartels, believing that their effect is to deprive consumers of the benefits of undistorted competition. It has resolved to deploy all the resources necessary to take effective action against them despite the major effort in terms of manpower and lengthy procedure that their identification and combating involves.[12] This attitude has been reflected by a number of factors, for example:

- increasing numbers of decisions prohibiting cartels;[13]
- ever-increasing fines where serious violations of the competition rules have been committed;
- the issue of a notice indicating that fines will increase the more serious the violation and the longer the duration (cartel members know that the clock is ticking);[14]

---

[7] [1991] OJ L152/1, [1994] 4 CMLR 454.

[8] [1985] OJ L35/1, [1985] 1 CMLR 481.

[9] Even the Chicago school accepts that the antitrust laws should be applied to deter hard-core cartels: see R.H. Bork, *The Antitrust Paradox* (Basic Books, 1978, reprinted with a new Introduction and Epilogue, 1993), 67.

[10] R.A. Posner, *Antitrust Law* (University of Chicago Press, 1976), 39.

[11] One of the major reasons for reforming the UK competition rules and for introducing the Chap. I prohibition into the UK Competition Act 1998 was to ensure that the UK's Office of Fair Trading could effectively combat the operation of cartels. Under the Restrictive Trade Practices Act 1976 the authorities had extremely limited investigatory powers and fines could not be imposed in respect of agreements operated in contravention of the Act.

[12] See, e.g., *XXIIIrd Report on Competition Policy* (Commission, 1993), pt. 209. See also M. Monti, 'Fighting Cartels Why and How? Why should we be concerned with cartels and collusive behaviour?' 3rd Competition Policy Conference, Stockholm, 11–12 Sept. 2000.

[13] See, e.g., *Nederlandse Federative Vereniging voor de Froothandel op Elektrotechnisch Gebied and Technische Unie (FEG and TU)* [2000] OJ L39/1; *British Sugar plc, Tate & Lyle plc, Napier Brown & Company Ltd, James Budgett Sugars Ltd (British Sugar)* [1999] OJ L76/1, [1999] 4 CMLR 1316, appeal pending, Cases T–202/98 etc. *Tate & Lyle v Commission*; *Pre-Insulated Pipe Cartel* [1999] OJ L24/1, [1998] 4 CMLR 402, appeal pending Case T–9/99 etc., *HFB Holdings v Commission*; *Greek Ferry Services* [1999] OJ L109/24, [1999] 5 CMLR 47, appeal pending Cases T–56/99 etc., *Marlines SA v Commission*, pending.

[14] The Commission's policy on fines will be discussed *infra* in Chap. 14.

- the issue of a notice seeking to encourage cartel members to come forward and confess and/or to co-operate with the Commission by offering reductions in fines;[15]
- the creation of a specific cartel unit (Unit E 1) within the competition directorate;[16] and finally
- the Commission's desire to abolish the notification and authorization system set up in Regulation 17 in order to enable the Commission to refocus its activities on the most serious infringements of competition law, especially the detection and prevention of cartels (see its White Paper on Modernisation and proposal for a Regulation to replace Regulation 17).[17]

(ii) TACIT COLLUSION

In some markets it seems that the players do not need actually to meet or communicate in order to be able to co-ordinate their behaviour. Market forces dictate that the undertakings set their prices 'as if' there had been some collusion between them.

The theory of oligopolistic interdependence suggests that undertakings operating on a market on which there are only a few players may align their conduct as a rational response to the market circumstances. Because there are only a few players on the market, their awareness of each other's presence is automatically heightened. An undertaking is bound to monitor the behaviour of its competitors since a reduction in price by a competitor may swiftly attract away the former's customers. Oligopolists may, therefore, recognize their interdependence and realize, without the need for communication, that the most efficient course of conduct is for them all to set their prices at a profit-maximizing level.

The Prisoners' Dilemma set out on pages 632–633 above provides an explanation of how this may occur. The model establishes that even without agreement A and B know that if they both choose a high price they will, collectively, maximize their profits (by raising their prices and restricting their output). However, A is aware that if B charges a high price, A can substantially increase its profits, at B's expense, by reducing its price and attracting away B's customers. B is also aware that it can achieve substantial profits by reducing its price and soliciting A's customers. In the event that both A and B end up lowering their prices or having a price war, prices will be driven down to (or possibly below) the level that would be charged in a competitive market. Each will charge a price established at a level which covers costs plus only a reasonable profit (and they will not maximize their profits).

The first game suggests that although both A and B know that they will both be better off if they behave 'as if' they were a monopolist or had agreed to charge high prices that they can increase their own individual profits by reducing price. Further that it may in fact be dangerous not to do so. A knows that if it does not reduce price, it takes the risk that it will lose customers if B chooses to do so. Consequently, both may reduce price and the result achieved is disadvantageous for both parties. Next time or next game, even if A and B do not meet and agree to charge high prices they may reconsider their situation independently and realize that they are both much better off if they decide to do so.

---

[15] See *supra* n. 13.

[16] Commission press release IP(98)1060.

[17] Commission White Paper on modernisation of the rules implementing Arts. 85 and 86 [now 81 and 82] of the EC Treaty [1999] OJ C132/1, [1999] 5 CMLR 208, paras. 13 and 42 and proposal for a Reg. implementing Arts. 81 and 82, COM (2000) 582. See Chaps. 4 and 16.

The interdependence of oligopolists and game theory thus suggests that on some oligopolistic markets the players will behave 'as if' they have agreed to act in a manner which maximizes the profits of the market players.

S. Bishop and M. Walker, *The Economics of EC Competition Law: Concepts, Application and Measurement* (Sweet & Maxwell, 1999), 80

Explicit and tacit collusion

4.08 Before looking at those characteristics which make collusion both possible and sustainable, a distinction should be made between explicit collusion and tacit or implicit collusion [or conscious parallelism]. While firms can collude explicitly, *e.g.* through meetings between members of various firms, the recognition of their interdependence may lead firms to collude tacitly. Tacit collusion exists where in the absence of any formal attempts to implement a collusive outcome, firms understand that if each firm competes less vigorously they might all be able to enjoy higher prices and higher profits. For example, a firm may realise that cutting prices will lead to rival firms following suit. Hence, the best the firm can do given the likely reactions of its rivals is to maintain prices at the current level.

The factors which imply tacit collusion is more likely are similar to those which make sustainable cartel behaviour more likely. For this reason, those industries in which firms have formed, or attempted to form, cartels are more often viewed as being prone to tacit collusion . . .

Studies by academic commentators have sought to test for tacit collusion . . . These studies conclude that interaction over time may enable firms to increase their profits relative to the one shot non-co-operative outcome . . . Nevertheless, total industry profit falls short of the monopoly or perfect cartel level. It has been argued that this suggests that co-ordination and communication difficulties are probably greater in practice than most theoretical treatments assume.

Thus empirical research suggests that undertakings operating in oligopolistic markets may realize their mutual interdependence and so be able to realize profits which are greater than those which would be achieved on a competitive market.[18] Although the profits achieved may not be as great as those which might arise were the parties to collude, the impact on consumer welfare as a whole will still be a detrimental one.

(iii) MARKETS PRONE TO EXPRESS COLLUSION

Certain markets are more prone to cartelization than others.[19] These markets, of course, display features which make it possible to establish and operate a cartel successfully. For example, cartelization may be more likely to occur where demand for the members' product is relatively inelastic and on markets in which co-ordination is relatively simply and cheating on the cartel can most easily be detected, punished and prevented:

---

[18] E. Green and R. Porter, 'Non-co-operative Collusion under Imperfect Price Information' (1984) 52 *Econometrica*, 87–100.

[19] See also the discussion of markets which are conducive to explicit and tacit collusion, *infra* in Chap. 12.

- *Inelastic demand*
  Undertakings will be able to increase prices and raise profits only where demand for their product is inelastic. Where demand for a product is elastic then price increases are more difficult.
- *Market concentration*
  The fewer the number of operators on the market, or controlling the market, the simpler it is to co-ordinate actions, the cheaper the costs of collusion, the easier it is to detect cheating and the easier it is to keep the arrangement secret. Further, the larger the market share that each undertaking has the greater the potential profits to be earned from successful collusion. The greater the anticipated rewards the more likely they are to outweigh the risks of detection.
- *Barriers to entry*
  Barriers to entry[20] are important to the successful operation of a cartel. In the absence of barriers, an increase in price will attract new competitors into the market.
- *Homogeneous goods*
  Where goods are homogeneous the costs of collusion are reduced and the likelihood of successful collusion increased. The possibility for non-price competition through product differentiation is, of course, reduced. Competition is not multidimensional but focuses almost solely on price. Many of the Commission's decisions prohibiting the operation of a cartel have been taken against undertakings whose products offer little scope for differentiation, for example, sugar, cement, cartonboard, pvc, soda ash and polypropylene.[21] In *BELASCO*[22] cartel members actually took steps, through standardization and joint advertising etc., to foster an impression in consumers that their products were homogeneous in order to limit the scope of competition by means of product differentiation.
- *Depressed conditions*
  Industries which suffer in recessions or from declining demand may be tempted to adopt price-fixing or other collusive agreements to maintain profits (see, e.g., the arguments raised in *Polypropylene*[23]).
- *Mechanisms for co-ordination*
  Because of the rewards which might result from cheating on a cartel, undertakings will be tempted to cheat on any cartel that they have concluded. An undertaking will be likely to cheat on the cartel only where it can do so for a relatively long period of time without detection. The effective operation of a cartel thus requires that some credible enforcement mechanism is in place. Further, cartel members usually, in addition to price fixing, also agree to share markets and/or to adhere to quotas. It may be easier to detect if firms are not complying with quotas or are selling to

---

[20] See *supra* Chap. 1 and 6 for a discussion of barriers to entry.

[21] See, e.g., *UK Sugar Cartel* [1999] OJ L76/1, [1999] 4 CMLR 1316, on appeal to the CFI, Case T–9/99 and *Polypropylene* [1988] OJ L230/1, [1988] 4 CMLR 347, appeals substantially dismissed both by the CFI and the ECJ: see, e.g., Case C–51/92P, *SA Hercules NV v. Commission* [1999] 5 CMLR 976 and Case C–199/92P, *Hüls AG v. Commission (Polypropylene)* [1999] 5 CMLR 1016.

[22] [1986] OJ L232/15, [1991] 4 CMLR 130, on appeal, Case 246/86, *Re Roofing Felt Cartel: BELASCO v Commission* [1989] ECR 2117, [1991] 4 CMLR 96.

[23] See *infra* 649. The fact that an agreement is intended to combat the effect of over-capacity does not deprive the agreement of its anti-competitive effect. It might, however, encourage the Commission to be more sympathetic when considering any fines to be imposed in respect of the breach of Art. 81(1).

customers outside their allotted territory. In *BELASCO*,[24] for example, the trade association of which the parties to the cartel were members took steps to monitor compliance with a price- and quota-fixing cartel. Indeed, it employed an accountant which fined undertakings which exceeded the quota allocated to it under the terms of the cartel agreement.

• *Dispersed buyers*

Where buyers are numerous and dispersed it is almost impossible to advertise price-cuts or reductions and, consequently, to cheat on the cartel without it being brought to the attention of the other members.

• *Demand patterns*

Cyclical changes in demand may lead to the breakdown of a cartel. In these circumstances undertakings may find it difficult to determine whether the decline in demand for their products is due to a reduction in demand as a whole or to another member cheating on the cartel. This uncertainty may cause the members to deviate from the terms of the cartel. Further, where large orders are put in for a product occasionally (rather than on a regular basis) there may be a greater temptation for cheating since the gains will obviously be greater.

S. Bishop and M. Walker, *The Economics of EC Competition Law: Concepts, Application and Measurement* (Sweet & Maxwell, 1999), 86

Cartels and collusion: main points

4.23 In many industries, firms have an incentive to form cartels. The success of a cartel depends largely on the elasticity of demand facing the cartel members. The less elastic the demand curve, the greater the increase in price that can be achieved.[25] For this to be the case, the ability of fringe firms outside the cartel to expand output or the scope for new entry must be limited.

However, firms also have a natural incentive to deviate from such cartel agreements once they are formed. Cartels can only be sustained over time if cartel members are able to detect and adequately punish firms which deviate from the cartel agreement. For this reason, cartels often introduce a number of measures designed to prevent cheating. These include agreeing to fix more than just price levels, *e.g.* dividing the market, fixing market shares or establishing trigger prices.

(iv) MARKETS PRONE TO TACIT COLLUSION

There are oligopolistic markets where both price and non-price competition is intense. The prisoners' dilemma does not explain why this is the case. It seems likely, however, that markets on which collusion is feasible are also the markets on which tacit collusion may be possible. In particular, it will be much more difficult for the undertakings to behave as if there is a co-operation agreement between them on markets in which there is product differentiation,[26] if a number of undertakings operate on the market or if barriers to entry are low.

---

[24] [1986] OJ L232/15, [1991] 4 CMLR 130, on appeal, Case 246/86, *Re Roofing Felt Cartel: BELASCO v Commission* [1989] ECR 2117, [1991] 4 CMLR 96.

[25] See *supra* Chap. 1.

[26] Parallel pricing will have little impact where the undertakings are also competing on factors such as the quality of their product and brand image.

Thus the industries more prone to 'tacit collusion' or oligopolistic parallel behaviour exhibit the same features as those prone to explicit collusion. Typically these are markets which are concentrated, on which homogenous products are produced, on which demand is stable and inelastic, on which barriers to entry are high, and on which deviation from parallelism is likely to result in costly price wars or the expansion of output.

C. COMPETITION LAW AND COLLUSION (EXPLICIT AND TACIT)

Where undertakings agree to fix or otherwise *collude* in fixing prices, restricting output, and/or sharing markets there will be sufficient collusion between the undertakings to trigger the operation of Article 81(1) (assuming of course that the other requirements of Article 81 are satisfied). The difficulty with tacit collusion is that although the impact of such co-ordination on the market is the same, or at least similar, as where it is explicit (inefficiency occurs), the parties have not in fact *agreed* or otherwise colluded in co-ordinating their behaviour.

How should the competition rules deal with this tacit collusion? Since the effects are similar to cases in which there is explicit collusion, should parallel behaviour or conscious parallelism, without any proof of actual collusion between the undertakings, be prohibited under Article 81? If it is not, what other action can be taken to deal with the problems arising on an oligopolistic market. It will be seen that Article 82 does not present an ideal tool for effective control of undertakings operating on an oligopolistic market. It may be, therefore, that the European Commission will have to consider other, alternative means of control.

2. CARTELS

A. INTRODUCTION

It is Article 81, of course, which prohibits the creation and operation of cartels. Article 81(1) prohibits all 'agreements between undertakings, decisions by associations of undertakings and concerted practices' which both affect trade between Member States and have as their object or effect the prevention, restriction, or distortion of competition.[27]

B. SCOPE OF ARTICLE 81

In order to ensure that detrimental collusion between undertakings does not escape the ambit of the competition rules, the requirements of Article 81(1) have been interpreted broadly.

---

[27] See *supra* Chap. 3.

In most cartel cases, in contrast with distribution cases, the question whether or not any established agreement, decision, or concerted practice has as its object or effect the prevention, restriction, or distortion of competition is usually fairly uncontroversial. The objects of most cartels are found to be to restrict competition. The difficulty for the Commission, however, is to establish the existence of an agreement, decision, or concerted practice. The meaning and interpretation of these concepts is thus of great importance. Further, other important questions arise relating to the burden and standard of proof.

C. PRICE FIXING, QUOTAS, MARKET SHARING, AND COLLUSIVE TENDERING

(i) GENERAL

Classic cartels are generally operated by fixing prices and/or by imposing quotas on the members and/or by sharing markets between them. Alternatively, cartel members may limit price competition and share the market between them by engaging in collusive tendering. The Commission is of the view that such agreements have as their object the restriction of competition.[28] This view has been endorsed both by the ECJ[29] and the CFI. In *European Night Services v Commission*[30] the CFI held that where an agreement contains obvious restrictions of competition the Commission is not obliged to consider the effect of any horizontal agreement in its market context. Provisions fixing prices or sharing markets are obvious restrictions of competition and will automatically be held to restrict competition within the meaning of Article 81(1). The effect of the agreement will, therefore, be relevant only when determining whether its impact on competition or trade is appreciable,[31] whether it meets the criteria for exemption set out in Article 81(3),[32] or, where a breach of the rules is established, to the determination of the fine, if any, imposed.[33]

The object of an agreement is not affected by the fact that the agreement has proved

---

[28] See, e.g., *BELASCO* [1986] OJ L232/15, [1991] 4 CMLR 130, on appeal, Case 246/86, *Re Roofing Felt Cartel: BELASCO v Commission* [1989] ECR 2117, [1991] 4 CMLR 96.

[29] See, e.g., Case 246/86, *Re Roofing Felt Cartel: BELASCO v. Commission* [1989] ECR 2117, [1991] 4 CMLR 96; Case 96/82, *IAZ International Belgium NV v. Commission* [1983] ECR 3369, [1984] 3 CMLR 276; and Case T–7/89, *SA Hercules NV v. Commission* [1991] ECR II–1711, [1992] 4 CMLR 84.

[30] Cases T–374, 375, 384 & 388/94 [1998] ECR II–3141, [1998] 5 CMLR 718.

[31] The Commission's Notice indicates that agreements concluded between undertakings with not more than 5% of the relevant market will, *prima facie*, be considered to be of minor importance for the purposes of Art. 81(1). However, where the agreement has as its object the fixing of prices, limiting production or sales, or sharing markets the applicability of Art. 81(1) cannot be ruled out (but the notice stresses that agreements between small and medium-sized undertakings are rarely capable of significantly affecting trade or competition within the common market). In practice, the Commission appears to take the view that agreements which contain these serious restrictions of competition will not be considered to be insignificant unless the parties to the agreement have much lower market shares. Perhaps where the market shares are below 1% of the market, Commission Notice on agreements of minor importance which do not fall under Art. 85(1), [now 81(1)] of the Treaty establishing the European Community [1997] OJ C372/13; see *supra* Chap. 3 and 4.

[32] Exemptions can, of course, currently be granted only to horizontal agreements which have been notified prospectively from the date of notification: see *supra* Chap. 4.

[33] Case 246/86, *Re Roofing Felt Cartel: BELASCO v. Commission* [1989] ECR 2117, [1991] 4 CMLR 96.

difficult to apply in practice (and may not, therefore, have had the effect of restricting competition).[34] Nor is it a defence that a participant always intended to ignore the terms of the agreement and that it did, in fact, cheat on the cartel. There are always strong incentives for individual members to cheat on a cartel,[35] and when cheating the undertaking inevitably relies on the existence of the agreement or concerted practice. If the others do not adhere to the terms of the cartel arrangement no gain can be made from the decision to cheat.[36] Further, it is no defence that the agreement has been rendered lawful by national legislation.[37]

(ii) PRICE-FIXING AGREEMENTS

a. SELLING PRICES

Article 81(1) specifically provides that agreements 'directly or indirectly fixing purchase or selling prices or any other trading conditions' may infringe Article 81(1) of the Treaty.

In *Dyestuffs*,[38] the ECJ stressed that: '[t]he function of price competition is to keep prices down to the lowest possible level . . . Although every producer is free to change his prices, taking into account in so doing the present or foreseeable conduct of his competitors, nevertheless it is contrary to the rules on competition contained in the Treaty for a producer to co-operate with his competitors, in any way whatsoever, in order to determine a co-ordinated course of action relating to a price increase and to ensure its success by prior elimination of all uncertainty as to each other's conduct regarding the essential elements of that action, such as the amount, subject-matter, date and place of the increases.'[39]

In many of the cartel cases investigated the Commission's final decision has condemned price-fixing arrangements between the cartel members. This of course is the most blatant form of cartel, an agreement or conspiracy to raise prices and to exploit the consumer. Some examples of such cases are summarized below.[40]

In *Cartonboard*[41] the Commission fined nineteen producers of cartonboard (used primarily for the manufacture of folding cartons for packaging food and non-food consumer goods) for their participation in a price-fixing cartel. The producers had met secretly but regularly in order to plan and implement uniform and regular price increases within the

---

[34] *Ferry Operators* [1997] OJ L26/23, [1997] 4 CMLR 789.

[35] See the discussion of the prisoners' dilemma, *supra* 632–633.

[36] See *BELASCO* [1986] OJ L232/15, [1991] 4 CMLR 130, on appeal, Case 246/86, *Re Roofing Felt Cartel: BELASCO v. Commission* [1989] ECR 2117, [1991] 4 CMLR 96.

[37] See *infra* 657–658.

[38] Cases 48, 49, 51–7/69, *ICI v. Commission (Dyestuffs)* [1972] ECR 619, [1972] CMLR 557.

[39] *Ibid.* paras. 115 and 118.

[40] See also Greek *Ferry Services* [1999] OJ L109/24, [1999] 5 CMLR 47, appeal pending Cases T–56/99 etc., *Marlines SA v. Commission* (price fixing of ro-ro services between Italy and Greece); *Pre-Insulated Pipe* Cartel [1999] OJ L24/1, [1998] 4 CMLR 402, appeal pending Case T–9/99 etc., *HFB Holdings v. Commission,* discussed *infra* 648; and *British Sugar plc, Tate & Lyle plc, Napier Brown & Company Ltd, James Budgett Sugars Ltd (British Sugar)* [1999] OJ L76/1, [1999] 4 CMLR 1316, appeal pending, Cases T–202/98 etc., *Tate & Lyle v. Commission, infra* n. 56.

[41] [1994] OJ L243/1, [1995] 5 CMLR 547. The decision was broadly upheld by the CFI. Appeals are pending before the ECJ: see, e.g., Case C–286/98P, *Stora* [1998] OJ C299/27.

Community, to plan and co-ordinate price initiatives in advance, to freeze market shares, to control output, and to organize the exchange of confidential information.[42]

The Commission found incriminating documentation that disclosed evidence of collusion at the premises of a number of the participants. The collusion was complex and long, having lasted at least since mid-1986 (although one of the undertakings, Stora, had informed the Commission that the parties had been co-operating since 1975, the Commission had no documentary evidence to corroborate these statements). The Commission did not consider it to be necessary for the collusion to be characterized as either exclusively an agreement or a concerted practice between the undertakings. The documents established that implementation of uniform price increases for each grade of cartonboard were closely monitored. Failure to co-operate would be the subject of discussion and laggards would be strongly urged to support the increases. Although not entirely watertight, the agreement caused considerable harm to competition.

The large fines imposed by the Commission (totalling approximately ECU 132,000,000) reflected the serious nature of the infringement. Although some of these fines were reduced on appeal, the reductions were not substantial.[43]

In *Dyestuffs*,[44] the Commission condemned a concerted practice affecting the parties' price behaviour. The Court affirmed the Commission's decision. The parallel price behaviour of the dyestuff producers was not explicable other than on the ground that it had been co-ordinated by means of a concerted practice.

In *Wood Pulp*, the Commission's finding that forty-one producers of bleached sulphate wood pulp and two trade associations had violated Article 81(1) by concerting on announced and actual transaction prices, was broadly annulled by the ECJ. Although the Court did not deny that such practices might amount to a breach of Article 81(1), it considered that the parallel conduct in question had not been proved to have resulted from the producers' concertation. In the absence of the existence of an agreement, decision, or concerted practice, the adoption of identical announced and transaction prices does not amount to an infringement of Article 81(1).[45]

Similarly, the CFI annulled the Commission's decision in *Flat Glass*. The decision had condemned three Italian undertakings for their participation in a scheme which, it alleged, involved price-fixing, quota-fixing, and agreements to exchange products.[46] However, the CFI annulled the Commission's decision in a judgment which was highly critical of the Commission's procedures.[47] The judgment shows that the CFI is not afraid to review the Commission's findings of fact and the circumstances of the decision in considerable detail.

The Commission's decision in *PVC*,[48] finding that producers of PVC had infringed Article

---

[42] In a series of cases, see in particular Case T–334/94, *Sarrio SA v. Commission* [1998] ECR II–1439, [1998] 5 CMLR 195, the CFI broadly upheld the fines imposed (one firm, Enzo, had its fine annulled but most of the fines on the ringleaders remained unchanged).

[43] The Commission's fining policy is discussed *infra* in Chap. 14.

[44] Cases 48, 49, 51–7/69, *ICI v. Commission (Dyestuffs)* [1972] ECR 619, [1972] CMLR 557.

[45] Cases C–89 etc/85, [1993]ECR I–1307, [1993] 4 CMLR 407.

[46] [1989] OJ L33/44, [1990] 4 CMLR 535.

[47] Cases T–68, 77–78/89, *Società Italiana Vetro (SIV) v. Commission* [1992] ECR II–1403, [1992] 5 CMLR 302.

[48] [1994] OJ L239/14, upheld by the CFI on appeal in Cases T–305–307, 313–316, 318, 325, 328–329 and 335/94, *Limburgse Vinyl Maatschappij NV v. Commission* [1999] ECR I–931 [1999] 5 CMLR 303 (*PVC Cartel*

81 by participating in an agreement and/or a concerted practice, was also annulled by the ECJ on procedural grounds. The Commission, however, subsequently re-adopted its decision.

In *Re Roofing Felt Cartel*, the Commission held[49] that the Belgian producers of roofing felt had formed a cartel to control that market by, amongst other things, adopting common price lists and minimum prices. The agreement was reinforced by policing, penalties for non-compliance, controlling the discounts which could be granted to customers, and fixing the prices of ancillary products etc. The agreement was adopted by resolutions of, and administered at, general meetings of the trade association, BELASCO. The Commission clearly asserted that in assessing an agreement it was not necessary to consider the effect of the agreement if it had been established to have the object of restricting competition. Further, agreements between members and non-members intended to restrict competition between the participants were expressly condemned by Article 81(1). The ECJ affirmed that the decisions of the general meeting fixing the prices were intended to restrict competition.

Both the Commission and the Court in this case rejected an argument raised that Belgian pricing controls left little room for price competition between the undertakings. Sufficient possibility remained for price competition. It is also clear that the Commission will take action against agreements which have subsequently been rendered lawful by national law.[50] In the latter case the Member State may also be in breach of its Treaty obligations.[51]

Article 81(1) also applies, of course, to agreements operated in the services sector. Although occasionally the Commission has tempered the rigorous application of the rules in certain service sectors, for example banking and insurance, in *Eurocheque: Helsinki Agreement*[52] the Commission fined French banks and Eurocheque for operating a scheme under which the same commission was charged for both Eurocheque transactions and for the use of Carte Bleu. The Commission considered that the scheme eliminated the positive features of the Eurocheque system (that it was free to the payee). Further, it eliminated competition between Eurocheques and Carte Bleu. Heavy fines were imposed.

b. TARGET PRICES AND INDIRECT PRICE FIXING

Not only are agreements to fix prices prohibited, but the discussion and implementation of target prices will be condemned:

[I]f a system of imposed selling prices is clearly in conflict with that provision [Article 81], the system of (target prices) is equally so. It cannot in fact be supposed that the clauses of the agreement concerning the determination of target prices are meaningless. In fact the fixing of a price, even one

---

II). The 1994 decision replaced the original 1990 one, [1989] OJ L74/1, [1990] 4 CMLR 345, annulled on appeal by the ECJ on procedural grounds: Cases C–137/92P, *Commission v. BASF* [1994] ECR I–2555 setting aside the judgment of the CFI in Case T–79/89 etc., *BASF v. Commission* [1992] ECR II–315, [1992] 4 CMLR 357 which had declared the decision non-existent. For this aspect of the case, see *infra* Chap. 14.

[49] [1986] OJ L232/15, [1991] 4 CMLR 130, on appeal, Case 246/86, *Re Roofing Felt Cartel: BELASCO v. Commission* [1989] ECR 2117, [1991] 4 CMLR 96.

[50] See, e.g., Case 136/86, *Bureau National Interprofessionnel du Cognac v. Aubert* [1987] ECR 4789, [1988] 4 CMLR 331 and *CNDS* [1993] OJ L203/27, [1995] 5 CMLR 495.

[51] See *supra* Chap. 8.

[52] [1992] OJ L95/50, [1993] 5 CMLR 323. But see *Uniform Eurocheques* [1985] OJ L35/43, [1985] 3 CMLR 434; *infra*, n. 88 and accompanying text.

which merely constitutes a target, affects competition because it enables all the participants to predict with a reasonable degree of certainty what the pricing policy pursued by their competitors will be.[53]

Other agreements which may directly or indirectly facilitate level pricing will also be condemned, for example, agreements fixing or prohibiting discounts, rebates[54] or other financial concessions,[55] or a collaborative strategy of higher pricing.[56]

In *Polypropylene*[57] the Commission fined producers of polypropylene for their participation in an agreement and/or concerted practice to implement price initiatives, to set target prices, and to operate production and sales quotas.[58] The complex of schemes and arrangements was held to constitute a single continuing 'agreement'. However, where producers had not expressed their definite assent to a particular course of action agreed by the others but had indicated their general support for the scheme in question, the overall agreement displayed characteristics of a concerted practice. Given the overtly anti-competitive object of the agreement the Commission held that it was not strictly necessary for an adverse effect upon competition to be demonstrated. However, it found evidence that the agreement did in fact produce an appreciable effect upon competitive conditions. It fined the undertakings a total of approximately ECU 57 million.

In a series of cases both the CFI and the ECJ have broadly dismissed the Polypropylene appeals.[59] However, in a few cases, where the Court found that the Commission had not sufficiently proved the period of time during which an undertaking had participated in the collusion, the amount of the fine was reduced.[60]

In *FENEX*,[61] the Commission held that tariffs recommended by a Dutch association to its members constituted a decision by an association of undertakings. The terms in which the recommendations were circulated (accompanied by circulars in mandatory terms etc.) had to be interpreted as a faithful reflection of the association's resolve to co-ordinate the

---

[53] Case 8/72, *Cementhandelaren v. Commission* [1972] ECR 977, [1973] CMLR 7.

[54] Case 311/85, *VZW Vereniging van Vlaamse Reisbureaus v. VZW Sociale Dienst van de Plaatselijke en Grewestelijke Overheidsdiensten* [1987] ECR 3801, [1988] 4 CMLR 755.

[55] E.g., *IFTRA Rules on Glass Containers* [1974] OJ L160/1, [1974] 2 CMLR D50.

[56] *British Sugar plc, Tate & Lyle plc, Napier Brown & Company Ltd, James Budgett Sugars Ltd (British Sugar)* [1999] OJ L76/1, [[1999] 4 CMLR 1316, appeal pending, Cases T–202/98 etc., *Tate & Lyle v. Commission*. In this case the Commission did not find that the parties had specifically fixed prices but that they had engaged in a collaborative and co-ordinative strategy of higher pricing.

[57] *Polypropylene* [1986] OJ l230/1, [1988] 4 CMLR 347, appeals substantially dismissed both by the CFI and the ECJ see, e.g., Case C–51/92P, *SA Hercules NV v. Commission* [1999] 5 CMLR 976 and Case C–199/92P, *Hüls AG v. Commission (Polypropylene)* [1999] 5 CMLR 1016.

[58] *Polypropylene* [1986] OJ L230/1, [1988] 4 CMLR 347, appeals substantially dismissed both by the CFI and the ECJ: see Case T–7/89 etc., *SA Hercules NV v. Commission* [1991] ECR II–1711, [1992] 4 CMLR 84 and Case C–51/92P etc., *SA Hercules/ Hüls/ICI/Shell v. Commission* [1999] 5 CMLR 976, 1016, 1110, 1142.

[59] See e.g., Case T–7/89 *SA Hercules NV v. Commission* [1991] ECR II–1711, [1992] 4 CMLR 84, Case T–11/89, *Shell International Chemical Co Ltd v. Commission* [1992] ECR II–757; Case T–13/89 *Imperial Chemical Industries plc v. Commission* [1992] ECR II–757; Case C–51/92P, *SA Hercules NV v. Commission* [1999] 5 CMLR 976; Case C–199/92P, *Hüls AG v. Commission* [1999] 5 CMLR 1016; Case C–200/92P, *Imperial Chemical Industries plc v. Commission* [1999] 5 CMLR 1110; Case C–234/92P, *Shell International Chemical Co Ltd v. Commission* [1999] 5 CMLR 1142.

[60] E.g. Case T–2/89, *Petrofina v. Commission* [1991] ECR II–1087 and Case T–11/89, *Shell v. Commission* [1991] ECR II–757.

[61] [1996] OJ L181/28, [1996] 5 CMLR 332.

conduct of its members on the relevant market. Although the Commission conceded that it was normal practice for a trade organization to provide management assistance to its members, it stressed that trade associations could not exercise any direct or indirect influence on competition, notably in the form of tariffs applicable to all undertakings regardless of their own cost price structure. The Commission concluded that the object of the horizontal practice in question was to affect the market significantly so that it fell within the scope of Article 81(1).

c. BUYING PRICES

Although rare, horizontal agreements restricting the parties' freedom to negotiate buying prices are also explicitly prohibited by Article 81.[62]

d. AGREEMENTS BETWEEN DISTRIBUTORS

It is, of course, an infringement of Article 81(1) for distributors of a product to agree its price amongst themselves. Further, a manufacturer may not seek to restrict price competition at the distributor's level.[63]

e. RESALE PRICE MAINTENANCE

The Commission has condemned horizontal agreements to impose resale prices in so far as they have an impact on inter-state trade. In particular, it has been unsympathetic to the arguments in favour of collective resale price maintenance in the book industry.[64] Both the Commission and the Court have also found that individual resale price maintenance infringes Article 81(1). Individual resale price maintenance is discussed in Chapter 9 which deals generally with distribution agreements.

f. SUPPLEMENTARY PROVISIONS

Price-fixing agreements are frequently supplemented by other devices aimed at strengthening the operation of the cartel.

(iii) OUTPUT RESTRICTIONS

A restriction in output automatically creates an imbalance between supply and demand and causes an increase in market prices. Conversely, volume control is an inevitable consequence of any price initiative adopted. Article 81(1)(b) specifically provides that agreements which 'limit or control production . . . or investment' may restrict competition within the meaning of that provision.

Many of the cases discussed above involved collusion to fix both prices and sales quotas.

---

[62] See e.g., *Zinc Producer Group* [1984] OJ L220/7, [1985] 2 CMLR 108.

[63] See *supra* Chap. 9.

[64] *VBVB/VBBB* [1982] OJ L54/36, [1982] 2 CMLR 344. Its view was upheld by the ECJ in Cases 43 and 63/82, *VBVB and VBBB v. Commission* [1984] ECR 19, [1985] 1 CMLR 27. See *Publishers' Association—Net Book Agreement* [1989] OJ L22/12, [1989] 4 CMLR 825 (Commission); Case T–66/89, *Publishers' Association v. Commission* [1992] ECR II–1995, [1992] 5 CMLR 120 (CFI), and Case C–360/92P, *Publishers' Association v. Commission* [1995] ECR I–23, [1995] 5 CMLR 33 (ECJ).

In many cases the implementation of quotas is easier to operate than adherence to a pricing policy: no undertaking can benefit from price-cutting if it is obliged to adhere to sales restrictions, and the adherence to quotas may be easier to monitor. Further, a decision to adhere to quotas may facilitate collusion where participants with different cost structures cannot agree on the prices to be charged for their products. The Organization of Petroleum Exporting Countries (OPEC) cartel, for example, operated simply by the members voluntarily restricting their outputs following the negotiation of quotas in 1973. As a result of the output restrictions, the world price of oil nearly quadrupled within a year. The increase in wealth to the participants was so enormous that, initially at least, there was little temptation to cheat on the cartel.

The *Quinine Cartel* was the first case in which the Commission fined undertakings for the operation of a cartel which raised prices by means of the restriction of output.[65] In particular, certain French companies had agreed not to manufacture synthetic quinidine. The parties contended that, in any event, the companies did not have either the expertise or the resources to manufacture quinidine. The Court dismissed those arguments:

The fact relied upon that, when the gentlemen's agreement was concluded, the French undertakings were not in a position to manufacture synthetic quinidine does not render lawful such a restriction which entirely precluded them from taking up this activity.[66]

In *BELASCO*, an accountant appointed by BELASCO monitored compliance with quotas at the end of each year. Undertakings which had exceeded these quotas were required to pay penalties.

The *Polypropylene*[67] cartel not only operated price initiatives and set target prices but operated production and sales quotas. The CFI in *Hercules v Commission* had no hesitation in holding that the object of meetings to fix target prices and sale volume targets was anti-competitive.[68]

In *Zinc Producer Group* the Commission held that an agreement to fix prices, to adhere to production quotas, and to refrain from the building of new production capacity without the consent of the Group infringed Article 81(1).[69] The purpose of the agreement was to substitute its common zinc producer price for the London Metal Exchange (LME) price. Production controls precluded producers from supplying surplus zinc to the LME or zinc producers at lower prices. The fact that the practices had been tolerated/approved by Member States could not be used as a defence to the operation of the EC competition rules.

(iv) MARKET SHARING

Market-sharing agreements also have restrictive effects on competition and Article 81(1)(b) and (c) specifically prohibits collusive practices which 'limit or control . . . markets' or 'share markets and sources of supply'. Exclusivity in a particular geographical area obviously

---

[65] *Quinine Cartel* [1969] OJ L192/5, [1969] CMLR D41.
[66] Case 41/69, *ACF Chemiefarma NV v. Commission* [1970] ECR 661.
[67] *Polypropylene* [1986] OJ 1230/1, [1988] 4 CMLR 347, appeals substantially dismissed both by the CFI and the ECJ: see, e.g., Case C–51/92P, *SA Hercules NV v. Commission* [1999] 5 CMLR 976 and Case C–199/92P, *Hüls AG v. Commission (Polypropylene)* [1999] 5 CMLR 1016.
[68] See *supra* 644.
[69] [1984] OJ L220/27, [1985] 2 CMLR 108.

grants an undertaking a monopoly within that area which it is free to exploit. No price competition between the parties to the agreement thus operates at all. From the perspective of the Commission, market-sharing agreements operated on national lines are viewed particularly seriously. In addition to restricting competition, such agreements thwart the objective of integrating the single market by dividing up the common market. The Commission is likely to punish such infringements particularly severely. The Commission has stated:

Market sharing agreements are particularly restrictive of competition and contrary to the achievement of a single market. Agreements or concerted practices for the purpose of market-sharing are generally based on the principle of mutual respect of the national markets of each Member State for the benefit of producers resident there. The direct object and result of their implementation is to eliminate the exchange of goods between the Member States concerned. The protection of their home market allows producers to pursue a commercial policy—particularly a pricing policy—in that market which is insulated from the competition of other parties to the agreement in other Member States, and which can sometimes only be maintained because they have no fear of competition from that direction.[70]

The Commission and Court have acted against all forms of geographical market sharing: whether through agreements to refrain from exporting from home markets; agreements to make sales only through the home manufacturer; agreements to limit sales to home markets; or agreements between EC and non-EC undertakings to protect the EC market from low-priced imports.

In *Cement*[71] the Commission found that Community cement producers had operated a systematic and well-policed policy of, amongst other things, dividing markets on the basis of the 'home market principle' (refraining from exporting to other Member States). The agreements showed that the parties made concerted efforts to stem cross-frontier flows and to reduce trade between Member States. A number of bilateral and multilateral agreements were concluded in order to back up the main agreement, for example, to exchange sensitive price information. The agreement or concerted practice which had as its object or effect the non-transhipment of products to home markets of Member States and the regulation of sales to other Member States' markets was clearly prohibited by Article 81(1), market sharing being expressly referred to in Article 81(1).

The Commission imposed fines totalling approximately ECU 248,000,000 on the cement producers. On appeal the CFI found that there *was* a single agreement between all the applicants that was designed to ensure no transhipment to the companies' home markets. However, the Court found that the Commission had not adequately proved the participation of all of the undertakings in the agreement, and in the case of others the duration of the participation was not as long as the Commission had found. The total fines were reduced to around Euro 110 million.[72]

In *Peroxygen Products*[73] the Commission fined producers of hydrogen peroxide a total of ECU 9 million (and one sole undertaking ECU 3 million) for operating agreements which included a 'home market' rule. The agreement provided that undertakings would confine

---

[70] *Commission's Ist Report on Competition Policy* (Commission, 1971), para. 2.

[71] [1994] OJ L343/1, [1995] 4 CMLR 327.

[72] Case T–25/95 etc., *Cimenteries CBR SA v. Commission*, 15 Mar. 2000. Some of the fines were annulled for procedural flaws: see *infra* Chap. 14.

[73] [1985] OJ L35/1, [1985] 1 CMLR 481.

their activities to their traditional home markets. It had eliminated all competition between the competitors and excluded virtually all trade between Member States (prices varied enormously between States).

In *Soda-Ash*[74] the Commission imposed large fines (of approximately ECU 7 million) on both ICI and Solvay, the two largest producers of synthetic soda ash in the Community, for the operation of an agreement under which ICI was exclusively to supply the UK and Ireland and Solvay was exclusively to supply continental Europe. Although the formal written agreement had been abandoned in 1972 (on the UK's accession to the Community) the Commission found that the agreement/concerted practice in fact continued unaltered. This decision was, however, annulled on procedural grounds.[75]

In *Siemens-Fanuc*[76] fines of ECU 1 million were imposed both on Siemens and Fanuc for their operation of a distribution agreement. Under the agreement, Fanuc agreed exclusively to supply a competitor, Siemens, with numerical controls (special purpose computers which control the sequence of motions and the operation of machine tools) in Europe. The Commission held that the market-sharing agreement restricted, distorted and prevented arrangements for selling goods in the common market. It neutralized the impact of sales of an important competitor of Siemens in Europe. An appreciable effect on competition was caused. The agreement resulted in the isolation of the common market from a potentially cheaper source.

(v) COLLUSIVE TENDERING

Collusive tendering occurs where undertakings collaborate on responses to invitations to tender for the supply of goods and services. The practice limits price competition between the parties and amounts to an attempt by the tenderers to share markets between themselves. Instead of competing to submit the lowest possible tender at the tightest possible margin, the parties may agree on the lowest offer to be submitted or agree amongst themselves who should be the most successful bidder. The practice will automatically infringe Article 81(1).

In a system of tendering, competition is of the essence. If the tenders submitted by those taking part are not the result of individual economic calculation, but of knowledge of the tenders by other participants or of concertation with them competition is prevented, or at least distorted and restricted.[77]

In the *Pre-Insulated Pipe Cartel*[78] the Commission imposed fines in excess of ECU 92 million on ten undertakings it had found to be engaged in market-sharing, price-fixing, and bid-rigging in the market for pipes used for district heating systems (contracts for the supply of pipes were almost all awarded on the basis of competitive tendering procedures). The parties had also tried to squeeze out of the market the only competitor which had refused to participate in the cartel and deliberately flouted the EU Public Procurement Rules. The large

---

[74] [1991] OJ L152/1, [1994] 4 CMLR 454.

[75] Case T–30/91, *Solvay SA v. Commission* [1995] ECR II–1775, [1996] 5 CMLR 57; see further *infra* Chap. 14.

[76] [1985] OJ L376/29, [1988] 4 CMLR 945.

[77] *Re The European Sugar Cartel* [1973] OJ L140/17, [1973] CMLR D65, para. 42.

[78] [1999] OJ L24/1, [1998] 4 CMLR 402; appeal pending Case T–9/99 etc., *HFB Holdings v. Commission*.

fines imposed reflected the deliberate nature, the gravity, and duration of the infringement (in particular, the fact that the parties had continued to operate the cartel after the Commission investigation had commenced).

(vi) EXEMPTIONS

a. THE POSSIBILITY OF AN EXEMPTION

Where parties to an agreement have not notified their agreement to the Commission for exemption the latter has no power to exempt the agreement from the operation of Article 81(1).[79] If the industry is, for example, in crisis or decline or where there is over-capacity the operation of Article 81(1) is not affected.

The fact that [a] . . . market was characterised over a period of several years by under-utilisation of capacity, with attendant losses by the producers, does not relieve the agreement of its anti-competitive object.[80]

If parties wish to complain that they have incurred or are incurring substantial losses in the face of a volatile, depressed market characterized by over-capacity and a sharp down-turn in demand, they should make sure that they notify their agreement to the Commission and do not take it upon themselves to engage in concerted action. Occasionally, the difficulties faced by undertakings have been taken into account as mitigation in assessing the fine.[81]

Where an agreement is notified for exemption the Commission must consider whether or not the conditions of Article 81(3) have been fulfilled.[82] Thus technically all agreements, even agreements which have the sole objective of fixing prices, setting quotas, and sharing markets, which are so serious as to cause them to have a restrictive object, are eligible for exemption under Article 81(3). In practice, however, these are the sorts of agreements which are almost totally prohibited under Article 81 and are extremely unlikely to receive an exemption.

b. PRICE–FIXING AGREEMENTS

The Commission is of the view that price-fixing agreements fall into 'the category of manifest infringements under Article [81(1)] which it is always impossible to exempt under Article [81(3)] because of the total lack of benefit to the consumer'.[83] Even in cases concerning 'crisis cartels'[84] the Commission will not extend its benevolent approach to terms fixing prices. If it is sceptical that any benefits really flow from a notified agreement, it may decide to withdraw the parties' immunity from fines.

Despite this robust view some restrictions on pricing have on rare occasions been accepted. Council Regulation 4056/86, for example, block exempting certain liner conference

---

[79] See *supra* Chap. 4. But see the Commission's proposals for a fully directly applicable system to replace the current notification system, *infra* Chap. 16.

[80] See *Polypropylene* [1986] OJ L230/1, [1988] 4 CMLR 347, para. 89; appeals substantially dismissed both by the CFI and the ECJ, see, e.g., Case C–51/92P, *SA Hercules NV v. Commission* [1999] 5 CMLR 976 and Case C–199/92P, *Hüls AG v. Commission (Polypropylene)* [1999] 5 CMLR 1016.

[81] See e.g., *Polypropylene* [1986] OJ L230/1, [1988] 4 CMLR 347, para. 108.

[82] Case T–17/93, *Matra Hachette v. Commission* [1994] ECR II–595, *supra* Chap. 4.

[83] *Commission's Xth Report on Competition Policy* (Commission, 1980), 115.

[84] See *supra* Chap 4 and *infra* 650–651.

agreements, refers to the 'stabilising effect of liner conferences' on pricing.[85] The Commission has also been prepared to exempt terms which limit price competition in the context of beneficial collaboration between undertakings, for example, research and development projects.[86] Further, it has on occasions adopted a more benevolent approach in certain sectors, for example the banking sector.[87] In *Uniform Eurocheques*,[88] the Commission was prepared to exempt for a limited period an agreement which fixed commissions for the cashing of Eurocheques. Although the uniformity of prices and conditions for Eurocheque services led to a restriction of competition between banks in different countries in cashing Eurocheques, the Commission found that the agreement (i) improved payment methods and (ii) benefited users (all currencies were available and interest-free credit was available whilst the cheques were being cleared). The restrictions were essential in the circumstances and did not lead to an elimination of competition. Customers using the facilities knew that they would be charged a uniform amount throughout the EC.

c. RESTRICTIONS ON OUTPUT

Again the Commission will rarely exempt agreements the sole object of which is to restrict output. However, where a restriction of output is ancillary to a beneficial research and development agreement the terms in such agreements may, in certain circumstances, be exempted.[89]

Where there is serious over-capacity in an industry, the Commission has also been sympathetic to parties that have notified 'crisis cartels' (for example, restructuring agreements) for exemption. One of the Commission's objectives is to ensure the elimination of over-capacity in an industry and to enable the industry to recover its profitability.[90] It has, therefore, on several occasions, permitted undertakings operating in industries suffering severe difficulties to conclude co-operation agreements providing, for example, for an orderly reduction in over-capacity where the economic effect of the improved rationalization outweighs the disadvantages of the reduced competition in the short term. However, it will not allow the restructuring to be achieved by unacceptable means such as price-fixing or market-sharing. Further, it will regard the restrictions as indispensable only if the agreement is concerned solely with the reduction of capacity and is limited from the outset to a period necessary for its setting up and implementation.

The Commission has permitted several agreements in the petro-chemical and thermoplastics sector. For example, in *ENI/Montedison*,[91] the Commission exempted for fifteen years an agreement between two large petrochemical groups for rationalization of their production capacities and transfer of certain businesses leading to a *de facto* specialization by each party. The Commission considered that the agreement would:

(i) improve production and distribution and promote technical and economic progress since the parties would, by concentrating on a narrower product range,

---

[85] For further discussion of liner conferences, see *infra* 684 ff and the discussion of Cases C–395 and 396/96P, *Compagnie Maritime Belge Transports SA v. Commission*, [2000] 4 CMLR 1076, *supra* Chap. 7.

[86] See *infra* Chap. 13.

[87] But see *Eurocheque: Helsinki Agreement* [1992] OJ L95/50, [1993] 5 CMLR 323, *supra* 643.

[88] [1985] OJ L35/43, [1985] 3 CMLR 434.

[89] See *infra* Chap. 13.

[90] *XXIst Report on Competition Policy* (Commission, 1991), 207 ff.

[91] [1987] OJ L5/13, [1988] 4 CMLR 444. See also the discussion of crisis cartels *supra* Chap. 4.

be able to slim down operations and concentrate on modernizing their plant; and

(ii) benefit consumers who would be ensured a continued supply of products, cost-saving in the medium term, and better products in the long term generated by the parties' ability to finance new research and development.

The radical reorganization could not be achieved without the restrictions and workable competition would not be eliminated by the agreement.

d. MARKET SHARING AGREEMENTS

It is particularly unlikely that an exemption will be forthcoming in cases of market sharing. The Commission has stated its opinion that:

in principle, exemption from the prohibition cannot be considered for market-sharing agreements. The elimination of a competitor from a market—either in whole or in part—cannot be justified objectively on economic or technical grounds or in the interests of the consumer.[92]

e. COLLUSIVE TENDERING

It is extremely unlikely that any such practice would benefit from an exemption under Article 81(3).[93]

D. RESTRICTIONS ON NON-PRICE TRADING CONDITIONS, ADVERTISING, AND PROMOTION

(i) GENERAL

Agreements relating to non-price trading conditions or relating to advertising or promotion may not have such a serious impact on competition as the agreements discussed in the section above, but they may, nonetheless, restrict important methods of competition between undertakings operating on the market. Although these types of agreements may well fall within Article 81(1) it is possible that, if notified, the agreements may merit an exemption under Article 81(3).

(ii) RESTRICTIONS ON NON-PRICE TRADING CONDITIONS

Because non-price competition may also be an important part of competition between undertakings Article 81(1)(a) prohibits, as incompatible with the common market, collusive practices which 'directly or indirectly fix . . . any other trading conditions'.

---

[92] *Ist Report on Competition Policy* (Commission, 1971), p 3.
[93] See, e.g., *Cast Iron and Steel Rolls* [1983] OJ L317/1, [1984] 1 CMLR 694.

a. UNIFORM TERMS AND CONDITIONS

The use of printed forms setting out standard terms and conditions to be applied by undertakings will not necessarily infringe Article 81(1). However, where the terms and conditions relate to 'important secondary aspects of competition',[94] that is, to any aspect of a supplier's offer which has economic value in the eyes of the customer, they may infringe Article 81(1).

In *Fabricants de Papiers Peints de Belgique*,[95] the Commission found that general conditions of sale concluded by Belgian manufacturers of wallpaper, which related to terms of delivery, returns policy, lengths of rolls, etc. infringed Article 81(1). No exemption was granted under Article 81(3).

b. CUSTOMER SERVICES

Prohibitions on parties to an agreement offering customers special services such as the loan of products or special delivery arrangements are likely to cause an infringement of Article 81(1).[96]

c. PRODUCT QUALITY

The adoption of a common quality label (establishing that products meet a minimum quality standard) will not necessarily infringe Article 81(1). However, a provision restricting suppliers from producing products of a different, inferior, standard (and limiting the quality of products supplied) will infringe Article 81(1).[97]

d. TECHNICAL DEVELOPMENT

Similarly, the adoption of a label identifying products that achieve a certain common technical standard will not infringe Article 81(1) where the quality mark is freely available and the parties are free to market products of a different or inferior standard.[98] There may, however, be an infringement of Article 81(1) where the agreement limits technical development[99] or is used to hinder imports, as in *IAZ*.

In *IAZ*[100] a Belgian trade association agreed with Belgian manufacturers and sole importers for washing machines and dishwashers that only appliances with a 'conformity' label could be connected to the mains. To receive a conformity label the appliances had to comply with technical standards laid down by Belgian law. In fact, the label was available only to Belgian manufacturers or sole importers of products. Thus parallel imports of the appliances were made impossible in practice.

---

[94] *Vimpoltu* [1983] OJ L200/44, [1983] 3 CMLR 619.

[95] [1974] OJ L 237/3, [1974] 2 CMLR D102.

[96] See e.g., *VCH* [1972] OJ L13/34, [1973] CMLR D16.

[97] *Belgian Association of Pharmacists* [1990] OJ L160/1; *European Council of Manufacturers of Domestic Appliances*, IP/00/148.

[98] Notice on Co-operation Agreements [1968] JO C75/3, para. II(8).

[99] See e.g., *Video Cassette Recorders* [1978] OJ L47/42, [1978] 2 CMLR 160.

[100] *Anseau* [1982] OJ L167/39, [1982] 2 CMLR 193; on appeal Case 96/82, *IAZ International Belgium NV v. Commission* [1983] ECR 3369, [1984] 3 CMLR 276.

e. EXEMPTION

The Commission has recognized that it may be advantageous for undertakings to have access to suitably drafted terms and conditions and/or the adoption of common quality or technical standards. On occasions it has, therefore, decided that Article 81(1) is not applicable to such agreements or has granted them an individual exemption.[101]

For example, in *European Council of Manufacturers of Domestic Appliances*[102] the Commission exempted an agreement concluded between 95 per cent of the producers and importers of washing machines operating on the EU market that restricted their freedom to manufacture or import the least energy-efficient washing machines. The agreement was found to restrict competition within the meaning of Article 81(1),[103] but was exempted on account of the important benefits and savings which would result to the consumer from the agreement. In particular, the agreement would result in the reduction of polluting emissions from electricity generation. This case seems to reflect the Community's increasing commitment to the environment.

(iii) RESTRICTIONS ON ADVERTISING AND PROMOTION

The advertising and promotion of a product may be an extremely important aspect of competition between undertakings. It may be a vital means of distinguishing the products, in the eyes of the consumer, from those of competitors and may draw attention to the different characteristics and qualities of the relevant products.

a. RESTRICTIONS ON THE PARTIES' ABILITY TO ADVERTISE

The Commission has indicated that restrictions on the ability of parties to an agreement to advertise is likely to be seen as a restriction on their competitive freedom and competition.[104]

b. JOINT ADVERTISING AND PROMOTION

In general, where parties agree jointly to advertise industry products or products of a common brand, there is no infringement of Article 81(1) so long as the parties are also free to advertise individually. However, different rules may apply in an oligopolistic market where product differentiation and advertising may play a more vital role.[105]

In *Milchförderúngsfonds*,[106] the German dairy industry established a milk promotion fund. The fund was financed by a voluntary levy on milk delivered to dairies. The purpose of the fund was to promote the export of milk products. Brand advertising campaigns and subsidized sales were conducted abroad. The Commission considered that the campaign distorted competition within Article 81(1) and artificially strengthened the position of

---

[101] *Concordato Incendio* [1990] OJ L15/27, [1991] 4 CMLR 199.

[102] IP/00/148. See also *EACEM* [1998] OJ C12/2. The Commission issued an Art. 19(3) Notice setting out its intention of taking a favourable view under Art. 81 of a notified agreement concluded between certain members of EACEM, an organization representing the European consumer electronics industry.

[103] It would result in a reduction of choice for consumers since fewer, cheaper washing machines would be on the market.

[104] Notice on Cooperation Agreements [1968] JO C75/3, para. 11(7).

[105] *Ibid.*, in particular, para. 11(7).

[106] [1985] OJ L35/35, [1985] 3 CMLR 101.

German exporters abroad. Although generic advertising, which did not commend the products solely on the ground of their national origin and did not disparage foreign products, would have benefited all exporters, brand-oriented advertising appreciably reduced the possibility of sales for competing brands. Individual manufacturers benefited from the campaign without having to suffer a corresponding cost which otherwise would have been reflected in the sales price.

In *BELASCO*,[107] Belgian manufacturers jointly advertised and promoted their products, which were sold under a common trademark, through the association, BELASCO. The Commission considered that the purpose of the standardization of the products and the joint advertising was to reinforce the other provisions of the agreement which provided for a common price list and sales quotas. The fostering of an impression in consumers that their products were homogeneous limited the scope of competition by means of product differentiation.

c. EXEMPTION

The Commission has on occasions accepted that it may be advantageous for undertakings to rationalize and co-ordinate their advertising efforts, particularly in the context of trade fairs.[108]

E. AGREEMENTS, DECISIONS AND CONCERTED PRACTICES

(i) GENERAL

The Commission's decisions and case law of the Court clearly establish that cartels fixing prices, output, sharing markets, or otherwise rigging the market are considered to be serious infringements of the competition rules which will infringe Article 81(1) and will only, in extremely rare circumstances, merit exemption. If detected, and in the absence of the agreement being notified,[109] a large fine may be imposed on the undertakings proved to have been party to the infringement.

As a result, undertakings, instead of trying to defend the legitimacy of the practices under Article 81, have tended more recently to be driven underground and to attempt to hide their participation in these types of arrangements. The challenge for the Commission is therefore to uncover the covert operation of such cartels and, where evidence is skimpy, to determine whether or not the parallel behaviour on the market results from explicit collusion, which is prohibited under Article 81, or tacit co-ordination, which is not.

---

[107] [1986] OJ L232/15, [1991] 4 CMLR 130.

[108] See e.g., *UNIDI* [1984] OJ L322/10, [1985] 2 CMLR 38.

[109] Even where the parties notify the agreement, the Commission may decide to suspend the parties' immunity from fines: see *Stichting Certicatie Kraaverhuurbedrijf and the Federatie van Nederlandse Krannverhuurbedrijven* [1995] OJ L312/79, [1996] 4 CMLR 565.

(ii) AGREEMENTS

The term agreement has been construed to catch all agreements concluded between undertakings whatever their form.[110] Oral, informal, and gentlemen's agreements are caught. No provision for constraints or penalties need be made. An agreement exists once the parties agree on 'good neighbour rules' or 'establish practice and ethics' or 'certain rules of the game which it is in the interests of all of us to follow'.[111] Complex schemes of arrangements may be characterized as a single continuing agreement if a sufficient consensus to adhere to a plan which limits the parties' commercial freedom can be established.

(iii) DECISIONS BY ASSOCIATIONS OF UNDERTAKINGS

a. THE MEANING OF DECISIONS BY ASSOCIATIONS OF UNDERTAKINGS

In Chapter 3 it was seen that the term 'association' has been construed broadly to catch the decisions of trade associations and other bodies. Further, associations, particularly trade associations, frequently provide the ideal forum for competitors to get together and to discuss matters which may be to their mutual interest. Thus activities of trade associations may also have to be scrutinized and monitored closely.

Such associations may provide a perfect vehicle through which undertakings in a specific industry co-ordinate action. The prohibition of not only agreements and concerted practices in Article 81(1) but also of *decisions* by associations of undertakings may facilitate the proof and prohibition of collusive devices operated through associations. The authorities have adopted a broad construction of the term 'decision'. For example, resolutions passed at an association meeting or an association's recommendations may constitute a decision by an association of undertakings where they manifest a resolve of the association to co-ordinate the conduct of its members. Article 81(1) applies to associations of undertakings where the activities of the associations are aimed at producing effects prohibited under the Article.[112]

b. MEDIUM FOR A CARTEL

Most blatantly, members have used trade associations as a convenient medium through which to meet and to formulate and administer an agreement or cartel. In *Re Belgian Roofing Felt Cartel*[113] an agreement was discovered between members of Belasco (Société Coopérative des Asphalteurs Belges) which was intended to ensure control of the Belgian roofing market. The parties had agreed, amongst other things, to adopt a common price list and minimum selling prices for roofing felt, to set quotas for sales on the Belgian market, and to advertise jointly their 'Belasco' products. The agreement was implemented by resolutions passed at the general meeting of Belasco. Belasco actively participated in the operations in a number of ways: in particular, it employed an accountant who was central in policing

---

[110] See *supra* Chap. 3.

[111] Cases 209–215, 218/78, *Van Landewyck v. Commission* [1980] ECR 3125, [1981] 3 CMLR 134, paras. 85 and 86 and *Cement* [1994] OJ L343/1, [1995] 4 CMLR 327, para. 45(6).

[112] *Cement* [1994] OJ L343/1, [1995] 4 CMLR 327, para. 44(2).

[113] Case 246/86, *Re Roofing Felt Cartel: BELASCO v. Commission* [1989] ECR 2117, [1991] 4 CMLR 96.

compliance with the agreement. The accountant monitored compliance with quotas at the end of each year. Penalties were levied on members which had exceeded their quotas. Further, Belasco financed the joint advertising of the 'Belasco' trade mark which fostered users' impression of a homogeneous product. Members were not, therefore, able to compete by differentiating their products.

c. TRADE ASSOCIATION RECOMMENDATIONS

An association that simply makes recommendations to its members will not necessarily escape the application of Article 81(1). Even though the recommendation has no binding effect, it will be prohibited if in reality the recommendation is intended to determine, or is likely to have the effect of determining, the members' conduct. In *IAZ*,[114] a recommendation made by an association of water-supply undertakings that its members should not connect 'unauthorized' appliances (without a conformity label supplied by another Belgian trade association) to the mains systems was held to be a binding decision capable of restricting competition within the meaning of Article 81(1). The practice discriminated against non-Belgian producers of the appliances. Similarly, in *FENEX*,[115] the Commission held that the recommendation of tariffs by a Dutch association to its member forwarding companies constituted a decision by an association of undertakings within the meaning of Article 81(1). Although the tariffs merely took the form of recommendations, the procedure for drawing up and circulating the tariffs was a habitual activity of the association and was accompanied by circulars drafted in more mandatory terms. The Commission concluded that the circulation of the tariffs had to be interpreted as a faithful reflection of the association's resolve to co-ordinate the conduct of its members on the relevant market.

d. MEDIUM FOR EXCHANGE OF INFORMATION

More subtly, the association may simply collect and disseminate sensitive information and facilitate its exchange between competitors. Were the association to be used, for example, as a vehicle for exchanging information on the prices that the members intended to charge for their products etc., the parties would inevitably be found to be operating a concerted practice.[116] Further, it will be seen from the *UK Agricultural Tractor Exchange* case[117] that, where members of an association operating within a tight oligopolistic market agree to distribute detailed market information between themselves, the agreement may well be found to restrict competition.

e. CERTIFICATION SCHEMES

The Commission will also be wary where members of an association operate certification schemes in case, in reality, the scheme is designed to exclude non-members from business

---

[114] *Anseau* [1982] OJ L167/39, [1982] 2 CMLR 193, on appeal Case 96/82, *IAZ International Belgium NV v. Commission* [1983] ECR 3369, [1984] 3 CMLR 276.

[115] [1996] OJ L181/28, [1996] 5 CMLR 332.

[116] See Cases 40–48, 50, 54–56, 111, 113–4/73, *Re the European Sugar Cartel; Cooperatiëve Vereniging 'Suiker Unie' UA v. Commission* [1975] ECR 1663, [1976] 1 CMLR 295.

[117] [1992] OJ L68/19, upheld on appeal, Case T–34/92 *Fiatagri and Ford New Holland v. Commission* [1994] ECR II–905, and Case T–35/92, *John Deere Ltd v. Commission* [1994] ECR II–957; on appeal to the ECJ Case C–7/95P, *John Deere Ltd v. Commission* [1998] ECR I–3111, [1998] 5 CMLR 311.

opportunities or to preclude foreign undertakings from penetrating the domestic market of the association's members.[118] The word 'decision', in addition to catching acts of the association which are binding on its members, may also, therefore, catch more informal methods of co-ordinating members' actions. Certification schemes may therefore be caught where they are utilized to exclude non-members or to exclude foreign imports from the market.[119] In *Stichting Certificatie Kraanverhuurbedrijf and the Federatie van Nederlandse Krannverhuurbedrijven v Commission*,[120] the Commission fined both FNK and SCK after an examination of agreements that they had notified.[121] Not only did the rules of FNK (the rules constituted a decision by an association of undertakings) providing for the charging of 'reasonable' rates by its members infringe Article 81(1), but SCK's rules on the certification of the crane-hire trade were also caught. The prohibition on the certificate holders from hiring cranes from non-affiliated firms without valid certification plates (and not affiliated to SCK) restricted competition between affiliated firms and substantially restricted access to the market by other firms.

The individual members themselves may be fined where membership coincides with participation in the agreement. Further, where the Commission finds that there has been a 'decision' by an association of undertakings, the association may be fined independently. In *Re Belgian Roofing Felt Cartel*[122] fines were imposed on both Belasco itself (ECU 15,000) and the individual members of the cartel (between ECU 50,000 and 420,000 each). In fixing those amounts, the Commission took account of the annual turnover of each undertaking concerned (and the turnover for supplies of roofing felt) and, in Belasco's case, its annual expenses.[123]

f. THE TRADE ASSOCIATION'S CONSTITUTION

The constitution and rules of a trade association may themselves qualify as a decision (and an agreement) within Article 81(1).[124]

g. GOVERNMENTAL INTERVENTION

The fact that a governmental body has either approved of or even imposed an obligation on an association to adopt a scale of compulsory tariffs for the association's members does not

---

[118] As in *Anseau* [1982] OJ L167/39, [1982] 2 CMLR 193, on appeal Case 96/82, *IAZ International Belgium NV v. Commission* [1983] ECR 3369, [1984] 3 CMLR 276. See also Case 8/72, *Vereeniging van Cementhandelaren v. Commission* [1972] ECR 977, [1973] CMLR 7.

[119] As shown in Case 96/82, *IAZ International Belgium NV v. Commission* [1983] ECR 3369, [1984] 3 CMLR 276.

[120] *Stichting Certificatie Kraanverhuurbedrijf and the Federatie van Nederlandse Krannverhuurbedrijven* [1995] OJ L312/79, [1996] 4 CMLR 565; on appeal Cases T–213/95 and T–18/96, *Stichting Certificatie Kraanverhuurbedrijf and the Federatie van Nederlandse Krannverhuurbedrijven v. Commission* [1997] ECR II–1739, [1998] 4 CMLR 259.

[121] After a preliminary examination of the agreements ([1994] OJ L117/30), the Commission had suspended the parties' immunity from fines that arises on the notification of an agreement to the Commission (Reg. 17 [1959–62] OJ Spec. Ed. 87, Art. 15(6)). For the suspension of immunity on fines see *infra* Chap. 14.

[122] [1986] OJ L232/15, [1991] 4 CMLR 130; on appeal Case 246/86, *Re Roofing Felt Cartel: BELASCO v. Commission* [1989] ECR 2117, [1991] 4 CMLR 96.

[123] For the Commission's fining policy generally, see *infra* Chap. 14.

[124] *National Sulphuric Acid* [1980] OJ L260/24, [1980] 3 CMLR 429.

alter any resolution's (or other decision's) status as a decision of an association of undertakings.[125]

(iii) CONCERTED PRACTICE

a. THE NATURE OF A CONCERTED PRACTICE

Because of its all-embracing nature, conduct which amounts to an agreement within the meaning of Article 81(1) may range from more formal agreements set out in writing to the most informal understanding resulting from a 'nod and a wink'. The latter may present elements of both an agreement and a concerted practice. It was seen in Chapter 3 above that the term 'concerted practice' is a difficult concept. Broadly, however, it provides a safety-net. Its aim is to ensnare 'colluders' not otherwise caught by Article 81 by forestalling the possibility of undertakings evading the application of that Article by colluding in a manner falling short of a definite agreement. Its meaning was explained by the ECJ in *ICI v Commission (Dyestuffs)*. The Court held that the term caught:

co-ordination between undertakings which, without having reached the stage where an agreement, properly so called has been concluded, knowingly substitutes practical co-operation between them for the risks of competition.[126]

The concept thus epitomizes the notion inherent in Article 81 that economic operators should determine the commercial policy that they intend to adopt on the market *independently*. The difficulty is that where undertakings enter into arrangements which the participants know to be contrary to the competition rules, they act surreptitiously, embarking on elaborate schemes such as those discovered in *Polypropylene*[127] and *PVC*.[128] Where unwritten, secret arrangements are involved it may be difficult to uncover any co-operation and to identify the moment at which consensus is reached. In such a case the parties will argue that, since there is no proof of an agreement, their conduct is not caught by Article 81(1). It is in these types of cases that the Commission may prefer to characterize the collusion as concerted practices rather than agreements.

b. THE DISTINCTION BETWEEN AGREEMENT AND CONCERTED PRACTICES

In the appeals from the Commission's decision in *Polypropylene*[129] the question arose

---

[125] *AICIA v. CNSD* [1993] OJ L203/27, [1995] 5 CMLR 495, paras. 42–44.

[126] Cases 48, 49, 51–7/69, *ICI v. Commission (Dyestuffs)* [1972] ECR 619, 655, [1972] CMLR 557, para. 64.

[127] *Polypropylene* [1986] OJ L230/1, [1988] 4 CMLR 347, appeals substantially dismissed both by the CFI and the ECJ: see e.g., Case C–51/92P, *SA Hercules NV v. Commission* [1999] 5 CMLR 976 and Case C–199/92P, *Hüls AG v. Commission (Polypropylene)* [1999] 5 CMLR 1016.

[128] [1994]OJ L239/14, upheld by the CFI on appeal: Cases T–305–307, 313–316, 318, 325, 328–329 & 335/94, *Limburgse Vinyl Maatschappij NV v. Commission* [1999] ECR II–931 [1999] 5 CMLR 303 (*PVC Cartel II*). The 1994 decision replaced the original 1990 one, [1989] OJ L 74/1, [1990] 4 CMLR 345, annulled on appeal by the ECJ on procedural grounds: Cases C–137/92P, *Commission v. BASF* [1994] ECR I–2555 setting aside the judgment of the CFI: Cases T–79/89 etc., *BASF v. Commission* [1992] ECR II–315, [1992] 4 CMLR 357 which had declared the decision non-existent. For this aspect of the case, see *infra* Chap. 14.

[129] *Polypropylene* [1986] OJ L230/1, [1988] 4 CMLR 347, appeals substantially dismissed both by the CFI and the ECJ: see e.g., Case C–51/92P, *SA Hercules NV v. Commission* [1999] 5 CMLR 976 and Case C–199/92P, *Hüls AG v. Commission (Polypropylene)* [1999] 5 CMLR 1016.

whether or not it mattered whether the parties' conduct was characterized as an agreement or a concerted practice. One of the arguments raised by some of the parties was that although an agreement would be caught by Article 81(1) even if it was not implemented, as intended, on the market, direct or indirect conduct which has not been implemented on a market does not amount to a concerted practice. An agreement, however informal and whether or not successful or acted upon, is a consensual act. In contrast, the word 'practice' in the concept concerted practice requires proof not only of concertation but *also* of the fact that steps have been taken to give effect to the concertation. There would, therefore, be no actual concerted *practice* if the parties only *plotted* to co-ordinate their behaviour but did not carry out that plot by conduct on the market. The arguments supporting this view and academic writings on this issue are fully reviewed in the Opinion of Advocate General Vesterdorf designated by the President of the CFI.[130]

In the *Polypropylene* appeal, the ECJ accepted that the concept of a concerted practice did require, in addition to concertation between the undertakings, 'subsequent conduct on the market, and a relationship of cause and effect between the two'.[131] However, once the Commission had adduced evidence of concertation it was for the undertaking to establish that concertation had not been followed by conduct on the market.

Case C-199/92P, *Hüls AG v Commission (Polypropylene)*, 8 July 1999, [1999] 5 CMLR 1016

Court of Justice

158. The Court of Justice has consistently held that a concerted practice refers to a form of co-ordination between undertakings which, without having been taken to a stage where an agreement properly so-called has been concluded, knowingly substitutes for the risks of competition practical co-operation between . . .

159. The criteria of co-ordination and co-operation must be understood in the light of the concept inherent in the provisions of the Treaty relating to competition, according to which each economic operator must determine independently the policy which he intends to adopt on the market . . .

160. According to that case law, although that requirement of independence does not deprive economic operators of the right to adapt themselves intelligently to the existing and anticipated conduct of their competitors, it does however strictly preclude any direct or indirect contact between such operators, the object or effect whereof is either to influence the conduct on the market of an actual or potential competitor or to disclose to such a competitor the course of conduct which they themselves have decided to adopt or contemplate adopting on the market,

---

[130] See [1991] ECR I–1711, 1923–1946, [1992] 4 CMLR 84, 141–164. The AG was appointed following the order of the ECJ referring this and other cases to the CFI soon after its establishment. It was the view of the AG that failed attempts to concert would not be caught by Art. 81(1). The CFI did not specifically address this point, since it took the view that having participated in and having obtained information from meetings with competitors an undertaking would be bound to take it into account, directly or indirectly, when determining its conduct on the market. The Court assumed that information acquired as a result of a concerted practice always influences the market conduct of the participants: see e.g., Case T–7/89, *SA Hercules NV v. Commission* [1991] ECR II–1711, [1992] 4 CMLR 84, para. 260.

[131] Case C–199/92P, *Hüls AG v. Commission* [1999] 5 CMLR 1016, para. 161.

where the object or effect of such contact is to create conditions of competition which do not correspond to the normal conditions of the market in question, regard being had to the nature of the products or services offered, the size and number of the undertakings and the volume of the said market . . .

161. It follows, first, that the concept of a concerted practice, as it results from the actual terms of Article [81(1)] E.C., implies, besides undertakings' concerting with each other, subsequent conduct on the market, and a relationship of cause and effect between the two.

162. However, subject to proof to the contrary, which the economic operators concerned must adduce, the presumption must be that the undertakings taking part in the concerted action and remaining active on the market take account of the information exchanged with their competitors for the purposes of determining their conduct on that market. That is all the more true where the undertakings concert together on a regular basis over a long period, as was the case here, according to the findings of the Court of First Instance.

163. Secondly, contrary to Hüls's argument, a concerted practice as defined above is caught by Article [81(1)] E.C., even in the absence of anti-competitive effects on the market.

164. First, it follows from the actual text of that provision that, as in the case of agreements between undertakings and decisions by associations of undertakings, concerted practices are prohibited, regardless of their effect, when they have an anti-competitive object.

165. Next, although the very concept of a concerted practice presupposes conduct by the participating undertakings on the market, it does not necessarily mean that that conduct should produce the specific effect of restricting, preventing or distorting competition.

166. Lastly, that interpretation is not incompatible with the restrictive nature of the prohibition laid down in Article [81(1)] E.C. . . . since, far from extending its scope, it corresponds to the literal meaning of the terms used in that provision.

167. Consequently, contrary to Hüls's argument, the Court of First Instance was not in breach of the rules applying to the burden of proof when it considered that, since the Commission had established to the requisite legal standard that Hüls had taken part in polypropylene producers' concerting together for the purpose of restricting competition, it did not have to adduce evidence that their concerting together had manifested itself in conduct on the market or that it had had effects restrictive of competition; on the contrary, it was for Hüls to prove that that did not have any influence whatsoever on its own conduct on the market.

It can also be seen from the extract above that the Court emphasized that the question whether or not the parties had engaged in a concerted practice was completely distinct from the question whether or not the agreement had restricted competition. Where the object of the concerted practice was clearly to restrict competition it was not necessary to show that the conduct had had the *effect* of restricting, preventing, or distorting competition.

The position thus appears to be that there is a distinction between co-operation identified as a concerted practice and co-operation identified as an agreement. The former requires not only concertation *but also* subsequent conduct. In practice, however, since there is a presumption that concertation has been followed by conduct this is unlikely to make a material difference. It is hard to envisage circumstances in which an undertaking can establish that its conduct was *not* influenced by information acquired through concerting with others. The most important question appears to be whether or not there was collusion. 'The importance of the concept of a concerted practice does not thus result so much from the distinction between it and an agreement as from the distinction between forms of collusion falling under Article [81(1)] and mere parallel behaviour with no element of concertation.'[132] It thus seems that '[i]n the context of a complex infringement which involves many producers seeking over a number of years to regulate the market between them' the Commission may be able to adopt a decision that classifies the infringement as either an agreement or a concerted practice.[133]

The following are examples of the type of conduct which might be used to establish that the parties involved have engaged in a 'concerted practice'.

c. DIRECT OR INDIRECT CONTACT

If parties (however informally or loosely) agree to let other players know in advance of their anticipated future business moves, this may well amount to concerted practice. As the ECJ held in *Suiker Unie*,[134] the criteria do not require the working out of an actual plan but preclude any:

direct or indirect contact between [competitors], the object or effect whereof is either to influence the conduct on the market of an actual or potential competitor or to disclose to such a competitor the course of conduct which they themselves have decided to adopt or contemplate adopting on the market.[135]

Although in such an instance there is no agreement, collusive devices are used by the parties to facilitate the co-ordination of their commercial behaviour. In *Suiker Unie*, documents established that the parties had in fact contacted each other and that they pursued the aim of removing in advance any uncertainty about the future conduct of their competitors.

In *PVC*,[136] the Commission considered that the term concerted practice was particularly apt to cover the involvement of some undertakings, for example Shell. Shell, whilst not a full member of the cartel, had co-operated with it. It was thus able to adapt its own market behaviour in the light of this contact.

An acute difficulty might be to determine whether or not the players have intended to let each other know in advance what their intended business moves will be. For example, can undertakings be said to have concerted if they exchange information which is freely available to the public generally. It might be argued that the exchange of sensitive information, such as price lists, which is available to the public and consequently to an undertaking's competitors should not be prevented under Article 81(1). Take, for example, four leading undertakings competing on a market which publish price lists setting out prices to be charged over the next quarter. Since each undertaking has only three main competitors, each will probably take steps to get hold of the others' price lists. For example, an employee may drive to the premises of the competitors and obtain price lists. Given the ease with which the information can be acquired can a decision by the undertakings to exchange this information be prohibited (after all it would save cost and pollution if the lists were simply put in the post)?

The purpose of Article 81(1) is, however, to ensure that where possible undertakings act

---

[132] *Polypropylene* [1986] OJ L230/1, [1988] 4 CMLR 347, para. 87.

[133] Cases T–305–307, 313–316, 318, 325, 328–329 and 335/94, *Limburgse Vinyl Maatschappij NV v. Commision* [1999] ECR I–931 [1999] 5 CMLR 303 (*PVC Cartel II*), paras. 696–697.

[134] Cases 40–48, 50, 54–56, 111, 113–4/73, *Re the European Sugar Cartel; Cooperatieve Vereniging 'Suiker Unie' UA v. Commission* [1975] ECR 1663, [1976] 1 CMLR 295.

[135] *Ibid.* para. 174.

[136] [1994] OJ L239/14.

'independently' so that a spirit of competition is fostered on the market. Thus it seems inevitable that the Commission will find that the exchange of information on prices to be charged is caught by Article 81(1). Even if the parties have not actually agreed to exchange the information the simple exchange will be prohibited since the behaviour of the undertakings will almost certainly eliminate 'the risks of competition and the hazards of competitors' spontaneous reactions by co-operation'.[137] Exchanges of information, the object or effect of which is to influence the conduct on the market of an actual or potential competitor, to disclose to a competitor the course of conduct which the sender has decided to adopt on a market or rendering the market artificially transparent will therefore be unacceptable.[138] Indeed, the Commission has taken steps generally to discourage the exchange of less sensitive information on oligopolistic markets. It takes the view that the exchange exacerbates the problems of, and increases transparency on, oligopolistic markets where there is already limited opportunity for competition.[139]

In contrast, Article 81(1) does not ordinarily preclude unilateral decisions adopted by undertakings independently, for example, a decision to send its price list to the press for publication. Such behaviour will be prohibited only if an agreement, an understanding, or direct or indirect contact between the parties (a concerted practice) is established.[140]

d. PARTICIPATION IN MEETINGS

In *Polypropylene*[141] although the Commission had concluded that an agreement existed between the undertakings, the CFI[142] confirmed that the Commission had been correct to classify the meetings in the alternative as a concerted practice. The clear purpose of the competing undertakings participating in meetings during which information was exchanged about, for example, the prices and sales volumes was to disclose to each other the course of conduct which each of the producers itself contemplated adopting on the market.[143] Participants clearly had the aim of eliminating any uncertainty about the future conduct of their competitors. They were bound to take into account the course of conduct upon which other participants had decided.

Any regular participant at this type of meeting which might suggest that it had not subscribed to the initiatives agreed would have to convince the Commission, or Court, that this was the case by means of corroborative evidence.[144] The fact that it had not put the initiatives into effect would be no defence. Evidence of prices or other behaviour which do not reflect those discussed at the meeting would not, therefore, be sufficient to convince the Court that it had not participated in the scheme.[145] It would have to be established that the

---

[137] Cases 48, 49, 51–7/69 *ICI v. Commission (Dyestuffs)* [1972] ECR 619, [1972] CMLR 557, para. 119.

[138] See also, Cases 40–48, 50, 54–56/73, *Re the European Sugar Cartel: Cooperatiëve Verniging 'Suiker Unie' UA v Commission* [1975] ECR 1663, [1976] 1 CMLR 295.

[139] See *infra*, 671 ff.

[140] See discussion *infra* 663 ff.

[141] *Polypropylene* [1986] OJ L230/1, [1988] 4 CMLR 347.

[142] The judgments of the ECJ focussed mainly on procedural arguments, but see e.g., Case C–199/92P, *Hüls AG v. Commission (Polypropylene)* [1999] 5 CMLR 1016, discussed *supra* 659.

[143] E.g., Case T–7/89, *Hercules NV v. Commission* [1992] ECR II–1711, [1992] 4 CMLR 84, para. 259.

[144] See e.g., Case 2/89, *Petrofina SA v. Commission* [1991] ECR II–1087, para. 128; Case T–14/89, *Montedipe v. Commission* [1992] ECR II–1155, [1993] 4 CMLR 110.

[145] Case T–3/89, *Atochem v. Commission* [1991] ECR II–867, para. 100.

undertaking did not have any anti-competitive intention when it attended the meetings, and that the other participants were aware of this.[146] In *Steel Beams*[147] the CFI also held, in the context of a decision taken under Article 65 of the ECSC Treaty, that undertakings participating in meetings in which anti-competitive activities are pursued will be taken, in the absence of proof to the contrary, to have participated in those activities.

Documentary evidence found at the premises of one cartel member may be used against other members of the cartel. However, the document must be an objective reflection of the meeting's content and be sufficiently precise. The fact that the note may be 'badly written, unsigned and undated is quite normal, since it is a note taken during a conversation . . . and the anti-competitive nature of the note was reason for its author to leave the least trace possible'.[148]

(iv) CONCERTED PRACTICES AND PARALLEL BEHAVIOUR

a. THE OLIGOPOLY PROBLEM

It has already been explained that in some markets it appears that players do not need actually to meet or communicate. Market forces dictate that the undertakings set their prices 'as if' there had been some collusion between them. Undertakings operating on a market on which there are only a few players may align their conduct as a rational response to the market circumstances. Because there are only a few players on the market, their awareness of each other's presence is automatically heightened. An undertaking is bound to monitor the behaviour of its competitors since a reduction in price by a competitor may swiftly attract away the former's customers. Oligopolists may, therefore, recognize their interdependence and realize, without the need for explicit communication, that the most efficient course of conduct is for them all to set their prices at a profit-maximizing level. The players behave 'as if' they have agreed to act in a manner which maximizes the profits of the market players.

It is generally the case that the markets on which oligopolistic parallel pricing might occur are also prone to cartelization.[149] Where a competition authority has been unable to collect sufficient evidence of explicit collusion it will be very difficult for it to know whether or not there has, in fact, been collusion (and the communication process hidden) or whether the parties have simply tacitly colluded or consciously adopted parallel behaviour.

Arguably, since the effect of tacit collusion and explicit collusion is the same in economic terms, both should be prohibited under the Treaty rules. It is important to know, therefore, the minimum degree of interaction between undertakings required for concertation to be proved, in particular, whether or not parallel behaviour or conscious parallelism, without any proof of explicit collusion, is prohibited under Article 81.[150] If it is not, and Article

---

[146] *Ibid., paras. 53–54.*

[147] Case T–141/94, *Thyssen Stahl AG v. Commission* [1999] 4 CMLR 810, para. 177.

[148] Case T–11/89, *Shell v. Commission* [1991] ECR II–757.

[149] See *supra* 636–639. Markets with too many firms for successful tacit collusion but sufficiently few firms to control cheating on a price agreement may provide the best prospects for cartel investigation.

[150] In a strict sense, oligopolists do not behave independently since their ability to co-ordinate their behaviour results from their mutual interdependence and the modification of their behaviour accordingly. Does this, however, amount to concertation and, therefore, to a concerted practice within the meaning of Art. 81(1)?

81(1) applies only if the parties have in fact collaborated, can the Commission prove the existence of such concertation by relying on economic evidence alone? Can parallel conduct ever be used to justify a finding that an agreement or concerted practice existed between the undertakings, and what proof must be adduced to show that a concerted practice has indeed taken place?

The answer to these questions has been clearly provided in the ECJ's judgment in *Wood Pulp*.[151] First, tacit co-ordination is not prohibited by Article 81(1). Secondly, although parallel behaviour may furnish proof of explicit collusion it will do so only if the behaviour cannot be explained by the conditions of competition on the market, for example, oligopolistic interdependence. Before looking at the Court's judgment in *Wood Pulp* it is, however, first useful to consider some of the Court's previous rulings, in particular its judgment in *Dyestuffs*, *Suiker Unie*, and *Züchner*.

b. THE *DYESTUFFS* CASE

In *Dyestuffs*, three general and uniform increases in the prices of dyestuffs had taken place within the common market over a period of years. The first, in 1964, took place on the markets in Italy, Holland, Belgium, and Luxembourg, the second in 1965 on the market in Germany, and in 1967 uniform increases took place in Germany, Holland, Belgium, Luxembourg, and France (the latter at a different rate, since prices had previously been frozen by the Government there).

In this case the Commission concluded that the increases had occurred as a result of a concerted practice operating between ten producers (it had discovered significant evidence of actual direct/indirect contact between the parties).[152]

The ECJ upheld the decision. The behaviour constituted a concerted practice prohibited by Article 81(1) of the Treaty. In particular, the Court relied upon the fact that price increases had been announced in advance (the announcements eliminating all uncertainty between them as regards their future conduct and the risk inherent in any independent change in conduct) and that the announcements rendered the market transparent as regards the rates of increases. Further, given the number of producers on the European dyestuffs market, it did not consider that it was possible to say, as the applicants had alleged, that the market was an oligopolistic one. Price competition should have been able to play a substantial role. It was not plausible, therefore, that the parallel conduct could have been brought into effect within a period of two to three days without prior concertation. The Court concluded that, taking into account the nature of the market in the products in question, the conduct of the undertakings was designed to replace both the risks of competition and the hazards of competitors' spontaneous reactions with co-operation.

There were suggestions and concern after the Court's judgment that its interpretation of the term 'concerted practice' would be used broadly to catch rational, and purely parallel, market behaviour.[153] The Court had relied mainly on market data to support its finding that the parties had co-operated, without conducting a thorough study of the market. In

---

[151] Cases C–89 etc/85 [1993] ECR I–1307, [1993] 4 CMLR 407.

[152] *Re Cartel in Aniline Dyes* [1969] CMLR D23.

[153] E.g., see V. Korah, 'Concerted Practices' (1973) 36 *MLR* 260; R. Joliet, 'La notion de pratique concertée et l'arrêt I.C.I. dans une perspective comparative' [1974] *CDE* 251.

particular, it characterized behaviour as apparently innocuous as making price announcements in advance as an impermissible means of indirect communication.[154]

The Commission had, however, in fact discovered significant evidence of actual direct/indirect contact between the parties. It had not relied on economic evidence of parallel behaviour alone. Apart from the similarity in rates and dates of increases, the Commission found proof of concertation from the similarity of the content of the orders sent by the producers to their subsidiaries or representatives on the various markets, to make the increases. The orders were on occasions sent on the same day (at the same hour), were couched in similar terms, and showed a very great similarity in drafting. Some messages contained exactly identical phrases which, the Commission concluded, could not be explained in the absence of a prior concert between the undertakings involved (especially since they had been sent on the same day or hour even). The Commission also discovered records of meetings of the producers in Basel and London. The records disclosed that not only was the question of prices discussed but that on occasions the dates and timings of intended price increases were announced.

Further, the ECJ specifically stated that 'parallel behaviour may not by itself be identified with a concerted practice' although it could provide 'strong evidence of such a practice if it leads to conditions of competition which do not correspond to the normal conditions of the market, having regard to the nature of the products, the size and number of the undertakings, and the volume of the said market'.[155] This would be the case, for example, where prices were stabilized at a level different from that to which competition would otherwise have led. A producer was thus 'free to charge his prices, taking into account in so doing the present or foreseeable conduct of his competitors'. In contrast, he was precluded from co-operating 'with his competitors, in any way whatsoever, in order to determine a co-ordinated course of action relating to a price increase to ensure its success by prior elimination of all uncertainty as to each other's conduct'.[156] However:

As Professor Joliet pointed out, the judgment was not so much worrying because of its definition of a concerted practice but more because it so easily assumed, without a detailed study of the market characteristics and without evidence of concertation, that parties had cooperated. Although the Court recognized the need to consider the specific features of the market in weighing the evidence, . . . it only did so superficially . . .[157]

c. *SUIKER UNIE* AND *ZÜCHNER*

In both *Suiker Unie*[158] and *Züchner*[159] the ECJ stressed that Article 81(1) did not prevent an undertaking from adapting its behaviour intelligently to the existing or anticipated conduct of competitors. In accordance with these judgments the Commission, in *Zinc Producer's Group*,[160] accepted the legitimacy of parallel/oligopolistic behaviour. It held that:

---

[154] See *infra* 669–671.

[155] Cases 48, 49, 51–7/69 [1972] ECR 619, [1972] CMLR 557, para. 66; see Annex 4.

[156] *Ibid.*, para. 118.

[157] G. van Gerven and E.N. Varona, 'The Wood Pulp Case and the Future of Concerted Practices' (1994) 31 *CMLRev.* 575, 590.

[158] Cases 40–48, 50, 54–56, 111, 113–4/73, *Re the European Sugar Cartel: Cooperatiëve Vereniging 'Suiker Unie' UA v. Commission* [1975] ECR 1663, [1976] 1 CMLR 295.

[159] Case 172/80, *Züchner v. Bayerische Vereinsbank* [1981] ECR 2021, [1982] 1 CMLR 313.

[160] [1984] OJ L220/27, [1985] 2 CMLR 108.

parallel pricing behaviour in an oligopoly producing homogeneous goods [would] not in itself be sufficient evidence of a concerted practice.[161]

Thus, parallel action explicable in terms of barometric price leadership (that is to say, linked to a change in the market conditions, for example, an increase in the price of the main raw material) would not be sufficient evidence of a concerted practice.

d. WOOD PULP

The ECJ in *Re Wood Pulp Cartel: Ahlström Oy v Commission (Wood Pulp II)*[162] delivered the clearest judgment so far on the relationship between conscious parallelism (or tacit collusion) and concerted practices. The Commission had investigated alleged restrictive practices and agreements between pulp producers operating on the bleached sulphate wood pulp market. The Commission found several breaches of Article 81(1) and levied fines on forty-three wood pulp producers.[163] In particular, it found that concertation between many of the Finnish, US, and Canadian undertakings with regard to both announced and transaction prices in the pulp market had led to prices which were both artificially high and rigid. The Commission considered that the parallel behaviour was not explicable as rational behaviour.[164] It could not be explained as independently chosen parallel conduct in a narrow oligopolistic market (the market was characterized by a large number of producers, customers, and products; the market was not inherently transparent, but was only so as a result of the producers' deliberately chosen strategy of making price announcements in advance and there was no clear price leader etc.). The parties sought annulment of the Commission's decision before the ECJ.

The Court annulled much of the Commission's decision and many of the fines on substantive grounds. It considered two separate points: first whether or not the price announcements were in themselves prohibited by Article 81(1)[165] and secondly whether they provided evidence of a concerted practice and concertation in advanced prices.

The Court reiterated its previous statements that parallel conduct could not be used to establish the existence of a concerted practice unless, taking account of the nature of the products, the size and the number of undertakings, and the volume of the market in question, it could not be explained otherwise than by concertation. Parallel behaviour would furnish proof of concertation only where it constituted the only plausible explanation for such conduct. Every producer was free to react intelligently to market forces and to alter its course of action, taking into account in so doing the present or foreseeable conduct of his competitors.

The Court was not prepared to reject, as the Commission had done, the protestations that the undertaking's behaviour was a consequence, not of a concerted practice, but of non-collusive interdependence or conscious parallelism. It commissioned two independent

---

[161] *Ibid.*, paras 75–76.

[162] Cases C–89, 104, 114, 116–117, 125–129/85 [1993] ECR I–1307, [1993] 4 CMLR 407.

[163] [1985] OJ L85/1, [1985] 3 CMLR 474.

[164] Although the Commission relied on some documentary evidence to supplement its finding this was excluded by the Court.

[165] See *infra* 669–671.

reports from economic experts to analyse the wood pulp market and the evidence involved. The reports were extremely damaging to the Commission's case. On the facts and relying on experts' reports, the Court found that the system of quarterly price announcements did not, of itself, amount to an infringement of Article 81(1)[166] and that this system and the parallelism of announced prices were not evidence of concertation. It could not be conclusively stated that the system of advance price announcements and parallel behaviour was a result of a concerted practice. The Commission had failed sufficiently to appreciate that the wood pulp market had oligopolistic tendencies, being characterized by oligopolies and oligopsonies (on the buying side), in particular pulp types. Also the market was inherently transparent. Paper manufacturers were in constant touch with a number of pulp suppliers and exchanged price information amongst themselves and the transparency was reinforced both by a number of common agents that operated throughout the market and an active trade press.

The system of advanced announced prices was, therefore, explicable as a rational response to the fact that the pulp market was a long-term one and met a legitimate business concern of customers.

Cases C–89, 104, 114, 116–117, 125–129/85, *Re Wood Pulp Cartel: Ahlström Oy v Commission (Wood Pulp II)* [1993] ECR 1–1307, [1993] 4 CMLR 407

Court of Justice

70. Since the Commission has no documents which directly establish the existence of concertation between the producers concerned, it is necessary to ascertain whether the system of quarterly price announcements, the simultaneity or near-simultaneity of the price announcements and the parallelism of price announcements as found during the period from 1975 to 1985 constitute a firm, precise and consistent body of evidence of prior concertation.

71. In determining the probative value of those different factors, it must be noted that parallel conduct cannot be regarded as furnishing proof of concertation unless concertation constitutes the only plausible explanation for such conduct. It is necessary to bear in mind that, although Article [81] ... prohibits any form of collusion which distorts competition, it does not deprive economic operators of the right to adapt themselves intelligently to the existing and anticipated conduct of their competitors (see *Suiker Unie*, ... paragraph 174).

72. Accordingly, it is necessary in this case to ascertain whether the parallel conduct alleged by the Commission cannot, taking account of the nature of the products, the size and the number of the undertakings and the volume of the market in question, be explained otherwise than by concertation.

...

126. Following that analysis, it must be stated that, in this case, concertation is not the only plausible explanation for the parallel conduct. To begin with, the system of price announcements may be regarded as constituting a rational response to the fact that the pulp market constituted a long-term market and to the need felt by both buyers and sellers to limit commercial risks. Further, the similarity in the dates of price announcements may be regarded as a direct result of the high degree of market transparency, which does not have to be described as artificial. Finally, the parallelism of prices and the price trends may be satisfactorily explained by the oligopolistic tendencies of the market and by the specific circumstances prevailing in certain periods. Accordingly, the parallel conduct established by the Commission does not constitute evidence of concertation.

127. In the absence of a firm, precise and consistent body of evidence, it must be held that

[166] See *infra* 670.

concertation regarding announced prices has not been established by the Commission. Article 1(1) of the contested decision must therefore be annulled.

e. CONCLUSIONS ON PARALLEL BEHAVIOUR

It is clear that purely parallel oligopolistic behaviour is not prohibited *per se* by Article 81(1). Parallel behaviour will, however, furnish proof of an agreement or concerted practice *only* if it is not the kind of behaviour which would be anticipated on the market involved (whether the parallel conduct alleged by the Commission cannot, taking into account the nature of the products, the size and number of the undertakings, and the volume of the market in question, be explained otherwise than by concertation) and if there is no other plausible explanation for the conduct.

A. Jones, 'Wood pulp: Concerted Practice and/or Conscious Parallelism' [1993] ECLR 273, 275–276

(a) Concertation and reciprocity

The width of the definition of a concerted practice has been a matter of controversy. There were suggestions that the concept as laid down in the earlier cases was too broad, being wide enough to catch rational market behaviour (eg oligopolistic interdependence or price leadership). There were worries that the Commission might find collusion on insufficient evidence and ignore commercial explanations of what had happened. The court's decision in *Wood pulp* makes it plain that this will not be permitted.

The ECJ referred to and approved its earlier ruling in *Suiker Unie*. Further, it stated that 'parallel conduct cannot be regarded as furnishing proof of concertation unless concertation constituted the only plausible explanation for such conduct. It is necessary to bear in mind that although Article [81] prohibits any form of collusion which distorts competition, it does not deprive economic operators of the right to adapt themselves intelligently to the existing and anticipated conduct of their competitors (see *Suiker Unie*). Accordingly, it is necessary in this case to ascertain whether the parallel conduct alleged by the Commission cannot, taking account of the nature of the products, the size and the number of the undertakings and the volume of the market in question, be explained otherwise than by concertation' . . .

The court considered the alleged infringements set out in the Commission's decision. The system of announcing price increases in advance did not *per se* amount to a concerted practice and actual concertation had not been proved . . . So, some conspiracy between operators needs to be shown. Although parallel behaviour may be evidence of this, it is not in itself either sufficient or prohibited under Article [81].

The ECJ's judgment appears, therefore, to confirm the opinion of Darmon AG in *Wood Pulp* that in the scheme of Article [81] a concerted practice does not refer to identical conduct between undertakings. Mere 'concomitant conduct does not constitute a concerted practice but may at best point, on the basis of further evidence, to the existence of an agreement between the parties concerned.' So, price signalling, for example, should not be considered *per se* to be a violation of Article [81(1)] unless the public exchanges of information established sufficient reciprocal communication to show concertation.

US authority supports this approach. The Supreme Court has refused to find that a Sherman Act offence of restraint of trade caused by 'contract, combination or conspiracy' has been committed on the basis of parallel behaviour alone. 'Circumstantial evidence of consciously parallel behaviour may have made heavy inroads into the traditional judicial attitude towards conspiracy, but 'conscious parallelism' has not yet read conspiracy out of the Sherman Act entirely.'

The ECJ's decision does not, however, give concrete guidance beyond that which can be extracted from the *Suiker Unie* judgment as to what must positively be demonstrated to establish a concerted practice. Some assistance is provided by Darmon AG's opinion. For him the concept required reciprocation of communication between competitors. Although this element had not been stressed sufficiently in earlier decisions of the ECJ it had become apparent in the more recent judgments. It was not necessary that the parties should jointly consider their future policies together, but what was necessary was a co-ordinated course of action which would be successful as a result of the 'prior elimination of all uncertainty as to each other's conduct regarding the essential elements of that action'. In Darmon AG's opinion, 'the concept of concerted practices refers to reciprocal communications between the competitors with the aim of giving each other assurances as to their conduct on the market'. He relied on an English decision,. . . as well as the decisions of the ECJ, to reinforce his conclusion that reciprocity is necessary.

Although the ECJ did not specifically refer to a need for reciprocity this seems implicit from its judgment. Not only was it stressed that Article [81(1)] prohibited *collusion* (parallel conduct alone was not sufficient to establish this) but in considering the quarterly price announcements it found that Article [81(1)] had not been proved to have been infringed. The parties' conduct did nothing to 'lessen each undertaking's uncertainty as to the future attitude of its competitors [since at] the time when each undertaking engages in such behaviour, it cannot be sure of the future conduct of the others.' Thus, the individual announcements did not amount to concertation even though, in practice, they may have served to remove uncertainty as to a competitor's conduct.

Actual communication between the parties appears, therefore, to be a requirement. Something more than simply monitoring a market since every producer is free to alter his course of action 'taking into account in so doing the present or foreseeable conduct of his competitors'. Undertakings can react intelligently to market forces. The ECJ appears to have heeded the Advocate General's advice against an extension of Article [81(1)] to cover unilateral conduct on a market.

(v) CONCERTED PRACTICES AND UNILATERAL PRICE ANNOUNCEMENTS IN ADVANCE

In *Dyestuffs* the ECJ considered that advance price communications provided, in the circumstances, proof of a concerted practice. It held that the announcements rendered the market artificially transparent and eliminated all uncertainty between the operators as regards the rates of increase, future conduct, and the risks inherent in an independent change of conduct. The Court commented:

. . . the undertakings taking the initiative . . . announced their intentions of making an increase some time in advance, which allowed the undertakings to observe each other's reactions on the different markets, and to adapt themselves accordingly. By means of these advance announcements the various undertakings eliminated all uncertainty between them as to their future conduct and, in doing so, also eliminated a large part of the risk usually inherent in any independent change of conduct on one or several markets. This was all the more the case since these announcements, which led to the fixing of general and equal increases in prices for the markets in dyestuffs, rendered the market transparent as regard the percentage rates of increase. Therefore, by the way in which they acted, the undertakings in question temporarily eliminated with respect to prices some of the preconditions for competition on the market which stood in the way of the achievement of parallel uniformity of conduct.[167]

---

[167] Cases 48, 49, 51–7/69, *ICI v. Commission (Dyestuffs)* [1972] ECR 619, [1972] CMLR 557, paras. 100–103.

This case must now be assessed in the light of its own particular facts and the judgment of the ECJ in *Wood Pulp*. In the latter case the Commission found concertation in respect of both announced and actual transaction prices. The ECJ, however, held that price announcements in advance did not, *per se*, constitute an infringement of Article 81(1).

64. In this case, the communications arise from the price announcements made to users. They constitute in themselves market behaviour which does not lessen each undertaking's uncertainty as to the future attitude of its competitors. At the same time when each undertaking engages in such behaviour, it cannot be sure of the future conduct of the others.

65. Accordingly, the system of quarterly price announcements on the pulp market is not to be regarded as constituting in itself an infringement of Article [81](1).

Further, the Court held that it had not been established that the system amounted to a means of indirect communication between the competitors. The announcements served the need of customers desiring the information to plan the cost of their paper products. This provided a plausible or alternative explanation for the parallel behaviour (see the discussion on parallel behaviour at 666–668 above).

In the light of these two cases it is conceivable that, where advanced price announcements or other price signalling do not correspond to a legitimate business justification, the conduct might be considered to be an illegal exchange of information[168] which amounts to indirect contact between the undertakings.[169]

G. van Gerven and E.N. Varona, 'The *Wood Pulp* Case and the Future of Concerted Practices' (1994) 31 CMLRev. 575, 595

It is clear that in deciding whether price signalling is illegal, one should not overlook the circumstances. In the *Wood pulp* case, it was established that (i) there was a clear lawful business justification for advance price communications, since the price of wood pulp constituted a major proportion of the cost of paper and it was the paper producers themselves which had requested prior announcement; (ii) the announcements were made to customers. If, given the high transparency of the market, firms become aware of the prospective pricing of their competitors, so be it. If a rival adapts its pricing to the information it has obtained, it merely 'adapts intelligently to existing or anticipated conduct of its competitors' as allowed by the *Dyestuffs* and *Suiker Unie* judgments.

Firstly, as Advocate Darmon pointed out in his opinion, if price signalling does not correspond to a legitimate business justification, such advance announcements may very well be considered as an illegal exchange of information. In the end, as so often in antitrust law, the decisive question in practice may be whether there is a valid business reason for the particular market conduct. In the *Wood pulp* judgment, the Court had no difficulty finding such a valid business reason for the price announcements and, therefore, it was easy and correct to conclude that the system of price announcements did not give rise to a concerted practice. However, price signalling, if not warranted by any legitimate explanation and clearly not in the individual (non-collusive) self-interest of the individual companies may constitute sufficient evidence of concertation.

Secondly, in *Wood pulp*, it appeared that the trade press was also very rapidly informed of the advance price announcements but the Court went out of its way to state that most of the wood pulp

---

[168] See the Opinion of Darmon AG in Cases C–89, 104, 114, 116–117, 125–129/85, *Re Wood Pulp Cartel: Ahlström Oy v. Commission(Wood Pulp II)* [1993] ECR I–1307, [1993] 4 CMLR 407, para. 251.

[169] For greater discussion, see G. van Gerven and E. Varona, 'The Wood Pulp Case and the Future of Concerted Practices' (1994), 31 *CMLRev.* 575.

producers did not send as a matter of course their announced prices to the trade press and that if, sporadically, this was done, such communications were made at the request of the press. Thus the Court implicitly rejected the Commission's claim that wood pulp producers had deliberately made the market transparent or increased transparency by talking to the press.

In the *Cartonboard* case, where the producers, twice a year, announced price increases several months in advance, the Commission took care to produce documentary evidence establishing that the undertakings had agreed the date and sequence of advance price increases.

The Commission will inevitably be sensitive to attempts by oligopolists to make the market artificially more transparent than it otherwise would be. The section below shows that the Commission is hostile to information exchanges on oligopolistic markets.

(vi) INFORMATION SHARING AGREEMENTS

a. EXCHANGE OF INFORMATION BETWEEN COMPETITORS

The dissemination and exchange of information between competitors and the creation of a transparent market may be harmless or even highly beneficial to the competitive structure of the market. Trade associations frequently collect industry data on prices, outputs, capacity, and investment and circulate information to their members. Detailed market data may make it easier for undertakings to plan their own business strategies (for example, data may avoid the creation of over-capacity in an industry based on false expectations). Further, the theory of perfect competition rests upon the assumption that there is perfect freedom of information. A market characterized by many buyers and sellers should, therefore, positively benefit from such transparency. Where information is available generally, consumers with complete knowledge of what is on offer may fully utilize their choice. Competition will be maximized. Where the exchange of opinion or experience is harmless or beneficial to competition, it will not infringe Article 81(1).[170]

However, information exchanges present a danger. The ECJ and the Commission have consistently stressed the importance of competitors acting independently. Information exchanges may exacerbate the problems of, and increase the transparency on, oligopolistic markets where there is already limited opportunity for competition. Particularly where sensitive market information is exchanged, the exchange is likely to be condemned under Article 81(1).[171] The exchange of information may thus make it easier for competitors to act in concert or to engage in tacit co-ordination.

Agreements to exchange information on prices to be charged or output to be produced (often through trade associations) will be caught by Article 81(1). Even if it cannot be established that an agreement which is restrictive of competition has been concluded, it has already been seen that Article 81(1) also prohibits behaviour which eliminates 'the risks of competition and the hazards of competitors' spontaneous reactions by co-operation'.[172] Exchanges of information, the object or effect of which is to influence the conduct on the

---

[170] See e.g., *Eudim* [1996] OJ C111/8. This case concerned an information exchange on the market for installation machines. The market was fragmented and there were around a million products on the market.

[171] See *supra* 661 ff.

[172] Cases 48, 49, 51–7/69, *ICI v. Commission (Dyestuffs)* [1972] ECR 619, [1972] CMLR 557, para. 119. See *supra* 661–662.

market of an actual or potential competitor, to disclose to a competitor the course of conduct which the sender has decided to adopt on a market or to render the market artificially transparent, will therefore be unacceptable.[173] Where, however, there is no direct or indirect contact between the parties (for example, where the producers provide a central statistical office with information) no agreement or concerted practice exists and no infringement of Article 81(1) is committed.

The difficulty is to distinguish between legitimate and anti-competitive exchanges. Two issues, in particular, are crucial to the making of such a determination: the type of information exchanged and the market structure.

b. THE TYPE OF INFORMATION EXCHANGED

Statistical information which enables undertakings to assess the level of demand and output in the market or the costs of its competitors may be beneficial and is not of itself objectionable.[174] Similarly, exchange of technical or other information that does not restrict the parties' freedom to determine their market behaviour independently should not be objectionable. However, information on individuals' pricing intentions, output predictions, research projects, or other business secrets will probably be unacceptable.

c. THE MARKET STRUCTURE

It has already been mentioned that information exchanges in competitive markets may be beneficial. However, information exchanges in markets which are prone to cartelization or which have oligopolistic tendencies are likely to be scrutinized by the Commission with care. Individualized market data may facilitate the identification of those cheating on a cartel. Alternatively, they may facilitate conscious parallel behaviour by enabling undertakings to react rapidly to one another's actions:

In assessing information agreements the Commission also pays close attention to the structure of the relevant market. The tendency for firms to fall in line with the behaviour of their competitors is particularly strong in oligopolistic markets. The improved knowledge of market conditions aimed at by information agreements strengthens the connection between the undertakings, in that they are enabled to react very efficiently to one another's actions, and thus lessens the intensity of competition.[175]

The effect of such exchanges is likely to be less serious (a) where consumers also have access to the information, and (b) where the agreement provides for post-notification of historic information rather than pre-notification of information. In *UK Agricultural Tractor Registration Exchange*, the Commission condemned the exchange of information relating to past transactions.[176] Where demand was stable, a forecast of a competitor's future actions could be largely determined on the basis of past transactions. The forecast would be more effective the more accurate and recent the information was. The exchange of information could,

---

[173] See also Cases 40–48, 50, 54–56/73, *Re the European Sugar Cartel: Cooperatiëve Verniging 'Suiker Unie' UA v. Commission* [1975] ECR 1663, [1976] 1 CMLR 295.

[174] Case T–334/94, *Sarrio SA v. Commission* [1998] ECR II–1439, [1998] 5 CMLR 195.

[175] Commission's *VII*[th] Report on Competition Policy (Commission, 1977), 7(2).

[176] [1992] OJ L 68/19, [1994] 3 CMLR 358; on appeal Case T–34/92, *Fiatagri & Ford New Holland v. Commission* [1994] ECR II–905 and Case T–35/92, *John Deere Ltd v. Commission* [1994] ECR II–957; on appeal to the ECJ, Case C–7/95P, *John Deere Ltd v. Commission* [1998] ECR I–3111, [1998] 5 CMLR 311.

however, truly be categorized as historic from a certain period of time (for example, if it was more than one year old).

d. NOTICE ON CO-OPERATION AGREEMENTS

The Commission has accepted that information exchanges may be beneficial. Indeed, it has issued a Notice concerning such co-operation.[177] The Notice sets out certain agreements which will be found to fall outside the ambit of Article 81(1). For example, where the sole object of the agreements is:

- to exchange opinion and experience, joint market research, joint comparative studies of industries;
- to co-operate in accounting.

The Notice specifically indicates that the Commission will be wary of agreements on an oligopolistic market for homogeneous products. Further, in *UK Agricultural Tractor Registration Exchange*,[178] the Commission stated that in more concentrated or oligopolistic markets there was already limited opportunity for competition and '[u]ncertainty and secrecy between suppliers [was] . . . vital'[179] to it.

e. AGREEMENT OR CONCERTED PRACTICE ESSENTIAL

The existence of an agreement to exchange information or a concerted practice is vital to the establishment of an infringement of Article 81(1). It is not sufficient that the information is readily available. As seen above, in *Wood Pulp*,[180] the ECJ found that there was no infringement of Article 81 where undertakings had announced their price increases in advance. The increases had been rapidly transferred between both buyers and sellers by means of publication in the trade press and by agents which dealt with a number of buyers and sellers. No agreement or concerted practice between the producers to exchange the information had, however, been established. The system of quarterly price announcements did not, of itself, infringe Article 81(1), and neither this system nor the parallelism of announced prices were evidence of a concerted practice operating between the undertakings.[181]

In contrast, where there is direct or indirect contact between parties, the Commission has held that:

It is contrary to the provisions of Article [81(1)]. . . for a producer to communicate to his competitors the essential elements of his price policy such as price lists, the discounts and terms of trade he applies, the rates and date of any change to them and the special exceptions he grants to specific customers.[182]

even if they had not concluded an agreement in the contractual sense. Obviously there is little incentive to make a price cut to attract business from a competitor if that information must be disclosed to the competitor.

---

[177] [1968] OJ C75/3. The Notice is, however, likely to be replaced by the Commission's Guidelines on Horizontal Cooperation. See the Draft Guidelines [2000] OJ C118/14, [2000] 5 CMLR 124, para 8.

[178] [1992] OJ L68/19, [1993] 4 CMLR 358.

[179] *Ibid.*, para. 37.

[180] Cases C–89, 104, 114, 116–117, 125–129/85, *Re Wood Pulp Cartel: Ahlström Oy (Wood Pulp II) v Commission (Wood Pulp II)* [1993] ECR I–1307, [1993] 4 CMLR 407.

[181] See *supra* 666–671.

[182] *IFTRA Rules on Glass Containers* [1974] OJ L160/1, [1974] 2 CMLR D50.

f. *COBELPA/VNP* AND *UK AGRICULTURAL TRACTOR REGISTRATION EXCHANGE*

In *Cobelpa/VNP*,[183] the Commission held that although there was nothing wrong in a trade association exchanging information on industry output and sales, in this case, where the information exchanged identified the output and sales of individual undertakings, the practice was prohibited. By exchanging information about matters normally regarded as confidential (especially where the information was not available to consumers) the parties were replacing practical co-operation for the normal risks of competition. It would make no difference that the information could have been obtained from elsewhere.[184]

In *UK Agricultural Tractor Registration Exchange*,[185] eight UK manufacturers and importers of agricultural tractors operated, through the Agricultural Engineers Association, an information exchange agreement called the UK Agricultural Tractor Registration Exchange. The information identified the volume of retail sales and market shares of each of the eight manufacturers individually. In condemning the agreement under Article 81(1) and refusing to exempt it under Article 81(3) (after an initial Commission investigation the Exchange had been notified with an application for negative clearance or an exemption under Article 81(3)) the Commission took account of the fact that:

- the market was highly concentrated, (the eight manufacturers/importers had approximately 87–88% of the relevant market);
- there were high barriers to entry into the market;
- there were insignificant extra-Community imports;
- the information exchanged was detailed and identified the exact retail sales and shares of the undertakings which were generally trade secrets between competitors; and
- the members met regularly.

First, the Commission held that the exchange of information prevented hidden competition by creating transparency on a market which was already highly concentrated and largely shielded from outside competition. Although it recognized that there were benefits of transparency in a competitive market, in this case the concentration of the market was not low and the market transparency was not in any way directed towards the benefit of consumers. The information in this case enabled each participant accurately to establish its rivals' market position and to see immediately if a rival increased its market share (for example, by price reductions or other marketing incentives). It limited price competition since competitors would be able to react quickly to changes in market positions (this would, of course, mean that there was little incentive for a potential initiator to take steps to improve its position). Information would thus limit the possibility of surprise or secrecy if a rival received information disclosing sensitive information about his competitors. It would then be able to react quickly and eliminate any possible advantage to be gained by the initiator.

Secondly, the information would also be likely to increase barriers to entry since participants would know immediately of new market entrants and would be able to react accordingly.

---

[183] [1977] OJ L242/10, [1977] 2 CMLR D28.
[184] See also *UK Agricultural Tractor Registration Exchange* [1992] OJ L68/19, [1993] 4 CMLR 358.
[185] *Ibid.*

The Commission's analysis was upheld by the CFI in *John Deere Ltd v Commission*.[186] The Court accepted that a truly competitive market would benefit from transparency but that exchanges of precise information at short intervals on a highly concentrated market would be likely to impair the competition which existed between the traders.

Cases T–35/92, *John Deere Ltd v Commission* [1994] ECR II–957

Court of First Instance

51. The Court observes that, as the applicant points out, the Decision is the first in which the Commission has prohibited an information exchange system concerning sufficiently homogeneous products which does not directly concern the prices of those products, but which does not underpin any other anti-competitive arrangement either. As the applicants correctly argue, on a truly competitive market transparency between traders is in principle likely to lead to the intensification of competition between suppliers, since in such a situation, the fact that a trader takes into account information made available to him in order to adjust his conduct on the market is not likely, having regard to the atomized nature of the supply, to reduce or remove for the other traders any uncertainty about the foreseeable nature of its competitors' conduct. On the other hand, the Court considers that, as the Commission argues this time, general use, as between main suppliers and, contrary to the applicant's contention, to their sole benefit and consequently to the exclusion of the other suppliers and of consumers, of exchanges of precise information at short intervals, identifying registered vehicles and the place of their registration is, on a highly concentrated oligopolistic market such as the market in question and on which competition is as a result already greatly reduced and exchange of information facilitated, likely to impair substantially the competition which exists between traders (see paragraph 81, below). In such circumstances, the sharing, on a regular and frequent basis, of information concerning the operation of the market has the effect of periodically revealing to all the competitors the market positions and strategies of the various individual competitors.

52. Furthermore, provision of the information in question to all suppliers presupposes an agreement, or at any rate a tacit agreement, between the traders to define the boundaries of dealer sales territories by reference to the United Kingdom postcode system, as well as an institutional framework enabling information to be exchanged between the traders through the trade association to which they belong and, secondly, having regard to the frequency of such information and its systematic nature, it also enables a given trader to forecast more precisely the conduct of its competitors, so reducing or removing the degree of uncertainty about the operation of the market which would have existed in the absence of such an exchange of information. Furthermore, the Commission correctly contends, at points 44 to 48 of the Decision, that whatever decision is adopted by a trader wishing to penetrate the United Kingdom agricultural tractor market, and whether or not it becomes a member of the agreement, that agreement is necessarily disadvantageous for it. Either the trader concerned does not become a member of the information exchange agreement and, unlike its competitors, then forgoes the information exchanged and the market knowledge which it provides; or it becomes a member of the agreement and its business strategy is then immediately revealed to all its competitors by means of the information which they receive.

53. It follows that the pleas that the information exchange agreement at issue is not of such a nature as to infringe the Community competition rules must be dismissed.

. . .

---

[186] Case T–34/92 [1994] ECR II–905.

81. Secondly, with regard to the type of information exchanged, the Court considers that, contrary to the applicant's contention, the information concerned, which relates in particular to sales made in the territory of each of the dealerships in the distribution network, is in the nature of business secrets. Indeed, this is admitted by the members of the agreement themselves, who strictly defined the conditions under which the information received could be disseminated to third parties, especially to members of their distribution network. The Court also observes that, as stated above (in paragraph 51), having regard to its frequency and systematic nature the exchange of information in question makes the conduct of a given trader's competitors all the more foreseeable for it in view of the characteristics of the relevant market as analyzed above, since it reduces, or even removes, the degree of uncertainty regarding the operation of the market, which would have existed in the absence of such an exchange of information, and in this regard the applicant cannot profitably rely on the fact that the information exchanged does not concern prices or relate to past sales. Accordingly, the first part of the plea, to the effect that there is no restriction of competition as a result of alleged 'prevention of hidden competition', must be dismissed.

An appeal before the ECJ against the judgment of the CFI was unsuccessful.[187]

g. EXEMPTIONS

The main question arising on the compatibility of information-sharing agreements with Article 81 has been whether or not they are caught by Article 81(1) at all. Where the agreement is prohibited by Article 81(1) an exemption under Article 81(3) will be rare. In *UK Agricultural Tractor Exchange*,[188] for example, the Commission rejected the parties' application for an exemption.

(viii) PROBLEMS OF DETECTION OF CARTELS

a. GENERAL

In many cases it is the detection of cartels, rather than the legal intricacies of Article 81, which presents the main difficulty for the Commission. Although the rules set out in Article 81 are strict and the Commission has established a strong policy of enforcing the rules, it does not appear to have led to the widespread abandonment of all cartels. Rather, undertakings wishing to conspire to fix prices, restrict output, etc. do not attempt to conclude formal legally enforceable agreements but are driven underground. The members will find some other means of enforcing their agreement/understanding amongst themselves. The Commission's task of proving the existence of the cartel is, therefore, an onerous one. The Commission's investigatory powers and the procedures which must be complied with when investigating a breach of Article 81 are dealt with in Chapter 14. Some of the difficulties involved in establishing an infringement are, however, outlined below.

It has already been seen that certain industries are particularly prone to cartelization. Where parallel market behaviour is detected by undertakings operating in such industries, investigations are more likely, therefore, to lead to the uncovering of a covert cartel.

---

[187] See Case C–7/95P *John Deere Ltd v. Commission* [1998] ECR I–3111, [1998] 5 CMLR 311.
[188] [1992] OJ L68/19, [1993] 4 CMLR 358.

b. COMMISSION'S INVESTIGATIVE POWERS

Regulation 17 confers on the Commission the power to enforce the competition rules. The Commission's powers of investigation and enforcement are discussed in Chapter 14. Broadly, however, the Commission can, on its own initiative, decide to investigate the activities of undertakings operating on a market. Alternatively, it may decide to investigate following a complaint.[189] The Commission has stated that it receives useful information from complainants and thus welcomes the lodging of complaints (in the period between 1988 and 1998 the Commission stated that 29 per cent of its work stemmed from complaints as compared with 13 per cent from own initiative investigations).[190] In *Cartonboard*, for example, the Commission received an informal complaint (not one lodged under Article 3) from British carton printers which alleged that they had observed a 'series of simultaneous and uniform price increases'.[191]

The extensive investigatory powers conferred on the Commission by Regulation 17 have been crucial to the Commission's ability to uncover the operation of covert cartels. Nonetheless, the Commission is seeking to obtain broader investigatory powers.[192]

c. THE BURDEN OF PROOF

The ECJ has confirmed that 'the presumption of innocence resulting in particular from Article 6(2) of the ECHR is one of the fundamental rights which . . . are protected in the Community legal order . . . It must also be accepted that . . . the presumption of innocence applies to the procedures relating to infringements of the competition rules applicable to undertakings that may result in the imposition of fines or periodic penalties payments'.[193] The burden is therefore clearly on the Commission to prove that an undertaking has infringed Article 81(1).

It is clear from the ECJ's judgment in *Wood Pulp* that, although the Commission may, in certain circumstances, be able to rely on parallel market behaviour as evidence of concertation it will not be able to do so where a 'plausible explanation' is provided for that conduct.[194] Despite the more relaxed approach of the ECJ in *Dyestuffs*, the decision in *Wood Pulp* established that the Commission will be required to examine the characteristics of the market carefully and to evaluate its evidence in the light of this analysis. The more recent cases reflect the court's increasing willingness (a) to embark on economic analysis,[195]

---

[189] Reg. 17 [1959–62] OJ Spec. Ed. 87.

[190] See *infra* Chap. 15 and the White Paper on Modernisation of the Rules Implementing Articles 85 and 86 [now 81 and 82] of the EC Treaty [1999] OJ C132/1, [1999] 5 CMLR 208, paras. 44 and 117. The difficulty is, however, to distinguish between legitimate and illegitimate complaints.

[191] [1994] OJ L243/1, [1994] 5 CMLR 547, para. 22.

[192] Its powers under Art. 14 to conduct dawn raids (to make unannounced, surprise, on-the-spot investigations of an undertaking's premises) has been extremely helpful in uncovering the operation of covert cartels. In *Cartonboard* [1994] OJ L243/1, [1994] 5 CMLR 547, the Commission unearthed useful information whilst conducting dawn raids. This was despite the fact that the documentation found suggested that 'dummy runs' of raids had been conducted by external lawyers and documentation removed from the premises for further investigation (although both the undertaking and its lawyer denied that documentation had in fact been removed)! See also the Commission's proposal for a Reg. implementing Arts. 81 and 82, COM (2000) 582, Arts. 19 and 20.

[193] Case C–199/92P, *Hüls AG v. Commission (Polypropylene)* [1999] 5 CMLR 1016, paras. 149–150 and para. 45.

[194] See *supra* 668.

[195] See e.g. Case C–234/89, *Delimitis v. Henninger Bräu* [1991] ECR I–935, [1992] 5 CMLR 210.

and (b) the CFI's willingness to scrutinize the Commission's finding of facts.[196] In *Wood Pulp* the ECJ's judgment describes the market characteristics in meticulous detail. In particular, it seems clear that the number of undertakings on the market, the homogeneity of the product, and the transparency of the market will be relevant to the analysis. Although the market structure may not often impose parallel behaviour it may be useful in providing plausible explanations for the behaviour. It can be seen from *Wood Pulp* itself that explanations may well be available outside a tight oligopoly situation. It thus seems unlikely that the Commission will be able to rely solely on economic evidence to establish the existence of a cartel. Rather, it will need to adduce other evidence to corroborate its case.[197] Indeed, in *Cartonboard* the Commission stated:

Had they been challenged, the producers could as a result of this elaborate scheme of deception have attributed the series of uniform, regular and industry-wide price increases in the cartonboard sector to the phenomenon of 'oligopoly behaviour'. They could argue that it made sense for all the producers to decide of their own volition to copy an increase initiated by one or other of the market leaders as soon as it became publicly known; unlawful collusion as such would not necessarily be indicated. Customers might well suspect and even accuse them of operating a cartel; and given the relatively large number of producers, economic theory would be stretched to its limits and beyond, but unless direct proof of collusion were forthcoming—and they went to some lengths to ensure it was not—the producers must have had hopes of defeating any investigation into their pricing conduct by the competition authorities by invoking the defence of oligopolistic interdependence.[198]

Although it seems that it will be rare that evidence of parallel behaviour alone will be relied upon to establish the existence of a concerted practice, it is unclear whether, on the proof of parallel behaviour, the burden shifts onto the accused to establish that there *is* a plausible explanation for the conduct. If the onus does not shift it is impossible to imagine how the Commission (or any other) could establish that there is no other plausible explanation for the parallel conduct. In *Wood Pulp*, the Advocate General appeared to consider, however, that '[t]he burden of proof cannot be shifted simply by a finding of parallel conduct. Unless the Court can be satisfied by a set of presumptions having a solid basis, concertation is not established.'[199] Where the Commission cannot rely on parallel or economic evidence alone, it will have to find admissible documents or other compelling evidence to establish its case.

d. STANDARD OF PROOF

It is, at the current state of development of EC law, unclear whether a breach of the competition rules has to be established, by the Commission, on the balance of probabilities or more conclusively (for example, beyond reasonable doubt). The ECJ has merely indicated that the Commission must produce 'sufficiently precise and coherent proof' to justify its view.[200]

---

[196] See e.g. Cases T–68 and 77–78/89, *Società Italiana Vetro SpA v. Commission* [1992] ECR II–1403, [1992] 5 CMLR 302.

[197] Cartel members thus have a strategic advantage in cartel investigations in the sense that, if guilty, they can nonetheless destroy incriminating evidence making the detection, prosecution, and final repression of the cartel extremely difficult.

[198] *Cartonboard* [1994] OJ L243/1, [1994] 5 CMLR 547, para. 73.

[199] [1993] ECR I–1307, [1993] 4 CMLR 407, Darmon AG, para. 195.

[200] Cases 29 and 30/83, *Compagnie Royale Asturienne des Mines SA and Rheinzink GmbH v. Commission* [1984] ECR 1679, [1985] 1 CMLR 688.

In *Suiker Unie*,[201] Advocate General Mayras was of the opinion that fines imposed were not criminal law sanctions. The Commission was merely carrying out an administrative, not judicial, function (Regulation 17 specifically provides that infringement of the competition rules do not attract criminal sanctions[202]). This may suggest that the ordinary civil standard of proof should apply.

In contrast in *Wood Pulp* Advocate General Darmon[203] expressed the opinion that a Commission decision was 'manifestly of a penal nature' (breach of the provisions potentially resulting in substantial fines of up to 10 per cent of an undertaking's turnover). This, and the Court's requirement that the breach should be sufficiently precise and coherent, suggest that the standard of proof should be an onerous one, perhaps even that adopted in criminal cases. As there is no Community criminal law, this issue may have to be resolved by reference to general principles of law and fundamental rights. This latter view accords with that of the European Commission of Human Rights. In *Société Stenuit v France*,[204] it was held that a company fined in proceedings under French competition law had faced a 'criminal charge' within the meaning of the Convention. The power to fine up to 5 per cent of a firm's annual turnover was quite clearly intended to be a deterrent. Given the importance that the ECJ in *Hüls AG v Commission (Polypropylene)*[205] attached to the presumption of innocence in the context of proceedings liable to culminate in the imposition of fines or periodic penalty payments it seems likely that this latter view will be the one that is upheld.

There will be no finding of an agreement or a concerted practice, therefore, unless the Commission can provide sufficient evidence to corroborate its allegations. It has been seen from cases such as *Dyestuffs*, *Polypropylene*, and *Cartonboard* that the Commission will generally attempt to fulfil its burden of proof by producing written evidence of concertation or direct communication between the undertakings. The Courts, in particular the CFI, are not afraid to annul the whole or parts of decisions where it considers that the Commission has not produced sufficient evidence to establish its case. The CFI will carefully scrutinize both the validity[206] and the merits[207] of the Commission's evidence and will, of course, exclude Commission evidence that has, for example, been doctored.[208]

In some cases, the Commission has relied on the evidence collected at the premises of one cartel-member[209] (even badly written, unsigned, and undated documents and other records

---

[201] Cases 40–48, 50, 54–56, 111, 113–4/73, *Re the European Sugar Cartel: Cooperatiëve Vereniging 'Suiker Unie' UA v. Commission* [1975] ECR 1663, 2065, [1976] 1 CMLR 295, 328.

[202] Reg. 17, Art. 15.

[203] [1993] ECR I–1307, [1993] 4 CMLR 407, Darmon AG, para. 451.

[204] (1992) 14 EHRR 509. The French judicial authorities were found not to have afforded a company fined under the French competition rules the protection of proceedings satisfying the requirements of Art. 6(1) of the European Convention on Human Rights (fair hearing).

[205] Case C–199/92P [1999] 5 CMLR 1016.

[206] Cases T–68 and 77–78/89, *Società Italiana Vetro SpA v. Commission* [1992] ECR II–1403, [1992] 5 CMLR 302 (the CFI excluded Commission evidence that had been doctored).

[207] In some of the *Polypropylene* cases, the CFI held that the Commission had not conclusively proved the participation of the undertakings for the entire duration of the cartel (e.g. Case T–2/89, *Petrofina v. Commission* [1991] ECR II–1088 and Case T–11/89, *Shell v. Commission* [1991] ECR II–757).

[208] Cases T–68 and 77–78/89, *Società Italiana Vetro SpA v. Commission* [1992] ECR II–1403, [1992] 5 CMLR 302. See generally *infra* Chap. 14.

[209] See e.g. *Cement* [1994] OJ L343/1, [1995] 4 CMLR 327; on appeal Cases T–25/95 etc, *Cimenteries CBR SA v. Commission*, 15 Mar. 2000.

of meetings) and the confessions of 'whistle-blowers' who have decided to co-operate with the Commission as against other members of the cartel.[210]

e. WHISTLE-BLOWERS

The difficulties the Commission may have in producing satisfactory evidence are evident. It has, therefore, publicized its desire to encourage undertakings to co-operate with it prior to or during cartel investigations. It has issued a formal notice setting out circumstances in which participants in cartels that co-operate with it may be able to avoid the imposition of a fine or receive a mitigated fine (the 'Leniency Notice').[211] This Notice is discussed in greater detail in Chapter 14 below but broadly it offers reductions in fines (of between 10 and 100 per cent) to undertakings which co-operate with the Commission and provide it with evidence. The sooner the undertaking co-operates the greater the reduction in fine which may be received. The conditions which the undertakings must fulfil to receive these reductions (especially the very significant reductions) are extremely onerous and the Commission has a broad discretion in determining what reduction should be granted (the maximum reduction available to a ringleader is 50 per cent). Nonetheless the Notice seeks to provide certainty for undertakings considering co-operating with the Commission.

Two major drawbacks of the notice are that it is difficult to know what the initial fine will be (before the reduction is applied) and that the Notice cannot give whistle-blowers immunity from the civil law consequences of its participation in an illegal agreement.[212]

f. GUIDELINES ON THE METHOD FOR THE SETTING OF FINES

The Commission has adopted guidelines on the setting of fines[213] which aim to improve transparency, to strengthen the coherence of the policy of the Commission as regards fines, whilst maintaining the deterrent character of the sanctions. The Commission's fining policy, both generally and in respect of cartels, is discussed in Chapter 14 below.

F. AN EFFECT ON INTER-STATE TRADE

It will also be necessary to establish that any agreement affects trade between Member States. In most cartel cases, even where the agreement operates only between producers in one Member State, inter-state trade is likely to be affected. In order to be successful, cartels will make it more difficult for undertakings, including undertakings from other Member States, to penetrate the market.[214] It is possible, however, that a cartel affecting only a local geographic market may not have an effect on inter-state trade.

---

[210] See, in particular, *Cartonboard* [1994] OJ L243/1, [1994] 5 CMLR 547.

[211] Commission Notice on the non-imposition or reduction of fines in cartel cases [1996] OJ C207/4, discussed *infra* in Chap. 14.

[212] Civil proceedings may, therefore, be commenced by a third party injured by the cartel's actions. Having provided evidence incriminating itself and others, a whistle-blower may have difficulty defending such proceedings successfully. Private enforcement of the competition rules is dealt with *infra* in Chap. 15.

[213] [1998] OJ C9/3, [1998] 4 CMLR 472, but see the more detailed discussion of the Commission's fining policy *infra* in Chap. 14.

[214] See *supra* Chap. 3.

3. OLIGOPOLY

A. OLIGOPOLY AND ARTICLE 81

The question whether parallel behaviour on a market can provide conclusive evidence of an agreement or concerted practice between undertakings operating on a market was set out in detail in the section above. It was seen that, broadly, although the ECJ in *Wood Pulp* decided that in certain circumstances parallel conduct could be used to establish the existence of a concerted practice it could only be so used where, taking account of the nature of the products, the size and the number of undertakings, and the volume of the market in question, it cannot be explained otherwise than by concertation. Parallel behaviour will furnish proof of concertation only where it constitutes the only *plausible explanation* for such conduct. Thus parallel behaviour *itself* is not prohibited by Article 81(1). It is prohibited only if it results from collusion. Conversely, every producer is free to react *independently* and intelligently to market forces and to alter his course of action, taking into account in so doing the present or foreseeable conduct of his competitors.

True parallel behaviour between oligopolists is not, therefore, caught by Article 81 of the Treaty. It has therefore become acutely important to know whether or not Article 82 applies to abuses committed by undertakings, such as oligopolists, which collectively hold a dominant position on a market.[215]

B. OLIGOPOLY AND ARTICLE 82

(i) 'ONE OR MORE UNDERTAKINGS'

a. THE ACCEPTANCE OF A CONCEPT OF COLLECTIVE OR JOINT DOMINANCE[216]—THE JUDGMENT IN *FLAT GLASS*

It has been seen in Chapter 5 that Article 82 prohibits as incompatible with the common market, in so far as trade between Member States is affected, '[a]ny abuse by one or more undertakings of a dominant position'. Article 82 thus lends itself to a broad interpretation, and the view that Article 82 might be used both to control the behaviour of a monopolist, or a single undertaking that is 'dominant', and also the 'abuses' of duopolists or oligopolists which collectively hold a dominant position on a market. It was also seen in Chapter 5 that, initially at least, it was believed that the term 'one or more undertakings' referred only to bodies which were within the same corporate group or which

---

[215] In particular, Community law does not provide for an investigatory procedure such as that set out in the UK's Fair Trading Act 1973, but see *infra* 695–697.

[216] The terms collective, joint, and oligopolistic dominance are used interchangeably. See generally on this subject R. Whish, 'Collective Dominance' in D. O'Keefe and M. Andenas (eds.), *Liber Amicorum for Lord Slynn* (Kluwer, 2000).

formed part of the same economic entity.[217] In *Hoffmann La-Roche v Commission*, the ECJ stated:

A dominant position must also be distinguished from parallel courses of conduct which are peculiar to oligopolies in that in an oligopoly the courses of conduct interact, while in the case of an undertaking occupying a dominant position the conduct of the undertaking which derives profits from that position is to a great extent determined unilaterally.[218]

Such an interpretation would however have been inconsistent with the interpretation of the term 'undertaking' adopted for the purposes of Article 81[219] and in *Flat Glass* the CFI confirmed that the term 'undertaking' had the same meaning within the context of both Article 82 and 81. Article 82 could apply where a dominant position was held collectively by one or more *economically independent* undertakings. The Article was not confined to the activities of one or more undertakings within the same corporate group.

Cases T–68, 77 and 78/89, *Società Italiana Vetro SpA v. Commission ('Flat Glass')* [1992] ECR II–1403, [1992] 5 CMLR 302

In *Flat Glass* the Commission found that three Italian producers of flat glass had all infringed Article 81(1) (by concluding agreements to fix prices and sales quotas for their products etc) and infringed Article 82 by abusing their collective dominant position (although the Commission did not adduce any evidence to establish the latter infringement above that relied on to establish the breach of Article 81).[220] On appeal, the Court of First Instance quashed the Commission's decision that there had been an abuse of a joint dominant position. It was not sufficient simply to recycle the facts constituting an infringement of Article 81 in order to deduce that their behaviour constituted an abuse of a collective dominant position.

The Court, however, finally expressed its view that Article 82 could apply to independent undertakings and that Article 82 was not confined to the activities of one or more undertakings within the same corporate group.

Court of First Instance

357. The Court notes that the very words of the first paragraph of Article [82] provide that 'one or more undertakings' may abuse a dominant position. It has consistently been held, as indeed all the parties acknowledge, that the concept of agreement or concerted practice between undertakings does not cover agreements or concerted practices among undertakings belonging to the same group if the undertakings form an economic unit ... It follows that when Article [81] refers to agreements or concerted practices between 'undertakings', it is referring to relations between two or more economic entities which are capable of competing with one another.

---

[217] Case 85/76, *Hoffmann-La Roche v. Commission* [1979] ECR 461, [1979] 3 CMLR 211, para. 39.

[218] *Ibid.*

[219] Case 15/74, *Centrafarm v. Sterling Drug* [1974] ECR 1147, [1974] 2 CMLR 480, para. 41, repeated in Case 30/87, *Bodson v. Pompes Funèbres des Régions Libérées* [1988] ECR 2479, [1989] 4 CMLR 984, para. 19. See discussion *supra* in Chap. 3. This seems to be a two pronged test, but in Case C–73/95P, *Viho Europe BV v. Commission* [1996] ECR I-5457, [1997] 4 CMLR 419, para. 16 the ECJ concentrated on the lack of freedom aspect. 'Parker and its subsidiaries thus form a single economic unit within which the subsidiaries do not enjoy real autonomy in determining their course of action in the market, but carry out the instructions issued to them by the parent company controlling them.' See also the Opinion of Fennelly AG in Cases C–395/96P, and 396/96P *Compagnie Maritime Belge Transports SA v. Commission*, 29 Oct. 1998, para. 24.

[220] [1989] OJ L33/44, [1990] 4 CMLR 535.

358. The Court considers that there is no legal or economic reason to suppose that the term 'undertaking' in Article [82] has a different meaning from the one given to it in the context of Article [81]. There is nothing in principle, to prevent two or more independent economic entities from being, on a specific market, united by such economic links that, by virtue of that fact, together they hold a dominant position *vis-à-vis* the other operators on the same market. This could be the case, for example, where two or more independent undertakings jointly have, through agreements or licences, a technological lead affording them the power to behave to an appreciable extent independently of their competitors, their customers and ultimately of their consumers (*Hoffmann-La Roche* [Case 102/77, [1978] ECR 1139], paragraphs [38] and [48]).

359. The Court finds support for that interpretation in the wording of Article 8 of Council Regulation 4065/86 . . . laying down detailed rules for the application of Articles [81] and [82] [EC] to maritime transport. Article 8(2) provides that the conduct of a liner conference benefiting from an exemption from a prohibition laid down by Article [81(1)] [EC] may have effects which are incompatible with Article [82] [EC]. A request by a conference to be exempted from the prohibition laid down by Article [81(1)] necessarily presupposes an agreement between two or more independent economic undertakings.

The Court thus clearly held in paragraph 358 that there is nothing, in principle, to prevent two or more independent economic entities from being, on a specific market, united by such economic links that, by virtue of that fact, together they hold a dominant position *vis-à-vis* the other operators on the same market. The Court gave examples of when such economic links would exist, for example, where two or more independent undertakings jointly have, through agreements or licences, a technological lead affording them the power to behave to an appreciable extent independently of their competitors, their customers, and ultimately of their consumer.

The judgment, despite recognizing that a joint dominant position can be held by independent economic entities, was not, however, as helpful as it might have been. The requirement in paragraph 358 that the entities be united by '*economic links*' arguably supports a wide view of Article 82. Such links may be derived from the structure of the market which dictates that the undertakings operating upon it may tacitly collude.[221] However, the Court, by subsequently referring to 'agreements or licences' operating between independent undertakings as an example of economic links, cast doubt on this broad view. The reference to such structural links between the parties caused speculation that Article 82 would not apply unless something more than mutual interdependence existed between the undertakings, perhaps an agreement or some other special relationship between the parties. This latter narrower view of the concept was supported by the Court's reliance on Article 8(2) of Council Regulation 4056/86 which provides that Article 82 may be applied to agreements between undertakings even though they have been exempted under the Regulation.[222]

If this latter position had been the correct one it is hard to see how the concept of an abuse of a joint dominant position could usefully have added to the Commission's armoury.

---

[221] [1986] OJ L378/1. See discussion of the kind of markets on which tacit collusion between undertakings operating on a market might be likely, *supra* 636–639.

[222] [1986] OJ L378/1. This Council Reg. lays down the substantive and procedural rules for the application of Arts. 81 and 82 to maritime transport services from or to a Community port (excluding tramp vessel services). Part of the Reg. (see especially Art. 3) provides exemption for 'liner conference agreements' from the Art. 81(1) prohibition. Art. 8(2) of the Reg. provides that the Commission may withdraw the benefit of the block exemption where it considers that an agreement benefiting from it has effects incompatible with Art. 82 and take measures to bring the infringement to an end.

Agreements between undertakings could, in any event, be controlled under Article 81 (the concept would be useful only to act against agreements between the undertakings which fall outside Article 81(1) or which are exempt from its operation). It seemed unlikely, therefore, that the Court intended to confine the term 'economic links' to circumstances in which an agreement existed between the undertakings. However, the judgment left it far from clear what exactly it did mean when it said that the undertakings should be united by 'economic links'. The question whether the Treaty provision would apply where the only link between the parties was the 'economic interdependence' which independent undertakings have with each other on an oligopolistic market was of enormous importance.

b. THE DEVELOPMENT OF THE CONCEPT OF COLLECTIVE DOMINANCE UNDER ARTICLE 82

Subsequent Commission decisions and Court judgments in the sphere of Article 82 did not initially add much clarity to the picture. Indeed, in subsequent cases the Commission appeared to proceed cautiously. In *French-West African Shipowners' Committees*,[223] *CEWAL*,[224] and *Trans-Atlantic Conference Agreement* (TACA)[225] the Commission used the concept of a joint dominant position in relation to shipowners that were members of shipowners' committees and which had concluded agreements regulating the operation of cargo trade on certain shipping routes. The parties in these cases were, therefore, clearly united by contractual links which amounted to economic links within the meaning set out by the Court.[226]

In *French-West African Shipowners' Committees*,[227] for example, the Commission imposed fines on shipowners that had participated in cargo-sharing systems on routes between France and eleven West African States. The Committee monitored the quota systems and imposed penalties on those that exceeded the quotas without approval. The Commission found that the agreements infringed Article 81(1) (since their object and effect were to share markets amongst the members and to limit the supply of transport services available, contrary to Article 81(1)(c) and (b) respectively) and could not be exempted under Article 81(3). Further, and because the objective of the agreements was not to fix common rates of the participants, it did not fall within the terms of the block exemption dealing with 'liner conferences' in Regulation 4056/86[228] (the Regulation provides a block exemption for carriers providing international carrier services that agree to operate on particular routes under certain terms and conditions). Nor was an individual exemption possible.

In addition to the Article 81 infringement, the Commission considered that the shipowners had infringed Article 82. As a result of the conference, the shipowners had presented themselves with a united front to shippers and, consequently, the position of the shipowners on the market for cargo between France and the eleven African States had to be assessed collectively. Since the committees had been set up by a group of shipowners covering

---

[223] [1992] OJ L134/1, [1993] 5 CMLR 446.
[224] [1993] OJ L34/20, [1995] 5 CMLR 198. The finding of joint dominance was upheld on appeal: Cases T–24/93 etc., *Compagnie Maritime Belge Transports SA v. Commission* [1997] 4 CMLR 273 and Cases C–395 and C–396/96P, *Compagnie Maritime Belge Transports SA v. Commission* [2000] 4 CMLR 1076.
[225] [1999] OJ L95/6: appeal pending, Case T–191/98 etc. [1999] OJ C71/33.
[226] See *French-West African Shipowners' Committees* [1992] OJ L134/1, [1993] 5 CMLR 446.
[227] [1992] OJ L134/1, [1993] 5 CMLR 446.
[228] [1986] OJ L378/1.

virtually the entire market, the agreement resulted in the creation of a collective dominant position to their advantage. Their practices, which endeavoured to eliminate effective competition for non-committee shipping lines, also constituted an abuse of a dominant position within the meaning of Article 82(b) by limiting the supply of liner services available to shippers. Both the practice of imposing penalties on shipowners which had exceeded their quotas and the application of conditions protecting their own interests against those of newcomers wishing to serve the routes infringed Article 82.

In this case the agreement was, therefore, crucial to the finding of a collective dominant position. It was the agreement which enabled the undertakings to present a 'united front' to shippers. Although it does not seem that it was strictly necessary to use Article 82, since Article 81 was applicable (Article 82 would only have been vital had the agreement been block exempted under Article 3 of Regulation No 4056/86), the case fitted neatly within CFI's formulation in *Flat Glass*. It gave the Commission a further opportunity to explore the operation of the concept of joint dominance. Had there been no agreement existing between the parties, it would have been necessary to take a much broader view of 'economic links'. The Commission also found that parties to a liner conference held a joint dominant position in *TACA*.[229]

Similarly in *CEWAL* (on appeal *Compagnie Maritime Belge*) the Commission found that members of a liner conference were jointly dominant on the group of shipping routes it operated between Northern Europe and Zaïre. This decision has broadly been upheld by both the CFI and the ECJ.[230] The latter judgment will be considered below since it sheds important light on the meaning of collective dominance for the purposes of Article 82. In addition, in *Irish Sugar* the Commission found Irish Sugar and one of its distributors to be collectively dominant. In this case the producer and the distributor were linked *vertically* by agreements and other factors which created a clear parallelism of interest, such as a significant equity holding which Irish Sugar had in the distributor.[231]

In *Almelo*, a ruling under Article 234 (then Article 177) of the Treaty, the ECJ simply stated that:

42. . . . in order for such a collective dominant position to exist, the undertakings in the group must be linked in such a way that they adopt the same conduct on the market . . .

43. It is for the national court to consider whether there exist between the regional electricity distributors in the Netherlands links which are sufficiently strong for there to be a collective dominant position in a substantial part of the common market'.[232]

This case lends support to the view that the purpose of requiring links between the undertakings is to determine whether the parties are likely to engage in a co-ordinated course of

---

[229] [1999] OJ L95/6: appeal pending, Case T–191/98 etc. [1999] OJ C71/33.

[230] [1993] OJ L34/2, [1995] 5 CMLR 198; on appeal Cases T–24/93 etc., *Compagnie Maritime Belge Transports SA v. Commission* [1996] ECR II–1019, [1997] 4 CMLR 273; on appeal Cases C–395/96P and C–396/96P *Compagnie Maritime Belge Transports SA v. Commission* 16 Mar. 2000. The CFI considered (paras. 62–65) that the parties were linked in such a way so as to adopt the same conduct on the market and, consequently, held a collective dominant position for the purposes of Art. 82. The ECJ has annulled certain parts of the decision relating to the fine.

[231] *Irish Sugar* [1997] OJ L258/1, [1997] 5 CMLR 666; on appeal Case T–228/97, *Irish Sugar plc v. Commission* [1999] 5 CMLR 1300. For a more detailed discussion of the case see *supra* Chap. 7. The relations between the parties were found not to be so close that they constituted a single economic entity: see *infra*.

[232] Case C–393/92, *Almelo v. NV Energiebedrijf Ijsselmij* [1994] ECR I–1477, paras. 42–43.

conduct on the market (such as tacit collusion). However, the judgment does not elaborate on what links were necessary between undertakings before they could be found, collectively, to hold a dominant position on the market.

Since then the Court has spoken again on the concept of collective dominance on a number of occasions.[233] Of particular importance have been two judgments given on the concept of collective dominance for the purposes of the Merger Regulation and two judgments given on the concept of collective dominance for the purposes of Article 82. Before going on to consider the latter, we will break the discussion for a moment and outline the developments that have occurred within the sphere of the Merger Regulation.

c. COLLECTIVE DOMINANCE AND THE MERGER REGULATION

It will be seen in Chapter 12 that the Court has had to decide whether or not the European Community Merger Regulation[234] authorizes the Commission to prohibit mergers which lead to the creation or strengthening of a *collective* dominant position. The discussion of this point will be dealt with in greater detail in that chapter. However a summary of that discussion is presented here since the rulings of the Court given in this context may be vital to the interpretation of 'collective dominance' for the purposes of Article 82.

Given the inability or difficulties that the Commission has in controlling the activities of undertakings tacitly colluding on an oligopolistic market, the Commission has, understandably, been keen to act to prevent mergers which would create a market situation ripe for collusion, express or tacit. The problem was that the wording of the Merger Regulation did not make it crystal clear that the Regulation could be applied to prevent mergers leading to the creation or strengthening of a collective dominant position.[235] The Commission, undeterred by this ambiguity, has taken the view that it does so apply and has applied the Regulation to such situations almost from the outset.[236] Finally, following its decision in *Kali und Salz*,[237] a challenge was made to its ability to apply the Regulation in this way and this point fell to be decided by the ECJ.[238] In *France v Commission, Société Commerciale des Potasses et de l'Azote v Commission*[239] the ECJ upheld the Commission's view, confirming that mergers leading to the creation of a collective dominant position did fall within the scope of the Merger Regulation.[240] Thus the Regulation could be relied upon to preclude mergers which 'lead to a situation in which effective competition in the relevant market is significantly impeded by the undertakings involved in the concentration and one or more other undertakings which together, in particular because of factors giving rise to a connection between them, are able to adopt a common policy on the market and act to a consider-

---

[233] The explanation of collective dominance in *Almelo* was reiterated by the Court on a number of occasions, particularly by the CFI in Cases T–24/93 etc., *Compagnie Maritime Belge Transports SA v. Commission* [1996] ECR II–1019, [1997] 4 CMLR 273. But see the ruling of the ECJ, *infra* 688.

[234] Reg. 4064/89 [1989] OJ L395/1, as amended by Reg. 1310/97 [1997] OJ L180/1.

[235] See *infra* Chap. 12.

[236] Case IV/M190, *Nestlé/ Perrier*. [1992] OJ L356/1 discussed *infra* Chap. 12.

[237] Case IV/M308 [1994] OJ L186/30; on appeal Cases C–68/94 and C–30/95, *France v. Commission, Société Commerciale des Potasses et de l'Azote (SCPA) v. Commission* [1998] ECR I–1375, [1998] 4 CMLR 829.

[238] See *infra* Chap. 12.

[239] Cases C–68/94 and C–30/95 [1998] ECR I–1375, [1998] 4 CMLR 829.

[240] *Ibid.*, para. 178.

able extent independently of their competitors, customers, and also of consumers'.[241] This judgment did not, however, clarify whether or not the merger provisions would apply to the creation of oligopolistic dominance in the absence of contractual or other, more formal, structural links between the 'collectively dominant' undertakings operating on the market.

In *Gencor Ltd v Commission*[242] the CFI confirmed that 'structural' links between the undertakings were not necessary for a finding of collective dominance. All that is necessary is a 'relationship of interdependence existing between the parties to a tight oligopoly' which would make alignment of conduct likely.

273. In its judgment in the *Flat Glass* case, the Court referred to links of a structural nature only by way of example and did not lay down that such links must exist in order for a finding of collective dominance to be made.

274. It merely stated . . . that there is nothing, in principle to prevent two or more independent economic entities from being united by economic links in a specific market and, by virtue of that fact, from together holding a dominant position *vis-à-vis* the other operators on the same market.

. . .

276. Furthermore, there is no reason whatsoever in legal or economic terms to exclude from the notion of economic links the relationship of interdependence existing between the parties to a tight oligopoly within which, in a market with the appropriate characteristics, in particular in terms of market concentration, transparency and product homogeneity, those parties are in a position to anticipate one another's behaviour and are therefore strongly encouraged to align their conduct in the market, in particular in such a way as to maximise their joint profits by restricting production with a view to increasing prices. In such a context, each trader is aware that highly competitive action on its part designed to increase its market share (for example a price cut) would provoke identical action by the others, so that it would derive no benefit from its initiative. All the traders would thus be affected by the reduction in price levels.

Although the Court did not explain exactly what it meant when it referred to 'structural' and 'economic' links there now seems no doubt that the relationship of interdependence existing between parties to a tight oligopoly constitutes an economic link sufficient for a finding of collective dominance within the meaning of the Merger Regulation. The important factor appears to be whether or not the market structure will provoke the undertakings *to align their conduct* on the market by restricting output and increasing prices and whether the links between the undertakings are such that tacit co-ordination on the market can be expected.

d. THE JUDGMENTS IN *IRISH SUGAR* AND *COMPAGNIE MARITIME BELGE*

The CFI in *Gencor* was dealing with interpretation of collective dominance for the purposes of the Merger Regulation. However, in reaching its decision it can be seen that in paragraph 273 the Court based its ruling upon the interpretation of the concept in the judgment of the CFI in *Flat Glass* (an Article 82 case).[243] It thus appears that the Court envisaged that the concept of joint dominance would be similarly interpreted for the purposes of both Article 82 and the Merger Regulation.

The view that the concepts will be defined in a similar way also gains support from the

---

[241] *Ibid.*, para. 221.
[242] Case T–102/96, *Gencor Ltd v. Commission* [1999] 4 CMLR 971.
[243] See extract *supra* 682–683.

judgment of the CFI in *Irish Sugar plc v Commission*.[244] The Court relied on the ECJ's confirmation in the merger case *France v Commission, Société Commerciale des Potasses et de l'Azote v Commission*[245] for its finding that:

a joint dominant position consists in a number of undertakings being able together, in particular because of factors giving rise to a connection between them, to adopt a common policy on the market and act to a considerable extent independently of their competitors, their customers, and ultimately consumers (Joined Cases C–68/94 and C–30/95 *France and Others v Commission* [1998] ECR I–1375, paragraph 221).[246]

In *Compagnie Maritime Belge* the ECJ also relied on the Court's ruling in *France v Commission* when defining collective dominance for the purposes of Article 82:

Court of Justice Cases C–395 and 396/96P, *Compagnie Maritime Belge Transports SA v Commission*, 16 March 2000 [2000] 4 CMLR 1076

32. The second and third grounds of appeal, which should be examined together, relate essentially to the issue whether the Commission is entitled to base a finding that there is abuse of a dominant position solely on circumstances or facts which would constitute an agreement, decision or concerted practice under Article [81(1)] of the Treaty, and therefore be automatically void unless exempted under Article [81(3)] of the Treaty.

33. It is clear from the very wording of Articles [81(1)] (a), (b), (d) and (e) and [82](a) to (d) of the Treaty that the same practice may give rise to an infringement of both provisions. Simultaneous application of Articles [81] and [82] of the Treaty cannot therefore be ruled out a priori. However, the objectives pursued by each of those two provisions must be distinguished.

34. Article [81] of the Treaty applies to agreements, decisions and concerted practices which may appreciably affect trade between Member States, regardless of the position on the market of the undertakings concerned. Article [82] of the Treaty, on the other hand, deals with the conduct of one or more economic operators consisting in the abuse of a position of economic strength which enables the operator concerned to hinder the maintenance of effective competition on the relevant market by allowing it to behave to an appreciable extent independently of its competitors, its customers and, ultimately, consumers (see Case 322/81 *Michelin v Commission* [1983] ECR 3461, paragraph 30).

35. In terms of Article [82] of the Treaty, a dominant position may be held by several 'undertakings'. The Court of Justice has held, on many occasions, that the concept of 'undertaking' in the chapter of the Treaty devoted to the rules on competition presupposes the economic independence of the entity concerned (see, in particular, Case 22/71 *Béguelin Import v G.L. Import Export* [1971] ECR 949).

36. It follows that the expression 'one or more undertakings, in Article [82] of the Treaty implies that a dominant position may be held by two or more economic entities legally independent of each other, provided that from an economic point of view they present themselves or act together on a

---

[244] In *Irish Sugar* [1997] OJ L258/1, [1997] 5 CMLR 666, the Commission fined Irish Sugar for a number of breaches of Art. 82 of the Treaty. In particular, it found 7 individual abuses by Irish Sugar on the market in granulated sugar intended for retail and for industry in Ireland. However, it found that for a period of 5 years some of the breaches had been of a collective dominant position held with a distributor. The decision imposed a fine of ECU 8,800,000. The CFI upheld the finding of joint dominance: Case T–228/97, *Irish Sugar plc v. Commission* [1999] 5 CMLR 1300.

[245] Cases C–68/94 and C–30/95 [1998] ECR I–1375, [1998] 4 CMLR 829.

[246] Case T–228/97, *Irish Sugar plc v. Commission* [1999] 5 CMLR 1300, para. 46.

particular market as a collective entity. That is how the expression 'collective dominant position', as used in the remainder of this judgment, should be understood.

37. However, a finding that an undertaking has a dominant position is not in itself a ground of criticism but simply means that, irrespective of the reasons for which it has such a dominant position, the undertaking concerned has a special responsibility not to allow its conduct to impair genuine undistorted competition on the common market (see *Michelin*, paragraph 57).

38. The same applies as regards undertakings which hold a collective dominant position. A finding that two or more undertakings hold a collective dominant position must, in principle, proceed upon an economic assessment of the position on the relevant market of the undertakings concerned, prior to any examination of the question whether those undertakings have abused their position on the market.

39. So, for the purposes of analysis under Article [82] of the Treaty, it is necessary to consider whether the undertakings concerned together constitute a collective entity *vis-à-vis* their competitors, their trading partners and consumers on a particular market. It is only where that question is answered in the affirmative that it is appropriate to consider whether that collective entity actually holds a dominant position and whether its conduct constitutes abuse.

40. In the contested judgment, the Court of First Instance was careful to examine separately those three elements, namely the collective position, the dominant position and the abuse of such a position.

41. In order to establish the existence of a collective entity as defined above, it is necessary to examine the economic links or factors which give rise to a connection between the undertakings concerned (see, inter alia, Case C–393/92 *Almelo* [1994] ECR I–1477, paragraph 43, and Joined Cases C–68/94 and C–30/95 *France and Others v Commission* [1998] ECR I–1375, paragraph 221).

42. In particular, it must be ascertained whether economic links exist between the undertakings concerned which enable them to act together independently of their competitors, their customers and consumers (see *Michelin*).

43. The mere fact that two or more undertakings are linked by an agreement, a decision of associations of undertakings or a concerted practice within the meaning of Article [81](1) of the Treaty does not, of itself, constitute a sufficient basis for such a finding.

44. On the other hand, an agreement, decision or concerted practice (whether or not covered by an exemption under Article [81(3)] of the Treaty) may undoubtedly, where it is implemented, result in the undertakings concerned being so linked as to their conduct on a particular market that they present themselves on that market as a collective entity *vis-à-vis* their competitors, their trading partners and consumers.

45. The existence of a collective dominant position may therefore flow from the nature and terms of an agreement, from the way in which it is implemented and, consequently, from the links or factors which give rise to a connection between undertakings which result from it. Nevertheless, the existence of an agreement or of other links in law is not indispensable to a finding of a collective dominant position; such a finding may be based on other connecting factors and would depend on an economic assessment and, in particular, on an assessment of the structure of the market in question.

This judgment devotes a number of paragraphs to the meaning and means of establishing the existence of collective dominance and is of great importance. Not only does it follow the pattern of earlier cases of not distinguishing between cases on collective dominance decided under Article 82 and those decided under the Merger Regulation, but it appears also to support the view that structural links between the parties will be unnecessary to a finding of collective dominance.

The Court starts by spelling out that a dominant position within the meaning of Article 82 can be held by two or more undertakings provided that they *present themselves or act together on a particular market as a collective entity*. It then states that the proof of the existence of a collective dominant position involves a two-stage process: it is necessary first to establish the existence of a collective entity and then, where the position is established, to establish that the collective entity holds a dominant position.

It was when discussing the means of establishing the existence of a collective entity that the Court relied on the ruling in *Almelo* and its own ruling in the merger case, *France v Commission*. These cases establish the necessity of 'economic links or factors which give rise to a connection between the undertakings concerned'. The Court held that such links could, but would not necessarily, be established by an agreement, decision, or concerted practice within the meaning of Article 81 concluded by the undertakings (even if exempted from the prohibition in Article 81(1) by Article 81(3)). The CEWAL agreement did in fact provide the requisite links. The Court stressed, however, in paragraph 45 that 'the existence of an agreement or of other links in law is not indispensable to a finding of a collective dominant position; such a finding may be based on other connecting factors and would depend on an economic assessment and, in particular, on an assessment of the structure of the market in question'.

e. SUMMARY

The concept of a collective dominant position is of enormous importance to both Article 82 and the Merger Regulation. The case law now establishes that the Merger Regulation may be applied to prevent concentrations which lead to the creation or strengthening of a collective dominant position and that Article 82 may be used to control abuses of an existing collective dominant position.

Although the Court has not explicitly said it, it also seems likely that the concept of a collective dominant position will be defined in the same way for the purposes of both the Merger Regulation and Article 82. The case law under each provision cross-references to case law derived from the other without distinction. Obviously the assessments in each case will be different: in the case of Article 82 the examination determines whether or not there has been an abuse of an existing collective dominant position;[247] in contrast the assessment under the Merger Regulation is prospective in nature, to determine whether or not the merger (or concentration for the purposes of the Regulation) *will* lead to the creation or strengthening of a collective dominant position and to a situation in which effective competition in the relevant market is impeded. In the context of both provisions, however, the Court has stressed the need to show that the entities do, or will, present themselves collectively because the links between them are such that they will be encouraged to align their conduct or to adopt a common policy on the market and to act to a considerable extent independently of their customers, competitors, and consumers.

The concept emerging thus appears to be that a collective dominant position will exist where the parties are, as a result of the economic links between them, able or encouraged to

---

[247] Occasionally there may be a complaint that an undertaking has threatened a breach of a dominant position and interim measures sought: see Chaps. 7 and 14.

adopt the same conduct and to align their behaviour on the relevant market.[248] Further, it is clear that, for the purposes of the Merger Regulation, a joint dominant position may be found in the absence of structural links (such as contractual links) between the parties. It may be held by parties within a tight oligopoly which are in a position to anticipate one another's behaviour and to align their conduct. The pattern of the case law and the judgment in *Compagnie Maritime Belge* indicate that a collective dominance will, in the context of Article 82, also be found in the absence of structural links between the undertakings.

(ii) ABUSE OF A COLLECTIVE DOMINANT POSITION

Now that the applicability of Article 82 to undertakings which hold a collective dominant position seems settled, a further, perhaps more difficult, question arises for the future. What conduct may amount to an abuse of a collective dominant position?

a. *FLAT GLASS*

In *Flat Glass*, the Commission had concluded that the undertaking's communication of, for example, identical prices to customers and granting of identical discounts constituted abuses within the meaning of Article 82. However, the CFI criticized the Commission for simply having recycled the facts of the Article 81 infringement to present an infringement of Article 82. Since then the Commission has been more careful to spell out the relevant market for the purposes of Article 82, the position of the undertakings on the market, and the abuses in the context of the express provisions of Article 82.

b. *FRENCH-WEST AFRICAN SHIPOWNERS' COMMITTEE AND CEWAL*

The conduct alleged to be abusive in *French-West African Shipowners' Committee*[249] *and CEWAL*[250] was broadly the same as that which the Commission had already held to infringe Article 81 (the attempt by the members of the committee to eliminate effective competition from non-committee shipowners). However, the Commission couched its analysis in terms of Article 82 and went further than a simple recycling of the facts constituting an infringement of Article 81(1). Nonetheless the fact remains that much of the conduct was anyway condemned under Article 81. In *Compagnie Maritime Belge* the Court upheld the Commission's finding of abuse in CEWAL, including the finding that the undertakings' putting on of fighting ships was an abuse for the purposes of Article 82.[251]

c. COLLECTIVE ABUSES

Clearly, if the power to prohibit abuses of a jointly held dominant position is to be of any force to the Commission, it will wish to condemn as 'abusive' behaviour, such as 'excessive pricing' by oligopolists perhaps, which is not dependent on the finding of an agreement or concerted practice (and which can, in any event, be condemned under Article 81).

It has been seen in Chapter 7 that Article 82 has been used to condemn a range of conduct. It prohibits both exploitative practices (such as excessive pricing or inertia) and

---

[248] But see the Commission's decision under the Merger Reg. in Case IV/M1524 *Airtours/First Choice* [2000] OJ L93/1 discussed *infra* Chap. 12.

[249] [1992] OJ L134/1.

[250] [1993] OJ L34/20.

[251] Cases C–395 and 396/96P, *Compagnie Maritime Belge Transports SA v. Comission* [2000] 4 CMLR 1076.

anti-competitive practices (such as predatory or discriminatory pricing, tying, refusals to supply, etc.). It is a crucial question whether or not these notions of abuse will be useful to control the behaviour of oligopolists.

Excessive pricing

A main cause for concern in an oligopolistic market is that undertakings will naturally emulate the economic effects of monopoly. Oligopolists may not, therefore, engage in price competition but may set their prices at a level which produces monopoly profits, restricts output,[252] and maximizes the profits of the oligopolists as a whole. Could this behaviour be caught by Article 82, which expressly provides that an abuse may consist of directly or indirectly imposing 'unfair selling prices'?

Apart from in the *Chiquita* decision, Article 82 has, in fact, rarely been used to condemn exploitative prices. Although the Commission in *Chiquita*[253] fined United Brands for, amongst other things, charging excessive prices for its 'Chiquita' bananas, the ECJ considered that the Commission had failed adequately to establish that excessive prices had in fact been charged. In each case, the Commission would have to establish that the accused was 'charging a price which is excessive because it has not reasonable relation to the economic value of the product supplied'. Further, '[t]his excess could, inter alia, be determined objectively if it were possible for it to be calculated by making a comparison between the selling price of the product in question and its cost of production'.[254] In practice this will be very hard to establish. It is very difficult to determine an objective way of establishing exactly what price covers costs plus a reasonable profit margin.[255]

It would thus seem possible in principle for the Commission to condemn oligopolists that have engaged in parallel pricing at a level that the Commission considers to be 'excessive'. However, as seen from the discussion in earlier Chapters, it will be an extremely difficult task to establish that excessive prices have been charged. In practice, the Commission has not sought to do so but has preferred to avoid acting as price regulator. In addition, it is arguably perverse to prohibit conduct which is 'natural' in some oligopolies as abusive and, consequently, to render the relevant undertakings open to large fines by way of penalties and/or to actions in national courts.[256]

Other collective abuses

It is hard to envisage what other abuses may be committed by undertakings indulging in non-collusive parallel behaviour. It seems hard to explain collective decisions refusing to supply an undertaking, or targeting a new entrant to the market, on the grounds of mutual interdependence. However, it could be argued, for example, that an abuse will have been committed by collectively dominant undertakings which are inefficient or which all impose exclusive purchasing commitments on their distributors.

---

[252] Case IV/M524 *Airtours/First Choice* [2000] OJ L93/1 discussed *infra* in Chap. 12.

[253] [1976] OJ L95/1, [1976] 1 CMLR D28. See *supra*, Chaps. 5 and 7.

[254] Case 27/76, *United Brands Co and United Brands Continental BV v. Commission* [1978] ECR 207, [1978] 1 CMLR 429, paras. 250 and 251.

[255] See the Commission's *Vth Report on Competition Policy* (Commission, 1975), at point 3. The Commission is, however, developing an approach to excessive pricing in the telecoms area: see M. Haag and R. Klotz, 'Commission Practice Concerning Excessive Pricing in Telecommunications' EC *Commission Competition Policy Newsletter* 1998/2, 35.

[256] See R. Whish and B. Sufrin, 'Oligopolistic Markets and EC Competition Law' [1992] *YEL* 59, 74–5.

b. ABUSE BY ONE OF THE COLLECTIVELY DOMINANT UNDERTAKINGS

In *Irish Sugar plc v Commission*[257] the CFI held that an *individual* undertaking could engage in conduct which constitutes an abuse of its dominant position held collectively with one or more undertakings:

Whilst the existence of a joint dominant position may be deduced from the position which the economic entities concerned together hold on the market in question, the abuse does not necessarily have to be the action of all the undertakings in question. It only has to be capable of being identified as one of the manifestations of such a joint dominant position being held. Therefore, undertakings occupying a joint dominant position may engage in joint or individual abusive conduct.[258]

This finding was, however, made in the context of a joint dominant position held by a dominant undertaking and its distributor. In this case Irish Sugar had such a close relationship with its distributor that it seems possible that they actually formed a single economic unit. Had the Commission made such a finding, it would have been unnecessary to invoke the concept of collective dominance.[259]

In contrast, it is less easy to envisage what conduct (other than exploitative abuses) which is traditionally seen as anti-competitive when indulged in by an individual dominant undertaking may also be found to be abusive when engaged in by one of a group of oligopolists. The granting of loyalty rebates, discriminatory pricing, or selective price-cutting by single dominant undertakings may be condemned (it may make it more difficult for competitors to gain access to the market).[260] On an oligopolistic market, however, the granting of rebates to customers, discriminatory pricing, or selective price-cutting by one of the undertakings may mean that price competition is in fact operating between the oligopolists.[261]

(iii) REMEDIES AND FINES

Under Regulation 17, the Commission has power only to require an undertaking to bring an infringement to an end (Article 3) and to impose fines on undertakings for any infringements committed (Article 15).[262] Article 3 has been interpreted widely. It could, for example, enable the Commission to order a 'demerger' where it considered that a 'merger'

---

[257] Case T–228/97 [1999] 5 CMLR 1300.

[258] *Ibid.*, para. 66.

[259] The various terms used in the contested decision to describe the applicant's position on the market before February 1990 are the result of the special nature of its links with SDL before that date. The Commission claims to have established the existence of infringements of Art. [82] of the Treaty from 1985 to February 1990 committed by the applicant alone, by SDL alone, or by both together. Having accepted the applicant's argument that it did not control the management of SDL, despite holding 51% of SDH's capital, the Commission decided that even if it was not possible to regard the applicant and SDL as a single economic entity, they had, together at least, held a dominant position on the market in question. Para. 110 of the statement of objections confirms that that was the Commission's view: 'To defend its market [the applicant] had recourse to different forms of abusive conduct which were used alternatively or in combination with one another whenever it was felt necessary throughout the period from 1985. Some of the relevant practices were carried out by [the applicant] itself; others, on the retail sugar market, by SDL, the commercial subsidiary of [the applicant]): Case T–228/97, *Irish Sugar plc v. Commission* [1999] 5 CMLR 1300, para. 28.

[260] See e.g. Case 85/76 *Hoffmann-La Roche v. Commission* [1979] ECR 461, [1979] 3 CMLR 211.

[261] See *TACA* [1999] OJ L95/6, [1999] 4 CMLR 1415.

[262] [1959–62] OJ Spec. Ed. 87. See *infra* Chap. 14.

constituted an abuse of a dominant or collective dominant position,[263] or to supply a customer where an undertaking had abused its dominant position by a refusal to supply.[264] It would not, however, enable the Commission, for example:

(i)   to order that the prices charged by the undertakings be reduced or otherwise controlled;

(ii) to look pragmatically for other problems causing price rigidity in the market and suggest solutions for resolving them; or

(iii) to make more dramatic orders such as 'divestiture' to alter and to improve the competitive structure of the market (currently it has power under Regulation 17 only to order an undertaking to sell a business or assets where, in acquiring those assets, it has committed an infringement of Article 81 or Article 82).[265]

(iv) CONCLUSIONS

It appears that Article 82 will be applicable to independent undertakings that are not linked together by some agreement or other special relationship. Even if Article 82 is applied to oligopolists linked only by their mutual interdependence, it has been seen that the concept of abuse, developed in relation to individually dominant firms, is not a mechanism ideally equipped to control the behaviour of oligopolists. Further, the action that the Commission may take under Regulation 17 on the finding of an infringement may not be the most appropriate means of dealing with the problems posed. It is far from clear that imposing fines on undertakings for behaving in an economically rational way is logical. In addition, the power to order an undertaking to bring its infringement to an end may be an ineffective means of dealing with the oligopoly problem.

It is, however, perhaps the lack of any other effective method of dealing with oligopolies rather than the appropriateness of Article 82 itself that has led the Commission to persist in the development of the concept of an abuse of a collective dominant position.

C. ALTERNATIVE METHODS FOR DEALING WITH OLIGOPOLISTIC MARKETS UNDER EC LAW

(i) MERGER REGULATION

Given that oligopolistic markets often do not function as effectively as one in which free competition operates, and given the difficulties involved in applying either Article 81 or Article 82 to the conduct of undertakings operating on such markets, it may be that the EC Merger Regulation holds the key. It seems sensible to ensure that the Merger Regulation is utilized to prevent mergers which create or strengthen a collective dominant position as a result of which competition in the common market is likely to be impeded. Prevention is

---

[263] See Case 6/72, *Continental Can v. Commission* [1973] ECR 215, [1973] CMLR 199, but see n. 265.

[264] See Cases 6 and 7/73, *Istituto Chioterapico Italiano SpA and Commercial Solvents v. Commission* [1974] ECR 223, [1974] 1 CMLR 309.

[265] See *supra* n. 263. But see the Commission's proposal for a Reg. implementing Arts. 81 and 82, Art. 7, COM (2000) 582 (the Commission wishes to be able to impose remedies of a structural nature). See Chaps. 5 and 14.

better than a cure. If the Commission prohibits mergers causing market imperfections it will have to worry less frequently about corrective measures.

The possibility that firms can engage in tacit collusion raises a difficult policy issue. How can one discriminate between anti-competitive tacit behaviour and normal effective competition? In other words, how is one to discriminate between a firm which is competing legitimately — *i.e.* doing the best it can given the actions of its rivals — and one which in some sense is not? . . . It should be recognised that the mere fact that firms recognise their interdependence with other firms is not sufficient grounds for inferring that observed outcomes are not the result of effective competition. Given the difficulties in discriminating between the two modes of competition, policy should not as a general rule attempt to intervene in a market on suspicions that firms are competing tacitly. Not only is it difficult to discriminate , but what is the regulatory remedy? This means that the principal policy weapon against tacit collusion should be exercised through merger control and is therefore preventive in nature rather than corrective . . .[266]

Since it is now clear that the Commission can rely on the Merger Regulation to control the creation or strengthening of a collective dominant position[267] a strict merger policy may, therefore, reduce some of the difficulties that arise in attempting to control oligopolistic markets and markets on which one undertaking only is found to be dominant.

Where a market is already an oligopolistic one the Merger Regulation will only be of use to ensure that the undertakings' positions on the market are not strengthened through merger. Other solutions may need to be found to deal with an oligopolistic market which already exists.

(ii) ARTICLE 12, REGULATION 17

Article 12(1) of Regulation 17 provides:

If in any sector of the economy the trend of trade between Member States, price movements, inflexibility of prices or other circumstances suggest that in the economic sector concerned competition is being restricted or distorted within the common market, the Commission may decide to conduct a general inquiry into that economic sector and in the course thereof may request undertakings in the sector concerned to supply the information necessary for giving effect to the principles formulated in Articles [81] and [82] of the Treaty and for carrying out the duties entrusted to the Commission.

This provision gives the Commission a wide discretion to decide whether or not to investigate markets that it considers to be malfunctioning. It need not have any evidence of, or even suspect, an infringement of either Article 81 or 82 before commencing an inquiry.

Unfortunately the Commission has no power to take any action to remedy any defects identified in an Article 12(1) investigation (although it may use any information gathered against a particular undertaking if it subsequently commences proceedings under Article 81(1)). It is perhaps for this reason that the provision has rarely been used for investigations (there have only been two reported examples of sector inquiries: one into margarine and another into the brewery sector).

Whish and Sufrin have argued that 'given the political will' the provision could form the:

---

[266] S. Bishop and M. Walker, *The Economics of EC Competition Law: Concepts, Application and Measurement* (Sweet & Maxwell, London, 1999), para. 4.09.

[267] See *supra* 686–687 and *infra* Chap. 12.

basis of a proper investigative system. Although there may be understandable concern about giving the Commission such large elements of discretion in respect of oligopolistic markets it is doubtful whether it is more worrying than the prospect of the Article [82] prohibition applied wholesale to the complex behaviour of oligopolies.[268]

(iii) CARTELS

Many oligopolistic markets have characteristics which make them particularly prone to cartelization. The Commission should ensure that it is particularly vigilant in these markets in case cartels are being operated.

(iv) INFORMATION SHARING AGREEMENTS

It has been seen that the Commission is wary of information-sharing agreements concluded between undertakings operating on a tight oligopolistic market. Such information exchanges may exacerbate the problems arising on such markets.

(v) OTHER AGREEMENTS

The Commission may scrutinize more carefully research and development and other beneficial collaboration agreements concluded between two or more participants operating on a concentrated market. In particular, it will be seen in Chapter 13 that some of the Community block exemptions applying to horizontal agreements do not apply to agreements concluded between undertakings with large market shares. The Commission will want to examine such agreements individually to ensure that they are not unduly restrictive of competition.[269]

4. CONCLUSIONS

The Commission has wide investigative powers which it can use to unearth covertly operated cartels. However, where the Commission is unable to find evidence of the existence of a cartel or where it considers that an oligopolistic market is functioning in an inefficient manner it is powerless to act under Article 81. The Commission may have power to prevent the creation or strengthening of a collective dominant position under the Merger Regulation but the Regulation does not enable it to regulate or control the behaviour of undertakings operating on an existing oligopolistic market.

Article 82 is being developed to enable the Commission to control the conduct of independent undertakings that are collectively dominant. Many are of the opinion that this solution is not a satisfactory one. However, if Article 82 is not used, the Commission may only take measures to ensure that restrictive agreements (for example, cartels, information-sharing agreements, or those dressed up as beneficial collaboration agreements) are not concluded by undertakings operating in such markets.

---

[268] R. Whish and B. Sufrin, 'Oligopolistic Markets and EC Competition Law' [1992] *YEL* 59, 83. In its proposal for a Reg. implementing Arts. 81 and 82, Art. 17, COM (2000) 582, the Commission proposes that it should retain its right to conduct general inquiries into sectors. There has been no proposal to the Member States that there should be a broader right to conduct investigations (which would require a Treaty amendment).

[269] See *infra* Chap. 13.

It is thus arguable that the powers set out in Article 12 Regulation 17 should be developed and widened in order to empower the Commission to launch inquiries into, and take measures in, sectors that it considers are not functioning satisfactorily. The Commission could then survey the industry as a whole, identify the causes of any market weaknesses, and make recommendations aimed at rectifying those weaknesses.

In the UK, for example, the Director General of Fair Trading has power under the Fair Trading Act 1973 to refer complex monopolies (where at least 25 per cent of the goods of a description (or the supply of a service) are supplied by, or to, two or more persons who conduct their affairs in any way to prevent, restrict, or distort competition) to the Competition Commission (formerly, the Monopolies and Merger Commission) for investigation. The Competition Commission then investigates. Where it concludes that the situation operates against the public interest it makes recommendations aimed, broadly, at improving the competitiveness of the relevant market (the Secretary of State for Trade and Industry decides whether or not to implement those recommendations). It may, for example, recommend the total or partial termination of an agreement; it may recommend that the prices to be charged for any specified goods or services on a market should be regulated; or recommend that any business, or part of a business, be disposed of (by the sale or any part of an undertaking or assets or otherwise).[270]

On some occasions the Competition Commission has even recommended that measures should be taken by or against bodies other than the market players (for example, where it considers that the market rigidity has been caused, partly at least, by advertising restrictions or other legal or regulatory barriers). The changes introduced to UK law by the Competition Act 1998 have not deprived the UK competition authorities of these useful powers under the Fair Trading Act.

Resort to such draconian remedies as price control and divestiture may not always be a suitable means of dealing with the problems arising on oligopolistic markets. However, it can also be seen that a more flexible system may have advantages over one focusing exclusively on the abusive conduct, or the behaviour, of the undertakings on the market. Dramatic changes in the Community rules would need to be made before such a system could be operated by the Commission. In the meantime, the temptation may be for the Commission to continue with its development of the concept of collective dominance.

5. FURTHER READING

A. BOOKS

BISHOP S., and WALKER M., *The Economics of EC Competition Law: Concepts, Application and Measurement* (Sweet & Maxwell, 1999) paragraphs 2.19–2.26 and paragraphs 4.06–4.23

CLARKE R., *Industrial Economics* (Blackwell, 1985), Chapter 3

SCHERER F.M., and MOSS D., *Industrial Market Structure and Economic Performance* (3rd edn., Houghton Mifflin 1990), Chapters 7 and 8

---

[270] See Fair Trading Act 1973, Sched. 8. See *supra* nn. 265 and 268.

B. ARTICLES

CARLE J., and JOHNSSON M., 'Benchmarking and EC Competition Law' [1998] *ECLR* 74

FRANZOSI M., 'Oligopoly and the Prisoners' Dilemma: Concerted Practices and As If Behaviour' [1988] *ECLR* 385

VAN GERVEN G., and VARONA E.N. 'THE WOOD PULP CASE AND THE FUTURE OF CONCERTED PRACTICES' (1994) 31 *CML Rev* 575

JOLIET R., 'La Notion de Pratique Concertée et l'Arrêt I.C.I. dans une perspective comparative' [1974] *CDE* 251

JONES A., 'Wood Pulp: Concerted Practice and/ or Conscious Parallelism' [1993] *ECLR* 273

KORAH V., 'Concerted Practices' (1973) 36 *MLR* 260

—— '*Gencor* v *Commission:* Collective Dominance' [1999] *ECLR* 337

WHISH R., 'Collective Dominance' in D. O'Keefe and M. Andenas (eds.), *Liber Amicorum for Lord Slynn* (Kluwer, 2000)

——, and SUFRIN B., 'Oligopolistic Markets and EC Competition Law' [1992] *YEL* 59

12

MERGERS

1. INTRODUCTION

A. WHAT IS A MERGER?

Broadly, a merger occurs where two or more formerly independent entities unite. Obviously, a number of different transactions and agreements concluded by undertakings could result in a unification of the independent undertakings' decision-making process. Every jurisdiction needs, therefore, to adopt a definition of what constitutes a merger for the purposes of any merger control legislation. The European Community Merger Control Regulation (the 'Merger Regulation'),[1] for example, applies to 'concentrations'. Broadly, there is a concentration where two or more previously independent undertakings merge their businesses *or* where there is a change in control of an undertaking (sole or joint control of an undertaking being acquired by another undertaking or undertakings).[2]

B. THE PURPOSES OF MERGER CONTROL

The purpose of merger control is to enable competition authorities to regulate changes in market structure by deciding whether two or more commercial companies may merge, combine, or consolidate their businesses into one.[3] It has already been seen that the Community authorities are hostile to anti-competitive agreements concluded between independent companies (especially horizontal ones).[4] Mergers naturally create a more permanent and lasting change on the market than agreements. It might be expected, therefore, that many mergers, especially horizontal mergers, would be forbidden. Mergers may raise severe competition concerns. In particular, they may result in the undertakings acquiring or strengthening a position of market power and, consequently, in an increase in the market price of the products or services on the relevant market. However, mergers also give the

---

[1] Reg. 4064/89 [1989] OJ L395/1, [1990] 4 CMLR 286, corrigendum [1990] OJ L257/1 (the Merger Reg.). The Merger Reg. was amended by Reg. 1310/97 [1997] OJ L180/1, corrigendum [1998] OJ L40/17.

[2] Merger Reg., *supra* n. 1, Art. 3. See discussion *infra* 717–726.

[3] For merger control to be effective, it is necessary to control both amicable agreements to merge and hostile takeovers.

[4] *Supra*, especially Chap. 11.

owner of a business the opportunity to sell it. Without this possibility, entrepreneurs might be reluctant to start a business. Further, mergers provide many other efficiency opportunities.

The reasons for not making mergers unlawful per se or for not even coming anywhere near such a rule are plain. Widespread prohibition of mergers would impose serious, if not intolerable, burdens upon owners of businesses who wished to liquidate their holdings for irreproachable personal reasons. Moreover, economic welfare is significantly served by maintaining a good market for capital assets . . . Most importantly, a policy of free transferability of capital assets tends to put them in the hands of those who will use them to their utmost economic advantage, thus tending to maximize society's total output of goods and services.

   Growth by merger . . . will often yield substantial economies of scale—in production, research, distribution, cost of capital and management. Entry by merger . . . may stimulate improved economic performance in an industry characterized by oligopolistic lethargy and inefficiency. Finally, acquisition of diversified line of business, by stabilizing profits, may minimize the risk of business failure and bankruptcy.[5]

The task of the competition authorities is to identify and to prohibit those mergers which have such an adverse impact on competition or society that any benefits resulting from them are outweighed or should be ignored. Although, therefore, the motives for, and benefits of, mergers are important, the key to effective merger control is to identify why and when a merger should be prohibited.

(i) THE MOTIVES FOR, AND ADVANTAGES OF, A MERGER

a. EFFICIENCY

In many cases the parties will state that the main motivation for their merger is that the merged entity will be more efficient. The entity may be able to exploit economies of scale in production (this argument will be strongest in the context of horizontal or, sometimes, vertical mergers where related operations are combined). Such economies will be of particular importance in a market in which the cost of production of a product is high in comparison to the size, or the anticipated size, of the market or where there is a minimum efficient scale of production.[6] The merger may also give rise to other operating efficiencies such as marketing efficiencies (arising, for example, from broader product lines, streamlining of the sale force, and the use of common advertising, etc.) or the ability to pool research development skills (giving rise to the opportunity for greater innovation).

   Mergers may, therefore, enable undertakings to increase these efficient levels of manufacture, research and development, and distribution more rapidly and more cheaply than they could by internal growth. They may also encourage management efficiency by ensuring that the most productive assets are managed by the most efficient managers (the merger may bring new and superior management to the business[7]).

---

   [5] D. Turner, 'Conglomerate Mergers and Section 7 of the Clayton Act' (1965) 78 Harv. LRev. 1313, 1317.
   [6] *Supra* Chap. 1.
   [7] The simple threat of a take-over may encourage the incumbent management of a company to strive for efficiency (rigid control of mergers will remove or greatly reduce this perceived threat). However, overconfident entrepreneurs may overestimate their ability to manage more complex undertakings or businesses in an unfamiliar field or market.

b. BARRIERS TO EXIT

It has already been noted that few people would go to the trouble to set up a business if they could not sell it when they had had enough or when they wished to realize capital profits from it. In particular, many smaller business owners may wish to sell their business if no obvious successor is available.

c. FAILING UNDERTAKINGS AND UNEMPLOYMENT

A merger may provide an escape route for a company facing an otherwise inevitable liquidation.[8] In a case such as this the possibility of selling the business to another may mean that productive assets are kept in production and that creditors, owners, and employees are protected from the adverse consequences of the undertaking's failure.

d. SINGLE MARKET INTEGRATION

Cross-border mergers may facilitate market integration. '[E]xternal growth by means of mergers and acquisitions can be a means of quickly realizing potential cost savings and integration gains offered by the internal market.'[9]

e. NATIONAL OR EUROPEAN CHAMPIONS

The desire to increase the scale of national and European companies may be a goal of national, or European, industrial policy.[10] Mergers affect the structure of a market and questions of industrial policy inevitably arise. The ability to restructure or to create national or European champions may, for example, mean that the parties can, in combination, survive and compete more effectively on international markets, contribute to technical and economic progress, and/ or facilitate cross-border trade.

(ii) THE ADVERSE CONSEQUENCE OF MERGERS

More important perhaps than focusing on the benefits of a merger is the answer to the question: why should mergers be prohibited?[11] When, and on what grounds, a competition authority should take steps to interfere with the market for corporate control and preclude a merger is a matter of great controversy. Failure to agree on this key issue was one of the factors which seriously delayed the introduction of any comprehensive system of merger regulation at the Community level. Should competition be the sole criterion relevant to a decision to clear or to prohibit a merger? Or should other wider policy issues, such as regional, industrial, or social policy, also be taken into account?

---

[8] See discussion *infra* at 801–805.

[9] 'Competition and Integration: Community Merger Policy' (1994) 57 *European Economy*, p. vii. The need for merger control at the Community level was, eventually, seen as a necessary complement to the 1992 single market programme: Commission's XVIIIth and XIXth *Reports on Competition Policy*, (Commission, 1988) and (Commission, 1989) and discussion *infra* at 708–712.

[10] See *infra* 798.

[11] It is not necessary to show that a merger creates efficiencies. It should be sufficient that it does not create the power to restrict output: see R.H. Bork, *The Antitrust Paradox* (Basic Books, 1978, reprinted with a new Introduction and Epilogue, 1993), chaps. 9–11.

a. A DAMAGING EFFECT ON THE COMPETITIVE STRUCTURE OF THE MARKET

There is a danger that undertakings may wish to merge in order to achieve or to strengthen their monopoly power.

In horizontal mergers, and especially in the massive consolidations that took place [in the US] around the turn of the century, the desire to achieve or strengthen monopoly power played a prominent role. Some 1887–1904 consolidations gained monopoly power by creating firms that dominated their industries. Others fell short of dominance, but transformed market structures sufficiently to curb the tendencies toward price competition toward which sellers gravitated in the rapidly changing market conditions of the time. As Thomas Edison remarked to a reporter concerning reasons for the formation of the General Electric Company in 1892:

Recently there has been sharp rivalry between [Thomson-Houston and Edison General Electric], and prices have been cut so that there has been little profit in the manufacture of electrical machinery for anybody. The consolidation of the companies . . . will do away with competition which has become so sharp that the product of the factories has been worth little more than ordinary hardware.

Those were days when businesspeople were not yet intimidated by the wrath of trustbusters or public opinion. Now they are more circumspect, and evidence of monopoly-creating intent is harder to find. Also, vigorous antitrust enforcement in the United States and, more recently, abroad has done much to curb competition-inhibiting mergers.[12]

Even if dominance or the acquisition of market power is not the motive for a merger, it may be its effect. A merger control system focusing exclusively on competition issues will adopt a strict policy against such mergers.

Horizontal mergers

A horizontal merger is one which occurs between undertakings operating at the same level of the economy. As Hovenkamp points out, such mergers have two important implications for the market on which the merging firms operate:

Because the horizontal merger involves two firms in the same market, it produces two consequences that do not flow from vertical or conglomerate mergers: 1) after the merger the relevant market has one firm less than before; 2) the post-merger firm ordinarily has a larger market share than either of the partners had before the merger.[13]

A merger between two or more firms which sell competing products may create or reinforce a position of dominance or create or reinforce a position of collective dominance:

These structural changes raise two potential competitive concerns. First, by eliminating the competitive constraint which currently exists between the parties, the merger may weaken to a significant degree the strength of the overall competitive constraints acting on one or both of the two parties. As a result, the prices charged by the merged entity may increase relative to their pre-merger level. A merger which has these characteristics is said to give rise to a situation of *single dominance* [the

---

[12] F.M. Scherer and D. Ross, *Industrial Market Structure and Economic Performance* (3rd edn. Houghton Mifflin, 1990) 160.

[13] H. Hovenkamp, *Federal Antitrust Policy: The Law of Competition and its Practice* (West Publishing, 1994), 445.

unilateral effect of the merger] . . . Secondly, the merger may lead to a reduction in the effectiveness of competition if the change in market structure creates a competitive environment more favourable to sustainable tacit collusion.[14]

We have already seen that markets dominated by a single or a few undertakings create severe problems for competition authorities.[15] It is difficult for those authorities to control the behaviour of a dominant undertaking and to detect abuses of its market power. An active merger policy seeks to avoid these difficulties by precluding undertakings from merging where the parties will obtain or strengthen a position of market power which might be exploited at the expense of customers and protected by anti-competitive behaviour. The US antitrust authorities, for example, will not, therefore, permit mergers which 'create or enhance market power or facilitate its exercise'.[16]

A merger between two or more previously independent undertakings which does not lead to the creation of an individual dominant position may nonetheless lead to a substantial increase in the concentration of a particular industry. This may lead to the creation or strengthening of a collective dominant position on an oligopolistic market and may consequently facilitate collusion, explicit or tacit,[17] between the undertakings operating on the relevant market. In Chapter 11 it was seen that where two or more undertakings are jointly dominant on a market, those firms may exercise market power (emulating the effect of monopoly) by either explicitly or tacitly co-ordinating their action.[18] Many competition authorities, therefore, adopt a merger policy which seeks to prevent undertakings from merging to create or strengthen a collective dominant position.[19] In the USA Hovenkamp states that one of the principal concerns of US merger policy has been that 'horizontal mergers may facilitate express or tacit collusion or Cournot-style oligopoly behaviour':

Merger policy is the most powerful weapon available in the American antitrust arsenal for combating tacit collusion or Cournot style oligopoly. Since we cannot go after oligopoly directly under [section 1 Sherman Act], we do the next best thing. We try to prevent (taking efficiencies and other factors into account) the creation of market structures that tend to facilitate Cournot or collusion-like outcomes.[20]

Various methods have been adopted by competition authorities to explain the principles upon which an authority measures market power. Since 1982 the merger authorities in the USA have used a concentration index to make preliminary assessments of the legitimacy of a

[14] S. Bishop and M. Walker, *The Economics of EC Competition Law: Concepts, Application and Measurement* (Sweet & Maxwell, London, 1999), 6.08.

[15] See generally *supra* Chapters 5–7 and Chap. 11.

[16] Horizontal Merger Guidelines, issued on 2 April 1992 (revised in 1997). The exercise of market power results in a misallocation of resources or a transfer of wealth from buyer to seller.

[17] See *infra* 771–789.

[18] The EC competition authorities are not particularly well equipped to deal effectively with problems raised on an oligopolistic market, and cartels are notoriously difficult to detect: *supra* Chap. 11.

[19] In the USA the 1992 Guidelines (revised in 1997) are concerned with higher concentration in markets which might facilitate 'co-ordinated interaction' among the remaining firms on the market. Various market factors are identified which may facilitate or impede reaching terms of co-ordination and monitoring and enforcing those terms: such as the availability of key information on market conditions, transactions and individual competitors; firm and product homogeneity; typical pricing or marketing practices; characteristics of buyers and sellers and typical transactions.

[20] H. Hovenkamp, *Federal Antitrust Policy: The Law of Competition and its Practice* (West Publishing Co, 1994), 445 and 447.

horizontal merger and the reduction in competition it will cause on a particular market. The Herfendahl–Hirschman index (the HHI) seeks to identify the concentration of a particular market by using numerical distinctions. Its aim is to prevent acquisitions which are likely to create monopoly or oligopoly power. The HHI seeks to measure the concentration in a way which reflects both the concentration levels on the market generally and the degree to which larger firms are dominant in the market.

The HHI operates by adding together the squares of the market shares of each of the undertakings operating in the market. The degree of concentration on the market is assessed by reference to the sum of those market shares. Where the HHI is under 1,000, the market is not perceived to be concentrated: if it is between 1,000 and 1,800 the market is moderately concentrated; and over 1,800 the market is highly concentrated.

In evaluating horizontal mergers, the market concentration (post-merger) and the increase in concentration resulting from the merger are assessed in order to create a presumption of the merger's legality or illegality:

(i)   There is an assumption that a merger does not raise any competition concerns if either the HHI is (post-merger) less than 1,000 or if the HHI is between 1,000 and 1,800 but the increase to the index is less than fifty;

(ii) Where (a) the HHI is above 1,800 and there is an increase of between fifty and 100 in the index or (b) where the HHI is between 1,000 and 1,800 and there is an increase in excess of 100 in the index, a challenge from the competition authorities is likely. The merger 'potentially raises significant competitive concerns';

(iii) Where the HHI is above 1,800 and the merger has led to an increase to the index in excess of 100 points the merger is presumed to be illegal.

The EC authorities have not adopted this method of measuring industry concentration. The HHI has some drawbacks.[21] In addition, because the wording of the EC Merger Regulation requires the Commission to assess whether or not the concentration leads to the creation or strengthening of a dominant position, the Commission is not able to put as much weight on concentration data as has been done in the USA. The Commission has, however, issued a notice setting out guidance on how it defines markets.[22] This notice indicates that the Commission is willing to take account of econometric and quantitative tests when defining a market.

Vertical mergers

The motive for vertical mergers, between firms at different levels of production in the economy, is usually to obtain a secure supply of a raw material or to secure an outlet for the sale of products. Vertical mergers may raise some competition concerns. The predominant fear is that vertical mergers may 'foreclose' the market or a source of supply to competitors.[23] For example, a merger between a manufacturer of a product and a supplier of an

---

[21] See S. Bishop and M. Walker, *The Economics of EC Competition Law: Concepts, Application and Measurement* (Sweet & Maxwell, 1999), 2.45–2.46; F. Fishwick, *Making Sense of Competition Policy* (Kogan Page, 1993), 86.

[22] [1997] OJ C362/5; *supra* Chap. 1.

[23] See C.J. Cook and C.S. Kerse, *E.C. Merger Control* (3rd edn., Sweet & Maxwell, London, 2000), 166. It is possible that vertical integration may raise barriers to entry: *supra* Chap. 6.

essential component for that product (backward integration) may have severe implications for competing manufacturers. The foreclosure effect will be acute where there are few or no other suppliers of the essential components. Similarly, the acquisition by a manufacturer of a distributor (forward integration) may make it more difficult for competitors to distribute their products.

A merger between undertakings involved at different stages of production is said to be a vertical merger. Vertical mergers often involve a supplier and actual or potential customer (*e.g.* a merger between a brewer and a chain of public houses). Vertical mergers can give rise to a number of competition issues, including the possibility of foreclosure or of creating a more favourable environment for collusive behaviour. As with vertical restraints, anti-competitive effects are likely only if there is horizontal market power at one or more of the vertical levels.[24]

In the USA, the competition authorities have, in recent times, rarely been interested in either vertical or conglomerate mergers since these mergers rarely lead to the increase of market power.[25]

Conglomerate mergers

Conglomerate mergers (involving concentrations which have no horizontal or vertical effect) do not result in an increase of market power but may frequently be motivated by the need for risk-reduction. An undertaking may wish to expand into another market where it is operating in a declining or cyclical industry or where it simply wishes to spread risk. However, where an undertaking is dominant in one market there may be concern that it will use its power in that market to engage in tying or, by cross-subsidizing, predatory pricing in another market (and perhaps thereby to acquire a dominant position in that other market[26]). This may be more likely where the relevant markets are related and the merged undertakings will be able to offer a wide portfolio of products.[27] Alternatively there may be a fear that conglomeracy will lead to a loss of potential competition. A merger of firms operating in different product or geographic markets may cause a loss of potential competition. Any threat that they may enter each other's markets is eliminated. This may be of particular importance where the undertakings operate in the same product but a different geographic market or where they operate in neighbouring product markets.

These arguments against conglomeracy have been criticized by Bork:

the most common charges leveled against conglomerate mergers are that they may: (1) create a 'deep pocket' that enables a firm to devastate its less affluent rivals; (2) lower costs; (3) raise barriers to entry; (4) frighten smaller companies into less vigorous rivalry; (5) create the opportunity to engage in reciprocal dealing; and (6) eliminate potential competition. Of these alleged dangers, only

---

[24] S. Bishop and M. Walker, *The Economics of EC Competition Law: Concepts, Application and Measurement* (Sweet & Maxwell, 1999), para. 6.09.

[25] Bork, in particular, has argued that antitrust should never interfere with vertical or conglomerate mergers. They never put together rivals and do not, therefore, create or increase the ability to restrict output through an increase in market share. See R.H. Bork, *The Antitrust Paradox*, (Basic Books, 1978, reprinted with a new Introduction and Epilogue, 1993), chaps. 11–12.

[26] See *supra* Chap. 7.

[27] For a discussion of 'portfolio power' see *infra* 767 ff.

the sixth, which is really a horizontal and not a conglomerate merger theory, has any possible validity, and that one will rarely be significant.[28]

Efficiency and/or other considerations?

A further matter of controversy is whether a finding that a merger has an adverse effect on competition should be final and fatal to the conclusion of the merger. It is arguable that, even where a position of market power is acquired or reinforced, a merger should be permitted if, for example: (1) it leads to greater efficiency (the cost savings resulting from the merger outweigh the detrimental impact of the merger on consumer welfare as a whole); (2) the merger is supported as a matter, for example, of industrial or social policy; or (3) the merger will save a firm which, otherwise, faces an inevitable failure. Whether or not such factors should be, or are, taken into account under the EC Merger rules will be considered below.

b. CONGLOMERATES AND BIG BUSINESS

Mergers may cause other worries, apart from competition ones, for authorities. Most of the factors that will be discussed in this section and sections (c) and (d) below would not, however, cause concern on the ground of strict economic theory unless it could *also* be shown that consumer welfare was adversely affected by the merger.

Some individuals believe that conglomeracy has implications for the freedom of society more generally. It is feared that too great economic concentration is anti-democratic and restricts individual freedom and enterprise.

[O]ur concern for the maintenance of effective competition extends beyond purely economic considerations. Competition is one of the foundations of an open society . . . it is therefore necessary to weigh against the gains from industrial concentration the socio-political consequences of concentrations of private power, which could discredit property owning democracy.[29]

In Chapter 1 it was seen that it has been argued that one of the goals of European competition should be the diffusion of economic power and the protection of individual freedom.

Private power can cross economic boundaries and poses the threat of an 'extra market' power which can change the rules of the game in favour of the dominant corporations. In such a situation, where relationships between firms and their socio-economic environment constitute a mixture of market and non-market bonds, the authorities aim at the dispersion of private power. Even if this entails some loss of economic efficiency, such a choice would not necessarily be irrational, because such costs may be outweighed by social or political advantages.[30]

It is these sentiments which have led some authorities to utilize competition law as a tool to protect not only the process of competition but competitors (and the freedom of enter-

---

[28] R.H. Bork, *The Antitrust Paradox*, (Basic Books, 1978, reprinted with a new Introduction and Epilogue, 1993), 249. Bork concludes his chap. by stating: 'We have now examined all the major theories of the ways in which conglomerate mergers may injure competition and found that none of them (with a minor exception for a theory that is really horizontal) bears analysis. The conclusion must be, therefore, that conglomerate mergers should not be prohibited by judicial interpretation of Section 7 of the Clayton Act.'

[29] A. Caincross *et al.*, *Economic Policy for the European Community* (Macmillan, 1974).

[30] A.P. Jacquemin and H.W. de Jong, *European Industrial Organisation* (Macmillan, 1997), 198–9.

prise). German competition law, in particular, reflects this political philosophy. Not only is tight control exercised over mergers but, for example, abuse by one firm of the dependence upon it of another is prohibited.

c. SPECIAL SECTORS AND FEAR OF OVERSEAS CONTROL

It may be believed that tighter control should be exercised over mergers which occur in particularly sensitive sectors. In these sectors it might be thought that a broader range of factors should be taken into account in determining whether or not a merger operates in the public interest. For example, interests of democracy may require the preservation of the 'plurality of the press' or national security may require that the ownership of certain industries such as oil and defence equipment do not pass overseas.

d. UNEMPLOYMENT

Mergers may mean asset-stripping, profits to shareholders, rationalization, and loss of jobs. Mergers which occur in depressed regions or in areas in which unemployment is already high may, therefore, cause concern for national authorities.

2. THE HISTORY OF THE EUROPEAN MERGER CONTROL REGULATION

A. THE INITIAL LACUNA

The original EEC Treaty, unlike the ECSC Treaty,[31] did not provide any specific provision for controlling mergers. Articles 81 and 82 EC focus on the control of the behaviour of undertakings rather than mergers which affect a lasting change to the structure of the market. An explanation for the different approach set out in the ECSC and the EEC Treaties may be that the former was a *traité-loi* whilst the latter was a *traité-cadre* (a framework document, to be fleshed out by implementing legislation). However, it is more likely that other factors were responsible for the omission of merger control from the EEC Treaty.

In particular, it seems likely that it would have been easier to agree on a rule which would affect only the specific industries dealt with by the ECSC Treaty. Indeed, the ability to control mergers in these sectors was perceived to be of vital importance given their political and military significance.[32] In contrast, it would have been more difficult to agree on rules which were to affect all other undertakings generally. Further, at the time, it seems to have been considered that the objectives set out in Article 2 of the EEC Treaty of economic

---

[31] See Art. 66(7) of the ECSC Treaty.

[32] The French in particular were keen to have in place rules which imposed constraints on the German war industry: S. Bulmer, 'Institutions and Policy Change: The Case of Merger Control' (1994) 72 Public Administration 423, 427–8.

expansion might be achieved by concentrating economic power rather than prohibiting mergers.[33]

B. THE DRIVE FOR MERGER CONTROL AT THE COMMUNITY LEVEL

The drive to introduce legislation at the Community level specifically focused on merger control was led by the Commission. In 1966 it first acknowledged, in its publication of its *Memorandum on the Concentration of Enterprises in the Common Market*,[34] that some form of EC merger control was necessary.[35] The Commission believed that its inability to control mergers inhibited its capability to operate effective competition control.[36] In 1973 the Commission first adopted a legislative proposal for a merger control regulation.[37] The dangers posed by market dominance were apparent to a number of the European States (merger control was introduced in the UK in 1965 (although it was not then a Member State), in Germany in 1973, and in France in 1977).

Any regulation on merger control had to be passed unanimously by the Council.[38] For a long time there was no consensus amongst the Member States that merger control was necessary at all. Those Member States that did recognize a need for merger control were reluctant to cede power to the Commission and to relinquish their economic sovereignty. Many Member States wished to retain control over changes in industrial structure in their territories. In addition, early drafts of the Merger Regulation gave the Commission a broad discretion in assessing whether or not a merger was in the Community interest. Member States were divided on what substantive criteria should be used to appraise Community mergers. The UK, for example, was adamant, at least in later negotiations, that only the effects on competition should be taken into account, fearing perhaps that any exception to this strict approach would be used to allow social and industrial policy considerations in through the back door.[39] There were, therefore, two major sticking points:[40]

---

[33] Undertakings might achieve industrial competitiveness by benefiting from economies of scale.

[34] EEC Competition Series Study No 3.

[35] See C. Overbury, 'Politics or Policy? The Demystification of EC Merger Control' [1992] *Fordham Corporate Law Institute* 561.

[36] Prior to the adoption of the Merger Reg. the Commission relied, where possible, on Arts. 82 and 81 to prohibit some mergers. See in particular the discussion of Case 6/72, *Europemballage Corp. and Continental Can Co. Inc.* v. *Commission* [1973] ECR 215, [1973] CMLR 199, *infra* 709–710.

[37] In the period between 1973 and 1989 a series of draft regs. was proposed and rejected by the Council: see [1973] OJ C92/1, [1982] OJ C36/3, [1984] OJ C51/8, [1988] OJ C130/4, [1989] OJ C22/14l.

[38] The legal basis for the EC Merger Reg. is Arts. 83 (ex Art. 87) and 308 (ex Art. 235) of the Treaty. The latter is discussed *supra* Chap. 2.

[39] In the 1980s the decision in the UK whether or not to refer a merger for investigation to the UK's (then) Monopolies and Mergers Commission (now the Competition Commission) was predominantly determined by competition factors. The 'Tebbitt Guidelines' stressed that merger policy was an important part of the Government's policy of promoting competition within the economy in the interests of consumers. It was therefore rare for intervention to occur unless a merger potentially raised problems on competition grounds. The German authorities were reluctant to cede control over mergers which might have anti-competitive effects on its markets: see the discussion of the German clause *infra* at 741–744.

[40] See B.E. Hawk and H.L. Huser, *European Community Merger Control* A Practitioner's Guide' (Kluwer Law International, 1996), 2–3.

1. *Jurisdiction.* Whether, and if so at what point, control should be relinquished by the Member States to the Commission and what the relationship between European and national law should be; and

2. *Appraisal criteria.* Should factors other than competition be taken into account in assessing whether a particular merger was compatible or incompatible with the common market?

C. THE CATALYST FOR THE EC MERGER REGULATION

(i) ARTICLES 81 AND 82 OF THE EC TREATY

a. ARTICLE 82

Frustrated by the lack of a specific provision enabling it to control mergers the Commission sought not only to persuade the Council to enact a specific merger control provision but it applied its existing tools to prevent them: it utilized Articles 82 and, subsequently, 81 of the Treaty to prevent takeovers and acquisitions of shareholdings in other undertakings.

In *Europemballage Corp. and Continental Can Co Inc* v. *Commission*[41] the ECJ upheld the Commission's view that Article 82 could be used to prevent a dominant undertaking from abusing its dominant position by acquiring a competitor and thereby strengthening that dominant position.[42] In this case the Court of Justice confirmed that an abuse for the purpose of that Article does not have to be attributable to, or dependent on, the existing dominant position. Breach is not dependent upon use of the dominant position. Rather, an abuse occurs 'if an undertaking in a dominant position strengthens such a position in such a way that the degree of dominance reached substantially fetters competition'.[43] Because the Commission adopts a low threshold in assessing whether or not an undertaking is dominant,[44] it appears that Article 82 was a reasonably effective weapon against mergers.[45] This view is expressed by Cook and Kerse in the extract below.

C. J. Cook and C. S. Kerse *E.C. Merger Control* (3rd edn., Sweet & Maxwell, 2000), 2–3

While the Commission's views on the use of Article 81 were to change its approach to the use of Article 82 to regulate concentrations remained fairly consistent, the Article was used on a number of occasions to exercise a significant measure of control, albeit often informal, over Community takeover

---

[41] Case 6/72 *Europemballage Corp. & Continental Can Co Inc* v. *Commission* [1973] ECR 215, [1973] CMLR 199.

[42] See *supra* Chap. 5.

[43] Case 6/72, *Europemballage Corp & Continental Can Co Inc* v. *Commission* [1973] ECR 215, [1973] CMLR 199, para. 26. The abuse thus results from a limitation of competition in a market which it already dominates.

[44] *Supra* Chapters 5–7.

[45] The extent to which Arts. 81 and 82 can be applied following the EC Merger Reg. (Council Reg. 4064/89 [1989] OJ L385/1, as amended by Council Reg. 1310/97 [1997] OJ L180/1) coming into force is discussed *infra* 748–750.

activity. The European Court of Justice bolstered the Commission's view when, in 1973, in *Continental Can*, . . . it found that the acquisition of a competitor could constitute an abuse of a dominant position falling within Article 82. It confirmed that Article 82 could apply to the acquisition of a competitor by a firm enjoying a dominant position:

> 'Abuse may . . . occur if an undertaking in a dominant position strengthens such a position in such a way that the degree of dominance reached substantially fetters competition, *i.e.* that only undertakings remain in the market whose behaviour depends on the dominant one.' [para 26]

The test for intervention under Article 82 is therefore a strict one. The Court suggested that an acquisition has to result in the virtual elimination of competition in that product market before Article 82 could be infringed . . . But *Continental Can* provoked the Commission soon after to propose a form of prior control over concentrations, and, significantly, the Commission took the opportunity to consider, albeit informally, a number of mergers under Article 82. It publicised its approach in its Tenth Report on Competition Policy. This achieved the results the Commission was looking for and prudent advisers tended increasingly to assess market concentration levels at Community and national level and, if the magic figure of 40 per cent was breached, to consider carefully at least informal approaches to the Competition Directorate. . . The latter part of the 1980s saw much greater use of such techniques as consortium bidding and financial leveraging to support a number of hostile acquisitions. The intervention of the Commission in a consortium bid for Irish Distillers showed the way for using the E.C. competition rules as a spoiling tactic.[46]

The use of Article 82 is, however, limited. It does not apply unless there is an abuse of an *existing* dominant position. The acquiring company must, therefore, have a dominant position before Article 82 can apply. It does not, *prima facie*, apply where two or more undertakings merge to create a dominant position[47] or where a dominant undertaking is acquired by a non-dominant undertaking.[48]

b. ARTICLE 81

The Commission initially appeared to accept that Article 81 would not be used to control mergers.[49] Indeed, Article 81 does not appear to be particularly suitable for the purpose. Because the Article strikes principally at *agreements* between independent undertakings it would be artificial to try and deal with many types of mergers under its provisions (in particular, hostile takeovers which are opposed by the target undertaking).[50] Notwithstanding the early views expressed by the Commission, it later sought to apply Article 81 as a

---

[46] Apart from its decision in *Continental Can* the Commission has, however, only once issued a decision prohibiting a merger transaction under Art. 82, *Warner-Lambert/ Gillette* [1993] OJ L116/21, [1993] 5 CLR 559, especially paras. 22–32.

[47] '[O]nly the strengthening of dominant positions and not their creation can be controlled under Art. [82] of the Treaty': Case T–102/96, *Gencor Ltd* v. *Commission* [1999] ECR II–753, [1999] 4 CMLR 971, para. 155; and see Case 6/72, *Europemballage and Continental Can* v. *Commission* [1973] ECR 215, [1973] CMLR 864, para. 26.

[48] C.J. Cook and C.S. Kerse, *E.C. Merger Control* (3rd edn. Sweet & Maxwell, London, 2000), 129 especially n. 19 and accompanying text.

[49] The Commission concluded in its *Memorandum on the Concentration of Enterprises in the Common Market*, EEC Competition Series Study No 3 (published in 1966), para. 58, that Art. 81 would not be applicable to agreements 'whose purpose is the acquisition of total or partial ownership of enterprises of the reorganization of the ownership of enterprises'.

[50] Further, the sanction of nullity set out in Art. 81(2) and the scheme for exempting agreements for a specified period of time set out in Art. 81(3) seem an inappropriate means of controlling and authorizing mergers.

weapon against mergers. In *BAT and Reynolds* v. *Commission*[51] the ECJ confirmed that Article 81 might apply to the acquisition by an undertaking of a minority shareholding in another.

36. It should be recalled that the agreements prohibited by Article [81] are those which have as their object or effect the prevention, restriction or distortion of competition within the Common Market.

37. Although the acquisition by one company of an equity interest in a competitor does not in itself constitute conduct restricting competition, such an acquisition may nevertheless serve as an instrument for influencing the commercial conduct of the companies in question so as to restrict or distort competition on the market on which they carry on business.

38. That will be true in particular where, by the acquisition of a shareholding or through subsidiary clauses in the agreement, the investing company obtains legal or de facto control of the commercial conduct of the other company or where the agreement provides for commercial co-operation between the companies or creates a structure likely to be used for such co-operation.

39. That may also be the case where the agreement gives the investing company the possibility of reinforcing its position at a later stage and taking effective control of the other company. Account must be taken not only of the immediate effects of the agreement but also of its potential effects and of the possibility that the agreement may be part of a long-term plan.

This judgment indicated that agreed share transactions could fall within Article 81(1). The difficulties raised and the ambiguities left unresolved by the judgment (in particular whether or not Article 81 might be applied more broadly to mergers) led to widespread concern in industry which complained both to the Commission and to Member States. The ambiguities 'were fully exploited by the Commission. The resulting uncertainty was used skilfully by the Commission, particularly by the then Competition Commissioner, Mr Peter Sutherland, to persuade Member States to return to the negotiating table on a new draft of the Regulation'.[52] Soon after this judgment the green light was given to the Commission to put forward another proposal for a merger regulation.

The subsequent adoption of the Merger Regulation means that the question whether the acquisition of sole control is also caught by Article 81(1) is likely never to be resolved. Where an undertaking acquires direct or indirect control of another a concentration is deemed to arise for the purposes of the Merger Regulation.[53] The objective of the Merger Regulation is that *it alone* shall apply to concentrations within the meaning of that Regulation and the Commission's powers to apply Articles 81 and 82 under Regulation 17 and the other implementing regulations are disapplied.[54] The judgment will still be important, however, where direct or indirect control is not acquired so that the Merger Regulation does not apply.[55]

Article 81 is also of importance to 'joint ventures' which are not concentrations for the purposes of the Merger Regulation.[56]

---

[51] Cases 142 & 156/84 [1987] ECR 4487, [1988] 4 CMLR 24.

[52] C.J. Cook and C.S. Kerse, *E.C. Merger Control* (3rd edn. Sweet & Maxwell, 2000), 3.

[53] Merger Reg., Art. 3(1), see discussion *infra* 717 ff.

[54] See, Merger Reg. Art. 22(1), but see discussion *infra* 740 ff. For Reg. 17 [1959–62] OJ Spec. Ed. 87, see *infra* Chap. 14.

[55] See, e.g., *British Telecom-MCI* [1994] OJ L52/51, [1995] 5 CMLR 301.

[56] See *infra* 721 ff.

c. THE RESIDUAL APPLICATION OF ARTICLES 81 AND 82

It is possible that irrespective of the existence of the Merger Regulation the Commission itself, the national courts and/ or the national competition authorities may in some circumstances still be empowered to act pursuant to the Treaty provisions. This possibility is discussed on pages 748–750 below.

(ii) THE INTERNAL MARKET

The Commission's White Paper, *Completing the Internal Market,*[57] did not make any reference to merger control. However, business restructuring was a natural result of the programme. Commission data showed that an increasing number of mergers were completed in the lead-up to 1992,[58] many between companies in different EC countries or between EC companies and enterprises outside the Community. The need for some form of EC merger control thus became apparent and its absence anomalous. Industry, in particular, became keen to have a level playing field (some Member States did not have merger rules, whilst the rules in other Member States differed dramatically) and to have to comply with only *one* set of merger rules.

A combination of Commission support, pressure from industry, the single market programme and increasing numbers of mergers led to the eventual realization that a system of European merger control was inevitable.

D. THE EC MERGER CONTROL REGULATION— COUNCIL REGULATION (EEC) 4064/89

The Merger Control Regulation was finally adopted by the Council of Ministers on 21 December 1989.[59] It came into force nine months later on 21 September 1990. Its legal basis is Article 83 (ex Article 87) and Article 308 (ex Article 235) of the Treaty. The Regulation sets out both substantive and procedural rules. The procedural requirements are fleshed out by Regulation 447/98 which deals with matters such as notification, time limits, and hearings.[60]

---

[57] COM(85)310.

[58] In 1982–3 there were 115 mergers, by 1988–9 the number had grown to 492 and to 622 in 1989–90: L. Tsoukalis, *The New European Economy Revisited* (2nd edn., Oxford University Press, 1993), 103.

[59] Council Reg. (EEC) 4064/89 of 21 Dec. 1989 on the control of concentrations between undertakings [1989] OJ L395/1, corrigendum [1990] OJ LL257/14 (hereinafter the Merger Reg.).

[60] Commission Reg. 447/98 [1998] OJ L61/1 of 1 Mar. 1998 on the notifications, time limits, and hearings provided for in Council Reg. 4064/89 on the control of concentrations between undertakings [1998] OJ L61/1. The Commission has procedural and investigatory powers similar to those applicable under Reg. 17. Provisions exist to protect business secrecy. Further, there are powers to request information from the parties to the concentration, Member States, and third parties and to conduct 'dawn raids' to acquire information. The Commission may impose fines on undertakings which do not comply with the provisions of the Merger Reg.: see *infra* 735 and 737.

Numerous Commission notices set out guidance on how the Commission interprets various aspects of the Regulations.[61]

Mergers falling within the scope of the Regulation are investigated and appraised by a division of the Competition Directorate called the Merger Task Force.

E. THE GREEN PAPER

In 1996 the Commission issued a Green Paper reviewing the Merger Regulation.[62] It conducted this review having received 376 notifications of mergers and having issued 357 final decisions under the Regulation. The Paper looked at several areas of merger control which might be in need of change or reform.

In particular, the Commission considered that a number of mergers that significantly affected trade in the Member States had escaped the ambit of the rules. It thus proposed that more mergers should be brought within the scope of the Merger Regulation. Additionally, or alternatively, it made proposals to deal with mergers which would not now fall within the Merger Regulation but which had, potentially, to be notified to the competition authorities in a number of EU/EEA or other States. The Commission also set out, for example, proposals to improve procedures and the treatment of joint ventures[63] and to find a more realistic way of assessing the turnover of financial institutions for the purposes of the regulation.

F. COUNCIL REGULATION (EC) 1310/97

In response to the Green Paper Council Regulation 1310/97,[64] which came into force on 1 March 1998, introduced some amendments to the Merger Regulation. Predictably, the Commission did not acquire sufficient support from the Member States to hand much greater control over mergers to Brussels. However, some compromise was reached in relation to mergers which would otherwise have to be notified to multiple national competition authorities.[65] Many of the other Green Paper proposals were also introduced in the regulation: for example, changes were introduced to the rules dealing with joint ventures[66] and to the rules setting out when concentrations involving credit and other financial institutions

---

[61] Although the notices do not have binding effect they are extremely useful indicators of the Commission's approach. See the Commission's Notice on the concept of full-function joint ventures [1998] OJ C66/1, [1998] 4 CMLR 581; Notice on the concept of concentration [1998] OJ C66/5, [1998] 4 CMLR 586; Notice on the concept of undertakings concerned [1998] OJ C66/14, [1998] 4 CMLR 599; Notice on calculation of turnover [1998] OJ C66/25, [1998] 4 CMLR 613, draft Notice regarding restrictions directly related and necessary to concentrations [2000] 4 CMLR 779, and draft Notice on Commitments [2000] 4 CMLR 794. The Commission's Notice on market definition is also of course of extreme importance.

[62] Community Merger Control, COM(96)19 final.

[63] See *infra* 721 ff.

[64] Council Reg. 1310/97 of 30 June 1997 [1997] OJ L180/1.

[65] See *infra* 727 ff.

[66] Reg. 1310/97, Art. 1(3); see *infra* 721 ff.

have a Community dimension.[67] The changes introduced by this Regulation to the Merger Regulation will, of course, be incorporated within the discussion of the rules and throughout the course of this chapter.[68]

G. THE FUTURE

The Commission is again reviewing the operation of the Meyer Regulation. In particular, it is carrying out the mandatory review of the jurisdiction thresholds set out in the Regulation.[69] Other proposals for change are under review. Further, the Commission has simplified the notification procedure for certain mergers. These proposals will be considered in the text below.

3. SCHEME OF THE MERGER REGULATION

The Merger Regulation applies to 'concentrations' with a 'Community dimension'. Both terms are defined in the Regulation itself.[70] The concept of a 'Community dimension' allocates responsibility over concentrations between the Commission and the Member States.[71] Broadly, with certain limited exceptions, concentrations that do not have a Community dimension are assessed under any applicable national competition legislation,[72] whilst concentrations with a Community dimension are assessed under the provisions of the Merger Regulation.[73] In the latter case, the Commission's decision under the terms of the Merger Regulation is decisive and, as a general rule, no other rule of national or Community competition law applies.[74] The basic scheme is, therefore, that concentrations with a Community dimension benefit from a 'one stop shop' and are not subject to assessment under the competition rules of the Member States.

Concentrations with a Community dimension must be notified to the Commission in accordance with the requirements set out in Form C/O. On notification, the Commission is

---

[67] Reg. 1310/97, Art. 1(4).

[68] For a summary of the main changes see, e.g., C. Ahlborn and V. Turner, 'Expanding Success? Reform of the E.C. Merger Regulation' [1998] ECLR 249.

[69] Merger Reg. Art. 1(4).

[70] See infra 717–726.

[71] It is underpinned by the same principles as those which underlie the principle of subsidiarity.

[72] Infra 746. The Commission does not have power to appraise the concentration either under the Merger Reg. or under Arts. 81 and 82 of the Treaty. A Member State can, however, request that the Commission examine, and render a decision on, a concentration which does not have a Community dimension where the Member State does not itself wish to investigate the merger: Art. 22(3), discussed infra 747–748.

[73] Infra 727.

[74] A Member State may, however, have jurisdiction over various aspects of a concentration which has a Community dimension: see Arts. 9, 21(3), Art. 296 EC and discussion infra 740–746. There is also a possibility that both Arts. 81 and 82 of the Treaty will have a residual role to play: see infra 748–750.

obliged to assess, within a period of one month,[75] whether or not that concentration falls within the scope of the Merger Regulation and, if so, whether it raises serious doubts about its compatiblity with the common market (the Phase I investigation).[76] Approximately 90–95 per cent of Community merger cases are dealt with in Phase I proceedings and, therefore, within a period of one month.[77] Where the Commission believes that the concentration raises serious doubts about its compatibility with the common market a second-phase investigation will be launched to analyse whether or not this is the case. The Phase II investigation must normally be concluded within a period of four months from the initiation of the Phase II proceedings.[78] In general, the operation of the concentration is suspended until the Commission's final decision. The Advisory Committee on Concentrations must be consulted before a final decision is taken.[79] The final decision is made by the College of Commissioners.[80]

These procedures and tight legal time limits are in stark contrast to those that apply under Regulation 17 with respect to Articles 81 and 82.[81] The requirement that merger decisions should be made quickly was crucial, however, in the negotiations leading up to the conclusion of the Merger Regulation. In particular, Member States were anxious that delays should not hamper the flexibility of undertakings seeking to engage in industrial restructuring.

There is a right of appeal from all Commission decisions to the CFI or, occasionally, direct to the CFI.[82] Despite the recognition of the need for speed in merger cases there is, however, no expedited appeals procedure. It may, therefore, take years before an appeal is heard against a Commission decision to prohibit a merger.[83]

Section 4 below sets out more fully when the Commission has jurisdiction over mergers and the procedures it adopts in appraising such mergers. Section 5 deals with the substantive appraisal of mergers and the difficult question of how it is determined whether or not a merger is compatible with the common market.

---

[75] The period is extended in certain circumstances: see Art. 10(1) and discussion *infra* 737.

[76] Merger Reg., Art. 6(1)(a)–(c). Broadly, this means that the Commission must determine whether (a) the concentration creates or strengthens a dominant position, (b) as a result of which effective competition in the common market (or a substantial part of it) would be significantly impeded, Art. 2(2) and 2(3). But see now the special rules for joint ventures previously classified as 'co-operative' joint ventures, but now falling within the ambit of the Merger Reg., *infra* 807–808.

[77] In its Green Paper the Commission stated that out of 357 decisions delivered, 31 had been under Art. 6(1)(a), 303 under Art. 6(1)(b), 19 under Art. 8(2), and 4 under Art. 8(3). 93.5% were, therefore, concluded in the course of Phase I proceedings. Statistics for the period 1990–8 are set out in J. Faull and A. Nikpay, *The EC Law of Competition* (Oxford University Press, 1999), para. 4.280 and statistics up to 30 Sept. 2000 are available on DG Comp. 5 website.

[78] Merger Reg., Art. 10(3).

[79] It must also be consulted, e.g., before a decision imposing a fine or penalty or ordering divestment is taken.

[80] In some particularly sensitive merger cases there is a fear that this factor allows political and other considerations to enter the decision-making process. This has led to some calls for the creation of an independent European cartel office or competition tribunal: see *infra* 799–801.

[81] *Supra* Chap. 4.

[82] See *infra* 809–810. The CFI has jurisdiction only to hear actions for judicial review brought by private individuals or companies. It does not have jurisdiction in actions brought by Community institutions or Member States under Art. 230. Where the appeal is made by a Member State the appeal is made straight to the ECJ: see Council Decision 93/350 [1993] L144/21 and *infra* n. 293.

[83] See *infra* 810.

AN OVERVIEW OF
THE EC MERGER REGULATION

Regulation 4064/89 (as amended by regulation 1310/97)
Art 1 The Merger Regulation applies to all concentrations with a Community dimension

There must be a Concentration
Art 3

Is there a Community dimension?
Art 1(2)(3)

Yes – Thresholds met	No – Thresholds not met
Commission has sole jurisdiction under the Merger Regulation – no national law applies Art 21(1)(2) Art 22(2)	National law applies Art 22(1)
But NB Art 9 – Distinct Markets Art 21(3) – Legitimate Expectations Art 223 EC – National Security Arts 81/82 EC – Residuary Role	But NB Art 22(3) – Reference to the Commission Art 22(1) – Joint ventures Arts 81/82 EC – Residuary Role
Concentration must be notified Suspension of operations Art 4 Art 7	Any relevant national procedures and appraisal applies
Phase I – Decision to be taken within 4–6 weeks Art 10(1) Art 6(1)(a)(b)(c)	
Phase II investigation only where concentration raises serious doubts Decision to be taken within four months Art 10(3)	
Concentration declared to be compatible or incompatible with the common market Art 8(2)(3)	
Appeal Art 230 EC	

4. JURISDICTION AND PROCEDURE

A. CONCENTRATIONS

(i) DEFINITION

The Merger Regulation seeks to govern concentrations bringing 'about a lasting change in the structure of the undertaking concerned'.[84] The term concentration is defined in Article 3 of the Merger Regulation.[85] It provides:

'1. A concentration shall be deemed to arise where:

    (a) two or more previously independent undertakings merge, or

    (b) —one or more persons already controlling at least one undertaking, or

—one or more undertakings

acquire, whether by purchase of securities or assets, by contract or by any other means, direct or indirect control of the whole or parts of one or more other undertakings.'

A concentration thus occurs where two or more undertakings merge their businesses *or* where there is a change in control of an undertaking. A Commission Notice on the concept of a concentration under Council Regulation 4064/89 provides guidance on how the Commission interprets the notion of a concentration.[86]

a. ARTICLE 3(1)(a)—MERGERS BETWEEN PREVIOUSLY INDEPENDENT UNDERTAKINGS

The Regulation does not define what is meant by the term 'merge'. The term is merely used to describe one type of concentration which falls within the ambit of the Regulation. It appears that the word is used 'narrowly'.

Were a very broad economically-oriented interpretation to the term 'merge' adopted, Article 3(1)(b) ff. would be rendered otiose. The purpose of Article 3(1)(a) appears therefore to be to catch undertakings which have fused their businesses ('legal' mergers), that is where 'one or more pre-existing undertakings, as a result of the transaction, cease to exist as individual economic entities'.[87] For example, the term merge describes the situation where two or more undertakings amalgamate into one business or where one undertaking acquires and completely absorbs another undertaking (which subsequently ceases to exist).[88]

---

[84] See Merger Reg., recital 23.

[85] As amended by Reg. 1310/97, Art. 1(3).

[86] [1998] OJ C66/5, [1998] 4 CMLR 586 (replacing the notice set out in [1994] OJ C385/5).

[87] J. Faull and A. Nikpay, *The EC Law of Competition* (Oxford University Press, 1999), para. 4.10. It is noted at para. 4.12 that '[p]erhaps surprisingly a relatively small proportion of cases notified under the Merger Reg. are mergers. Overall, in the first eight years of application (1990–1997) fewer than 3 per cent of all notified agreements fell in this category.'

[88] See C.J. Cook and C.S. Kerse, *E.C. Merger Control* (3rd edn. Sweet & Maxwell, 2000), 27 and Commission Notice on the concept of a concentration [1998] OJ C66/5, [1998] 4 CMLR 586, paras. 6 and 7.

C.J. Cook and C.S. Kerse, *E.C. Merger Control* (3rd edn., Sweet & Maxwell, 2000), 27 and 29

There is no definition or explanation in the Regulation of what is meant by the term 'merge'. 'Merger' in the Regulation (for example in Article 4(2)) is used merely to refer to the type of concentration falling within Article 3(1)(a). The absence of definition here is in stark contrast to the case of concentration by the acquisition of control, dealt with in Article 3(1)(b), where three paragraphs are spent clarifying the concept. A wide economically-oriented definition of 'merger' would render Article 3(1)(b) to 4 largely, if not completely, redundant. It would appear, therefore, that 'merger' in Article 3(1)(a) is to be given a narrow meaning, the primary intention being to refer to a merger in the technical sense of *'fusion'*. This is the sense in which the term 'merger' is used the in the Third Directive on Company Law. A merger will occur where all the rights and liabilities of one or more companies are transferred to another company (which may have been formed for the purpose). The members of the acquired company or companies receive shares in the acquiring company with or without an additional cash payment. Following the transfer of the assets and liabilities, the acquired company or companies as a general rule cease to exist . . .

. . . A narrow approach to the term 'merger' is reflected in the Commission's implementation and application of the Regulation . . . In the notification form, Form CO (s.2, para. 2.1(a)) reference is made to a 'full legal merger'. It is unclear whether 'merger' covers anything less, such as a partial acquisition of assets or some form of economic concentration

. . . It must be recognised, however, that the practical effect of the distinction between mergers within Article 3(1)(1) and other concentrations is minimal. [A concentration consisting of a merger within Article 3(1)(a) must be notified jointly (Article 4(2))].

b. ARTICLE 3(1)(b)—ACQUISITION OF CONTROL

Decisive influence

Article 3(1)(b) applies where there is a change in control of an undertaking, for example: where an undertaking acquires sole control of another (even if the acquiring company previously jointly controlled the company, this still constitutes a change in control[89]), two or more undertakings acquire *joint* control of another (even if one of them previously had sole control of that other) or two or more undertakings establish a joint venture company[90] in respect of which they exercise joint control. Control is acquired where an undertaking, or undertakings, gains the ability to affect the strategic decision of another or others. The acquisition of control is defined in Article 3(3) of the Regulation:

For the purposes of this Regulation, control shall be constituted by rights, contracts or any other means which, either separately or in combination and having regard to the considerations of fact or law involved, confer the possibility of exercising decisive influence on an undertaking, in particular by:

  (a) ownership or the right to use all or part of the assets of an undertaking;
  (b) rights or contracts which confer decisive influence on the composition, voting or decisions of the organs of an undertaking.

---

[89] Case IV/M23, *ICI/Tioxide* [1991] 4 CMLR 792.
[90] See discussion *infra* 721–726 and Chap. 13.

The Regulation is thus intended to catch transactions which lead to an undertaking or undertakings acquiring *decisive influence* over another.[91] Control may be gained over a particular undertaking *or* by the acquisition of assets of an undertaking,

Commission Notice on the concept of concentration under Council Regulation (EEC) No 4064/89 on the control of concentrations between undertakings [1998] OJ C66/5, [1998] 4 CMLR 586

9. Whether an operation gives rise to an acquisition of control depends on a number of legal and/or factual elements. The acquisition of property rights and shareholders' agreements are important, but are not the only elements involved: purely economic relationships may also play a decisive role. Therefore, in exceptional circumstances, a situation of economic dependence may lead to control on a *de facto* basis where, for example, very important long-term supply agreements or credits provided by suppliers or customers, coupled with structural links, confer decisive influence. . . .

There may also be acquisition of control even if it is not the declared intention of the parties. . . Moreover, the Merger Regulation clearly defines control as having 'the possibility of exercising decisive influence' rather than the actual exercise of such influence.

11. The object of control can be one or more undertakings which constitute legal entities, or the assets of such entities, or only some of those assets. . . The assets in question which could be brands or licences, must constitute a business to which a market turnover can be clearly attributed.

Sole control

Control, or decisive influence, is generally acquired through an acquisition of more than 50 per cent of the share capital (and with it, more than 50 per cent of the voting rights) of another undertaking. However, it will always be necessary to look at other factors. Even an undertaking with more than 50 per cent of the share capital will not acquire control if, for example, a minority shareholder is able to veto all strategic decisions made by the business.

Conversely, control may be gained where a share of less than 50 per cent is acquired, for example: where the remainder of the shares are widely dispersed;[92] where special rights are attached to the shareholding (a majority of the voting rights are nonetheless conferred on the shareholder or the shareholder has power to appoint more than half of the management team); or where the right to affect the commercial strategy and financial management of the company is conferred by a management or shareholders' agreement (for example, where the consent of a particular shareholder is necessary for all strategic decisions made by the company[93]). It is thus important to consider a number of factors, for example, all sharehold-ings, special rights, and veto rights attached to the shareholding or set out in a management or shareholding agreement.

---

[91] Legal control (a controlling interest) is not therefore necessary.

[92] See, e.g., Case IV/M25, *Arjomari/Wiggins Teape* [1990] OJ C321/16 where a 39% shareholding was found to confer sole control because no other entity had more than a 4% shareholding

[93] In Case IV/M17, *MBB/Aerospatiale* [1992] 4 CMLR M70, Aerospatiale and MBB formed a joint venture to carry out their helicopter businesses. Although Aerospatiale received 60% of equity (and MBB only 40%) the Commission found the parties had joint control of the joint venture. All strategic decisions for the joint venture required unanimous consent of both partners.

The Commission explains the concept of sole control in its Notice on the meaning of concentration.

Commission Notice on the concept of concentration under Council Regulation (EEC) No 4064/89 on the control of concentrations between undertakings [1998] OJ C66/5, [1998] 4 CMLR 586

Sole control

13. Sole control is normally acquired on a legal basis where an undertaking acquires a majority of the voting rights of a company. It is not in itself significant that the acquired shareholding is 50% of the share capital plus one share. . . or that it is 100%. . . .

Joint control

Similar factors must be taken into account when assessing whether or not one or more undertakings have acquired *joint control* of another or have formed a joint venture of which they each have joint control. It is necessary to consider not only the size of the undertakings' shareholdings but also factors such as the voting rights attached to the shareholdings and shareholder and management agreements etc.

Commission Notice on the concept of concentration under Council Regulation (EEC) No 4064/89 on the control of concentrations between undertakings [1998] OJ C66/5, [1998] 4 CMLR 586

21. Joint control may exist even where there is no equality between the two parent companies in votes or in representation in decision-making bodies or where there are more than two parent companies. This is the case where minority shareholders have additional rights which allow them to veto decisions which are essential for the strategic commercial behaviour of the joint venture. . . These veto rights may be set out in the statute of the joint venture or conferred by agreement between its parent companies. The veto rights themselves may operate by means of a specific quorum required for decisions taken at the shareholders' meeting or by the board of directors to the extent that the parent companies are represented on this board. It is also possible that strategic decisions are subject to approval by a body, e.g. supervisory board, where the minority shareholders are represented and form part of the quorum needed for such decisions.

22. These veto rights must be related to strategic decisions on the business policy of the joint venture. They must go beyond the veto rights normally accorded to minority shareholders in order to protect their financial interests as investors in the joint venture. This normal protection of the rights of minority shareholders is related to decisions on the essence of the joint venture, such as changes in the statute, an increase or decease in the capital or liquidation. A veto right, for example, which prevents the sale or winding-up of the joint venture does not confer joint control on the minority shareholder concerned. . .

23. In contrast, veto rights which confer joint control typically include decisions and issues such as the budget, the business plan, major investments or the appointment of senior manage-

ment. The acquisition of joint control, however, does not require that the acquirer has the power to exercise decisive influence on the day-to-day running of an undertaking. The crucial element is that the veto rights are sufficient to enable the parent companies to exercise such influence in relation to strategic business behaviour of the joint venture. Moreover, it is not necessary to establish that an acquirer of joint control of the joint venture will actually make use of its decisive influence. The possibility of exercising such influence and hence, the mere existence of the veto rights, is sufficient.

24. In order to acquire joint control, it is not necessary for a minority shareholder to have all the veto rights mentioned above. It may be sufficient that only some, or even one such right, exists. Whether or not this is the case depends upon the precise content of the veto right itself and also the importance of this right in the context of the specific business of the joint venture.

. . .

34. In the case where a new joint venture is established, as opposed to the acquisition of minority shareholdings in a pre-existing company, there is a higher probability that the parent companies are carrying out a deliberate common policy. This is true, in particular, where each parent company provides a contribution to the joint venture which is vital for its operation (e.g. specific technologies, local know-how or supply agreements). In these circumstances, the parent companies may be able to operate the joint venture with full co-operation only with each other's agreement on the most import- ant strategic decisions even if there is no express provision for any veto rights. The greater the number of parent companies involved in such a joint venture, however, the more remote is the likelihood of this situation occurring.

(ii) JOINT VENTURES

a INTRODUCTION

It has been seen from the discussion above that a concentration may occur where two or more undertakings form a *joint venture* which they jointly control. The difficulty with the concept of a 'joint venture' is that it covers a wide spectrum of activities,[94] which includes an agreement to merge completely the activities of the partner companies on a particular market and to cease to operate in that market themselves. This may make it difficult to know when these joint ventures should be dealt with under merger rules, which deal with trans- actions which lead to structural changes on a market, and when they should be dealt with under cartel rules, such as Article 81, which focus on agreements concluded between under- takings operating on a particular market.

In EC law, joint ventures are dealt with under the merger rules only where they amount to a 'concentration' within the meaning of Article 3. The definition of a 'concentrative' joint venture and its interpretation have been of critical importance, as the procedural and sub- stantive rules applying under the merger rules and under Article 81 respectively are extremely different. There has been much concern in industry about the difference in treatment that joint ventures falling within the scope of the Merger Regulation and those falling to be assessed under Article 81 receive.

Broadly, joint ventures amounting to a 'concentration' for the purposes of the Merger Regulation have been perceived to receive significantly more favourable treatment. Apart

---

[94] See *infra* Chap. 13.

from the fact that the substantive analysis conducted of the joint venture is different,[95] these joint ventures benefit from favourable procedural rules. For example, (1) where the concentration has a Community dimension the parties benefit from a '*one stop shop*'. National merger (and other competition) rules do not apply. Where the concentration does not have a Community dimension then, broadly, no Community law applies at all;[96] and (2) decisions taken under the Merger Regulation must be made within strict legal deadlines. Most decisions are made within one month of notification. The remainder are generally made within five months.

In contrast, for joint ventures falling to be assessed under Article 81: (1) the application of Article 81 does not preclude the application of national law (although national law must respect the principle of supremacy[97]), and (2) no legal time limits apply in the context of Article 81. Indeed the procedural restrictions are such that even though the Commission endeavours to take a view of the compatibility of a joint venture with Article 81 within a period of two months it can do so only by administrative letter. No formal decision is possible. An administrative letter does not give the parties the same degree of legal certainty as a formal decision, since it is not binding on either the national courts or national authorities of the Member States.[98]

These difficulties and inequalities have led to a number of changes in the treatment of joint ventures over the years. The Commission has, for example, sought to alter the way in which it deals with joint ventures under Article 81 and it has adopted as broad as possible an interpretation of a 'concentration' for the purposes of the Merger Regulation.[99] In its Green Paper in 1996 it set out proposals to improve further the treatment of joint ventures. In response, the Council, in Regulation 1310/97, amended the definition set out in the Merger Regulation of a concentrative joint venture. These changes came into effect on 1 March 1998.

b. CONCENTRATIVE JOINT VENTURES PRIOR TO 1 MARCH 1998

Article 3(2) of the Merger Regulation sets out when joint ventures constitute a concentration. This used to read as follows:

An operation, including the creation of a joint venture, which has as its object or effect the co-ordination of the competitive behaviour of undertakings which remain independent shall not constitute a concentration within the meaning of paragraph 1(b).

The creation of a joint venture performing on a lasting basis all the functions of an autonomous economic entity, which does not give rise to co-ordination of the competitive behaviour of the parties amongst themselves or between them and the joint venture, shall constitute a concentration within the meaning of paragraph 1(b).

---

[95] The creation or strengthening of a dominant position test applied in the Merger Reg. (see Art. 2 discussed *infra* 750 ff) catches fewer transactions than the 'restriction of competition' test under Art. 81. The former focuses on the impact that a concentration will have on the structure of the market whilst Art. 81 focuses on the restrictive nature of an agreement concluded between independent undertakings.

[96] *Infra* at 746–748 ff.

[97] *Infra* Chap. 15. In the Proposal for a new Reg. implementing Arts. 81 and Art. 82, COM (2000) 582, Art. 3 the Commission proposes that national competition laws should be excluded where Arts. 81 and 82 apply.

[98] See *supra* Chap. 4. Although the Commission has indicated that it will make its decisions within this 2-month period, it has no legal obligation to do so.

[99] These matters are dealt with in greater detail *infra* in Chap. 13.

Three requirements had to be met (a Commission Notice[100] set out guidance on how the provision was interpreted):

(i) The parent companies had to acquire joint control of the joint venture;

(ii) The joint venture had to be formed on a lasting basis to carry out the functions of an autonomous economic entity (*the positive condition*); and

(iii) The joint venture was not to have as its object or effect the co-ordination of the competitive behaviour of independent undertakings likely to result in a restriction of competition within the meaning of Article 81(1) (*the negative condition*).

c. 'FULL FUNCTION' JOINT VENTURES FALLING WITHIN THE MERGER REGULATION SUBSEQUENT TO 1 MARCH 1998

The definition set out in Article 3(2) has now been altered:

The creation of a joint venture performing on a lasting basis all the functions of an autonomous economic entity shall constitute a concentration within the meaning of paragraph 1(b).[101]

It can be seen from this alteration that the Regulation now omits all reference to co-ordination of the competitive behaviour of the parents. It is now necessary for a joint venture to satisfy only the first two requirements set out above: that is, to show that the parent companies have acquired joint control of the joint venture and that the joint venture is formed on a lasting basis to carry out the functions of an autonomous economic entity. The Commission has issued a new notice setting out guidance on what amounts to such a *full-function* joint venture for the purposes of the Merger Regulation.[102]

Joint control

Joint ventures are undertakings jointly controlled by two or more undertakings. The meaning of joint control is explained above and is dealt with, not in the Commission's Notice on full-function joint ventures,[103] but in the Notice on the meaning of concentration.[104]

An autonomous economic entity

The Commission explains the meaning of an autonomous or 'full-function' joint venture in paragraphs 11 and 12 of the notice. It stresses the importance of the joint venture bringing about a lasting change to the structure of the undertakings involved and the ability of the joint venture itself to act autonomously on the market.

---

[100] Commission Notice on the distinction between concentrative and co-operative joint ventures under Council Reg. 4064/89 of 21 Dec. 1989 on the control of concentrations between undertakings [1994] OJ C385/1. The 1994 Notice replaced a notice on the same subject adopted by the Commission in 1990 [1990] OJ C203/10.

[101] As amended by Art. 1(3) of Reg. 1310/97 [1997] OJ L180/1.

[102] [1998] OJ C66/1, [1998] 4 CMLR 581.

[103] Commission Notice on the notion of full-function joint ventures [1998] OJ C66/1, [1998] 4 CMLR 581, paras. 3, 9, and 10.

[104] Commission Notice on the concept of concentration under Council Reg. (EEC) No 4064/89 on the control of concentrations between undertakings [1998] OJ C66/5, [1998] 4 CMLR 586, paras. 18–39.

Commission Notice on the notion of full-function joint ventures under Council Regulation (EEC) No 4064/89 on the control of concentrations between undertakings [1998] OJ C66/1, [1998] 4 CMLR 581

11. Article 3(2) provides that the joint venture must perform, on a lasting basis, all the functions of an autonomous economic entity. Joint ventures which satisfy this requirement bring about a lasting change in the structure of the undertakings concerned. They are referred to in this Notice as 'full-function' joint ventures.

12. Essentially this means that a joint venture must operate on a market, performing the functions normally carried out by undertakings operating on the same market. In order to do so the joint venture must have a management dedicated to its day-to-day operations and access to sufficient resources including finance, staff, and assets (tangible and intangible) in order to conduct on a lasting basis its business activities within the area provided for in the joint venture agreement.

Subsequent paragraphs set out the kinds of factors which are taken into account when determining whether or not such a full-function joint venture has been created. The notice indicates, for example, that a full-function joint venture will not have been created if the joint venture 'only takes over one specific function within the parent companies' business activities without access to the market, such as joint ventures limited to R & D or production'.[105] Paragraph 14 deals with the difficult position which exists where one of the parent companies operates up or downstream for the joint venture.

The notice also points out that the fact that the agreement contains clauses providing for the dissolution of the joint venture, for example, on its failure or on disagreement between the parents, does not necessarily mean that the joint venture has not been established on a lasting basis. Further, an agreement which lasts for a finite period long enough to affect the structure of the market will be established on a lasting basis, but one established for a short finite period will not.[106] Some examples of joint ventures which are not full-function and which are consequently subject to Article 81 are set out in Chapter 13.

Commission Notice on the notion of full-function joint ventures under Council Regulation (EEC) No 4064/89 on the control of concentrations between undertakings [1998] OJ C66/1, [1998] 4 CMLR 581

13. A joint venture is not full-function if it only takes over one specific function within the parent companies' business activities without access to the market. This is the case, for example, for joint ventures limited to R & D or production. Such joint ventures are auxiliary to their parent companies' business activities. This is also the case where a joint venture is essentially limited to the distribution or sales of its parent companies' products and, therefore, acts principally as a sales agency. However, the fact that a joint venture makes use of the distribution network or outlet of one or more of its

---

[105] Commission Notice on the notion of full-function joint ventures [1998] OJ C66/1, [1998] 4 CMLR 581, para. 13. Para. 14 deals with the position where one or more of the parent companies operates in upstream or downstream markets.

[106] Commission Notice on the notion of full-function joint ventures [1998] OJ C66/1, [1998] 4 CMLR 581, para. 15.

parent companies normally will not disqualify it as 'full-function' as long as the parent companies are acting only as agents of the joint venture . . .

14. The strong presence of the parent companies in upstream or downstream markets is a factor to be taken into consideration in assessing the full-function character of a joint venture where this presence leads to substantial sales or purchases between the parent companies and the joint venture. The fact that the joint venture relies almost entirely on sales to its parent companies or purchases from them only for an initial start-up period does not normally affect the full-function character of the joint venture. Such a start-up period may be necessary in order to establish the joint venture on a market. It will normally not exceed a period of three years, depending on the specific conditions of the market in question. . . .

Where sales from the joint venture to the parent companies are intended to be made on a lasting basis, the essential question is whether, regardless of these sales, the joint venture is geared to play an active role on the market. In this respect the relative proportion of these sales compared with the total production of the joint venture is an important factor. Another factor is whether sales to the parent companies are made on the basis of normal commercial conditions . . .

In relation to purchases made by the joint venture from its parent companies, the full-function character of the joint venture is questionable in particular where little value is added to the products or services concerned at the level of the joint venture itself. In such a situation, the joint venture may be closer to a joint sales agency. However, in contrast to this situation where a joint venture is active in a trade market and performs the normal functions of a trading company in such a market, it normally will not be an auxiliary sales agency but a full-function joint venture. A trade market is characterised by the existence of companies which specialise in the selling and distribution of products without being vertically integrated in addition to those which are integrated, and where different sources of supply are available for the products in question. In addition, many trade markets may require operators to invest in specific facilities such as outlets, stockholding, warehouses, depots, transport fleets and sales personnel. In order to constitute a full-function joint venture in a trade market, an undertaking must have the necessary facilities and be likely to obtain a substantial proportion of its supplies not only from its parent companies but also from other competing sources . . .

15. Furthermore, the joint venture must be intended to operate on a lasting basis. The fact that the parent companies commit to the joint venture the resources described above normally demonstrates that this is the case. In addition, agreements setting up a joint venture often provide for certain contingencies, for example, the failure of the joint venture or fundamental disagreement as between the parent companies . . . This may be achieved by the incorporation of provisions for the eventual dissolution of the joint venture itself or the possibility for one or more parent companies to withdraw from the joint venture. This kind of provision does not prevent the joint venture from being considered as operating on a lasting basis. The same is normally true where the agreement specifies a period for the duration of the joint venture where this period is sufficiently long in order to bring about a lasting change in the structure of the undertakings concerned (12), or where the agreement provides for the possible continuation of the joint venture beyond this period. By contrast, the joint venture will not be considered to operate on a lasting basis where it is established for a short finite duration. This would be the case, for example, where a joint venture is established in order to construct a specific project such as a power plant, but it will not be involved in the operation of the plant once its construction has been completed.

The relevance of co-ordination of competitive behaviour

The removal of the *negative* condition from Article 3(2) means that the complex determination of whether or not a joint venture has as its object or effect the co-ordination of the competitive behaviour of independent undertakings does not have to be made at the jurisdictional stage. It is still of importance to know whether a joint venture enables the co-ordination of the competitive behaviour of independent undertakings, however.

First, although all full-function joint ventures may be appraised under the procedures set out in the Merger Regulation there will be a different *substantive* appraisal for joint ventures which have co-ordinative aspects. The basic appraisal made in the case of each joint venture will be same, but the co-ordinative aspects of joint ventures will be assessed additionally for their compatibility with the common market in accordance with the criteria set out in Article 81 of the Treaty.[107]

Secondly, in derogation from the general rule, the Commission will be able to apply Article 81 to a joint venture which enables the co-ordination of the competitive behaviour of independent undertakings but which does *not* have a Community dimension.[108] It will not, therefore, fall to be assessed only under national provisions.

d. PARTIAL-FUNCTION JOINT VENTURES FALLING TO BE ASSESSED UNDER ARTICLE 81

The determination of whether or not a joint venture falls within the jurisdiction of the Merger Regulation or that of Article 81 has been simplified by the removal of the requirement that the joint venture should not have co-ordinative aspects. Nonetheless it may still be difficult to assess whether or not there is joint control or whether the joint venture is full-function, created on a lasting basis. If the undertakings notify a joint venture in accordance with Form CO when the joint venture does not, in fact, amount to a concentration, the Commission may treat the notification as if it has been made pursuant to Article 81.[109] It will be remembered, however, that in its White Paper on modernisation the Commission has proposed abolishing the notification system for agreements. Recognizing the difficulties that this may cause for parties to joint ventures, the Commission has suggested that, if the notification procedure is abolished, partial-function production joint ventures should be brought within the procedural framework of the Merger Regulation.[110]

For the more immediate future, the Commission is taking steps to improve the position of joint ventures still falling for assessment under Article 81. The application of Article 81 to joint ventures is dealt with in Chapter 13.

(iii) ARTICLE 3(5)

Article 3(5) of the Merger Regulation sets out several circumstances in which a concentration shall be deemed not to arise. These deal with shares held by financial institutions on a temporary basis, the acquisition of control by liquidators or other administrators, and operations carried out by financial holding companies.

---

[107] 'To the extent that the creation of a joint venture constituting a concentration pursuant to Art. 3 has as its object or effect the co-ordination of the competitive behaviour of undertakings that remain independent, such co-ordination shall be appraised in accordance with the criteria of Art. [81(1)] and (3) of the Treaty, with a view to establishing whether or not the operation is compatible with the common market': Merger Reg., Art. 2(4) as amended by Art. 1(3) of Reg. 1310/97.

[108] Merger Reg., Art. 22(1) (as amended by Art, 1(12) of Reg. 1310/97).

[109] In accordance with Form A/B, Sep Reg. 447/98 [1998] OJ L61/1, Art. 5.

[110] White Paper on modernisation of the rules implementing Articles 85 and 86 [now 81 and 82] of the EC Treaty [1999] OJ C132/1, [1999] OJ 5 CMLR 208, paras. 79–81.

B. COMMUNITY DIMENSION[111]

(i) THE INITIAL TEST

The Merger Regulation aims to apply to concentrations which create significant structural changes the impact of which extend beyond the national borders of any one Member State.[112] It is concentrations with a *Community dimension* which fall for appraisal under the terms of the Merger Regulation. Broadly, whether or not a merger has a Community dimension is assessed by reference to the turnover of the parties involved. Since the notification of concentrations with a Community dimension is compulsory, the jurisdiction test incorporated within the Merger Regulation is intended to be one which can be applied relatively easily. The corollary of having a simple jurisdictional test is that concentrations between undertakings which obviously do not impede effective competition in the common market may be brought within the Regulation and be subject to mandatory notification. Thus many mergers will be notifiable even if they have no effect on competition. The requirement that they should impede competition within the common market is relevant only to the substantive assessment of whether or not the concentration is compatible with the common market.[113] The Commission is aware of the huge inconvenience and cost that this imposes and has taken steps to ameliorate the situation of undertakings in such a position. The Commission has issued a Notice setting out a simplified procedure for concentrations that do not raise competition concerns.[114] In such cases a full-form notification is not necessary, and where the Commission is satisfied that the concentration qualifies for the simplified procedure it adopts a short-form decision.[115]

The thresholds are set out in Article 1(2) and (3). The latter was added on the amendment of the Regulation by Regulation 1310/97.

The initial test contained in the Merger Regulation is that which is still set out in Article 1(2). Only if this test is not satisfied is it necessary for an undertaking to consider whether or not the thresholds set out in Article 1(3) are satisfied.

Council Regulation 4064/89 of 21 December 1989 on the control of concentrations between undertaking [1989] OJ L395/1, Article 1

1. Without prejudice to Article 22, this Regulation shall apply to all concentrations with a Community dimension as defined in paragraphs 2 and 3.

2. For the purposes of this Regulation, a concentration has a Community dimension where: —

---

[111] See generally M. Broberg, *The European Commission's Jurisdiction to Scrutnise Mergers* (Kluwer, Deventer, 1998).

[112] Merger Reg., recital 9.

[113] The Commission has power to prohibit only concentrations that create or strengthen a dominant position in the common market or a substantial part of it: Art. 2(3) of the Merger Reg. The wide jurisdiction means, however, that parties to a concentration falling under the Merger Reg. but with no potential effect in the Community will still have to incur the costs of notification.

[114] Commission's Notice on a simplified procedure for treatment of certain concentrations under Council Reg. (EEC) No. 4064/89 [2000] OJ C217/32.

[115] *Ibid.*, especially paras. 10–13.

(a)   the combined aggregate worldwide turnover of all the undertakings concerned is more than
[Euro] 5,000 million; and

(b)   the aggregate Community-wide turnover of each of at least two of the undertakings concerned is more than [Euro] 250 million.

unless each of the undertakings concerned achieves more than two-thirds of its aggregate
Community-wide turnover within one and the same Member State.

This test thus looks to the worldwide and Community-wide turnover in Euro of all or some
of the parties involved in the concentration (approximately £3,000 million and £150 million
respectively[116]). Where the turnovers of the parties are not sufficiently high to meet those
thresholds the concentration will not satisfy the test set out in Article 1(2). Similarly, jurisdiction is denied even where the thresholds are met if the *proviso* applies. Where each of the
undertakings involved achieves more than two-thirds of its Community turnover within
one and the same Member State there is no Community dimension, so that the concentration *prima facie* falls to be assessed at the national level.

The purpose of the proviso is to exclude concentrations the effects of which are felt
primarily in one Member State. The application of this proviso has occasionally led to
peculiar results. For example, two competing bids made for the take-over of Midland Bank
by Lloyds Bank and Hong Kong and Shanghai Bank respectively fell to be assessed under
different merger regimes. The former bid did not have a Community dimension (and fell
within the jurisdiction of the UK authorities). The latter did have a Community dimension
and fell to be assessed under the EC Merger rules (and, consequently, on account of the
speed with which the Commission decisions are made may have had an advantage over the
competing bid).[117]

(ii) THE GREEN PAPER

The thresholds set in Article 1(2) are in stark contrast to those set out by the Commission in
its original draft proposal in May 1989. It recommended that the worldwide turnover should
be set at ECU 1,000 million, the Community-wide turnover at ECU 100 million, and that
jurisdiction should then only be denied if more than *three-quarters* of the aggregate
Community-wide turnover was achieved in one and the same Member State. The reluctance
of many of the Member States to relinquish merger control to the Commission, however,
meant that the thresholds were finally set at the high levels set out in Article 1(2). The
Commission's fears that it would have no work if the turnovers were set at such unrealistic
levels were not realized.[118] However, it still believed that significant mergers with cross-
border effects fell outside these thresholds. Not only did it think that the actual thresholds

---

[116] The thresholds were originally expressed in ECU. However Council Reg. 1103/97 [1997] OJ L162/1,
provides that as from 1 January 1999 all references to ECU in Community legal intruments shall be read as
references to Euro.

[117] The UK could, however, have made use of the Dutch clause (Art 22(3) of the Merger Reg.; see *infra*
747) and requested the Commission to appraise the Lloyds Bank bid even though the concentration did not
have a Community dimension. Alternatively, it could possibly have requested, under the German clause (Art
9) the referral of the Hong Kong and Shanghai Bank bid back to it: see *infra* 740, especially the discussion of
Case IV/M180, *Steetley/Tarmac plc* [1992] 4 CMLR 337.

[118] The Merger Reg. came into force almost at the peak of merger activity.

excluded too many mergers which might have an important impact within the Community but the Commission believed that the two-thirds proviso enabled mergers with important cross-border effects to escape. At the time of the Green Paper the Commission noted that Siemens, for example, produced two-thirds of its turnover in one Member State but still had significant operations outside of its home market.[119]

The Commission was unhappy about these thresholds from the start. As a compromise, Article 1(3) of the original Merger Regulation anticipated a review, and a lowering, of the thresholds by the end of 1993. Severe opposition from a number of Member States, including Germany, the UK, and France, meant that any such review was likely to be redundant. The Commissioner for Competition at the time, Karel van Miert, thus decided not to conduct a review at this stage. The question whether the thresholds should be lowered was, however, raised in the Green Paper published in 1996.

In the Green Paper the Commission put forward a strong case in support of its proposal to lower both the worldwide and Community-wide thresholds. It stressed that many mergers with important cross-border effects were escaping the provisions of the Merger Regulation because the thresholds were not met. Further, trans-national mergers which did not meet the thresholds were likely to meet the notification requirements of more than one Member State (there were at that time thirteen systems of merger control within the EEA alone[120]) and, consequently, to have to bear the additional costs and efforts of these notifications. These costs are compounded by the enormous differences between each of the national systems of merger control.[121] This situation meant undertakings restructuring within the Community did not have a level playing field. As a result of the problems caused by multiple notifications and multiple procedures, the Commission view gained support from much of European industry.

The Commission thus proposed a lowering of the thresholds in Article 1(2)(a) and (b) to ECU 2,000 million (worldwide turnover) and ECU 100 million (Community-wide turnover) respectively. Realizing that these stark reductions in thresholds might be too much for the Member States to swallow (particularly in the light of some controversial merger decisions which may not have been welcomed by the authorities of certain Member States[122]) an alternative was suggested. If the Council could not be persuaded to agree to the suggested reductions, it proposed that concentrations which exceeded these thresholds *and* which would otherwise be notifiable to several national competition authorities should be held to have a Community dimension.

---

[119] See the Green Paper on Communtiy Merger Control COM(96)19 final, para. 48.

[120] Since then both the Netherlands and Finland have enacted merger control legislation. In the EU only Luxembourg and Denmark do not now have merger rules.

[121] In some Member States notification is obligatory; in others (such as the UK) it is generally not obligatory (in the Consultation Document which sets out proposals to reform the UK system of mergers, the Government sets out its intention, subject to responses, to retain the voluntary notification system: DTI, *Mergers: A Consultation Document on Proposals for Reform*, Aug. 1999, http://www.dti.gov.uk/cacp/cp/mergercon/index.htm, s. 6, paras. 3–8); in others there are no merger rules (Luxembourg and Denmark). Turnover thresholds triggering a notification vary from Member State to Member State and deadlines for investigating the impact of a merger range from six months to much longer. In some Member States the final decisions are taken by administrative or ministerial organizations, in others independent competition authorities.

[122] See the discussion, e.g., of Case IV/M53 *Aérospatiale-Alenia/de Havilland* [1991] OJ L334/42, [1992] 4 CMLR M2, *infra* 799–800.

(iii) ARTICLE 1(3) OF THE MERGER REGULATION AS AMENDED BY COUNCIL REGULATION 1310/97

In the face of strong opposition from several Member States[123] the Commission never put forward such ambitious proposals to the Council as those it set out in its Green Paper. A compromise solution was eventually reached, however, on the passing of Council Regulation 1310/97. The latter Regulation does not alter the thresholds set out in Article 1(2) of the Merger Regulation. However, it amends the Merger Regulation so that it now applies to concentrations with a Community dimension as defined in paragraph 1(2) *and* 1(3). Paragraph 1(3) provides that a concentration which satisfies lower worldwide and Community-wide turnovers then those set out in Article 1(2) may be caught if two additional criteria are satisfied. Broadly, these two factors seek to catch concentrations which are likely to have a significant impact in three or more Member States and which are therefore likely to be subject to the merger rules of those three or more Member States.[124] It also contains a proviso excluding concentrations that meet the thresholds where two-thirds of the Community-wide turnover of all of the undertakings involved is achieved in one and the same Member State. It provides:—

Council Regulation 4064/89 of 21 December 1989 on the control of concentrations between undertakings [1989] OJ L395/1, Article 1

3. For the purposes of this Regulation, a concentration that does not meet the thresholds laid down in paragraph 2 has a Community dimension where:

(a) the combined aggregate worldwide turnover of all the undertakings concerned is more than [Euro] 2 500 million;

(b) in each of at least three Member States, the combined aggregate turnover of all the undertakings concerned is more than [Euro] 100 million;

(c) in each of at least three Member States included for the purpose of point (b), the aggregate turnover of each of at least two of the undertakings concerned is more than [Euro] 25 million; and

(d) the aggregate Community-wide turnover of each of at least two of the undertakings concerned is more than [Euro] 100 million

unless each of the undertakings concerned achieves more than two-thirds of its aggregate Community-wide turnover within one and the same Member State.

Article 1(4) of the Merger Regulation provides for a further review of these thresholds. Further, Article 1(5) provides that the Council may review the thresholds acting by *qualified majority.*

---

[123] In particular, the UK and Germany (the countries with the strongest national competition authorities and most unwilling to cede power in this area of Brussels) wished to keep merger control under the jurisdiction of their own national competition authorities.

[124] Reg. 1310/97, Art. 1(1)(a) and (b). The test was not set, however, by reference to the number of notifications which had to be made. It would have been excessively complicated to do it in this way, especially as some Member States do not have compulsory notification. The jurisdictional test seeks to be as easy to apply as possible.

Council Regulation 4064/89 of 21 December 1989 on the control of concentrations between undertakings [1989] OJ L395/1, Article 1

4. Before 1 July 2000 the Commission shall report to the Council on the operation of the thresholds and criteria set out in paragraphs 2 and 3.

5. Following the report referred to in paragraph 4 and on a proposal from the Commission, the Council, acting by qualified majority, may revise the thresholds and criteria mentioned in paragraph 3.

Since unanimity is not required, this may make it easier for the Commission to persuade the Council to lower the thresholds in Article 1(3). It is unlikely, however, to succeed in persuading the Council to lower the thresholds set out in Article 1(2). The Commission has commenced the review process. In its report to the Council on the application of the Merger Regulation thresholds (June 2000) the Commission stated its view that an important number of transactions with significant cross-border effects remain outside the Community merger rules. The Commission concluded in the report that a more in-depth analysis of the appropriate mechanism for establishing Community jurisdiction in merger cases is necessary.

Concentrations that do not have a Community dimension are, as a general rule, dealt with at the national level under any applicable national merger rules.[125]

(iv) CALCULATION OF TURNOVER AND UNDERTAKINGS CONCERNED

Despite the aim of the Regulation to provide a clear, simple jurisdictional test the quantification of 'turnover' and the identification of the 'undertakings concerned' is not as easy as it might at first seem.[126] The meaning of turnover and undertakings concerned is set out in the Regulation itself and clarified in Commission notices.

The definition of turnover is set out in Article 5. The Commission's Notice on calculation of turnover seeks to 'elucidate certain procedural and practical questions which have caused doubt or difficulty' in the text.

Article 5(1) defines turnover as 'the amount derived by the undertakings concerned in the previous financial year from the sale of products and provisions of services falling within the undertaking's ordinary activities'.[127] Article 5(2) sets out rules which apply where only part of an undertaking is taken over or acquired, and Article 5(3) sets out special turnover rules which apply, for example, to credit and financial institutions and insurance undertakings.[128]

Turnover is assessed by reference not only to the turnover of the undertakings concerned but also to certain affiliated companies. The Commission's Notice on the concept of undertakings concerned clarifies the Commission's interpretation of the term 'undertakings concerned', guided by reference to cases previously notified to the Commission. Article 5(4) of the Merger Regulation provides that turnover is calculated not only by reference to those

---

[125] But see *infra* 746–748.
[126] See M. Broberg, *The European Commission's Jurisdiction to Scrutnise Mergers* (Kluwer, 1998), chaps. 4–6.
[127] Sales tax, VAT, and sales rebates are ignored.
[128] See M. Broberg, *The European Commission's Jurisdiction to Scrutnise Mergers* (Kluwer, 1998), Chap. 6.

undertakings concerned but also to the turnover of all those entities which they control or by whom they are controlled, and to other connected undertakings.[129]

(v) THE LONG ARM OF THE EC MERGER REGULATION

a. INTERNATIONAL AND GLOBAL MERGERS

The quantitative jurisdictional tests incorporated within the Merger Regulation look not to the effect of the concentration on inter-state trade or on competition but to the size of the undertakings involved. So long as the Community-wide turnovers are satisfied, mergers between non-EC undertakings will be caught even though the undertakings' business is principally carried on outside the EC, even though the merger is completed outside the EC, and even though the merger may have been cleared in another jurisdiction. There is no exemption for mergers occurring outside the EU or any requirement that any of the undertakings involved is established or has substantial operations in any part of the EU.[130] The Commission's scrutiny of some mergers has, therefore, been extremely politically sensitive in nature.

In 1997, for example, the Commission considered a merger announced in December 1996 between Boeing and McDonnell Douglas.[131] The merger was instigated with the encouragement of the US authorities (the Clinton administration) and had been approved by the US Federal Trade Commission in July 1997.[132] The concentration had a Community dimension and was notifiable to the Commission under EC rules irrespective of the fact that neither party had any facilities or assets in the Community. The Commission was hostile to the merger, believing that it would lead to the strengthening of Boeing's dominant position on the relevant market within the EU. In the end a political storm was saved by Boeing's offer of commitments to the Commission which resolved its competition concerns. Similarly, in *Gencor/Lonrho*[133] a concentration concluded between a South African (Gencor) and UK (Lonrho) company merging business activities based in South Africa had a Community dimension and was notifiable under the EC merger rules. In this case the Commission actually prohibited the merger even though the South African Competition Board did not consider that the operation gave rise to competition concerns under South African law.

These two cases raise some important issues. The first is to what extent does the Commission have *jurisdiction* to apply the Merger Regulation extraterritorially to concentrations between foreign entities. The second is what steps have the Community authorities taken to

---

[129] The definition of control is different from that which applies in relation to Art. 3 of the Merger Reg. It is set out in Art. 5(4) of the Reg.

[130] In earlier drafts of the Merger Reg. it was a requirement that at least one of the undertakings was established in the Community and had substantial operations in one of the Member States: see Commission Proposal for a Reg. of the Council on the control of concentrations between undertakings, [1973] OJ C/92/1, Art. 1(1), [1982] OJ C36/3, [1988] OJ C130 4.

[131] Case IV/M877 [1997] OJ L336/16, [1997] 5 CMLR 270. The extraterritorial aspects of this case are discussed in greater detail *infra* in Chap. 17.

[132] The merger was cleared on 1 July 1997 without conditions: see US Federal Trade Commission Press Releases of 1 July 1997: *FTC Allows Merger of the Boeing Company and McDonnell Douglas Corporation* 23 Sept. 1997.

[133] Case IV/M619 [1997] OJ L11/30, [1996] 4 CMLR 742.

co-operate with the competition authorities of other States involved in the investigation of the same case and to avoid the taking of conflicting decisions.

b. EXTRATERRITORIALITY

In an appeal to the CFI, *Gencor Limited* v. *Commission*,[134] the Commission's decision prohibiting the merger, in particular its jurisdiction over the case, was challenged. This involved an assessment of whether the Regulation itself authorized the Commission to take jurisdiction over a merger between undertakings which did not have production facilities within the Community. Further, the Court had to consider whether the test set out in the Regulation itself was compatible with international law. The Court held that the Regulation did authorize jurisdiction and was compatible with public international law. The extraterritorial aspects of this case and the extraterritorial application of the EC merger rules are discussed in Chapter 17. It should be noted, however, that in practice the Commission might have difficulty actually enforcing compliance with the rules against undertakings which are not present in the European Union.

c. INTERNATIONAL CO-OPERATION

In 1991 a co-operation agreement was concluded between the USA and the EC. This agreement, broadly, imposes obligations on the respective US and EC competition authorities to notify each other when its enforcement activities may impact on the activities of the other, to exchange information, to assist each other, to co-operate in the enforcement of each other's competition rules, and to consider each other's important interests. Many of the notifications made under this agreement have been in respect of mergers. The parties seek to co-operate on matters such as the relevant market and to avoid conflicting decisions or remedies. A co-operation agreement has also been concluded with Canada. International co-operation is also discussed in Chapter 17.

The one-stop shop principle set out in the Merger Regulation means, in practice, that in many cases multiple notifications to the authorities of the Member States are avoided.[135] Further, the Commission and the Member States are bound by a duty of co-operation.[136] Article 19 of the Merger Regulation reinforces this duty by requiring the Commission to liaise with the authorities of the Member States in particular ways: for example, by transmitting copies of notifications, liaising with the authorities of the Member States when carrying out its procedures, and consulting the Advisory Committee.[137]

(vi) RECIPROCITY

Article 24 of the Merger Regulation makes provision for the Member States to inform the Commission 'of any general difficulties encountered by their undertakings with concentrations . . . in a non-member country'. Further it provides for the Commission to draw up reports on this issue.

---

[134] Case T–102/96 [1999] ECR II–753, [1999] 4 CMLR 971.
[135] See *infra* 740–746.
[136] Art. 10 (ex Art. 5) of the Treaty.
[137] See *infra* n. 176.

Where it appears that certain non-Member States do not permit or otherwise make it difficult for EU undertakings to carry out mergers in circumstances in which undertakings in that State would be permitted to carry out a merger in the EU, 'the Commission may submit proposals to the Council for an appropriate mandate for negotiation with a view to obtaining comparable treatment for Community undertakings'.[138]

C. CONCENTRATIONS WITH A COMMUNITY DIMENSION

(i) NOTIFICATION, SUSPENSION, INVESTIGATION AND OTHER PROCEDURE

a. NOTIFICATION

The general rule is that concentrations with a Community dimension benefit from a one stop shop. They must be notified to the Commission for assessment under the Merger Regulation and no other Community or national law applies.[139]

The Merger Regulation does not start with any presumption in favour of, or against, concentrations.[140] It does require, however, to ensure effective control,[141] the notification of concentrations with a Community dimension. Parties to a transaction may fear that news of their intentions will become public as a result of such notification. The Commission is, however, bound by a general duty of confidentiality, set out in Article 286 (ex Article 213(b)) of the Treaty, and may not disclose business secrets.[142] Further, Article 17(2) of the Merger Regulation specifically provides that, subject to specified limited exceptions, 'the Commission and the competent authorities of the Member States, their officials and other servants shall not disclose information they have acquired through the application of this Regulation of the kind covered by the obligation of professional secrecy'.

Notifications must be made to the Commission within a time period set out in Article 4.

Council Regulations 4064/89 of 21 December 1989 on the control of concentrations between undertakings [1989] OJ L395/1, Article 4

1. Concentrations with a Community dimension . . . shall be notified to the Commission not more than one week after the conclusion of the agreement, or the announcement of the public bid, or the acquisition of a controlling interest. That week shall begin when the first of those events occurs.

Which parties to the concentration are obliged notify is dependent on the type of trans-

---

[138] Merger Reg., Art. 24(3).

[139] But see *infra* 740–746.

[140] Contrast the position in the UK. The Fair Trading Act 1973 sets out a presumption that mergers operate in the public interest (*cf* water mergers).

[141] Merger Reg., recital 17.

[142] See *infra* Chap. 14.

action that occurs.[143] Form CO, which is set out in an Annex to the Implementing Regulation, Regulation 447/98, sets out how the notification should be made. The Regulation and Form CO set out the information and documents which must be furnished to the Commission. Like Form A/B,[144] Form CO is also not a form but a pattern, divided into twelve sections, which prescribes how the information requested must be presented. A large amount of information is required (to enable the Commission to comply with the tight deadlines imposed on it). Thus background information is required (section 1) and information relating to: details of the concentration (section 2); ownership and control (section 3); personal and financial links and previous acquisitions (section 4); supporting documentation (section 5); market definitions (section 6); information on affected markets (sections 7 and 8); general market information (section 9); co-operative effects of joint ventures (section 10); and general matters (section 11). Section 12 requires the notification to be accompanied with a declaration signed by representatives of the undertakings.

It can be seen from this list that notification is costly and time-consuming to complete. Failure to recognize the time and effort involved in the notification could disrupt the completion of the deal between the merging undertakings. Further, if all the requisite information is not supplied the notification will be 'incomplete' and a decision from the Commission will be delayed.[145] Pre-notification discussions with the Commission may minimize the possibility of an incomplete notification and a simplified procedure applies for certain concentrations that do not raise competition concerns.[146]

The Commission has power under Article 14(1)(a) and (b) of the Merger Regulation to impose fines of between Euro 1,000 and Euro 50,000 on a party that fails to notify a concentration or that supplies incorrect or misleading information in a notification.[147] Further it has power under Articles 11–13 of the Regulation to request information and inspect premises in order to determine whether or not a breach of the rules has been committed.[148] The Commission may impose fines for furnishing incomplete or misleading information.[149] It was not, however, until 1998 that the Commission first imposed fines on an undertaking, Samsung, which had failed to notify a concentration in due time. Samsung had acquired control over an American firm, AST Research Inc., without the Commission's authorization in breach of Community rules. The Commission imposed a fine of ECU 33,000. It took into account the fact that the concentration had had no damaging effect on competition and that Samsung had recognised the breach and fully co-operated with the Commission. However, in the Commission's view a fine was necessary as a warning to other companies and because the notification was very late. Samsung was an important company with significant interests in Europe which would, undoubtedly, have been aware of the competition rules.[150] Fines have been imposed in subsequent case and it seems likely that

---

[143] Merger Reg., Art. 4(2).

[144] See *supra* Chap. 4.

[145] The tight time limits imposed on the Commission for assessing the concentration do not start to run until notification is complete.

[146] See [2000] OJ C217/32, *supra* 714 and 727, and e.g., the *Best Practice Guidelines* produced by the European Competition Lawyers' Forum (available on the Competition Directorate website).

[147] Merger Reg., Art. 14(1)(a) and (b). It also has power to order a reversal of the concentration, *infra* 739.

[148] See discussion *infra* 737 and Chap. 14.

[149] Case IV/29.895, *Telos* [1982] OJ L58/19, [1982] 1 CMLR 267.

[150] Case IV/M920 [1999] OJ L225/12, [1998] 4 CMLR 494.

fines may be greater in the future.[151] The fine is likely to be larger the more serious the impact the non-notified concentration has on competition.

In *Gencor/Lonrho*[152] the Commission took the view that the parties' notification of the concentration to it meant that it had submitted to the Community jurisdiction.[153]

b. SUSPENSION

It was a condition of German support of the Merger Regulation that a concentration should be suspended pending investigation of the concentration. Article 7 of the Merger Regulation originally provided for an automatic suspension period of three weeks. A concentration could not be put into effect 'before its notification or within the first three weeks following its notification'. Although the Commission used to be able to take a decision to extend this suspension period, it was a peculiar period to have adopted because the Commission has a period of one month, following notification, in which to make its preliminary assessment of the concentration's compatibility with the common market.[154] In practice, this meant that it had to make a firm assessment of whether it was likely to open stage two proceedings within three weeks, so that it could decide whether or not to extend the suspension period.

Regulation 1310/97 has amended Article 7 with the purpose of harmonizing the duration of the suspensory period with the duration of the investigation. Article 7(1) now provides that a concentration shall not be put into effect 'either before its notification or until it has been declared compatible with the common market pursuant to a decision under Article 6(1)(b) or Article 8(2)'.[155] There is, therefore, an automatic suspension of the concentration until it has been declared to be compatible with the common market.[156] The Commission has power however to permit derogations from this suspensory effect.[157]

The Commission also has power under Article 14(2)(b) to impose penalties of up to 10 per cent of turnover on those intentionally or negligently breaching the suspensory provisions.

Undertakings which do not notify a concentration with a Community dimension to the Commission or which do not comply with the suspensory period risk having to reverse their concentration if the Commission later finds that the concentration is not compatible with the common market.[158]

---

[151] In 1999, the Commission imposed a fine of Euro 219,000 on another firm, Case IV/M969, *AP Moller*, [1999] OJ L183/29, [1999] 4 CMLR 392 for failing to notify three concentrations which it had effected. The breach had occurred prior to the Samsung decision, Moller had voluntarily informed the Commission of its breach and the concentrations were later cleared.

[152] Case IV/M619 [1997] OJ L11/42, [1996] 4 CMLR 742.

[153] See discussion *supra* 732 and *infra* Chap. 17.

[154] See Merger Reg., Arts 6(1) and 10(1).

[155] As amended by Reg. 1310/97, Art. 1(6). The Commission can grant a derogation from the suspensory period. The effects of the suspension on the parties and third parties and the threat to competition posed by the concentration will be taken into account in taking this decision: Merger Reg., Art. 7(4).

[156] See the exception that applies in relation to public bids set out in Art. 7(3).

[157] Merger Reg., Art. 7(4), but see Art. 14(2)(a).

[158] See *ibid.*, Art. 8(4).

c. PHASE I INVESTIGATION

The Commission must examine notifications as soon as they are received.[159] Decisions must be taken within one month of the day of complete notification.[160] Details of notification must be published in the Official Journal in order to give third parties the opportunity to react.[161]

When making its assessment the Commission may obtain further information from the parties, or third parties (such as customers, suppliers or competitors), by means of a request[162] or an inspection (including unannounced on the spot investigations).[163] It has power under Articles 14 and 15 to impose both fines and periodic penalty payments for a number of offences, such as a failure to respond to an Article 11 letter.[164]

At the end of the one month period the Commission must adopt a decision under Article 6. This may take one of several forms.

Article 6(1)(a)

Where the notified transaction does not in fact fall within the Merger Regulation at all, it does not amount to a concentration with a Community dimension, the Commission may issue a decision to that effect. If the transaction does not amount to a concentration the notification may be treated as a notification under Article 81.[165]

Article 6(1)(b)

The Commission may declare the concentration, and restrictions directly related and necessary to the implementation of the concentration,[166] to be compatible with the common market.

Alternatively, the Commission may declare the concentration to be compatible with the common market subject to the acceptance of commitments by the parties.[167] Where commitments are offered the period for assessing the concentration is extended from one month to six weeks.[168]

Section 6(1)(c)

Where the Commission has serious doubts about the concentration's compatibility with the common market it must issue a decision to that effect and initiate proceedings launching a second phase investigation. It has already been seen above that this is in fact a rare occurrence and that a great majority of cases (approximately 95 per cent) are dealt with in Phase I

---

[159] *Ibid.*, Art. 6(1).

[160] *Ibid.*, Art. 10(1). For more detailed provisions relating to the calculation of the one month period see the implementing Reg., Reg. 447/98.

[161] Merger Reg., Art. 4(3).

[162] *Ibid.*, Art. 11. The time limits for replying to such request for information are inevitably short since the Commission itself is complying with tight time constraints.

[163] *Ibid.*, Arts 12 and 13. The power to carry out dawn raids is equivalent to those set out in Reg. 17 [1959–62] OJ Spec. Ed. 87, discussed *infra* in Chap. 14. An inspection is unlikely, given the time constraints under which the Commission is operating.

[164] See also *supra* n. 150.

[165] See Chaps. 4 and 13.

[166] See *infra* 809.

[167] See discussion of commitments, *infra* at 789–791.

[168] Merger Reg., Art. 10(1); see also *infra* n. 183.

proceedings within a period of one month (or six months where commitments are offered or an Article 9 reference requested).[169]

Article 10(6)

Where the Commission fails to adopt a decision within the prescribed periods the concentration 'shall be deemed to have been declared to be compatible with the common market'.

d. PHASE II

The Commission has a period of four months in which to make its assessment in Phase II proceedings.[170] Again, if no decision is taken within the prescribed period the concentration is deemed to be compatible with the common market.[171] Within this short period several steps must usually be taken within stipulated periods of time.

The Commission may first make further requests for information. Then a statement of objections is served on the notifying parties. This lets the parties know the Commission's objections to the concentration.[172] Parties then have an opportunity to respond to the statement; they have a right to access to the file[173] and to attend and speak at the oral hearing.[174] Further, other involved parties and third parties[175] may have a right to receive the statement of objections, to respond to it, to have access to the file, to attend the oral hearing, and to speak at it.

J. Faull and A. Nikpay, *The EC Law of Competition* (Oxford University Press, 1999), 266–7

Non-confidential version and communication to third parties

4.244 On the dispatch of the Statement of Objections, the Commission will require that the notifying parties identify any business secrets contained in the Statement of Objections in order that they may be eliminated. This is necessary in order to allow the Commission to inform other involved parties of the objections (Article 13(2)) and, similarly, any third parties identified in accordance with Article 18(4) of the Merger Regulation of the same objections (Article 16(1)).

4.245 The notifying parties, other involved parties, and third parties may respond to the Statement of Objections in writing. However, a response is not obligatory. In addition, the Commission services have adopted a policy of making such parties' responses available to the other parties, after an elimination of business secrets. While the notifying parties may wish to have their response distributed, in order to present their view of the effects of the operation, the Commission cannot enforce such action.

---

[169] See *supra* n. 77.

[170] Merger Reg., Art. 10(3). This period can be extended in certain circumstances, e.g., to allow for information to be collected: Art. 10(4).

[171] *Ibid.*, Art. 10(6).

[172] *Ibid.*, Art. 18(1) and (2).

[173] The Commission's Notice on the access to the file is discussed *infra* in Chap. 14.

[174] Procedure and enforcement under Reg. 17 are discussed in detail *infra* in Chap. 14.

[175] See also on the rights of third parties, Cases C–68/94 and C–30/95, *France v. Commission, Société Commerciale des Potasses et de l'Azote (SCPA) v. Commission* [1998] ECR I–1375, [1998] 4 CMLR 829; *infra* 776–778.

Rights of notifying, involved, and third parties, management and union bodies

4.246. The rights of the notifying parties to be heard is established in Article 18(1) of the Merger Regulation; similarly Article 18(4) allows the Commission to hear other third parties and specifically members of the administrative or management bodies of the undertakings concerned and representatives of their employees. The right of representatives of employee's organizations to be heard has been confirmed in two cases . . . brought before the Court of First Instance concerning the acquisition of Perrier by *Nestlé*.

The Implementing Regulation is, however, more specific as regards the various parties' rights as Table 1 shows.

Table 1

	Receipt of Statement of Objections	Right of response to Statement	Access to File	Attendance at Oral Hearing	Right to speak at Oral hearing
Notifying parties	Yes	Yes	Yes	Yes	Yes
Involved parties	After deletion of business secrets	Yes	In so far as is necessary in order to exercise their rights of defence	Yes	Yes
Third parties	Limited to 'nature and subject matter of the procedure'	Yes	No	Yes	Yes

Before a second phase decision is adopted the Advisory Committee on concentrations must be consulted.[176] At the end of the proceedings the Commission may under Article 8 of the Merger Regulation either:

(a) declare the concentration and restrictions related and necessary to the concentration to be compatible with the common market,

(b) declare the concentration and ancillary restrictions to be compatible with the common market but only subject to the performance of certain stipulated commitments[177] (the decision can subsequently be revoked if the parties breach the commitments[178]),

(c) declare the merger to be incompatible with the common market (Article 8(3)).[179]

If the parties have already completed the transaction the Commission has power under Article 8(4) of the Treaty to order divestiture and the reversal of the concentration.

---

[176] The Advisory Committee must also be consulted prior to a Commission decision imposing fines pursuant to Merger Reg., Arts. 14 and 15. See *supra* Chap. 2 for the role of Advisory Committees.

[177] Merger Reg., Art. 8(2). Commitments are discussed *infra* 789–791.

[178] Merger Reg., Art. 8(5). It may also revoke decisions which are based on incorrect information.

[179] This has rarely been done. Up to the end of 1998 only 13 Art. 8(3) or (4) prohibitions had been ordered: see J. Faull and A. Nikpay, *The EC Law of Competition* (Oxford University Press, 1999), para. 4.280.

(ii) A ONE-STOP SHOP?

a. EXCLUSIVE COMPETENCE OF THE COMMISSION UNDER THE MERGER REGULATION

Article 21(1) and (2) provides:

1. Subject to review by the Court of Justice, the Commission shall have sole jurisdiction to take the decisions provided for in this Regulation.

2. No Member State shall apply its national legislation on competition to any concentration that has a Community dimension.

The basic scheme of the Merger Regulation is that parties to a concentration with a Community dimension benefit from a 'one-stop shop'. The parties must notify their concentration to the Commission for assessment under the Merger Regulation. The general rule is that the Merger Regulation alone and no other Community law applies to concentrations (Regulation 17 and the other legislation authorizing the Commission to apply Articles 81 and 82 is disapplied[180]) and that national law does not apply to concentrations with a Community dimension. The decision of the Commission under the Merger Regulation is decisive. There is no need to obtain approval for the concentration from any national competition authority. The one-stop shop held one of the greatest appeals of a Community merger scheme to both the Commission and the business community.

Notwithstanding this basic starting point there are circumstances in which the merger, or aspects of the merger, may be referred to a national authority for assessment under its domestic law. Further, it may be that there are circumstances in which Articles 81 and 82 can be applied to a concentration by the Commission itself or by a national court or national competition authority.

b. ARTICLE 9—DISTINCT MARKETS

Objectives of Article 9

Article 21(2) states that the prohibition on a Member State applying its national competition legislation to a concentration with a Community dimension is without prejudice to the Member States' ability to take action under the 'distinct market' provisions of Article 9. Article 9 of the Merger Regulation is known as the 'German clause', it having been included at the particular insistence of the Germans.

It has already been noted that Germany was particularly opposed to the introduction of any form of EC merger control and that, in particular, it feared that EC competition law would not be applied stringently enough. Article 9 was added at a late stage in the negotiations to meet the Germans' objections over loss of control. It provides for the referral, at the request of a national authority, of a merger, or aspects of a merger, to that authority where the concentration threatens competition in a 'distinct' market in that authority's State. Article 9 was intended to meet the particular fear that the Commission's action may be less rigorous than national merger control would be. It also seeks to deal with the fear that

---

[180] Merger Reg., Art. 22(1).

local or regional issues might not be addressed by the criteria set out for the assessment of concentrations in Article 2 of the Merger Regulation.[181]

Article 9 accepts, therefore, that there might be room for domestic law to apply to a concentration which, although innocuous from a Community perspective, has more serious repercussions in a Member State or a small part of a Member State.

Council Regulation 4064/89 of 21 December 1989 on the control of concentrations between undertakings [1989] OJ L395/1, Article 9

1. The Commission may, by means of a decision notified without delay to the undertakings concerned and the competent authorities of the other Member States, refer a notified concentration to the competent authorities of the Member State concerned in the following circumstances.

2. Within three weeks of the date of receipt of the copy of the notification a Member State may inform the Commission, which shall inform the undertakings concerned, that:

(a) a concentration threatens to create or to strengthen a dominant position as a result of which effective competition will be significantly impeded on a market within that Member State, which presents all the characteristics of a distinct market, or

(b) a concentration affects competition on a market within that Member State, which presents all the characteristics of a distinct market and which does not constitute a substantial part of the common market.[182]

3. If the Commission considers that, having regard to the market for the products or services in question and the geographical reference market within the meaning of paragraph 7, there is such a distinct market and that such a threat exists, either:

(a) it shall itself deal with the case in order to maintain or restore effective competition in the market concerned, or

(b) it shall refer the whole or part of the case to the competent authorities of the Member State concerned with a view to the application of that State's national competition law.

If, however, the Commission considers that such a distinct market or threat does not exist it shall adopt a decision to that effect which it shall address to the Member State concerned.

In cases where a Member State informs the Commission that a concentration affects competition in a distinct market within its territory that does not form a substantial part of the common market, the Commission shall refer the whole or part of the case relating to the distinct market concerned, if it consider that such a distinct market is affected.

Request

Despite the background to the adoption of Article 9, the Article in fact concedes little authority to the Member States. A Member State may express concern about the effect of a merger in its territory, but if the concentration has a Community dimension and potentially impedes competition in the common market or a substantial part of it, the Commission is

---

[181] Art. 2 of the Merger Reg. only permits the Commission to take action against concentrations which would impede competition in 'the common market or in a substantial part of it'.

[182] Reg. 1310/97, Art. 1(8) introduced this new para. 2(b). Member States now need to demonstrate only that the concentration affects competition on a distinct market within that State. It does not have to be proved that the concentration threatens to create or strengthen a dominant position.

the sole arbiter of whether or not the matter should be referred to the Member State under Article 9.

Where the Commission receives a request from a Member State in accordance with Article 9(2),[183] the Commission must determine (1) whether the distinct market exists and (2) whether competition in that market would be significantly impeded. Even where these conditions are satisfied, the Commission may nonetheless decide to deal with the case itself in order to maintain or restore effective competition on the market concerned. Alternatively, it may make the requested reference.[184]

If the Commission does make a reference to the national authority it merely delegates power to investigate the aspects of the merger that affect competition in that distinct market.[185] This may mean that the whole concentration is referred for assessment to the national authority. Alternatively, the Commission itself may deal with some aspects of the merger and refer only the aspects relating to the 'distinct market' to the Member State.[186]

Distinct markets which do not constitute a substantial part of the common market

Where a Member State informs the Commission that a concentration affects competition in a distinct market within its territory which does not form a substantial part of the common market,[187] the Commission is *required* to refer the whole or part of the case relating to the distinct market back, if it considers that such a distinct market is affected.

Distinct market

Whether a distinct market exists is determined with regard to the market for the products or services in question and, in particular, the geographical reference market. The meaning of a geographical reference market is given in Article 9(7):

7. The geographical reference market shall consist of the area in which the undertakings concerned are involved in the supply and demand of products or services, in which the conditions of competition are sufficiently homogeneous and which can be distinguished from neighbouring areas because, in particular, conditions of competition are appreciably different in those areas. The assessment should take account in particular of the nature and characteristics of the products or services concerned, of the existence of entry barriers or of consumer preferences, of appreciable difference of the undertakings' market shares between the area concerned and neighbouring areas or of substantial price differences.

---

[183] The Member State's request must be made within three weeks of receipt of a copy of the notification. The one-month period in which the Commission must make its preliminary investigation (Merger Reg., Art. 9(2) set out above) and the Commission's period for assessing whether or not to proceed against a merger is increased from one month to six weeks: Art. 10(1).

[184] Merger Reg., Art. 9(3).

[185] The Member State is obliged to act promptly and to complete its examination within 4 months of referral from the Commission: Merger Reg., Art. 9(6). Further Art. 9(8) provides that 'the Member State concerned may take only the measures strictly necessary to safeguard or restore effective competition on the market concerned'.

[186] See Case IV/M180, *Steetley plc/Tarmac* [1992] 4 CMLR 337 discussed *infra* 743.

[187] Art. 2(3) of the Merger Reg. only authorizes the Commission to declare incompatible with the common market only concentrations which significantly impede effective competition on that market or a substantial part of it.

Success of claims

At first the Commission made requested references relatively infrequently. Initially at least the German clause was not, therefore, a particularly effective compromise of the principle that the Commission should have sole jurisdiction over concentrations with a Community dimension.[188] Ironically, the first four applications made by Germany under Article 9 were rejected.[189]

Since 1996, however, references back have been made much more frequently. The first case in which the Commission agreed to make a reference back was *Steetley plc/Tarmac*.[190] In this case competing bids had been made for Steetley plc by Tarmac and Redland. Only the Tarmac bid had a Community dimension and the Redland bid fell to be assessed under domestic law (under the UK Fair Trading Act 1973). The concentration between Steetley and Tarmac would have pooled the building material activities of the undertakings. In particular, the undertakings had very high market shares for bricks and clay tiles in some parts of England. The Commission agreed that the concentration would lead to particular local problems in the market for the manufacture and sale of bricks in the North East and South West of England and in relation to the manufacture of clay tiles throughout Great Britain.[191] The brick markets were therefore regional (the cost of transporting such heavy products being high relative to the cost of the products) and trade flows in clay tiles between Great Britain and the rest of the Community were low (although the tiles were lighter and could be transported more easily throughout the country significant barriers to entry to the market remained—adequate clay reserves were necessary to manufacture the tiles). The economic implications were therefore substantially limited to the UK. The Commission issued a decision referring these aspects of the merger back to the UK to be assessed under the provisions of the Fair Trading Act.[192] On the same day it issued a decision finding that the remaining aspects of the concentration were compatible with the common market.[193] In the end the Redland bid for Steetley was successful (its bid was not referred to the MMC). The UK's Monopolies and Mergers Commission never therefore considered the effect of the Tarmac bid on the public interest.

In *McCormick/CPC/Ostmann* a German request under Article 9 was finally successful.[194] This was only on account of a Commission error, however! The German authorities wished to consider a concentration affecting the German herb and spice market. It considered that features of the distinct market meant that there would be no likely entrants onto the market, and that the merger threatened to create a dominant position as result of which competition

---

[188] Although in practice it means that the national competition authorities of the Member States will be likely to scrutinize all concentrations affecting competition within their jurisdiction so that they may determine whether or not a request should be made.

[189] See Case IV/M165, *Alcatel/AEG Kabel* [1992] OJ C6/23; Case IV/M12, *Varta/Bosch* [1991] OJ L320/26, [1992] 5 CMLR M1; Case IV/M222, *Mannesmann/Hoesch* [1993] OJ L114/34; and Case IV/M238, *Siemens/Phillips* (subsequently abandoned).

[190] Case IV/M180 [1992] 4 CMLR 337.

[191] The Commission also considered the fact that a competing bid was being assessed at the domestic level. It is hard, however, to see how this was a relevant factor to be taken into account under Art. 9.

[192] For the powers of the UK authorities with respect to Art. 9 see EEC Merger Reg. (Distinct Market Investigations) Regulations 1990 SI 1990/1715.

[193] Case IV/M180, not published.

[194] Case No IV/M330, not published.

would be significantly impeded. The Commission agreed that the German herb and spice market did constitute a distinct market within the meaning of Article 9 but intended to assess the merger itself. However, because of an error in the calculation of the time limits set out in Article 10(1) it was unable to launch a Phase II investigation (if the Commission fails to take a decision in accordance with the deadlines set out in Article 10(1) the concentration is 'deemed to have been declared compatible with the common market'[195]). The examination of the concentration would not, therefore, have been possible unless the notification had been referred to the German authorities. Soon after the reference the parties abandoned the concentration.

In many cases a decision to make a reference to a national authority will sound the death knell for the concentration. The decision to make the reference is unlikely to be requested or made unless the concentration is considered to pose particular risks for a distinct national market. In *Holdercim/Cedest*,[196] however, the French authorities cleared aspects of a concentration which had been referred to it under Article 9. The remaining aspects were cleared by the Commission after a preliminary assessment under Article 6(1)(b).

Appeal
Any Member State can appeal from a Commission decision taken under Article 9 in accordance with the ordinary provisions of the Treaty.

c. ARTICLE 21(3)—LEGITIMATE INTERESTS

Article 21(3) recognizes that there are some matters which are so sensitive to the national interest that the Member States should be entitled to retain control over them themselves. Under Article 21(3), a Member State may take steps to protect 'legitimate interests' which are not protected under the Merger Regulation itself:

3. Notwithstanding paragraphs 1 and 2, Member States may take appropriate measures to protect legitimate interests other than those taken into consideration by this Regulation and compatible with the general principles and other provisions of Community law.

Public security, plurality of the media and prudential rules shall be regarded as legitimate interests within the meaning of the first subparagraph.

Any other public interest must be communicated to the Commission by the Member State concerned and shall be recognised by the Commission after an assessment of its compatibility with the general principles and other provisions of Community law before the measures referred to above may be taken. The Commission shall inform the Member State concerned of its decision within one month of that communication.

The provision does *not* enable a Member State to clear a merger which the Commission has prohibited under the Merger Regulation. It is defensive in nature. It enables a Member State to protect its legitimate interests[197] by scrutinizing, and, if necessary,

---

[195] Merger Reg., Art. 10(6).

[196] Case IV/M460, not published.

[197] In Case IV/1616 *Banco Santander Central Hispano/A Champalimaud*, not published, the Commission rejected the Portuguese authorities' opposition to a concentration within the financial services sector which the authorities claimed would interfere with matters essential to the Portuguese economy and financial system.

prohibiting mergers which may raise concerns other than pure competition ones (even were the Commission to consider that the merger was compatible with the common market).[198]

In *Newspaper Publishing*,[199] for example, although the proposed acquisition of Newspaper Publishing plc (publisher of the Independent) by Promotora de Informaciones SA, Editoriale l'Espresson SpA and Mirror Group Newspapers plc fell within the scope of the Merger Regulation, the UK was able to take steps to protect its legitimate interests, in this case the plurality of the media. The Commission cleared the merger but noted that the UK Secretary of State would also have to grant formal consent under the UK Fair Trading Act. The Commission made it clear that any measures adopted by the UK authorities would, however, have to be objectively the least restrictive to achieve the end pursued (they would, therefore, have to comply with the Community principle of proportionality). The UK is one of many States that consider that media ownership may require a different approach from that ordinarily applicable in domestic competition law.[200]

It is clear from the third paragraph of Article 22(3) that Member States may take steps to protect a 'public interest', other than those specifically referred to in the Article. In *Lyonnaise des Eaux SA/ Northumbrian Water Group* the Commission accepted that the regulation of the UK water industry constituted a legitimate interest.

Following the privatization of the UK water industry, the Director General of Water Services seeks to maintain competitive pressures on water suppliers (which enjoy a monopoly in the provision of local or regional services) by making comparisons of, for example, the relative operating and capital costs of the different water enterprises. In order to achieve this task a sufficient number of independent providers must be maintained. Thus mergers between water enterprises above a certain size are, in contrast to the general rule applying in the UK, automatically referable to the UK's Competition Commission. In accepting the legitimate interests of the UK the Commission held, however, that the UK authorities should not, in their scrutiny of the concentration, take account of factors which properly fell for assessment by the Commission:

the control exercised by the UK authorities is aimed at ensuring that the number of independently controlled water companies is sufficient to allow the Director General of Water Services to exercise his regulatory functions . . . in order not to go beyond the interest pursued by the UK regulatory legislation other issues in relation to mergers between water companies can only be taken into account to the extent that they affect the control regime set out above . . .[201]

[198] In that sense it is rather different from other provisions in Community law which recognize that Member States may wish to act to protect essential interests such as public policy or security or protection of the health and life of humans. Art. 30 (ex Art. 36) of the Treaty, for example, permits the Member States, in specified circumstances, to derogate from the fundamental objective of creating an internal market characterized by the abolition of obstacles to the free movement of goods (Arts. 3(1)(c) (ex Art. 3(c)) and 28 (ex Art. 30) EC Treaty).

[199] Case IV/M423, not published.

[200] The UK has special rules governing newspaper mergers: see ss 57–62 of the Fair Trading Act 1973. The Government proposes to carry forward these special measures even if other reform of the merger rules occurs: DTI, *Mergers: A Consultation Document on Proposals for Reform*, Aug. 1999, http://www.dti.gov.uk/cacp/cp/mergercon/index.htm, ss. 5, paras 12–16.

[201] Case No IV/M567 [1996] 4 CMLR 614.

d. ARTICLE 296 OF THE EC TREATY—ESSENTIAL INTERESTS OF
SECURITY

Article 296(1)(b) of the Treaty provides that nothing in the Treaty shall preclude the
application by Member States of measures 'it considers necessary for the protection of the
essential interests of its security which are connected with the production of or trade in
arms, munitions and war material'. Recital 28 to the Merger Regulation makes it clear that
the Regulation does not affect the Member States' ability to act under this Article. The
ability of Member States to act under Article 296 is not, therefore, affected by the reference
in Article 21(3) to matters of 'public security'. Article 296 thus enables a Member State to
request parties to a concentration not to notify military aspects of a merger to the
Commission.

In the competing bids for VSEL plc (a builder of UK Trident submarines), for example,
British Aerospace plc and GEC notified their competing bids (which amounted to concentrations) to the Commission only in so far as they related to the non-military activities of
VSEL (only 2.5 per cent of the business). The UK, relying on Article 296(1)(b), had
instructed the competitors not to notify the acquisition of the military activities. The Commission cleared the non-defence activities of the undertakings and stated that it was satisfied
with the measures taken by the UK under Article 296. There was no need to take steps under
Article 299 in order to ensure that the measures taken under Article 296 did not have the
effect of distortion competition in the common market.[202]

The Commission later accepted that Article 296 applied to the military aspects of a
proposed merger between Marconi Electronic Systems (a part of GEC) and British Aerospace plc. Again it cleared the non-military aspects of the concentration.[203]

D. CONCENTRATIONS WITHOUT A COMMUNITY DIMENSION

(i) NATIONAL LAW APPLIES

Article 22(1) provides that the Merger Regulation alone applies to 'concentrations' and takes
away the Commission's powers under Regulation 17 etc. to implement Articles 81 and 82. As
Regulation 17 and the other implementing Regulations, do not apply to concentrations, and
because the general rule is that the Merger Regulation applies only to concentrations which

---

[202] See for example, M.528 British Aerospace/VSEL. Ultimately the GEC bid prevailed even though on
investigation the Monopolies and Mergers Commission recommended that the British Aerospace bid should
be cleared but that the GEC bid would operate against the public interest, see *GEC/VSEL* Cm 2852 (1995).
The UK Secretary of State (who makes the final decision after the recommendations of the Competition
Commission (formerly the Monopolies and Mergers Commission) did not, however, accept opinion of
majority and did not act to prevent the GEC bid. There are, however, proposals to reform the UK merger
rules.

[203] Case IV/M1438 *British Aerospace/GEC Marconi* OJ [1999] C241/8, see also Case IV/M.820 *British
Aerospace/Lagadère SCA* [1996] 5 CMLR 523.

have a Community dimension,[204] the general principle is that national law *only* applies to concentrations which do not have a Community dimension.[205]

1. This Regulation alone shall apply to concentrations as defined in Article 3 and Regulations No 17, (EEC) No 1017/68, (EEC) No 4056/86 and (EEC) No 3975/87 shall not apply, except in relation to joint ventures that do not have a Community dimension and which have their object or effect the co-ordination of the competitive behaviour of undertakings that remain independent.

(ii) JOINT VENTURES

Article 22(1) itself makes it clear that there is an exception to this general position that national law only applies to concentrations which do not have a Community dimension.

It will be remembered that Regulation 1310/97 amended the definition of concentration in Article 3, bringing within the scope of the Merger Regulation all full-function ventures, even those which might lead to the co-ordination of the competitive behaviour of independent undertakings.[206] Previously these joint ventures would have been appraised under Article 81.[207] These joint ventures with a Community dimension are now appraised under the Merger Regulation.[208] If, however, such a joint venture does *not* have a Community dimension the Commission is still able to apply Article 81 of the Treaty to the joint venture using its powers under Regulation 17.

(iii) ARTICLE 22(3)

Article 22(3), or the Dutch clause,[209] also derogates from the general rule. It provides:

3. If the Commissions finds, at the request of a Member State or at the joint request of two or more Member States, that a concentration as defined in Article 3 that has no Community dimension within the meaning of Article 1 creates or strengthens a dominant position as result of which effective competition would be significantly impeded within the territory of the Member State or States making the joint request, it may, insofar as that concentration affects trade between Member States, adopt the decisions provided for in Article 8(2), second subparagraph, (3) and (4).

The Article provides a mechanism by which a Member State can request the Commission to apply the provisions of the Merger Regulation to a concentration which does not have a Community dimension but which, nonetheless, affects trade between Member States. A Member State might make such a request where, for example, it has no, or inadequate, merger rules in place, it has inadequate resources to deal with the concentration, a competing bid has a Community dimension which will be considered by the Commission[210] or the Member State considers that the case is one which is primarily of Community interest.

---

[204] Merger Reg., Art. 1(1).

[205] The prohibition in Art. 21(2) on a Member State applying its national legislation on competition applies only where the concentration has a Community dimension. But see discussion *infra* on the residual role of Arts. 81 and 82 of the Treaty.

[206] See, *supra* 723–726.

[207] See *infra* Chap. 13.

[208] A different substantive test applies: *infra* 806–808.

[209] The clause having been inserted at the request of the Dutch.

[210] See *supra* n. 117 and accompanying text.

Three of the four requests which had been made to the Commission prior to the end of 1999 were made by Member States which did not, at that time, have merger control rules.[211] In *Kesko/Tuko*,[212] for example, the Finnish Office of Free Competition requested the Commission to examine the acquisition of Tuko Oy by Kesko Oy. Although the concentration did not have a Community dimension (both undertakings achieved more than two thirds of their respective Community-wide turnover in Finland) the Commission found that the concentration affected trade between Member States within the meaning of Article 22(3). It could, therefore, assess the concentration following the Member State's request under Article 22(3) request. The Commission ultimately prohibited the concentration. The acquisition having already taken place the Commission ordered Kesko under Article 8(4) of the Merger Regulation to divest itself of the Tuko business.[213] Kesko was required to find a purchaser which had to be a viable existing or prospective competitor, independent of and unrelated to the Kesko group, and with sufficient financial resources to enable it to maintain and develop the business as an active competitive force in competition with Kesko's business.[214]

Since 1997 the supsensory provisions set out in Article 7 of the Merger Regulation apply to concentrations which have not been put into effect on the date on which the Commission informs the parties that a request under Article 22(3) has been made.[215]

Once a reference is made to the Commission the Member State retains no control over the Commission's investigation.[216] The Commission is empowered only to take action to maintain or restore effective competition within the territory of the Member State or States at the request of which it intervenes.[217]

E. A RESIDUAL ROLE FOR ARTICLES 81 AND 82 OF THE TREATY

(i) THE RELEVANCE OF ARTICLES 81 AND 82 OF THE TREATY

Prior to the enactment of the Merger Regulation the Commission made use of both Articles 81 and 82 to prohibit transactions which would now amount to a concentration within the meaning of the Merger Regulation.[218] Subject to the special provisions for co-ordinative

---

[211] The only Member States which do not have merger control rules now are Luxembourg and Denmark: *supra* n. 120. Merger rules were adopted in Finland only at the end of 1998. The fourth was made by Belgium which wished the Commission to intervene in the *British Airways/Dan Air* merger (Case IV/M278 [1993] 5 CMLR M61). The Belgian authorities did not under its national law have jurisdiction to preclude a merger between two UK companies. The Commission cleared the merger unconditionally.

[212] Case No IV/M784 [1997] OJ L174/47.

[213] See *supra* 739.

[214] The Commission's original decision was upheld by the CFI, Case T–22/97, *Kesko Oy* v. *Commission* [2000] 4 CMLR 335.

[215] Merger Reg., Art. 22(4).

[216] Case T–221/95 *Endemol Entertainment Holding BV* v. *Commission*, [1999] ECR II–1299, [1999] 5 CMLR 611, para. 42.

[217] Merger Reg., Art. 22(5).

[218] See *supra* 709–711.

full-function joint ventures,[219] Article 22(1) disapplies Regulation 17 and the other implementing legislation and clearly intends, subject to the provisos discussed in sections C and D above, that the Merger Regulation alone should apply to concentrations with a Community dimension and that national law alone should apply to concentrations which do not. The purpose is to exclude the possible application of Article 81 or 82 to *concentrations* all together.

The difficulty is that the Regulation cannot disapply the application of Article 81 and 82, which are Treaty provisions, but disapplies only the implementing legislation which delegates responsibility for the enforcement of the rules to the Commission.

A question which arises is to what extent can the national courts apply Articles 81 and 82. Further, to what extent is the Commission, and/or national competition authority, authorized to intervene in 'concentration' cases by Articles 85 and 84 of the Treaty respectively?[220]

(ii) APPLICATION IN THE NATIONAL COURTS

The case law indicates that whilst Article 82 has direct effect and is applicable by national courts,[221] in contrast Article 81 is not directly effective, in the absence of implementing legislation.[222]

It is possible therefore that, irrespective of the principle of a one-stop shop and the principle that in the absence of a Community dimension Community law does not apply, a private individual may challenge before a national court the compatibility of a concentration with Article 82 of the Treaty. In practice this is most likely to occur where the concentration does not have a Community dimension.

(iii) THE COMMISSION AND NATIONAL COMPETITION AUTHORITIES

It is also possible that both the Commission and the national competition authorities have power to apply Articles 81 and 82 using their residual powers set out in Article 85 and Article 84 of the Treaty respectively.[223]

It seems clear that Article 85 does authorize the Commission to investigate a breach of Article 81 or 82 on its own initiative or at the request of a Member State. Thus it could in theory investigate a breach of these provisions in respect of a concentration which does not have a Community dimension.[224] Because, however, the implementing regulations are suspended the Commission would have to operate without the powers set out therein, for

---

[219] See *supra* 747.

[220] These provisions are discussed *supra* in Chap. 2.

[221] Case 66/86, *Ahmed Saeed Flugreisen* v. *Zentrale zur Bekämpfung Unlauteren Wettbewerbs ev* [1989] ECR 803, [1990] 4 CMLR 102; see especially paras. 19–21, 30–33, and Cases 209–213/84, *Ministère Public* v. *Asjes* (*Nouvelles Frontières*) [1986] ECR 1425, [1986] 3 CMLR 173.

[222] *Ibid.* But see the Commission's White Paper on Modernisation of the rules implementing Articles 85 and 86 [now Arts. 81 and 82] of the EC Treaty [1999] OJ C132/1, [1999] CMLR 208, which proposes taking steps to make Art. 81 directly effective in its entirety: *infra* Chap. 16.

[223] These provisions are discussed *supra*, in Chap. 2.

[224] It is difficult to see why it would wish to do so where the concentration does have a Community dimension since it will in any event be investigating under the Merger Reg.

example, the power to request information and the power to impose fines on those found to be in breach. It may, however, propose appropriate measures to bring an infringement to an end, and if the infringement is not brought to an end, it may issue a reasoned decision and authorise a Member State to take measures to remedy the situation.

Article 84 authorizes the competition authorities of the Member States to act when no implementing legislation applies. Where a concentration does not have a Community dimension then neither the provisions of the Merger Regulation nor of Regulation 17 (save in the case of joint ventures with co-ordinative aspects[225]) apply.[226] Where, however, a concentration has a Community dimension it seems, since the parties are obliged to notify such concentrations to the Commission, that their jurisdiction is denied under Article 84.[227]

5. SUBSTANTIVE APPRAISAL OF CONCENTRATIONS UNDER THE EC MERGER REGULATION

A. BACKGROUND

The disagreement between the Member States on the factors to be taken into account in assessing the compatibility of a merger with the common market was an important reason for the delay in the introduction of the Merger Regulation. A first glance at the Merger Regulation itself suggests a victory for those in favour of a strict competition-based approach.[228] Article 2(1) obliges the Commission to assess whether a notified concentration is compatible with the common market. Article 2(2) and (3) defines when this will, and will not, be the case:

2. A concentration which does not create or strengthen a dominant position as a result of which effective competition would be significantly impeded in the common market or in a substantial part of it shall be declared compatible with the compatible.

3. A concentration which creates or strengthens a dominant position as a result of which effective competition would be significantly impeded in the common market or in a substantial part of it shall be declared incompatible with the common market.

The provisions indicate that the essential objective of the regulation is the maintenance and development of effective competition and the preservation of the competitive structure of

---

[225] *Supra* 747.

[226] Consequently it seems that both Arts. 81 and 82 could be applied.

[227] *Supra* Chap. 2.

[228] The UK and Germany, in particular, were in favour of a test based solely on competition issues. See *supra* 708.

the common market. In *Gencor Limited* v. *Commission* the CFI confirmed that the purpose of the Merger Regulation was:

to ensure that the restructuring of undertakings does not result in the creation of positions of economic power which may significantly impede effective competition in the common market. Community jurisdiction is therefore founded, first and foremost, on the need to avoid the establishment of market structures which may create or strengthen a dominant position, and not on the need to control directly possible abuses of a dominant position.[229]

Concentrations which lead to the acquisition or strengthening of a dominant position and which result in a significant impediment to competition are prohibited. In contrast to the position under Article 81, there is no possibility of an exemption. In contrast to the position under Article 82 the Merger Regulation focuses on the *creation* or *strengthening* of market power, and not the abuse of an *existing* position of market power. Thus in contrast to both Articles 81 and 82, the analysis is *prospective* in nature looking not to past events, but to the effect a concentration will have on competition if implemented.[230] The merger rules aim to preclude the creation of a dominant position and, consequently, the need for the application of Article 82.

Article 2(1) sets out the criteria to be used in appraising whether or not the concentration is compatible with the common market.

In making this appraisal, the Commission shall take into account:

(a) the need to maintain and develop effective competition within the common market in view of, among other things, the structure of all the markets concerned and the actual or potential competition from undertakings located either within or outwith the Community;

(b) the market position of the undertakings concerned and their economic and financial power, the alternatives available to suppliers and users, their access to supplies or markets, any legal or other barriers to entry, supply and demand trends for the relevant goods and services, the interests of the intermediate and ultimate consumers, and the development of technical and economic progress provided that it is to consumers' advantage and does not form an obstacle to competition.

Article 2(4) sets out an additional test against which any co-ordinative aspects of full-function joint ventures must be assessed. This test is discussed in Section E below.

The sections below will examine how the Commission determines whether or not a concentration will lead to the creation or strengthening of a dominant position within the meaning of Article 2(2) and (3). Further, they will examine whether or not factors other than competition, such as industrial and social policy, are relevant to the decision-making process.

---

[229] Case T–102/96 [1999] ECR II–753 [1999] 4 CMLR 971, para. 106. Thus although the elimination of the risk of future abuses may be a legitimate concern of any competent competition authority, it is not the main objective in exercising control over concentrations at Community level.

[230] If the undertakings have complied with the provisions of the Merger Reg. they will have notified the concentration prior to having carried it out. Where the concentration does not have a Community dimension but the Member State decides to request the Commission to look at the concentration (Art. 22(3)) the parties may already have completed the transaction: see Case IV/M784, *Kesko/Tuko* n. 212 and accompanying text.

B. IS THE CONCENTRATION COMPATIBLE WITH THE COMMON MARKET?

(i) A DOMINANT POSITION AND A SIGNIFICANT IMPEDIMENT TO EFFECTIVE COMPETITION

In order to assess whether or not a merger is compatible with the common market the Commission must determine whether or not the concentration:

  (1) creates or strengthens a dominant position;
  (2) as a result of which effective competition would be significantly impeded in the common market or in a substantial part of it.

Before a merger can be declared incompatible with the common market it is thus clear from Article 2(3) that it is first necessary to show that a dominant position will be created or strengthened. If it is not created or strengthened then the concentration should be declared compatible with the common market.[231] Since a finding of dominance necessarily implies adverse consequences for competition, it may seem a moot point whether or not the requirement that the dominant position should significantly impede competition in the common market, or a substantial part of it, adds anything.[232]

It now seems clear, however, that the two tests must be applied separately. A causal link between the creation and strengthening of the dominant position and the impact on competition must be established.[233] Thus a concentration, for example, which leads to the strengthening of a dominant position by a tiny amount may be cleared on the ground that that strengthening does not result in effective competition being significantly impeded. Similarly a concentration which leads to the creation or strengthening of a dominant position may be cleared if, in the absence of the concentration, competition would in any event be significantly impeded[234] or if the dominance is likely to be temporary (it will not impede effective competition). Cook and Kerse explain the practice of the Commission and the Court in this respect:

C. J. Cook and C. S. Kerse, *E.C. Merger Control* (3rd edn., Sweet & Maxwell, 2000), 128–9

As regards the relationship between the two limbs of the test of compatibility in Article 2(1) the Commission has not adopted a mechanistic approach in applying the Regulation. The requirement

---

[231] Art 2(2). But see *infra* 806 ff.

[232] 'Sir Leon Brittan argued that the importance of the distinction between dominance and impeding effective competition lay with the 'dynamic factor of time' in that a sizeable market share held for a short duration in a market with few barriers to entry would not really be a threat to effective competition. . . A more conventional argument would be that a firm in such a position cannot properly be described as dominant': T. A. Downes and D. S. MacDougall, 'Significantly Impeding Effective Competition: Substantive Appaisal under the Merger Regulation.' [1994] *ELR* 286, 289; L. Brittan, *Competition Policy and Merger Control in the Single European Market* (Hersh Lauterpacht Memorial Lectures) (Grotius, 1991), 36.

[233] Cases C–68/94 and C–30/95 *France v. Commission, Société Commerciale des Potasses et de l'Azote (SCPA) v. Commission* [1998] ECR I–1375, [1998] 4 CMLR 829, paras. 110–124.

[234] See the discussion of the failing firm defence, *infra* 801–805.

that the dominant position must significantly impede competition is in practice a two-part composite test, and is a formulation broadly consistent with existing case law under Article 82. At the same time the Commission has the flexibility and discretion it clearly needs when making assessments under Article 2. It is doubtful, moreover, whether it is helpful to think in terms of the shifting of the burden of proof, or the creation of a presumption against the notifying party once the criterion of dominance is established. For example, an undertaking with a 40 per cent share of a product market in the Community may acquire a competitor with a 2 per cent share of the same market. Clearly, there is some aggregation of market share but such a concentration would be unlikely of itself to result in competitive detriment because the reality is that no significant competition has been eliminated as a result of the concentration. This approach has been made more apparent in commission decisions under the Regulation in recent years. Its correctness has now been confirmed by the European Court in *Kali und Salz*. The Court interpreted the second limb of the compatibility test as emphasising the need for a causal link between the creation or strengthening of a dominant position and a significant detrimental impact on effective competition, observing. . .

> 'The introduction of that criterion is intended to ensure that the existence of a causal link between the concentration and the deterioration of the competitive structure of the market can be excluded only if the competitive structure resulting from the concentration would deteriorate in similar fashion even if the concentration did not proceed.'

The apparent flexibility of the second limb of the compatibility test can also be seen in the practice of the Commission. In *Mannesmann/Hoesch*, for example, the Commission concluded that the merged entity would occupy a dominant position on the German market for certain types of gas pipeline but found that the dominance would be short-lived because of the imminent introduction of mandatory competitive tendering by the companies' traditional customers. The strengthening of the existing dominant position would not, therefore, hinder effective competition. Interestingly the issue of the enduring nature of the joint venture's dominance, which might well have been subsumed within the analysis of the dynamics of the markets concerned, or of dominance itself, appears to have been dealt with under the second rather than the first limb of the compatibility test. It is questionable, however, whether the result would have been different if the Commission had not been able to rely on the second limb of the test. It could equally well have based its conclusion on a prediction as to how the relevant market would evolve in the near future, and this approach has been preferred in other cases.

(ii) A DOMINANT POSITION—SINGLE-FIRM DOMINANCE

a. THE DEFINITION OF A DOMINANT POSITION

By focusing on the 'creation or strengthening of a dominant position' the Merger Regulation adopts language reminiscent of that used in Article 82. Indeed, the concept of a dominant position is interpreted by the Commission in accordance with the Court's case law under Article 82.

J. Faull and A. Nikpay *The EC Law of Competition* (Oxford University Press, 1999), 241

4.141 For the purpose of the Merger Regulation the Commission employs the definition of dominance as defined by the European Court of Juste in past Article 82 cases:

> 'The dominant position referred to (in Article 86 [now Article 82] relates to a position of economic strength enjoyed by an undertaking which enables it to prevent effective competition being maintained

> on the relevant market by giving it the power to behave to an appreciable extent independently of its competitors, customers and ultimately of its consumers. [Case 27/76 *United Brands Company* v. *Commission* [1978] ECR 207]'

and

> such a position does not preclude some competition, which it does where there is a monopoly or quasi-monopoly, but enables the undertaking which profits by it, if not to determine, at least to have an appreciable influence on the conditions under which that competition will develop, and in any case to act largely in disregard of it so long as such conduct does not operate to its detriment. [Case 85/76 *Hoffmann-La Roche & Co AG* v. *Commission* [1979] ECR 461]

The key difference of course, as noted above, is that in Article 82 cases the analysis is retrospective in nature. In the context of the Merger Regulation the analysis is forward-looking and may be more complex. In particular in the context of joint ventures it will be difficult to show that the creation or strengthening of a position of *joint* dominance will result in effective competition in the common market being significantly impeded

It was seen in Chapter 6 that in determining whether or not an undertaking has a dominant position for the purposes of Article 82 it is necessary first to define the relevant market (both its product and geographic dimensions) and then to assess the position of the relevant undertaking on that market. Similarly, in merger cases the definition of the market is crucial to enable the Commission to attain meaningful information regarding the market power that the merged parties will acquire. The Commission considers that dominance will 'usually arise when a firm or group of firms would account for a large share of the supply in any given market, provided that other factors analysed in the assessment (such as entry barriers, capacity of reaction of customers, etc) point in the same direction'.[235]

b. THE RELEVANT MARKET

[A] proper definition of the relevant market is a necessary precondition for any assessment of the effect of a concentration on competition.[236]

The Commission's notice on the definition of the relevant market for the purpose of Community competition law[237] sets out how the Commission goes about determining the relevant market for the purposes of its merger decisions. In particular it stresses its use of the SSNIP test. The notice and the SSNIP test were discussed in detail in Chapter 1. In this chapter we will consider more specifically how the Commission has defined the market for the purposes of its merger decisions. Since the Commission adopted 883 final decisions under the Merger Regulation between 1990 and 1998[238] there is significant guidance on market definition in most spheres.[239]

---

[235] Commission Notice on the definition of the relevant market for the purposes of Community competition law [1997] OJ C372/5, para. 10.

[236] Cases C–68/94 and C–30/95 *France* v. *Commission, Société Commerciale des Potasses et de l'Azote (SCPA)* v. *Commission* [1998] ECR I–1375, [1998] 4 CMLR 829, para. 143.

[237] [1997] OJ C372/5, discussed *supra* in Chap. 1.

[238] J. Faull and A. Nikpay (eds.), *The EC Law of Competition* (Oxford University Press, Oxford, 1999), para. 4.280.

[239] Although only Phase II decisions are generally reported in the Official Journal the Phase I decisions are available, in the language of notification, from a number of sources, in particular, on the Competition Directorate's home page and on CELEX, http://europa.eu.int/comm/competition/index_en.html.

Section 6 of Form CO asks the parties to identify any affected markets and the amount of information required in a notification establishes how much importance is attached to economic analysis in making this assessment. The undertaking notifying the concentration will generally argue that the market is a wide one (in which the combined market shares of the parties will, of course, be lower). In some cases an accurate assessment of the market will not be necessary, because even on the assumption of the narrowest possible market the merger will not lead to the creation or strengthening of a dominant position.

Relevant product market

It will be remembered that '[a] relevant product market comprises all those products and/ or services which are regarded as interchangeable or substitutable by the consumer, by reason of the products' characteristics their prices and their intended use'.[240] It will also be remembered that, in making its assessments of dominance, the Commission places most emphasis on demand-side substitution. This entails a determination of the range of products which are viewed as substitutes by the consumers.

The Commission in determining the relevant market makes use, where possible, of the SSNIP test 'by postulating a hypothetical small, non-transitory change in relative prices and evaluating the likely reaction of customers to that increase'.[241] The test has greatest utility in the application of the merger rules since the practical problem presented by the *Cellophane fallacy* does not ordinarily apply.[242] In addition, supply-side factors are relevant where suppliers can switch production to the relevant products in the short term without incurring significant additional costs or risks (where the effect if immediate).[243]

As indicated in its Notice on market definition the Commission relies on a range of evidence in support of a particular definition of a market. Thus evidence of past behaviour, quantitative tests, the views of customers and competitors, consumer preference, physical characteristics, price and switching costs, etc. may be relevant.

In *Aérospatiale-Alenia/de Havilland*,[244] for example, the Commission placed must emphasis on demand-side factors, the evidence of customers and competitors, in reaching its conclusion on the relevant product market.[245] The proposed concentration, by which Aérospatiale SNI and Alenia-Aeritalia e Selenia SpA would jointly acquire the de Havilland division from Boeing Company, affected the turbo-prop commuter aircraft market. The parties argued that there was one market for all aircraft of between twenty and seventy seats. The Commission concluded, however, that three separate markets were affected by the concentration. The turbo-prop commuter aircraft market was divided into three distinct markets, between commuters with twenty to thirty-nine seats; forty to forty-nine seats; and sixty seats and over.

---

[240] Commission Notice on the definition of the relevant market for the purposes of Community competition law [1997] OJ C372/5, para. 7 (this definition was adapted by reference to the definition set out in Form CO).

[241] *Supra* Chap. 1.

[242] *Ibid.* The Commission's practice in defining markets for the purposes of the Merger Reg. is the inspiration behind the SSNIP test set out in the Notice [1997] OJ C372/5.

[243] See, e.g., Case IV/M214, *ICI/ Du Pont* [1992] OJ L7/13.

[244] Case IV/M53 [1991] OJ L334/42, [1992] 4 CMLR M2.

[245] It considered supply-side factors in assessing whether or not potential competitors would exercise a restraining influence over the concentration (i.e. in assessing whether or not the high market shares which would be realized by the merger were indicative of market power, see discussion *infra* 762–763).

Similarly, in consumer product markets it may be expected that the greatest emphasis will be placed on demand-side factors. In *Procter & Gamble/VP Schickedanz*[246] the Commission, in finding that separate markets exist for tampons and sanitary towels, placed much emphasis on consumer preferences and consumer behaviour which was affected by many factors other than price (such as cultural, psychological, and physical differences).

In *Nestlé/Perrier*[247] the Commission relied on a wider range of factors in defining the relevant product market. The case concerned a public bid notified by Nestlé SA for 100 per cent of the shares of Source Perrier SA. The proposed concentration primarily affected the business of bottling water originating from a natural spring or source ('source water').[248] Nestlé submitted that there was no separate market for bottled source water. Rather, the relevant market was non-alcoholic refreshment beverages, including both bottled source water and soft drinks.[249] The Commission, in concluding that the relevant product was that of bottled source water, relied on price correlation analsyis. Further, it relied partly on supply-side factors in support of its conclusion that it would be difficult to justify an exclusion of sparkling and flavoured source water from the relevant product market. Most companies marketing still and source water also marketed sparkling and flavoured source waters, and a bottler of sourced water could easily switch production to a sparkling or flavoured source water. The Commission did not consider, however, that the assessment of the case would differ whether or not sparkling and flavoured waters were included or excluded from the market.

Case IV/M190, *Nestlé/Perrier* [1992] OJ L356/1, [1993] 4 CMLR M17

Commission

B. Distinction between still source waters and sparkling and flavoured waters

20. The assessment of the proposed merger would not be materially different whether sparkling and flavoured source waters are excluded form the relevant product market or not. Several demand factors indicate that sparkling and flavoured waters could be excluded from the relevant product market. There are a number of differences between still source waters and sparkling and flavoured waters, in terms of physical characteristics, taste, intended use, volumes consumed and price levels. In certain exceptional cases, the companies concerned position sparkling and flavoured waters closer to soft drinks in terms of packaging, marketing and price. The sparkling water Perrier (3.8 % of the market) and certain flavoured waters (less than 1 %) constitute examples of such exceptions.

However, it is not possible to exclude competitive interactions between sparkling flavoured and still source waters. Most companies marketing still source waters also market sparkling source waters, and to a lesser extent, flavoured source waters. A bottler of still source water can easily switch production to a sparkling or flavoured source water, at least from a technical point of view.

For these reasons, it might be difficult to justify a radical exclusion of sparkling and flavoured source water from the relevant product market. However, still sparkling and flavoured waters certainly

---

[246] Case IV/M430 [1994] OJ L354/32, [1994] 5 CMLR 146.

[247] Case IV/M190 [1992] OJ L356/1, [1993] 4 CMLR M17.

[248] Nestlé agreed that if it succeeded in acquiring control over Perrier it would sell the Volvic source of Perrier to BSN (the third major supplier on the French source water market).

[249] See the discussion of the case set out *supra* in Chap. 6.

constitute different categories of products, or segments, within the overall market of bottled source water. In the present case the assessment of the proposed merger would in any event not materially differ even if sparkling and flavoured waters were excluded.

In *Mannesmann/Vallourec/Ilva*[250] the Commission also defined the relevant product market by reference to both demand and supply-side factors. Under the proposed concentration the three parties, Mannesmann AG, Vallourec SA, and Ilva SpA, intended to operate their seamless stainless steel tube businesses through a holding company which would be jointly controlled by the parties. In concluding that the stainless steel tubes were in a distinct market from carbon steel tubes (with a lower chronium content) the Commission took account both of the views of customers and the fact that the manufacturing process for the tubes was very different. Further, in ruling out welded steel tubes from the market the Commission focused on differences in end use, price (seamless tubes were, in general twice the price of welded ones) and manufacturing techniques. However, in holding that hot- and cold-finished seamless steel tubes were in the same market the Commission stressed the fact that both products were produced by the same producers and bought by the same customers as part of packages. This was despite the fact that the price for cold-finished tubes was signficantly higher than for hot-finished ones (cold-finishing being more labour intensive) and that the manufacturing techniques for the two differed.

In *Kali und Salz/MDK/Treuhand*[251] Kali und Salz and Mitteldeutsche Kali AG (MdK, owned by Treuhand) were to combine their potash and rock-salt activities. The Commission concentrated primarily on the effects of the concentration on the market for potash. Although there were two distinct categories of customers for the potash (producers that acquired the potash in powder form to make, in combination with other plant nutrients, compound fertilisers and farmers who purchased granulated potash for direct agricultural application) the Commission drew the market broadly. Irrespective of these different customer needs and irrespective of the fact that granulated potash was 10 per cent more expensive than the potash in its powder form it concluded that they were both part of the same market. Producers could make both forms of potash and could, without difficulty, change the balance of output of the two products.

The relevant geographic market

'The relevant geographic market comprises the area in which the undertakings concerned are involved in the supply and demand of products and services, in which the conditions of competition are sufficiently homogeneous and which can be distinguished from neighbouring areas because the conditions of competition are appreciably different in those areas.'[252] The objective of defining the market is to determine the area in which undertakings will genuinely be competitors of the concentration.

As in the assessment of the relevant product market, both demand and supply side substitution will be relevant in assessing the area comprising the geographic market:

---

[250] Case IV/M315 [1994] OJ L102/15, [1994] 4 CMLR 529.

[251] Case IV/M308 [1994] OJ L186/30, [1994] 4 CMLR 526; on appeal Cases C–68/94 and C–30/95, *France v. Commission, Société Commerciale des Potasses et de l'Azote (SCPA) v. Commission* [1998] ECR I–1375, [1998] 4 CMLR 829.

[252] Commission Notice on the definition of the relevant market for the purposes of Community competition law [1997] OJ C372/5, para. 8

whether it is national/ EU/EEA, worldwide, or some other. The Commission has relied in its merger decisions on evidence such as current geographical pattern of purchases, past evidence of diversion of orders to other areas, basic demand characteristics, views of customers and competitors, trade-flows and barriers, and switching costs when defining the geographic market. The Commission will also take account of the process of market integration in defining markets. In many cases this process may mean that in a short period the market may become wider than past figures suggest.[253]

Obviously, the parties will, again, wish to argue for as wide a geographic market as possible. Indeed, some markets may be worldwide. This may be more likely in the case of highly technical products with high capital costs which require huge research and development and manufacturing costs (especially where the cost is very high relative to the cost of transport). In *Aérospatiale/Alenia/de Havilland*, for example, the Commission concluded that the geographical market for the commuter aircraft was worldwide, excluding China and eastern Europe.

2. Geographical reference market

20. The commuter markets from an economic point of view are considered to be world markets. There are no tangible barriers to the importation of these aircraft into the Community and there are negligible costs of transportation.

In *Mannesmann/Vallourec/Ilva*,[254] however, the Commission rejected the parties' allegation that the market for seamless steel tubes was worldwide. The Commission did not consider that the parties' evidence, based on price correlations between Western European and the United States and figures establishing that more than 10 per cent of production was exported from Western Europe, established that the market was worldwide. Rather, it concluded that the market was Western Europe (the EC and EFTA countries). In this area there were no tariff barriers to trade, a high level of trade between the different countries, low transport costs, and similar structures of supply and demand.

In view of the single market project and the aim of breaking down barriers to trade between Member States, it is perhaps to be expected that many markets will be at least Community-wide rather than national. Nevertheless, particularly in consumer product markets, the market has often been found by the Commission to be national. This has been the case even where there are no legal barriers to entry and where it would not be anticipated that other barriers to entry would exist.[255] In some markets technical barriers to entry may still exist. In others the reason for a national market may be that transport costs are high relative to the cost of the product or due to consumer brand loyalty, national buying preferences, or a lack of effective cross-border distribution and marketing infrastructures. Markets may have evolved on national lines over hundreds of years and be unlikely to change in the near future. In *Nestlé/Perrier* a combination of the factors set out above led the Commission to conclude that the geographic market was France.

---

[253] IV/M165, *Alcatel/AEG Kabel* [1992] OJ C6/23.

[254] Case IV/M315 [1994] OJ L102/15, [1994] 4 CMLR 529.

[255] See also discussion *supra* in Chap. 6 and, e.g., Case IV/M43, *Magneti Marelli/CEAC* [1991] OJ L222/38, [1992] 4 CMLR M61.

Case IV/M190, *Nestlé/Perrier* [1992] OJ L356/1, [1993] 4 CMLR M17

Commission

Relevant geographic market

21. In view of the structural elements set out below, and after examination of the competitive environment in the source water markets in the Community, the Commission has concluded that the relevant geographic market within which the power of the new entity has to be assessed is France. Several factors indicate that the parties to the concentration are and will be able to determine their competitive behaviour in France without suffering significant competitive constraints from outside France.

. . .

However, in view of the different competitive environment prevailing in each Member State, the practical impossibility of the development of parallel imports and the absence of Community competitors capable of overcoming the strong barriers to entry into the French market, the Commission concludes that the relevant geographic market is France.

A. Competitive environment in the Community

23. The competitive environment in the bottled source water market is very heterogeneous throughout the Community. Demand presents different characteristics in each Member State, trade flows are negligible in terms of consumption and supply is highly fragmented in most Member States.

. . .

B. French exports and the threat of parallel imports

28. Bottled source water is a relatively inexpensive and bulky merchandise with a high impact of transport costs. It is not likely, even if margins would be high, that a parallel importer could move throughout the various Member States the large volumes required to earn significant revenue and profits. Moreover, it has to be noted that, as a rule, exports of the French mineral waters are carried out through subsidiaries of the main suppliers. For instance, all export activity of Vittel to Belgium and Germany is carried out through Vittel's subsidiaries in those countries (Societe Vittel Import and Vittel Mineralwasser GmbH respectively). This arrangement allows for a certain degree of control of the water exported to these two countries.
. . ., [T]he Commission considers that the conditions prevailing in the source water market show that the parties' exports and the threat of parallel imports do not and will not constrain the parties' competitive behaviour in the relevant geographic market.

C. Barriers to entry isolating the French market

29. In addition to the different competitive conditions prevailing in France on the one hand and the rest of the Community on the other hand, there are strong barriers to entry into the French market of bottled source water. These barriers (see recitals 30 to 34) in themselves clearly indicate that France constitutes a separate geographical market, where French suppliers are able to impose appreciable non-transitory price increases without suffering any external competitive constraint.

30. Absence of imports

In spite of the absence of tariff and legal barriers to trade, imports of bottled source water into France are negligible (between 1 and 2 % of total French consumption) and show no increasing trend. This is easily explained by the market structure prevailing in other Member States. Imports from remote areas or imports of glass bottles are practically excluded for reasons of price. It is important to remember that mineral and spring waters have to be bottled at the source and therefore can be produced only at one specific location. To the extent that there might be foreign sources located near France their transport costs might be absorbed. However, even if that were to be the case, the absence of imports is also explained by several other factors.

31. Distribution logistics

French mineral water producers generate large enough volumes to transport water by train in complete wagons. Their logistics and that of most of their main customers are adapted to this competitive type of transport. Even companies located near France (such as Spa) would suffer a transport cost disadvantage to export to France, since they would have to either transport by truck or develop the necessary logistics and generate sufficient volume to take advantage of transport by train.

32. Access to distribution

The French market is a mature market in terms of the number of brands and range of products. According to industry sources, access to the French retail market with a new source water brand additional to the well-established national brands is difficult; only brands with an established name can reasonably expect to survive in the medium to long term, rendering entry into the market a high-risk strategy. In addition, water shelf space in retail stores is necessarily limited, and it might in certain cases prove difficult to replace an existing brand.

33. Advertising (sunk) costs

The French water market is characteried by the predominance of brands. The combined advertising budget of the three national French suppliers—Nestle, Perrier and BSN—amounted to over FF 680 million in 1991. Heavy advertising by the three established suppliers has existed for several years. The establishment of a new brand would require heavy investment and could take a long time. In addition, the multiplicity of existing brands makes the establishment of a new one more difficult (access to the media at the appropiate moment) and involves a high level of risk, in particular in view of the national image attached to brands belonging to Nestle, Perrier and BNS.

34. Additional barriers to entry

The high degree of concentration in the French source water market, with three companies holding 82 % of the market share by value, constitutes an additional barrier to entry and increases the risks associated with new entry (see recital 98).

The apparent failure of past attempts to enter the French market, together with the absence of imports confirms the actual economic impact of the barriers mentioned above. According to Perrier, there were 15 attempts at entry during the last five years. Only four are still present in the French market: Ferrarelle, which belongs to BSN, San Pellegrino, where Perrier holds a 20 % stake and has three of the nine members of the board of management, and Apollinaris and San Benedetto, which remain insignificant in terms of sales. According to food distributors' sources, while certain brands might enjoy an initial acceptance by the French consumer, consumers in general return to the well-known national brands in the short or medium term. The fact that the Belgian company Spadel directs its export effort to the UK rather than to France, in spite of the geographical situation of its source, further shows to the difficulties of penetrating the French market.

Similarly in *Kali und Salz/MDK/Treuhand*[256] the Commission found that there were two relevant geographical potash markets. There was one market for Germany alone and another for the Community apart from Germany. The reasons for concluding that Germany constituted a separate market hinged on both historical factors (consumers had long-established supply relationships with German suppliers) and other factors (such as the relatively high transport cost within Germany).

In some cases, however, the Commission will take account of the fact that barriers to entry into national markets are likely to be broken down in view of Community initiatives. Thus in *Alcatel/Telettra*[257] the Commission permitted Alcatel to acquire a controlling interest in Telettra even though the concentration would lead to the acquisition of an aggregate market of 80 per cent of the Spanish market in the supply of microwave and line transmissions. The Commission took into account the fact that it was, at that time, taking steps to liberalize the telecommunications equipment market throughout the Community. This meant that in due course the Spanish monopsonistic purchaser, Telefonica, would be able to purchase products from both local and foreign sources.

C. A DOMINANT POSITION—HORIZONTAL MERGERS

According to the Court's case law it is the merged entities' ability to act independently and free of competitive constraint on the relevant market which is critical to a determination of dominance. In Chapter 6 it was seen that a number of factors are crucial in the assessment of dominance: the market share that will be acquired; the size of this share and the market power of the undertaking relative to that of the other competitors; and barriers to entry into the market (or other factors indicating dominance). Where the parties acquire a large share of the market it will be vital to know whether or not that undertaking will be able to exploit that position or whether any such attempt would cause potential competitors to enter the market.

In Chapter 6 the assessment of both the Commission's decisions and the judgments of the ECJ made in relation to Article 82 showed that those institutions have been criticized in many cases for placing, in their assessment of whether or not an undertaking holds a dominant position, too much emphasis on the market shares of the undertaking involved. High market shares are almost equated with dominance.[258] The ECJ has held on several occasions that high market shares are, save in exceptional circumstances, evidence of a dominant position.[259] Further, in *AKZO* the ECJ held that 50 per cent of the market was sufficient to constitute a high market share for these purposes.[260]

Although the higher the market share the closer the scrutiny a concentration is likely to receive, the Commission appears, in its merger decisions, to adopt a more realistic approach.

---

[256] Case IV/M308 [1994] OJ L186/30, [1994] 4 CMLR 526; on appeal Cases C–68/94 and C–30/95, *France v. Commission, Société Commerciale des Potasses et de l'Azote (SCPA) v. Commission* [1998] ECR I–1375, [1998] 4 CMLR 829.

[257] Case IV/M42 [1991] OJ L122/48, [1991] 4 CMLR 778.

[258] This approach fails to take sufficient account of the fact that market shares reveal little or nothing about market power. An undertaking may have high market shares because it is the most efficient producer or because it is dominant in the market.

[259] Case 85/76, *Hoffmann-la Roche & Co AG v. Commission* [1979] ECR 461, [1979] 3 CMLR 211.

[260] Case C–62/86, *AKZO Chemie BV v. Commission* [1991] ECR I–3359, [1993] 5 CMLR 215.

J. Faull and A. Nikpay (eds.), *The EC Law of Competition* (Oxford University Press, 1999), 243

4–146 In the assessment the Commission weighs a number of factors such as market position, countervailing buyer power, and potential competition simultaneously against each other in reaching a conclusion on whether a dominant position is created or strengthened. In academic economics literature, methods have been suggested by means of which market power can be assessed quantitatively, for example, by estimating the residual demand elasticity of an undertaking following a concentration. The main problem is that these analyses normally require a large amount of data, and still in most cases can only be expected to give a certain indication of whether a merger significantly increase market power. While the Commission will use quantitative evidence, whenever it is available and sufficiently sound, the assessment of dominance is still, in the large majority of cases a qualitative analysis based on a mix of quantitative and qualitative evidence. The Commission will normally first assess current competition between existing competitors. If need be the Commission will subsequently analyse countervailing buyer power and potential competition.

The Commission commences by identifying the likely market shares that the parties to the concentration will acquire, and takes careful account of the effect that the concentration will have on the market (especially when contrasted with the market shares of their competitors). The Commission recognizes that in certain industries market shares may be volatile,[261] or that high market shares and potential dominance may be met by rigorous competition faced from another competitor on the market:

A market share as high as 90 per cent is, in itself, a very strong indicator of the existence of a dominant position. However, in certain rare circumstances even such a high market share may not necessarily result in dominance. In particular, if sufficient active competitors are present on the market, the company with the large market share may be prevented from acting to an appreciable extent independently of the pressure typical of a competitive market.[262]

Similarly, high market shares may be met by the countervailing exercise of market power of a purchaser from the merged entity. This power may be sufficient to counteract any otherwise anticipated anti-competitive effects of a merger. In *Enso/Stora*,[263] for example, the Commission considered that even though the parties would acquire a market share of 60 per cent in the market for liquid packaging board they would not acquire a dominant position since they would face a very concentrated buying situation. In particular, Tetra Pak purchased 60 per cent of the packaging board and would be likely to set up an alternative source of supply if the new entity sought to exploit its position of market power.

Countervailing purchaser power was also relevant in *Alcatel/Telettra*.[264] In this case the

---

[261] In Case IV/M354, *American Cyanamid/Shell* [1993] OJ C273/6 the Commission considered that 'an analysis focusing on market shares alone is not particularly probative in a dynamic and R&D-intensive industry'.

[262] Case IV/M68, *Tetra Pak/Alfa Laval* [1991] OJ L290/35, 38–9 [1992] 4 CMLR M81. Case IV/M12, *Varta/Bosch* [1991] OJ L320/26, [1992] 5 CMLR M1 the merged entity held 44% of the German battery market. However, a competitor, with only 5–10% of the market would provide strong competition on account of its reputation and resources. Similarly, in Case IV/M4, *Renault/Volvo* [1990] OJ C281/2 Renault would acquire 54% of the French market. Although Mercedes only had 18%, it had the reputation and resources to be able to exercise sufficient competitive restraint on Renault. However, some competitors may not provide effective competition and may be unlikely to do so in the future: Case IV/M190, *Nestlé/Perrier*. [1992] OJ L356/1.

[263] Case IV/M1225, not published.

[264] Case IV/M42 [1991] OJ L122/48, [1991] 4 CMLR 778.

Commission cleared a merger which gave the parties market shares of 83 per cent. The Commission considered that two main factors meant that the concentration would not be enabled to impede competition in the common market. Telefonica, the only purchaser, would be able to exert a downward pressure on prices.[265] Further, the Commission's initiative to erode barriers to cross-border trade in this sphere meant that Telefonica would seek products elsewhere if the concentration sought to charge excessive prices (high market shares in a market are unlikely to be significant in an opening market).

The Commission recognizes therefore that if no barriers to entry exist large market shares do not in themselves create a problem. If the parties can establish evidence of entry and exit into the market, the Commission may accept that new entry will occur if the merged enterprise seeks to earn monopoly profits.[266] Clear evidence that a position of market strength will only be temporary and will be quickly eroded because of a high probability of strong market entry should similarly lead to a finding that the concentration is compatible with the common market.[267] An appraisal of the relevant market will, therefore, normally be necessary to determine whether factors such as advertising, economies of scale, intellectual property rights, brand image, or national regulations and buying preferences operate as barriers to entry.[268] The Commission has even taken account of competition from manufacturers operating outside the geographic market in support of a conclusion that the constraining competition from these manufacturers meant that the proposed concentration would not strengthen or create a collective dominant position.[269]

In looking at barriers to entry and the possibility of potential competition it seems that the Commission considers only potential competitors which are likely to enter the market within a relatively short time-frame.

J. Faull and A. Nikpay (eds.), *The EC Law of Competition* (Oxford University Press, 1999), 245–6

4.153 The assessment of whether potential competition is a constraining force on companies in a given market relies basically on the assessment of entry barriers for the likely potential entrants. If entry barriers are low and consequently entry is easy and rapid then, normally, potential competition would be considered in the assessment of the degree of effective competition in a market. On the other hand, if entry barriers are high, and consequently entering the market will be difficult and slow, then potential competition would not be considered as a source of competition.

4.154 The assessment of potential competition depends on the specific case. However, the Commission has normally only accepted taking potential competition into account, if potential competitors could enter the market within one year. . . In *Boeing/McDonnell-Douglas* it was in particular noted that research and development costs for a new large get aeroplane amounted to some US $10 billion and production involved large-scale advantages in the form of learning curve effects. Finally, in

---

[265] See also Case IV/M4, *Renault/Volvo* [1990] OJ C281/2 where the Commission found that large fleet buyers would exercise downward pressure on truck and bus prices.

[266] Case IV/M42, *Alcatel/Telettra* [1991] OJ L122/48, [1991] 4 CMLR 778.

[267] See, e.g., Case IV/M477, *Mercedes-Benz/Kässbohrer* [1995] OJ L211/1, [1995] 4 CMLR 600; cf. Case IV/M774, *Saint Gobain/Wacker-Chemie/NOM* [1997] OJ L247/1, [1997] 4 CMLR 25.

[268] Whether or not something amounts to a barrier to entry will, of course, have to be analysed in the context of each relevant market; for a greater discussion of barriers see *supra* Chaps. 1 and 6.

[269] Case IV/M315, *Mannesmann/Vallourec/Ilva* [1994] OJ L102/15. For a possible explanation of this conclusion see *infra* 799–801.

Kesko/Tuko, . . . it was even concluded that the merger led to an increase in entry barriers (and consequently a decrease in potential competition.

4.155 Entry barriers vary from market to market and can take numerous forms such as regulatory barriers, for example, concerning packaging, or purely economic barriers, such as the need to build brands requiring heavy advertising expenditures, access to distribution, access to technology, or high research and development costs. In its assessment of entry barriers the Commission has attached importance to the existence of sunk costs. . . A typical example has been the case where it was necessary to build a brand in order to compete in a market; such brand building required heavy advertising expenditure. These expenditures would be sunk costs and would therefore increase the risk of entering a market. . . The impact of sunk costs as an entry barrier could be even higher in cases where the market leader already has high market shares, since the market leader may be able to increase further its advertising expenditures and thereby raise entry barriers for potential entrants.

In *Aérospatiale/Alenia/de Havilland* the Commission considered existing competition, countervailing purchasing power, and barriers to entry on the market. It found that the concentration would lead to the parties acquiring very large shares on the forty to fifty-nine seat market (about 64 per cent worldwide and about 72 per cent Community-wide) and on the overall commuter market generally (approximately 50 per cent worldwide and 65 per cent Community-wide). However, before concluding that the concentration was incompatible with the common market, the Commission took account of the relative strength of the competitors (which was weak) and the bargaining ability of the customers (which was limited). Further, it looked at other structural factors. In its view the general trend towards larger aircraft meant that the parties' position would be stronger than that reflected in the market shares. The parties would therefore acquire a dominant position in the commuter markets of forty seats and over and on the overall market of aircraft of twenty to seventy seats.

In addition the Commission went on to consider the likelihood of new entry into the market. It stated that 'a concentration which leads to the creation of a dominant position may, however, be compatible with the common market . . . if there exists strong evidence that this position is only temporary and would be quickly eroded because of high probability of strong market entry. With such market entry the dominant position is not likely to significantly impede effective competition . . . In order to assess whether the dominant position of ATR/de Havilland is likely to significantly impede effective competition therefore, it is necessary to assess the likelihood of new entry into the market.'[270] On the facts it considered that new entry was likely to occur only after a period of time. Similarly, it attached importance to the fact that the risk of entering the market was extremely high, in particular because of the high sunk costs involved.

Case IV/M53, *Aérospatiale-Alenia/de Havilland* [1991] OJ L334/42, [1992] 4 CMLR M2

Commission

54. Any theoretical attractiveness of entry into the commuter market by a new player must be put into perspective taking into account the forecast demand and the time and cost considerations to enter the market.

Based on the parties' figures, the overall market potential for 20 to 70-seat commuter aircraft over the next 20 years is estimated at around • units, including the backlog of around 700 units. It is

[270] Case IV/M53 [1991] OJ L334/42, [1992] 4 CMLR M2, para. 53.

expected that the current level of demand will be maintained only until the mid-1990s, and thereafter decline and stabilise. The average annual level of demand from the mid-1990s onwards could then be estimated at around • units compared to the current rate of some • units.

It follows that in terms of increase in annual deliveries the market appears to have therefore already reached maturity.

55. Even for a company currently active in a related industry not already present on the commuter market—in practice this would seem to be limited to large jet aircraft manufacturers—it would be very expensive to develop a new commuter from scratch. According to the study submitted buy the parties, there are high sunk initial costs of entering the regional aircraft market and delays in designing, testing and gaining regulatory approval to sell the aircraft. These are important for several reasons. The critical point is that with substantial fixed and sunk costs of entering the industry, these markets will be viable only for a limited number of producers. Furthermore, once a manufacturer is committed to the design and production of an aircraft, it is extremely costly and lengthy to adjust that design and production to unanticipated changes in market demand for aircraft. Critical design features of the aircraft include its size, weight, engine specifications with attendant pay-load, fuel efficiency and distance capacity. The magnitude of the initial sunk development costs of the aircraft constitutes a significant risk associated with commitment to a particular aircraft. If the manufacturers errs in design, these initial costs are not recoverable.

In terms of time, the study states that it takes approximately two to three years of marketing research to determine which plane is required to meet the anticipated needs of the market. This involves forecasting changes in aircraft technology as well as forecasting the evolving nature of the market. From the point of initial research and development to the point of producing and delivering aircraft, an additional four years would likely elapse. The total time lag involved is of the order of six to seven years. This does not include any time required to construct or acquire plant facilities necessary for aircraft construction.

The study concludes that there is no doubt that the presence of substantial and fixed entry costs significantly reduces the entry response by others to any successful aircraft by one manufacturer.

56. It follows from the above that a new entrant into the market would face high risk. Furthermore, given the time necessary to develop a new aircraft and the foreseeable development of the market as described above, a new manufacturer may come too late into the market to catch the expected period of relatively high demand. Any new market entry at this stage could only come when the market would have declined from current levels and have stabilised. It is therefore doubtful whether a break-even level of sales could be achieved by a new entrant since even existing competitors are not yet at break-even point in their product cycles.

57. For these reasons it is considered that it would not be rational to now enter the commuter aircraft market. This is accepted by the parties. The parties argue however that some newly industrialised countries would decide nonetheless to support the development of a local commuter industry. Even if some time in the future such a local commuter industry were established in the way the parties suggest, it is considered unlikely that significant inroads into the international markets could occur in this way. Such an uncertain possibility would not in any case be sufficient to justify a conclusion that the dominant position of ATR/de Havilland is only temporary.

As to market entry in the foreseeable future, furthermore, there is no known development programme by a company not yet on the market other than as assessed below. All competitors contacted considered that it is not probable that there will be another entrant into the market because, given the current structure of the market, the level of development costs is out of all proportion to any possible return.

In 1994 Ridyard summarized the reasons for this decision and the pattern he considered to be emerging from the Commission's merger decisions.

D. Ridyard, 'Economic Analysis of Single Firm and Oligopolistic Dominance' [1994] ECLR 255, 256–7

The main features that appear to have led the Commission to its finding of incompatibiltiy in the *ATR/de Havilland* are the gap between the post-merger firm and its nearest competitor (Saab, whose share was some 19 per cent, would have been less than half the size of the combined group), the high sunk costs required for entry and the maturity of the market. Together, these factors combined to increase the risks and reduce the likelihood of new entry into the market, and the Commission also concluded that the scale and product range benefits that would have been enjoyed by the merged group increased the scope for anti-competitive exclusionary behaviour against existing competitors.
. . .

Cases where high shares have been declared compatible

The pattern to emerge from *ATR/de Havilland* and *Du Pont/ICI* is one of single firm dominance being concerned principally with the existence of a gap in size and industrial capability between the post-merger firm and its nearest rivals. The impression that this is the key to the Commission's idea of dominance is further strengthened by looking at some of the cases where high market shares have been declared compatible with the Common Market. . . .

   These decisions highlight the extent to which the Commission has relied on the industrial capabilities of the rivals to the post-merger firm . . .

d. VERTICAL MERGERS

Although concentrations with vertical effects on the market are rarer and of less concern than those with horizontal effects,[271] the Commission does of course consider the detrimental effects which may result from vertical integration. The key concern is foreclosure, and in *Skanska/Scancem*,[272] for example, the Commission declared as incompatible with the common market the acquisition by Skanska, a Swedish construction company, of Scancem, a Swedish buildings materials group. In particular, Scancem had 90 per cent of the Swedish market for the supply of cement. The Commission was worried about the loss of competition which would result from the acquisition. Not only would Skanska be unlikely to search for alternative supplies of cement outside the Swedish market, but it would have a clear advantage over Scancem's customers which were also its competitors. Since the concentration had been completed prior to notification, Skanska was required to divest itself of its shareholding in Scancem.

   The Commission has not ordinarily been concerned with vertical mergers which have no foreclosure effects.[273]

---

[271] *Supra* 704–705.
[272] Case IV/M1157 [1999] OJ L183/10.
[273] J. Faull and A. Nikpay (eds.), *The EC Law of Competition* (Oxford University Press, 1999), para. 4.157.

e. CONGLOMERATE MERGERS AND PORTFOLIO POWER

At first sight it seems hard to see how a conglomerate merger between undertakings which do not operate on the same relevant market or on upstream or downstream markets may lead to the creation or strengthening of a dominant position. In a number of decisions, however, the Commission indicated that an increase in 'portfolio power' may lead to the creation or strengthening of a dominant position.[274] Although the meaning and extent of the concept are still uncertain it introduces the possibility that a concentration which does not have either a horizontal or vertical effect may be prohibited.

In *Guinness/Grand Metropolitan*,[275] for example, the concentration had an impact on certain separate spirits markets. Although there was some horizontal overlap in the relevant markets in which the parties operated, the merger also led to an extension of the complementary products and range of spirits offered. The Commission permitted the merger only once the parties agreed to end its distribution arrangements for Bacardi rum in Greece even though the merger did not increase the parties' market shares on this market.

The Commission's decision in *Guinness/Grand Metropolitan* has been criticized not for its adoption of the concept of portfolio power but for failing to identify with sufficient clarity what is wrong with an undertaking's acquisition of a wider portfolio of products. For example, some paragraphs of the Commission's decision indicate that the Commission objected to the economies of scale and scope offered to the parties from the increased range of products that the merger allowed.[276] Such benefits would, however, not harm but benefit consumers and intervention on these grounds would give the Commission a broad discretion. An objection to portfolio power on the ground that it would give the merged entity greater power to tie products would be less controversial.[277]

The following extract explains portfolio power and some of the potential problems that may arise from the Commission's failure to set out adequately and with sufficient clarity its concerns about portfolio power:

S. Bishop and M. Walker, *The Economics of EC Competition Law: Concepts, Application and Measurement* (Sweet & Maxwell, 1999), 159–60

6.41 ... The issue of portfolio power arises in those mergers where customers (usually, large retailers) typically purchase a range of the affected products. The underlying principle in the application of the concept of portfolio power is that the market power which can be derived from a range of products in separate markets is greater than the sum of its parts. In other words, being present in each of five separate relevant markets gives a firm a better competitive position than being present in only one.

---

[274] See Case IV/M833, *The Coca-Cola Company/Carlsberg A/S* [1998] OJ L145/41; Case IV/M938, *Guinness/Grand Metropolitan* [1998] OJ L288/24.

[275] Case IV/M938 [1998] OJ L288/24.

[276] [1998] OJ L288/24, para. 40.

[277] In Chap. 7 it was seen that an undertaking may be able to use its dominant position to tie other products to its sales in the dominated market.

6.42 To examine the logic of these arguments consider the following example of a merger between Firm A and Firm B . . . Firm A operates in markets I, II and III while firm B operates in markets III, IV, and V. It is agreed that all five markets are distinct relevant markets. A single hypothetical single supplier in each of these market[s] could therefore profitably increase price. Table 6.2 provides the pre-merger market shares of the two parties and the impact post-merger.

Table 6.2 Portfolio power

	Market				
	I	II	III	IV	V
A	30	30	10	0	0
B	0	0	10	40	40
Post-merger	30	30	20	40	40

The only overlap of the merger is in market III but this gives rise to a post-merger market share of only 20 per cent. It is assumed that on the basis of a standard competition analysis, this merger does not give rise to any detrimental competitive outcomes.

Underlying the basic notion of 'portfolio power' is the idea that the market power deriving from a portfolio of brands exceeds the sum of its parts. In its general discussion of portfolio power concept in *Guinness/Grand Metropolitan*, the Commission states that the holder of a wide portfolio of products will:

'. . . have greater flexibility to structure his prices, promotions and discounts, he will have greater potential for tying, and he will be able to realise economies of scale and scope in his sales and marketing activities. Finally, the implicit (or explicit) threat of refusal to supply is more potent.' [[1998] OJ L288/ 24, paragraph 40]

It is important to distinguish those concerns of the Commission which have no sound economic basis from those which may enjoy economic support. The Commission's *Guinness/Grand Metropolitan* decision is troubling for a number of reasons. It is difficult to see how 'portfolio power' that arises via the realisation of economies of scale and scope can be considered to be anti-competitive, particularly if the costs of other suppliers are unaffected. Similar arguments can apply to the Commission's concern that the combined entity might provide a more convenient service to some consumers.

But this does not necessarily imply that there are no potential concerns. If an extended portfolio increases the scope for tying, makes more potent the threat to refuse to deal, and consequently increases the ability to secure promotional support for secondary brands, then 'portfolio power' cannot be summarily dismissed. Such concerns are similar to the so-called post-Chicago theories on vertical restraints, whereby firms with market power can use that power to foreclose market access and raise rivals' costs or dampen competition.

6.43 However, if the only economically defensible manifestation of 'portfolio power' is closely associated with tying, a more focused and appropriate analysis might result if it is described as tying. The introduction of a new enforcement 'buzzword' does little to advance the quality of analysis and could act as an excuse for excessive and unwarranted intervention.

Mainstream economic theory acknowledges that tying purchases of products in a potentially competitive market to products in which the tying supplier has market power can in certain circumstances foreclose the market to rivals and damage competition. Distilling that theory into a practical and robust policy framework, however, is not trivial. In particular, economic theory does not suggest that tying is always, or even nearly always, anti-competitive, and simplistic arguments that monopoly power can be automatically extended from one market to another through tying have been discredited. For these reasons, a merger that made tying more likely would not necessarily harm competition. Instead, even if it can be assumed that market power exists in some market, it is then necessary to show how the portfolio extension caused by the merger increases the seller's leverage in a way that will foreclose the market to rivals and enhance the post-merger firm's dominance.

6.44 While it is wrong to dismiss 'portfolio power' summarily as being without economic foundation, the uncritical acceptance of this concept should be resisted. Such acceptance would create an unjustified prejudice against any augmentation of the product range of multi-product firms. Economic theory suggest that the number of demonstrable cases of mergers creating 'portfolio power' with adverse effects for competition will be small.

(iii) COLLECTIVE OR JOINT DOMINANCE[278]

a. GENERAL

It has been seen in Chapter 11 that some oligopolistic markets are prone to both explicit and tacit collusion. Undertakings operating on an oligopolistic market may agree to act in their own best interest. Similarly, undertakings may recognize their interdependence and that if they compete less vigorously they may be able to enjoy higher prices and profits. Even in the absence of an agreement or other collusion between them the undertakings may therefore raise prices and the same or a similar outcome as if they had explicitly colluded may arise. The undertakings may behave 'as if' they have colluded, with the consequent adverse impact on efficiency and consumer welfare as a whole.

A difficult problem for competition authorities is how they should control the behaviour of undertakings operating on such a market. Since they have not actually colluded or concerted Article 81(1) does not prohibit the tacit co-ordination engaged in by the undertakings on the market. The Commission has, consequently, sought to develop Article 82 so that it may prohibit the abuse of a dominant position held collectively by one or more undertakings. However, Article 82 provides less than an ideal tool for controlling the behaviour of undertakings operating on an oligopolistic market.[279] Given this lacuna the question whether the Merger Regulation can be utilized to prevent mergers which lead to the creation or strengthening of a collective dominant position has assumed great importance. If a vigorous preventive merger control policy is adopted, then, of course, there will be less need for later control of a corrective nature.

S. Bishop and M. Walker, *The Economics of EC Competition Law: Concepts, Application and Measurement* (Sweet & Maxwell, 1999), 149–50

Oligopolistic Dominance

6.21 Horizontal mergers may also lead to a reduction in effective competition if the structural change caused by the merger creates conditions more favourable to co-ordinated behaviour between

---

[278] The terms collective, joint, and oligopolistic dominance are used interchangeably. See generally on this subject R. Whish, 'Collective Dominance' in D. O'Keefe and M. Andenas (eds.), *Liber Amicorum for Lord Slynn* (Kluwer, Deventer, 2000), i.

[279] See *supra* Chap. 11.

the remaining firms competing in the relevant market. This source of competitive concern is known as oligopolistic dominance. It has been argued that the indirect effect of an increase in concentration on the form of competition post-merger may be a more significant factor than the direct effects of concentration and indeed it is arguable that this effect is still the primary focus of the DoJ/FTC Merger Guidelines.

The increased prices which follow a shift to a more collusive market environment are termed co-ordinated effects because they result not from the actions of individual firms but rather from the realisation amongst all firms that the returns to co-ordinated behaviour are greater. Unlike unilateral effects, co-ordinated effects rely on other firms as well as the merged firm modifying their behaviour following the merger.

Example of co-ordinated effects

6.22 Suppose that there are currently four firms in an industry. They each have one manufacturing plant. They each sell 100 units at a price of 1. Fixed costs are 40 and unit costs are 0.6. This implies that total industry output is 400 and each firm make zero profits. Each plant is operating at full capacity. Now suppose that two of the firms merge and that this allows the three remaining firms to move from a position of effective competition to one of tacit collusion. This might allow the firms to reduce output profitability to only 80 per manufacturing plant and to raise prices by 20 per cent. In this case, each plant would now make a profit of 8 (revenues of 96 less total costs of 88). Each plant is now run at below full capacity (*i.e.* spare capacity of 20 per plant) and so each firm has an incentive to raise its output and so lower its price below the cartel price. However, if the probability of detection is very high, then the firms will prefer to collude rather than to 'cheat'.

In this hypothetical example, the key to this result was the fact that the movement from four to three firms made tacit collusion possible.

In the USA because 'the Sherman Act has turned out to be woefully inadequate instrument for going after oligopoly or other collusion-like behaviour' merger policy has taken on an important role in preventing 'the creation of markets structures that tend to facilitate Cournot or collusion-like outcomes'.[280] Similarly, it is arguable that the European Commission should act vigorously against concentrations which lead to the creation or strengthening of a collective dominant position on an oligopolistic market where a collusion-like outcome is likely. Unfortunately, the text of the Merger Regulation left it unclear whether or not the Commission is actually permitted to do so.

D. Ridyard, 'Economic Analysis of Single Firm and Oligopolistic Dominance' [1994] *ECLR* 255, 258

The oligopoly 'blind spot'

... [B]ecause the compatibility test contained in Article 2(3) of the Regulation allows the Commission to object to mergers if and only if they create or strengthen a dominant position, the most natural interpretation is that the Regulation exists to prevent single firms from achieving a position of market dominance. During the first year of the Regulation, it appeared that the Commission was indeed powerless to prevent mergers that led to high concentration but no outright market leader.

---

[280] H. Hovenkamp, *Federal Antitrust Policy: The Law of Competition and its Practice* (West Publishing Co, 1994), 447. In the USA this was, for many years, a principal concern of merger policy.

It is obvious to any experienced anti-trust observer, however, that a merger control policy that was confined strictly to this narrow objective would contain a serious blind spot when it came to mergers in highly concentrated oligopolistic markets. In the extreme case, a merger bringing together numbers two and three behind a market leader with 51 per cent of the market may add 1,200 point to a pre-merger Herfindahl-Hirxchman Index (HHI) . . . of 3,800 and still not create a dominant firm. Under the US Horizontal Mergers Guidelines, this merger would clearly fall into the high risk category . . . The same conclusion holds under German merger control, where post-merger three-firm concentration ratios in excess of 50 per cent give rise to a presumption that competition is threatened. In UK mergers policy, where the legal provisions are open-ended, there are clear instance of mergers being declared against the public interest even when they do not lead to outright dominance . . .'

The concept of collective dominance has, therefore, been central to the debate not only about the scope of Article 82 but also about the scope and effectiveness of the Merger Regulation. It was only in 1998 that the ECJ finally had the opportunity to clarify that the Merger Regulation *can* be applied to prevent a concentration which leads to the creation or strengthening of a collective dominant position.[281]

b. COLLECTIVE DOMINANCE AND ARTICLE 82

In *Flat Glass* the CFI confirmed that Article 82 applied to a situation in which a dominant undertaking was held by two or more independent entities united together by 'economic links'.[282] The case law and Commission practice in the context of Article 82, however, did little to clarify what the Court meant when it stated that the undertakings had to be united by economic links.[283] It was uncertain whether or not the concept of collective dominance was intended to be confined to independent undertakings united together by some contractual or other structural (such as cross-shareholdings) arrangements or whether it intended to refer also to independent undertakings united only by the structure of the market.

In the context of the Merger Regulation it has also become important to know whether or not that Regulation applics to concentrations which lead to the creation or strengthening of a collective dominant position, and, if so, whether or not the concept of collective dominance will be developed in the same way as it has in the context of Article 82 and, if so, whether it will apply only to undertakings which are united together by structural links. It has taken a number of years of application of the Merger Regulation for these questions to be answered.

c. COLLECTIVE DOMINANCE AND THE MERGER REGULATION

In contrast to the position under Article 82 the text of the Merger Regulation lends no support for the view that it should apply to concentrations which lead to the creation or strengthening of a collective dominant position. It simply refers to concentrations which lead to the creation or strengthening of *a* dominant position. The main reason for doubting the ability of the Merger Regulation to apply to such concentrations thus hinged on the wording of the Regulation itself. If it was intended that the Regulation should apply to

---

[281] See discussion of Cases C–68/94 and C–30/95 *France* v. *Commission, Société Commerciale des Potasses et de l'Azote (SCPA)* v. *Commission* [1998] ECR I–1375, [1998] 4 CMLR 829, *infra* 773–779.

[282] See *supra* Chap. 11.

[283] But see Cases C–395–396/96P *Compagnie Maritime Belge* v. *Commission* [2000] 4 CMLR 1076, *supra* Chap. 11.

prevent the creation or strengthening of a collective dominant position or a dominant position held by one or more independent undertakings why was this not spelt out in the legislation?[284]

The lack of textual support did not deter the Commission from its view that the Merger Regulation authorized it to act against concentrations which led to the creation or strengthening of a collective dominant position. The Commission proceeded as a matter of expediency, recognizing that a system of merger control which did not allow it to prevent concentration, or the further concentration of an industry, would be seriously flawed. If concentrations could be conducted which would result in highly concentrated markets, ripe for explicit or tacit collusion, there would be a serious gap in its ability effectively to apply a coherent system of antitrust enforcement.[285] Although wary of the difficulties of proof that would be involved in establishing that, as a result of the collective dominant position, effective competition could not be expected[286] the Commission thus took the view that the Merger Regulation did operate to prevent the creation or strengthening of a collective dominant position.[287]

Nestlé/Perrier was the first case in which the Commission took commitments as condition for clearing a concentration (between Nestlé and Perrier) which it considered would 'create a duopolistic dominant position which would significantly impede effective competition position on the French bottled water market'.[288]

---

[284] Recital 15 of the Merger Reg. makes little sense if it applies to collective dominance. The recital indicates that concentrations are not liable to impede effective competition and may be presumed to be compatible with the common market where the market share of the undertakings concerned does not exceed 25% either in the common market or a substantial part of it. See the arguments raised in Case T–102/96 *Gencor Ltd* v. *Commission* [1999] ECR II–753 [1999] 4 CMLR 971, report for the hearing, paras 110–127.

[285] See Commission's *XVI Report on Competition Policy* (Commission, 1986), 285 and discussion *supra* at 769–771.

[286] It cannot simply be assumed that an oligopolistic market will not operate competitively: Case IV/M165, *Alcatel/AEG Kabel* [1992] OJ C6/23 and *infra* 781 ff. In contrast, in Germany, for example, there is a presumption that competition is threatened by collective dominance if the three largest firms have a combined market share of at least 50% or if the top five have a combined share of two-thirds of the market: § 22(3) of the Gesetz gegen Wettbewerbsbeschrankungen (GWB, the German law against restrictions on competition).

[287] It first introduced the concept in Case IV/M165, *Alcatel/AEG Kabel* [1992] OJ C6/23 but nonetheless cleared the merger.

[288] Given the insufficient competitive counterweight from local mineral and spring waters, the increased dependency of retailers and wholesalers on the portfolio of brands of Nestlé and BSN, the absence of effective price-constraining potential competition from newcomers, [1992] OJ L356/1, para. 108. Nestlé and Perrier between them held 60% of the French bottled water market whilst another undertaking, BSN, had 22% of the market. The remainder of the market was shared by a number of much smaller companies. In support of its conclusion on dominance, the Commission relied on the fact that price competition on the market was already weak, the price of bottled water was relatively inelastic, that the reduction from three to two suppliers would make anti-competitive competitive parallel behaviour leading to collective abuses much easier, the mineral water suppliers in France had developed instruments of transparency which facilitated a tacit co-ordination of pricing policies and that the reciprocal dependence of Nestlé and BSN would create a strong common interest and incentive to maximise profits by engaging in anti-competitive parallel behaviour. '[A]ny competitive action by one would have a direct and significant impact on the activity of the other supplier and most certainly provoke strong reactions with the result that such action could considerably harm both suppliers in their profitability without improving their sales volumes. Their reciprocal dependency thus creates a strong common interest and incentive to maximise profits by engaging in anti-competitive parallel behaviour.'

In a number of subsequent cases the Commission launched Phase II investigations into concentrations which it believed would lead to the creation or strengthening of a collective dominant position.[289] It thus continually reiterated its view that it has the right to challenge collective as well as single dominance in merger cases (although it did not, in any of these cases, actually preclude the merger[290]). The Commission's decision in *Kali und Salz/MdK/ Treuhand*,[291] however, led to an appeal by third parties on the question whether or not the Merger Regulation applied to such cases. In that case the Commission had found that the concentration created or led to the creation of a market-leading duopoly on the Community (except Germany) market for potash. Two entities would enjoy a dominant position: Kali und Salz (K+S)/MdK (the merging parties) and Société Commerciale des Potasses et de l'Azote (SCPA). The Court of Justice summarised the findings of the Commission in particular that:

— the potash market is a mature market characterised by a largely homogeneous product and the lack of technical innovation . . .;

— the market circumstances are very transparent, so that information on production, demand, sales and prices is generally available . . .;

— exceptionally close links have existed for a long time between K+S and SCPA, which might in themselves suggest that there is no effective competition between those undertakings which, moreover, account for about 53% of the Community market apart from Germany, calculated on the basis of sales, including not only sales from K+S and SCPA's own production but also by SCPA of potash imported directly from non-member countries, which has to be channelled through SPCA, thus giving it control over supplies from outside the Community . . .;

— despite over-production in Germany, there is still only a small flow of potash supplies from K+S to France which is not channelled through SCPA, France being by far the largest potash-consuming State in the Community . . .;

— K+S and MdK, which will form a joint undertaking following the concentration, and SCPA account for 5%, 25% and 20% respectively of total potash production in the Community . . .;

— MdK is the second largest potash producer in the Community, even though utilisation of the undertaking's capacity is currently only around 50% . . .;

— following the concentration, the K+S/MdK and SCPA grouping will hold a total market share, calculated on the basis of sales, of about 60% . . .;

— supply outside the grouping is fragmented . . .;

— the other producers do not have the sales base necessary to survive on the market against a K+S/MdK and SCPA duopoly . . .'[292]

To prevent the Commission from declaring that the concentration between K+S and MdK was incompatible with the common market, the parties offered the Commission certain

---

[289] See, e.g. Case IV/M358, *Pilkington/SIV* [1994] OJ L158/24, [1994] 4 CMLR 405 and Case IV/M315, *Mannesmann/Vallourec/Ilva* [1994] OJ L102/15, [1994] 4 CMLR 529.

[290] As a result no appeal was immediately forthcoming before the ECJ.

[291] Case IV/M308 [1994] OJ L186/30; on appeal Cases C–68/94 and C–30/95 *France* v. *Commission, Société Commerciale des Potasses et de l'Azote (SCPA)* v. *Commission* [1998] ECR I–1375, [1998] 4 CMLR 829.

[292] Cases C–68/94 and C–30/95, *France* v. *Commission, Société Commerciale des Potasses et de l'Azote (SCPA)* v. *Commission* [1998] ECR I–1375, [1998] 4 CMLR 829, para. 219.

commitments. Those commitments affected not only the parties to the concentration, but also SCPA. Their aim was broadly to bring to an end to the co-operation between K+S/MdK and SCPA. For example, the parties to the concentration agreed to withdraw from an export company in which SCPA was a shareholder and to terminate co-operation with SCPA as a distribution partner in the French market. The Commission was satisfied by this offer to sever links between the duopolistic parties. It was partly as a result of these conditions imposed and conditions offered that the affected third party, SCPA, EMC (its parent company), and France brought actions for annulment, or partial annulment of the Commission's decision under Article 230 (then Article 173) of the Treaty. Because one of the appellants was a Member State the appeal was brought straight before the ECJ.[293] The appellants considered that the Commission had made an incorrect assessment of the effect of the concentration on the Community market apart from Germany. In addition, they disputed the applicability of the Regulation to collective dominant positions. There was no textual or historical justification for such a finding. On the contrary, certain aspects of the Merger Regulation would be inconsistent with such a ruling. In particular, the Regulation provided no procedural safeguards for a third party, such as SCPA, which might be (and was in this case) affected by the procedure. Although third parties *could* be heard under the Regulation there was no obligation upon the Commission to do so. The arguments of the parties are summarized in the following extract from the Court's judgment:

Cases C–68/94 and C–30/95, *France* v. *Commission, Société Commerciale des Potasses et de l'Azote* v. *Commission* [1998] ECR I–1375, [1998] 4 CMLR 829

Court of Justice

2. Applicability of the Regulation to collective dominant positions

152. The French Government and the applicant companies submit that the Regulation does not authorise the Commission to apply it in cases where there is a collective dominant position. On this point, they observe that the wording of the Regulation, in particular Article 2 thereof, unlike Article [82] of the EC Treaty does not expressly refer to collective dominant positions. Whereas Article [82] of the Treaty prohibits 'abuse by one or more undertakings of a dominant position', Article 2 of the Regulation regards as compatible with the common market concentrations which do not create or strengthen an anticompetitive dominant position, and as incompatible those which do.

153. Moreover, the legal bases of the Regulation do not justify the interpretation adopted by the Commission. It is not a measure for the application of Article [82] of the Treaty. According to the French Government, the Regulation is based primarily on Article [308] of the EC Treaty, and while it is also based on Article [84] of the Treaty, which empowers the Council to adopt appropriate regulations or directives to give effect to the principles set out in Articles [81] and [82], that is precisely because, although the Court had decided that Article [82] may be used to control certain concentrations (Case 6/72 *Europemballage and Continental Can* v. *Commission* [1973] ECR 215),

---

[293] Case IV/M308 [1994] OJ C199/5. Appeals by private parties are usually heard before the CFI. However, procedures by Member States are heard before the ECJ. In view of the fact that the cases before the ECJ and the CFI called into question the validity of the same action, the CFI declined jurisdiction over the *SCPA* case in order to enable the ECJ to rule on the application for annulment.

it reduces the scope thereof, by providing in particular in Article 22(1) that 'this Regulation alone shall apply to concentrations as defined in Article 3'.

154. Furthermore, there is nothing in the legislative history of the Regulation to support the view that the legislature intended it also to cover collective dominant positions. To accept that such positions are covered by the Regulation would amount to adopting a very wide and, above all, very uncertain scope for prohibitions or conditional authorisations. The French Government therefore considers that if the Community legislature, one of whose essential concerns was to ensure legal certainty for undertakings, had wished to introduce that concept in the Regulation, it would have done so expressly, as in Article [82] of the Treaty.

155. EMC and SCPA submit that the interpretation of the Regulation put forward by the Commission has the effect of distorting its scheme. In support of that argument, they submit that that interpretation may lead to the Regulation being applied even where the market share of the undertakings concerned does not exceed 25% either in the common market or in a substantial part of it, contrary to the 15th recital in the preamble to the Regulation. According to that recital, an indication that concentrations are not liable to impede effective competition and may therefore be presumed to be compatible with the common market exists in particular where the market share of the undertakings concerned does not exceed 25% either in the common market or in a substantial part of it.

156. Finally, the lack of adequate procedural safeguards for third parties confirms, in the applicants' view, that the Regulation is not designed to be used as a framework for the application of the concept of a collective dominant position. Thus undertakings which are not parties to the concentration being examined under the Regulation but which in the Commission's view constitute an oligopoly together with the undertakings involved in the concentration are not at the outset given any specific information to indicate what the consequences of the procedure in progress might be for them. The French Government observes that while the Commission or the competent authorities of the Member States do indeed, under the first sentence of Article 18(4) of the Regulation, have the possibility of hearing third parties and hence, if appropriate, the representatives of undertakings not involved in the concentration, that step is not compulsory, and if it is taken, it is informal and does not offer the safeguards prescribed for hearings of parties to the concentration. Furthermore, since third parties who are regarded as sharing in a collective dominant position are not informed of the decision the Commission intends to take, by the same token they are deprived of the opportunity to make effective use of the possibility, provided for in the second sentence of Article 18(4) of the Regulation, of applying to be heard.

A momentary blow to the Commission's view that the Merger Regulation prohibits the creation or strengthening of a collective dominant position was dealt on the delivery of the Opinion of the Advocate General in this case. Advocate General Tesauro expressed the view that the Merger Regulation did not entitle the Commission to take collective dominance or oligopolistic dominance into account in its application of Article 2. However, this aspect of the Advocate-General's opinion was not followed by the ECJ which confirmed that the Regulation did apply to collective dominant positions.

d. THE JUDGMENTS IN *FRANCE* V. *COMMISSION* AND *GENCOR LTD* V. *COMMISSION*

In *France* v. *Commission, Société Commerciale des Potasses et de l'Azote (SCPA)* v. *Commission*[294] the Court annulled the Commission's decision on the facts, finding that the

---

[294] Cases C–68/94 and C–30/95, *France v. Commission, Société Commerciale des Potasses et de l'Azote (SCPA) v. Commission* [1998] ECR I–1375, [1998] 4 CMLR 829.

Commission had not established that the concentration would in fact give rise to a collective dominant position on the market.[295] Nonetheless, the judgment is of enormous significance since the ECJ held, applying an interpretation of the Regulation in accordance with 'its purpose and general structure', that 'collective dominant positions do not fall outside the scope of the Regulation'.[296] A concentration which creates or strengthens a dominant position on the part of the parties concerned with an entity not involved in the concentration may be declared incompatible with the common market.

In upholding a broad view of the Merger Regulation the Court adopted, in its construction, a teleological approach adopting a view which best reflected the Community's aims and objectives. The Court considered that a textual and historical examination of the Regulation was not conclusive on the question but that it was necessary to interpret the Regulation with reference to its purpose and general structure. In particular, since the Regulation was intended to apply to all concentrations in so far as they were likely to prove incompatible with the system of undistorted competition envisaged by the Treaty, it was essential that concentrations which created or strengthened a dominant position on the part of parties concerned with an entity not involved in the concentration be prohibited by the Regulation. Conversely, a narrow interpretation of the Regulation would have meant that competition in the common market could be distorted and that the Regulation would be deprived of much of its effect. Neither the lack of procedural safeguards for third parties nor the argument based on the fifteenth recital, setting out a presumption that concentrations would be compatible with the common market if the undertakings concerned had a combined market share of less than 25 per cent, could cast doubt on the applicability of the regulation to cases of a collective dominant position. In particular, Community law required, irrespective of the provisions in the Regulation, that an individual whose interests would be adversely affected by proceedings had a right to be heard.

Cases C–68/94 and C–30/95, *France* v. *Commission, Société Commerciale des Potasses et de l'Azote* v. *Commission* [1998] ECR I–1375, [1998] 4 CMLR 829

Court of Justice

165. The Court finds, first of all, that the applicants' submission, to the effect that the choice of legal bases in itself militates in favour of the argument that the Regulation does not apply to collective dominant positions, cannot be accepted. As the Advocate General observes in point 83 of the Opinion, Articles [84] and [308] of the Treaty can in principle be used as the legal bases of a regulation permitting preventive action with respect to concentrations which create or strengthen a collective dominant position liable to have a significant effect on competition.

166. Second, it cannot be deduced from the wording of Article 2 of the Regulation that only

---

[295] This was the first case in which the ECJ annulled a Commission decision under the Merger Reg. Following the annulment, the Commission re-examined the concentration and cleared it following a Phase I investigation: see N. Hacker, 'The Kali+Salz Case—the Re-examination of a Merger after an Annulment by the Court' Commission's *Competition Policy Newsletter* 1998/3, 46.

[296] Cases C–68/94 and C–30/95, *France* v. *Commission, Société Commerciale des Potasses et de l'Azote (SCPA)* v. *Commission* [1998] ECR I–1375, [1998] 4 CMLR 829, para. 178. See the view of the appellants, set out *supra* at 774.

concentrations which create or strengthen an individual dominant position, that is, a dominant pos- ition held by the parties to the concentration, come within the scope of the Regulation. Article 2, in referring to 'a concentration which creates or strengthens a dominant position', does not in itself exclude the possibility of applying the Regulation to cases where concentrations lead to the creation or strengthening of a collective dominant position, that is, a dominant position held by the parties to the concentration together with an entity not a party thereto.

167. Third, with respect to the travaux préparatoires, it appears from the documents in the case that they cannot be regarded as expressing clearly the intention of the authors of the Regulation as to the scope of the term 'dominant position'. In those circumstances, the travaux préparatoires provide no assistance for the interpretation of the disputed concept (see, to that effect, Case 15/60 *Simon* v. *Court of Justice* [1961] ECR 115).

168. Since the textual and historical interpretations of the Regulation, and in particular Article 2 thereof, do not permit its precise scope to be assessed as regards the type of dominant position concerned, the provision in question must be interpreted by reference to its purpose and general structure (see, to that effect, Case 11/76 *Netherlands* v. *Commission* [1979] ECR 245, paragraph 6).

169. As may be seen from the first and second recitals in its preamble, the Regulation is founded on the premiss that the objective of instituting a system to ensure that competition in the common market is not distorted is essential for the achievement of the internal market by 1992 and for its future development.

170. It follows from the sixth, seventh, tenth and eleventh recitals in the preamble that the Regula- tion, unlike Articles [81] and [82] of the Treaty, is intended to apply to all concentrations with a Community dimension in so far as they are likely, because of their effect on the structure of competi- tion within the Community, to prove incompatible with the system of undistorted competition envis- aged by the Treaty.

171. A concentration which creates or strengthens a dominant position on the part of the parties concerned with an entity not involved in the concentration is liable to prove incompatible with the system of undistorted competition which the Treaty seeks to secure. Consequently, if it were accepted that only concentrations creating or strengthening a dominant position on the part of the parties to the concentration were covered by the Regulation, its purpose as indicated in particular by the abovementioned recitals would be partially frustrated. The Regulation would thus be deprived of a not insignificant aspect of its effectiveness, without that being necessary from the perspective of the general structure of the Community system of control of concentrations.

172. Neither the argument based on the lack of procedural safeguards nor the argument based on the 15th recital in the preamble to the Regulation can cast doubt on its applicability to cases where a collective dominant position is the result of a concentration.

173. As to the first argument, it is true that the Regulation does not expressly provide that undertak- ings, not involved in the concentration, which are regarded as the external members of the dominant oligopoly must be given an opportunity to make their views known effectively where the Commission intends to attach to the 'authorisation' of the concentration conditions or obligations specifically affecting them. The same applies in a situation where the Commission intends to attach conditions or obligations affecting third parties to a concentration which will lead simply to the creation or strengthening of an individual dominant position.

174. In any event, even on the assumption that a finding by the Commission that the proposed concentration creates or strengthens a collective dominant position involving the undertakings con- cerned on the one hand and a third party on the other may in itself adversely affect that third party, it must be borne in mind that observance of the right to be heard is, in all proceedings liable to culminate in a measure adversely affecting a particular person, a fundamental principle of

Community law which must be guaranteed even in the absence of any rules governing the procedure (see, to that effect, Case 85/76 *Hoffmann-La Roche* v. *Commission* [1979] ECR 461 and Case C–32/95 *P Commission* v. *Lisrestal and Others* [1996] ECR I–5373, paragraph 21).

175. Given the existence of that principle, and the purpose of the Regulation as explained above, the fact that the Community legislature did not expressly provide in the Regulation for a procedure safeguarding the right to be heard of third party undertakings alleged to hold a collective dominant position together with the undertakings involved in the concentration cannot be regarded as decisive evidence of the Regulation's inapplicability to collective dominant positions.

176. As to the second argument, the presumption that concentrations are compatible with the common market if the undertakings concerned have a combined market share of less than 25%, as stated in the 15th recital in the preamble, is not developed in any way in the operative part of the Regulation.

177. The 15th recital in the preamble to the Regulation must, having regard in particular to the realities of the market underlying this recital, be interpreted as meaning that a concentration which does not give the undertakings concerned a combined share of at least 25% of the reference market is presumed not to create or strengthen an anticompetitive dominant position on the part of those undertakings.

178. It follows from the foregoing that collective dominant positions do not fall outside the scope of the Regulation.

This judgment did not, however, like *Flat Glass*, clarify whether or not the merger provisions would apply to the creation of oligopolistic dominance in the absence of links, such as contractual links, between the members of the oligopoly. The Court stressed that the key to collective dominance was the parties' ability to adopt a common policy on the market and to act independently of their competitors, customers, and consumers. Although this did not appear to limit a finding of collective dominance to a position where there were contractual or other arrangements between the parties, such as those in existence between K+S/MdK and SCPA, the Court did not expressly state what the position would have been had no such links existed.

C. J. Cook and C. S. Kerse, *E. C. Merger Control* (3rd edn., Sweet & Maxwell, 2000), 169

5.7 . . . From the perspective of preserving effective competition in markets in the European Union the Court's teleological approach is difficult to fault . . . It also minimises the symmetry between E.C. and national merger and monopoly controls, some of which have special provisions for dealing with oligopolies. . . . There remain, however, a number of practical difficulties . . . in using the Regulation to control the development of uncompetitive oligopolies.

The CFI in *Gencor Ltd* v. *Commission*[297] shed further light on this point. This case concerned a decision by two companies, Gencor Ltd (a South African company) and Lonrho Plc (a UK company), to merge their business activities in the platinum group metal ('PGM') sector. Although the platinum businesses were both based in South Africa (and the South African Competition Board did not consider that the operation gave rise to competition policy concerns under South African law) the Commission nevertheless issued a decision

---

[297] Case T–102/96 *Gencor Limited* v. *Commission* [1999] ECR II–753 [1999] 4 CMLR 971.

prohibiting the merger. It considered that the merger would create a duoply between the merged entity and Anglo American Corporation of South Africa Ltd ('AAC'), which through its associated company, Amplats, was the remaining competitor on the market. Further, the anti-competitive effects of that duopoly would be felt on the relevant markets within the EU and EEA.[298] In this case no contractual or other structural links existed between the parties.

The applicant sought annulment of the Commission's decision. After reiterating that 'collective dominant positions do not fall outside the scope of the Regulation, as the Court of Justice indeed itself held . . . in *France and Others v. E.C. Commission* (paragraph 178))' the Court rejected the applicant's claim that, in order that a finding of collective dominance be made, 'structural' links had to exist between the undertakings involved.

Case T–102/96, *Gencor Limited* v. *Commission* [1999] ECR II–753 [1999] 4 CMLR 971

Court of First Instance

273. In its judgment in the *Flat Glass* case, the Court referred to links of a structural nature only by way of example and did not lay down that such links must exist in order for a finding of collective dominance to be made.

274. It merely stated . . . that there is nothing, in principle to prevent two or more independent economic entities from being united by economic links in a specific market and, by virtue of that fact, from together holding a dominant position *vis-à-vis* the other operators on the same market.

. . .

276. Furthermore, there is no reason whatsoever in legal or economic terms to exclude from the notion of economic links the relationship of interdependence existing between the parties to a tight oligopoly within which, in a market with the appropriate characteristics, in particular in terms of market concentration, transparency and product homogeneity, those parties are in a position to anticipate one another's behaviour and are therefore strongly encouraged to align their conduct in the market, in particular in such a way as to maximise their joint profits by restricting production with a view to increasing prices. In such a context, each trader is aware that highly competitive action on its part designed to increase its market share (for example a price cut) would provoke identical action by the others, so that it would derive no benefit from its initiative. All the traders would thus be affected by the reduction in price levels.

277. That conclusion is all the more pertinent with regard to the control of concentrations, whose objective is to prevent anti-competitive market structures from arising or being strengthened. Those structures may result from the existence of economic links in the strict sense argued by the applicant or from market structures of an oligopolistic kind where each undertaking may become aware of common interests and, in particular, cause prices to increase without having to enter into an agreement or resort to a concerted practice.

278. In the [present] case, therefore, the applicant's ground of challenge alleging that the Commission failed to establish the existence of structural links is misplaced.

279. The Commission was entitled to conclude, relying on the envisaged alteration in the structure of

---

[298] See *infra* 782 and Chap. 17.

the market and on the similarity of the costs of Amplats[299] and [Implats[300]/LPD[301]], that the proposed transaction would create a collective dominant position and lead in actual fact to a duopoly constituted by those two undertakings

The case is illuminating in a number of respects. In particular, by referring to *Flat Glass* when considering the links required between undertakings before a finding of collective dominance can be made the Court clearly indicates that the concept will be dealt with in the same way for the purposes of both Article 82 and the Merger Regulation. For this reason, the Court's judgment is also of great importance when considering the scope of Article 82.[302]

In addition, the Court establishes that the contractual links given as examples of economic links in *Flat Glass* are not necessary to support a finding of collective dominance. Although the Court does not fully explain the difference between the 'structural' and 'economic links' it refers to in its judgment there seems little doubt that the market structure itself (the relationship of interdependence existing between parties to a tight oligopoly) may suffice to establish the economic links required for a finding of collective dominance. The key question, therefore, appears now to be do, or will, the links between the parties facilitate collusion, tacit or explicit, between them? If so, it does not matter whether the links are purely economic and provided by market structures of an oligopolistic kind or 'structural' provided by contracts or licences concluded between the undertakings or by shareholdings which one of the undertakings has in the other. If this is correct then the latter 'structural links' are just simply one type of link which may be used to establish the broader economic links essential to a finding of collective dominance. This view is set out in the extract from Faull and Nikpay below:

J. Faull and A. Nikpay (eds.), *The EC Law of Competition* (Oxford University Press, 1999), 249

4.164 In the judgment given by the Court of First Instance on 25 March 1999 in *Gencor* v. *Commission*, . . . the Court confirmed the Commission's decision and dismissed the appeal. In the judgment the Court accepted that the Commission can look at factors such as market transparency, product homogeneity, a moderate level of growth, a low rate of technological change, high barriers to entry, etc

---

[299] Amplats was controlled by AAC. Through this associated company, Amplats, which is the leading supplier worldwide, AAC was the main competitor of Gencor and Lonrho in the PGM sector.

[300] 'Impala Platinum Holding Ltd ("Implats") is a company incorporated under South African law bringing together Gencor's activities in the platinum group metal ("PGM") sector': Case T–102/96, *Gencor Ltd* v. *Commission* [1999] 4 CMLR 971, para. 2.

[301] 'Eastern Platinum Ltd . . . and Western Platinum Ltd . . ., generally known under the mane of Lonrho Platinum Division ('LPD'), are companies incorporated under South African law which bring together Lonrho's activies in the PGM Sector': Case T–102/96, *Gencor Ltd* v. *Commission* [1999] 4 CMLR 971, para. 4.

[302] See *supra* Chaps. 6 and 11. Similarly, in Case T–228/97, *Irish Sugar plc* v. *Commission* [1999] 5 CMLR 1300 (a case on the concept of dominant position within the context of Art. 82) the CFI, para. 46, in upholding the Commission's finding of an abuse of a collective dominant position relied on the ECJ's ruling in *France* v. *Commission*, (a decision taken within the context of the Merger Reg.) that 'a joint dominant position consists in a number of undertakings being able together, in particular because of factors giving rise to a connection between them, to adopt a common policy on the market and act to a considerable extent independently of their competitors, their customers, and ultimately consumers (Cases C–68/94 and C–30/95, *France* v. *Commission, Société Commerciale des Potasses et de l'Azote (SCPA)* v. *Commission* [1998] ECR I–1375, [1998] 4 CMLR 829, para. 221)'.

in its analysis of whether a market is prone to tacit co-ordination. Furthermore, of particular interest is that the Court interpreted the judgment in . . . *Flat Glass* . . . as far as the role of structural links between members of an oligopoly is concerned. The Court explicitly said that the reference to structural links in *Flat Glass* was merely by way of example, and that structural links are not necessary for a finding of oligopolistic dominance. Therefore, according to this judgment, it can be concluded that the focus of analysis in the assessment of oligopolistic dominance is the likelihood of tacit co-ordination and not whether there are structural links between the members of an oligopoly.

d. ESTABLISHING THE EXISTENCE OF A COLLECTIVE DOMINANT POSITION

Even though the Commission's view that the Merger Regulation permits it to control mergers which lead to the creation or strengthening of a collective dominant position has been vindicated before the Court, the Commission still has an onerous burden to discharge to establish that that position has in fact been created or strengthened. It will have to establish that competition in the relevant market subsequent to the merger will be significantly impeded by the collectively dominant undertakings' ability to adopt a common policy on the market and 'to a considerable extent independently of their competitors, their customers, and also of their consumers'. It must be established not only that the market will become a concentrated one but that the parties will engage in explicit or tacit collusion on the market.

In *France* v. *Commission* the French Government and SCPA submitted that, if the regulation did apply to collective dominant positions, the Commission's reasoning concerning the alleged creation of a dominant duopoly had been based on an assessment which was wrong in fact or law and which was inadequate. The ECJ upheld this limb of the applicant's appeal. It held that the Commission's analysis of the concentration and of its effects on the market in question was flawed in certain respects which affected the economic assessment of the concentration.[303] Without having to establish whether, in the absence of the flaws, the Commission's findings would have provided a sufficient basis for the conclusion that a collective dominant position existed, it held that the Commission had not shown to the necessary legal standard that the concentration would give rise to a collective dominant position which was liable to impede significantly effective competition in the relevant market. In particular, a market share of 60 per cent (which would be held by K+S/MdK and SCPA after the concentration, they had 23 per cent and 37 per cent shares respectively) did not of itself point conclusively to the existence of a collective dominant position on the part of the undertakings. Further, an essential factor relied upon by the Commission in support of its finding of collective dominance was the structural links between K+S and SCPA. These had not, however, been shown to be as tight or binding as the Commission had sought to make out. Further, the Commission had not succeeded in showing that there was no effective competitive counterweight to the grouping allegedly formed by K+S/MdK and SCPA.

221. In the case of an alleged collective dominant position, the Commission is, therefore, obliged to assess, using a prospective analysis of the reference market, whether the concentration which has been referred to leads to a situation in which effective competition in the relevant market is significantly impeded by the undertakings involved in the concentration and one or more other undertakings which together, in particular because of factors giving rise to a connection between them, are able to

---

[303] See, in particular, paras. 179–250.

adopt a common policy on the market and act to a considerable extent independently of their competitors, their customers, and also of consumers.

None of the other factors relied upon could be regarded as lending decisive support to the Commission's conclusion.

This case makes it clear that the Commission's decisions finding collective dominance will have to be rigorously supported by evidence other than that relating to market shares. In drawing attention to the failures of the Commission, however, the Court did not clearly set out what kind of evidence might be helpful in establishing a position of collective dominance or the factors giving rise to a connection between the undertakings which will enable them to adopt a *common policy* on the market. This problem will be especially acute when there are no contractual or structural links which exist between the collectively dominant parties. In one of the Competition Policy Newsletters it is expressly recognized that the thing now to be assessed in cases of collective dominance 'is the likelihood of tacit co-ordination in the market'.[304]

In *Gencor/Lonrho* the Commission carefully set out the factors supporting its finding that a collective dominant position would be created on the platinum market. In *Gencor Limited* v. *Commission*[305] the CFI affirmed that these factors had been correctly relied upon. Some of the factors which were important to its finding were set out in paragraph 141 of the Commission's decision:

141. (a) on the demand side, there is moderate growth, inelastic demand and insignificant countervailing buyer power. Buyers are therefore highly vulnerable to a potential abuse;
(b) the supply side is highly concentrated with high market transparency for a homogenous product, mature production technology, high entry barriers (including high sunk costs) and suppliers with financial links and multi-market contacts. These supply side characteristics make it easy for suppliers to engage in parallel behaviour and provide them with incentives to do so, without any countervailing checks from the demand side.

Obviously the relevant factors may vary from market to market. This checklist, however, seems to 'be based upon the standard "textbook" characteristics which are thought to facilitate tacit collusion in a market'.[306] In Chapter 11 the factors which are likely to make a market prone to explicit or tacit co-ordination were discussed. Broadly, these characteristics are similar and are dependent upon the ability of the undertakings: (1) to raise prices and restrict output without attracting new entrants to the market (this is likely to be possible where the demand for the product is relatively inelastic, market shares are stable, and there are barriers to entry to the market); (2) to co-ordinate their behaviour (this is facilitated where the market is concentrated, demand is stable, and goods are homogenous so that product differentiation is not possible); (3) to detect cheating on the cartel (this will be facilitated where products are homogenous, buyers are dispersed, and the market is concentrated); and (4) to punish those cheating on the collusion (for example, by a costly price war or by the undertakings expanding output).[307]

---

[304] P. Christensen and P. Owen 'Comment on judgment of the CFI of 25 March 1999 in the Merger Case IV/M619—Gencor/Lourho' [1999] Competition Policy Newsletter 2/19, 23.

[305] Case T–102/96 [1999] ECR II–753, [1999] 4 CMLR 971.

[306] The Lexecon *Competition Memo* of Nov. 1999.

[307] See also S. Bishop and M. Walker, *The Economics of EC Competition Law: Concepts, Application and Measurement* (Sweet & Maxwell, 1999), paras. 6.23–25.

In *Price Waterhouse/Coopers & Lybrand*[308] the Commission authorized a merger between two of the 'big six' firms of accountants on the ground that there was no conclusive proof that the merger would create or strengthen a position of collective dominance. At the time of investigation, however, two of the other big six firms were also proposing to merge (KPMG and Ernst & Young) and had notified their concentration to the Commission. This of course would have led to a reduction from six to four firms rather than from six to five. If this had been the case it seems likely that both mergers would have been prohibited (in fact the negotiations between KPMG and Ernst & Young collapsed).[309] In the extract below, Cook and Kerse examine this decision:

C. J. Cook and C. S. Kerse, *E.C. Merger Control* (3rd edn., Sweet & Maxwell, 2000), 172

5.7.5 Price Waterhouse/Coopers & Lybrand . . . — *Oligopolistic Markets*

In its second stage examination in *Price-Waterhouse/Coopers & Lybrand*, the Commission had to consider whether a merger of two of the so-called 'Big Six' accountancy firms . . . would create or strengthen a position of collective dominance. The Commission recognised as a general principle that 'collective dominance involving more than three of four suppliers is unlikely simply because of the complexity of the interrelationships involved, and the consequent temptation to deviate' . . . In such a market no enduring uncompetitive stability could exist. This is a somewhat dogmatic and surprising statement to make at this stage in the evolution of the regulation of oligopolies under the Regulation.

The Commission went on to emphasise the difficulties it faced in establishing oligopolistic dominance in the light of the judgment of the Court in *Kali und Salz*, handed down a matter of weeks before the decision. Of that judgment it said:

'. . . [the Court] has emphasised that there is a strong burden of proof on the Commission in the case of an oligopolistic market which the Commission holds to be subject to collective dominance.

The Court held that a high level of concentration in an oligopolistic market is not in itself a deciding factor as to the existence of collective dominance. In addition, the Court's judgment implies that evidence of the lack of effective competition between a group of suppliers held to be collectively dominant must be very strong, as must evidence of the weakness of competitive pressure from other suppliers (If there are any such in the market in question).'

The Commission indicated that had the proposed merger of KPMG and Ernst & Young . . . gone ahead it would have considered the possibility that a dominant duopoly would be created in the market for accounting and auditing services for major national and international companies and would have considered the possibility that a dominant duopoly would be created in the market for accounting and auditing services for major national and international companies and would have considered the PW/Coopers merger in the light of the plans of KPMG and Ernst & Young . . . In concluding that it had 'no conclusive proof' (a high standard for the Commission to impose on itself) that a position of oligopolistic or duopolistic dominance would be created or strengthened as a result of the merger, the Commission noted particularly 'the non-emergence of any two clear leading firms following the merger' . . . The strategical lesson is perhaps not to be second in the consolidation stakes in already concentrated markets! . . .

---

[308] Case IV/M1016 [1999] OJ L50/27, [1999] 4 CMLR 665.
[309] *Ibid.*, para. 110.

In *Airtours/First Choice*[310] the Commission adopted a controversial decision prohibiting the acquisition by Airtours of First Choice which appears to diverge from its previous practice. The Commission held that the concentration would lead to the creation or strengthening of a collective dominant position on the UK foreign package holiday (the 'FPH') market. The dominant position would be held by Airtours/First Choice (32 per cent), Thomson (27 per cent), and Thomas Cook (20 per cent). The remainder of the market was highly fragmented which meant that no effective restraint on the competitive conduct of the larger players would be exercised.

In reaching its decision the Commission appeared to expand the concept of collective dominance and to find its existence in circumstances beyond those which have so far been identified with collectively dominant positions. The Commission held in paragraph 54 of its decision that it was not necessarily essential to show that the parties would adopt a common policy on the market. Rather, it appeared to take the view that the ability to engage in explicit or tacit co-ordination is not essential. It was sufficient that each individual undertaking operating on the oligopolistic market had sufficient market power on that market to enable it to act independently.[311] Nonetheless the Commission did consider that tacit co-ordination between the parties would occur. That tacit co-ordination would, however, not occur in relation to price but in relation to output or capacity on the market. For this reason the checklist of factors relied upon by the Commission to support its finding of collective dominance[312] was not perhaps as convincing as that relied upon in earlier cases.[313] Arguably, the characteristics of the UK's FPH market did not make the Commission's finding of collective dominance conclusive. Further, the Commission considered the need for the undertakings to be able to punish those cheating or not conforming on the market to be unnecessary.

Case IV/M1524, *Airtours/First Choice* [2000] OJ L93/1

52. Airtours argued at the hearing that collective dominance could be thought of as a cartel, but without an explicit agreement, cartel meetings etc. Airtours then went on to expla[i]n that such a 'tacit cartel' would be unstable in the British market for short-haul foreign package holidays because there would be no retaliatory mechanism which would prevent any of the participants in the tacit cartel from cheating (see recital 55)

53. As set out by the Commission in previous cases, and confirmed by the Court of First Instance of the European Communities most recently in the merger case Gencor/Lonrho . . . active collusive conduct of any kind is not a prerequisite for collective dominance to occur. It is sufficient that adaptation to market condition causes an anti-competitive market outcome. As the Commission's Decision in the Gencor/Lonrho case (at recital 140) states, a collective dominant position 'can occur where a mere adaptation by members of the oligopoly to market conditions causes anti-competitive parallel behaviour whereby the oligopoly becomes dominant. Active collusion would not therefore be required for members of the oligopoly to become dominant and to behave to an appreciable extent independently of their remaining competitors, their customers and, ultimately, the consumers'.

---

[310] Case IV/M1524, *Airtours/First Choice* [2000] OJ L93/1.

[311] See especially para. 54.

[312] See especially para. 87 ff.

[313] Although the Commission stated, relying on its decisions in *Gencor/Lonrho* and *Price Waterhouse/ Coopers & Lybrand*, in a footnote to para. 87 that '[t]he characteristics listed are substantially those employed in previous Commission Decisions in Merger Reg. cases where oligopoly . . . was an issue'.

54. Furthermore . . . it is not a necessary condition of collective dominance for the oligopolists always to behave as if there were one or more explicit agreements (e.g. to fix prices or capacity, or share the market) between them. It is sufficient that the merger makes it rational for the oligopolists, in adapting themselves to market conditions, to act, individually, in ways which will substantially reduce competition between them, and as a result of which they may act, to an appreciable extent, independently of competitors, customers and consumers.

55. In its Statement of Objections, the Commission identified . . . certain features of market structure and operation which had been identified as making anti-competitive outcomes, and in particular, collective dominance more likely. Airtours considers that, in effect, none of these indicators are present and that, furthermore, it would be impossible for the major suppliers to retaliate in the event that one of them tried to win market share from the others by increasing capacity and offering lower prices. However, the Commission did not suggest, nor does it consider that all of the features have to be present and/or aggravated by the merger in order for collective dominance to arise in a given case. Nor does it regard a strict retaliation mechanism, such as that proposed by Airtours in its reply to the Statement of Objections . . . as a necessary condition for collective dominance in this case; where as here, there are strong incentives to reduce competitive action, coercion may be unnecessary. However, in any case, as set out below, the Commission does not agree that there is no scope for retaliation in this market. Rather there is considerable scope for retaliation, which will only increase the incentives to behave in an anti-competitive parallel way.

56. In this particular case, the Commission has come to the conclusion that the substantial concentration in the market structure, the resulting increase in its already considerable transparency, and the weakened ability of the smaller tour operators, and of potential entrants to compete will make it rational for the three major players that would remain after the merger to avoid or reduce competition between them, in particular by constraining overall capacity. This does not mean that the Commission believes that there will be no competition in the market after the merger. Even in cases involving single dominance or tight cartels competition is rarely completely eliminated. In this particular case, as further discussed below, capacity is basically set prior to the selling season. A distinction, therefore, has to be made between the setting of capacity pre-season and the sale of capacity during the selling season. Constraining overall capacity in the pre-season does not exclude certain competitive actions during the selling season, for example, various types of promotions. However, constraining the overall amount of capacity put onto the market ensures that the market will be kept tight. If capacity is constrained, prices and profits will be higher than otherwise, whatever competition takes place during the selling season. The Commission has reached the overall conclusion that the merger would result in a market structure which would create an incentive for the three remaining large operators to constrain capacity in this way.

The parties argued that it was a requirement that collectively dominant undertakings should be able to adopt a common policy on the market, that the concentration would not facilitate tacit co-ordination on the FPH market, and that retaliation could not be taken against any undertaking which did not accede to the co-ordination. In their view a finding of collective dominance was not possible. The extract below from a memorandum by Lexecon (which acted as one of Airtours' economic advisers) sets out some of these arguments and criticizes the Commission's decision.

The Lexecon Competition Memo (Lexecon Ltd., November 1999) The Airtours case

In the *Airtours* decision, no economic case was put forward that unilateral effects would have been significant (which is not surprising given the merged firm's post-merger market share of 32%) and the case for higher post-merger prices through tacit collusion was very weak. Arguments against post-merger tacit collusion include the following points. First, the requirements of the standard 'checklist' for collective dominance are not satisfied in the UK FPH market. Second, there is no effective punishment mechanism, which in economics is a key requirement for tacit collusion to operate.

The Checklist

The checklist routinely applied by the Commission in joint dominance cases seeks to evaluate the market in question against certain characteristics, which are deemed to facilitate tacit co-ordination. Yet in the Airtours case there were several ways in which the requirements of the checklist were not met, as the following examples show.

• Product homogeneity

Holidays vary by type, location, departure time and quality. With such highly differentiated products and a multitude of prices, co-ordinating on price alone would not be feasible. This was not contested by the Commission. Co-ordinating on capacity is generally viewed as more difficult than on price because of the time lags involved and would have been rendered even harder in the FPH market by the variety of holiday types on offer.

• Stable and Symmetric market shares

Stable shares help a collusive arrangement, because output is most easily 'allocated' on the basis of current market shares. However market shares in the UK FPH market are relatively volatile. Airtours and Thomas Cook have both grown markedly in recent years, and large firms have left the market. The Commission's view was that market shares are less volatile if the effects of historical acquisitions are stripped out, but this is not relevant for assessing the scope for future co-ordination.

• Stable demand

FPH capacity is set 18 months in advance, and firms' capacity levels are not transparent. Demand, in contrast, is highly dependent on disposable income which can be difficult to predict well ahead of time. Demand can also be volatile within the FPH market, particularly as a result of external shocks (such as terrorist activity). These factors make co-ordination problematic.

• High Barriers to entry

Barriers to entry in the FPH market are low, as the MMC recognised in its recent report on the UK FPH market. Arguably, barriers to expansion are also low: retail space, aircraft and hotels are all available to firms seeking to expand. Moreover, empirical evidence showed that smaller firms were able to offer substitute products to those of the larger firms at competitive prices and were able to purchase inputs at comparable rates.

These and other factors were part of a wider economic analysis which suggested that the conditions usually deemed necessary for collective dominance to be sustainable are not present in the UK FPH market . . .

Punishment

Economic analysis shows that the ability to 'punish' firms who deviate from an implicit agreement is an *essential* requirement for tacit co-ordination to be sustainable. Short-lived but bloody price wars (not to be confused with end-of season sales of a 'perishable' good like a package holiday) are the standard mechanism through which deviating firms are brought back into line in a tacitly collusive market.

Indeed the whole underlying logic of the 'checklist' applied by the Commission is to capture the incentive to deviate from potential future co-ordination, and the scope for punishing such deviations through harsh competition in the market.

In the UK FPH market capacity is set 18 months in advance and can only be modestly increased in the short run. This means that there is no credible punishment mechanism to sustain co-ordination. Fixed capacity means that the firm implementing punishment will be unable to serve additional customers if it cuts prices. . . .

Conclusion

Collective dominance is an important instrument in merger control. However, it can be used effectively and fairly only if there is a clear understanding of the concept. Prior to the *Airtours* case it was understood that it related to the ability of firms to tacitly co-ordinate.

The *Airtours* assessment was a 'forced fit' in terms of collective dominance, as market conditions in FPH were not conducive to the establishment of tacit co-ordination. TO get around this the Commission has shifted the goalposts as to what constitutes collective dominance. This has damaged the credibility of the concept. The Commission should avoid the temptation to use an ill-defined approach to collective dominance simply to block mergers it does not like. Clarification is required: the Commission need to issue a Notice on the subject so that companies can obtain clear guidance as to how the law will be applied.

However, Motta has suggested that the finding of collective dominance may be supportable by economic evidence and that, even in the case of uncertainty, it may be preferable to prohibit a merger and pursue a strict merger policy in concentrated markets.[314] In particular mergers between undertakings which do not create a dominant position or leave a situation in which the parties remaining on the concentrated market are likely to collude may, nonetheless, cause economic efficiency. The doctrine of 'unilateral effects' predicts that such mergers, which produce no efficiency gains, will be detrimental. They will lead to increases in prices.[315]

M. Motta, 'E.C. Merger Policy and the Airtours Case' [2000] 4 *ECLR 199*, 206–7

To summarise, it is conceivable that firms might tacitly collude on capacities, but whether the probability that this will indeed happen is high enough to justify a decision . . . blocking a merger resorting to joint dominance is not so clear. The overall line of reasoning of the Commission makes

---

[314] See *supra* 701 ff.

[315] M. Motta, 'E.C. Merger Policy and the Airtours Case' [2000] 4 *ECLR* 199, 199–202. 'Consider for instance a situation where very few firms would be left in the industry after a merger, but none of them has enough market power to be considered dominant and it is also very unlikely that they will collide (i.e. they are not jointly dominant). In such a situation, economic theory suggests that, if there are no efficiency gains, the merging firms will unilaterally increase their prices, and that the merger will be detrimental . . .', 201. It may be for this reason that the Commission in para. 54 of its decision focussed on the ability of the collectively dominant undertakings to act unilaterally on a market.

economic sense, . . . but it is not water-tight either. The features of the industry are not such that joint dominance is uncontroversial. . .

Yet even if joint dominance (*i.e.* collusion after the merger) is far from certain, economic analysis suggests that blocking the merger has been the right decision. Contrary to the Merger Regulation, an approach inspired by economic thinking would not require the Commission to prove to a high likelihood of dominance, but it would centre the assessment on the extent to which the merger would lead to price increases. The Airtours/First Choice merger would then have little chance of going ahead. It occurs in an industry which shows very high concentration . . . and the remaining firms or potential entrants are unlikely to discipline the major operators. Only considerable efficiency gains might outweigh the negative impact of a merger in such a concentrated sector. However, efficiency gains are unlikely to occur from this merger: '. . . the merger is only expected to lead to overall synergies of less than 1% of the overall costs of the combined entity. Furthermore, the cost savings mostly relate to overhead and other fixed costs.'[para. 146]

Whether the merger does or does not give rise to joint dominance might be discussed, but it seems hard to deny that this merger would decrease economic efficiency, at least on the basis of information contained in the Commission decision. If the Merger Regulation had covered the concept of unilateral effects, the decision of prohibition taken by the Commission would have been less open to discussion. By having to rely on the concept of joint dominance, the decision is more controversial.

A possible interpretation of this decision is that, whether consciously or not, by extending the use of the joint dominance concept to this 'border-line' case, the Commission is trying to cope with a distortion of the Merger Regulation which does not prohibit mergers detrimental to welfare unless they create or reinforce dominance. To avoid further distortions, however, the Commission should also take into account efficiency gains. Otherwise, lowering the standards of proof on joint dominance might result in some beneficial mergers being blocked.

Better still, the Commission might ask for a modification in the Merger Regulation so as to allow for the prohibition of welfare detrimental mergers even when they do not create or strengthen dominance. Otherwise, it might have to rely increasingly on the concept of joint dominance (with uncertain outcomes in the court, where to prove the existence of collusion after the merger is not likely to be straightforward) to prohibit mergers which do not create single firm dominance, whereas it would be fairly easy to prove the merger is likely to have adverse effects on welfare.

e. CONCLUSIONS ON COLLECTIVE DOMINANCE AND THE MERGER REGULATION

Just as the Court's case law has begun to shed light on the relevance and meaning of the concept of collective dominance within the concept of the Merger Regulation the Commission's decision in *Airtours* has introduced new uncertainty. The case is now on appeal to the CFI which will have to clarify the meaning of collective dominance and indicate the factors which are essential to the proof of its existence. It may be, however, that there is pressure to adopt a broad view of the concept so that the Commission will be enabled to preclude mergers in markets that are becoming increasingly concentrated.

C.J. Cook and C.S. Kerse, *E.C. Merger Control* (3rd edn., Sweet & Maxwell, 2000), 174–5

5.7.7   Karel van Miert, then Competition Commissioner, recently expressed the view that the trend of consolidation in European industry had gone far enough. Certainly had the Court ruled that the Regulation was confined to the control of single firm dominance. . . the scope for preserving competitive structures in E.U. markets would have been very narrow. As it is, the Commission has a very demanding task to assess the risk of collective dominance in sufficient depth within the four week stage one timetable to justify the opening of a second stage inquiry. Oligopoly is a very common market structure, and the rapid pace of consolidation through cross-border deals in the E.U. and worldwide present the Commission with a monumental task.

Moreover, the regulation of oligopolies raises both structural and behavioural issues. In the United Kingdom, for example, the monopoly provisions of the Fair Trading Act provide the possibility of examining markets which tend toward oligopoly, whereas under German anti-trust law, special merger control rules apply in concentrated markets. Arguably, if it is the underlying characteristics of a market which pre-dispose companies to behave uncompetitively, measures should be applied to the industry as a whole. Under the Regulation, however, even if a case of collective dominance is established remedies can be applied only to the parties of the notified concentration. . . . If the merger itself creates the collective dominance then prohibiting the concentration should be an adequate remedy, but if the conclusion is that the merger strengthens an existing oligopoly the Commission has no powers to do more, though it could conceivably use a combination of Articles [81] and [82] to regulate any market characteristics which could be attributed to infringements of those provisions. The Commission has not, however, undertaken such industry-wide examinations in the past; Articles [81] and [82] were not designed with this kind of case in mind although there are some indications that the Commission is re-examining how they might be used to police markets in which there are few competitors.

It will be interesting to see how the Commission uses it newly-recognised power. To examine markets in the four weeks allowed for in stage one in order to judge whether the notified concentration might create or strengthen a position of collective dominance presents a considerable challenge. . . . Careful consideration also needs to be given to the remedies which are appropriate where the Commission concludes that a concentration creates or strengthens such a position. Since it is the inherent characteristics of a market which allows an uncompetitive oligopoly to emerge and flourish the acceptance of commitments from the parties to the notified concentration may not be a sufficient remedy. It might well be argued that if a market is predisposed to oligopoly, only the preservation of an adequate number of independent firms in that market will guarantee effective competition. This would suggest that outright prohibitions of operations which reduce the number of competitors below a safe level may be the most appropriate, proportionate and logical remedy. In the absence of any anti-monopolisation provision in E.C. competition law similar to that in the U.S. Sherman Act it will be interesting to see how the Commission develops its approach toward collective dominance in applying the Regulation.

C. COUNTERVAILING BENEFITS. CAN A MERGER BE CLEARED WHERE IT LEADS TO THE CREATION OR STRENGTHENING OF A DOMINANT POSITION?

(i) CONDITIONS AND UNDERTAKINGS

In many cases where the Commission considers that a concentration will give rise to a dominant position or a collective dominant position, the parties may agree to modify the original concentration plan and to offer commitments to the Commission. It is crucial, however, that the commitments offered are sufficient to prevent the dominant position from being created or strengthened or to prevent effective competition from being impeded.[316] Under Article 8(2) of the Merger Regulation the Commission is authorized to accept commitments from parties to modify their concentration in order to ensure its compatibility with the common market. Regulation 1310/97 also gave the Commission power to accept and enforce undertakings given at the end of Phase I proceedings (Article 6(1a) and 6(1b)).[317] Commitments must be offered within specified periods of time[318] and Regulation 1310/97 indicates that transparency should be maintained and that Member States and interested third parties should be consulted.[319] The Commission generally prefers to find a solution along these lines than to have to prohibit the merger outright. The parties' ability to influence the outcome of the decision is, therefore, strong. The Commission has issued a draft Notice on commitments which provides guidance on the types of commitments which may be suitable to resolve the competition concerns raised by a concentration and the procedure governing such commitments.[320] The draft reflects the Commission's experience regarding their assessment, acceptance, and implementation.

Commitments concluded may relate to the *structure* of the concentration or to the *behaviour* of the parties. The only requirement is that the commitments 'are capable of rendering the notified transaction compatible with the common market'.[321] In some situations, therefore, remedies may be difficult, if not impossible.[322]

In practice, structural remedies are more common. Behavioural remedies are extremely difficult to control and enforce.[323] Further, in many cases a structural remedy will be the only possible means of solving the structural problem caused by the creation of the dominant undertaking.[324] Structural remedies frequently involve the merged undertaking's divesting themselves of some part of the business.[325]

In *Nestlé/Perrier*, for example, the Commission concluded that the proposed merger would create a dominant position as a result of which effective competition would be impeded in a substantial part of the common market. However, the commitments offered by Nestlé enabled the Commission to declare the concentration to be compatible with the

---

[316] The Commission does not, otherwise, have power to authorize a concentration which has been found to be incompatible with the common market.

[317] 'Where the Commission finds that, following modification by the undertakings concerned, a notified concentration no longer raises serious doubts within the meaning of para. 1 (c), it may decide to declare the concentration compatible with the Common Market pursuant to para. 1(b).
The Commission may attach to its decision under para. 1(b) conditions and obligations intended to ensure that the undertakings concerned comply with the commitments they have entered into vis-à-vis the commission with a view to rendering the concentration compatible with the Common Market . . .'

[318] Reg. 447/98, Art. 18(1) and (2). Commitments must be offered within three weeks of notification in Phase I proceedings and within three months of the initiation of proceedings in Phase II proceedings.

[319] Reg. 1310/97, recital 8. See also Cases C–68/94 and C–30/95, *France* v. *Commission, Société Commerciale des Potasses et de l'Azote (SCPA)* v. *Commission* [1998] ECR I–1375, [1998] 4 CMLR 829; *supra* 775.

[320] [2000] 4 CMLR 794.

[321] Case T–102/96, *Gencor Ltd* v. *Commission* [1999] ECR II–753, [1999] 4 CMLR 971, para. 318.

[322] Commission's draft Notice on commitments [2000] 4 CMLR 794, para. 26.

[323] See Case IV/M490, *Nordic Satellite Distribution* [1990] OJ L53/21, [1995] CMLR 258 where the Commission rejected the undertakings offered by the parties on these grounds.

[324] See Case IV/M469, *MSG Media Service GmbH* [1994] OJ L364/1, [1994] 5 CMLR 499, para. 99.

[325] The Commission refers to three main types of commitment in its draft Notice on commitments [2000] 4 CMLR 794: the first is divestiture, the second is termination of exclusive agreements, and the third is to give access to infrastructure of key technology.

common market. Broadly, Nestlé promised to sell several minor brands, not to BSN, but to a third party. This was intended to facilitate the entry of a viable competitor with adequate resources in the bottled water market, or to increase the capacity of an existing competitor, so that such a competitor could effectively compete with Nestlé and BSN on the French bottled water market.[326] (In this case behavioural remedies were also taken with the aim of reducing the transparency of the market.) The Commission has on other occasions accepted a commitment to divest a major brand within a period after the concentration in order to ensure that effective competition is maintained on the relevant market by the creation of another viable competitor to the concentration.[327] Usually tight deadlines are set within which the divestiture must occur. However, as the Commission points out in its draft notice '[s]uitable remedies are not limited to divestiture commitments . . . the possibility cannot automatically be ruled out that other types of commitments, for instance not to use a trademark for a certain period, or to make part of the production capacity of the entity arising from the concentration available to third-party competitors, or, more generally to grant access to essential facilities on non-discriminatory terms, may themselves also be capable of preventing the emergence or strengthening of a dominant position'.[328] Thus a promise to terminate exclusive dealing arrangements to facilitate market entry by ensuring that competitors have access to necessary infrastructure or key technology (through, for example, licensing agreements) may also be sufficient to prevent the merger creating or strengthening a dominant position. Sometimes a package of commitments will be appropriate.[329]

Behavioural commitments were offered and accepted in the *Boeing/McDonnell Douglas* case.[330] Such commitments are often appropriate in cases involving the creation of a collective dominant position. In *Kali und Salz/MdK/Treuhand*,[331] for example, the parties to the concentration offered to sever links with its main competitor, SCPA (which were considered to facilitate anti-competitive behaviour on the oligopolistic market).[332]

In some cases a concentration has been saved by a third party to the transaction. In *Alcatel/Telettra*,[333] for example, the Spanish telecommunications company, Telefonica, agreed to sell its interests in the parties to the concentration in order to persuade the Commission that the undertakings' potential market power would be counteracted by the countervailing exercise of monopolistic demand.

(ii) TECHNICAL AND ECONOMIC PROGRESS

The requirement set out in Article 2(1)(b) of the Merger Regulation that the Commission should, in appraising the merger take into account 'the development of technical and

---

[326] [1992] OJ L356/1, [1993] 4 CMLR M17, paras 136–138.

[327] See also, e.g., Case IV/M430, *Procter and Gamble/ VP Schickedanz* [1994] OJ L354/32, [1994] 5 CMLR 499.

[328] Draft Commission Notice on commitments [2000] 4 CMLR 794, para. 11.

[329] *Ibid.*, paras 23–25.

[330] Case IV/M877 [1997] OJ L336/16, [1997] 5 CMLR 270. Further, the Commission also required Boeing to make some of its intellectual property rights available, through licences, to competitors.

[331] Case IV/M308 [1994] OJ L186/30; on appeal Cases C–68/94 and C–30/95, *France v. Commission, Société Commerciale des Potasses et de l'Azote (SCPA)* v. *Commission* [1998] ECR I–1375, [1998] 4 CMLR 829.

[332] Their imposition was one of the factors which caused SCPA and France to challenge, successfully, the legitimacy of the Commission's decision, see *supra* 775 ff.

[333] Case IV/M42, *Alcatel/Telettra* [1991] OJ L122/48, [1991] 4 CMLR 778.

economic progress provided that it is to consumers' advantage and does not form an obstacle to competition' raises two related problems. First to what extent does this wording allow for the acceptance of an 'efficiency' defence for concentrations which lead to the creation or strengthening of a dominant position? Secondly, to what extent does the provision allow for industrial policy considerations to be taken into account by the Commission in appraising concentrations under Article 2.

a. AN EFFICIENCY DEFENCE?

It is important to know whether or not the Merger Regulation admits an 'efficiency defence' to redeem a concentration which increases concentration and leads to dominance but which results in significant cost savings and economies of scale (which favour restructuring).

The most difficult problem in determining an appropriate merger policy is that the field of mergers cannot be divided into mergers that encourage collusion or increase market power on the one hand, and mergers that create efficiency on the other. Many mergers do both an once . . . Horizontal mergers can create substantial efficiencies even as they facilitate collusion or enlarge market power. Courts and other policy makers have entertained three different positions concerning efficiency and the legality of mergers:

1) mergers should be evaluated for their effect on market power or likelihood of collusion, and efficiency considerations should be largely irrelevant;

2) mergers that create substantial efficiencies should be legal, or there should be at least a limited 'efficiency defense' in certain merger cases;

3) a merger should be condemned *because* they create efficiencies, in order to protect competitors of the post-merger firm.[334]

In the USA the rule that mergers should be prohibited because they create efficiencies has been abandoned. Instead the authorities appear to be receptive to arguments based on the efficiencies and cost savings of a merger.[335] However, the onus of proving qualifying efficiencies rests on the parties to the merger.[336]

The US Merger Guidelines[337] indicate that the defence may apply where (1) efficiencies relied upon are merger-specific (they will not be achieved in the absence of the merger); (2) the efficiencies are achieved in the same market as the market in which the anti-competitive effects of the merger are likely to be felt; (3) the efficiencies are cognizable—they are verifiable and measurable; and finally that (4) the efficiencies outweigh reverse the merger's potential harm to consumers in the relevant market by, for example, preventing price increases in that market. The guidelines indicate that the more anti-competitive the merger under the concentration analysis the stronger the evidence of efficiencies must be.

Arguably, the acceptance of such a defence is supported on the ground of economic theory so that no conflict between competition and industrial policy arises. Rather, on

---

[334] H. Hovenkamp, *Federal Antitrust Policy: The Law of Competition and its Practice* (West Publishing Co, 1994), 446 and 450–1.

[335] Efficiency defences have been recognized in Australia and Canada.

[336] Department of Justice and Federal Trade Commission Horizontal Merger Guidelines (1992, amended 1997).

[337] 1992 Guidelines, (revised in 1997), para. 4.

grounds of strict economic theory, the defence should be permissible since the costs savings give rise to an increase in consumer welfare as a whole.

An increase in consumer welfare

The argument raised in support of such a defence is outlined by Hovenkamp:

H. Hovenkamp, *Federal Antitrust Policy: The Law of Competition and its Practice* (West Publishing Co, 1994), 453–5

12.2b The Welfare 'Tradeoff' Model and the Efficiency Defense

The rule that mergers should be condemned because they create efficiency has been implicitly abandoned. . . . The opposite position is that mergers should be legal when they create substantial efficiencies—or alternatively, that there should be an 'efficiency defense' in merger cases. Although the trail is still somewhat ambiguous, the courts seem to be heading in the direction of adopting such a rule. Importantly, the rule comes into play *only* after the merger has been found presumptively anticompetitive by structural and behavioral analysis. . . . If a merger poses no competitive threat to begin with, then analysis of possible efficiencies is unnecessary.

The argument for an 'efficiency defense' in merger cases is illustrated by the graph in Figure 1. . . . The graph illustrates a merger that give the post-merger firm measurably more market power than it had before the merger. As a result, the firm reduces output from Q_1 to Q_2 on the graph, and increases price from P_1 to P_2. Triangle A_1 represents the monopoly 'deadweight loss' created by this increase in market power. . . .

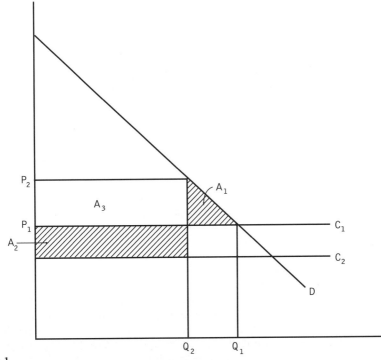

Table 1

At the same time, the merger produces measurable economies, which show up as a reduction in the firm's costs from C_1 to C_2, Rectangle A_2 represents efficiency gains that will result from these economies. If A_2 is larger than A_1 the merger produces a *net* efficiency gain, even though it permits the firm to raise its price above its marginal cost. Furthermore, A_2 is often larger than A_1. The efficiency gains illustrated by A_2 are spread over the entire output of the post-merger firm. The deadweight losses in A_1 are spread over only the reduction in output. If the post-merger firm reduced its output by 10%, each of the 90% of units still being produced would contribute to the efficiency gains; the deadweight loss, however, would accrue over only the 10% reduction.

Williamson concluded that in a market with average elasticities of demand and supply, a merger that produced 'nontrivial' economies of 1.2% would be efficient even if it resulted in a price increase of 10% . . .

Williamson's analysis is vulnerable to some criticism. First, his description of triangle A_1 in the figure as the efficiency costs of a merger probably understates the true social cost. Rectangles A_2plus A_3 represent potential monopoly profits to the post-merger firm. A profit-maximizing firm will be willing to spend substantial resources in an effort to acquire or retain a certain amount of monopoly power. . . . If a particular merger will give a firm $1,000,000 in additional monopoly profits, the firm will spend up to $1,000,000 in order to accomplish the merger and then retain its monopoly position. It could spend this money in highly inefficient ways, such as espionage, predatory pricing against a potential take-over target, or vexatious litigation. At the extreme $A_2 + A_3$ are not increased profits to the post-merger firm at all, but funds inefficiently spent in order to give the firm its market position. Importantly, the anticompetitive risk in the merger case is not increased likelihood of single-firm monopoly, but increased likelihood of collusion. The costs of managing a cartel or oligopoly can be quite high in relation to the profits that it produces. . . . A cartel or oligopoly that occasions a price increase of 10% would very likely produce much smaller gains in profitability. . . .

The second problem with Williamson's analysis is more ideological than economic. Williamson is willing to balance an absolute output reduction and price increase against any efficiency saving. Suppose that two firms selling widgets at a competitive price of $1.00 merge. As a result of the merger the post-merger firm has enough market power to reduce output and increase the price of widgets to $1.05. In addition, the firm's marginal costs drop from $1.00 per widget to 95¢ per widget. In this case the efficiency gains which are measured across all widgets produced, will probably be larger than the deadweight loss from monopoly pricing, which is measured across only the reduction in output. However, the merger results in an *actual* output reduction and an *actual* price increase for consumers. Although the overall effect of the merger is efficient, all the benefits of the increased efficiency accrue to the post-merger firm in the form of higher profits. . . . Such a merger rule would undoubtedly be politically unacceptable, even though the rule promotes efficiency. If the requirement were, not efficiency gains generally but rather efficiencies sufficiently large to result in lower prices, then a much larger efficiency gain would be needed to offset a given increase in market power. . . .

A third problem with Williamson's analysis is that it may encourage us to make a false comparison. Deadweight losses must be traded against efficiency gains *only* if the efficiencies cannot be attained by alternative means. Most efficiency gains can be realized through mechanisms other than merger. One knows the true consequence of an efficiency defense only by comparing these alternatives as well. For example, suppose a merger permits a firm to make plants operate more efficiently by specializing production across numerous plants. These reductions amount to, say, $2 million per year. The merger also facilitates a monopoly price increase of $1 million per year. So far the merger looks efficient. But why couldn't the firm have built the extra plants itself? In that case the consumers will have the benefit of the operating efficiencies and there will be *no* offsetting monopoly price increase. Of course, adding the new plants to the capacity that the acquired firm already has may be unprofitable, but that presents an empirical question. Importantly, the welfare tradeoff that results from the Williamson merger analysis is the correct 'tradeoff' only if we know that the least costly way of achieving the productive efficiencies is through merger. This means that courts must scrutinize efficiency claims carefully to ensure themselves that the efficiencies cannot be achieved through less anticompetitive means.

Questions about the availability of alternatives are vexing, and explain why the efficiency defense has been successful so infrequently. Suppose that the claimed efficiency is that the acquirer needs to modernize and the cheapest way to do so is to acquire another firm's recently built modern plant. . . . Unquestionably, modernization is efficient and anything that reduces the cost of modernization must be efficient as well. But the defense makes sense only if the acquired firm's plant has excess capacity; . . . if it does not, then the post-merger firm must continue to use the old plants as well or perhaps reduce output to the level previously produced by the acquired firm alone. The argument might be that adding to the existing modern plant is cheaper than building a second free-standing plant, but adding would require the two firms to be one. However, then we would want to know why the *acquired* firm cannot simply enlarge its capacity on its own: that is, competition rather than merger most usually solves such problems. The same limitations generally apply to the claim that the merger is efficient because the acquired firm is poorly managed and the acquisition will place it in the acquiring firm's more capable hands. . . . We should assume that the market for managers is competitive. In that case, the acquired firm should be able to find better management on its own, or through a merger that is less threatening to competition. . . . Many claimed efficiencies, although genuine, can be obtained through alternative means, unless the market in which efficiencies are claimed is working very poorly.

A fourth problem with Williamson's proposal is that courts are simply unable to make the measurements that his analysis would require. Efficiencies, Judge Posner has written, are an 'intractable subject for litigation'. . . . Courts are not up to measuring marginal costs or elasticities of supply or demand with anything approaching the precision required by such an 'efficiency defense'. Our knowledge that mergers can produce both economies and monopoly pricing is fairly secure. However, quantifying either of these in a particular merger case is impossible. Most mergers found illegal under current law probably create efficiencies. They are condemned, however, because no court is capable of balancing the increase in market power or the potential for collusion against the economies achieved. Judges must necessarily make decisions based on the information they can obtain and understand. When a merger involves companies having a small share of the market, they infer that the potential for monopolistic pricing or collusion is trivial; therefore, the merger must be calculated to increase the efficiency of the post-merger firm. If the merger involves firms large enough to threaten competitive pricing significantly, however, then the alternative explanation of monopoly or collusion and the difficulty of measuring any resulting efficiencies warrant condemnation. . . .

Most of the courts that have considered the efficiency defense have been skeptical. Some have rejected evidence of efficiencies. . . . Some have required proof that the efficiencies could not have been obtained by other means than an anticompetitive merger. . . . A few have recognized the defense. . . .

Broadly, Williamson establishes that in some cases mergers which enable the parties to acquire market power and, consequently, to restrict output and raise prices may nonetheless lead to an increase in consumer welfare. Although consumers lose output (and deadweight loss occurs) in some cases, where efficiency gains are large, that loss is offset by a greater gain in cost or resource savings. To determine whether or not this is the case a comparison must be made in each case of deadweight loss relative to cost savings. Although this may lead to a shift in income from purchasers to managers and owners (all the benefits of the merger accrue to the merging undertakings in the form of higher profits), the welfare of consumers as a class (which includes those managers and owners) is increased.

Supporters of such a theory suggest that efficiency gains from mergers are generally overlooked (in particular, in some industries (such as defence and banks) where the scope for economies of scale are great). It has, however, been disputed whether comparisons between deadweight loss and cost savings can, in reality, be made and the sums calculated mathematically.[338] Arguably, until this can be done it is impossible to decide whether or not an efficiency defence should be accepted. More particularly, it has been suggested that the comparison should not be made at all. Huge cost savings would be necessary to offset any associated price increases[339] and, instead, a rigorous merger policy would be more likely to bring about an increase in economic welfare. Public policy should thus concentrate on preserving and fostering competition for the ultimate benefit of consumers.

The merger regulation

It appears from the text of Article 2 of the Merger Regulation that it leaves little or no scope for the trade off of efficiencies where a concentration leads to the creation or strengthening of a dominant position. The Regulation does not expressly provide an efficiency defence and allows in Article 2(1)(b) only for 'technical and economic progress' to be taken into account as part of the appraisal. Although efficiency considerations may lead to an increase in consumer welfare as a whole, it is hard to see how, as required by Article 2(1)(b), the technical and economic progress is to the consumers' advantage (the consumer would have to pay monopoly prices, post-merger) or that the merger does not form an obstacle to competition.[340] It could possibly be argued that, since the merger increases consumer welfare as a whole, the dominant position created or strengthened does not result in a significant impediment to effective competition within the common market, but this view is not reflected in the cases.

Efficiency arguments were raised in *Aérospatiale-Alenia/de Havilland*.[341] The parties argued that an important objective of the merger was to reduce costs. The Commission did not specifically state that efficiency considerations were relevant to the assessment, but considered the arguments 'without prejudice' to their relevance. The Commission concluded that the concentration would lead to the creation of a dominant position which would significantly impede effective competition within the common market and dismissed the efficiency arguments raised as negligent or unrelated to the merger.[342] The Commission's view that any advantages had to accrue to consumers and that, since the concentration led to the creation of a dominant position, it would be harmful to customers, suggests that the defence cannot be entertained under the current wording of Article 2. In fact, the parties claim that efficiency gains arose from the merger instead of acting as an offsetting factor to

[338] See R. H. Bork, *The Antitrust Paradox* (Basic Books, 1978, reprinted with a new Introduction and Epilogue, 1993).

[339] F. M. Scherer and D. Ross, *Industrial Market Structure and Economic Performance* (3rd edn. Houghton Mifflin, 1990) 174: statistical evidence supporting the hypotheses that profitability and efficiency increase following mergers is at best weak.

[340] See, e.g., A. Jacquimin, 'Mergers and European Policy' in P. H. Admiraal (ed.), *Merger and Competition Policy in the European Community* (Blackwell, 1990), 36.

[341] Case IV/M53 [1991] OJ L334/42, [1992] 4 CMLR M2.

[342] Similarly, in Case IV/M126, *Accor/Wagon-Lits* [1992] OJ L204/1, [1993] 5 CMLR M13, the Commission indicated that efficiencies could not be taken into account unless it could be established that cost savings would be passed on to customers. On the facts there was, in any event, insufficient evidence of efficiencies. However, the Commission held that, even if there had been, it could not be established that the efficiencies would outweigh the anti-competitive effects of the concentration. The demand for motorway catering services was highly inelastic, so there was no indication that any benefits would be passed on to customers.

mitigate the adverse competitive effects of the merger, appear to have 'merely strengthened the Commission's view that the merged group would enjoy benefits that would be out of the reach of its competitors. It anything, the "efficiency defence" seems in this case to have reduced the chances of clearance for the deal'.[343] This approach may mean that parties are unwilling to raise efficiency savings out of fear that the enhanced position of the new undertaking will be taken as making it even harder for other undertakings to compete with it.

There is no case in which the Commission has actually applied the efficiency defence to clear a merger leading to the creation or strengthening of a dominant position on account of its efficiency benefits.[344] The extract from Faull and Nikpay below indicates that the Commission may believe that is not entitled to do so:

In some merger proceedings the parties have brought forward arguments related to technical and economic progress in its decision in the case . . . The Commission has in some of these cases included a discussion of the impact of technical and economic progress in its decision in the case . . . However, the Merger Regulation does not allow for an efficiency defence in the sense that the negative effects of a merger are weighed up against the positive effects of the merger. The Merger Regulation only allows efficiency considerations to be included in the assessment 'provided that it is to the consumer's advantage and does not form an obstacle to competition.' (Article 2(1)(b)).[345]

If this is correct, it might be argued that the Regulation is too rigid.[346] The Regulation may have been drafted tightly to preclude broad industrial policy concerns infiltrating the assessment process but changes could be made to permit mergers which lead to significant cost savings even where they result in the enhancement of competitive advantages of the firms involved. Whether or not it is believed that an efficiency defence should be provided for in the Merger Regulation depends, of course, on the acceptance of Williamson's theory.

b. INDUSTRIAL POLICY

Article 2 of the merger regulation

A merger control system focusing exclusively on competition issues would adopt a strict policy to preclude mergers which impede effective competition by creating a dominant position. However, a more positive or interventionist industrial policy which promotes structural adjustment may, in some cases, require a more lenient approach. Industrial policy may support industrial restructuring where it is necessary for the undertakings to survive in a global market, to encourage cross-border concentration, to encourage technical progress, to protect certain industries, or to protect employment.

An original draft of the Merger Regulation gave the Commission power to exempt concentrations which led to the creation or strengthening of a dominant position but which resulted in technical and economic progress to the benefit of consumers. However, many

---

[343] D. Ridyard, 'Economic Analysis of Singel Firm and Oligopolistic Dominance' [1994] ECLR 255, 256–7.

[344] 'However, commentators have often suggested that the commission is perfectly aware of the importance of efficiency gains, and that it has taken them into account *implicitly*, for instance at the stage of determination of market dominance': M. Motta, 'E.C. Merger Policy and the Airtours Case' [2000] *ECLR* 199, 203, relying on P. D. Camesasca, 'The Explicit Efficiency Defence in Merger Control: Does it Make the Difference?' [1999] *ECLR* 26–7.

[345] J. Faull and A. Nikpay, *The EC Law of Competition* (Oxford University Press, 1999), para. 4.167.

[346] See, e.g., M. Motta, *E.C. Merger Policy and the Airtours Case* [2000] 4 ECLR 199, 202.

Member States objected to the inclusion of such a defence on the ground that the Regulation would be used as an adjunct to industrial policy with the objective of supporting European winners. Although industrial policy may no longer be applied in such a protectionist way as it was in many Member States in the 1960s and 1970s,[347] it was still feared that EU industrial policy, aimed at safeguarding and ensuring 'the competitiveness of European industry', might support the creation of a Eurochampion in circumstances where that Eurochampion would be dominant and impede effective competition within the common market.[348]

The final text of the Merger Regulation does not allow for such an exemption for mergers. Technical and economic progress is just one factor to be taken into account in the overall appraisal. In the view of the Commissioner responsible for competition at the time the Merger Regulation was passed, Sir Leon Brittan, the wording of Article 2(1) would not open the back door to industrial policy considerations. In particular, the Article permits technical and economic progress to be taken into account only 'provided that it is to the consumers' advantage and does not form an obstacle to competition'. There thus seems little opportunity for benefits to be taken into account where the dominance of an undertaking hinders effective competition.

In *MSG Media Service GmbH*[349] the Commission refused to clear a joint venture formed between two German media companies and the German state telecommunications company to operate in the pay-TV market. MSG was to provide administrative and technical services for the provision of pay-TV and multimedia and interactive services (services hitherto unavailable in the market place). The Commission rejected the argument that the creation of the joint venture would contribute to technical and economic development, the development of digital TV. It pointed out that the reference to tehnical and economic progress was subject to the reservation that no obstacle to competition be formed. In this case the concentration was likely to seal off the market and lead to an early creation of a dominant position. The concentration would therefore substantially hinder effective competition on the future market for pay-TV.

Conversely, the Commission appears to have been antagonized by the parties' reliance on technical and economic progress, and it may be that this argument actually weakened their case. The technical advantages enhanced the lead of the parties to the concentration over their competitors and reinforced the finding of dominance (since competitors were unlikely to have access to such advanced technology).

That is not to say that the Commission will never authorize the creation of an undertaking which could be characterized as a European winner or Eurochampion. The Commission may be prepared to clear such a concentration where it is possible to do so on competition grounds. In *Aérospatiale/MBB*, for example, the Commission declared a concentration which would lead to the undertakings acquiring an EU market share of approaching 70 per cent compatible with the common market. The market in that case was, however, worldwide and the concentration would be subjected to severe competitive pressure from manufactures outside the Community, in particular in the USA.

---

[347] Shielding European firms from competition abroad.

[348] There was also a fear that the defence may be used, e.g., to resist take-overs by non-EC companies, in order to assist a takeover of the same target company by another EC enterprise.

[349] Case IV/M469 [1994] OJ L364/1, [1994] 5 CMLR 499.

The political element—the college of commissioners

The final decision to clear or prohibit a concentration following a Phase II merger investigation is made by the College of Commissioners and not simply the Commissioner responsible for competition.[350] This inevitably means that in controversial or politically charged cases lobbying of the Commissioners takes place. This has led to concern that, even where the Merger Task Force concentrates exclusively on competition criteria in its assessment of the concentration, that these competition factors will be overridden by other policy considerations when the final decision is taken.

Some high-profile merger cases appear to have caused a clash between proponents of industrial policy and supporters of a competition policy based strictly on competition factors alone. The discussion above indicates that such considerations may not, legitimately, be taken into account under the terms of the Merger Regulation itself. However, supporters of the view that competition criteria alone are, and should be, relevant consider that these factors may have influenced some of the final decisions taken by the College of Commissioners. It has thus been suggested that an independent European Cartel Office should be created, which would be seen to operate independently and free from political constraints.[351]

The case of *Aérospatiale-Alenia/de Havilland*[352] caused considerable political controversy. It seems that the concentration was supported by the French and Italian Governments,[353] the Commissioner for Industry, Martin Bangemann, and the then President of the Commission, Jacques Delors. It seems likely, therefore, that the French and Italian Commissioners faced pressure to ensure that the concentration was cleared. It appears that Martin Bangemann considered that the industrial advantages of the merger exceeded its drawbacks, but that the Competition Commissioner, Sir Leon Brittan, was opposed to the merger, believing that it would lead to the creation of a dominant position which would operate as a significant impediment to competition.[354] Faced with this controversy, Brittan seemed to face an

---

[350] See *supra* Chap. 2.

[351] Discussions in favour of an independent European Cartel Office (ECO) were revived, mainly out of fear that merger decisions would be taken not on competition grounds but on the grounds of short-term political considerations. The main support for the ECO has come from Germany. The former head of the German Bundeskartellamt, Wolfgang Kartte, is a strong supporter of an independent competition tribunal, e.g. It has been suggested that the ECO could be modelled on the German competition authority, the Bundeskartellamt. Although the issue was raised at the 1996–7 Intergovernmental Conference no changes were agreed in the Amsterdam Summit. The basic objective would be to establish an ECO to promote competition and to allow competition criteria to override political, social, and all other policy considerations. The view of the Commission is that it is more independent than other Community agencies. Further, if it exceeds or abuses its powers an appeal can be made to the CFI or ECJ, using the procedure in Art. 230. In the view of the need for agreement from all 15 Member States and for, amongst many other things, complicated Treaty amendments it perhaps seems unlikely that the ECO dream will ever by realised. See also *infra*, Chap. 14.

[352] Case IV/M53 [1991] OJ L334/42, [1992] 4 CMLR M2.

[353] From the point of view of the French and Italian Governments the merger would lead to the creation of a powerful Franco-Italian global competitor (if successful, the merger would have given the French and Italian firms 50% of the world market and around 65% of the EU market) which would have positive effects in those States, for example, on employment. These were the market shares even if the relevant product market was the overall 20–70 seat market.

[354] The concentration would not face effective competition from existing competitors and there was no realistic possibility of new competitors entering the market in the foreseeable future.

uphill struggle.[355] In the end, however, the Commissioners voted with Brittan to prohibit, for the first time, a merger under the provisions of the Merger Regulation.[356] The decision was, however, not a universally popular one and met with wide coverage in the media. Although the case represented a victory for a competition-driven merger policy, it may have increased the hostility of some Member States to the Merger Regulation and their reluctance to agree to any reduction in the Regulation's thresholds.[357]

The Commission's second prohibition of a merger was also a controversial one. It has been seen that the Commission prohibited the concentration in *MSG Media Service GmbH*.[358] It did so on the ground that the joint venture would create a durable dominant position in the market for administrative and technical services which would prevent future competition in this market and that this position would further strengthen the position of the parents in the markets for pay and cable TV. Again it seems that the Competition Commissioner faced strong opposition to the decision not only from, then, DGIII (Industry) but also from, then, DGXIII (Telecommunications, Information Market and Exploitation of Research).[359] The final decision to block the merger came under fierce attack for impeding the development of the European multi-media sector.

In *Mannesmann/Vallourec/Ilva*[360] it appears that the will of the College of Commissioners finally won the day. In this case, it seems that the Merger Task Force wished to prohibit the merger which it considered would lead to the creation of a collective dominant position (held by the concentration, DMV, and its main competitor, Sandvik) on the Western European market for seamless steel tubes.[361] A majority of the Advisory Committee on Concentrations agreed with the Commission's draft decision to this effect.[362] However, again the case caused political controversy and the deal was strongly supported by the Commissioner responsible for industry. The College of Commissioners was deadlocked.[363] Since the Commission had not voted to prohibit the merger, the decision was rewritten to avoid clearance by default (which would have occurred had the Commissioners failed to deliver a formal decision in time).[364]

The Commission does not, of course, accept that there has been any internal difference in opinion on policy. Rather, it is suggested that the Commissioners' differences in opinion have been over market definition. In the Commission's view, merger decisions are based on competition principles but are also in conformity with industrial policy principles:

---

[355] In many cases the outcome of the case may, therefore, depend on the political weight and effectiveness of the Commissioner responsible for Competition.

[356] The vote was only narrowly won, by 9–7 (one abstention).

[357] See *supra* 729.

[358] Case IV/M469 [1994] OJ L364/1, [1994] 5 CMLR 499.

[359] It was believed that the merger would lead to the creation of a European-based world telecommunications player.

[360] IV/M315 [1994] OJ L102/15, [1994] 4 CMLR 529.

[361] [1994] OJ L102/15, [1994] 4 CMLR 529.

[362] [1994] OJ C111/6.

[363] It seems it was split 8–8 for/against the merger (with one abstention).

[364] It is perhaps because of these events that the Commission's decision may appear to make rather curious reading. Having concluded that the market was a Western European one (and not worldwide, as the parties had alleged) the Commission finally decided to clear the merger on the ground that competition from *Japanese* and *Eastern European* producers would be likely to enter the market if DMV and Sandvik were to engage in anti-competitive parallel pricing.

[T]he Commission has aimed to apply the Regulation in conformity with its fundamental objectives: allowing concentrations which bring about necessary corporate reorganisations in the Community as a result of the opening of national markets to Community and world markets, while prohibiting or modifying concentrations which are likely to result in lasting damage to effective competition in the common market or a substantial part of it.[365]

c. CONCLUSIONS ON TECHNICAL AND ECONOMIC PROGRESS AND INDUSTRIAL POLICY

The Merger Task Force does not appear, overtly at least, to allow industrial or efficiency criteria to prevail in merger policy. Rather, such criteria and other political factors are likely to arise, if it all, at the final stage, the decision of the College of Commissioners. '[T]he industrial policy issue may be less important than the danger of "agency capture".'[366] It is clear, however, that the Commission does not seek to prevent mergers as an aim of its merger control. Instead, it seeks, where possible, to facilitate mergers, if necessary by persuading the parties to modify parts of the concentration and/or by accepting obligations and conditions.

(iii) THE FAILING FIRM DEFENCE

The failing firm defence is well established in US antitrust case law and referred to in the US Horizontal Merger Guidelines.[367] The defence provides an escape route for a firm facing an otherwise inevitable liquidation. Historically, it appears to have been adopted to ensure the protection of the creditors, owners, and/or employees of small businesses and as such is concerned not with efficiency but with distributive justice. It has been suggested, however, that 'a strong argument can be made that a narrowly applied failing company defense is economically efficient . . . The failing company defense could be efficient when it (1) enables a failing firm and its creditors to avoid the high administrative costs of bankruptcy; and (2) it keeps on the market productive assets that are worth keeping in production and would likely to be taken out of production were it not for the merger. Offsetting these advantages is the social cost of any monopoly pricing that flows from the merger itself, less the social cost that would flow from any monopoly created if the failing firm simply went out of business'.[368] It has thus been held in the USA that the defence may be raised where an undertaking can establish that the failing company will fail to meet its financial obligations in the future, will be unable to reorganize successfully, and has unsuccessfully sought reasonable, less anti-competitive alternative offers (i.e. an acquisition by a smaller competitor or non-competitor).[369] This position is broadly adopted by the 1992 Guidelines:

'A merger is not likely to create or enhance market power or facilitate its exercise if the following circumstances are met: 1) the allegedly failing firm would be unable to meet its financial obligations in the near future; 2) it would be unable to reorganize successfully under Chapter 11 of the Bankruptcy Act; 3) it has made unsuccessful good-faith efforts to elicit reasonable alternative offers of

---

[365] *Community Merger Control: Report from the Commission on the Implementation of the Merger Regulation*, COM(93)385, 4.

[366] See W. Sauter *Competition Law and Industrial Policy in the EU* (Clarendon Press, Oxford, 1997), 140.

[367] See *supra* n. 337.

[368] H. Hovenkamp, *Federal Antitrust Policy: The Law of Competition and its Practice* (West Publishing Co, 1994), para. 12.8, 494–5.

[369] See, e.g., *Citizen Publishing Co.* v. *United States*, 394 US 131, 138, 89 S Ct. 927, 931 (1969).

acquisition of the assets of the failing firm that would both keep its tangible and intangible assets in the relevant market and pose a less severe danger to competition than does the proposed merger: and 4) absent the acquisition, the assets of the failing firm would exit the relevant market.'[370]

The language of the Merger Regulation does not, at first sight, seem to leave room for a failing firm defence. The question whether or not an undertaking with large market shares could combine activities with its only, or main, failing competitor was raised in *Kali und Salz/MdK/Treuhand.*[371]

It has already been seen that the case concerned the combination of the potash and rock-salt activities of Kali und Salz and Mitteldeutsche Kali AG (MdK, owned by Treuhand). Although the Commission found that the concentration would acquire enormous shares on the potash market in Germany and the magnesium products market of 98 per cent and 100 per cent respectively, it concluded that the concentration did not lead to the creation or strengthening of a dominant position within the meaning of Article 2(2) of the Merger Regulation. It was not the merger that could be said to be the cause of the deterioration in the competitive structure. Even if the merger was prohibited, the acquiring undertaking would inevitably achieve or reinforce its dominant position to the same extent. The parties established (the onus being on them to do so) that: (1) the acquired undertaking, MdK, would have inevitably have been forced out of the market (it was in a critical economic position following the collapse of the relevant markets); (2) the acquiring undertaking, Kali und Salz, would inevitably acquire the market share since it was the only other relevant participator on the respective markets; and (3) no less anti-competitive purchase was possible (although tenders had been invited all other alternatives had practically been ruled out). The failing company defence thus succeeded and the Commission's approach was upheld by the ECJ on appeal.[372] The Court affirmed that these three conditions had to be satisfied. It stated:

Cases C–68/94 and C–30/95, *France* v. *Commission, Société Commerciale des Potasses et de l'Azote (SCPA)* v. *Commission* [1998] ECR I–1375, [1998] 4 CMLR 829

Court of Justice

100. The Commission concedes that in the contested decision it did not adopt the American 'failing company defence' in its entirety. However, it fails to see how that could affect the lawfulness of its decision.

101. It considers, moreover, that it has shown to the necessary legal standard that the criteria it used for the application of the 'failing company defence' were indeed satisfied in the present case.

---

[370] 1992 Guidelines, (revised in 1997), para. 5.1. The Guidelines also recognize a failing division defence.

[371] Case IV/M308 [1994] OJ L186/30, [1994] 4 CMLR 526; on appeal Cases C–68/94 and C–30/95, *France* v. *Commission, Société Commerciale des Potasses et de l'Azote (SCPA)* v. *Commission* [1998] ECR I–1375, [1998] 4 CMLR 829.

[372] An approach similar to that of the USA has, therefore, been adopted. In the USA it is not, however, necessary to show that, absent the merger, the acquiring firm would have acquired the failing firm's market share (it remains to be seen whether or not the Commission will insist on this requirement in all cases). The Commission in para. 112 of its decision recognizes that the conditions it set out in para. 111 are not identical to those set out in US law. It did not however wish simply to ape the US position.

102. With respect to the likelihood that MdK would soon be forced out unless it was acquired by another operator, the Commission observes that in points 76 and 77 of the contested decision it stated that Treuhand could not be expected to use public funds to cover the long-term debts of an undertaking which was no longer economically viable, and that even if it does not happen immediately, for social, regional and general policy reasons, it is very probable that MdK will close down in the near future.

103. It is also not disputed that MdK's share of the market in Germany will in all probability be absorbed by K + S.

104. As regards the condition that there should be no less anticompetitive alternative to the acquisition of MdK, the Commission refers to points 81 to 90 of the contested decision. It considers, moreover, that the French Government has not shown how the criticisms of the MdK trade unions could call into question its assessment. After all, the Commission was not satisfied with the finding that the tendering procedure had not permitted another purchaser to be found, but had itself carried out a further inquiry.

105. With respect to the absence of conditions for authorisation of the concentration on the German market, the Commission observes that the French Government does not specify what commitments K+S and MdK could have entered into in order to open the German market to competition. The argument which the French Government attempts to base on the Nestlé/Perrier decision is immaterial. In that decision, according to the Commission, it was possible to authorise the concentration in view of certain commitments relating to the structure of competition in the relevant product market. In the present case, however, in order to open the German market to competition, it would be necessary to attack not the structure of competition but the behaviour of buyers. In the Commission's opinion, even if the means to open the German market could have been structural, no solution to the acquisition of MdK with a lesser effect on competition was available.

106. The German Government submits that, under Article 2(3) of the Regulation, a concentration may be prohibited only if it will worsen conditions of competition. There is no causal link between the concentration and its effect on competition where the identical worsening of conditions of competition is to be expected even without the concentration. That will be the case when the three conditions applied by the Commission are satisfied.

107. The German Government submits that, contrary to the French Government's contention, the Commission has shown to the necessary legal standard that the conditions it laid down were satisfied. First, MdK is not viable on its own, that is to say, it is not possible to restructure the undertaking while preserving its autonomy in the market. In point 76 of the contested decision, the Commission gave solid reasons for considering that with Treuhand's 100% ownership being maintained MdK was not likely to be rescued in the long term. Second, there is no doubt that MdK's market share would automatically be absorbed by K + S, since K+S would be alone on the relevant market after MdK had been forced out, and that is an essential condition in this context. Third, the German Government submits that the Commission gave exhaustive reasons as to why no alternative means of acquiring MdK was available.

108. As to the approval of the concentration on the German market without conditions or obligations, the German Government observes that in the absence of a causal link between the concentration and the strengthening of a dominant position, one of the conditions for imposing a prohibition under Article 2(3) of the Regulation was not fulfilled. The concentration therefore had to be authorised without obligations or conditions.

109. The Court observes at the outset that under Article 2(2) of the Regulation, a 'concentration

which does not create or strengthen a dominant position as a result of which effective competition would be significantly impeded in the common market or in a substantial part of it shall be declared compatible with the common market'.

110. Thus if a concentration is not the cause of the creation or strengthening of a dominant position which has a significant impact on the competitive situation on the relevant market, it must be declared compatible with the common market.

111. It appears from point 71 of the contested decision that, in the Commission's opinion, a concentration which would normally be considered as leading to the creation or reinforcement of a dominant position on the part of the acquiring undertaking may be regarded as not being the cause of it if, even in the event of the concentration being prohibited, that undertaking would inevitably achieve or reinforce a dominant position. Point 71 goes on to state that, as a general matter, a concentration is not the cause of the deterioration of the competitive structure if it is clear that:

—the acquired undertaking would in the near future be forced out of the market if not taken over by another undertaking,

—the acquiring undertaking would gain the market share of the acquired undertaking if it were forced out of the market,

—there is no less anticompetitive alternative purchase.

112. It must be observed, first of all, that the fact that the conditions set by the Commission for concluding that there was no causal link between the concentration and the deterioration of the competitive structure do not entirely coincide with the conditions applied in connection with the United States 'failing company defence' is not in itself a ground of invalidity of the contested decision. Solely the fact that the conditions set by the Commission were not capable of excluding the possibility that a concentration might be the cause of the deterioration in the competitive structure of the market could constitute a ground of invalidity of the decision.

113. In the present case, the French Government disputes the relevance of the criterion that it must be verified that the acquiring undertaking would in any event obtain the acquired undertaking's share of the market if the latter were to be forced out of the market.

114. However, in the absence of that criterion, a concentration could, provided the other criteria were satisfied, be considered as not being the cause of the deterioration of the competitive structure of the market even though it appeared that, in the event of the concentration not proceeding, the acquiring undertaking would not gain the entire market share of the acquired undertaking. Thus, it would be possible to deny the existence of a causal link between the concentration and the deterioration of the competitive structure of the market even though the competitive structure of the market would deteriorate to a lesser extent if the concentration did not proceed.

115. The introduction of that criterion is intended to ensure that the existence of a causal link between the concentration and the deterioration of the competitive structure of the market can be excluded only if the competitive structure resulting from the concentration would deteriorate in similar fashion even if the concentration did not proceed.

Until the end of 1999 this was the only case in which the Commission has accepted the defence applied (but not the only case in which it has been pleaded[373]). It appears that the

---

[373] See, e.g., Case IV/M774, *Saint-Gobain/Wacker-Chemie-NOM* [1997] OJ L247/1, [1997] 4 CMLR 25.

defence does not apply where only part of a firm is failing[374] 'or to companies having entered a so-called 'death spiral''.[375]

Although the Court and Commission have referred to the failing firm defence, in reality it is not a defence. Rather, it appears that where it is established that the creation or strengthening of an acquiring firm's dominant positions is a result, not of the concentration, but of market circumstances (the fact that the acquired firm would otherwise have failed and that the acquiring firm would inevitably have picked up the market share (there being no possible alternative purchasers etc.)) so that the concentration is compatible with the common market (Article 2(2) of the Merger Regulation). The chain of causation between the concentration and the creation or strengthening of the dominant position is broken.

(iv) SOCIAL AND OTHER CONSIDERATIONS

Following the Commission's decision to clear the merger in *Nestlé/Perrier* a challenge was made to the decision by the trade unions in the Perrier group. It was argued before the CFI that the Commission had failed to take account of the employment consequences of the merger. Recital 13 to the Merger Regulation states that the assessment of the compatibility of a merger should be made 'within the general framework of the fundamental objectives referred to in Article 2 of the E.C. Treaty, including that of strengthening the Community's economic and social cohesion referred to in Article [157 (ex Article 130a)]'. Although this requirement is set out only in the Treaty recitals and seems hard to reconcile with the test set out in Article 2 of the Merger Regulation, the Court's judgment in this case indicates that the Commission may be obliged to ensure that the appraisal of a concentration is conducted within the framework of Article 2 of the Treaty:

Case T–12/93, *Comité Central d'Entreprise de la Société Anonyme Vittel* v. *Commission* [1995] ECR II–1247

Court of First Instance

38. For that purpose it must be noted to begin with that in the scheme of Regulation No 4064/89, the primacy given to the establishment of a system of free competition may in certain cases be reconciled, in the context of the assessment of whether a concentration is compatible with the common market, with the taking into consideration of the social effects of that operation if they are liable to affect adversely the social objectives referred to in Article 2 of the Treaty. The Commission may therefore have to ascertain whether the concentration is liable to have consequences, even if only indirectly, for the position of the employees in the undertakings in question, such as to affect the level or conditions of employment in the Community or a substantial part of it.

39. Article 2(1)(b) of Regulation No 4064/89 requires the Commission to draw up an economic balance for the concentration in question, which may, in some circumstances entail considerations of a social nature, as is confirmed by the thirteenth recital in the preamble to the regulation, which states that the 'the Commission must place its appraisal within the general framework of the achievement of the fundamental objectives referred to in Article 2 of the Treaty, including that of

---

[374] *Ibid.*

[375] J. Faull and A. Nikpay (eds.) *The EC Law of Competition* (Oxford University Press, 1999), para. 1.66 citing Case IV.M877 *Boeing McDonnell-Douglas* [1997] OJ L336/16, [1997] 5 CMLR 270.

strengthening the Community's economic and social cohesion, referred to in Article 130a'. In that legal context, the express provision in Article 18(4) of the regulation, giving specific expression to the principle stated in the nineteenth recital that the representatives of the employees of the undertakings concerned are entitled, upon application, to be heard, manifests an intention to ensure that the collective interests of those employees are taken into consideration in the administrative procedure.

40. In those circumstances, the Court considers that, in the scheme of Regulation No 4064/89, the position of the employees of the undertakings which are the subject of the concentration may in certain cases be taken into consideration by the Commission when adopting its decision. That is why the regulation makes individual mention of the recognized representatives of the employees of those undertakings, who constitute a closed category clearly defined at the time of adoption of the decision, by expressly and specifically giving them the right to submit their observations in the administrative procedure. Those organizations, who are responsible for upholding the collective interests of the employees they represent, have a relevant interest with respect to the social considerations which may in appropriate cases be taken into account by the Commission in the context of its appraisal of whether the concentration is lawful from the point of view of Community law.

It seems unlikely that any similar claim will be successful as a result of the Court's finding that any prejudice to the applicants was not attributable to the Commission's decision because the employee's rights on the transfer of a business were protected by the Community's Acquired Rights Directive (Directive 77/187/EEC).[376]

Given that the final decision to prohibit or clear the merger is taken by the College of Commissioners as a whole, it cannot conclusively be stated that employment and/or other considerations will influence the final decision taken.[377]

D. CAN A MERGER BE PROHIBITED WHERE IT DOES NOT LEAD TO THE CREATION OR STRENGTHENING OF A DOMINANT POSITION AS A RESULT OF WHICH COMPETITION IN A SUBSTANTIAL PART OF THE COMMON MARKET WOULD BE SIGNIFICANTLY IMPEDED?

(i) GENERAL

It is clear from the Merger Regulation that a concentration which does not lead to the creation or strengthening of a dominant position, as a result of which effective competition would be significantly impeded in the common market or in a substantial part of it, is compatible with the common market.[378] It is possible, however, that in such cases steps may nonetheless be taken by the authorities of the individual Member States to preclude the merger or aspects of the merger.

---

[376] [1977] OJ L61/27.
[377] See discussion *supra* 799–801.
[378] Merger Reg., Art. 2(2).

(ii) LEGITIMATE INTERESTS

It has already been seen that a Member State may, under, Article 21(3) of the Merger Regulation, take steps to protect legitimate interests which are not taken into consideration under the Regulation itself. Thus even if a concentration with a Community dimension is cleared by the Commission, a Member State may rely on applicable provisions of national law to prohibit a merger in so far as is necessary to protect public security, the plurality of the press, or any other legitimate interests. The national authority in making its assessment may take account only of factors which are not taken into account under Article 2 of the Merger Regulation. Further, any steps taken by a national authority must comply with the principles of Community law, in particular the principle of proportionality.

(iii) ESSENTIAL INTERESTS OF SECURITY

It has also been seen that Member States may, under Article 296 (ex Article 223) of the Treaty, take such measure it considers necessary to protect essential interests of security connected with the production or trade in arms etc.

(iv) DISTINCT MARKETS

In addition, Article 9 allows a Member State to request that a concentration, or aspects of a concentration, be referred to it where that merger leads to the creation or strengthening of a dominant position as a result of which effective competition would be impeded in that State (or a part of it) which presents all the characteristics of a distinct market.

E. JOINT VENTURES WITH CO-OPERATIVE ASPECTS

All jointly controlled full-function joint ventures established on a lasting basis which have a Community dimension fall for assessment under the Merger Regulation. In the case of joint ventures it is necessary first to determine whether or not they lead to the creation or strengthening of a dominant position as a result of which effective competition in the common market is significantly impeded.[379] Secondly, it is necessary to determine whether the joint venture will lead to the co-ordination of the competitive behaviour of undertakings which remain independent on any particular market (these joint ventures would previously have fallen for assessment not under the Merger Regulation but under Article 81[380]). This may well occur if two or more of the parents compete in an upstream or downstream market or in the joint venture in its market . If the object or effect of the joint venture is to co-ordinate the independent undertakings' behaviour Article 2(4) of the Merger Regulation provides that these co-ordinative aspects of the joint venture will be appraised in accordance with criteria set out in Article 81(1) and (3):

---

[379] Merger Reg., Art. 2(2) and (3).
[380] See *supra* 721 ff.

4. To the extent that the creation of a joint venture constituting a concentration pursuant to Article 3 has its object or effect the co-ordination of the competitive behaviour of undertakings that remain independent, such co-ordination shall be appraised in accordance with the criteria of Article [81(1)] and (3) of the Treaty, with a view to establishing whether or not the operation is compatible with the common market.

In making this appraisal, the Commission shall take into account in particular:

—whether two or more parent companies retain to a significant extent activities in the same market as the joint venture or in a market which is downstream of upstream from the joint venture or in a neighbouring market closely related to this market,

—whether the co-ordination which is the direct consequence of the creation of the joint venture affords the undertakings concerned the possibility of eliminating competition in respect of a substantial part of the products or services in question.[381]

Although Article 2(4) has not yet generated much decisional practice it seems that the appraisal made under Article 2(4) is made in accordance with the way in which it used to assess co-operative joint ventures under Article 81.[382] Further, there must be a causal link between the setting up of the joint venture and the appreciable restriction of competition on the market.[383] It may be however that the Commission has so far taken a more realistic approach to the co-ordinative aspects of the joint venture than it has previously done in its Article 81(1) decisions.[384] For example, in *Telia/Telenor/Schibsted*[385] the Commission considered a joint venture for the provision of various Internet services. The Commission considered that the parents remained active on two markets in which co-ordinated behaviour might be possible. In particular both Telia and Telor remained present on the market to provide 'dial-up' internet access. Although the parents already had joint market shares of between 35 per cent and 65 per cent of the market it was concluded that co-ordinated behaviour between the parents was not likely. These market shares were not significant on the growing market for dial up Internet access in Sweden. The market was characterized by high growth, low barriers to entry, and low switching costs. On the other market, the website production market, the parent companies and the joint venture had less than 10 per cent of the market. Any co-ordination on such a market would not would not amount to appreciable restriction of competition.[386]

---

[381] As amended by Reg. 1310/97, Art. (2).

[382] See *infra* Chap. 13. This approach was explained in the Commission Notice on the distinction between concentrative and co-operative joint ventures [1994] OJ C385/1. Note the new Commission Notice on the notion of full-function joint ventures, see discussion *supra* 724.

[383] See, e.g., Case IV/JV2, *ENEL/DT/FT* (1998, not reported). This case concerned a joint venture for fixed telephony in Italy. The Commission concluded that the likelihood of any co-ordination between the parents on the mobile market outside the joint venture (e.g. in France and Germany) would be due not to the joint venture at issue but to links and joint ventures previously concluded between the parties.

[384] See *supra* Chap. 4 and *infra* Chap. 13.

[385] Case IV/JV1 [1999] 4 CMLR 216.

[386] Interestingly, in this case the Commission appears to have accepted that there may be no appreciable restriction of competition where the parties have shares of up to 10% of the relevant market, but see *supra* Chap. 4 and *infra* Chap. 13.

F. ANCILLARY RESTRAINTS—RESTRICTIONS DIRECTLY RELATED AND NECESSARY TO THE CONCENTRATION

Ancillary restraints are clauses the presence of which is vital to the particular transaction since the transaction, in its absence, would not take place. For example, it is usually a condition of a sale of a business that the vendor covenants not to compete with the business for a period of time. Otherwise the goodwill of the business may be rendered valueless.[387] Similarly, in joint ventures the parents may agree to license intellectual property rights to the joint venture.

The Commission may clear ancillary restraints concluded in agreements between undertakings in its decision to clear the concentration as a whole. The concentration and ancillary restraints are therefore considered together. A decision of compatibility with the common market should, therefore, cover 'restrictions directly related and necessary to the implementation of the concentration' in both Phase II and Phase I proceedings.[388] No separate and time-consuming notification under Article 81 is necessary. The Commission issued a Notice on ancillary restraints[389] which is to be replaced by a Notice regarding restrictions directly related and necessary to concentrations.[390]

6. APPEALS

The ordinary provisions in the EC Treaty authorizing the review by the ECJ of Community acts and Community institutions' failure to act apply.[391] A party to a concentration may, therefore, institute proceedings against Commission merger decision under Article 230 of the Treaty. Appeals go initially to the CFI and subsequently, on points of law, to the ECJ.[392] Article 21(1) clearly envisages such a right of appeal. It provides:

1. Subject to review by the Court of Justice, the Commission shall have sole jurisdiction to take the decisions provided for in this Regulation.

Further, third parties, to whom a merger decision is not addressed, may appeal if it can be established that that the decision 'is of direct and individual concern to the third party'. Thus a challenge to a merger decision has successfully been commenced by employees of a company involved in a merger,[393] by a competitor of the merging parties,[394] and by a

---

[387] See, e.g., the discussion of non-compete clauses *supra*, in Chap. 4.

[388] Merger Regulation, Art. 8(2). See also Art. 6(1).

[389] [1990] OJ C203/5.

[390] See the draft Notice [2000] 4 CMLR 779; see also [2000] 4 CMLR 788 (explanatory guidelines).

[391] See *infra* Chap. 14.

[392] But see *supra* n. 293 and accompanying text.

[393] Case T–12/93 *Comité Central d'Entreprise de la Société Anonyme Vittel v. Commission* [1995] ECR II–1247.

[394] Case T–2/93, *Air France v. Commission* [1994] ECR II–323.

third party affected by commitments given in a merger decision.[395] The Court has warned, however, that it will not take an interventionist approach. Rather, it takes full account of the wide discretion that the Regulation imposes on the Commission and the complex economic assessments required.[396]

[I]t should be observed that the basic provisions of Regulation 4064/89, in particular Article 2 thereof confer a discretion on the Commission, especially with respect to assessments of an economic nature. Consequently, review by the Community judicature of the exercise of that discretion, which is essential for defining the rules on concentrations, must take account of the discretionary margin implicit in the provisions of an economic nature which form part of the rules on concentrations (Joined Cases C68/94 and & 30/95 *France and Others* v. *EC Commission*: [1998] ECR 1375, [1998] 4 CMLR 829, paras [223] and [224].[397]

The appeals procedures is discussed more fully in Chapter 14. An important question which arises specifically in merger cases is whether there should be a fast-track procedure for appeals, as in Austria, for example. Although the Commission has to proceed within very tight time limits under the Regulation itself it may be years before a review of its decision is conducted by the Court. This, of course, puts the Commission in a powerful position.[398]

7. FURTHER READING

A. BOOKS

BRITTAN, L., *Competition Policy and Merger Control in the Single European Market* (Hersh Lauterpacht Memorial Lectures) (Grotius, 1991)

BROBERG, M., *The European Commission's Jurisdiction to Scrutinise Mergers* (Kluwer, 1998)

COOK, C. J., and KERSE, C. S., *EC Merger Control* (3rd edn., Sweet & Maxwell, 2000)

HAWK, B. E., and HUSER, H. L., *European*

Community Merger Control, A Practitioner's Guide (Kluwer Law International, 1996)

HOVENKAMP, H., Federal Antitrust Policy: The Law of Competition and its Practice (West Publishing Co, 1994)

SAUTER, W., *Competition Law and Industrial Policy in the EU* (Oxford University Press, 1997), 132–41

B. ARTICLES

BRIGHT, B., 'The European Merger Control Regulation: Do Member States still have an

Independent Role in Merger Control?' [1991] *ECLR* 139

---

[395] Cases C–68/94 and C–30/95, *France* v. *Commission, Société Commerciale des Potasses et de l'Azote (SCPA)* v. *Commission* [1998] ECR I–1375, [1998] 4 CMLR 829, paras. 173–175.

[396] Cases C–68/94 and C–30/95, *France* v. *Commission, Société Commerciale des Potasses et de l'Azote (SCPA)* v. *Commission* [1998] ECR I–1375, [1998] 4 CMLR 829, paras. 223–224.

[397] Case T–221/95, *Endemol Entertainment Holding BV* v. *Commission* [1999] ECR II–1299 [1999] 5 CMLR 611.

[398] This fact may encourage the undertakings involved to give commitments to persuade the Commission to authorize the merger. Further, the parties will have to observe a prohibition or commitments imposed until the Commission's decision is suspended or annulled.

BRITTAN, L., 'The Law and Policy of Merger Control in the EEC' (1990) 15 *ELRev.* 351

CAMESASCA, D., 'The Explicit Efficiency Defence in Merger Control: Does it Make the Difference?' [1999] *ECLR* 26

DOWNES, T. A., and MacDOUGALL, D. S., 'Significantly Impeding Effective Competition: Substantive Appraisal under the Merger Regulation' [1994] *ELR* 286

GOYDER, D., 'The Implementation of the Merger Control Regulation: New Wine in Old Bottles' [1992] *Current Legal Problems* 117

HACKER, N., 'The Kali+Salz Case – the Re-examination of a Merger after an Argument by the Court', Commission's *Competition Policy Newsletter* 1998/3, 40.

JACQUIMIN, A., 'Mergers and European Policy' in P. H. Admiral (ed.), *Merger and Competition Policy in the European Community* (Blackwell, 1990)

MOTTA, M., 'EC Merger Policy and the Airtours Case' [2000] *ECLR* 199

RIDYARD, D., 'Economic Analysis of Single Firm and Oligopolistic Dominance' [1994] *ECLR* 255

TURNER, D., 'Conglomerate Mergers and Section 7 of the Clayton Act' (1965) 78 *Harv. LR* 1313

WHISH, R., 'Collective Dominance' in D. O'Keefe and M. Andenas (eds.), *Liber Amicorum for Lord Slynn* (Kluwer, 2000)

13

JOINT VENTURES AND OTHER BENEFICIAL HORIZONTAL ARRANGEMENTS

1. INTRODUCTION

Co-operation between firms at the same level of the market is not necessarily anti-competitive. Outside the realm of hard-core cartel arrangements involving price-fixing, market-sharing, and quotas,[1] horizontal agreements may promote economic efficiency and integration. Co-operation may enable economies of scale to be achieved, new products or services to be brought onto the market, and/or new markets to be penetrated. Competition authorities will wish to allow or even encourage such beneficial arrangements while remaining steadfast against agreements and concerted practices which rig prices and markets.

Non-cartel-type co-operation between undertakings can take a wide variety of forms. It ranges from temporary arrangements at one level of activity, such as the research and development (R&D) stage, to what is in effect a merger uniting the undertakings' entire operations in a particular area of interest. Sometimes the parties to the arrangements are actual or potential competitors in the field in which they are co-operating, but sometimes they bring to the collaborative enterprise skills or resources which are complementary rather than parallel. Competition authorities, in judging whether the arrangements restrict competition, and if so whether they should be permitted, will be concerned not only with reductions of competition between the parties themselves but also with effects on third parties.

These types of co-operative arrangements are very common. Firms frequently look for 'partners' for particular operations, either in the short or long term. Notably, modern technological developments (and the liberalization of hitherto regulated markets) have led to an increase in collaborative arrangements as companies active in rapidly developing markets such as telecommunications, information technology, and the media decide to pool their resources and expertise in order to make the next leap forward feasible.

EC competition policy towards horizontal co-operation between undertakings has changed over the years, and one cannot assume that the same attitude towards a particular

[1] See Chap. 11.

arrangement would be taken now as in the past. The Commission's thinking about what amounts to a 'restriction of competition' in this context has developed, and there have also been changes in the procedures dealing with co-operation between undertakings. In 1997[2] the Commission announced the launch of a review of its policy towards horizontal arrangements with the object of clarifying the instruments, such as regulations and notices, in this field. The review was intensified in 1998 and the Commission decided that the existing provisions needed to be improved and updated.[3] A set of draft guidelines on horizontal co-operation and drafts of new block exemptions for R&D agreements and specialization agreements were put out for public consultation on 27 April 2000.

This chapter considers first a particular *form* of horizontal arrangement, the joint venture. It then considers how Article 81 applies to types of co-operation such as R&D and special-ization. It will be seen that in this area of competition law there are very few judgments of the Court. This is because, on the whole, the Commission has permitted the co-operation to take place, although sometimes after requiring that the plans be amended. Undertakings given the go-ahead have therefore not challenged the Commission in the Court, preferring if necessary to comply with the Commission's requirements and get on with the project. The result is that in this area of competition law the Commission has had an even freer hand than usual.

2. JOINT VENTURES

A. WHAT IS A JOINT VENTURE?

The term 'joint venture' could be used to describe virtually any commercial arrangement involving two or more firms.[4] It is normally used in competition law, however, to describe an arrangement by which two or more undertakings (the 'parents'), in order to achieve a particular commercial goal, integrate part of their operations, and put them under joint control.

According to the Commission's 1993 Notice on co-operative joint ventures[5] all joint ventures 'embody a special, institutionally fixed form of cooperation between undertakings. They are versatile instruments at the disposal of the parents, with the help of which different goals can be pursued and attained.' In the Notice on the concept of a full-function joint venture[6] the Commission says that joint ventures encompass a broad range of operations from merger-like operations to co-operation for particular functions such as R&D, produc-tion, and distribution. However, it identifies the essential feature as joint control by two or more other undertakings. The entity set up by the parents may take the form of a jointly

---

[2] Commission, *XXVIIth Report on Competition Policy* (Commission, 1997) pts 46 and 47. The review was provoked by the imminent expiry of the relevant block exemptions: see *infra* 831–833.

[3] Commission, *XXVIIIth, Report on Competition Policy* (Commission, 1998), pts 54 and 55.

[4] See J. Faull and A. Nikpay (eds.), *The EC Law of Competition* (Oxford University Press. 1999), para. 6.47.

[5] [1993] OJ C43/2, para. 1.

[6] [1998] OJ C66/1, para. 3.

controlled subsidiary company, but it may only be a joint committee or a partnership. In every case, however, the parents each put resources into the enterprise: finance, intellectual property rights, know-how, personnel, premises, or equipment for example.

B. COMPETITION CONCERNS IN RESPECT OF JOINT VENTURES

The competition concerns over joint ventures concern, first, the relations between the parents. A joint venture, unlike a full-scale merger, leaves the parents as economically independent undertakings. Their common links to the joint venture, however, may lead them to engage in collusion in matters outside the ambit of the joint venture, so-called 'spill-over effects'. If this happens the efficiency gains and other advantages derived from the activities of the joint venture may be offset by restrictions of competition in other respects. Secondly, there is the matter of a reduction of actual or potential competition between the parents or between the parents and the joint venture within the ambit of the joint venture. This needs to be weighed against the competitive gains from the new presence on the market. Thirdly, a joint venture may have the effect of foreclosing the market to competition. As in other areas of competition law, the question whether the undertakings concerned have market power plays an important part.

C. JOINT VENTURES AND THE MERGER REGULATION

(i) THE TREATMENT OF JOINT VENTURES PRIOR TO THE MERGER REGULATION

Before the Merger Regulation[7] came into force in 1990, joint ventures were dealt with under Article 81 unless they involved the transfer of assets to the new entity to an extent which amounted to a 'partial merger'.[8] This concept was described in the *VIth Report on Competition Policy*:[9]

Even where the transfer of assets is limited only to a part of the total business previously engaged in independently by the parent companies, the transfer may in exceptional cases be treated in the same way as a merger. But such exceptional cases can be taken to arise only where the parent companies completely and irreversibly abandon business in the area covered by the joint venture, and provided that the pooling of certain areas of business does not weaken competition in other areas, and particularly in related areas, where the firms involved remain formally independent of each other.

Such transactions fell into a gap in the competition rules: Article 81(1) was not applied to them, Article 82 did not apply unless one of the parties was strengthening an already

---

[7] Council Reg. 4064/89 on the control of concentrations between undertakings. [1989] OJ L395/1; see *supra* Chap. 12.

[8] As in *SHV/Chevron* [1975] OJ L38/14, [1975] 1 CMLR D68.

[9] (Commission, 1976), pt 55.

dominant position,[10] and there was no other Community merger control.[11] In the case of other joint ventures Article 81 applied.

(ii) THE TREATMENT OF JOINT VENTURES UNDER THE MERGER REGULATION PRIOR TO 1 MARCH 1998

a. GENERAL

The treatment of joint ventures changed when the Merger Regulation (ECMR)[12] came into force in 1990.

As explained in Chapter 12 the scheme set up by the Merger Regulation is that concentrations with a Community dimension are dealt with by the Competition DG according to the procedure set up by the Regulation, while concentrations without a Community dimension are subject only to national regulation. What is meant by a 'concentration' is defined in Article 3 and encompasses some joint ventures, but not all. The types of joint venture to which the Merger Regulation applies has changed since 1990, principally when the Regulation was amended in 1997.[13]

b. THE DISTINCTION BETWEEN CONCENTRATIVE AND CO-OPERATIVE JOINT VENTURES

As explained in Chapter 12 the original version of the Merger Regulation created a distinction between 'concentrative' and 'co-operative' joint ventures. Only the former were dealt under the Merger Regulation as concentrations. Article 81 continued to apply to 'co-operative' joint ventures.

According to the original version of Article 3(2) of the ECMR, a joint venture was *not* a concentration if it had 'as its object or effect the coordination of the competitive behaviour of undertakings which remain independent'. Such joint ventures were called 'co-operative'. However, a joint venture *did* constitute a concentration if it performed 'on a lasting basis all the functions of an autonomous economic entity, which does not give rise to coordination of the competitive behaviour of the parties among themselves or between them and the joint venture'. Such joint ventures were called 'concentrative'.

Therefore two conditions had to be fulfilled if the joint venture was to be deemed concentrative, one positive and one negative. The positive condition was that the joint venture must perform on a lasting basis all the functions of an autonomous economic entity. The negative one was that there must be an absence of the co-ordination of economic behaviour between the parties *inter se* or between them and the joint venture.

The Commission recognized from the start that the distinction between these two types of joint venture would be difficult to draw in practice and it issued a Notice (known as the

---

[10] Under the principle in Case 6/72, *Europemballage Corp. & Continental Can Co Inc* v. *EC Commission* [1973] ECR 215, [1973] CMLR 199.

[11] See *SHV/Chevron* [1975] OJ L38/14, [1975]1 CMLR D68; *Zip Fasteners*, Commission's *VIIth, Report on Competition Policy* (Commission, 1978) pt 29; J. Temple Lang, 'Joint Ventures under the EEC Treaty Rules on Competition' (1978) 13 *Irish Jurist* 132.

[12] Council Reg. 4064/89 on the control of concentrations between undertakings, [1989] OJ L395/1 (amended [1990] OJ L257/13).

[13] By Council Reg. 1310/97 [1997] OJ L180/1.

Interface Notice) to give guidance.[14] The distinction was absolutely crucial because it had both procedural and substantive consequences, as set out in Chapter 12.[15]

The advantages of a joint venture being treated as concentrative encouraged parties to structure deals so that they fell within the Merger Regulation. In recognition of the attractions of the fixed time-limits in the Merger Regulation, the Commission introduced a 'fast-track' procedure as from 1 January 1993 whereby companies which notify a 'structural' type of joint venture[16] will get a comfort letter or a 'warning' letter within two months of the Commission receiving complete notification.[17] This, however, is not binding, but only a matter of internal discipline and does not apply to later stages in the process.

c. THE CRITERIA FOR A CONCENTRATIVE JOINT VENTURE

The positive criteria for a concentrative joint venture were that it had to perform on a lasting basis all the functions of an autonomous economic entity. The meaning of this was explained in the 1990 Interface Notice. However, the requirement of 'autonomy' as set out in the Notice created problems in practice as regards the joint venture's relationship with its parents, and in a number of decisions under the Merger Regulation the Commission in effect rendered the Notice a dead letter in that respect. When the Notice was replaced by a new one in 1994[18] it stressed the need for the joint venture to be 'full-function' rather than concentrating on the idea of autonomy.

The negative criterion was that the joint venture should not have as its object or effect the co-ordination of the competitive behaviour of undertakings which remained independent. This was at the heart of the distinction between the two categories of joint venture and caused many joint ventures to fail to qualify as concentrative. The 1990 Notice made it clear that the co-ordination referred to in Article 3(2) included co-ordination between the parents and the joint venture. This, again, proved difficult in practice because if strictly applied if would have caught many joint ventures which would otherwise have qualified as concentrative. The Commission, however, came to the view that such vertical co-ordination was not of such concern and the 1994 Notice sidelined the issue, paragraph 8 saying that co-ordination between the parents and the joint venture would make a joint venture cooperative rather than concentrative only in so far as that co-ordination was an instrument for producing or reinforcing co-ordination *between the parents.*

d. THE REASON FOR THE CONCENTRATIVE/CO-OPERATIVE DISTINCTION: THE PROBLEM OF THE CO-ORDINATION OF COMPETITIVE BEHAVIOUR BETWEEN THE PARENTS

The distinction between concentrative and co-operative joint ventures was based on the idea that mergers merit favourable treatment[19] because they generate greater efficiencies and

---

[14] Commission Notice on co-operative and concentrative joint venture [1990] OJ C203/6.

[15] See *supra* Chap. 12.

[16] One which involves an important change in the structure of the parties' assets.

[17] See Commission's *XXII Report on Competition Policy*, (Commission , 1992), pts 122–124. The procedure was later incorporated into Reg. 3385/94 [1994] L337/28, containing the revised Form A/B.

[18] Notice on the distinction between concentrative and co-operative joint ventures (the 1994 Interface Notice) [1994] OJ C385/1.

[19] See *supra* Chap. 12.

other economic benefits than those produced by lesser degrees of integration between undertakings. Unless a dominant position is created or strengthened, those efficiencies can be expected to be fully exploited for the benefit of consumers.[20] Although a merger replaces two or more undertakings with only one, that one will act on the market as an independent entity and does not pose the same dangers to the competitive process as collusion between undertakings.

The Merger Regulation did not therefore accord the 'privilege' of being treated as a concentration to transactions which were 'partial function' and/or for a limited duration and did not create a 'full-function' joint venture. However, because of the negative criteria in Article 3(2), it also excluded from the privilege those joint ventures which *were* full-function but which would lead to the co-ordination of their parents' conduct in areas which had *not* been merged and where the parents remained competitors. The argument was that such transactions lead to anti-competitive effects which are not compensated for by the creation of efficiencies. There is also the question of situations where the parents continue to operate in the same market as the joint venture, as the parents can be expected to co-ordinate their competitive behaviour with the joint venture which again leads to losses in efficiencies.

Nevertheless, these arguments are not universally accepted. Hawk, a leading American commentator, was highly critical of the concentrative/co-operative distinction.

B. Hawk, 'A Bright Line Shareholding Test to End the Nightmare under the EEC Merger Regulation' (1993) 30 *CMLRev.* 1155, 1160–1

... the theory of joint ventures underlying the existing CC distinction views limited duration, partial function and other 'cooperative' joint ventures as creating greater risks of competitive harm and fewer opportunities for competitive benefits than full mergers and acquisitions. In reality, virtually all joint ventures falling within the existing 'cooperative' category present fewer (and certainly no greater) risks of competitive harm and equivalent opportunities for competitive benefits as full mergers and acquisitions involving the same parties.

As a result, the CC distinction exhibits two fundamental defects. First, it treats 'like' transactions (i.e. those having similar economic effects) differently, without any credible legal or economic justification . . . Second, by applying stricter 'cartel' rules to 'cooperative' joint ventures, the CC distinction deters formation of desirable joint ventures, thereby ultimately leading to less competitive market structures in European industries: firms are encouraged to merge their competing operations fully and permanently rather than engage in limited duration/partial function or other 'cooperative' joint ventures that create fewer long term risks of competitive harm, yet present equivalent opportunities for economic integration as full mergers and acquisitions . . .

The answer to this is that the Merger Regulation did not treat like phenomena differently because transactions which do not result in a complete and lasting integration of the parents' activities in a particular area are *not* equivalent to transactions which do. Nevertheless, the Commission was not happy with the rigid dividing line in Article 3(2) which dispatched what were in fact often very similar transactions down different procedural tracks to be judged by different tests. In the Green Paper on the Review of the Merger Regulation in

---

[20] See the discussion in J. Faull and A. Nikpay (eds.), *The EC Law of Competition* (Oxford University Press, 1999), paras. 6.56–6.67.

1996, following a consultation with industry and Member States, it suggested that changes should be made.[21] Some of the options put forward were merely for procedural changes, but in the end the Commission chose a more radical solution.

(iii) THE TREATMENT OF JOINT VENTURES AFTER THE COMING INTO FORCE OF REGULATION 1310/97 ON 1 MARCH 1998

Council Regulation 1310/97[22] amended the Merger Regulation in several respects.[23] As far as joint ventures are concerned, it altered the system radically by deleting the parts of Article 3(2) containing the negative criteria and adding a new paragraph to Article 2 on the appraisal of concentrations. Article 3(2) now reads:

The creation of a joint venture performing on a lasting basis all the functions of an autonomous economic entity shall constitute a concentration within the meaning of paragraph 1(b).

This means that there is still a distinction drawn between types of joint venture but the line is drawn in a different place. The crucial question now is simply: is it full-function. *All* full-function joint ventures are now treated as concentrations. The Commission, however, has not abandoned the belief that the possible co-ordination of the competitive behaviour of the parents needs to be considered under Article 81. The new Article 2(4) of the Merger Regulation subjects the co-ordinative aspects to Article 81, but this appraisal is done within the Merger Regulation procedure, rather than under Regulation 17.[24]

The application of the Merger Regulation, including Article 2(4), to full-function joint ventures is discussed in Chapter 12.

D. THE ASSESSMENT OF JOINT VENTURES UNDER ARTICLE 81

(i) GENERAL

Despite more transactions being drawn into the scope of the Merger Regulation by the 1997 amendments there nevertheless remain many joint ventures which are not full-function. In respect of these the question is still whether they fall within Article 81(1), and if so whether they qualify for exemption. It must always be remembered that any restriction of competition arising from the joint venture must be *appreciable* under the normal criteria for the application of Article 81(1), and it was partly on the this point that the CFI annulled the Commission decision in *European Night Services*,[25] discussed below.

As explained below,[26] the Commission previously took a very interventionist approach to joint ventures based on a fear of co-ordination between the parents and on the loss of

---

[21] COM(96)19 final, paras. 100–121.
[22] [1997] OJ L180/1.
[23] For the amendments generally, see Chap. 12.
[24] [1959–62] OJ Spec.Ed. 87.
[25] Cases T–374–375, 384 & 388/94, *European Night Services* v. *Commission* [1998] 5 CMLR 718.
[26] See *infra* 819–821.

potential competition. However, the *XIIIth Competition Policy Report* signalled a change of policy which was applied in subsequent cases.

An early Notice on co-operation agreements in 1968[27] stated that there were certain forms of co-operation between undertakings which would not normally fall within Article 81(1). This was in effect incorporated into the Notice which the Commission issued in 1993. This Notice concerned the assessment of co-operative joint ventures pursuant to Article 81[28] and summarized the Commission's administrative practice to date in order to inform undertakings 'about both the legal, and economic criteria which will guide the Commission in the future application of Article [81](1) and Article [81](3) to cooperative joint ventures'.[29] The Notice remained relevant even after the 1997 Merger Regulation amendments, although some of its references to full-function joint ventures had to be read in the light of those changes.

In 1985 the Commission adopted two block exemption regulations relevant, *inter alia*, to joint ventures. These were Regulation 417/85 on specialization agreements,[30] and Regulation 418/85 on R&D agreements.[31] As explained below, both Regulations have been of limited use because of their limited provisions. They originally expired at the end of 1997 but were extended until the end of 2000.

The review of horizontal agreements which the Commission inaugurated in 1997 encompasses joint ventures along with other co-operative arrangements. As we see below, the Draft Guidelines issued by the Commission in April 2000 do not deal with joint ventures as a separate species of agreement, but consider them according to their subject-matter.

(ii) THE DEVELOPMENT OF THE COMMISSION'S POLICY TOWARDS THE APPLICATION OF ARTICLE 81 TO JOINT VENTURES

Until the early 1980s the Commission's practice was to hold that joint ventures were, caught by Article 81(1), but then to exempt them under Article 81(3). It was invariably impressed by the benefits the joint venture offered, but considered that there was a restriction of competition involved which brought the joint venture within the prohibition. The concern about the loss of potential competition was vividly illustrated by the *Vacuum Interrupters* decision where the Commission found that the formation of a joint venture infringed Article 81(1) on the basis of the hypothetical possibility that despite all the evidence to the contrary the parents *might* each have proceeded alone, and *might* each have ultimately produced a commercial product which they could have sold in other Member States in competition with each other if a market had developed for it there.

---

[27] [1968] JO C75/3, rectified [1968] JO C84/14.

[28] [1993] OJ C43/2.

[29] *Ibid.*, para. 7.

[30] [1985] OJ L53/1 as amended by Commission Reg. 151/93 [1993] OJ L21/8 and extended by Commission Reg. 2236/97 [1997] OJ L306/12.

[31] [1985] OJ L53/5 as amended by Commission Reg. 151/93 [1993] OJ L21/8 and extended by Commission Reg. 2236/97 [1997] OJ L306/12.

AEI/Reyrolle Parsons re Vaccum Interrupters [1977] OJ L48/32, [1977] 1 CMLR D67

Two UK companies, AEI and Reyrolle Parsons, formed a jointly owned subsidiary company, Vacuum Interrupters Ltd, to develop, produce and sell a particular type of vacuum interrupter, a product to be incorporated into circuit-breakers in switchgear apparatus. Both parents had been researching the product for ten years, but its construction and operation were complex and difficult and neither had been able to bring the product to the market. The agreement provided for the parents to cease independent work on the interrupter. As the Commission said (paragraph 10): 'Each of the companies found the cost of development was very substantial and each recognised that if vacuum interrupters were to be brought to commercial use at a price which would make them competitive with the conventional forms of switchgear, a collaboration and pooling of the resources available was essential in order that the heavy expenditure involved by the individual companies would be reduced'.

Commission

15. Prior to the signing of the agreement of 25 March 1970 neither Associated Electrical Industries Ltd. nor Reyrolle Parsons Ltd. were manufacturing vacuum interrupters. However, their experience in the field of heavy electrical equipment and their ability to manufacture components therefore, the extent and quality of their R&D work, some of which was concentrated in the field of vacuum interrupters, their skill in producing electrical equipment generally and the natural growth of their activities in the field of manufacture of electrical equipment might well have led them to extend their range of products to include vacuum interrupters, thereby making them direct competitors in the relevant product market. They must therefore be assumed to be potential competitors and the agreement of 25 March 1970 to have been concluded between potentially competing manufacturers.

16. The object and effect of the agreement is to restrict competition within the common market. There is not at present even one manufacturer of components for electrical equipment within the area of the common market which makes and sells vacuum interrupters. When two companies, each of which is a potential manufacturer and which are each within the common market, merge their activity in the fields of research, development, manufacture and sale by establishing a joint venture concerned with this one product on such terms that they deprive themselves of the possibility of developing and selling that product independently of and in competition with each other, there is a restriction of competition.

However, the joint venture scheme had obvious advantages and the Commission exempted it under Article 81(3):

22. . . .

(1) The availability of vacuum interrupters enables switchgear manufacturers to design, develop and manufacture electric circuit breakers which have technical advantages over existing air and liquid apparatus.

(2) The agreement makes provision for the financial resources and technical support necessary to enable the R&D of vacuum interrupters to be carried out in depth.

(3) The users of switchgear incorporating vacuum interrupters receive benefits therefrom.

(4) The agreement enables the vacuum type interrupter to be developed, manufactured, and sold to consumers within the EEC on a competitive basis with those which will be available for import into the EEC from the United States and Japan when a market for the vacuum interrupter is established within the Member States of the EEC.

(5) The technical and financial effort required to produce the vacuum interrupter as a commercially viable product within a useful period of time would not have been achieved if
both of the parties had relied solely on their own resources

Decisions of this kind were subject to considerable criticism for finding restrictions of
potential competition based on unrealistic assumptions. Further, exempting transactions
like *Vacuum Interrupters* under Article 81(3) was theoretically inconsistent with their coming within Article 81(1) in the first place. One of the criteria for the application of Article
81(3) is that the agreement does not impose on undertakings restrictions which are not
indispensable to the attainment of the agreement's (beneficial) objectives. Yet if the parents
were able to enter the market independently, how could their coming together be
indispensable?

The Commission re-evaluated its attitude towards the potential competition issue and in
the Commission's *XIIIth Report on Competition Policy* (Commission, 1983) signalled a new
approach. It set out a checklist of questions it would ask in future in gauging whether there
really *was* a restriction of potential competition:

55. In determining whether Article [81(1)] is applicable to a joint venture between undertakings
at the same level of economic activity, the restrictive effects on competition in the relevant
market and on inter-State trade must be first examined. In this context, it must be determined
whether the cooperation agreement has the object or effect of appreciably restricting competition between the founding undertakings or between them and other undertakings. If the
participating undertakings are clearly and actually competitors, Article [81(1)] will apply, if
the restrictive effect on competition in the relevant market and the effect on inter-State trade
are perceptible.

The Commission maintains the position that in judging the effects of joint ventures under
Article [81(1)] in specific cases, all relevant factors must be taken into account which determine not only actual but also potential competition. It is determined to make its assessment
of potential competition in the most realistic way possible. This does not mean that the
application of the competition rules will vary according to business-cycle fluctuations, but
signifies the Commission's conviction that a realistic approach to potential competition is
called for.

To evaluate in an individual case whether the formation of a joint venture in the production
field restricts potential competition, the Commission may use the following checklist of questions with respect to each of the partners. The basic point is that the degree of potential
competition depends largely on the nature of the product manufactured or the services offered
by the joint venture.

The following individual questions may be relevant:

Input of the joint venture

Does the investment expenditure involved substantially exceed the financing capacity of each partner? Does each partner have the necessary technical know-how and sources of supply of input
products?

Production of the joint venture

Is each partner familiar with the process technology? Does each partner itself produce inputs for or
products derived from the joint venture's product and does it have access to the necessary production
facilities?

Sales by the joint venture

Is the actual or potential demand such that it would be feasible for each of the partners to manufacture the product on its own? Does each have access to the necessary distribution channels for the joint venture's product?

Risk factor

Could each partner bear the technical and financial risks associated with the production operations of the joint venture alone?

In applying these objective criteria the Commission will be guided by what in its opinion could reasonably be expected of the participating firms in the light of all relevant economic factors. Clearly, the weight given to the various criteria in assessing potential competition will vary from case to case.

Regardless of the practical interpretation given to the concept of potential competition, the Commission will continue to apply Article [81] as has been the practice hitherto and in accordance with the case law of the Court, wherever it finds that the formation of the joint venture involves restrictions of competition between the partners or between them and third parties.

An important concern under Article [81(3)] will be whether the provisions of the agreement in question, in subject matter, geographical scope or time, go beyond what is necessary for the setting up and operation of the joint venture. Particular scrutiny will be necessary where the partners for example accept unqualified bans on their competition with one another, or supply and purchasing restrictions, which go beyond what is required for the joint venture. The same applies where the formation of the joint venture is taken by the partners as an occasion for placing restrictions on distribution arrangements. The Commission has already given general approval for some such restrictions within the limits set out by the block exemption regulation for specialization agreements. In its proposed block exemption regulation on joint R&D, it is also seeking general criteria for permitted restrictions in this context.

Cases involving restrictions of competition not covered by block exemption regulations are subject to individual examination. The Commission is fully aware of the difficulties this entails for joint venture partners and has therefore taken steps to simplify and expedite its examination procedure. (. . .)

The result of this change of heart was seen in a number of subsequent decisions. *Optical Fibres* is considered to be the first manifestation of the new policy in practice:

Optical Fibres [1986] OJ L236/30

This concerned three joint ventures set up between a US company, Corning Glass Works, on the one hand and respectively BICC in the UK (a 50/50 unlimited partnership), Siemens in Germany (a joint venture company owned 50/50) and COFOCO in France (a joint venture company owned 40/60). The joint ventures were set up to develop, produce and sell optical fibres and optical cables for use in the European telecommunications market. Corning had experience in optical fibre manufacture but none in cables and the European partners had no experience in optical fibres. There were no clauses restricting competition between Corning and the other parties and they were all free to do independent research and development in optical fibres although in reality there was no prospect of the European companies doing this.

Commission

46. The individual joint venture agreements do not as such restrict competition between Corning and its partners. When the agreements were concluded, the parties were not actual or potential competitors in the market for optical fibres or optical cables. The production of optical fibres and optical cables are different activities. Corning had no experience in cable manufacture, while Corning's

partners had no experience in glass manufacture which could have led to an invention competitive with Corning's. In spite of the parties' considerable financial resources, the entry by Corning into the optical cables market or by Corning's partners into the optical fibres market was not a natural and reasonably foreseeable extension of their respective business activities. The cooperation between Corning and its partners is rather of a complementary nature which does not give rise to restriction or distortion of competition at the level of the cooperating parties. Moreover, the agreements do not foreclose market access by third parties or have any other foreseeable anti-competitive impact on their activities. The various amendments made to the original agreements ensure that competition is maintained and that third parties do not suffer from discrimination or market partitioning. In addition, by virtue of the conditions and obligations attached to this Decision, competition is safe-guarded and the Commission is in a position to monitor future developments.

47. There is neither restriction nor distortion of competition between the parents and the joint venture. The agreements provide that the parents are free to engage in independent R&D of optical fibres. Furthermore, the individual joint venture agreements do not contain obligations which go beyond what would be admitted in simple licensing agreements between non-competitors. Thus the parties are free to engage in independent R&D of optical fibres, although in practice they depend on a continuous transfer of technology from Corning. In addition, there is no obligation on the joint ventures to grant exclusive licenses to Corning in respect of improvements or innovations.

48. The principal restrictions and distortions of competition in this case are to be found rather in the relationship between the joint ventures. The joint ventures have substantially the same business activity, namely the production and marketing of optical fibres. These joint ventures are therefore directly competing companies. The agreements taken together give rise to the creation of a network of inter-related joint ventures with a common technology provider in an oligopolistic market. Corning is one of the major producers and distributors of optical fibres in the world. Its partners are cable makers with large market shares in their respective home countries. The joint ventures therefore bring together companies with strong positions in the optical fibres and cables markets. Although the joint ventures are free to make active and passive sales into each other's territories, only passive sales are permitted in territories where Corning has an exclusive licensee. Corning has interests, whether through joint ventures, subsidiaries or licensees, in several Member States. Its financial stake and key technical and financial personnel representation in the joint ventures, the success of which depends on rapid access to Corning's technology, ensure that Corning is in a position to influence and coordinate the joint venture's conduct.

It can be seen from paragraphs 46 and 47 that the Commission did not consider that there was a restriction of competition between Corning and its partners. Neither side was able to develop and put on to the market the joint venture product without the collaboration of the other, and the individual joint venture agreements were therefore outside Article 81(1). What concerned the Commission was the setting up of the network of three joint ventures. This aspect of the operation *was* within Article 81(1) and needed exemption under Article 81(3). Exemption was given (for fifteen years) after modifications were made to the agreements to ensure competition between the joint ventures and to reduce Corning's control over them.[32]

---

[32] See also *Mitchell Cotts/Solfitra* [1987] OJ L41/31, [1988] 4 CMLR 111 (parents neither actual nor potential competitors, but the distribution arrangements brought it within Art. 81(1) because they raised barriers to entry).

In *ODIN*[33] however, the liberal policy led to a negative clearance. Metal Box (UK) and Elopak (Norway) set up a 50/50 jointly owned company called ODIN. Metal Box manufactured a range of metal, plastic, and polythene containers, bottles and other packaging, and various closures and seals. Elopak's expertise was in cartons for the dairy and food industries. The joint venture was to develop a new form of paperboard-based package with a separate laminated metal lid to be used for UHT-treated foods with a long shelf-life. The parties were not existing competitors and neither of them had all the technology required for the new product or the technical knowledge to develop it separately. The agreement did not contain ancillary restrictions[34] beyond those necessary to make the joint venture work. *Konsortium ECR 900*[35] concerned a co-operative joint venture between three undertakings for the development, manufacture, and distribution of a telecommunication system. It was held not to be caught by Article 81(1) because the undertakings could not have done it individually in the time required by the relevant tender deadline, the financial expenditure and staff resources required were too great for individual action, and as there were only fifteen potential customers the parties could not have borne the financial risk individually.

(iii) THE 1993 NOTICE ON THE ASSESSMENT OF CO-OPERATIVE JOINT VENTURES

The Commission adopted the 1993 Notice in order to aid undertakings and their advisers by setting out its current approach to the application of Article 81 to the assessment of joint ventures. In the Notice the Commission set out its policy of making a realistic economic analysis before finding that the joint venture restricts competition within Article 81(1).

The Notice stated (paragraph 15) that Article 81(1) will not normally apply to joint ventures formed by undertakings within the same group,[36] joint ventures of minor economic importance within the meaning of the Notice on agreements of minor importance,[37] and joint ventures with activities neutral to competition within the meaning of the 1968 Notice on co-operation agreements.[38] The categories set out in the 1968 Notice were:

1. Agreements having as their sole object: (a) an exchange of opinion or experience, (b) joint market research, (c) the joint carrying out of comparative studies of enterprises or industries, (d) the joint preparation of statistics and calculation models.

2. Agreements having as their sole object: (a) cooperation in accounting matters, (b) joint provision of credit guarantees, (c) joint debt collecting associations, (d) joint business or tax consultant agencies.

3. Agreements having as their sole object: (a) the joint implementation of R&D projects, (b) the joint placing of R&Ds contracts, (c) the sharing out of R&D projects among participating enterprises.

4. Agreements which have as their sole object the joint use of production facilities and storing and transporting equipment.

---

[33] *Metal Box/Elopak (ODIN)* [1990] OJ L209/15, [1991] 4 CMLR 832.
[34] For ancillary restrictions, see further *infra* 830.
[35] [1990] OJ L228/31, [1992] 4 CMLR 54.
[36] Because of the single economic entity doctrine: see *supra* Chap. 3.
[37] This should now be read as a reference to the 1997 Notice: see *supra* Chap. 3.
[38] [1968] JO C75/3, rectified [1968] JO C84/14.

5. Agreements having as their sole object the setting up of consortia for the joint execution of orders, where the participating enterprises do not compete with each other as regards the work to be done or where each of them by itself is unable to execute the orders.

6. Agreements having as their sole object: (a) joint selling arrangements, (b) joint after sales and repairs service, provided the participating enterprises are not competitors with regard to the products or services covered by the agreement.

7. Agreements having joint advertising as their sole object.

8. Agreements having as their sole object the use of a common label to designate a certain quality, where the label is available to all competitors on the same conditions.

The Commission stressed, however, that these matters are not fixed, but form part of the development of Community law and must be construed in the light of the Court's case law and Commission decisions.

The 1993 Notice set out (in paragraphs 17–42) the criteria for establishing whether the joint venture restricted competition in cases not covered by the above. Four main issues were to be considered when assessing whether Article 81(1) applied: (i) the restriction of actual or potential competition, both between the parents as between themselves and between the parents and the joint venture; (ii) the effect on third parties; and (iii) any network effect.[39] The 'spill-over' effect was not separately addressed in the 1993 Notice although the Commission continued to consider it an issue of major importance.[40] Further, the Notice considered how the criteria applied to two different groups of joint ventures, those between non-competitors and those between competitors (actual or potential). As far as the first group was concerned, the Commission stated that they 'rarely cause problems for competition'[41] (as in the *ODIN* case, above) and the main issue was whether market access for third parties was significantly affected.[42] The Commission recognized (paragraph 42) that even joint ventures between competitors will not be caught by the Article 81(1) prohibition where the parties could not enter the market individually (as was the case in *Konsortium ECR 900*).

If a joint venture, in the light of the above, *does* fall within Article 81(1) the four criteria in Article 81(3) must be applied to it in the usual way. It is possible that the joint venture could fall within a block exemption. Those mentioned in the Notice as relevant (paragraphs 43–51) are the block exemption for R&D agreements, Regulation 418/85,[43] the block exemption for specialization agreements, Regulation 417/85,[44] and the two intellectual property licensing block exemptions[45] which have now been replaced by Regulation 240/96 on technology transfer agreements.[46] For the reasons discussed below, these block exemptions are of limited utility in respect of joint ventures, and once found to be within Article 81(1) the transaction will usually have to be individually assessed under Article 81(3).

---

[39] It was the network effect which brought the *Optical Fibres* transaction within Art. 81(1).

[40] See J. Faull and A. Nikpay (eds.), *The EC Law of Competition* (Oxford University Press, paras., 1999), 6.88–6.105. And see the *Exxon/Shell* decision [1994] OJ, L144/20, where the spill-over was on the same market as the joint venture; it could also occur on adjacent markets (both product or geographic).

[41] 1993 Notice [1993], OJ C43/2 para. 32.

[42] *Ibid.*, para. 32.

[43] [1985] OJ L53/5, as amended by Group Exemptions (Amendment) Reg. 151/93 [1993] OJ L21/8.

[44] [1985] OJ L53/1, as amended by Group Exemptions (Amendment) Reg. 151/93 [1993] OJ L21/8.

[45] Reg. 2349/84 [1984] OJ L219/15, on patent licensing and 556/89 [1989] OJ L61/1, on know-how licensing.

[46] [1996] OJ L31/2.

Paragraphs 52–64 of the Notice deal with the principles upon which the Commission bases in its decision in applying the Article 81(3) criteria. The Notice considers various types of joint venture agreement in turn: R&D (paragraph 59), joint sales (paragraph 60), joint purchasing (paragraph 61), and production joint ventures (paragraphs 62–63). The general principles upon which the Commission proceeds are stated to be:

54. In order to fulfil the first two conditions of Article [81(3)] the JV must bring appreciable objective advantages for third parties, especially consumers, which at least equal the consequent detriment to competition.

55. Advantages in the above-mentioned sense, which can be pursued and attained with the aid of a JV, include, in the Commission's opinion, in particular, the development of new or improved products and processes which are marketed by the originator or by third parties under licence. In addition, measures opening up new markets, leading to the sales expansion of the undertaking in new territories or the enlargement of its supply range by new products, will in principle be assessed favourably. In all these cases the undertakings in question contribute to dynamic competition, consolidating the internal market and strengthening the competitiveness of the relevant economic sector. Production and sales increases can also be a pro-competitive stimulant. On the other hand, the rationalization of production activities and distribution networks is rather a means of adapting supply to a shrinking or stagnant demand. It leads, however, to cost savings which, under effective competition, are usually passed on to customers as lower prices. Plans for the reduction of production capacity, however, lead mostly to price rises. Agreements of this latter type will be judged favourable only if they serve to overcome a structural crisis, to accelerate the removal of unprofitable production capacity from the market and thereby to reestablish competition in the medium term.

56. The Commission will give a negative assessment to agreements which have as their main purpose the coordination of actual or potential competition between the participating undertakings. This is especially so for joint price fixing, the reduction of production and sales by establishing quotas, the division of markets and contractual prohibitions or restrictions on investment. JVs which are created or operated essentially to achieve such aims are nothing but classic cartels the anticompetitive effects of which are well known.

57. The pros and cons of a JV will be weighed against each other on an overall economic balance, by means of which the type and the extent of the respective advantages and risks can be assessed. If the parents are economically and financially powerful and have, over and above that a high market-share, their exemption applications will need a rigorous examination. The same applies to JVs which reinforce an existing narrow oligopoly or belong to a network of JVs.

58. The acceptance pursuant to Article [81(3)](a) of restrictions on the parents or the JV depends above all on the type and aims of the cooperation. In this context, the decisive factor is usually whether the contractual restriction on the parties' economic freedom is directly connected with the creation of the JV and can be considered indispensable for its existence. It is only for the restriction of global competition that Article [81(3)](b) sets an absolute limit. Competition must be fully functioning at all times. Agreements which endanger its effectiveness cannot benefit from individual exemption. This category includes JVs which, through the combination of activities of the parents, achieve, consolidate or strengthen a dominant position.

(iv) THE APPLICATION OF ARTICLE 81(1) AND (3) TO JOINT VENTURES AFTER THE 1993 NOTICE: SOME EXAMPLES

Every co-operative joint venture is different and its assessment will turn on the individual facts. Despite the policy reflected in the Notice, the Commission has sometimes still engaged in economic analysis under Article 81(3) rather than under Article 81(1). The judgment of the CFI in *European Night Services*,[47] however, showed that the Commission cannot rely on granting exemption under Article 81(3) as a substitute for analysis under Article 81(1).

European Night Services was a significant case because the CFI annulled the Commission decision. The Commission found that a joint venture between four railway companies to provide overnight passenger rail services between the UK and the Continent through the Channel Tunnel restricted competition between the parents, between the parents and the joint venture, and *vis-à-vis* third parties and that these effects were exacerbated by a network of joint ventures set up by the parents. The joint venture was exempted, however, although subject to conditions unacceptable to the parties. The CFI held that the Commission had not shown why Article 81(1) applied. It had not identified the relevant market properly, had not applied the appreciability criteria properly, and had demonstrated insufficient economic reasoning: for example, the holding that potential competition was restricted was based on 'a hypothesis unsupported by any evidence or any analysis of the structures of the relevant market from which it might be concluded that it represented a real, concrete possibility.'[48] The exemption conditions were flawed as well, as the Commission had applied the essential facilities inappropriately[49] and had given the exemption for too short a time in view of the long-term investment required.

In *P&O/Stena*[50] P&O Ferries and Stena Lines formed a joint venture to provide cross channel ferry services on the Short French Sea[51] and the Belgian Strait.[52] There were two markets involved: that for tourist passenger services on the short sea routes and that for unitized freight services between England and mainland Europe. The Commission held that the joint venture was within Article 81(1) because the parties were actual competitors. There was, however, no appreciable risk of spill-over. The Commission then turned to Article 81(3). It held that the criteria were fulfilled in respect of the freight market. In respect of the tourist market the Commission had little difficulty in holding that the first three criteria were fulfilled. The problems lay in the fourth, that there should be no elimination of competition in respect of a substantial part of the products in question. The Commission's doubt was that the creation of the joint venture would lead to a duopolistic market structure between the joint venture and Eurotunnel. After analysing the situation it concluded that the joint venture and Eurotunnel were likely to compete rather than to act in parallel to raise prices. Given that the market conditions were likely to change, however, because of the abolition of duty-free sales in 1999 the Commission limited the duration of the exemption to three years.

---

[47] Cases T–374–375, 384 & 388/94, *European Night Services* v. *Commission* [1998] ECR II–3141 [1998] 5 CMLR 718; see further *supra* Chap. 4.

[48] *Ibid.*, para. 142.

[49] See *supra* Chap. 7.

[50] [1999] OJ L163/61, [1999] 5 CMLR 682 (being in the maritime transport sector, notification was under Art. 12 of Reg. 4056/86 [1986] OJ L378/4).

[51] Dover, Folkestone, Ramsgate, Newhaven/Calais, Dieppe, Boulogne, and Dunkirk.

[52] Ramsgate/Ostend.

P&O/Stena Line [1999] OJ L163/61, [1999] 5 CMLR 682

Commission

39. The formation of the joint venture constitutes a restriction of competition within the meaning of Article [81(1)] because the parties were actual competitors on the relevant markets on which the joint venture operates.

40. That restriction of competition is appreciable. The parties have a high combined market share (even if their combined market share on the Short Sea declined following the market entry of Eurotunnel). The joint venture is a full function joint venture which operates in the same freight transport market as its parents, and in a neighbouring passenger transport market to those in which its parents operate.

41. The formation of the joint venture has an effect on trade between Member States given the importance of the parties in the Short Sea tourist market and in the Anglo/Continental freight market . . .

. . .

61. The first and second conditions of Article [81(3)] require an assessment of the efficiencies and other benefits that can be expected from merging the parties' separate ferry operations on the Short Sea, and the extent to which those efficiencies will benefit consumers.

62. The creation of the joint venture will bring about benefits, notably the improved frequency to be offered by the joint venture, continuous loading, and estimated cost savings of £[. . .] million. The overall positive benefits will arise even were the joint venture to decide to stop operating on the Newhaven/Dieppe route.

7.2 Allowing consumers a fair share of the resulting benefit

63. Customers can be expected to benefit from the improved frequency and continuous loading. Customers can be expected to benefit from the cost savings to the extent that the joint venture will be faced by effective competition.

7.3 No restrictions which are not indispensable

64. The third condition of Article [81(3)] requires consideration of whether less restrictive alternatives are available to achieve the benefits of the proposed joint venture.

65. The Commission considers that lesser forms of co-operation between P&O and Stena, such as joint scheduling, interlining or pooling, would be unlikely to lead to the benefits to be achieved by the joint venture. In particular, any form of co-operation less than a joint venture would not achieve the savings in administration and marketing, which represent a significant part (£[. . .] million) of the estimated £[. . .] million costs savings.

66. Under the agreement, P&O and Stena undertake not to be involved directly or indirectly (other than through the joint venture) with the provision of ferry services calling at any port on the English coastline between (and including) Newhaven and (but excluding) Harwich or on the European mainland coastline between (and including) Dieppe and (but excluding) Zeebrugge. The joint venture's activities are limited to the provision of ferry services on the Dover/Calais, Dover/Zeebrugge and Newhaven/Dieppe routes. These restrictions can be regarded as necessary for the creation of the joint venture.

7.4 No elimination of competition in respect of a substantial part of the products in question

67. The fourth condition of Article [81(3)] requires an assessment of whether the proposed joint

venture can be expected to be faced with effective competition in the Short Sea tourist passenger market.

68. In its 'letter of serious doubts' the Commission stated its concern that the creation of the joint venture could lead to a duopolistic market structure conducive to parallel behaviour of the joint venture and Eurotunnel. This issue is addressed in the following section.

. . .

127. The Commission considers that characteristics of the market are such that the joint venture and Eurotunnel can be expected to compete with each other rather than to act in parallel to raise prices. First, although a more concentrated market structure is brought about by the creation of the joint venture, with Eurotunnel and the joint venture each having similar large market shares, market shares have not been stable in recent years. Secondly, Eurotunnel and the joint venture are unlikely both to face significant capacity restraints and they have different cost structures. Thirdly, other ferry operators can, at least until 1999, be expected to provide competition. The proposed joint venture can therefore be expected to be faced with effective competition in the Short Sea tourist passenger market. The Commission therefore considers that the fourth condition of Article [81(3)] of the Treaty is fulfilled.

128. An important change in market conditions will occur when duty-free concessions are abolished in mid-1999. The effects of the loss of revenue from duty-free sales is uncertain. It seems likely that ticket prices will rise . . . and some operators have stated that prices will be likely to rise in the order of 30 to 40 per cent. . . . Price increases would, however, decrease the number of tourist passengers and operators have strong incentives to limit any price increases by reducing costs and to developing alternative sources of revenue.

129. The abolition of duty-free concessions may have knock-on effects on competition between the joint venture and Eurotunnel in one or more of the following ways. First, Eurotunnel might find its Le Shuttle tourist service capacity constrained if demand for cross-Channel travel were to increase more strongly than it has projected and notwithstanding possible price increases due to the loss of duty-free revenues. Secondly, to the extent that operators are not successful in developing revenue sources to replace duty-free sales, they will have less incentive to maximise load factors in order to increase revenues. Thirdly, the extent to which the other ferry operators will after 1999 be able to provide effective competition to the joint venture and Eurotunnel is uncertain.

130. The Commission therefore considers it appropriate in this case to limit the duration of the exemption to three years from the date of implementation of the agreement, that is from 10 March 1998. This will enable the Commission to assess the impact of the joint venture on the Short Sea tourist market after the 2000 summer season, by which time the full effects of the end of duty-free concessions on market conditions can be expected to be known.

In *ATLAS*[53] the Commission dealt with a joint venture between the French and German national telephone operators designed to provide a range of complex communications packages. The Commission granted an exemption to the joint venture despite the substantial elimination of competition between the parents which it involved. It considered that consumers would benefit from the earlier provision of improved technology and that the joint venture would enable better technical harmonization. The exemption was, however, made

---

[53] [1996] OJ L239/29, [1997] 4 CMLR 89.

subject to stringent conditions and the Commission has been described as granting the exemption 'in such a way as to use the leverage of the exemption request to forward its own policy priorities on the two governments concerned, thus possibly enabling liberalization of French and German telecommunications markets to occur more quickly than would otherwise be the case'.[54]

The Commission's currently realistic application of Article 81(1) to a joint venture was shown in two cases in 1999 concerning telecommunications in France: *Re Cégétel: Vivendi/ BT/Mannesmann/SBC International*[55] and *Re Telecom Développement: SNCF/Cégétel*.[56] These decisions were considered in Chapter 4.[57]

(v) ANCILLARY RESTRAINTS

Ancillary restraints are contractual restrictions between the parties which accompany the creation of the joint venture. Restraints which are essential to the functioning of a joint venture which is not within Article 81(1) itself will also not be caught. If the joint venture is exempted under Article 81(3) the ancillary restraints will be exempted as well. In paragraph 66 of the 1993 Notice the Commission says that it is a question of distinguishing between additional agreements which are directly related to and necessary for the establishment and functioning of the joint venture in so far as they cannot be disassociated from it without jeopardizing existence, and those which are simply concluded at the same time as the joint venture's creation without having those features. Examples of the former have included in decided cases: exclusive purchasing obligations on the parents of the joint venture at least for a start-up period,[58] non-competition obligations on the parents for the joint venture's lifetime,[59] and a restriction on the joint venture producing or dealing in products which compete with the parents.[60] Guidance on the matter can also be obtained from the Notice on Restrictions Ancillary to Concentrations.[61]

---

[54] D. Goyder, *EC Competition Law*, (3rd edn., Oxford University Press, Oxford, 1998), 456.
[55] [1999] OJ L218/14, [2000] 4 CMLR 106.
[56] [1999] OJ L218/24, [2000] 4 CMLR 124.
[57] See *supra* Chap. 4.
[58] e.g. in *Rockwell/Iveco* [1983] OJ L224/19, [1983] 3 CMLR 709.
[59] e.g. *GEC/Weir* [1977] OJ L327/26, [1978] 1 CMLR D42.
[60] e.g. *Mitchell Cotts/Sofiltra* [1987] L41/31, [1988] 4 CMLR 111.
[61] See Chap. 12.

3. RESEARCH AND DEVELOPMENT AGREEMENTS, SPECIALISATION AGREEMENTS, AND THE 1985 BLOCK EXEMPTIONS

A. GENERAL

The Commission singled out two particular types of horizontal agreement for special treatment and in 1985 adopted two block exemptions, Regulations 417/85 on specialization agreements[62] and Regulation 418/85 on R&D agreements.[63] The Commission proposes to replace these Regulations with new block exemptions which will come into force when the extended life of Regulations 417/85 and 418/85 expires at the end of 2000. This chapter therefore concentrates on the proposed replacements.[64]

The Commission also proposes to adopt a new set of guidelines on the assessment of horizontal agreements. The draft of these, which is discussed and partly reproduced below,[65] contains a statement on the Commission's current thinking on the application of Article 81 to specialization and R&D agreements.

B. SPECIALIZATION AGREEMENTS

Specialization agreements are those by which the parties agree to specialize in manufacture by allocating the manufacture of certain products amongst themselves. Such agreements will normally involve a diminution of competition but they can contribute to efficiencies in that they may reduce costs and/or increase output. If competition on the market is not eliminated, in that competition from other manufacturers remains, they can often be exempted as they bring benefits to consumers.

There are various forms of specialization agreement. The classic example is *Jaz/Peter*.[66] Both parties manufactured clocks. Under the agreement Jaz in France was to continue making only electric clocks and domestic alarm clocks and Peter in Germany was to make large mechanical alarm clocks. They agreed that they would each supply the other with their products and spare parts, that they could both sell the whole range of the products in their respective territories, and that they would not buy the products covered by the agreement from third parties. The agreement was exempted: the rationalization of production would

---

[62] [1985] OJ L53/1 as amended by Commission Reg. 151/93 [1993] OJ L21/8 and extended by Commission Reg. 2236/97 [1997] OJ L306/12.

[63] [1985] OJ L53/5 as amended by Commission Reg. 151/93 [1993] OJ L21/8 and extended by Commission Reg. 2236/97 [1997] OJ L306/12.

[64] See *infra* 842–848.

[65] See *infra* 833–842.

[66] [1969] OJ L195/5, [1970] CMLR 129.

lead to lower prices.[67] *ACEC/Berliet*[68] was a different type of arrangement. The parties agreed to collaborate in bus manufacture, and the production and development of the individual components was divided between them. ACEC was to make the transmission systems and Berliet the basic bus structure. This agreement was also exempted.

Regulation 417/85[69] provides a block exemption for various types of specialization agreements, including the format in *Jaz/Peter* and *ACEC/Berliet*. It does not, however, cover arrangements of the kind in *Prym/Beka*[70] where one party gives up manufacture of a product altogether and agrees to obtain its future supplies of the product from the other, because there is a lack of mutuality. Although not as complex as the R&D exemption, Regulation 417/85 applies only where the products do not represent more than 20 per cent of the market in the common market or a substantial part of it (but 10 per cent if the parties, or a third party on their behalf are also entrusted with the distribution of the products) and the aggregate turnover of the parties concerned does not exceed Euros 1,000 million.

C. RESEARCH AND DEVELOPMENT AGREEMENTS

R&D agreements may be structured in various ways and may or may not involve a joint venture. Some of the cases discussed above, for example *Konsortium ECR 900* and *ODIN*, were R&D agreements. They may be between companies but sometimes they involve a company co-operating with an academic institution or research institute. Faull and Nikpay explain why R&D arrangements are attractive to companies.

J. Faull and A. Nikpay (eds.), *The EC Law of Competition* (Oxford University Press, 1999), 372

6.124   In many industries a company's level of innovation has become a key competitive factor. From pharmaceuticals to computing and electronics it is not just price and quality that give firms a competitive edge but their technical know-how and ability to develop new products.

6.125   Co-operation at the level of research and development is therefore increasingly important to many companies. The costs, and risks, associated with R&D can be very high, therefore many companies choose to co-operate to spread these risks. There are also potentially enormous benefits in avoiding expensive duplication of effort and in the cross-fertilization of ideas and experience that come from R&D co-operation. It is for these reasons that the Commission has taken a generally positive view of R&D co-operation.

6.126   Co-operation in R&D can take place at many levels. In some cases the co-operation is in fundamental research projects far from the market often in collaboration with universities or publicly funded research programmes. In other cases the R&D is basically no more than incremental improvements to existing products and may be an adjunct to a joint production arrangement.

---

[67] The 10-year exemption was renewed in 1978: *Jaz-Peter (No 2)* [1978] OJ L61/17, [1978] 2 CMLR 186.

[68] [1968] OJ L201/7, [1968] CMLR D35.

[69] [1985] OJ L53/1, as amended by Commission Reg. 151/93 [1993] OJ L21/8 and Commission Reg. 2236/97 [1997] OJ L306/12.

[70] [1973] OJ L296/24, [1973] CMLR D250.

Not only does the Commission have few problems with agreements simply limited to joint R&D, but the Community positively encourages co-operative projects through various research programmes.[71] Most of the difficulties arise when the parties wish to go beyond collaboration at the R&D stages and extend their co-operation into the stages of commercial exploitation and distribution.

The block exemption on R&D agreements, Regulation 418/85,[72] has been little used. Overall, it contains detailed provisions with which few agreements comply. Further, it provides a limited exemption only for a very basic type of R&D, whereas most collaborative arrangements are more complex. Indeed, many R&D agreements which fall within the block exemption would not be caught by Article 81(1) at all. In particular, there is only very limited exemption for co-operation in the distribution stage. Also, it applies only if certain preconditions are fulfilled, and it contains market share criteria.

4. THE DRAFT COMMISSION GUIDELINES ON HORIZONTAL CO-OPERATION AND THE DRAFT NEW BLOCK EXEMPTIONS

A. GENERAL

The review of the application of Article 81 to horizontal co-operation upon which the Commission embarked in 1997[73] resulted in the publication in April 2000 of a draft set of guidelines, similar to those it had recently adopted on vertical restraints.[74] These accompanied the publication of the drafts of two new block exemptions, the replacements for those discussed above. The publication of *two* draft block exemptions caused surprise in some quarters since it had been widely believed that the Commission intended to produce one 'umbrella' block exemption on horizontal agreements, in the same way that it had just produced an umbrella exemption for vertical agreements. When adopted in their final version the guidelines will replace the 1968 Notice on co-operation agreements between enterprises and the 1993 Notice on the assessment of joint ventures which are discussed above.

The guidelines are not limited to R&D and specialization. They deal with a number of types of agreement which 'potentially generate efficiency gains' i.e. R&D, production (which

---

[71] Art. 163(2)) (ex Art. 130(f)(2)) of the Treaty calls upon the Community to encourage undertakings, including small and medium sized undertakings, in their research and technological development activities of high quality, and to support their efforts to cooperate with one another. The Fifth Framework Programme for Research, Technological Development and Demonstration Activities was launched on 25.2.1999 (OJ [1999] L26/46).

[72] [1985] OJ L53/5, as amended by Commission Reg. 151/93 [1993] OJ L21/8 and Commission Reg. 2236/97 [1997] OJ L306/12.

[73] See *supra* 813.

[74] See *supra* Chap. 9.

includes specialization), purchasing, commercialization, standardization, and environ-mental.[75] These types of agreement are dealt with in different sections, and where the agreement contains elements falling under more than one head the applicable section is to be determined according to the 'centre of gravity of the cooperation'.[76] The guidelines apply whether or not the transaction involves the formation of a joint venture and they apply to co-operation over both products and services.[77] The guidelines do not cover 'more complex arrangements such as strategic alliances that combine a number of different areas and instruments of cooperation in varying ways'. Nor do they apply to the extent that sector-specific rules apply.[78]

The purpose of the guidelines is 'to provide an analytical framework for the most common types of horizontal co-operation' (although the Commission says that given the enormous variety in types and combinations of horizontal co-operation and market circum-stances it is impossible to provide specific answers to every possible scenario)[79] and to 'form a complement' to the new block exemptions.[80] After a statement of the scope of the guide-lines the Commission discusses the basic principles underlying the assessment of horizontal co-operation under Article 81. It then considers the application of Article 81 to specific types of horizontal agreement. The application of Article 81(3) is discussed in the light of the draft block exemptions.[81] The Commission has illustrated the guidelines with a number of examples, many of them based on agreements with which they have dealt in the past.

It should be noted that the guidelines have been drawn up against the background of the Commission's proposals for modernizing the implementation of the competition rules.[82] As explained in Chapter 16, this will put more responsibility on undertakings to ensure that their agreements do comply with the rules.[83] The guidelines will therefore be important in helping them to do this.

B. THE POLICY OF THE GUIDELINES

The Commission begins by recognizing the basic tension between the benefits of co-operation and the need to protect competition.

2.   Companies need to respond to increasing competitive pressure and a changing market place driven by globalisation, the speed of technological progress and the generally more dynamic nature of markets. Cooperation can be a means to share risk, save costs, pool know how and launch innovation faster. In particular for small and medium sized enterprises cooperation is an important means to adapt to the changing market place.

---

[75] Draft guidelines [2000] OJ C118/14, para. 10. They do not deal with agreements on information exchanges or on minority shareholdings, which are to be addressed separately.

[76] *Ibid.*, para. 12.

[77] *Ibid.*, para. 13.

[78] *Ibid.*, para. 13.

[79] *Ibid.*, para. 7.

[80] *Ibid.*, para. 8.

[81] See *infra* 842–848.

[82] White Paper on modernisation of the rules implementing Articles. 85 and 86 [now 81 and 82] of the EC Treaty [1999] OJ C132/1.

[83] Although note the special proposals in respect of production joint ventures, *infra* 848.

3. Horizontal co-operation may, however, also lead to competition problems. This is the case if the parties to a co-operation agree to fix prices, output or share markets, or if the co-operation enables the parties to maintain, gain or increase market power and thereby causes negative market effects with respect to prices, output, innovation or the variety and quality of goods.

4. The Commission, while recognising the economic benefits that can be generated by co-operation, has to ensure that effective competition is maintained. Article 81 provides the legal framework for a balanced assessment taking into account both anti-competitive effects as well as economic benefits.

The Commission states that as most horizontal co-operation agreements do not have as their *object* a restriction of competition it is necessary to analyse the agreement in its economic context. It considers that some agreements are not normally caught by Article 81(1):

23. Some categories of agreements do not fall under Article 81(1) because of their very nature. This is normally true for co-operation that does not imply a co-ordination of the parties' competitive behaviour in the market such as

— co-operation between non-competitors,

— co-operation between competing companies that can not independently carry out the project or activity covered by the co-operation,

— co-operation concerning an activity far removed from the marketing level.

These categories of co-operation could only come under Article 81(1) if they involve firms with significant market power and are likely to cause foreclosure problems vis-à-vis third parties.

The Commission compares the above with agreements which usually do fall under Article 81(1):

24. Another category of agreements can be assessed from the outset as normally falling under Article 81(1). This concerns co-operation agreements that have the object to restrict competition by means of price fixing, output limitation or sharing of markets or customers. These restrictions are considered to be the most harmful, because they directly interfere with the outcome of the competitive process. Price fixing and output limitation directly lead to customers paying higher prices or not receiving the desired quantities. The sharing of markets or customers reduces the choice available to customers paying higher prices or not receiving the desired quantities. The sharing of markets or customers reduces the choice available to customers and therefore also leads to higher prices or reduced output. It can therefore be presumed that these restrictions have negative market effects. They are therefore almost always prohibited.

25. This does, however, not apply if such a provision is necessary for the functioning of an otherwise non-restrictive or exemptable agreement. An example would be a production joint venture which also markets the jointly manufactured goods. It is inherent to the functioning of such a joint venture that decisions on output and prices are taken jointly by the parties to such an agreement. In this case, the inclusion of provisions on prices or output does not automatically cause the agreement to fall under Article 81(1). The provisions on prices or output will have to be assessed together with the other effects of the joint venture on the market following the framework described below to determine the applicability of Article 81(1).

Paragraph 25 shows the Commission taking an economic approach to the application of Article 81(1).[84]

---

[84] See *supra* Chap. 4.

It will be noted that in paragraph 23 above the Commission refers to the possible anti-competitive effect of agreements involving firms with significant market power. The issue of market power is a central theme of the guidelines. The market position of the parties is the major factor in determining whether or not the agreement falls within Article 81(1):

27. The starting point for the analysis is the position of the parties in the markets affected by the co-operation. This determines whether or not they are likely to maintain, gain or increase market power through the co-operation., i.e. have the ability to cause negative market effects as to prices, output, innovation or the variety or quality of goods and services. To carry out this analysis the relevant market(s) have to be defined by using the methodology of the market definition notice of the Commission. Where specific types of markets are concerned such as purchasing or technology markets, these guidelines will provide additional guidance.

28. If the parties together have a weak market position, a restrictive effect of the co-operation is unlikely and no further analysis is required. Given the variety of co-operation types and the different effects they may cause in different market situations, it is impossible to give a general market share threshold above which sufficient market power for causing restrictive effects can be assumed.

29. In addition to the combined market shares. The parties' individual market shares must be taken into account. A high combined market normally cannot be seen as indicating a restrictive effect on competition in the market if one of two parties has only insignificant market shares.

30. Where the combined market position is strong and the addition of market shares not insignificant, the market concentration, i.e. the position and number of competitors, may have to be taken into account as an additional factor to assess the impact of the co-operation on market competition. As an indicator the Herfindahl-Hirshman Index ('HHI'), which sums up the squares of the individual market shares of all competitors,[85] can be used: With an HHI below 1000 the market concentration can be characterized as low, 1000 and 1800 as moderate and above 1800 as high.

Once an agreement is within Article 81(1) it is then a question, of course, of seeing whether it can be exempted under Article 81(3). The Commission rehearses the Article 81(3) criteria, and refers to the revised block exemptions for R&D and specialization agreements. It is able to adopt block exemptions for those categories because under certain conditions the criteria can be assumed to be fulfilled. The 'combination of complementary skills or assets can be the source of substantive efficiencies'.[86]

---

[85] A market consisting of four firms with shares of 30%, 25%, 25% and 20%, has a HHI of 2550 (900 + 625 + 625 + 400) pre-co-operation. If the first two market leaders would co-operate, the HHI would change to 4050 (3025 + 625 + 400) post-co-operation. The HHI post-co-operation is decisive for the assessment of the possible market effects of a co-operation. (Commission's own fn.).

[86] Draft Guidelines [2000] OJ C118/14, para. 38.

C. THE TREATMENT OF VARIOUS CATEGORIES OF AGREEMENTS UNDER THE GUIDELINES

(i) RESEARCH AND DEVELOPMENT AGREEMENTS

The Commission acknowledges that R&D agreements *may* cause competition problems but starts from the position that they can bring significant benefits:

41. Co-operation in R&D may reduce duplicative, unnecessary costs, lead to significant cross fertilisation of ideas and experience and thus result in products and technologies being developed more rapidly than would otherwise be the case. As a general rule R&D co-operation tends to increase overall R&D activities.

42. Small and Medium-sized Enterprises (SMEs) form a dynamic and heterogeneous community which is confronted by many challenges, including the growing demands of larger companies for which they often work as sub-contractors. In R&D intensive sectors, fast growing SMEs, more often called 'start-up companies', also aim at becoming a leader in fast developing market segments. To meet those challenges and to remain competitive, SMEs need constantly to innovate. Through R&D co-operation there is a likelihood that overall R&D by SMEs will increase and that they will be able to compete more vigorously with stronger market players.

The guidelines distinguish between agreements that normally do not fall within Article 81(1), those almost always do, and those which may do.

The first category comprises agreements relating to co-operation in R&D 'at a rather theoretical stage, far removed from the marketing of possible results'[87] and agreements between non-competitors:

53. Moreover, R&D co-operation between non-competitors does generally not restrict competition. The competitive relationship between the parties has to be analysed in the context of affected existing markets and/or innovation. If the parties are not able to carry out the necessary R&D independently, there is no competition to be restricted. This can apply, for example, to firms bringing together complementary skills, technologies and other resources. The issue of potential competition has to be assessed on a realistic basis. For instance parties cannot be defined as potential competitors simply because the co-operation enables them to carry out the R&D activities. The decisive question is whether each party independently has the necessary means as to assets, know how and other resources.

Further, R&D co-operation 'which does not include the joint exploitation of possible results by means of licensing, production and/or marketing rarely falls under Article 81(1)'. It causes competition problems only if effective competition with respect to innovation is significantly reduced.[88]

The second category, agreements that almost always fall within Article 81(1), concerns co-operation which is a tool to engage in a disguised cartel.[89]

In the third category are agreements which cannot be assessed from the outset as non-restrictive of competition but have to be analysed in their economic context. The guidelines

---

[87] *Ibid.*, para. 52.

[88] *Ibid.*, para. 55. co-operation which is a tool to engage in a disguised cartel.

[89] *Ibid.*, para. 56.

specifically mention R&D co-operation set up at a stage close to the market launch and which is agreed between competitors.[90]

Turning to the question of market structure, the guidelines state that the negative effects of R&D co-operation are likely to occur only where there is market power:

58. R&D co-operation can cause negative market effects in three respects: First, it may restrict innovation, secondly it may cause the co-ordination of the parties' behaviour in existing markets and thirdly, foreclosure problems may occur at the level of the exploitation of possible results. These types of negative market effects, however, are only likely to emerge when the parties to the co-operation have significant power on the existing markets and/or competition with respect to innovation is significantly reduced. Without market power there is no incentive to co-ordinate behaviour on existing markets or to reduce or slow down innovation. A foreclosure problem may only arise in the context of co-operation involving at least one player with significant market power for a key technology and the exclusive exploitation of results.

The guidelines consider the application of Article 81(3) to R&D co-operation and say that the block exemption applies where there are no hard-core restrictions and only a limited degree of market power. The new block exemption is discussed below.[91]

The guidelines then set out how the Commission appraises the application of Article 81(3) to agreements which fall within Article 81(1) but are outside the block exemption because the market share thresholds are exceeded. The guidelines distinguish between the improvement of existing products and the creation of new ones, but admit that most cases lie somewhere in between.

61. If the R&D is directed at the improvement or refinement of existing products/technology possible effects concern the relevant market(s) for these existing products/technology. Effects on prices, output and/or innovation in existing markets are, however, only likely if the parties together have a strong position, entry is difficult and few other innovation activities are identifiable. Furthermore, if the R&D only concerns a relatively minor input of a final product, effects as to competition in these final products are, if at all, very limited. In general, a distinction has to be made between pure R&D agreements and more comprehensive co-operation involving different stages of the exploitation of results (i.e. licensing, production, marketing). As said above, pure R&D agreements rarely come under Article 81(1). This is in particular true for R&D directed towards a limited improvement of existing products/technology. If in such a scenario, the R&D co-operation includes joint exploitation only by means of licensing, restrictive effects such as foreclosure problems are unlikely. If, however, joint production and/or marketing of the slightly improved products/technology are included, the co-operation has to be examined more closely. First, negative effects as to prices and output in existing markets are more likely if strong competitors are involved in such a situation. Secondly, the co-operation may come closer to a production agreement because the R&D activities may, de facto, not form the centre of gravity of such a collaboration.

62. If the R&D is directed at an entirely new product (or technology) which creates its own new market, price and output effects on existing markets are rather unlikely. The analysis has to focus on possible restrictions of innovation concerning for instance, the quality and variety of possible future products/technology or the speed of innovation. Those restrictive effects can arise where two or more of the few firms engaged in the development of such a new product, start to co-operate at a stage where they are each independently rather near to the launch of

---

[90] *Ibid.*, para. 57.
[91] See *infra* 842–848.

the product. In such a case, innovation may be restricted even by a pure R&D agreement. In general, however, R&D co-operation concerning entirely new products is pro-competitive. This principle does not change significantly, if the joint exploitation of the results, even joint marketing, is involved. Indeed, the issue of joint exploitation in these situations is only relevant where foreclosure from key technologies play a role. Those problems would, however, not arise where the parties grant licences to third parties.

63. Most R&D agreements will lie somewhere in between the two situation described above. They may therefore have effects on innovation as well as repercussions on existing markets. Consequently, both the existing market and the effect on innovation may be of relevance for the assessment with respect to the parties' combined positions, concentration ratios, number of players/innovators and entry conditions. In some cases there can be restrictive price/output effects on existing markets and a negative impact on innovation by means of slowing down the speed of development. For instance, if significant competitors on an existing technology market co-operate to develop a new technology which may one day replace existing products, this co-operation is likely to have restrictive effects if the parties have significant market power on the existing market (which would give an incentive to exploit it), and if they also have a strong position with respect to R&D. A similar effect can occur, if the major player in an existing market co-operates with a much smaller or even potential competitor who is just about to emerge with a new product/technology which may endanger the incumbent's position.

The Guidelines then apply these principles to a number of example scenarios.

(ii) PRODUCTION AGREEMENTS

'Production agreements' in this context means unilateral or reciprocal specialization,[92] joint production, and sub-contracting agreements. Subcontracting agreements are those whereby one party entrusts the production of a product to another party. They are vertical agreements and may be covered by the block exemption, Regulation 2790/1999,[93] unless they are between competitors, in which case these guidelines apply. If they are between non-competitors and involve the transfer of know-how to the sub-contractor the 1979 Notice applies.[94]

The guidelines state that production agreements between non-competitors are not normally caught by Article 81(1).[95] However, agreements between competitors are not necessarily caught either:

82. Even production agreements between competitors do not necessarily come under Article 81(1). First, co-operation between firms which compete on markets closely related to the market directly concerned by the co-operation, cannot be defined as restricting competition, if the co-operation is the only commercially justifiable possibility to enter a new market, to launch a new product or service or to carry out a specific project.

83. Secondly, an effect on the parties' competitive behaviour as market suppliers is highly unlikely if the parties have a small proportion of their total costs in common. For instance, a low degree of commonality in total costs can be assumed, where two or more companies agree

---

[92] See *supra* 831–832.
[93] [1999] OJ L336/21.
[94] Notice on sub-contracting agreements [1979] OJ C1/2.
[95] Draft Guidelines [2000] OJ C118/14, para. 81.

to specialise or to jointly produce an intermediate product which only accounts for a small proportion of the production costs of the final product and, consequently, the total costs. A low degree of commonality of total costs can also be assumed where the parties jointly manufacture a final product, but only a small proportion as compared to the total output of the final product. Even if a significant proportion is jointly manufactured, the degree of commonality of total costs may nevertheless be low or moderate, if the co-operation concerns heterogeneous products which require a costly marketing.

As with R&D agreements, the guidelines distinguish between agreements which almost always fall under Article 81(1) because they fix prices, limit output, or share customers[96] and those which have to be assessed in their economic context. Again, the Commission takes the starting point for the analysis as the position of the parties in the market as 'without market power the parties to a production agreement do not have an incentive to co-ordinate their competitive behaviour as suppliers'. Further, 'there is no effect on competition in the market without market power of the parties, even if the parties would co-ordinate their behaviour.'[97]

The revised block exemption, as we see below, applies only to parties with a combined market share of below 20 per cent. For agreements caught by Article 81(1) but not covered by the block exemption the guidelines state:

90. If the parties' combined market share is larger than 20%, the likely impact of the production agreement on the market must be assessed. In this respect market concentration as well as market shares will be a significant factor. The higher the combined market share of the parties, the higher the concentration in the market concerned. However, a moderately higher market share than allowed for in the block exemption does not necessarily imply a high concentration ratio. For instance, a combined market share of the parties of slightly more than 20% may occur in a market with a moderate concentration (HHI below 1800). In such a scenario a restrictive effect is unlikely. In a more concentrated market, however, a market share of more than 20% is likely to cause a competition restriction (......). The picture may nevertheless change, if the market is very dynamic with new participants entering the market and market positions changing permanently.

91. For joint production, network effects, i.e. links between a significant number of competitors, can also play an important role. In a concentrated market the creation of an additional link may tip the balance and make collusion in this market likely, even if the parties have a significant, but still moderate combined market share (......).

92. Under specific circumstances a co-operation between potential competitors may also raise competition concerns. This is, however, limited to cases where a strong player in one market co-operates with a realistic potential entrant, for instance, with a strong supplier of the same product or service in a neighbouring geographic market. The reduction of potential competition creates particular problems if actual competition is already weak and threat of entry is a major source of competition.

The Guidelines also consider co-operation in upstream markets:

93. Joint production of an important component or other input to the parties' final product can cause negative market effects under certain circumstances:

— Foreclosure problems (......) provided that the parties have a strong position on the

---

[96] For the exceptions to this see *ibid.* para. 84.
[97] Draft Guidelines [2000] OJ C118/14, para. 86. The English in this sentence is slightly strange.

relevant input market (non-captive use) and that switching between captive and non-captive use would not occur in the presence of a small but permanent relative price increase for the product in question.

— Spill-over effects (......) provide that the input is an important component of costs and that the parties have a strong position in the downstream market for the final product.

As with R&D agreements, the guidelines set out a number of hypothetical examples, showing how Article 81(3) would be applied to various situations.

(iii) PURCHASING AGREEMENTS

Purchasing agreements concern the joint buying of products. Often, as the guidelines say, they are concluded by small and medium sized enterprises:

106. This chapter focuses on agreements concerning the joint buying of products. Joint buying can be carried out by a jointly controlled company or by a company in which many firms hold a small stake or by a contractual arrangement or even looser form of co-operation.

107. Purchasing agreements are often concluded by small and medium sized enterprises to achieve similar volumes and discounts as their bigger competitors. These agreements between small and medium sized enterprises are therefore normally pro-competitive. Even if a moderate degree of market power is created, this may be outweighed by economies of scale provided the parties really bundle volume. Joint buying occurs in many sectors; most frequently it seems to occur in the retail sector.

182. For instance, environmental agreements, which may phase out or significantly affect an important proportion of the parties' sales as regards their products or production process, may fall under Article 81(1) when the parties hold a significant proportion of the market. The same applies to agreements whereby the parties allocate individual pollution quotas.

183. Similarly, agreements whereby parties holding important market shares in a substantial part of the common market appoint an undertaking as exclusive provider of collection and/or recycling services for their products, may also appreciably restrict competition, provided other actual or realistic potential providers exist.

In applying Article 81(3) (there is no block exemption) the Commission not surprisingly takes a positive stance. It is a particularly interesting example of the weighing up of benefits of the agreement against the restriction of competition.

185. Environmental agreements caught by Article 81(1) may attain economic benefits which, either at individual or aggregate consumer level, outweigh their negative effects on competition. To fulfil this condition, there must be net benefits in terms of reduced environmental pressure resulting from the agreement, as compared to a baseline where no action is taken. In other words, the expected economic benefits must outweigh the costs . . .

186. Such cost include the effects of lessened competition along with compliance costs for economic operators and/or effects on third parties. The benefits might be assessed in two stages. Where consumers individually have a positive rate of return from the agreement under reasonable payback periods, there is no need for the aggregate environmental benefits to be objectively established. Otherwise, a cost-benefit analysis may be necessary to assess whether net benefits for consumers in general are likely under reasonable assumptions.

The example the Commission gives in this section is of an agreement between washing-machine manufacturers not to manufacture or import into the EU products which do not comply with certain environmental criteria. This example is clearly based on the exemption given on 11 February 2000 to an agreement to this effect between virtually all the European producers and importers of washing-machines.[98]

5. THE DRAFT BLOCK EXEMPTION REGULATIONS

A. THE FORMAT OF THE BLOCK EXEMPTIONS

As explained above, two separate draft block exemptions were published in April 2000, one on R&D and one on specialization. Like the new block exemption for vertical agreements, Regulation 2790/1999,[99] the drafts eschew a 'white list' of exempted clauses and concentrate instead on the 'black list' of restrictions or clauses which are not exempted. As in the case of Regulation 2790/1999 the block exemptions contain market share thresholds. They apply only to agreements where the participating undertakings' share of the relevant market is below a certain figure. Each draft contains the same explanation of this in the recitals:[100]

It is appropriate to move away from the approach of listing exempted clauses and to place greater emphasis on defining the categories of agreements which are exempted up to a certain level of market power and on specifying the restrictions or clauses which are not to be contained in such agreements. This is consistent with an economics based approach which assesses the impact of agreements on the relevant market.

In the block exemptions market share is used as a proxy for market power.

B. THE DRAFT BLOCK EXEMPTION ON SPECIALIZATION AGREEMENTS

Article 1 of the draft defines the type of agreement to which it relates:

1. Pursuant to Article 81(3) of the Treaty and subject to the provisions of this Regulation, it is hereby declared that Article 81(1) of the Treaty shall not apply to the following agreements entered into between two or more undertakings and which relate to the conditions under which those undertakings specialize in the production of products:

    (a) unilateral specialization agreements, by virtue of which one party agrees to cease pro-duction of certain products or to refrain from producing these products and to purchase

---

[98] Commission Press Release IP/00/148.

[99] [1999] OJ L336/21.

[100] Para. 5 in the specialization draft block exemption [2000] OJ C118/10 and para. 7 in that on R&D [2000] OJ C118/4.

them from a competitor, while the competitor agrees to produce and supply these products; or

(b) reciprocal specialisation agreements, by virtue of which two or more parties on a reciprocal basis accept to cease or refrain from producing certain but different products and to purchase these products from the other parties, who accept to supply them; or

(c) joint production agreements, by virtue of which two or more parties agree to produce certain products jointly.

This exemption shall apply to the extent that such agreements (hereinafter referred to as specialisation agreements) contain restrictions of competition falling within the scope of Article 81(1) of the Treaty.

The exemption therefore covers two types of specialization properly so called, unilateral specialization (the *Prym/Beka* situation which was not covered by Regulation 417/85[101]) and reciprocal specialization. It also covers agreements for joint production. Further, it encompasses ancillary provisions 'such as those concerning the assignment or use of intellectual property rights' which do not constitute the primary object of the agreement.[102] The two types of specialization, however, are exempted only if the agreement contains cross purchase and supply obligations. Recital 12 explains that this is to ensure that the benefits of specialization materialize without one party leaving the market downstream of production. Article 2(a) allows the related purchase and supply obligations to be exclusive,[103] and Article 2(b) provides exemption for provisions whereby the parties arrange for joint distribution or for distribution by a (non-competitor) third party.

The 'products' referred to in Article 1 means goods or services, including intermediate and final goods and services, but does not include distribution or rental services.[104]

Article 3 provides that the block exemption applies only where the participating undertakings[105] do not have a combined market share which exceeds 20 per cent of the relevant market. The rules for calculating the market share threshold are laid down in Article 6. The primary criterion is market sales value; if these data are not available recourse may be had to 'other reliable market information', including market sales volumes.[106] The block exemption contains a market share threshold because the Commission considers, as it states in Recital 13, that '[i]t can be presumed that, where the participating undertakings' share of the relevant market does not exceed 20%, specialisation agreements of the category defined in this Regulation will, as a general rule, give rise to economic benefits in the form of

---

[101] See *supra*.

[102] If provisions concerning patents or know-how were the primary object of the agreement they might be covered by block exemption Reg. 240/96 [1996] OJ L31/2, on technology transfer agreements.

[103] An 'exclusive supply obligation' is defined (Art. 5(7)) as an obligation not to supply a competitor with the product to which the specialization agreement relates. Note that this is different from the definition of exclusive supply obligation in the block exemption on for vertical agreements, Reg. 2790/1999, Art. 1(c) of which provides that it means 'any direct or indirect obligation causing the supplier to sell the goods or services specified in the agreement only to one buyer inside the Community for the purposes of a specific use or for resale'.

[104] Specialization draft block exemption [2000] OJ C118/10, Art. 5(3).

[105] As usual, 'participating undertakings' is defined (Art. 5(1)) as the parties to the agreement and their connected undertakings. 'Connected undertakings' is defined in Art. 5(2).

[106] Specialization draft block exemption [2000] OJ C118/10, Art. 6(a). Note that Art. 6 provides for some marginal relief in that the 20% may be exceeded by 5% for up to two years without the benefit of the exemption being lost.

economies of scale or scope or better production technologies, while allowing consumers a fair share of the resulting benefits'.[107]

Article 4 contains the 'black list' of three hard-core restrictions, the presence of which in an agreement prevents the application of the block exemption:

1. The exemption provided for in Article 1 shall not apply to agreements which, directly or indirectly, in isolation or in combination with other factors under the control of the parties, have as their object:

    (a) the fixing of prices,
    (b) the limitation of output or sales,
    (c) the allocation of markets or customers:

2. Paragraph 1 does not apply to:

    (a) provisions on the agreed amount of products in the context of Article 1, paragraph 1(a) and (b), or the setting of the capacity and production volume of a production joint venture in the context of Article 1, paragraph 1(c).

    (b) the fixing of prices that a production joint venture charges to its immediate customers, provided that the joint venture also carries out the distribution of these products so that the price fixing by the joint venture is the effect of integrating the various functions.

The proviso makes it clear that Article 4 does not outlaw provisions limiting the number of products subject to the specialization, or the amount to be produced by a production joint venture. It is also permissible to fix the prices charged by a production joint venture which also distributes the products.

The draft contains, as usual, a provision allowing the Commission to withdraw the benefit of the block exemption from a particular agreement where it finds that the agreement's effects are incompatible with Article 81(3). Unlike Regulation 2790/1999 on vertical agreements, there is no provision for *Member States* to withdraw it in respect of their own territory.[108]

The main differences between the new draft exemption and the existing Regulation, 417/85, can be summed up as:

- there is no white list of exempted clauses in the draft. The block exemption will apply to all restrictions of competition except those listed in Article 4;
- there is no turnover threshold, only the market share threshold of 20 per cent;
- the agreement must contain a cross supply obligations;
- exclusive supply and purchase obligations are permitted;
- the new block exemption will apply to both products and services;
- the new block exemption applies to unilateral as well as reciprocal specialization;
- a limit on capacity and production may be set;
- prices may be fixed where a production joint venture carries out distribution;
- ancillary provisions can be included;
- the draft does not contain an opposition procedure.

[107] See also the importance accorded to market power in the Draft Guidelines [2000] OJ C118/14, *supra* 840.

[108] Reg. 2790/1999, [1999] OJ L336/21 Art. 7; see *supra* Chap. 9. The provision does not appear in the R&D draft, discussed *infra*, either. Note that the White Paper on modernisation of the rules implementing Articles 85 and 86, [now 81 and 82] of the EC Treaty [1999] OJ C132/1 proposes that Member States should have the power to withdraw the benefit of block exemptions: see *infra* Chap. 16.

C. THE DRAFT BLOCK EXEMPTION ON RESEARCH AND DEVELOPMENT AGREEMENTS

As with the revised specialization exemption, the new draft block exemption for R&D agreements follows the same basic format as the existing Regulation, 418/85, except that there are no 'white' clauses, only 'black' ones. There is a more extensive list of blacklisted clauses than in the specialization draft.

Article 1 defines the scope of the exemption:

Article 1

Scope

1. Pursuant to Article 81(3) of the Treaty and subject to the provisions of this Regulation, it is hereby declared that Article 81(1) of the Treaty shall not apply to agreements entered into between two or more undertakings which relate to the conditions under which those undertakings pursue:

    (a) joint research and development of products[109] or processes and joint exploitation of the results of that research and development;

    (b) joint exploitation of the results of research and development of products or processes jointly carried out pursuant to a prior agreement between the same undertakings; or

    (c) joint research and development of products or processes excluding joint exploitation of the results.

    This exemption shall apply to the extent that such agreements (hereinafter referred to as research and development agreements) contain restrictions of competition falling within the scope of Article 81(1).

2. The exemption provided for in Paragraph 1 shall also apply to provisions contained in research and development agreements which do not constitute the primary object of, but are directly related to and necessary for their implementation, such as an obligation not to carry out independently or together with third parties research and development in the field to which the agreement relates or in a closely connected field during the execution of the agreement.

This does, however, not apply to provisions which have the same object or effect as the restrictions of competition enumerated in Article 5, paragraph 1.

'Exploitation of the results' is defined in Article 4 as meaning 'the manufacture, selling, distribution or promotion of the contract products or the application of the contract processes or the assignment or licensing of intellectual property rights or the communication of know-how required for such manufacture or application'. Under Article 1(2) ancillary provisions are exempted.

Article 2 contains a list of conditions which must be fulfilled before the agreement may benefit from the block exemption. One of the conditions contained in the corresponding list in Regulation 418/85, that there had to be a framework programme defining the objectives of the work and the field in which it is to be carried out, has been deleted. It is specifically

---

[109] 'Product', as in the specialization draft, covers services (Art. 4(4)).

provided that academic or research bodies may agree to confine their use of the results of the work to further research.

Article 2

Conditions of exemption

1. The exemption provided for in Article 1 shall apply subject to the conditions set out in paragraphs 2 to 5.

2. All the parties have access to the results of the work. However, research institutes or academic bodies may agree to confine their use of the results for the purposes of further research.

3. Where the agreement provides only for joint research and development, each party must be free to exploit the results of the joint research and development and any pre-existing know-how necessary therefor independently.

4. Any joint exploitation must relate to results which are protected by intellectual property rights which substantially contribute to technical or economic progress and the results must be decisive for the manufacture of the contract products or the application of the contract processes.

5. Undertakings charged with manufacture by way of specialisation in production must be required to fulfil orders for supplies from all the parties, except where the agreement also provides for joint distribution.

Article 3 provides that where the parties are not competing manufacturers of products capable of being improved or replaced by the contract products, the exemption can last for the duration of the R&D stage and, where the results are jointly exploited, for five years from the time that the products concerned are put on the market in the common market. It can then *continue* to apply so long as the participating undertakings do not attain a share of the relevant market which exceeds 25 per cent. If, however, the parties are competing manufacturers the exemption covers them only if their combined market share does not exceed 25 per cent at the time of the agreement.[110]

Article 5 contains the blacklisted clauses. It is important to note that, by Article 5(2), it *is* permissible to set production targets for a production joint venture, and where a distribution joint venture is involved sales targets and sales prices may be fixed.

Article 5

Agreements not covered by the exemption

1. The exemption provided for in Article 1 shall not apply to agreements which, directly or indirectly, in isolation or in combination with other factors under the control of the parties, have as their objects:

    (a) the restriction of the freedom of the participating undertakings to carry out research and development independently or in co-operation with third parties in a field unconnected with that to which the research and development relates or, after its completion, in the field to which it relates or in a connected field;

---

[110] The provision about the calculation of market share, Art. 6, is the same as that in the specialization draft block exemption. There is a similar marginal relief provision too: the 25% may be exceeded by up to 5% for up to two years without the befit of the exemption being lost.

(b) the prohibition to challenge after completion of the research and development the validity of intellectual property rights which the parties hold in the common market and which are relevant to the research and development or, after the expiry of the agreement, the validity of intellectual property rights which the rights hold in the common market and which protect the results of the research and development;

(c) the limitation of output or sales;

(d) the fixing of prices;

(e) the restriction of the customers that the participating undertakings may serve, after the end of five years from the time the contract products are first put on the market within the common market;

(f) the prohibition to make passive sales for the contract products in territories reserved for other parties;

(g) the prohibition to put the contract products on the market or to pursue an active sales policy for them in territories within the common market that are reserved for other parties after the end of five years from the time the contract products are first put on the market within the common market;

(h) the requirement not to grant licences to third parties to manufacture the contract products or to apply the contract processes where the exploitation by the parties themselves of the results of the joint research and development is not provided for or does not take place;

(i) the requirement to refuse to meet demand from users or resellers in their respective territories who would market the contract products in other territories within the common market, or

(j) the requirement to make it difficult for users or resellers to obtain the contract products from other resellers within the common market, and in particular to exercise intellectual property rights or take measures so as to prevent users or resellers from obtaining, or from putting on the market within the common market, products which have been lawfully put on the market within the European Community by another party or with its consent.

2. Paragraph 1 does not apply to:

(a) the setting of production targets where the exploitation of the results includes the joint production of the contract products;

(b) the setting of sales targets and the fixing of prices charged to immediate customers where the exploitation of the results includes the joint distribution of the contract products.

Provision is made in Article 7 for the Commission to withdraw the benefit of the exemption should it have effects incompatible with Article 81(3). The situations mentioned in particular are: the limitation of the scope for third parties to carry out R&D in the field because of limited research capacity elsewhere; the substantial restriction of the access of third parties to the market for the products; the failure of the parties to exploit the R&D for no objectively valid reason; lack of effective competition in respect of the products; and the elimination as a result of the existence of the agreement of effective competition in R&D on a particular market.

The main differences between the new draft exemption and the existing Regulation, 418/85,[111] can be summed up as:

---

[111] [1985] OJ L53/5.

- there is no white list of exempted clauses in the draft. The block exemption will apply to all restrictions of competition except those listed in Article 5;
- ancillary provisions are exempted;
- there is a single market share threshold of 25 per cent whether or not joint distribution is involved;
- production targets can be set for a production joint venture;
- sales targets and prices can be set for distribution joint ventures;
- there is no condition about setting a framework programme defining objectives;
- there is no opposition procedure.

6. PRODUCTION JOINT VENTURES AND THE MODERNIZATION PROPOSALS

As explained in Chapters 4 and 16, the Commission's White Paper on Modernization[112] proposes the abolition of the notification and exemption procedure. The White Paper does, however, concede that this may result in too much uncertainty for partial-function production joint ventures as 'operations of this kind generally require substantial investment and farreaching integration of operations, which makes it difficult to unravel them afterwards at the behest of a competition authority'.[113] It therefore proposes that such joint ventures should be subject to the Merger Regulation, as full-function production joint ventures are. This would only be so if no block exemption applied.[114] Partial – function production joint ventures would be subject to both the Merger Regulation's Article 2(3) dominance test and the Article 81 test under Article 2(4).[115]

7. CONCLUSION

The Draft Guidelines and the draft revised block exemptions were put out to public consultation in April 2000. Although as a result of this consultation the Commission may change some of the detail, it is unlikely to change the main thrust of its proposals as they are the outcome of a lengthy consideration of its whole policy towards horizontal co-operation agreements. The policy set out in the Draft Guidelines is to take a realistic view, based on economic analysis, of whether an agreement really does restrict competition in the first place, and to focus on market power as the main concern for the competition authorities.

---

[112] White Paper on modernisation of the rules implementing Arts. 85 and 86 [now 81 and 82] of the EC Treaty [1999] OJ C 132/1.

[113] *Ibid.*, para. 79.

[114] *Ibid.*, para. 80.

[115] *Ibid.*, para. 81. For the application of the tests under the Merger Reg., Reg. 4064/89 [1989] OJ L395/1. see *supra*, Chap. 12.

8. FURTHER READING

BRODLEY, J., 'Joint Ventures and Antitrust Policy' (1982) 95 *Harv. LR* 1521

HAWK, B., 'A Bright Line Shareholding, Test to End the Nightmare under the EEC Merger Regulation' (1993) 30 *CMLRev* 1155

KATTAN, J., 'Antitrust Analysis of Technology Joint Ventures: Allocative Efficiency and the Rewards of Innovation' (1993) 61 *Antitrust LJ* 937

KITCH, E., 'The Antitrust Economics of Joint Ventures' (1987) 54 *Antitrust LJ* 957

14

ENFORCEMENT BY THE COMMISSION

1. INTRODUCTION

As explained in Chapter 2, the Commission has the central role in the application and enforcement of EC competition law. The national courts and competition authorities also play a role, which will increase if the Commission proposals for modernization are implemented.[1] In this chapter we consider enforcement by the Commission under Regulation 17. For a detailed treatment, reference should be had to practitioners' books.[2] In the next chapter we look at enforcement through other channels.

Whatever happens in the future as a consequence of the Commission's modernization proposals, the system hitherto has been a highly centralized one.

Enforcement by the Commission comprises two main strands. First, there is detection, investigation, and decision-making in respect of anti-competitive conduct and agreements which are not notified. Secondly there is its role in respect of agreements which *are* notified in order to obtain a negative clearance or Article 81(3) exemption. Regulation 17 lays down the procedures which the Commission must follow before adopting decisions in either situation.[3]

The Commission plays the part of law-maker, policeman, investigator, prosecution, judge and jury. It performs the activities both of fact-finding and of legal evaluation.[4] Inevitably, this arrangement is subject to criticism. However, the Commission's exercise of its powers of enforcement is subject to judicial review by the Court. Moreover, the Court has developed an extensive jurisprudence on the place of general principles of law and fundamental rights in the Community legal order. The Court's jurisprudence draws, *inter alia*, on the European Convention on Human Rights, (ECHR) which has a special significance in Community law,[5]

---

[1] Commission White Paper on Modernization of the rules implementing Art. 85 and 86, [now 81 and 82] of the EC Treaty [1999] OJ C132/1, [1999] 5 CMLR 208. See *infra* Chap.16.

[2] See P. Freeman and R. Which (eds.), *Butterworths Competition Law*, (Butterworths, looseleaf) Division X; C.S Kerse, *EC Anitrust Procedure* (4th edn., Sweet and Maxwell, London, 1998); L.O.Blanco, *EC Competition Procedure* (Oxford University Press, Oxford, 1996).

[3] For the notification and exemption system, see *supra* Chap. 4. The procedure followed in cases of merger notifications is contained in Council Reg. 4064/89 [1989] OJ L395/1 and Commission Reg. 447/98 [1998] OJ L61/1: see *supra* Chap. 12.

[4] See A. Pera and M Todino, 'Enforcement of EC Competition Rules: Need for a Reform'? [1996] Fordham Corporate Law Institute 125, 144.

[5] Although the Community is not formally bound by the Convention and the Court has held that the

and the cases discussed in the following sections show how the Court has sought to reconcile human rights and the protection of those subject to the Commission's investigations and penalties with the tasks entrusted to the Commission. It should be noted, in particular, that the ECJ has held that the presumption of innocence is a general principle of Community law.[6] Nevertheless, many of the issues raised in the cases stem from the very nature of the Commission's multiplicity of roles. The Commission is sensitive to criticisms of its role, particularly in the light of calls to remove competition law enforcement from the Commission entirely and to entrust it to a separate independent agency.[7]

2. REGULATION 17

Council Regulation 17[8] is the implementing legislation which confers upon the Commission power to enforce the competition rules in all areas of the economy other than transport.[9] A synopsis of the contents of Regulation 17 is given below. The full text appears in the Appendix.

Article 1   The effect of the Article 81(1)EC and Article 82 EC prohibitions.

Article 2   The Commission's power to give negative clearances.

Article 3   The Commission's power to order the termination of infringements. Member States and 'natural or legal persons who claim a legitimate interest' may request the Commission to do this.

Article 4–9   The notification of agreements and granting of exemptions. Article 4(1) is the basic provision and Article 4(2) (as amended by Regulation 1216/99[10]) creates the category of 'non-notifiable' agreements. Article 8 deals with

---

Community as such cannot accede to the Convention without an amendment to the Treaty (*Opinion 2/94* [1996] ECR I–1759, [1996] 2 CMLR 265) the Court consistently refers to the Convention as a source of Community law, and acts now as if it *were* formally bound. For the development of the Court's jurisprudence on human rights see e.g. Case 4/73 *Nold* v. *Commission* [1974] ECR 491; Case 44/79, *Hauer* v. *Land Rheinland-Pfalz* [1979] ECR 1213; Case 222/84, *Johnston* v. *Chief Constable of the RUC* [1986] ECR 1651, [1986] 3 CMLR 240; Case C–260/89, *Elliniki Radiophonia Tileorasi* (*ERT*) v. *DEP* [1991] ECR I–2925. Art. 6 of the Treaty on European Union (as amended by the Treaty of Amsterdam) says that the Union shall respect fundamental rights, as guaranteed by the European Convention and as they result from the constitutional traditions common to the Member States, as general principles of Community law.

[6] Case C–199/92P, *Hüls AG* v. *Commission* (*Polypropylene*) [1999] 5 CMLR 1016, para. 149. The ECJ says that this results in particular from Art. 6(2) of the ECHR; 'Everyone charged with a criminal offence shall be presumed innocent until proved guilty according to law'. However, the Court maintains that fines imposed by the Commission in competition cases are not of a criminal nature: see *infra* 859.

[7] These calls have come particularly from Germany, but see the arguments against: C-D Ehlermann, 'Reflections on a European Cartel Office' (1995) 32 *CMLRev.* 471, *infra* 942–944.

[8] [1959–62] OJ Spec. Ed. 87.

[9] The Reg. applying the competition rules in the transport sector are now Council Reg. 1017/68 [1968] OJ Spec. Ed. 302, as regards land and inland waterways, Council Reg. 4056/86 [1986] OJ L378/4, as regards maritime transport, and Council Reg. 3975/87 [1987] OJ L374/1, in the aviation sector.

[10] [1999] OJ L148/5.

the duration and revocation of exemptions. Article 9(1) says that only the Commission has power to grant exemptions under Article 81(3)EC.

Article 10   Liaison by the Commission with the authorities in the Member States and the role of the Advisory Committee on Restrictive Practices and Monopolies.[11]

Article 11   Power of the Commission to request information from Member States and undertakings and to demand information from undertakings.

Article 12   Power of the Commission to carry out inquiries into sectors of the economy.

Article 13   Investigations by the authorities of Member States pursuant to a request by the Commission.

Article 14   Powers of the Commission to carry out investigations on the premises of undertakings.

Article 15   Fines. Under Article 15(2) the Commission can impose fines for breaches of the competition rules. These are up to 1 million Euros or 10 per cent of the undertaking's previous year's turnover if greater.

Article 16   Periodic penalty payments which can be imposed for defiance of the Commission and failure to comply with Commission decisions.

Article 17   The Court's review of penalties pursuant to Article 229 EC.

Article 18   The currency in which fines are expressed.

Article 19   Hearings.

Article 20   The keeping of professional and business secrets by the Commission.

Article 21   Publication of Commission decisions.

Article 22   Special provisions in relation to Article 4(2).

Article 23   Transitional provisions relating to decisions of the authorities of Member States.

Article 24   The Commission's power to adopt implementing provisions on the details of applications, notifications, and hearings.

Article 25   Arrangements for agreements brought within the competition rules by virtue of accessions of new Member States.

It is important to note that neither the Treaty Articles or Regulation 17 imposes a *duty* to notify the Commission about any agreements or practices.[12] Notification brings with it certain advantages, discussed in Chapter 4, but the obligation on undertakings is to not infringe the Treaty. It is not an obligation to notify.

---

[11] See *supra* Chap. 2.

[12] Compare this with the position as regards mergers under Reg. 4064/89, [1989] OJ L395/1, Art. 4: see *supra* Chap. 12.

3. THE GENESIS OF ENFORCEMENT BY THE COMMISSION

The Commission's enforcement of the competition rules is triggered in one of three ways. First, parties may notify agreements to the Commission under Regulation 17, Article 4(1), seeking negative clearance[13] or exemption.[14] Secondly, under Regulation 17, Article 3(1), the Commission may on its own initiative commence an investigation into a matter *not* notified to it. Thirdly, it may commence an investigation upon receiving a complaint (or, in the words of the Regulation 'upon application'), also under Regulation 17, Article 3(1). In the White Paper on Modernization[15] the Commission stated that in the period 1988–98 58 per cent of the Commission's work stemmed from notifications, 29 per cent from complaints, and 13 per cent from own-initiative investigations. It is this imbalance towards dealing with notifications which has partly prompted the Commission's proposal in the White Paper to make the whole of Article 81 directly applicable and to abolish the centralized notification procedure.

The Commission must comply with the principle of business secrecy which governs the conduct of all proceedings relating to undertakings and their business concerns. Commission investigations should be confidential.[16]

4. FACT-FINDING[17]

A. GENERAL

The Commission's enforcement procedure falls into two stages. First, there is a preparatory fact-finding stage. Secondly, if there is evidence of an infringement the Commission opens a formal procedure.

In the fact-finding stage, the Commission has extensive investigatory powers under Regulation 17, Articles 11 and 14. These can be used to obtain information and are particularly crucial when the Commission is looking into matters which have not been notified to it. The exercise of the powers is often hotly contested by the undertakings subjected to them. The rights of the parties are for the most part not expressly contained in Regulation 17 itself but have been spelt out in the case law of the Court when the Commission's actions have been

---

[13] Technically the parties make an 'application' for negative clearance: Reg. 17, [OJ Spec. Ed. 87 Art. 2.

[14] Or, in the case of conduct which might be caught by Art. 82, negative clearance only.

[15] Commission White Paper on modernisation of the rules implementing Articles 85 and 86 [now 81 and 82] of the EC Treaty [999] OJ C132/1, [1999] 5 CMLR 208 at para. 44, discussed *infra* in Chap. 17.

[16] Art. 287 (ex Art. 214). The Commission breached this when it announced to the press the fine it intended to impose on Volkswagen before the decision was adopted: Case T–62/98, *Volkswagen* v. *Commission*, [2000] 5 CMLR 853, paras 279–282.

[17] The Commission has published a guide for undertakings, *Dealing with the Commission* (Commission, 1997).

challenged, often on the grounds that the Commission has acted in breach of the general principles of law or of fundamental rights.

Under Regulation 17, Article 11, the Commission may request undertakings to supply it with information. When agreements are notified to the Commission the parties have to supply considerable information on Form A/B[18] although Article 11 can be used to acquire additional information. In the case of complaints complainants should provide the Commission with any relevant information they possess. However, where the Commission investigates suspected infringements of the competition rules, either following a complaint or on its own initiative, it is frequently looking for information which the parties would rather not give it and which they may have taken active steps to conceal. Under Article 11 the Commission may turn to the undertakings under investigation and to other undertakings such as customers, competitors, or suppliers of the allegedly infringing firms and request them, and ultimately require them, to supply information.

Article 14 enables the Commission to conduct investigations on the undertakings' premises. It can exercise these powers immediately, and does not have to make a prior request for information under Article 11. The Court has emphazised that Regulation 17 imposes on undertakings the obligation to co-operate actively with the investigative measures.[19]

B. ARTICLE 11 REQUESTS FOR INFORMATION

Article 11 provides a two-stage process, an 'informal' one in Article 11(3) and a 'formal' one in Article 11(5). The Commission has to go through the Article 11(3) stage before proceeding to Article 11(5). This differs from the Article 14 investigation, where the Commission can advance to the more extreme procedure immediately.

Article 11(1) says that in carrying out its duties the Commission may obtain 'all necessary information' from Member States' governments and competent authorities and from undertakings.[20] The meaning of 'necessary information' was considered by the Court in SEP.[21] The CFI stated that the term 'necessary information' in Article 11(1) must be interpreted by reference to the purposes for which the powers of investigation in question were conferred upon the Commission. The requirement for a correlation between the request for information and the presumed infringement is met if, at this stage of the procedure, the request can be legitimately considered to be related to the presumed infringement.[22] The ECJ upheld this.[23] Although it is not easy, therefore, to show that the information requested is outside the leeway allowed to the Commission, it does mean that the Commission cannot go on a complete 'fishing expedition' and that the Court would be prepared to hold in an appropriate case that it had exceeded its powers.[24]

---

[18] See *supra* Chap. 4.

[19] Case 374/87, *Orkem SA* v. *Commission* [1989] ECR 3283, [1991] 4 CMLR 502, paras. 22 and 27.

[20] And associations of undertakings.

[21] Case T–39/90, *SEP* v. *Commission* [1991] ECR II–1497, [1992] 5 CMLR 33.

[22] *Ibid., para. 29.*

[23] Case C–36/92P, *SEP* v. *Commission* [1994] ECR I–1911.

[24] See also Case 155/79, *AM&S Ltd* v. *Commission* [1982] ECR 1575, [1982] 2 CMLR 264 and Case 374/87, *Orkem SA* v. *Commission* [1989] ECR 3283, [1991] 4 CMLR 502.

Article 11(3) gives undertakings the chance to provide information 'voluntarily' by responding to a 'request'. The Commission invariably stipulates a time limit (otherwise it cannot proceed to Article 11(5)). There is no *duty* to comply with the request, although the intentional or negligent provision of *incorrect* information can be penalized with a fine under Regulation 17, Article 15(1)(b). The level of fine is low, Euro 100 to 5,000,[25] but the real spur to accuracy is often a desire to co-operate with the Commission and not to make the situation worse.

If undertakings do not comply with the Article 11(3) request the Commission can proceed to demand the information by decision by Article 11(5):

Regulation 17 [1956–62] OJ spec ed., 87 Article 11(5)

Where an undertaking or association of undertakings does not supply the information requested within the time limit fixed by the Commission, or supplies incomplete information, the Commission shall by decision require the information to be supplied. The decision shall specify what information is required, fix an appropriate time limit within which it is to be supplied and indicate the penalties provided for by Article 15(1)(b) and Article 16(1)(c) and the right to have the decision reviewed by the Court of Justice.

The fact that in the end the Commission can demand the information by using Article 11(5) is another reason for complying with the Article 11(3) request. An Article 11 request is not precluded by the fact that the Commission has already carried out an Article 14 inspection and is using Article 11 to obtain documents which it failed to obtain during the inspection.[26] The *Scottish Football Association* case demonstrates how undertakings served with an Article 11(3) request are expected to co-operate if the Commission is not to proceed to an Article 11(5) decision:

Case T–46/92, *The Scottish Football Association* v. *Commission* [1994] ECR II–1039

On 5 December 1991 the Commission sent the Scottish Football Association (SFA) an Article 11(3) letter following a complaint from the European Sports Network that the SFA was intending to prevent it from broadcasting Argentinian football matches in Scotland. The Commission asked the SFA certain specific questions about its correspondence with the Argentinian FA and communications with FIFA. The SFA wrote back expressing 'some surprise' at the letter, explaining in general terms its policy about broadcasts, and saying it was 'happy to meet you at any time to explain our views'. The Commission did not reply but ten weeks later adopted an Article 11(5) decision requiring the information requested in the December letter. The SFA complied with the decision, but challenged it as well, *inter alia* on the grounds that the Commission had acted disproportionately and excessively by threatening it in a formal decision with the imposition of penalties when it could have achieved its objective just by asking the SFA simply to supplement its original answers. The Commission argued that it was justified as treating the SFA's response as a refusal since it had implied that 'the Argentinian matter' was not the Commission's business, ignored two of the five questions and only offered to discuss generalities and not the specific questions put.

---

[25] It was set in 1962. The White Paper on Modernization of the rules implementing Articles 85 and 86 [now 81 and 82] of the EC Treaty [1999] OJ C182/1 (para. 124) proposes an increase to Euros 1,000 to 50,000.

[26] Case 374/87, *Orkem SA* v. *Commission* [1989] ECR 3283, [1991] 4 CMLR 502, para. 14.

Court of First Instance

29. First, the plea advanced by the applicant does not concern the inherent legality of the request for information addressed to it, since the applicant does not challenge the Commission's power to put to it the four questions concerned. Its sole complaint is that the Commission acted prematurely and excessively in adopting the decision threatening it with periodic penalties instead of continuing to exchange informal correspondence with it.

30. Next, as regards the question whether in adopting the contested decision in the circumstances of this case the Commission correctly applied Article 11 of Regulation No 17, it should be remembered that, according to the case-law of the Court of Justice, that article lays down, for the exercise by the Commission of its power to request the information it considers necessary, a two-stage procedure, the second stage of which, involving the adoption by the Commission of a decision specifying the information required, may only be initiated if the first stage, in which a request for information is sent, has been tried without success (Case 136/79 *National Panasonic v Commission* [1980] ECR 2033, paragraph 10).

31. As regards the ways in which the Commission should 'try' the first stage of the preliminary investigation procedure, the Court of Justice has held that Regulation No 17 confers on the Commission wide powers of investigation and imposes on the individuals concerned the obligation to co-operate actively in the investigative measures, which means that they must make available to the Commission all information relating to the subject-matter of the investigation (Case 374/87 *Orkem v Commission* [1989] ECR 3283, paragraphs 22 and 27). Consequently, the applicant's argument that the contested decision could only have been justified if it had manifestly obstructed the Commission in carrying out its task must be rejected. Given that individuals concerned have such an obligation to co-operate actively in the initial investigation procedure, a passive reaction may in itself justify the adoption of a formal decision under Article 11(5) of Regulation No 17.

32. It is in the light of those considerations that the responses which the applicant gave in its letter of 14 January 1992 to the request for information of 5 December 1991 must therefore be considered. The Court observes in that regard that the applicant, stated, in response to the first question, that it did not have to have any legal basis to justify writing to the Argentinian Football Association and, in response to the second question, that it did not have the information requested; instead of replying to the third question, it offered to give general oral explanations; and it did not provide at all the correspondence between the applicant and the Argentinian Football Association requested by the fourth question. In the Court's view, those responses cannot be regarded as active co-operation on the part of the applicant.

33. Furthermore, the applicant stated that 'we honestly think that as to the Argentinian matter, the Commission need not be troubled about an exchange of correspondence between two fraternal associations . . .'. Considered objectively, that remark constitutes a polite but explicit refusal to co-operate with the Commission in the matter. In those particular circumstances, the Commission was under no obligation either to pursue lengthy informal correspondence or to engage in oral discussions with the applicant, which had provided only part of the information requested. It was entitled to proceed to the second stage of the preliminary investigation procedure, involving a request for information by way of a decision, and that step cannot be regarded as excessive.

34. It follows from all the foregoing considerations that the Commission correctly applied Article 11 of Regulation No 17 and that the plea of breach of the principle of proportionality must therefore be dismissed.

However, *Orkem* established that the duty actively to co-operate with the Commission does not mean that the undertaking has to incriminate itself by admitting to infringements of the competition rules.

Case 374/87, *Orkem SA* v. *Commission* [1989] ECR 3283, [1991] 4 CMLR 502

Like *Hoechst*, discussed below, this case arose out of the investigations conducted by the Commission into alleged cartels in the thermoplastics industry. The questions required to be answered asked for (1) factual information about a meeting, (2) clarification on 'every step or concerted measure which may have been envisaged or adopted to support such price initiatives', (3) the 'details of any system or method which made it possible to attribute sales or targets or quotas to the participants' and (4) 'details of any methods facilitating annual monitoring of compliance with any system of targets in terms of volumes or quotas'. The undertaking challenged the decision claiming that the Commission had infringed the general principle that no-one may be compelled to give evidence against himself, a principle which was part of Community law as it was recognised by the Member States, by Article 6 of the European Convention on Human Rights and by paragraph 3(g) of the International Covenant on Civil and Political Rights, 1966.

Court of First Instance

20. The rule necessary for the application of Articles [81] and [82], introduced by the Council, prescribe two successive but clearly separate procedures: first, a preparatory investigation procedure, and secondly, a procedure involving submissions by both parties initiated by the statement of objections.

21. The sole purpose of the preliminary investigation procedure is to enable the Commission to obtain the information and documentation necessary to check the actual existence and scope of a specific factual and legal situation (*National Panasonic . . .*).

22. For that purpose, Regulation 17 conferred on the Commission wide powers of investigation and imposed on undertakings the obligation to co-operate in the investigative measures.

23. Thus, Article 11(1) of Regulation 17 empowers the Commission to obtain all necessary information from undertakings and Article 11(5) authorizes it to require, by decision, that information be supplied to it where an undertaking does not supply the information requested, or supplies incomplete information.

24. If the Commission considers that the information thus obtained justifies such a course of action, it sends a statement of objections to the undertaking concerned, thus initiating the *inter partes* procedure governed by Commission Regulation 99/63 on the hearings provided for in Article 19(1) and (2) of Council Regulation 17.

25. For the purposes of the *inter partes* procedure, Article 19 of Regulation 17 and Regulation 99/63 provide in particular that the undertaking concerned is entitled to make known in writing and, if appropriate, orally its views on the objections raised against them (see also the judgments in Case 85/76, *Hoffmann-la Roche v. EC.Commission . . .* and Joined cases 10–103/80, *Musique Diffusion Francasise And Others v. E.C.Commission . . . .* In any decision which the Commission might be prompted to adopt on conclusion of the procedure, it will be entitled to set out only those objections on which the undertaking concerned has had an opportunity of making known its views.

26. In the course of the preliminary investigation procedure, Regulation 17 expressly accords only certain guarantees to the undertaking under investigation. Thus, a decision requiring information to be supplied may be taken only after a prior request has proved unsuccessful. Similarly, a decision fixing the definitive amount of a fine or penalty payment, in a case where the undertaking concerned fails to supply the information required by the decision, may be adopted only after the undertaking in question has been given an opportunity to make its views known.

27. On the other hand, Regulation 17 does not give an undertaking under investigation any right to evade the investigation on the ground that the results thereof might provide evidence of an infringe-

ment by it of the competition rules. On the contrary, it imposes on the undertaking an obligation to co-operate actively, which implies that it must make available to the Commission all information relating to the subject-matter of the investigation.

28. In the absence of any right to remain silent expressly embodied in Regulation 17, it is appropriate to consider whether and to what extent the general principles of Community law, of which fundamental rights form an integral part and in the light of which all Community legislation must be interpreted, require, as the applicant claims, recognition of the right not to supply information capable of being used in order to establish against the person supplying it, the existence of an infringement of the competition rules.

29. In general, the laws of the member-States grant the right not to give evidence against oneself only to a natural person charged with an offence in criminal proceedings. A comparative analysis of national law does not therefore indicate the existence of such a principle, common to the laws of the Member-States, which may be relied upon by legal persons in relation to infringements in the economic sphere, in particular infringements of competition law.

30. As far as Article 6 of the European Convention is concerned, although it may be relied upon by an undertaking subject to an investigation relating to competition law, it must be observed that neither the wording of that Article nor the decisions of European Court of Human Rights indicate that it upholds the right not to give evidence against oneself.

31. Article 14 of the International Covenant, which upholds, in addition to the presumption of innocence, the right (in paragraph 3(g)) not to give evidence against oneself or to confess guilt, relates only to persons accused of a criminal offence in court proceedings and thus has no bearing on investigations in the field of competition law.

32. It is necessary, however, to consider whether certain limitations on the Commission's powers of investigation are implied by the need to safeguard the rights of the defence which the Court has held to be fundamental principle of the Community order (Case 322/82, *Michelin v. E.C. Commission*...

33. In that connection, the court observed recently in its judgment in Joined Cases 46/87 & 227/88 *Hoechst v. E.C. Commission* ..., that whilst it is true that the rights of the defence must be observed in administrative procedures which may lead to the imposition of penalties, it is necessary to prevent those rights from being irremediably impaired during preliminary inquiry procedures which may be decisive in providing evidence of the unlawful nature of conduct engaged in by undertakings and for which they may be liable. Consequently, although certain rights of the defence relate only to contentious proceedings which follow the delivery of the statement of objections, other rights must be respected even during the preliminary inquiry.

34. Accordingly, whilst the Commission is entitled, in order to preserve the useful effect of Article 11(2) and (5) of Regulation 17, to compel an undertaking to provide all necessary information concerning such facts as may be known to it and to disclose to it, if necessary, such documents relating thereto as are in its possession, even if the latter may be used to establish, against it or another undertaking, the existence of anti-competitive conduct, it may not, by means of a decision calling for information, undermine the rights of defence of the undertaking concerned.

35. Thus, the Commission may not compel an undertaking to provide it with answers which might involve an admission on its part of the existence of an infringement which it is incumbent upon the Commission to prove.

On this basis, the Court annulled the decision in respect of all the questions listed above except the first one. The Court drew a distinction (paragraphs 34 and 35) between a right to compel the undertaking to provide factual information which can be used to establish a breach of the rules, and a right to compel it to admit to the breach. The Commission has the former but not the latter right.

The problem is that this may not be in line with the interpretation by the European Court of Human Rights of Article 6 of the ECHR, which guarantees the right to a fair trial.[27] The Court denied in *Orkem* (see paragraph 30) that Article 6 included the right not to provide evidence against oneself. In *Funke*,[28] however, the European Court of Human Rights held that as a result of Article 6 anyone charged with a criminal offence within the meaning of that Article had the right 'to remain silent and not to contribute to incriminating himself'. This included the right not to produce incriminating documents. The basic question is whether competition infringements are criminal offences. Regulation 17, Article 15(4), expressly states that fines under that Article 'shall not be of a criminal law nature', and in *Orkem* the Court considered that competition investigations do not involve a criminal offence (paragraph 31). However, it cannot be assumed that EC competition proceedings are not 'criminal' for the purposes of the ECHR. The definition of a 'criminal charge' is a matter of Convention law.[29] The competition rules are of general application and fines for breaches of the substantive rules can be considerable, running into many millions of Euros, and serve as both a sanction and a deterrent.[30] These are relevant factors in determining whether the matter is a 'criminal charge'.[31] Moreover, in *Société Stenuit* v. *France* the European Commission on Human Rights held in its Opinion that a fine imposed on undertakings by the French competition authorities was criminal in nature.[32]

In *Saunders* v. *United Kingdom*[33] the European Court of Human Rights held that the use in the case against Ernest Saunders in the *Guinness* criminal trial of incriminating statements obtained from him by DTI inspectors under their compulsory powers was oppressive, and impaired his ability to defend himself by undermining his right to remain silent. The result was an infringement of Article 6(1). However, the judgment suggested that compulsorily obtaining incriminating documents by a warrant would be justified, which is a watering down of *Funke*.

The CFI followed the approach of the ECJ in the *PVC II Cartel* cases.[34] It considered that an absolute right of silence would hinder the Commission. As far as Article 11(1) requests

---

[27] See A. Riley, 'Saunders and the Power to Obtain Information in Community and United Kingdom Competition Law' (2000) 25 *ELRev.* 264.

[28] *Funke* v. *France*, Series A, No 256–A, (1993) 16 EHRR 297, para. 44.

[29] *Engel* v. *Netherlands* Series A, No. 22 (1979–80) 1 EHRR 647.

[30] See *infra* 901–918.

[31] See *Bendenoun* v. *France* Series A, No. 284 (1994) 18 EHRR 54. *Funke* involved possible infringements of French foreign currency regulations; *Benedenoun* involved possible infringements of French tax law.

[32] (1992) 14 EHRR 509: *Stenuit* did not proceed to a judgment by the European Court of Human Rights as the applicant and the French authorities settled the matter. See also Judge Vesterdorf (acting as Advocate-General) in Case T–1/89, *Rhône-Poulenc SA* v. *Commission* [1991] ECR II–867, 885, who wondered whether the penalties were criminal.. The applicants raised *Stenuit* in Case T–348/94, *Enso Española* v. *Commission* [1998] ECR II–1875, but the CFI did not expressly deal with it. And see the CFI in Cases T–25/95 etc. *Cimenteries CBR SA* v. *Commission*, judgment of 15 Mar. 2000, [2000] 5 CMLR 204, para. 718.

[33] *Saunders* v. *United Kingdom* (1997) 23 EHRR 313. This judgment would still allow procedures such as taking DNA samples or breath tests because they are not material which has an 'independence from the will' of the suspect.

[34] See also Case T–34/93 *Société Générale* v. *Commission* [1995] ECR II–545, [1996] 4 CMLR 665 and Case T–31/91, *Solvay* v. *Commission* [1995] ECR II–1821.

for information were concerned, the CFI did not consider that the possible of a penalty for supplying *inaccurate* information meant that undertakings were under an obligation to reply.

Joined Cases T–305–307, 313–316, 318, 325, 328–329 and 335/94, *Limburgse Vinyl Maatschappij NV and others* v *Commission* judgment 20 April 1999 [1999] 5 CMLR 303

Court of First Instance

448. The recognition of the absolute right of silence, as argued for by the applicants, would go beyond what is necessary to preserve the defence rights of undertakings and would constitute an unjustified hindrance to the Commission in the accomplishment of its task under Article [85] of the Treaty of ensuring compliance with the competition rules in the Common Market. The Court would point out, in particular, that both in their replies to the requests for information and in the administrative procedure which follows where, in appropriate cases, the Commission decides to open that procedure, undertakings have every opportunity to put their point of view, especially concerning the documents which they may have been led to produce or replies which they have given to the Commission's questions.

449. The Commission may not, however, by a decision to request information, undermine the undertaking's defence rights. Thus it may not compel an undertaking to provide it with answers which might involve an admission on its part of the existence of an infringement which it is incumbent on the Commission to prove . . .

. . .

455. Secondly, an undertaking is not under an obligation to reply to a request for information under Article 11(1) of Regulation No 17, as opposed to decisions requiring information.

456. In those circumstances, the undertakings are free to reply or not to the questions put to them under that provision. That conclusion is not affected by the fact that a penalty is stipulated in the first part of the sentence of Article 15(1)(b) of Regulation No 17. Such a penalty applies only where, having agreed to reply, the undertaking provides inaccurate information.

457. Therefore, by making requests for information under Article 11(1) of Regulation No 17, the Commission cannot be regarded as compelling an undertaking to provide it with answers which might involve an admission on its part of the existence of an infringement which it is incumbent upon the Commission to prove.

The CFI repeated the above in *Cement*, although it prefaced it with a reference to *Funke* which it did not elaborate upon:[35]

The Court points out that the Commission may not compel an undertaking involved in a proceeding finding an infringement of Article [81](1) and/or Article [82] of the Treaty 'to provide answers which might involve an admission on its part of the existence of an infringement which it is incumbent on the Commission to prove' (Case 374/87 *Orkem v Commission* . . . . paragraph 35; Case T–34/93 *Société Générale v Commission* . . . . paragraph 74; see, by analogy, the judgment of the European Court of Human Rights *Funke v France*, Series A, No 256-A, p. 22).

---

[35] Cases T–25/95 etc., *Cimenteries CBR SA* v. *Commission*, judgment of 15 Mar. 2000, [2000] 5 CMLR 204, para. 732.

In its White Paper on Modernization[36] the Commission ignores any problems about non-incrimination and expresses satisfaction with Article 11:

116. Experience has shown that requests for information addressed by the Commission to undertakings under Article 11 do not raise any major difficulty. The principle that undertakings
are bound to reply has repeatedly been upheld by the Court of Justice, which has allowed an
exception only in the case of directly incriminating questions.[37]

The White Paper also proposes a power of the Commission to summon company representatives or employees to Brussels to answer questions. This may also raise human rights problems.[38]

C. ARTICLE 14 INVESTIGATIONS

Article 14(1) gives the Commission powers to carry out 'all necessary investigations' into undertakings. This involves a power to:

- examine the books and other business records;
- take copies of or extracts from the books and business records;
- ask for oral explanations on the spot;
- enter any premises, land and means of transport of undertakings.

Under Article 14(2) the Commission can carry out the inspection at the premises simply on production of an 'authorization in writing' . The inspectors may either give advance notice of their arrival or come without warning. So long as they carry only the Article 14(2) 'authorization' there is no legal obligation to submit to the inspection. Under Article 14(3), however, undertakings *must* submit to procedures ordered by decision of the Commission.[39] The undertaking must actively co-operate. In *Fabbrica Pisani* the Commission said:[40]

the obligation on undertakings to supply all documents required by Commission inspectors must
be understood to mean not merely giving access to all files, but actually producing the specified
documents required.

The most notorious form of Commission inspection is where the inspectors arrive with-
out warning, armed with an Article 14(3) decision. The ECJ held in *National Panasonic*[41] that they are entitled to do this without going through the 'voluntary' Article 14(2) procedure first. Article 14 therefore differs in this respect from Article 11. Although popularly known as 'dawn raids' unannounced inspections take place during normal business hours.

---

[36] Commission White Paper on modernisation of the rules implementing Art. 85 and 86 [now 81 and 82] of the EC Treaty [999] OJ C132/1, [1999] 5 CMLR 208.

[37] The only amendment the Commission proposes is to provide that lawyers may reply on their clients' behalf.

[38] See *infra* 871.

[39] Case 5/85, *AKZO* v. *Commission* [1986] ECR 2585, [1987] 3 CMLR 716; Cases 46/87 and 227/88, *Hoechst AG* v. *Commission* [1989] ECR 2859, [1991] 4 CMLR 410.

[40] [1980] OJ L75/30, [1980] 2 CMLR 354.

[41] Case 136/79, *National Panasonic* v. *Commission* [1980] ECR 2033, [1980] CMLR 169.

There may, however, be simultaneous surprise arrivals at undertakings across the Community where, for example, the Commission suspects the existence of a cartel or abuses of a dominant position. The *Polypropylene* cartel investigation,[42] for example, involved ten simultaneous raids. Julian Joshua, now Deputy Head of the Cartel Unit in the Competition DG, explained in 1983 why the apparently draconian powers of the Commission in Article 14(3) are necessary:[43]

More often, the most serious cartels are not modified at all. They are operated in conditions of strict secrecy. Communication between participants is kept to a minimum and knowledge of the arrangements confined to certain key employees. Meetings take place in safe countries or under the cover of a seemingly innocent trade association. There may even be emergency arrangements to shred documents and warn other participates by coded telex messages in the event of an investigation. Sometimes the cartel rules provide for members to deny all knowledge of documents or their contents even when these are found in the safe. In such circumstances resort to surprise must be a legitimate and essential precaution.

Article 14(3) decisions are taken by the Commissioner responsible for competition. This delegation by the College of Commissioners is valid as it does not involve a matter of principle.[44]

D. THE RIGHTS OF UNDERTAKINGS WHICH ARE THE SUBJECT OF ARTICLE 11 AND ARTICLE 14 PROCEDURES

In *National Panasonic* an undertaking subjected to the first unannounced Article 14(3) investigation claimed that the procedure infringed its fundamental rights. It relied in particular on Article 8 of the ECHR. It also claimed that in this case the principle of proportionality was infringed.

Case 136/79, *National Panasonic* v. *Commission* [1980] ECR 2033, [1980] CMLR 169

Commission officials arrived at Panasonic's offices in Slough at 10.00 am. The directors asked if the inspection could be delayed to await the arrival of their solicitor, who was in Norwich. The officials waited until 10.45 am and then began. The solicitor did not arrive until 1.45 pm and the inspection finished at 5.30 pm. Panasonic subsequently challenged the validity of the decision ordering the inspection in the Court of Justice and asked that all the documents taken by the Commission should be returned or destroyed.

Court of Justice

17. The applicant then claims that by failing previously to communicate to it beforehand the decision ordering an investigation in question, the Commission has in this instance infringed fundamental rights of the applicant, in particular the right to receive advance notification of the intention to apply a decision regarding it, the right to be heard before a decision adversely affecting it is taken

---

[42] See *Polypropylene Cartel* [1986] OJ L230/1, [1988] 4 CMLR 347.
[43] J.M. Joshua: 'The Element of Surprise' (1983) 8 *ELRev*, 3, 5.
[44] Case 53/85, *AKZO* v. *Commission* 5/85, [1986] ECR 2585, [1987] 3 CMLR 716.

and the right to use the opportunity given to it under Article [242] of the Treaty to request a stay of execution of such a decision. The applicant relies in particular on Article 8 of the European Convention for the Protection of Human Rights and Fundamental Freedoms of 4 November 1950 whereby 'everyone has the right to respect for his private and family life, his home and his correspondence'. It considers that those guarantees must be provided *mutatis mutandis* also to legal persons.

18. As the Court stated in its judgment of 14 May 1974 in Case 4/73, *J. Nold, Kohlen-und Baustoffgrosshandlung v Commission of the European Communities* [1974] ECR 491 at p.507, fundamental rights form an integral part of the general principles of law, the observance of which the Court of Justice ensures, in accordance with constitutional traditions common to the Member States and with international treaties on which the Member States have collaborated or of which they are signatories.

19. In this respect it is necessary to point out that Article 8 (2) of the European Convention, in so far as it applies to legal persons, whilst stating the principle that public authorities should not interfere with the exercise of the rights referred to in Article 8(1), acknowledges that such interference is permissible to the extent to which it 'is in accordance with the law and is necessary in a democratic society in the interests of national security, public safety or the economic well-being of the country, for the prevention of disorder or crime, for the protection of health or morals, or for the protection of the rights and freedom of others.'

20. In this instance, as follows from the seventh and eighth recitals of the preamble to Regulation No 17, the aim of the powers given to the Commission by Article 14 of that regulation is to enable it to carry out its duty under the EEC Treaty of ensuring that the rules on competition are applied in the common market. The function of these rules is, as follows from the fourth recital of the preamble of the Treaty, Article 3[(1)(g)] and Articles [81] and [82], to prevent competition from being distorted to the detriment of the public interest, individual undertakings and consumers. The exercise of the powers given by the Commission by Regulation No 17 contributes to the maintenance of the system of competition intended by the Treaty which undertakings are absolutely bound to comply with. In these circumstances, it does not therefore appear that Regulation No 17, by giving the Commission powers to carry out investigations without previous notification, infringes the right invoked by the applicant.

21. Moreover, as regard more particularly the argument that the application was in this instance denied the right to be heard before a decision was taken regarding it, it is necessary to state that the exercise of such a right of defence is chiefly incorporated in legal or administrative procedures for the termination of an infringement or for a declaration that an agreement, decision or concerted practice is incompatible with Article [81], such as the procedures referred to by Regulation No 99/63/EEC. On the other hand, the investigation procedure referred to in Article 14 of Regulation No 17 does not aim at terminating an infringement or declaring that an agreement, decision or concerted practice is incompatible with Article [81]; its sole objective is to enable the Commission to gather the necessary information to check that the actual existence and scope of a given factual and legal situation. Only if the Commission considers that the data for the appraisal thereof collected in this way justify the initiation of a procedure under Regulation No 99/63/EEC must the undertaking or association of undertakings concerned be heard before such a decision is taken pursuant to Article 19(1) of Regulation No 17 and to the provisions of Regulation No 99/63/EEC. Precisely this substantive difference between the decisions taken at the end of such a procedure and decisions ordering an investigation explains the wording of Article 19(1) which, in listing the decisions which the Commission cannot take before giving those concerned the opportunity of exercising their right of defence, does not mention that laid down in Article 14(3) of the same regulation.

22. Finally, the argument that the absence of previous information deprived the applicant of the opportunity of exercising its rights under Article [242] of the Treaty to request the Court for a stay of execution of the decision in question is contradicted by the very provisions of Article [242]. That article presupposes in fact that a decision has been adopted and that it is effective whereas the previous notification, which the applicant complains that the Commission did not send it, should have preceded the adoption of the contested decision and could not have been binding.

23. In view of these considerations, the second submission is not well founded.

(d) The violation of the principle of proportionality

28. The applicant points out in addition that the principle of proportionality, as established by the case-law of the Court of Justice, implies that a decision ordering an investigation adopted without the preliminary procedure may only be justified if the situation is very grave and where there is the greatest urgency and the need for complete secrecy before the investigation is carried out. It points out, finally, that the contested decision violates such a principle by not indicating in the statement of the reasons upon which it is based that any of those facts exists.

29. The Commission's choice between an investigation by straightforward authorization and an investigation ordered by a decision does not depend on the facts relied upon by the applicant but on the need for an appropriate inquiry, having regard to the special features of the case.

30. Considering that the contested decision aimed solely at enabling the Commission to collect the necessary information to appraise whether there was any infringement of the Treaty, it does not therefore appear that the Commission's action in this instance was disproportionate to the objective pursued and therefore violated the principle of proportionality.

31. For all these reasons, since the last submission cannot be accepted either, it is necessary to dismiss the application as unfounded.

The ECJ therefore rejected National Panasonic's claims and held that an unannounced Article 14(3) inspection does not infringe the inspected undertaking's fundamental right.

The application of Article 8(1) of the ECHR was considered again in *Hoechst*. The position of undertakings faced with unannounced Article 14(3) inspections and the powers of the Commission in respect thereof were considered at length by the Court. The case arose from a dawn raid in the course of the Commission's investigations into the PVC and polyethylene cartels. Hoechst, unusually, simply refused to admit the Commission inspectors when they arrived.

Cases 46/87 and 227/88, *Hoechst AG* v. *Commission* [1989] ECR 2859, [1991] 4 CMLR 410

The Commission suspected the existence of cartel arrangements between certain suppliers and producers of polyethylene and PVC. On 15 January 1987 it adopted a decision providing for an Article 14(3) investigation into Hoechst. On 20 January the Commission inspectors arrived at Hoechst's offices but Hoechst refused to allow the investigation to go ahead. It claimed that the investigation was an unlawful search, and insisted that the inspectors noted its objections in writing. The inspectors tried twice more, on 22 and 23 January, but the same thing happened. The Commission sent Hoechst a telex calling upon it to submit to the investigation and setting a periodical penalty in the event of non-compliance of 1,000 ECUs per day, and on 3 February it adopted a decision imposing that penalty. The Commission had sought the assistance of the Bundeskartellamt (the Federal Cartel

Office) under Regulation 17, Article 14(5) and (6) and the Bundeskartellamt applied to the local district court (the Amtsgericht, Frankfurt am Main) for a search warrant. On 12 February the Amtsgericht refused the warrant on the grounds that no facts had been put before it which justified the suspicions of the existence of a cartel. Hoechst applied to the Court of Justice for suspension of both the decision ordering the investigation and the decision imposing the periodic penalty but the President of the Court dismissed the application. The Bundeskartellamt applied to the Amtsgericht for a search warrant in the Commission's own name and this was granted on 31 March. The investigation was finally carried out at Hoechst's premises on 2 and 3 April. On 26 May the Commission adopted a decision fixing the definitive amount of the periodic penalty at 55,000 ECUs (i.e. 1,000 a day from 6 February to 1 April). Hoechst brought actions before the Court of Justice under Article 234 alleging that the decisions of 15 January, 3 February and 26 May were all void. The following extract deals with the question of the decision of 15 January ordering the Article 14(3) investigation.

Court of Justice

12. It should be noted, before the nature and scope of the Commission's powers of investigation under Article14 of Regulation No 17 are examined, that that article cannot be interpreted in such a way as to give rise to results which are incompatible with the general principles of Community law and in particular with fundamental rights.

13. The Court has consistently held that fundamental rights are an integral part of the general principles of law the observance of which the Court ensures, in accordance with constitutional traditions common to the Members States, and the international treaties on which the Member States have collaborated or of which they are signatories (see, in particular, the judgment of 14 May 1974 in Case 4/73 *Nold v Commission* [1974] ECR 491). The European Convention for the Protection of Human Rights and Fundamental Freedoms of 4 November 1950 (hereinafter referred to as 'the European Convention on Human Rights') is of particular significance in that regard (see, in particular, the judgment of 15 May 1986 in Case 222/84 *Johnston v Chief Constable of the Royal Ulster Constabulary* [1986] ECR 1651).

14. In interpreting Article 14 of Regulation No 17, regard must be had in particular to the rights of the defence, a principle whose fundamental nature had been stressed on numerous occasions in the Court's decisions (see, in particular, the judgment of 9 November 1983 in Case 322/81 *Michelin v Commission* [1983] ECR 3461, paragraph 7).

15. In that judgment, the Court pointed out that the rights of the defence must be observed in administrative procedures which may lead to the imposition of penalties. But it is also necessary to prevent those rights from being irremediably impaired during the preliminary inquiry procedures including, in particular, investigations which may be decisive in providing evidence of the unlawful nature of conduct engaged in by undertakings for which they may be liable.

16. Consequently, although certain rights of the defence relate only to the contentious proceedings which follow the delivery of the statement of objections, other rights, such as the right to legal representation and the privileged nature of correspondence between lawyer and client (recognized by the Court in the judgment of 18 May 1982 in Case 155/79 *AM & S v Commission* [1982] ECR 1575) must be respected as from the preliminary-inquiry stage.

17. Since the application has also relied on the requirements stemming from the fundamental right to the inviolability of the home, it should be observed that, although the existence of such a right must be recognized in the Community legal order as a principle common to the laws of the Member States in regard to the private dwellings of natural persons, the same is not true in regard to undertakings, because there are not inconsiderable divergences between the legal systems of the Member States in regard to the nature and degree of protection afforded to business premises against intervention by the public authorities.

18. No other inference is to be drawn from Article 8(1) of the European Convention on Human Rights which provides that: 'Everyone has the right to respect for his private and family life, his home and his correspondence'. The protective scope of that article is concerned with the development of man's personal freedom and may not therefore be extended to business premises. Furthermore, it should be noted that there is no case-law of the European Court of Human Rights on that subject.

19. None the less, in all the legal systems of the Member States, any intervention by the public authorities in the sphere of private activities of any person, whether natural or legal, must have a legal basis and be justified on the grounds laid down by law, and , consequently, those systems provide, albeit in different forms, protection against arbitrary or disproportionate intervention. The need for such protection must be recognized as a general principle of Community law. In that regard, it should be pointed out that the Court has held that it has the power to determine whether measures of investigation taken by the Commission under the ECSC Treaty are excessive (judgment of 14 December 1962 in Joined Cases 5 to 11 and 13 to 15/62 *San Michele and Others v Commission* [1962] ECR 449).

20. The nature and scope of the Commission's powers of investigation under Article 14 of Regulation No 17 should therefore be considered in the light of the general principles set out above.

21. Article 14(1) authorizes the Commission to undertake all necessary investigations into undertakings and associations of undertakings and provides that: 'To this end the officials authorized by the Commission are empowered:

(a) to examine the books and other business records;

(b) to take copies of or extracts from the books and business records;

(c) to ask for oral explanations on the spot;

(d) to enter any premises, land and means of transport of undertakings'.

22. Article 14(2) and (3) provide that investigations may be carried out upon production of an authorization in writing or of a decision requiring undertakings to submit to the investigation. As the Court has already decided, the Commission may choose between those two possibilities in the light of the special features of each case (judgment of 26 June 1980 in Case 1365/79 *National Panasonic v Commission* [1980] ECR 2033). Both the written authorizations and the decisions must specify the subject-matter and purpose of the investigation. Whichever procedure is followed, the Commission is required to inform, in advance, the competent authority of the Member State in whose territory the investigation is to be carried out and, according to Article 14(4), that authority must be consulted before the decision ordering the investigation is adopted.

23. According to Article 14(5), the Commission's officials may be assisted in carrying out their duties by officials of the competent authority of the Member State in whose territory the investigation is to be made. Such assistance may be provided either at the request of that authority or of the Commission.

24. Finally, according to Article 14(6), the assistance of the national authorities is necessary for the carrying out of the investigation where it is opposed by an undertaking.

25. As the Court pointed out in the abovementioned judgment of 26 June 1980 (paragraph 20), it follows from the seventh and eighth recitals in the preamble to Regulation No 17 that the aim of the powers given to the Commission by Article 14 of that regulation is to enable it to carry out its under the EEC Treaty of ensuring that the rules on competition are applied in the common market. The function of those rules is, as follows from the fourth recital in the preamble to the Treaty, Article 3(1)

and Articles [81] and [82], to prevent competition from being distorted to the detriment of the public interest, individual undertakings and consumers. The exercise of the powers given to the Commission by Regulation No 17 thus contributes to the maintenance of the system of competition intended by the Treaty with which undertakings are absolutely bound to comply. The eighth recital states that for that purpose the Commission must be empowered, throughout the common market, to require such information to be supplied and to undertake such investigations 'as are necessary' to bring to light any infringement of Articles [81] and [82].

26. Both the purpose of Regulation No 17 and the list of powers conferred on the Commission's officials by Article 14 thereof show that the scope of investigations may be very wide. In that regard, the right to enter any premises, land and means of transport of undertakings is of particular import-ance inasmuch as it is intended to permit the Commission to obtain evidence of infringements of the competition rules in the places in which such evidence is normally to be found, that is to say, on the business premises of undertakings.

27. That right of access would serve no useful purpose if the Commission's officials could do no more than ask for documents or files which they could identify precisely in advance. On the contrary, such a right implies the power to search for various items of information which are not already known or fully identified. Without such a power, it would be impossible for the Commission to obtain the information necessary to carry out the investigation if the undertakings concerned refused to co-operate or adopted an obstructive attitude.

28. Although Article 14 of Regulation No 17 thus confers wide powers of investigation on the Commission, the exercise of those powers is subject to conditions serving to ensure that the rights of the undertakings concerned are respected.

29. In that regard, it should be noted first that the Commission is required to specify that subject-matter and purpose of the investigation. That obligation is a fundamental requirement not merely in order to show that the investigation to be carried out on the premises of the undertakings concerned is justified but also to enable those undertakings to assess the scope of their duty to co-operate while at the same time safeguarding the rights of the defence.

30. It should also be pointed out that the conditions for the exercise of the Commission's investiga-tive powers vary according to the procedure which the Commission has chosen, the attitude of the undertakings concerned and the intervention of the national authorities.

31. Article 14 of Regulation No 17 deals in the first place with investigations carried out with the co-operation of the undertakings concerned, either voluntarily, where there is a written authorization, or by virtue of an obligation arising under a decision ordering an investigation. In the latter case, which is the situation here, the Commission's officials have, *inter alia*, the power to have shown to them the documents they request, to enter such premises as they choose, and to have shown to them the contents of any piece of furniture which they indicate. On the other hand, they may not obtain access to premises of furniture by force or oblige the staff of the undertaking to give them such access, or carry out searches without the permission of the management of the undertaking.

32. The situation is completely different if the undertakings concerned oppose the Commission's investigation. In that case, the Commission's officials may, on the basis of Article 14(6) and without the co-operation of the undertakings, search for any information necessary for the investigation with the assistance of the national authorities, which are required to afford them the assistance necessary for the performance of their duties. Although such assistance is required only if the undertaking expresses its opposition, it may also be requested as a precautionary measure, in order to overcome any opposition on the part of the undertaking.

33. It follows from Article 14(6) that it is for each Member State to determine the conditions

under which the national authorities will afford assistance to the Commission's officials. In that regard, the Member States are required to ensure that the Commission's action is effective, while respecting the general principles set out above. It follows that, within those limits, the appropriate procedural rules designed to ensure respect for undertakings' rights are those laid down by national law.

34. Consequently, if the Commission intends, with the assistance of the national authorities, to carry out an investigation other than with the co-operation of the undertakings concerned, it is required to respect the relevant procedural guarantees laid down by national law.

35. The Commission must make sure that the competent body under national law has all that it needs to exercise its own supervisory powers. It should be pointed out that that body, whether judicial or otherwise, cannot in this respect substitute its own assessment of the need for the investigations ordered for that of the Commission, the lawfulness of whose assessments of fact and law is subject only to review by the Court of Justice. On the other hand, it is within the powers of the national body, after satisfying itself that the decision ordering the investigation is authentic, to consider whether the measures of constraint envisaged are arbitrary or excessive having regard to the subject-matter of the investigation of those measures.

36. In the light of the foregoing, it must be held that the measures which the contested decision ordering the investigation permitted the Commission's officials to take did not exceed their powers under Article 14 of Regulation No 17. Article 1 of that decision merely requires the applicant 'to permit officials authorized by the Commission to enter its premises during normal office hours, to produce for inspection and to permit copies to be made of business documents related to the subject-matter of the enquiry which are requested by the said officials and to provide immediately any explanations which those officials may seek'.

It can be seen therefore that this judgment established:

- the right to inviolability of the home does not apply to business premises;
- rights such as the right to legal representation and the legal privilege of correspondence between lawyer and client must be respected from the preliminary inquiry stage; [45]
- the Commission's powers in the investigation depend on whether the undertaking co-operates. If the undertaking is willing to submit, the Commission officials have power to have shown to them the documents they request, and to enter such premises they choose and have shown to them the contents of particular furniture they indicate. They are *not* entitled forcibly to enter premises or furniture or carry out searches without the undertaking's consent. If the undertaking does not submit to the investigation Article 14(6) comes into play and the Commission has to rely on the assistance of the Member State, which under Article 14(6) is bound to provide assistance.[46]

The Court may, however, have been over-sanguine in saying that the principle of the inviolability of the home in Article 8(1) of the ECHR does not apply to commercial premises. In *Niemitz*[47] the European Court of Human Rights said that the words 'private life' and

---

[45] Legal privilege was first recognized in Case 155/79, *AM&S Ltd* v. *Commission* [1982] ECR 1575, [1982] 2 CMLR 264; see *infra* 872–876.

[46] See *infra* 869 for the position on this in the UK. Art. 14(6) stipulates that the *Member State* concerned must assist, not just its competent authority.

[47] *Niemitz* v. *Germany*, Series A, No 251–B, (1993) 16 EHRR 97, para. 31.

'home' in Article 8(1) included certain professional or business activities or premises. In that case a lawyer's office was protected. The Court said this interpretation was necessary because otherwise unequal treatment could arise, in that self—employed persons may carry on professional activities at home and private activities at their place of work.

The duty to submit to an Article 14(3) investigation is a continuing one, and entails both allowing the inspection to begin and co-operating thereafter. Nevertheless, the limited nature of the Commission officials' powers, and their reliance on national authorities and national procedures, was sharply demonstrated in *Hoechst*. At the time of *Hoechst* the enforcement of the Commission's powers in the UK was by way of application in the name of the Attorney-General to the High Court for an injunction, defiance of which would be a contempt of court.[48] Under the Competition Act 1998, however, the powers of the Director General of Fair Trading to enter premises with a warrant from the High Court in England and Wales or a Court of Session in Scotland using reasonable force as necessary are also applicable in the event of the obstruction of a Commission investigation with which the DGFT is assisting.[49] In effect, therefore, Article 14(3) investigations in the UK are possible by forcible entry. It appears from Article 14(6) that Member States are obliged to afford assistance only when the undertaking has actually opposed the investigation whereas section 62(1) of the Competition Act contemplates the issue of a warrant when an investigation 'is being, *or is likely to be*, obstructed' (emphasis added).

The Commission is unhappy about its reliance on national procedures and national authorities to overcome obstruction by undertakings under investigation. There are particular problems when it is conducting investigations in several Member States simultaneously. In the White Paper the Commission proposes two options for remedying this: centralizing the judicial review element in the hands of the ECJ or harmonizing and simplifying national procedures.

White paper on modernisation of the rules implementing articles 85 and 86 [now 81 and 82] of the EC Treaty [1999] OJ C132/1

110. When the Commission wishes to carry out investigations under Article 14(3), the national authorities assisting it must, in most Member States . . ., secure authorisation from a judge in order to overcome any opposition on the part of the undertaking . . . When there are several undertakings involved, investigations most often have to be conducted in several Member States, and authorisation has therefore to be sought from several judges, whose role is confined to satisfying themselves that the decision ordering the investigation is authentic and that the investigation envisaged is not arbitrary or excessive. . .

111. There are several possible ways to ensure that the investigations are simultaneous and consistent, and to strengthen the guarantees offered to undertakings under investigation. The element of judicial review could be centralised, and entrusted to one of the Community courts. This method of safeguarding the rights of undertakings under investigation would have the advantage of greatly simplifying investigation procedures, and resolving once and

---

[48] See G. Borrie and N. Lowe, *The Law of Contempt* (3rd edn., Butterworths, 1996) Chap. 14.

[49] Competition Act 1998 ss. 61–64. These provisions also apply to an investigation carried out by the DGFT under EC law at the request of the European Commission and to a 'Director's investigation' which is a special investigation carried out by the DGFT in connection with a Commission investigation.

for all the problems of inconsistency and lack of simultaneity. Another possibility would be to harmonise and simplify the procedural law in the Member States, so as to ensure that in any Member States where orders were needed they could be obtained rapidly and simultaneously. The second option is a great deal more complex, and would require far-reaching amendment of judicial procedural law in certain Member States.

The Commission recognizes the difficulty in achieving the second option and its preference is for the first one. The summary of observations on the White Paper[50] records that three Member States opposed centralisation in Luxembourg, two thought the reform unnecessary and one thought the centralization option more realistic than harmonisation of national laws.[51]

There is some doubt about the extent of the Commission's right to 'ask for oral explanations on the spot' under Article 14(1). There is a surprising lack of authority on what this covers.[52] A request under Article 11 must *ex hypothesi* be in writing and the undertaking is given a time in which to reply. There is an argument that if Article 14(1)(c) allowed wide—ranging questions to be put orally to the undertaking during an inspection it would undermine these Article 11 safeguards.[53] The generally accepted view is that Article 14 encompasses asking questions directly arising from the books and records being examined and asking for explanations of such matters as the references, terms, and abbreviations appearing in them, but that it does not authorize a general interrogation of officers or employees of the undertaking. Article 14 does not specify who should answer the oral questions put to the undertaking but a failure by the undertaking to put forward a suitable person may be construed as a refusal to co-operate. Unlike some systems of national competition law, however, no obligation or liability affixes to individuals as such.[54] The Commission considers that its present powers place too great a fetter on the investigators. The White Paper proposes amending Article 14 to make it clear that the undertaking's representatives or staff can be asked any questions that are justified and related to the investigation's purpose, and that the Commission can demand full and precise answers. The Commission also proposed that it should acquire the right to subpoena witnesses to appear before it in Brussels.

---

[50] Summary of observations on the White Paper on reform of Reg. 17, published by the Commission, 29 Feb. 2000.

[51] *Ibid.*, para. 7.2.

[52] As the Commission's guide, *Dealing with the Commission* (Commission, 1997), para. 5.6, recognizes. There was some consideration of it in Case 136/79, *National Panasonic v. Commission* [1980] ECR 2033, [1980] CMLR 169 but no decisive ruling by the Court.

[53] See P. Freeman and R. Whish (eds.), *Butterworths Competition Law* (Butterworths, looseleaf), Division X, para. 573.

[54] Cf the position in the UK under the Competition Act 1998 s. 26, which refers to 'any person' being required by the DGFT to produce documents or supply information (a provision which during the passage of the legislation conjured up visions in one member of the House of Lords of the inspectors 'shimmying up to the cleaning lady': Lord Kingsland, HL, 17 Nov. 1997, col. 388) and provides for penalties against individuals in some situations.

White paper on modernisation of the rules implementing articles 85 and 86 [now 81 and 82] of the EC Treaty [1999] OJ C132/1

112. During investigations, the right of authorised Commission officials to ask questions of an undertaking's representatives or staff which are not directly related to documents found on the premises has sometimes been questioned. In addition, the system of administrative penalties for supplying incorrect information is silent on this point.

113. It is therefore proposed that Article 14 of Regulation 17 should be amended to make it quite clear that in the course of an investigation the authorised Commission officials are empowered to ask the undertaking's representatives or staff any questions that are justified by and related to the purpose of the investigation, and to demand a full and precise answer. A further provision could be introduced under which the authorised officials would be empowered to draw up official minutes of the answers given in the course of the investigation. These minutes would be included in the file, and could be used at later stages of the procedure. As a corollary to this new provision, the answers given in the course of investigations would be brought within the scope of the penalties for supplying incorrect information.

114. In order to increase the effectiveness of its enquiries the Commission should also be empowered to summon to its own premises any person likely to be able to provide information that might be helpful to its enquiries, and to take minuted statements . . . .. This possibility could be used with respect to the undertakings that are the subject of the procedure: it would serve to complement Article 14 by allowing persons to be questioned who were not present at the time of the investigation. It could also be used with respect to complainants and third parties.

Comments submitted by industry and by lawyers on the above proposals were unenthusiastic.[55] Concern was expressed about the position of the individual staff concerned, and their need for independent legal advice. Commission investigations are often complex and concern events of some years before. It is thought unreasonable that staff are expected to give 'full and precise' answers without warning. Further, the White Paper does not state what would happen if an individual refused to go to Brussels to be questioned pursuant to the proposed power in paragraph 114, or whether any penalty would be imposed upon him or her, or upon the undertaking. Moreover, there are again serious questions about the possible incompatibility of these proposals with the ECHR.[56]

E. LEGAL ADVICE

Article 14 says nothing about an undertaking's right to have legal advisers present during the investigation. The Court said in paragraph 16 of *Hoechst* that an undertaking has a right to legal representation in the investigation stage. When conducting the unannounced investigation in *National Panasonic*, however, the Commission was prepared to wait for some time for the undertakings' legal advisers to arrive, but after a while proceeded in their absence. The Court held that Panasonic's fundamental rights had not been infringed in the

---

[55] Summary of observations on the White Paper on reform of Reg. 17, published by the Commission, 29 Feb. 2000, para. 7.4.

[56] See *supra* 859. The Draft Reg. does not contain a provision about summonsing persons to Brussels: see Proposal for a new Reg. implementing Art. 81 and 82 COM (2000) 582.

investigation, although it did not expressly avert to the legal adviser point. The Commission's guide says that the investigation must not be 'unduly delayed', but that it has a policy 'of allowing firms a reasonable time to secure the services of an in-house legal adviser or lawyer of its choice'. During any wait the undertaking's management has to ensure that business records remain as they were on the officials' arrival and the officials have to be allowed to enter and remain in the offices of their choice.[57] In other words, there must be no opportunity for the operation of the paper-shredder.

As noted above, the comments on the White Paper from industry and lawyers have stressed the importance of the availability of legal advice to persons required to answer questions according to the proposals discussed above.[58]

F. LEGAL PRIVILEGE

Regulation 17 is also silent on the issue whether documents can be withheld from the Commission on grounds of legal privilege. Legal privilege is an established principle in English law. It means that confidential communications passing between lawyer and client with a view to giving or securing legal advice are privileged so far as the client is concerned, and protected from disclosure.[59] The leading case on this in EC law is *AM&S*, in which a UK undertaking argued that it was entitled to keep from the Commission correspondence with its legal advisers that would have been privileged under English law. The case raised two main issues: first, whether legal privilege does apply in EC competition cases, and if so, whether it is a *Community* principle or a matter of recognizing the rule in the Member State concerned; secondly, if legal privilege is recognized, how procedurally is it to be dealt with? It is not attractive to the investigated undertakings for the Commission inspectors to look at documents and then decide they are to be disregarded, whatever 'Chinese walls' the Commission erects internally between the inspectors and those deciding on the existence or otherwise of an infringement.

Case 155/79, *AM&S Ltd* v. *Commission* [1982] ECR 1575, [1982] 2 CMLR 264

On 20 February 1979 Commission officials arrived in the centre of Bristol at the offices of AM&S for an unannounced Article 14(2) investigation. The investigation proceeded for two days and at the end the Commission inspectors left with copies of about 35 documents, leaving behind a written request for certain other documents to be supplied. The Managing Director in response to this sent a further seven files of documents on 26 March but with a letter saying that certain of the requested documents, set out in an appendix were not being produced because the undertaking's lawyers felt that they were covered by legal privilege. Without any further communication the Commission adopted a decision on 6 July under Article 14(3) demanding that the undertaking submit to an inspection and in

---

[57] *EC Commission, Dealing with the Commission* (Commission, 1997), para. 5.5.

[58] Summary of observations on the White Paper on reform of Reg. 17, published by the Commission, 29 Feb. 2000, para. 7.4.

[59] For a statutory formulation see e.g. the Police and Criminal Evidence Act 1984, s. 10(1) and see the discussion of the concept in English law generally in C. Tapper (ed.), *Cross & Tapper on Evidence* (9th edn., Butterworths, 1999) 438–61.

particular produce the excluded documents. In the preamble to the decision the Commission stated that although Community competition law did not provide for protection for legal papers nonetheless it was willing not to use certain communications between the undertaking and its lawyers as evidence and that '[w]hen the Commission comes across such papers it does not copy them'. It was for the Commission, subject to review by the Court, to decide whether a given document should be used or not. The Commission inspectors arrived in Bristol and served the decision on 25 July and carried out a further investigation. The undertaking still refused to disclose all the disputed documents but finally, after further correspondence and a meeting with the Commission in Brussels, it disclosed all except one. On 4 October the undertaking commenced an action under Article 230 claiming that the decision of 6 July was void insofar as it required the disclosure of legally privileged documents.

The Court of Justice received evidence from several Member States and from the Consultative Committee of the Bars and Law Societies of the European Community. Advocate General Warner presented in his Opinion a survey of the position on legal privilege in all Member States.

Court of Justice

15. The purpose of Regulation No 17 of the Council which was adopted pursuant to the first subparagraph of Article [83(1)] of the Treaty, is, according to paragraph (2) (a) and (b) of that article, 'to ensure compliance with the prohibitions laid down in Article [81(1)] and in Article [82]' of the Treaty and 'to lay down detailed rules for the application of Article [81(3)]'. The regulation is thus intended to ensure that the aim stated in Article 3 (1)(g) of the Treaty is achieved. To that end it confers on the Commission wide powers of investigation and of obtaining information by providing in the eighth recital in its preamble that the Commission must be empowered, throughout the Common Market, to require such information to be supplied and to undertake such investigations 'as are necessary' to bring to light infringements of Articles [81 and [82] of the Treaty.

16. In Articles 11 and 14 of the regulation, therefore, it is provided that the Commission may obtain 'information' and undertake the 'necessary' investigations, for the purpose of proceedings in respect of infringements of the rules governing competition. Article 14(1) in particular empowers the Commission to require production of business records, that is to say, documents concerning the market activities of the undertaking, in particular as regards compliance with those rules. Written communications between lawyer and client fall, in so far as they have a bearing on such activities, within the category of documents referred to in Articles 11 and 14.

17. Furthermore since the documents which the Commission may demand are, as Article 14(1) confirms, those whose disclosure it considers 'necessary' in order that it may bring to light an infringement of the Treaty rules on competition, it is in principle for the Commission itself, and not the undertaking concerned or a third party, whether an expert or an arbitrator, to decide whether or not a document must be produced to it.

(b) *Applicability of the protection of confidentiality in Community Law*

18. However, the above rules do not exclude the possibility of recognizing, subject to certain conditions, that certain business records are of a confidential nature. Community law, which derives from not only the economic but also the legal interpenetration of the Member States, must take into account the principles and concepts common to the laws of those States concerning the observance of confidentiality, in particular, as regards certain communications between lawyer and client. That confidentiality serves the requirements, the importance of which is recognized in all of the Member States, that any person must be able, without constraint, to consult a lawyer whose profession entails the giving of independent legal advice to all those in need of it.

19. As far as the protection of written communications between lawyer and client is concerned, it

is apparent from the legal systems of the Member States that, although the principle of such protection is generally recognised, its scope and the criteria for applying it vary, as has, indeed, been conceded both by the application and by the parties who have intervened in support of its conclusions.

20. Whilst in some of the Member States the protection against disclosure afforded to written communications between lawyer and client is based principally on a recognition of the very nature of the legal profession, inasmuch as it contributes towards the maintenance of the rule of law, in other Member States the same protection is justified by the more specific requirement (which, moreover, is also recognized in the first-mentioned States) that the rights of the defence must be respected.

21. Apart from these differences, however, there are to be found in the national laws of the Member States common criteria inasmuch as those law protect, in similar circumstances, the confidentiality of written communications between lawyer and client provided that, on the one hand, such communications are made for the purposes and in the interests of the client's rights of defence and, on the other hand, they emanate from independent lawyers, that is to say, lawyers who are not bound to the client by a relationship of employment.

22. Viewed in that context Regulation No 17 must be interpreted as protecting, in its turn, the confidentiality of written communications between lawyer and client subject to those two conditions, and thus incorporating such elements of that protection as are common to the laws of the Member States.

23. As far as the first of those two conditions is concerned, in Regulation No 17 itself, in particular in the eleventh recital in its preamble and in the provisions contained in Article 19, care is taken to ensure that the rights of the defence may be exercised to the full, and the protection of the confidentiality of written communications between lawyer and client is an essential corollary to those rights. In those circumstances, such protection must, if it is to be effective, be recognized as covering all written communications exchanged after the initiation of the administrative procedure under Regulation No 17 which may lead to a decision on the application of Articles [81] and [82] of the Treaty or to a decision imposing a pecuniary sanction on the undertaking. It must also be possible to extend it to earlier written communications which have a relationship to the subject-matter of that procedure.

24. As regards the second condition, it should be stated that the requirement as to the position and status as an independent lawyer, which must be fulfilled by the legal adviser from whom the written communications which may be protected emanate, is based on a conception of the lawyer's role as collaborating in the administration of justice by the courts and as being required to provide, in full independence, and in the overriding interests of that cause, such legal assistance as the client needs. The counterpart of that protection lies in the rules of professional ethics and discipline which are laid down and enforced in the general interest by institutions endowed with the requisite powers for that purpose. Such a conception reflects the legal traditions common to the Member States and is also to be found in legal order of the Community, as is demonstrated by Article 17 of the Protocols on the Statutes of the Court of Justice of the EEC and the EAEC, and also by Article 20 of the Protocol on the Statute of the Court of Justice of the ECSC.

25. Having regard to the principles of the Treaty concerning freedom of establishment and the freedom to provide services the protection thus afforded by Community law, in particular in the context of Regulation No 17, to written communications between lawyer and client must apply without distinction to any lawyer entitled to practice his profession in one of the Member States, regardless of the Member State in which the client lives.

26. Such protection may be not be extended beyond those limits which are determined by the scope of the common rules on the exercise of the legal profession as laid down in Council Directive 77/249/EEC of 22 March 1977 (OJ L 78, p.17), which is based in its turn on the mutual recognition by all the Member States of the national legal concepts of each of them on this subject.

27. In view of all these factors it must therefore be concluded at although Regulation No 17, and in particular Article 14 thereof, interpreted in the light of its wording, structure and aims, and having regard to the laws of the Member States, empowers the Commission to require, in the course of an investigation within the meaning of that article, production of the business documents the disclosure of which it considers necessary including written communications between lawyer and client, for proceedings in respect of any infringements of Articles [81] and [82] of the Treaty, that power is, however, subject to a restriction imposed by the need to protect confidentiality, on the conditions defined above, and provided that the communications in question are exchanged between an independent lawyer, that is to say one who is not bound to his client by a relationship of employment, and his client.

28. Finally, it should be remarked that the principle of confidentiality does not prevent a lawyer's client from disclosing the written communications between them if he considers that it is in his interests to do so.

(c) *The procedures relating to the application of the principle of confidentiality*

29. If an undertaking which is the subject of an investigation under Article 14 of Regulation No 17 refuses, on the ground that it is entitled to protection of the confidentiality of information, to produce, among the business records demanded by the Commission, written communications between itself and its lawyer, it must nevertheless provide the Commission's authorised agents with relevant material of such a nature as to demonstrate that the communications fulfil the conditions for being granted legal protection as defined above, although it is not bound to reveal the contents of the communications in question.

30. Where the Commission is not satisfied that such evidence has been supplied, the appraisal of those conditions is not a matter which may be left to an arbitrator or to a national authority. Since this is a matter involving an appraisal and a decision which affect the conditions under which the Commission may act in a field as vital to the functioning of the Commission may act in a field as vital to the functioning of the common market as that of compliance with the rules on competition, the solution of disputes as to the application of the protection of the confidentiality of written communications between lawyer and client may be sought only at Community level.

31. In that case it is for the Commission to order, pursuant to Article 14 (3) of Regulation No 17, production of the communications in question and, if necessary, to impose on the undertaking fines or periodic penalty payments under that regulation as a penalty for the undertaking's refusal either to supply such additional evidence as the Commission considers necessary or to produce the communications in question whose confidentiality, in the Commission's view, is not protected in law.

32. The fact that by virtue of Article [242] of the EEC Treaty any action brought by the undertaking concerned against such decisions does not have suspensory effect provides an answer to the Commission's concern as to the effect of the time taken by the procedure before the Court on the efficacy of the supervision which the Commission is called upon to exercise in regard to compliance with the Treaty rules on competition, whilst on the other hand the interests of the undertaking concerned are safeguarded by the possibility which exists under Articles [242] and [243] of the Treaty, as well as under Article 83 of the Rules and Procedure of the Court, of obtaining an order suspending the application of the decision which has been taken, or any other interim measure.

The Court thus held that EC law does recognize legal privilege. This judgment, holding that the Community legal order should recognize a principle contained in some form in nearly every Member State, is a famous example of the development of the jurisprudence on the general principles of law.[60] Legal privilege in EC law is, however, a *Community* concept and the Court held that in Community law it is subject to conditions: the communication must be with[61] an independent lawyer, not an in-house lawyer bound to the undertaking by an employment relationship; the lawyer must be entitled to practise in one of the Member States; and the documents must be made for the purposes and in the interests of the clients' rights of defence. That last condition (paragraphs 21 and 23) sounds restrictive, but the Court interpreted it broadly in *AM&S* itself, and in practice it has not caused difficulty, as the Commission accepts that earlier communications with a relationship to the subject-matter of the proceedings are also covered.

The limitation of privilege to external lawyers (paragraph 24) is grounded in the role of the lawyer as a collaborator in the administration of justice and the fact that in some Member States different rules of professional discipline apply once a lawyer is operating in an employment relationship. The limitation was softened by the CFI holding in *Hilti*[62] that a report made and circulated within the undertaking of the legal advice received from an external legal adviser is privileged. On the other hand, in *John Deere*[63] the Commission examined advice from in-house lawyers and concluded therefrom that the undertaking was aware that it was infringing Article 81. It took this into account when imposing the fine. Representations were made by in-house lawyers in submissions on the White Paper strongly arguing that privilege should be extended to them. In the system of non-notification proposed by the White Paper undertakings will be more heavily reliant on legal advice, and the lawyers said that such an extension would promote effective compliance with the competition rules. They argued that all lawyers must act ethically as defined in the rules of professional ethics and discipline.[64]

In *AM&S* the Court reserved to itself the determination of whether any particular document is protected. The procedure is for the undertaking claiming that documents are privileged to provide the inspectors with proof of that fact without revealing their contents.[65] If the inspectors are not convinced the Commission may take a decision under Regulation 17, Article 14(3), requiring the production of the document or further evidence of its status. Such a decision may be challenged by the undertaking under Article 230 and so the Court will ultimately decide the matter.

---

[60] See generally, T. Tridimas, *The General Principles of EC Law* (Oxford University Press, 1999).

[61] The judgment is worded with reference to communications *from* the lawyer, but the right does encompass communications in both directions.

[62] Case T–30/89A, *Hilti AG* v. *Commission* [1990] 4 CMLR 602.

[63] [1985] OJ L35/58, [1985 2 CMLR 554.

[64] Summary of observations on the White Paper on reform of Reg. 17, published by the Commission, 29 Feb. 2000, para. 7.7.

[65] The fact that they emanated from an independent lawyer can be established by showing the inspectors the top of the headed notepaper.

5. THE SECOND STAGE OF THE PROCEDURE

A. GENERAL: THE RIGHT TO A HEARING

If the Commission finds evidence of an infringement it opens a formal procedure. Before taking Regulation 17 decisions granting, refusing, or revoking exemptions, granting negative clearance, finding an infringement of the Treaty, or imposing fines or periodic payments the Commission must, by Article 19(1), grant the undertakings concerned the opportunity of being heard on matters to which the Commission has taken objection.[66] The ECJ has held that the right to a hearing means in the first place that parties must be told the case against them. It said in *Transocean Marine Paint*[67] that this is an application of the general rule that a person whose interests are perceptibly affected by a decision made by a public authority must be given the opportunity to make his views known, and to make his views known he must know the case against him. The Commission satisfies this obligation in competition cases by sending the undertakings a document called the Statement of Objections. The undertakings may then make submissions in reply and are offered the opportunity of an oral hearing. These procedures are now contained in Commission Regulation 2842/98 (the Hearing Regulation), replacing Regulation 99/63.[68] If at the end of the proceedings the Commission finds that the competition rules have been infringed it may adopt a decision under Regulation 17, Article 3, and may impose a penalty under Article 15.

Considerable problems arise over the content of the rights of defence during these procedures, particularly where the rights of undertakings to know the case against them conflict with the Commission's duty to preserve the confidentiality of business secrets. Above all there is the pervasive problem of the Commission's multi-faceted role. Undertakings repeatedly appeal against Commission decisions on the ground that the competition procedures are contrary to Article 6 (1) of the ECHR which provides that 'in the determination of his civil rights and obligations or of any criminal charge against him, everyone is entitled to a fair and public hearing within a reasonable time by an independent and impartial tribunal'. The Court has held that the Commission is not a tribunal within Article 6, as its decisions are those of an administrative authority.[69] However, it has also been held that the

---

[66] It also hears other natural or legal persons: see Art. 19(2) of reg. 17. Note that there is no duty to give parties a hearing where the Commission is simply replacing a decision ruled invalid for procedural defects at the final, authentication stage with another which relies on the same evidence as that which was annulled: see Cases T–3050307, 313–316, 318, 328–329, & 335/94, *Re the PVC Cartel II: Limburgse Vinyl Maatschappij NV and others* v. *Commission* [1999] 5 CMLR 303.

[67] Case 17/74, *Transocean Marine Paint Association* v. *Commission (No 2)* [1974] ECR 1063, [1974] 2 CMLR 459 where the decision concerned was an Art. 81(3) exemption which was subject to conditions to which the addressee objected. The right to be heard, in all proceedings liable to culminate in a measure adversely affecting a particular person, is a fundamental principle of Community law: see Cases C–68/94 & 30/95, *France & SCPA* v. *Commission* [1998] ECR I–1375, [1998] 4 CMLR 829, para. 174.

[68] [1963–64] OJ Spec. Ed. 47. The new Hearing Reg., Commission Reg. 2842/98 [1998] OJ L354/18, takes into account the case law of the Court and other developments since 1963.

[69] Joined Cases 209–215 and 218/78, *Van Landewyck* v. *Commission* [1980] ECR 3125, [1981] 3 CMLR 134 para. 81; *Musique Diffusion Française* v. *Commission* [1983] ECR 1823, [1983] 2 CMLR 221 at para. 7; Case T–11/89, *Shell* v. *Commission* [1992] ECR II–757, para. 39.

requirements of Article 6(1) are satisfied by the right of the parties to challenge Commission decisions in the Court. The CFI has held itself to be an independent and impartial court, established in order particularly to improve the judicial protection of individuals by making a close inspection of complex facts.[70]

In the following sections we consider the procedure from the sending of the Statement of Objections to review by the Court. It should be noted, however, that in many cases matters are settled *informally*[71] without the need for a formal procedure and decision.

B. THE STATEMENT OF OBJECTIONS

By Article 3(1) of Regulation 2842/98[72] (the Hearing Regulation) 'the Commission shall inform the parties in writing of the objections raised against them'. By Article 2(2) Commission decisions can deal only with objections in respect of which the parties have had the opportunity to make their views known. The Statement of Objections sets out the facts as understood by the Commission, a legal analysis explaining why it considers Article 81 or 82 to be infringed (or in the case of a notified agreement, why an Article 81(3) exemption is being refused), and any proposed remedy the Commission is contemplating adopting. It cannot fine parties unless it has expressed an intention to do so in the Statement of Objections.[73] It must state the duration of the infringement.[74] The parties are invited to reply within a set time limit (Regulation 2842/98, Article 3(4)).[75] The Commission can send the parties fresh documents on which it intends to rely, after the initial Statement of Objections, so long as it gives the necessary time for the parties to comment on them.[76]

In order for the parties to make their views known, the Commission must reveal the documents on which it intends to rely. The current arrangements for doing this contained in the Commission's 1997 Notice on access to the file.[77] This says that the Statement of Objections will be accompanied only by evidence and documents on which the objections are based[78] but that parties will be invited to examine *all* the relevant files at the Commis-

---

[70] Case T–348/94, *Enso Española* v. *Commission* [1998] ECR II–1875, paras. 57–63; Joined Cases T–25/95 etc., *Cimenteries CBR SA* v. *Commission*, judgment of 15 Mar. 2000, [2000] 5 CMLR 204, paras. 718–719. For the Court's exercise of judicial review, see *infra* 925–937.

[71] See *infra* 921–922.

[72] [1998] OJ L354/18.

[73] In Joined Cases T–25/95 etc *Cimenteries CBR SA* v. *Commission*, judgment of 15 Mar. 2000, [2000] 5 CMLR 204 the CFI annulled the fines on associations of undertakings where the Commission had not announced in the Statement of Objections its intention to fine the associations as distinct from their individual members. On the other hand, the ECJ annulled the fines on the individual members of a liner conference in Cases C–395 and 396/P, *Compagnie Maritime Belge and others* v. *Commission* [2000] 4 CMLR 1076, because the Commission had announced an intention to fine only the conference, not the individual shipping lines.

[74] Cases 100–103/80, *Musique Diffusion Française* v. *Commission* (*Pioneer*) [1983] ECR 1823, [1983] 2 CMLR 221.

[75] The minimum time set down in Reg. 2842/98 is two weeks, but the period is usually two months and may be three: see Commissions *XXIIIrd Report on Competition Policy* (Commission, 1993), pt 207.

[76] Case 107/82, *AEG-Telefunken* v. *Commission* [1983] ECR 3151, [1984] 3 CMLR 325; Cases T–3050307, 313–316, 318, 328–329, & 335/94, *Re the PVC Cartel II: Limburgse Vinyl Mij NV and others* v. *Commission* [1999] 5 CMLR 303, para. 497.

[77] [1997] OJ C23/3; see *infra* 897–891.

[78] Section II.C.2.: this is a change to previous practice.

sion's premises (although if the file is not too bulky the undertaking can be sent 'all the accessible documents'[79] as an alternative to visiting Brussels). If the undertaking accompanies its reply to the Statement of Objections by other documents the Commission can subsequently rely on them even though they were not referred to in the Statement of Objections.[80] The Statement of Objections is not a reviewable act against which an action for annulment can be brought, as it is only a preparatory act and can be challenged in an action brought against the act concluding the proceedings.[81]

C. THE HEARING OFFICER

In 1982 the Commission decided to meet some of the criticisms of its position as investigator, prosecutor, and judge, and of the lack of objectivity in its decision-making process by establishing the position of Hearing Officer.[82] Originally, his role was to preside over the oral hearing, but in 1994 it was extended to cover the whole of the Commission's administrative procedure.[83] Since 1994 the Hearing Officer also has jurisdiction in relation to hearings provided for in the Merger Regulation.[84]

The rationale for creating the post in 1982 was to inject an element of disinterested objectivity into the Commission's decision-making process. Nevertheless, the Hearing Officer is part of the Competition DG, although he is not a member of any of the operational Directorates and has direct access to the Commissioner responsible for competition.[85]

D. ACCESS TO THE FILE

(i) GENERAL

There is a problem about how far the parties are entitled to examine all the evidence in the Commission's 'file' on which the Statement of Objections is based so that they may know

---

[79] For the meaning of this, see *infra* 888.

[80] Case T–11/89, *Shell* v. *Commission* [1992] ECR II–757.

[81] Case 60/81, *IBM* v. *Commission* [1981] ECR 2639, [1981] 3 CMLR 635.

[82] See EC Commission *XIth Report on Competition policy* (Commission, 1981), paras. 26 and 27 and the *XIIth Report* (Commission, 1982), pts 36 and 37. The original terms of reference of the Hearing Officer, [1982] OJ C215/2, were reformulated in 1990 because of the need to take on board hearings in transport cases: see EC Commission *XXth Report on Competition Policy* (Commission, 1990), 312–314, and revised in 1994: Commission Decision 94/810 on the terms of reference of hearing officers in competition procedures before the Commission, [1994] OJ L330/67. See generally M. van der Woude, 'Hearing Officers and EC Antitrust Procedures; The Art of Making Subjective Procedures More Objective' (1996) 33 *CMLRev*, 531.

[83] When the post was created in 1982 the rules on hearings were contained in Reg. 99/63 [1963–64] OJ Spec. Ed. 47 but this was replaced by Reg. 2842/98, which takes account of the 1994 terms of reference: see recital 2 of Reg. 2842/98 [1998] OJ L354/18.

[84] Reg. 4064/89 [1989] OJ L395/1: see the 1994 Terms of Reference, Art. 1(1). The Hearing Officer equally has jurisdiction in respect of hearings in the transport sector, which since Reg. 2842/98 are all subject to the same set of rules.

[85] 1994 Terms of Reference, Art. 1(3).

the case against them. It appears from the judgment in *Hercules*[86] that 'access to the file' is an integral part of the right to be heard and not a right in itself:

75. . . . access to the file in competition cases is intended in particular to enable the addressees of Statements of Objections to acquaint themselves with the evidence in the Commission's file so that on the basis of that evidence they can express their views effectively on the conclusions reached by the Commission in its Statement of Objections . . .

76. Thus the general principles of Community law governing the right of access to the Commission's file are designed to ensure effective exercise of the rights of the defence, including the right to be heard provided for in Article 19(1) of Regulation 17 and Articles 3 and 7 to 9 of Commission Regulation 99/63 of 25 July 1963[87] on the hearings provided for in Article 19(1) and (2) of Regulation 17.

(ii) THE RIGHT OF PARTIES TO KNOW THE CASE AGAINST THEM

The extent of the right of access to the file has changed over the years. Initially the Court expressed the right of the parties quite conservatively[88] but more recently has insisted on the parties being properly apprised of the details of the case against them.[89] In the *XXIIth Report* the Commission said it intended to 'go beyond the requirements laid down by the Court of Justice and improve the exercise of the rights of defence in the course of administrative procedures' and lay down a procedure for organizing the file and allowing undertakings to inspect it at the Commission's offices.[90] The CFI held in *Hercules*[91] that, although the Commission had imposed on itself rules exceeding the requirements laid down by the ECJ, it now had to follow them. Accordingly:

54. It follows that the Commission has an obligation to make available to the undertakings involved in Article [81(1)] proceedings all documents, whether in their favour or otherwise, which it has obtained in the course of the investigation, save where the business secrets of other undertakings, the internal documents of the Commission or other confidential information are involved.[92]

The Commission's procedure was subsequently revised, and the present version is in the 1997 Notice on access to the file.[93] The revision was made largely, as the Notice says, to

---

[86] Case C–51/92P *Hercules Chemicals NV* v. *Commission* (*Polypropylene*) [1999] 5 CMLR 976 at paras. 75–76; see also Case C–185/95P *Baustahlgewebe GmbH* v. *Commission* [1999] 4 CMLR 1203 at para. 89 and Cases T–10–12, 14–15/92, *Cimenteries CBR SA* v. *Commission* [1992] ECR II–2667, [1992] 4 CMLR 243 at para. 38; note that the principles governing access to the Commission's file do not, as such, apply to Court proceedings, which are governed by the EC Statute of the ECJ and the Rules of Procedure of the CFI: see C–185/95P, *Baustahlgewebe* at para. 90).

[87] Now Art. 3–5 and 10–12 of Reg. 2842/98 [1998] OJ L354/18.

[88] See Cases 56 & 58, *Etablissements Consten SA & Grundig-Verkaufs-GmbH* v. *Commission* [1966] ECR 299, [1966] CMLR 418; Case s 43 and 63/82, *VBVB and VBBB* v. *Commission* [1984] ECR 19, [1985] 1 CMLR 27.

[89] See e.g. Case C–185/95P, *Baustahlgewebe GmbH* v. *Commission* [1999] 4 CMLR 1203, paras. 89–90, Case C–51/92P, *Hercules Chemicals NV* v. *Commission* (*Polypropylene*) [1999] 5 CMLR 976, paras. 75–79.

[90] Commission' *XXIIth Report on Competition Policy* (Commission, 1982) pts 34 and 35.

[91] Case T–7/89, *Hercules* v. *Commission* [1991] ECR II–1711.

[92] *Ibid.*, para. 54.

[93] The Notice [1997] OJ C23/3 pre–dates the most recent version of the Hearing Reg., 2842/98 [1998] OJ L354/18, but both are emanations from the Commission and the Notice must be considered to be compatible with the Reg.. The Notice explains how the file is organized and the documents numbered: Section II.A.1.4.

ensure compatibility of the procedures with the requirements laid down by the Court, particularly by the CFI in *Solvay* (the *Soda Ash* cases[94]).

In *Solvay* the CFI annulled the Commission decisions because of the Commission's failure properly to disclose to the parties documents which might have been useful in their defence. The Court said that it is important that the undertakings have disclosed to them documents which tend to exonerate them (exculpatory documents) as well as those which tend to incriminate them (inculpatory). It is not for the Commission alone to decide what documents are useful to the defence.[95] In the *Solvay* judgment the CFI introduced the 'general principle of equality of arms' between the Commission and the undertakings being investigated. This means that the undertakings' knowledge of the file used in the proceedings is the same as that of the Commission.

Cases T–30/91, *Solvay SA* v. *Commission* [1995] ECR II–1775, [1996] 5 CMLR 57

Court of First Instance

81. In that context the Commission observes that although its officials themselves examined and re-examined all the documents in its possession, they found no evidence which might exculpate the applicant, so that there was no point in disclosing them. In that regard, it should be stated that in the defended proceedings for which Regulation 17 provides it cannot be for the Commission alone to decide which documents are of use for the defence. Where, as in the present case, difficult and complex economic appraisals are to be made, the Commission must give the advisers of the undertaking concerned the opportunity to examine documents which may be relevant so that their probative value for the defence can be assessed.

82. That is particularly true where parallel conduct is concerned, which is characterised by a set of actions that are prima facie neutral, where documents may just as easily be interpreted in a way favourable to the undertakings concerned as in an unfavourable way. The Court considers that in such circumstances any error made by the Commission's officials in categorizing as 'neutral' a given document which, as an item of irrelevant evidence, will not then be disclosed to the undertakings, must not be allowed to impair their defence. The opposite view, for which the Commission contends, would mean that such an error could not be discovered in time, before adoption of the Commission's decision, except in the exceptional case where the undertakings concerned co-operated spontaneously, which would present unacceptable risks for the sound administration of justice . . .

83. Having regard to the general principle of equality of arms, which presupposes that in a competition case the knowledge which the undertaking concerned has of the file used in the proceeding is the same as that of the Commission, the Commission's view cannot be upheld. The Court considers that it is not acceptable for the Commission alone to have had available to it, when taking a decision on the infringement, the documents marked "V", and for it therefore to be able to decide on its own whether or not to use them against the applicant, when the applicant had no access to them and was therefore unable likewise to decide whether or not it would use them in its defence. In such a situation, the rights of defence which the applicant enjoys during the administrative procedure would be excessively restricted in relation to the powers of the Commission, which would then act as both the

---

94 Cases T–30/91, *Solvay SA* v. *Commission* [1995] ECR II–1775, [1996] 5 CMLR 57 and Case T–36/91, *ICI* v. *Commission* [1995] ECR II–1847, applied in Cases T–305–307, 313–316, 318, 328–329, & 335/94, *Re the PVC Cartel II: Limburgse Vinyl Mij NV and others* v. *Commission* [1999] 5 CMLR 303; see *infra* 883–884.

95 *Ibid.*, para. 81.

authority notifying the objections and the deciding authority, while having more detailed knowledge of the case-file than the defence.

The actual circumstances in *Solvay* were commented on by, *inter alia*, the former Director-General:

C.D. Ehlermann and B.J. Drijber, 'Legal Protection of Enterprises: Administrative Procedure, in Particular Access to the File and Confidentiality' [1996] 7 ECLR 375, 381

A first point concerns the attitude of the parties concerned in the course of the investigation and during the administrative procedure. ICI and Solvay had both requested confidential treatment of their documents *vis-à-vis* other producers. However, once it had received the statement of objections, ICI without lifting that claim of confidentiality asked for unrestricted access to the documents coming from other producers, including Solvay. It in fact asked a double standard to be applied. With the benefit of hindsight it may be easy to say that the Commission should have ignored ICI's and Solvay's general requests for confidential treatment, except for (an undefined category of) 'certain sensitive information' . . . But one easily understands the Commission's hesitations to concede to requests for disclosure from companies which themselves claimed that all their own material was (and is) highly confidential.

The procedural position of Solvay is even more striking. That company never made a request to see the Commission's file; it apparently felt it was sufficiently informed by the vast annexes to the statement of objections. Apart from some quibbles about the status of a limited number of documents produced at the oral hearing held in June 1990 (which Solvay had not thought worth attending), there had not been any procedural problems. In what may be seen as an attempt to ensure that the outcome of the two cases T–30/91 and T–36/91 would be the same, the CFI excused Solvay for not having requested access to the file at the appropriate moment by putting the blame on the Commission: such a request would have been futile anyhow since Solvay was aware that the Commission had already refused an identical request from ICI . . . In general, such reasoning is difficult to accept. It would potentially reward companies which intentionally fail to ask for access at the appropriate stage.

The CFI was generous to the applicants on yet another point. Its conclusion that the rights of the defence had been violated was to a large extent based on the link it construed between the Article [81] case and the two Article [82] cases. It is true that the other party's strength could be a plausible explanation for not selling outside one's 'own' territory. However obvious the argument may seem now, neither of the parties used it in their defence to the statement of objections or indeed in their application to the CFI. Significantly, at the oral hearing before the Commission, an expert witness explained that it was not economically feasible to ship soda ash across the Channel to France but that transport costs were no obstacle to making shipments to customers in Norway.

Another practical aspect relates to the meaning of the principle of 'equality of arms', as interpreted by the CFI . . . One may wonder whether a company is really put in a disadvantageous position if it has not been shown all the documents the Commission has it its possession. First, the Commission can hardly avoid gathering, during inspections, lots of paper which on examination prove to be devoid of any relevance for its case. The reason is very simple: due to time and other constraints, the number and the nature of the documents seized during an inspection are largely fortuitous. Much irrelevant material (although falling within the inspection mandate) will be seized, whereas potentially relevant material may be overlooked. Second, it is fair to assume that the companies themselves best know the industry, the market and their own behaviour in that market. For these obvious reasons, the companies are normally much better informed than the Commission. In a context so different from the traditional criminal law procedures, the argument derived from the principle of equality of arms should therefore be taken with a pinch of salt.

It is clear, however, that there is no absolute right of access to the file, in that breach of the principle laid down in *Solvay* will not always lead to annulment of the decision. It will depend on whether, in the Court's view, the undertaking's ability to defend itself was prejudiced, as can be seen from *PVC Cartel II*.

Cases T–305–307, 313–316, 318, 328–329, & 335/94, *Re the PVC Cartel II: Limburgse Vinyl Maatschappij NV and others* v. *Commission* [1999] 5 CMLR 303

Court of First Instance

1011. The purpose of providing access to the file in competition cases is to enable the addressees of statements of objections to examine evidence in the Commission's file so that they are in a position effectively to express their views on the conclusions reached by the Commission in its statement of objections on the basis of that evidence. Access to the file is thus one of the procedural safeguards intended to protect the rights of the defence. Respect for the rights of the defence in all proceedings in which sanctions may be imposed is a fundamental principle of Community law which must be respected in all circumstances, even if the proceedings in question are administrative proceedings. The proper observance of that general principle requires that the undertaking concerned be afforded the opportunity during the administrative procedure to make known its views on the truth and relevance of the facts, charges and circumstances relied on by the Commission (Case T–30/91, *Solvay*, . . ., Case T–36/91, *ICI*, . . . Case T–37/91, *ICI*, . . . and the case law cited therein).

1012. In the adversarial proceedings for which Regulation 17 provides, it cannot be for the Commission alone to decide which documents are of use for the defence (Case T–30/91, *Solvay*, . . . Case T–36/91, *ICI* . . .). Having regard to the general principle of equality of arms, the Commission cannot be permitted to decide on its own whether or not to use documents against the applicants, where the latter had no access to them and were therefore unable to take the relevant decision whether or not to use them in their defence (Case T–30/91, *Solvay* . . ., Case T–36/91, *ICI* . . .).

1013. Such an infringement of the rights of the defence is, moreover, an objective one and does not depend upon whether the Commission's officials acted in good or bad faith (Case T–30/91, *Solvay* . . ., Case T–36/91, *ICI* . . .).

1014. In any event, the defence of one undertaking cannot depend upon the goodwill of another undertaking which is supposed to be its competitor and against which the Commission has made similar allegations. Since the Commission is responsible for the proper investigation of a competition case, it may not delegate that task to the undertakings, whose economic and procedural interests often conflict. Consequently, in determining whether the rights of the defence were infringed, it does not matter that the impugned undertakings have been authorised to exchange documents. Such co-operation between undertakings, which cannot be taken for granted, cannot in any case relieve the Commission of its own duty to ensure that during the investigation of an infringement of competition law the defence rights of the undertakings concerned are respected (Case T–30/91, *Solvay*, . . . Case T–36/91, *ICI* . . .).

1015. However, as the Commission has emphasized, access to the file cannot extend to internal documents of the institution, the business secrets of other undertakings and other confidential information (*BPB Industries And British Gypsum* . . .).

1016. According to a general principle which applies during the course of the administrative procedure and which is expressed in Article 214 of the Treaty and various provisions of Regulation 17, undertakings have a right to protection of their business secrets. However, that right must be weighed against safeguarding the rights of the defence (Case T–30/91, *Solvay* . . ., Case T–36/91 *ICI* . . .).

1017. In those circumstances, the Commission cannot use a general reference to confidentiality to justify a total refusal to divulge documents on its file. Moreover, in this case it does not seriously maintain that all the information contained in those documents was confidential. The Commission would therefore have been able to prepare (or have prepared) a non-confidential version of the documents in question or, should that prove difficult, to have drawn up a sufficiently precise list of the documents concerned so as to allow the undertaking to determine, in the light of full knowledge of the facts, whether the documents described could be relevant to its defence (Case T–30/91, *Solvay* . . .; Case T–36/91, *ICI* . . .).

1018. In this case, no non-confidential version of the documents in question has been prepared. Moreover, even if the Commission did in fact supply the applicants with a list of the documents in its file, that list was of no use to the applicants because it merely indicated in a general way the undertaking from which the corresponding pages of the administrative file came.

1019. In the light of all those factors, the Court finds that during the administrative procedure in this case the Commission did not give the applicants proper access to the file.

1020. However, that is not sufficient of itself to warrant annulment of the Decision.

1021. An alleged infringement of the rights of the defence must be examined in relation to the specific circumstances of each particular case, because it is effectively the objections raised by the Commission which determined the infringement which the undertaking concerned is alleged to have committed. It is therefore necessary to consider whether the applicant's ability to defend itself was affected by the conditions in which it had access to the Commission's administrative file. In that respect, it is sufficient for a finding of infringement of defence rights for it to be established that non-disclosure of the documents in question might have influenced the course of the procedure and the content of the decision to the applicant's detriment (Case T–30/91, *Solvay* . . .; Case T–36/91, *ICI* . . .; see also, in the area of State aids, Case 259/85, *France v. E.C. Commission* . . .).

1022. If that were so, the administrative procedure would be defective and the Decision would have to be annulled. Any infringement of the rights of the defence occurring during the administrative procedure cannot be remedied in the proceedings before the Court of First Instance, whose review is restricted to the pleas raised and which cannot therefore be a substitute for a thorough investigation of the case in the course of the administrative procedure. If during the administrative procedure the applicants had been able to rely on documents which might exculpate them, they might have been able to influence the assessment of the college of Commissioners (Case T–30/91, *Solvay* . . .; Case T–36/91, *ICI* . . .).

On the facts the CFI decided that the non-disclosure did not prejudice the defence. As the Court said in *Hercules*,[96] the undertaking concerned does not have to show that, if it *had* had

---

[96] Case C–51/92P, *Hercules Chemicals NV v. Commission* (*Polypropylene*) [1999] 5 CMLR 976, para. 81.

access to other documents the Commission decision would have been different in content, but only that it would have been able to use those documents for its defence. Nevertheless, in *Hercules* the ECJ decided that the CFI had not erred in finding that in that case the applicant could not have relied on the disputed documents for its defence. In the light of these cases a definitive statement of the position as regards access to the file was set out by the CFI in the *Cement* appeal:[97]

247. Consequently, where an applicant submits, in the context of an application for annulment, that its rights of defence have been infringed because it was not given access during the administrative procedure to a document in the investigation file which, it claims, could have been useful in its defence, the Court must require that document to be disclosed to the Court. It must then examine that document for any relationship with the objections upheld against the applicant in the contested decision. If there is no objective link between the document and the objection upheld in the contested decision, the outcome of the administrative procedure could not have been different for the applicant if it had had access to that document during that procedure. In such circumstances, the plea by that applicant must be rejected. If, on the other hand, there is an objective link between the document in question and one of the objections upheld against the applicant in the contested decision, the Court must assess whether, in the light of the evidence adduced by the Commission in support of the objections referred to in the contested decision, the document would have had any even a small chance of altering the outcome of the administrative procedure if the applicant had been able to rely on it during that procedure. If, in the light of the evidence as a whole, the Court considers that the document would have had such a chance of altering the outcome to the administrative procedure, it will find that the rights of the defence have been infringed . . .

Here the CFI required only a 'small chance' of the undisclosed document altering the outcome. In *Cement*, findings against two undertakings were annulled on grounds of non-disclosure.[98]

(iii) CONFIDENTIALITY

There is a fundamental tension between the rights of the parties to know the case against them and the Commission's obligation to preserve confidentiality. A general duty of confidentiality is laid down in the Treaty itself. Article 287 (ex Article 214) says:

The members of the institutions of the Community, the members of committees, and the officials and other servants of the Community shall be required, even after their duties have ceased, not to disclose information of the kind covered by the obligation of professional secrecy, in particular information about undertakings, their business relations or their cost components.

Regulation 17, Article 20 specifically provides for confidentiality in the context of competition proceedings, where it is a particular issue because of the highly sensitive information which the Commission is likely to obtain during an investigation. Article 20 states:

---

[97] Joined Cases T–25/95 etc., *Cimenteries CBR SA v. Commission*, judgment of 15 Mar. 2000, [2000] 5 CMLR 204, para. 247.

[98] In relation to one undertaking, Cedest, the CFI held that an undisclosed memo shed fresh light on what its representative had actually said at a meeting.

1.   Information acquired as a result of the application of Articles 11, 12,[99] 13,[100] and 14 shall
     be used only for the purposes of the relevant request or investigation.

2.   Without prejudice to the provisions of Articles 19 and 21, the Commission and the competent
     authorities of the Member States, their officials and other servants shall not disclose informa-
     tion acquired by them as a result of the application of this Regulation and of the kind covered
     by the obligation of professional secrecy.

Both Articles 19(3) and 20, which deal with the publication of Commission decisions,
provide that regard shall be had 'to the legitimate interest of undertakings in the protection
of their business secrets'.

It will be seen from this that the Treaty and Regulation 17, Article 20, refer to 'professional
secrecy' and Regulation 17, Articles 19(3) and 20, to 'business secrets'. Regulation 2842/98
speaks of 'business secrets and other confidential information'.[101] What exactly is covered
by these terms is not clear,[102] as the Commission admitted in the 1997 Notice.[103] Business
secrets seems to encompass information not in the public domain which is commercially
important,[104] and confidential information includes matters which would identify
'whistleblowers'.[105]

The basic principle, laid down in *Hoffmann-La Roche*, is that the Commission cannot use
to an undertaking's detriment facts or documents which it cannot disclose, where the
absence of disclosure adversely affects the undertaking's opportunity to be heard:

Case 85/76, *Hoffmann-La Roche* v. *Commission* [1979] ECR 461, [1979] 3 CMLR 211

Court of Justice

14. The said Article 20 [of Regulation 17] by providing undertakings from whom information has
been obtained with a guarantee that their interests which are closely connected with observance of
professional secrecy, are not jeopardized enables the Commission to collect on the widest possible
scale the requisite data for the fulfilment of the task conferred upon it by Articles [81] and [82] of
the Treaty without the undertakings being able to prevent it from doing so, but it does not nevertheless allow it to use, to the detriment of the undertakings involved in a proceeding referred to in
Regulation 17, facts, circumstances or documents which it cannot in its view disclose if such a refusal
of disclosure adversely affects that undertaking's opportunity to make known effectively its views on
the truth or implications of those circumstances on those documents or again on the conclusions
drawn by the Commission from them.

---

[99] Enquiries into sectors of the economy.

[100] Investigations by national competition authorities at the Commission's request.

[101] [1998] OJ L354/18 Art. 3(2) and (5), Art. 12(3) and (4), Art. 13(1).

[102] See P. Freeman and R Which (eds.) *Butterworths Competition Law* (Butterworths, looseleaf), Division
X, para. 1359–70.

[103] Section I.A.1.

[104] See the 1997 Notice, Section I.A.1.: '[b]usiness secrets need no longer be protected when they are
known outside the firm (or group or association of firms) to which they relate. Nor can facts remain business
secrets if, owing to the passage of time or for any other reason, they are no longer commercially important'.

[105] *Ibid.*, Section I.A.2. The Commission's notorious failure to conceal the identity of the whistleblower
Stanley Adams from Hoffmann-La Roche rendered the Commission liable to him in damages under Art.
288(2) (ex Art. 215(2)): Case 145/83, *Adams* v. *Commission* [1985] ECR 3539, [1986] 1 CMLR 506.

There are provisions on confidentiality in the Hearing Regulation of 1998.[106] Article 13 puts the onus on the parties to identify confidential material which they do not want disclosed:

(1) Information, including documents, shall not be communicated or made accessible in so far as it contains business secrets of any party, including the parties to which the Commission has addressed objections, applicants and complainants and other third parties, or other confidential information or where internal documents of the authorities are concerned. The Commission shall make appropriate arrangements for allowing access to the file, taking due account of the need to protect business secrets, internal Commission documents and other confidential information.

(2) Any party which makes known its views under the provisions of this Regulation shall clearly identify any material which it considers to be confidential, giving reasons, and provide a separate non-confidential version by the date set by the Commission. If it does not do so by the set date, the Commission may assume that the submission does not contain such material.

The 1997 Notice sets out the practical arrangements for giving access to the Commission's file while preserving confidentiality. It essentially relates to the rights of undertakings which are the subject of investigations into alleged infringements, rather than to third parties such as complainants.[107] It states:[108]

Access to the file is an important procedural stage in all contentious competition cases (prohibitions with or without a fine, prohibitions of mergers, rejections of complaints etc.). The Commission's task in this area is to reconcile two opposing obligations, namely that of safeguarding the rights of the defence and that of protecting confidential information concerning firms.

As far as business secrets are concerned the Commission says:[109]

Where business secrets provide evidence of an infringement or tend to exonerate a firm, the Commission must reconcile the interest in the protection of sensitive information, the public interest in having the infringement of the competition rules terminated, and the rights of the defence. This calls for an assessment of:

(i) the relevance of the information to determining whether or not an infringement has been committed;

(ii) its probative value;

(iii) whether it is indispensable;

(iv) the degree of sensitivity involved (to what extent would disclosure of the information harm the interests of the firm?);

(v) the seriousness of the infringement.

Each document must be assessed individually to determine whether the need to disclose it is greater than the harm which might result from disclosure.

Where confidential information is concerned it concludes that:

---

[106] [1998] OJ L354/18.
[107] Introduction to the1997 Notice on access to the file [1997] OJ C23/3.
[108] *Ibid.*, Introduction.
[109] Section I.A.1.

as a rule the confidential nature of documents is not a bar to their disclosure if the information in question is necessary in order to prove an alleged infringement ('inculpatory documents') or if the papers invalidate or rebut the reasoning of the Commission set out in its statement of objections.

A distinction is made between communicable and non-communicable documents. 'Non-communicable documents' consist of those categories singled out in *Hercules*[110] (business secrets, internal documents of the Commission and other confidential information) and communicable documents are everything else. The file is organized with each document enumerated and labelled 'accessible', 'non-accessible', and 'partially accessible'. The Hearing Officer has jurisdiction to determine whether or not particular documents fall within the protected category. All undertakings providing information to the Commission (voluntarily or not) are asked to detail what they regard as confidential or business secrets and to provide 'a non-confidential version of their confidential documents'.[111] If disclosure is contemplated and the undertaking does not supply a 'reasonably coherent' non-confidential version[112] but continues to object to disclosure, the matter goes to the Hearing Officer for a decision under Article 5(4) of Decision 94/810.[113] His decision can be challenged immediately before the Court of First Instance, and the Commission cannot proceed to disclosure before the action has been heard and the decision confirmed.

Both business secrets and confidential information are placed in the 'non-accessible document' part of the file. Other documents are in the 'accessible' part. The Commission's internal documents are 'inaccessible'.[114] These are *not* disclosed. The Commission's rationale for this protection is that internal documents are not, by their nature, the sort of evidence on which the Commission can rely in its assessment of a case, and that it is important that Commission departments can express themselves freely.[115] These arrangements, which mean that the internal documents are placed in a separate file and do not form part of the 'investigation file' at all, have been criticized on the grounds that they are a backward step and may conceal from the parties documents relevant to their defence, and that it is difficult to invoke the Hearing Officer's jurisdiction without an indication of the contents of the file.[116]

(iv) ARTICLE 82 CASES

The Commission considers that in Article 82 cases there is a special problem about evidence from third parties. In *BPB Industries and British Gympsum Ltd*[117] the Court accepted that

---

[110] Case–7/89, *Hercules* v. *Commission* [1991] ECR II–1711, [1992] 4 CMLR 84, para. 54, *infra*.

[111] Notice, [1997] OJ C23/3 Section II.A.1.2.

[112] *Ibid.*, Section II.A.1.3. In Section II.B.1(c), which deals with arrangements for access to the file in merger cases, parties are asked for 'a *reasonably coherent* non-confidential version' (emphasis added) in the first place.

[113] Commission Decision 94/810, [1994] OJ L330/67 on the terms of reference of hearing officers, the 'Hearing Officer Mandate'.

[114] Notice, [1997] OJ L23/3 Section I.A.3.

[115] *Ibid.*

[116] See M. Levitt, 'Commission Notice on Internal Rules of Procedure for Access to the File' [1997] *ECLR* 187.

[117] Case C–310/93P, *BPB Industries and British Gypsum Ltd* v. *Commission* [1995 ECR I–865, [1997] 4 CMLR 238.

the Commission was entitled to keep such correspondence confidential because of the fear of retaliation from the dominant firm. This point is included in the Notice:[118]

By definition, firms in a dominant position on a market are able to place very considerable economic or commercial pressure on their competitors or on their trading partners, customers or suppliers.

The Court of First Instance and the Court of Justice thus acknowledged the legitimacy of the reluctance displayed by the Commission in revealing certain letters received from customers of the firm being investigated.

Although it is of value to the Commission for giving a better understanding of the market concerned, the information does not in any way constitute inculpatory evidence, and its disclosure to the firm concerned might easily expose the authors to the risk of retaliatory measures.

This attitude is criticized by Levitt,[119] who points out (i) that whether the undertaking *is* in fact dominant may be one of the things which is in dispute, (ii) that the so-called 'economic or commercial pressure' may be no more than an unrealized fear of potential retaliation unrelated to the actual abuse allegation, and (iii) that the *BPB Industries* judgment on which the Commission relies predates and is irreconcilable with the *Soda Ash* judgments, where the CFI did not consider the undertaking's rights of defence, were any the less because an alleged infringement of Article 82 was concerned.

(v) CONFIDENTIALITY AND COMPLAINANTS

It was held in *AKZO*,[120] that business secrets are accorded 'very special protection' and cannot be disclosed to third parties who have lodged complaints.[121] Otherwise, as the Court said, competitors could obtain access to other undertaking's secrets simply by lodging a complaint:

Case 53/85, *AKZO* v. *Commission* [1986] ECR 1965, [1987] 1 CMLR 231

ECS complained to the Commission about the alleged predatory pricing of AKZO. The Commission sent AKZO a statement of objections and a copy of it to ECS. ECS then asked the Commission for copies of the documents in the annexes to the statement of objections so that it could exercise its right to be heard under Regulation 17, Article 19(2). The Commission disclosed a number of documents to it. AKZO claimed that the Commission had breached its duty to preserve AKZO's business secrets.

Court of Justice

26. In the first place, it must be borne in mind that Article [287] of the Treaty requires the officials and other servants of the institutions of the Community not to disclose information in their possession of the kind covered by the obligation of professional secrecy. Article 20 of Regulation No 17/62 which implements that provision in regard to the rules applicable to undertakings, contains in

---

[118] Section II.D.2.
[119] M. Levitt, 'Commission Notice on Internal Rules of Procedure for Access to the File' [1997] *ECLR* 187.
[120] Case 53/85, *AKZO* v. *Commission* [1986] ECR 1965, [1987] 1 CMLR 231.
[121] For complaints generally, see *infra* Chap. 15.

paragraph (2) a special provision worded as follows: 'Without prejudice to the provisions of Articles 19 and 21, the Commission and the competent authorities of the Member States, their officials and other servants shall not disclose information acquired by them as a result of the application of this regulation and of the kind covered by the obligation of professional secrecy.'

27. The provisions of Articles 19 and 21, the application of which is thus reserved, deal with the Commission's obligations in regard to hearings and the publication of decisions. It follows that the obligation of professional secrecy laid down in Article 20(2) is mitigated in regard to third parties on whom Article 19(2) confers the right to be heard, that is to say in regard, in particular, to a third party who has made a complaint. The Commission may communicate to such a party certain information covered by the obligation of professional secrecy in so far as it is necessary to do so for the proper conduct of the investigation.

28. However, that power does not apply to all documents of the kind covered by the obligation of professional secrecy. Article 19(3) which provides for the publication of notices prior to the granting of negative clearance or exemptions, and Article 21 which provides for the publication of certain decisions, both require the Commission to have regard to the legitimate interest of undertakings in the protection of their business secrets. Business secrets are thus afforded very special protection. Although they deal with particular situations, those provisions must be regarded as the expression of a general principle which applies during the course of the administrative procedure. It follows that a third party who has submitted a complaint may not in any circumstances be given access to documents containing business secrets. Any other solution would lead to the unacceptable consequence that an undertaking might be inspired to lodge a complaint with the Commission solely in order to gain access to its competitors' business secrets.

29. It is undoubtedly for the Commission to assess whether or not a particular document contains business secrets. After giving an undertaking an opportunity to state its views, the Commission is required to adopt a decision in that connection which contains an adequate statement of the reasons on which it is based and which must be notified to the undertaking concerned. Having regard to the extremely serious damage which could result from improper communication of documents to a competitor, the Commission must, before implementing its decision, give the undertaking an opportunity to bring an action before the Court with a view to having the assessments made reviewed by it and to preventing disclosure of the documents in question.

30. In this case, the Commission gave the undertaking concerned an opportunity to make its position known and adopted a decision containing an adequate statement of the reasons on which it was based and concerning both the confidential nature of the documents at issue and the possibility of communicating them. At the same time, however, by an act which cannot be severed from that decision, the Commission decided to hand over the documents to the third party who had made the complaint even before it notified its findings to that undertaking. It thus made it impossible for the undertaking to avail itself of the means of redress provided by Article [230] in conjunction with Article [242] of the Treaty with the view to preventing the implementation of a contested decision.

31. That being the case, the decision which the Commission notified to the applicant by letter of 18 December 1984 must be declared void without there being any need to determine whether the documents communicated to the intervener did in fact contain business secrets.

The Court's order to the Commission to recover the documents meant that ECS was unable to rely on them in national proceedings.

It is clear from *AKZO* that complainants cannot have the same access to the file as alleged infringers. This is embodied in Section D.1. of the Notice. A complainant who has been told of the intention to reject his complaint[122] may request access to the documents on which the Commission based the rejection but cannot have access to the confidential information or business secrets of the firm complained about, or of any third parties, which the Commission has acquired in the course of its investigations.

(vi) CONFIDENTIALITY AND NATIONAL PROCEEDINGS

Problems have arisen over how far information gained by the Commission can be used in national proceedings, either in courts or in competition investigations. In *Spanish Banks*[123] the ECJ held that national competition authorities cannot use as evidence the information and documents supplied to them by the Commission pursuant to its obligations under Regulation 17, Article 10.[124] On the other hand, they are not obliged to suffer 'acute amnesia', so they may decide on the basis of what they have learned to open a national investigation of their own, although the facts must be proved again *de novo* according to national procedural rules. In *Postbank*,[125] the Commission sent to firms which were bringing actions in a national court a copy of a Statement of Objections so that the firms could prepare to take part in a Commission hearing. It stipulated that the Statement could not be used in the national court. The CFI, however, held that this restriction could not be imposed as the Commission had a duty of sincere co-operation with national courts stemming from Article 10 of the Treaty.[126] This covered even the transmission of confidential material.

The Commission White Paper on Modernization[127] recognizes that the *Spanish Banks* interpretation of Regulation 17, Article 20, creates problems for the proposed decentralization of competition law enforcement.[128]

E. THE ORAL HEARING

The right to be heard is primarily exercised in writing, but Regulation 2842/98, Article 5 gives the parties a right to an oral hearing if they request it in their written comments on the Statement of Objections.[129] The oral hearing is controlled and supervised by the Hearing Officer.[130] Third parties such as complainants may be heard in addition to the

---

[122] See *infra* Chap. 15.

[123] Case C–67/91, *Dirección General de Defensa de las Competencia* v. *Asociación España de Banca Privada (AEB) and others (Spanish Banks)* [1992] ECR 4785.

[124] See *infra* 924.

[125] Case T–353/94 *Postbank* v. *Commission* [1996] ECR II–921.

[126] And see the judgment of the ECJ in Case C–234/89, *Stergios Delimitis* v. *Henninger Bräu* [1991] ECR 1–935, [1992] 5 CMLR 210 and the Notice on co-operation between national courts and the commission [1993] OJ C39/6.

[127] White Paper on Modernisation of the rules implementing Articles 85 and 86 [now 81 and 82] of the EC Treaty [1999] OJ C132/1, para 96.

[128] See *infra* Chap. 16.

[129] [1998] OJ L354/18. For a full description of the oral hearing, see C.S. Kerse, *EC Antitrust Procedure* (4th edn., Sweet & Maxwell Chap. 4.

[130] 1994 Terms of Reference [1994] OJ L330/67, Art. 7(2).

parties.[131] The oral hearing is not a formal 'trial'. It may last anything from a day to two or three weeks, depending on the complexity of the case. Regulation 2842/98, Article 12(2) provides that the persons being heard may be 'assisted by' their legal advisers. It does not say 'represented by' because it is considered necessary that someone from the undertaking itself (although that can be an in-house lawyer) is present to provide relevant information about the organization.[132]

Regulation 2842/98, Article 12 provides that the statements made at the hearing shall be tape-recorded and the record made available to each person who has been heard.[133] Business secrets and other confidential information are deleted.

The Hearing Officer is not a judge. It is not his function to come to a decision, but to report to the Director-General on the hearing and the conclusions to be drawn from it.[134] It is advice for the Commission, which is not bound to follow it.[135] The Hearing Officer's report is not made available to the parties, and they have no right to see it or comment on it.[136]

6. COMMISSION DECISIONS IN INFRINGEMENT PROCEEDINGS

A. GENERAL

The Commission may take a final decision ordering the termination of infringements of the competition rules and may take procedural decisions during the course of its investigation, as seen in the sections above. It may also take interim measures in order to prevent irreparable damage occurring before it can come to a final decision. It is usual to speak of 'the Commission' when discussing the conduct of EC competition policy, meaning the policy and actions of the Competition DG. However, it is important to remember that unless the taking of particular acts of management or administration has been delegated to a single Commissioner decisions are collegiate acts of the whole Commission.[137] When the Commission adopts an infringement decision, therefore, the Commissioner responsible for

---

[131] Reg. 2842/98, Art. 8.

[132] See Case 49/69, *BASF* v. *Commission* (*Dyestuffs*) [1972] ECR 619, [1972] CMLR 557.

[133] [1998] OJ L354/18. Reg. 99/63 [1963–64] OJ Spec. Ed. 47, merely provided for the taking of minutes.

[134] *Ibid.,* Art. 8.

[135] Cases T–305–307, 313–316, 318, 328–329, & 335/94, *Re the PVC Cartel II: Limburgse Vinyl Mij NV and others* v. *Commission* [1999] 5 CMLR 303, para. 375.

[136] Case 322/81, *Nederlandsche Banden-Industrie Michelin* v. *Commission* [1983] ECR 3461, [1985] 1 CMLR 282; Cases T–305–307, 313–316, 318, 328–329, & 335/94, *Re the PVC Cartel II: Limburgse Vinyl Mij NV and others* v. *Commission* [1999] 5 CMLR 303, paras. 375–377.

[137] This aspect of decisions was stressed by the CFI in the *Cement* appeal. Two of the applicants claimed a breach of the principle of impartiality, in that the same Commission official had carried out the investigation, acted as rapporteur, drawn up the Statement of Objections, and prepared the draft decision. The CFI held that the principle was not breached because the contested decision was actually taken by the College of Commissioners, not by the official: Joined Cases T–25/95 etc., *Cimenteries CBR SA* v. *Commission,* judgment of 15 Mar. 2000, [2000] 5 CMLR 204 para. 721.

competition lays the draft before the whole College at one of its meetings and the measure is adopted by the College.[138]

This section deals with the content of decisions other than the imposition of fines: fines are dealt with in Section 7 below.

B. FINAL DECISIONS

Regulation 17, Article 3(1) says under the heading 'Termination of Infringements':

Where the Commission, upon application or upon its own initiative, finds that there is infringement of Article [81] or Article [82] of the Treaty, it may by decision require the undertakings or associations of undertakings concerned to bring such infringement to an end.

A decision finding an infringement may therefore order undertakings to bring the infringement to an end where it has not definitely been terminated already. These are called 'cease and desist orders'. The decision may also contain a 'like effects order' whereby the parties are prohibited from entering into similar arrangements, as for example in *Welded Steel Mesh*, a cartel case, where Article 2 of the decision stated:[139]

The undertakings named in Article 1 which are still involved in the welded steel mesh sector in the Community shall forthwith bring the said infringements to an end (if they have not already done so) and shall henceforth refrain in relation to their welded steel mesh operations from any agreement or concerted practice which may have the same object or effect.

On the other hand, in *Langnese-Iglo*[140] the Court held that the Commission was not entitled to forbid the undertaking from entering into exclusive purchasing agreements in the future. It was an Article 81 proceeding, and whether or not an exclusive purchasing agreement is restrictive of competition and can be exempted depends on the circumstances and context. The refusal of exemption could relate only to existing agreements.

The Court established in *Cementhandelaren*[141] that the Commission is justified in taking a decision after an infringement has terminated so that the decision is in effect only a declaration that the past conduct did infringe.

Article 3(1) does not expressly state whether the Commission can take decisions ordering the parties to take *positive* steps in order to bring the infringement to an end. The Court, however, held in *Commercial Solvents* that it can:[142]

[Article 3] must be applied in relation to the infringement which has been established and may include an order to do certain acts or provide certain advantages which have been wrongfully withheld as well as prohibiting the continuation of certain actions, practices or situations which are contrary to the Treaty.

---

[138] The failure of the College to adopt an authenticated version of the decision was one reason for the annulment of the *PVC* decision in Cases C–137/92P, *Commission v. BASF and others* [1994] ECR I–2555: *infra* 931.

[139] [1989] OJ L260/1, [1991] 4 CMLR 13.

[140] Cases T–7 & 9/93, *Lagnese-Iglo & Schöller Lebensmittel v. Commission* [1995] ECR II–1533, [1995] 5 CMLR 602, upheld by the ECJ in Case C–279/95P, *Languese-Iglo v. Commission*, [1998] ECR I–5609, [1998] 5 CMLR 933.

[141] Case 8/72, *Cementhandelaren v. Commission* [1972] ECR 977, [1973] CMLR 7.

[142] Cases 6, 7/73, *Istituto Chemioterapico Italiano Spa and Commercial Solvents Corp v. EC Commission* [1974] ECR 223, [1974] 1 CMLR 309, para. 45.

In *Commercial Solvents* the dominant undertaking was ordered to supply a certain amount of raw material to the complainant, which involved the parties entering into contractual relations. Many subsequent Article 82 cases on refusal to supply and essential facilities have also involved ordering a dominant undertaking to supply or to share facilities.[143] Where infringements of Article 81 are concerned, the CFI has said that the Commission does not have the power to order a party to enter into a contractual relationship where there are other ways of making the party end the infringement.

Case T–24/90 *Automec srl* v. *Commission* (*No 2*) [1992] ECR II–2223, [1992] 5 CMLR 431

Automec was an Italian car dealer which had had a distributorship agreement with BMW. When BMW discontinued the agreement Automec brought an action in the Italian courts and lodged a complaint with the Commission, alleging that BMW's behaviour infringed Article 81 and asking the Commission for an injunction compelling BMW to resume supplies of its cars. The Commission rejected the complaint, *inter alia* on the ground that it had no power to issue such an order under Article 81(1). Automec appealed to the Court of First Instance.[144]

Court of First Instance

51. As the freedom to contract must remain the rule, the Commission cannot in principle be acknowledged to possess, in the framework of its powers of injunction to put an end to infringements of Article [8(1)1], a power to order a party to enter into a contractual relationship where as a general rule the Commission has suitable means at its disposal for compelling an enterprise to end an infringement.

52. In particular there is no justification for any such restriction on the freedom to contract where several means exist for ending an infringement. This is the case with regard to infringements of Article [81(1)] arising from the application of a distribution system. Such infringements can also be discontinued by giving up or altering the distribution system. Under these circumstances the Commission undoubtedly has power to find the existence of the infringement and order the parties concerned to end it, but it is not for the Commission to impose upon the parties its own choice among the different potential courses of action which all conform to the Treaty.

53. In the circumstances of the particular case, therefore, it must be found that the Commission was not empowered to adopt specific injunctions compelling BMW to supply the applicant and to permit it to use BMW trade marks. It follows that the Commission has not broken Community law by refusing the application for the adoption of such injunctions on the ground that it had no power to do so.

54. The Commission's power to adopt a decision capable of producing practical effects equivalent to those of the injunctions sought by the applicant and the option, which was open to the Commission, of redefining Automec's application as an application for the adoption of such a decision are not such as to cast doubt on this conclusion. The Commission did not seek to rely on its lack of power to justify the rejection of the entire complaint, but only to justify the refusal to adopt the measures specifically requested. In so far the subject-matter of the complaint goes beyond this specific application, the question is not raised in the first part of the decision but the second.

---

[143] See *supra* Chap. 7.
[144] For the other aspects of this case, see *infra* Chap. 15.

The other means for ending the infringement in this type of situation are presumably the withdrawal or refusal of exemption and a fine.[145]

The Commission may order an undertaking to amend its contractual terms and may restrict its future pricing policies. The terms of the order in *Tetra Pak II*, where the dominant undertaking was found to have infringed Article 82 by predatory and discriminatory pricing and by imposing unfair terms on its customers, illustrate this.[146]

Tetra Pak II [1992] OJ L72/1, [1992] 4 CMLR 551

Article 3

In particular, Tetra Pak shall take the following measures:

1. Tetra Pak shall amend or where appropriate, delete from its machine purchase/lease contracts and carton supply contracts the clause listed under numbers (i) to (xxviii) so as to eliminate the aspects which have been found by the Commission to be abusive. The new contracts shall be submitted to the Commission;

2. Tetra Pak shall ensure that any differences between the prices charged for its products in the various member-States result solely from the specific market conditions. Any customer within the Community shall be supplied by any Tetra Pak subsidiary it chooses, and at the price it practises;

3. Tetra Pak shall not practise predatory or discriminatory prices and shall not grant to any customer any form of discount on its products or more favourable payment terms not justified by an objective consideration. Thus, discounts on cartons should be granted solely according to the quantity of each order, and orders for different types of carton may not be aggregated for that purpose;

4. Tetra Pak may not refuse orders, at prevailing prices, on the ground that the orderer is not an end-user of Tetra Pak products;

5. Tetra Pak shall inform any customer purchasing or leasing a machine of the specifications which packaging cartons must meet in order to be used on its machines.

Article 4

During the period of five years beginning 1 January 1992, Tetra Pak shall, within the first six months of each year, give the Commission a report allowing it to establish if the actions taken by Tetra Pak pursuant to this Decision have indeed brought the infringements detailed in Article 1 to an end.

It will be noted, however, that this ordered Tetra Pak not to practise predatory or discriminatory pricing rather than imposing price control in the shape of minimum or maximum prices.[147] The Commission has also ordered the parties to notify third parties that they are free to terminate or renegotiate contracts with them.[148]

---

[145] See C.S. Kerse, *EC Antitrust Procedure* (4th edn., Sweet & Maxwell, 1998), para. 6.19; Cases 25–26/84, *Ford* v. *Commission (No 2)* [1985] ECR 2725, [1985] 3 CMLR 528.

[146] For the substantive aspects of these case, see *supra* Chap. 7.

[147] *Cf.* the interim measures in *ECS/AKZO* [1983] OJ L252/13, [1983] 3 CMLR 694, where minimum prices *were* imposed.

[148] See *Astra* [1993] OJ L20/23, [1994] 5 CMLR 226 (a joint venture to which exemption under Art. 81(3) was refused); *TACA* [1999] OJ L95/1, [1999] 4 CMLR 1559 (infringements of Art. 81(1), Art. 82, and Reg. 1017/68 [1968] OJ Spec. Ed. 302, on transport by rail, road and inland waterway).

The power to order positive measures in appropriate cases does not appear to include a general power to order divestiture. Article 82 is infringed by an abuse, not by the dominant position *per se* and Regulation 17, Article 3 provides only for the Commission to order the termination of the *infringement*. It does not give a power to restructure the market to prevent future abuses.[149] However, in *Continental Can*[150] the Commission decision held that an undertaking had committed an abuse by acquiring another company and required it to dispose of it. The decision was annulled on substantive grounds, and so the order was never enforced. In this case, however, the order to divest related to the very subject-matter of the abuse. For the question of the effect of Article 81(2) on proprietary rights, see Chapter 15.

C. PROCEDURAL DECISIONS

As seen above, the Commission, in the course of its investigations, may take decisions about procedural matters. Thus, information may be demanded by decision under Regulation 17, Article 11(5), and an inspection may be ordered under Regulation 17, Article 14(3). Failure to comply with such decisions may be penalized by fines.[151] The question of the confidentiality of documents is settled by decision under Article 5(4) of Decision 94/810.[152]

D. INTERIM MEASURES

Regulation 17 does not expressly provide powers for the Commission to take interim measures in relation to possible infringements of Articles 81 and 82. However, if the Commission did not have such powers there would be a serious lacuna. Commission proceedings can be very protracted and irreparable damage might occur before it could take a final decision under Regulation 17, Article 3. In *Camera Care*, therefore, the Court held that the Commission *can* take interim decisions.

---

[149] See J. Faull and A. Nikpay (eds.), *The EC Law of Competition* (Oxford University Press, Oxford, 1999), para. 3.350; C.S. Kerse, *EC Antitrust Procedure* (4th edn., Sweet & Maxwell, London, 1998), para. 6.19. Compare the powers of the Secretary of State under the Fair Trading Act 1973, Sched. 8 Pt II to order structural remedies. The Commission has proposed that it should have power to order structural remedies in the Draft Reg. COM [2000] 582, Art. 7(1)

[150] Case 6/72, *Europemballage Corp & Continental Can Co Inc* v. *EC Commission* [1973] ECR 215, [1973] CMLR 199; see *supra* Chaps. 6, 7 and 12.

[151] See *infra* 900.

[152] The Hearing Officer's terms of reference [1994] OJ L330/67. The jurisdiction of the Hearing Officer to take decisions in this respect means that the power to adopt a challengeable act has been delegated by the Commission to a single official. Such delegation is permitted where it does not involve a matter of principle: see Case T–450/93, *Listeral* [1994] ECR II–1177 and generally M. van der Woude, 'Hearing Officers and EC Antitrust Procedures; The Art of Making Subjective Procedures More Objective' (1996) 33 *CMLRev*. 531. *Cf.* the delegation of Reg. 17 Art. 14(3) decisions to a single *Commissioner*, the validity of which was confirmed in Case 53/85, *AKZO* v. *Commission* [1986] ECR 1965, [1987] 1 CMLR 231.

Case 792/79R, *Camera Care* v. *Commission* [1980] ECR 119, [1980] 1 CMLR 334

Camera Care sold and repaired cameras. It complained to the Commission, alleging that it was being denied supplies of Hasselblad cameras by Hasselblad and its distributors who were operating the distribution system in a way which hindered inter-Member State trade in Hasselblad equipment and maintained differential price levels. It asked the Commission to take interim measures to protect its position while the matter was being investigated, but the Commission considered it had no power to do so. Camera Care appealed to the Court of Justice against the Commission's decision refusing interim relief.

Court of Justice

14. It is obvious that in certain circumstances there may be a need to adopt interim protective measures when the practice of certain undertakings in competition matters has the effect of injuring the interests of some Member States, causing damage to other undertakings, or of unacceptably jeopardizing the Community's competition policy. In such circumstances it is important to ensure that, whilst inquiries are being carried out, no irreparable damage is caused such as could not be remedied by any decision which the Commission might take at the conclusion of the administrative procedure.

15. Although it is true that, from the point of view of both the efficacy of competition law and the protection of the legitimate interests of the Member States or undertakings concerned, the adoption of protective measures may seem to be necessary in certain circumstances, the provisions of Regulation No 17 must nevertheless be examined to see whether they can accommodate this legal requirement.

16. It is as well to observe on this point that Article 3 of the Regulation entitles the Commission to take two types of action in order to bring to an end any infringements that it finds: first, the Commission may take 'decisions' which, according to Article [249] of the Treaty, are binding upon those to whom they are addressed and which, according to Articles 15 and 16 of Regulation No 17, may be accompanied by fines and periodic penalty payments; secondly, before taking a binding decision, the Commission is always entitled under Article 3(3) to address to the undertakings concerned 'recommendations for termination of the infringement'. The object of this last provision is to enable the Commission to inform the undertakings concerned of its assessment of the situation with regard to Community law in order to persuade them to comply with its point of view without immediately resorting to legal enforcement. It cannot, however, be construed as a limitation upon the practical ways in which the power to take a decision, which is the core of Article 3, may be exercised.

17. As regards the right to take decisions conferred upon the Commission by Article 3(1), it is essential that it should be exercised in the most efficacious manner best suited to the circumstances of each given situation. To this end the possibility cannot be excluded that the exercise of the right to take decisions conferred upon the Commission should comprise successive stages so that a decision finding that there is an infringement may be preceded by any preliminary measures which may appear necessary at any given moment.

18. From this point of view the Commission must also be able, within the bounds of its supervisory task conferred upon it in competition matters by the Treaty and Regulation No 17, to take protective measures to the extent to which they might appear indispensable in order to avoid the exercise of the power to make decisions given by Article 3 from becoming ineffectual or even illusory because of the action of certain undertakings. The powers which the Commission holds under Article 3(1) of Regulation No 17 therefore include the power to take interim measures which are indispensable for the effective exercise of its functions and, in particular, for ensuring the effectiveness of any decisions

requiring undertakings to bring to an end infringements which it has found to exist.

19. However, the Commission could not take such measures without having regard to the legitimate interests of the undertaking concerned by them. For this reason it is essential that interim measures be taken only in cases proved to be urgent in order to avoid a situation likely to cause serious and irreparable damage to the party seeking their adoption, or which is intolerable for the public interest. A further requirement is that these measures be of a temporary and conservatory nature and restricted to what is required in the given situation. When adopting them the Commission is bound to maintain the essential safeguards guaranteed to the parties concerned by Regulation No 17, in particular by Article 19. Finally, the decisions must be made be made in such a form that an action may be brought upon them before the Court of Justice by any party who considers he has been injured.

20. As the President of the Court has indicated, in the context of the ECSC Treaty, in his interlocutory order of 22 October 1975 in Case 109/75R (*National Carbonising Company*, [1975] ECR 1193), it is in accordance with the key principles of the Community that any interim measures which prove to be necessary should be taken by the Community institution which is given the task of receiving complaints by governments or individuals, of making enquiries and of taking decisions in regard to infringements which are found to exist, whilst the role of the Court of Justice consists in undertaking the legal review of the action taken by the Commission in these matters. In this regard, the rights of those concerned are safeguarded by the fact that if interim measures decided upon by the Commission adversely affect the legitimate interests of any party the person concerned may always obtain the revision of the decision made, by the appropriate judicial recourse, applying if necessary for emergency measures under Article [242] or Article [243] of the EEC Treaty.

The *Camera Care* judgment is a striking example of the Court's teleological interpretative technique: it reasoned that the Commission needed to be able to take interim measures in order to carry out its tasks. It therefore held that Article 3(1) included such powers even though they were not mentioned.

Certain conditions must be fulfilled before interim measures are taken:[153]

- there must be a *prima facie* infringement of the competition rules;
- it must be a situation of proven urgency where there would otherwise be serious and irreparable damage to the party seeking the measures or damage which would be intolerable to the public interest; this includes damage such as the complainant suffering a long-term competitive disadvantage and is not limited to situations which are irremediable by the final Commission decision, such as where without the measures the complainant would go out of business;[154]
- the measures must be of a temporary and conservatory nature only and restricted to what is required in the particular situation to preserve the *status quo*; the measures have to accord, like all Community acts, with the principle of proportionality;
- the legitimate rights of the party on which the measures are being imposed must be observed and the 'essential guarantees' provided for by Regulation 17, especially Article 19 on the right to be heard, must be maintained;

---

[153] See also Cases 228–229/82R, *Ford Werke AG* v. *Commission* [1982] ECR 3091, [1982] 3 CMLR 673; Case T–44/90 *La Cinq SA* v. *Commission* [1992] ECR II–1.

[154] Case T–44/90, *La Cinq supra* n. 153, paras. 78–83.

• the measures must be in a form which is subject to review by the Court, i.e. in the form of a reasoned decision.

In *Boosey & Hawkes*[155] the complainant undertakings claimed that without interim measures they would be forced to cease trading. The interim measures therefore ordered the dominant undertaking to maintain supplies to them on the terms and conditions on which the parties had previously done business. In *Sealink/B&I*[156] Sealink was ordered to return to its previous published timetable. In *Sea Containers/Stena*[157] the Commission held that there was a *prima facie* case that the shipping company had abused its dominant position as controller of a port by refusing reasonable access to another ferry operator, but refused interim measures on the ground that there was not sufficient urgency. Since the initial application the complainant had been offered and had accepted an offer of access so there was no danger of serious and irreparable harm occurring.

7. FINES AND PERIODIC PENALTY PAYMENTS

A. GENERAL

Regulation 17 empowers the Commission to take decisions to impose fines on undertakings and associations of undertakings both for substantive infringements of the competition rules (Article 15(1)) and for procedural infringements (Article 15(2)). The Commission may also impose periodic penalty payments, in order to compel undertakings to do what the Commission requires by penalizing defiance. Regulation 17 provides for fines and penalties to be levied only on *undertakings*: it does not impose liability on natural persons such as company directors and executives, unlike in US antitrust and under the UK Competition Act 1998.[158]

The lack of detail in the fining provisions of Regulation 17 with regard to substantive infringements and the broad discretion left to the Commission led to controversy, particularly in the light of the Commission's multiplicity of roles in the enforcement regime. In EC

---

[155] *BBI/Boosey & Hawkes* [1987] OJ L286/36, [1988] 4 CMLR 67.

[156] *Sealink/B&I Holyhead: Interim Measures* [1992] 5 CMLR 255, where the decision ordering the interim measures contained the Commission's first explicit statement of the essential facilities doctrine in Community law (see *supra* Chap. 7): as in *Boosey & Hawkes* the case did not go to a final decision.

[157] [1994] OJ L15/8, [1995] 4 CMLR 84.

[158] S. 1 of the Sherman Act makes violations thereof a felony: for fines in US antitrust generally see G. Spratling, 'Fines in Criminal Antitrust Cases' in P. Slot and A. McDonnell (eds.), *Procedure and Enforcement in EC and US Competition Law* (Sweet and Maxwell, 1993) 76–87. Under US law prison sentences can be imposed on executives. In 1999 executives from Archer Daniels Midland Company were convicted in connection with a cartel and sentenced to prison terms of 24 to 30 months. In UK law penalties may be imposed on individuals for certain procedural offences: see the Competition Act 1998 ss 42–44. The proposals in the White Paper on modernisation [1999] OJ L132/1 in respect of summoning individuals to Brussels raised questions about how this would be enforced: see *supra* 871.

competition law the prosecutor fixes the fine. However, Article 229 of the EC Treaty (ex Article 172) provides that regulations may give the ECJ 'unlimited jurisdiction with regard to the penalties provided for in such regulation'. Pursuant to this Regulation 17, Article 17 states:

The Court of Justice shall have unlimited jurisdiction within the meaning of Article [229] of the Treaty to review decisions whereby the Commission has fixed a fine or periodic penalty payment; it may cancel, reduce or increase the fine or periodic penalty payment imposed.

This jurisdiction is dealt with below.[159]

Regulation 17 originally expressed the monetary amounts in units of account but these should now be read as referring to Euro.[160]

B. FINES FOR PROCEDURAL INFRINGEMENTS

Regulation 17, Article 15(1) says:

The Commission may by decision impose on undertakings or associations of undertakings fines of from [Euro] 100 to 5000 where, intentionally or negligently:

   (a) they supply incorrect or misleadingly information in an application pursuant to Article 2 or in a notification pursuant to Articles 4 or 5; or

   (b) they supply incorrect information in response to a request made pursuant to Article 11 (3) or (5) or to Article 12, or do not supply information within the time limit fixed by a decision taken under Article 11 (5); or

   (c) they produce the required books or other business records in incomplete form during investigations under Article 13 or 14, or refuse to submit to an investigation ordered by decision issued in implementation of Article 14 (3).

Under this provision the Commission imposes fines for failure to co-operate with its investigations under Regulation 17, Articles 11 and 14 or for supplying incorrect or misleading information.[161] In the White Paper the Commission says that the figures of 1,000 to 5,000 Euros, being unchanged since 1962 'are too small today to have any real dissuasive effect' and proposes raising them.[162]

---

[159] See *infra* 937–938.

[160] Pursuant to Art. 2(1) of Council Reg. 1103/97 [1997] OJ L162/1 on certain provisions relating to the introduction of the Euro. Previously to that fines were expressed in ECUs (and in the national currency most closely connected to the undertaking concerned as payment could not be made in ECUs). For the problems of expressing fines in ECUs, where the exchange rate with national currency fluctuated, see e.g. Cases T–305–307, 313–316, 318, 328–329, & 335/94. *Re the PVC Cartel II: Limburgse Vinyl Mij NV and others v. Commission* [1999] 5 CMLR 303 at paras. 1225–1235. Prior to 1980 the Community used units of account instead of ECUs. By Council Reg. 3368/80 [1980] OJ L345/1 all references to units of account in Community legal instruments were to read as references to ECUs.

[161] See *supra* 854–861. It also applies to failures to co-operate with investigations of Member States under Reg. 17, Art. 13 see *infra* 923.

[162] Commission White Paper on modernisation of the rules implementing Articles 85 and 86 [now 81 and 82], para. 124 suggested Euro 1,000 to 50,000. The Draft Reg proposes a sum not exceeding 1% of the previous years' turnover (Art. 22).

C. PERIODIC PENALTY PAYMENTS

Periodic penalty payments may be imposed at a daily rate for defiance of the Commission. Regulation 17, Article 16(1) says:

The Commission may by decision impose on undertakings or associations of undertakings periodic penalty payments of from [Euro] 50 to 1000 per day, calculated from the date appointed by the decision, in order to compel them:

    (a)   to put an end to an infringement of Article [81] or [82] of the Treaty, in accordance with a decision taken pursuant to Article 3 of this Regulation;

    (b)   to refrain from any act prohibited under Article 8 (3);

    (c)   to supply complete and correct information which it has requested by decision taken pursuant to Article 11 (5);

    (d)   to submit to an investigation which it has ordered by decision taken pursuant to Article 14 (3).

As with procedural fines, the Commission thinks that the present levels are two low and proposes increasing them.[163] It also proposes a 'second category' of periodic penalty payments, to be imposed on undertakings which fail to comply with obligations imposed by a decision.[164]

D. FINES FOR SUBSTANTIVE INFRINGEMENTS

(i) BROAD DISCRETION CONFERRED ON THE COMMISSION BY REGULATION 17, ARTICLE 15(2)

Regulation 17, Article 15(2), provides for the imposition of fines for substantive infringements:

The Commission may by decision impose on undertakings or associations of undertakings fines of from [Euro] 1,000 to 1,000,000, or a sum in excess thereof but not exceeding 10% of the turnover in the preceding business year of each of the undertakings participating in the infringement where, either intentionally or negligently:

    (a)   they infringe Article [81] or Article [82] of the Treaty; or

    (b)   they commit a breach of any obligation imposed pursuant to Article 8(1).[165]

In fixing the amount of the fine, regard shall be had both to the gravity and to the duration of the infringement.

This crucial provision, which confers upon the Commission its power to punish violations of the competition rules, says only three things:

---

[163] *Ibid.*, para. 125. The Draft Reg. proposes a maximum sum of 5% of daily average turnover (Art. 23).

[164] *Ibid.*, para. 126. This would bring the penalty provisions into line with the analogous provision in Art. 15(2) of the Merger Reg., 4064/89 [1989] OJ L395/1. See the Draft Reg Art. 23(1)(c).

[165] This concerns the breach of obligations attached to Art. 81(3) exemption decisions.

- fines can only be imposed for intentional or negligent infringements;
- the maximum fine is Euro one million or 10% of turnover if greater (although it does not specify what turnover is to be taken into account);
- in fixing the fine regard is to be had to both the gravity of the infringement and to its duration.

In addition it will be recollected that according to Article 15(4) these fines are not criminal penalties.

(ii) INTENTIONAL OR NEGLIGENT INFRINGEMENT

Article 15(2) provides that the Commission may impose a fine only where the infringement was intentional or negligent. An undertaking, however, can act only through human agency and the intentions and negligence in issue are in effect those of its human directors and employees. EC competition law has not concerned itself with theories of vicarious liability or become involved in the kind of agonizing over the imputation of the employees' conduct to the company which featured in UK cases under the Restrictive Trade Practices Act.[166] In EC law the undertaking is responsible for the conduct of its directors and employees and undertakings should have in place, and enforce, compliance programmes to prevent infractions of the rules.[167]

'Intentional' means an intention to restrict competition, not an intention to infringe the rules. In *PVC Cartel II* the CFI said:[168]

For an infringement of the competition rules of the Treaty to be regarded as having been committed intentionally, it is not necessary for an undertaking to have been aware that it was infringing those rules; it is sufficient that it could not have been unaware that its conduct was aimed at restricting competition . . .

In *Miller International*[169] the undertaking claimed that it had not intentionally infringed Article 81(1) by prohibiting exports and that its lawyers had not pointed out the infringement. The Court dismissed this:[170]

17. The applicant has requested in the alternative that the fine of 70 000 u.a. should be annulled or reduced.

It has maintained that it did not intentionally commit the infringements of which it is accused and furthermore that those infringements were not serious.

---

[166] *Director General of Fair Trading* v. *Pioneer Concrete (UK) (Ltd)*, *Re Ready Mixed Concrete (Supply of) No 2* [1995] 1 AC 456, [1995] 1 All ER 135.

[167] See W. Wils, 'The Undertaking as Subject of EC Competition Law and the Imputation of Infringements to Natural or Legal Persons' (2000) 25 *ELRev.* 99, 109–11.

[168] Cases T–305–307, 313–316, 318, 328–329, & 335/94, *Re the PVC Cartel II: Limburgse Vinyl Mij NV and others* v. *Commission* [1999] 5 CMLR 303, para. 1111; see also Cases 100–103/80 *Musique Diffusion Française SA* v. *Commission (Pioneer)* [1983] ECR 1825, [1983] 3 CMLR 221, para. 221; Case T–65/89, *BPB Industries and British Gypsum Ltd* v. *Commission* [1993] ECR–II 389, [1993] 5 CMLR 32, paras. 165–166; Case T–143/89, *Ferriere Nord* v. *Commission* [1995] ECR II—917, para. 41.

[169] Case 19/77, *Miller International Schallplatten GmbH* v. *Commission* [1978] ECR 131, [1978] 2 CMLR 334.

[170] *Ibid.*, para. 18.

It claims that in adopting the clauses prohibiting exports it did not intentionally infringe the prohibitions contained in Article 81[(1)] of the Treaty.

This lack of awareness is said to be demonstrated by the opinion of a legal adviser consulted by the applicant concerning the drafting of its terms and conditions of sale, which opinion, produced as an annex to its reply, does not mention the fact that a clause prohibiting exports might be incompatible with Community law.

18. As is clear from the foregoing as a whole, the clauses in question were adopted or accepted by the applicant and the latter could not have been unaware that they had as their object the restriction of competition between its customers.

Consequently, it is of little relevance to establish whether the applicant knew that it was infringing the prohibition contained in Article 81.

In this connection, the opinion of a legal adviser, on which it relies, is not a mitigating factor.

It must thus be held that the acts prohibited by the Treaty were undertaken intentionally and in disregard of the provisions of the Treaty.

Even if the infringement is not characterized as intentional it is likely to be held negligent. The Court has never defined negligence for this purpose but the Commission and the Court expect experienced commercial entities to understand what they are doing. Their attitude to claims of ignorance or inadvertence can be illustrated by *United Brands* and *Sandoz*. In *United Brands* the undertaking claimed that it did not know it was in a dominant position for the purposes of Article 82 and did not know its conduct constituted an abuse. The Court responded:[171]

298. The applicant submits that it did not know that it was in a dominant position, still less that it had abused it, especially as, according to the case-law of the Court to date, only undertakings which were pure monopolies or controlled an overwhelming share of the market have been held to be in a dominant position.

299. UBC is an undertaking which, having engaged for a very long time in international and national trade, has special knowledge of anti-trust laws and has already experienced their severity.

300. UBC, by setting up a commercial system combining the prohibition of the sale of bananas while still green, discriminatory prices, deliveries less than the amounts ordered, all of which was to end in strict partitioning of national markets, adopted measures which it knew or ought to have known contravened the prohibition set out in Article [82] of the Treaty.

301. The Commission therefore had good reason to find that UBC's infringements were at the very least negligent.

In *Sandoz* the undertaking, a major pharmaceutical producer, sent invoices to its customers with 'export prohibited' printed on them. The company said it had used these invoices for many years, since before the inception of the Community, and had simply omitted to amend them. The Commission did not absolve it of liability.

---

[171] Case 27/76, *United Brands* v. *Commission* [1978] ECR 207, [1978] 1 CMLR 429, paras. 298–301.

Sandoz [1987] OJ L222/28, [1989] 4 CMLR 628[172]

Commission

34. . . . the invoices in question were adopted by Sandoz PF which could not have been unaware that the export ban had as its object the restriction of competition on trade between member — States. Consequently, it is of little relevance to establish whether or not Sandoz PF knew that it was infringing the prohibition contained in Article [81]. Therefore it can only be concluded that the acts prohibited by that Article were undertaken intentionally. However, even if Sandoz PF's thesis of a 'mere oversight' were to be accepted, this would not exclude its liability and would represent a grave form of negligence.

35. As explained above, Sandoz PF has stated that it was as a result of a 'mere oversight' that the invoice in question bore the words 'export prohibited', and that anyway the company had taken no steps to enforce the prohibition. However, on this point, it must be recalled that the words 'export prohibited' were found on the top right hand corner of the invoice in use until 31 December 1983, and were then moved to the bottom centre of the new invoice introduced from 1 January 1984, after the corporate name was changed. It is precisely because the words in question were moved that an actual recurrence of the 'mere oversight' is scarcely plausible. Indeed, it is rather difficult to imagine that the new invoice form, on which several significant changes were made compared to the earlier one, was examined and checked so superficially by the competent departments of Sandoz PF as to let slip an 'oversight' of such clear and evident commercial and legal importance, particularly to an important subsidiary of a multinational group.

36. As regards the Sandoz PF comment on the removal of the words 'export prohibited' which, at least up to 1970, still appeared on it drug packaging, it must first be stressed that, rather than strengthening the validity of the 'oversight' argument, the fact that the packaging was brought into line with the EEC rules is evidence of another occasion on which Sandoz PF should have brought the invoice into line with such rules. It must also be pointed out that even before 1970 it was clear that Community law did not permit undertakings to prohibit exports between the member-States. Therefore, the fact that Sandoz PF also retained this prohibition until the said date on the individual drugs packagings it distributed, as well as its invoices, is an aggravating and not an extenuating circumstance.

Since both intention and negligence produce liability to fines it is usually unnecessary to decide into which category the infringement falls, except that intentional infringements attract heavier fines.

There are rare instances where ignorance has led to non-imposition of a fine[173] and the Commission may in particular consider that an undertaking has not been negligent where it condemns a practice as an infringement of the competition rules for the first time.[174]

---

[172] Upheld by the ECJ, Case 277/87, *Sandoz Prodotti Farmaceutici SpA* v. *Commission* [1990] ECR I–45.

[173] See *Bayer Dental* [1990] OJ L351/46, [1992] 4 CMLR 61; *Stainless Steel* [1990] OJ L220/28 and the other cases discussed by L. Gyselen in 'The Commission's Fining Policy in Competition Cases—"Questo è il catalogo"' in P. Slot and A. McDonnell (eds).*Procedure and Enforcement in EC and US Competition Law* (Sweet and Maxwell, 1993) 63–75.

[174] See e.g. *Vegetable Parchment* [1978] OJ L70/54, [1978] 2 CMLR 334. On the other hand, the arguable novelty of the developments in Art. 82 did not save United Brands, (see *supra* 903) or Hoffmann-La Roche in Case 85/76, *Hoffmann-La Roche* v. *Commission* [1979] ECR 461, [1979] 3 CMLR 211; nor did it save Tetra Pak in Case C–333/94P, *Tetra Pak International SA* v. *Commission* [1996] ECR I—5951, [1997] 4 CMLR 662.

(iii) DEVELOPMENT OF THE COMMISSION'S FINING POLICY

As is noted above, Regulation 17 contains no detailed provisions about the amount or purpose of fines. It merely gives a maximum (and minimum) amount related to turnover, says that gravity and duration should be taken into account, and states that the fines are not of a criminal nature. To what turnover the 10 per cent figure relates is not specified. There is no indication in the Regulation whether the purpose of the fines is deterrence, punishment, ensuring that the offence does not pay, or some combination of these and perhaps other factors. In its *XIIIth Report on Competition Policy*, however, the Commission said that the purpose was twofold: 'to impose a pecuniary sanction on the undertaking for the infringement and prevent a repetition of the offence, and to make the prohibition in the Treaty more effective'.[175]

The Commission first imposed a fine in 1969 in the *Quinine Cartel*.[176] The amount was 500,000 units of account.[177] For the next ten years the level of fines was 'relatively light'.[178] Change came in 1979 when the Commission indicated in *Pioneer* that it intended to reinforce the deterrent effect of fines by raising their general level in cases of serious infringements. It fined one culprit over four million units of account.[179] The undertakings appealed and the Court confirmed the legality of the Commission's policy and strategy.

Cases 100–103/80, *Musique Diffusion Française SA* v. *Commission* (*Pioneer*) [1983] ECR 1825, [1983] 3 CMLR 221

Court of Justice

106. It follows that, in assessing the gravity of an infringement for the purpose of fixing the amount of the fine, the Commission must take into consideration not only the particular circumstances of the case but also the context in which the infringement occurs and must ensure that its action has the necessary deterrent effect, especially as regards those types of infringement which are particularly harmful to the attainment of the objectives of the Community.

107. From that point of view, the Commission was right to classify as very serious infringements prohibitions on exports and imports seeking artificially to maintain price differences between the markets of the various member-States. Such prohibitions jeopardize the freedom of intra-Community trade, which is a fundamental principle of the Treaty, and they prevent the attainment of one of its objectives, namely the creation of a single market.

108. It was also open to the Commission to have regard to the fact that practices of this nature, although they were established as being unlawful at the outset of Community competition policy, are still relatively frequent on account of the profit that certain of the undertakings concerned are able to derive from them and, consequently, it was open to the Commission to consider that it was appropriate to raise the level of fines so as to reinforce their deterrent effect.

---

[175] (Commission, 1983), pt. 62.

[176] [1969] OJ L192/5, [1969] CMLR D241.

[177] The fines are expressed in units of account, ECUs or Euro, depending on when they were imposed. For present purposes these terms can be considered interchangeable: see n. 160 *supra*.

[178] According to the Commission in the *XIIIth Report on Competition Policy* (Commission, 1983), pt 63.

[179] *Pioneer* [1980] OJ L60/21, [1980] 1 CMLR 457.

109. For the same reasons, the fact that the Commission, in the past, imposed fines of a certain level for certain types of infringement does not mean that it is estopped from raising that level within the limits indicated in Regulation 17 if that is necessary to ensure the implementation of Community competition policy. On the contrary, the proper application of the Community competition rules requires that the Commission may at any time adjust the level of fines to the needs of that policy.

. . .

120. In assessing the gravity of an infringement regard must be had to a large number of factors, the nature and importance of which vary according to the type of infringement in question and the particular circumstances of the case. Those factors may, depending on the circumstances, include the volume and value of the goods in respect of which the infringement was committed and the size and economic power of the undertaking and, consequently, the influence which the undertaking was able to exert on the market.

121. It follows that, on the one hand, it is permissible, for the purpose of fixing the fine, to have regard both to the total turnover of the undertaking, which gives an indication, albeit approximate and imperfect, of the size of the undertaking and of its economic power, and to the proportion of that turnover accounted for by the goods in respect of which the infringement was committed, which gives an indication of the scale of the infringement. On the other hand, it follows that it is important not to confer on one or the other of those figures an importance disproportionate in relation to the other factors and, consequently, that the fixing of an appropriate fine cannot be the result of a simple calculation based on the total turnover. That is particularly the case where the goods concerned account for only a small part of the figure. It is appropriate for the Court to bear in mind those considerations in its assessment, by virtue of its powers of unlimited jurisdiction, of the gravity of the infringements in question.

This confirmed that the Commission was justified in suddenly raising the level of fines and in using fines to deter other undertakings from infringing. It will be seen from paragraphs 120 and 121 that the Commission must take into account a number of factors, depending on the nature of the infringement and the circumstances of the case. In paragraph 119 the Court said that 'turnover' in Article 15(2) means the *total* turnover of the undertaking or group, and not just that of the products in respect of which the infringement was committed. On the other hand, the Commission must have regard to the latter turnover when fixing the fine, because it gives an indication of the scale of the infringement. The Commission explained its policy in the light of its 'vindication' by the *Pioneer* judgment in the *XIIIth Report*.[180]

The Commission has discretion in fixing the size of fines, subject to the general power of judicial review by the Court of Justice. In assessing the fine, the Commission takes into account all relevant facts of the case as to the gravity and duration of the infringement and whether it was deliberate or merely negligent.

It also endeavours to observe the principle of proportionality in its fining policy, i.e., to relate the fine to the infringement, the size of the undertaking concerned and its responsibility for the infringement.

The complexity of the factors to be weighed means that the assessment of fines, rather than being a mathematical exercise based on an abstract formula, involves a legal and economic appraisal of each case on the basis of the above principles.

---

[180] *XIIIth Report on Competition Policy* (Commission, 1983), pt 64.

It will be appreciated that this policy gave the Commission a very wide discretion, allowing it to 'individualize' the fine to each infringing undertaking.[181] The Commission increasingly took into account the Community turnover in the product concerned in the infringement and stated the importance of this factor in the *Cement Cartel* press release, where it said 'calculation is normally based on the Community turnover in the product concerned'.[182] In addition it took into account a number of other factors, either in mitigation or as aggravation, such as profits from the infringement in so far as these were calculable,[183] the economic circumstances faced by the undertakings,[184] the degree of co-operation with the Commission,[185] the knowledge and intention of the parties, the nature and gravity of the restriction,[186] the duration of the infringement,[187] the responsibility of each of the undertakings concerned where they are acting in concert, the actual effect of the infringement, uncertainty about the illegality of the conduct concerned, the adoption of a compliance programme,[188] and the willingness of the infringer to accept undertakings to remedy the situation.

In the XXIst Competition Policy Report the Commission said that in future it would continue to move closer to the maximum fine laid down in Regulation 17.[189] From the mid-1980s onwards the size of fines increased markedly. In 1992 a fine of 75 million ECUs, approximately 2.5 per cent of its overall turnover, was imposed on Tetra Pak for abuse of a dominant position[190] and forty-one participants in the *Cement Cartel* were fined a total of 248 million ECUs (including one fine of over 32 million ECUs) in 1994.[191] In 1996 the Commission, in pursuance of its desire to obtain hard evidence of the existence of cartels, introduced a Notice offering leniency over fines to cartel participants which informed on it to the Commission.[192]

(iv) CRITICISMS OF THE COMMISSION'S FINING POLICY

The fining policy described above was criticized for its lack of transparency. It was often felt

---

[181] The CFI said in Case T–150/89, *Martinelli* v. *Commission* [1995] ECR II–1165, para. 69, that the Commission could not be expected to apply a precise mathematical formula to fining calculations. And see also Case 322/81 *Nederlandsche Banden-Industrie Michelin* v. *Commission* [1983] ECR 3461, [1985] 1 CMLR 282, paras. 17–21.

[182] Press release IP/1108 of 30 Nov. 1994.

[183] See e.g *Eurocheque: Helsinki Agreement* [1992] OJ L95/50, and *infra* 909.

[184] E.g., in *Polypropylene Cartel* [1986] OJ L230/1, [1988] 4 CMLR 347.

[185] *Ibid.*, in regard to ICI.

[186] Art. 15(2) obliges the Commission to take gravity into account.

[187] Also stipulated in Art. 15(2).

[188] For whether these mitigate or aggravate the offence, see *infra* 917.

[189] (Commission, 1992) at pt 139.

[190] *Tetra Pak II* [1992] OJ L/72/1, [1992] 4 CMLR 551, upheld on appeal Case T–83/91, *Tetra Pak Rausing* v. *Commission* [1994] ECR II–755, [1997] 4 CMLR 726 and Case C–333/94P, *Tetra Pak International SA* v. *Commission* [1996] ECR I–5951, [1997] 4 CMLR 662: the fact that it was the first time that the Commission had held that an undertaking dominant on one market could abuse it by its conduct on the other did not reduce the size of the fine.

[191] Some of these fines were reduced on appeal where the Commission had not proved the length of the infringement it alleged: Joined Cases T–25/95 etc., *Cimenteries CBR SA* v. *Commission*, judgment of 15 Mar. 2000 [2000] 5 CMLR 204.

[192] See *infra* 919–921.

that the Commission plucked figures from the air in what could only be described as a lottery[193] and that the increasingly swingeing fines were based on no discernible methodology. The absence of a proper 'tariff', or to put it in the Commission's words, the rejection of 'a mathematical exercise based on an abstract formula' was contrasted unfavourably with the normal position in most national legal systems in relation to both civil damages and criminal sanctions. In the USA, the federal sentencing guidelines apply to criminal antitrust. The debate about the desirability of more certainty in fining practice involves, *inter alia*, assessing which is the best deterrent, certainty or uncertainty. If undertakings know what infringements will cost them, will they engage in a cost-benefit analysis and, deciding that they will on balance gain or lose, then act accordingly? Will they be deterred only if they face unknown amounts? Such questions are not, of course, unique to competition laws and there is a large literature on deterrence and criminal law and the economics of crime deterrence.[194] Some commentators and Commission officials believe in the value of uncertainty. Gyselen states that 'obviously tarification would seriously jeopardize the main objective of a fine. It would take away its deterrent effect. If companies knew in advance how much they have to pay they would operate a cost-benefit analysis with respect to the contemplated infringement'.[195] This was the view of the then Director-General of DG IV giving evidence to the House of Lords Select Committee. The report states that he did not believe it was possible or advisable to establish a tariff formula which one could calculate in advance and suggested that 'the risk of being caught is not that big and people would calculate whether they should or should not violate the law in view of the tariff'.[196] Others argue the reverse. Wils says:[197]

> ... the basic assumption underlying all attempts to deter infringements by imposing fines is that companies indeed operate a cost-benefit analysis. If deterrence works, it does so by altering the potential offender's balance of expected cost and benefit in such a way as to induce him to refrain from the undesirable action.

Wils also argues that relating the amount of the fine to turnover (which was not *required* by the Court in *Pioneer*) rather than the harm caused or the benefit gained, is not economically justified:

W.P.J. Wils, 'The Commission's new method for calculating fines in antitrust cases' (1998) 23 *ELRev* 252 255–6.

If there is no legal reason to calculate fines as a percentage of turnover, an economic justification is not easy to find either. To achieve effective deterrence, fines should optimally be equal to the harm

---

[193] See I. Van Bael, 'Fining à la Carte: The Lottery of EU Competition Law' [1995] 4 *ECLR* 237.

[194] See W.P.J. Wils, 'EC Competition Fines: To Deter or Not to Deter' [1995] *Yearbook of European Law* 17 and the literature cited there: some of Wils' conclusions are summarized in the article in (1998) 23 *ELRev.*, 252 an extract from which appears *infra*.

[195] Gyselen, 'The Commission's Fining Policy in Competition Cases—'Questo è il catalogo" in P. Slot and A. McDonnell eds. *Procedure and Enforcement in EC and US Competition Law* (Sweet and Maxwell, 1993) 63 at 64.

[196] Enforcement of Community Competition Rules, HL Session 1993–94, 1st Report, Select Committee on the European Communities, 23, para. 62.

[197] W.P.J.Wils, 'The Commission's New Method for Calculating Fines in Antitrust Cases' (1998) 23 *ELRev.* 252 at 256.

caused by the infringement, or alternatively equal to the benefit gained by the violator plus some safety margin, divided by the probability of detection and punishment. . . . Where it is not possible to evaluate these factors directly, the turnover accounted for by the goods in respect of which the infringement was committed might be regarded as a proxy. It would be an extremely crude approximation, though. . . . Take the simple case of a price cartel. A first element of the harm is the transfer from consumers to producers, which equals the price increase caused by the cartel multiplied by the quantity of products bought. By taking turnover as a basis (which is quantity times price, not quantity times price increase), one makes abstraction of the degree to which the price was artificially raised, obviously an essential determinant of harm. A second component of the harm is the dead-weight welfare loss attributable to the misallocation of resources, . . . which is proportional to the price increase and to the concomitant decrease in cartel production. . . . Again turnover, which does not capture the changes in price and quantity, misses much of the essence. As to measuring other components of harm, such as productive inefficiencies or wasteful efforts to create and continue the cartel, turnover does not seem particularly suited either.

In the end, the method of calculation of fines as a percentage of the relevant turnover creates an illusion of scientific rigour, as there is no good reason for fines to be proportional to turnover nor any criterion to select the percentage figure to apply to the turnover . . .

In 1992, the Commission announced a new emphasis on the benefit gained through the infringement:[198]

The financial benefit which companies infringing the competition rules have derived from their infringements will become an increasingly important consideration. Wherever the Commission can ascertain the level of this ill-gotten gain, even if it cannot do so precisely, the calculation of the fine may have this as a starting-point. When appropriate, that amount could then be increased or decreased in the light of the other circumstances of the case, including the need to introduce an element of deterrence or penalty in the sanction imposed on the participating companies.

Despite this, turnover remained the first consideration.[199]

Another problem with using the turnover criterion is that it makes the reasoning which led the Commission to a particular figure even more opaque, given that turnover is usually a unpublishable business secret. It has been argued that the obfuscation surrounding the calculation of fines has been partly responsible for the stream of challenges to the Commission's decisions before the Court.[200] Given that undertakings usually appeal on substantive and other procedural grounds as well, it is not clear that improved transparency in fining will stem that tide. However, the difficulties in determining how the Commission reached a particular figure were notably striking in cartel cases, where numerous participants were fined widely differing amounts and the reasons for the variations were unclear.

Decisions levying fines can be challenged before the Court. As the Commission has to observe the normal general principles of Community law these decisions can be challenged on grounds, *inter alia*, of lack of adequate reasoning, lack of proportionality, and discrimination[201] (the last is relevant to the different treatment of cartel participants). However, the

---

[198] Commission's *XXIst Report on Competition Policy*, at para. 139.

[199] As was seen in the *Cement Cartel* Press Release IP/1108 of 30 Nov. 1994, *supra* n. *Eurocheque: Helsinki Agreement* [1992] OJ L95/50 was a rare case in which the Commission emphasized the profit made from the infringement. See also *Soda ash-Solvay/ICI* [1991] OJ L152/1.

[200] See R. Richardson, 'Guidance Without Guidance—A European Revolution in Fining Policy? The Commission's New Guidelines on Fines' [1999] 7 *ECLR* 360.

[201] See *infra* 929–932.

Court, having been reluctant in *Pioneer* to trammel the Commission's discretion, has continued to take a comparatively 'hands off' approach. The Court has not been slow to annul decisions on substantive grounds or for procedural infringements, but although it *has* been willing to annul or reduce fines it has been comparatively tolerant of the Commission in the fining area.[202]

There was no major change in the Court's policy in this regard after the inauguration of the CFI. A good example of the attitude of the CFI to fines is *Tréfilunion* in 1995.[203] There, one of the participants in the *Welded Steel Mesh Cartel*[204] claimed that the reasoning which led to the calculation of its fine was inadequate. The CFI accepted that it should not be necessary for an undertaking to have to bring court proceedings in order to ascertain how the fine was calculated, but still upheld the decision. It also upheld the Commission's decision in *PVC Cartel II*, where some undertakings argued that the decision contained no specific information explaining the level of fines imposed on each of them and that the Commission had failed to specify the objective standards used to assess the liability of the undertakings and their respective importance.

Cases T–305–307, 313–316, 318, 328–329, & 335/94, Re the PVC Cartel II: Limburgse Vinyl Maatschappij NV and others v. Commission [1999] ECR II–931 [1999] 5 CMLR 303

Court of First Instance

1172. It is settled case law that the statement of reasons required by Article [253] of the Treaty, which constitutes an essential procedural requirement within the meaning of Article [230] of the Treaty, must be appropriate to the measure at issue and disclose clearly and unequivocally the reasoning followed by the institution which adopted it in such a way as to enable the persons concerned to ascertain the reasons for the measure and to enable the competent court to exercise its power of review. The requirements to be satisfied by the statement of reasons depend on the circumstances of each case, and in particular the content of the measure, the nature of the reasons given and the interest which the addressees of the measure or other parties to whom it is of direct and individual concern, may have in obtaining explanations. It is not necessary for the reasoning to go into all the relevant facts and points of law, since the question whether the statement of reasons meets the requirements of Article [253] of the Treaty must be assessed with regard not only to its wording but also to its context and to all the legal rules governing the matter in question (see *inter alia* C–367/95 P, *E.C. Commission v. Sytraval and Brink's France* . . .).

1173. Although, in the case of a decision imposing fines on several undertakings for an infringement of Community competition rules, the scope of the duty to state reasons must be assessed *inter alia* in the light of the fact that the gravity of the infringement depends on a large number of factors, such as the particular circumstances of the case, its context and the dissuasive effect of fines, no binding or exhaustive list of the criteria to be applied has been drawn up (*SPO* . . .).

        . . .

---

[202] E.g., the unprecedentedly high 75 million ECUs fine in *Tetra Pak II* was not reduced: see Case T–83/91 *Tetra Pak Rausing* v. *Commission* [1994] ECR II–755, [1997] 4 CMLR 726 and Case C–333/94P *Tetra Pak International SA* v. *Commission* [1996] ECR I–5951, [1997] 4 CMLR 662.

[203] Case T–148/89 etc., *Tréfilunion* v. *Commission* [1995] ECR II–1063.

[204] [1989] OJ L260/1, [1991] 4 CMLR 13.

1179. Interpreted in the light of the detailed account in the Decision of the factual allegations made against each addressee of the Decision, Points 51 to 54 of the Decision contain a sufficient and relevant indication of the factors taken into account by the Commission in assessing the gravity and duration of the infringement committed by each of the undertakings in question.

1180. It is certainly desirable, in order to enable undertakings to define their position with full knowledge of the facts, for them to be able to determine in detail, in accordance with such system as the Commission might consider appropriate, the method whereby the fine imposed upon them in a decision establishing an infringement of Community competition rules has been calculated, without their being obliged, in order to do so, to bring court proceedings against the decision (*Tréfilunion . . .*).

1181. However, such calculations do not constitute an additional and subsequent ground for the Decision, but merely translate into figures the criteria set out in the Decision which are capable of being quantified.

1182. Pursuant to Articles 64 and 65 of its Rules of Procedure it is for the Court of First Instance to ask the Commission, if the Court considers it necessary in order to examine the applicants' pleas, for specific explanations of the various criteria applied by the Commission and referred to in the Decision.

1183. Indeed, in the course of the actions challenging the 1988 decision the Court asked the Commission to produce explanations at the hearing concerning the calculation of the fines imposed. For that purpose the Commission produced a table, which was annexed to the applications in the current proceedings.

1184. Consequently, the applicants' pleas that the Decision did not adequately state reasons concerning the criteria taken into account for the purposes of determining the fine must be dismissed.

It will be seen from paragraphs 1183–1184 that the Court considered as part of the reasons a document produced by the Commission for the Court when the previous *PVC* decision was challenged.[205]

(v) THE COMMISSION'S 1998 GUIDELINES ON THE METHOD OF SETTING FINES

Conscious of the problems surrounding its fining policy the Commission published a Notice in January 1998, the guidelines on the method of setting fines. The Commission did not thereby surrender its discretion. Rather it set out a methodology which it would henceforth follow, which still allows a very wide margin of discretion. The Notice does not mean that fines can now be precisely calculated with mathematical accuracy and much of it, in particular as regards aggravating and attenuating circumstances, reflects the previous practice of the Commission and the rulings of the Court.

The Notice goes back to the two criteria stipulated in Regulation 17, gravity and duration, and bases the calculation of fines on these.

---

[205] *PVC Cartel I* [1989] OJ L74/1, [1990] 4 CMLR 345, annulled in Cases C–137/92P etc., *Commission* v. *BASF and others* [1994] ECR I—2555; see *infra* 931.

Guidelines on the method of setting fines imposed pursuant to Article 15(2) of Regulation No 17 and Article 65(5) of the ECSC treaty [1998] OJ C9/3

The principles outlined here should ensure the transparency and impartiality of the Commission's decisions, in the eyes of the undertakings and of the Court of Justice alike, while upholding the discretion which the Commission is granted under the relevant legislation to set fines within the limit of 10% of overall turnover. This discretion must, however, follow a coherent and non-discriminatory policy which is consistent with the objectives pursued in penalizing infringements of the competition rules.

The new method of determining the amount of a fine will adhere to the following rules, which start from a basic amount that will be increased to take account of aggravating circumstances or reduced to take account of attenuating circumstances.

1. Basic amount

The basic amount will be determined according to the gravity and duration of the infringement, which are the only criteria referred to in Article 15 (2) of Regulation No 17.

A. Gravity

In assessing the gravity of the infringement, account must be taken of its nature, its actual impact on the market, where this can be measured, and the size of the relevant geographic market.

Infringements will thus be put into one of three categories: minor infringements, serious infringements and very serious infringements.

— *minor infringements*:

> These might be trade restrictions, usually of a vertical nature, but with a limited market impact and affecting only a substantial but relatively limited part of the Community market.

> Likely fines: [Euro] 1 000 to ECU 1 million.

— *serious infringements*:

> These will more often than not be horizontal or vertical restrictions of the same type as above, but more rigorously applied, with a wider market impact, and with effects in extensive areas of the common market. There might also be abuse of a dominant position (refusals of supply, discrimination, exclusion, loyalty discounts made by dominant firms in order to shut competitors out of the market, etc.)

> Likely fines: [Euro] 1 million to [Euro] 20 million.

— *very serious infringements*:

> These will generally be horizontal restrictions such as price cartels and market-sharing quotas, or other practices which jeopardize the proper functioning of a single market, such as the partitioning of national markets and clear-cut abuse of a dominant position by undertakings holding a virtual monopoly. . . .

> Likely fines: above [Euro] 20 million.

Within each of these categories, and in particular as far as serious and very serious infringements are concerned, the proposed scale of fines will make it possible to apply differential treatment to undertakings according to the nature of the infringement committed.

It will also be necessary to take account of the effective economic capacity of offenders to cause significant damage to other operators, in particular consumers, and to set the fine at a level which ensures that it has a sufficiently deterrent effect.

Generally speaking, account may also be taken of the fact that large undertakings usually have legal and economic knowledge and infrastructures which enable them more easily to recognize that their conduct constitutes an infringement and be aware of the consequences stemming from it under competition law.

Where an infringement involves several undertakings (e.g. cartels), it might be necessary in some cases to apply weightings to the amounts determined within each of the three categories in order to take account of the specific weight and, therefore, the real impact of the offending conduct of each undertaking on competition, particularly where there is considerable disparity between the sizes of the undertakings committing infringements of the same type.

Thus, the principles of equal punishment for the same conduct may, if the circumstances so warrant, lead to different fines being imposed on the undertakings concerned without this differentiation being governed by arithmetic calculation.

B. Duration

A distinction should be made between the following:

— infringements of short duration (in general, less than one year): no increase in amount,

— infringements of medium duration (in general, one to five years): increase of up to 50% in the amount determined for gravity,

— infringements of long duration (in general, more than five years): increase of up to 10% per year in the amount determined for gravity.

This approach will therefore point to a possible increase in the amount of the fine.

Generally speaking, the increase in the fine for long-term infringements represents a considerable strengthening of the previous practice with a view to imposing effective sanctions on restrictions which have had a harmful impact on consumers over a long period. Moreover, this new approach is consistent with the expected effect of the notice of 18 July 1996 on the non-imposition or reduction of fines in cartel cases . . . .[206] The risk of having to pay a much larger fine, proportionate to the duration of the infringement, will necessarily increase the incentive to denounce it or to co-operate with the Commission.

The basic amount will result from the addition of the two amounts established in accordance with the above:

x gravity + y duration = basic amount

2. *Aggravating circumstances*
The basic amount will be increased where there are aggravating circumstances such as:

— repeated infringement of the same type by the same undertaking(s),

— refusal to co-operate with or attempts to obstruct the Commission in carrying out its investigations,

— role of leader in, or instigator of the infringement,

---

[206] This Notice [1996] OJ C207/4 (mentioned also in Section 2) is that concerned with the lenient treatment offered to cartel participants who reveal matters to the Commission : see *infra* 919–921.

— retaliatory measures against other undertakings with a view to enforcing practices which constitute an infringement,

— need to increase the penalty in order to exceed the amount of gains improperly made as a result of the infringement when it is objectively possible to estimate that amount,

— other.

3. *Attenuating circumstances*

The basic amount will be reduced where there are attenuating circumstances such as:

— an exclusively passive or 'follow-my-leader' role in the infringement,

— non-implementation in practice of the offending agreements or practices,

— termination of the infringement as soon as the Commission intervenes (in particular when it carries out checks),

— existence of reasonable doubt on the part of the undertaking as to whether the restrictive conduct does indeed constitute an infringement,

— infringements committed as a result of negligence or unintentionally,

— effective co-operation by the undertaking in the proceedings, outside the scope of the Notice of 18 July 1996 on the non-imposition or reduction of fines in cartel cases,

— other.

The Guidelines therefore provide that the Commission will first decide a base sum, set not by turnover[207] but according to the gravity and duration of the infringement. There are three levels of gravity—minor, serious and very serious.

Minor infringements 'might be' behaviour with a limited market impact and affecting only a relatively limited part of the Community market. The Commission specifically mentions vertical restrictions here. Fines are likely to be no more than Euro one million.

Serious infringements are likely to be the same type of behaviour but 'more rigorously applied' with a wider impact on the market and geographically. However, they may also include abuses of a dominant position. Fines are likely to be between Euro one million and 20 million.

Very serious infringements will generally be price-fixing and market-sharing cartels and other practices which jeopardize the single market, and 'clear-cut' abuses of a dominant position by undertakings with a 'virtual monopoly'—this is another indication of the Commission's increasing tendency to identify what has been termed 'super-dominance'.[208] Fines are likely to be over Euro 20 million. The very serious infringements are the kind of cases which have always attracted the most swingeing fines, and the Guidelines cite some of the most notorious, such as *Cartonboard, Cement,* and *Tetra Pak II.*

In the coda to Section 1.A. on gravity, the Commission confirms its freedom to apply different fines to undertakings involved in the same infringing conduct to take into account the 'real impact' of each undertaking's behaviour. This is particularly relevant to cartels. The Commission also stresses the necessity of producing a sufficient deterrent effect and of taking account of an undertaking's capacity to cause damage to others.

---

[207] Although of course the 10% of total turnover laid down in Reg. 17, Art. 15(2), can never be exceeded.
[208] See *supra* Chaps. 5 and 7.

The second element in assessing the base figure is duration. There are three categories: short (generally less than a year), medium (generally one to five years), and long (generally over five years). The scheme is that the figure determined for gravity is increased by up to 50 per cent for medium length infringements, but up to 10 per cent *per year* for long infringements.

The final base figure is reached by adding the gravity and duration elements together, which the Commission represents as a simple equation. The base amount can then be increased by 'aggravating circumstances' (section 2) or reduced by 'attenuating circumstances' (section 3). Examples of each category are given, and these reflect the Commission's existing practice. Three things in particular should be noted. First, in section 2 the Commission mentions increasing the base amount in order to exceed the gains from the infringement. Secondly, there is no mention of the effect of the adoption or existence of a compliance programme.[209] Thirdly, Sections 2 and 3 both contain the category 'other' which serves to underline the discretion which the Commission still reserves to itself and which arguably reduces legal certainty.

In the final section of the Notice the Commission makes four 'General Comments'. The first relates to the maximum turnover ceiling in Article 15(2). The other three are:

5. General comments

. . .

(b) Depending on the circumstances, account should be taken, once the above calculations have been made, of certain objective factors such as a specific economic context, any economic or financial benefit derived by the offenders (see Twenty-first report on competition policy, point 139), the specific characteristics of the undertakings in question and their real ability to pay in a specific social context, and the fines should be adjusted accordingly.

(c) In cases involving associations of undertakings, decisions should as far as possible be addressed to and fines imposed on the individual undertakings belonging to the association. If this is not possible (e.g. where there are several thousands of affiliated undertakings), and except for cases falling within the ECSC Treaty, an overall fine should be imposed on the association calculated according to the principles outlined above but equivalent to the total of individual fines which might have been imposed on each of the members of the association.

(d) The Commission will also reserve the right, in certain cases, to impose a 'symbolic' fine of [Euro] 1 000, which would not involve any calculation based on the duration of the infringement or any aggravating or attenuating circumstances. The justification for imposing such a fine should be given in the text of the decision.

Paragraph (b) again raises the issue of profits from the infringement but also says that the 'real ability' of undertakings to pay should be taken into account. This allows for any reluctance of the Commission to fine at a level which would cause the undertaking's bankruptcy, for example, if this was thought undesirable.[210] Paragraph (c) deals with the method

---

[209] A compliance programme is a policy adopted and implemented by a company to ensure that its officers and employees do nothing which could amount to an infringement of the competition rules.

[210] But note that the CFI held in the *Cement* appeal, Cases T–25/95 etc., *Cimenteries CBR SA v. Commission*, judgment of 15 Mar. 2000, [2000] 5 CMLR 204, para. 4925, that the Commission is not required to take into account the loss-making situation of an undertaking when determining its fine, since that may give an unjustified competitive advantage to the undertakings least well adapted to market conditions.

of fining associations of undertakings[211] and (d) provides for the imposition of 'symbolic' fines of Euro 1,000 unrelated to the calculation method set out in the rest of the Notice. Such a symbolic fine was imposed on the organizers of the 1998 Football World Cup Finals for infringing Article 82 by discriminating on grounds of nationality in the sale of tickets.[212]

One commentator represents the formula for calculating fines under the Notice as follows:[213]

Decisions then contain up to six figures: an amount x in ECUs determined on the basis of gravity, an amount y in ECUs for medium or long duration, a single percentage figure i on account of one or more aggravating circumstances, a single percentage figure j reflecting all attenuating circumstances (other than co-operation under the notice of July 18, 1996) and a percentage figure k in case of application of the notice of July 18, 1996, as well as the final figure of the fine f.,

which gives:

$$[x + y] \times [(100 + i - j) \div 100] \times [(100 - k) \div 100] = f.$$

(vi) EFFECT AND APPLICATION OF THE GUIDELINES

The Guidelines do not affect the level at which the Commission pitches fines, or the overall amount, but simply set out the method of calculation. The most significant change is the move from turnover to gravity and duration as the basic elements of the calculation. Turnover may still be relevant as a factor in assessing the 'effective economic capacity' and size of an undertaking, but it has lost its pole position.

It is still impossible for undertakings to compute precisely the fine they are incurring. The Notice contains many variables and many matters which are a matter of discretionary assessment by the Commission,[214] and the language of the Notice is imprecise—full of 'might be', 'generally speaking', 'in general', 'particularly'.

The application of the Notice is illustrated by a number of decisions taken shortly after its promulgation. In *Volkswagen*[215] the Commission imposed the highest ever fine on a single undertaking, 102 million ECUs.[216] In *TACA*[217] it imposed a total of 273 million ECUs on fifteen members of a liner conference, including one fine of over 41 million ECUs, two of 27.5 million ECUs and four of over 20 million ECUs. In *British Sugar*[218] the fines totalled 50.2 million ECUs, including 39.6 million imposed on one undertaking.

---

[211] There is a problem with fining associations of undertakings, as although the turnover to be considered is that of the members of the association, Reg. 17, Art. 15 does not provide for the members to be jointly and severally liable. This can cause problems in collecting the fine (see Joined Cases T–213/95 and T–18/96, *SCK and FNK* v. *Commission* [1997] ECR I–1739). The Commission's White Paper on Modernization [1999] OJ C132/1, paras. 127–128, proposes that the new implementing Reg. should provide for such liability.

[212] [2000] 4 CMLR 963.

[213] W.Wils, 'The Commission's New Method for Calculating Fines in Antitrust Cases' (1998) 23 *ELRev.* 252, nn. 20 and 21.

[214] See eg., the decision to add 20% for aggravating circumstances in *Volkswagen* [1998] OJ L124/60, [1998] 5 CMLR 33.

[215] [1998] OJ L124/60, [1998] 5 CMLR 33 (the decision was dated 28 Jan. 1998, the Guidelines on Fines were published in the Official Journal on 14 Jan. 1998[1998] OJ C9/3).

[216] It was reduced by the CFI on appeal to 90 million ECUs, but only because part of the decision was annulled.

[217] *TACA* (*Transatlantic Conference Agreement*) [1998] OJ L95/1, [1999] 4 CMLR 1415.

[218] *British Sugar* [1999] OJ L76/1, [1999] 4 CMLR 1316.

Volkswagen concerned the car-maker's actions in preventing exports of its cars from Italy to other Member States. The Commission considered this compartmentalization of the common market to be a 'very serious' offence meriting a fine of 50 million ECUs. It found the infringement to have lasted for over ten years, and the duration element was fixed at 35 million, giving a total base figure of ECU 85 millions. Aggravating features included continuing despite warnings from the Commission while representing to the Commission that the infringements had ended, and putting pressure on dealers to comply with the policy. This meant that an increase of 20 per cent in the basic amount 'appears justified'.[219] That added 17 million to the ECU 85 millions base, making 102 million ECUs in all. There were no exenuating circumstances. The dealers were considered 'victims' who had acted under duress, often to their own disadvantage,[220] and were not fined. The CFI reduced the fine to ECU 90 millions because it held that the Commission had not proved that the infringements lasted for more than three years. It did *not* reduce the fine proportionately because the shorter duration did not diminish the gravity of the infringement.[221]

The TACA was fined for infringing Article 81(1) by fixing prices and other terms and conditions ('serious') and for infringing Article 82 by altering the competitive structure ('very serious').[222] In calculating the fines the Commission took into account the value of the services directly affected (ECU 3.2 billions assessed by reference to turnover), and the profits of the TACA members and the price increases. The duration was two to three years and this resulted in an increase of 25 per cent. The fines imposed varied between the members because the Commission divided them into four groups according to size and graduated the fines accordingly. This was in line with the coda to Section 1.A. of the Notice.

British Sugar concerned concerted practices on the British sugar market aimed at price co-ordination between the two producers active there and two merchants. In view of what they were trying to do the infringement was categorized as intentional[223] and 'serious'.[224] British Sugar, with the larger share of the market, was fined 18 million ECUs for gravity and Tate & Lyle ECU 10 millions. The merchants, in a position of dependence on the producers, were fined ECU 1.5 millions each. The duration was 'medium' (four years) which resulted in another ECU 7.2 millions for British Sugar, 4 million for Tate & Lyle and 0.5 million each for the merchants. British Sugar's fine was increased by 75 per cent (ECU 18.9 millions) for aggravating circumstances which included being the ringleader and, interestingly, for acting contrary to its own compliance programme, the adoption of which had been taken into account in mitigation when British Sugar's conduct was the subject of a previous Article 82 action.[225] The fact that this infringement overlapped with the earlier one and occurred on the same market also aggravated the offence. Tate & Lyle, on the other hand, was given a reduction of 50 per cent for co-operating with the Commission's investigation.[226]

---

[219] *Volkswagen* [1998] OJ L124/60, [1998] S CMLR 33, para. 221.

[220] *Ibid.*, para 208.

[221] Case T–62/98, *Volkswagen AG* v. *Commission*, [2000] 5 CMLR 853, para. 347.

[222] See Chap. 11.

[223] For the question of intention, see *supra* 902.

[224] *British Sugar* [1999] OJ L76/1, [1999] 4 CMLR 1316, para. 193: while the Commission concluded that the collusion consisted in a 'collaborative strategy of higher pricing' it admitted that there was insufficient evidence to state that prices were jointly fixed.

[225] *Napier Brown-British Sugar* [1988] OJ L284/41, [19990] 4 CMLR 196: see *supra* Chap. 7.

[226] By analogy with the Notice on the non-imposition of fines in cartel cases [1996] OJ C207/4, as the events preceded the publication of that Notice: see *infra* 921.

In the *Pre-Insulated Pipe Cartel*[227] a fine of ECU 70 millions was imposed on one under-taking (50 million for gravity and 20 million for duration) for the organization of the cartel 'conceived, approved and directed at a senior level of group management as were the measures to deny and conceal its existence and to continue its operation for nine months after the investigation'.[228] It would have been ECU 100 millions had it not been given a 30 per cent reduction under the Leniency Notice for co-operating with the investigation.[229] The cartel concerned district heating pipes and the fine appeared to exceed the turnover of that division of the undertaking.

As explained above, the CFI can change the fine imposed by the Commission and the ECJ can change the fine set by the CFI. In *Baustahlgewebe*[230] the CFI reduced the fine of ECU 4.5 millions set by the Commission to 3 million because it annulled the decision in respect of one of the agreements which the Commission had found the undertaking had entered into, and the ECJ[231] reduced it by another 50,000 to reflect the unacceptably excessive duration of the proceedings before the CFI.

(vii) LIABILITY FOR FINES

The question of the liability of successor undertakings for infringements is considered in Chapter 3. The way in which this can result in liability for an 'innocent' company is demon-strated by *British Sugar*. British Sugar's management was replaced soon after the infringing events and the company was later acquired by another. This was irrelevant to the calculation of the fine and the Commission reiterated the principle that the purchaser of a company acquires its liabilities, including that arising from infringements of the competition rules.[232]

(viii) THE PAYMENT AND COLLECTION OF FINES

The payment of fines is enforceable pursuant to Article 256 (ex Article 192) of the Treaty which provides that enforcement of decisions of the Council or Commission which impose a pecuniary obligation on persons other than States shall be governed by the rules of civil procedure in force in the State in the territory of which it is carried out. Member States must designate a relevant national authority for enforcement purposes.[233] Decisions normally give the undertakings concerned three months in which to pay the fine and specify a bank account into which it is to be paid. They normally state that interest becomes payable after the specified time.[234] A challenge to the decision before the Court does not operate to

---

[227] [1999] 4 CMLR 402.

[228] *Ibid.*, para. 169.

[229] Notice on the non-imposition of fines in cartel cases [1996] OJ C207/4.

[230] Case T–145/89, *Baustahlgewebe GmbH* v. *Commission* [1995] ECR II–987.

[231] Case C–185/95P, *Baustahlgewebe GmbH* v. *Commission* [1998] ECR I–8417, [1999] 4 CMLR 1203.

[232] *British Sugar* [1999] OJ L76/1, para. 211. And see W.Wils, 'The Undertaking as Subject of EC Competi-tion Law and the Imputation of Infringements to Natural or Legal Persons' (2000) 25 *ELRev.* 99, 114–16.

[233] The UK has designated the High Court (the Court of Session in Scotland) pursuant to the European Communities (Enforcement of Community Judgments) Order SI 1972/1590. Fines are enforced as if they were judgments of the UK courts.

[234] The payment of interest was approved by the ECJ in Case 107/82, *AEG-Telefunken* v. *Commission* [1983] ECR 3151, [1984] 3 CMLR 325; see also the CFI in Case T–275/94, *Groupement des Cartes Bancaires CB* v. *Commission* [1995] ECR II–216.

suspend the payment of the fine but the Commission usually agrees to defer enforcing it pending the outcome of the appeal if the undertakings agree to pay interest on it and provide a bank guarantee.

(ix) NOTICE ON THE NON-IMPOSITION OR REDUCTION OF FINES IN CARTEL CASES

In 1996 the Commission published a Notice sometimes called the 'Leniency Notice' or 'Whistleblower's' Notice'[235] stating that in the event of participants in cartels giving information to the Commission and co-operating with it in the investigation they can expect a reduction in the fine which would otherwise be imposed, or even no fine at all. The Commission has serious problems in detecting cartels and in proving them to the standard required by the Court, particularly where oligopolistic industries are concerned and the participants plead the 'oligopoly defence'.[236]

Although the Commission has the Regulation 17, Article 14(3) inspection powers described above,[237] obtaining direct evidence of a cartel is much easier if some of the participants can be induced to turn 'Queen's evidence'. In *Cartonboard* one of the ringleaders 'spontaneously admitted' the infringement and provided detailed evidence to the Commission.[238] Its fine was reduced by two-thirds to ECU 11.25 millions, representing 3 per cent of its turnover in the Community cartonboard market for the relevant year, rather than the 9 per cent suffered by the other ringleaders.[239] The Notice puts such a practice on a systematic footing and offers undertakings involved in cartels certain specific degrees of leniency in return for co-operation at various stages of the investigation. It is an unabashed attempt to encourage 'whistleblowing' by appealing to undertakings' self-interest.

The Notice identifies certain stages at which the undertaking can offer information and/or co-operation and stipulates what reduction in the fine can be expected at each stage and the conditions which must be fulfilled. It is modelled on (although significantly different from) the US Department of Justice's Corporate Leniency Policy Notice.[240] There are three levels of co-operation and therefore reduction.

Notice on the non-imposition or reduction of fines in cartel cases [1996] OJ C207/4, [1996] 5 CMLR 362

B. *Non-imposition of a fine or a very substantial reduction in its amount*

An enterprise which:

(a) informs the Commission about a secret cartel before the Commission has undertaken an

---

[235] Commission Notice on the non-imposition of fines in cartel cases [1996] OJ C204/14.

[236] See *supra* Chap. 11.

[237] See *supra* 861–862.

[238] [1994] OJ L243/1, [1994] 5 CMLR 547, para. 171.

[239] See the discussion in the CFI judgments in the appeals from the decision, e.g. Case T–319/94, *Fiskeby Board AB* v. *Commission*, [1998] ECR II–1331 paras. 86–104.

[240] 10 Aug. 1993. It relates only to corporate immunity from the *criminal* penalties which apply in US antitrust. See S. Hornsby and J. Hunter, 'New Incentives for "Whistleblowing": Will the EC Commission's Notice Bear Fruit?' [1997] *ECLR* 38.

investigation, ordered by decision, of the enterprises involved, provided that it does not already have sufficient information to establish the existence of the alleged cartel;

(b)   is the first to adduce decisive evidence of the cartel's existence;

(c)   puts an end to its involvement in the illegal activity no later than the time at which it discloses the cartel;

(d)   provides the Commission with all the relevant information and all the documents and evidence available to it regarding the cartel and maintains continuous and complete co-operation throughout the investigation;

(e)   has not compelled another enterprise to take part in the cartel and has not acted as an instigator or played a determining role in the illegal activity,

will benefit from a reduction of at least 75% of the fine or even from total exemption from the fine that would have been imposed if they had not co-operated.

C. *Substantial reduction in a fine*

Enterprises which both satisfy the conditions set out in Section B, points (b) and (e) and disclose the secret cartel after the Commission has undertaken an investigation ordered by decision on the premises of the parties to the cartel which has failed to provide sufficient grounds for initiating the procedure leading to a decision, will benefit from a reduction of 50% to 75% of the fine.

D. *Significant reduction in a fine*

1.   Where an enterprise co-operates without having met all the conditions set out in Sections B or C, it will benefit from a reduction of 10% to 50% of the fine that would have been imposed if it had not co-operated.

2.   Such cases may include the following:

      — before a statement of objections is sent, an enterprise provides the Commission with information, documents or other evidence which materially contribute to establishing the existence of the infringement;

      — after receiving a statement of objections, an enterprise informs the Commission that it does not substantially contest the facts on which the Commission bases its allegations.

It will be seen from this how onerous are the conditions which must be fulfilled before the maximum reduction of at least 75 per cent applies. The undertaking must approach the Commission *before* the latter commences an investigation by decision, must be the *first* to adduce decisive evidence, and the Commission must not already have sufficient evidence to establish the cartel's existence. This requires some degree of guesswork by the undertaking (how does it know it is the first and whether or not the Commission has sufficient evidence already?) and faith in the Commission's judgement of what is decisive and sufficient.[241] There is a wide discretion given to the Commission in the amount of the reduction: under the lowest level of co-operation, D, it can be between 10 per cent and 50 per cent, a huge variation when tens of millions of Euro are in issue. The Notice was published before the Guidelines on setting fines, but even under the Notice the Commission still has considerable discretion in setting the base figure for gravity, so undertakings cannot know at the time they may contemplate whistleblowing from what they can expect a reduction. However,

---

[241] See the comments by S. Hornsby and J. Hunter, 'New Incentives for "Whistleblowing": Will the EC Commissioners Notice Bear Fruit' [1997] *ECLR* 38, who suggest that the degree of uncertainty in the Notice may be counter-productive.

although not technically legislation, Section E.1. recognizes that it creates legitimate expect-ations so the Commission must honour it,[242] but only so long as the undertaking continues to meet all the criteria and to co-operate. The Notice does not affect undertakings' civil liability, and as a final sting in the tail the Commission says (Section E.4) that if it reduces the fine in accordance with the Notice and the undertaking then contests the facts for the first time in an appeal to the CFI, it will request the Court to *increase* the fine.

The Notice was applied in the *Pre-Insulated Pipe Cartel*.[243] One of the ringleaders came under Section D because it had co-operated only from when the Commission had sent out detailed requests for information under Article 11. Its fine was reduced by 30 per cent rather than the maximum 50 per cent available under Section D. It is clear from the treatment of two other companies that the Commission does require some active co-operation for Sec-tion D to apply, and it described those two companies as being 'on the borderline between active co-operation with the Commission and merely admitting what could not be denied'.[244] They received a 20 per cent reduction. Another company received no reduction because, despite some ultimate co-operation, it had been guilty of a 'systematic attempt to mislead the Commission as to the true relationship between the companies in the group' which 'constituted a deliberate obstruction of the Commission's investigations'. In *British Sugar*[245] the Notice was applied by analogy to events which preceded it[246] and Tate & Lyle was considered to have met the conditions in Section B (a)–(c), but not (d) because it had not 'maintained continuous and complete co-operation with the Commission throughout the investigation'. It was therefore treated as falling within D.2. and given a 50 per cent reduction, in view of the value of the information it had provided.[247]

8. INFORMAL SETTLEMENTS

A. GENERAL

In many cases the Commission does not proceed to a formal decision but terminates the matter informally. Comfort letters in respect of notified agreements were dealt with in Chapter 4. In some cases there is an 'administrative closure of the file' where the Commis-sion ceases to pursue the matter, for example because it concludes that there is no infringe-ment of the rules or because any infringement is insignificant and does not merit the expenditure of resources upon it.[248] Cases may also be terminated informally because the

---

[242] Legitimate expectation being a general principle of Community law, breach of which is a ground for the annulment of a decision under Art. 234: see *infra* 931–932.

[243] [1999] 4 CMLR 402.

[244] *Ibid.*, para. 180.

[245] [1999] 4 CMLR 1316.

[246] So the Notice was applied by extension *ratione temporis*: see *ibid.*, para. 212.

[247] *Ibid.*, paras. 217–218. Tate and Lyle appealed against this finding. It claims that the Commission's assertion that it had failed to maintain continuous and complete co-operation was incorrect: Case T–202/98, *Tate & Lyle* v. *Commission* (pending).

[248] For the position of complainants when the complaint is not pursued, see *infra* Chap. 14.

Commission and the parties have come to a settlement. This is usually because the companies have made enough concessions to satisfy the Commission, and the latter considers that nothing will be gained by pursuing a formal proceeding any further. The settlement may be reached before or after the Statement of Objections.

B. SETTLEMENTS AND UNDERTAKINGS

Settlements which include the parties giving undertakings to the Commission have become increasingly important as part of the enforcement mechanism. Several important cases have been terminated in this way, such as *IBM*,[249] *Microsoft*,[250] *Digital*,[251] and *Deutsche Telekom Tariffs*.[252] This procedure can be attractive to both sides. Undertakings can involve positive measures of the type included in decisions, but if they relate to the future the Commission is not thereby estopped from taking proceedings in respect of past conduct.[253] One disadvantage to the development of the law, however, is that it can mean that highly contentious matters are not fought out to the end and never reach the Court. *IBM*, for example, concerned access to technology, *Microsoft* concerned licensing terms, and the *Digital* settlement involved the assumption that Digital was not entitled to tie its software packages together, even though it was not dominant in the primary market.[254] Settlements are frequently publicized, in Commission press releases, in law reports, and in the Commission's annual reports, and inevitably they can attain the status of precedent. Clearly they are valuable guidance to other companies on what is acceptable to the Commission but of their nature they involve compromise and concession.

9. THE ROLE OF NATIONAL COMPETITION AUTHORITIES IN THE COMMISSION'S ENFORCEMENT PROCEDURES

A. GENERAL

The Commission encourages the participation of the national authorities in the enforcement of EC law. As explained in Chapter 2 it has long wished to decentralize enforcement and the 1997 Notice on co-operation between national competition authorities and the Commission[255] attempted to strengthen the relationship between national and Community

---

[249] [1984] 3 CMLR 147.

[250] Commission Press Release IP(94)653 [1994] 5 CMLR 143.

[251] Commission Press Release IP/97/868.

[252] Commission's *XXVIIth Report on Competition Policy* (Commission, 1997), pt 77.

[253] See the discussion in C.S. Kerse, *EC Antitrust Procedure* (4th edn., Sweet & Maxwell, 1998), para. 6.64.

[254] See the discussion of these cases *supra* in Chap. 7.

[255] [1997] OJ C313/3.

enforcement. The 1999 White Paper proposals would give national competition authorities a greatly enhanced role. The present involvement of national competition authorities in various aspects of the Commission's enforcement procedures has been noted at in the relevant points in the previous sections of this chapter. This section summarizes this involvement.

B. INVESTIGATIONS AND HEARINGS

Under Regulation 17, Article 11(2) the Commission has to inform the national authorities of requests to undertakings to provide information under that Article: it must 'forward a copy of the request to the competent authority of the Member State in whose territory the seat of the undertaking or association of undertakings is situated'. It must likewise, under Article 11(6), forward copies of Article 11(5) decisions demanding information.

Under Article 14(2) the Commission 'in good time before the investigation' must tell the national authorities when it is going to conduct an Article 14(2) investigation and inform them of the identity of the investigating officials. According to Article 14(4) the Commission can take a decision ordering an Article 14(3) 'dawn raid' only after 'consultation with' the national authority on whose territory it is to take place. This consultation does not have to be in writing; in an emergency a telephone conversation will suffice.[256] The obligation is only to consult, and not to follow any advice or opinion of the national authority. The national authority's officials may be asked to assist the Commission officials in carrying out the investigation (Article 14(5)) and may be involved in the Member State 'affording the necessary assistance' to them under Article 14(6) where the undertaking opposes the investigation.[257]

Regulation 17, Article 19 provides for the hearing of parties and third persons and states in paragraph 2 if the Commission *or the competent authorities of the Member States* consider it necessary they shall hear third persons. Article 11(2) of the Hearing Regulation[258] says that the Commission shall invite the competent authorities of the Member States to take part in the oral hearing.

Regulation 17, Article 13 contains a little-used power for the Commission to request the competent authorities of the Member States not to *assist* with investigations but*themselves* to carry out Article 14(1) and (3) investigations, which the Commission thinks are necessary. The national officials may be assisted by Commission officials. This procedure was first used in the UK in 1992 during investigations into the PVC cartel.[259]

---

[256] Case 53/85 *AKZO* v. *Commission* [1986] ECR 1965, [1987] 1 CMLR 231, paras. 20–23.

[257] See *supra* 868–869.

[258] Reg. 2842/98 [1998] OJ L354/18.

[259] Under s. 61 of the Competition Act 1998 a 'Director's investigation' is one conducted by the Director General of Fair Trading at the request of the Commission and a 'Director's special investigation' is one conducted at the request of the Commission in connection with a Commission investigation.

C. GIVING AND RECEIVING INFORMATION

Regulation 17, Article 10(1) provides that the Commission shall send to the competent authorities of the Member States copies of applications for negative clearance, of notifications for exemption and of 'the most important documents' lodged with it for the purpose of establishing infringements. Article 10(2) says that the Commission should carry out its procedures in close and constant liaison with the competent authorities, which have the right to express their views on the Commission's procedure. The Commission sends to the competent authorities copies of a number of other documents, including Statements of Objections, reasons for not following up a complaint, Article 15(6) preliminary decisions withdrawing immunity from fines, written submissions by the undertakings and third parties on these documents, and records of hearings. Member States are also informed about the transmission of information under international co-operation agreements such as the EC/US Co-operation Agreements of 1995 and 1998.[260] For the issue of confidentiality in respect of information sent by the Commission to national authorities see the *Spanish Banks* case, above.[261]

Regulation 17, Article 11(1) states that in carrying out its duties the Commission 'may obtain all necessary information from the Governments and competent authorities of the Member States the Member States'.

D. EXEMPTIONS

As explained in Chapter 2 the Member States have a duty to enforce the competition rules before the coming into force of implementing legislation empowering the Commission, and by Regulation 17, Article 9(3), remain competent to apply Articles 81(1) and 82 until the Commission has initiated a proceeding. They may not grant Article 81(3) exemptions. They can, however, insist on the Commission opposing an agreement claiming the benefit of an opposition procedure.[262] The competent authorities are given a new power by Article 7 of the block exemption on vertical restraints, Regulation 2790/99, which allows them to *withdraw* the benefit of the block exemption from an agreement in respect of their territory or part of it which 'has all the characteristics of a distinct geographic market'.[263]

---

[260] See *infra* Chap. 17.

[261] Case C–67/91 *Dirección General de Defensa de las Competencia* v. *Asociación España de Banca Privada* (*AEB*) *and others* (*Spanish Banks*) [1992] ECR 4785; see *supra* 891. For the problems with this in connection with the White Paper proposals, see *infra* Chap. 16.

[262] See *supra* Chap. 4

[263] For Reg. 2790/1999 [1999] OJ L336/21, see *supra* Chap. 9.

10. SECTOR INQUIRIES

Regulation 17, Article 12 provides for the Commission to conduct general inquiries into a sector of the economy if:

the trend of trade between Member States, price movements, inflexibility of prices or other circumstances suggest that in the economic sector concerned competition is being restricted or distorted within the common market. . . .

To this end the Commission has the powers to require information and carry out inspections contained in Articles 11 and 14 and the Commission may request national authorities to carry out investigations under Article 13. This provision has rarely been used in the past, but in the White Paper on Modernization the Commission states that it would be more important if notification was abolished, because detection of infringements would rely largely on surveillance of the market.[264]

11. JUDICIAL REVIEW

A. GENERAL

Commission competition decisions can be challenged before the Court in an action for annulment under Article 230 (ex Article 173).[265] Although these actions are colloquially called 'appeals' they are in fact judicial review proceedings. The details of judicial review differ between EC law and national laws but the essence is the same: the legality of action taken by administrative authorities is determined by an independent, impartial judicial body. Being judicial review it is not the function of the Court to substitute its own judgment for that of the Commission but to ensure that the Commission keeps within the bounds of its powers and discretions and observes the law. It does not entail a rehearing. The question of the intensity of the review in which the Court engages in Article 230 actions is an issue across all areas of Community law but particularly so in competition law, where the delegation of powers by the Council to the Commission is so extensive. Since 1989 Article 230 actions in competition cases have gone to the CFI with an appeal on a point of law to the ECJ. The CFI has examined the factual basis for the Commission's decisions with particular rigour. As the Commission is not a tribunal for the purposes of Article 6(1) of the ECHR the supervision by the Court must satisfy the requirement for a fair and public hearing before an independent and impartial tribunal if the competition proceedings are to comply with the Convention.[266]

---

[264] White Paper on modernisation of the rules implementing Articles 85 and 86 [now 81 and 82]of the EC Treaty [1999] OJ C132/1, para. 115.

[265] Art. 232 (ex Art. 175), providing for an action for failure to act, is of limited application in competition law, as elsewhere, but can be relevant with regard to complainants: see further *supra* Chap. 15.

[266] See *supra* 877 and *infra* 941.

Under Article 229 (ex Article 172) the Court has 'unlimited jurisdiction' in respect of fines and penalties imposed by the Commission in competition cases.

B. ARTICLE 230

Article 230 says:

The Court of Justice shall review the legality of acts adopted jointly by the European Parliament and the Council, of acts of the Council, of the Commission and of the ECB, other than recommendations and opinions, and of acts of the European Parliament intended to produce legal effects *vis-à-vis* third parties.

It shall for this purpose have jurisdiction in actions brought by a Member State, the Council or the Commission on grounds of lack of competence, infringement of an essential procedural requirement, infringement of this Treaty or of any rule of law relating to its application, or misuse of powers.

The Court of Justice shall have jurisdiction under the same conditions in actions brought by the European Parliament, by the Court of Auditors and by the ECB for the purpose of protecting their prerogatives.

Any natural or legal person may, under the same conditions, institute proceedings against a decision addressed to that person or against a decision which, although in the form of a regulation or a decision addressed to another person, is of direct and individual concern to the former.

The proceedings provided for in this Article shall be instituted within two months of the publication of the measure, or of its notification to the plaintiff, or, in the absence thereof, of the day on which it came to the knowledge of the latter, as the case may be.

The issues which arise from this provision are:

- is there a challengeable act?
- does the natural or legal person wishing to make the challenge have standing to do so?
- are there grounds for annulling the act?

There is a short time limit (two months from publication or notification) for bringing an action. The limit is strictly adhered to. The position of addressees who do not appeal is illustrated by that of the undertakings in *Wood Pulp* which were not party to the challenge.[267]

C. *LOCUS STANDI*—WHO CAN BRING AN ACTION

The Member States and the Council and Commission are 'privileged applicants' who have standing to challenge any act.[268] Any other natural or legal person has limited standing, able only to challenge a decision actually addressed to it, or a decision which is of 'direct and individual concern' to it although in the form of a regulation or a decision addressed to *another* person.[269]

---

[267] Case C–51/92P, *Commission* v. *Assidomän Kraft Products AB and others* [1999] 5 CMLR 1253: see *infra* 934.

[268] Art. 230(2). By para. (3) the Parliament, the Court of Auditors, and the European Central Bank may bring actions to protect their prerogatives.

[269] *Ibid.*, para. 4.

There is no problem about parties who seek to challenge acts of the Commission which are addressed to them. The problems arise concerning the rights of persons to challenge acts in the form of regulations or decisions addressed to other persons, and the issue has generated a large body of case law.[270] Competition cases do not usually involve the thorny questions when private persons may challenge regulations or challenge decisions addressed to Member States enabling the latter to take further action. They normally involve the simpler question when a person may challenge a decision addressed to another person, such as the grant of an Article 81(3) exemption. The test formulated by the ECJ for deciding when a person is directly and individually concerned in a decision addressed to another is whether that decision 'affects them by reason of certain attributes which are peculiar to them or by reason of circumstances in which they are differentiated from all other persons and by virtue of these factors distinguishes them individually just as in the case of the person addressed'.[271]

The Court first allowed standing to a non-addressee of a decision in *Metro I*,[272] in respect of a party who had complained under Regulation 17, Article 3(2) (b), and who objected to the granting of an exemption. In *Metro II*[273] it widened the 'complainant' category to cover a party who had not *formally* complained but who had taken part in the Commission's proceedings both before and after the publication of the Article 19(3) notice, and been recognized by the Commission as having a 'legitimate interest'. The applicant in both *Metro* cases was a retailer who was excluded by the provisions of SABA's exempted selective distribution system from distributing SABA products. *Métropole*[274] shows how widely the CFI is prepared to cast the standing net. Antena 3, a TV service, was refused admission to the EBU as an active member before the Commission adopted a decision exempting the EBU's rules. Antena 3 brought an action to have the decision annulled. The Commission argued that it was not individually and directly concerned and had not submitted observations following the publication of the Article 19(3) notice. The CFI, however, held that taking part in the administrative proceedings was not a prerequisite for being accorded standing, and that its application to join the EBU distinguished Antena 3 in the same way as if it were an addressee of the decision.

On the other hand, in *Kruidvat*[275] the Commission denied standing to a retailer who wished to challenge the Article 81(3) exemption of Givenchy's selective distribution network. It had taken no part in the Commission proceedings, had not complained to the Commission, had not applied to become a member of Givenchy's network, and did not wish to be one.[276] It was simply a competitor of Givenchy's authorized distributors. The Commission said that to grant Kruidvat standing would be to 'allow a practically limitless number of actions from unforeseeable sources to be brought'. The CFI agreed and said

---

[270] See P. Craig and G. de Búrca, *EU Law: Text, Cases and Materials* (2nd edn., Oxford University Press, 1998), chap. 11.

[271] Case 25/62, *Plaumann & Co v. Commission* [1963] ECR 95, [1964] CMLR 29.

[272] Case 26/76, *Metro-SB-Grossmärkte GmbH v. Commission (No 1)* [1977] ECR 1875, [1978] 2 CMLR 1.

[273] Case 75/84, *Metro-SB-Grossmärkte GmbH v. Commission (No 2)* [1986] ECR 3021, [1987] 1 CMLR 118.

[274] Cases T–528, 542, 543, 546/93, *Métropole Télévision v. Commission* [1996] ECR II–652, [1996] 5 CMLR 386.

[275] Case T–87/92 *BVBA Kruidvat v. Commission* [1996] ECR II–1851, [1997] 4 CMLR 1046.

[276] Its parent company was a member of a trade association which *had* participated, although the views of the association and of Kruidvat materially differed.

that individual concern could not be established on the basis that the legality of the decision might affect indirectly related national proceedings. The distinction between this case and *Métropole* is that in the latter the applicant was actually being denied access to the market, and it is submitted that a party in that position is likely to be accorded standing.[277]

D. WHICH ACTS CAN BE CHALLENGED

It is not just formal decisions which can be challenged, but also other 'acts' taken by the Commission in the course of its procedures. This is important in competition proceedings, where parties may receive letters signed by senior officials, rather than actual decisions.

The basic principle, laid down in *ERTA*,[278] is that Article 230 covers 'all measures adopted by the institutions which are intended to have legal force'. This was applied in *IBM*[279] where an undertaking wished to challenge the Statement of Objections. The Court said:

9.   Any measure the legal effects of which are binding on, and capable of affecting the interests of, the applicant by bringing about a distinct change in his legal position is an act or decision which may be the object of an action under Article [230] for a declaration that it is void.

The test here is: does the act change the applicant's legal position? The Statement of Objections does not do so; it is merely a preparatory act and any irregularity can be dealt with in a challenge to the act which concludes the proceedings. For the same reasons an Article 19(3) notice, whereby the Commission indicates it intends to adopt a favourable position with regard to a notified agreement and invites third party comments, cannot be challenged.[280] However, an Article 15(6) communication withdrawing the immunity from fines may be challenged,[281] as may interim decisions.[282] Where complaints are concerned, 'Article 6' letters cannot be challenged but the final rejection of the complaint can be, even if it is only in the form of a letter.[283]

E. THE GROUNDS OF REVIEW

(i) GENERAL

Article 230 provides four grounds of challenge, although they are all really encompassed in the third one, the infringement of the Treaty or of any rule of law relating to its application. The fourth ground, misuse of powers (*détournement de pouvoir*) means that the Community institution has used its powers other than for the purpose for which they were conferred. A challenge on this ground very rarely succeeds as the burden on the applicant is a heavy one,

---

[277] See C.S. Kerse, *EC Antitrust Procedure* (4th edn., Sweet & Maxwell, 1998), para. 9.05.
[278] Case 22/70, *Commission* v. *Counci,l Re ERTA* [1971] ECR 263, [1971] CMLR 335.
[279] Case 60/81, *IBM* v. *Commission* [1981] ECR 2639, [1981] 3 CMLR 635.
[280] Case T–74/92, *Ladbroke* v. *Commission* [1995] ECR II–115, para 72.
[281] Cases 8–11/66, *SA Cimenteries CBR* v. *Commission* [1967] ECR 75.
[282] Case T–19/91 *Vichy* v. *Commission* [1992] ECR II–415, para. 68.
[283] See *infra* Chap. 15.

and one has never succeeded in a competition case.[284] Given the large degree of overlap, the Court often does not specify under which heading the reasons for an annulment fall.

(ii) LACK OF COMPETENCE

This is the EC equivalent of the English concept, *ultra vires*. It covers: the lack of competence of the Community to act at all, because no Treaty provision has empowered it to do so; the lack of competence of the institutions to act under a particular empowering provision; and the lack of competence of the particular institution or official to take the challenged act.

In the competition field the best example of the first situation is challenges made to the extraterritorial application of the competition rules. Undertakings outside the Community have argued that the Community could not apply its rules to them because they were outside the jurisdiction. These challenges have not succeeded.[285]

The second situation is exemplified in the challenges brought by Member States to directives adopted by the Commission on the basis of Article 86(3), where they claimed that the Commission should instead have used the harmonization of laws provisions, which would have involved going through the Council where the States could have influenced proceedings.[286]

The third situation has arisen in competition cases where parties have alleged that the power to take decisions was unlawfully delegated. The delegation to the Commissioner responsible for competition of the power to take decisions ordering 'dawn raid' inspections under Regulation 17, Article 14(3) was unsuccessfully challenged in *AKZO*,[287] and the delegation of the signing of documents such as Statements of Objections has likewise been upheld.[288] However, a challenge to the adoption of a final Decision finding an infringement by a single Commissioner succeeded in the *PVC* cartel case where a challenge to a decision on both competence and infringement of an essential procedural requirement grounds spectacularly succeeded.[289]

The issue of lack of competence is a matter of public interest and should therefore be raised by the Court of its on motion.[290]

(iii) INFRINGEMENT OF AN ESSENTIAL PROCEDURAL REQUIREMENT

Infringement of an essential procedural requirement covers situations where a measure has been passed without complying with the legislative process laid down by the Treaty,[291] or

---

[284] Although it has been pleaded: see e.g. Case 5/85, *AKZO Chemie BV* v. *Commission* [1986] ECR 2585, [1987] 3 CMLR 716; Case, T–5/93, *Roger Tremblay* v. *Commission* [1995] ECR II–185.

[285] See Chap. 17.

[286] See Case C–202/88, *France* v. *Commission* (*Telecommunications Equipment*) [1991] ECR I–1223; Cases C–271, 281 & 289/90, *Spain, Belgium & Italy* v. *Commission* (*Telecommunications Services*) [1992] ECR I–5833: see *supra* Chap. 8.

[287] Case 5/85, *AKZO Chemie BV* v. *Commission* [1986] ECR 2585, [1987] 3 CMLR 716: see *supra* **.

[288] See Case 48/69, *ICI* v. *Commission* (*Dyestuffs*) [1972] ECR 619, [1972] CMLR 557.

[289] Cases T–79/89 etc., *BASF and others* v. *Commission* [1992] ECR II–315, [1992] 4 CMLR 357, on appeal to the ECJ, Cases C–137/92P etc., *Commission* v. *BASF and others* [1994] ECR I–2555: see *infra* 931.

[290] Cases T–79/89 etc., *BASF and others* v. *Commission* [1992] ECR II–315, [1992] 4 CMLR 357, para. 31.

[291] As where Parliament is not consulted: Case 138/79 *Roquette Frères* v. *Council* [1980] ECR 3333.

with the rules of procedure of the relevant institution,[292] or with a general principle of law concerned with procedure,[293] or where the measure does not contain an adequate statement of reasons contrary to Article 253 (ex Article 190). Inadequate statements of reasons and breaches of general principles of law guaranteeing procedural rights are also infringements of the Treaty or of any rule relating to its application but, as explained above, the Court is not concerned with categorization. The only issue is whether there is a defect which requires the act's annulment.

The Court annuls acts only for breach of an *essential* procedural requirement, and what amounts to such is a matter for the Court. A requirement is essential if the failure to observe it might have affected the final outcome of the act. On this basis the wrongful revelation of confidential material to the complainant in *AKZO*[294] was not a reason for annulling the Commission decision. An adequate statement of reasons is essential because it is necessary for the review process. As the ECJ said in *Germany v. Commission*:[295]

In imposing upon the Commission the obligation to state reasons for its decisions, Article [253] is not taking mere formal considerations into account but seeks to give an opportunity to the parties of defending their rights, to the Court of exercising its supervisory functions and to Member States and to all interested nationals of ascertaining the circumstances in which the Commission has applied the Treaty.

What amounts to adequate reasons depends on the context of the act. In an interlocking series of regulations the acts may refer to each other and the reasoning of the institutions may be deduced from them as a whole. In competition cases, where the Commission has wide discretion and a power of appraisal, the reasoning is of fundamental importance because in reviewing the decision the Court must be able to establish whether the factual and legal matters upon which the exercise of the power of appraisal depended were present.[296] The Commission has to deal properly with the parties' arguments. In the *Net Book Agreement* the Publishers' Association (PA) had argued that the resale price maintenance on books provided for in the Net Book Agreement should be allowed. It put forward as evidence the judgments of the UK Restrictive Practices Court (RPC) which permitted RPM on books in the UK and set out the benefits of such pricing. The ECJ annulled the decision because the Commission had not adequately dealt with this evidence.[297]

Challenges to competition decisions frequently plead procedural defects as grounds for annulment. The CFI annulled the *Soda-ash* decisions,[298] for example, on grounds that insufficient access to the Commission's file prejudiced the parties' right to be heard. The

---

[292] Case 68/86, *United Kingdom* v. *Council* [1988] ECR 855, [1988] 2 CMLR 543, and note the application of this in the *PVC cartel* case: Cases C–137/92P, *Commission* v. *BASF and others* [1994] ECR I–2555, discussed *infra* at 931.

[293] Such as the *audi alteram partem* rule giving parties a right to a hearing: Case 17/74, *Transocean Marine Paint* v. *Commission* [1974] ECR 1063, [1974] 2 CMLR 459: see the discussion *supra* 878.

[294] See *supra* 889–890.

[295] Case 24/62, *Germany* v. *Commission* [1963] ECR 63, [1963] CMLR 347.

[296] See K. Lenaerts and P. Van Nuffel, *Constitutional Law of the European Union* (Sweet & Maxwell,1999), paras. 14–085.

[297] Case C–360/92P, *Publishers' Association* v. *Commission* [1995] ECR II–23, [1995] 5 CMLR 33 setting aside the CFI judgment, Case T–66/89 *Publishers' Association* v. *Commission* [1992] ECR II–1995, [1992] 5 CMLR 120.

[298] Cases T–30/91 *Solvay SA* v. *Commission* [1995] ECR II–1775, [1996] 5 CMLR 57.

most celebrated case of annulment on procedural grounds (and of lack of competence), however, is the *PVC* case. There the CFI found differences in both the statement of reasons and the operative part of the decision between the version adopted by the College of Commissioners at its relevant meeting and the version notified to the undertakings concerned. The differences went beyond mere corrections of grammar and syntax. The Commission was unable to produce an authenticated version of the decision as adopted by the College. A draft in only three languages was available at the meeting, and the Competition Commissioner was authorized to adopt the measure in the other official Community languages, including those of undertakings to which the decision was addressed. Further, the Competition Commissioner whose signature appeared on the decision notified to all the addressees had left office some days before the notified version appeared to have been finalized. The CFI considered these procedural defects, including the breach of the principle of collegiate responsibility, so serious that it did not merely annul the decision, it declared it *non-existent*.[299] On appeal the ECJ held that the flaws were not so fundamental as to render the act non-existent. It put aside the judgment of the CFI, held that the decision existed, but annulled it.[300]

The Commission responded to the final annulment by adopting a new decision six weeks later. The undertakings again appealed, *inter alia* on the grounds that this breached the principle of double jeopardy, *non bis in idem*, and that the Commission had denied them the right to be heard by not sending a new Statement of Objections and holding new hearings. The CFI held that *non bis in idem* did not apply when the annulment was only on procedural grounds, and that given that the Court had not found any defects in the preparatory stages of the Commission's procedure, there was no need to repeat those stages. A right to be heard was necessary only in respect of matters which were not in the original decision.[301]

(iv) INFRINGEMENT OF THE TREATY OR ANY RULE OF LAW RELATING TO ITS APPLICATION

As noted above, this ground is so wide that it covers the other three grounds as well. 'The Treaty' means the Treaties establishing the Communities together with the Protocols, and Treaties and Acts of Accession. 'Any rule of law relating to its application' covers all the other

---

[299] Cases T–79/89 etc., *BASF* v. *Commission* [1992] ECR II–315, [1992] 4 CMLR 357.

[300] Cases C–137/92P, *Commission* v. *BASF and others* [1994] ECR I–2555. The *LdPE cartel* (low-density polyethylene) decision [1989] OJ L74/21, [1990] 4 CMLR 382 was annulled on similar grounds in Cases T–80/89 etc., *BASF* v. *Commission* [1995] ECR II–729. After the *PVC* judgment two of the undertakings concerned in the *Polypropylene Cartel*, who were challenging that decision in an action before the CFI in which the oral proceedings had already been closed, asked the CFI to reopen those proceedings so that they could enter pleas based on the *PVC* arguments. They claimed that the CFI had wrongfully failed to raise those issues of its own motion. The CFI refused and this was upheld by the ECJ: see Case C–234/92P, *Shell International Chemical Company Ltd* v. *Commission* [1999] 5 CMLR 1142 at paras. 66–68. The CFI did, however, annul a Commission decision in Cases T–31–32/91, *Solvay* v. *Commission* [1995] ECR II–1821 on non—authentication grounds. The applicants raised the plea after the close of the written procedure in the case, having read statements by Commission officials in the *Financial Times* and the *Wall Street Journal* that the Commission had been following the procedure condemned in the *PVC* case for the past 25 years. The annulment was upheld by the ECJ, Joined Cases C–287–288/95P, *Commission* v. *Solvay*, judgment 6 Apr. 2000.

[301] Cases T–305–307, 313–316, 318, 328–329, & 335/94, *Re the PVC Cartel II: Limburgse Vinyl Maatschappij NV and others* v. *Commission* [1999] 5 CMLR 303.

binding provisions of the Community legal order, including the general principles of law and human rights developed in the Court's jurisprudence, and provisions of international law, particularly principles of customary international law and agreements the Community itself has concluded.

The Court will therefore annul a decision where the Commission has misinterpreted the law or failed to abide by general principles of law such as proportionality, legitimate expectation, the presumption of innocence, or legal certainty.[302] The rights to due process described in the sections above and the right to confidentiality are such principles. However, this ground of annulment goes beyond misinterpreting or misapplying the law: it also covers the Court finding that the Commission committed a 'manifest error of appraisal'[303] and that the evidence relied on or the facts established by the Commission do not support the finding of law. This is crucial in competition cases, for it means that the Court *does* look at the facts, not to rehear the case but to see whether the factual basis of the Commission decision was correct or sufficient. It annuls decisions where it finds that the Commission drew the wrong conclusions from the facts. The Court can play an active role in fact-finding by ordering measures of inquiry such as experts' reports.

Continental Can was an early case where the Court annulled the decision because the Commission had failed to establish why a particular type of container should be considered a relevant market. This meant there was no basis for its finding of dominance and the application of Article 82, even though the Court confirmed the Commission's extensive interpretation of Article 82 to cover mergers.[304] In *Wood Pulp II*[305] the Court appointed experts to produce a report on parallelism of prices in the wood pulp industry, whether the documents relied on by the Commission justified their conclusions on the pricing and whether there was a distinction between the documents gathered before and after the Statement of Objections. A second experts' report into the structure and characteristics of the market was commissioned. These reports, particularly the finding that the market *was* oligopolistic, were crucial to the Court's judgment and it (largely) annulled the decision.

The CFI was established largely to relieve the ECJ of having to deal with complex issues of fact. In competition cases it has been assiduous in its examination of the factual basis of decisions. A leading example of this was its treatment of the *Italian Flat Glass* decision in *Società Italiana Vetro*[306] where the CFI subjected the Commission's documentary evidence to careful scrutiny and in the main found it seriously wanting. Two other striking examples of annulment are *Métropole*[307] and *European Night Services*.[308] In the former it annulled a decision because the Commission had not properly examined whether the fourth criterion for Article 81(3) exemption relating to the indispensability of restrictions was satisfied, and

---

[302] Legal certainty was cited in the *PVC* judgments (supra) as being infringed when the Commission did not follow its own rules of procedure and could not produce the authenticated decision.

[303] Case 42/84, *Remia & Nutricia* v. *Commission* [1985] ECR 2566, [1987] 1 CMLR 1, para. 34.

[304] Case 6/72, *Europemballage Corp & Continental Can Co Inc* v. *EC Commission* [1973] ECR 215 [1973] CMLR 199.

[305] Cases C–89/85 etc., *A. Ahlström Oy* v. *Commission* [1993] ECR I–1307, [1993] 4 CMLR 407; see *supra* Chap. 11.

[306] Cases T–68/89 etc., *Società Italiana Vetro Spa* v. *EC Commission* [1992] ECR II–1403, [1992] 5 CMLR 302.

[307] Cases T–528 etc./93, *Métropole Télévision* v. *Commission* [1996] ECR II–652, [1996] 5 CMLR 386.

[308] Cases T–374–375, 384 & 388/94, *European Night Services* v. *Commission* [1998] 5 CMLR 718; see *supra* Chap. 4.

had taken into account the criteria in Article 86(2) despite having decided that Article did not apply. The latter decision was annulled because the Commission had not analysed whether there *was* a restriction of competition, had applied the *de minimis* test in too mechanistic a manner, had unsatisfactorily defined the market, and had applied the essential facilities doctrine without explaining why the resources at issue could be considered essential facilities.

It is not only the CFI which takes this rigorous approach to the Commission's decisions. In the 1998 judgment on the Commission's application of the Merger Regulation to the *Kali—Salz* merger the ECJ took the view that the Commission's analysis of the post-merger market did not stand up to examination and that its evidence of the structural links between the parties was unconvincing. It therefore quashed the decision.[309]

On the other hand, the Court does not interfere with the exercise of the Commission's discretion in what are essentially matters of economic policy. This means that ultimately its control over competition policy is limited.[310] In addition, the Court itself is committed to interpreting Community law in a way which gives effect to the objectives of the Treaty. The great leaps forward which the Commission has made in the interpretation of the competition provisions have invariably been confirmed by the Court: the extension of the 'abuse' concept to cover mergers,[311] the development of the doctrine of collective dominance,[312] the idea that abuse and dominant position may be on different markets,[313] and the original finding that Article 81(1) applied equally to horizontal and vertical restraints.[314]

F. THE EFFECTS OF ANNULMENT

Article 231 (ex Article 174) says that if the action is well-founded, the ECJ shall 'declare the act concerned to be void'. However, if articles of the decision are severable, the Court can declare some void and leave others. This is often done. The Court cannot, however, substitute its own decision for that of the Commission. So, in *European Night Services*[315] the CFI refused to annul the conditions which the Commission had attached to the Article 81(3) exemption and leave the applicants with an unconditional decision. It annulled the decision completely.

Article 233 (ex Article 176) says:

---

[309] Cases C–68/94 & 30/95, *France & SCPA* v. *Commission* [1998] ECR I–1375, [1998] 4 CMLR 829; see *supra* Chap. 12.

[310] See V. Korah, *An Introductory Guide to EC Competition Law and Practice* (6th edn., Hart Publishing, 1997), 319–23.

[311] Case 6/72, *Europemballage Corp & Continental Can Co Inc* v. *EC Commission* [1973] ECR 215, [1973] CMLR 199, although the decision was annulled because the Commission had not defined the market sufficiently, see *supra* Chap. 6.

[312] Cases C–68/94 & 30/95, *France & SCPA* v. *Commission* [1998] ECR I–1375, [1998] 4 CMLR 829; see *supra* Chap. 11 and Chap. 12.

[313] Case C–333/94P, *Tetra Pak International SA* v. *Commission* [1996] ECR I–5951, [1997] 4 CMLR 662, see *supra* Chap. 7

[314] Cases 56 & 58, *Etablissements Consten SA & Grundig-Verkaufs-GmbH* v. *Commission* [1966] ECR 299, [1966] CMLR 418; see *supra* Chap. 3.

[315] Cases T–374–375, 384 & 388/94, *European Night Services* v. *Commission* [1998] 5 CMLR 718.

The institution or institutions whose act has been declared void or whose failure to act has been declared contrary to this Treaty shall be required to take the necessary measures to comply with the judgment of the Court of Justice.

This does not, however, mean that the Commission has to refund the fine of parties who did *not* challenge a decision annulled at the suit of other addressees. Twenty-eight of the thirty-six addresses of the *Wood Pulp* decision[316] brought an action for annulment. The ECJ annulled or reduced the fines imposed on the applicants.[317] Subsequently the other addressees requested the Commission to refund to them the fines they had paid pursuant to the annulled articles. The Commission refused. The ECJ upheld this: a decision finding an infringement of the competition rules addressed to each undertaking concerned individually can be annulled only as regards the addressees who have successfully challenged it before the Court. The other addressees had not challenged the decision within the two-month time-limit and it continued to be valid and binding on them.[318]

G. APPEALS FROM COURT OF FIRST INSTANCE TO THE COURT OF JUSTICE

An appeal lies from the CFI to the ECJ on a point of law. The ECJ does not enquire into the CFI's findings of fact. A point of law means the grounds of lack of competence of the CFI, a breach of procedure before it adversely affecting the interests of the applicant, or the infringement of Community law by the CFI.[319]

In *Baustahlgewebe*[320] the applicant claimed that the time the proceedings had taken before the CFI breached its right to legal process within a reasonable time. The ECJ accepted it had jurisdiction to consider this plea and held it was well-founded, as the CFI proceedings had involved taken thirty-two months between the end of the written procedure and the decision to open the oral procedure and twenty-two months between the oral procedure and the judgment. As the delay had not prejudiced the outcome of the proceedings, however, the ECJ merely reduced the three million ECUs fine by 50,000 ECUs.

The appellant has to state the errors alleged to have been made by the CFI. It is not sufficient for it simply to repeat the arguments it raised before that Court.[321] The ECJ cannot be asked to review the facts found by the CFI, to raise matters of fact which were not found by the CFI, or to consider the assessment of evidence adduced before the CFI unless the CFI committed an error of law.[322] The ECJ explained the respective roles of the ECJ and the CFI in *John Deere*.[323]

---

[316] [1985] OJ L85/1, [1985] 3 CMLR 474.

[317] Cases C–89/85 etc., *A. Ahlström Oy* v. *Commission* [1993] ECR I–1307, [1993] 4 CMLR 407.

[318] Case C–51/92P, *Commission* v. *AssiDomän Kraft Products AB and others* [1999] 5 CMLR 1253.

[319] Art. 51 of the Statute of the ECJ.

[320] Case C–185/95P, *Baustahlgewebe GmbH* v. *Commission* [1998] ECR I–8417, [1999] 4 CMLR 1203.

[321] Case C–19/95P, *San Marco* v. *Commission* [1996] ECR I–4435.

[322] Case C–53/92P, *Hilti* v. *Commission* [1994] ECR I–666, [1994] 4 CMLR 614.

[323] see also Case C–185/95P *Baustahlgewebe GmbH* v. *Commission* [1998] ECR I–8417, [1999] 4 CMLR 1203.

Cases C–7/95P, *John Deere* v. *Commission* [1998] ECR I–3111, [1998] 5 CMLR 311

Court of Justice

18. Article [225 E.C]. and Article 51 of the E.C. Statute of the Court of Justice state that an appeal is to be limited to points of law and must be based on the grounds of lack of competence of the Court of First Instance, breach of procedure before it which adversely affects the interest of the appellant or infringement of Community law by the Court of First Instance. Article 112(1)(c) of the Court's Rules of Procedure provides that an appeal must contain the pleas in law and legal arguments relied on.

19. It follows from those provisions that an appeal must indicate precisely the contested elements of the judgment which the appellant seeks to have set aside, and also the legal arguments specifically advanced in support of the appeal (see the order in Case C–19/95P, *San Marco v. E.C. Commission* . . .).

20. That requirement is not satisfied by an appeal confined to repeating or reproducing word for word the pleas in law and arguments previously submitted to the Court of First Instance, including those based on facts expressly rejected by that court; in so far as such an appeal does not contain any arguments specifically contesting the judgment appealed against, it amounts in reality to no more than a request for re-examination of the application submitted to the Court of First Instance, which under Article 49 of the E.C. Statute the Court of Justice does not have jurisdiction to undertake (see to this effect, in particular the order in *San Marco v. E.C. Commission* . . .).

21. It also follows from the foregoing provisions that an appeal may be based only on grounds relating to the infringement of rules of law, to the exclusion of any appraisal of the facts. The Court of First Instance has exclusive jurisdiction, first, to establish the facts except where the substantive inaccuracy of its findings is apparent from the documents submitted to it and, second, to assess those facts. When the Court of First Instance has established or assessed the facts, the Court of Justice has jurisdiction under Article [225] of the Treaty to review the legal characterisation of those facts by the Court of First Instance and the legal conclusions it has drawn from them (see, in particular, the order in *San Marco v. E.C. Commission* . . .).

22. The Court of Justice thus has no jurisdiction to establish the facts or, in principle, to examine the evidence which the Court of First Instance accepted in support of those facts. Provided that the evidence has been properly obtained and the general principles of law and the rules of procedure in relation to the burden of proof and the taking of evidence have been observed, it is for the Court of First Instance alone to assess the value which should be attached to the evidence produced to it (see, in particular, the order in *San Marco v. E.C. Commission* . . .). The appraisal by the Court of First Instance of the evidence put before it does not constitute, save where the evidence has been fundamentally misconstrued, a point of law which is subject, as such, to review by the Court of Justice (judgment in Case C–53/92P, *Hilti v. E.C. Commission* . . .).

This was elaborated upon in *Hüls AG*, one of the appeals from the *Polypropylene* decision:

Case C–199/92P, *Hüls AG* v. *Commission* (*Polypropylene*) judgment 8 July 1999, [1999] 5 CMLR 1016

Court of Justice

58. Pursuant to Article 225 E.C. (ex Article 168A) and the first paragraph of Article 51 of the E.C. Statute of the Court of Justice, an appeal is limited to points of law and may rely only on the grounds listed exhaustively therein, to the exclusion of any fresh appraisal of the facts. According to the Commission, Hüls's appeal does not enable it to be clearly determined whether the breaches of procedure allegedly committed by the Court of First Instance are criticised as a breach of the applicable rules of evidence or from the point of view of the specific application of the rules of evidence to the facts, which cannot constitute a ground of appeal in itself. Hüls does not adequately specify the rule of law that the Court of First Instance is alleged to have infringed.

59. According to the Commission, Hüls is criticising the fact, first, that the Court of First Instance relied *inter alia* on evidence that was undetermined by other evidence and, secondly, that it was in breach of the principle that the benefit of the doubt must be given or the presumption of innocence. Hüls did not claim that the Court of First Instance had not examined or had distorted evidence, which could constitute a breach that the Court should examine, but rather it criticised the assessment of the facts by the Court of First Instance.

60. The same applies to the alleged breach of the rule of presumption of innocence. Where the Court of First Instance assesses various items of contradictory evidence and, after reflection, reaches a conclusion as to the finding of facts, that conclusion is not subject to review by the Court of Justice, unless it is clear from the file that that finding is objectively wrong. Only the legal characterisation of a fact and, in consequence, determination of the applicable rule of law may constitute the subject-matter of an appeal. Review by the Court of Justice concerns the question whether the facts found, after assessment of the evidence by the Court of First Instance, justify application of that rule of law. That should not, however, be confused with review of findings of fact and the assessment of items in evidence, which is what Hüls does.

61. Hüls states that it has explained in detail how the Court of First Instance was in breach of substantive provisions of Community law and clearly explained that no assessment of items of evidence was involved. On the contrary, it claimed that the Court of First Instance did not fully investigate the facts and based itself on presumptions which were contradicted by contrary presumptions. That method of proceedings runs counter not only to principles of logic and experience, but also to the obligation of the Court of First Instance to undertake an inquiry and to obtain evidence.

62. Hüls expressly raised disregard of the principle that the benefit of the doubt must be given, which, it states, is a principle of law. It also relied on Article 6 of the Convention for the Protection of Human Rights and Fundamental Freedoms of 4 November 1950 ('ECHR'), which forms part of Community law pursuant to Article F(2) of the Treaty on European Union (now, after amendment, Article 6(2) E.U.). Hüls claims that failure to comply with the obligation of inquiry constitutes a breach of the presumption of innocence, which applies also to administrative law penalties, such as fines in cases of infringement of the competition rules.

63. According to Hüls, the Court of Justice must review the judgments of the Court of First Instance with regard to breaches of the law of evidence, and of principles of logic and common experience. The application of provisions of competition law to situations in which the facts do not allow for such application is a question of law, just like the question whether the facts found are sufficient to constitutes a breach of Article 81 E.C. To apply that provision to facts which do not form

a sufficient basis for such a breach is an infringement of the competition rules. Breach of the applicable rules of evidence leads also, by enlarging their scope, to breaches of the competition provisions,. The Court of First Instance committed such an error when it confirmed the existence of a concerted practice without finding on the market conduct by Hüls corresponding to such a practice. In conclusion, the questions concerning the degree of proof, the relevance and exhaustive nature of the facts found in relation to their legal consequences are points of law subject to review by the Court. The appeal is therefore wholly admissible.

64. In that regard, it should be borne in mind that, pursuant to Article 225 E.C. and the first paragraph of Article 51 of the E.C. Statute of the Court of Justice, an appeal may rely only on grounds relating to the infringement of rules of law, to the exclusion of any appraisal of the facts. The appraisal by the Court of First Instance of the evidence put before it does not constitute, save where the clear sense of that evidence has been distorted, a point of law which is subject, as such, to review by the Court of Justice (Case C–53/92P, Hiltiv Commission . . .)

65. It follows that, inasmuch as they relate to the assessment by the Court of First Instance of the evidence adduced, the appellant's complaints cannot be examined in an appeal. However, it is incumbent on the Court to verify whether, in making that assessment, the Court of First Instance committed an error of law by infringing the general principles of law, such as the presumption of innocence and the applicable rules of evidence, such as those concerning the burden of proof. . . .

66. Pleas in law alleging that the grounds of the contested judgment are inadequate or contradictory are also admissible in an appeal. . . .

This does not mean that the ECJ always rubber-stamps the CFI's judgment.[324] Also, although upholding the CFI, the ECJ may phrase its own judgment in different terms. This happened in *Magill* where the CFI's attempts to struggle with the intellectual property rights/competition interface were side-stepped by the ECJ which gave a judgment in much narrower terms.[325]

H. APPEALS AGAINST PENALTIES: ARTICLE 229

As discussed above[326] the Commission has a very wide discretion in setting fines under Regulation 17, Article 15. Regulation 17, Article 17 gives the Court a power to cancel, reduce, or increase the fines or periodic penalty pursuant to Article 229.

The distinction between the Court's powers under Article 229 and under Article 230 is that under the former the Court may actually *change* the Commission's decision. It may cancel, increase, or reduce the fine (it has never yet *increased* a fine). Under Article 230,

---

[324] E.g., it set aside the CFI's judgment upholding the Commission decision in the *Net Book Agreement* case, Case C–360/92P, *Publishers' Association* v. *Commission* [1995] ECR II—23, [1995] 5 CMLR 33; replaced the CFI's finding of a non-existent act in *PVC I* with a finding of an act which should be annulled: Cases C–137/92P, *Commission* v. *BASF and others* [1994] ECR I–2555; and set aside the CFI judgment against the Commission in Case C–51/92P, *AssiDomän Kraft Products AB and others* [1999] 5 CMLR 1253.

[325] Cases T–69–70/89, 76/89, *RTE, ITP, BBC* v. *EC Commission* [1991] ECR II–485, [1991] 4 CMLR 586 and Cases C241–241/91 P, *RTE & ITP* v. *Commission* [1995] ECR I–743, [1995] 4 CMLR 718: see *supra* Chaps. 7 and 10.

[326] See *supra* 899–918.

however, the Court is limited to reviewing the legality of the decision and annulling all or part of it on the grounds laid down in the Article but cannot substitute its own judgment for that of the Commission.

It is necessary to distinguish between the functions of the ECJ and the CFI in respect of fines. Article 229 actions go first to the CFI with an appeal to the ECJ. The ECJ holds firmly that it is for the CFI to examine how the Commission assessed the gravity of the infringement and to decide whether the fine should be changed. The ECJ will not substitute its own assessment for that of the CFI. It stated in *Ferriere Nord*:[327]

31. As regards the allegedly unjust nature of the fine, it is important to point out that it is not for this Court, when ruling on questions of law in the context of an appeal, to substitute, on grounds of fairness, its own assessment for that of the Court of First Instance exercising its unlimited jurisdiction to rule on the amount of fines imposed on undertakings for infringements of Community law (Case C–310/93 P, *BPB Industries and British Gypsum* v. *E.C. Commission* . . .). In contrast, the Court of Justice does have jurisdiction to consider whether the Court of First Instance has responded to a sufficient legal standard to all the arguments raised by the appellant with a view to having the fine abolished or reduced.

As was seen above[328] the Court has often reduced or cancelled fines, but it has been tolerant of the Commission's general approach. It approved the change to higher fines for the sake of deterrence in *Pioneer*[329] and did not demur from the ever higher level of fines imposed during the 1990s.

I. INTERIM MEASURES BY THE COURT UNDER ARTICLE 230

Bringing an Article 230 action for annulment does not automatically suspend the contested act. However, Article 242 (ex Article 185) states:

Actions brought before the Court of Justice shall not have suspensory effect. The Court of Justice may, however, if it considers that circumstances so require, order that application of the contested act be suspended.

Also, Article 243 (ex Article 186) provides that in any cases before it, the Court may prescribe any necessary measures. The President of the CFI normally hears applications for suspension. His or her decision may be appealed to the ECJ.[330]

In order for a decision to be suspended the applicants must show that the main action is admissible and that suspension is urgently needed to prevent them suffering irreparable damage which could not be remedied in the event of their winning the main action. On this

---

[327] Case C–219/95, *Ferriere Nord* v. *Commission* [1997] ECR I–865; [1997] 5 CMLR 575; see also Case C–310/93P, *BPB Industries and British Gypsum Ltd* v. *Commission* [1995] ECR I–865, [1997] 4 CMLR 238 at para. 34; and Case C–185/95P, *Baustahlgewebe GmbH* v. *Commission* [1999] 4 CMLR 1203 at paras. 128–129.

[328] See *supra* 909–910.

[329] Cases 100–103/80, Musique Diffusion Française SA v. *Commission* (*Pioneer*) [1983] ECR 1825, [1983] 3 CMLR 221.

[330] The Commission appealed in *Atlantic Container Line* when the President suspended its decision: Case C–149/95P(R), *Commission* v. *Atlantic Container Line and others* [1995] ECR I–2165.

basis suspension was ordered, *inter alia*, in *United Brands*,[331] *Magill*,[332] *Net Book Agreement*,[333] *ADALAT*,[334] *Atlantic Container Line*, and *Van den Bergh*.[335]

The President has to balance the harm to the applicant from non-suspension (foreseeable with a sufficient degree of probability)[336] with any harm which will be suffered by other parties if the suspension is granted. In *Adalat*, for example, the President considered that as a result of the order the applicant, Bayer, might be obliged to lower the prices of the drug in issue, risking major and irrecoverable losses of profit and the risk that the pharmaceutical base of one subsidiary 'might be deprived of its economic basis, resulting in the dismissal of many employees' and that this would be disproportionate in relation to the interests of wholesalers in Spain and France in increasing their exports.[337]

In *Van den Bergh* the Commission's decision prohibited a distribution system for impulse ice-cream which involved freezer exclusivity and which was the subject of proceedings before the Irish courts. The Irish High Court decided that the distribution system did not infringe but expressed its intention to seek an Article 234 ruling from the ECJ. Meanwhile the Commission's decision was appealed to the CFI. The President of the CFI said that the contradiction between the decision and the judgment was 'contrary to the general principle of legal certainty' and that in the circumstances the Commission's interest in having the infringement brought to an end could not prevail over the applicant's interest in not running the risk of jeopardising its distribution system or over the interest in limiting the effects of a contradiction in the application of the provisions of the Treaty.[338] He therefore granted a suspension.

The CFI may suspend the obligation to give a bank guarantee ensuring payment of the fine but this is done only in very exceptional circumstances.[339]

12. CONCLUSIONS

The Commission's multi-faceted role in the enforcement of the competition rules is subject to constant criticism by commentators, very often practitioners who have acted for the undertakings on the receiving end of the enforcement process. It is defended, equally robustly, by Commission officials. One needs to make allowances for partisanship but, even so, there is obviously a serious issue to be tried.

Montag argues that the Commission officials are asked to fulfill fundamentally contradictory functions:

---

[331] Case 27/76R, *United Brands* v. *Commission* [1976] ECR 425, [1976] 2 CMLR 147.

[332] Cases 76–77 and 91/89R, *RTE and others* v. *Commission* [1989] ECR 1141, [1989] 4 CMLR 749.

[333] Case 56/89R, *Publishers' Association* v. *Commission* [1989] ECR 1693, [1989] 4 CMLR 816.

[334] Case T–41/96R, *Bayer* v. *Commission* [1996] ECR II–407, [1996] 5 CMLR 290.

[335] Case T–65/98R, *Van den Bergh Foods Ltd* v. *Commission* [1998] 5 CMLR 475.

[336] Case C–280/93R, *Commission* v. *Germany* [1993] ECR I–3667.

[337] [1996] ECR II–407 at paras. 59–60.

[338] *Van den Bergh* at paras. 72–73.

[339] See Case T–295/94R, *Buchmann* v. *Commission* [1994] ECR II—1265 (one of several applications for such interim measures by the undertakings fined in the *Cartonboard Cartel* [1994] OJ L243/1, [1994] 5 CMLR 547).

F. Montag: 'The case for radical reform of the infringement procedure under regulation 17' [1996] *ECLR* 428, 429–430

The first issue to be examined in determining the need for reform of the anti-trust infringement procedure is the question of whether the procedure allows for the full observance of fundamental principles of law designed to protect the individual. Such principles must be observed by the Commission in infringement proceedings against undertakings since they are part of Community law within the meaning of Article [220] EC Treaty. . . . One of these is the principle *in dubio pro reo* according to which, until proven to have committed an alleged violation of the law, the individual accused is deemed not to have committed it.

Commission decisions imposing significant fines frequently raise doubts as to the impartial and unbiased handling of the matter by the Commission. In particular, this is the case where the wording of the final decision is almost identical to the wording of the Statement of Objections issued by the Commission at the beginning of the second stage of the proceedings. . . . Unfortunately, cases in which this occurs are not the exception but appear rather to be the rule. The consequence of this practice is that undertakings will inevitably be given the impression that their defence has not been heard.

It is unlikely that this means that undertakings have almost no relevant defences to present in the proceedings. A survey of the close resemblance between the Statements of Objections and decisions adopted instead, more realistically, leads to the conclusion that the parties' rights in proceedings before the Commission are of little practical value. Undertakings do in fact have the opportunity of an oral hearing before an independent Hearing Officer . . . but it is difficult to know whether the conclusions of the hearing play a role in the decision taken by the Commission. . . . The same is true for the written submission in answer to the Statement of Objections. It is often not possible to deduce from the reasons for a decision that points in the submission were taken into account by the Commission in reaching its final decision.

It is submitted that the described problem is primarily due to the contradictory functions which the Commission officials handling infringement cases are obliged to perform under Regulation 17. These officials are responsible for the case from the time an investigation is opened until the Commission adopts a decision. They carry out the preliminary investigation which ends with the drafting of the Statement of Objections, act as a quasi-prosecutor during the infringement proceedings and, finally, are responsible for drafting the Commission's decision.

The longer the proceedings lasts—and this can be years . . .—the more entrenched the barriers of defence between the undertaking and the Commission administrators involved tend to become. Commission officials, who often investigate for years and thereby invest significant time and personal energy in the file, want, in the end, to bring the procedure—from their point of view—to a successful conclusion. In the event of the staff changes, due, for example to movement within the Commission, successive administrators tend to defend the conclusions of their predecessors set out in the Statement of Objections. After all, who would want to stab a colleague in the back, especially if one can profit from the predecessor's work and from the expertise he acquired on the job by accepting his advice and getting the job done? Thus, it is understandable in human terms that Commission officials sometimes want to push through what they perceive to be 'their' case. And it explains why arguments put forward by the parties often appear to fall on deaf ears.

As a result, undertakings are faced with a situation which, as an inevitable consequence, leads to a reversal of the burden of proof in the administrative proceedings as well as in any ensuring court proceedings and therefore to a serious infringement of the principle of *in dubio pro reo*. As has been shown, for the reasons just outlined, the Commission rarely changes its position during the course of the administrative procedure and simply relies on large passages in the Statement of Objections when writing its decision. This negatively affects not only the decision imposing fines, but also the position of the undertakings if they appeal the decision to the Court of First Instance. When facts disputed by an undertaking appear as 'established' in the final decision, the only way these can be challenged is by attempting to disprove them in subsequent court action. Experience in proceedings before the Court of First Instance shows that the principle *in dubio prodecisione* takes precedence over the principle *in dubio pro reo*, because the court only examines the Commission decision for defects. Moreover, the courts are renowned for their reluctance to interfere with the wide discretion of the Commission in the application of Regulation 17.... In the administrative proceeding the principle is of little value to the undertaking concerned due to the various interests which have been outlined, and ensuring court proceedings cannot, due to the peculiarities of Article [230] of the Treaty, completely remedy this problem.... This means that the fundamental legal maxim *in dubio pro reo* is effectively undermined throughout the infringement proceeding.

Others take the view that the review provided for by Article 230 is sufficient to guarantee the rights of the parties. The discussion which took place at the XVIIth FIDE (Fédération internationale de droit européen) Congress concluded that the judicial review by the Court does satisfy Article 6(1) of the ECHR.[340] Even if the 'fair hearing' requirements of Article 6(1) are satisfied, however, there are several outstanding problems of inconsistencies between the case law of the ECJ and that of the Strasbourg court in relation to the Commission's investigative process.[341] Toth argues that these discrepancies are unavoidable, given the existence of two 'supreme' courts and the different objectives of the body of laws they apply:

A.G. Toth, 'The European Union and human rights: the way forward' (1997) 34 *CMLRev* 491, 500

....although there exists one single system of substantive fundamental rights in Europe, there are two distinct systems of remedies in operation, each headed by a judicial body which is the supreme authority in its own field and which is totally independent of the other. The co-existence of two Supreme Courts, the Court of Justice and the ECHR, each having independent power to interpret and apply the same text, the Convention, carries with it the possibility of conflicting interpretations, which is the surest way to undermine legal certainty and confidence in the system. Conflicting interpretations are likely to occur because both Courts follow the same 'teleological' method. The ECHR interprets the Convention according to the Convention's objectives, while the Court of Justice interprets it according to the Community's objectives. ... However, the two sets of objectives do not necessary coincide. The Convention's aim is to protect the *individual* as a human being, while the Community's aim is to further economic and social integration. In many areas, such as competition law, State aids, etc., the EC Treaty deals with *undertakings* as economic entities, whose basic rights may need different types of protection from those afforded to individuals.

This explains certain divergencies in the Convention's interpretation that have already come to light. Thus, when in the *Hoechst* case ... the Court of Justice held that Article 8(1) of the European Convention, which protects the right to respect for private and family life, home and correspondence,

---

[340] K. Lenaerts and J. Vanhamme, 'Procedural Rights of Private Parties in the Community Administrative Process' (1997) 34 *CMLRev.* 531.

[341] See *supra* e.g. 859–860 and D. Spielman, 'Human Rights Case Law in the Strasbourg and Luxembourg Courts: Conflicts, Inconsistencies, and Complementaries in P. Alston (ed.), *The EU and Human Rights* (Oxford University Press, Oxford, 1999); R. Lawson, 'Confusion and Conflict? Diverging Interpretations of the European Convention on Human Rights in Strasbourg and Luxembourg' in R. Lawson and M. de Blois, *The Dynamics of the Protection of Human Rights in Europe: Essays in Honour of Henry G. Schermers* (Martinus Nijhoff, The Hague, 1994); P. Weatherill and S. Beaumont, *EU Law* (3rd edn., Penguin, 1999) 900–2.

applies only to the private dwellings of natural persons but not to the business premises of under-takings, its reasons were that 'the protective scope of that article is concerned with the development of man's personal freedom and may not therefore be extended to business premises'. By contrast, in the *Niemietz* case . . . the ECHR's opinion was that to interpret the words 'private life' and 'home' as including certain professional or business activities or premises 'would be consonant with the essential object and purpose of Article 8, namely to protect the individual against arbitrary interfer-ence by the public authorities'. In *Orkem*, . . . while recognizing that Article 6 of the European Convention, which guarantees the right to a fair trial, may be relied on by an undertaking subject to an investigation relating to competition law, the Court of Justice denied that that Article includes the right not to give evidence against oneself. In contrast, in the *Funke* case . . . the ECHR upheld the right of anyone charged with a criminal offence, within the meaning of Article 6 'to remain silent and not to contribute to incriminating himself'. These discrepancies are due to the fact that the Court of Justice has interpreted and applied the provisions of the Convention with regard to undertakings, in the context of competition proceedings, and having special regard to the objectives and rules of EC competition law, . . . while the ECHR has interpreted and applied the same provi-sions with respect to private individuals, in the context of criminal proceedings, and in accordance with the objectives of the Convention itself. Such differences are virtually unavoidable in the present system where the Court of Justice is not only not bound by the rulings of the ECHR but, in the absence of an appropriate mechanism, is unable to seek any preliminary advice or opinion before interpreting a provision which the ECHR has not interpreted previously, as in the two cases cited above.

The European Council at Cologne in June 1999 decided that the Union needed its own 'Charter' of fundamental rights. The Tampere Council of October 1999 set up a body to prepare a draft of this to present to the Council in December 2000. At present it is not clear what the status of such a Charter would be,[342] but it should be an opportunity for clarifying the issues surrounding the compatibility of the Community's administrative procedures with the rights of those subjected to them.

The two proposals which are repeatedly made for reforming competition procedure are to put the whole thing into the hands of an independent European competition authority (a European Cartel Office) quite separate from the Commission, or to leave the investigation process with the Commission but give the decision-making and fining stages to the CFI. The first of these suggestions was much mooted before the 1996 Intergovernmental Conference, particularly by Germany.[343] The arguments in favour of this are explained by Ehlermann in the following passage.

C-D Ehlermann, 'Reflections on the ECO' (1995) 32 *CMLRev* 471, 474, 479–480

The objectives and motives of the (German) proponents of a European Cartel Office are clear and straightforward.

What they want is more competition, not less; that is they are anxious to see the competition principle strengthened within the European Union. It is felt that an authority which has a remit confined to competition matters and is independent of the Commission will, in the long run, be far more likely to apply the existing rules, particularly the Merger Control Regulation, in a purely competition-oriented

---

[342] See R. White, Editorial, (2000) 25 *ELRev*. 97.
[343] And see G. Amato, *Antitrust and the Bounds of Power* (Hart Publishing, Oxford, 1997), Chap. 8.

manner than the Commission, a political and collegiate body with general competences. The proponents of a European Cartel Office are willing to accept that appeals against the Office's decisions may be lodged with the Commission (mirroring the *Ministererlaubnis*), as they have faith in the salutary effect of public discussion: separating the Office's basic decision-making power from the Commission's power to hear appeals creates the much sought-after transparency which is currently lacking.

At least some of the proponents of an independent European competition authority are also counting on an acceleration of the current decision-making process, and claim that a European Cartel Office would work more quickly and more efficiently than the Commission.

The call for greater transparency is, of course, not restricted to the field of competition but encompasses the Community's decision-making process generally. It is one of the many aspects of the constitutional debates triggered or at least intensified in most of the Member States by the Maastricht Treaty. It must therefore be taken particularly seriously.

But the desire to see greater transparency in Commission decision-making also has a politically sensitive core, one rarely conceded in public: some of the larger Member States in particular are not impressed by the Commission as a decision-making body. They do not feel that it looks after their interests very well.

In the field of competition this is especially true of Germany, which is apprehensive about the influence of industrial policy. Here, Germany's fears are directed at the Commission as a collegiate body, not at DG IV. In neighbouring France the opposite is true, and DG IV is viewed there as a greater danger. For this reason, few people in France will ever have seriously toyed with the idea of transforming DG IV into an independent cartel authority.

. . .

An independent European Cartel Office would be a kind of political orphan. Its decisions could meet with stiff resistance in countries where the public is less committed to the competition principle than in Germany. Non-political and purely subject-related decisions might not be perceived as an advantage but as a disadvantage, for example by isolating competition policy from other policies and making it independent. . . . If this were to lessen acceptance of the Office's decisions, the new Office would be tempted to adapt to its environment, with its resolve to take courageous decisions weakening. This would do a disservice to competition policy and the competition principle, especially at a time when the extension of competition law to new areas (e.g. air and sea transport, telecommunications, posts, electricity and gas, banks and insurance) requires political courage.

Just as important as the effects on the future cartel authority with its first—instance competences are the probable consequences which independent handling of this policy area will have on the Commission's existing structure: only a small part of the Commission's powers in the field of competition will be transferred to the European Cartel Office. The Commission will not only have to hear appeals on competition cases handled by the Cartel Office. It will retain its responsibility for applying the rules of competition to the conduct of Member States (monitoring of state aid, elimination or restriction of state monopolies). And of course it will still have responsibility for all those tasks, other than competition in the narrower sense, set out in the Treaties, e.g. agricultural and transport policy, commercial policy, regional policy, research policy, environmental policy, social policy and general economic policy.

DG IV is of course very much the leading department in ensuring that the Member States observe the rules of competition. And it influences the Commission's other activities in the same way as any other participating Directorate General. Even if DG IV were to continue looking after the remaining tasks in the competition area in the narrow sense (monitoring of state aids and control of monopolies, appeals against the Cartel Office) after a European Cartel Office had been set up, its position would presumably be much weaker than it is today. This would have a generally negative effect on the competition-promoting thrust of the Commission's activities, at least until such time as one of the other Directorates General had become the Commission's competition conscience.

The proponents of an independent European competition authority will presumably not be keen to pay this price. But they will probably point out that hiving off these functions will lessen the influence of the other Directorates General on DG IV. Other DGs, particularly the Directorate General for Industry, also have a hand in merger control, although the Commission member responsible has no right of assent or veto. German critics of the existing decision-making structure in competition cases have regarded this form of participation as harmful to purely competition-based merger control.

As natural as this fear might originally have been, these days it is unfounded. Involving other DGs in the preparation of decisions has proved to be a useful challenge to DG IV, obliging it to produce well—reasoned drafts. The conflict of arguments has not weakened DG IV, but strengthened it.

The Commission is naturally not prepared to surrender its role as the guardian of the Treaty's competition rules.[344] In the White Paper on modernization[345] it reaffirms its central position in the direction of competition policy. The reforms now proposed are not to take competition enforcement into some separate body, or to split investigations from decision-making, but to decentralise to national courts and authorities. These proposals are discussed in Chapter 16.

13. FURTHER READING

A. BOOKS

AMATO, G., *Antitrust and the Bounds of Power* (Hart Publishing, 1997), Chapter 8.

BLANCO, L.O., *EC Competition Procedure* (Oxford University Press, 1996)

CRAIG, P., and DE BÚRCA, G., *EU Law: Text, Cases and Materials* (2nd edn., Oxford University Press, 1998), Chapter 11

KERSE, C.S., *EC Antitrust Procedure* (4th edn., Sweet and Maxwell, 1998)

LENAERTS K., and ARTS, D., *Procedural Law of the European Union* (Sweet & Maxwell, 1999)

—— VAN NUFFEL, P., *Constitutional Law of the European Union* (Sweet & Maxwell, 1999)

TRIDIMAS, T., *The General Principles of EC Law* (Oxford University Press, 1999)

WEATHERILL, S., and BEAUMONT, P., *EU Law* (3rd edn., Penquin, 1999) 900–902

---

[344] See K. van Miert (then Commissioner for Competition), 'The Proposal for a Europ. Competition Agency', in *Competition Policy Newsletter*, 2–2 (Commission, 1996).

[345] White Paper on modernisation of the rules implementing Articles 85 and 86 [now 81 and 82] of the EC Treaty [1999] OJ C132/1.

B. ARTICLES

DOHERTY, S., 'Playing Poker with the Commission: Rights of Access to the Commission's File in Competition Cases' [1994] *ECLR* 8

EHLERMANN, C.-D., 'Reflections on a European Cartel Office' (1995) 32 *CMLRev.* 471

—— DRIJBER, B.J., 'Legal Protection of Enterprises: Administrative Procedure in Particular Access to the File and Confidentiality' [1996] *ECLR* 375

GYSELEN, L., 'The Commission's Fining Policy in Competition Cases—"Questo è il catalogo"' in P.J. Slot and A. McDonnell (eds.), *Procedure and Enforcement in EC and US Competition Law* (Sweet and Maxwell, 1993) 63–75

KERSE, C.S., 'Procedures in EC Competition Cases: The Oral Hearing' [1994] *ECLR* 40

LAVOIE, C., 'The Investigative Powers of the Commission with Respect to Business Secrets under Community Competition Rules' (1992) *ELRev.* 20

HORNSBY, S. and HUNTER, J., 'New Incentives for "Whistleblowers": Will the EC Commission's Notice Bear Fruit?' [1997] *ECLR* 38

LAWSON, R., 'Confusion and Conflict? Diverging Interpretations of the European Convention on Human Rights in Strasbourg and Luxembourg' in R. Lawson and M. de Blois, *The Dynamics of the Protection of Human Rights in Europe: Essays in Honour of Henry G. Schermers* (Martinus Nijhoff, 1994)

LENAERTS, K., and VANHAMME J., 'Procedural Rights of Private Parties in the Community Administrative Process' (1997) 34 *CMLRev.* 531

LEVITT, M., 'Commission Notice on Internal Rules of Procedure for Access to the File' [1997] *ECLR* 187

MONTAG, F., 'The Case for Radical Reform of the Infringement Procedure under Regulation' [1998] *ECLR* 428

PERA, A., and TODINO, M., 'Enforcement of EC Competition Rules: Need for a Reform?' [1996] *Fordham Corporate Law Institute* 125

RICHARDSON, R., 'Guidance Without Guidance—A European Revolution in Fining Policy? The Commission's New Guidelines on Fines' [1999] *ECLR* 360

RILEY, A., 'Saunders and the Power to Obtain Information in Community and United Kingdom Competition Law' (2000) 25 *ELRev.* 264

SPIELMAN, D., 'Human Rights Case Law in the Strasbourg and Luxembourg Courts: Conflicts, Inconsistencies, and Complementaries' in P. Alston (ed.) *The EU and Human Rights* (Oxford University Press, 1999)

SPRATTLING, G., 'Fines in Criminal Antitrust Cases' in P. Slot and A McDonnell (eds.) *Procedure and Enforcement in EC and US Competition Law* (Sweet and Maxwell 1993). 76–87

TOTH, A.G., 'The European Union and Human Rights: The Way Forward' (1997) 34 *CMLRev.* 491

BAEL, Ivo van., 'Fining à la Carte: The Lottery of EU Competition Law' [1995] *ECLR* 237

WILS, W.P.J., 'EC Competition Fines: To Deter or Not to Deter' [1995] *YEL* 17

—— 'The Commission's New Method for Calculating Fines in Antitrust Cases' (1998) *ELRev.* 252

—— 'The Undertaking as Subject of EC Competition Law and the Imputation of Infringements to Natural or Legal Persons' (2000) 25 *ELRev.* 99

WOUDE, M., VAN DER, 'Hearing Officers and EC Antitrust Procedures: The Art of Making Subjective Procedures more Objective' (1996) *CMLRev.* 531

15

PROCEEDINGS AT THE NATIONAL LEVEL AND COMPLAINTS BY PRIVATE PARTIES

1. INTRODUCTION

An entity which believes that another undertaking has committed, or is committing, a breach of Community competition law may wish to take action to ensure that the undertaking in breach complies and is punished in respect of that breach. In addition, it may hope to recover in respect of any loss suffered in consequence of the breach of the rules.

Such an entity essentially has two choices. It may complain to the Commission[1] and hope that the Commission acts on the complaint. The Commission has power to take interim measures and to issue a decision ordering the termination of a breach of the law. Alternatively it may bring proceedings in the national court seeking a declaration that an agreement infringes the competition rules and is unenforceable, an injunction to prevent future breaches, and/or other remedies in respect of a breach. Both Articles 81(1) and 82 are directly effective and confer rights on individuals that can be relied on before a national court.

Obviously a complaint to the Commission is the cheaper of the two options and causes least inconvenience to the individual. The Commission is, however, trying to encourage greater private enforcement of the competition rules at the national level. It wishes to preserve its resources for cases in which a point of particular 'Community' interest is raised (it has the resources to issue only a small number of decisions each year[2]).[3] It may, therefore, decline to act on the complaint. Further, where the Commission finds an infringement of the rules it has power only to order a guilty undertaking to bring its infringement to an end[4] and to fine an undertaking in respect of any breach committed.[5] It does not have power to

---

[1] It may also be possible to lodge a complaint with a national competition authority, see *infra* 1004 ff.
[2] *Supra* Chap. 4.
[3] See *infra* 950 ff and the Commission's White Paper on modernisation of the rules implementing Articles 85 and 86 [now 81 and 82] of the EC Treaty [1999] OJ C132/1, [1999] 5 CMLR 208.
[4] Reg 17, [1959–1962], OJ Spec. Ed. 87, Art. 3(1).
[5] *Ibid.*, Art. 15.

award damages or other compensation to those which have suffered as a result of the breach. Where an undertaking seeks compensation or another remedy a private action will, therefore, be the only satisfactory option.[6]

2. COMPLAINTS TO THE COMMISSION

A. GENERAL

Although the procedure governing complaints is informal, Regulation 17 itself envisages that complaints will be made to the Commission. It makes it clear that individuals with a sufficient interest may complain to the Commission. Further, the Commission has drafted a form on which complaints can be notified. Complaints have now become an established part of the enforcement procedure. Indeed, in its White Paper on Modernisation the Commission estimates that almost 30 per cent of new cases it deals with result from complaints and that many of its own-initiative investigations begin with information sent to the Commission informally.[7] If the Commission's proposals in its White Paper on Modernisation come to fruition, so that a change is made to a completely directly applicable system, the Commission envisages that complaints will become an increasingly important part of the new procedure.[8] The Commission intends to encourage and facilitate the lodging of complaints so that its (and/or a relevant national competition authority's) attention will be drawn to the most serious breaches of the competition rules.

One of the difficulties of this procedure and of encouraging more complaints is that, in many cases, they may be lodged by disgruntled entities losing out on the competitive process rather than by entities really suffering as a result of a breach of the EC competition rules. The Commission must distinguish between legitimate and illegitimate complaints and is not bound to investigate all complaints. In fact, it will be seen below that it is not bound to investigate even if it considers that there has been a breach of the competition rules.

B. STANDING

Regulation 17[9] provides that only Member States and 'natural or legal persons who claim a legitimate interest' have standing to complain about a breach of the competition rules.

---

[6] An individual could of course commence private proceedings following proceedings by the Commission. The ability of that individual to rely on a Commission decision or other documents might facilitate those private proceedings, see *infra* n. 67.

[7] White Paper on modernization of the rules implementing Articles. 85 and 86 [now 81 and 82] of the EC Treaty [1999] OJ C132/1, [1999] 5 CMLR 208, para. 117.

[8] For a discussion of the proposals set out in the White Paper, see *infra* Chap. 16.

[9] [1959–62] OJ Spec. Ed. 87.

Article 3

Termination of infringements

1. Where the Commission, upon application or upon its own initiative, finds that there is infringement of Article [81] or Article [82] of the Treaty, it may by decision require the undertakings or associations of undertakings concerned to bring such infringement to an end.

2. Those entitled to make application are:

(a) Member States;
(b) natural or legal persons who claim a legitimate interest.

The interpretation of the phrase 'direct and individual concern' in Article 230 (ex Article 173) of the Treaty is linked to the interpretation given to 'natural or legal person who claims a legitimate interest' in Article 3(2). Article 230 enables individuals who are not addressees of a competition, or other, decision to challenge that decision in judicial review proceedings if the decision is of direct and individual concern to them. In *Metro* v. *Commission* the ECJ considered that it was essential that a person with a legitimate interest under Regulation 17 'should be able, if their request is not complied with either wholly or in part, to institute proceedings in order to protect their legitimate interests. In those circumstances, the applicant must be considered to be directly and individually concerned within the meaning of the second paragraph of Article [230], by the contested decision'.[10]

The requirement that an individual should have a legitimate interest does not present a major obstacle to potential complainants. An applicant which directly suffers, or will suffer, injury or loss as a result of the infringement is likely to have standing for the purposes of Article 3(2). It has been held, for example, that an individual: who has been excluded, or threatened with exclusion, from a distribution network;[11] who believes that he was negotiating with members of a cartel;[12] or which believes himself to be a victim of abusive behaviour by a dominant undertaking,[13] has a legitimate interest within the meaning of Article 3(2). In *BEMIM* v *Commission*[14] the CFI held that a trade association had a legitimate interest where the conduct complained of was liable to affect adversely the interests of the members that it was entitled to represent. Even if an individual does not have a legitimate interest within the meaning of Regulation 17 it is not prevented from drawing the Commission's attention to conduct it believes to be in breach of Community rules. The Commission would then, of course, be free to determine on its own initiative[15] whether or not it should investigate or commence proceedings against perpetrators of conduct which may be anti-competitive.

---

[10] Case 26/76, *Metro SB-Grosmärtke GmbH & Co KG* v. *Commission* [1977] ECR 1875, [1978] 2 CMLR 1, para. 13. For a discussion of Art. 230 see *supra*, Chap. 14

[11] Case 210/81, *Demo-Studio Schmidt* v. *Commission* [1983] ECR 3045, [1984] 1 CMLR 63.

[12] See, e.g., *Building and Construction Industry in the Netherlands* [1992] OJ L92/1, [1993] 5 CMLR 135 (a complaint about collusive tendering lodged by a local authority).

[13] See, e.g., Cases 6 and 7/73, *Istituto Chemioterapico Italiano SpA and Commercial Solvents Corp* v. *Commission* [1974] ECR 223, [1974] 1 CMLR 309 (complaint by Zoja, *Zoja-CSC/ICI* [1972] OJ L299/51, [1973] CMLR D50); Case C–62/86, *AKZO Chemie BV* v. *Commission* [1991] ECR I–3359, [1993] 5 CMLR 215, complaint lodged by ECS; see *supra* Chaps. 6 and 7.

[14] Case T–144/92 [1995] ECR II–147, [1996] 4 CMLR 305; see in particular para. 28.

[15] Reg 17, Art. 3(1), see *supra* Chap. 14.

C. THE PROCEDURE

Complainants may submit a complaint on Form C. Although they are not obliged to use this form complainants must provide the Commission with sufficient detail of the alleged breach, the parties involved, and the markets affected by the breach. In addition, since the Commission has expressed its intention to investigate only infringements with a sufficient Community interest,[16] it is essential that the complainant should indicate why the Community interest is affected and impress on the Commission why it should take action.

D. THE OBLIGATIONS ON THE COMMISSION

On receipt of a complaint the Commission is bound to collect information which enables it to determine whether it should reject the complaint or conduct an investigation. There is no time limit within which the Commission must deal with the complaint; it is necessary only that it should do so within a reasonable period.[17] The Commission recognizes that this position may not be satisfactory for individuals who believe that they are being injured by a breach of the competition rules and need to know quickly whether or not the Commission will act upon their complaint. In its White Paper on Modernisation the Commission has proposed that a time limit should be introduced within which it should be obliged to inform the complainant whether or not it intends to proceed.[18] If the complaint is rejected the complainant may then turn to a national competition authority or the national courts instead.

E. REJECTION OF THE COMPLAINT

(i) INTRODUCTION

The Commission may on investigation consider that no breach of the EC competition rules has occurred. Alternatively, it may consider that a breach has occurred but that the case raises insufficient Community interest to warrant the time and resources which would be involved in investigation. Although the Commission has a duty

to examine carefully the facts and points of law brought to its notice by the complainant in order to decide whether they disclose conduct liable to distort competition in the Common Market and affect trade between Member States[19]

it does not have a duty to proceed to final decision on the alleged breach of the rules.

---

[16] See *infra* 950 ff.

[17] White Paper on Modernisation of the Rules Implementing Articles 85 and 86 [now 81 and 82] of the EC Treaty OJ [1999] C 132/1, [1999] 5 CMLR 208, para. 120.

[18] It has proposed a period of four months. However, it also recognizes that the current procedures involved in rejecting a complaint are too cumbersome and should be simplified.

[19] Case T–575/93 *Koelman* v. *Commission* [1996] ECR II–1, [1996] 4 CMLR, para. 39.

(ii) THE COMMUNITY INTEREST

In *Automec Srl v. Commission (Automec II)*[20] the CFI held that the Commission is entitled to prioritize cases before it. It may reject complaints on the ground that they do not raise a sufficient Community interest. Save where the subject matter of the complaint falls within the exclusive purview of the Commission,[21] the rights conferred upon complainants do not, therefore, include a right to obtain a decision as regards the existence or otherwise of the alleged infringement. Rather, it has been accepted that the Commission is bound, in fulfilling its functions under the Treaty, to apply different degrees of priority to the cases arising before it. The Commission is entitled to assess whether the complaint raises sufficient Community interest to warrant an investigation.

Case T–24/90 *Automec Srl* v. *Commission (Automec II)* [1992] ECR II–2223, [1992] 5 CMLR 431

This case concerned a complaint lodged by Automec Srl, a private company, which had been a distributor of BMW vehicles for BMW Italia SpA in Treviso. On the expiry of its dealership in 1984, BMW Italia declined to renew the contract (although the applicant continued selling BMWs which it obtained from other BMW dealers). Automec brought proceedings before the national courts to compel BMW to continue the contractual relationship and subsequently, in 1988, lodged a complaint with the Commission under Article 3(2) of Regulation 17. In particular, it contended that since it met the qualitative criteria agreed by BMW with the Commission for the lawful operation of its selective distribution system[22] BMW was obliged to supply it with vehicles and spare parts on the terms applicable to other dealers. In 1988 the Commission sent Automec a letter stating that it had no power to grant its application. Automec commenced judicial review proceedings before the Court of First Instance seeking annulment of the letter and seeking damages from the Commission in respect of loss suffered in consequence of the Commission's failure to commence proceedings against BMW (*Automec I*). Subsequent to the commencement of these proceedings further letters were exchanged between the Commission and Automec. In February 1990 the Commissioner responsible for competition sent the applicant a letter rejecting the complaint. The letter stated that there was not a sufficient Community interest to justify examining the facts raised by the complaint. In 1990 the applicant brought further proceedings before the Court of First Instance seeking annulment of the February 1990 decision of the Directorate-General for Commission.

Court of First Instance

71. The Court considers that the question raised by this plea asks in substance what the Commission's obligations are when it receives an application under Article 3 of Regulation No 17 from a natural or legal person.

72. It is appropriate to point out that Regulations Nos 17 and 99/63 confer procedural rights on persons who have lodged a complaint with the Commission, such as the right to be informed of the reasons for which the Commission intends to reject their complaint and the right to submit observations in this connection. Thus the Community legislature has imposed certain specified obligations upon the Commission. However, neither Regulation No 17 nor Regulation No 99/63 contain express provisions relating to the action to be taken concerning the substance of a complaint and any obligations on the part of the Commission to carry out investigations.

---

[20] Case T–24/90 [1992] ECR II–2223, [1992] 5 CMLR 431.
[21] E.g., for the withdrawal of an exemption granted under Art. 81(3) of the Treaty.
[22] *Bayerische Motoren Werke AG* [1975] OJ L29/1, [1975] 1 CMLR D44.

73. In determining the Commission's obligations in this context, the first point to note is that the Commission is responsible for the implementation and orientation of Community competition policy (see the judgment of the Court of Justice in Case C–234/89 *Delimitis v Henninger Bräu AG* [1991] ECR I–935, at I–991). For that reason, Article [85(1)] of the Treaty gave the Commission the task of ensuring that the principles laid down by Articles [81] and [82] were applied, and the provisions adopted pursuant to Article [83] have conferred wide powers upon it.

74. The scope of the Commission's obligations in the field of competition law must be examined in the light of Article [85(1)] of the Treaty, which, in this area, constitutes the specific expression of the general supervisory task entrusted to the Commission by Article [211] of the Treaty. However, as the Court of Justice has held with regard to Article [226] of the Treaty in Case 247/87 *Star Fruit v Commission* [1989] ECR 291, at 301, that task does not mean that the Commission is bound to commence proceedings seeking to establish the existence of any infringement of Community law.

75. In that regard, the Court observes that it appears from the case-law of the Court of Justice (judgment in *GEMA*, [Case 125/78, *GEMA v Commission* [1979] ECR 3173] at 3189) that the rights conferred upon complainants by Regulations Nos 17 and 99/63 do not include a right to obtain a decision, within the meaning of Article [249] of the Treaty, as regards the existence or otherwise of the alleged infringement. It follows that the Commission cannot be required to give a decision in that connection unless the subject-matter of the complaint falls within its exclusive purview, as in the case of the withdrawal of an exemption granted under Article [81(3)] of the Treaty.

76. As the Commission is under no obligation to rule on the existence or otherwise of an infringement it cannot be compelled to carry out an investigation, because such investigation could have no purpose other than to seek evidence of the existence or otherwise of an infringement, which it is not required to establish. In that regard, it should be noted that, unlike the provision contained in the second sentence of Article [85(1)] in relation to applications by Member States, Regulations Nos 17 and 99/63 do not expressly oblige the Commission to investigate complaints submitted to it.

77. In that connection, it should be observed that, in the case of an authority entrusted with a public service task, the power to take all the organizational measures necessary for the performance of that task, including setting priorities within the limits prescribed by the law—where those priorities have not been determined by the legislature—is an inherent feature of administrative activity. This must be the case in particular where an authority has been entrusted with a supervisory and regulatory task as extensive and general as that which has been assigned to the Commission in the field of competition. Consequently, the fact that the Commission applies different degrees of priority to the cases submitted to it in the field of competition is compatible with the obligations imposed on it by Community law.

78. That assessment does not conflict with the judgments of the Court of Justice in *Demo-Studio Schmidt*, [Case 210/81 *Demo-Studio Schmidt* v. *Commission* [1983] ECR 3045], in Case 298/83 *CICCE v Commission* [1985] ECR 1105 and in Joined Cases 142 and 156/84 *BAT and Reynolds* v *Commission* [1987] ECR 4487. In the judgment in *Demo-Studio Schmidt*, the Court of Justice held that the Commission 'was under a duty to examine the facts put forward' by the complainant, without prejudging the question whether the Commission could refrain from investigating the complaint because, in that case, the Commission had examined the facts set out in the complaint and had rejected it on the ground that there was nothing to suggest the existence of an infringement. Likewise this question did not arise in the later cases of *CICCE* (cited above) and *BAT and Reynolds* (cited above).

79. However, although the Commission cannot be compelled to conduct an investigation, the

procedural safeguards provided for by Article 3 of Regulation No 17 and Article 6 of Regulation No 99/63 oblige it nevertheless to examine carefully the factual and legal particulars brought to its notice by the complainant in order to decide whether they disclose conduct of such a kind as to distort competition in the common market and affect trade between Member States (see the judgments in *Demo-Studio Schmidt, CICCE* and *BAT and Reynolds,* cited above).

. . .

84. The next point to consider is whether it is legitimate, as the Commission has argued, to refer to the Community interest in a case as a priority criterion.

85. In this connection, it should be borne in mind that, unlike the civil courts, whose task is to safeguard the individual rights of private persons in their relations *inter se,* an administrative authority must act in the public interest. Consequently, the Commission is entitled to refer to the Community interest in order to determine the degree of priority to be applied to the various cases brought to its notice. This does not amount to removing action by the Commission from the scope of judicial review, since, in view of the requirement to provide a statement of reasons laid down by Article [253] of the Treaty, the Commission cannot merely refer to the Community interest in the abstract. It must set out the legal and factual considerations which led it to conclude that there was insufficient Community interest to justify investigation of the case. It is therefore by reviewing the legality of those reasons that the Court can review the Commission's action.

86. In order to assess the Community interest in further investigation of a case, the Commission must take account of the circumstances of the case, and in particular of the legal and factual particulars set out in the complaint referred to it. The Commission should in particular balance the significance of the alleged infringement as regards the functioning of the common market, the probability of establishing the existence of the infringement and the scope of the investigation required in order to fulfil, under the best possible conditions, its task of ensuring that Articles [81] and [82] are complied with.

Soon after this judgment the Commission issued a 'Notice on cooperation between national courts and the Commission in applying Articles 85 and 86 [now 81 and 82] of the EEC [now EC] Treaty' (the 'Cooperation Notice'). In this Cooperation Notice the Commission stressed that it will concentrate on cases with 'particular political, economic or legal significance for the Community'[23] and that it will be unwilling to take action where the Community provisions can be enforced before the national courts.

Notice on cooperation between national courts and the Commission in applying Articles 85 and 86 [now 81 and 82] of the EEC [now EC] Treaty [1993] OJ C39/6, [1993] 4 CMLR 12

13. As the administrative authority responsible for the Community's competition policy, the Commission must serve the Community's general interest. The administrative resources at the Commission's disposal to perform its task are necessarily limited and cannot be used to deal with all the cases brought to its attention. The Commission is therefore obliged, in general, to take all organizational measures necessary for the performance of its task and, in particular, to establish priorities [Case T–24/90 *Automec II,* paragraph 77].

14. The Commission intends, in implementing its decision-making powers, to concentrate on notifications, complaints and own-initiative proceedings having particular political, economic or legal

---

[23] Notice on cooperation between national courts and the Commission in applying Articles 85 and 86 [now 81 and 82] of the EEC [now EC] Treaty [1993] OJ C39/6, [1993] 4 CMLR 12, para. 14.

significance for the Community. Where these features are absent in a particular case, notifications will normally be dealt with by means of comfort letter and complaints should, as a rule, be handled by national courts or authorities.

15. The Commission considers that there is not normally a sufficient Community interest in examining a case when the plaintiff is able to secure adequate protection of his rights before the national courts [Case T–24/90 *Automec II*, paras. 91–94]. In these circumstances the complaint will normally be filed.

(iii) THE COMMISSION IS OBLIGED TO MAKE A FORMAL REJECTION OF THE COMPLAINT

Where the Commission decides not to act on a complaint three successive steps must be taken. First it must notify the complainant of this decision in a letter. This communication is know as an 'Article 6' letter since it is made pursuant to Article 6 of Regulation 2842/98.[24] Regulation 99/63). Following this communication the complainant must be given the opportunity to be heard. Once the Commission has taken account of the complainant's views it must then proceed to a formal decision.[25]

It is clear that these steps are not discretionary. Even though Regulation 17 does not specifically state that a formal rejection of a complaint is necessary,[26] the ECJ has confirmed that once the Article 6 letter has been served and the complainant has submitted his observations, the Commission must either initiate a procedure or adopt a definitive decision rejecting the complaint.

Case T–186/94 *Guérin Automobiles* v. *Commission* [1995] ECR II–1753, [1996] 4 CMLR 685, paragraph 34

[I]t should be emphasized that, having submitted within the time stipulated in the letter of 13 June 1994 comments in response to the Article 6 notification, the applicant is henceforth entitled to obtain a definitive decision from the Commission on its complaint; and that decision may, if the applicant sees fit, be challenged in an action for annulment before this court . . .

Although, therefore, the Commission cannot be required in every case to proceed to a formal decision on the compatibility of the conduct complained of with the competition rules it must, if it is not going to investigate, formally reject the complaint before closing its file.

The Commission considers that this procedure is too cumbersome and time-consuming (approximately half of the decisions it takes each year are rejections of complaints). It has thus proposed that the system should be simplified and more flexible arrangements should be made for hearing the complainant and the undertaking(s) complained against.[27]

---

[24] Commission Reg. 2842/98 of 22 Dec. 1998 on the hearing of parties in certain proceedings under Articles 85 and 86 [now 81 and 82] of the EC Treaty [1998] OJ L354/18.

[25] Case T–64/89, *Automec Srl* v. *Commission* (*Automec I*) [1990] ECR II–367, [1991] 4 CMLR 177.

[26] In the transport sector the regs. specifically state that a complaint must be rejected where the Commission considers that there are no grounds for action, see Reg. 1017/68 [1968]OJ Spec. Ed. 302, Art. 11(3); Reg. 4056/86 [1986] OJ L378/4, Art. 11(3); and Reg. 3975/8 [1989] OJ L374/1, Art. 4(2).

[27] White Paper on Modernisation, [1999] OJ C132/1, [1999] 5 CMLR 208, para. 121.

F. ACTING ON A COMPLAINT

(i) FACT FINDING AND OPENING A FORMAL PROCEDURE

The Commission may determine whether or not to act on a complaint by using its investigatory powers to collect information and evidence relating to the breach. If it then considers it to be worthwhile it may open a procedure by issuing a Statement of Objections. The Commission's fact-finding powers and the opening of a formal procedure are discussed in Chapter 14 above. A few points of importance to a complainant will, however, be reiterated here. In particular, the complainant will wish to know what rights he has during the course of the investigation, whether the Commission is able to take interim measures to prevent the alleged breach of the competition rules and what action the Commission may take if it finally issues a decision finding a breach of the rules.

(ii) THE RIGHTS OF THE COMPLAINANT IN THE COURSE OF AN INVESTIGATION

When acting on a complaint the Commission generally informs the undertakings being investigated of the allegations set out in the complaint. Since the Commission is bound by a general duty of confidentiality[28] the complainant should be sure to mark any business secrets or other confidential information which it does not wish the Commission to disclose. The complainants right to protect its confidential information is discussed in Chapter 14 above.

A complainant has a right to be heard both where the Commission decides to reject his complaint[29] and where the Commission decides to conduct an investigation.[30] The complainant is entitled to make its views known in writing and may be given the opportunity to make oral submissions if it so requests.[31] In practice, the Commission strives to keep the complainant fully informed, especially if it intends to take a negative clearance or exemption decision or to negotiate a settlement with the undertakings complained of.[32] In *BAT and Reynolds v. Commission*[33] the ECJ held that although the procedural rights of a complainant were not as extensive as those being investigated by the Commission, complainants had to 'be given the opportunity to defend their legitimate interests in the course of the administrative proceedings'.

A complainant's right of access to the file is much more limited than that of an undertaking complained of.[34] In *Matra Hachette v. Commission*[35] the CFI indicated that the right to full disclosure applied only to undertakings which were likely to be penalized by a Commission decision taken pursuant to Article 81 or 82. In contrast the right of third party

---

[28] Art 287 of the Treaty and Reg. 17, Art. 20 *supra* n. 9, discussed *supra* Chap. 14.

[29] Reg 2842/98 [1998] OJ L354/18 , Art. 6; *supra* 953.

[30] *Ibid.*, Art. 7.

[31] Reg 2842/98, Art. 8.

[32] Cases 142 & 156/84 *BAT and Reynolds v. Commission* [1987] ECR 4487, [1988] 4 CMLR 24.

[33] *Ibid.*, para. 20.

[34] See discussion *supra* in Chap. 14.

[35] Case T–17/93 [1994] ECR II–595; see especially para. 34.

complainants was simply to participate in the administrative procedure. In practice, however, complainants are informed of the contents of the file and given access to those documents which are not confidential[36] and kept informed of responses made by undertakings to the complaints lodged against them.[37]

(iii) REMEDIES

a. TERMINATION OF THE INFRINGEMENT, NEGATIVE CLEARANCE OR EXEMPTION

It was seen in Chapter 14 that, following an investigation, the Commission can take a final decision ordering that an infringement be brought to an end.[38] This usually takes the form of a cease and desist order but *positive* measures can be ordered by the Commission where necessary to terminate or to reverse the infringement.[39] In *Automec II*, however, the Court of First Instance indicated that the Commission did not have power to insist on contractual arrangements when other suitable means were at its disposal to compel the termination of the infringement.[40] When dealing with an agreement which has been notified to it, the Commission may also grant the agreement an exemption or issue a decision stating that the agreement does not infringe Article 81(1) at all.[41]

If the Commission does find that an undertaking has infringed Article 81 or 82 it may impose fines on any undertaking involved in the breach.[42] The Commission cannot compensate an undertaking which has suffered loss in consequence of a breach. In its Guidelines on the methods of setting fines, however, the Commission indicates that a number of factors are relevant to its determination of the final fine imposed. For example, the Commission seeks to ensure that the fine imposed exceeds any amount gained improperly as a result of the infringement *and* that the capacity of the offender to cause damage to others is taken into account.[43]

b. INTERIM RELIEF

Of enormous importance to a complainant is the Commission's ability to grant interim relief. Although Regulation 17 itself does not specifically confer power on the Commission to grant such relief it was seen in Chapter 14 that the ECJ in *Camera Care* confirmed that Article 3(1) did entitle the Commission to take interim measures.[44]

In *Sea Containers Ltd/Stena Sealink—Interim Measures*,[45] for example, the applicant applied to the Court seeking an order that the Commission should grant interim measures

---

[36] The Commission's *XIIth Report on Competition Policy* (Commission, 1982), pt 35.

[37] See, e.g., the Commission's *XIIIth Report on Competition Policy* (Commission, 1983), pt 7.

[38] Reg. 17, Art. 3.

[39] *Supra* Chap. 14.

[40] Case T–24/90 [1992] ECR II–2223, [1992] 5 CMLR 431, para. 51. This aspect of *Automec II* is discussed in Chap. 14.

[41] *Supra* Chap. 4.

[42] Reg, 17 Art. 15(2); *supra* Chap. 14

[43] The Guidelines [1998] OJ C9/3 are set out in Chap. 14.

[44] Case 792/79R, *Camera Care* v. *Commission* [1980] ECR 119, [1980] 1 CMLR 334. See also the Commission's proposal for a Reg. implementing Arts. 81 and 82, Art. 8, COM(2000)582, 27 Sept. 2000.

[45] [1994] OJ L15/8, [1995] 4 CMLR 84; see *supra* Chap. 8.

against Stena Sealink Line and Stena Sealink Port which it considered to be committing an abuse of a dominant position contrary to Article 82. The Court rejected the application. Although the Court held that the applicant had established a sufficient *prima facie* case of an infringement it held that the measures were not required urgently, arising from the danger of serious and irreperable harm.

G. JUDICIAL REVIEW PROCEEDINGS

(i) AN OMISSION TO ACT

Where the Commission is in breach of an obligation to act it is possible, under Article 232 (ex Article 175) of the Treaty, to bring proceedings in respect of its failure to act. Before such proceedings can be brought it is essential that the Commission should have been called upon to act and have failed to adopt a measure in relation to the complainant which that complainant was legally entitled to claim by virtue of the rules of Community law.

Article 232

Should the European Parliament, the Council or the Commission, in infringement of this Treaty, fail to act, the Member States and the other institutions of the Community may bring an action before the Court of Justice to have the infringement established.

The action shall be admissible only if the institution concerned has first been called upon to act. If, within two months of being so called upon, the institution concerned has not defined its position, the action may be brought within a further period of two months.

Any natural or legal person may, under the conditions laid down in the preceding paragraphs, complain to the Court of Justice that an institution of the Community has failed to address to that person any act other than a recommendation or an opinion.

Since a complainant cannot insist that the Commission should commence an investigation it cannot bring proceedings under Article 232 in respect of its failure to launch such an investigation. However, because the Commission is obliged to issue a formal rejection of a complaint, a complainant can bring Article 232 proceedings where such a final decision has not been taken. Once the Commission informs a complainant that it has decided to close its file and has formally rejected a complaint that complainant may, if it so wishes, bring judicial review proceedings under Article 230 (ex Article 173) of the Treaty challenging the validity of that decision.

(ii) REVIEW OF ACTS

a. STANDING

A complainant may wish to bring proceedings to annul a Commission decision rejecting its complaint or any decision made subsequent to an investigation. The procedure for bringing judicial review proceedings under Article 230 of the Treaty is described in detail in Chapter 14 above. A few points of importance are made here, however.

The Court takes the view that if an individual has standing to complain to the Commission pursuant to Article 3(2)(b) of Regulation 17 it will also have standing to institute proceedings where its complaint is rejected. Complainants are directly and individually concerned within the meaning of Article 230 of the Treaty. The Court has taken a broad view of individuals which are directly and individually concerned within the field of the EC competition rules.[46]

b. A REVIEWABLE ACT

Only legally binding measures intended to have legal force can be challenged under Article 230.[47] The formal rejection of a complaint is a reviewable act within the meaning of Article 230. However, the Article 6 letter and preliminary investigations are not and may not be challenged. In some cases it may be difficult to determine whether or not the Commission has gone beyond the investigation procedure, which is not open to challenge, or whether the Commission has actually given a final decision which is susceptible to challenge under Article 230.[48]

Final decisions adopted by the Commission may clearly be annulled under Article 230.

c. GROUNDS FOR ANNULMENT

The grounds for annulment are the ordinary grounds set out in Article 230 of the Treaty itself, lack of competence, infringement of an essential procedural requirement, infringement of the Treaty or any rule of law or misuse of power.[49]

In *Automec II* the CFI considered whether the Commission had been right to rule that the case had insufficient Community interest to warrant further investigation.[50] This judgment makes it clear that the Court will ensure that the Commission evaluates the factual and legal considerations with due care and that proper reasons are given for its rejection of a complaint. A complaint will, however, be legitimately rejected if the complainant can get effective protection of his rights before a national court.

H. COMPLAINTS AND THE MERGER REGULATION

On account of the different procedural structure of the Merger Regulation,[51] and in particular the tight time limits within which decisions must be made, the complaints procedure is more formal when made within the context of this regulation.

---

[46] See *supra* Chap. 14. Contrast the position where an individual wishes to challenge the enactment of Regs. or decisions in other circumstances. In these cases the Community Courts have taken an extremely strict approach to standing: see P. Craig and G. de Búrca, *EU Law: Text, Cases and Materials* (2nd edn., Oxford University Press, Oxford, 1998), 466–73.

[47] *Supra* Chap. 14.

[48] See also, e.g., Case T–37/92, *BEUC* [1995] ECR II–285, [1995] 4 CMLR 167 and Case C–39/93P, *SFEI* v. *Commission* [1994] ECR I–2681.

[49] *Supra* Chap. 14.

[50] Case T–24/90, *Automec Srl* v. *Commission (Automec II)* [1992] ECR II–2223, [1992] 5 CMLR 431.

[51] Council Reg. 4064/89 [1989] OJ L395/1, as amended by Council Reg. 13110/97 [1997] OJ L180/1.

Broadly, third parties with a sufficient interest (which, for example, believe that they would be adversely affected by a decision to authorize a merger[52]) and members of the administration or management of the undertakings concerned or recognized workers' representatives of those undertakings are entitled on application to be heard by the Commission.[53] Not all entities entitled to complain may have full standing under Article 230, however. For example, in *Comité Central d'Entreprise de la SA des Grands Sources v. Commission* the CFI held that although the unions did have standing under Article 230 they could not challenge the substance of the decision made by the Commission under the regulation, which was not of direct concern to them.[54]

3. PROCEEDINGS IN THE NATIONAL COURTS

A. GENERAL

There has, within the European Community, been very little 'antitrust litigation' brought by private individuals to enforce the EC competition rules. This position is in stark contrast to that which exists in the USA where there is a culture of such litigation which, arguably, has contributed to the success of the antitrust rules. Indeed, one US commentator has stated his view that:

no antitrust regulation system has any realistic chance of success without it. Government antitrust authorities will never have the resources to prosecute all infringements which should be pursued and should not be in the business of awarding compensation. My own experience in private antitrust litigation—mostly for the defence—has brought me to the belief that society, and even the best firms, benefit from the constraints on behaviour which exist and are perceived to exist from the presence of a viable private enforcement system. To those who believe that private enforcement is wasteful, I reply that this is sometimes true, but it is better than the alternative of inadequate private enforcement. If we are to have private antitrust laws, we should have effective ones which are enforced.[55]

The European Commission is in favour of, and is seeking to encourage, greater private

---

[52] Cases C–68/94 and C–30/95 *France v. Commission* [1998] ECR I–1375, [1998] 4 CMLR 829.

[53] Merger Reg., Art. 18(4), Reg. 447/98 [1998] OJ L106/1, Arts. 11–17.

[54] Case T–96/92 [1995] ECR II–1213. They could, however, insist that procedural rights conferred upon them were respected. See also *Comité Central d'Entreprise de la Société Anonyme Vittel and Comité d'Etablissement de Peirval and Fédération Générale Agroalimentaire v. Commission* [1995] ECR II–1247 and *infra* Chap. 12.

[55] C.A. Jones, *Private Enforcement of Antitrust Law in the EU, UK and USA* (Oxford University Press, Oxford, 1999), p. xii. He also comments at p. xi. of the preface that he was prompted to write the book partly as a result of his astonishment to learn that 'antitrust litigation as known to most of the American antitrust bar essentially did not exist in Europe'. The purpose of his book is thus to 'encourage the private antitrust litigation in the UK and the EC' (p. xii).

enforcement of Community competition law before the national courts. The Commission believes that increased enforcement at the national level will both heighten awareness of, and respect for, the Community provisions and free the Commission's own resources for complex cases which raise new or difficult problems from a legal or economic point of view. In addition, it believes that national proceedings will, in many cases, provide a quicker and more efficient means of bringing infringements to an end.[56] In order to encourage such proceedings it has been seen that the Commission has indicated that it will not ordinarily act where the rights conferred by the competition law provisions can be protected at the national level. The Commission has also stressed in its Cooperation Notice the advantages that would result to individuals where private proceedings are brought. In particular a private litigant may be able to recover compensation in respect of loss, to obtain interim measures, to pursue remedies for breach of national law, and to recoup the costs of the proceedings.

Notice on cooperation between national courts and the Commission in applying Articles 85 and 86 [now 81 and 82] of the EEC [now EC] Treaty [1993] OJ C 39/6, [1993] 4 CMLR 12

15. The Commission considers that there is not normally a sufficient Community interest in examining a case when the plaintiff is able to secure adequate protection of his rights before the national courts [Case T–24/90 *Automec II*, paras. 91–94]. In these circumstances the complaint will normally be filed.

16. In this respect the Commission would like to make it clear that the application of Community competition law by the national courts has considerable advantages for individuals and companies:

— the Commission cannot award compensation for loss suffered as a result of an infringement of Article [81] or Article [82]. Such claims may be brought only before the national courts. Companies are more likely to avoid infringements of the Community competition rules if they risk having to pay damages or interest in such an event,

— national courts can usually adopt interim measures and order the ending of infringements more quickly than the Commission is able to do,

— before national courts, it is possible to combine a claim under Community law with a claim under national law. This is not possible in a procedure before the Commission,

— in some Member States, the courts have the power to award legal costs to the successful applicant. This is never possible in the administrative procedure before the Commission.

The Cooperation Notice also sets out general guidance for national courts dealing with cases which raise a point of Community competition law. Despite this clear policy, there has

---

[56] See the Commission's *XV Report on Competition Policy* (Commission, 1985), pt 39.

still been no case in which damages have been awarded by an English court to compensate for loss arising from an infringement of Article 81 or 82 of the Treaty.[57]

It is unclear why such a small volume of litigation has arisen in the English courts (and in Europe generally), especially when contrasted with the relatively large volumes of litigation arising before the US courts. Common suggestions for the difference in approach and the comparative success of private enforcement of the rules in the US are founded on factors such as:

(1) the existence of wider discovery powers;
(2) the availability of treble damages;[58]
(3) the ability to bring class actions;
(4) the fact that US citizens are generally more litigious; and
(5) the differences in the competition provisions.

A key factor, however, appears to be the perception of individuals and the difference in the way that the two sets of rules have developed.

C.A. Jones, *Private Enforcement of Antitrust Law in the EU, UK and USA* (Oxford University Press, Oxford 1999), 85

[T]he US enforcement system was explicitly created with public-private pluralism in mind. The litigation-oriented US system has for decades relied on a ratio of private to public suits ranging from 10 to 1 to 20 to 1, and there has never been any expectation[59] that the Antitrust Division of the US Department of Justice would shape antitrust law in the manner of the Commission.

In contrast, the Community system has resulted in the Commission having virtually exclusive control of competition regulation. The Community's centralized administrative system of antitrust and the lack of explicit provision for private enforcement have made it extremely difficult for such actions to gain a significant foothold in Community jurisprudence. Some have argued that in the Community system there can be no place (read 'should be' no place) for private actions.

It must be correct that the main reason for the dearth of private litigation is the fact that the Commission, historically, wished to retain control over, and to mould, EC competition

---

[57] Successful actions have, however, been brought in Germany and France: see e.g., *Metro-Cartier Düsseldorf* Court of Appeal, 20 Dec. 1988 and *Euro Garage* v. *Renault*, Cour d'Appel, de Paris, 23 Mar. 1989.

[58] 'It is thought by some in Europe that private antitrust actions under Community law will never be of importance due to the absence of the legislative provision for treble damages which so ubiquitously characterizes the remedy provisions of the Sherman Act. It is submitted that the perceived superiority of the treble damages provisions of US law over damages rules available in Europe is exaggerated. In fact, . . . other components of the damage system in the USA are such that 'treble' damages under US law are essentially mythical and that comparable results are in fact obtainable in Europe, especially in the UK, without a treble damages multiplier': C.A. Jones, *Private Enforcement of Antitrust Law in the EU, UK and USA* (Oxford University Press, 1999), 199. That author also notes (at 35–6) that the model for the treble damages formula adopted in the USA was an English Statute of Monopolies 1623 (now repealed). He points out the irony in this 'in view of the distaste for US antitrust treble damages actions reflected in some British judgments and statutes' (see in particular *Midland Bank plc* v. *Laker Airways Ltd* [1986] 1 QB 689 and the Protection of Trading Interests Act 1980).

[59] It is pointed out that one of the main purposes of the dual enforcement system in the USA was to prevent political and budgetary considerations from affecting enforcement resources and legal principles: C.A. Jones, *Private Enforcement of Antitrust Law in the EU, UK and USA* (Oxford University Press, 1999), 89.

policy. It has taken the leading role in enforcement actions and has only in relatively recent times sought to encourage more enforcement at the national level. In particular, this policy was encouraged and made possible by the Council's decision to confer exclusive power on the Commission to grant individual exemptions to agreements under Article 81(3). By adopting a broad interpretation of Article 81(1) the Commission has been able to reserve for itself the primary role in assessing agreements for their compatibility with Article 81. The wide view of Article 81(1) has excluded national courts and national competition authorities from this task. This 'bifurcation of Article 81 . . . and the exclusive allocation in Regulation 17 of the power of exemption to the Commission . . . have the effect of excluding the national courts of the Member States from 'what the legal system of the United States understands by antitrust analysis'.[60] In the USA this has not been possible since the prohibition of contracts in restraint of trade set out in section 1 of the Sherman Act 1890 can be applied in its entirety by the US courts. No part of it is reserved exclusively to the US enforcement authorities.

There is no doubt that greater private enforcement would have a significant effect on the application of the EC competition rules. In particular, it would mean that: (1) the enforcement of the rules is not left to Commission when its resources and inclination permit; (2) the legal principles, in particular the interpretation of Article 81, would be more heavily influenced by the courts (national and, through Article 234 references, the ECJ) than is currently the case; (3) victims would be able to obtain remedies in respect of breaches of the rules; and (4) the threat of private proceedings would serve as an extra deterrent discouraging breaches of the rules.

Given the Commission's unwillingness to deal with cases which it considers can be dealt with adequately at the national level and in view, in particular, of its proposals set out in the White Paper on Modernisation its draft Regulation that Article 81(3) should be made directly applicable, it seems inevitable that numbers of proceedings before the national courts will have to increase. The sections below set out the difficulties confronting potential applicants and the issues that may have to be resolved if increased litigation is to become a reality.

B. THE PROBLEMS WITH PRIVATE ACTION

It has already been noted that, in comparison with the position in the USA, there is not a culture of private enforcement of the competition rules within the European Community. The discussion in section A above suggests that one of the key reasons for this has been the perception that the Commission is responsible for competition policy and the enforcement of the rules. Indeed, in its *Thirteenth Report on Competition Policy* the Commission complained that there was a 'widespread misconception on the part of the public in Europe that only the Commission can enforce Articles [81] and [82]'.[61]

In addition, however, it seems that private litigation has been deterred by a number of other obstacles confronting an individual considering action. Some commentators have even gone as far as to argue that private enforcement of the competition rules should not be

---

[60] C.A. Jones, *Private Enforcement of Antitrust Law in the EU, UK and USA* (Oxford University Press, 1999), 85; see also *supra* Chap. 4.

[61] EC Commission, *XIII Report on Competition Policy* (Commission, 1983), pt 217.

encouraged.[62] This point of view is summarized by Jones in the following extract from his book.

C.A. Jones, *Private Enforcement of Antitrust Law in the EU, UK and USA* (Oxford University Press, 1999), 88–9

In an article representative of this school of thought, then Professor, now Advocate General, Jacobs listed several objections to the practice of national courts taking final decisions in damages actions based on the antitrust rules.[63] The principal 'practical' objections put forth seem to be that (1) lack of resources at Community level is not a relevant reason for deciding an issue principle; (2) compensation of victims for violations of Community antitrust is not a sufficient justification where breaches of national competition law do not ordinarily give rise to actions for damages; (3) courts are not appropriate agencies to decide complex issues of fact and policy present in the competition field; (4) the co-existence of two systems of antitrust law, national and Community, means that a right to damages would turn on the 'relatively insignificant criterion' of whether there exists an actual or potential effect on interstate trade-which is regarded as 'making a nonsense of the assertion of a claim to damages in national courts in cases where there would be no such claim for breach of the domestic antitrust law'; . . . (5) it may be difficult for plaintiffs to meet their burden of proof, especially with regard to obstacles to discovery of documents; (6) it is uncertain who would have standing to sue and there would be the risk of multiple actions by different parties in different Member States with the possibility of conflicting results; (7) there would be a risk of forum-shopping if plaintiffs sought to sue in the jurisdiction offering the best prospects for success and the highest available damages award; and (8) prospective plaintiffs might consider that in the absence of treble damages and class actions, the damages recovered might not justify the total risks of litigation.

It seems likely that many of the factors discussed in the extract above have inhibited proceedings, for example: the cost and risk of litigation (this may well deter many smaller undertakings from acting); the complex economic evidence which may have to be raised to establish a breach of the rules (most cases will require markets to be defined etc.); the fact that some national courts are not used to antitrust arguments and may not, consequently, be the most appropriate or understanding forum for the hearing; the fact that the breach may have to be proved to a standard which is higher than on the balance of probabilities;[64] and the need to establish a causal link between the damage suffered by the applicant and the infringement of the competition rules. Further, action may be deterred by other inhibitions, such as: the difficulty of gathering the requisite evidence, especially where it is situated in another Member State or States;[65] the fact that

---

[62] F.G. Jacobs 'Civil Enforcement of EEC Antitrust Law' (1984) 82 *Mich. L Rev.* 1364.

[63] The author does not intend to imply that these views are still held by Jacobs AG today.

[64] In *Masterfoods v. HB Ice Cream* [1992] 3 CMLR 830 the Irish High Court took the view that the requisite standard is balance of probabilities. But, because of the possibility of fines, it is possible that a breach of the competition rules is closer to criminal proceedings, which would demand the breach to be proved to a higher standard: see discussion *supra* in Chap. 12, and see the view of the English High Court in *Shearson Lehmann* v. *McLaine Watson* [1989] 3 CMLR 429 (a high degree of probability is required).

[65] In Case T–5/93 *Tremblay* v. *Commission* [1995] ECR II–185, the CFI acknowledged that difficulties would arise where a national court did not have sufficient powers to ensure all the evidence, whether situated locally or abroad, is gathered. In contrast the Commission has wide powers to gather evidence and may unearth extremely useful evidence when conducting dawn raids (Reg. 17, Art. 14(3). This breadth of information is unlikely to come to light when using the ordinary national civil disclosure rules.

proceedings are likely to be lengthy and protracted (especially if an Article 234 (ex Article 177) reference to the ECJ is necessary); the possibility that the defendant may invoke a privilege against self-incrimination,[66] the uncertainty whether, and if so when, the applicant may rely on Commission documents and Commission decisions in national proceedings;[67] and difficulties which result from the possibility of dual enforcement. National courts have an obligation to ensure that their decisions do not conflict with any decision which might be given at the Community level, so in many cases the national court will have to stay proceedings or take interim measures pending the Commission decision.[68]

In England these problems have been compounded by the reluctance of the courts to grant interim relief, the general uncertainty surrounding the question of what remedies, if any, are available to compensate those which have suffered as a result of another's breach of the competition rules, and the far from enthusiastic response with which those pleading a breach of the competition rules have been met.

C. COMPLAINT *V.* PRIVATE ACTION: THE PROS AND CONS

IN FAVOUR OF A COMPLAINT	IN FAVOUR OF A PRIVATE ACTION
National proceedings are expensive and the outcome uncertain.	The Commission will not act on all complaints. It can reject complaints.
National courts may be unfamiliar with the economic issues raised by competition law cases.	The Commission may be reluctant to grant interim relief.
Breaches of the competition rules may be difficult to establish (particularly when dealing with Article 82). Legal difficulties in proving a breach may be compounded by evidential and procedural problems.	The Commission cannot compensate an entity in respect of loss suffered in consequence of a breach of the competition rules.
The ECJ has not ruled whether specific remedies are necessary to protect the Community rights of entities harmed by a breach of the competition rules.	The Commission cannot award costs to a complainant.
English law is not clear on what remedies are available to individuals harmed by a breach of the competition rules.	An entity is in control of the private action. The action is not dependent upon the view of the Commission and proceedings been taken by it.
Complaining to the Commission is relatively cheap.	National courts may order interlocutory remedies. English courts may grant an interim injunction. However, if such an injunction is granted a cross undertaking in damages will have to be given.

Where the Commission acts on a complaint it may, in some circumstances, grant interim relief. The complainant will not have to give a cross-undertaking in damages if subsequent proceedings are unsuccessful.

National courts may award remedies in respect of a breach, e.g. injunction/ damages/ restitution

The Commission will put an end to infringements of the rules and may impose significant fines on parties found to be in breach. It does not have to show that the breach caused any damage to another entity.

National courts may be able to award costs to successful parties.

Where an entity wishes to object to a Commission decision which has been granted its only option will be to bring judicial review proceedings before the CFI.

There may also be a breach of national law.

D. THE ENFORCEABILITY OF AGREEMENTS INFRINGING ARTICLE 81 OR 82

(i) ARTICLE 81

a. THE SANCTION OF NULLITY

The incompatibility of a contract with Article 81 can of course be raised in national proceedings. The ECJ has made it plain that the effect of Article 81(2) is that, in the absence on an exemption, clauses in an agreement prohibited by Article 81(1) are void. Further, the agreement as a whole is void if those clauses cannot be severed from the remaining provisions of the contract.[69]

Both Article 81(1) and (2) are directly effective[70] and must be applied by the national courts. The position of those courts when applying Article 81(2) is, however, considerably complicated by the fact that the Commission currently has the exclusive right to grant

---

[66] The protection given to a defendant under English law (see *Rio Tinto Zinc* v. *Westinghouse Electric Corp.* [1978] AC 547) is significantly greater than that granted to an undertaking being investigated by the Commission for a breach of one of the Treaty competition rules: see *supra* Chap. 14.

[67] It now seems to be accepted by the English courts that a Commission decision cannot be challenged by the parties to an action, see e.g., *Iberian UK Ltd* v. *BPB Industries plc* [1997] 4 CMLR 33. Further, it seems that litigants may rely on other Commission documents, such as a statement of objections, in national proceedings, see Case T–353/94 *Postbank* v. *Commission* [1996] ECR II–921, [1997] 4 CMLR 33 (subject to compliance with the *AKZO* procedure). *Cf.* the judgment in Case C–67/91, *Dirección General de Defensa de las Competencia* v. *Asociación España de Banca Privada (AEB) and others (Spanish Banks)* [1992] ECR I–4820, *infra* n. 217 and accompanying text.

[68] See discussion of enforceability of agreements *infra*.

[69] Case 56/65, *Société La Technique Minière* v. *Maschinêbau Ulm GmbH* [1966] ECR 234, [1966] CMLR 357; Case 319/82, *Société de Vente de Ciments et Bétons de l'Est SA* v. *Kerpen & Kerpen GmbH & Co KG* [1983] ECR, [1985] 1 CMLR 511. See *supra* Chap. 3.

[70] See Case 234/89, *Delimitis* v. *Henninger Bräu* [1991] ECR I–935, [1992] 5 CMLR 210, para. 45 and Case 127/73, *BRT* v. *SABAM* [1974] ECR 51, [1974] 2 CMLR 238.

exemptions under Article 81(3). Although a national court can apply the provisions of a block exemption and consider whether or not an agreement falls within it, it may not apply the criteria set out in Article 81(3) to determine whether an agreement which infringes Article 81(1) otherwise merits an exemption. Where the nullity of an agreement or a provision in an agreement under Article 81 is raised in national proceedings the national court should, therefore, determine whether or not the relevant agreement benefits from provisional validity, whether it has been exempted from the application of Article 81(3), or whether it is possible that the Commission may clear or exempt the agreement in the future.

b. PROVISIONAL VALIDITY

A national court should take cognizance of the fact that 'old' agreements, concluded prior to the adoption of Regulation 17, enjoy provisional validity, and are treated as valid so long as they were notified to the Commission by 1 November 1962. Such an agreement benefits from provisional validity until the Commission holds otherwise.[71] A national court may not, therefore, declare automatically void under Article 81(2) agreements which have been duly notified and which were in existence prior to the adoption of Regulation 17. Although old agreements are extremely rare, it is possible that agreements which become subject to the Treaty competition rules by virtue of a Member State's accession also enjoy provisional validity.[72]

c. NOTIFIED AND NON-NOTIFIABLE AGREEMENTS

The national court must respect any individual exemption granted to an agreement and apply the provisions of any relevant block exemption to determine whether or not the agreement is exempted under that Regulation. The national court must also proceed with caution where the parties to the agreement have notified it to the Commission or if the agreement is a non-notifiable agreement.[73] In these circumstances a finding by the national court that the agreement infringes Article 81(1) and is consequently void risks conflicting with a Commission decision clearing or exempting the agreement.

In *Delimitis* v. *Henninger Bräu*[78] the ECJ stressed that national courts have a duty to avoid decisions which would conflict with one by the Commission. It set out guidance for national courts dealing with cases raising the possibility of nullity under Article 81(2). Broadly, the position is that the national court may proceed if:

(1) the agreement clearly does not infringe Article 81(1);[75]

---

[71] [1959–62] OJ Spec. Ed. 87. See Case 48/72, *Brasserie de Haecht* v. *Wilkin Jansen* [1973] ECR 77, [1973] CMLR 287, and Cases 253/78, 1–3, 37 and 99/79 *Lancôme* v. *Etos BV* [1980] ECR 2511, [1981] 2 CMLR 164.

[72] *Supra* Chap. 4. Notice on cooperation between national courts and the Commission in applying Articles 85 and 86 [now 81 and 82] of the EEC [now EC] Treaty [1993] OJ C39/6, [1993] 4 CMLR 12, para. 31. But see C.S. Kerse, *EC Antitrust Procedure* (4th ed)n., Sweet & Maxwell, 1998), para. 10.07.

[73] Non-notifiable agreements may be granted an exemption retrospectively to the date that the agreement was concluded.

[74] Case C–234/89 [1991] ECR I–935, [1992] 5 CMLR 210.

[75] In this case there is scarcely any risk of the Commission taking a conflicting decision: Case 234/89, *Delimitis* v. *Henninger Bräu* [1991] ECR 1–935, [1992] 5 CMLR 210, para. 50. The national court may, of

(2) the agreement infringes Article 81(1) but benefits from an individual or block exemption;[76] or

(3) the agreement clearly infringes Article 81(1) and will undoubtedly not be exempted by the Commission under Article 81(3).[77]

Where, however, the national court considers that the agreement may infringe Article 81(1) but that an exemption may be forthcoming, the national court should ordinarily stay the proceedings or adopt interim measures pursuant to its national rules of proceeding (even if a comfort letter indicates that the Commission believes that the agreement merits exemption[78]).

In determining what course of action to take the national court may, so long as its procedures allow it, make contact with the Commission and request information from it. In particular, it may seek information on whether a notification has been made, the status of Commission proceedings, points of law, and factual data. Where appropriate the Commission could be asked to proceed to a decision on the agreement's compatibility with Article 81. The Commission has indicated in its Cooperation Notice that it will give priority to cases which are the subject of national proceedings and which have been suspended pending a Commission decision.[79]

Case C–234/89, *Delimitis* v. *Henninger Bräu* [1991] ECR 1–935, [1992] 5 CMLR 210

It will be remembered that this case involved a contractual dispute between a café proprietor and a publican. In the course of those proceedings the compatibility of the brewery agreement with Article 81 was raised. The Court of Justice set out guidelines for the national court on how to assess the agreement's compatibility with Article 81.

Court of Justice

The jurisdiction of the national court to apply Article [81] to an agreement not enjoying the protection of an exemption regulation

43. In its final question the national court asks what assessment it is to make under Community competition rules in regard to an agreement which does not satisfy the conditions for the application of Regulation No 1984/83. That question raises a general problem of a procedural nature concerning the respective powers of the Commission and national courts in the application of those rules.

---

course, seek guidance from the ECJ on the compatibility of the agreement before it with Art. 81(1) using the procedure set out in Art. 234. This is what happened in *Delimitis* itself. A national court may wish to take account of a Commission comfort letter which states its view that the agreement does not infringe Art. 81(1). Such a letter does not, however, prevent a national court from reaching a different conclusion, Cases 253/78, 1–3, 37 and 99/79, *Lancôme* v. *Etos BV* [1980] ECR 2511, [1973] CMLR 287.

[76] The national court may not rely on a Commission comfort letter stating its view that the agreement would benefit from an exemption pursuant to Art. 81(3): Case C–234/89, *Delimitis* v. *Henninger Bräu* [1991] ECR 1–935, [1992] 5 CMLR 210.

[77] Case 234/89, *Delimitis* v. *Henninger Bräu* [1991] ECR 1–935, [1992] 5 CMLR 210, para. 50.

[78] *Supra* n. 76.

[79] Commission Notice on Cooperation between national courts and the Commission in applying Articles 85 and 86 [now 81 and 82] of the EEC [now EC] Treaty [1993] OJ C39/6, [1993] 4 CMLR 12, paras 40–41.

44. In that respect it should be stressed, first of all, that the Commission is responsible for the implementation and orientation of Community competition policy. It is for the Commission to adopt, subject to review by the Court of First Instance and the Court of Justice, individual decisions in accordance with the procedural rules in force and to adopt exemption regulations. The performance of that task necessarily entails complex economic assessments, in particular in order to assess whether an agreement falls under Article [81(3)]. Pursuant to Article 9(1) of Regulation No 17 of the Council of 6 February 1962, First regulation implementing Articles 85 and 86 [now 81 and 82] of the EEC [now EC] Treaty (Official Journal, English Special Edition 1959–62, p. 87), the Commission has exclusive competence to adopt decisions in implementation of Article [81(3)].

45. On the other hand, the Commission does not have exclusive competence to apply Articles [81(1)] and [82]. It shares that competence with the national courts. As the Court stated in its judgment in Case 127/73 (*BRT v SABAM* [1974] ECR 51), Articles [81(1)] and [82] produce direct effect in relations between individuals and create rights directly in respect of the individuals concerned which the national courts must safeguard.

46. The same is true of the provisions of the exemption regulation (judgment in Case 63/75, *Fonderies Roubaix* [1976] ECR 111). The direct applicability of those provisions may not, however, lead the national courts to modify the scope of the exemption regulations by extending their sphere of application to agreements not covered by them. Any such extension, whatever its scope, would affect the manner in which the Commission exercises its legislative competence.

47. It now falls to examine the consequences of that division of competence as regards the specific application of the Community competition rules by national courts. Account should here be taken of the risk of national courts taking decisions which conflict with those taken or envisaged by the Commission in the implementation of Articles [81(1)] and [82], and also of Article [81(3)]. Such conflicting decisions would be contrary to the general principle of legal certainty and must, therefore, be avoided when national courts give decisions on agreements or practices which may subsequently be the subject of a decision by the Commission.

48. As the Court has consistently held, national courts may not, where the Commission has given no decision under Regulation No 17, declare automatically void under Article [81(2)] agreements which were in existence prior to 13 March 1962, when that regulation came into force, and have been duly notified (judgment in Case 48/72 *Brasserie De Haecht v Wilkin Jansen* [1973] ECR 77; and judgment in Case 59/77 *De Bloos v Bouyer* [1977] ECR 2359). Those agreements in fact enjoy provisional validity until the Commission has given a decision (judgment in Case 99/79 *Lancôme v Etos* [1980] ECR 2511).

49. The contract at issue in the main proceedings was entered into on 14 May 1985 and there is nothing in the file to indicate that that contract represents an exact reproduction of a standard contract concluded before 13 March 1962 and duly notified (judgment in Case 1/70 *Rochas* [1970] ECR 515). The contract would not therefore appear to enjoy provisional validity. Nevertheless, in order to reconcile the need to avoid conflicting decisions with the national court's duty to rule on the claims of a party to the proceedings that the agreement is automatically void, the national court may have regard to the following considerations in applying Article [81].

50. If the conditions for the application of Article [81(1)] are clearly not satisfied and there is, consequently, scarcely any risk of the Commission taking a different decision, the national court may continue the proceedings and rule on the agreement in issue. It may do the same if the agreement's incompatibility with Article [81(1)] is beyond doubt and, regard being had to the exemption regulations and the Commission's previous decisions, the agreement may on no account be the subject of an exemption decision under Article [81(3)].

51. In that connection it should be borne in mind that such a decision may only be taken in respect of an agreement which has been notified or is exempt from having to be notified. Under Article 4(2) of Regulation No 17, an agreement is exempt from the notification obligation when only undertakings from a single Member State are parties to it and it does not relate to imports or exports between Member States. A beer supply agreement may satisfy those conditions, even if it forms an integral part of a series of similar contracts (judgment in *Bilger v Jehle*, [Case 43/69 *Bilger* v. *Jehle* [1970] ECR 127]).

52. If the national court finds that the contract in issue satisfies those formal requirements and if it considers in the light of the Commission's rules and decision-making practices, that that agreement may be the subject of an exemption decision, the national court may decide to stay the proceedings or to adopt interim measures pursuant to its national rules of procedure. A stay of proceedings or the adoption of interim measures should also be envisaged where there is a risk of conflicting decisions in the context of the application of Articles [81(1)] and [82].

53. It should be noted in this context that it is always open to a national court, within the limits of the applicable national procedural rules and subject to Article [287] of the Treaty, to seek information from the Commission on the state of any procedure which the Commission may have set in motion and as to the likelihood of its giving an official ruling on the agreement in issue pursuant to Regulation No 17. Under the same conditions, the national court may contact the Commission where the concrete application of Article [81(1)] or of Article [82] raises particular difficulties, in order to obtain the economic and legal information which that institution can supply to it. Under Article [10] of the Treaty, the Commission is bound by a duty of sincere cooperation with the judicial authorities of the Member State, who are responsible for ensuring that Community law is applied and respected in the national legal system (Order of 13 July 1990 in Case C–2/88, *Zwartveld* [1990] ECR I–3365, paragraph 18).

54. Finally, the national court may in any event, stay the proceedings and make a reference to the Court for a preliminary ruling under Article [234] of the Treaty.

55. The reply to the Oberlandesgericht's last question should therefore be that a national court may not extend the scope of Regulation No 1984/83 to beer supply agreements which do not explicitly meet the conditions for exemption laid down in that regulation. Nor may a national court declare Article [81(1)] of the Treaty inapplicable to such an agreement under Article [81(3)]. It may, however, declare the agreement void under Article [81(2)] if it is certain that the agreement could not be the subject of an exemption decision under Article [81(3)].

The English courts seem to have accepted that an action raising the validity of an agreement should be stayed where the agreement has been notified to the Commission. In *MTV Europe* v. *BMG Records*,[80] for example, the Court of Appeal granted a stay on proceedings brought by an independent third party against seven parties to an agreement. In this case the agreement had been notified to the Commission. Sir Thomas Bingham MR recognized the uncertainty which would be created were an inconsistent decision to be made by the Commission on the one hand and the national court on the other. The Court accepted, however, that some preparation of action for trial could be made in the meantime.

---

[80] [1997] 1 CMLR 867. See also *Williams* v. *Welsh Rugby Union* [1999] EuLR 195 and *Philips Electronics* v. *Ingman Ltd* [1998] 2 CMLR 839.

d. AGREEMENTS WHICH MAY NOT BE EXEMPTED UNDER ARTICLE 81(3)

The position is different where it appears that an agreement may be prohibited by Article 81(1) and:

- the agreement does not benefit from and individual or group exemption;
- there has been no application for an individual exemption and/or negative clearance; and
- the agreement does not fall within the category of non-notifiable agreements set out in Article 4(2) of Regulation 17.

In this case the national court will have to consider whether or not the agreement is prohibited by Article 81(1). If it is uncertain it may consult the Commission or make an Article 234 reference to the ECJ. If the national court concludes that the agreement does not infringe Article 81(1) it can make a declaration to that effect. If, however, the national court believes that the agreement or provisions within it infringe Article 81(1) it cannot[81] grant the agreement an individual exemption or authorize an agreement which falls outside of a block exemption only to a marginal extent.[82] In these circumstances it would, therefore, be obliged to find that the contractual provisions infringing the agreement are void (in accordance with Article 81(2)) even if it considers that the agreement would have been exempted had it been notified correctly. The national rules of severance will have to be applied to determine whether or not the offending provisions can be severed from the remaining provisions of the agreement.

e. NULLITY AND SEVERANCE

Although the effect of Article 81(2) has clearly been spelt out by Community law, the ECJ has held that the question whether the prohibited clauses can actually be severed from the remaining provisions in the contract is a matter for national, not Community, law. This approach has been criticized since it means that the enforceability of a contract will vary depending on which Member State's rules are applicable. Arguably, the impact of Article 81(2) should have a uniform impact throughout the Community.[83]

Where the applicable law is English law,[84] English contractual rules on severance will have to be applied. Broadly, the English courts will sever parts of a contract where sufficient consideration remains to support the agreement and it is possible to sever by running a blue pencil through that offending part. The courts will not make a new contract or rewrite the contract for the parties, for example, by adding or re-arranging words. Nor will a court strike out words of a contract if so doing would leave a contract of an entirely different scope or intention.[85]

---

[81] But see the Commission's White Paper on Modernisation of the Rules Implementing Articles 85 and 86 [now 81 and 82] of the EC Treaty [1999] OJ C132/1, [1999] 5 CMLR 208, discussed *infra* in Chap. 16.

[82] Case C–234/89 *Delimitis* v. *Henninger Bräu* [1991] ECR 1–935, [1992] 5 CMLR 210, paras. 39 and 46. The position will be different, however, if the Commission's proposals for modernization became a reality, see Chaps. 4 and 16.

[83] See e.g., R. Whish, *The Enforceability of Agreements under EC and UK Competition Law* in F. Rose (ed.), *International Commercial Law* (LLP, London, 2000). The applicability of national rules may in some circumstances be constrained by the Community principle of effectiveness (discussed *infra* at 000).

[84] The applicable law should be determined by the Rome Convention on the Law Applicable to Contractual Obligations, 1980, consolidated version with First and Second Protocols [1998] OJ C27/31.

[85] See, e.g., *Goldsoll* v. *Goldman* [1914] 2 Chap. 603.

In *Chemidus Wavin Ltd* v. *TERI*[86] the Court of Appeal considered the severance rules in the context of a licence agreement containing clauses which, arguably, contravened Article 81(1). Buckley LJ stated that:

in applying Article [81] to an English contract, one may well have to consider whether, after the excisions required by the Article of the Treaty have been made from the contract, the contract could be said to fail for lack of consideration or on any other ground, or whether the contract would be so changed in its character as not to be the sort of contract that the parties intended to enter into at all.[87]

The compatibility of an agreement, or clauses within it, with Article 81 has now been raised in a number of cases before the English courts. It would be fair to say, however, that such arguments have not received a warm reception. Rather, the cases have been marked by an air of scepticism about the merits of the 'Euro-defence' and a reluctance to accept that Article 81 applies.[88]

The compatibility of a beer tie agreement with Article 81(1) has been raised in a series of cases involving disputes between brewers and their publican tenants (the beer tie cases). Broadly, the cases have raised the question whether the tenancy agreements concluded between the parties are compatible with Article 81(1). It has been accepted in these beer tie cases that an exclusive purchasing commitment (beer tie) within a tenancy agreement might infringe Article 81(1).[89] The courts have, however, held that the rules of severance allow the severance of the tie, if invalid, from the remainder of the agreement.[90] This has enabled the courts to hold that the provisions in the agreement which do not infringe Article 81(1) (including the tenant's obligation to pay rent) are unaffected by the prohibition. It has also been considered that that the contractual provisions prohibited by Article 81(1) are not only void but *also* illegal.

f. NULLITY AND ILLEGALITY

In *Gibbs Mew plc* v. *Gemmell*[91] the Court of Appeal considered that contractual provisions offending Article 81(1) are both void and illegal for the purposes of the (English) *in pari delicto* rule. Broadly, this rule is a principle of public policy which prevents a court from lending 'its aid to a man who founds his cause of action upon an immoral or illegal act'.[92] This finding has caused the defeat of claims for damages or restitution brought by the tenant against the brewer in the beer tie cases. The impact of the plea of illegality on the claims is discussed below.[93]

---

[86] [1978] 3 CMLR 514.

[87] [1978] 3 CMLR 514, 520.

[88] See, e.g., *Society of Lloyd's* v. *Clementson* [1995] 1 CMLR 693; *Higgins* v. *Marchant & Eliot Underwriting Ltd* [1996] 3 CMLR 313; *Oakdale (Richmond) Ltd* v. *National Westminster Bank plc* [1997] EuLR 7, 40 affirmed [1997] 3 CMLR 815.

[89] See, in particular, *Gibbs Mew plc* v. *Gemmell* [1991] 1 EGLR 43; *Courage Ltd* v. *Crehan* [1992] 2 EGLR 145; and *Trent Taverns Ltd* v. *Sykes* [1998] Eu. LR 571, affirmed [1999] Eu. LR 492.

[90] See *Inntrepreneur Estates Ltd* v. *Mason* [1993] 2 CMLR 293 and *Inntrepreneur Estates (GL) Ltd* v. *Boyes* [1993] 2 EGLR 112.

[91] [1999] 1 EGLR 43.

[92] *Holman* v. *Johnson* (1775) 1 Cowp. 341, 343, *per* Lord Mansfield. For a more detailed discussion of the rules see R. Goff and G. Jones, *The Law of Restitution* (15th edn., Sweet & Maxwell, London 1998), chap. 24.

[93] See *infra* 995 ff.

g. TRANSIENT NULLITY

An agreement infringes Article 81(1) only if all five of its elements are satisfied.[94] It is possible that, as events change over a period of time, an agreement which does not infringe Article 81(1) will subsequently be found to infringe Article 81(1) and vice versa. Suppose, for example, a small, local undertaking concludes an agreement which does not infringe Article 81(1) on account of its minor importance. The undertaking has an extremely small share of the market.[95] Suppose, however, that that undertaking is subsequently taken over by a larger undertaking so that the agreement now does have an appreciable effect on competition and trade. The agreement which, previously, fell outside Article 81(1) now becomes subject to its prohibition. The agreement which was valid consequently becomes void. In *Passmore* v. *Morland plc* the reverse scenario occurred and the English Court of Appeal held that the reverse can occur: an agreement which was initially void can become valid (and possibly void again) as the agreement falls within and without the Article 81(1) prohibition.

Passmore v. *Morland plc* [1999] 3 All ER 1005, 1014–15

This action concerned another beer tie case. It involved a tenancy agreement concluded initially between a brewer, Inntrepreneur Pub Co (IPC) (a relatively large brewer), and Passmore which imposed an obligation on Passmore to purchase all of his beer requirements from IPC. Later IPC sold the pub and the reversion of the lease was acquired by Morland, a much smaller brewer. The compatibility of the agreement with Article 81(1) was raised.

The claimant accepted that applying the test set out by the Court of Justice in *Delimitis* v. *Henninger Bräu*[96] it was likely that an agreement concluded *de novo* with Morland would have been compatible with Article 81(1).[97] It was argued, however, that since the agreement when concluded with IPC infringed Article 81(1) and was absolutely void it was not possible to assign that lease once it had been established that the lease was invalid.

The Court of Appeal disagreed. It held that the nullity set out in Article 81(2) was transient according to the agreement's compatibility with Article 81(1)

Court of Appeal

Chadwick LJ

[Article 81(1)] only prohibits agreements and concerted practices which have a particular offensive economic objective or effect; . . .in order to decide whether it is within the prohibition, each agreement, or clause in an agreement, has to be examined in the factual context in which it is to be operated. . .

It follows that an agreement which is not within Article [81(1)] at the time when it is entered into—because, in the circumstances prevailing in the relevant market at that time, it does not have the effect of preventing, restricting or distorting competition—may, subsequently and as the result of a change in those circumstances, come within Article [81(1)]—because, in the changed circumstances, it does have that effect . . .

It must follow, also, by a parity of reasoning, that an agreement which is within the prohibition in

---

[94] See *supra* Chap. 3.

[95] Art. 81(1) prohibits only agreements which have an appreciable effect on competition and trade; see *supra* Chap. 3.

[96] Case C–234/89 [1991] ECR 1–935, [1992] 5 CMLR 210, *supra* Chap. 4.

[97] Morland owned relatively few pubs. Applying the test set out in *Delimitis*, therefore, the agreement would escape the Art. 81(1) prohibition. Although the market was foreclosed, the contribution of Morland's agreements to the foreclosure effect would be insignificant.

Article [81(1)] at the time when it is entered into—because, in the circumstances prevailing in the relevant market at that time, it does have the effect of preventing, restricting or distorting competition—may, subsequently and as the result of a change in those circumstances, fall outside the prohibition contained in that article—because, in the changed circumstances, it no longer has that effect.

The meaning and effect to be given to Article [81(2)]

Article [81(2)] has to be construed in conjunction with Article [81(1)]. In particular Article [81(2)] has to be construed in the light of an appreciation that the prohibition of Article [81(1)] is not an absolute prohibition; but rather a prohibition which arises when, and continues for so long as (and only for so long as), it is needed in order to promote the freedom of competition within the common market which is the stated objective of Article [81(1)]. The prohibition is temporaneous (or transient) rather than absolute; in the sense that it endures for a finite period of time—the period of time for which it is needed—rather than for all time . . .

(ii) ARTICLE 82

a. VOID AND UNENFORCEABLE?

Article 82 contains no declaration of nullity equivalent to that set out in Article 81. This omission is not surprising, however, since Article 82 does not explicitly prohibit agreements but focuses on a much wider range of conduct than Article 81 (all aspects of a dominant undertaking's behaviour[98]). Nevertheless, the Article implicitly prohibits many contracts and contractual terms and the effect in relation to sanctioned agreements is, despite being couched in different terms, similar to that of Article 81. It is to be expected, therefore, that the effect on the agreement would be the same.

In principle, it would seem that Article 82 should also render a contract, or severable terms of a contract, affected by its prohibition void[99] or, at the very least, unenforceable.[100]

A national court should therefore refuse to enforce a contractual provision that is in breach of Article 82. Article 82 is directly effective and no part of the application of Article 82 is reserved exclusively to the Commission. The Commission does not have the power to exempt abusive conduct from the prohibition of Article 82[101] (in contrast to the position in relation to Article 81). A national court may wish to suspend proceedings, however, if the Commission is investigating the same matter. In these circumstances a finding by the national court that conduct does or does not infringe Article 82 risks being incompatible

---

[98] The Art. sets out a non-exhaustive list of abuses which may take many forms, e.g. refusing to supply, charging excessive, discriminatory or predatory prices, or imposing unfair trading terms on a business partner.

[99] See R. Whish, *Frontiers of Competition Law* (ed Dr Julian Lonbay, Wiley, 1994) Chap. 5. A contractual clause may, in certain circumstances, be found to contravene the prohibitions of both Arts. 81(1) and 82.

[100] Art. 82 does not impose a multilateral prohibition against the parties entering into or implementing an agreement which offends the prohibition (as Art. 81 does) but imposes only a unilateral prohibition against the abuse of a dominant position. Thus it is arguable that a clause in a contract concluded in contravention of Art. 82 is, in contrast to one included in an agreement contravening Art. 81, not void but merely unenforceable. This was the argument raised by counsel for the claimant in *Gibbs Mew plc* v. *Gemmell* [1999] 1 EGLR 43.

[101] The national court will, however, have to determine whether there is an objective justification for the conduct engaged in by the dominant undertaking: see *supra* Chaps. 5 and 7.

with a subsequent ruling of the Commission.[102] The national court can, of course, refer any questions relating to the interpretation of Article 82 to the ECJ for a preliminary ruling using the procedure set out in Article 234.

b. ILLEGALITY

The question whether a contract or contractual provision is illegal for the purposes of the *in pari delicto* rule is more complex when dealing with Article 82, since Article 82 does not prohibit both parties from concluding the contract. However, even if the agreement is found to be illegal, that characterization should deny only a claim brought by the dominant undertaking. The rule should not prevent recovery where the applicant can establish that the parties were not *in pari delicto* (of equal fault). Rather, the duty of observing the law is placed squarely on the shoulders of the dominant party to the contract and is, in some circumstances at least, imposed to protect the other party from exploitation.

The effect of the *in pari delicto* rule on restitutionary and damages claims will be discussed in greater detail in section E below.

(iii) THE COMMISSION'S COOPERATION NOTICE

The Commission has summarized the obligations on the national court when dealing with a plea of nullity or unenforceability under Article 81 or Article 82 in its Co-operation Notice.

Notice on cooperation between national courts and the Commission in applying Articles 85 and 86 [now 81 and 82] of the EEC [now EC] Treaty [1993] OJ C39/6, [1993] 4 CMLR 12

1. Application of Article [81 (1)] and (2) and Article [82]

20. The first question which national courts have to answer is whether the agreement, decision or concerted practice at issue infringes the prohibitions laid down in Article [81(1)] or Article [82]. Before answering this question, national courts should ascertain whether the agreement, decision or concerted practice has already been the subject of a decision, opinion or other official statement issued by an administrative authority and in particular by the Commission. Such statements provide national courts with significant information for reaching a judgment, even if they are not formally bound by them. It should be noted in this respect that not all procedures before the Commission lead to an official decision, but that cases can also be closed by comfort letters. Whilst it is true that the Court of Justice has ruled that this type of letter does not bind national courts, it has nevertheless stated that the opinion expressed by the Commission constitutes a factor which the national courts may take into account in examining whether the agreements or conduct in question are in accordance with the provisions of Article [81] . . .

21. If the Commission has not ruled on the same agreement, decision or concerted practice, the national courts can always be guided, in interpreting the Community law in question, by the case-law of the Court of Justice and the existing decisions of the Commission. It is with this in view that the Commission has, in a number of general notices. . ., specified categories of agreements that are not caught by the ban laid down in Article [81 (1)].

---

[102] See Case 234/89, *Delimitis v Henninger Bräu* [1991] ECR 1–935, [1992] 5 CMLR 210.

22. On these bases, national courts should generally be able to decide whether the conduct at issue is compatible with Article [81(1)] and Article [82]. Nevertheless, if the Commission has initiated a procedure in a case relating to the same conduct, they may, if they consider it necessary for reasons of legal certainty, stay the proceedings while awaiting the outcome of the Commission's action. . . A stay of proceedings may also be envisaged where national courts wish to seek the Commission's views in accordance with the arrangements referred to in this Notice. . . Finally, where national courts have persistent doubts on questions of compatibility, they may stay proceedings in order to bring the matter before the Court of Justice, in accordance with Article [234] of the Treaty.

23. However, where national courts decide to give judgment and find that the conditions for applying Article [81(1)] or Article [82] are not met, they should pursue their proceedings on the basis of such a finding, even if the agreement, decision or concerted practice at issue has been notified to the Commission. Where the assessment of the facts shows that the conditions for applying the said Articles are met, national courts must rule that the conduct at issue infringes Community competition law and take the appropriate measures, including those relating to the consequences that attach to infringement of a statutory prohibition under the civil law applicable.

2. Application of Article [81(3)]

24. If the national court concludes that an agreement, decision or concerted practice is prohibited by Article [81(1)], it must check whether it is or will be the subject of an exemption by the Commission under Article [81(3)]. Here several situations may arise.

25. (a) The national court is required to respect the exemption decisions taken by the Commission. Consequently, it must treat the agreement, decision or concerted practice at issue as compatible with Community law and fully recognize its civil law effects. In this respect mention should be made of comfort letters in which the Commission services state that the conditions for applying Article [81(3)] have been met. The Commission considers that national courts may take account of these letters as factual elements.

26. (b) Agreements, decisions and concerted practices which fall within the scope of application of a block exemption regulation are automatically exempted from the prohibition laid down in Article [81(1)] without the need for a Commission decision or comfort letter. . .

27. (c) Agreements, decisions and concerted practices which are not covered by a block exemption regulation and which have not been the subject of an individual exemption decision or a comfort letter must, in the Commission's view, be examined in the following manner.

28. The national court must first examine whether the procedural conditions necessary for securing exemption are fulfilled, notably whether the agreement, decision or concerted practice has been duly notified in accordance with Article 4 (1) of Regulation No 17. Where no such notification has been made, and subject to Article 4 (2) of Regulation No 17, exemption under Article [81(3)] is ruled out, so that the national court may decide, pursuant to Article [81(2)], that the agreement, decision or concerted practice is void.

29. Where the agreement, decision or concerted practice has been duly notified to the Commission, the national court will assess the likelihood of an exemption being granted in the case in question in the light of the relevant criteria developed by the case law of the Court of Justice and the Court of First Instance and by previous regulations and decisions of the Commission.

30. Where the national court has in this way ascertained that the agreement, decision or concerted practice at issue cannot be the subject of an individual exemption, it will take the measures necessary to comply with the requirements of Article [81(1)] and (2). On the other hand, if it takes the view that individual exemption is possible, the national court should suspend the proceedings while

awaiting the Commission's decision. If the national court does suspend the proceedings, it neverthe-less remains free, according to the rules of the applicable national law, to adopt any interim measures it deems necessary.

31. In this connection, it should be made clear that these principles do not apply to agreements, decisions and concerted practices which existed before Regulation No 17 entered into force or before that Regulation became applicable as a result of the accession of a new Member State and which were duly notified to the Commission. The national courts must consider such agreements, decisions and concerted practices to be valid so long as the Commission or the authorities of the Member States have not taken a prohibition decision or sent a comfort letter to the parties informing them that the file has been closed . . .

32. The Commission realizes that the principles set out above for the application of Articles [81] and [82] by national courts are complex and sometimes insufficient to enable those courts to perform their judicial function properly. This is particularly so where the practical application of Article [81(1)] and Article [82] gives rise to legal or economic difficulties, where the Commission has initiated a procedure in the same case or where the argeement, decision or concerted practice concerned may become the subject of an individual exemption within the meaning of Article [81(3)]. National courts may bring such cases before the Court of Justice for a preliminary ruling, in accord-ance with Article [234]. They may also avail themselves of the Commission's assistance according to the procedures set out below.

(iv) CONCLUSIONS

It is clear that contractual provisions offending the prohibition under Article 81(1) are void and unenforceable. Article 81 may, therefore, be used as a shield in national proceedings. Similarly, it is to be expected that Article 82 can be used in an identical way. It is not clear, however, from the Treaty or any other Community enactment that Articles 81 or 82 can be used as a sword. It still remains to be clarified whether, and if so when, those provisions confer rights on individuals and whether, and if so when, breach of those rights demands a specific remedy, such as a right to damages, restitution, or an injunction.

E. NATIONAL REMEDIES AND THE PRINCIPLE OF NATIONAL PROCEDURAL AUTONOMY

(i) THE PRINCIPLES OF NATIONAL PROCEDURAL AUTONOMY, EQUIVALENCE AND EFFECTIVENESS

The principles of direct effect and supremacy make it possible for Community provisions to be enforced directly by private parties at the national level. The fact that Article 81(1), 81(2), and Article 82 are directly effective has meant that private individuals can commence pro-ceedings before the national courts against those that have infringed the provisions. It has already been seen that a private litigant may question an agreement's compatibiltiy with the competition rules. Further, he may additionally, or alternatively, seek some form of redress in respect of a breach of the rules, perhaps damages to compensate him in respect of loss, restitution, or an injunction to prevent future breaches of the rules.

It was seen in Chapter 2 that where an individual seeks to vindicate or protect his Community rights before a national court, the general principle is that of 'national procedural autonomy', national law sets out the rules governing proceedings. In principle, the protection given to Community rights and the availability of any remedy for breach of the competition rules are dependent on the procedural, evidential, and substantive rules applicable in each particular Member State. The law of each Member State should, *prima facie*, determine what remedies are available to those injured by a breach of the competition rules. It was also seen in Chapter 2 that the position is not, in reality, that simple. The ECJ has taken steps to ensure that national courts provide *real* protection of individuals' Community rights. Some limits are, therefore, imposed on the national courts' freedom of action. National rules (1) must not be less favourable than those relating to similar claims of a domestic nature (the principle of equivalence or non-discrimination); and (2) must not make it virtually impossible or excessively difficult to exercise the right that the national courts are obliged to protect (the principle of effectiveness).

(ii) NATIONAL COURTS MUST GUARANTEE EFFECTIVE PROTECTION OF COMMUNITY RIGHTS

The principles of equivalence and effectiveness have imposed important limitations on the freedom of national courts when acting within the sphere of Community law. A national court must disapply rules which are 'discriminatory' or which make it virtually impossible for an individual to enforce its Community right.[103] Further, national courts must actually ensure real and effective judicial protection of the Community rights.[104] '[T]he full effectiveness of Community law would be impaired if individuals were unable to obtain redress when their rights were infringed by a breach of Community law.'[105]

(iii) A COMMUNITY RIGHT TO A SPECIFIC REMEDY

In some cases the ECJ has held that the full effectiveness of Community law requires that a *specific* remedy should be available to remedy a *specific* breach of Community law. For example, in certain circumstances a Member State is obliged to compensate individuals who have been injured by its breach of Community law. Further, a Member State is required, in principle, to repay charges levied in breach of Community law.[106]

Although national courts are not required to grant *new* remedies,[107] this obligation

---

[103] See Case 37/76, *Rewe-Zentral Finanz eG and Rewe-Zentral AG* v. *Landwirtschaftskammer für das Saarland* [1976] ECR 1989, [1977] 1 CMLR 533.

[104] Case 14/83, *Von Colson and Kamann* v. *Land Nordrhein-Westfalen* [1984] ECR 1891, especially para. 23. In accordance with the duty of co-operation, set out in Art. 10 of the EC Treaty, see Case 33/76 *Rewe-Zentral Finanz eG and Rewe-Zentral AG* v. *Landswirtschaftskammer für das Saarland* [1976] ECR 1989, [1977] 1 CMLR 533, para. 5. Community law is thus capable of having a substantial impact on the Member States' national legal order and the rights of their citizens. 'By contrast with ordinary international treaties, the EEC Treaty has created its own legal system which . . . became an integral part of the legal systems of the Member States and which their courts are bound to apply': Case 6/64, *Costa* v. *ENEL* [1964] ECR 585, 593–4, [1964] CMLR 425.

[105] Cases C–46 and 48/93 *Brasserie du Pêcheur SA* v. *Germany* and *R* v. *Secretary of State for Transport, ex parte Factortame Ltd* [1996] ECR I–1029, [1996] 1 CMLR 889, para. 20.

[106] *Infra* 995.

[107] Case 158/80, *Rewe-Handelsgesellschaft Nord mbH* v. *Hauptzollamt Kiel* [1981] ECR 1805, [1981] 1 CMLR 449.

means that national rules may have to be adapted or extended to ensure that a remedy is available where it is required by Community law. National defences and procedural limitations to the claim will apply in so far as those rules comply with the Community principles of equivalence and effectiveness.[108]

The sections below consider the remedies available to protect Community rights in English law. They also consider whether or not there is a Community right to damages, restitution, or an injunction and the compatibility of the English rules with the obligations, if any, set out in Community law.

F. DAMAGES ACTIONS—THIRD PARTIES' CLAIMS

(i) THE POSITION IN ENGLISH LAW

a. GENERAL

It is possible to envisage a number of situations in which an individual might wish to recover damages against an undertaking which has breached the provisions of Community competition law. For example an applicant may wish to recover in respect of loss suffered as a result of:

(1) having purchased goods from a member of a cartel (in breach of Article 81(1)) at an inflated price over a period of years;

(2) having purchased at excessive prices from a dominant undertaking (in breach of Article 82) over a period of years;

(3) having been wrongfully excluded from a market by a dominant undertaking (acting in breach of Article 82);

(4) having been able to purchase its products only from a French distributor because the producer's policy is to deter distributors from making sales outside of their own allotted territories (the agreement infringes Article 81(1)). Prices are much lower in the UK.

Although it is expected that an individual which has suffered loss as a result of another undertaking's or other undertakings' breach of Article 81 or 82 will be able to recover damages in respect of that loss, this point has not yet been finally settled. No English court has yet granted damages to an individual which has suffered loss in consequence of another's breach of Article 81 or 82 of the Treaty.[109] It is still not clear that an undertaking which commits a breach of one of the directly effective competition provisions set out in the Treaty commits a wrong which is actionable in tortious proceedings. Nor is it clear, if damages are available, whether the basis of the claim is breach of statutory duty or some other tort, such as unlawful interference with trade, *or* whether a new tort should be recognized which reflects the Community nature of the claim. Whatever the correct basis of the claim it may

---

[108] For a fuller explanation of the relationship between the principles of national procedural autonomy and the principles of equivalence and effectiveness see, e.g., A. Jones, *Restitution and European Community Law* (LLP, London, 2000), 6–13.

[109] *Supra* n. 57 and accompanying text.

be that the conditions of liability will have to be developed to meet the requirements, if any, imposed by Community law. Those requirements are discussed below.

b. THE BASIS OF THE CLAIM

Breach of statutory duty

In English law not every breach of a statutory duty gives rise to a private action for damages suffered in consequence. However, what little English authority exists suggests that the correct cause of action is breach of statutory duty. This cause of action was favoured, obiter, by four of the members of the House of Lords in *Garden Cottage Foods Ltd* v. *Milk Marketing Board*[110] and by Morritt J in *Plessey Co plc* v. *General Electric Co plc and Siemens*.[111]

Garden Cottage Foods Ltd v. *Milk Marketing Board* [1984] AC 130, 141

This case concerned an action commenced by Garden Cottage Foods Ltd against the Milk Marketing Board (MMB). MMB had changed its distribution policy and was refusing to supply the claimant. The claimant alleged that MMB was acting in breach of Article 82 and that the breach was causing the claimant severe loss. The claimant could only purchase products through another distributor and consequently could not compete effectively on the market. The claimant sought an injunction restraining MMB from abusing its dominant position and refusing to supply it. The judge at first instance refused the injunction on the ground that damages would be an adequate remedy and the injunction would unduly prejudice MMB and its distributors.[112] The Court of Appeal upheld the claimant's appeal and granted the injunction since, in particular, the court was uncertain that a claim, based on a breach of Article 82, was one which would sound in damages at all. An injunction might therefore be the only remedy which would protect the claimant. The possibility of the award of an injunction thus turned partly on the question whether damages, if available, would be an adequate remedy. The House of Lords held, Lord Wilberforce dissenting, that if an action for a breach of Article 82 did lie based on a breach of statutory duty that action would give rise to a remedy in damages and would not merely give rise to a remedy by way of injunction. The judge had, therefore, been entitled to refuse an injunction and the Court of Appeal had been wrong to interfere with the judge's discretion not to grant it.

House of Lords

Lord Diplock

This article of the [EC] Treaty was held by the European Court of Justice in *Belgische Radio en Televisie v SV SABAM* (Case 127/73) [1974] ECR 51, 62 to produce direct effects in relations between individuals and to create direct rights in respect of the individuals concerned which the national courts must protect. This decision of the European Court of Justice as to the effect of article [82] is one which section 3(1) of the European Communities Act 1972 requires your Lordships to follow. The rights which the article confers upon citizens in the United Kingdom accordingly fall within section 2(1) of the Act. They are without further enactment to be given legal effect in the United Kingdom and enforced accordingly.

A breach of the duty imposed by article [82] not to abuse a dominant position in the common market or in a substantial part of it, can thus be categorised in English law as a breach of statutory

---

[110] [1984] AC 130.

[111] [1988] ECC 384; see also the beer tie cases discussed *infra* 992 ff.

[112] See discussion of injunctions, *infra* 1002 ff.

duty that is imposed not only for the purpose of promoting the general economic prosperity of the common market but also for the benefit of private individuals to whom loss or damage is caused by a breach of that duty.

If this categorisation be correct, and I can see none other that would be capable of giving rise to a civil cause of action in English private law on the part of a private individual who sustained loss or damage by reason of a breach of a directly applicable provision of the [EC] Treaty, the nature of the cause of action cannot, in my view, be affected by the fact that the legislative provision by which the duty is imposed takes the negative form of a prohibition of particular kinds of conduct rather than the positive form of an obligation to do particular acts.

In *Garden Cottage Foods* Lord Diplock (with whom three of the members of the House agreed) took the view that since Article 82 was directly effective it created rights in those suffering loss or damage in consequence of its breach which the English courts were bound to protect. Although he did not consider it to be totally clear that a breach of Article 82 gave rise to a civil cause of action, he considered that if it did, it should be a cause of action which sounded in damages. In his view the correct cause of action was breach of statutory duty (in this case Article 82 incorporated into UK law by virtue of section 2 of the European Communities Act 1972). That prohibition was imposed not only for the purpose of promoting economic prosperity but also for the benefit of individuals to whom loss and damage is caused by a breach of that duty.[113] Subsequent cases have tended to assume that the basis of the claim is breach of statutory duty.[114]

If this is correct and the cause of action is breach of statutory duty, then the claimant will have to show that:

(1) the loss suffered is within the scope of the statute, ie that the statute imposes a duty for the benefit of the individual harmed;[115]

(2) the statute gives rise to a civil cause of action;[116]

(3) that there has been a breach of statutory duty (generally liability is strict once the breach of duty is established);[117] and

(4) the breach has caused the loss complained of.[118]

[113] Lord Wilberforce, dissenting, did not agree. He considered it to be unclear that damages should be available in respect of a breach of Art. 82 and was not willing to resolve that difficult question in the course of interlocutory proceedings.

[114] In the beer tie cases the publican-tenants founded their action on the brewers' breach of statutory duty, see *infra* 992 ff.

[115] Arguably, the simple direct effect of Arts. 81 and 82 causes this requirement to be satisfied: see discussion *infra* 988 ff.

[116] As far as English law is concerned the courts have taken the view that a statute does not generally do so where the rights can be protected in some other way, for example, where a penalty is imposed in respect of its breach. The Community provisions are, of course, also enforced by the European Commission which has power to fine undertakings found to be in breach of the rules. It seems, however, that the question whether a breach of Art. 81 or 82 is intended to give rise to a civil cause of action is a question of Community law which may be answered by the ECJ, see *infra* 982 ff.

[117] In rare cases the courts have accepted that the statute requires that some element of fault should be established before liability is imposed (see, e.g., *Read v Croydon Corporation* [1938] 4 All ER 631). At first sight, it seems that liability in the case of a breach of Art. 81 or 82 would be imposed strictly. Neither provision requires unreasonable behaviour or an intent to contravene the prohibitions (intention is occasionally required in the context of Art. 82, see e.g., the discussion of predatory pricing *supra* in Chaps. 5 and 7). Arguably, however, this may impose liability too readily. It would impose liability strictly and equally (jointly and several liability) on each of the parties to the breach. Again, however, the substantive requirements of this offence are likely to be dictated by Community not national rules, see *infra* 982 ff.

[118] The damage would not have occurred but for the breach.

How these provisions are interpreted will depend upon whether the matter is left entirely to national law or whether national rules have to be shaped to comply with substantive rules set out by Community law.

Unlawful interference with trade or business

Some commentators have questioned the suitability of breach of statutory duty as the correct cause of action. The broad objection is that liability should not be imposed strictly in respect of every breach of the competition rules which causes damage to another. An alternative solution is that the basis of the claim should be unlawful interference with trade or business. This tort would at least require the claimant to show that the defendant's unlawful act was specifically addressed to it or intended to harm it.[119]

Conspiracy

In the context of Article 81 another possible claim might be one based on the tort of civil conspiracy. However, it seems likely that the conditions necessary to establish a breach of statutory duty will be easier to satisfy.[120]

A new tort or the direct applicability of the provision

It has been suggested that, rather than trying to squeeze proceedings within one of the existing causes of action, it might be preferable to recognize a new tort which would reflect the Community basis of the claim. If necessary, such a tort could be moulded appropriately to comply with the requirements, if any, of Community law.[121] In *Application des Gaz SA* v. *Falks Veritas Ltd*[122] Lord Denning suggested that the English courts might recognize new torts where the competition provisions were breached, such as the tort of 'undue restriction of competition within the common market' and 'abuse of dominant position within the common market'. This view was not, however, favoured by Lord Diplock in *Garden Cottage Foods* and has had little support generally.

Garden Cottage Foods Ltd v. *Milk Marketing Board* [1984] AC 130, 144–5

House of Lords

Lord Diplock

In a previous decision of the Court of Appeal, *Application des Gaz SA v Falks Veritas Ltd* [1974] Ch. 381, 396, Lord Denning MR had stated that 'articles [81] and [82] are part of our law. They create new torts or wrongs.' The issue in that case, however, which was one for breach of copyright in a drawing of a tin for holding liquid gas, was whether a defendant could plead breaches by the plaintiff of article [81] or [82] as a defence to the plaintiff's claim. The court was unanimous in holding that the defendant could so plead but only the Master of the Rolls expressed any view as to whether those articles created new torts or wrongs in English law. It was unnecessary for the purposes of that case to do more than to decide that it was arguable that those articles could be used as a shield, whether or not they could also be used as a sword; and in the *Valor International* case [1978] 3 CMLR 87,

---

[119] See *Barretts & Baird (Wholesale)* v. *IPCS* [1987] IRLR 3, 6.
[120] See M. Brealey and M. Hoskins, *Remedies in EC Law* (2nd edn., Sweet & Maxwell, 1998), 127.
[121] See *infra* 982 ff.
[122] [1974] Chap. 381.

Roskill LJ, who had been a member of the court in the *Falks Veritas* case, pointed this out and said, at p 100, that there were—

'many questions which will have to be argued in this court or elsewhere in this country or at Luxembourg, before it can be stated categorically . . . that articles [81] and [82] create new torts or wrongs'.

In *Bourgoin SA* v. *MAFF* Mann J considered this view now to be obsolete.[123]

Alternatively, it has been argued that the cause of action is simply the direct applicability of the prohibitions. One of these solutions might be more appealing if the English courts were required to grant damages in order to comply with their obligations set out in Community law.

The mystery of the basis of the claim

It seems astonishing that nearly thirty years after the UK joined the European Community uncertainty still surrounds the question whether or not damages are available in respect of a breach of the Community competition rules and, if so, how an action for damages should be framed. It is obvious that if private actions are to be encouraged it is essential to know what the correct cause of action, if any, is. The problems facing those contemplating proceedings to recover damages are summarized below.

R. Whish, 'The Enforcement of EC Competition Law in the Domestic Courts of Member States' [1994] *ECLR 60*, 64–5

If damages are available in the United Kingdom for breaches of Articles [81] and [82], a difficult question is how the action should be framed.

Lord Denning expressed the view in *Application des Gaz v Falks Veritas Ltd* . . . that there were two new torts in English law, 'undue restriction of competition within the Common Market' and 'abuse of a dominant position within the Common Market'. This approach has not found favour in subsequent years, and one finds that UK courts have looked for a 'traditional' peg on which to hang the action: in the lead is the tort of breach of statutory duty, although one or more of the economic torts may be considered by some to be more appropriate.

In *Garden Cottage Foods* Lord Diplock was of the view that the action should be for breach of statutory duty, the relevant statute being section 2 European Communities Act, which gives effect to directly applicable provisions of Community law. However it is not obvious that this action is appropriate where the competition rules are broken. For example, the 'abuse' of a dominant position is an objective concept . . . and a dominant undertaking may abuse its position without intention or even recklessness. It is not obvious that an action for breach of statutory duty should lie in these circumstances, since it could render dominant undertakings liable to actions for damages on a very strict basis. This could be a particularly severe problems where, for example, a privatised utility, accused for example of discrimination under Article [82(c)] of the Treaty, is faced with actions by several million customers claiming to have been treated less favourably than others. Familiar warnings of floodgates come to mind in such circumstances.

One might overcome some of the anxieties about this by refining the tort of breach of statutory duty in the context of infringements of Articles [81] and [82]: for example one could require a finding of recklessness or at least negligence before establishing liability for breach . . . or one could impose a strict rule on causation in order to exclude plaintiffs who are not harmed directly but only,

[123] [1986] 1 QB 716, 734.

as it were, peripherally by an infringement. It may be that case law of the ECJ under Article [288], which deals with liability of Community institutions in non-contractual matters, would be supportive of such an approach.

A second problem with the breach of statutory duty solution is that the normal rule in domestic law is that, where a financial penalty is available under a statute, there is no right to bring an action for breach of statutory duty; . . . as infringement of Article [82] can be penalized under Regulation 17/62, it could be argued that there should not also be a right to bring an action for breach of statutory duty.

If one has scruples about the use of the tort of breach of statutory duty, a more discriminating cause of action might be the tort of wrongful interference: liability there requires an intention on the part of the defendant to harm the plaintiff, although this does not have to have been the defendant's predominant motive. . . This approach may enable the domestic court to distinguish particularly reprehensible cases, where a plaintiff ought to be compensated by the defendant, from those where the harm suffered by the plaintiff is an incidental effect of the defendant's infringement of the competition rules. However there is a possibility that a requirement of super-added fault as a determinant of liability to damages could in itself be inconsistent with Community law: in the context of unlawful discrimination this was the judgment of the ECJ in *Dekker*. . .

A more radical solution to this conundrum, although one that would reopen the floodgates argument, would be to recognize that the direct applicability of Treaty Articles is sufficient, in and of itself, to provide a cause of action. As Nicholas Green has put it, in striking language,

> the Court makes it clear that the cause of action is direct applicability and the task of the court is simply to 'protect' the rights individuals enjoy under that cause of action. The national court is servant to the needs of the Community master. But the latter does not, like some legal chameleon, shed its Community guise and don a national visage simply because it makes an appearance in the national courts . . .

This solution would be more appealing than Lord Denning's, which would create a series of distinct torts based on each Treaty Article.

An answer to the cause of action mystery is urgently needed. Otherwise, uncertainty will persist and effective enforcement of Articles [81] and [82] will be impeded.

Unfortunately, six years later the cause of action mystery has still not been solved. It may be, however, that the answer to this question will be determined, indirectly at least, by the ECJ. Although it is true that the Treaty itself 'is noticeably lacking in express provision for the use of Articles 81 and 82 . . . as "swords" '[124] this does not mean that there is no Community right to damages in cases involving infringements of these provisions. On the contrary, the national courts are charged with an obligation to provide an 'effective remedy' to all individuals whose Community rights have been infringed by another's breach of Community law.

(ii) A COMMUNITY RIGHT TO DAMAGES?

a. THE *FRANCOVICH* PRINCIPLE

It was explained above that national courts must ensure that remedies are available to individuals which are sufficient to ensure real and effective protection of their Community rights. Individuals' rights cannot be fully protected simply by the principles of direct effect and supremacy. Rather the full and complete implementation of the Treaty and full

---

[124] C.A. Jones, *Private Enforcement of Antitrust Law in the EU, UK and USA* (Oxford University Press, 1999), 45.

effectiveness of Community law require that individuals should be entitled to obtain redress when their Community rights are infringed.

In some cases the requirement that a remedy must be adequate, real and effective may leave a national court free to determine how best to protect those rights.[125] In some cases, it may leave the national court a choice between two or more possible remedies[126] and in others the requirement may mean that a national court must ensure that a specific remedy is available to remedy a specific wrong.

In *Francovich* v. *Italy*,[127] the ECJ held that, where certain conditions are fulfilled, a Member State *must* make reparation for loss arising in consequence of its breach of Community law. Individuals have a right to seek compensation in national courts from a Member State for loss or damage caused by its breach of Community law where the requirements of Community law are satisfied. In this case the ECJ did not, therefore, leave the determination of the procedural and substantive rules to the national courts. Rather, it made clear that where the Community requirements were satisfied Community law *required* a remedy to be available. Compensation is obligatory as a matter of Community law.

This 'Community remedies' principle departs significantly from the notion that Community law provides the substantive rule and national law the procedures and remedies. After *Francovich*, it may no longer be vitally important whether *national* law recognizes a damages remedy for breaches of competition rules, because *Francovich* has explicitly forged a *Community* law damages remedy of apparently wide scope which the national courts will be required to recognize and enforce. The procedural autonomy of Member States is now subject to the '*Francovich* reservation' that there is a right to compensation founded directly on Community law. *Francovich* arguably renders moot much of the debate over whether a 'new' national remedy is being created or an existing one adapted, by declaring the existence of a Community remedy which must be available in the national courts.[128]

Case law subsequent to *Francovich* has clarified the conditions for liability under this principle. Of particular importance is the ECJ's ruling in *Brasserie du Pêcheur and Factortame*.[129]

Cases C–46 and C 48/93, *Brasserie du Pêcheur SA* v. *Germany and R* v. *Secretary of State for Transport, ex parte Factortame Ltd* [1996] ECR I–1029, [1996] 1 CMLR 889

27. Since the Treaty contains no provision expressly and specifically governing the consequences of breaches of Community law by Member States, it is for the Court, in pursuance of the task conferred on it by Article [220] of the Treaty of ensuring that in the interpretation and application of the Treaty the law is observed, to rule on such a question in accordance with generally accepted methods of interpretation, in particular by reference to the fundamental principles of the Community legal system and, where necessary, general principles common to the legal systems of the Member States.

---

125 Case 34/67, *Lück* v. *Hauptzollamt Köln* [1968] ECR 245.

126 See Case C–271/91, *Marshall* v. *Southampton and South-West Hampshire Area Health Authority (Teaching) (No 2)* [1993] ECR I–4367, [1993] 3 CMLR 293.

127 Cases C–6 & 9/90 [1991] ECR I–5357, [1993] 2 CMLR 66.

128 C. A. Jones, *Private Enforcement of Antitrust Law in the EU, UK and USA* (Oxford University Press, 1999), 72.

129 Cases C–46 and 48/93, *Brasserie du Pêcheur SA* v. *Germany and R* v. *Secretary of State for Transport, ex parte Factortame Ltd* [1996] ECR I–1029, [1996] 1 CMLR 889.

51. . . . Community law confers a right to reparation where three conditions are met: the rule of law infringed must be intended to confer rights on individuals; the breach must be sufficiently serious; and there must be a direct causal link between the breach of the obligation resting on the State and the damage sustained by the injured parties.

b. THE EXTENSION OF THE *FRANCOVICH* PRINCIPLE?

It is clear that where a Member State has acted in breach of Community law, Community law requires that State to make reparation in respect of its breach where the three substantive conditions set out in *Brasserie du Pêcheur and Factortame* are satisfied. Thus a Member State that:

(1) has infringed a rule of Community law which is intended to confer rights on an applicant;

(2) which is sufficiently serious; and

(3) in circumstances in which there is a direct causal link between its breach and the applicant's loss;

must compensate the applicant in respect of that loss. A question that follows is to what extent does this *Francovich* principle apply horizontally to cases where an *undertaking* which is not a State entity has committed a breach of the competition rules? Does a similar principle require such an undertaking to make reparation? Is a Community right to damages (similar to that set out by the Court in the series of cases commencing with *Francovich*) available in respect of breaches of the Community competition provisions?

It is argued by Jones, in the extract from his book set out below, that the principle of horizontal direct effect[130] dictates that the *Francovich* principle *does* apply to all breaches of Community law, whether committed by a Member State or any other entity.

C.A. Jones, *Private Enforcement of Antitrust Law in the EU, UK and USA* (Oxford University Press, 1999), 75–8

6.3 The 'Sons' of *Francovich*: private damages actions for breach of the competition rules

The first case raising the application of the *Francovich* Community damages remedy to directly effective provisions was *Banks*, . . . a competition law case in which a private company claimed that British Coal had abused its dominant position as a supplier of coal for producing electricity in violation of Articles 4(d), 60 and/or 65 ECSC and, in the alternative, Articles 85, 86 and 232(1) (now 81, 82 and 305) EC. On a preliminary reference from the High Court, the ECJ decided that the applicable Treaty provisions were those of the ECSC, the ECSC provisions were not directly effective, and the national courts could not entertain actions for damages absent a Commission decision on compatibility with Article 65 ECSC. . . Advocate General van Gerven addressed the issue, not reached by the Court in light of its disposition of the direct effects question, of the application of the *Francovich* case to an action for damages against third parties for infringement of directly effective competition rules.

The Advocate General agreed with the Commission's view that the existence of direct effect (in *Francovich* there was not a directly effective provision) 'constitutes an *a fortiori* argument . . . for

---

[130] See *supra* Chap. 2.

the application of the Community right to damages. On the question whether the *Francovich* principle extended to 'horizontal' actions by one individual or undertaking against another in respect of the breach of a directly effective provision, the Advocate General took the view that it did . . . [131][131]

The ECJ addressed some of these issues in a non-competition law context . . .
None of these decisions definitively addressed the horizontal application of Community competition rules, but the language used by the Court makes this application abundantly clear: Articles 85(1)–(2) and 86 (now 81 and 82) create directly effective Community rights, and the right to damages is a necessary corollary of the principle of direct effect. The right of reparation arises equally with respect to loss and damage caused by private parties breaching Community law as it does from Member States breaching Community law. As private parties have no legislative discretion, it must be the case that a mere breach of Community competition law suffices to give rise to a right of reparation on the part of one suffering loss or damage from the breach.

The Court of Justice seems to have confirmed this conclusion in its recent judgement in *Guérin* . . . a case concerning a French car dealer's complaint that Volvo France had breached Article 81 . . . and wrongfully terminated Guérin's dealership agreement. In the context of an action complaining of the Commission's failure to act, or in the alternative for annulment, the Court said :

> It must also be noted that any undertaking which considers that it has suffered damage as a result of restrictive practices may rely before the national courts, particularly where the Commission decides not to act on a complaint, on the rights conferred on it by Article [81(1)] and Article [82] . . . of the Treaty, which produce direct effects in relations between individuals [[1994] ECR I–1503, paragraph 39].

The author thus supports his conclusion that the principle of *Francovich* should apply to cases where there has been a breach of Community law which has horizontal direct effect by referring both to the Opinion of the Advocate General in *Banks* and to the ECJ's own judgment in *Guérin*. The conclusion is also supported by the ECJ's ruling in *GT-Link A/S v. De Danske Statsbaner (DSB)*.[132]

In *Banks v. British Coal Corporation*[133] the Advocate General explicitly stated his view that the *Francovich* principle should extend to horizontal actions between two private undertakings. National courts should be required to ensure that damages are available to compensate victims of breaches of the competition provisions. The obligation to impose liability on those which had acted in breach of Community law is a natural extension of the principle developed by the ECJ in *Francovich*.

Case C–128/92 *Banks* v. *British Coal Corporation* [1994] ECR I–1209, [1994] 5 CMLR 30

The case concerned an action brought by Banks a private company engaged in the production of coal under licences for its extract issued by British Coal, a statutory corporation created by the Coal Industry Nationalisation Act 1946. Banks considered that British Coal had acted in breach of the ECSC Treaty competition rules, and, in the alternative, the EC Treaty rules. It thus commenced proceedings before the High Court of Justice of England and Wales seeking damages. The High Court referred a number of questions to the Court of Justice for a preliminary ruling under Article 42 ECSC

---

[131] See *infra* 986–987.
[132] Case C–242/95 [1997] ECR I–4449, [1997] 5 CMLR 601.
[133] Case C–128/92 [1994] ECR I–1209, [1994] 5 CMLR 30.

and Article 234 EC. Amongst other things it asked whether a national court had the power *or was obliged* under Community law to award damages in respect of breach of the EC Treaty competition rules. The Court of Justice found that the applicable rules were those set out in the ECSC Treaty and that it was not required to answer the question. Under that Treaty the Commission had sole jurisdiction to find whether the ECSC provisions had been infringed (the provisions did not confer rights which were directly enforceable by private parties in proceedings before the national courts and were not directly effective[134]). Consequently, a national court could 'not entertain an action for damages in the absence of a Commission decision adopted in the exercise of that jurisdiction.'[135] It was not, therefore, required to answer the question. The Advocate General did consider the question, however.

Advocate general Van Gerven

43. The general basis established by the Court in the *Francovich* judgment for State liability also applies where an *individual* infringes a provision of Community law to which he is subject, thereby causing loss and damage to another individual. The situation then falls within the terms stated by the Court in paragraph 31 of the *Francovich* judgment . . . namely breach of a right which an individual derives from an obligation imposed by Community law on another individual. Once again, the full effect of Community law would be impaired if the former individual or undertaking did not have the possibility of obtaining reparation from the party who can be held responsible for the breach of Community law-all the more so, evidently, if a directly effective provision of Community law is infringed: in that regard the Court has already pointed out in *Simmenthal* that such provisions are;

> 'a direct source of . . . duties *for all those affected thereby,* whether Member States or individuals, who are parties to legal relationships under Community law.'. . .

It has been generally acknowledged for some considerable time (and, in particular, since the *BRT* judgment. . .) that such provisions of Community law as have direct effect in relation to individuals include Articles [81] and [82] of the [EC] Treaty: as shown earlier in this Opinion the same is true of Article 4, 65(1) and 66(7) of the ECSC Treaty. When an undertaking subject to those rules infringes them, it can be held responsible for that infringement, according to the reasoning in the *Francovich* judgment, and it must be held liable for the loss and damage resulting from that breach of Community law.

44. In a field such as competition law, moreover, there are powerful additional arguments which militate in favour of undertakings having the possibility under Community law of obtaining reparation for loss and damage which they sustain as a result of a failure by other undertakings to fulfil their obligations under Community law. I shall confine myself to two of those arguments.

To begin with, recognition of such a right to obtain reparation constitutes a *logical conclusion of the horizontal direct effect* of the rules concerned: the rulings in *Simmenthal* and *Factortame* . . . offer no solution where a national court has to adjudicate not on a rule of national legislation or administrative law which it can refrain from applying, but on a situation governed by private law in which one or more undertakings infringe a rule of competition, as a result of which a third party suffers loss and damage. The only effective method whereby the national court can in those circumstances fully safeguard the directly effective provisions of Community law which have been infringed is by restoring the rights of the injured party by the award of damages. Even a declaration that the legal relationship between the parties is void—for which there is an express basis in Community law—is not capable of making good the loss and damage (already) suffered by a third party.

In addition, such a rule on reparation plays a significant role in making *the Community rules of competition more operational,* particularly since the Commission, as guardian of those rules, itself

---

[134] Case C–128/92 [1994] ECR I–1209, [1994] 5 CMLR 30, paras. 15–19.
[135] *Ibid.*

acknowledges that it is dependent on the cooperation of the national courts in enforcing them. . . Individual actions for damages have for some time proved useful for the enforcement of federal anti-trust rules in the United States as well. . .

45. I conclude from the foregoing that the right to obtain reparation in respect of loss and damage sustained as a result of an undertaking's infringement of Community competition rules which have direct effect is based on the Community legal order itself. Consequently, as a result of its obligation to ensure that Community law is fully effective and protect the rights thereby conferred on individuals, the national court is under an obligation to award damages for loss sustained by an undertaking as a result of the breach by another undertaking of a directly effective provision of Community competition law.

This view is also supported by the ECJ's judgment in *GT-Link A/S* v. *De Danske Statsbaner (DSB)*.[136] In this case the Court held that where the conditions set out in *Brasserie du Pêcheur and Factortame* are satisfied, an individual can claim reparation of loss caused by a state entity's or public undertaking's breach of Article 86 of the Treaty, read in conjunction with Article 82. In this case the public undertaking had levied charges from the applicant in breach of Article 82.[137] This case clearly establishes that the liability of a Member State to make reparation for its breaches of Community law applies where the breach has been of a Community provision which also has horizontal direct effect. Although in this case the Court was clearly dealing with the liability of the State, the Court also stressed the rights conferred upon the individual by Article 82.[138] This right not to have to pay unfair charges levied by a dominant undertaking in breach of Article 82 must be the same whether or not the charges had been levied by a state or non-state entity (the right not to be exploited by an undertaking in a dominant position).[139] Article 82 imposes obligations on both public and *private* entities.[140] It seems natural, therefore, that the ruling should apply more broadly to breaches committed by private undertakings.[141]

If it is correct that the *Francovich* principle requires an individual to make reparation in respect of loss it will still be necessary for any applicant to show that:

(1) the competition rules confers rights upon it;
(2) that the breach is sufficiently serious; and
(3) a causal link between the damage and the loss suffered.

Points (1) and (2) are questions of Community law. Point (3), however, is to be determined by national rules in so far as those rules comply with the Community principles of equivalence and effectiveness.

---

[136] Case C–242/95 [1997] ECR I–4449, [1997] 5 CMLR 601.

[137] *Ibid.*, para. 60 set out *infra* 996.

[138] *Ibid.*, para. 57.

[139] Although dealing with duties demanded by a public undertaking, the Court, in reaching its conclusion that the charges should be repaid, clearly looked to and stressed the rights conferred on individuals by Art. 82, see discussion *infra* 995–996.

[140] It will be remembered that Arts. 81 and 82 apply, broadly, to undertakings entity engaged in economic activities, see *supra* Chap. 3.

[141] Indeed the case suggests that, at least in the context of Art. 82, it will do so. In particular, it would not seem satisfactory to draw a distinction between actions brought against state and non-state entities especially as the distinction between the two is 'so precarious and so difficult to employ' that it may be inadvisable to apply it: Opinion of Van Gerven AG in Case C–128/92, *Banks & Co Ltd* v. *British Coal Corp.* [1994] ECR I–1209, [1999] 5 CMLR 30, para. 41.

c. THE CONDITIONS OF LIABILITY

When do the competition rules confer rights upon an applicant?

In *GT-Link* the Court stressed the rights conferred by Article 82 on an individual which had been obliged to pay charges levied in breach of that prohibition. It seems obvious that Article 82 should confer rights on an individual in these circumstances. In that case the payer of the charge had been exploited by the undertaking holding a dominant position. One of the undisputed objectives of Article 82 is to preclude undertakings with market power from exploiting that dominant position by charging excessive prices (monopoly prices).[142] Similarly, it would seems clear that Article 81 is designed to prevent undertakings exploiting their customers by, for example, engaging in a price-fixing cartel. No doubt, therefore, Article 81 is designed to confer rights on individuals which have been obliged to pay more for a product or service in consequence of a horizontal price-fixing agreement. Even if it is accepted that Articles 82 and 81 confer rights on individuals in these circumstances,[143] it must still be considered whether the competition provisions confer rights on individuals in other cases.

It is less obvious, for example, that Article 82 is intended to confer rights on a competitor of a dominant undertaking which acts in breach of Article 82 by tying its customers to it. Such conduct might cause damage to the competitor which is unable to gain access to the market. If, however, the purpose of applying Article 82 is to protect not those competitors but the competitive process[144] (the conduct enables the dominant undertaking to preserve and exploit its dominant position) can Article 82 be said to confer rights on the competitor?

Similar arguments can be raised in the context of Article 81, especially where an individual suffers loss in consequence of its *own* adherence to a prohibited term in the agreement.[145] Some English courts, for example, appear to have taken the view, in the context of a claim for breach of statutory duty, that the prohibition set out in Article 81(1) is *not* imposed for the benefit of a 'co-contractor', a party to the prohibited agreement.[146]

Although this type of argument may seem appealing at first, it can also be seen that were the ECJ to start engaging in this kind of discussion the case law would quickly become full of tortuous distinctions which turn upon the (often disputed) objectives of the competition rules.[147] In *GT-Link* the Court did not consider the objectives of Article 82 but concluded simply 'that even within the framework of Article [86], Article [82] has direct effect and confers on individuals rights which the national courts must protect'.[148] In *Guérin Autombiles* v. *Commission*,[149] the Court stated that 'any undertaking which considers that it has

---

[142] Such behaviour is expressly prohibited by Art. 82(a): see *supra* Chap. 5.

[143] See *supra* Chap. 5.

[144] See *supra* Chap. 1.

[145] See the section on co-contractors, *infra* 991.

[146] In *Inntrepreneur Estates (CPC) plc* v. *Milne* (unreported, 30 July 1993), e.g., Mitchell J seemed to consider that where two parties entered into a prohibited agreement the statutory duty, if it existed, not to enter into agreements contravening Art. 81 applied to both parties. He accepted, however, 'that a *third party* might have a cause of action against either party to the agreement because of the contravention of Art. [81]'. See the discussion of actions brought by co-contractors, *infra* 991.

[147] See *supra* Chap. 1.

[148] Case C–242/95, *GT-Link A/S* v. *De Danske Statsbaner (DSB)* [1997] ECR I–4449, [1997] 5 CMLR 601, para. 57.

[149] Case C–282/95P [1997] ECR I–1503, [1997] 5 CMLR 447, para. 39.

suffered damage as a result of restrictive practices may rely before the national courts . . . on the rights conferred on it by Article [81(1)] and Article [82] of the Treaty, which produce direct effects in relations between individuals'. Similarly, in *BRT* v. *SABAM* the Court simply held that '[a]s the prohibitions of Articles [81(1)] and [82] tend by their very nature to produce direct effects in relations between individuals, these Articles create direct rights in respect of the individuals concerned which the national courts must safeguard'.[150] These cases do not, therefore, indicate that the rights should be conferred only on individuals whom the provision was specifically designed to protect. Rather, the rights arise from the simple direct effect of the Community provision.[151]

This suggests that damages should, *prima facie*, be available to all individuals who have suffered loss in consequence of another's breach of the competition rules. Restrictions on liability, if any, may, however, be imposed by other means. The ECJ may, for example, stipulate, as it has in the case of state liability, that damages be available only where there has been a sufficiently serious breach of the Community rules. Alternatively, the ECJ may allow the national courts to apply stringent (non-discriminatory) rules of causation or defences that would bar an unmeritorious claim.

A sufficiently serious breach?

Opinions are likely to differ on the question whether or not liability in respect of a breach of the Community competition rules should be imposed strictly or whether other factors should be relevant. The view might be taken that although, for example, a breach of Article 82 is committed whenever the requirements of Article 82 are fulfilled, independent of any intent,[152] liability for damages should not be so readily awarded. Liability should not arise save where an undertaking commits a reckless or negligent breach of the rules.[153]

In the *Francovich* cases liability has been imposed only where a Member State has committed a sufficiently serious breach of the rules. However, this limitation has been imposed on public policy grounds to protect Member States when acting within spheres in which they have wide legislative discretion. Where a State is not acting within its legislative discretion, liability is imposed strictly.[154] A precise extension of the *Franovich* principle, therefore, suggests that liability would be strict.[155]

Causation

The above discussion indicates that, assuming an extension of the *Francovich* principle, the ECJ is likely to take the view that an individual who commits a breach of the Community competition rules is, in principle, bound to compensate another that has suffered in consequence of that breach. The claim is however brought at the national level, and the question whether the breach caused the loss is determined not by Community but national law. It

---

[150] Case 127/73 [1974] ECR 51, [1974] 2 CMLR 238, para. 16.

[151] Since the Arts. not only impose obligations on undertakings, but confer rights on individuals, they impose a duty to benefit particular individuals: see M. Brealey and M. Hoskins, *Remedies in EC Law* (2nd edn., Sweet & Maxwell, London, 1998), 221.

[152] But see, e.g., discussion of predatory pricing *supra* in Chap. 7.

[153] See R. Whish, 'The Enforcement of EC Competition Law in the Domestic Courts of Member States' [1994] 2 *ECLR* 60, 62–65.

[154] Case C–5/94, *R* v. *Ministry of Agriculture, Fisheries and Food, ex parte Hedley Lomas (Ireland) Ltd* [1996] ECR I–2553, [1996] 2 CMLR 391.

[155] See the view of Jones set out in the extract of his book reproduced *supra* 984–985.

may be that in some cases a finding that liability should be strict may be tempered by national rules on causation.

Take, for example, the claim of a French purchaser of a product which has suffered loss in consequence of a UK distributor's refusal to supply purchasers outside the UK (see example (4) set out on page 977 above). The purchaser has, consequently, been forced to purchase from a French distributor which charges a greater price. In this case both the producer and the UK distributor are parties to a distribution agreement, imposing an export ban, which contravenes Article 81(1). They are, therefore, both potentially liable, jointly and severally, in respect of the loss suffered if the UK distributor: (a) had reluctantly accepted the export ban imposed in the agreement; or (b) had acquiesced, expressly or implicitly, in the producer's policy to deter parallel trading.[156] It may perhaps seem harsh to allow recovery against the distributor in circumstances such as these. If, however, liability is strict, it will be imposed by virtue of the distributor's simple participation in a contract prohibited by Article 81(1). Such a distributor could, however, attempt to rely on national rules of causation to establish that its breach was not the cause of the loss (this will of course be dependent upon national rules). In England, for example, a claimant seeking damages in respect of a defendant's breach of statutory duty must establish that the damage was caused, both in fact and as a matter of law, by the defendant's breach of statutory duty. Liability will not be imposed even if the loss would not have occurred but for the defendant's conduct if the *legal* cause of the damage was in fact some other more important factual cause.[157]

d. OTHER DEFENCES

Other national rules limiting or barring the claim (limitation periods, for example) may be applied so long as they comply with the Community principles of equivalence and effectiveness.

(iii) THE IMPACT OF COMMUNITY LAW ON THE ENGLISH RULES

It seems likely that the national courts will be required as a matter of Community law to ensure that damages are, in principle, available to an individual who has suffered as a result of another's infringement of the competition rules. If this is the case, national law must still supply the tools to ensure that the action is successful.

The English courts will, therefore, have to determine the correct means for dealing with the claim. The national courts could accept that the cause of action is the direct applicability of Community law itself or, as suggested by Lord Denning, recognize the existence of a new tort. These torts could then be shaped in such a way as to ensure recovery in all circumstances in which it is required by Community law. An English court would, however, be

---

[156] See the discussion of agreements and unilateral action *supra* in Chap. 3, especially Case T–41/96 Bayer AG v. Commission, Judgment of 26 Oct. 2000.

[157] E.g., if the main cause of the damage is attributable to the producer: see *Clerk and Lindsell on Torts* (17th edn., Sweet & Maxwell, 1995), 11–27.

more likely to find that the correct basis of the claim was one recognized by English law moulded, if necessary, to reflect the Community nature of the claim.[158]

In *R* v. *Secretary of State for Transport, ex parte Factortame*[159] the English courts appeared to accept that an individual who suffers loss as a result of the State's breach of Community law can bring an action for breach of statutory duty. It was recognized, however, that the action was *sui generis* since the substantive conditions of liability were determined primarily by Community, not national, law. This case may suggest that if the English courts are obliged to ensure that an award of damages is in principle available in respect of breaches of EC competition law, the basis of the claim may also be found to be breach of statutory duty.[160] The four requirements that: the loss is within the scope of the statute; the statute gives rise to a civil cause of action; there has been a breach of the statutory duty; and the breach has caused the loss will, however, have to be interpreted in such a way that liability is imposed where required by Community law. As in *Factortame*, therefore, the action will be *sui generis* since the substantive conditions of liability will be dictated, partially at least, by Community, not national, law.

Whether or not the English rules governing causation or other rules operating to limit or bar the claim[161] can be applied will be dependent upon their being compatible with the Community principles of equivalence and effectiveness. A point of particular importance is whether the English rules on illegality would prevent the effective protection of an individual's Community rights.

G. ACTIONS BETWEEN CO-CONTRACTORS—TORTIOUS AND RESTITUTIONARY CLAIMS

(i) GENERAL

A party to a contract which has been concluded in breach of Article 81 or 82 might wish to bring an action for damages against the other party to the contract. For example:

(a) a distributor may wish to recover in respect of loss suffered in consequence of an export ban imposed upon it in a distribution agreement concluded with a producer; or

(b) a ferry operator may wish to recover in respect of loss suffered as a result of the decision of a port owner (which runs a competing ferry service) only to allow it to offer its ferry services between 2 and 5 am in the morning.

Alternatively, a party to a contract or contractual provision prohibited by Article 81 or 82

---

[158] See the extract from R. Whish 'The Enforcement of EC Competition Law in the Domestic Courts of Member States' [1994] *ECLR* 60, set out *supra* 981–982.

[159] In *R* v. *Secretary of State for Transport, ex parte Factortame* [1997] Eu. LR 475 where the national court had to ensure that damages were available where the conditions set out by the ECJ in Cases C–46/93 and 48/93, *Brasserie du Pêcheur SA* v. *Germany and R* v. *Secretary of State for Transport, ex parte Factortame Ltd* [1996] ECR I–1029, [1996] 1 CMLR 889 were satisfied. The decision of the Divisional Court was affirmed by both the Court of Appeal, [1998] 3 CMLR 192, and the House of Lords, [1999] 3 WLR 1062.

[160] But see *supra* 978 ff.

[161] Such as the application of a limitation period or a defence such as *volenti non fit injuria* or contributory negligence.

might claim to be entitled to recover not damages but benefits conferred under a prohibited contractual provision. Take, for example, the following scenarios:

(1) A tenancy agreement is concluded between a brewer and its publican-tenant. Under that agreement the publican is obliged to purchase beer and other drinks from the brewer or another named supplier. The publican receives beer in accordance with the agreement. However, the publican believes that the exclusive purchasing agreement is void and refuses to make payment for the beer. The brewer wishes to recover in respect of the beer which the tenant has received but has not paid for;

(2) A and B set up a joint venture. A possesses intellectual property rights necessary for the successful operation of the joint venture. B therefore makes an initial payment of £1 million to A. A wishes to abandon the agreement which it considers infringes Article 81(1). B wishes to recover the £1 million paid; or

(3) take C, the owner of a port, who, contrary to Article 82, charges D an excessive rate to operate his ferry services from the port. Can D recover all or any part of the excessive payments made?

In accordance with the principle of national procedural autonomy national rules *prima facie* govern the claim. Those rules must of course comply with the Community principles of effectiveness and equivalence.

(ii) THE POSITION IN ENGLISH LAW—THE PRINCIPLE OF ILLEGALITY

Even if the English courts were to find that an action were *prima facie* available to an individual injured by another's breach of the competition rules a claim brought by a party to a prohibited contract may be barred by the principle of illegality.

The illegality of an agreement concluded in contravention of Article 81 has become an important issue in a number of the beer-tie cases.[162] In many of these cases the tenants have alleged that the commitment imposed in the tenancy agreement obliging them to purchase beer[163] from the brewer, or some other named-supplier (the tie) is in breach of Article 81(1).[164] Consequently, they argued that they were entitled to damages[165] in respect of their loss suffered in consequence of the void beer tie (the actions were based on the brewer's breach of statutory duty) or to recover the payments made pursuant to the void contract (the restitutionary claim).

The English courts have given short shrift to the claims. The courts have questioned whether, in the context of a breach of Article 81, any tortious action for damages for breach of statutory duty lies at all,[166] and whether, if available, any such statutory duty, is owed to a

---

[162] Discussed *supra* 970 ff.

[163] And perhaps other drinks.

[164] See *supra* 970.

[165] They have therefore claimed the difference between the contract price of the beer and its market value and other consequential loss.

[166] In *Inntrepreneur Estates (CPC) plc* v. *Milne*, unreported, 30 July 1993, Mitchell J considered the case of a breach of statutory duty only on the hypothesis that the duty existed. Further in *Matthew Brown plc* v. *Campbell* [1998] Eu.LR 530 Michael Tugendhat QC, sitting as a Deputy High Court judge, felt that the existence of the statutory duty had not been accepted.

claimant/ co-contractor.[167] Further, a number of objections have been raised to the restitutionary claims and it is now settled that they will fail.[168] A variety of reasons have been given for this conclusion.[169]

The major obstacle to both actions has, however, been that the claim is based on an illegal act. The English courts[170] have generally refused to assist a claimant whose action is founded on an illegal act: *ex turpi causa non oritur actio*[171] and to allow a party to a prohibited contract either to enforce that contract or to bring any other action based upon it: *in pari delicto potior est conditio defendentis*.[172]

The objection, that a contract is immoral or illegal as between plaintiff and defendant . . . is founded in general principles of policy, which the defendant has the advantage of . . . as between him and the plaintiff . . . The principle of public policy is this: *ex dolo malo non oritur actio*. No Court will lend its aid to a man who founds his cause of action upon an immoral or an illegal act. If, from the plaintiff's own stating or otherwise, the cause of action appears to arise *ex turpi causa*, or the transgression of a positive law of this country, there the Court says he has no right to be assisted.[173]

The term 'illegal' has developed broadly to discourage all contracts that are contrary to public policy. 'For an agreement to be illegal it need not be in breach of the criminal law'[174] but contracts which are, for example, immoral or expressly or implicitly forbidden by statute may also be characterized as illegal for the purposes of the rule. The fact that a breach of the EC competition rules does not attract criminal sanctions[175] has not, therefore, precluded the characterization of the contract as illegal for the purposes of the rule. In *Gibbs Mew Plc* v. *Gemmel* Peter Gibson LJ stated that 'English law does not allow a party to an illegal agreement to claim damages from the other party for loss caused to him by being a party to the illegal agreement'.[176]

Although the principles of illegality have developed differently in the context of tortious

---

[167] Some of the cases suggest any action for breach of statutory duty could not be brought by a party to a contract who was also in breach. A party to a contract would not be someone to whom the duty contemplated by the statute was owed (a requirement for establishing a breach of statutory duty).

[168] See, in particular, *Gibbs Mew plc* v. *Gemmell* [1999] 1 EGLR 43.

[169] In *Courage Ltd* v. *Crehan* [1999] 2 EGLR 145, e.g., it was concluded that the contracts for the sale of beer were separate from the tenancy agreement which incorporated the beer tie and were, consequently, unaffected by the nullity. The contract was not 'so closely connected with the breach of Art. [81] so that it should be regarded as springing from, or founded on, the agreement rendered illegal by Art. [81]': [1999] 2 EGLR 145, 155. Further, in some of the cases the courts have in addition, or alternatively, been reluctant to allow a restitutionary claim where the claimant is unable to return non-monetary benefits received in return for payment. In *Gibbs Mew plc* v *Gemmell* [1991] 1 EGLR 43, for example, the Court of Appeal held that a publican could not be entitled to restitution of money paid under a void beer tie when the drinks received in return for payment could not be restored. For a more detailed discussion of the restitutionary aspect of these cases see A. Jones, *Restitution and European Community Law* (LLP, London, 2000) Chapter 6.

[170] See the discussion of the beer tie cases, *supra* 970.

[171] 'No court will lend its aid to a man who founds his action upon an immoral or illegal act.'

[172] 'Where both parties are equally wrongful the position of the defendant is stronger.'

[173] *Holman* v. *Johnson* (1775) 1 Cowp. 341, 343, *per* Lord Mansfield. The rule is a principle not of justice but of policy.

[174] *Gibbs Mew plc* v. *Gemmell* [1999] 1 EGLR 43, 49.

[175] Reg 17 [1959–62] OJ Spec. Ed. 87, Art. 15(4).

[176] [1999] 1 EGLR 43, 49.

and restitutionary claims[177] a number of exceptions apply generally to the illegality rule.[178] One of the most important exceptions is that the principle does not apply if the claimant is a member of the vulnerable class for whose protection the illegality was created.[179]

In *Gibbs Mew* Peter Gibson LJ took the view that Article 81(1) was not intended, even partially, to protect parties to the contract and to ensure equality of bargaining power but was designed[180] to protect competition between the parties to the contract and third party competitors. It was concerned not with 'inequality of bargaining power between the parties to the illegal agreement but . . . the effect of the agreement on competition'.[181] The Court of Appeal adopted a similar approach in *Courage Ltd* v. *Crehan*.[182]

The principle of *in pari delicto* should not, however, operate as a bar to a claim brought by an individual injured by a dominant undertaking's breach of Article 82. It seems unlikely that such a claim can be said to be founded on an illegal act (the Article 82 prohibition applies only to the dominant undertaking). In any event, since the duty of observing the prohibition is imposed solely on the dominant undertaking the parties are not *in pari delicto*.[183] In *Gibbs Mew Plc* v. *Gemmel* Peter Gibson LJ considered that one of the objectives of Article 82 was to ensure fairness between the parties so that the illegality bar might not apply.[184] Similarly in *Courage Ltd* v. *Crehan*, Morritt LJ considered that the purpose of Article 82 was to protect against the consequences of unequal bargaining power and to prohibit unfair trading terms.[185]

It appears therefore that as far as English law is concerned a claim brought by a party to a contract prohibited by Article 81 will be precluded by its illegality (see example (a) and (1) and (2) on pages 991–992 above).[186] But any claim successfully raised by a party to a contractual provision prohibited by Article 82 would not be so prohibited (example (b) and (3)).

It is therefore important to know whether or not it is compatible with Community law for a court to bar a claim based on a clause of a contract prohibited by Article 81(1) on account of its illegality.

---

[177] See, generally, N. Enonchong, *Illegal Transactions* (LLP, 1998).

[178] See R. Goff and G. Jones *The Law of Restitution* (15th ed) (Sweet & Maxwell, 1998), chap. 24 and Enonchong, *supra* n. 177, (LLP, 1998), Part III.

[179] 'Where contracts . . . are prohibited by positive statutes, for the sake of protecting one set of men from another set of men: the one, from their situation and condition, being liable to be oppressed or imposed upon by the other: then the parties are not in pari delicto; and in furtherance of those statutes the person injured after the transaction is finished and completed may bring his action and defeat the contract': *Browning* v. *Morris* (1778) 2 Cowp. 790, 792, *per* Lord Mansfield.

[180] In the context of vertical agreements at least.

[181] [1999] 1 EGLR 43, 50.

[182] [1999] 2 EGLR 145, 149.

[183] This argument would, however, remain subject to the contention that the purpose of Art. 82 is to protect a wider economic and public interest beyond the protection of individuals harmed by the action.

[184] See also the ECJ's judgment in Case C–242/95, *GT-Link A/S* v. *De Danske Statsbaner (DSB)* [1997] ECR I–4449, [1997] 5 CMLR 601, discussed *supra* 987.

[185] [1999] 2 EGLR 145, 149.

[186] There are of course other exceptions which may exclude the application of the principle. E.g., it will not apply where the claimant has withdrawn from the contract within the *locus poenitentiae*: *Hastelow* v. *Jackson* (1828) B&C 221, 226 (this might perhaps be relevant e.g. in situation (2) in our examples above). This rule encourages the abandonment of contracts contrary to public policy but does not apply once the contract has been partly performed: *Kearley* v. *Thompson* (1890) 24 QBD 742.

(iii) ILLEGALITY AND COMMUNITY LAW

a. A COMMUNITY REMEDY

Whether or not the English courts have, in denying the tenants' tortious and restitutionary claims, acted in breach of their Community obligations is dependent upon two questions: first, whether, as a matter of Community law, national courts are required *in principle* to ensure that an individual can recover in respect of loss caused by another's breach of Community law or whether an individual is entitled to recover a benefit conferred under a contract which is in breach of the Community competition rules; secondly, if they are, whether or not the application of the defence of illegality is compatible with the Community principle of effectiveness (since the rule is not discriminatory it complies with the Community principle of equivalence).

It has been seen that the ECJ has not yet ruled whether or not a national court is obliged to ensure that damages are, in principle, available to compensate an individual who has suffered loss as a result of an undertaking's (or undertakings') breach of the Community competition provisions. Nonetheless, it seems likely that the *Francovich* principle will be extended to require private individuals to make reparation in respect their breaches of the Community rules.

Similarly, the ECJ has not ruled on the question whether or not an individual who has received a benefit in breach of the Community competition rules should make restitution. However, in a series of cases the ECJ has held that a *Member State* is obliged in principle to repay charges levied in breach of Community law. Further, a national agency must seek repayment of money paid out in breach of Community rules.[187] In *Amministrazione delle Finanze dello Stato* v. *San Giorgio SpA*, for example, the ECJ held that the applicant's right to restitution is a 'consequence of and an adjunct to' the rights conferred on that individual by Community law. As in the case of damages, it is important to know whether this principle applies more widely. Is an undertaking which has received a benefit in breach of the Treaty competition provisions also required, in principle, to make restitution?[188]

In *GT-Link* the ECJ held that a state entity which imposes a charge on an individual in breach of the Community competition provisions is obliged to repay those charges.

Case C–242/95 *GT-Link A/S* v. *De Danske Statsbaner (DSB)* [1997] ECR I–4449, [1997] 5 CMLR 601

This case concerned shipping and goods duties levied on a ferry operator, GT-Link A/S by De Danske Statsbaner (DSB). DSB was a state-owned undertaking which operated Danish state railways and owned the port of Gedser from which GT-Link operated its ferry services. GT-Link brought proceedings in the Danish courts to recover the duties which it considered had been levied in breach of Community law, particularly, Article 86, read in conjunction with Article 82. The commercial port had not imposed the port duties on its own ferry route or on that of its co-operation partner.

The Court of Justice found that the duties would be in breach of Article 86(1), read in conjunction with Article 82, if they were unfair or if they were discriminatory (if in exempting its own ferry services, and reciprocally those of some its trading partners, from payment of duties, DSB had

---

[187] See, e.g., Cases 205–215/82, *Deutsche Milchkontor GmbH* v. *Germany* [1983] ECR 2633.
[188] Case 199/82 [1983] ECR 3595, [1985] 2 CMLR 658.

applied dissimilar conditions to equivalent services). It was for the national court to determine whether the charges levied were in breach of the competition rules. Further, if they were unlawfully levied, Article 86(2) could not be used to justify the charges. A public undertaking could not levy port charges in breach of Community law which were not necessary to the particular task assigned to it. The Court of Justice then ruled on the question whether GT-Link had a right to recover any charges which had been levied in breach of Community law.

Court of Justice

56. By this question the national court asks whether, if the duties at issue in the main proceedings are held to be incompatible with Article [86(1)], read in conjunction with Article [82], Community law confers on persons or undertakings who have been required to pay such charges the right to claim reimbursement or compensation.

57. The first point to note in that context is that even within the framework of Article [86], Article [82] has direct effect and confers on individuals rights which the national courts must protect (Case 155/73 *Sacchi* [1974] ECR 409, paragraph 18, and *Merci Convenzionali Porto di Genova* [Case C–179/90 [1991] ECR I–5889], paragraph 23).

58. Second, the Court has consistently held (see, most recently, Joined Cases C–192/95 to C–218/95 *Comateb and Others v Directeur Général des Douanes et Droits Indirects* [1997] ECR I–165, paragraph 20) that entitlement to repayment of charges levied by a Member State in breach of the rules of Community law is a consequence of, and an adjunct to, the rights conferred on individuals by the Community provisions prohibiting such charges. The Member State is therefore in principle required to repay charges levied in breach of Community law, except where it is established that the person required to pay such charges has actually passed them on to other persons (*Comateb*, paragraph 21, and cases cited therein).

59. The same reasoning applies in any event where duties are levied by a public undertaking which is responsible to the Danish Ministry of Transport and whose budget is governed by the Budget Law . . .

60. It should be emphasized, however, that traders may not be prevented from applying to the courts having jurisdiction, in accordance with the appropriate procedures of national law, and subject to the conditions laid down in Joined Cases C–46/93 and C–48/93 *Brasserie du Pêcheur and Factortame* [1996] ECR I–1029, for reparation of loss caused by the levying of charges not due, irrespective of whether those charges have been passed on (*Comateb*, paragraph 34).

61. In the light of those considerations the answer to the seventh question must be that persons or undertakings on whom duties incompatible with Article [86(1)] in conjunction with Article [82] of the Treaty have been imposed by a public undertaking which is responsible to a national ministry and whose budget is governed by the Budget Law are in principle entitled to repayment of the duty unduly paid.

In this case the Court stressed that 'the right to repayment was a consequence of, and an adjunct to, the rights conferred on individuals by the Community provisions'. It is to be expected, therefore, that the conclusion would have been the same had the proceedings been brought against a private entity acting in breach of Article 82. An English court is then obliged to ensure that a ferry operator (see example (3) on page 992 above) can, in principle, recover the charges demanded in breach of Article 82.

It is less clear, however, that an individual should be entitled as a matter of Community law to recover benefits conferred on an undertaking pursuant to a contract infringing Article 81. In contrast to Article 82, Article 81 imposes a multilateral prohibition on *all* parties to the contract and benefits conferred under such a contract are not exacted with the same degree of coercion or pressure that can be exercised by a Member State or a dominant undertaking. However, if an individual which has paid a benefit under a contractual term prohibited by Article 82 *or* 81 is entitled, in principle, to recover, valuable advantages may result.

In other spheres of Community law the ECJ has recognized that the ability of an individual to recover sums paid in breach of Community law ensures that Community rules are observed and that breaches of the rules are deterred. Further, the recipient of the sums is not permitted to retain an enrichment received in breach of Community law. Similarly, in the context of the competition rules recovery may have the effect of enforcing the competition rules *and*, crucially, ensuring that an undertaking must relinquish any enrichment received unlawfully in breach of those rules. The extract below sets out these arguments more fully.

A. Jones, *Restitution and European Community Law* (LLP, 2000), 191–92

The case-law of the Court of Justice suggests . . . that any individual affected by a breach of the competition rules has rights which the national courts must protect. . . Further, . . . the finding that a public authority must repay charges levied in breach of Community law (set out in cases such as *GT-Link* and *Amministrazione delle Finanze dello Stato v SpA San Giorgio*. . .) is not only dictated by the need to protect individual rights; restitution is required to ensure that the Community rules are observed and that entities cannot retain an enrichment received unlawfully in breach of those rules. The right to recover is essential, more broadly, to prevent unjust enrichment and to ensure compliance with Community law. In the absence of an obligation to repay there would be little incentive to comply with the rules and infringements would be encouraged. . . Furthermore, . . . the right to recover aids or subsidies paid out in breach of Community law is required in order to uphold the principle of legality. Restitution ensures that the 'status quo' prior to the breach of Community law is restored and that breaches are not encouraged. . .

Similarly, in the context of Article 81 there may be a strong public interest in repayment. An obligation to repay ensures that an undertaking must relinquish any enrichment received under a contractual clause infringing the competition rules. If there is something abhorrent in the nature of a public authority (with draconian remedies) demanding sums contrary to Community law, it is also wrong that a private wrongdoer should retain benefits received under a prohibited agreement. . . Further, the right to recover benefits will encourage individuals to bring private proceedings to enforce the competition rules. . . The competition rules are central to the objectives of the Community, especially the goal of creating a system in which competition in the internal market is not distorted. . . The Commission is unable to police compliance with the Community competition provisions throughout the whole community. Greater private enforcement of the rules at the national level would ensure that Community resources were freed to concentrate on more serious breaches of the rules. . .

Even a restitutionary action brought by a dominant undertaking requesting payment in respect of goods or services conferred under a void contractual provision would have the effect of enforcing Article 82 and the competition rules. Recovery would also ensure that a non-dominant undertaking could not retain money or escape paying a fair price for goods or services conferred under the contract.

b. THE DEFENCE OF ILLEGALITY

If the Court decides that the damages and/or the restitution claim should in principle be available then it will be bound to have to answer a number of further questions, relating to the compatibility with Community law of national rules operating to limit or bar such the claims. It has already become important to know whether an English court is entitled to apply a principle, such as the *in pari delicto* rule, to bar a claim for damages.

In *Courage Ltd* v. *Crehan* the English Court of Appeal recognized that the question of whether, and if so when, an individual must make recompense in respect of its breach of the Treaty competition rules might not be purely a matter of national law. Further, that the answer to such a question might be affected by the fact that the claim is commenced by one of the parties to the prohibited conduct.

This case was an appeal from several joined cases. The facts of the *Crehan* case were complicated but essentially involved a lease for a demise of a public house for a period of twenty years. Under the terms of the lease the tenant was obliged to purchase all his requirement of certain beers from specified undertakings and no-one else and to purchase minimum amounts of those beers. The tenant fell behind in its obligation to pay rent and the brewer commenced proceedings against him. The tenant alleged that the beer tie was void, being concluded in breach of Article 81, and that he had suffered loss as a result of adhering to this tie. The price that he was obliged to pay as a tied tenant was substantially higher than those charged to the brewers' customers which were not subject to the tie. The Court of Appeal concluded that:[189]

So far as English law is concerned, it is common ground that where a defendant is sued under an agreement that is prohibited under Article [81], he may rely on that prohibition as a defence, and that a person who is not a party to a prohibited agreement may sue those who are parties to it for the damage caused to him by their operation of the agreement. . .

This court has ruled that 'English law does not allow a party to an illegal agreement to claim damages from the other party for loss caused to him by being a party to the illegal agreement. That is so whether the claim is for restitution or damages' [see *Gibbs Mew plc* v. *Gemmell* [1998] Eu. LR 588, 606]. That ruling was based on *Tinsley v Milligan* [1994] 1 AC 340.

The English Court recognized, however, that Community law might require the court to protect rights conferred on a party to a contract prohibited by Article 81(1) and to award damages to an injured party. It thus made a reference to the ECJ requesting a preliminary ruling from the ECJ on four questions. These questions seek to establish whether Article 81 confers rights on a party to a (tied house) contract concluded in breach of that provision and, if so, whether such an individual should, in principle be entitled to damages. If damages should in principle be available it has asked whether, and if so when, the national court may nonetheless deny the claim on account of its illegality?

Courage Ltd v. *Crehan* [1999] 2 EGLR 145

Court of Appeal

1. Is Article 81 EC (ex Article 85) to be interpreted as meaning that a party to a prohibited tied house agreement may rely upon that article to seek relief from the courts from the other contracting party?

2. If the answer to question 1 is yes is the party claiming relief entitled to recover damages alleged to arise as a result of his adherence to the clause in the agreement which is prohibited under Article 81?

---

[189] [1999] 2 EGLR 145, 151.

3. Should a rule of national law which provides that Courts should not allow a person to plead and/or rely upon his own illegal actions as a necessary step to recovery of damages be allowed as consistent with Community law?

4. If the answer to Question 3 is that in some circumstances such a rule may be inconsistent with Community law what circumstances should the national court take into consideration.

It seems likely that the ECJ will find that Articles 81 and 82 confer rights on *any* individual harmed by another's breach of the competition rules.[190] Any other conclusion would be excessively complex and cause unclear and unsatisfactory distinctions to be drawn. Article 81 should, therefore, confer rights on a party to a prohibited tied house agreement who may rely upon the Article when seeking relief from the other contracting party before a national court.

Further, it also seems likely that the ECJ will find that the *Francovich* duty to make reparation applies horizontally to all those that have committed a breach of Community rules.[191] This would mean that in principle a party to a contract should be entitled to claim damages from another party to the contract. Where a breach of the Community competition provisions has occurred the availability of damages should, in principle, be governed by Community, not national, law.[192]

A restitutionary claim was raised and abruptly dismissed in the *Crehan* case. For this reason the Court of Appeal did not ask the ECJ whether or not Community law required a party to restore benefits conferred under a contractual provision prohibited by Article 81 and whether any such right could be denied on account of the illegality of the claim. It is, however, regrettable that this reference was not made, since the nature of the two claims is distinct. The purpose of the restitutionary claim is to prevent a party to a prohibited contract from retaining an enrichment received pursuant to a void contractual provision. In contrast, the purpose of the tortious claim is to award damages to a party to a contract in respect of its own adherence to the void provision. The question, 'should a rule of national law which provides courts should not allow a person to plead and/or rely upon his own illegal actions as a necessary step to recovery of damages be allowed as consistent with Community law?' (question 3), might not necessarily provoke the same answer as the question 'should a rule of national law which provides that courts should not allow a person to plead and/or rely upon his own illegal actions as a necessary step to a claim for restitution be allowed as consistent with Community law?'.

The answer to the court's third question is dependent upon whether the application of the English rules on illegality complies with the Community principle of effectiveness. This will depend partly on the Court's reason for finding that damages (or restitution) must, in principle, be available and partly on the rationale underlying the English principle of illegality.

In the context of a restitutionary claim it has been argued above that a right to restitution would serve the important function of enforcing the Community rules, ensuring compliance with them, and ensuring that an undertaking must relinquish an enrichment received in breach of them. The policy considerations lying behind the English principle of illegality

---

[190] *Supra* 982 ff.
[191] *Supra* 982 ff.
[192] *Supra* 982 ff.

hinge on the need to protect the public 'through deterrence from crime and other illegal conduct'.[193] However, the strict application of the rules frequently allows an undertaking which has acted illegally to retain an enrichment even if he is equally, or more, at fault, as between the parties responsible for the violation. In addition it may result in the imposition of a penalty on the claimant greater than, or in addition to, that which would have been imposed on him in respect of his infringement of the competition rules. The principle produces injustice.

First, one guilty party suffers, while another of equal guilt is rewarded. Secondly, the penalty is usually utterly disproprotionate to the offence.[194]

The extract below assesses why the strict application of the illegality defence to a restitutionary claim may be incompatible with the Community principle of effectiveness.

A. Jones, *Restitution and European Community Law* (LLP, 2000), 193–4

D. Defences

A case has been made supporting the view that, as a matter of Community law, benefits conferred under a contract contravening Article 81 or Article 82 should, in principle, be recoverable. The English courts may, therefore, have to ensure that, in principle, a restitutionary action exists. . . Were this to be the case the national court would only be able to apply the principle of *in pari delicto* if it complied with the Community principles of equivalence and effectiveness.

In . . . the context of restitutionary claims, the Court of Justice has on the whole been reluctant to interfere with national rules which are genuine attempts to weigh the policy in favour of restitution against a policy protecting other legitimate interests (such as the protection of legal certainty etc). In accordance with the principle of national procedural autonomy, it has preferred to leave it to the Member State to determine how best to give effect to the competing interests raised by the claim. . . Many Member States have rules in place which deny recovery where benefits have been conferred under an illegal or immoral agreement.[[195]] It might be thought, therefore, that the Court of Justice would leave it to the individual Member State to determine whether or not, in its view, the policy pursued by such a rule militated against recovery.

The Court of Justice, however, always insists that in weighing competing interests sufficient weight must be given by the national court to the Community interest in recovery. In this case it would seem that the application of a defence such as the *in pari delicto* rule would undermine the important function performed by the restitutionary claim. The private action enforces the competition rules and deprives an individual of an enrichment received in contravention of those rules . . . Although a Court may consider that the conduct of some claimants seems more reprehensible than that of others it is suggested that an attempt to adopt rules which would distinguish between the different degrees of moral culpability of the claimant would be impossible to apply in practice. Further, it must not be forgotten that the fact that an individual is permitted to recover in restitutionary proceedings does not mean that he will not be punished for the breach of the competition rules laws that he has committed. A contravention of the rules having been established, that individual will be vulnerable to action in respect of its violation. The Commission may fine an undertaking that has committed a serious infringement of the rules. . . Further, a third party damaged by the breach might commence an action

---

[193] N. Enonchong, *Illegal Transactions* (LLP, 1998), 15.

[194] J. H. Wigmore, (1891) 25 *Am. L Rev* 712.

[195] See the *Application of Articles 85 and 86 [now 81 and 82] of the EC Treaty by National Courts in the Member States* (Commission, 1997), especially the sections dealing with Germany, France and Spain.

for damages before a national court. The right to recover ensures, however, that the applicant will not be arbitrarily penalized for contravention of the rules.

It is suggested, therefore, that were the Court of Justice to find that the benefits should, in principle, be recovered it would go on to find that the *in pari delicto* rule would operate as an unnecessary and unacceptable bar to the proceedings.

In our view a blanket defence of illegality should *not* be applied to defeat all claims to recover benefits conferred under a contract in breach of Article 81(1). Rather, it would be better in each case to determine whether or not the policy against illegal contracts would be better served by allowing or denying the claim.[196] Similarly, in the context of tortious proceedings it should be considered whether or not the policy against illegal contracts would be better served by allowing or denying the tortious claim. Arguably, the allowance of both claims will contribute to the enforcement of the Community rules and encourage compliance with them. It may also encourage the Commission to commence proceedings and fine those in breach. It is arguable, however, that the allowance of the tortious claim would be more likely than the restitutionary claim to encourage the conclusion of prohibited contracts. It may be, therefore, that in the context of the former claim, which aims to compensate the applicant, the illegality plea may have greater relevance.[197]

(iv) THE FUTURE OF CLAIMS BETWEEN CO-CONTRACTORS

It seems clear that the English courts in the beer tie cases were unwilling to allow the tenant to get out of a 'bad bargain'[198] and to avoid their contractual obligations (in many of the cases the tenants had fallen into arrears with their rents). In *Trent Taverns Ltd* v. *Sykes* Steel J stated that 'Article [81] is not concerned with furnishing a remedy for an improvident

---

[196] 'The question is always whether allowing the claim in unjust enrichment would make nonsense of the law's condemnation of the illegal conduct in question and of its refusal to enforce the illegal contract': P. Birks, 'Recovering Value Transferred under an Illegal Contractor [2000]' *Theoretical Inquiries in Law* 155, 202.

[197] In some cases the allowing of the tortious claim may permit a party to a prohibited contract to benefit whether or not the illegal contract is carried out. Suppose, e.g., A and B operate a price-fixing cartel and B's customer sets up his own source of supply, causing extreme damage to B. If B could sue A, claiming damages from A in respect of A's breach of Art. 81(1), he might be encouraged to operate the cartel which that provision was designed to prevent. If the cartel is successful he will win, but if it fails he can recover his loss from A. The following example also shows why the principle of in pari delicto may have greater force in the context of a tortious claim. Take our example (1) above. A brewer supplies beer pursuant to a contract containing a prohibited beer tie. Since Art. 81(2) renders the prohibited tie void the brewer cannot rely on the contract to recover the payment due pursuant to that contract. It seems reasonable, however, that the tenant should not be able entirely to escape its obligation to pay for the beer. Otherwise it would be enriched as a result of its own breach of the competition rules. The brewer should, therefore, be entitled to recover in the context of a restitutionary claim, a *quantum valebat*, in respect of the beer supplied under the void contractual provision. It seems wrong, however, that the brewer should be entitled to recover damages suffered by it in consequence of the tenant's adherence to the void contractual provision. This might entitle the brewer to recover in respect not only of beer supplied pursuant to the void contract but also the consequential loss caused to it by the tie. E.g., the brewer may be able to establish that, as a result of the tie, the tenant has purchased less beer (the higher prices charged by the tenant having led to reduced sales). See the discussion in *Perma Mufflers Inc* v. *International Parts Corporation*, 392 US 134 (1968).

[198] In *Gibbs Mew plc* v. *Gemmell* [1999] 1 EGLR 43, 48, Peter Gibson LJ expressed his 'clear view that Mr Gemmell did receive exactly what he bargained for, and is merely complaining of what he now sees as a bad bargain. Art. [81] provides no remedy for that'.

agreement'.[199] The courts were no doubt also aware that many of the brewers had been negotiating with the Commission and were likely to receive confirmation from the Commission that their agreement did not infringe Article 81(1) or merited an individual exemption.

It seems unlikely that many claims will be brought between co-contractors in the future. If the Commission begins to take a less broad view of Article 81(1) fewer cases will arise.[200] Further, many cases between parties to vertical agreements will now be prevented since the Commission may exempt such agreements retrospectively, to the date that the agreement was concluded,[201] and a broader block exemption applies. Finally, the national courts may be more willing to apply the provisions of Article 81 if they are able to apply Article 81(3) as well as Article 81(1) and (2). If the Commission's proposals to modernize the current system of enforcement are adopted the national courts will become free to do so.

H. INTERIM INJUNCTIONS

(i) GENERAL

An individual suffering in consequence of a breach of the competition rules might request an injunction to prevent the undertaking or undertakings committing a breach of the rules in future. The injunction sought might be final or interim, pending resolution of the final dispute between the parties. The availability of an interim injunction will be of particular importance to an undertaking which believes that it is being driven out of the market, for example, by a dominant undertaking's predatory behaviour in breach of Article 82.

(ii) THE POSITION IN ENGLISH LAW

The English High Court has jurisdiction to grant both final and interim injunctions where the court considers it to be 'just and equitable' to do so.[202] In *Garden Cottage Foods* v. *Milk Marketing Board*[203] the court considered, but declined, to grant an interim injunction to prevent the MMB's alleged abuse of a dominant position.

Broadly, an interim injunction will be granted where the guidelines set out by the House of Lords in *American Cyanamid Co* v. *Ethicon*[204] are satisfied. In determining whether or not to grant the injunction the court will take account of the following factors:

(i)   Whether or not the claimant's case is frivolous or vexatious, there must be a serious issue to be tried;

(ii) Whether damages would be an adequate remedy for either party (in *Garden Cottage Foods* Parker J, at first instance, held that damages would be an adequate remedy for the claimant in that case were the breach to be established (the loss of

---

[199] [1999] Eu. LR 571, 578.

[200] *Supra* Chap. 4.

[201] Reg. 17 [1959–62] OJ Spec.Ed. 87, Arts. 4(2) and 6(2), *supra* Chap. 4. Notification to the Commission will, therefore, effectively bring a halt to national proceedings.

[202] The principles which govern a court's decision whether or not to grant an injunction differ depending upon whether the injunction sought is final or interim.

[203] [1984] AC 130.

[204] [1975] AC 396.

profit could easily be calculated and the MMB could pay)). If the injunction is granted the claimant will usually be required to give a cross-undertaking in damages to the defendant;

(iii) Whether on the balance of convenience the injunction should be granted;

(iv) Whether there are other special factors. The injunction will not be granted if, for example, it would result in summary judgment for the claimant.[205]

(iii) A COMMUNITY RIGHT TO AN INJUNCTION

The ECJ held in *R v. Secretary of State for Transport, ex parte Factortame Ltd*[206] that a national court must ensure that interim measures are available where necessary to protect putative Community rights:

19. In accordance with the case-law of the Court, it is for the national courts, in application of the principle of cooperation laid down in Article [10] of the [EC] Treaty, to ensure the legal protection which persons derive from the direct effect of provisions of Community law. . .

20. The Court has also held that any provision of a national legal system and any legislative, administrative or judicial practice which might impair the effectiveness of Community law by withholding from the national court having jurisdiction to apply such law the power to do everything necessary at the moment of its application to set aside national legislative provisions which might prevent, even temporarily, Community rules from having full force and effect are incompatible with those requirements, which are the very essence of Community law. . . .

21. . . . the full effectiveness of Community law would be just as much impaired if a rule of national law could prevent a court seised of a dispute governed by Community law from granting interim relief in order to ensure the full effectiveness of the judgment to be given on the existence of the rights claimed under Community law. It follows that a court which in those circumstances would grant interim relief, if it were not for a rule of national law, is obliged to set aside that rule.

(iv) THE IMPACT OF COMMUNITY LAW ON THE ENGLISH RULES

The question whether or not an interim injunction should be available in *Factortame* arose in the context of a dispute over the compatibility of provisions of the Merchant Shipping Act 1988 with Community law. The provisions had been adopted to prevent Spanish fishermen from fishing under the UK's fishing quota introduced under Community fishing conservation measures. The fishermen alleged that the provisions were in breach of Community rules on free movement and challenged the validity of the registration conditions in judicial review proceedings before the English Divisional court.[207] Pending final judgment interim relief was sought. The question whether an interim injunction could or should be granted to suspend the operation of the statute fell to be decided by the House of Lords.

Although the English courts undoubtedly have power to grant interim injunctions the difficulty in this case was that the injunction was sought against the Crown and sought to

---

[205] See, e.g., *Plessey Co plc* v. *General Electric Co plc* [1988] ECC 384, where the award of the interim injunction would have precluded any take-over bid.

[206] Case 213/89 [1990] ECR I–2433, [1990] 3 CMLR 1.

[207] The Divisional Court made a reference to the ECJ requesting guidance on whether the legislation was incompatible with Community law: *R v. Secretary of State for Transport, ex parte Factortame Ltd* [1989] 2 CMLR 353. The ECJ made it clear that they were, Case C–221/89 *R v. Secretary of State for Transport, ex parte Factortame Ltd* [1991] ECR I–3905, [1991] 3 CMLR 589.

suspend the operation of an Act of Parliament. If purely a matter of domestic law these factors would have meant that the injunction was not available. In *R* v. *Secretary of State for Transport, ex parte Factortame*, set out above, the ECJ made it clear that interim relief should be available where the only obstacle to the granting of the relief was a rule of national law. When the matter reverted to the House of Lords the injunction was granted.[208]

The difficulty for the House of Lords in this case was that it did not believe that it had jurisdiction to grant an injunction at all. In contrast, in private claims the courts have jurisdiction to grant interim relief as long as it is satisfied, applying the *American Cyanamid* principles, that it is just and equitable to do so. An English court will have to take care when applying these principles in the context of a claim alleging a breach of the Community competition rules, that it ensures that an interim injunction is granted where necessary to give effective protection to the claimant's Community rights. The principles set out in *American Cyanamid* should enable a court to do so. Indeed, they appear to impose less stringent requirements on a claimant than those which must be satisfied by a claimant seeking interim relief from the Commission.[209]

Although the English courts have refused relief on a number of occasions, in *Cutsforth* v. *Mansfield Inns*[210] the High Court granted interim relief to a supplier of juke boxes. The claimant alleged that a clause in a tenancy agreement which obliged the defendant's tenants to use juke boxes only from specific suppliers was in breach of Article 81. The High Court held that there was a serious issue to be tried and that if the injunction was not granted the claimant would be likely to go out of business. Damages would not be an adequate remedy. Consequently, the balance of covenience favoured the grant of the injunction.

4. ENFORCEMENT BY NATIONAL AUTHORITIES

A. COMPLAINING TO A NATIONAL COMPETITION AUTHORITY

It was seen in Chapter 2 that in certain circumstances national competition authorities are authorized to apply Articles 81 and 82 of the Treaty.[211] It was also seen, however, that in

---

[208] *R* v. *Secretary of State for Transport, ex parte Factortame Ltd* [1990] AC 603. A question which arose was whether or not the English court would have *to create a new remedy* in order to comply with its obligation to give effective protection to Community law. Lord Bridge appeared to believe only that it was necessary *to create jurisdiction* to comply with the ECJ's ruling and the Court's ruling vested the English court with that jurisdiction. In contrast, the ECJ appeared to consider that the English court did have jurisdiction to grant the injunction but was precluded from exercising it by a common law rule (it side-stepped the complaint that the ECJ was, contrary to Case 158/80, *Rewe-Handelsgesellschaft Nord mbH* v. *Hauptzollamt Kiel* [1981] ECR 1805, [1981] 1 CMLR 449, actually requiring the creation of a new remedy). It was not necessary for the national courts to create jurisdiction to exercise a remedy where none existed before. The national court merely had to set aside and to refuse to apply a rule which prevented it from exercising its jurisdiction to issue an injunction.

[209] See *supra* 955–956 and Chap. 14.

[210] [1986] I CMLR I.

[211] See Art. 84 of the Treaty and Reg. 17, Art. 9(3).

practice the national competition authorities have not played a great role in the enforcement of the Community competition rules. Only eight of the fifteen Member States have conferred power on their competition authorities to apply the EC rules. Further, those authorities have been deterred from exercising those powers by a number of factors, in particular their inability to grant Article 81(3) exemptions.[212]

Nonetheless the Commission, in accordance with its desire to see greater enforcement at the national level, is seeking to encourage complainants to complain to a relevant national authority. In its Notice on cooperation between national competition authorities and the Commission in handling cases falling within the scope of Articles 85 [now 81] or 86 [now 82] of the EC Treaty[213] the Commission explains the different roles played by the Commission and the national authorities. It also seeks to explain why the Commission encourages the participation of national authorities in competition law enforcement.

Notice on cooperation between national competition authorities and the Commission in handling cases falling within the scope of Articles 85 [now 81] or 86 [now 82] of the EC Treaty [1997] OJ C313/3

1. In competition policy the Community and the Member States perform different functions. Whereas the Community is responsible only for implementing the Community rules, Member States not only apply their domestic law but also have a hand in implementing Articles [81] and [82] of the EC Treaty.

2. This involvement of the Member States in Community competition policy means that decision[s] can be taken as closely as possible to the citizen (Article [1] of the Treaty on European Union). The decentralized application of Community competition rules also leads to a better allocation of tasks. If, by reason of its scale or effects, the proposed action can best be taken at Community level, it is for the Commission to act. Otherwise, it is for the competition authority of the Member State concerned to act.

3. Community law is implemented by the Commission and national competition authorities, on the one hand, and national courts, on the other, in accordance with the principles developed by the Community legislature and by the Court of Justice and the Court of First Instance of the European Communities. . .

4. As administrative authorities, both the Commission and national competition authorities act in the public interest in performing their general task of monitoring and enforcing the competition rules. . . Relations between them are determined primarily by this common role of protecting the general interest. Although similar to the Notice on cooperation with national courts, this Notice accordingly reflects this special feature.

. . .

6. The Commission is convinced that enhancing the role of national competition authorities will boost the effectiveness of Articles [81] and [82] of the Treaty and, generally speaking, will bolster the application of Community competition rules throughout the Community. In the interests of

---

[212] *Supra* Chap. 2 and *infra* 1007–1008.
[213] [1997] OJ C313/3.

safeguarding and developing the single market, the Commission considers that those provisions should be used as widely as possible. Being closer to the activities and businesses that require monitoring, national authorities are often in a better position than the Commission to protect competition.

7. Cooperation must therefore be organized between national authorities and the Commission. If this cooperation is to be fruitful, they will have to keep in close and constant touch.

The Commission recognizes that not all national authorities have powers to apply Articles 81 and 82, and states in paragraph 10 that the advantages of national enforcement can still be obtained by authorities applying their domestic law (on the assumption that the result will be similar).

The notice draws attention to the specific advantages which may accrue to a complainant where a complaint is made to a national authority rather than the Commission. Such an authority may also be able to pursue proceedings under national rules, better understand the workings of national markets and be in a better position to detect breaches of the rules carried out in its Member State.

Commision notice on cooperation between national competition authorities and the Commission in handling cases falling within the scope of Articles 85 [now 81] or 86 [now 82] of the EC Treaty [1997] OJ C313/3

12. Member States' competition authorities often have a more detailed and precise knowledge than the Commission of the relevant markets (particularly those with highly specific national features) and the businesses concerned. Above all, they may be in a better position than the Commission to detect restrictive practices that have not been notified or abuses of a dominant position whose effects are essentially confined to their territory.

13. Many cases handled by national authorities involve arguments based on national law and arguments drawn from Community competition law. In the interests of keeping proceedings as short as possible, the Commission considers it preferable that national authorities should directly apply Community law themselves, instead of making firms refer the Community-law aspects of their cases to the Commission.

The Commission is, however, aware of the difficulties which will follow if the national authority has insufficient powers to investigate complaints, to take interim measures and to impose penalties on an undertaking found to be in breach. The Notice thus indicates that any national competition authority taking on such a case should have adequate powers to ensure the protection of those being injured by a breach of the competition rules.

25. A national authority having sufficient resources in terms of manpower and equipment and having had the requisite powers conferred on it, also needs to be able to deal effectively with any cases covered by the Community rules which it proposes to take on. The effectiveness of a national authority's action is dependent on its powers of investigation, the legal means it has at its disposal for settling a case—including the power to order interim measures in an emergency—and the penalties it is empowered to impose on businesses found guilty of infringing the competition rules. Differences between the rules of procedure applicable in the various Member States should not, in the Commission's view, lead to outcomes which differ in their effectiveness when similar cases are being dealt with.

B. CASE ALLOCATION

The ability of both the national competition authorities and the Commission to apply Articles 81(1), (2), and 82 may lead to complications. The Notice thus sets out 'guidelines on case allocation'.[214] It states that, in principle, national authorities should handle cases 'the effects of which are felt mainly in their territory and which appear upon preliminary examination unlikely to qualify for exemption under Article [81](3)'. However, it continues that 'the Commission reserves the right to take on certain cases displaying a particular Community interest'.[215] The Commission also wishes to retain cases which raise a new point of law which 'has not yet been the subject of a Commission decision or a judgment of the Court of Justice or Court of first Instance'.[216]

A significant limitation on the ability of the national authorities to act is that such authorities may not use evidence collected by the Commission in the course of any of their investigations. They 'are not entitled to use as evidence, for the purposes of applying either national rules or the Community competition rules, unpublished information contained in replies to requests for information sent to firms under Article 11 of Regulation no 17 or information obtained as a result of any inspections carried out under Article 14 of that Regulation. This information can nevertheless be taken into account, where appropriate, to justify instituting national proceedings'.[217]

The Commission's White Paper on Modernisation and subsequent draft Regulation makes proposals to ensure that greater enforcement can be conducted by the national authorities.

5. PROPOSALS FOR MODERNIZATION

It has been seen in sections 3 and 4 above that the Commission's desire to encourage greater enforcement at the national level has been thwarted. This has been partly due to the inability of these bodies fully to apply Article 81(3). The Commission has been reluctant in the past to give up its exclusive power to grant exemptions. In its White Paper on Modernisation the Commission finally recognised the need to relinquish this exclusive right. The Commission has followed up the proposals in the White Paper by adopting a draft Regulation which would not reserve the sole right to grant exemptions to the Commission but which proposes that Article 81 should become directly applicable in its entirety.[218] The regulation thus envisages that both the national courts and the national competition authorities should play

---

[214] Notice on cooperation between national competition authorities and the Commission in handling cases falling with the scope of Articles 85 [now 81] and 86 [now 82] of the EC Treaty [1997] OJ C313/3, paras. 23–36.

[215] *Ibid.*, para. 26.

[216] *Ibid.*, para. 34.

[217] *Ibid.*, para. 47, relying on Case C–67/91, *Dirección General de Defensa de las Competencia v. Asociación España de Banca Privada (AEB) and others (Spanish Banks)* [1992] ECR I–4785.

[218] White Paper on Modernisation [1999] OJ C132/1, [1999] 5 CMLR 208 and proposal for a Reg. implementing Arts. 81 and 82, COM(2000)582.

a more active part in the enforcement of Articles 81 and 82. Indeed the draft Regulation requires Member States to designate an authority to apply Articles 81 and 82 and to empower it to act.[219] The White Paper is discussed in Chapter 16.

6. THE RELATIONSHIP BETWEEN EC AND NATIONAL COMPETITION LAW

A. THE APPLICATION OF NATIONAL COMPETITION RULES

Although national competition authorities and national courts may be able to apply Community competition rules a question which also arises is to what extent can they apply, concurrently, their own *domestic, national* competition rules. It is clear that the fact that an agreement or conduct may infringe Article 81 or 82 of the Treaty does not currently preclude the application of national competition provisions.[220] An important question which arises therefore is to what extent can a national authority apply its national rules to circumstances which might also be affected by the Community provisions. In the context of the Merger Regulation the division of responsibilities between the Community and national authorities has been more clearly defined.

C.S. Kerse, *EC Antitrust Procedure* (4th edn., Sweet & Maxwell, 1998), 445–6

Avoidance of conflict

10.28   Community competition law and national competition laws may overlap in their fields of application . . . Whilst national laws may be designed to deal with the same sorts of circumstances (*i.e.* restrictive practices, cartels, dominant positions) and may be cast in similar terms as Community law, their purposes will, generally, be specific to the Members State in question and may not, however necessarily, reflect the same interests and objectives as the Community's . . . The application of two or more concurrent systems of competition law need not necessarily give rise to conflicts. . . .

The broad jurisdictional demarcation line between the Community rules and national competition law is said to be 'the effect upon trade between Member States'. Indeed in those national systems modelled on Articles [81] and [82] this criterion may be varied and refer to the effect on trade in the Member State concerned. Thus in *Consten and Grundig*, the Court said: . . . 'The concept of an agreement "which may affect trade between Member

---

[219] Proposal for a Council Reg. implementing Arts. 81 and 82, Arts. 5 and 36, COM(2000)582.
[220] Case 14/68, *Walt Wilhelm v. Bundeskartellamt* [1969] ECR 1, [1969] CMLR 100 but see *infra* 1016.

States" is intended to define, in the law governing cartels, the boundary between the areas respectively covered by Community law and national law'. Only if an agreement affects trade between Member States is it capable of falling within the prohibition of Article [81(1)]. In practice the different fields of application, whether territorial or substantive, of national and Community law may be blurred, in good part as a consequence of the wide interpretation the Court has given to the notion of effect on trade between Member States. There is frequently overlap and potentially duplication of procedures and the possibility of conflict. While the Merger Control Regulation has drawn a clear dividing line (by reference to 'Community dimension' as expressly defined) between cases falling within the jurisdiction of the Commission and those remaining with national authorities, no such rule applies in relation to competition laws generally . . . To date the Community has largely adopted a case-by-case approach, guided by the Court of Justice in a small number of rulings, the leading case being *Walt Wilhelm* . . . The practical emphasis has shifted towards increased co-operation between Community and national regimes, including the employment of domestic competition laws by national authorities to compensate for the limited resources of the Commission.

The danger of applying conflicting rules will of course be minimized where the national competition rules are modelled on Community law.[221] In other cases, there may be greater difficulty. It is important to know, therefore, whether or not a national competition authority or court can, for example: (1) authorize an agreement prohibited by Article 81 or behaviour which infringes Article 82; or (2) condemn conduct which is not prohibited by Community law (for example, because an agreement does not infringe Article 81(1) or benefits from an exemption under Article 81(3)).

B. THE PRINCIPLE OF SUPREMACY AND THE DUTY OF CO-OPERATION

(i) WALT WILHELM

Where there is a conflict between a directly effective provision of Community law and national law the former must prevail.[222] In addition authorities of a Member State have a duty to 'facilitate the achievement of the Community's tasks' and to 'abstain from any measure which could jeopardise the attainment of the objectives of this Treaty'.[223]

It is clear consequently that although national authorities have *concurrent* responsibility for the enforcement of competition rules they may apply their rules only in so far as the Community principle of supremacy is satisfied and so long as they comply with their obligation of solidarity to the Community objectives. In *Walt Wilhelm* v.

---

[221] In a number of Member States the rules are similar to and modelled on the Community rules. This is the case, e.g., in Spain, Italy, Belgium, Ireland, Denmark, the Netherlands, and the UK. In the UK, however, some of the previous rules have been retained, see e.g. the Fair Trading Act 1973.

[222] *Supra* Chap. 2.

[223] Art 10 of the Treaty provides that 'Member States shall take all appropriate measured . . . to ensure fulfilment of the obligations arising out of this Treaty or resulting from action taken by the institutions of the Community. They shall facilitate the achievement of the Community's tasks.' It thus imposes an obligation of solidarity on the national authorities in respect of the Community project.

Bundeskartellamt[224] the ECJ held that national law may be applied so long as its application does not 'prejudice the full and uniform application of Community law or the effects of measures taken or to be taken to implement it'.

The ability of a national authority to act is dependent upon the exact circumstances which arise.

(ii) COMMUNITY PROHIBITION

In *Walt Wilhelm* the ECJ held that, subject to the proviso set out above, national authorities could take action against entities being investigated under the Community competition rules. An infringement of the Community competition rules and the imposition of a fine does not therefore mean that an undertaking cannot *also* be pursued under national competition rules.[225]

Case 14/68, *Walt Wilhelm* v. *Bundeskartellamt* [1969] ECR 1, [1969] CMLR 100

In this case the German Bundeskartellamt (Federal Cartel Bureau) fined the applicants under paragraph 38, jointly with paragraph 1, of the GWB (Gesetz gegen Wettbewerbsbeschränkungen—the German law against restraint of competition of 27 July 1957) in respect of an agreement to fix and increase the price of aniline.

The Commission also commenced proceedings to verify the compatibility with the Article 81 of the price increases in aniline.

The parties challenged the Bundeskartellamt's decision before the Kammergericht (Kartellsenat), Berlin. The alleged that it was not entitled to take proceedings in respect of a breach of law which was simultaneously the subject of parallel proceedings before the Commission. The Kammergericht asked the Court for a preliminary ruling under Article 234 of the Treaty. In particular, it asked:

1. Is it in accordance with Article [81(1)] and (3) of the [EC] Treaty and Article 9 of Regulation No 17 of 6 February 1962 (on cartels), and with the prevailing general principles of Community law, to apply concurrently to a situation capable of fulfilling the conditions set out in Article [81(1)] of the [EC] Treaty not only the prohibition prescribed by that Article but also the restrictive provisions contained in the cartel law of a Member State, in this instance paragraph 1 together with paragraph 38(1) (i) of the GWB (the German Law against Restraint of Competition), when the Commission of the European Communities has already asserted its jurisdiction under Article 3 of the [EC] Treaty through action taken under Article 14 of Regulation No 17 (on cartels) (Case No IV/26.267/E1 of the Commission of the European Communities)?

2. Or is this impossible because of the risk of its resulting in a double sanction imposed by the Commission of the European Communities and by the national authority with jurisdiction in cartel matters—in this case, the Bundeskartellamt?

3. Does Article [10] of the [EC] Treaty, in conjunction with Article [3(1)(g)] of the [EC] Treaty and with Article 9 of Regulation No 17 (on cartels) make this impossible in particular

---

[224] Case 14/68 [1969] ECR 1, [1969] CMLR 100, para. 9.

[225] Although the Court indicated in *Walt Wilhelm Bundeskartellaust* [1969]ECR I, [1969] CMLR 100, that the principle of natural justice might require any previous sanction imposed to be taken into account when a second sanction is imposed.

because Member States must refrain from applying their own law regarding competition when the uniform legal assessment of a case would otherwise be placed at risk and/ or when there would thereby result a distortion of competition in the common market to the detriment of those subject to that law?

Court of justice

I— The first and third questions

In the first question the national court asks whether, when a procedure has already been initiated by the Commission under Article 14 of Regulation No 17 of 6 February 1962, it is compatible with the Treaty for the national authorities to apply to the same facts the prohibitions laid down by the national law on cartels. This request is elaborated in particular in the third question, relating to the risk of a different legal assessment of the same facts and to the possibility of distortions of competition in the common market to the detriment of those subject to the said national law. In this respect reference is made to Article 9 of Regulation No 17, to Articles [81], [3(1)(g)] and [10] of the [EC] Treaty and to the general principles of Community law.

3. Article 9(3) of Regulation No 17 is concerned with the competence of the authorities of the Member States only in so far as they are authorized to apply Articles [81(1)] and [82] of the Treaty directly when the Commission has taken no action of its own. This provision does not apply where the said authorities are acting in pursuance not of the said articles but only of their internal law. Community and national law on cartels consider cartels from different points of view. Whereas Articles [81] regards them in the light of the obstacles which may result for trade between Member States, each body of national legislation proceeds on the basis of the considerations peculiar to it and considers cartels only in that context. It is true that as the economic phenomena and legal situations under consideration may in individual cases be interdependent, the distinction between Community and national aspects could not serve in all cases as the decisive criterion for the delimitation of jurisdiction. However, it implies that one and the same agreement may, in principle, be the object of two sets of parallel proceedings, one before the Community authorities under Article [81] of the [EC] Treaty, the other before the national authorities under national law.

4. Moreover this interpretation is confirmed by the provision in Article [83(2)(e)], which authorizes the Council to determine the relationship between national . . . laws and the Community rules on competition; it follows that in principle the national cartel authorities may take proceedings also with regard to situations likely to be the subject of a decision by the Commission. However, if the ultimate general aim of the Treaty is to be respected, this parallel application of the national system can only be allowed in so far as it does not prejudice the uniform application throughout the Common Market of the Community rules on cartels and the full effect of the measures adopted in implementation of those rules.

[5.] Any other solution would be incompatible with the objectives of the Treaty and the character of its rules on competition. Article [81] of the [EC] Treaty applies to all the undertakings in the Community whose conduct it governs either by prohibitions or by means of exemptions, granted—subject to conditions which it specifies—in favour of agreements which contribute to improving the production or distribution of goods or to promoting technical or economic progress. While the Treaty's primary object is to eliminate by this means the obstacles to the free movement of goods within the common market and to confirm and safeguard the unity of that market, it also permits the Community authorities to carry out certain positive, though indirect, action with a view to promoting a harmonious development of economic activities within the whole Community, in accordance with Article 2 of the Treaty. Article [83(2)(e)], in conferring on a Community institution the power to determine the relationship between national laws and the Community rules on competition, confirm the supremacy of Community law.

6. The [EC] Treaty has established its own system of law, integrated into the legal system of the Member States, and which must be applied by their courts. It would be contrary to the nature of such a system to allow Member States to introduce or to retain measures capable of prejudicing the practical effectiveness of the Treaty. The binding force of the Treaty and of measures taken in application of it must not differ from one state to another as a result of internal measures, lest the functioning of the Community system should be impeded and the achievement of the aims of the Treaty placed in peril. Consequently, conflicts between the rules of the Community and national rules in the matter of the law on cartels must be resolved by applying the principle that Community law takes precedence.

7. It follows from the foregoing that should it prove that a decision of a national authority regarding an agreement would be incompatible with a decision adopted by the Commission at the culmination of the procedure initiated by it, the national authority is required to take proper account of the effects of the latter decision.

8. Where, during national proceedings, it appears possible that the decision to be taken by the Commission at the culmination of a procedure still in progress concerning the same agreement may conflict with the effects of the decision of the national authorities, it is for the latter to take the appropriate measures.

9. Consequently, and so long as a regulation adopted pursuant to Article [83(2)(e)] of the Treaty has not provided otherwise, national authorities may take action against an agreement in accordance with their national law, even when an examination of the agreement from the point of view of its compatibility with Community law is pending before the Commission, subject however to the condition that the application of national law may not prejudice the full and uniform application of Community law or the effects of measures taken or to be taken to implement it.

II — The second question

10. In the second question the Kammergericht asks whether 'the risk of its resulting in a double sanction imposed by the Commission of the European Communities and by the national authority with jurisdiction in cartel matters . . .' renders impossible the acceptance for one set of facts of two parallel procedures, the one Community and the other national.

11. The possibility of concurrent sanctions need not mean that the possibility of two parallel proceedings pursuing different ends is unacceptable. Without prejudice to the conditions and limits indicated in the answer to the first question, the acceptability of a dual procedure of this kind follows in fact from the special system of the sharing of jurisdiction between the Community and the Member States with regard to cartels. If, however, the possibility of two procedures being conducted separately were to lead to the imposition of consecutive sanctions, a general requirement of natural justice, such as that expressed at the end of the second paragraph of Article 90 of the ECSC Treaty, demands that any previous punitive decision must be taken into account in determining any sanction which is to be imposed. In any case, so long as no regulation has been issued under [Article 83(2)(e)], no means of avoiding such a possibility is to be found in the general principles of Community law; this leaves intact the reply given to the first question.

The principle of supremacy does dictate, however, that an agreement prohibited under Article 81 or conduct prohibited under Article 82 cannot be authorized at the national level.[226]

---

[226] The fact that an agreement has been authorized at the national level does not preclude the Commission from subsequently finding that the agreement in fact infringes Art. 81: see Case C–360/92P, *Publishers' Association* [1995] ECR I–23, [1995] 5 CMLR 33.

(iii) COMMUNITY AUTHORISATION

a. GENERAL

The position is more complex where conduct is not prohibited under Community law but where a national authority wishes to apply national rules prohibiting the conduct. In this case it is necessary to differentiate between different scenarios. It will be important to know whether or not the conduct is authorized because it is an agreement which has been exempted, individually or *en block* or because it does not infringe Article 81(1) or Article 82 at all.

b. INDIVIDUAL EXEMPTION

There is no case law which sets out whether or not a national authority can condemn an agreement which has been granted an individual exemption by the Commission pursuant to Article 81(3) or clear it subject only to compliance with more stringent conditions and obligations than those imposed by the Commission.

In *Walt Wilhelm* the ECJ did not have to consider this position. In that case the Commission was investigating the existence of a cartel and the German court wished to know whether or not this investigation precluded the German Bundeskartellamt from taking action under German law which prohibited restraints of competition. It has been seen that the Court in this case held that parallel action by a national authority is permissible so long as its does not prejudice the full and uniform application of Community law.

Arguably, an exemption is merely permissive in nature and should not preclude a national authority from applying more stringent national rules.[227] However, it could also be argued that the Commission's decision to grant an individual exemption forms part of its coherent competition policy and is designed to encourage certain types of agreements. As the Commission has taken 'certain positive, though indirect, action with a view to promoting a harmonious development of economic activities within the whole Community' (see paragraph 5 of *Walt Wilhelm* set out above at 1011) its actions should not be thwarted by the application of conflicting, more stringent, national rules.

c. BLOCK EXEMPTION

Similarly uncertainty surrounds the question whether or not a national competition authority should be able to apply stricter national rules to agreements which benefit from a Community block exemption. The argument that the exemption is merely permissive in nature and should not preclude the application of more stringent national rules is arguably stronger in the context of block exemptions. An agreement which is exempted under the provisions of a group exemption has not, after all, been assessed individually by the Commission.[228]

It has been seen, however, that in practice many more agreements are likely to benefit

---

[227] See e.g., the UK MMC Report on *The Supply in the UK for retail sale of Fine Fragrances*, Cm 2380, (HMSO, 1993).

[228] See the UK's MMC report on *The Supply of Beer* (HMSO, 1989) Cm 651 and the resultant orders, Supply of Beer (Loan Ties etc.) Order 1989 SI 1989/2258 and the Supply of Beer (Tied Estate) Order 1989 SI 1989/2390).

from a block exemption than an individual exemption and that the Commission has sought to mould competition policy through the adoption of block exemption. Arguably, therefore, the 'principle of primacy of Community law requires that an agreement protected by an exempting regulation cannot be prohibited, on the basis of more restrictive national provisions, by the national authorities'.[229]

Some of the arguments for and against a national authority being able to apply stricter provisions of national law where a Community exemption has been granted are set out below:

C.S. Kerse, *EC Antitrust Procedure* (4th edn., Sweet & Maxwell, 1998)

Community exemption

10.33   The Co-operation Notice accepts that the position is 'less clear' as to whether national authorities are allowed to apply more strict national competition law where the situation they are assessing has been the subject of an individual exemption decision or is covered by the block exemption... Advocates of the so-called double barrier theory (*Zweischrankentheorie*) argue that an agreement is only lawful if it passes the tests laid down by both national law and Community law. It is based on a complete philosophy of competition, of which prohibition is considered the material instrument, and exemptions are tolerated but are by no means indispensable. The Commission has said that the Court of Justice rejected this theory in *Walt Wilhelm*... It did not in fact do so expressly but, as will be shown below, there must be serious doubt about the validity of the theory in Community law, at least in its purest form.

It has been suggested that the Court's reference to 'certain positive, though indirect action' of Community institutions means or includes exemption... Given the context in which the phrase appears the argument is compelling. There is, however, an alternative interpretation.... This is that the positive action referred to means other measures under the Treaty such as directives ... addressed to Member States to harmonise national laws. Even so, it might still be argued that a national prohibition cannot override the effect of a Community exemption because the application of national laws must not interfere with the uniform application throughout the Community of the competition rules. (Indeed it is a consistent theme of the Court's case law that the Treaty imposes a duty on Member States not to adopt or maintain in force any measure which could deprive Articles [81] and [82] of their effectiveness...). As the Commission argued in the *Volkswagen* case, the uniform application of Community law would be frustrated every time an exemption was made dependent on the relevant national rules. Differential treatment in the Member States would detract from the uniform application of Community law. The full effectiveness of an act giving effect to the Treaty would also be disregarded...

But in *Walt Wilhelm* Advocate-General Roemer commented:...

---

[229] Opinion of Tesauro AG in Case C–266/93, *Bundeskartellamt v. Volkswagen and VAG Leasing* [1995] ECR I–3479, paras. 44–60. The new Verticals Reg. Reg. 2790/1999 [1999] OJ L336/21, gives the Member States power to withdraw the benefit of the exemption in certain circumstances in respect of activities occurring in its territory. Nonetheless the power of withdrawal must not be exercised in a way that prejudices the uniform application throughout the common market of the Community competition rules or the full effect of the measures adopted in implementation of those rules (recital 14).

'If national authorities thwart the Community exemption through the application of a national rule of prohibition, they no more threaten the objectives of the Treaty than do the parties to an agreement when they refrain from applying it, which can occur at any time. This conclusion applies as a general rule because in principle cartels cannot be considered as instruments of the organisation of the Common Market'.

Indeed, in the absence of a Community provision which requires the performance of an exempted agreement, it may, at least at first sight, be surprising that a Member State could be considered to be under an obligation to relax its national law to permit such performance.

d. COMFORT LETTERS

Comfort letters issued by the Commission are not binding acts.[230] It would seem unlikely therefore that the grant of a comfort letter would preclude a national authority from taking a stricter view of an agreement under domestic law. Since, however, many more agreements are operated in reliance on comfort letters than in reliance on an exemption it may be that the effect of comfort letters on the application of domestic rules should be dealt with in the same way as exemptions.

e. NO INFRINGEMENT OF ARTICLE 81(1) OR ARTICLE 82

What is the position where Article 81 or 82 does not apply to conduct at all? Can more stringent national rules prohibit the operation of an agreement or conduct authorized or permitted under Community law. Arguably when an agreement or conduct falls outside the Community rules there is no conflict where national rules apply and there is no interference with the full and uniform application of Community law.[231] It is possible in the context of Article 81, however, that the answer to this question will depend partly upon why the agreement does not infringe Article 81. If the agreement does not affect trade (the Community has no jurisdiction over the case) or the agreement is of minor importance (because of the insignificant impact at the Community level)[232] then it seems entirely appropriate that national rules should apply. It seems from the Court's judgment in *Perfumes*[233] that in these circumstances at least national authorities are free to apply domestic law. Where, however, an agreement does not infringe Article 81(1) because the agreement has been found not to have as its object or effect the prevention, restriction, or distortion of competition then the position is less clear. It could be argued that this finding constitutes a positive step taken which aims, as in the case where an exemption is granted, to promote and permit certain types of agreements.

(iv) CO-OPERATION BETWEEN THE NATIONAL AND COMMUNITY AUTHORITIES

A positive means of minimizing conflicts between the national and Community authorities is for those authorities to co-operate as closely as possible. Some practical arrangements are

---

[230] See *supra* Chap. 4.
[231] C.S. Kerse, *EC Antitrust Procedure* (4th edn., Sweet & Maxwell, 1998), para. 10.32.
[232] See *supra* Chap. 3.
[233] Cases 253/78 and 1–3, 37 & 99/79, *Procureur de la République v. Giry and Guérlain* [1980] ECR 2327, [1981] 2 CMLR 99.

set out in the Commission's Notice on co-operation between national competition authorities and the Commission[234] for communication and the allocation of cases between the two authorities.

(v) THE MERGER REGULATION

It was seen in Chapter 12 above that the Merger Regulation[235] sets out rules which allocate responsibility for mergers between the Community and national authorities. The basic rule is that the Merger Regulation alone applies to a concentration with a Community dimension. No national competition law may be applied. The Regulation itself, however, sets out some exceptions to this rule.

C. THE FUTURE

In its proposal for a new Regulation implementing Articles 81 and 82 (which would replace Regulation 17) the Commission has suggested that all agreements or abuses of a dominant position which affect trade between Member States shall be governed solely by Community law to the exclusion of national law.[236] Although this proposal must be seen in context, as part of an attempt to modernize the enforcement of the EC competition rules more generally, the proposal would radically alter the current position. The proposal is, therefore, likely to provoke strong reactions and debate.

7. FURTHER READING

A. BOOKS

BREALEY, M., and HOSKINS, M., *Remedies in EC Law* (2nd edn., Sweet & Maxwell, 1998)

EUROPEAN COMMISSION, *The Application of Articles 85 & 86 of the EC Treaty by National Courts in the Member States* (Commission, 1997)

JONES, A., *Restitution and European Community Law* (LLP, 2000), Chapter 6

JONES, C. A., *Private Enforcement of Antitrust Law in the EU, UK and USA* (Oxford University Press, 1999)

SLOT, P. J., and MACDONNELL, A., *Procedure and Enforcement in EC and US Competition Law* (Sweet & Maxwell, 1993)

B. ARTICLES

JACOBS, F. G., 'Civil Enforcement of EEC Antitrust Law' (1984) 82 *Mich LR* 1364

BAEL, I. van, 'The Role of the National Courts' [1994] *ECLR* 3

WHISH, R., 'The Enforcement of EC Competition Law in the Domestic Courts of Member States' [1994] *ECLR* 60

—— 'Frontiers of Competition Law' (ed. J. Lonbay) (Wiley, 1994), Chapter 5

—— 'The Enforceability of Agreements under EC and UK Competition Law' in F. D. Rose (ed.), *Lex Mercatoria: Essays in International Commercial Law in Honour of Francis Reynolds* (LLP, 2000) 297–319

---

[234] [1997] OJ C313/3.

[235] Council Reg. 4064/89 [1989] OJ L395/1, as amended by Council Reg. 1310/97 [1997] OJ L180/1.

[236] Proposal for a Reg. implementing Arts. 81 and 82, Art. 3, COM(2000)582, and *infra* Chap. 16.

16

THE COMMISSION'S WHITE PAPER ON MODERNISATION OF THE RULES IMPLEMENTING ARTICLES 81 AND 82 OF THE EC TREATY

1. INTRODUCTION

It cannot have escaped the notice of the reader of this book that in 1999 the Commission adopted a White Paper on modernisation of the rules implementing Articles 85 and 86 [now Article 81 and 82] of the EC Treaty.[1] In many chapters of this book the White Paper, published on 28 April 1999,[2] has been referred to and some of its proposals discussed.[3] In this chapter we seek to outline, as a whole, the main proposals set out in that Paper and to deal with some of the difficult questions that they raise.

For a long time the Commission has been considering the need for changes to the current enforcement mechanisms and has been promoting greater decentralization of enforcement through the national courts and competition authorities.[4] The White Paper seeks essentially to deal with the problems of enforcement which have arisen since the adoption in 1962 of Regulation 17.[5] It is this Regulation, of course, which confers powers of supervision and enforcement on the Commission. The Commission recognizes that the current system may soon become unworkable. The thrust of the White Paper is thus to make suggestions either for improvement of that system or for its radical reform.

It has been seen that the main problems with the current enforcement system hinge on a number of factors:

- The need for prior notification of agreements for exemption under Article 81;[6]
- The fact that the Commission alone has power to grant individual exemptions under

---

[1] [1999] OJ C132/1, [1999] 5 CMLR 208.

[2] In contrast to a Commission Green Paper which merely sets out options and establishes a consultation process, the White Paper presents a statement of the Commission's policy. *Cf.* the Green Paper on Vertical Restraints, COM(96)721 final.

[3] See especially Chap. 2, 4, and 15.

[4] See *supra* Chap. 15.

[5] [1959–62] OJ Spec. Ed. 87.

Article 81(3) to agreements contravening Article 81(1). It is thus difficult for national courts and national competition authorities to participate in the enforcement of Article 81;[7]

- The fact that individuals have a perception that the Commission alone enforces the competition rules. Thus individuals prefer to complain to the Commission rather than bring private proceedings before the national courts;[8]
- The fact that a national competition authority may be unwilling or unable to enforce the EC competition rules;[9]
- The fact that the Commission has limited resources. If precious resources are spent dealing with exemptions for agreements then less resources are available for the detection and prohibition of more serious violations of the rules.

Although the system may have worked in 1962 the position is very different today. In 1962 the idea of a centralized authorization system was an appealing one. The centralized system would, and did, enable the Commission to create a 'culture of competition' in Europe and ensure the integration of national markets. At the time this system was devised there were only six Member States and it could not perhaps have been foreseen how quickly the Community would expand and how broadly Articles 81 and 82 would be interpreted. The discussion in previous chapters of this book established that the system set up in 1962 has not been able to cope with the growing Community. It has imposed a great burden on both business and the Commission and has had to be operated in a very different way from that envisaged. The Commission in the White Paper recognizes this fact, commenting that what seemed appropriate in 1962 'is no longer appropriate for the Community of today with 15 Member States, 11 languages and over 350 million inhabitants'. In its view a centralized prior authorization system in Brussels is no longer possible.[10] The Commission thus proposes steps to make greater enforcement at the national level possible and to free its resources for cases raising a particular Community interest and/or a serious infringement of the rules, especially participation in cross-border cartels and abuses of a dominant position.

White paper on modernisation of the rules implementing articles 85 and 86 [now Articles 81 and 82] of the EC Treaty [1999] OJ C132/1, [1999] 5 CMLR 208

8. The role of the Commission in this new environment has changed. At the beginning the focus of its activity was on establishing rules on restrictive practices interfering directly with the goal of market integration. As law and policy have been clarified, the burden of enforcement can now be shared more equitably with national courts and authorities, which have the advantage of proximity to citizens and the problems they face. The Commission has now come to concentrate more on ensuring effective competition by detecting and stopping cross-border cartels and maintaining competitive market structures. It has also risen to the chall-

---

[6] *Supra* Chap. 4.
[7] *Supra* Chaps. 4 and 15.
[8] *Supra* Chap. 15.
[9] *Supra* Chaps. 2 and 15.
[10] White Paper on modernization, *supra* n. 1, C7, para. 40.

enges of merger control, liberalisation of hitherto monopolised markets and international cooperation.

9. The Commission can cope with all these developments only by focussing its attention on the most important cases and on those fields of activity where it can operate more efficiently than national bodies. To this end it has already adopted various measures such as the 'de minimis' Notice for agreements of minor importance and block exemption regulations.

10. However, these measures are not sufficient to meet the new challenges outlined above. It is no longer possible to maintain a centralised enforcement system requiring a decision by the Commission for restrictive practices which fulfil the conditions of Article [81(3)]. To make such an authorisation system work in the Community of today and tomorrow would require enormous resources and impose heavy costs on companies. It is essential to adapt the system so as to relieve companies from unnecessary bureaucracy, to allow the Commission to become more active in the pursuit of serious competition infringements and to increase and stimulate enforcement at national level. Our Community requires a more efficient and simpler system of control.

A key difficulty faced by the Commission is its lack of resources. The Commission (or rather, the Competition Directorate) does not have, and seems unlikely ever to be granted, adequate resources by the Member States to carry out the tasks entrusted to it. With the prospect of ten or more new Community members looming on the horizon, the Commission seems aware that the present system, already under strain, will not be able to cope. Something has to change. The Commission's solution is that if the Member States are not prepared to dedicate adequate means for the *Commission* to apply and enforce the competition rules then the Member States must themselves become responsible, at least in part, for their enforcement. The White Paper presents this change, however, as desirable as a matter of principle rather than as a mere matter of expediency.

The White Paper does discuss the option of modernizing the system by changing the interpretation of Article 81(1) 'so as to include the analysis of the harmful and beneficial effects of an agreement in the assessment of Article [81](1)'. The Commission rejected this idea because it would mean Article 81(3) being 'cast aside', whereas 'that provision in fact contains all the elements of a rule of reason.'[11] It states that such an approach would also risk diverting Article 81(3) from providing a legal framework for the economic assessment of restrictive practices into allowing 'the application of the competition rules to be set aside because of political considerations'.[12] This last comment is very interesting in view of the debate about the matters to be taken into account under Article 81(3), which is pertinent to the viability of the proposals in the White Paper.[13] The other objection in the White Paper to improving the present system by changing the interpretation of Article 81(1) is that it would be dependent on the case law of the Court. Even if it upheld the new interpretation, the process of modernization could take many years.[14]

---

[11] See *supra.* Chap. 4.
[12] White Paper on Modernization, *supra* n. 1, paras. 56–57.
[13] See Chap. 4 and *infra* 1035 ff.
[14] White Paper on modernisation, *supra* n. 1, para. 57.

2. SUMMARY OF PROPOSALS

We have already outlined the main proposals set out in the White Paper in Chapter 4. It will be remembered that the simple solution put forward by the Commission in the White Paper is more revolutionary than expected. The proposal is:

- to abolish the notification and authorization system;
- to abandon its monopoly over the grant of Article 81(3) exemptions; and
- to move to a fully *directly applicable* system in which Article 81 can be applied in its entirety by the national courts and the national competition authorities.

The Commission does not therefore propose merely sharing power to grant Article 81(3) exemptions with the national competition authorities, but instead proposes the complete abolition of the centralized notification and authorization system for Article 81(3) exemptions set up by Article 9(1) of Regulation 17. The system would be replaced by a fully directly applicable system within which national courts and national competition authorities would be free to apply both Article 81 and 82 in their entirety. 'Article 81 would then become *a unitary norm comprising a rule establishing the principle of prohibition unless certain conditions are met.*'[15] The Commission discussed, but rejected, the possibility of trying to improve the current system set out in Regulation 17.

White paper on modernisation of the rules implementing articles 85 and 86 [now 81 and 82] of the EC Treaty [1999] OJ C132/1, [1999] 5 CMLR 208

11. In the White Paper, the Commission discusses several options for reform. It proposes a system which meets the objectives of rigorous enforcement of competition law, effective decentralisation, simplification of procedures and uniform application of law and policy development throughout the EU.

12. The proposed reform involves the abolition of the notification and exemption system and its replacement by a Council Regulation which would render the exemption rule of Article [81(3)] directly applicable without prior decision by the Commission. Article [81] as a whole would be applied by the Commission, national competition authorities and national courts, as is already the case for Articles [81(1)] and [82].

13. This reform would allow the Commission to refocus its activities on the most serious infringements of Community law in cases with a Community interest. It would pave the way for decentralised application of the EC competition rules by national authorities and courts and eliminate unnecessary bureaucracy and compliance costs for industry. It would also stimulate the application of the EC competition rules by national authorities.

14. In the new system, the Commission would keep a leading role in determining EC competition policy. It would continue to adopt Regulations and Notices setting out the principal rules of interpretation of Articles [81] and [82]. The Commission would also continue to adopt

---

[15] Commission's own emphasis, White Paper on Modernisation, *supra* n. 1, para. 69.

prohibition decisions and positive decisions to set out guidance for the implementation of these provisions. It is also envisaged that production joint ventures involving sizeable investments would not be included in the new system, but submitted instead to the procedural rules of the Community merger regulation.

The White Paper also proposes strengthening the Commission's powers of investigation, strengthening the complaints system, and these other changes to the enforcement regime. Many of these proposals have now been incorporated by the Commission in a draft Regulation which, if adopted, will replace Regulation 17.[16]

3. THE DECENTRALIZED APPLICATION OF THE COMPETITION RULES

A. ARTICLE 81(3) TO BECOME DIRECTLY APPLICABLE

At the heart of the White Paper is the unexpectedly radical proposal to make Article 81(3) a 'directly applicable exception'. The decision whether or not an agreement fulfills the criteria in Article 81(3) would no longer be taken by the Commission after notification of the agreement by the parties. Instead, the decision would be able to be made by a national court if the matter were relevant to litigation before it, by a national competition authority, or by the Commission itself, but *not* after a notification. Undertakings would, therefore, be deprived of the comfort of being able to notify and receive assurance of the compatibility of their agreement with Article 81. Instead they would be left to judge for themselves the legitimacy of their arrangements.[17] In place of a prior authorization system there would be what the White Paper calls 'intensified *ex post* control' which would include strengthening the Commission's powers of enquiry, and making it easier to lodge complaints.[18]

The proposal to render Article 81(3) directly applicable raises a number of interesting issues concerning its compatibility with the Treaty and the suitability of the Article 81(3) criteria for adjudication by national courts and competition authorities. These matters are considered below.[19]

B. THE ROLE OF THE COMMISSION IN THE NEW SYSTEM

The proposals envisage a new division of responsibilities, but the central, guiding role will remain with the Commission. It will be aided in its duty of enforcing Article 81 by the national courts and the national competition authorities. It will, nonetheless, retain control

[16] Proposal for a Reg. implementing Arts. 81 and 82, COM (2000) 582, 27 Sept. 2000 (the draft Reg.). The reg. also incorporates a number of other dramatic changes to the current system.

[17] Unless the transaction is a partial-function production joint venture; *ibid.*, para. 79. See *supra* Chap. 4, 12 and 13.

[18] White Paper on Modernization, *supra* n. 1, para. 108.

[19] *Infra.*

over competition policy.[20] It will do this by retaining the sole right to propose legislative texts, adopt regulations (including block exemptions,[21] and issue notices and guidelines; by continuing to adopt prohibition decisions (in increasing numbers) which will set out important precedents,[22] and by sometimes adopting 'positive decisions' where necessary to clarify the law.[23] The Commission also proposes[24] the adoption of a new kind of decision, which will be issued on the termination of proceedings that would have resulted in a prohibition decision if suitable commitments had not been offered by the parties. The possibility of fines and periodic penalty payments would have to be introduced in order to ensure that such commitments are complied with.[25]

1. Competition policy to be determined by the commission

83. Decentralisation must not be allowed to result in inconsistent application of Community competition law. Competition policy will thus continue to be determined at Community level, both by means of the adoption of legislative texts and individual decisions. The Commission, as guardian of the Treaties and guarantor of the Community interest subject to the supervision of the Court of Justice, has a special role to play in the application of Community law and in ensuring the consistent application of the competition rules.

84. In a directly applicable exception system, the legislative framework is of primary importance. The application of the rules must be sufficiently reliable and consistent to allow businesses to assess whether their restrictive practices are lawful. The Commission would keep the sole right to propose legislative texts, in whatever form – regulations, notices, guidelines etc. – and would act whenever necessary in order to ensure consistency and uniformity in the application of the competition rules.

85. Block exemptions are the first of these legislative texts. Given the importance of legislation in the new directly applicable exception system, legal certainty for undertakings demands that an agreement exempted by a block exemption should not then be held contrary to national law. This can be achieved by invoking Article [83(2)(e)]: a Community regulation should be enacted to prevent national legislation from prohibiting or varying the effects of agreements exempted by Community regulation. Some Member States have already entered this principle in their own legislation. For example, the Belgian Law No 91/2790 of 5 August 1991 provides that Community exemptions are a bar to action by the Belgian authorities, and that agreements so exempted need not be notified under domestic law. Danish law excludes restrictive practices covered by a Community exemption regulation from the scope of the prohibition that it lays down. Spanish and UK laws make similar provision.

86. The Commission also intends to draw up more notices and guidelines to explain its policy and provide guidance for the application of the Community competition rules by national authorities. These instruments are particularly well suited to the interpretation of rules of an

---

[20] White Paper on Modernisation, *supra* n. 1. paras. 83–90.

[21] As a constitutive act is no longer necessary under Art. 81(3) they will really be block clearances rather than block exemptions.

[22] As it would be concentrating on the most serious restrictions of competition rather than scrutinizing notified agreements which tend to be innocuous, the number of individual prohibition decisions can be expected to increase substantially: White Paper on Modernisation, *supra* n. 1, para. 87.

[23] *Ibid.*, paras. 88 and 89.

[24] *Ibid.*, para. 90.

[25] The Commission does not specifically say so, but a similar practice is adopted under the Merger Reg, Reg. 4064/89 [1989] OJ L395/1; see *supra* Chap. 12.

economic nature, because they make it easier to take account of the range of criteria that are relevant to an examination under the competition rules. They might not be binding on national authorities, but they would make a valuable contribution to the consistent application of Community law, because in its decisions in individual cases the Commission would confirm the approach they set out. Provided those individual decisions were upheld by the Court of Justice, then, notices and guidelines would come to form part of the rules that must be applied by national authorities.

87. In a directly applicable exception system, Commission policy on competition would continue to be reflected in prohibition decisions in individual cases, and these would be of great importance as precedents. As the Commission would be concentrating its attention on the most serious restrictions, the number of individual prohibition decisions can be expected to increase substantially.

88. It is true that the Commission would no longer adopt exemption decisions under Article [81(3)] as it does now, but it should nevertheless be able to adopt individual decisions that are not prohibition decisions. Where a transaction raises a question that is new, it may be necessary to provide the market with guidance regarding the Commission's approach to certain restrictions in it. Positive decisions of this kind would therefore be taken in exceptional cases, on grounds of general interest.

89. These positive decisions would confine themselves to a finding that an agreement is compatible with Article [81] as a whole, whether because it falls outside Article [81(1)], or because it satisfies the tests of Article [81(3)]. They would be of a declaratory nature, and would have the same legal effect as negative clearance decisions have at present.

90. In the course of procedures that might otherwise end with a prohibition, it can happen that the undertakings concerned propose to give the Commission undertakings that would overcome the objections raised against their agreement. It is useful that the Commission should be able to make such commitments binding, both in order to oblige the undertakings to comply with them and to enable the parties and others to rely on them before their national courts. In the new Regulation applying Articles [81] and [82], therefore, the Commission intends to make provision for a new kind of individual decision, subject to the ordinary publication requirements, in which the Commission would take note of the commitments entered into by the parties and render them binding. Such a decision would allow the procedure to be terminated while ensuring that the commitments were respected. As a corollary to this change, a clause would be included in the system of penalties in the Regulation providing for fines and periodic penalty payments in the event of failure on the part of undertakings to meet such commitments.

C. THE ROLE OF THE NATIONAL COMPETITION AUTHORITIES AND NATIONAL COURTS

The Commission wishes to see the national competition authorities and the national courts play an enhanced role in the application of the Community competition rules. It would be vital, therefore, for all national competition authorities to be given the power, as a matter of domestic law, to apply Community law. At the time the White Paper was published seven Member States (including the UK) had not conferred such power on their competition authorities.[26]

---

[26] White Paper on Modernisation, *supra* n. 1, paras. 91–98. The draft Reg. states that national competition authorities shall have power to apply Arts. 81 and 82 (see Arts. 5 and 36).

It was seen in Chapter 2 that the role of the national competition authorities with authority to apply not only national competition rules but the Community rules has been curtailed and frustrated, in particular, by their inability to apply Article 81(3). Under the Commission's proposals all the national competition authorities would be expected to apply both Article 81(1) and (3). They would be able to investigate cases and apply Community law, either in response to complaints or on their own initiative, and would be able to assess whether or not a restrictive practice meets the Article 81(3) criteria.[27] The authorities will not of course have power to grant exemptions since the new system will not admit the possibility of exemptions.

In addition, if the Commission relinquishes its monopoly over the exemption process and if Article 81(3) is held to be directly effective, a national court will be able to rule (a) whether or not an agreement before it infringes Article 81(1); (b) where it does, whether or not it satisfies the criteria of Article 81(3) and so merits exemption; and (c) where it does not merit exemption, that the agreement as a whole, or its severable restrictions, is void under Article 81(2). Although the courts will not be able to grant an *exemption* to an agreement which satisfies the criteria of Article 81(3) (individual exemptions will no longer exist) they will be able to rule on the compatibility of the agreement with those criteria.

D. THE NEED FOR CONSISTENT AND UNIFORM APPLICATION OF THE COMPETITION RULES

The Commission recognizes that the most urgent matter to address in respect of its proposals is to ensure that they do not jeopardize the consistent and uniform application of the competition rules. Decentralization should not be accompanied by divergent application among the various Member States. One major problem, which the Notice does not address, is the uncertainty surrounding the factors to be taken into account when making the Article 81(3) assessment. This is discussed below.[28]

B. Consistent and uniform application of the competition rules

1. Risk of inconsistencies and principles for their resolution

101. Decentralised application of the competition rules and abandonment of the prior authorisation system must not be allowed to stand in the way of the maintenance of conditions of competition that are consistent throughout the Community. The principle of the primacy of Community law prevents the application of national law from undermining the full and uniform application of Community law and the effectiveness of measures implementing it. But where Community law is being applied by several bodies at once (Commission, national authorities and national courts), there are potential conflicts of two kinds:

(1) A national authority or court may take a favourable approach to a restrictive practice prohibited by the Commission (by rejecting a complaint on the ground that the agreement is not caught by Article [81(1)] or that it satisfies the tests of Article [81(3)], or by a judgment ordering its enforcement);

---

[27] *Ibid.*, para. 93.
[28] *Infra* 1035–1036.

(2) An authority may prohibit a restrictive practice, or a court may refuse to enforce it, despite a positive approach taken by the Commission (rejection of a complaint against it or a positive decision).

The Commission sanguinely says, in paragraph 102, that although parallel application of Articles 81(1) and 82 has existed since 1962 this 'has given rise to very few problems'. This has mainly, however, been due to the fact that comparatively few actions have been brought in national courts,[29] that in many Member States the competition authorities have not had power under national law to apply the Community rules, and that in those States where the authorities do have power to apply the Community provisions it has been rare for them to do so.[30] The very existence of the centralized authorization system has operated to reduce the problems at national level.

In paragraph 102 the Commission sets out four 'principles for the resolution of conflicts':

102. It should be pointed out, first of all, that parallel application of Article 8[1](1) and Article [82] has existed since 1962, and has given rise to very few problems. The principles for resolution of conflicts are as follows:

(1) The Court of Justice held in Delimitis,[31] that once the Commission has initiated procedures, and a fortiori when it has adopted a decision no longer open to appeal or which has been confirmed on appeal, the national courts are bound to avoid conflicting decisions, if necessary by suspending the proceedings before them to ask the Commission for information, or by making a reference for a preliminary ruling under Article [234] of the Treaty; the same principle can by analogy be applied to national competition authorities, although the avenue of a reference under Article [234] is not open to them;

(2) When a national authority has adopted a positive decision which is either no longer open to appeal or which has been confirmed on appeal, or a court has delivered a positive judgment (for example rejection of a complaint on the ground that a restrictive practice satisfies the tests of Article [81](3)) which is either no longer open to appeal or has been confirmed on appeal, the Commission can always intervene to prohibit the agreement, subject only to the principle of res judicata that applies to the dispute between the parties themselves, which has been decided once and for all by the national court;

(3) Where an authority or a national court takes a negative decision in respect of a restrictive practice, the Commission believes that it should not normally seek to intervene otherwise than as an intervener on a reference for a preliminary ruling under Article [234], if any such reference is made;

(4) For as long as a decision of a national authority or court is still open to appeal or the decision on appeal is pending, the Commission may at any time adopt a contrary decision. In that case the principle that conflicting decisions must be avoided will apply to the appeal body.

103. If conflicts should arise between the different bodies applying Community competition law, these principles should allow them to be resolved. It may also be necessary to strengthen the principle that the application of national or Community law by national courts or authorities should be consistent with the application of Community competition law by the Commission, subject to the supervision of the Court of Justice. But it would nevertheless be advisable to establish mechanisms to avoid such conflicts in the first place.

---

[29] See *supra* Chap. 15.
[30] See *supra* Chap. 2.
[31] Case C–234/89 *Stergios Delimitis v. Henninger Bräu* [1991] ECR 1–935, [1992] 5 CMLR 210; see *supra* Chap. 15.

It can be seen from this that the Commission considers that many problems of conflict can be solved by the recognition of the principle of the supremacy of Community law and by use of the Article 234 (ex Article 177) reference procedure. It rather brushes aside in (1) the difficult fact that national competition authorities cannot make Article 234 references.[32] It is made clear that any decision of the Commission must always override any national decision. By 'positive' decisions the Commission means cases where the national court or authority finds that the agreement *is* compatible with the competition rules, and 'negative' decisions are cases where they find that it is *not.* The Commission states that it may intervene to prohibit an agreement approved by a national authority in a positive decision[33] but that it will not ordinarily intervene where negative decisions are adopted, except in the context of an Article 234 action. The Commission is clearly more concerned about the 'wrong' authorization of anti-competitive agreements than it is about the 'wrong' prohibition of harmless ones. The Commission's summary of observations submitted on the White Paper[34] recorded that most of the respondents from industry and some Member States were opposed to the Commission having such a power of prohibition.[35]

The Commission says (paragraph 103) that the best strategy is to establish mechanisms for the avoidance of conflicts in the first place. In paragraphs 104–107 it suggests some mechanisms which it believes will ensure consistent application of the rules and the 'preservation of the unity of competition policy'. In paragraph 104 it refers to the existing Article 226, (ex Article 169) and 234 procedures[36] but says that what are needed are flexible and rapid mechanisms for *day-to-day* co-operation between the Commission and the national courts and authorities. It then considers, first, co-operation with the national competition authorities, and secondly, co-operation with the courts.

E. CO-OPERATION WITH NATIONAL COMPETITION AUTHORITIES

105. As regards competition authorities, it is proposed that the amended Regulation No 17 should include an obligation to inform the Commission of cases in which Articles [81] and [82] are applied by the competition authorities of the Member States; this would correspond to the obligation imposed on the Commission by Article 10 of the present Regulation.[37] The Commission would have to be informed of the initiation of procedures and before their termination. The Commission would also have to be informed if an authority planned to withdraw the benefit of a block exemption. Information of this kind together with any correspondence that might take place with the national authorities should ensure that the

---

[32] They are not 'courts or tribunals' within the meaning of Art. 234: See Case 246/80, *C. Broekmeulen* v. *Huisarts Registratie Commissie* [1981] ECR 2311, [1982] 1 CMLR 91.

[33] Or where a positive judgment has been given by a national court, although it would respect the principle of *res judicata* between the parties.

[34] White Paper on the reform of Reg. 17: Summary of the observations, DG Comp. Doc., 29 Feb. 2000.

[35] *Ibid.*, Para. 6.4.

[36] See *supra* Chap. 2.

[37] Here the Commission notes that German law already provides that the Commission is to be informed of cases of application of Community law so as to enable it to state a view: s 50(3) of the Restriction of Competition Act (Gesetz gegen Wettbewerbsbeschränkungen, as amended).

consistency of competition policy can be preserved without requiring machinery to impose solutions to conflicts in the application of Community law. But the Commission would still have the possibility of taking a case out of the jurisdiction of the national competition authorities, by means of a mechanism equivalent to that in Article 9(3) of the present Regulation No 17. To ensure consistency between proceedings under Community law and proceedings under domestic law, the national authorities would also be required to inform the Commission, on their own initiative or at the Commission's request, of any proceedings they were conducting under national law that might have implications for Community proceedings.

106. The proper functioning of the network between the Commission and the Member States clearly implies a reinforcement of the role of the Advisory Committee on Restrictive Practices and Dominant Positions. It would become a full-scale forum in which important cases would be discussed irrespective of the competition authority dealing with them. It would continue to be consulted on legislation drafted by the Commission and on draft Commission decisions in the same way as today, but the Commission, acting on its own initiative or at the request of a Member State, could also be empowered to ask the Committee for its opinion on cases of application of Community law by national authorities. In the context of pre-accession strategy, the Commission will devote particular attention to the development of competition in the candidate countries and will provide their competition authorities with increased assistance.

The Commission proposes here that there should be close interaction between itself and the national authorities. National authorities would have to inform the Commission of the initiation of proceedings and of any plan to withdraw the benefit of a block exemption.[38] The Commission's view that the exchange of such information and subsequent correspondence between it and the national competition authority would preserve the consistency of competition policy presumably implies that the Commission envisages telling the national authorities its view of the matter and expecting them to comply. An important point is that the Commission reserves the right to take a case out of the jurisdiction of a national authority.[39] This will presumably increase the pressure on the national competition authority to adhere to the Commission's view. The national authorities will also be under an obligation to inform the Commission of proceedings being conducted under *national* law that might have implications for Community proceedings, although the Commission does not state what the outcome of this obligation would be.

The Commission stresses, at paragraph 85, the importance that block exemptions will play in the proposed new system and says that a Community regulation should specifically provide that Member States should not be able to prohibit under national law agreements that benefit from exemption under a Community block exemption.[40] However, paragraph 95 of the White Paper says that Member States must have the power to withdraw the benefit

---

[38] The Commission points to Reg. 17 [1959–62], OJ Spec. Ed. 87, Art. 10 as currently obliging the *Commission* to inform *Member States* about certain matters, such as notified agreements. See draft Reg. COM (2000) 582, Arts. 11–13.

[39] The Commission draws an analogy with Reg. 17 [1959–62] OJ Spec. Ed. 87, Art. 9(3) which provides that national authorities are able to apply Art. 81(1) and 82 as long as the Commission has not started any procedure. The difference is, of course, that Art. 9(3) of Reg. 17 is in the context of the present centralized system, where the application of the rules by the Commission is the norm.

[40] See *supra* Chap. 15.

of a block exemption regulation from particular agreements where, in their territory, the criteria for the satisfaction of Article 81(3) are not met.[41]

The proposals in the White Paper would involve a significant amount of information passing between the Commission and the national authorities. The Commission considers[42] that this would necessarily entail confidential information passing, both between the Commission and national authorities and between the national authorities *inter se*. The Commission recognizes that Regulation 17, Article 20, currently prevents confidential information gathered by the Commission being passed on to national authorities for use by them in their national enforcement proceedings, because of the decision in *Spanish Banks*.[43]

Paragraph 106 proposes strengthening the role of the Advisory Committee,[44] which would become a 'full-scale forum' for discussing important cases whichever authority, national or the Commission, was dealing with them. The White Paper does not suggest, however, that the Committee's opinions should be *binding*.

F. DIVIDING RESPONSIBILITIES BETWEEN THE COMMISSION AND THE NATIONAL COMPETITION AUTHORITIES

Although the proposals envisage that the Commission and the national competition authorities will share responsibility for the enforcement of the rules neither Article 81 nor Article 82, in contrast to the Merger Regulation,[45] set out obvious means for allocating that responsibility. The Commission notes that there will be cases in which a national authority, acting on a complaint, may realize that another national authority could more appropriately deal with the case, or that the Commission should deal with it because the matter requires investigation in several Member States. Conversely, the Commission may commence investigating a situation the effects of which it subsequently considers are felt primarily in one Member State. In all these situations the White Paper proposes that the authorities should be able to pass the case on to be dealt with by whichever is the more appropriate authority.[46] However, simply relying on the Commission and the national authorities to pass cases around among themselves on the basis of what they feel to be

---

[41] Provision has already been made for this in respect of block exemptions falling within Reg. 19/65, by Reg. 1215/1999 [1999] OJ L148/1, Art. 1(4) (amending Reg. 19/65 [1965] OJ Spec. Ed. 85, Art. 7) allowing a national authority to withdraw the benefit of a block exemption where there is an effect on a distinct market' in that Member State. Art. 6 of the new block exemption on vertical restraints: Reg. 2790/1999 [1999] OJ L336/21, expressly provides this power.

[42] In paras. 92 and 96–97. See draft Reg. COM (2000) 582, Art. 12.

[43] Case C–67/91, *Direción General de Defensa de las Competencia* v *Asociación España de Banca Privada (AEB) and others (Spanish Banks)* [1992] ECR 4785: see *supra* Chap. 14.

[44] See *supra* Chap. 2 for its present role.

[45] Council Reg. 4064/89 [1989] OJ L395/1, amended by Council Reg. 1310/97 [1997] OJ L180/1. See *infra* Chap. 12. The general scheme under the Merger Reg. is that the Commission should deal with concentrations which have a 'Community dimension' and that national competition authorities should have responsibility for concentrations which do not have a community dimension. The Merger Reg. itself sets out certain defined exceptions to this position, however.

[46] Including any relevant confidential information, which would mean a change in the *Spanish Banks* rule n. 43 *supra*.

appropriate is no substitute for some principles of jurisdiction. It is possible that jurisdiction could be allocated on the basis of 'Schwerpunkttheorie', or the centre of gravity of the agreement. It seems essential that some rules relating to jurisdiction be adopted to ensure that undertakings do not face proceedings in respect of the same agreement or conduct before one or more competition authorities. The White Paper does recognize the danger of double jeopardy. It therefore states at paragraph 98 that separate penalties should not be imposed by a national authority and the Commission and that separate commitments should not have to be entered into to satisfy objections raised at the two levels.

G. CO-OPERATION WITH THE NATIONAL COURTS

Until recently there has been comparatively little litigation concerning Article 81 before the national courts.[47] This has been partly due at least to their inability to make a complete assessment of an agreement's compatibility with Article 81 and because they will adjourn proceedings where an agreement has been notified to the Commission.[48] As the Commission recognizes in paragraph 100 of the White Paper, this means in practice that undertakings can bring proceedings to a halt through notification. The abolition of the notification system, and the national courts' ability to apply Article 81(3), should prevent this happening, although proceedings may still be disrupted where a defendant lodges a complaint with the Commission.[49] The Commission considers (paragraph 100) that the ability of national courts to apply Article 81(3) in its entirely would be advantageous to undertakings. The parties to agreements would have greater legal certainty and third parties would be able to obtain damages more quickly. The judgments of national courts would be *res judicata* (subject to any appeal), and would be entitled to recognition in all other Member States of the EU and Contracting States of the EEA under the Brussels and Lugano Conventions respectively.

However, the question of the relationship between the national courts and the Commission is even more delicate than that of the relationship between competition authorities and the Commission.

In contrast with the position with regard to national competition authorities, an existing formal avenue for dialogue and co-operation between the national courts and the ECJ is provided by the Article 234 (ex Article 177) preliminary reference procedure. It is apparent from the White Paper that the Commission does not consider that this procedure would be adequate to ensure consistency in interpretation were greater delegation to the national courts to occur. In particular, since a reference to the ECJ inevitably causes delay (of at least eighteen months) a national court will obviously be reluctant to make a reference save in

---

[47] Although there were at the end of 1999 some hundreds of cases on beer ties pending before the UK courts.

[48] See *supra* Chap. 15.

[49] If the Commission, perhaps well over a year later, decides not to proceed with the complaint (under the principle in *Automec* (Case T–24/90, *Automec* v. *Commission (No 2)* [1992] ECR II–2223, [1992] 5 CMLR 431)) it may by then be pointless for the claimant to pursue the action.

cases of absolute expediency.[50] Further, it is only final courts which are actually obliged to make a reference, and where reference is made the ECJ only 'interprets' Community law, leaving the national court free to apply the ruling to the facts in front of it.[51]

In the White Paper the Commission proposes steps to 'support' national courts when interpreting and applying the EC competition rules:

107. As regards national courts, in order to maintain consistency of interpretation when the application of the rules is decentralized, and to lend support to the national courts in the exercise of their functions, mechanisms would have to be set up for cooperation between the Commission and the courts. It is vital, first of all, that the Commission should be aware of proceedings in which Articles [81] and [82] are invoked before the courts, so that it is made aware of any problems of textual interpretation or lacunae in the legislative framework. It is therefore proposed that the regulation should require courts to supply such information. A similar obligation already exists in German law, for example (. . .). The Commission should also be allowed, subject to the leave of the court, to intervene in judicial proceedings that come to its attention as a result of information supplied in this way. Allowing it to intervene as amicus curiae would be an effective way of helping to maintain consistency in the application of the law. It is consequently proposed that a specific provision to this effect should be included in the regulation. It is also proposed that the amended Regulation No 17 should incorporate the rules now set out in the Commission notice on cooperation between the Commission and national courts, which provides that in the course of proceedings before them courts may address themselves to the Commission to ask for information of a procedural, legal or economic nature. Moreover, in certain Member States, there exist cooperation mechanisms between national courts hearing a competition law question and national competition authorities (for example, the possibility for the Bundeskartellamt to intervene in Germany, or for the Conseil de la Concurrence to give expert testimony in France).

In this paragraph the Commission makes three specific suggestions: that national courts should be required to inform the Commission of proceedings before it involving Article 81 or 82; that the Commission should be entitled to intervene as *amicus curiae* in national proceedings; and that national courts should be encouraged to seek the advice of, or information from, the Commission in relation to procedural, legal, or economic matters.[52] At the end of paragraph 107 the Commission points approvingly to the existing mechanism in some Member States providing for co-operation between national courts seised of a competition law question and national competition authorities.

These proposals are far-reaching and would, if implemented, grant the Commission a much greater input than it currently has in national proceedings. They would inevitably

---

[50] Changes to Community competition procedures will not, however, be happening in a vacuum. The 2000 Intergovernmental Conference is examining the need for reform to prepare the EU institutions for the accession of new Member States. Reform of the Court is being considered in this context, and the problem of the excessive workload of the Court is one of the major issues under review. The Commission's contribution to the IGC, *Reform of the Community Courts* COM (2000) 109 was made on 1 Mar., 2000. One of the Commission's proposals is that preliminary references in very specialized areas of law should be entrusted to the CFI. The Commission gives cases on intellectual property rights as an example, but there is considerable support in many quarters for competition case references going to the CFI instead of to the ECJ. See Summary of observations on the White Paper, DG Comp. Doc., 29 Feb. 2000, para. 5.5.

[51] Although the line between interpretation and application is famously difficult to draw.

[52] House of Lords Select Committee [Sub-committee E] on the European Communities, Session 1999–2000, Fourth Report, 29 Feb. 2000, para. 87. See draft Reg. COM (2000) 582, Art. 15.

involve some measure of procedural harmonization.[53] For example, it may be that not all Member States' legal systems are currently able to accept the *amicus curiae* system. A majority of the Member States expressed reservations about the *amicus* proposal, generally on the grounds that it may be difficult to reconcile such intervention with the independence of national courts.[54] Further, it seems likely that national courts would also be required to ensure that certain specific remedies and procedures were available in actions raising the EC competition rules: for example declaratory actions, class actions, interlocutory relief, remedies against unlawfully obtained advantages, and proceedings being conducted without delays. The Faculty of Advocates has said that the proposal about intervention by the Commission raises 'delicate questions as to the role of the national courts and seems to envisage a more pro-active or inquisitorial role for domestic courts and judges than has hitherto been the norm within the Anglo-Celtic legal systems of England, Scotland and Ireland'.[55]

An obvious difficulty is that divergent decisions may be made by the national courts of the different Member States. It may be that specialized courts or judges may be required to deal specifically with competition cases.[56] The greatest problem arising from the delegation of responsibility for the interpretation of Article 81(3) to the national courts may relate, however, to the uncertainty surrounding the factors to be taken into account when making the Article 81(3) assessment and the fact that the provision may be inherently unsuited to judicial interpretation at Member State level.

4. THE IMPLICATIONS OF AND THE PROBLEMS PRESENTED BY THE PROPOSALS

A. THE RESPONSE

It was seen in Chapter 4 that the radical proposals set out in the White Paper triggered heated debate. Responses to the proposals were submitted by individuals, companies, trade associations, lawyers, Community and national institutions,[57] and Member States. The Commission published a summary of the observations it received, including views presented in conference papers.[58] In the UK the White Paper was examined by the House of Lords Select Committee on the European Union, which published a wide-ranging report

---

[53] Summary of observations on the White Paper, DG Comp. Doc. 29 Feb. 2000, para. 5.3.

[54] *Ibid.*, para. 87.

[55] House of Lords Select Committee [Sub-Committee E] on the European Communities, Session 1999–2000, Fourth Report, 29 Feb. 2000, para. 87.

[56] See *infra* 1035–1036.

[57] A detailed investigation conducted by the European Parliament has broadly been supportive of the Commission's proposals: '*Report on the Commission White Paper on modernization of the rules implementing Articles 85 and 86 of the EC Treaty*', Final A5–0069/1999 (the Parliament reported on 30 Nov. 1999).

[58] Summary of Observations on the White Paper, DG Comp. Doc. 29 Feb. 2000.

together with accompanying evidence.[59] The responses to the proposals varied, and ranged from general opposition to general support. In Chapter 4 it was seen that some businesses have been critical of the proposal to abolish the notification system in its entirety, mainly because they fear a loss of legal certainty.[60] Further, the legality, and hence feasibility, of the Commission's proposed solution has been doubted, in particular by the German government.[61] It has questioned whether Article 81(3) can be applied directly and whether the notification system can, consequently, be eliminated. Other concerns centre on the suitability of the Article 81(3) criteria for determination at national level and, above all, whether it will be possible to maintain the consistent enforcement of the competition rules.

B. IS AN END TO THE NOTIFICATION AND AUTHORIZATION SYSTEM NECESSARY OR DESIRABLE

It was noted in Chapter 4 that the proposal to go beyond the simple termination of the Commission's monopoly over the grant of individual exemptions has provoked concern. Under the proposed new scheme there will be no possibility, save in the case of joint ventures,[62] of notifying to the Commission and receiving assurance that the agreement complies with the Community rules. Rather, undertakings will be required to become 'self-reliant' and to 'make their own assessment of the compatibility of their restrictive practices with Community law, in the light of the legislation in force and the case-law.[63] These proposals may, however, lead to significant uncertainty for undertakings concluding complex and costly agreements.

None of the fourteen Member States which submitted observations to the Commission was in favour of keeping the current centralized system.[64] Two, however, favoured decentralizing the grant of Article 81(3) exemptions to national competition authorities and opposed the Commission's proposal to abandon the notification and authorization system altogether. The other twelve supported the Commission's proposal to abandon the system, and of these six expressly opposed decentralization of the granting of exemptions to national authorities.[65] The greatest opposition has come from the German Government,

---

[59] House of Lords Select Committee [Sub committee E] on the European Communities, Session 1999–2000, Fourth Report, 29 Feb. 2000.

[60] The CBI's Position Paper of 29 Sept. 1999 was critical of many features of the proposals, in particular on decentralization and the abolition of notification.

[61] See *infra* 1033 ff.

[62] The Commission says that for such transactions prior authorization may be essential because 'operations of this kind generally require substantial investment and far-reaching integration of operations which makes it difficult for them to unravel afterwards at the behest of a competition authority'. It has thus proposed that partial-function joint ventures be brought within the framework of the Merger Reg. [1989] OJ L395/1: White Paper on Modernisation, *supra* n. 1, paras. 70–81, and see Chap. 13 *supra*. This is, however, an admission by the Commission that there is no substitute for the security of authorization. There has been comment from industry and from lawyers about why this particular category should be singled out, as there are other types of transactions which may involve equally involve large investment and be difficult to unravel: see Summary of observations on the White Paper, DG Comp. Doc. 29 Feb. 2000, para. 4.2.

[63] White Paper on Modernisation, *supra* n. 1, para. 77.

[64] Summary of observations on the White Paper, DG Comp. Doc. 29 Feb. 2000, para. 2.3.

[65] *Ibid.*, Paras. 2.2, 4.1.

which believes that the present procedural arrangements are in urgent need of reform,[66] but favours a fourfold solution whereby: notification is retained but made 'leaner'; the application of Article 81 is decentralized to national competition authorities (but not to national *courts*); the Commission's procedures are accelerated and simplified; and deadlines for taking exemption decisions are introduced.[67]

The Commission's summary of observations records that a 'large majority' of the responses from associations of undertakings favoured the abolition of the present notification system, because of the administrative burden it imposes. However, there was particular opposition from companies in the retail sector which considered that relying on *ex post* control would encourage abuse and be detrimental to small and medium-sized undertakings. Lawyers' responses were divided. Some emphasized the heavy burden of notification and some stressed the chilling effect of the present system, in that it can discourage companies from potentially beneficial projects. On the other hand, some lawyers said that it was difficult for them to give proper advice about the fulfilment of the Article 81(3) criteria, a point which goes back to the question whether only the Commission is equipped to deal with Article 81(3).[68] It is clear from the evidence given to the House of Lords Select Committee that there is a wide variety of views across industry and the legal profession, and within Member States and not just between them.[69]

(i) IS THE PROPOSAL TO MAKE ARTICLE 81(3) DIRECTLY APPLICABLE FEASIBLE?

A. *L'EXCEPTION LÉGALE?*

Fundamental to the Commission's proposals is the possibility that Article 81(3) can be applied directly by the national courts and the national competition authorities. It has been argued, however, that the language of Article 81(3) does not admit such a possibility. An important question, therefore, is whether Article 81(3) *can* be applied directly as a legal exception to the prohibition in Article 81(1) or whether it requires a positive act or decision by a public body, such as the Commission, before Article 81(1) can be rendered inapplicable.

The Commission's view, of course, is that Article 81(3) can be directly applied as an exception to the Article 81(1) prohibition. This is referred to as the doctrine '*de l'exception légale*'. In the White Paper the Commission states that the delegations from the original six future Member States who drafted the EC Treaty could not decide between a directly applicable system and an authorization system, as some favoured one and some the other. Article 81(3) was therefore deliberately drafted to allow for either possibility.[70] It was only on the adoption of Regulation 17 that the Community legislator finally chose an authorization system.

---

[66] The President of the German Federal Cartel Office described the present regime as 'fossilized': House of Lords Select Committee [Sub-Committee E] on the European Communities, Session 1999–2000, Fourth Report, 29 Feb. 2000, para. 16.

[67] *Ibid.*, para. 22.

[68] See *infra* 1035–1036.

[69] See e.g. the mixed views of French industry: House of Lords Select Committee Report, *supra* n. 66, para. 18.

[70] White Paper on Modernisation, *supra* n. 1, paras. 11 and 12.

It is arguable, however, that the language of Article 81 does not support such a construction. Rather, since Article 81(2) specifically provides that any agreement which infringes Article 81(1) is void and Article 81(3) states only that the provisions of Article 81(1) '*may . . . be declared* inapplicable' a constitutive act of a public authority is required to lift the Article 81(1) prohibition.

Although there has hitherto been little discussion of this issue since the adoption of Regulation 17, the view that a constitutive act is required has received support over the years. For example, in *De Geus* v. *Bosch*,[71] Advocate General Lagrange took the view that the 'constitutive decision' theory best accorded with the wording of Article 81(3) and the theory depending on *l'exception légale* would have required a different text, for example: '[t]he provisions of paragraph (1) shall be deemed not to apply' or simply 'shall not apply'.[72] Similarly, Professor Deringer, the head of the committee responsible for the drafting of Regulation 17, considers that the task of disapplying Article 81(1) is a normative activity to be conducted by an administrative, not a judicial, body.[73] He pointed out to the Select Committee that the Commission cited no evidence in the White Paper to support its contention that the question was deliberately left open in 1957.[74] Further, in *Ahmed Saeed* the ECJ indicated that Article 81(3) itself required an act or decision before the Article 81(1) prohibition could be declared inapplicable and that Regulation 17 merely conferred the power on the Commission to do this.[75]

The main proponent of the view that Article 81(3) does not allow for a directly applicable exception is the German Government. Apart from the issue of the wording of the Treaty, its main arguments are that Article 81(3) does not fulfill the criteria for direct effect and that the Commission has previously acknowledged that Article 81(3) makes it possible to have regard to non-competition – related considerations.[76] These arguments are discussed below.[77]

A definitive ruling of the ECJ may be necessary, therefore, before it can be said with

---

[71] Case 13/61 *De Geus* v. *Bosch* [1962] ECR 45, [1962] CMLR 1, the first ever reference to the ECJ for a preliminary ruling under Art. 234 (Art. 177 as it then was).

[72] [1962] ECR 45 at 67. The AG stated that personally he thought that the *exception légale* was particularly suited to the needs of the application of the Treaty, since it would ensure that the question of prohibition and that of any possible exemption from prohibition would be examined at the same time, by the same authority or court, and mean that there would be no difficulty over the effects of the automatic nullity. He did not, however, think that this was what the Treaty provided.

[73] A. Deringer, 'The Distribution of Powers in the Enforcement of the Rules of Competition under the Rome Treaty' [1963] 1 *CMLRev*, 30, 34.

[74] House of Lords Select Committee [Sub-Committee E] on the European Communities, Session 1999–2000, Fourth Report, 29 Feb. 2000, para 31.

[75] Case 66/86, *Ahmed Saeed Flugreisen and Silver Line Reisebüro GmbH* v. *Zentrale zur Bëkampfung Unlauteren Wettbewerbs eV* [1989] ECR 803, [1990] 4 CMLR 102; see also Cases 209 213/84 *Ministère Public* v. *Lucas Asjes (Nouvelles Frontières)* [1986] ECR 1455, [1986] 3 CMLR 173. In *Ahmed Saeed* the ECJ spoke of the implementing legislation being adopted 'with a view to organising the Commission's powers to grant exemptions under Art. 81(3) and hence to conduct the competition policy sought by the Treaty' (para. 20). This clearly suggests that it interpreted Art. 81(3) as itself embodying an authorization system, which Reg. 17 carried out, rather than a situation where the implementing legislation could make the choice about the nature of Art. 81(3).

[76] Summary of observations on the White Paper, DG Comp. Doc. 29 Feb. 2000, para. 3.2. The arguments were set out in the submissions of the German Monopolkommission.

[77] *Infra* 1035–1036. The other argument of the Monopolkommission is the fact that group exemption reg. have to be limited to categories of agreements, which means that a global exemption cannot be issued, whereas the effect of the legal exception rule would be that of a global block exemption reg.

assurance that the Commission's proposals do not require a Treaty amendment. What is clear, however, is that the Court is unlikely to feel bound by the strict wording of Article 81 itself of by the views of those that drafted the Treaty or Regulation 17. On the contrary, it is more likely to interpret Article 81 teleologically in a way which it considers will achieve the Treaty's aims and objectives and ensure effective enforcement of the competition rules.

b. IS ARTICLE 81(3) CAPABLE OF DIRECT EFFECT?

In its White Paper the Commission states that the switch to a directly applicable system 'can be achieved by a Council Regulation, based on Article [83] of the Treaty, which would stipulate that all national authorities or courts before which the applicability of Article [81(1)] of the Treaty was invoked would also consider the applicability of Article [81(3)]'.

Neither the Council nor the Commission, however, has power to determine whether or not a Treaty provision or other Community act has direct effect. A Community measure is capable of direct effect only if it meets the criteria set out in the jurisprudence of the Court. Article 81(3) will, therefore, be directly applicable only if it is capable of direct effect, that is if it is sufficiently precise and unconditional or 'justiciable'.[78] This would be a matter for the Court to decide.

It was seen in Chapter 4 that Article 81(3) confers considerable discretion on the authority (hitherto the Commission) determining whether or not an agreement satisfies its four criteria. Further, it was seen that it is arguable that Article 81(3) authorizes the entity applying it to take account of a wide range of factors, not just economic but also social, cultural, industrial, and environmental ones. The breadth of the criteria that might possibly be considered when making the assessment under Article 81(3) may be relevant to the question whether the provision is capable of direct effect. A conclusion that Article 81(3) requires the weighing of competing public and private interests may lead to a finding that the provision is not justiciable and so incapable of direct effect. Rather, it requires the act of a public body to weigh these competing interests. It seems therefore that the debate over the scope or the purpose of Article 81(3) is relevant to the legitimacy of the Commission's proposals. The suitability of Article 81(3) for direct application by the national courts and national competition authorities cannot be addressed in a vacuum and without asking what is the purpose of Article 81(3). The Commission suggests in the White Paper that broader socio-political factors should not be relevant to the Article 81(3) assessment.[79] However, these statements are hard to reconcile both with some of the Commission's own decisions[80] and the Court's repeated insistence that Community law must be interpreted in the light of the objectives of the Treaty.[81]

---

[78] See Case 26/62, *Van Gend en Loos* v. *Nederandse Administrative der belastingen* [1963] ECR 1, [1963] CMLR 105; Case 43/75, *Defrenne* v. *SABENA (No 2)* [1976] ECR 455, [1976] 2 CMLR 98, and Chap. 2 *supra*. In Case 127/73, *BRT* v. *SABAM* [1974] ECR 51 the ECJ said that Art. 81(1) and 82 'tend by their very nature to produce direct effects in relations between individuals'. Some opinion at the time thought that these Art were so special that they alone could modify relations between individuals. Pescatore argues that direct applicability is the normal characteristic of Community law, and that it simply comes down to a question of justiciability: see P. Pescatore, 'The Doctrine of "Direct Effect": An Infant Disease of Community Law' (1983) 8 *ELRev* 155.

[79] White Paper on Modernisation, *supra* n. 1, paras. 56–57.

[80] See *supra* Chap. 4.

[81] See *supra* Chaps. 1 and 2.

Even if Article 81(3) is limited to the consideration of purely competition factors there is still doubt in many quarters whether courts are suitable fora for determining whether the criteria are fulfilled. The question is not just whether the direct application of Article 81(3) by national courts is legally possible, but whether it is practically possible. The application of Article 81(3) requires complex economic analysis and the fear is that national courts would apply Article 81(3) inconsistently and incoherently.[82] The responses to the White Paper therefore revealed more misgivings over decentralization to the national courts than over decentralization to national competition authorities.[83] In the House of Lords Select Committee two English High Court judges[84] stated that they did not see judges and national courts as suitable fora for the determination of the issues raised by Article 81(3). Laddie J said that 'the sort of feeling that judges can decide economic issues to my mind is wholly misplaced . . . They cannot make value judgments except in a very limited field, certainly not in relation to general economic questions.' He did not consider that the criteria were sufficiently precise for justiciability: '[t]he court should not have any part to play, it seems to me, in deciding whether an agreement or a course of conduct contributes to improving the production or distribution of goods or promoting technical or economic progress'.[85]

The UK Government's view is that it sees no problem in principle in UK courts applying Article 81 as a whole, although it acknowledges that certain practicalities need further consideration.[86] This view is shared by some lawyers and others who argue that, in the light of the guidance offered by nearly forty years of cases and decisions, the application of Article 81(3) is no more difficult (and perhaps less difficult) than the application of Article 81(1), which has always been directly applicable and which entails judges asking that most intractable of questions: is this a restriction of competition?

There has been some support for the idea that if decentralization to national courts does occur it should be to specialized courts. Three Member States are in favour of this suggestion, as are some parts of industry and the legal profession.[87] One difficulty with this would be the jurisdiction of such courts, as competition questions can arise in a wide range of cases.

5. CONCLUSIONS AND THE FUTURE

Surprisingly perhaps, the position might have been less complex if the Commission had simply proposed the abolition of Article 81(3). This would have put an end to the problems resulting from the bifurcation of the Treaty and an end to the controversy surrounding the role of Article 81(3). The dispute could then simply centre around the question of what factors should be relevant in the determination of whether an agreement restricts

---

[82] Particularly in view of the future expansion of the European Union to take in Central and Eastern European countries; see Summary of observations on the White Paper, DG Comp. Doc. 29 Feb. 2000, para 5.2.

[83] *Ibid.*, para 5.2.

[84] Ferris and Laddie JJ.

[85] House of Lords Select Committee [Sub-Committee E] on the European Communities, Session 1999–2000, Fourth Report 29 Feb. 2000, para. 59.

[86] *Ibid.*, para 57.

[87] Summary of observations on the White Paper, DG Comp. Doc. 29 Feb. 2000, para. 5.2.

competition for the purposes of Article 81(1). Such a step would, of course, require a Treaty amendment.

The White Paper therefore proposes not a Treaty amendment or a change in interpretation of Article 81(1) but a bold and imaginative move which the Commission considers can be accomplished by a Council regulation. The draft Regulation[88] adopted by the Commission on 27 September 2000 sets out how the Commission considers this regulation should be framed. Article 1 of the draft Regulation provides that Article 81, like Article 82, should be directly applicable in its entirety. Articles 4–6 thus require that Articles 81 and 82 should be applied by the Commission, the competition authorities of the Member States and the national courts. Articles 11–16 seek to ensure that the rules are applied coherently and consistently by those bodies. It is clear from the latter provisions that the Commission envisages playing an active and central role in national proceedings.

The Commission believes that the greater participation of the national bodies in the enforcement of the rules will enable it to refocus its efforts on the detection of serious infringements of the EC competition rules. In order to facilitate this the draft Regulation strengthens the Commission's investigatory powers[89] and broadens the remedies that may be imposed in infringement cases.[90]

The Commission also takes the opportunity in the draft Regulation to make other important changes to the regime currently set out in Regulation 17. If this Regulation, or a similar one, is adopted by the Council it is clear that the application of Articles 81 and 82 will never be quite the same again.

6. FURTHER READING

ARTICLES

DERINGER, A., 'The Distribution of Powers in the Enforcement of the Rules of Competition under the Rome Treaty' [1963] 1 *CMLRev.* 30

WHISH, R., and SUFRIN, B., 'Community Competition Law: Notification and Exemption— Goodbye to All That' in D. Hayton (ed), *Law's Future(s): British Legal Developments in the 21st Century* 135–59.

---

[88] Proposal for a Reg. implementing Arts. 81 and 82, COM(2000)582.
[89] *Ibid.*, especially Arts. 19 and 20.
[90] *Ibid.*, Article 7.

17

EXTRATERRITORIALITY, INTERNATIONAL ASPECTS, AND GLOBALIZATION

1. INTRODUCTION

Restrictions on competition and abusive conduct which affect trade between Member States may originate outside the Community. Foreign firms established outside the Community may, for example, fix prices in the Community or divide the common market between them. A firm established outside the Community may hold a dominant position in the common market and may engage in behaviour which is an abuse under Article 82. Further, concentrations involving non-EC undertakings may have consequences for competition inside the Community. It is important to know, therefore, to what extent the EC competition rules can be applied to undertakings established and acting outside its borders. How far does the jurisdiction of the EC competition authorities reach?

This is a problem which faces all competition authorities and, as we see below, it has much exercised the American courts. From the point of view of the State in whose territory the consequences of the anti-competitive conduct is felt it is obviously unsatisfactory if it is powerless to take action against those who target it from outside. However, matters may look quite different from the standpoint of the country in which the offending parties are located. As Lord Wilberforce said in *Rio Tinto Zinc Corp.* v. *Westinghouse Electric Corp.*, 'it is axiomatic that in anti-trust matters the policy of one state may be to defend what it is the policy of the other state to attack'.[1] It is notable that the USA, despite its stringent antitrust laws, expressly permits export cartels under the Webb-Pomerene Act.

While most States agree, at least officially, that murder, kidnap, and rape are criminal activities deserving of punishment, the belief that anti-competitive behaviour is also contrary to the public good depends on the acceptance of a certain set of economic and political beliefs.[2] Despite Fukuyama's 'end of history'[3] the entire world has not yet embraced free market capitalism. Even in the States with competition law regimes, the detail of the laws may vary, or the authorities' application of them in a specific situation may differ. For example, in the case of the *Boeing/McDonnell Douglas* merger dispute the EC and US

---

[1] [1978] AC 547, 617.
[2] See *supra* Chap. 1.
[3] F. Fukuyama, *The End of History and the Last Man* (Hamish Hamilton, 1992).

authorities had different views despite the close co-operation between the two jurisdictions in competition matters and the existence of similar laws. If States apply their competition laws extraterritorially undertakings may find themselves subject to a number of competing and irreconcilable actions, there may be conflict between national authorities, and other States may feel that their sovereignty is infringed.

This issue is part of a broader debate about the rights of States to take jurisdiction outside their territory, i.e. *extraterritorially*. Extraterritoriality is a controversial topic of much complexity in international law.[4] International law usually distinguishes between two types of jurisdiction. On the one hand there is what is variously called prescriptive, legislative, or subject-matter jurisdiction: the right of States to make their laws applicable to persons, territory, or situations. On the other hand there is enforcement jurisdiction, which is the capacity to take executive action to enforce compliance with those laws.

Within the context of competition law the issue of extraterritoriality has become increasingly important as what is called the 'globalization' of the world economy advances. It becomes more and more impossible to isolate the effects of transactions which take place on that global market. A need for a solution to the problems has become more urgent. A number of remedies have been proposed, including the conclusion of bilateral and multilateral international arrangements to deal with the matter. The EU has been an enthusiastic proponent of international co-operation in competition law matters. The Competition Commissioner, Karel Van Miert, explained in the Foreword to the 1998 Competition Report, how he perceived the problem:[5]

The ever-increasing integration of the world economy is creating an unprecedented inter-dependence between countries. Over the past decade, with the successful conclusion of the Uruguay Round, we have seen an acceleration in the progressive dismantling of trade barriers. Business is taking advantage of this openness, and there has been a huge growth in the volume of trade. In many industries, companies are competing in worldwide markets, and are becoming larger and multinational as a result. The past year has seen a series of so-called 'mega-mergers' between companies based in different parts of the world, creating new corporations of truly global dimensions. Where companies are not already present in several countries, they often form strategic alliances which enable them to penetrate foreign markets together with international partners. This is particularly true in high-technology sectors such as the telecommunications, information technology, entertainment, air transport and pharmaceutical industries. The Commission has had to keep pace with the increasing globalisation of markets and, to an increasing extent, its analyses of competition problems take into account market data from outside the European Union.

It is not surprising to find that, in these circumstances, competition problems are also taking on global dimensions. Anticompetitive behaviour, including restrictive arrangements between companies and abuses of market dominance, does not respect borders. The emergence of ever-larger multinational companies, with the technological means and resources to do business on a global level, brings with it the danger that they may be tempted to take measures – either unilaterally or in collusion with other firms – which restrict competition or abuse their market power on these global markets. If anticompetitive behaviour is allowed to go unchecked, it is no exaggeration to say that many of the benefits that have been achieved in terms of opening markets across the globe could be negated. The enhanced opportunities which trade liberalisation has provided for the interpretation of markets around the world could very well be seriously undermined by restrictive commercial

---

[4] See *infra* 1046–1047.
[5] Commission's *XXVIIIth Report on Competition Policy* (Commission, 1998), 3–4.

behaviour. Such practices may be resorted to by companies seeking to protect their traditional, often national, markets from foreign competitors.

National or regional competition authorities are ill-equipped to grapple with the problems posed by commercial behaviour occurring beyond their borders. Information may be difficult to obtain, and decisions, once taken, may be impossible to enforce. Although new competition legislation has been introduced in many countries in recent years, some behaviour might not be unlawful in the country where it is being carried out, or the authorities there may be unwilling to condemn it. Alternatively, incoherent or even directly contradictory conclusions might be reached by different enforcement authorities, both of which may claim jurisdiction over the same subject matter. Such divergent treatment not only entails the risk of precipitating a dispute between countries or trading blocks, as was illustrated by the initial disagreement between the US and the EU over the proposed Boeing/ MDD merger last year, but is also a source of considerable uncertainty and cost for companies engaging in global transactions.

In this chapter we consider first how the problem has been dealt with in the USA and EC, and subsequently we consider some of the solutions which have been adopted or proposed.

2. THE POSITION IN US LAW

A. GENERAL

It is difficult to consider the question of extraterritoriality in EC competition law without first looking at the position in US law. Because the Sherman Act dates from 1890 its extraterritorial reach inevitably became an issue before the EEC even existed.[6] Two particular factors have meant that the extraterritorial application of US antitrust law remains a controversial topic: first, the USA's customary aggressive stance in defence of its own interests[7] and, secondly, the fact that private individuals can recover 'treble damages' for breaches of the antitrust laws and that US law provides for far-ranging pre-trial discovery.[8] The 'effects doctrine' propounded in the US courts has provided the central concept around which the discussion of extraterritoriality in competition law is usually conducted.

---

[6] See R.Y. Jennings, *'Extraterritorial Jurisdiction and the United States Antitrust Laws'* (1957) 33 *BYIL*, 146.

[7] The antitrust laws are not the only area in which US attempts at extraterritorial jurisdiction have proved controversial. The USA sought jurisdiction over technological exports from other States to the Communist bloc (see the US Export Administration Act) and took measures against non-US companies involved in the construction of the West Siberian pipeline. US legislation imposing sanctions on Iran, Libya, and Cuba has also purported to have extraterritorial reach; there has been particular opposition by other countries to the extension of sanctions against Cuba by the Cuban Democracy Act of 1992 (which led to the UK adopting an Order under the Protection of Trading Interests Act 1980 (see *infra* 1045–1046)). The 1992 Act was further controversially extended by the 'Helms-Burton' Act in 1996 which provided for actions in US courts against those, including foreign nationals or companies, who were 'trafficking' in property expropriated from US nationals by Cuba. The D'Amato Act in 1996 imposed sanctions or companies participating in the development of oil resources in Libya or Iran.

[8] See *infra* 1045–1046.

B. THE EFFECTS DOCTRINE

In the first half-century following the enactment of the Sherman Act the US courts were diffident about applying the rules extraterritorially. In the *American Banana* case[9] Justice Oliver Wendell Holmes said in the Supreme Court that 'the general and almost universal rule is that the character of an act as lawful or unlawful must be determined wholly by the law of the country where the act is done'. Later cases retreated from this self-denying ordinance,[10] and in the *Alcoa* case[11] in 1945 Judge Learned Hand laid down what is known as the 'effects doctrine'. The case concerned a cartel of aluminium producers based in Switzerland which fixed production quotas to boost prices. The court (the Second Circuit Court of Appeals) held that the Sherman Act applied to a Canadian company which had participated in the cartel. Judge Learned Hand said that the Sherman Act *did* apply to agreements concluded outside the USA which were intended to affect US imports and did actually affect them.

Not surprisingly, the extraterritorial application of US antitrust laws met with hostility from other States.[12] The American courts have not been altogether insensitive to this. In *Timberlane*[13] the Ninth Circuit Court of Appeals considered the notion of 'international comity' in this context. 'Comity' means living peacefully with other nations in mutual respect and accommodating their interests or, as one authority puts it, the 'rules of politeness, convenience and goodwill observed by States in their mutual intercourse without being legally bound by them'.[14] In *Timberlane* Judge Choy recognized the effects doctrine as laid down in *Alcoa*, but considered that its application had to be balanced against the interests of international comity. The case concerned an action by an American company alleging that the defendants in Honduras had conspired to exclude it from the Honduran lumber market, from where it planned to export to the USA (the allegations included claims that Honduran government officials had been bribed). Judge Choy said that three questions had to asked:

Timberlane Lumber Co. v. *Bank of America,* 549 F. 2d 597 at 613 (9th Cir.1976)

Judge Choy

Despite its description as 'settled law', ALCOA's assertion has been roundly disputed by many foreign commentators as being in conflict with international law, comity and good judgment. Nevertheless American courts have firmly concluded that there is some extra-territorial jurisdiction under the Sherman Act. Even among American courts and commentators, however, there is no consensus on how far the jurisdiction should extend . . .

There is no agreed black-letter rule articulating the Sherman Act's commerce coverage in the international context . . . The effects test by itself is incomplete because it fails to consider the other

---

9 *American Banana Co.* v. *United Fruit Co.*, 213 US 347, 356, 29 SCt. 511, 512 (1909).

10 See *United States* v. *Sisal Sales Corp.*, 274 US 268, 47 SCt. 592 (1927).

11 *United States* v. *Aluminum Co. of America*, 148 F, 2d 416 (2d Cir. 1945).

12 For the particular problems with regard to their enforcement, see *infra* 1045–1046.

13 *Timberlane Lumber Co.* v. *Bank of America*, 549 F 2d 597 (9th Cir. 1976).

14 Oppenheim's *International Law* (ed. R.Y. Jennings and A. Watts) (9th edn.), (Longman, 1992), i, 34 n. 1.

nation's interests; nor does it expressly take into account the full nature of the relationships between the actors and this country . . .

A tripartite analysis seems to be indicated. As acknowledged above, the antitrust laws require in the first instance that there be *some* effect—actual or intended—on American foreign commerce before the federal courts may legitimately exercise subject-matter jurisdiction under those statutes. Second, a greater showing of burden or restraint may be necessary to demonstrate that the effect is suf- ficiently large to present cognizable injury to the plaintiffs and therefore a civil violation of the antitrust laws . . . Third, there is the additional question, which is unique to the international setting, of whether the interests of and links to the United States, including the magnitude of the effect on American commerce, are sufficiently strong, *vis-à-vis* those of other nations, to justify an assertion of extra-territorial authority . . .

In answering this third question, which was necessary because 'at some point the interests of the United States are too weak and the foreign harmony incentive for restraint too strong to justify an extraterritorial assertion of jurisdiction', he said that the following factors should be taken into account:

the degree of conflict with foreign law or policy, the nationality or allegiance of the parties and the locations or principal places of business of corporations, the extent to which enforcement by either state can be expected to achieve compliance, the relative significance of effects on the United States as compared with those elsewhere, the extent to which there is explicit purpose to harm or affect American commerce, the foreseeability of such effect, the relative importance to the violations charged of conduct within the United States as compared with conduct abroad.

The criteria were expanded in *Mannington Mills*,[15] where the plaintiff claimed that the defendant had infringed its export business by fraudulently obtaining foreign patents and the court added to the *Timberlane* list of factors to be brought into the balancing exercise.[16]

Timberlane and *Mannington Mills* do not *deny* jurisdiction to the US courts in the inter- ests of comity, but merely hold that it should not be *exercised* where the interests of the USA in asserting jurisdiction are outweighed by the interests of comity.[17]

In 1982 Congress approved the Foreign Trade Antitrust Improvements Act (FTAIA) which amended the Sherman Act. The Act stipulates that as regards foreign commerce *other than import commerce* the antitrust laws will not apply unless the conduct has a *direct, substantial, and reasonably foreseeable* effect on US commerce. In other words, the Act exempts export transactions from the Sherman Act unless for some particular reason they injure the American economy. Despite the 'export trade' context of this provision it has

---

[15] Accord *Mannington Mills Inc. v. Congoleum Corp.*, 595 F, 2d 1287 (3rd Cir.1979).

[16] The additional criteria were: the possible effect on foreign relations if the court exercises jurisdiction; if the relief is granted, whether a party will be put in the position of being forced to perform an act illegal in either country or be under conflicting requirements by both countries; whether an order for relief would be acceptable in the USA if made by a foreign nation under similar circumstances; whether a treaty with the affected nations has addressed the issue.

[17] Such a balancing act had earlier been advocated by Kingman Brewster, who called it a 'jurisdictional rule of reason' in *Antitrust and Americal Business Abroad* (McGraw-Hill, 1958). Note that in the *Timberlane* case itself the Court of Appeals said that, as there was no indication of a conflict with the law and policy of the Honduran government, the trial judge could not have dismissed the action on jurisdictional grounds. Some commentators hold, however, that comity *deprives* the courts of jurisdiction (see the discussion in H. Hov- enkamp, *Federal Antitrust Policy* (West Publishing Co, St Paul, Minn., 1994), 702). This was the approach taken by Justice Scalia, dissenting, in *Hartford Fire Insurance*, 509 US 764, 113 S Ct. 2891 (1993), discussed *infra*.

inevitably come to be seen as a statutory formulation of the effects doctrine. The test it contains—direct, substantial, reasonably foreseeable—is very much like the *Alcoa* formula, except that it adds forseeability.[18] It does not address any *Timberlane*-type balancing exercise.

On the other hand, the American Law Institute's *Third Restatement of the Foreign Relations Law of the United States*[19] sets out the principles of extraterritorial jurisdiction in terms of the *Timberlane/Mannington Mills* balancing act.

In *Hartford Fire Insurance*[20] in 1993 the Supreme Court recognized the claims of comity, but took a robust approach to applying the effects doctrine nevertheless. Re-insurers based in London agreed with parties in the USA to boycott certain types of insurers, which meant that some types of insurance cover were not available in the USA. The Supreme Court, by a majority, held that the Sherman Act could be applied to the acts of the British insurers. Justice Souter, delivering the majority opinion, said that 'it is well established by now that the Sherman Act applies to foreign conduct that was meant to produce and did in fact produce some substantial effect in the United States'.[21] He looked to the FTAIA formulation as expressing the effects doctrine, and said that in the light of that the court should first decide whether it had jurisdiction. Then it could be determined whether jurisdiction should be declined on comity grounds. In this case there was no reason to decline it. He took the view that although the UK *allowed* the conduct, it did not *compel* it.[22] There was therefore no conflict between British and American policy, and no reason for comity concerns to override the effects doctrine.

However, if international comity is only to prevent the USA taking jurisdiction in such narrowly drawn conflict situations it will rarely prevail. Further, it should be noted that when dealing with internal inconsistencies between federal antitrust law and the laws of US states, it is accepted that immunity from the former may sometimes arise as a consequence of the latter, even where the individual or undertaking concerned *could* comply with both.[23] The disregard of another jurisdiction which merely *permits* rather than *compels* conduct which is contrary to the first State's antitrust laws also arises in EC law. It is vividly demonstrated by the merger case, *Gencor*, discussed below.[24]

In *Hartford Fire Insurance* a strong dissent was voiced by Justice Scalia. His view was that comity is an integral part of determining whether the court has jurisdiction in the first place, rather than something to be taken into account when deciding whether to *exercise* jurisdiction.[25] Hovenkamp comments that Scalia took a 'private' view of the litigation, although

---

[18] Foreseeability indicates that the 'intent' in *Alcoa* 274 US 268, 47 S Ct. 592 (1927) is objective rather than subjective.

[19] (American Law Institute, 1995) at sec. 403. The American Law Institute is a private body, but the Restatements are accorded great respect.

[20] *Hartford Fire Insurance Co.* v. *California*, 509 US 764, 113 S Ct. 2891 (1993).

[21] *Ibid.* at 796 (US).

[22] The 'foreign sovereign compulsion defence' (the US courts do not hold private individuals liable for acts they were compelled to perform by a foreign sovereign on that sovereign's territory) therefore did not apply. (The USA also recognizes 'foreign sovereign immunity' whereby foreign governments have immunity in the courts, although this does not usually cover commercial activities).

[23] A. Robertson and M. Demetriou, '*But That was in Another Country . . .*': *The Extraterritorial Application of US Antitrust Laws in the US supreme Court* (1994) 43 ICLQ 417, 421–2.

[24] Case T–102/96, *Gencor Ltd* v. *Commission* [1999] ECR II–753 [1999] 4 CMLR 971, discussed *infra* at 1059–1066.

[25] See also the minority opinion by Judge Adams in *Mannington Mills* 595 F, 2d. 1287 (3d Cir. 1979).

antitrust law expresses the substantive economic policy of the United States and 'American "public" policy is entitled to be given as much weight by an American court as is the policy of a foreign sovereign, at least where American interests covered by the policy are substantially affected'.[26] He criticises *Timberlane* and *Mannington Mills* as giving rise to a situation where 'numerous factors are to be balanced in some unspecified way'.[27] F.A.Mann, writing in 1984,[28] also disapproved of the 'balancing interests' idea. He considered that if a court has jurisdiction it must exercise it. If, on the other hand, international law says it has no jurisdiction that is the end of the matter. One cannot, however, have a court which has a discretion whether or not to exercise its own jurisdiction.

In 1995 the Department of Justice and the Federal Trade Commission issued a set of Antitrust Enforcement Guidelines for International Operations.[29] These explain, *inter alia*, that the agencies will take comity into account when deciding to bring an action or seek particular remedies. The Guidelines list a number of factors (similar to those in *Timberlane*) that will be considered when making the decision. Once the decision is made, however, this represents 'a determination by the Executive Branch that the importance of antitrust enforcement outweighs any relevant foreign policy concerns'. The Guidelines warn that the courts should not 'second-guess' its judgment 'as to the proper role of comity concerns under these circumstances'.

The effects doctrine was applied in *Nippon Paper*,[30] where the Antitrust Division of the Department of Justice commenced *criminal* proceedings under the Sherman Act against a Japanese company for a cartel fixing the price at which fax paper should be sold in the USA.[31] The conspirators were all Japanese and all the activities of the cartel—the meetings, monitoring, and the sales to distributors with instructions about the resale price in the USA—took place in Japan. In contrast to the position in *Hartford Fire Insurance* the conduct was *illegal* under Japanese law (although the Japanese Government intervened in the case as an *amicus* on behalf of the defendant undertakings). The First Circuit Court of Appeals held that the US courts did have jurisdiction. The court said that *Hartford Fire* had 'stunted' the concept of comity in antitrust cases. It looked at the Restatement and the test of 'reasonableness' but considered that the Japanese undertakings should not, in these circumstances, be sheltered from prosecution by principles of comity:

We see no tenable reason why principles of comity should shield [the Japanese undertakings] from prosecution. We live in an age of international commerce, where decisions reached in one corner of the world can reverberate around the globe in less time than it takes to tell the tale. Thus, a ruling in [the Japanese undertakings'] favor would create perverse incentives for those who would use nefarious means to influence markets in the United States, rewarding them for enacting as many territorial firewalls as possible between cause and effect.[32]

---

[26] H. Hovenkamp, *Federal Antitrust Policy* (West Publishing Co., 1994) 699.

[27] See also Judge Wilkey in *Laker Airways Ltd* v. *Sabena*, 731 F 2d 909 (DC Cir. 1984).

[28] F.A. Mann, 'The Doctrine of International Jurisdiction Revisited After Twenty Years' (1984) 186 *RdC* 9, the sequel to the celebrated 1964 article, 'The Doctrine of Jurisdiction in International Law' (1964) 111 RdC 1.

[29] Antitrust and Trade Reg. Rep. (BNA), Special Supplement (6 Apr. 1995).

[30] *United States* v. *Nippon Paper Industries Co.*, 109 F, 3d (1st Cir. 1997).

[31] See R.M. Reynolds, J. Sicilian, P.S. Wellman, 'The Extraterritorial Application of the US Antitrust Laws to Criminal Conspiracies' [1998] *ECLR* 151; J. Griffin, 'Reactions to U.S. Assertions of Extraterritorial Jurisdiction' [1998] *ECLR* 64, 68.

[32] *Ibid.*, at 9.

This was the first case in which extraterritorial *criminal* jurisdiction had been taken under the Sherman Act. It showed that the USA has lost none of its enthusiasm for the application of its antitrust laws beyond its borders.

C. REACTIONS OF OTHER COUNTRIES TO THE US EFFECTS DOCTRINE

Other countries have tended to react unfavourably to US claims of extraterritorial jurisdiction based on the effects doctrine.[33] This is because of both the nature of the US provisions and the procedures and enforcement mechanisms the US law employs. In the USA, in contrast to the EC, the antitrust laws are predominantly enforced by private suits in the civil courts and not just by the antitrust authorities. The authorities do not have a strong influence over the courts or a claimant's decision to bring proceedings before the courts. For instance, the 1995 Guidelines state that the authorities will not bring an action unless they have weighed up the antitrust enforcement versus comity issues and decided that the former outweigh the latter. It is unlikely that a private plaintiff will go through the same process. Some countries have enacted 'blocking statutes' as a defence to what they consider excessive US claims to jurisdiction. The two greatest objections are that treble damages and extraterritorial discovery are available.

US law provides for successful plaintiffs in antitrust action to recover punitive, 'treble' damages. The Clayton Act[34] provides:

Except as provided in subsection(b) [suits by foreign governments], any person who shall be injured in his business or property by reason of anything forbidden in the antitrust laws may sue therefor in any district court of the United States in the district in which the defendant resides or is found or has an agent, without respect to the amount in controversy, and shall recover threefold the damages by him sustained, and the cost of suit, including a reasonable attorney's fee . . .

Some countries' blocking statutes prevent the recovery of treble damages from their nationals.[35] Section 5 of the UK's Protection of Trading Interests Act 1980 describes such awards as 'penal' and forbids their enforcement in UK courts under the usual reciprocal enforcement procedures.[36] Further, section 6 sets out a 'clawback' provision enabling British citizens or companies or persons carrying on business in the UK to bring an action in the UK courts to recover the non-compensatory part of any such damages they have paid.

The other main bone of contention is US pre-trial discovery, which confers wide-ranging powers on US plaintiffs wishing to search for evidence abroad. The House of Lords reacted with hostility in *Rio Tinto Zinc*[37] to letters rogatory requesting the High Court to require directors and employees of a British company to give oral evidence before an examiner in London and to require the company to produce the documents contained in a lengthy schedule. The request was in connection with a private antitrust suit in Virginia. The House

---

[33] There has also been almost universal opposition to the extraterritorial application of measures taken in pursuit of American foreign policy, noted *supra* at n. 7.

[34] S.4 of 15 USC Sec.15.

[35] See *supra* Chap. 15, n. 58 and accompanying text.

[36] See *supra* Chap. 15.

[37] *Rio Tinto Zinc Corp.* v. *Westinghouse Electric Corp.* [1978] AC 547.

decided that the US court's request for assistance fell within the exceptions to the obligation to assist in requests for discovery by foreign courts contained in the Evidence (Proceedings in Other Jurisdictions) Act 1975, and consequently refused discovery. Section 2 of the Protection of Trading Interests Act empowers the Secretary of State to prohibit persons within the UK from complying with demands by foreign tribunals and authorities for commercial documents or information not located within the jurisdiction of the State concerned.

3. INTERNATIONAL LAW

Given the controversy the US effects doctrine has generated, it is important to determine whether or not it is in conformity with international law.[38] There is no clear answer to this. The US government considers that the effects doctrine, whereby it asserts jurisdiction based on 'direct, substantial, and reasonably foreseeable' effects within the United States *is* in accordance with international law. Other governments disagree.[39]

It is generally accepted that the two undoubted bases for criminal jurisdiction[40] in international law are nationality and territory. There are two aspects to territoriality: subjective and objective. Subjective territoriality gives a State jurisdiction over acts which originated within its territory but were completed abroad. Objective territoriality gives a State jurisdiction over acts which originated abroad but were completed, at least partially, within its own territory. Objective territoriality was recognized by the Permanent Court of International Justice in the *Lotus* case.[41] However, there is continuing uncertainty about what *Lotus* actually decided. Brownlie states: '[i]n most respects the Judgment of the Court is unhelpful in its approach to the principles of jurisdiction, and its pronouncements are

---

[38] There is an enormous literature on jurisdiction in international law, a complex issue of which the question of jurisdiction in competition law is but a small part. See e.g. M. Akehurst, 'Jurisdiction in International Law' (1972–3) 46 BYIL, 145; F.A. Mann, 'The Doctrine of International Jurisdiction Revisited After Twenty Years' (1984) 156 Rdc 9; F.A. Mann, 'The Doctrine of Jurisdiction in International Law' (1964) 111 Rdc 3; D.W. Bowett, 'Jurisdiction: Changing Problems of Authority over Activities and Resources' (1982) 53 BYIL, R.Y. Jennings and A.D. Watts (eds.), *Oppenheim's International Law* (9th edn., (Longman, 1992)), i, 456; O. Schachter, *International Law in Theory and Practice* (Nijhoff, 1991) chap. XII; R. Higgins, *Problems and Process* (Oxford University Press, 1994) chap. 4. With particular reference to antitrust law, see K.M. Meessen, 'Antitrust Jurisdiction under Customary International Law' (1984) 78 *AJIL* 783; P.J. Slot and E. Grabandt, 'Extraterritoriality and Jurisdiction' (1986) 23 *CMLRev.* 545; P.M. Roth, 'Reasonable Extraterritoriality: Correcting the "Balance of Interests"' (1992) 41 *ICLQ* 245.

[39] See J. Griffin, 'Reactions to U.S. Assertions of Extraterritorial Jurisdiction' [1998] *ECLR* 64, 68.

[40] It is not clear whether there is any significant difference between jurisdiction in criminal, civil, and monetary matters: see e.g. I. Brownlie, *Principles of Public International Law* (5th edn.,) (Oxford University Press, Oxford, 1998), 313; M. Akehurst, 'Jurisdiction in International Law' (1972–3) 46 *BYIL* 145, 177.

[41] (1927), PCIJ, Ser.A, no. 10, 23. The case arose from a collision on the high seas between a French ship and a Turkish ship which led to Turkey instituting criminal proceedings against the officers of the watch on the French ship when it put into a Turkish port. The PCIJ held that international law did not *prevent* Turkey instituting proceedings: it was not asked whether international law *authorized* it to do so. See J. Griffin, 'Reactions to US Assertions of Extraterritorial Jurisdiction' [1998] *ECLR* 64, 68.

characterized by vagueness and generality'.[42] The important point here is whether the effects doctrine is validly derived from the principle of objective territoriality recognized in *Lotus* or whether it is an illegitimate extension which is inconsistent with the principle of the sovereignty of nations. The US position is, of course, the former.[43]

Further possible principles of jurisdiction are the passive personality principle, by which States claim jurisdiction over aliens who have committed acts abroad harmful to their nationals, and the protective or security principle[44] by which they claim jurisdiction over aliens for acts committed abroad which harm the security of the State. The latter principle is capable of indefinite expansion and could potentially be used to justify jurisdiction over economic acts.

It should be noted that private international law (conflict of laws), as well as public international law, is relevant to jurisdiction questions in competition cases. Private international law attempts to regulate whether a particular State has jurisdiction to try an issue and which law will be applied in determining it.

The position in international law was surveyed by Advocate General Darmon in his opinion in the leading EC case, *Wood Pulp I*.[45] He concluded that the effects doctrine was not contrary to international law and that it should be adopted by Community law:

57. ... there is no rule of international law which is capable of being relied upon against the criterion of the direct, substantial and foreseeable effect. Nor does the concept of international comity, in view of its uncertain scope, militate against the criterion either.

58. In the absence of any such prohibitive rule and in the light of widespread State practice, I would therefore propose that in view of its appropriateness to the field of competition, it be adopted as a criterion for the jurisdiction of the Community.

As we shall see below, the ECJ considered that its taking of jurisdiction in *Wood Pulp* was 'covered by the territoriality principle as universally recognised in public international law'.[46] This may well be unduly sanguine. While there is undoubtedly a territoriality principle in international law, what it covers is far from certain. It appears, however, to be developing in the direction of a formulation which demands a 'substantial and genuine connection' between the subject-matter and the source of the jurisdiction and an observance of the principle of non-intervention in the domestic or territorial jurisdiction of other States.[47]

---

[42] Brownlie, *Principles of Public International Law*, (5th edn.,) (Oxford University Press, 1998), 305.

[43] See the *Alcoa* case (*supra* n. 11) itself. F.A. Mann,' The Doctrine of International Jurisdiction Revisited after Twenty Years', (1984) 186 RdC9 concluded that although the effects doctrine is recognized by several countries, it does not seem to be regarded as a principle of international law.

[44] See the *Cutting* case (1886), J.B. Moore, Digest of International Law, vol II (1906). A further principle, not relevant here, is the universality principle, where jurisdiction is taken over aliens as a matter of international public policy for crimes such as piracy or aircraft hijacking. Jurisdiction over those who commit war crimes is sometimes seen as part of the universality principle, but may be a separate head of jurisdiction; see I. Brownlie, *Principles of Public International Law* (5th edn., Oxford University Press, 1998) 305.

[45] Cases 89, 104, 114, 116, 117 and 125–129/85, *A. Ahlström Oy* v. *Commission* [1988] ECR 5193, [1988] 4 CMLR 901 (*Wood Pulp I*), paras. 19–32 and 47–58 of the Opinion.

[46] *Ibid.*, para. 18.

[47] See, F.A. Mann, 'The Doctrine of Jurisdiction in International Law' (1964) III RdC1; Brownlie, *supra* n. 42.

4. THE POSITION IN EC LAW

A. GENERAL

Articles 81 and 82 are silent on the question whether or not they apply extraterritorially. At first the development of the single economic entity doctrine[48] precluded the need for resolving the issue. However, the point finally had to be dealt with in *Wood Pulp*.[49] The Merger Regulation,[50] while not expressly addressing the extraterritoriality question, contains a jurisdiction threshold which may catch concentrations between undertakings based outside the EC so long as the EC turnover thresholds set out in the Regulation are satisfied.[51] The discussion below establishes that the CFI has dealt with the question of extraterritoriality in respect of mergers differently from the ECJ in respect of Articles 81 and 82.

B. THE *DYESTUFFS* CASE

In 1972 in *Béguelin*,[52] a case concerning a Japanese manufacturer whose distribution arrangements with its French distributor compartmentalized the common market on national lines the ECJ held that the agreement infringed Article 81(1). As one of the parties to the agreement was clearly within the Community, and in the context of the case the imposition of a penalty on the Japanese undertaking did not arise, jurisdiction could be asserted without the question of an effects doctrine having to be faced.

In the *Dyestuffs* case[53] the question whether EC law had an effects doctrine was raised for the first time. The Commission investigated an alleged cartel among the producers of aniline dyes. It found *inter alia* that ICI, a company incorporated and having its headquarters in the UK which was not at that time a member of the Community, had engaged in concerted practices contrary to Article 81(1) by virtue of the instructions it had given to its Belgian subsidiary. It imposed a fine of 50,000 units of account on ICI.[54] In paragraph 28 of the Decision the Commission said:

Under Article [81](1) of the Treaty instituting the [EC] all agreements between undertakings, all decisions by associations of undertakings and all concerted practices which may affect trade between Member States and the object or effect of which is to prevent, restrict or distort competition within the Common Market shall be prohibited as incompatible with the Common Market. The competition rules of the Treaty are, consequently, applicable to all restrictions of competition which produce within the Common Market effects set out in Article [81](1). There is therefore no need to examine

---

[48] See *supra* Chap. 3.

[49] Cases 89, 104, 114, 116, 117 and 125–129/85, *A. Ahlström Oy* v. *Commission* [1988] ECR 5193, [1988] 4 CMLR 901.

[50] Council Reg. 4064/89 [1989] OJ L395/1, as amended by Council Reg. 131./97 [1997] OJ L180/1.

[51] For the Community dimension threshold generally, see *supra* Chap. 12.

[52] Case 22/71, *Béguelin Import Co* v. *GL Import Export* [1971] ECR 949, [1972] CMLR 81.

[53] Case 48/69 *ICI* v *Commission (Dyestuffs)* [1972] ECR 619, [1972] CMLR 557. The case was also an important early decision on concerted practices: see *supra* Chap. 11.

[54] *Re the Cartel in Aniline Dyes* [1969] JO L195/11, [196] CMLR D23.

whether the undertakings which are the cause of these restrictions of competition have their seat within or outside the Community.

It will be noted that here the Commission applies an 'effects' doctrine without any further amplification. The UK government, provoked by the Decision, despatched an *aide-mémoire* to the Commission setting out its views on the matter. It disapproved of jurisdiction being taken on the basis of an effects doctrine.[55]

Statement of Principles According to Which, in The View of The United Kingdom Government, Jurisdiction May Be Exercised Over Foreign Corporations in Anti-trust Matters

The basis on which substantive jurisdiction may be exercised in anti-trust matters

(1) On general principles, substantive jurisdiction in anti-trust matters should only be taken on the basis of either
    (a) the territorial principle, or
    (b) the nationality principle.
There is nothing in the nature of anti-trust proceedings which justifies a wider application of these principles than is generally accepted in other matters; on the contrary there is much which calls for a narrower application.

(2) The territorial principle justifies proceedings against foreigners and foreign companies only in respect of conduct which consists in whole or in part of some activity by them in the territory of the State claiming jurisdiction. A State should not exercise jurisdiction against a foreigner who or a foreign company which has committed no act within its territory. In the case of conspiracies the assumption of jurisdiction is justified:
    (a) if the entire conspiracy takes place within the territory of the State claiming jurisdiction; or
    (b) if the formation of the conspiracy takes place within the territory of the State claiming jurisdiction even if things are done in pursuance of it outside its territory; or
    (c) if the formation of the conspiracy takes place outside the territory of the State claiming jurisdiction, but the person against whom the proceedings are brought has done things within its territory in pursuance of the conspiracy.

(3) The nationality principle justifies proceedings against nationals of the State claiming jurisdiction in respect of their activities abroad only provided that this does not involve interference with the legitimate affairs of other States or cause such nationals to act in a manner which is contrary to the laws of the State in which the activities in question are conducted.

ICI appealed against the Commission decision, *inter alia* on the jurisdiction point. It claimed that the Commission had no power to apply the competition rules to an undertaking established outside the (then) EEC. In reply the Commission relied not just on an elaboration of the effects doctrine but also on the claim that, although the subsidiaries within the Community had separate legal personality in law, the reality was that they were merely carrying out the parent's orders, so that subsidiaries appeared 'as mere extensions of ICI in the Common Market'.[56]

---

[55] 20 Oct. 1969. The text is in E. Lauterpacht (ed.), *British Practice in International Law* (1967), 58 and is set out in Brownlie, *supra* n. 42, 317.
[56] Case 48/69 *ICI* v. *Commission (Dyestuffs)* [1972] ECR 619, 627.

Advocate General Mayras recommended that the Commission's decision should be upheld on the basis of the 'effects doctrine'. He reviewed the national laws of the Member States on this issue, the international law arguments, and, of course, US law. He said that the conditions necessary for taking extraterritorial jurisdiction were that the agreement or concerted practice must create a *direct and immediate* restriction of competition, that the effect of the conduct must be *reasonably foreseeable,* and that the effect produced on the territory must be *substantial.* The Advocate General justified this adoption of what amounted to an effects doctrine not just by reference to principle, but also on grounds of pragmatism.[57]

Just as it would be quite wrong to reduce the concept of a concerted practice to so narrow a meaning that it would no longer connote anything more than a particular expression of the concept of an agreement, the obvious risk being that Article [81](1) would not be given the effective scope intended by the authors of the Treaty, so—subject to a reservation concerning powers of enforcement – that article would be drained of a large part of its meaning and at any rate its force would be dissipated if the Community authorities were denied the use in relation to any undertaking outside the Common Market of the powers that that same Article [81] confers on them.

Surely the Commission would be disarmed if, faced with a concerted practice the initiative for which was taken and the responsibility for which was assumed exclusively by undertakings outside the Common Market, it was deprived of the power to take any decision against them? This would also mean giving up a way of defending the Common Market and one necessary for bringing about the major objectives of the European Economic Community.

He drew a distinction, however, between prescriptive and enforcement jurisdiction. He considered that the *imposition* of fines is part of the legislative (prescriptive) jurisdiction, whereas their *recovery* (or other measures, such as the annulment of contracts) amounts to enforcement jurisdiction. He was prepared to accept that the decision taken by the Commission might not be capable of enforcement:[58]

the courts or administrative authorities of a State—and, *mutatis mutandis,* of the Community—are certainly not justified under international law in taking coercive measures or indeed any measure of inquiry, investigation or supervision outside their territorial jurisdiction where execution would inevitably infringe the internal sovereignty of the State on the territory of which they claimed to act.

In its judgment the ECJ did not take up its Advocate General's espousal of an effects doctrine. Instead it upheld the Commission's decision on the basis of what has become known as the single economic entity doctrine. It is explained in Chapter 3 that Community law has developed this doctrine by which parents and subsidiaries are considered to be one undertaking for the purposes of the application of the competition rules. In *Dyestuffs* the Court relied on this concept to impute the conduct of the subsidiary to the parent and to hold that the Commission did have jurisdiction over the UK company.

---

[57] *Ibid.,* 696.
[58] *Ibid.,* 695.

Case 48/69, *ICI* v. *Commission (Dyestuffs)* [1972] ECR 619, [1972] CMLR 557

The Court of Justice

130 By making use of its power to control its subsidiaries established in the Community, the applicant was able to ensure that its decision was implemented on that market.

131 The applicant objects that this conduct is to be imputed to its subsidiaries and not to itself.

132 The fact that a subsidiary has separate legal personality is not sufficient to exclude the possibility of imputing its conduct to the parent company.

133 Such may be the case in particular where the subsidiary, although having separate legal personality, does not decide independently upon its own conduct on the market, but carries out, in all material respects, the instructions given to it by the parent company.

134 Where a subsidiary does not enjoy real autonomy in determining its course of action in the market, the prohibitions set out in Article [81(1)] may be considered inapplicable in the relationship between it and the parent company with which it forms one economic unit.

135 In view of the unity of the group thus formed, the actions of the subsidiaries may in certain circumstances be attributed to the parent company.

136 It is well-known that at the time the applicant held all or at any rate the majority of the shares in those subsidiaries.

137 The applicant was able to exercise decisive influence over the policy of the subsidiaries as regards selling prices in the Common Market and in fact used this power upon the occasion of the three price increases in question.

138 In effect the Telex messages relating to the 1964 increase, which the applicant sent to its subsidiaries in the Common Market, gave the addressees orders as to the prices which they were to charge and the other conditions of sale which they were to apply in dealing with their customers.

139 In the absence of evidence to the contrary, it must be assumed that on the occasion of the increases of 1965 and 1967 the applicant acted in a similar fashion in its relation with its subsidiaries established in the Common Market.

140 In the circumstances the formal separation between these companies, resulting from their separate legal personality, cannot outweight the unity of their conduct on the market for the purposes of applying the rules on competition.

141 It was in fact the applicant undertaking which brought the concerted practice into being within the Common Market.

142 The submission as to lack of jurisdiction raised by the applicant must therefore be declared to be unfounded.

The Court therefore held here that the subsidiary did not have 'real autonomy' but acted on its parent's instructions, so that the infringing conduct in the EEC could be treated as having been committed by the subsidiary as an agent of the parent.[59]

The application of the single economic entity doctrine to take what is in effect

---

[59] F.A. Mann argued that the facts of the case did not support this conclusion: (1973) 22 *ICLQ* 35 and 'Reponsibility of Parent Companies for Foreign Subsidiaries' in C. Olmstead (ed.), *Extra-territorial Application of Laws and Responses Thereto* (ESC Publishing, Oxford 1984), 156.

extraterritorial jurisdiction has its opponents. At the time of *Dyestuffs* the UK was among them. In the *aide-mémoire* to the Commission[60] the UK government disputed the disregarding of the legal separation between parent and subsidiary:

The basis on which personal jurisdiction may be exercised over foreign corporations

(1) Personal jurisdiction should be assumed only if the foreign company 'carries on business' or 'resides' within the territorial jurisdiction.

(2) A foreign company may be considered to 'carry on business' within the jurisdiction by an agent only if the agent has legal power to enter into contracts on behalf of the principal.

(3) A foreign parent company may not be considered to 'carry on business' within the jurisdiction by a subsidiary company, unless it can be shown that the subsidiary is the agent for the parent in the sense of carrying on the parent's business within the jurisdiction.

(4) The separate legal personalities of a parent company and its subsidiary should be respected. Such concepts as 'enterprise entity' and 'reciprocating partnership' when applied for the purpose of asserting personal jurisdiction over a foreign parent company by reason of the presence within the jurisdiction of a subsidiary (and a foreign subsidiary by reason of its parent company) are contrary to sound legal principle in that they disregard the distinction of personality between parent and subsidiary.

(5) The normal rules governing the exercise of personal jurisdiction should not be extended in such a manner as to extend beyond proper limits the exercise of substantive jurisdiction in respect of the activities of foreigners abroad. Nor can the assertion of extended personal jurisdiction be justified on the basis that it is necessary for the enforcement of legislation which in itself exceeds the proper limits of substantive jurisdiction.

(6) There is no justification for applying a looser test to methods of personal service in anti-trust matters than is permissible in relation to other matters.

The UK has, however, since dropped its hostility to this concept and the Competition Act 1998 receives it fully into UK law, along with the other jurisprudence of the Court on the competition rules.[61] However, it is worth noting that many countries continue to have particular concerns about the application of a similar concept in US law. As Griffin explains.[62]

Nearly all nations agree that nationality can be a valid basis for asserting extraterritorial jurisdiction. However, U.S. assertions of jurisdiction based upon the control exercised by an American parent over a subsidiary incorporated and operating abroad are not accepted as valid under international law by a number of nations. These nations contend that despite the American parent's majority ownership or its possession of effective working control, under international law nationality is properly determined by the place of incorporation. . . . Moreover, according to one knowledgeable British official,[63] 'even where nationality is a legitimate basis for extraterritorial jurisdiction it must remain subject to the primacy of the laws and policies of the territorial state.'. . . U.S. officials typically respond to these contentions with the assertion that they cannot permit 'technicalities' such as the place of incorporation and inconsistent policies of host states to be used by American companies to evade their obligations under U.S. law. . . .

---

[60] See *supra* n. 55. The Court of Appeal had rejected the single economic entity concept in a Restrictive Trade Practices Act case, *Schweppes Ltd v Registrar of Restrictive Trading Agreements* [1965] 1 All ER 195, LR 5 RP 103.

[61] Competition Act 1998, s. 60.

[62] J. Griffin, 'Reactions to US Assertions of Extraterritorial Jurisdiction' [1998] *ECLR* 64, 69.

[63] The reference is to William M. Knighton, *Nationality and Extraterritorial Jurisdiction: Us Law Abroad*, Remarks before the International Law Institute of the Georgetown University Law Center 2, 13 Aug. 1981.

In *Dyestuffs* the ECJ neither approved nor disapproved the views of its Advocate General on the effects doctrine. It clearly preferred to proceed on the other available ground which was less controversial. Its silence on the point, however, encouraged the Commission's belief that Community law did recognize the effects doctrine.

C. THE *WOODPULP* CASE

Finally, a case came before the ECJ in which the existence or otherwise of an effects doctrine, or something similar, in EC law had to be addressed. This was *Wood Pulp I*, a leading case on cartels which is discussed in Chapter 11. The full facts are set out there, but can be summarized as follows. The Commission investigated alleged price-fixing in the wood pulp industry. It found that a cartel existed, and held that forty-one producers and two trade associations (Finncell and KEA) had engaged in concerted practices contrary to Article 81(1). It imposed fines on thirty-six of the addressees.[64] All forty-three producers and trade associations concerned had their registered offices outside the EC. Most, if not all, of the producers had 'branches, subsidiaries, agencies or other establishments within the Community'.[65]

Many of the addressees appealed. There were two grounds: first that the Commission had no jurisdiction to apply its competition law to the addressees and, secondly, that they had not participated in concerted practices. The Court decided to hear the plea about the jurisdiction first.[66]

As already noted[67] Advocate General Darmon engaged in a lengthy survey of the relevant international and US law and the scholarly literature and concluded that the Community was entitled to take, and should take, jurisdiction in this case on the basis of the effects doctrine. The Court, however, couched its judgment in slightly different terms:

Cases 89, 104, 114, 116, 117 and 125–129/85, *A. Ahlström Oy* v *Commission* [1988] ECR 5193, [1988] 4 CMLR 901[68]

Court of Justice

11. In so far as the submission concerning the infringement of Article [81] of the Treaty itself is concerned, it should be recalled that that provision prohibits all agreements between undertakings and concerted practices which may affect trade between member-States and which have as their object or effect the restriction of competition within the Common Market.

12. It should be noted that the main sources of supply of wood pulp are outside the Community, in Canada, the United States, Sweden and Finland and that the market therefore has global dimensions.

---

[64] *Wood Pulp* [1985] OJ L85/1, [1985] 3 CMLR 474.

[65] Only some of them did according to para 79 of the Decision, [1988] OJ L85/1, but later, in its rejoinder before the Court, the Commission stated that all of them did: see W. van Gerven, 'EC Jurisdiction in Antitrust Matters: The Wood Pulp Judgment' [1989] *Fordham Corporate Law Institute* 451, 464.

[66] This is therefore colloquially known as *Wood Pulp I*. The judgment on the substantive issue is known as *Wood Pulp II* (Cases C–89/85 etc., *A. Ahlström Oy* v. *Commission* [1993] ECR I–1307, [1993] 4 CMLR 407).

[67] *Supra* 1047.

[68] See generally W van Gerven, EC Jurisdiction in Antitrust Matters: The Wood Pulp Judgment [1989] Fordham Corporate Law Institute 451. Professor van Gerven was at the time of delivering this paper an AG at the ECJ.

Where wood pulp producers established in those countries sell directly to purchasers established in the Community and engage in price competition in order to win orders from those customers, that constitutes competition within the Common Market.

13. It follows that where those producers concert on the prices to be charged to their customers in the Community and put that concertation into effect by selling at prices which are actually coordinated, they are taking part in concertation which has the object and effect of restricting competition within the Common Market within the meaning of Article [81] of the Treaty.

14. Accordingly, it must be concluded that by applying the competition rules in the Treaty in the circumstances of this case to undertakings whose registered offices are situated outside the Community, the Commission has not made an incorrect assessment of the territorial scope of Article [81]

15. The applicants have submitted that the decision is incompatible with public international law on the grounds that the application of the competition rules in this case was founded exclusively on the economic repercussions within the Common Market of conduct restricting competition which has adopted outside the Community.

16. It should be observed that an infringement of Article [81], such as the conclusion of an agreement which has had the effect of restricting competition within the Common Market, consists of conduct made up of two elements, the formation of the agreement, decision or concerted practice and the implementation thereof. If the applicability of prohibitions laid down under competition law were made to depend on the place where the agreement, decision or concerted practice was formed, the result would obviously be to give undertakings an easy means of evading those prohibitions. The decisive factor is therefore the place where it is implemented.

17. The producers in this case implemented their pricing agreement within the Common Market. It is immaterial in that respect whether or not they had recourse to subsidiaries, agents, sub-agents, or branches within the Community in order to make their contacts with purchasers within the Community.

18. Accordingly the Community's jurisdiction to apply its competition rules to such conduct is covered by the territoriality principle as universally recognised in public international law.

19. As regards the argument based on the Infringement of the principle of non-interference, it should be pointed out that the applicants who are members of KEA have referred to a rule according to which where two States have jurisdiction to lay down and enforce rules and the effect of those rules is that a person finds himself subject to contradictory orders as to the conduct he must adopt, each State is obliged to exercise its jurisdiction with moderation. The applicants have concluded that by disregarding that rule in applying its competition rules the Community has infringed the principle of non-interference.

20. There is no need to enquire into the existence in international law of such a rule since it suffices to observe that the conditions for its application are in any event not satisfied. There is not, in this case, any contradiction between the conduct required by the United States and that required by the Community since the Webb-Pomerene Act[69] merely exempts the conclusion of export cartels from the application of United States antitrust laws but does not require such cartels to be concluded.

21. It should further be pointed out that the United States authorities raised no objections

---

[69] The Webb-Pomerene Act 1918 is a US statute which allows American exporters to act together in export markets in ways which would otherwise violate the Sherman Act.

regarding any conflict of jurisdiction when consulted by the Commission pursuant to the OECD Council Recommendation of 25 October 1979 concerning Co-operation between Member Countries on Restrictive Business Practices affecting International Trade. . . .

22. As regards the argument relating to disregard of international comity, it suffices to observe that it amounts to calling in question the Community's jurisdiction to apply its competition rules to conduct such as that found to exist in this case and that, as such, that argument has already been rejected.

23. Accordingly it must be concluded that the Commission's decision is not contrary to Article [81] of the Treaty or to the rules of public international law relied on by the applicants.

Significantly, this judgment avoided talking about 'effects'. Given the terms in which the Commission decision, the arguments before the Court, and the Advocate General's opinion had been couched, this avoidance of specific reference to the effects doctrine must have been deliberate. Instead, the Court talked about 'implementation' (paragraphs 16 and 17).

It will be noted that the judgment above (which comprises the entirety of the section on jurisdiction) falls into distinct parts. First, paragraphs 11–14 deal with whether or not the Commission infringed *the Treaty* by applying the competition rules to the individual under-takings.[70] The ECJ held that it had not, as it had correctly assessed the territorial scope of Article 81. Secondly, paragraphs 15–18 consider whether the Commission had infringed *international* law. The Court held that it had not done this either, as the taking of juris-diction was covered by the 'universally recognized' territoriality principle (paragraph 18). Thirdly, paragraphs 19–22 reject the argument based on a possible 'non-interference' prin-ciple by saying that the US legislation did not *require* export cartels to be entered into, but merely tolerated them. This is the same position as that reached by the Supreme Court in *Hartford Fire* in respect of the UK legislation.

In paragraph 16 the Court divided the infringing conduct into two elements, the forma-tion of the agreement and its implementation. It did not matter where the formation of the agreement took place: the decisive factor was the place where it was 'implemented'.

The crucial question is what is meant by 'implementation' and how, if at all, this differs from the effects doctrine? The first thing to note is that the Court said in paragraph 17 that it was immaterial whether or not the producers used subsidiaries, agents, sub-agents, or branches inside the Community. This means that 'implementation' covers *direct sales* to Community purchasers and does not depend on the sellers establishing some form of marketing organization within the Community. Jurisdiction is taken simply because of sales into the Community. Some commentators believe that this is not justified in international law. Van Gerven, for example, has argued:[71]

Accepting this type of conduct [i.e. setting up a marketing organisation and using it to give effect to a cartel] does not, I believe, unduly stretch the underlying strict territoriality and is, therefore, as indicated above, compatible with public international law. That cannot be said, however, of conduct which amounts to selling directly to purchasers within the Community, even when selling takes place through authorized but independent distributors or dealers that are doing business on their own

---

[70] As far as the applicant trade association, KEA, was concerned, the Court annulled the decision because it held that KEA had not played a separate role in the implementation of the price-fixing agreements: judgment [1988] ECR 5193 paras. 24–28).

[71] W. van Gerven, 'EC Jurisdiction in Antitrust Matters: The Wood Pulp Judgment' [1989] *Fordham Corporate Law Institute* 451, 470.

behalf. Selling from abroad to purchasers and/or independent distributors or dealers within the regulating State cannot, I submit, reasonably be qualified as conduct of the 'parent' itself, or conduct imputable to it within the Common Market, because it does not constitute a sufficiently close and relevant link with the regulating State that is compelling enough to justify jurisdiction on its part. If the mere fact of selling directly in the territory (without requiring any permanent presence in the form of a sales organization, be it only a sales agent or sales representative) amounts to implementing conduct, then such a loose 'point of contact' can confer jurisdiction upon many States, thereby depriving the point of contact of its true content. . . . The mere statement that the exercise of jurisdiction in such circumstances is permitted by the strict territoriality test, is of course, no proof of sufficient respect for that principle. It follows therefrom that I am not in a position to subscribe to the Court's statement in the *Wood Pulp* judgment that '[i]t is immaterial . . . whether or not [the undertakings] had recourse to subsidiaries, agents, sub-agents, or branches within the Community' . . .

A second point to note is that the preponderant view is that 'implementation' would *not* cover negative behaviour such as agreements concluded outside the Community by which undertakings agree not to sell within the Community, or agree not to purchase from Commission producers.[72] However, such conduct could, it is argued, fall within the effects doctrine.[73]

In *Wood Pulp*, therefore, the Court confirmed that Article 81[74] could be applied extraterritorially, but did so by enunciating a Community concept of extraterritorial jurisdiction based on implementation rather than by adopting the effects doctrine as developed in US law. However, it is now necessary to consider the *Wood Pulp* judgment in the light of the case law under the Merger Regulation, to which we turn below.

D. THE MERGER REGULATION

(i) THE TERMS OF THE MERGER REGULATION

As is explained in Chapter 12, the EC Merger Regulation[75] provides that the Commission has sole jurisdiction[76] over concentrations with a 'Community dimension'.[77] The meaning of a 'Community dimension' is set out in Article 1. Under Article 1(2) a concentration will have a Community dimension if the worldwide (Euro 5,000 million) and Community-wide (Euro 250 million) turnover thresholds are met. There is a proviso which excludes concentrations in which the undertakings concerned achieve at least two-thirds of the Community-wide turnover in the same Member State. An alternative set of thresholds was

---

[72] See e.g. Griffin, *supra* n. 62, 68; Van Gerven, *supra* n. 71, 471. Van Gerven's view is also that any attempt to encompass such conduct within 'implementation' would be contrary to international law as there would not be a sufficiently close link to support jurisdiction.

[73] Griffin, *supra* n. 62, 68.

[74] And presumably also Art. 82.

[75] For the Merger Reg. [1989] OJ L395/1, as amended by Council Reg. 1310/97 [1997] OJ L180/1, generally, see *supra* Chap. 12.

[76] Subject to certain exceptions, discussed in Chap. 12, such as Art. 9 which allows for concentrations to be referred back to national authorities.

[77] For a full analysis of the 'Community dimension' see M. Broberg, *The European Commission's Jurisdiction to Scrutinise Mergers* (Kluwer, 1998).

introduced by Regulation 1310/97[78] Further, it should be noted that Recital 11 of the Regulation states that a Community dimension exists 'where the concentrations are effected by undertakings which do not have their principal fields of activities in the Community but which do have substantial operations there'.[79]

Article 1 does not, however, expressly say anything about where the undertakings concerned are incorporated, or carry on business, or whether the undertakings must have assets in the Community. Its criteria relate only to a worldwide turnover figure and a much smaller Community-wide turnover figure. Article 5, which deals with the calculation of turnover, says that '[t]urnover in the Community or in a Member State, shall comprise products sold and services provided to undertakings or consumers, in the Community or in that Member State as the case may be'.[80] The main reason for the Regulation not directly addressing the jurisdiction issue seems to be that the Council Working Group was dealing with the details of the Regulation at the time *Wood Pulp I* was before the Court. In the light of the problems raised in that case express references to jurisdiction were deleted from the final version.[81]

As a result of this jurisdictional test it was inevitable that undertakings established abroad would be drawn into the net of Community merger control by involvement in transactions with Community undertakings. The way that the Community dimension threshold is formulated, however, can also catch transactions which involve *only* undertakings located outside the Community with few assets inside it, and transactions which have minimal impact inside the Community. The broad jurisdiction is unlikely to cause great problems in most cases, in that the concentration concerned will clearly not be incompatible with the common market under the test in Article 2.[82] In a number of cases, involving for example Japanese banks, foreign undertakings have notified the Commission and duly got their Article 6(1) clearance within a month.[83] Even so, non-EC undertakings may object to the Commission's jurisdiction, particularly where the Commission is unhappy about a concentration.

(ii) THE *BOEING/MCDONNELL DOUGLAS* CASE

The practical and diplomatic problems of taking jurisdiction over mergers involving undertakings established outside the Community were dramatically illustrated by the *Boeing/ McDonnell Douglas* saga.[84]

Boeing and McDonnell Douglas (MDC) were both US aircraft manufacturers. In February 1997 the Commission received notification pursuant to the Merger Regulation of a concentration by which Boeing would acquire control of MDC. The merger would create the world's largest aerospace manufacturer. The transaction clearly had a Community dimension within Article 1. The Commission had serious doubts about it and opened a

---

[78] The object of this additional set of criteria was to provide for concentrations which did not reach the Art. 1(2) thresholds and which might otherwise fall to be dealt with by several national merger authorities in the EC.

[79] Recital 11 was discussed in the *Gencor* judgment discussed *infra* at 1059–1066: see Case T–102/96, *Gencor Ltd* v. *Commission* [1999] ECR II–753, [1999] 4 CMLR 971 at paras. 83–85.

[80] Merger, Reg., Art. 5(1), second para.

[81] See C.J. Cook and C.S. Kerse, *EC Merger Control* (3rd edn., (Sweet and Maxwell, 2000), 11–12.

[82] See Chap. 12.

[83] See e.g. *Kyowa/Saitama Banks* [1992] 4 CMLR 1186; *Matsushita/MCA* [1992] 4 CMLR M36.

[84] The Commission's final decision in this case is at [1997] OJ L336/16.

Phase II investigation under Article 6(1)(c).[85] It was concerned that the number of large commercial jet aircraft manufacturers would be reduced from three to two (the other one being Airbus Industrie) and that Boeing's dominant position would be strengthened. It communicated its concerns to the US Federal Trade Commission pursuant to the EC–US Co-operation Agreement.[86] On 1 July 1997 the FTC cleared the merger and on 13 July informed the Commission that, *inter alia*, a decision prohibiting the proposed merger could harm important US defence interests.[87] However, the Commission continued with its objections. This led to a confrontation with the USA, with high-level political intervention including the involvement of President Clinton and threats by Vice-President Gore to wage commercial war against the EC. At the last moment the Commission cleared the merger, after Boeing had given certain undertakings,[88] and the storm died down. The undertakings related to the cessation of existing and future exclusive supply deals, the 'ring-fencing' of MDC's commercial aircraft activities, the licensing of patents to other jet aircraft manufacturers, commitments not to abuse relationships with customers and suppliers, and a commitment to report annually to the Commission.

The Commission issued a bullish Press Release, expressing satisfaction at this outcome:[89]

These commitments are considered adequate to resolve the identified competition problems, and the Commission has therefore decided to declare the operation compatible with the common market subject to conditions and obligations. The Commission has reached its decision after a rigorous analysis based on EU merger control law, and in accordance with its own past practice and the jurisprudence of the European Court. The Commission expects Boeing to comply fully with its decision, in particular as regards the commitments made by Boeing to resolve the competition problems identified by the Commission. The Commission will strictly monitor Boeing's compliance with these commitments. The EU Merger Regulation allows for appropriate measures to be taken by the Commission in the event of non-compliance by Boeing . . .

In arriving at this decision the Commission has taken into account concerns expressed by the U.S. Government relating to important US defence interests. The Commission took the US Government's concerns into consideration to the extent consistent with EU law, and has limited the scope of its action to the civil side of the operation, including the effects of the merger on the commercial jet aircraft market resulting from the combination of Boeing's and MDC's large defence and space interests.

In fact, the commitments were widely perceived in the Community as being weak and almost impossible to enforce, while US commentators and Boeing's lawyers claimed they were merely aimed at protecting and benefiting Airbus.[90] The Director General for

---

[85] See *supra* Chap. 12 for Commission proceedings under the Merger Reg.

[86] Art. VI. This agreement is discussed further, *infra*.

[87] [1997] OJ L336/16, para. 12.

[88] *Ibid.*, paras. 115–119.

[89] IP (1997) 729 of 30 July 1997 [1997] 5 CMLR 253.

[90] See M. Furse, *Competition Law of the UK and EC* (Blackstone Press, 1999), 305–6; A. Kaczorowska, 'International Competition Law in the Context of Global Capitalism [2000] *ECLR* 117, 118. Bill Bishop, however, argues that there were very good reasons for blocking the merger, as it took the industry from three players to two, where there was evidence that the third player exerted a significant downward effect on prices. He concludes that 'the actual result was a compromise making little economic sense since customers were not protected by it at all. But by the light of international politics it was all too easy to understand the result': B. Bishop, 'Editorial, The Boeing/McDonnell Douglas Merger' [1997] *ECLR* 417.

Competition, writing in the aftermath of the affair, expressed general satisfaction that in dealing with the case 'the European Commission obtained positive results for European competition policy on the one hand and for our co-operation with the US on the other' but admitted that 'diverging approaches of the competition authorities in Brussels and Washington made it impossible to reach commonly accepted solutions'.[91]

The matter showed that, despite the existence of bilateral co-operation arrangements[92] between broadly like-minded competition authorities, there will be clashes once the authorities attempt to apply their laws to third parties beyond their borders. It should be noted that the USA, the home of the effects doctrine, did *not* dispute the EC's assumption of extraterritorial jurisdiction, but expected that its assertions of the importance of the deal to its national interests would be deferred to by the Commission.[93] The implications of the situation had the merger actually been prohibited by the EC but allowed in the USA did not have to be faced.[94] The whole affair highlighted both the need for, and the problems of, international co-operation in competition law, which are further discussed below.[95]

(iii) THE *GENCOR* CASE

In *Boeing/McDonnell Douglas* the Commission ultimately permitted the merger. However, in *Gencor/Lonrho* in 1996 it prohibited a merger in the South African platinum and rhodium industry,[96] on the ground that it would create a position of oligopolistic dominance.[97] One of the parties appealed, *inter alia*, on the ground that the Commission had no jurisdiction over the transaction.[98]

The case concerned a proposed merger between the platinum and rhodium mining interests in South Africa of Gencor and LPD. Both were companies incorporated in South Africa, although LPD was a subsidiary of Lonrho, which was incorporated in London. LPD's sales worldwide were made through Lonrho's Belgian subsidiary. Platinum group metal (PGM) is sold throughout the world, mainly in Japan (approximately 50 per cent of world demand), and North America and Western Europe (approximately 20 per cent each).[99] Approximately 70–75 per cent of the world supply of PGM comes from South Africa and 22–25 per cent from Russia[100] (although South Africa has 90 per cent of the world reserves).

---

[91] A. Schaub, 'International Co-operation in Antitrust Matters: Making the Point in the Wake of the Boeing/MDD Proceedings' [1998] *Competition Policy Newsletter* no. 1, 2, 3–4.

[92] See *infra* 1067–1070.

[93] See, generally, A. Bavasso, 'Boeing/McDonnell Douglas: Did the Commission Fly Too High? [1998] *ECLR* 243.

[94] Although there was talk at the time of huge fines and the seizing of Boeing planes in Europe.

[95] See *infra* 1071–1073.

[96] Case IV/M 619 [1997] OJ. L11/30, [1999] 4 CMLR 1076.

[97] For this aspect of the case see *supra* Chap. 11 and 12.

[98] Once the Commission had blocked the merger there was no possibility of the transaction going ahead, since under the agreement between the parties it was a condition precedent that clearance from the Commission should be obtained by a certain date. The entire purchase agreement had therefore lapsed. Nevertheless, the CFI held that the action for annulment was still admissible since the applicant had an interest in having the legality of the decision addressed to it examined by the Community judicature: Case T–102/96, *Gencor Ltd v. Commission* [1999] ECR II–753, [1999] 4 CMLR 971, paras. 40–46.

[99] For the exact figures from 1991–5 see Table 5 in, Case IV/M619, *Gencor/Lonrho* [1997] OJ L11/30, [1999] 4 CMLR 1076.

[100] *Ibid.*, Table 2.

In South Africa the largest producer was Anglo-American, which was also incorporated there. The companies' sales figures were deleted from the published decision as business secrets, but it seems that Anglo-American probably had 35–50 per cent of world sales and LPD and Gencor 15–17 per cent each.[101]

All of the Gencor's and LPD's production was in South Africa. The proposed merger was notified to the South African authorities, which found that there were no competition problems. The Deputy Foreign Minister told the Commission that he would not contest the Commission's policy, but that the South African government considered that two equally matched competitors (as Anglo-American and Gencor-Lonrho would be) were preferable to the prevailing situation of one dominant firm (Anglo-American).[102] The merger had a Community dimension because of the worldwide and Community-wide turnover of Gencor and Lonrho. The Commission found the merger to be incompatible with the common market on account of the effect which the creation of the dominant duopoly position would have on *sales* of PGM in the Community.

Gencor contested the Commission's assumption of jurisdiction before the CFI. It argued[103] that the Merger Regulation is applicable only if the activities forming the subject-matter of the concentration are located within the Community. The location of the concentration was South Africa, and if the *Wood Pulp* test was applied the concentration was implemented in South Africa, not the Community. South Africa had approved the merger. Moreover, Gencor claimed, even if the test for jurisdiction *was* whether the merger had an immediate and substantial effect on competition within the Community, that test was not satisfied either: 'the Commission cannot claim jurisdiction on the basis of future and hypothetical behaviour in which undertakings in the relevant market might engage and which might or might not fall within its purview under the Treaty'.[104] The CFI, however, upheld the Commission's decision:

Case T–102/96, *Gencor Ltd* v. *Commission* [1999] ECR II–753, [1999] 4 CMLR 971

Court of First Instance

78. The Regulation, in accordance with Article 1 thereof, applies to all concentrations with a Community dimension, that is to say to all concentrations between undertakings which do not each achieve more than two-thirds of their aggregate Community-wide turnover within one and the same Member State, where the combined aggregate worldwide turnover of those undertakings is more than ECU 5000 million and the aggregate Community-wide turnover of at least two of them is more than ECU 250 million.

79. Article 1 does not require that, in order for a concentration to be regarded as having a Community dimension, the undertakings in question must be established in the Community or that the production activities covered by the concentration must be carried out within Community territory.

80. With regard to the criterion of turnover, it must be stated that, as set out in paragraph 13 of the contested decision, the concentration at issue has a Community dimension within the meaning of

---

[101] See the figures extrapolated from the information in the decision in E. Fox, 'The Merger Regulation and its Territorial Reach', [1999] *ECLR* 334, 334.

[102] Para. 19 of the judgment.

[103] [1999] ECR II–753, 4 CMLR 971, paras. 48–63 of the judgment.

[104] *Ibid.*, para. 61.

Article 1(2) of the Regulation. The undertakings concerned have an aggregate worldwide turnover of more than ECU 10 000 million, above the ECU 5000 million threshold laid down by the Regulation. Gencor and Lonrho each had a Community-wide turnover of more than ECU 250 million in the latest financial year. Finally, they do not each achieve more than two-thirds of their aggregate Community-wide turnover within one and the same Member State.

81. The applicant's arguments to the effect that the legal bases for the Regulation and the wording of its preamble and substantive provisions preclude its application to the concentration at issue cannot be accepted.

82. The legal bases for the Regulation, namely Articles [83] and [308] of the Treaty, and more particularly the provisions to which they are intended to give effect, that is to say Articles 3[(1)(g)] and [81] and [82] of the Treaty, as well as the first to fifth, ninth and eleventh recitals in the preamble to the Regulation, merely point to the need to ensure that competition is not distorted in the common market, in particular by concentrations which result in the creation or strengthening of a dominant position. They in no way exclude from the Regulation's field of application concentrations which, while relating to mining and/or production activities outside the Community, have the effect of creating or strengthening a dominant position as a result of which effective competition in the common market is significantly impeded.

83. In particular, the applicant's view cannot be founded on the closing words of the 11th recital in the preamble to the Regulation.

84. That recital states that 'a concentration with a Community dimension exists . . . where the concentrations are effected by undertakings which do not have their principal fields of activities in the Community but which have substantial operations there'.

85. By that reference, in general terms, to the concept of substantial operations, the Regulation does not, for the purpose of defining its territorial scope, ascribe greater importance to production operations than to sales operations. On the contrary, by setting quantitative thresholds in Article 1 which are based on the worldwide and Community turnover of the undertakings concerned, it rather ascribes greater importance to sales operations within the common market as a factor linking the concentration to the Community. It is common ground that Gencor and Lonrho each carry out significant sales in the Community (valued in excess of ECU 250 million).

86. Nor is it borne out by either the 30th recital in the preamble to the Regulation or Article 24 thereof that the criterion based on the location of production activities is well founded. Far from laying down a criterion for defining the territorial scope of the Regulation, Article 24 merely regulates the procedures to be followed in order to deal with situations in which non-member countries do not grant Community undertakings treatment comparable to that accorded by the Community to undertakings from those non-member countries in relation to the control of concentrations.

87. The applicant cannot, by reference to the judgment in *Wood Pulp*, rely on the criterion as to the implementation of an agreement to support its interpretation of the territorial scope of the Regulation. Far from supporting the applicant's view, that criterion for assessing the link between an agreement and Community territory in fact precludes it. According to *Wood Pulp*, the criterion as to the implementation of an agreement is satisfied by mere sale within the Community, irrespective of the location of the sources of supply and the production plant. It is not disputed that Gencor and Lonrho carried out sales in the Community before the concentration and would have continued to do so thereafter.

88. Accordingly, the Commission did not err in its assessment of the territorial scope of the

Regulation by applying it in this case to a proposed concentration notified by undertakings whose registered offices and mining and production operations are outside the Community.

2. Compatibility of the contested decision with public international law

89. Following the concentration agreement, the previously existing competitive relationship between Implats and LPD, in particular so far as concerns their sales in the Community, would have come to an end. That would have altered the competitive structure within the common market since, instead of three South African PGM suppliers, there would have remained only two. The implementation of the proposed concentration would have led to the merger not only of the parties' PGM mining and production operations in South Africa but also of their marketing operations throughout the world, particularly in the Community where Implats and LPD achieved significant sales.

90. Application of the Regulation is justified under public international law when it is foreseeable that a proposed concentration will have an immediate and substantial effect in the Community.

91. In that regard, the concentration would, according to the contested decision, have led to the creation of a dominant duopoly on the part of Amplats and Implats/LPD in the platinum and rhodium markets, as a result of which effective competition would have been significantly impeded in the common market within the meaning of Article 2(3) of the Regulation.

92. It is therefore necessary to verify whether the three criteria of immediate, substantial and foreseeable effect are satisfied in this case.

93. With regard, specifically, to the criterion of immediate effect, the words 'medium term' used in paragraphs 206 and 210 of the contested decision in relation to the creation of a dominant duopoly position are, contrary to the applicant's assertion, entirely unambiguous. They clearly refer to the time when it is envisaged that Russian stocks will be exhausted, enabling a dominant duopoly on the part of Amplats and Implats/LPD to be created on the world platinum and rhodium markets and, by the same token, in the Community as a substantial part of those world markets.

94. That dominant position would not be dependent, as the applicant asserts, on the future conduct of the undertaking arising from the concentration and of Amplats but would result, in particular, from the very characteristics of the market and the alteration of its structure. In referring to the future conduct of the parties to the duopoly, the applicant fails to distinguish between abuses of dominant position which those parties might commit in the near or more distant future, which might or might not be controlled by means of Articles [81] and/or [82] of the Treaty, and the alteration to the structure of the undertakings and of the market to which the concentration would give rise. It is true that the concentration would not necessarily lead to abuses immediately, since that depends on decisions which the parties to the duopoly may or may not take in the future. However, the concentration would have had the direct and immediate effect of creating the conditions in which abuses were not only possible but economically rational, given that the concentration would have significantly impeded effective competition in the market by giving rise to a lasting alteration to the structure of the markets concerned.

95. Accordingly, the concentration would have had an immediate effect in the Community.

96. So far as concerns the criterion of substantial effect, it should be noted that, as held in paragraph 297 below, the Commission established to the requisite legal standard that the concentration would have created a lasting dominant duopoly position in the world platinum and rhodium markets.

97. The applicant cannot maintain that the concentration would not have a substantial effect

in the Community in view of the low sales and small market share of the parties to the concentration in the EEA. While the level of sales in western Europe (20% of world demand) and the Community market share of the entity arising from the concentration (...) % in respect of platinum) were already sufficient grounds for the Community to have jurisdiction in respect of the concentration, the potential impact of the concentration proved even higher than those figures suggested. Given that the concentration would have had the effect of creating a dominant duopoly position in the world platinum and rhodium markets, it is clear that the sales in the Community potentially affected by the concentration would have included not only those of the Implats/LPD undertaking but also those of Amplats (approximately 35% to 50%), which would have represented a more than substantial proportion of platinum and rhodium sales in western Europe and a much higher combined market share held by Implats/LPD and Amplats (approximately ... % to 65%).

98. Finally, it is not possible to accept the applicant's argument that the creation of the dominant position referred to by the Commission in the contested decision is not of greater concern to the Community than to any other competent body and is even of less concern to it than to others. The fact that, in a world market, other parts of the world are affected by the concentration cannot prevent the Community from exercising its control over a concentration which substantially affects competition within the common market by creating a dominant position.

99. The arguments by which the applicant denies that the concentration would have a substantial effect in the Community must therefore be rejected.

100. As for the criterion of foreseeable effect, it follows from all of the foregoing that it was in fact foreseeable that the effect of creating a dominant duopoly position in a world market would also be to impede competition significantly in the Community, an integral part of that market.

101. It follows that the application of the Regulation to the proposed concentration was consistent with public international law.

102. It is necessary to examine next whether the Community violated a principle of non-interference or the principle of proportionality in exercising that jurisdiction.

103. The applicant's argument that, by virtue of a principle of non-interference, the Commission should have refrained from prohibiting the concentration in order to avoid a conflict of jurisdiction with the South African authorities must be rejected, without it being necessary to consider whether such a rule exists in international law. Suffice it to note that there was no conflict between the course of action required by the South African Government and that required by the Community given that, in their letter of 22 August 1995, the South African competition authorities simply concluded that the concentration agreement did not give rise to any competition policy concerns, without requiring that such an agreement be entered into (see, to that effect, *Wood Pulp*, paragraph 20).

104. In its letter of 19 April 1996 the South African Government, far from calling into question the Community's jurisdiction to rule on the concentration at issue, first simply expressed a general preference, having regard to the strategic importance of mineral exploitation in South Africa, for intervention in specific cases of collusion when they arose and did not specifically comment on the industrial or other merits of the concentration proposed by Gencor and Lonrho. It then merely expressed the view that the proposed concentration might not impede competition, having regard to the economic power of Amplats, the existence of other sources of supply of PGMs and the opportunities for other producers to enter the South African market through the grant of new mining concessions.

105. Finally, neither the applicant nor, indeed, the South African Government in its letter of 19 April 1996 have shown, beyond making mere statements of principle, in what way the proposed

concentration would affect the vital economic and/or commercial interests of the Republic of South Africa.

106. As regards the argument that the Community cannot claim to have jurisdiction in respect of a concentration on the basis of future and hypothetical behaviour, namely parallel conduct on the part of the undertakings operating in the relevant market where that conduct might or might not fall within the competence of the Community under the Treaty, it must be stated, as pointed out above in connection with the question whether the concentration has an immediate effect, that, while the elimination of the risk of future abuses may be a legitimate concern of any competent competition authority, the main objective in exercising control over concentrations at Community level is to ensure that the restructuring of undertakings does not result in the creation of positions of economic power which may significantly impede effective competition in the common market. Community jurisdiction is therefore founded, first and foremost, on the need to avoid the establishment of market structures which may create or strengthen a dominant position, and not on the need to control directly possible abuses of a dominant position.

107. Consequently, it is unnecessary to rule on the question whether the letter of 22 August 1995 from the South African Competition Board constituted a definitive position on the concentration, on whether or not the South African Government was an authority responsible for competition matters and, finally, on the scope of South African competition law. There is accordingly no need to grant the application for measures of organisation of procedure or of inquiry made by the applicant in its letter of 3 December 1996.

108. In those circumstances, the contested decision is not inconsistent with either the Regulation or the rules of public international law relied on by the applicant.

109. For the same reasons, the objection, based on Article [241] of the Treaty, that the Regulation is unlawful because it confers upon the Commission competence in respect of the concentration between Gencor and Lonrho must be rejected.

110. As regards the reasoning in the contested decision justifying Community jurisdiction to apply the Regulation to the concentration, it must be held that the explanations contained in paragraphs 4, 13 to 18, 204 to 206, 210 and 213 of the contested decision satisfy the obligations incumbent on the Commission under Article [253] of the Treaty to give reasons for its decisions so as to enable the Community judicature to exercise its power of review, the parties to defend their rights and any interested party to ascertain the conditions in which the Commission applied the Treaty and its implementing legislation.

111. Accordingly, both pleas of annulment which have been examined must be rejected, without it being necessary to grant the application for measures of organisation of procedure or of inquiry made by the applicant in its letter of 3 December 1996.

It can be seen from the extract above, that in paragraphs 78–88 the CFI looked first at the Regulation itself. It concluded that it does not matter where the PGM *production* took place, because not only does Article 1 not require that the production should take place in the Community (paragraph 79), it actually accords *greater* importance to *sales*. Further, in the second half of paragraph 87 it returned to the *Wood Pulp* judgment and said that the criterion of the implementation of an agreement is satisfied by *mere sale in the Community*. This point answers the doubt raised in respect of the *Wood Pulp* judgment by Van Gerven, above:[105] mere selling *does* equal implementation.

---

[105] See *supra* 1055–1056.

In paragraphs 89–111, the CFI considered whether the decision was in accordance with public international law. It concluded that it was. In the most significant passage, paragraph 90, the CFI seems unequivocally to adopt the effects doctrine by saying that the Regulation's application is justified in international law *when it is foreseeable that a proposed concentration will have an immediate and substantial effect in the Community.*

Gencor is a striking demonstration of the implications of the effects doctrine. The EC forbade a merger involving producer undertakings in a non-member country because of the sales of the product (less than a quarter of the worldwide total) in the Community. The interests of South Africa did not come into the equation because South Africa did not *require* the transaction to take place. This raised the non-interference issue discussed in *Wood Pulp* (and in *Hartford Fire*). The CFI concluded that there is no conflict of jurisdiction between a State which prohibits something and a State which allows it (rather than requires it). The difficulty with this is that merger control invariably operates only to forbid certain concentrations, not to require them, and the prohibiting jurisdiction will always trump the other. As Fox argues in the passage below, the *Gencor* transaction between the mining companies was likely to have a more serious impact on the economy of South Africa than on consumers in the EC. The affair has more than a whiff of neo-imperialism about it. One cannot but help contrast the outcome in this case with that in *Boeing/McDonnell Douglas* when the EC locked horns with the USA, a rather more formidable opponent in these matters than South Africa.

E. Fox, 'The Merger Regulation and its Territorial Reach' [1999] *ECLR* 334, 335–6

The market for platinum is a world market. If the concentration created a market structure that facilitated interdependence and thereby would produce higher prices, the price-raising effect would be equally felt in every country where platinum was sold. The E.U. was one of the three largest consuming regions; and the merging companies sold their platinum in the E.U. Moreover, if the merger was anti-competitive, South Africa might have profited from it, for consumption was predominantly abroad and the South African economy would probably have gained more than South African consumers would lose. . . . A sound competition law system would certainly allow a directly and substantially harmed jurisdiction to reprehend an anti-competitive transaction, particularly where it is likely to escape condemnation at home and is not justified by considerations such as defence.

Even so, there are remarkable aspects about this judgment. First, the Court of First Instance's expressed understanding of appropriate jurisdiction corresponds precisely with the United States' understanding of appropriate jurisdiction (and with the U.S. understanding of the effects test): that a jurisdiction may regulate conduct that has an immediate [or direct], substantial and foreseeable effect on the regulating jurisdiction's commerce. . . . 'Immediate' is a concept with elasticity; it is enough that the structural conditions for harm have been set in place. Restraint in the exercise of jurisdiction may be required in the event of a direct conflict of the laws of two jurisdictions; but the home nation's permissive stance and the regulating nation's prohibitory stance are not such a conflict. . . .

Second, as for E.C. law itself, the meaning of 'implemented' in *Woodpulp* has been an important undecided issue. Does the requirement that an offending act or agreement must be 'implemented' in the regulating jurisdiction add anything to the requirement that an act or agreement must have direct effects within the regulating jurisdiction? The Court of First Instance stated that 'implementation . . .

is satisfied by mere sale within the Community ...' ... If 'implementation' in a *merger* case is satisfied by mere sales in the jurisdiction of the merged firm's products, then implementation means effects, because the way that the anti-competitive nature of a merger is evidenced is through sales of the product of the merged firm.

To be sure, the worldwide sales subsidiary of the Lonrho parent was in Brussels; but if the consolidation of mining in South Africa were to trigger duopoly behaviour of Gencor/Lonrho with Anglo-American and thereby limit output in South Africa, this would be so no matter where the sales office was based. It is therefore unlikely that lack of a sales office in the Community would defeat the implementation requirement. . . .

Third, challenging issues lurk beneath the surface. Was there really no conflict between E.C. law and South African law? . . . Should it count for anything that the home authority vetted the concentration and found that a strong number two firm would be better for competition than a clearly dominant firm? What if the South African Government had taken a strong stand in favour of 'its' merger, as did the U.S. Government in *Boeing/McDonnell Douglas*? Should the most prohibitory jurisdiction always prevail? . . . Should a big consuming jurisdiction prevail, in any event, where the home jurisdiction is not a major consuming market and the home country's producers stand to gain more than its consumers stand to lose if the merger is anti-competitive? On the other hand, if every consuming nation can abort a merger—and some may even err in good faith in their effort to predict competitive harm—are international mergers excessively vulnerable?

South Africa's diplomatic stance (*ie* no opposition) made resolution of the jurisdictional problem in *Gencor* an easy one—compared with what have been the case if South Africa had fought for 'its' merger.

The fact is, however, that we now live in a world of mutual, liberal extraterritoriality. Mutually expansive scope for national law will not always be frictionless. *Gencor*, combined with *Boeing*, the parallel U.S. initiatives, and the cases yet to come, will force us sooner or later to face the question: does the world need an international merger protocol?

5. INTERNATIONAL CO-OPERATION

A. GENERAL

Faced with the globalization of the economy and with the problems of the application and enforcement of competition laws which are illustrated above, attention is increasingly turning to the desirability of international agreements as at least a partial solution. Agreements which are actually in place at the moment are mainly bilateral ones between major trading partners, but there has also been activity at the level of international organizations. The USA concluded bilateral agreements with Germany in 1976, Australia in 1982, and Canada in 1984 and 1995. These were all inspired by the OECD[106] Recommendation of (originally) 1967.[107] The 1991 Agreement between the USA and the EC, however, goes further than these agreements because it includes so-called 'positive comity' provisions.

---

[106] Organization for Economic Co-operation and Development.
[107] See *infra* 1071.

B. BILATERAL AGREEMENTS

(i) THE EC-US CO-OPERATION AGREEMENT

a. THE CONTENT OF THE 1991 AND 1998 AGREEMENTS

In 1991 the Commission concluded an agreement with the US authorities about co-opera-tion over the enforcement of their competition laws.[108] The authority of the Commission to enter into the agreement was subsequently challenged by France, supported by Spain and the Netherlands, and the ECJ found that the Commission did not have the power to to conclude (as distinct from negotiate) agreements with foreign countries.[109] The agreement was finally approved by means of a joint decision of the Council and Commission in 1995.[110]

The Agreement provides for: the reciprocal notification of cases under investigation by either authority, where they may affect the important interests of the other party (Article II); exchanges of information and periodic meetings between competition officials from each country (Article III); and rendering each other assistance and co-ordinating their enforce-ment activities (Article IV). The most significant provisions, however, are Articles V and VI. Article V is the 'positive comity' Article, providing the possibility for one authority to request the other to take enforcement action, and Article VI provides for 'traditional' or 'negative' comity, i.e. for each authority to take into account the important interests of the other in the course of its enforcement activities. (This concept was introduced above, in the context of the US cases, and it should be noted that Article VI seems to be less restrictive than the version which appears in *Hartford Fire Insurance*.)

Agreement between the Government of the USA and the Commission of the European Communities regarding the Application of their Competition Laws, 1991

Article V

Cooperation regarding anticompetitive activities in the territory of one Party that adversely affect the interests of the other Party

1. The Parties note that anticompetitive activities may occur within the territory of one Party that, in addition to violating that Party's competition laws, adversely affect important inter-ests of the other Party. The Parties agree that it is in both their interests to address anticom-petitive activities of this nature.

2. If a Party believes that anticompetitive activities carried out on the territory of the other Party are adversely affecting its important interests, the first Party may notify the other Party

---

[108] Agreement between the Government of the USA and the Commission of the European Communities regarding the application of their Competition Laws, 23 Sept. 1991 [1991] 4 CMLR 823, 30 ILM 1487.

[109] Case C–327/91, *France* v. *Commission* [1994] ECR I–3641, [1994] 5 CMLR 517.

[110] [1995] OJ L95/45.

and may request that the other Party's competition authorities initiate appropriate enforcement activities. The notification shall be as specific as possible about the nature of the anticompetitive activities and their effects on the interests of the notifying Party, and shall include an offer of such further information and other cooperation as the notifying Party is able to provide.

3.   Upon receipt of a notification under paragraph 2, and after such other discussion between the Parties as may be appropriate and useful in the circumstances, the competition authorities of the notified Party will consider whether or not to initiate enforcement activities, or to expand ongoing enforcement activities, with respect to the anticompetitive activities identified in the notification. The notified Party will advise the notifying Party of its decision. If enforcement activities are initiated, the notified Party will advise the notifying Party of their outcome and, to the extent possible, of significant interim developments.

4.   Nothing in this Article limits the discretion of the notified Party under its competition laws and enforcement policies as to whether or not to undertake enforcement activities with respect to the notified anticompetitive activities, or precludes the notifying Party from undertaking enforcement activities with respect to such anticompetitive activities.

Article VI

Avoidance of conflicts over enforcement activities

Within the framework of its own laws and to the extent compatible with its important interests, each Party will seek, at all stages in its enforcement activities, to take into account the important interests of the other Party. Each Party shall consider important interests of the other Party in decisions as to whether or not to initiate an investigation or proceeding, the scope of an investigation or proceeding, the nature of the remedies or penalties sought, and in other ways, as appropriate. In considering one another's important interests in the course of their enforcement activities, the Parties will take account of, but will not be limited to, the following principles:

1.   While an important interest of a Party may exist in the absence of official involvement by the Party with the activity in question, it is recognized that such interests would normally be reflected in antecedent laws, decisions or statements of policy by its competent authorities.

2.   A Party's important interests may be affected at any stage of enforcement activity by the other Party. The Parties recognize, however, that as a general matter the potential for adverse impact on one Party's important interests arising from enforcement activity by the other Party is less at the investigative stage and greater at the stage at which conduct is prohibited or penalized, or at which other forms of remedial orders are imposed.

3.   Where it appears that one Party's enforcement activities may adversely affect important interests of the other Party, the Parties will consider the following factors, in addition to any other factors that appear relevant in the circumstances, in seeking an appropriate accommodation of the competing interests:

     (a) the relative significance to the anticompetitive activities involved of conduct within the enforcing Party's territory as compared to conduct within the other Party's territory;

     (b) the presence or absence of a purpose on the part of those engaged in the anticompetitive activities to affect consumers, suppliers, or competitors within the enforcing Party's territory;

(c) the relative significance of the effects of the anticompetitive activities on the enforcing Party's interests as compared to the effects on the other Party's interests;

(d) the existence or absence of reasonable expectations that would be furthered or defeated by the enforcement activities;

(e) the degree of conflict or consistency between the enforcement activities and the other Party's laws or articulated economic policies; and

(f) the extent to which enforcement activities of the other Party with respect to the same persons, including judgments or undertakings resulting from such activities, may be affected.

The Competition Commissioner, writing in the *XXVIIIth Report on Competition Policy* said that this amounted to 'a commitment by the EU and the USA to cooperate with respect to antitrust enforcement, and not to act unilaterally and extraterritorially unless the avenues provided by comity have been exhausted'.[111]

The successful operation of the Agreement persuaded the parties to strengthen the positive comity provisions. In 1998, therefore, they signed the EU–US Positive Comity Agreement[112] which entered into force on 4 June 1998. This spells out more clearly the circumstances in which a request for positive comity will be made and the manner in which such requests should be treated. Article III provides:

Positive Comity

The competition authorities of a Requesting Party may request the competition authorities of a Requested Party to investigate and, if warranted, to remedy anticompetitive activities in accordance with the Requested Party's competition laws. Such a request may be made regardless of whether the activities also violate the Requesting Party's competition laws, and regardless of whether the competition authorities of the Requesting Party have commenced or contemplate taking enforcement activities under their own competition laws.

Article IV provides for investigations by the requesting party to be deferred or suspended in reliance on the requested party's enforcement. The effect of the 1998 Agreement is to create a presumption, as described by the Commission in its report on the application of the co-operation agreement for 1998:[113]

The 1998 EC/US Positive Comity Agreement, like the 1991 Agreement, does not alter existing law, nor does it require any change in existing law. However, it does create a presumption that when anticompetitive activities occur in the whole or in a substantial part of the territory of one of the parties and affect the interests of the other party, the latter 'will normally defer or suspend its enforcement activities in favour of' the former. This is expected to happen particularly when these anticompetitive activities do not have a direct, substantial and reasonably foreseeable impact on consumers in the territory of the party deferring or suspending its activities.

The presumption of deferral will only occur if the party in the territory of which the restrictive activities are occurring has jurisdiction over these activities and is prepared to deal actively and expeditiously with the matter. When dealing with the case that party will keep its counterpart closely

---

[111] Commissions *XXVIIth Report on Competition Policy* (Commission, 1998), Foreword, 5.
[112] [1998] OJ L173/28, [1999] 4 CMLR 502.
[113] At para. 3. See the *XXVIIIth Report on Competition Policy* (Commission, 1998), 315.

informed of any developments in the procedure, within the limits of its internal rules protecting confidentiality.

The new Agreement constitutes an important development, since it represents a commitment on the part of the European Union and the United States to cooperate with respect to antitrust enforcement in certain situations, rather than to seek to apply their antitrust laws extraterritorially.

It is important to note that because the EC merger rules do not allow for the deferral or suspension of action which the agreement envisages the EC merger rules are not within the 1998 agreement.[114]

b. THE APPLICATION OF THE AGREEMENTS

Both the EC and US authorities consider that their co-operation works well and has made a very positive contribution to competition law enforcement. Around forty cases a year are notified in each direction. The 1991 procedures worked particularly successfully in respect of the investigation into Microsoft in 1994.[115] The US Department of Justice (DOJ) and the Commission actively co-operated. However, there is a major drawback in the operation of the agreement. Articles VII of the 1991 Agreement and V of the 1998 Agreement provide for the maintenance of the confidentiality of information acquired by the authorities in the course of their investigations. Further, Articles IX and VII, respectively, provide that nothing in the agreements is to be interpreted in a manner which is inconsistent with the parties' existing laws. This greatly limits the information which the authorities may exchange.[116] It is notable that in the 1994 investigation Microsoft, which was happy to have the US and EC investigations combined as it was easier for the company to deal with the two authorities together, agreed to waive its rights to confidentiality and to allow information exchanges between the Commission and the DOJ.[117]

The existence of the co-operation agreement did not, however, prevent the 1997 dispute over the *Boeing/McDonnell Douglas* merger.[118] In that case the authorities *did* consult each other. In accordance with the provisions of the agreement the Commission and the Federal Trade Commission carried out the necessary notifications and consultations, and the Commission took into account the US concerns over its defence interests. In the end, however, as the Director General recognized, '[p]rocedures of notification and consultation and the principles of traditional and positive comity allow us to bring our respective approaches closer in cases of common interest but there exist no mechanism for resolving conflicts in cases of substantial divergence of analysis.'[119]

(ii) THE EC–CANADA CO-OPERATION AGREEMENT

Encouraged by the success of its agreement with the USA, the EC entered into a similar agreement with Canada which came into force on 29 April 1999. In particular, the Agree-

---

[114] Art. II(4)(a).

[115] Although because of the case brought by France (see *supra* n. 109) the agreement was not officially in force.

[116] See *supra* Chap. 14 for the question of confidentiality in EC competition procedure.

[117] See further C, Cocuzza and M. Montini, '*International Antitrust Co-operation in a Global Economy* [1998] *ECLR* 156; J. Parisi, *Enforcement Co-operation Among Antitrust Authorities* [1999] *ECLR* 133.

[118] See *supra* 1057–1059.

[119] Schaub, *supra* n. 91, 4.

ment contains (Articles V and VI), provisions similar to Articles V and VI of the 1991 Agreement including the principle of positive comity.[120]

C. MULTILATERAL CO-OPERATION

(i) GENERAL

There have been initiatives within various international fora aimed at formulating mechanisms for increasing co-operation over competition laws and avoiding conflicts. These are briefly described here. In (iv) below we consider the problems inherent in such multilateral international arrangements and ask whether it is possible to envisage the creation of an international competition law authority or a global merger authority.

(ii) UNCTAD AND THE OECD

The United Nations' Set of Multilaterally Agreed Equitable Principles and Rules for the Control of Restrictive Business Practices were adopted in 1980 under the auspices of UNCTAD[121] but provide only a voluntary, non-binding Code. In 1967 the OECD adopted a Recommendation that its member countries should co-operate with each other in the enforcement of their national competition laws.[122] This provides: for one country to notify another when the latter's important interests are affected by the former's investigation or enforcement; for countries to share information and to consult; for them to co-ordinate parallel investigations; for countries to assist one another in obtaining information inside each other's territory; and for countries to consider dealing with anti-competitive behaviour affecting their interests but occurring in another country's territory by requesting the latter's authorities to take action (positive comity). The bilateral agreements described in Section B above reflect these provisions but the 1991 EC–US Agreement was the first to include the 'positive comity' principle. In May 1998 the OECD (Committee of Competition Law and Policy) adopted a recommendation on hardcore cartels, aimed at strengthening the effectiveness and efficiency of the member countries' enforcement of their competition laws against such cartels.

(iii) THE WTO

The most significant developments currently, however, are taking place in relation to the World Trade Organization (WTO). When the WTO was being negotiated in 1993 a Draft International Antitrust Code was drawn up by a group of experts at the Max Planck Institute. This would have established an international antitrust regime.[123] The parties to the

---

[120] [1999] OJ L175, [1999] 5 CMLR 713.

[121] The United Nations Conference on Trade and Development.

[122] Amended, *inter alia* in 1995: OECD Doc.C(95)130/FINAL.

[123] For the details, see C Cocuzza and M Montini, 'International Antitrust Co-operation in a Global Economy' [1998] ECLR 156, 160–1; E.U. Petersmann, International Competition Rules for Governments and for Private Business (1996) 30 *J. World Trade* 5.

WTO did not agree to its adoption, however, and no agreement on international competition law was annexed to the WTO Charter. Promoted by the EC, the matter was later taken up at the First Ministerial Conference of the parties to the WTO in Singapore in 1996 and a Working Group on Trade and Competition Policy was set up in 1997. The first Chair of this Group was Professor Jenny of the French competition authority, Chair of the OECD Competition Law and Policy Committee.

In 1997 and 1998 the Working Group worked on a checklist of issues, of which the main elements were: the relationship between the objectives, principles, concepts, scope, and instruments of trade and competition policy and their relationship with development and economic growth; stocktaking and analysis of existing instruments, standards, and activities regarding trade and competition policy, including of experience with their application; and the interaction between trade and competition policy. In 1999 the Group examined three further topics: the relevance of the fundamental WTO principles of national treatment, transparency, and most-favoured-nation treatment to competition policy and vice versa; approaches to promoting co-operation and communication among members, including in the field of technical co-operation; and the contribution of competition policy to achieving the objectives of the WTO, including the promotion of international trade.

Ultimately, the question which has to be addressed is whether a multilateral framework on competition policy should be set up under the auspices of the WTO. The EU is at present a keen advocate of this. Its views were set out in a Discussion Document in March 1999, in preparation for the 1999 WTO Ministerial Conference in Seattle. The Document set outs its objectives as:

a) The introduction of a competition law by significant trading partners which still lack one, and agreement that competition law should in principle cover all the sectors of the economy;

b) Ensuring that competition law, and its enforcement, are based on core principles of efficiency, transparency, non-discrimination etc.;

c) Promoting a stricter enforcement policy in relation to anti-competitive practices with a significant impact on international trade and investment;

d) Promoting cooperation in the application of competition law to anti-competitive practices with an international dimension and limiting the risk of conflict arising from extraterritorial enforcement and fact-finding;

e) Reducing unnecessary costs and uncertainties for business arising from the application of different competition laws to the same international transactions.

Although many members of the WTO would like to see more co-operation among States in addressing anti-competitive practices, most have serious reservations about a multilateral framework. The USA, until recently, favoured the approach of bilateral or regional agreements rather than more wide-ranging multilateral structures.[124] In any event, the Seattle Ministerial Conference was suspended and the proposals about competition were not taken forward.

---

[124] Possibly because of its wariness of international organizations which have a limiting effect on their members' freedom of action. In September 2000 the US Assistant Attorney General, Antitrust Dept, DOJ, endorsed the idea of a multilateral organization (*not* within the WTO) to deal with international mergers: J. Klein, Time for a Global Competition Initiative, EC Merger Control, 10th Anniversary Conference, Brussels, 14 September 2000.

(iv) A GLOBAL COMPETITION LAW REGIME

The WTO provides the most obvious framework for the establishment of some type of international competition regime and its existing dispute – settlement mechanism provides a possible model. However, the problems currently facing the WTO vividly demonstrate how difficult it is to reach international consensus in the economic field when States are in such different stages of development and have such different interests. The requirement of the WTO is that all member states, except the very poorest, subscribe to its rights and obligations in exchange for trade liberalization. Prominent among the organization's short-comings, however, is that its rules do not sufficiently allow for socio-cultural and environmental criteria to be considered, and at least one voice has warned that it is essential to take account of socio-cultural divergences in any set of competition rules which are adopted at an international level.[125] Some developing countries have come to view the WTO as a 'rich man's club', run for the benefit of the world's most powerful trading blocs, although the bitterest disputes to date have been between the USA and the EC. Both caution and pragmatism would suggest that the present problems in the WTO need to be dealt with before a competition law element is added. However, more and more countries are adopting competition law regimes[126] and the capacity for conflict between them, should they all take extraterritorial jurisdiction, increases exponentially.

In the meantime, we live in what one EC official called a bipolar world, in which American antitrust is not the only show in town.[127] EC and US competition authorities have learned, on the whole, to co-operate bilaterally to their mutual advantage, but questions remain. There is the issue raised in *Gencor*, for example, whether the interests of consumers in America and Europe are necessarily identical to the interests of producer nations. The EC, however, remains committed to the belief that competition policy can deliver benefits to the whole global economy and that international co-operation is essential to enable it fully to do this. In the words of Faull:

I am not making extravagant moral claims for competition policy, but I do suggest that, if properly implemented, it undermines some of the less savoury features of the economies whose bubbles are bursting. Of course, competition policy is no guarantee against recession, stock market crashes, corruption, fraud or organised crime. However, in a competitive market, the commercial decisions most likely to prove successful are those taken on the basis of economic analysis and judgment, not in pursuit of patronage, preference or preferment. We should be advocating a role for competition policy in reconstructing the economies in crisis. Then we can start to build a network of competition among authorities all over the word, united around common international standards, concentrating on the defence of competition in domestic markets and working together to bring competition to world trade as well.

---

[125] W. Pape, 'Socio-Cultural Differences and International Competition Law' (1999) 5 *ELJ* 438.

[126] The EU Discussion Paper for the 1999 Ministerial Conference (see *supra* 1072) gave the figure as 70 WTO members with such regimes, with further countries proceeding to put one in place.

[127] Jonathan Faull, speaking at the Fordham Corporate Law Institute, New York, 22–23 Oct. 1998.

6. FURTHER READING

A. BOOKS

BROWNLIE, I., *Principles of Public International Law* (5th edn. Oxford University Press, 1998)

COOK, C.J., and KERSE, C.S., *EC Merger Control* (3rd edn., Sweet and Maxwell, 2000)

HIGGINS, R., *Problems and Process* (1994), Chapter 4.

JENNINGS R.Y., and WATTS A., (eds.) *Oppenheim's International Law* (9th edn.), (Longman, 1992), i.

SCHACHTER, O., *International Law in Theory and Practice* (Nijhoff, 1991), Chapter XII

B. ARTICLES

AKEHURST, M., 'Jurisdiction in International Law' (1972–3) 46 *BYIL*, 145

BAVASSO, A., 'Boeing/McDonnell Douglas: Did the Commission Fly Too High?' [1998] *ECLR* 243

BISHOP, B., 'Editorial, The Boeing/McDonnell Douglas Merger" [1997] *ECLR* 417

BOWETT, D.W., 'Jurisdiction: Changing Problems of Authority over Activities and Resources' 1982 53 BYIL 1

COCUZZA C., and MONTINI, M., 'International Antitrust Co-operation in a Global Economy' [1998] *ECLR* 156

CHARLTON, H., 'EC Competition Law: The New Regime under the EEA Agreement' [1994] *ECLR* 55

COLLINS, L., 'Blocking and Clawback Statutes' [1986] *JBL* 372 and 452

FERRY, J.E., 'Towards Completing the Charm: The Woodpulp Judgment' [1989] *ECLR* 58

FOX, E., 'The Merger Regulation and its Territorial Reach' [1999] *ECLR* 334

GERVEN, W. van, 'EC Jurisdiction in Antitrust Matters: The Wood Pulp Judgment' [1989] *Fordham Corporate Law Institute* 451

GRIFFIN, J., 'Reactions to U.S. Assertions of Extraterritorial Jurisdiction' [1998] *ECLR* 64

JENNINGS, R.Y., 'Extraterritorial Jurisdiction and the United States Antitrust Laws' (1957) 33 *BYIL* 146

KACZOROWSKA, A., 'International Competition Law in the Context of Global Capitalism' [2000] *ECLR* 117

LANGE D.F.G., and SANDAGE J.B., 'The Wood Pulp Decision' (1989) 26 *CMLRev.* 137

MANN, F.A., 'The Doctrine of Jurisdiction in International Law' (1964) 111 *RdC* 1

—— 'Casenote', (1973) 22 *ICLQ* 35

—— 'Responsibility of Parent Companies for Foreign Subsidiaries' in C. Olmstead (ed), *Extra-territorial Application of Laws and Responses Thereto* (ESC Publishing, 1984), 156

—— 'The Doctrine of International Jurisdiction Revisited After Twenty Years,' (1984) 186 *RdC* 9

MEESSEN, K.M., 'Antitrust Jurisdiction under Customary International Law' (1984) 78 *AJIL* 783

PAPE, W., 'Socio-Cultural Differences and International Competition Law' (1999) 5 *ELJ* 438

PARISI, J., 'Enforcement Co-operation Among Antitrust Authorities' [1999] *ECLR* 133

PETERSMANN, E.U., 'International Competition Rules for Governments and for Private Business' (1996) 30 *Journ. World Trade Law* 5

REYNOLDS, R.M., SICILIAN, J., and WELLMAN, P.S. 'The Extraterritorial Application of the US Antitrust Laws to Criminal Conspiracies' [1998] *ECLR* 151

ROBERTSON A., and DEMETRIOU, M., '"But that was in Another Country"': The Extraterritorial Application of US Antitrust Laws in the US Supreme Court' (1994) 43 *ICLQ* 417

ROTH, P.M., 'Reasonable Extraterritoriality:

Correcting the "Balance of Interests"' (1992) 41 *ICLQ* 245

SLOT P.J., and GRABANDI, E., 'Extraterritoriality and Jurisdiction' (1986) 23 *CMLRev.* 545

TORREMANS, P., 'Extraterritorial Application of EC and US Competition Law' (1996) 21 *ELRev.* 280

APPENDIX 1

GLOSSARY OF ECONOMIC TERMS

The following is a glossary of some of the economic terms used in competition law.

Absolute territorial protection

Absolute territorial protection is a situation where a dealer in goods of a particular brand in a particular territory is protected from competition from other sellers. It means that there is no other authorized dealer in that territory, customers there cannot obtain the goods from dealers in other territories or from third parties importing the goods into the protected territory, and parallel importing is not possible. It applies similarly in the context of licences of intellectual property rights. Absolute territorial protection is seldom achievable and will normally infringe the competition rules.

Arbitrage

Arbitrage is the exploitation of price differences by buying where prices are low and selling where they are higher.

Barriers to entry and exit

Barriers to entry are factors which prevent a firm entering a market and competing with the existing (incumbent) supplier. *Barriers to exit* are factors which make it difficult for firms to leave markets. The exact definition of barriers to entry is a matter of much controversy, and is discussed in Chapter 1.

Chicago school

Free-market and monetarist economic thinking developed from ideas emanating from the University of Chicago. Its school of antitrust analysis stemmed from work done there during the 1960s. Its radical ideas became very influential, particularly in the USA during the Reagan presidency. The leading proponents include George Stigler, Robert Bork, and Richard Posner. It holds that efficiency should be the only goal of antitrust laws, in particular the maximization of allocative efficiency, and that classical price theory can define the circumstances in which this will occur. The Chicago school holds that most markets are competitive, even with relatively few suppliers; monopoly tends to be self-correcting and government regulation provides the only real barriers to entry; economies of scale are present in more industries than previously thought; firms are profit-maximizers; and vertical restraints should not usually be regulated. This leads to a belief in minimal intervention by antitrust law. Chicago holds that the decision that efficiency should be the only goal of antitrust is non-ideological and non-political. Chicago ideas remain influential although some of the economic models on which they are based have now been questioned.

Concentration ratio

The *concentration ratio* describes how concentrated a market is, i.e. whether an industry is dominated by a few large firms or made up of many small firms. There can be a number of concentration ratios for any market, depending on how many firms are brought into the calculation. The two-firm concentration ratio relates to the market shares of the two leading firms, the three-firm concentration ratio relates to the market shares of the leading three firms, and so on. The formula called the *Herfindahl-Hirschman Index*, or *HHI*, takes account of *all* the firms in the market. The index is given by the sum of the squares of the market shares of all the firms. The formula is used, *inter alia*, by the US Department of Justice in its control of mergers.

Contestable markets

A theory which stems from W.J. Baumol in the early 1980s. Unlike perfect competition it focuses not on how many firms are in the market, but on the ease with which firms can enter and leave markets. In a perfectly contestable market entry and exit are costless and hit-and-run entry possible. The term is used to describe markets where potential competition may exert an influence on the way incumbent firms behave.

Economies of scale

Economies of scale are factors which cause the average cost of producing a commodity to fall when more of it is produced. *Minimum efficient scale (MES)* is the scale of production at which further increases in scale would not lead to lower costs in the production of each unit.

Economic efficiency

In economic terms *efficiency* means a situation in which no one can be made any better off without someone being made worse off (known as *pareto optimal* after the Italian economist Vilfredo Pareto who developed the theory). *Productive efficiency* means that output is being produced at the lowest possible cost. *Allocative efficiency* means that resources are allocated to the production of goods and services in the way that society most values.

Free-rider

Free-riding is taking advantage of something for which someone else has paid or of something which someone else has done. It is a feature of human life in general, but in competition law particularly arises in connection with dealers who sell goods at low prices by keeping down their own costs and who leave the expenses of promoting and advertising the goods to others. The latter therefore incur higher costs and have to sell at higher prices, but are then undercut by the free-riders who have taken advantage of their investment. Parallel importers (see below) may free-ride on the investment of the authorized dealers in the country of import.

Game theory

A branch of economics which represents decision-making as if it were a game with players, pay-offs, and strategies. It attempts to predict the outcome of situations by looking at the state of knowledge of the 'players' and their knowledge of the past. It is particularly relevant to the behaviour of oligopolistic markets.

Harvard school

A school of antitrust analysis stemming from the structure ▸ conduct ▸ performance paradigm developed in the 1930s. This means that the structure of the market leads to certain types of conduct from the undertakings on that market which leads to them performing in certain ways, i.e. the number of firms on the market, their concentration etc. determine the way in which firms compete, and this in turn determines their performance (i.e. profitability).

Horizontal and vertical agreements

A *horizontal agreement* is one entered into between parties who operate at the same level of the market e.g. an agreement between competing manufacturers or between competing retailers.
A *vertical agreement* is one entered into by parties operating at different levels of the market, e.g. between a manufacturer and the shop which sells its products.

Input

An input is a factor of production, i.e. any good or service used to produce a firm's output.

Inter-brand and intra-brand competition

Inter-brand competition is competition between different brands of the same goods, e.g. between Chanel and Christian Dior perfume.

Intra-brand competition is competition between those operating at the same level of the market in relation to the same brand, such as different distributors of the same brand, e.g. competition between Selfridges and John Lewis in the sale of Chanel perfume.

Long and short run (in relation to costs)

The *long run* is the period long enough for the firm to adjust all its inputs to a change in conditions.

The *short run* is the period in which the firm can only partially adjust its inputs to a change in conditions.

Marginal cost

Marginal cost is the increase in a firm's total costs caused by producing one extra unit.

Marginal revenue

This is the increase in the total revenue a firm receives from the sale of one extra unit of output.

Market power

This is the ability of a firm to exercise significant influence over price and output in a particular market. It is the central concept in competition law.

Monopoly

A monopoly is a market in which there is only one supplier.

A *statutory monopoly* is where there is only one supplier because of state regulation.

A *natural monopoly* is a market in which there are very large economies of scale and the (efficient) existence of more than one producer is precluded, e.g utilities which require a network of pipes or cables.

'Monopoly' is sometimes used as a general term to include situations where there *is* more than one supplier but a particular supplier has significant market power.

New industrial organization economics

This is a modern industrial organization theory which concentrates less on market structure and more on strategic issues and the strategic behaviour of firms.

Oligopoly

An oligopoly is a market in which there is no single dominant firm but a few firms share the market between them. Each firm will recognize that the price it can command depends not just on its own output but on the actions of the others.

Parallel importing

Parallel importing is buying goods in one Member State and selling them in another where they are more expensive. It undermines the distribution arrangements of suppliers whose goods are placed on the market at different prices in different Member States. A parallel importer will buy the goods in the State where they are cheaper and sell them in the State of import at a price which undercuts the supplier's authorized distributors. Absolute territorial protection (above) means that a territory is protected from the activities of parallel importers.

Perfect competition

Perfect competition is a market state in which there is a multitude of buyers and sellers of a homogeneous product, all with perfect information, and there are no barriers to entry or exit. Buyers and sellers are all so small that none of them has any individual impact on the market price. Each seller is assumed to wish to maximize profits and so will expand production until marginal cost equals market price. There is productive and allocative efficiency (see above) and consumer welfare is maximized.

Price elasticity of demand and cross-price elasticity of demand

Price elasticity of demand is the extent to which demand is sensitive to price. It is measured by dividing the percentage change in the quantity of a good demanded by the corresponding percentage change in its price. Demand is said to be elastic if price elasticity is more negative than -1 and inelastic if it is between -1 and 0. *Cross-price elasticity of demand* is the extent to which a change in the price of one product affects the demand for *another*. It is measured by the percentage change in the quantity of good y demanded divided by the corresponding percentage change in the price of good x. The cross-elasticity is positive if the rise in the price of x results in a rise in demand for y. It will therefore tend to be positive where x and y are substitutes for one another. It is negative if the rise in the price of x leads to a fall in the demand for y: that will tend to happen when x and y are complementary to each other (such as cars and petrol).

Relevant market

Competition law revolves around the idea of *relevant markets*. Markets are defined in order to determine which products and services are in competition with each other. For the purpose of competition law a relevant market comprises all the products and services which provide reasonable substitutes for one another. There are three aspects to the relevant market: product/service, geographic, and temporal.

Resale price maintenance

This is a restriction placed by a supplier on the price at which its distributors may sell the supplier's goods. It usually involves the stipulation of a *minimum* price.

Sunk costs

Sunk costs are costs which were incurred in the past and are irrecoverable (i.e. bygones are bygones).

Exogenous sunk costs are those which must be incurred by any one entering the market, e.g. the acquisition of a plant of minimum efficient scale.

Endogenous sunk costs are those stemming from decisions by the firm within its discretion, e.g. the level of advertising expenditure.

Further reading:

G. Bannock, R. Barder, and E. Davis (eds.) *Penguin Dictionary of Economics* (6th edn; Penguin, 1998)

D. Begg, S. Fischer, and R. Dornbusch, *Economics* (5th edn; (McGraw-Hill, 1997)

APPENDIX 2

TREATY ESTABLISHING THE EUROPEAN COMMUNITY

Article 2 (ex Article 2) The Community shall have as its task, by establishing a common market and an economic and monetary union and by implementing common policies or activities referred to in Articles 3 and 4, to promote throughout the Community a harmonious, balanced and sustainable development of economic activities, a high level of employment and of social protection, equality between men and women, sustainable and non-inflationary growth, a high degree of competitiveness and convergence of economic performance, a high level of protection and improvement of the quality of the environment, the raising of the standard of living and quality of life, and economic and social cohesion and solidarity among Member States.

TITLE VI. (EX TITLE V) COMMON RULES ON COMPETITION, TAXATION AND APPROXIMATION OF LAWS
Chapter 1: Rules on Competition

SECTION 1: RULES APPLYING TO UNDERTAKINGS

Article 81 (ex Article 85) 1. The following shall be prohibited as incompatible with the common market: all agreements between undertakings, decisions by associations of undertakings and concerted practices which may affect trade between Member States and which have as their object or effect the prevention, restriction or distortion of competition within the common market, and in particular those which:

(a) directly or indirectly fix purchase or selling prices or any other trading conditions;
(b) limit or control production, markets, technical development, or investment;
(c) share markets or sources of supply;
(d) apply dissimilar conditions to equivalent transactions with other trading parties, thereby placing them at a competitive disadvantage;
(e) make the conclusion of contracts subject to acceptance by the other parties of supplementary obligations which, by their nature or according to commercial usage, have no connection with the subject of such contracts.

2. Any agreements or decisions prohibited pursuant to this Article shall be automatically void.

3. The provisions of paragraph 1 may, however, be declared inapplicable in the case of:

— any agreement or category of agreements between undertakings;
— any decision or category of decisions by associations of undertakings;
— any concerted practice or category of concerted practices,

which contributes to improving the production or distribution of goods or to promoting technical or economic progress, while allowing consumers a fair share of the resulting benefit, and which does not:

(a) impose on the undertakings concerned restrictions which are not indispensable to the attainment of these objectives;
(b) afford such undertakings the possibility of eliminating competition in respect of a substantial part of the products in question.

Article 82 (ex Article 86) Any abuse by one or more undertakings of a dominant position within the common market or in a substantial part of it shall be prohibited as incompatible with the common market insofar as it may affect trade between Member States.

Such abuse may, in particular, consist in:

(a) directly or indirectly imposing unfair purchase or selling prices or other unfair trading conditions;
(b) limiting production, markets or technical development to the prejudice of consumers;
(c) applying dissimilar conditions to equivalent transactions with other trading parties, thereby placing them at a competitive disadvantage;
(d) making the conclusion of contracts subject to acceptance by the other parties of supplementary obligations which, by their nature or according to commercial usage, have no connection with the subject of such contracts.

Article 83 (ex Article 87) 1. The appropriate regulations or directives to give effect to the principles set out in Articles 81 and 82 shall be laid down by the Council, acting by a qualified majority on a proposal from the Commission and after consulting the European Parliament.

2. The regulations or directives referred to in paragraph 1 shall be designed in particular:

(a) to ensure compliance with the prohibitions laid down in Article 81(1) and in Article 82 by making provision for fines and periodic penalty payments;
(b) to lay down detailed rules for the application of Article 81(3), taking into account the need to ensure effective supervision on the one hand, and to simplify administration to the greatest possible extent on the other;
(c) to define, if need be, in the various branches of the economy, the scope of the provisions of Articles 81 and 82;
(d) to define the respective functions of the Commission and of the Court of Justice in applying the provisions laid down in this paragraph;
(e) to determine the relationship between national laws and the provisions contained in this Section or adopted pursuant to this Article.

Article 84 (ex Article 88) Until the entry into force of the provisions adopted in pursuance of Article 83, the authorities in Member States shall rule on the admissibility of agreements, decisions and concerted practices and on abuse of a dominant position in the common market in accordance with the law of their country and with the provisions of Article 81, in particular paragraph 3, and of Article 82.

Article 85 (ex Article 89) 1. Without prejudice to Article 84, the Commission shall ensure the application of the principles laid down in Articles 81 and 82. On application by a Member State or on its own initiative, and in cooperation with the competent authorities in the Member States, who shall give it their assistance, the Commission shall investigate cases of suspected infringement of these principles. If it finds that there has been an infringement, it shall propose appropriate measures to bring it to an end.

2. If the infringement is not brought to an end, the Commission shall record such infringement of the principles in a reasoned decision. The Commission may publish its decision and authorise Member States to take the measures, the conditions and details of which it shall determine, needed to remedy the situation.

Article 86 (ex Article 90) 1. In the case of public undertakings and undertakings to which Member States grant special or exclusive rights, Member States shall neither enact nor maintain in force any measure contrary to the rules contained in this Treaty, in particular to those rules provided for in Article 12 and Articles 81 to 89.

2. Undertakings entrusted with the operation of services of general economic interest or having the character of a revenue-producing monopoly shall be subject to the rules contained in this Treaty, in particular to the rules on competition, insofar as the application of such rules does not obstruct the performance, in law or in fact, of the particular tasks assigned to them. The development of trade must not be affected to such an extent as would be contrary to the interests of the Community.

3. The Commission shall ensure the application of the provisions of this Article and shall, where necessary, address appropriate directives or decisions to Member States.

REGULATION NO 17

First Regulation implementing Articles 85 and 86 [now 81 and 82] of the Treaty

[1959–62] OJ Spec.Ed 87

as last amended by Decision 95/1/EC. [1995] OJ L1/1 and by Regulation 1216/99 OJ L148/5[1]

THE COUNCIL OF THE EUROPEAN ECONOMIC COMMUNITY,

Having regard to the Treaty establishing the European Economic Community, and in particular Article [83] thereof;
Having regard to the proposal from the Commission;
Having regard to the Opinion of the Economic and Social Committee;
Having regard to the Opinion of the European Parliament;
Whereas, in order to establish a system ensuring that competition shall not be distorted in

---

[1] Regulation 17 contains references to units of accounts. These should now be read as references to Euro by virtue of Council Regulation 3308/80 [1980] OJ L345/1 and Council Regulation 1103/97 [1997] OJ L162/1.

the common market, it is necessary to provide for balanced application of Articles [81] and [82] in a uniform manner in the Member States;

Whereas in establishing the rules for applying Article [81(3)] account must be taken of the need to ensure effective supervision and to simplify administration to the greatest possible extent;

Whereas it is accordingly necessary to make it obligatory, as a general principle, for undertakings which seek application of Article [81(3)] to notify to the Commission their agreements, decisions and concerted practices;

Whereas, on the one hand, such agreements, decisions and concerted practices are probably very numerous and cannot therefore all be examined at the same time and, on the other hand, some of them have special features which may make them less prejudicial to the development of the common market;

Whereas there is consequently a need to make more flexible arrangements for the time being in respect of certain categories of agreement, decision and concerted practice without prejudging their validity under Article [81];

Whereas it may be in the interest of undertakings to know whether any agreements, decisions or practices to which they are party, or propose to become party, may lead to action on the part of the Commission pursuant to Article [81(1)] or Article [82];

Whereas, in order to secure uniform application of Articles [81] and [82] in the common market, rules must be made under which the Commission, acting in close and constant liaison with the competent authorities of the Member States, may take the requisite measures for applying those Articles;

Whereas for this purpose the Commission must have the co-operation of the competent authorities of the Member States and be empowered, throughout the common market, to require such information to be supplied and to undertake such investigations as are necessary to bring to light any agreement, decision or concerted practice prohibited by Article [81(1)] or any abuse of a dominant position prohibited by Article [82];

Whereas, in order to carry out its duty of ensuring that the provisions of the Treaty are applied, the Commission must be empowered to address to undertakings or associations of undertakings recommendations and decisions for the purpose of bringing to an end infringements of Articles [81] and [82];

Whereas compliance with Articles [81] and [82] and the fulfilment of obligations imposed on undertakings and associations of undertakings under this Regulation must be enforceable by means of fines and periodic penalty payments;

Whereas undertakings concerned must be accorded the right to be heard by the Commission, third parties whose interests may be affected by a decision must be given the opportunity of submitting their comments beforehand, and it must be ensured that wide publicity is given to decisions taken;

Whereas all decisions taken by the Commission under this Regulation are subject to review by the Court of Justice under the conditions specified in the Treaty; whereas it is moreover desirable to confer upon the Court of Justice, pursuant to Article [229], unlimited jurisdiction in respect of decisions under which the Commission imposes fines or periodic penalty payments;

Whereas this Regulation may enter into force without prejudice to any other provisions that may hereafter be adopted pursuant to Article [83];

HAS ADOPTED THIS REGULATION:

Article 1
Basic provision

Without prejudice to Articles 6, 7 and 23 of this Regulation, agreements, decisions and concerted practices of the kind described in Article [81(1)] of the Treaty and the abuse of a dominant position in the market, within the meaning of Article [82] of the Treaty, shall be prohibited, no prior decision to that effect being required.

Article 2
Negative clearance

Upon application by the undertakings or associations of undertakings concerned, the Commission may certify that, on the basis of the facts in its possession, there are no grounds under Article [81(1)] or Article [82] of the Treaty for action on its part in respect of an agreement, decision or practice.

Article 3
Termination of infringements

1. Where the Commission, upon application or upon its own initiative, finds that there is infringement of Article [81] or Article [82] of the Treaty, it may by decision require the undertakings or associations of undertakings concerned to bring such infringement to an end.

2. Those entitled to make application are:

(a)   Member States;
(b)   natural or legal persons who claim a legitimate interest.

3. Without prejudice to the other provisions of this Regulation, the Commission may, before taking a decision under paragraph 1, address to the undertakings or associations of undertakings concerned recommendations for termination of the infringement.

Article 4
Notification of new agreements, decisions and practices

1. Agreements, decisions and concerted practices of the kind described in Article [81(1)] of the Treaty which come into existence after the entry into force of this Regulation and in respect of which the parties seek application of Article [81 (3)] must be notified to the Commission. Until they have been notified, no decision in application of Article [81(3)] may be taken.

2. Paragraph 1 shall not apply to agreements, decisions or concerted practices where:

(1)   the only parties thereto are undertakings from one Member State and the agreements, decisions or practices do not relate either to imports or to exports between Member States;

[(2)   (a)   the agreements or concerted practices are entered into by two or more undertakings, each operating, for the purposes of the agreement, at a different level of the production or distribution chain, and relate to the conditions under which the parties may purchase, sell or resell certain goods or services;

(b)   not more than two undertakings are party thereto, and the agreements only impose restrictions on the exercise of the rights of the assignee or user of industrial property rights, in particular patents, utility models, designs or trade marks, or of the person entitled under a contract to the assignment, or grant, of the right to use a method of manufacture or knowledge relating to the use and to the application of industrial processes;][2]

(3) they have as their sole object:

(a) the development or uniform application of standards or types; or
(b) joint research and development;
(c) specialisation in the manufacture of products, including agreements necessary for achieving this:
— where the products which are the subject of specialisation do not, in a substantial part of the common market, represent more than 15% of the volume of business done in identical products or those considered by consumers to be similar by reason of their characteristics, price and use, and
— where the total annual turnover of the participating undertakings does not exceed 200 million unit of account.

These agreements, decisions and practices may be notified to the Commission.

Article 5
Notification of existing agreements, decisions and practices

1. Agreements, decisions and concerted practices of the kind described in Article [81(1)] of the Treaty which are in existence at the date of entry into force of this Regulation and in respect of which the parties seek application of Article [81(3)] shall be notified to the Commission before 1 August 1962.
2. Paragraph 1 shall not apply to agreements, decisions or concerted practices falling within Article 4 (2); these may be notified to the Commission.

Article 6
Decisions pursuant to Article [81 (3)]

1. Whenever the Commission takes a decision pursuant to Article [81(3)] of the Treaty, it shall specify therein the date from which the decision shall take effect. Such date shall not be earlier than the date of notification.

2. The second sentence of paragraph 1 shall not apply to agreements, decisions or concerted practices falling within Article 4 (2) and Article 5 (2), nor to those falling within Article 5 (1) which have been notified within the time limit specified in Article 5 (1).

Article 7
Special provisions for existing agreements, decisions and practices

1. Where agreements, decisions and concerted practices in existence at the date of entry into force of this Regulation and notified before 1 August 1962 do not satisfy the requirements of Article [81(3)] of the Treaty and the undertakings or associations of undertakings concerned cease to give effect to them or modify them in such manner that they no longer fall

---

[2] Article 4(2)(2) was amended by Council Regulation 1216/99 [OJ] 1999 L148/5.

within the prohibition contained in Article [81(1)] or that they satisfy the requirements of Article [81(3)], the prohibition contained in Article [81(1)] shall apply only for a period fixed by the Commission. A decision by the Commission pursuant to the foregoing sentence shall not apply as against undertakings and associations of undertakings which did not expressly consent to the notification.

2. Paragraph 1 shall apply to agreements, decisions and concerted practices falling within Article 4 (2) which are in existence at the date of entry into force of this Regulation if they are notified before 1 January 1964.

Article 8
Duration and revocation of decisions under Article [81 (3)]

1. A decision in application of Article [81(3)] of the Treaty shall be issued for a specified period and conditions and obligations may be attached thereto.

2. A decision may on application be renewed if the requirements of Article [81(3)] of the Treaty continue to be satisfied.

3. The Commission may revoke or amend its decision or prohibit specified acts by the parties:

(a) where there has been a change in any of the facts which were basic to the making of the decision;
(b) where the parties commit a breach of any obligation attached to the decision;
(c) where the decision is based on incorrect information or was induced by deceit;
(d) where the parties abuse the exemption from the provisions of Article [81(1)] of the Treaty granted to them by the decision.

In cases to which subparagraphs (b), (c) or (d) apply, the decision may be revoked with retroactive effect.

Article 9
Powers

1. Subject to review of its decision by the Court of Justice, the Commission shall have sole power to declare Article [81(1)] inapplicable pursuant to Article [81(3)] of the Treaty.

2. The Commission shall have power to apply Article [81(1)] and Article [82] of the Treaty; this power may be exercised notwithstanding that the time limits specified in Article 5 (1) and in Article 7 (2) relating to notification have not expired.

3. As long as the Commission has not initiated any procedure under Articles 2, 3 or 6, the authorities of the Member States shall remain competent to apply Article [81(1)] and Article [82] in accordance with Article 88 of the Treaty; they shall remain competent in this respect notwithstanding that the time limits specified in Article 5 (1) and in Article 7 (2) relating to notification have not expired.

Article 10
Liaison with the authorities of the Member States

1. The Commission shall forthwith transmit to the competent authorities of the Member

States a copy of the applications and notifications together with copies of the most important documents lodged with the Commission for the purpose of establishing the existence of infringements of Articles [81] or [82] of the Treaty or of obtaining negative clearance or a decision in application of Article [81(3)].

2. The Commission shall carry out the procedure set out in paragraph 1 in close and constant liaison with the competent authorities of the Member States; such authorities shall have the right to express their views upon that procedure.

3. An Advisory Committee on Restrictive Practices and Monopolies shall be consulted prior to the taking of any decision following upon a procedure under paragraph 1, and of any decision concerning the renewal, amendment or revocation of a decision pursuant to Article [81(3)] of the Treaty.

4. The Advisory Committee shall be composed of officials competent in the matter of restrictive practices and monopolies. Each Member State shall appoint an official to represent it who, if prevented from attending, may be replaced by another official.

5. The consultation shall take place at a joint meeting convened by the Commission; such meeting shall be held not earlier than fourteen days after dispatch of the notice convening it. The notice shall, in respect of each case to be examined, be accompanied by a summary of the case together with an indication of the most important documents, and a preliminary draft decision.

6. The Advisory Committee may deliver an opinion notwithstanding that some of its members or their alternates are not present. A report of the outcome of the consultative proceedings shall be annexed to the draft decision. It shall not be made public.

Article 11
Requests for information

1. In carrying out the duties assigned to it by Article [85] and by provisions adopted under Article [83] of the Treaty, the Commission may obtain all necessary information from the Governments and competent authorities of the Member States and from undertakings and associations of undertakings.

2. When sending a request for information to an undertaking or association of undertakings, the Commission shall at the same time forward a copy of the request to the competent authority of the Member State in whose territory the seat of the undertaking or association of undertakings is situated.

3. In its request the Commission shall state the legal basis and the purpose of the request and also the penalties provided for in Article 15 (1) (b) for supplying incorrect information.

4. The owners of the undertakings or their representatives and, in the case of legal persons, companies or firms, or of associations having no legal personality, the persons authorised to represent them by law or by their constitution shall supply the information requested.

5. Where an undertaking or association of undertakings does not supply the information requested within the time limit fixed by the Commission, or supplies incomplete information, the Commission shall by decision require the information to be supplied. The decision shall specify what information is required, fix an appropriate time limit within which it is to

be supplied and indicate the penalties provided for in Article 15 (1) (b) and Article 16 (1) (c) and the right to have the decision reviewed by the Court of Justice.

6. The Commission shall at the same time forward a copy of its decision to the competent authority of the Member State in whose territory the seat of the undertaking or association of undertakings is situated.

Article 12
Inquiry into sectors of the economy

1. If in any sector of the economy the trend of trade between Member States, price movements, inflexibility of prices or other circumstances suggest that in the economic sector concerned competition is being restricted or distorted within the common market, the Commission may decide to conduct a general inquiry into that economic sector and in the course thereof may request undertakings in the sector concerned to supply the information necessary for giving effect to the principles formulated in Articles [81] and [82] of the Treaty and for carrying out the duties entrusted to the Commission.

2. The Commission may in particular request every undertaking or association of undertakings in the economic sector concerned to communicate to it all agreements, decisions and concerted practices which are exempt from notification by virtue of Article 4(2) and Article 5(2).

3. When making inquiries pursuant to paragraph 2, the Commission shall also request undertakings or groups of undertakings whose size suggests that they occupy a dominant position within the common market or a substantial part thereof to supply to the Commission such particulars of the structure of the undertakings and of their behaviour as are requisite to an appraisal of their position in the light of Article [82] of the Treaty.

4. Article 10 (3) to (6) and Articles 11, 13 and 14 shall apply correspondingly.

Article 13
Investigations by the authorities of the Member States

1. At the request of the Commission, the competent authorities of the Member States shall undertake the investigations which the Commission considers to be necessary under Article 14 (1), or which it has ordered by decision pursuant to Article 14 (3). The officials of the competent authorities of the Member States responsible for conducting these investigations shall exercise their powers upon production of an authorisation in writing issued by the competent authority of the Member State in whose territory the investigation is to be made. Such authorisation shall specify the subject matter and purpose of the investigation.

2. If so requested by the Commission or by the competent authority of the Member State in whose territory the investigation is to be made, the officials of the Commission may assist the officials of such authorities in carrying out their duties.

Article 14
Investigating powers of the Commission

1. In carrying out the duties assigned to it by Article [85] and by provisions adopted under Article [83] of the Treaty, the Commission may undertake all necessary investigations into

undertakings and associations of undertakings. To this end the officials authorised by the Commission are empowered:

(a)   to examine the books and other business records;
(b)   to take copies of or extracts from the books and business records;
(c)   to ask for oral explanations on the spot;
(d)   to enter any premises; land and means of transport of undertakings.

2. The officials of the Commission authorised for the purpose of these investigations shall exercise their powers upon production of an authorisation in writing specifying the subject matter and purpose of the investigation and the penalties provided for in Article 15 (1) (c) in cases where production of the required books or other business records is incomplete. In good time before the investigation, the Commission shall inform the competent authority of the Member State in whose territory the same is to be made of the investigation and of the identity of the authorised officials.

3. Undertakings and associations of undertakings shall submit to investigations ordered by decision of the Commission. The decision shall specify the subject matter and purpose of the investigation, appoint the date on which it is to begin and indicate the penalties provided for in Article 15 (1) (c) and Article 16 (1) (d) and the right to have the decision reviewed by the Court of Justice.

4.   The Commission shall take decisions referred to in paragraph 3 after consultation with the competent authority of the Member State in whose territory the investigation is to be made.

5. Officials of the competent authority of the Member State in whose territory the investigation is to be made may, at the request of such authority or of the Commission, assist the officials of the Commission in carrying out their duties.

6. Where an undertaking opposes an investigation ordered pursuant to this Article, the Member State concerned shall afford the necessary assistance to the officials authorised by the Commission to enable them to make their investigation. Member States shall, after consultation with the Commission, take the necessary measures to this end before 1 October 1962.

Article 15
Fines

1. The Commission may by decision impose on undertakings or associations of undertakings fines of from 100 to 5000 units of account where, intentionally or negligently:

(a)   they supply incorrect or misleading information in an application pursuant to Article 2 or in a notification pursuant to Articles 4 or 5 ; or
(b)   they supply incorrect information in response to a request made pursuant to Article 11(3) or (5) or to Article 12, or do not supply information within the time limit fixed by a decision taken under Article 11(5); or
(c)   they produce the required books or other business records in incomplete form during investigations under Article 13 or 14, or refuse to submit to an investigation ordered by decision issued in implementation of Article 14 (3).

2. The Commission may by decision impose on undertakings or associations of undertakings fines of from 1000 to 1 000 000 units of account, or a sum in excess thereof but not exceeding 10% of the turnover in the preceding business year of each of the undertakings participating in the infringement where, either intentionally or negligently:

(a)   they infringe Article [81(1)] or Article [82] of the Treaty; or
(b)   they commit a breach of any obligation imposed pursuant to Article 8 (1).

In fixing the amount of the fine, regard shall be had both to the gravity and to the duration of the infringement.

3. Article 10(3) to (6) shall apply.

4. Decisions taken pursuant to paragraphs 1 and 2 shall not be of a criminal law nature.

5. The fines provided for in paragraph 2 (a) shall not be imposed in respect of acts taking place:

(a)   after notification to the Commission and before its decision in application of Article [81(3)] of the Treaty, provided they fall within the limits of the activity described in the notification;
(b)   before notification and in the course of agreements, decisions or concerted practices in existence at the date of entry into force of this Regulation, provided that notification was effected within the time limits specified in Article 5 (1) and Article 7 (2).

6. Paragraph 5 shall not have effect where the Commission has informed the undertakings concerned that after preliminary examination it is of opinion that Article [81(1)] of the Treaty applies and that application of Article [81(3)] is not justified.

Article 16
Periodic penalty payments

1. The Commission may by decision impose on undertakings or associations of undertakings periodic penalty payments of from 50 to 1000 units of account per day, calculated from the date appointed by the decision, in order to compel them:

(a)   to put an end to an infringement of Article [81] or [82] of the Treaty, in accordance with a decision taken pursuant to Article 3 of this Regulation;
(b)   to refrain from any act prohibited under Article 8 (3);
(c)   to supply complete and correct information which it has requested by decision taken pursuant to Article 11(5);
(d)   to submit to an investigation which it has ordered by decision taken pursuant to Article 14 (3).

2. Where the undertakings or associations of undertakings have satisfied the obligation which it was the purpose of the periodic penalty payment to enforce, the Commission may fix the total amount of the periodic penalty payment at a lower figure than that which would arise under the original decision.

3. Article 10(3) to (6) shall apply.

Article 17
Review by the Court of Justice

The Court of Justice shall have unlimited jurisdiction within the meaning of Article [229] the Treaty to review decisions whereby the Commission has fixed a fine or periodic penalty payment; it may cancel, reduce or increase the fine or periodic penalty payment imposed.

Article 18
Unit of account

For the purposes of applying Articles 15 to 17 the unit of account shall be that adopted in drawing up the budget of the Community in accordance with Articles [277] and [279] of the Treaty.

Article 19
Hearing of the parties and of third persons

1. Before taking decisions as provided for in Articles 2, 3, 6, 7, 8, 15 and 16, the Commission shall give the undertakings or associations of undertakings concerned the opportunity of being heard on the matters to which the Commission has taken objection.

2. If the Commission or the competent authorities of the Member States consider it necessary, they may also hear other natural or legal persons. Applications to be heard on the part of such persons shall, where they show a sufficient interest, be granted.

3. Where the Commission intends to give negative clearance pursuant to Article 2 or take a decision in application of Article [81(3)] of the Treaty, it shall publish a summary of the relevant application or notification and invite all interested third parties to submit their observations within a time limit which it shall fix being not less than one month. Publication shall have regard to the legitimate interest of undertakings in the protection of their business secrets.

Article 20
Professional secrecy

1. Information acquired as a result of the application of Articles 11,12,13 and 14 shall be used only for the purpose of the relevant request or investigation.

2. Without prejudice to the provisions of Articles 19 and 21, the Commission and the competent authorities of the Member States, their officials and other servants shall not disclose information acquired by them as a result of the application of this Regulation and of the kind covered by the obligation of professional secrecy.

3. The provisions of paragraphs 1 and 2 shall not prevent publication of general information or surveys which do not contain information of undertakings.

Article 21
Publication of decisions

1. The Commission shall publish the decisions which it takes pursuant to Articles 2, 3, 6, 7 and 8.

2. The publication shall state the names of the parties and the main content of the decision; it shall have regard to the legitimate interest of undertakings in the protection of their business secrets.

Article 22
Special provisions

1. The Commission shall submit to the Council proposals for making certain categories of agreement, decision and concerted practice falling within Article 4 (2) or Article 5 (2) compulsorily notifiable under Article 4 or 5.

2. Within one year from the date of entry into force of this Regulation, the Council shall examine, on a proposal from the Commission, what special provisions might be made for exempting from the provisions of this Regulation agreements, decisions and concerted practices falling within Article 4 (2) or Article 5 (2).

Article 23
Transitional provisions applicable to decisions of authorities of the Member States

1. Agreements, decisions and concerted practices of the kind described in Article [81(1)] of the Treaty to which, before the entry into force of this Regulation, the competent authority of a Member State has declared Article [81(1)] to be inapplicable pursuant to Article [81(3)] shall not be subject to compulsory notification under Article 5. The decision of the competent authority of the Member State shall be deemed to be a decision within the meaning of Article 6; it shall cease to be valid upon expiration of the period fixed by such authority but in any event not more than three years after the entry into force of this Regulation. Article 8 (3) shall apply.

2. Applications for renewal of decisions of the kind described in paragraph 1 shall be decided upon by the Commission in accordance with Article 8(2).

Article 24
Implementing provisions

The Commission shall have power to adopt implementing provisions concerning the form, content and other details of applications pursuant to Articles 2 and 3 and of notifications pursuant to Articles 4 and 5, and concerning hearings pursuant to Article 19 (1) and (2).

Article 25

1. As regards agreements, decisions and concerted practices to which Article [81] of the Treaty applies by virtue of accession, the date of accession shall be substituted for the date of entry into force of this Regulation in every place where reference is made in this Regulation to this latter date.

2. Agreements, decisions and concerted practices existing at the date of accession to which Article [81] of the Treaty applies by virtue of accession shall be notified pursuant to Article 5 (1) or Article 7 (1) and (2) within six months from the date of accession.

3. Fines under Article 15 (2) (a) shall not be imposed in respect of any act prior to notifica-

tion of the agreements, decisions and practices to which paragraph 2 applies and which have been notified within the period therein specified.

4. New Member States shall take the measures referred to in Article 14(6) within six months from the date of accession after consulting the Commission.

5. The provisions of paragraphs 1 to 4 still apply in the same way in the case of the accession of the Hellenic Republic, the Kingdom of Spain and of the Portuguese Republic.

6. The provisions of paragraphs 1 to 4 still apply in the same way in the case of the accession of Austria, Finland and Sweden. However, they do not apply to agreements, decisions and concerted practices which at the date of accession already fall under Article 53 of the EEA Agreement.

This Regulation shall be binding in its entirety and directly applicable in all Member States.

PROPOSAL FOR A

COUNCIL REGULATION ON THE IMPLEMENTATION OF THE RULES ON COMPETITION LAID DOWN IN ARTICLES 81 AND 82 OF THE TREATY AND AMENDING REGULATIONS (EEC) NO 1017/68, (EEC) NO 2988/74, (EEC) NO 4056/86 AND (EEC) NO 3975/87 ("REGULATION IMPLEMENTING ARTICLES 81 AND 82 OF THE TREATY")

(Text with EEA relevance)

The council of the european union,
HAVING REGARD to the Treaty establishing the European Community, and in particular Article 83 thereof,
HAVING REGARD to the proposal from the Commission,[3]
HAVING REGARD to the opinion of the European Parliament[4],
HAVING REGARD to the opinion of the Economic and Social Committee[5],
Whereas:

(1) If a system is to be established which ensures that competition in the common market is not distorted, Articles 81 and 82 must be applied effectively and uniformly in the

---

[3] OJ C
[4] OJ C.
[5] OJ C.

Community Council Regulation No 17 of 6 February 1962, First Regulation implementing Articles 85 and 86 of the Treaty[6], has allowed a Community competition
policy to develop that has helped to disseminate a competition culture within the
Community. In the light of experience, however, that Regulation should now be
replaced by legislation designed to meet the challenges of an integrated market and a
future enlargement of the Community.

(2) In particular, there is a need to rethink the arrangements for applying the exception
from the prohibition on agreements, which restrict competition, laid down in Article
81(3). Under Article 83(2) (b), account must be taken in this regard of the need to
ensure effective supervision, on the one hand, and to simplify administration to the
greatest possible extent, on the other.

(3) The centralised scheme set up by Regulation No 17 no longer secures a balance
between those two objectives. It hampers application of the Community competition
rules by the courts and competition authorities of the Member States, and the system
of notification it involves prevents the Commission from concentrating its resources
on curbing the most serious infringements. It also imposes considerable costs on
undertakings.

(4) The present system should therefore be replaced by a directly applicable exception
system in which the competition authorities and courts of the Member States have the
power to apply not only Articles 81(1) and 82, which have direct applicability by virtue
of the case-law of the Court of Justice of the European Communities, but also Article
81(3).

(5) It should be specified here that, in line with the case-law developed in the framework
of Regulation No 17, the burden of proving that the conditions of Article 81(3) are
fulfilled rests on the party seeking to rely on that provision. That party is usually best
placed to prove that the conditions of that paragraph are fulfilled.

(6) In order to ensure that the Community competition rules are applied effectively, the
competition authorities of the Member States must be associated more closely with
their application. To this end, they must be empowered to apply Community law.

(7) National courts have an essential part to play in applying the Community competition
rules. When deciding disputes between private individuals, they protect the subjective
rights under Community law, for example by awarding damages to the victims of
infringements. The role of the national courts here complements that of the competition authorities of the Member States. They must therefore be allowed to apply Articles
81 and 82 of the Treaty in full.

(8) In order to ensure that the same competition rules apply to businesses throughout the
Community, provision must be made pursuant to Article 83(2) (e) to regulate the
relationship between Articles 81 and 82 and national competition law by excluding the
application of national law to agreements, decisions and practices within the scope of
Articles 81 and 82.

(9) Although, in the new system, application of the rules will be decentralised, the uniformity of Community law requires that the rules be laid down centrally. To this end,

---

[6] OJ 13 21.2.1962, p. 204/62; Regulation as last amended by Regulation (EC) No 1216/1999 (OJ L 148,
15.6.1999, p. 5).

the Commission must be given a general power to adopt block exemption regulations in order to enable it to adapt and clarify the legislative framework. This power must be exercised in close cooperation with the competition authorities of the Member States. It must be without prejudice to the existing rules in Council Regulations (EEC) No 1017/68[7], (EEC) No 4056/86[8] and (EEC) No 3975/87[9].

(10) As the system of notification will now come to an end, it may be expedient, in order to improve transparency, to require registration of certain types of agreement. The Commission should accordingly be empowered to require registration of certain types of agreement. If any such requirement is introduced, it must not confer any entitlement to a decision on the compatibility with the Treaty of the agreement registered, and must not be prejudicial to effective action against infringements.

(11) For it to ensure that the provisions of the Treaty are applied, the Commission must be able to address decisions to undertakings or associations of undertakings for the purpose of bringing to an end infringements of Articles 81 and 82. Provided there is a legitimate interest in doing so, the Commission must also be able to adopt decisions which find that an infringement has been committed in the past even if it does not impose a fine. This Regulation should also make explicit provision for the Commission's power to adopt decisions ordering interim measures, which has been acknowledged by the Court of Justice.

(12) Where, in the course of proceedings which might lead to an agreement being prohibited, undertakings offer the Commission commitments such as to meet its objections, the Commission should be able to adopt decisions which make those commitments binding on the undertakings concerned, without settling the question of the applicability of Article 81 or Article 82, so that the commitments can be relied upon by third parties before national courts and failure to comply with them can be punished by the imposition of fines and periodic penalty payments.

(13) In exceptional cases where the public interest of the Community so requires, it may also be expedient for the Commission to adopt a decision of a declaratory nature finding that the prohibition in Article 81 or Article 82 does not apply, with a view to clarifying the law and ensuring its consistent application throughout the Community.

(14) If the Commission and the competition authorities of the Member States are to form together a network of public authorities applying the Community competition rules in close cooperation, arrangements for information and consultation must be set up and the exchange of information must be allowed between the members of the network even where the information is confidential, subject to appropriate guarantees for undertakings.

(15) If the competition rules are to be applied consistently and, at the same time, the network is to be managed in the best possible way, it is essential to retain the rule that

---

[7] OJ L 175, 23.7.1968, p.1; Regulation as last amended by the Act of Accession of Austria, Finland and Sweden.

[8] OJ L 378, 31.12.1986, p.4; Regulation as amended by the Act of Accession of Austria. Finland and Sweden.

[9] OJ L 374, 31.12.1987, p.1; Regulation as last amended by Regulation (EC) No 2410/92 (OJ L 240, 24.8.1992, p.18).

the competition authorities of the Member States are automatically relieved of their competence if the Commission initiates its own proceedings

(16) To ensure that cases are dealt with by the most appropriate authorities within the network, a general provision should be laid down allowing a competition authority to suspend or close a case on the ground that another authority is dealing with it or has already dealt with it, the objective being that each case should be handled by a single authority. This provision must not prevent the Commission from rejecting a complaint for lack of Community interest, as the case-law of the Court of Justice has acknowledged it may do, even if no other competition authority has indicated its intention of dealing with the case.

(17) The Advisory Committee on Restrictive Practices and Dominant Positions set up by Regulation No 17 has functioned in a very satisfactory manner. It will fit perfectly into the new system of decentralised application. It is necessary, therefore, to build upon the rules laid down by Regulation No 17, while improving the effectiveness of the organisational arrangements. To this end, it would be expedient to allow opinions to be delivered by written procedure. The Advisory Committee should also be able to act as a forum for discussing cases handled by the competition authorities of the Member States, so as to help safeguard the consistent application of the Community competition rules.

(18) Consistency in the application of the competition rules also requires that arrangements be established for cooperation between the courts of the Member States and the Commission. In particular, it will be useful to allow national courts to ask the Commission for information or for its opinion on points concerning the application of Community competition law. The Commission and the competition authorities of the Member States must also be able to submit written or oral observations to courts called upon to apply Article 81 or Article 82. Steps must therefore be taken to ensure that the Commission and the competition authorities of the Member States are kept sufficiently well informed of proceedings before national courts.

(19) In order to ensure compliance with the principles of legal certainty and the uniform application of the Community competition rules in a system of parallel powers, conflicting decisions must be avoided. When the Commission has adopted a decision, therefore, the competition authorities and courts of the Member States must use every effort to avoid contradicting it. In this context, it should be recalled that the courts may refer questions to the Court of Justice for a preliminary ruling.

(20) The Commission must be empowered throughout the Community to require such information to be supplied and to undertake such inspections as are necessary to detect any agreement, decision or concerted practice prohibited by Article 81 or any abuse of a dominant position prohibited by Article 82. The competition authorities of the Member States must cooperate actively in the exercise of these powers.

(21) The detection of infringements of the competition rules is growing ever more difficult, and, in order to protect competition effectively, the Commission's powers of investigation need to be supplemented. The Commission must in particular be empowered to interview any persons who may be in possession of useful information and to record the statements made. In the course of an inspection, authorised Commission officials must be empowered to affix seals and to ask for any information relevant to the subject matter and purpose of the inspection.

(22) It is expedient to clarify, in keeping with the case-law of the Court of Justice, the limits to the power of review that the national courts may exercise when asked, under national law, to order measures allowing assistance from law enforcement authorities in order to overcome opposition on the part of an undertaking to an inspection ordered by decision.

(23) Experience has shown that business records are often kept in the homes of directors or other people working for an undertaking. In order to safeguard the effectiveness of inspections, therefore, authorised Commission officials should be empowered to enter any premises where business records may be kept, including private homes. However, the exercise of this latter power must be subject to the authorisation of the judicial authority.

(24) In order to help the competition authorities of the Member States to apply Articles 81 and 82 effectively, it is expedient to enable them to assist one another by carrying out fact-finding measures.

(25) Compliance with Articles 81 and 82 and the fulfilment of the obligations imposed on undertakings and associations of undertakings under this Regulation must be enforceable by means of fines and periodic penalty payments. To that end, appropriate levels of fine should also be laid down for infringements of the procedural rules.

(26) The rules on periods of limitation for the imposition of fines and periodic penalty payments were laid down in Council Regulation (EEC) No 2988/74[10], which also concerns penalties in the field of transport. In a system of parallel powers, the acts, which may interrupt a limitation period, should include procedural steps taken independently by the competition authority of a Member State. To clarify the legal framework, Regulation (EEC) No 2988/74 should therefore be amended to prevent it applying to matters covered by this Regulation, and this Regulation should include provisions on periods of limitation.

(27) The undertakings concerned must be accorded the right to be heard by the Commission, third parties whose interests may be affected by a decision must be given the opportunity of submitting their observations beforehand, and the decisions taken must be widely publicised. While ensuring the rights of defence of the undertakings concerned, in particular, the right of access to the file, it is essential that business secrets be protected. The confidentiality of information exchanged in the network must likewise be safeguarded.

(28) Since all decisions taken by the Commission under this Regulation are subject to review by the Court of Justice in accordance with the Treaty, the Court of Justice should, in accordance with Article 229 thereof be given unlimited jurisdiction in respect of decisions by which the Commission imposes fines or periodic penalty payments.

(29) The principles laid down in Articles 81 and 82 of the Treaty, as they have been applied by Regulation No 17, have given a central role to the Community bodies.

This central role should be retained, whilst associating the Member States more closely with the application of the Community competition rules. In accordance with the principles of subsidiarity and proportionality as set out in Article 5 of the Treaty, this

---

[10] OJ L 319,. 29.11.1974, p.1.

Regulation confines itself to the minimum required in order to achieve its objective, which is to allow the Community competition rules to be applied effectively, and does not go beyond what is necessary for that purpose.

(30) As the case-law has made it clear that the competition rules apply to transport, that sector should be made subject to the procedural provisions of this Regulation. Regulations (EEC) No 1017/68, (EEC) No 4056/86 and (EEC) No 3975/87 should therefore be amended in order to delete the specific procedural provisions they contain.

(31) In order to take account of the new arrangements established by this Regulation, the following Regulations should be repealed: Council Regulation No 141 of 26 November 1962 exempting transport from the application of Regulation No 17[11], Council Regulation No 19/65/EEC of 2 March 1965 on application of Article 85(3) of the Treaty to certain categories of agreements and concerted practices[12], Council Regulation (EEC) No 2821/71 of 20 December 1971 on application of Article 85(3) of the Treaty to categories of agreements, decisions and concerted practices[13], Council Regulation (EEC) No 3976/87 of 14 December 1987 on the application of Article 85(3) of the Treaty to certain categories of agreements and concerted practices in the air transport sector[14], Council Regulation (EEC) No 1534/91 of 31 May 1991 on the application of Article 85(3) of the Treaty to certain categories of agreements, decisions and concerted practices in the insurance sector[15], and Council Regulation (EEC) No 479/92 of 25 February 1992 on the application of Article 85(3) of the Treaty to certain categories of agreements, decisions and concerted practices between liner shipping companies (consortia)[16],

HAS ADOPTED THIS REGULATION:

Chapter I: Principles

Article 1
Direct applicability

Agreements, decisions and concerted practices caught by Article 81(1) of the Treaty which do not satisfy the conditions of Article 81(3), and the abuse of a dominant position referred to in Article 82, shall be prohibited, no prior decision to that effect being required.

---

[11] OJ 124, 28.11.1962, p. 2751/62; Regulation as last amended by Regulation No 1002/67/EEC (OJ 306, 16.12.1967, p. 1).

[12] OJ 36, 6.3.1965, p. 533/65; Regulation as last amended by Regulation (EC) No 1215/1999 (OJ L 148, 15.6.1999, p. 1).

[13] OJ L 285, 29.12.1971, p. 46; Regulation as last amended by the Act of Accession of Austria, Finland and Sweden.

[14] OJ L 374, 31.12.1987, p. 9; Regulation as last amended by the Act of Accession of Austria, Finland and Sweden.

[15] OJ L 143, 7.6.1991, p. 1.

[16] OJ L 55, 29.2.1992, p. 3; Regulation as amended by the Act of Accession of Austria, Finland and Sweden.

Article 2
Burden of proof

In any national or Community proceedings for the application of Article 81 and Article 82 of the Treaty, the burden of proving an infringement of Article 81(1) or of Article 82 shall rest on the party alleging the infringement. A party claiming the benefit of Article 81(3) shall bear the burden of proving that the conditions of that paragraph are fulfilled.

Article 3
Relationship between Articles 81 and 82 and national competition laws

Where an agreement a decision by an association of undertakings or a concerted practice within the meaning of Article 81 of the Treaty or the abuse of a dominant position within the meaning of Article 82 may affect trade between Member States, Community competition law shall apply to the exclusion of national competition laws.

Chapter II: Powers

Article 4
Powers of the Commission

1. For the purpose of applying Articles 81 and 82 of the Treaty, the Commission shall have the powers provided for by this Regulation.

2. The Commission may, by regulation, determine types of agreements, decisions of associations of undertakings and concerted practices caught by Article 81(1) of the Treaty which must be registered by undertakings. In that event, it shall also determine the procedures for such registration and the penalties applicable in the event of failure to comply with the obligation. Registration of an agreement, a decision of an association or a concerted practice shall confer no entitlement on the registering undertakings or associations of undertakings and shall not form an obstacle to the application of this Regulation.

Article 5
Powers of the competition authorities of the Member States

The competition authorities of the Member States shall have the power in individual cases to apply the prohibition in Article 81(1) of the Treaty where the conditions of Article 81(3) are not fulfilled, and the prohibition in Article 82. For this purpose, acting on their own initiative or on a complaint, they may take any decision requiring that an infringement be brought to an end, adopting interim measures, accepting commitments or imposing fines, periodic penalty payments or any other penalty provided for in their national law. Where on the basis of the information in their possession the conditions for prohibition are not met they may likewise decide that there are no grounds for action on their part.

Article 6
Powers of the national courts

National courts before which the prohibition in Article 81(1) of the Treaty is invoked shall also have jurisdiction to apply Article 81(3).

Chapter III: Commission decisions

Article 7
Finding and termination of infringement

1. Where the Commission, acting on a complaint or on its own initiative, finds that there is an infringement of Article 81 or of Article 82 of the Treaty, it may by decision require the undertakings and associations of undertakings concerned to bring such infringement to an end. For this purpose, it may impose on them any obligations necessary, including remedies of a structural nature. If it has a legitimate interest in doing so, it may also find that an infringement has been committed in the past.

2. Those entitled to lodge a complaint for the purposes of paragraph 1 are Member States and natural or legal persons who can show a legitimate interest.

Article 8
Interim measures

1. In cases of urgency due to the risk of serious and irreparable damage to competition, the Commission, acting on its own initiative may, on the basis of a *prima facie* finding of infringement, by decision order interim measures.

2. A decision under paragraph 1 shall apply for a maximum of one year but shall be renewable.

Article 9
Commitments

1. Where the Commission intends to adopt a decision requiring that an infringement be brought to an end and the undertakings concerned offer commitments such as to meet the Commission's objections, the Commission may by decision make those commitments binding on the undertakings. Such a decision shall be adopted for a specified period.

2. Irrespective of whether or not there has been or still is an infringement of Article 81 or Article 82 of the Treaty, such a decision shall terminate the proceedings.

3. The Commission may reopen the proceedings:

(a) where there has been a material change in any of the facts on which the decision was based;
(b) where the undertakings concerned act contrary to their commitments; or
(c) where the decision was based on incomplete, incorrect or misleading information.

Article 10
Finding of inapplicability

For reasons of the Community public interest, the Commission, acting on its own initiative, may by decision find that, on the basis of the information in its possession, Article 81 of the Treaty is not applicable to an agreement, a decision of an association of undertakings or a concerted practice, either because the conditions of Article 81(1) are not fulfilled, or because the conditions of Article 81(3) are satisfied.

The Commission may likewise make such a finding with reference to Article 82 of the Treaty.

Chapter IV: Cooperation with National Authorities and Courts

Article 11
Cooperation between the Commission and the competition authorities of the Member States

1. The Commission and the competition authorities of the Member States shall apply the Community competition rules in close cooperation.

2. The Commission shall forthwith transmit to the competition authorities of the Member States copies of the most important documents it has collected with a view to applying Articles 7 to 10.

3. Where a matter involving the application of Article 81 or Article 82 of the Treaty is referred to the competition authorities of the Member States or where they act on their own initiative to apply those Articles, they shall inform the Commission accordingly at the outset of their own proceedings.

4. Where competition authorities of Member States intend to adopt a decision under Article 81 or Article 82 of the Treaty requiring that an infringement be brought to an end, accepting commitments or withdrawing the benefit of a block exemption regulation, they shall first consult the Commission. For that purpose, they shall no later than one month before adopting the decision provide the Commission with a summary of the case and with copies of the most important documents drawn up in the course of their own proceedings. At the Commission's request, they shall provide it with a copy of any other document relating to the case.

5. The competition authorities of the Member States may consult the Commission on any other case involving the application of Community law.

6. The initiation by the Commission of proceedings for the adoption of a decision under this Regulation shall relieve the competition authorities of the Member States of their competence to apply Articles 81 and 82 of the Treaty.

Article 12
Exchange of information

1. Notwithstanding any national provision to the contrary, the Commission and the competition authorities of the Member States may provide one another with and use in evidence any matter of fact or of law, including confidential information.

2. Information provided under paragraph 1 may be used only for the purpose of applying Community competition law. Only financial penalties may be imposed on the basis of information provided.

Article 13
Suspension or termination of proceedings

1. Where competition authorities of two or more Member States have received a complaint or are acting on their own initiative under Article 81 or Article 82 of the Treaty against the same agreement, decision of an association or practice, the fact that one authority is dealing

with the case shall be sufficient grounds for the others to suspend the proceedings before them or to reject the complaint. The Commission may likewise reject a complaint on the ground that the competition authority of a Member State is dealing with the case.

2. Where the competition authority of a Member State or the Commission has received a complaint against an agreement, decision of an association or practice which has already been dealt with by another competition authority, it may reject it.

Article 14
Advisory Committee

1. An Advisory Committee on Restrictive Practices and Dominant Positions shall be consulted prior to the taking of any decision under Articles 7, 9, 10, 22 and 23(2).

2. The Advisory Committee shall be composed of representatives of the competition authorities of the Member States. Each Member State shall appoint a representative who, if prevented from attending, may be replaced by another representative.

3. The consultation may take place at a meeting convened by the Commission, which shall supply the chairman, not earlier than fourteen days after dispatch of the notice convening it. The Member States may accept a period of notice of less than fourteen days. The Commission shall attach to the notice convening the meeting a summary of the case, together with an indication of the most important documents, and a preliminary draft decision. The Advisory Committee shall deliver an opinion on the Commission's preliminary draft decision. It may deliver an opinion even if some members are absent and are not represented.

4. Consultation may also take place by written procedure. In that case, the Commission shall determine a date by which the Member States are to put forward their observations. However, if any Member State so requests, the Commission shall convene a meeting.

5. The opinion of the Advisory Committee shall be delivered in writing and appended to the draft decision. The Advisory Committee may recommend publication of the opinion. The Commission may carry out such publication. The decision to publish shall take account of the legitimate interest of undertakings in the protection of their business secrets.

6. Acting on its own initiative or at the request of a Member State, the Commission may include a case being dealt with by the competition authority of a Member State on the agenda of the Advisory Committee for discussion before the final decision is adopted.

Article 15
Cooperation with national courts

1. In proceedings for the application of Article 81 or Article 82 of the Treaty, courts of the Member States may ask the Commission for information in its possession or for its opinion on questions concerning the application of the Community competition rules.

2. Courts of the Member States shall send the Commission copies of any judgments applying Article 81 or Article 82 of the Treaty within one month of the date on which the judgment is delivered.

3. For reasons of the Community public interest, the Commission may, on its own initiative, submit written or oral observations to courts of the Member States on the subject of

proceedings in which questions concerning the application of Article 81 or Article 82 of the Treaty arise. It may have itself represented by competition authorities of Member States. Acting on their own initiative, competition authorities of Member States may likewise submit written or oral observations to the national courts of their Member State.

To this end, the Commission and the competition authorities of the Member States may request the national courts to transmit to them any documents necessary.

Article 16
Uniform application of Community competition law

In accordance with Article 10 of the Treaty and the principle of the uniform application of Community law, national courts and the competition authorities of the Member States shall use every effort to avoid any decision that conflicts with decisions adopted by the Commission.

Chapter V: Powers of Investigation

Article 17
Inquiries into sectors of the economy

1. If, in any sector of the economy, the trend of trade between Member States, the rigidity of prices or other circumstances suggest that competition is being restricted or distorted within the common market, the Commission may conduct a general inquiry into that sector and, in the course of that inquiry, may request undertakings in the sector concerned to supply the information necessary for giving effect to Articles 81 and 82 of the Treaty and may carry out any inspections necessary for that purpose.

The Commission may in particular request any undertaking or association of undertakings in the sector concerned to communicate to it all agreements, decisions and concerted practices.

2. Articles 18 to 23 shall apply by analogy.

Article 18
Requests for information

1. In order to carry out the duties assigned to it by this Regulation, the Commission may request all necessary information from the governments and competition authorities of the Member States and from undertakings and associations of undertakings.

2. In its request for information the Commission shall state the legal bases of the request, the time-limit within which the information is to be provided, the purpose of the request, and the penalties provided for in Articles 22 and 23 for supplying incorrect, incomplete or misleading information.

3. The owners of the undertakings or their representatives and, in the case of legal persons, companies or firms, or associations having no legal personality, the persons authorised to represent them by law or by their constitution shall supply the information requested.

Lawyers duly authorised to act may supply the information on behalf of their clients. The latter shall remain fully responsible if the information supplied is incomplete, incorrect or misleading.

4 Where an undertaking or association of undertakings does not supply the information requested within the time-limit fixed or supplies incomplete information, the Commission shall by decision require the information to be supplied. The decision shall specify what information is required and fix an appropriate time-limit within which it is to be supplied. It shall indicate the penalties provided for in Article 22(1) (a), and indicate or impose the penalties provided for in Article 23(1) (d). It shall also indicate the right to have the decision reviewed by the Court of Justice of the European Communities.

Article 19
Power to take statements

In order to carry out the duties assigned to it by this Regulation, the Commission may interview any natural or legal person that may be in possession of useful information, in order to ask questions relating to the subject-matter of an investigation and recording the answers.

Article 20
The Commission's powers of inspection

1. In order to carry out the duties assigned to it by this Regulation, the Commission may conduct all necessary inspections of undertakings and associations of undertakings.

2. The officials authorised by the Commission to conduct an inspection are empowered:

(a) to enter any premises, land and means of transport of the undertakings and associations of undertakings concerned;

(b) to enter any other premises, including the homes of directors, managers and other members of staff of the undertakings and associations of undertakings concerned, in so far as it may be suspected that business records are being kept there;

(c) to examine the books and other business records, irrespective of the medium on which they are stored;

(d) to take copies of or extracts from the documents examined;

(e) to seal any premises or business records during the inspection;

(f) to ask any representative or member of staff of the undertaking or association of undertakings for information relating to the subject-matter and purpose of the inspection and to record the answers.

3. The officials authorised by the Commission to conduct an inspection shall exercise their powers upon production of a written authorisation specifying the subject matter and purpose of the inspection and the penalties provided for in Article 22 in cases where production of the required books or other business records is incomplete or where the answers to questions asked under paragraph 2 of this Article are incorrect, incomplete or misleading. In good time before the inspection, the Commission shall give notice of the inspection to the competition authority of the Member State in whose territory it is to be conducted.

4. Undertakings and associations of undertakings are required to submit to inspections ordered by decision of the Commission. The decision shall specify the subject matter and purpose of the inspection, appoint the date on which it is to begin and indicate the penalties provided for in Articles 22 and 23 and the right to have the decision reviewed by the Court of Justice. The Commission shall take such decisions after consulting the competition authority of the Member State in whose territory the inspection is to be conducted.

5. Officials of the competition authority of the Member State in whose territory the inspection is to be conducted shall, at the request of that authority or of the Commission, actively assist the officials of the Commission. To this end, they shall enjoy the powers specified in paragraph 2.

6. Where the officials authorised by the Commission find that an undertaking opposes an inspection ordered pursuant to this Article, the Member State concerned shall afford them the necessary assistance, requesting where appropriate the assistance of the police, so as to enable them to conduct their inspection.

If national law requires authorisation from the judicial authority before the assistance of the police can be called upon, such authorisation may be applied for as a precautionary measure.

7. Where the officials authorised by the Commission wish to exercise the power provided for by paragraph 2(b), authorisation from the judicial authority must be obtained beforehand.

8. The lawfulness of the Commission decision shall be subject to review only by the Court of Justice. The power of review of the national court shall extend only to establishing that the Commission decision is authentic and that the enforcement measures envisaged are neither arbitrary nor excessive having regard to the subject matter of the inspection. The national court may not review the necessity for the inspection or require information other than that out in the Commission decision.

Article 21
Investigations by competition authorities of Member States

1. The competition authority of a Member State may in its own territory carry out any fact-finding measure under its national law on behalf and for the account of the competition authority of another Member State in order to establish whether there has been an infringement of Article 81 or Article 82 of the Treaty. It shall transmit the information collected to the requesting authority in accordance with Article 12 of this Regulation.

2. At the request of the Commission, the competition authorities of the Member States shall undertake the inspections which the Commission considers to be necessary under Article 20(1) or which it has ordered by decision pursuant to Article 20(4). The officials of the competition authorities of the Member States who are responsible for conducting these inspections shall exercise their powers upon production of a written authorisation issued by the competition authority of the Member State in whose territory the inspection is to be conducted. Such authorisation shall specify the subject matter and purpose of the inspection.

If so requested by the Commission or by the competition authority of the Member State in whose territory the inspection is to be conducted, the officials of the Commission may assist the officials of the authority concerned.

Chapter VI: Penalties

Article 22
Fines

1. The Commission may by decision impose on undertakings and associations of undertakings fines not exceeding 1% of the total turnover in the preceding business year where, intentionally or negligently:

(a)   they supply incorrect, incomplete or misleading information in response to a request made pursuant to Article 17 or Article 18(1) or (4), or do not supply information within the time-limit fixed by a decision adopted pursuant to Article 18(4);

(b)   they produce the required books or other business records in incomplete form during inspections under Article 20 or Article 21(2), or refuse to submit to inspections ordered by a decision adopted pursuant to Article 20(4);

(c)   they refuse to answer a question asked in accordance with Article 20(2) (f) or give an incorrect, incomplete or misleading answer;

(d)   seals affixed by authorised officials of the Commission in accordance with Article 20(2) (e) have been broken.

2. The Commission may by decision impose on undertakings and associations of undertakings fines not exceeding 10% of the total turnover in the preceding business year of each of the undertakings participating in the infringement where, either intentionally or negligently:

(a)   they infringe Article 81 or Article 82 of the Treaty; or

(b)   they contravene a decision ordering interim measures under Article 8 of this Regulation; or

(c)   they fail to comply with a commitment made binding by a decision pursuant to Article 9 of this Regulation.

3. In fixing the amount of the fine, regard shall be had both to the gravity and to the duration of the infringement.

4. Where a fine is imposed on an association of undertakings under this Regulation and the association is not solvent, the Commission may require payment of the fine by any of the undertakings which were members of the association at the time the infringement was committed. The amount required to be paid by each individual member cannot exceed 10% of its total turnover in the preceding business year.

5. Decisions taken pursuant to paragraphs 1 and 2 shall not be of a criminal law nature.

Article 23
Periodic penalty payments

1. The Commission may, by decision, impose on undertakings or associations of undertak-

ings periodic penalty payments not exceeding 5% of the average daily turnover in the preceding business year per day and calculated from the date appointed by the decision, in order to compel them:

(a) to put an end to an infringement of Article 81 or Article 82 of the Treaty, in accordance with a decision taken pursuant to Article 7 of this Regulation;
(b) to comply with a decision ordering interim measures taken pursuant to Article 8;
(c) to comply with a commitment made binding by a decision pursuant to Article 9;
(d) to supply complete and correct information which it has requested by decision taken pursuant to Article 18(4);
(e) to submit to an inspection which it has ordered by decision taken pursuant to Article 20.

2. Where the undertakings or associations of undertakings have satisfied the obligation which the periodic penalty payment was intended to enforce, the Commission may fix the definitive amount of the periodic penalty payment at a figure lower than that which would arise under the original decision. Article 22(4) shall apply by analogy.

Chapter VII: Limitation Periods

Article 24
Limitation periods for the imposition of penalties

1. The powers conferred on the Commission by Articles 22 and 23 shall be subject to the following limitation periods:

(a) three years in the case of infringements of provisions concerning requests for information or the conduct of inspections;
(b) five years in the case of all other infringements.

2. Time shall begin to run on the day on which the infringement is committed. However, in the case of continuing or repeated infringements, time shall begin to run on the day on which the infringement ceases.

3. Any action taken by the Commission or by the competition authority of a Member State for the purpose of the investigation or proceedings in respect of an infringement shall interrupt the limitation period for the imposition of fines or periodic penalty payments. The limitation period shall be interrupted with effect from the date on which the action is notified to at least one undertaking or association of undertakings which has participated in the infringement. Actions which interrupt the running of the period shall include in particular the following:

(a) written requests for information by the Commission or by the competition authority of a Member State;
(b) written authorisations to conduct inspections issued to its officials by the Commission or by the competition authority of a Member State;

(c)   the initiation of proceedings by the Commission or by the competition authority of a Member State;

(d)   notification of the statement of objections of the Commission or of the competition authority of a Member State.

4.   The interruption of the limitation period shall apply for all the undertakings or associations of undertakings which have participated in the infringement.

5.   Each interruption shall start time running afresh. However, the limitation period shall expire at the latest on the day on which a period equal to twice the limitation period has elapsed without the Commission having imposed a fine or a periodic penalty payment. That period shall be extended by the time during which limitation is suspended pursuant to paragraph 6.

6.   The limitation period for the imposition of fines or periodic penalty payments shall be suspended for as long as the decision of the Commission is the subject of proceedings pending before the Court of Justice.

Article 25
Limitation period for the enforcement of penalties

1. The power of the Commission to enforce decisions taken pursuant to Articles 22 and 23 shall be subject to a limitation period of five years.

2. Time shall begin to run on the day on which the decision becomes final.

3. The limitation period for the enforcement of penalties shall be interrupted:

(a)   by notification of a decision varying the original amount of the fine or periodic penalty payment or refusing an application for variation;

(b)   by any action of the Commission or of a Member State, acting at the request of the Commission, designed to enforce payment of the fine or periodic penalty payment.

4. Each interruption shall start time running afresh.

5. The limitation period for the enforcement of penalties shall be suspended for so long as:

(a)   time to pay is allowed;

(b)   enforcement of payment is suspended pursuant to a decision of the Court of Justice.

Chapter VIII: Hearings and Professional Secrecy

Article 26
Hearing of the parties, complainants and others

1. Before taking decisions as provided for in Articles 7, 8, 22 and 23(2), the Commission shall give the undertakings or associations of undertakings which are the subject of the proceedings the opportunity of being heard on the matters to which the Commission has taken objection. The Commission shall base its decisions only on objections on which the

parties concerned have been able to comment. Complainants shall be associated closely with the proceedings.

2. The rights of defence of the parties concerned shall be fully respected in the proceedings. They shall be entitled to have access to the file, subject to the legitimate interest of undertakings in the protection of their business secrets. That legitimate interest may not constitute an obstacle to the disclosure and use by the Commission of information necessary to prove an infringement.

The right of access to the file shall not extend to confidential information and internal documents of the Commission or the competition authorities of the Member States. In particular, any correspondence between the Commission and the Competition Authority of the Member States, or between the latter, *inter alia*, documents drawn up pursuant to Articles 8 and 11 are excluded.

3. If the Commission or the competition authorities of the Member States consider it necessary, they may also hear other natural or legal persons. Applications to be heard on the part of such persons shall, where they show a sufficient interest, be granted.

Article 27
Professional secrecy

1. Without prejudice to Articles 12 and 15, information collected pursuant to Articles 17 to 21 shall be used only for the purpose for which it was acquired.

2. Without prejudice to Articles 11, 12, 14, 15 and 26, the Commission and the competition authorities of the Member States, their officials and other servants shall not disclose information acquired or exchanged by them pursuant to this Regulation and of the kind covered by the obligation of professional secrecy.

Chapter IX: Block Exemptions

Article 28
Adoption of block exemption regulations

1. In accordance with Article 81(3) of the Treaty, the Commission may, by regulation, declare that Article 81(1) is not applicable to categories of agreements, decisions by associations of undertakings or concerted practices, subject to the conditions in paragraphs 2 to 5 of this Article.

2. Exemption regulations must define the categories of agreements, decisions or concerted practices to which they apply and specify in particular the restrictions, which are not exempted, and any conditions that must be fulfilled.

3. Exemption regulations must be limited in time.

4. Before adopting an exemption regulation, the Commission must publish a draft thereof and invite all interested parties concerned to submit their comments within the time-limit it lays down, which may not be less than one month.

5. Before publishing a draft exemption regulation and before adopting such a regulation, the Commission shall consult the Advisory Committee on Restrictive Practices and Dominant Positions.

Article 29
Withdrawal in individual cases

1. Where, in any particular case, the Commission, acting on its own initiative or on a complaint, finds that agreements, decisions or concerted practices to which a block exemption regulation applies nevertheless have certain effects which are incompatible with Article 81(3) of the Treaty, it may withdraw the benefit of the regulation.

2. Where in any particular case agreements, decisions or concerted practices to which a block exemption regulation applies have effects which are incompatible with Article 81(3) of the Treaty in the territory of a Member State, or in a part thereof, which has all the characteristics of a distinct geographic market, the competition authority of that Member State may withdraw the benefit of the regulation in question in respect of that territory.

Article 30
Regulations ending the application of a block exemption

A block exemption regulation adopted pursuant to Article 28 may specify the circumstances which may lead to the exclusion from its scope of certain types of agreement, decision or concerted practice that are applied on a particular market. Where those circumstances obtain, the Commission may establish this by way of regulation, and fix a period on the expiry of which the block exemption regulation will no longer be applicable to the relevant agreements, decisions or concerted practices on that market. That period must not be less than six months. Article 28(4) and (5) shall apply by analogy.

Chapter X: General Provisions

Article 31
Publication of decisions

1. The Commission shall publish the decisions, which it takes pursuant to Articles 7 to 10, 22 and 23.

2. The publication shall state the names of the parties and the main content of the decision, including any penalties imposed. It shall have regard to the legitimate interest of undertakings in the protection of their business secrets.

Article 32
Review by the Court of Justice

The Court of Justice shall have unlimited jurisdiction to review decisions whereby the Commission has fixed a fine or periodic penalty payment. It may cancel, reduce or increase the fine or periodic penalty payment imposed.

Article 33
Exclusions

This Regulation shall not apply to agreements, decisions and concerted practices or to the abuse of a dominant position within the meaning of Article 82 of the Treaty in the following areas:

(a) international sea transport of the tramp service type;
(b) sea transport between ports in the same Member State;
(c) air transport between the Community and third countries.

Article 34
Implementing provisions

The Commission shall be authorised to take such measures as may be appropriate in order to apply this Regulation. The measures may concern *inter alia:*

(a) the introduction of a registration requirement for certain types of agreement;
(b) the form, content and other details of complaints lodged pursuant to Article 7 and the procedure for rejecting complaints;
(c) the practical arrangements for the exchange of information and consultations provided for in Article 11;
(d) the practical arrangements for the hearings provided for in Article 26.

Chapter XI: Transitional and Final Provisions

Article 35
Transitional provisions

1. Applications made to the Commission under Article 2 of Regulation No 17, notifications made under Articles 4 and 5 of that Regulation and the corresponding applications and notifications made under Regulations (EEC) No 1017/68, (EEC) No 4056/86 and (EEC) No 3975/87 shall lapse as from the date of application of this Regulation.

The validity of decisions applying Article 81(3) of the Treaty adopted by the Commission under those Regulations shall come to an end no later than the date of application of this Regulation.

2. Procedural steps taken under Regulation No 17 and Regulations (EEC) No 1017/68, (EEC) No 4056/86 and (EEC) No 3975/87 shall continue to have effect for the purposes of applying this Regulation.

Article 36
Designation of competition authorities of Member States

The Member States shall designate the competition authorities responsible for the application of Articles 81 and 82 of the Treaty, and shall take the measures necessary to empower those authorities to apply those Articles before ***.

Article 37
Amendment of Regulation (EEC) No 1017/68

Regulation (EEC) No 1017/68 is amended as follows:

(1)   Article 2 is deleted.
(2)   In Article 3(1), the words "The prohibition laid down in Article 2" are replaced by the words "The prohibition in Article 81(1) of the Treaty".
(3)   Articles 5 to 29 are deleted.
(4)   In Article 30, paragraphs 2 and 3 are deleted.

Article 38
Amendment of Regulation (EEC) No 2988/74

In Regulation (EEC) No 2988/74, the following Article 7a is inserted:
"*Article 7a*

Exclusion
This Regulation shall not apply to measures taken under Council Regulation (EC) No . . .*
____

*OJ L . . ."

Article 39
Amendment of Regulation (EEC) No 4056/86

Regulation (EEC) No 4056/86 is amended as follows:

(1)   Article 7 is amended as follows:
(a)   Paragraph 1 is replaced by the following:

> "1. *Breech of an obligation*
>
> Where the persons concerned are in breach of an obligation which, pursuant to Article 5, attaches to the exemption provided for in Article 3, the Commission may, in order to put an end to such breach and under the conditions laid down in Council Regulation (EC) No. . .: *
>
> – address recommendations to the persons concerned;
>
> – in the event of failure by such persons to observe those recommendations and depending on the gravity of the breach concerned, adopt a decision that either prohibits them from carrying out or requires them to perform certain specific acts, or withdraws the benefit of the block exemption which they enjoyed.
>
> *   OJ L . . ."

(b)   Paragraph 2 is amended as follows:

(i)   In point (a), the words "under the conditions laid down in Section II" are replaced by the words "under the conditions laid down in Regulation (EC) No . . ./. . .";

(ii)   The second sentence of the second subparagraph of point (c) (i) is replaced by the following:

"At the same time it shall decide, in accordance with Article 9 of Regulation (EC)

No .../..., whether it accepts commitments offered by the undertakings concerned with a view, *inter alia*, to obtaining access to the market for non-conference lines."

(2) In Article 8, paragraph 1 is deleted.

(3) Article 9 is amended as follows;

(a) In paragraph 1, the words "Advisory Committee referred to in Article 15" are replaced by the words "Advisory Committee referred to in Article 14 of Regulation (EC) No. . ./ . . .";

(b) In paragraph 2, the words "Advisory Committee as referred to in Article 15" are replaced by the words "the Advisory Committee referred to in Article 14 of Regulation (EC) No . . ./. . .".

(4) Articles 10 to 25 are deleted.

(5) In Article 26, the words "the form, content and other details of complaints pursuant to Article 10, applications pursuant to Article 12 and the hearings provided for in Article 23(1) and (2)" are deleted.

Article 40
Amendment of Regulation (EEC) No 3975/87

Articles 3 to 19 of Regulation (EEC) No 3975/87 are deleted.

Article 41
Repeals

Regulations No 17, No 141, No 19165/EEC, (EEC) No 2821/71, (EEC) No 3976/87, (EEC) No 1534/91 and (EEC) No 479/92 are hereby repealed.

References to the repealed Regulations shall be construed as references to this Regulation.

Article 42
Entry into force

This Regulation shall enter into force on the twentieth day following that of its publication in the *Official Journal of the European Communities*.

It shall apply from xxx.

This Regulation shall be binding in its entirety and directly applicable in all Member States.

Done at Brussels,

For the Council
The President

COUNCIL REGULATION OF 21 DECEMBER 1989 ON THE CONTROL OF CONCENTRATIONS BETWEEN UNDERTAKINGS (4064/89/EEC)[17]

The Council of the European Communities,
HAVING REGARD to the Treaty establishing the European Economic Community, and in particular Arts. [83] and [308] thereof,

(1) Whereas, for the achievement of the aims of the Treaty establishing the European Economic Community, Art. [3(1)(g)] gives the Community the objective of instituting 'a system ensuring that competition in the common market is not distorted';

(2) Whereas this system is essential for the achievement of the internal market by 1992 and its further development;

(3) Whereas the dismantling of internal frontiers is resulting and will continue to result in major corporate reorganisations in the Community, particularly in the form of concentrations;

(4) Whereas such a development must be welcomed as being in line with the requirements of dynamic competition and capable of increasing the competitiveness of European industry, improving the conditions of growth and raising the standard of living in the Community;

(5) Whereas, however, it must be ensured that the process of reorganisation does not result in lasting damage to competition; whereas Community law must therefore include provisions governing those concentrations which may significantly impede effective competition in the common market or in a substantial part of it;

(6) Whereas Arts. [81] and [82], while applicable, according to the case-law of the Court of Justice, to certain concentrations, are not, however, sufficient to control all operations which may prove to be incompatible with the system of undistorted competition envisaged in the Treaty;

(7) Whereas a new legal instrument should therefore be created in the form of a Regulation to permit effective control of all concentrations from the point of view of their effect on the structure of competition in the Community and to be the only instrument applicable to such concentrations;

(8) Whereas this Regulation should therefore be based not only on Art. [83] but, principally, on Art. [308] of the Treaty, under which the Community may give itself the additional powers of action necessary for the attainment of its objectives, including

---

[17] OJ 1990 L 257/14 (corrigendum to OJ 1989 L 395/1), as last amended by Regulation 1310/97/EC, OJ 1997 L 180/1. Pursuant to Article 2 of the latter Regulation, it shall not apply to any concentration which was the subject of an agreement or announcement or where control was acquired within the meaning of Article 4(1) of Regulation 4064/89/EEC, before 1 March 1998 and it shall not in any circumstances apply to any concentration in respect of which proceedings were initiated before 1 March 1998 by a Member State's authority with responsiblity for competition.

with regard to concentrations on the markets for agricultural products listed in Annex II to the Treaty;

(9)   Whereas the provisions to be adopted in this Regulation should apply to significant structural changes the impact of which on the market goes beyond the national borders of any one Member State;

(10) Whereas the scope of application of this Regulation should therefore be defined according to the geographical area of activity of the undertakings concerned and be limited by quantitative thresholds in order to cover those concentrations which have a Community dimension; whereas, at the end of an initial phase of the application of this Regulation, these thresholds should be reviewed in the light of the experience gained;

(11) Whereas a concentration with a Community dimension exists where the combined aggregate turnover of the undertakings concerned exceeds given levels worldwide and within the Community and where at least two of the undertakings concerned have their sole or main fields of activities in different Member States or where, although the undertakings in question act mainly in one and the same Member State, at least one of them has substantial operations in at least one other Member State; whereas that is also the case where the concentrations are effected by undertakings which do not have their principal fields of activities in the Community but which have substantial operations there;

(12) Whereas the arrangements to be introduced for the control of concentrations should, without prejudice to Art. [86(2)] of the Treaty, respect the principle of non-discrimination between the public and the private sectors; whereas, in the public sector, calculation of the turnover of an undertaking concerned in a concentration needs, therefore, to take account of undertakings making up an economic unit with an independent power of decision, irrespective of the way in which their capital is held or of the rules of administrative supervision applicable to them;

(13) Whereas it is necessary to establish whether concentrations with a Community dimension are compatible or not with the common market from the point of view of the need to maintain and develop effective competition in the common market; whereas, in so doing, the Commission must place its appraisal within the general framework of the achievement of the fundamental objectives referred to in Art. 2 of the Treaty, including that of strengthening the Community's economic and social cohesion, referred to in Art. [158]a;

(14) Whereas this Regulation should establish the principle that a concentration with a Community dimension which creates or strengthens a position as a result of which effective competition in the common market or in a substantial part of it is significantly impeded is to be declared incompatible with the common market;

(15) Whereas concentrations which, by reason of the limited market share of the undertakings concerned, are not liable to impede effective competition may be presumed to be compatible with the common market; whereas, without prejudice to Arts. [81] and [82] of the Treaty, an indication to this effect exists, in particular, where the market share of the undertakings concerned does not exceed 25% either in the common market or in a substantial part of it;

(16) Whereas the Commission should have the task of taking all the decisions necessary to establish whether or not concentrations with a Community dimension are compatible with the common market, as well as decisions designed to restore effective competition;

(17) Whereas to ensure effective control undertakings should be obliged to give prior notification of concentrations with a Community dimension and provision should be made for the suspension of concentrations for a limited period, and for the possibility of extending or waiving a suspension where necessary; whereas in the interests of legal certainty the validity of transactions must nevertheless be protected as much as necessary;

(18) Whereas a period within which the Commission must initiate proceedings in respect of a notified concentration and periods within which it must give a final decision on the compatibility or incompatibility with the common market of a notified concentration should be laid down;

(19) Whereas the undertakings concerned must be afforded the right to be heard by the Commission when proceedings have been initiated; whereas the members of the management and supervisory bodies and the recognised representatives of the employees of the undertakings concerned, and third parties showing a legitimate interest, must also be given the opportunity to be heard;

(20) Whereas the Commission should act in close and constant liaison with the competent authorities of the Member States from which it obtains comments and information;

(21) Whereas, for the purposes of this Regulation, and in accordance with the case-law of the Court of Justice, the Commission must be afforded the assistance of the Member States and must also be empowered to require information to be given and to carry out the necessary investigations in order to appraise concentrations;

(22) Whereas compliance with this Regulation must be enforceable by means of fines and periodic penalty payments; whereas the Court of Justice should be given unlimited jurisdiction in that regard pursuant to Art. [229] of the Treaty;

(23) Whereas it is appropriate to define the concept of concentration in such a manner as to cover only operations bringing about a lasting change in the structure of the undertakings concerned; whereas it is therefore necessary to exclude from the scope of this Regulation those operations which have as their object or effect the coordination of the competitive behaviour of undertakings which remain independent, since such operations fall to be examined under the appropriate provisions of the Regulations implementing Arts. [81] and [82] of the Treaty; whereas it is appropriate to make this distinction specifically in the case of the creation of joint ventures;

(24) Whereas there is no coordination of competitive behaviour within the meaning of this Regulation where two or more undertakings agree to acquire jointly control of one or more other undertakings with the object and effect of sharing amongst themselves such undertakings or their assets;

(25) Whereas this Regulation should still apply where the undertakings concerned accept restrictions directly related and necessary to the implementation of the concentration;

(26) Whereas the Commission should be given exclusive competence to apply this Regulation, subject to review by the Court of Justice;

(27) Whereas the Member States may not apply their national legislation on competition to concentrations with a Community dimension, unless this Regulation makes provision therefor; whereas the relevant powers of national authorities should be limited to cases where, failing intervention by the Commission, effective competition is likely to be significantly impeded within the territory of a Member State and where the competition interests of that Member State cannot be sufficiently protected otherwise by this Regulation; whereas the Member States concerned must act promptly in such cases; whereas this Regulation cannot, because of the diversity of national law, fix a single deadline for the adoption of remedies;

(28) Whereas, furthermore, the exclusive application of this Regulation to concentrations with a Community dimension is without prejudice to Art. [296] of the Treaty, and does not prevent the Member States from taking appropriate measures to protect legitimate interests other than those pursued by this Regulation, provided that such measures are compatible with the general principles and other provisions of Community law;

(29) Whereas concentrations not covered by this Regulation come, in principle, within the jurisdiction of the Member States; whereas, however, the Commission should have the power to act, at the request of a Member State concerned, in cases where effective competition could be significantly impeded within that Member State's territory;

(30) Whereas the conditions in which concentrations involving Community undertakings are carried out in non-member countries should be observed, and provision should be made for the possibility of the Council giving the Commission an appropriate mandate for negotiation with a view to obtaining non-discriminatory treatment for Community undertakings;

(31) Whereas this Regulation in no way detracts from the collective rights of employees as recognised in the undertakings concerned,

HAS ADOPTED this Regulation:

Article 1 Scope 1. Without prejudice to Art. 22, this Regulation shall apply to all concentrations with a Community dimension as defined in paragraphs 2 and 3.

2. For the purposes of this Regulation, a concentration has a Community dimension where:

(a) the combined aggregate worldwide turnover of all the undertakings concerned is more than ECU 5000 million; and

(b) the aggregate Community-wide turnover of each of at least two of the undertakings concerned is more than ECU 250 million,

unless each of the undertakings concerned achieves more than two-thirds of its aggregate Community-wide turnover within one and the same Member State.

3. For the purposes of this Regulation, a concentration that does not meet the thresholds laid down in paragraph 2 has a Community dimension where:

(a) the combined aggregate worldwide turnover of all the undertakings concerned is more than ECU 2 500 million;

(b) in each of at least three Member States, the combined aggregate turnover of all the undertakings concerned is more than ECU 100 million;

(c) in each of at least three Member States included for the purpose of point (b), the aggregate turnover of each of at least two of the undertakings concerned is more than ECU 25 million; and

(d) the aggregate Community-wide turnover of each of at least two of the undertakings concerned is more than ECU 100 million;

unless each of the undertakings concerned achieves more than two-thirds of its aggregate Community-wide turnover within one and the same Member State.

4. Before 1 July 2000 the Commission shall report to the Council on the operation of the thresholds and criteria set out in paragraphs 2 and 3.

5. Following the report referred to in paragraph 4 and on a proposal from the Commission, the Council, acting by a qualified majority, may revise the thresholds and criteria mentioned in paragraph 3.

Article 2 Appraisal of concentrations 1. Concentrations within the scope of this Regulation shall be appraised in accordance with the following provisions with a view to establishing whether or not they are compatible with the common market. In making this appraisal, the Commission shall take into account:

(a) the need to maintain and develop effective competition within the common market in view of, among other things, the structure of all the markets concerned and the actual or potential competition from undertakings located either within or outwith the Community;

(b) the market position of the undertakings concerned and their economic and financial power, the alternatives available to suppliers and users, their access to supplies or markets, any legal or other barriers to entry, supply and demand trends for the relevant goods and services, the interests of the intermediate and ultimate consumers, and the development of technical and economic progress provided that it is to consumers' advantage and does not form an obstacle to competition.

2. A concentration which does not create or strengthen a dominant position as a result of which effective competition would be significantly impeded in the common market or in a substantial part of it shall be declared compatible with the common market.

3. A concentration which creates or strengthens a dominant position as a result of which effective competition would be significantly impeded in the common market or in a substantial part of it shall be declared incompatible with the common market.

4. To the extent that the creation of a joint venture constituting a concentration pursuant to Article 3 has as its object or effect the coordination of the competitive behaviour of undertakings that remain independent, such coordination shall be appraised in accordance with the criteria of Article [81(1) and (3)] of the Treaty, with a view to establishing whether or not the operation is compatible with the common market.

In making the appraisal, the Commission shall take into account in particular:

— whether two or more parent companies retain to a significant extent activities in the same market as the joint venture or in a market which is downstream or upstream from that of the joint venture or in a neighbouring market closely related to this market,

— whether the coordination which is the direct consequence of the creation of the joint venture affords the undertakings concerned the possibility of eliminating competition in respect of a substantial part of the products or services in question.

Article 3 Definition of concentration 1. A concentration shall be deemed to arise where:

(a) two or more previously independent undertakings merge, or

(b) one or more persons already controlling at least one undertaking, or one or more undertakings

acquire, whether by purchase of securities or assets, by contract or by any other means, direct or indirect control of the whole or parts of one or more other undertakings.

2. The creation of a joint venture performing on a lasting basis all the functions of an autonomous economic entity shall constitute a concentration within the meaning of paragraph 1(b).

3. For the purposes of this Regulation, control shall be constituted by rights, contracts or any other means which, either separately or in combination and having regard to the considerations of fact or law involved, confer the possibility of exercising decisive influence on an undertaking, in particular by:

(a) ownership or the right to use all or part of the assets of an undertaking;

(b) rights or contracts which confer decisive influence on the composition, voting or decisions of the organs of an undertaking.

4. Control is acquired by persons or undertakings which:

(a) are holders of the rights or entitled to rights under the contracts concerned; or

(b) while not being holders of such rights or entitled to rights under such contracts, have the power to exercise the rights deriving therefrom.

5. A concentration shall not be deemed to arise where:

(a) credit institutions or other financial institutions or insurance companies, the normal activities of which include transactions and dealing in securities for their own account or for the account of others, hold on a temporary basis securities which they have acquired in an undertaking with a view to reselling them, provided that they do not exercise voting rights in respect of those securities with a view to determining the competitive behaviour of that undertaking or provided that they exercise such voting rights only with a view to preparing the disposal of all or part of that undertaking or of its assets or the disposal of those securities and that any such disposal takes place within one year of the date of acquisition; that period may be extended by the Commission on request where such institutions or companies can show that the disposal was not reasonably possible within the period set;

(b) control is acquired by an office-holder according to the law of a Member State relating to liquidation, winding up, insolvency, cessation of payments, compositions or analogous proceedings;

(c) the operations referred to in paragraph 1(b) are carried out by the financial holding companies referred to in Art. 5(3) of the Fourth Council Directive 78/660/EEC of 25 July 1978 on the annual accounts of certain types of companies,[18] last amended by

---

[18] OJ 1978 L 222/11.

Directive 84/569/EEC,[19] provided however that the voting rights in respect of the holding are exercised in particular in relation to the appointment of members of the management and supervisory bodies of the undertakings in which they have holdings, only to maintain the full value of those investments and not to determine directly or indirectly the competitive conduct of those undertakings.

Article 4 Prior notification of concentrations 1. Concentrations with a Community dimension defined in this Regulation shall be notified to the Commission not more than one week after the conclusion of the agreement, or the announcement of the public bid, or the acquisition of a controlling interest. That week shall begin when the first of those events occurs.

2. A concentration which consists of a merger within the meaning of Art. 3(1)(a) or in the acquisition of joint control within the meaning of Art. 3(1)(b) shall be notified jointly by the parties to the merger or by those acquiring joint control as the case may be. In all other cases, the notification shall be effected by the person or undertaking acquiring control of the whole or parts of one or more undertakings.

3. Where the Commission finds that a notified concentration falls within the scope of this Regulation, it shall publish the fact of the notification, at the same time indicating the names of the parties, the nature of the concentration and the economic sectors involved. The Commission shall take account of the legitimate interest of undertakings in the protection of their business secrets.

Article 5 Calculation of turnover 1. Aggregate turnover within the meaning of Art. 1(2) shall comprise the amounts derived by the undertakings concerned in the preceding financial year from the sale of products and the provision of services falling within the undertakings' ordinary activities after deduction of sales rebates and of value added tax and other taxes directly related to turnover. The aggregate turnover of an undertaking concerned shall not include the sale of products or the provision of services between any of the undertakings referred to in paragraph 4.

Turnover, in the Community or in a Member State, shall comprise products sold and services provided to undertakings or consumers, in the Community or in that Member State as the case may be.

2. By way of derogation from paragraph 1, where the concentration consists in the acquisition of parts, whether or not constituted as legal entities, of one or more undertakings, only the turnover relating to the parts which are the subject of the transaction shall be taken into account with regard to the seller or sellers.

However, two or more transactions within the meaning of the first subparagraph which take place within a two-year period between the same persons or undertakings shall be treated as one and the same concentration arising on the date of the last transaction.

3. In place of turnover the following shall be used:

(a)   for credit institutions and other financial institutions, as regards Article 1(2) and (3), the sum of the following income items as defined in Council Directive 86/635/EEC of 8 December 1986[20] on the annual accounts and consolidated accounts of banks and

---

[19] OJ 1985 L 314/28.
[20] OJ 1986 L 372/1.

other financial institutions, after deduction of value added tax and other taxes directly related to those items, where appropriate:

   (i) interest income and similar income;
  (ii) income from securities:
       —income from shares and other variable yield securities,
       —income from participating interests,
       —income from shares in affiliated undertakings;
 (iii) commissions receivable;
  (iv) net profit on financial operations;
   (v) other operating income.

   The turnover of a credit or financial institution in the Community or in a Member State shall comprise the income items, as defined above, which are received by the branch or division of that institution established in the Community or in the Member State in question, as the case may be;

(b)   for insurance undertakings, the value of gross premiums written which shall comprise all amounts received and receivable in respect of insurance contracts issued by or on behalf of the insurance undertakings, including also outgoing reinsurance premiums, and after deduction of taxes and parafiscal contributions or levies charged by reference to the amounts of individual premiums or the total volume of premiums; as regards Article 1(2)(b) and (3)(b), (c) and (d) and the final part of Article 1(2) and (3), gross premiums received from Community residents and from residents of one Member State respectively shall be taken into account.

4. Without prejudice to paragraph 2, the aggregate turnover of an undertaking concerned within the meaning of Art. 1(2) and (3) shall be calculated by adding together the respective turnovers of the following:

(a)   the undertaking concerned;
(b)   those undertakings in which the undertaking concerned, directly or indirectly:
       — owns more than half the capital or business assets, or
       — has the power to exercise more than half the voting rights, or
       — has the power to appoint more than half the members of the supervisory board, the
          administrative board or bodies legally representing the undertakings, or
       — has the right to manage the undertakings' affairs;
(c)   those undertakings which have in the undertaking concerned the rights or powers listed in (b);
(d)   those undertakings in which an undertaking as referred to in (c) has the rights or powers listed in (b);
(e)   those undertakings in which two or more undertakings as referred to in (a) to (d) jointly have the rights or powers listed in (b).

5. Where undertakings concerned by the concentration jointly have the rights or powers listed in paragraph 4(b), in calculating the aggregate turnover of the undertakings concerned for the purposes of Art. 1(2) and (3):

(a)   no account shall be taken of the turnover resulting from the sale of products or the provision of services between the joint undertaking and each of the undertakings concerned or any other undertaking connected with any one of them, as set out in paragraph 4(b) to (e);

(b)   account shall be taken of the turnover resulting from the sale of products and the provision of services between the joint undertaking and any third undertakings. This turnover shall be apportioned equally amongst the undertakings concerned.

Article 6 Examination of the notification and initiation of proceedings 1. The Commission shall examine the notification as soon as it is received.

(a)   Where it concludes that the concentration notified does not fall within the scope of this Regulation, it shall record that finding by means of a decision.

(b)   Where it finds that the concentration notified, although falling within the scope of this Regulation, does not raise serious doubts as to its compatibility with the common market, it shall decide not to oppose it and shall declare that it is compatible with the common market.

The decision declaring the concentration compatible shall also cover restrictions directly related and necessary to the implementation of the concentration.

(c)   Without prejudice to paragraph 1(a), where the Commission finds that the concentration notified falls within the scope of this Regulation and raises serious doubts as to its compatibility with the common market, it shall decide to initiate proceedings.

1a.   Where the Commission finds that, following modification by the undertakings concerned, a notified concentration no longer raises serious doubts within the meaning of paragraph 1(c), it may decide to declare the concentration compatible with the common market pursuant to paragraph 1(b).

The Commission may attach to its decision under paragraph 1(b) conditions and obligations intended to ensure that the undertakings concerned comply with the commitments they have entered into vis-à-vis the Commission with a view to rendering the concentration compatible with the common market.

1b.   The Commission may revoke the decision it has taken pursuant to paragraph 1(a) or (b) where:

(a)   the decision is based on incorrect information for which one of the undertakings is responsible or where it has been obtained by deceit, or

(b)   the undertakings concerned commit a breach of an obligation attached to the decision.

1c.   In the cases referred to in paragraph 1(b), the Commission may take a decision under paragraph 1, without being bound by the deadlines referred to in Article 10(1).

2. The Commission shall notify its decision to the undertakings concerned and the competent authorities of the Member States without delay.

Article 7 Suspension of concentrations 1. A concentration as defined in Article 1 shall not be put into effect either before its notification or until it has been declared compatible with the common market pursuant to a decision under Article 6(1)(b) or Article 8(2) or on the basis of a presumption according to Article 10(6).

[para. 2 repealed]

3. Paragraph 1 shall not prevent the implementation of a public bid which has been notified to the Commission in accordance with Art. 4(1), provided that the acquirer does not exercise the voting rights attached to the securities in question or does so only to maintain the full value of those investments and on the basis of a derogation granted by the Commission under paragraph 4.

4. The Commission may, on request, grant a derogation from the obligations imposed in paragraphs 1 or 3. The request to grant a derogation must be reasoned. In deciding on the request, the Commission shall take into account inter alia the effects of the suspension on one or more undertakings concerned by a concentration or on a third party and the threat to competition posed by the concentration. That derogation may be made subject to conditions and obligations in order to ensure conditions of effective competition. A derogation may be applied for and granted at any time, even before notification or after the transaction.

5. The validity of any transaction carried out in contravention of paragraph 1 shall be dependent on a decision pursuant to Article 6(1)(b) or Article 8(2) or (3) or on a presumption pursuant to Article 10(6).

This Article shall, however, have no effect on the validity of transactions in securities including those convertible into other securities admitted to trading on a market which is regulated and supervised by authorities recognized by public bodies, operates regularly and is accessible directly or indirectly to the public, unless the buyer and seller knew or ought to have known that the transaction was carried out in contravention of paragraph 1.

Article 8 Powers of decision of the Commission 1. Without prejudice to Art. 9, all proceedings initiated pursuant to Art. 6(1)(c) shall be closed by means of a decision as provided for in paragraphs 2 to 5.

2. Where the Commission finds that, following modification by the undertakings concerned if necessary, a notified concentration fulfils the criterion laid down in Article 2(2) and, in the cases referred to in Article 2(4), the criteria laid down in Article [81(3)] of the Treaty, it shall issue a decision declaring the concentration compatible with the common market.

It may attach to its decision conditions and obligations intended to ensure that the undertakings concerned comply with the commitments they have entered into vis-à-vis the Commission with a view to rendering the concentration compatible with the common market. The decision declaring the concentration compatible with the common market shall also cover restrictions directly related and necessary to the implementation of the concentration.

3. Where the Commission finds that a concentration fulfils the criterion defined in Article 2(3) or, in the cases referred to in Article 2(4), does not fulfil the criteria laid down in Article 85(3) of the Treaty, it shall issue a decision declaring that the concentration is incompatible with the common market.

4. Where a concentration has already been implemented, the Commission may, in a decision pursuant to paragraph 3 or by separate decision, require the undertakings or assets brought together to be separated or the cessation of joint control or any other action that may be appropriate in order to restore conditions of effective competition.

5. The Commission may revoke the decision it has taken pursuant to paragraph 2 where:

(a) the declaration of compatibility is based on incorrect information for which one of the undertakings is responsible or where it has been obtained by deceit; or

(b) the undertakings concerned commit a breach of an obligation attached to the decision.

6. In the cases referred to in paragraph 5, the Commission may take a decision under paragraph 3, without being bound by the deadline referred to in Art. 10(3).

Article 9 Referral to the competent authorities of the Member States 1. The Commission may, by means of a decision notified without delay to the undertakings concerned and the competent authorities of the other Member States, refer a notified concentration to the competent authorities of the Member State concerned in the following circumstances.

2. Within three weeks of the date of receipt of the copy of the notification a Member State may inform the Commission, which shall inform the undertakings concerned, that:

(a) a concentration threatens to create or to strengthen a dominant position as a result of which effective competition will be significantly impeded on a market within that Member State, which presents all the characteristics of a distinct market, or

(b) a concentration affects competition on a market within that Member State, which presents all the characteristics of a distinct market and which does not constitute a substantial part of the common market.

3. If the Commission considers that, having regard to the market for the products or services in question and the geographical reference market within the meaning of paragraph 7, there is such a distinct market and that such a threat exists, either:

(a) it shall itself deal with the case in order to maintain or restore effective competition on the market concerned; or

(b) it shall refer the whole or part of the case to the competent authorities of the Member State concerned with a view to the application of that State's national competition law.

If, however, the Commission considers that such a distinct market or threat does not exist it shall adopt a decision to that effect which it shall address to the Member State concerned.

In cases where a Member State informs the Commission that a concentration affects competition in a distinct market within its territory that does not form a substantial part of the common market, the Commission shall refer the whole or part of the case relating to the distinct market concerned, if it considers that such a distinct market is affected.

4. A decision to refer or not to refer pursuant to paragraph 3 shall be taken:

(a) as a general rule within the six-week period provided for in Art. 10(1), second sub-paragraph, where the Commission, pursuant to Art. 6(1)(b), has not initiated proceedings; or

(b) within three months at most of the notification of the concentration concerned where the Commission has initiated proceedings under Art. 6(1)(c), without taking the preparatory steps in order to adopt the necessary measures under Art. 8(2), second sub-paragraph, (3) or (4) to maintain or restore effective competition on the market concerned.

5. If within the three months referred to in paragraph 4(b) the Commission, despite a

reminder from the Member State concerned, has not taken a decision on referral in accordance with paragraph 3 nor has taken the preparatory steps referred to in paragraph 4(b), it shall be deemed to have taken a decision to refer the case to the Member State concerned in accordance with paragraph 3(b).

6. The publication of any report or the announcement of the findings of the examination of the concentration by the competent authority of the Member State concerned shall be effected not more than four months after the Commission's referral.

7. The geographical reference market shall consist of the area in which the undertakings concerned are involved in the supply and demand of products or services, in which the conditions of competition are sufficiently homogeneous and which can be distinguished from neighbouring areas because, in particular, conditions of competition are appreciably different in those areas. This assessment should take account in particular of the nature and characteristics of the products or services concerned, of the existence of entry barriers or of consumer preferences, of appreciable differences of the undertakings' market shares between the area concerned and neighbouring areas or of substantial price differences.

8. In applying the provisions of this Article, the Member State concerned may take only the measures strictly necessary to safeguard or restore effective competition on the market concerned.

9. In accordance with the relevant provisions of the Treaty, any Member State may appeal to the Court of Justice, and in particular request the application of Art. 186, for the purpose of applying its national competition law.

10. This Article may be re-examined at the same time as the thresholds referred to in Article 1.

Article 10 Time limits for initiating proceedings and for decisions 1. The decisions referred to in Art. 6(1) must be taken within one month at most. That period shall begin on the day following that of the receipt of a notification or, if the information to be supplied with the notification is incomplete, on the day following that of the receipt of the complete information.

That period shall be increased to six weeks if the Commission receives a request from a Member State in accordance with Art. 9(2), or where, after notification of a concentration, the undertakings concerned submit commitments pursuant to Article 6(1 a), which are intended by the parties to form the basis for a decision pursuant to Article 6(1)(b).

2. Decisions taken pursuant to Art. 8(2) concerning notified concentrations must be taken as soon as it appears that the serious doubts referred to in Art. 6(1)(c) have been removed, particularly as a result of modifications made by the undertakings concerned, and at the latest by the deadline laid down in paragraph 3.

3. Without prejudice to Art. 8(6), decisions taken pursuant to Art. 8(3) concerning notified concentrations must be taken within not more than four months of the date on which proceedings are initiated.

4. The periods set by paragraphs 1 and 3 shall exceptionally be suspended where, owing to circumstances for which one of the undertakings involved in the concentration is

responsible, the Commission has had to request information by decision pursuant to Art. 11 or to order an investigation by decision pursuant to Art. 13.

5. Where the Court of Justice gives a Judgement which annuls the whole or part of a Commission decision taken under this Regulation, the periods laid down in this Regulation shall start again from the date of the Judgment.

6. Where the Commission has not taken a decision in accordance with Art. 6(1)(b) or (c) or Art. 8(2) or (3) within the deadlines set in paragraphs 1 and 3 respectively, the concentration shall be deemed to have been declared compatible with the common market, without prejudice to Art. 9.

Article 11 Requests for information 1. In carrying out the duties assigned to it by this Regulation, the Commission may obtain all necessary information from the Governments and competent authorities of the Member States, from the persons referred to in Art. 3(1)(b), and from undertakings and associations of undertakings.

2. When sending a request for information to a person, an undertaking or an association of undertakings, the Commission shall at the same time send a copy of the request to the competent authority of the Member State within the territory of which the residence of the person or the seat of the undertaking or association of undertakings is situated.

3. In its request the Commission shall state the legal basis and the purpose of the request and also the penalties provided for in Art. 14(1)(c) for supplying incorrect information.

4. The information requested shall be provided, in the case of undertakings, by their owners or their representatives and, in the case of legal persons, companies or firms, or of associations having no legal personality, by the persons authorised to represent them by law or by their statutes.

5. Where a person, an undertaking or an association of undertakings does not provide the information requested within the period fixed by the Commission or provides incomplete information, the Commission shall by decision require the information to be provided. The decision shall specify what information is required, fix an appropriate period within which it is to be supplied and state the penalties provided for in Arts. 14(1)(c) and 15(1)(a) and the right to have the decision reviewed by the Court of Justice.

6. The Commission shall at the same time send a copy of its decision to the competent authority of the Member State within the territory of which the residence of the person or the seat of the undertaking or association of undertakings is situated.

Article 12 Investigations by the authorities of the Member States 1. At the request of the Commission, the competent authorities of the Member States shall undertake the investigations which the Commission considers to be necessary under Art. 13(1), or which it has ordered by decision pursuant to Art. 13(3). The officials of the competent authorities of the Member States responsible for conducting those investigations shall exercise their powers upon production of an authorisation in writing issued by the competent authority of the Member State within the territory of which the investigation is to be carried out. Such authorisation shall specify the subject-matter and purpose of the investigation.

2. If so requested by the Commission or by the competent authority of the Member State

within the territory of which the investigation is to be carried out, officials of the Commission may assist the officials of that authority in carrying out their duties.

Article 13 Investigative powers of the Commission 1. In carrying out the duties assigned to it by this Regulation, the Commission may undertake all necessary investigations into undertakings and associations of undertakings.

To that end the officials authorised by the Commission shall be empowered:

(a)   to examine the books and other business records;
(b)   to take or demand copies of or extracts from the books and business records;
(c)   to ask for oral explanations on the spot;
(d)   to enter any premises, land and means of transport of undertakings.

2. The officials of the Commission authorised to carry out the investigations shall exercise their powers on production of an authorisation in writing specifying the subject-matter and purpose of the investigation and the penalties provided for in Art. 14(1)(d) in cases where production of the required books or other business records is incomplete. In good time before the investigation, the Commission shall inform, in writing, the competent authority of the Member State within the territory of which the investigation is to be carried out of the investigation and of the identities of the authorised officials.

3. Undertakings and associations of undertakings shall submit to investigations ordered by decision of the Commission. The decision shall specify the subject-matter and purpose of the investigation, appoint the date on which it shall begin and state the penalties provided for in Arts. 14(1)(d) and 15(1)(b) and the right to have the decision reviewed by the Court of Justice.

4. The Commission shall in good time and in writing inform the competent authority of the Member State within the territory of which the investigation is to be carried out of its intention of taking a decision pursuant to paragraph 3. It shall hear the competent authority before taking its decision.

5. Officials of the competent authority of the Member State within the territory of which the investigation is to be carried out may, at the request of that authority or of the Commission, assist the officials of the Commission in carrying out their duties.

6. Where an undertaking or association of undertakings opposes an investigation ordered pursuant to this Article, the Member State concerned shall afford the necessary assistance to the officials authorised by the Commission to enable them to carry out their investigation. To this end the Member States shall, after consulting the Commission, take the necessary measures within one year of the entry into force of this Regulation.

Article 14 Fines 1. The Commission may by decision impose on the persons referred to in Art. 3(1)(b), undertakings or associations of undertakings fines of from ECU 1000 to 50000 where intentionally or negligently:

(a)   they fail to notify a concentration in accordance with Art. 4;
(b)   they supply incorrect or misleading information in a notification pursuant to Art. 4;
(c)   they supply incorrect information in response to a request made pursuant to Art. 11 or fail to supply information within the period fixed by a decision taken pursuant to Art. 11;

(d) they produce the required books or other business records in incomplete form during investigations under Arts. 12 or 13, or refuse to submit to an investigation ordered by decision taken pursuant to Art. 13.

2. The Commission may by decision impose fines not exceeding 10% of the aggregate turnover of the undertakings concerned within the meaning of Art. 5 on the persons or undertakings concerned where, either intentionally or negligently, they:

(a) fail to comply with an obligation imposed by decision pursuant to Art. 7(4) or 8(2), second subparagraph;
(b) put into effect a concentration in breach of Art. 7(1) or disregard a decision taken pursuant to Art. 7(2);
(c) put into effect a concentration declared incompatible with the common market by decision pursuant to Art. 8(3) or do not take the measures ordered by decision pursuant to Art. 8(4).

3. In setting the amount of a fine, regard shall be had to the nature and gravity of the infringement.

4. Decisions taken pursuant to paragraphs 1 and 2 shall not be of criminal law nature.

Article 15 Periodic penalty payments 1. The Commission may by decision impose on the persons referred to in Art. 3(1)(b), undertakings or associations of undertakings concerning periodic penalty payments of up to ECU 25000 for each day of delay calculated from the date set in the decision, in order to compel them:

(a) to supply complete and correct information which it has requested by decision pursuant to Art. 11;
(b) to submit to an investigation which it has ordered by decision pursuant to Art. 13.

2. The Commission may by decision impose on the persons referred to in Art. 3(1)(b) or on undertakings periodic penalty payments of up to ECU 100000 for each day of delay calculated from the date set in the decision, in order to compel them:

(a) to comply with an obligation imposed by decision pursuant to Art. 7(4) or Art. 8 (2), second subparagraph, or
(b) to apply the measures ordered by decision pursuant to Art. 8(4).

3. Where the persons referred to in Art. 3(1)(b), undertakings or associations of undertakings have satisfied the obligation which it was the purpose of the periodic penalty payment to enforce, the Commission may set the total amount of the periodic penalty payments at a lower figure than that which would arise under the original decision.

Article 16 Review by the Court of Justice The Court of Justice shall have unlimited jurisdiction within the meaning of Art. 172 of the Treaty to review decisions whereby the Commission has fixed a fine or periodic penalty payments; it may cancel, reduce or increase the fine or periodic penalty payments imposed.

Article 17 Professional secrecy 1. Information acquired as a result of the application of Arts. 11, 12, 13 and 18 shall be used only for the purposes of the relevant request, investigation or hearing.

2. Without prejudice to Arts. 4(3), 18 and 20, the Commission and the competent authorities of the Member States, their officials and other servants shall not disclose information they have acquired through the application of this Regulation of the kind covered by the obligation of professional secrecy.

3. Paragraphs 1 and 2 shall not prevent publication of general information or of surveys which do not contain information relating to particular undertakings or associations of undertakings.

Article 18 Hearing of the parties and of third persons 1. Before taking any decision provided for in Arts. 7(4), Art. 8(2), second subparagraph, and (3) to (5) and Arts. 14 and 15, the Commission shall give the persons, undertakings and associations of undertakings concerned the opportunity, at every stage of the procedure up to the consultation of the Advisory Committee, of making known their views on the objections against them.

2. By way of derogation from paragraph 1, a decision to grant a derogation from suspension as referred to in Article 7 (4) may be taken provisionally, without the persons, undertakings or associations of undertakings concerned being given the opportunity to make known their views beforehand, provided that the Commission gives them that opportunity as soon as possible after having taken its decision.

3. The Commission shall base its decision only on objections on which the parties have been able to submit their observations. The rights of the defence shall be fully respected in the proceedings. Access to the file shall be open at least to the parties directly involved, subject to the legitimate interest of undertakings in the protection of their business secrets.

4. In so far as the Commission or the competent authorities of the Member States deem it necessary, they may also hear other natural or legal persons. Natural or legal persons showing a sufficient interest and especially members of the administrative or management bodies of the undertakings concerned or the recognised representatives of their employees shall be entitled, upon application, to be heard.

Article 19 Liaison with the authorities of the Member States 1. The Commission shall transmit to the competent authorities of the Member States copies of notifications within three working days and, as soon as possible, copies of the most important documents lodged with or issued by the Commission pursuant to this Regulation. Such documents shall include commitments which are intended by the parties to form the basis for a decision pursuant to Articles 6(1)(b) or 8(2).

2. The Commission shall carry out the procedures set out in this Regulation in close and constant liaison with the competent authorities of the Member States, which may express their views upon those procedures. For the purposes of Art. 9 it shall obtain information from the competent authority of the Member State as referred to in paragraph 2 of that Article and give it the opportunity to make known its views at every stage of the procedure up to the adoption of a decision pursuant to paragraph 3 of that Article; to that end it shall give it access to the file.

3. An Advisory Committee on concentrations shall be consulted before any decision is taken pursuant to Art. 8(2) to (5), 14 or 15, or any provisions are adopted pursuant to Art. 23.

4. The Advisory Committee shall consist of representatives of the authorities of the Member States. Each Member State shall appoint one or two representatives; if unable to attend, they may be replaced by other representatives. At least one of the representatives of a Member State shall be competent in matters of restrictive practices and dominant positions.

5. Consultation shall take place at a joint meeting convened at the invitation of and chaired by the Commission. A summary of the case, together with an indication of the most important documents and a preliminary draft of the decision to be taken for each case considered, shall be sent with the invitation. The meeting shall take place not less than 14 days after the invitation has been sent. The Commission may in exceptional cases shorten that period as appropriate in order to avoid serious harm to one or more of the undertakings concerned by a concentration.

6. The Advisory Committee shall deliver an opinion on the Commission's draft decision, if necessary by taking a vote. The Advisory Committee may deliver an opinion even if some members are absent and unrepresented. The opinion shall be delivered in writing and appended to the draft decision. The Commission shall take the utmost account of the opinion delivered by the Committee. It shall inform the Committee of the manner in which its opinion has been taken into account.

7. The Advisory Committee may recommend publication of the opinion. The Commission may carry out such publication. The decision to publish shall take due account of the legitimate interest of undertakings in the protection of their business secrets and of the interest of the undertakings concerned in such publication's taking place.

Article 20 Publication of decisions 1. The Commission shall publish the decisions which it takes pursuant to Art. 8(2) to (5) in the *Official Journal of the European Communities.*

2. The publication shall state the names of the parties and the main content of the decision; it shall have regard to the legitimate interest of undertakings in the protection of their business secrets.

Article 21 Jurisdiction 1. Subject to review by the Court of Justice the Commission shall have sole jurisdiction to take the decisions provided for in this Regulation.

2. No Member State shall apply its national legislation on competition to any consideration that has a Community dimension.
    The first subparagraph shall be without prejudice to any Member State's power to carry out any enquiries necessary for the application of Art. 9(2) or after referral, pursuant to Art. 9(3), first subparagraph, indent (b), or (5), to take the measures strictly necessary for the application of Art. 9(8).

3. Notwithstanding paragraphs 1 and 2, Member States may take appropriate measures to protect legitimate interests other than those taken into consideration by this Regulation and compatible with the general principles and other provisions of Community law.
    Public security, plurality of the media and prudential rules shall be regarded as legitimate interests within the meaning of the first subparagraph.
    Any other public interest must be communicated to the Commission by the Member State concerned and shall be recognised by the Commission after an assessment of its compatibility with the general principles and other provisions of Community law before the

measures referred to above may be taken. The Commission shall inform the Member State concerned of its decision within one month of that communication.

Article 22   Application of the Regulation   1. This Regulation alone shall apply to concentrations as defined in Article 3, and Regulations No. 17,[21] (EEC) No. 1017/68[22] (EEC) No. 4056/86[23] and (EEC) No. 3975/87[24] shall not apply, except in relation to joint ventures that do not have a Community dimension and which have their object or effect the coordination of the competitive behaviour of undertakings that remain independent.

[para. 2 repealed]

3. If the Commission finds, at the request of a Member State or at the joint request of two or more Member States, that a concentration as defined in Article 3 that has no Community dimension within the meaning of Article 1 creates or strengthens a dominant position as a result of which effective competition would be significantly impeded within the territory of the Member State or States making the joint request, it may, insofar as that concentration affects trade between Member States, adopt the decisions provided for in Article 8(2), second subparagraph, (3) and (4).

4. Articles 2(1)(a) and (b), 5, 6, 8 and 10 to 20 shall apply to a request made pursuant to paragraph 3. Article 7 shall apply to the extent that the concentration has not been put into effect on the date on which the Commission informs the parties that a request has been made.

   The period within which proceedings may be initiated pursuant to Article 10(1) shall begin on the day following that of the receipt of the request from the Member State or States concerned. The request must be made within one month at most of the date on which the concentration was made known to the Member State or to all Member States making a joint request or effected. This period shall begin on the date of the first of those events.

5. Pursuant to paragraph 3 the Commission shall take only the measures strictly necessary to maintain or store effective competition within the territory of the Member State or States at the request of which it intervenes.

Article 23   Implementing provisions   The Commission shall have the power to adopt implementing provisions concerning the form, content and other details of notifications pursuant to Art. 4, time limits pursuant to Arts. 7, 9, 10 and 22, and hearings pursuant to Art. 18.

   The Commission shall have the power to lay down the procedure and time limits for the submission of commitments pursuant to Articles 6(1a) and 8(2).

Article 24   Relations with non-member countries   1. The Member States shall inform the Commission of any general difficulties encountered by their undertakings with concentrations as defined in Art. 3 in a non-member country.

---

[21] OJ Sp. Ed. 1959–62, 87.
[22] OJ 1968 L 175/1.
[23] OJ 1986 L 378/4.
[24] OJ 1987 L 374/1.

2. Initially not more than one year after the entry into force of this Regulation and thereafter periodically the Commission shall draw up a report examining the treatment accorded to Community undertakings, in the terms referred to in paragraphs 3 and 4, as regards concentrations in non-member countries. The Commission shall submit those reports to the Council, together with any recommendations.

3. Whenever it appears to the Commission, either on the basis of the reports referred to in paragraph 2 or on the basis of other information, that a non-member country does not grant Community undertakings treatment comparable to that granted by the Community to undertakings from that non-member country, the Commission may submit proposals to the Council for an appropriate mandate for negotiation with a view to obtaining comparable treatment for Community undertakings.

4. Measures taken under this Article shall comply with the obligations of the Community or of the Member States, without prejudice to Art. 307 of the Treaty, under international agreements, whether bilateral or multilateral.

Article 25   Entry into force   1. This Regulation shall enter into force on 21 September 1990. 2. This Regulation shall not apply to any concentration which was the subject of an agreement or announcement or where control was acquired within the meaning of Art. 4(1) before the date of this Regulation's entry into force and it shall not in any circumstances apply to any concentration in respect of which proceedings were initiated before that date by a Member State's authority with responsibility for competition.

3. As regards concentrations to which this regulation applies by virtue of accession, the date of accession shall be substituted for the date of entry into force of this Regulation. The provision of paragraph 2, second alternative, applies in the same way to proceedings initiated by a competition authority of the new Member States or by the EFTA Surveillance Authority.

[final provisions omitted]

INDEX